New 1996-97 Edition

PACIFIC NORTHWEST CAMPING

The Complete Guide to More Than 45,000
Campsites in Washington and Oregon

by Tom Stienstra

Foghorn Press
BOOKS BUILDING COMMUNITY™

ISBN 0-935701-94-X

51995

9 780935 701944

CREDITS

Research Editor	Janet Connaughton
Assistant Research Editors	Nan Bovee, Ashley Price, Nancy Sanchez
Editorial/Production Manager	Ann-Marie Brown

Publishing Manager	Rebecca Poole Forée
Production Manager	Michele Thomas
Editorial Assistant	Aimee Larsen
Production Assistant	Alexander Lyon
Acquisitions Editor	Judith Pynn
Cover Design	Stuart L. Silberman, Michele Thomas
Cover Photo	James W. Kay/West Stock

The Color of Commitment

Foghorn Press has always been committed to printing on recycled paper, but up to now, we hadn't taken the final plunge to use 100-percent recycled paper because we were unconvinced of its quality. And until now, those concerns were valid. But the good news is that quality recycled paper is now available. We are thrilled to announce that Foghorn Press books are printed with Soya-based inks on 100-percent recycled paper, which has a 50-percent post-consumer waste content. The only way you'd know we made this change is by looking at the hue of the paper—a small price to pay for environmental integrity. You may even like the color better. We do. And we know the earth does, too.

Printed in the United States of America

New 1996-97 Edition

PACIFIC NORTHWEST CAMPING

The Complete Guide to More Than 45,000 Campsites in Washington and Oregon

by Tom Stienstra

Foghorn Press
BOOKS BUILDING COMMUNITY™

TABLE OF CONTENTS

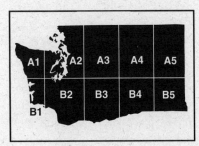

Washington, pages 89-378

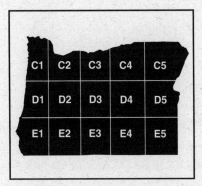

Oregon, pages 379-685

HOW TO USE THIS BOOK

You can search for your ideal camping spot in two ways:

1) If you know the name of the campsite you'd like to visit, or the name of the corresponding geographical area (town name, national or state forest name, national or state park name, lake or river name, etc.), use the index beginning on page 686 to locate it, and turn to the corresponding page. If you are looking for a specific campsite name, you'll find that all campsites are listed in the index in capital letters.

2) If you'd like to camp in a particular part of the state, and want to find out what camps are available there, use the Washington and Oregon state maps on the following page or in the back of this book. Find the area you'd like to camp in (such as A5 for the Spokane, Washington area or E2 for Ashland, Oregon), then turn to the corresponding pages in the book.

Washington, pages 89-378 (maps A1-B5)

Oregon, pages 379-685 (maps C1-E5)

•*See the bottom of every page for reference to corresponding maps.*

Note to RVers

Those of you with recreational vehicles will find *Pacific Northwest Camping* easy to use. Every camp listing that has RV sites also has an easy-to-spot RV symbol. Just flip the pages of the book and look for this symbol: **RV**. Occasionally you will find a campground listing that mentions RV sites but does not feature the RV symbol. This occurs in listings in which the camps have access routes that may not be safe for RVs.

Note to Tent Campers

Remember that an RV symbol by a camp listing does not mean that the camp is an exclusive RV resort or unsuitable for tent campers. Many campgrounds offer quality campsites for both tenters and RVers.

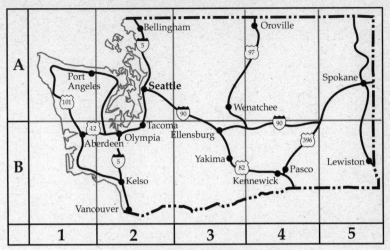

Washington map page 90

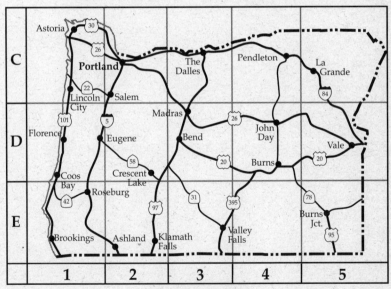

Oregon map page 380

INTRODUCTION

Going on a camping trip can be like trying to put hiking boots on an octopus. You've tried it too, eh? Instead of the relaxing, exciting sojourn that was intended, a camping trip can turn into a scenario called You Against The World. It can turn out to be about as easy as fighting an earthquake.

But it doesn't have to be that way and that's what this book is all about. If you give it a chance, it can put the mystery, excitement and fun back into your camping vacations—and remove the fear of snarls, confusion and occasional temper explosions of volcanic proportions that keep people at home, locked away from the action.

Mystery? There are hundreds of hidden, rarely used campgrounds listed and mapped in this book that you have never dreamed of. Excitement? At many of them you'll find the sizzle with the steak, the hike to a great lookout, the big fish at the end of the line. Fun? The how-to section of this book can help you take the futility out of your trips and put the fun back in. Add it up, put it in your cash register and you can turn a camping trip into the satisfying adventure it is meant to be, whether it's just an overnight quicky or a month-long expedition.

It has been documented that 95 percent of American vacationers use only five percent of the available recreation areas. With this book, you can leave the herd to wander and be free, and join the inner circle, the Five Percenters who know the great, hidden areas used by so few people. To join the Five Percent Club, you should take a hard look at the maps for the areas you wish to visit and the corresponding listings of campgrounds. As you study the camps, you will start to feel a sense of excitement building, a feeling that you are about to unlock a door and venture into a world that is rarely viewed. When you feel that excitement, act on it. Parlay that energy into a great trip.

The campground maps and listings can serve in two ways: 1) If you're on the road late in the day and you are stuck for a spot for the night, you can likely find one nearby; or 2) If you are planning in advance, you can tailor a vacation to fit exactly into your plans, rather than heading off, and hoping—maybe praying—it turns out all right.

For the latter, you may wish to obtain additional maps, particularly if you are venturing into areas governed by the U.S. Forest Service or Bureau of Land Management. Both are federal agencies and have low-cost maps available that detail all hiking trails, lakes, streams and backcountry camps reached via logging roads. How to obtain these and other maps is described in the Resource Guide on pages 81 to 86.

Backcountry camps listed in this book are often in primitive and rugged settings, but provide the sense of isolation that you may want for a trip. They also provide good jump-off points for backpacking trips, if that is your calling. These camps are also often free, and we have listed hundreds of them.

At the other end of the spectrum are the developed parks for motor homes, parks that offer a home away from home with everything from full hookups to a grocery store and laundromat. These spots are just as important as the remote camps with no facilities. Instead of isolation, an RV park provides a place to shower and get outfitted for food and clean clothes. For motor home cruisers, it is a place to stay in high style while touring the area. RV parks range in price from $8 to $20 per night, depending on location, and an advance deposit may be necessary in summer months.

Somewhere between the two extremes—the remote, unimproved camps and the lavish motor home parks—are hundreds and hundreds of campgrounds that provide a compromise: beautiful settings and some facilities, with a small overnight fee. Piped water, vault toilets and picnic tables tend to come with the territory, along with a fee that usually ranges from $7 to $15, with the higher-priced sites located near population centers. Because they offer a bit of both worlds, they are in high demand. Reservations are usually advised, and at state parks, particularly during the summer season, you can expect company. This does not mean you need to abandon them in hopes of a less confined environment. For one thing, most state parks have set up quotas so that you don't feel like you've been squeezed in with a shoehorn, and for another, the same parks are often uncrowded during the off-season or on weekdays.

Prior to your trip, you will want to get organized, and that's where you must start putting socks on that giant octopus. The key to organization for any task is breaking it down to its key components, then solving each element independent of the others. Remember the octopus. Grab a moving leg, jam on a boot and make sure it's on tight before reaching for another leg. Do one thing at a time, in order, and all will get done quick and right.

In the stories that follow, we have isolated the different elements of camping, and you should do the same when planning for your trip. There are separate stories on each of the primary ingredients for a successful trip: 1) Food and cooking gear; 2) Clothing and weather protection; 3) Hiking and foot care and how to choose the right boots and socks; 4) Sleeping gear; 5) Combatting bugs and some common sense first-aid; 6) Catching fish, avoiding bears and camp fun; 7) Outdoors with kids; 8) Weather prediction. We've also included sections on boat-in and desert camping and ethics in the outdoors, as well as a camping gear checklist.

Now you can become completely organized for your trip in just one week, spending just a little time each evening. Getting organized is an unnatural act for many. By splitting up the tasks, you take the pressure out of planning and put the fun back in.

As a full-time outdoors writer, the question I get asked more than any other is, "Where are you going this week?" All of the answers are in this book.

FOOD & COOKING GEAR

It was a warm, crystal clear day, the kind of day when if you had ever wanted to go skydiving, you would go skydiving. That was exactly the case for my old pal Foonsky, who had never before tried the sport. But a funny thing happened after he jumped out of the plane and pulled on the rip cord for the first time: His parachute didn't open.

In total free-fall, Foonsky watched the earth below getting closer and closer. Not one to panic, he calmly pulled the rip cord on the emergency parachute. But nothing happened then either. No parachute, no nothing.

The ground was getting closer and closer, and as he tried to search for a soft place to land, Foonsky detected a small object shooting up toward him, getting larger as it approached. It looked like a camper.

Foonsky figured this could be his last chance, so as they passed in mid-flight, he shouted, "Hey, do you know anything about parachutes?"

The other fellow just shouted back as he headed off into space, "Do you know anything about lighting camping stoves?"

Well, Foonsky got lucky and his parachute opened. As for the other fellow, well, he's probably in orbit like a NASA weather satellite. If you've ever had a mishap lighting a camping stove, you know exactly what I'm talking about.

When it comes to camping, all gear is not created equal. Nothing is more important than lighting your stove easily and having it reach full heat without feeling like you're playing with a short fuse to a miniature bomb. If your stove does not work right, your trip can turn into a disaster, regardless of how well you have planned the other elements. In addition, a bad stove will add an underlying sense of foreboding to your day. You will constantly have the inner suspicion that your darn stove is going to foul up again.

Camping Stoves

If you are buying a camping stove, remember this one critical rule: Do not leave the store with a new stove unless you have been shown exactly how to use it.

Know what you are getting. Many stores that specialize in

outdoor recreation equipment now provide experienced campers/ employees who will demonstrate the use of every stove they sell, and while they're at it, describe their respective strengths and weaknesses.

Never buy a stove that uses kerosene for fuel. Kerosene is smelly and messy, provides low heat, needs priming, and in America, is virtually obsolete as a camp fuel. As a test, I tried using a kerosene stove once. I could scarcely boil a pot of water. In addition, some kerosene leaked out when the stove was packed, and it ruined everything it touched. The smell of kerosene never did go away. Kerosene remains popular in Europe only because the campers haven't heard much of white gas yet, and when they do, they will demand it.

That leaves white gas or butane as the best fuels, and either one can be right for you, depending on your special preferences.

White gas is the most popular, because it can be purchased at most outdoor recreation stores, at many supermarkets, and is inexpensive and effective. It burns hot, has virtually no smell, and evaporates quickly if it should spill. If you get caught in wet, miserable weather and can't get a fire going, you can use it as an emergency fire starter, although its use as such should be sparing and never on an open flame.

White gas is a popular fuel both for car campers who use the large, two-burner stoves equipped with a fuel tank and a pump, and for hikers who use a lightweight backpacking stove. On the latter, lighting can require priming with a gel called priming paste, which some people dislike. Another problem with white gas is that it can be extremely explosive.

As an example, I once almost burned off my beard completely in a mini-explosion while lighting one of the larger stoves designed for car camping. I was in the middle of cooking dinner when the flame suddenly shut down. Sure enough, the fuel tank was empty, and after refilling it, I pumped the tank 50 or 60 times to regain pressure. When I lit a match, the sucker ignited from three feet away. The resulting explosion was like a stick of dynamite going off, and immediately the smell of burning beard was in the air. In the quick flash of an erred moment, my once thick, dark beard had been reduced to a mass of little, yellow, burned curly-Qs.

My error? After filling the tank, I forgot to shut the fuel cock off while pumping up the pressure in the tank. As a result, when I pumped the tank, the stove burners were slowly producing the gas/air mixture, filling the air space above the stove. The strike of a match even from a few feet away and ka-boom!

That problem can be solved by using stoves that use bottled

butane fuel. Butane requires no pouring, pumping or priming, and stoves that use butane are the easiest to light of all camping stoves. Just turn a knob and light—that's it. On the minus side, because it comes in bottles, you never know precisely how much fuel you have left, and when a bottle is empty, you have a potential piece of litter. Never litter. Ever.

The other problem with butane as a fuel is that it just plain does not work well in cold weather, or when there is little fuel left in the cartridge. Since you cannot predict mountain weather in spring or fall, you can use more fuel than originally projected. That can be frustrating, particularly if your stove starts wheezing with several days left in your trip. In addition, with most butane cartridges, if there is any chance of the temperature falling below freezing, you often have to sleep with the cartridge to keep it warm, or otherwise forget using it come morning.

Personally, I prefer using a small, lightweight stove that uses white gas so I can closely gauge fuel consumption. My pal Foonsky uses one with a butane bottle because it lights so easily. We have contests to see who can boil a pot of water faster and the difference is usually negligible. Thus, other factors are important when choosing a stove.

Of the other elements, ease of cleaning the burner is the most important. If you camp much, especially with the smaller stoves, the burner holes will eventually become clogged. Some stoves have a built-in cleaning needle; a quick twist of a knob and you're in business. On the other hand, others require disassembling and a protracted session using special cleaning tools. If a stove is difficult to clean, you will tend to put off doing it, and your stove will sputter and pant while you get humiliated watching the cold pot of water sitting on it.

Before making a purchase, have the salesman show you how to clean the burner head. Except in the case of the large, multi-burner family camping stoves, which rarely require cleaning, this test can do more to determine the long-term value of a stove than any other factor.

Building Fires

One summer expedition took me to the Canadian wilderness in British Columbia for a 75-mile canoe trip on the Bowron Lake Circuit, a chain of 13 lakes, six rivers and seven portages. It is one of the truly great canoe trips of the world, a loop trip that ends just a few hundred feet from its starting point. But at the first camp at Kibbee Lake, my camp stove developed a fuel leak at the base of the burner and the nuclear-like blast that followed just about turned Canada into a giant crater.

As a result, the final 70 miles of the trip had to be completed without a stove, cooking on open fires each night. The problem was compounded by the weather. It rained eight of the ten days. Rain? In Canada, raindrops the size of silver dollars fall so hard they actually bounce on the lake surface. We had to stop paddling a few times in order to empty the rainwater out of the canoe. At the end of the day, we'd make camp, and then came the test. Either make a fire or go to bed cold and hungry.

With an ax, at least we had a chance for success. As soaked as all the downed wood was, I was able to make my own fire-starting tinder from the chips of splitting logs; no matter how hard it rains, the inside of a log is always dry.

In miserable weather, matches don't stay lit long enough to get the tinder started. Instead, we used either a candle or the little, wax-like fire-starter cubes that stay lit for several minutes. From those, we could get the tinder going. Then we added small, slender strips of wood that had been axed from the interior of the logs. When the flame reached a foot high, we added the logs, with the dry interior of them facing in. By the time the inside of the logs had caught fire, the outside would be drying from the heat. It wasn't long before a royal blaze was brightening the rainy night.

That's a worst case scenario and hopefully you will never face anything like it. Nevertheless, being able to build a good fire and cook on it can be one of the more satisfying elements of a camping trip. At times, just looking into the flames can provide a special satisfaction at the end of a good day.

However, never expect to build a fire for every meal, or in some cases, even to build one at all. Many state and federal campgrounds have been picked clean of downed wood, or forest fire danger forces rangers to prohibit fires altogether during the fire season. In either case, you either use your camp stove or you go hungry.

But when you can build a fire, and the resources are available to do so, it will add to the quality of your camping trip. Of the camp-grounds listed in this book, the sites that allow you to build fires will usually already have fire rings available. In primitive areas where you can make your own, you should dig a ring eight inches deep, line the edges with rock, and clear all the needles and twigs in a five-foot radius. The next day, when the fire is dead, you can discard the rocks, fill over the black charcoal with dirt, then scatter pine needles and twigs over it. Nobody will even know you camped there. That's the best way I know to keep a secret spot a real secret.

When you start to build a campfire, the first thing you will notice is that no matter how good your intentions, your fellow campers will not be able to resist moving the wood around. Watch. You'll just be getting ready to add a key piece of wood at just the right spot, and your companion will stick his mitts in, confidently believing he has a better idea. He'll shift the fire around and undermine your best thought-out plans.

So I make a rule on camping trips. One person makes the fire and everybody else stands clear, or is involved with other camp tasks, like gathering wood, getting water, putting up tents or planning dinner. Once the fire is going strong, then it's fair game; anyone adds logs at their discretion. But in the early, delicate stages of the campfire, it's best to leave it to one person.

Before a match is struck, a complete pile of firewood should be gathered. Then start small, with the tiniest twigs you can find, and slowly add in larger twigs as you go, criss-crossing them like a miniature tepee. Eventually, you will get to the big chunks that will produce high heat. The key is to get one piece of wood burning into another, which then burns into another, setting off what I call the "chain of flame." Conversely, single pieces of wood, set apart from each other, will not burn.

On a dry, summer evening, at a campsite where plenty of wood is available, about the only way you can blow the deal is to get impatient and try to add the big pieces too quickly. Do that and you'll just get smoke, not flames, and it won't be long before every one of your fellow campers is poking at your fire. It will drive you crazy, but they just won't be able to help it.

Cooking Gear

I like traveling light, and I've found all I need for cooking is a pot, small frying pan, metal pot grabber, fork, knife, cup and matches. If you want to keep the price of food low and also cook customized dinners each night, a small pressure cooker can be just the ticket. (See "Keeping the Price Down" on page 18.) I keep all my gear in one small bag, which fits into my pack. If I'm camping out of my four-wheel drive rig, the little bag of cooking gear is easy to keep track of. Going simple, not complicated, is the key to keeping a camping trip on the right track.

You can get more elaborate by purchasing complete cook kits with plates, a coffee pot, large pots and other cookware, but what really counts is having one single pot you're happy with. It needs to be just the right size, not too big or small, and stable enough so it won't tip over, even if it is at a slight angle on a fire, full of water at a full boil. Mine is just six inches wide and four-and-a-half inches deep. It holds better than a quart of water and has served well for several hundred camp dinners.

The rest of your cook kit is easy to complete. The frying pan should be small, light-gauge aluminum, teflon-coated, with a fold-in handle so it's no hassle to store. A pot grabber is a great addition. It's a little aluminum gadget that will clamp to the edge of pots and allow you to lift them and pour water with total control, without burning your fingers. For cleanup, take a small bottle filled with dish cleaner and a plastic scrubber, and you're in business.

A Sierra Cup, which is a wide aluminum cup with a wire handle, is an ideal cup to carry because you can eat out of it as well as use it for drinking. This means no plates to clean after dinner, so cleanup is quick and easy. In addition, if you go for a hike, you can clip it to your belt with its wire handle.

If you want a more formal setup, complete with plates, glasses, silverware and the like, you can end up spending more time preparing and cleaning up from meals than you do enjoying the country you are exploring. In addition, the more equipment you bring, the more loose ends you will have to deal with, and loose ends can cause plenty of frustration. If you have a choice, choose simple.

And remember what Thoreau said: "A man is rich in proportion to what he can do without."

Food and Cooking Tricks

On a trip to the Bob Marshall Wilderness in western Montana, I woke up one morning, yawned, and said, "What've we got for breakfast?"

The silence was ominous. "Well," finally came the response, "we don't have any food left."

"What!?"

"Well, I figured we'd catch trout for meals every other night."

On the return trip, we ended up eating wild berries, buds and yes, even roots (not too tasty). When we finally landed the next day at a suburban pizza parlor, we nearly ate the wooden tables.

Running out of food on a camping trip can do more to turn reasonable people into violent grumps than any other event. There's no excuse for it, not when a system for figuring meals can be outlined with precision and little effort. You should not go out and buy a bunch of food, throw it in your rig and head off for yonder. That leaves too much to chance. And if you've ever been in the woods and real hungry, you'll know to take a little effort to make sure a day or two of starvation will not occur. A three-step process offers a solution:

1—Make a general meal-by-meal plan and make sure your companions like what is on it.

2—Tell your companions to buy any specialty items (like a special brand of coffee) on their own and not to expect you to take care of everything.

3—Put all the food on your living room floor and literally figure every day of your trip meal-by-meal, bagging the food in plastic bags as you go. You will know exact food quotas and will not go hungry.

Fish for meals? There's a guaranteed rule for that: If you expect to catch fish for meals, you will most certainly get skunked. If you don't expect to catch fish for meals, you will probably catch so many they'll be coming out of your ears. I've seen it a hundred times.

Keeping the Price Down

"There must be some mistake," I said with a laugh. "Who ever paid $750 for some camp food?"

But the amount was as clear as the digital numbers on the cash register: $753.27.

"How is this possible?" I asked the clerk at the register.

"Just add it up," she responded, irritated.

Then I started figuring. The freeze-dried backpack dinners cost $6 apiece. A small pack of beef jerky went for $2, the beef sticks for 75 cents, granola bars for 50 cents apiece. Then multiply it by four hungry men, including Foonsky, for 21 days. This food was for a major expedition—four guys hiking 250 miles over three weeks from Mount Whitney to Yosemite Valley.

The dinners alone cost close to $500. Add in the usual goodies— the jerky, granola bars, soups, dried fruit, oatmeal, Tang, candy and coffee—and I was handed a bill that felt like an earthquake.

A lot of campers have received similar shocks. In preparation for their trips, campers shop with enthusiasm. Then after hearing the price, they pay the bill in horror.

Well, there are solutions, lots of them. You can eat gourmet style in the outback without having your wallet cleaned out. But it means do-it-yourself cooking, more planning, and careful shopping. It also means transcending the push-button "I-want-it-now" attitude that so many people try to take with them to the mountains.

The secret is to bring along a small pressure cooker. A reader,

Mike Bettinger of San Francisco, passed this tip on to me. Little pressure cookers weigh about two pounds, and for backpackers and backcountry campers, that may sound like a lot. But when three or four people are on a trip, it actually saves weight.

The key is that it allows campers to bring items that are difficult to cook at high altitudes, such as brown and white rice, red, black, pinto and lima beans, and lentils. You pick one or more for a basic staple and then add a variety of freeze-dried ingredients to make a complete dish. Available are packets of meat, vegetables, onions, shallots and garlic. Sun-dried tomatoes, for instance, reconstitute wonderfully in a pressure cooker. Add herbs, spices and maybe a few rainbow trout and you will be eating better out of a backpack than most people eat in their homes.

"In the morning, I have used the pressure cooker to turn dried apricots into apricot sauce to put on the pancakes we made with sourdough starter," Bettinger said. "The pressure cooker is also big enough for washing out cups and utensils. The days when backpacking meant eating terrible freeze-dried food are over. It doesn't take a gourmet cook to prepare these meals, only some thought beforehand."

Now when Foonsky, Mr. Furnai, Rambob and me sit down to eat such a meal, we don't call it "eating." We call it "hodgepacking," or "time to pack your hodge." After a particularly long day on the trail, you can do some serious hodgepacking.

If your trip is a shorter one, like for a weekend, that means you can bring more fresh food to add some sizzle to the hodge. You can design a hot soup/stew mix that is good enough to make and eat at home.

You start by bringing a pot of water to a full boil, then adding pasta, ramen noodles or macaroni. While it simmers, cut in a potato, carrot, onion and garlic clove, and let it cook for about 10 minutes. When the vegetables have softened, add in a soup mix or two, maybe some cheese, and you are just about in business. But you can still ruin it and turn your hodge into slodge. Make sure you read the directions on the soup mix to determine cooking time. It can vary widely. In addition, make sure you stir the whole thing up, otherwise you will get these hidden dry clumps of soup mix that can taste like garlic sawdust.

How do I know? Well, it was up near Kearsage Pass in the Sierra Nevadas, where, feeling half-starved, I dug into our nightly hodge. I will never forget that first bite—I damn near gagged to death. Foonsky laughed at me, until he took his first bite (a nice big one), then turned green.

Another way to trim food costs is to make your own beef jerky, the trademark staple of campers for more than 200 years. But hey, a tiny, little packet of beef jerky costs $2. On that 250-mile expedition, I spent $150 on jerky alone. Never again. Now we make our own and get big strips of jerky that taste better than anything you can buy.

Foonsky settled on the following recipe, starting with a couple pieces of meat, lean top round, sirloin or tri-tip. At home, cut it in 3/16-inch strips across the grain, trimming out the membrane, gristle and fat. Marinate the strips for 24 hours, placing them in a glass dish. The fun begins in picking a marinade. Try two-thirds teriyaki sauce, one-third Worcestershire. You can customize the recipe by adding pepper, ground mustard, bay leaf, red wine vinegar, garlic and, for the brave, Tabasco sauce. After a day or so, squeeze out each strip of meat with a rolling pin, lay them in rows on a cooling rack over a cookie sheet, place them in an oven and dry them at 125 degrees for 12 hours. Thicker pieces can take as long as 18 to 24 hours.

That's it. The hardest part is cleaning the cookie sheet when you are done. The easiest part is eating your own homemade jerky while sitting at a lookout on a mountain ridge. The do-it-yourself method for jerky may take a day or so, but it is cheaper and can taste better than anything you can buy pre-made.

If all this still doesn't sound like your idea of a gourmet but low-cost camping meal, well, you are forgetting the main course: rainbow trout. Remember: If you don't plan on catching them for dinner, you'll probably snag more than you can finish in one night's hodgepacking.

Some campers go to great difficulties to cook their trout, bringing along frying pans, butter, grills, tin foil and more, but all you really need is some seasoned salt and a campfire.

Rinse the gutted trout off, and while it's still wet, sprinkle a good dose of seasoned salt on it, both inside and out. Clear any burning logs to the side of the campfire, then lay the trout right on the coals, turning it once so both sides are cooked. Sound ridiculous? Sound like you are throwing the fish away? Sound like the fish will burn up? Sound like you will have to eat the campfire ash? Wrong on all counts. The fish cooks perfectly, the ash doesn't stick, and after cooking trout this way, you may never fry a trout again.

But if you can't convince your buddies, who may insist the trout should be fried, then make sure you have butter to fry them in, not oil. And also make sure you cook them all the way through, so the meat strips off the backbone in two nice, clean fillets. The fish should end up looking like Sylvester the Cat just dipped it in his mouth, leaving only the head, tail and a perfect skeleton.

You can supplement your eats with sweets, nuts, freeze-dried fruits and drink mixes. In any case, make sure you keep the dinner menu varied. If you and your buddies look into your dinner cups and groan, "Ugh, not this again," you will soon start dreaming of cheeseburgers and french fries on your trip instead of hiking, fishing and finding beautiful campsites.

If you are car camping and have a big ice chest, you can bring virtually anything to eat and drink. If you are on the trail, and don't mind paying the price, the new era of pre-made freeze-dried dinners provide another option.

Some of the biggest advances in the outdoors industry have come in freeze-dried dinners now available for campers. Some of them are almost good enough to serve in restaurants. Sweet-and-sour pork over rice, tostadas, Burgundy chicken . . . it sure beats the poopy goop we used to eat, like the old, soupy chili mac dinners that tasted bad and looked so unlike "food" that consumption was near impossible, even for my dog, Rebel. Foonsky usually managed to get it down, however, but just barely.

To provide an idea of how to plan a menu, consider what my companions and I ate while hiking 250 miles on California's John Muir Trail:

• Breakfast—Instant soup, oatmeal (never get plain), one beef or jerky stick, coffee or hot chocolate.

• Lunch—One beef stick, two jerky sticks, one granola bar, dried fruit, half cup of pistachio nuts, Tang, one small bag of M&Ms.

• Dinner—Instant soup, one freeze-dried dinner, one milk bar, rainbow trout.

What was that last item? Rainbow trout? Right! Lest you plan on it, you can catch them every night.

Clothing & Weather Protection

What started as an innocent pursuit of a perfect campground evolved into one heck of a predicament for Foonsky and me.

We had parked at the end of a logging road and then bushwhacked our way down a canyon to a pristine trout stream. On my first cast, a little flip into the plunge pool of a waterfall, I caught a 16-inch rainbow trout, a real beauty that jumped three times. Magic stuff.

Then just across stream, we saw it. The Perfect Camping Spot. On a sandbar on the edge of the forest, there lay a flat, high and dry spot above the river. Nearby was plenty of downed wood collected by past winter storms that we could use for firewood. And, of course, this beautiful trout stream was bubbling along just 40 yards from the site.

But nothing is perfect, right? To reach it, we had to wade across the river, although it didn't appear to be too difficult. The cold water tingled a bit, and the river came up surprisingly high, just above the belt. But it would be worth it to camp at The Perfect Spot.

Once across the river, we put on some dry clothes, set up camp, explored the woods, and fished the stream, catching several nice trout for dinner. But late that afternoon, it started raining. What? Rain in the summertime? Nature makes its own rules. By the next morning, it was still raining, pouring like a Yosemite waterfall from a solid gray sky.

That's when we noticed The Perfect Spot wasn't so perfect. The rain had raised the river level too high for us to wade back across. We were marooned, wet and hungry.

"Now we're in a heck of a predicament," said Foonsky, the water streaming off him.

Getting cold and wet on a camping trip with no way to get warm is not only unnecessary and uncomfortable, but it can be a fast ticket to hypothermia, the Number One killer of campers in the woods. By definition, hypothermia is a condition where body temperature is lowered to the point where it causes illness. It is particularly dangerous because the afflicted are usually unaware it is setting in. The first sign is a sense of apathy, then a state of confusion, which can lead eventually to collapse (or what appears to be sleep), then death.

You must always have a way to get warm and dry in short order, regardless of any conditions you may face. If you have no way of getting dry, then you must take emergency steps to prevent hypothermia. Those steps are detailed in the following pages on first-aid.

But you should never reach that point. For starters, always have different sets of clothes tucked away, so no matter how cold and wet you might get, you always have something dry. On hiking trips, I always carry a second set of clothes, sealed to stay dry, in a plastic garbage bag. I keep a third set waiting back at the truck.

If you are car camping, your vehicle can cause an illusory sense of security. But with an extra set of dry clothes stashed safely away, there is no illusion. The security is real. And remember, no matter how hot the weather is when you start on your trip, always be prepared for the worst. Foonsky and I learned the hard way.

So both of us were soaking wet on that sandbar, and with no other choice, we tried holing up in the tent for the night. A sleeping bag with Quallofil™, or another polyester fiber fill, can retain warmth even when wet, because the fill is hollow and retains its loft. So as miserable as it was, we made it through the night.

The rain finally stopped the next day, and the river dropped a bit, but it was still rolling big and angry. Using a stick as a wading staff, Foonsky crossed about 80 percent of the stream before he was dumped, but he made a jump for it and managed to scramble to the river bank. He waved for me to follow. "No problem," I thought.

It took me 20 minutes to reach nearly the same spot where Foonsky had been dumped. The heavy river current was above my belt and pushing hard. Then, in the flash of an instant, my wading staff slipped on a rock. I teetered in the river current, and was knocked over like a bowling pin. I became completely submerged. I went tumbling down the river, heading right toward the waterfall. While underwater, I looked up at the river surface and can remember how close it appeared, yet how out of control I was. Right then, this giant hand appeared, and I grabbed it. It was Foonsky. If it wasn't for that hand, I would have sailed right over the nearby waterfall.

My momentum drew Foonsky right into the river, and we scrambled in the current, but I suddenly sensed the river bottom under my knees. On all fours, the two of us clambered ashore. We were safe.

"Thanks ol' buddy," I said.

"Man, we're wet," he responded. "Let's get to the rig and get some dry clothes on."

Dressing in Layers

After falling in the river, Foonsky and I looked like a couple of cold swamp rats. When we eventually reached the truck and finally started getting into warm clothes, a strange phenomenon hit both of us. Now that we were warming up, we started shivering and shaking like old engines trying to start. Shivering is the body's built-in heater. That's how the body tries to warm itself, producing as much heat as if you were jogging.

To retain that heat, you should dress in "layers." The interior layer, what you wear closest to your skin, and the exterior layer, what you wear to repel the weather, are the most important.

In the good ol' days, campers wore long underwear made out of wool, which was scratchy, heavy and often sweaty. Well, times have changed. You can now wear long underwear made of polypropylene, a synthetic material that is warm, light, and wicks dampness away from your skin. It's ideal to wear in a sleeping bag on cold nights, during cool evenings after the sun goes down, or for winter snow sports. Poly shirts come in three weights: light, medium and heavy. The medium weight is ideal for campers. The light weight clings too much to your body. We call it Indian Underwear, because it keeps creeping up on you. And the heavy weight is too warm and bulky. For most folks, the medium is just right.

The next layer of clothes should be a light cotton shirt or a long-sleeve cotton/wool shirt, or both, depending on the coolness of the day. For pants, many just wear blue jeans when camping, but blue jeans can be hot, tight, and once wet, they tend to stay that way. Putting on wet blue jeans on a cold morning is a torturous way to start the day. I can tell you that from experience since I have suffered that fate a number of times. A better choice are pants made from a cotton/canvas mix, which are available at outdoors stores. They are light, have a lot of give, and dry quickly. If the weather is quite warm, shorts that have some room to them can be the best choice.

Vests and Parkas

In cold weather, you should take the layer system one step further with a warm vest and a parka jacket. Vests are especially useful because they provide warmth without the bulkiness of a parka. The warmest vests and parkas are either filled with down, Quallofil™, or are made with a cotton/wool mix. Each has its respective merits and problems. Down fill provides the most warmth for the amount of weight, but becomes useless when wet, taking on a close resemblance to a wet dish rag. Quallofil™ keeps much of its heat-retaining quality even when wet, but is expensive. Vests made of cotton/wool mixes are the most attractive and also are quite warm, but they can be as heavy as a ship's anchor when wet.

Sometimes the answer is combining the two. One of my best camping companions wears a good-looking, cotton/wool vest, and a parka filled with Quallofil™. The vest never gets wet, so weight is not a factor.

Rain Gear

One of the most miserable nights I ever spent in my life was on a camping trip where I didn't bring my rain gear or a tent. Hey, it was early August, the temperature had been in the 90s for weeks, and if anybody told me it was going to rain, I would have told them to consult a brain doctor. But rain it did. And as I got more and more wet, I kept saying to myself, "Hey, it's summer, it's not supposed to rain." Then I remembered one of the Ten Commandments of camping: forget your rain gear and you can guarantee it will rain.

To stay dry, you need some form of water-repellent shell. It can be as simple as a $5 poncho made out of plastic or as elaborate as a Gore-Tex™ rain jacket and pants set that costs $300. What counts is not how much you spend, but how dry you stay.

Some can do just fine with a cheap poncho, and note that ponchos can serve other uses in addition to a rain coat. Ponchos can be used as a ground tarp, as a rain cover for supplies or a backpack, or in a pinch, can be roped up to trees to provide a quick storm ceiling if you don't have a tent. The problem with ponchos is that in a hard rain, you just don't stay dry. First your legs get wet, then they get soaked. Then your arms follow the same pattern. If you're wearing cotton, you'll find that once part of the garment gets wet, the water will spread until, alas, you are dripping wet, poncho and all. Before long you start to feel like a walking refrigerator.

One high-cost option is buying a Gore-Tex™ rain jacket and pants. Gore-Tex™ is actually not a fabric, as is commonly believed, but a laminated film that coats a breathable fabric. The result is a lightweight, water repellent, breathable jacket and pants. They are perfect for campers, but they cost a fortune.

Some hiking buddies of mine have complained that the older Gore-Tex™ rain gear loses its water-repellent quality over time. However, manufacturers insist that this is the result of water seeping through seams, not leaks in the jacket. At each seam, tiny needles have pierced through the fabric, and as tiny as the holes are, water will find a way through. An application of Seam Lock™, especially at major seams around the shoulders of a jacket, can usually end the problem.

If you don't want to spend the big bucks for Gore-Tex™ rain gear, but want more rain protection than a poncho affords, a coated nylon jacket is the compromise that many choose. They are inexpensive, have the highest water-repellent quality of any rain gear, and are warm, providing a good outer shell for your layers of clothing. But they are not without fault. These jackets don't breathe at all, and if you zip them up tight, you can sweat like an Eskimo.

My brother, Rambob, gave me a $20 nylon jacket prior to a mountain climbing expedition. I wore that $20 special all the way to the top with no complaints; it's warm and 100% waterproof. The one problem with nylon is when the temperatures drop below freezing. It gets so stiff that it feels like you are wearing a straight jacket. But at $20, it seems like a treasure, especially compared to the $180 Gore-Tex™ jackets. And its value increases every time it rains.

Other Gear... And a Few Tips

What are the three items most commonly forgotten on a camping trip? A hat, sunglasses and chapstick. A hot day is unforgiving without them.

A hat is crucial, especially when you are visiting high elevations. Without one you are constantly exposed to everything nature can give you. The sun will dehydrate you, sap your energy, sunburn your head, and in worst cases, cause sunstroke. Start with a comfortable hat. Then finish with sunglasses, chapstick and sunscreen for additional protection. They will help protect you from extreme heat.

To guard against extreme cold, it's a good idea to keep a pair of thin ski gloves stashed away with your emergency clothes, along with a wool ski cap. The gloves should be thick enough to keep your fingers from stiffening up, but pliable enough to allow full movement, so you don't have to take them off to complete simple tasks, like lighting a stove. An alternative to gloves are glovelets, which look like gloves with no fingers. In any case, just because the weather turns cold doesn't mean that your hands have to.

And if you fall into a river like Foonsky and I did, well, I hope you have a set of dry clothes waiting back at your rig. Oh, and a hand reaching out to you.

HIKING & FOOT CARE

We had set up a nice little camp in the woods, and my buddy, Foonsky, was strapping on his hiking boots, sitting against a big Douglas fir.

"New boots," he said with a grin. "But they seem pretty stiff."

We decided to hoof it down the trail for a few hours, exploring the mountain wildlands that are said to hide Bigfoot and other strange creatures. After just a short while on the trail, a sense of peace and calm seemed to settle in. The forest provides you the chance to be purified with clean air and the smell of trees, freeing you from all troubles.

But it wasn't long before the look of trouble was on Foonsky's face. And no, it wasn't from seeing Bigfoot.

"Got a hot spot on a toe," he said.

Immediately we stopped. He pulled off his right boot, then socks, and inspected the left side of his big toe. Sure enough, a blister had bubbled up, filled with fluid, but hadn't popped. From his medical kit, Foonsky cut a small piece of moleskin to fit over the blister, then taped it to hold it in place. A few minutes later, we were back on the trail.

A half hour later, there was still no sign of Bigfoot. But Foonsky stopped again and pulled off his other boot. "Another hot spot." Another small blister had started on the little toe of his left foot, over which he taped a Band-Aid to keep it from further chafing against the inside of his new boot.

In just a few days, ol' Foonsky, a strong, 6-foot-5, 200-plus pound guy, was walking around like a sore-hoofed horse that had been loaded with a month of supplies and then ridden over sharp rocks. Well, it wasn't the distance that had done Foonsky in; it was those blisters. He had them on eight of his ten toes and was going through Band-Aids, moleskin and tape like he was a walking emergency ward. If he used any more tape, he would've looked like a mummy from an Egyptian tomb.

If you've ever been in a similar predicament, then you know the frustration of wanting to have a good time, wanting to hike and explore the area at which you have set up a secluded camp, only to be turned gimp-legged by several blisters. No one is immune—all are created equal before the blister god. You can be forced to bow to it unless you get your act together.

That means wearing the right style boots for what you have in mind and then protecting your feet with a careful selection of socks. And then, if you are still so unfortunate as to get a blister or two, it means knowing how to treat them fast so they don't turn your walk into a sore-footed endurance test.

What causes blisters? In almost all cases, it is the simple rubbing of your foot against the rugged interior of your boot. That can be worsened by several factors:

1—A very stiff boot, or one in which your foot moves inside the boot as you walk, instead of the boot flexing as if it was another layer of skin.

2—Thin, ragged or dirty socks. This is the fastest route to blisters. Thin socks will allow your feet to move inside of your boots, ragged socks will allow your skin to chafe directly against the boot's interior, and dirty socks will wrinkle and fold, also rubbing against your feet instead of cushioning them.

3—Soft feet. By themselves, soft feet will not cause blisters, but in combination with a stiff boot or thin socks, they can cause terrible problems. The best way to toughen up your feet is to go barefoot. In fact, some of the biggest, toughest-looking guys you'll ever see from Hells Angels to pro football players have feet that are as soft as a baby's butt. Why? Because they never go barefoot and don't hike much.

Selecting the Right Boots

One summer I hiked 400 miles, including 250 miles in three weeks, along the crest of California's Sierra Nevada, and another 150 miles over several months in an earlier general training program. In that span, I got just one blister, suffered on the fourth day of the 250-miler. I treated it immediately, and suffered no more. One key is wearing the right boot, and for me, that means a boot that acts as a thick layer of skin that is flexible and pliable to my foot. I want my feet to fit snugly in them, with no interior movement.

There are three kinds of boots: mountaineering boots, hiking boots and canvas walking shoes. Either select the right one for you or pay the consequences.

The stiffest of the lot is the mountaineering boot. These boots are often identified by mid-range tops, laces that extend almost as far as the toe area, and ankle areas that are as stiff as a board. The lack of "give" in them is what endears them to mountaineers. Their stiffness is preferred when rock climbing, walking off-trail on craggy surfaces, or hiking down the edge of stream beds where walking across small rocks can cause you to turn your ankle. Because these boots don't give on rugged, craggy terrain, they reduce ankle injuries and provide better traction.

The drawback to stiff boots is that if careful selection of socks is not made and your foot starts slipping around in them, you will get a set of blisters that would raise even Foonsky's eyebrows. But if you just want to go for a walk, or a good tromp with a backpack, then hiking shoes or backpacking boots will serve you better.

Canvas walking shoes are the lightest of all boots, designed for day walks or short backpacking trips. Some of the newer models are like rugged tennis shoes, designed with a canvas top for lightness and a lug sole for traction. These are perfect for people who like to walk but rarely carry a backpack. Because they are flexible, they are easy to break in, and with fresh socks, they rarely cause blister problems. And because they are light, general hiking fatigue is greatly reduced.

On the negative side, because canvas shoes have shallow lug soles, traction can be far from good on slippery surfaces. In addition, they provide less than ideal ankle support, which can be a problem in rocky areas, such as along a stream where you might want to go trout fishing. Turn your ankle and your trip can be ruined.

My preference is for a premium backpacking boot, the perfect medium between the stiff mountaineering boots and the soft canvas hiking shoes. The deep lug bottom provides traction, the high ankle coverage provides support, yet the soft, waterproof leather body gives each foot a snug fit. Add it up and that means no blisters. On the negative side, they can be quite hot, weigh a ton, and, if they get wet, take days to dry.

There are a zillion styles, brands and price ranges of boots to choose from. If you wander about, comparing all their many features, you will get as confused as a kid in a toy store. Instead, go into the store with your mind clear with what you want, then find it and buy it. If you want the best, expect to spend $60 to $80 for canvas walking shoes, from $100 to $140 and sometimes more for hiking or mountaineering boots. This is one area you don't want to scrimp on, so try not to yelp about the high cost. Instead, walk out of the store believing you deserve the best, and that's exactly what you just paid for.

If you plan on using the advice of a shoe salesman for your purchase, first look at what kind of boots he is wearing. If he isn't even wearing boots, then any advice he might tender may not be worth a plug nickel. Most people I know who own quality boots, including salesmen, will wear them almost daily if their job allows, since boots are the best footwear available. However, even these well-meaning folks can offer sketchy advice. Every hiker I've ever met will tell you he wears the world's greatest boot.

Instead, enter the store with a precise use and style in mind. Rather than fish for suggestions, tell the salesman exactly what you want, try two or three different brands of the same style, and always try on the matching pair of boots simultaneously so you know exactly how they'll feel. If possible, walk up and down stairs with them. Are they too stiff? Are your feet snug yet comfortable, or do they slip? Do they have that "right" kind of feel when you walk?

If you get the right answers to those questions, then you're on your way to blister-free, pleasure-filled days of walking.

Socks

The poor gent was scratching his feet like ants were crawling over them. I looked closer. Huge yellow calluses had covered the bottom of his feet, and at the ball and heel, the calluses were about a quarter of an inch thick, cracking and sore.

"I don't understand it," he said. "I'm on my feet a lot, so I bought a real good pair of hiking boots. But look what they've done to my feet. My feet itch so much I'm going crazy."

People can spend so much energy selecting the right kind of boot that they virtually overlook wearing the right kind of socks. One goes with the other.

Your socks should be thick enough to provide a cushion for your feet, as well as a good, snug fit. Without good socks, you might try to get the boot laces too tight and that's like putting a tourniquet on your feet. You should have plenty of clean socks on hand, or plan on washing what you have on your trip. As socks are worn, they become compressed, dirty and damp. Any one of those factors can cause problems.

My camping companions believe I go overboard when it comes to socks, that I bring too many and wear too many. But it works, so that's where the complaints stop. So how many do I wear? Well, would you believe three socks on each foot? It may sound like overkill, but each has its purpose, and like I said, it works.

The interior sock is thin, lightweight, and made out of polypropy-lene or silk synthetic materials designed to transport moisture away from your skin. With a poly interior sock, your foot stays dry when it sweats. Without a poly sock, your foot can get damp and mix with dirt, which can cause a "hot spot" to start on your foot. Eventually you get blisters, lots of them.

The second sock is for comfort, and can be cotton, but a thin wool-based composite is ideal. Some made of the latter can wick moisture away from the skin, much like polypropylene does. If wool itches your feet, a thick cotton sock can be suitable, though cotton collects moisture and compacts more quickly than other socks. If you're on a short hike though, cotton will do just fine.

The exterior sock should be made of high quality, thick wool—at least 80 percent wool. It will cushion your feet, provide that "just right" snug fit in your boot, and in cold weather, give you some additional warmth and insulation. It is critical to keep the wool sock clean. If you wear a dirty wool sock over and over again, it will compact and lose its cushion, start wrinkling while you hike, and your feet will catch on fire from the blisters that start popping up.

A Few More Tips

If you are like most folks, that is, the bottom of your feet are rarely exposed and quite soft, you can take additional steps in their care. The best tip is keeping a fresh foot pad in your boot made of sponge rubber. Another cure for soft feet is to get out and walk or jog on a regular basis prior to your camping trip.

If you plan to use a foot pad and wear three socks, you will need to use these items when sizing boots. It is an unforgiving error to wear thin cotton socks when buying boots, then later trying to squeeze all this stuff, plus your feet, into your boots. There just won't be enough room.

The key to treating blisters is fast work at the first sign of a hot spot. But before you remove your socks, first check to see if the sock has a wrinkle in it, a likely cause of the problem. If so, either change socks or pull them tight, removing the tiny folds, after taking care of the blister. Cut a piece of moleskin to cover the offending toe, securing the moleskin with white medical tape. If moleskin is not available, small Band-Aids can do the job, but these have to be replaced daily, and sometimes with even more frequency. At night, clean your feet and sleep without socks.

Two other items that can help your walking is an Ace bandage and a pair of gaiters.

For sprained ankles and twisted knees, an Ace bandage can be like an insurance policy to get you back on the trail and out of trouble. Over the years, I have had serious ankle problems and have relied on a good wrap with a four-inch bandage to get me home. The newer bandages come with the clips permanently attached, so you don't have to worry about losing them.

Gaiters are leggings made of plastic, nylon or Gore-Tex™ which fit from just below your knees, over your calves, and attach under your boots. They are of particular help when walking in damp areas, or in places where rain is common. As your legs brush against ferns or low-lying plants, gaiters will deflect the moisture. Without them, your pants will be soaking wet in short order.

Should your boots become wet, a good tip is never to try to force dry them. Some well-meaning folks will try to speed-dry them at the edge of a campfire or actually put the boots in an oven. While this may dry the boots, it can also loosen the glue that holds them together, ultimately weakening them until one day they fall apart in a heap.

A better bet is to treat the leather so the boots become water repellent. Silicone-based liquids are the easiest to use and least greasy of the treatments available.

A final tip is to have another pair of lightweight shoes or moccasins that you can wear around camp, and in the process, give your feet the rest they deserve.

SLEEPING GEAR

One mountain night in the pines on an eve long ago, my dad, brother and I had rolled out our sleeping bags and were bedded down for the night. After the pre-trip excitement, a long drive, an evening of trout fishing and a barbecue, we were like three tired doggies who had played too much.

But as I looked up at the stars, I was suddenly wide awake. The kid was still wired. A half hour later? No change—wide awake.

And as little kids can do, I had to wake up ol' dad to tell him about it. "Hey, Dad, I can't sleep."

"This is what you do," he said. "Watch the sky for a shooting star and tell yourself that you cannot go to sleep until you see at least one. As you wait and watch, you will start getting tired, and it will be difficult to keep your eyes open. But tell yourself you must keep watching. Then you'll start to really feel tired. When you finally see a shooting star, you'll go to sleep so fast you won't know what hit you."

Well, I tried it that night and I don't even remember seeing a shooting star, I went to sleep so fast.

It's a good trick, and along with having a good sleeping bag, ground insulation, maybe a tent or a few tricks for bedding down in a pickup truck or motor home, you can get a good sleep on every camping trip.

Some 20 years after that camping episode with my dad and brother, we made a trip to the Planetarium at the Academy of Sciences in San Francisco to see a show on Halley's Comet. The lights dimmed, and the ceiling turned into a night sky, filled with stars and a setting moon. A scientist began explaining phenomenons of the heavens.

After a few minutes, I began to feel drowsy. Just then, a shooting star zipped across the Planetarium ceiling. I went into a deep sleep so fast it was like I was in a coma. I didn't wake up until the show was over, the lights were turned back on, and the people were leaving.

Feeling drowsy, I turned to see if ol' Dad had liked the show. Oh yeah? Not only had he gone to sleep too, but he apparently had no intention of waking up, no matter what. Just like a camping trip.

Sleeping Bags

Question: What could be worse than trying to sleep in a cold, wet sleeping bag on a rainy night without a tent in the mountains?

Answer: Trying to sleep in a cold, wet sleeping bag on a rainy night without a tent in the mountains, when your sleeping bag is filled with down.

Water will turn a down-filled sleeping bag into a mushy heap. Many campers do not like a high-tech approach, but the state-of-the-art polyfiber sleeping bags can keep you warm even when wet. That factor, along with temperature rating and weight, is key when selecting a sleeping bag.

A sleeping bag is a shell filled with a heat-retaining insulation. By itself, it is not warm. Your body provides the heat, and the sleeping bag's ability to retain that heat is what makes it warm or cold.

The old-style canvas bags are heavy, bulky, cold and, when wet, useless. With other options available, their use is limited. Anybody who sleeps outdoors or backpacks should choose otherwise. Instead, buy and use a sleeping bag filled with down or one of the quality poly-fills. Down is light, warm and aesthetically pleasing to those who don't think camping and technology mix. If you choose a down bag, be sure to keep it double wrapped in plastic garbage bags on your trips in order to keep it dry. Once wet, you'll spend your nights howling at the moon.

The polyfiber-filled bags are not necessarily better than those filled with down, but they can be. Their one key advantage is that even when wet, some poly-fills can retain up to 80 to 85 percent of your body heat. This allows you to sleep and get valuable rest even in miserable conditions. And my camping experience is that no matter how lucky you may be, there comes a time when you will get caught in an unexpected, violent storm and everything you've got will get wet, including your sleeping bag. That's when a poly-fill bag becomes priceless. You either have one and can sleep, or you don't have one and suffer. It is that simple. Of the synthetic fills, Quallofil™ made by Dupont is the leader of the industry.

But as mentioned, just because a sleeping bag uses a high-tech poly-fill doesn't necessarily make it a better bag. There are other factors.

The most important are a bag's temperature rating and weight. The temperature rating of a sleeping bag refers to how cold it can get before you start actually feeling cold. Many campers make the mistake of thinking, "I only camp in the summer, so a bag rated at 30 or 40 degrees should be fine." Later, they find out it isn't so fine, and all it takes is one cold night to convince them of that. When selecting the right temperature rating, visualize the coldest weather you might ever confront, and then get a bag rated for even colder weather.

For instance, if you are a summer camper, you may rarely experience a night in the low 30s or high 20s. A sleeping bag rated at 20 degrees would be appropriate, keeping you snug, warm and asleep. For most campers, I advise bags rated at zero or ten degrees.

If you buy a polyfilled sleeping bag, never leave it squished in your stuff sack between camping trips. Instead, keep it on a hanger in a closet or use it as a blanket. One thing that can reduce a polyfilled bag's heat-retaining qualities is if you lose the loft out of the tiny hollow fibers that make up the fill. You can avoid this with proper storage.

The weight of a sleeping bag can also be a key factor, especially for backpackers. When you have to carry your gear on your back, every ounce becomes important. To keep your weight to a minimum, sleeping bags that weigh just three pounds are available, although expensive. But if you hike much, it's worth the price. For an overnighter, you can get away with a four or four-and-a-half-pound bag without·much stress. However, bags weighing five pounds and up should be left back at the car.

I have two sleeping bags: a seven-pounder that feels like I'm in a giant sponge, and a little three-pounder. The heavy-duty model is for pickup truck camping in cold weather and doubles as a blanket at home. The lightweight bag is for hikes. Between the two, I'm set.

Insulation Pads

Even with the warmest sleeping bag in the world, if you just lay it down on the ground and try to sleep, you will likely get as cold as a winter cucumber. That is because the cold ground will suck the warmth right out of your body. The solution is to have a layer of insulation between you and the ground. For this, you can use a thin Insulite™ pad, a lightweight Therm-a-Rest™ inflatable pad, or an air mattress. Here is a capsule summary of them:

•**Insulite™ pads**—They are light, inexpensive, roll up quick for transport, and can double as a seat pad at your camp. The negative side is that in one night, they will compress, making you feel like you are sleeping on granite.

•**Therm-a-Rest™ pads**—They are a real luxury, because they do everything an Insulite pad does, but also provide a cushion. The negative side to them is that they are expensive by comparison, and if they get a hole in them, they become worthless without a patch kit.

•**Air mattress**—These are okay for car campers, but their bulk, weight and the amount of effort necessary to blow them up make them a nuisance.

A Few Tricks

When surveying a camp area, the most important consideration should be to select a good spot to sleep. Everything else is secondary. Ideally, you want a flat spot that is wind-sheltered, on ground soft enough to drive stakes into. Yeah, and I want to win the lottery, too.

Sometimes that ground will have a slight slope to it. In that case, always sleep with your head on the uphill side. If you sleep parallel to the slope, every time you roll over in your sleep, you'll find yourself rolling down the hill. If you sleep with your head on the downhill side, you'll get a headache that feels like an ax is embedded in your brain.

When you've found a good spot, clear it of all branches, twigs and rocks, of course. A good tip is to dig a slight indentation in the ground where your hip will fit. Since your body is not flat, but has curves and edges, it will not feel comfortable on flat ground. Some people even get severely bruised on the sides of their hips when sleeping on flat, hard ground. For that reason alone, they learn to hate camping. Instead, bring a spade, dig a little depression in the ground for your hip, and sleep well.

After the ground is prepared, throw a ground cloth over the spot, which will keep much of the morning dew off you. In some areas, particularly where fog is a problem, morning dew can be quite heavy and get the outside of your sleeping bag quite wet. In that case, you need overhead protection, such as a tent or some kind of roof, like that of a poncho or tarp, with its ends tied to trees.

Tents and Weather Protection

All it takes is to get caught in the rain once without a tent and you will never go anywhere without one again. A tent provides protection from rain, wind and mosquito attacks. In exchange, you can lose a starry night's view, though some tents now even provide moon roofs.

A tent can be as complex as a four-season, tubular-jointed dome with a rain fly, or as simple as two ponchos snapped together and roped up to a tree. They can be as cheap as a $10 tube tent, which is nothing more than a hollow piece of plastic, or as expensive as a $500 five-person deluxe expedition dome model. They vary greatly in size, price and put-up time. If you plan on getting a good one, then plan on doing plenty of shopping and asking lots of questions. The key ones are: Will it keep me dry? How hard is it to put up? Is it roomy enough? How much does it weigh?

With a little bit of homework, you can get the right answers to these questions.

• ***Will it keep me dry?*** On many one-person and two-person tents, the rain fly does not extend far enough to keep water off the bottom sidewalls of the tent. In a driving rain, water can also drip from the rain fly and to the bottom sidewalls of the tent. Eventually the water can leak through to the inside, particularly through the seams where the tent has been sewed together.

You must be able to stake out your rain fly so it completely covers all of the tent. If you are tent shopping and this does not appear possible, then don't buy the tent. To prevent potential leaks, use a seam water proofer like Seam Lock™, a glue-like substance, to close potential leak areas on tent seams. On the large umbrella tents, keep a patch kit handy.

Another way to keep water out of your tent is to store all wet garments outside the tent, under a poncho. Moisture from wet clothes stashed in the tent will condense on the interior tent walls. If you bring enough wet clothes in the tent, by the next morning you can feel like you're camping in a duck blind.

• ***How hard is it to put up?*** If a tent is difficult to erect in full sunlight, you can just about forget it at night. Some tents can go up in just a few minutes, without requiring help from another camper. This might be the kind of tent you want.

The way to compare put-up time of tents when shopping is to count the number of connecting points from the tent poles to the tent, and also the number of stakes required. The fewer, the better. Think simple. My tent has seven connecting points and, minus the rain fly, requires no stakes. It goes up in a few minutes. If you need a lot of stakes, it is a sure tip-off to a long put-up time. Try it at night or in the rain, and you'll be ready to cash your chips and go for broke.

Another factor is the tent poles themselves. Some small tents have poles that are broken into small sections that are connected by bungee cords. It takes only an instant to convert them to a complete pole.

Some outdoor shops have tents on display on their showroom floor. Before buying the tent, have the salesman take the tent down and put it back up. If it takes him more than five minutes, or he says he "doesn't have time," then keep looking.

• ***Is it roomy enough?*** Don't judge the size of a tent on floor space alone. Some tents small on floor space can give the illusion of roominess with a high ceiling. You can be quite comfortable in them and snug.

But remember that a one-person or two-person tent is just that. A two-person tent has room for two people plus gear. That's it. Don't buy a tent expecting it to hold more than it is intended to.

• *How much does it weigh*? If you're a hiker, this becomes the preeminent question. If it's much more than six or seven pounds, forget it. A 12-pound tent is bad enough, but get it wet and it's like carrying a piano on your back. On the other hand, weight is scarcely a factor if you camp only where you can take your car. My dad, for instance, used to have this giant canvas umbrella tent that folded down to this neat little pack that weighed about 500 pounds.

Bivouac Bags

If you like going solo and choose not to own a tent at all, a bivvy bag, short for bivouac bag, can provide the weather protection you require. A bivvy bag is a water-repellent shell in which your sleeping bag fits. They are light and tough, and for some, are a perfect alternative to a heavy tent. On the down side, however, there is a strange sensation when you try to ride out a rainy night in one. You can hear the rain hitting you, and sometimes even feel the pounding of the drops through the bivvy bag. It can be unsettling to try and sleep under such circumstances.

Pickup Truck Campers

If you own a pickup truck with a camper shell, you can turn it into a self-contained campground with a little work. This can be an ideal way to go: it's fast, portable, and you are guaranteed a dry environment.

But that does not necessarily mean it is a warm environment. In fact, without insulation from the metal truck bed, it can be like trying to sleep on an iceberg. That is because the metal truck bed will get as cold as the air temperature, which is often much colder than the ground temperature. Without insulation, it can be much colder in your camper shell than it would be on the open ground.

When I camp in my rig, I use a large piece of foam for a mattress and insulation. The foam measures four inches thick, is 48 inches wide and 76 inches long. It makes for a bed as comfortable as anything one might ask for. In fact, during the winter, if I don't go camping for a few weeks because of writing obligations, I sometimes will throw the foam on the floor, lay down the old sleeping bag, light a fire and camp right in my living room. It's in my blood, I tell you.

Motor Homes

The problems motor home owners encounter come from two primary sources: lack of privacy and light intrusion.

The lack of privacy stems from the natural restrictions of where a "land yacht" can go. Without careful use of the guide portion of this book, motor home owners can find themselves in parking lot settings, jammed in with plenty of neighbors. Because motor homes often have large picture windows, you lose your privacy, causing some late nights, and come daybreak, light intrusion forces an early wake-up. The result is you get shorted on your sleep.

The answer is always to carry inserts to fit over the inside of your windows. This closes off the outside and retains your privacy. And if you don't want to wake up with the sun at daybreak, you don't have to. It will still be dark.

First Aid & Insect Protection

The mountain night could not have been more perfect, I thought as I lay in my sleeping bag.

The sky looked like a mass of jewels and the air tasted sweet and smelled of pines. A shooting star fireballed across the sky, and I remember thinking, "It just doesn't get any better."

Just then, as I was drifting into sleep, this mysterious buzz appeared from nowhere and deposited itself inside my left ear. Suddenly awake, I whacked my ear with the palm of my hand, hard enough to cause a minor concussion. The buzz disappeared. I pulled out my flashlight and shined it on my palm, and there, lit in the blackness of night, lay the squished intruder. A mosquito, dead amid a stain of blood.

Satisfied, I turned off the light, closed my eyes, and thought of the fishing trip planned for the next day. Then I heard them. It was a squadron of mosquitos, flying landing patterns around my head. I tried to grab them with an open hand, but they dodged the assault and flew off. Just 30 seconds later another landed in my left ear. I promptly dispatched the invader with a rip of the palm.

Now I was completely awake, so I got out of my sleeping bag to retrieve some mosquito repellent. But while en route, several of the buggers swarmed and nailed me in the back and arms. Later, after applying the repellent and settling snugly again in my sleeping bag, the mosquitos would buzz a few inches from my ear. After getting a whiff of the poison, they would fly off. It was like sleeping in a sawmill.

The next day, drowsy from little sleep, I set out to fish. I'd walked but 15 minutes when I brushed against a bush and felt this stinging sensation on the inside of my arm, just above the wrist. I looked down: A tick had his clamps in me. I ripped it out before he could embed his head into my skin.

After catching a few fish, I sat down against a tree to eat lunch and just watch the water go by. My dog, Rebel, sat down next to me and stared at the beef jerky I was munching as if it was a T-bone steak. I finished eating, gave him a small piece, patted him on the head, and said, "Good dog." Right then, I noticed an itch on my arm where a mosquito had drilled me. I unconsciously scratched it. Two days later, in that exact spot, some nasty red splotches started popping up. Poison oak. By petting my dog and then scratching my arm, I had transferred the oil residue of the poison oak leaves from Rebel's fur to my arm.

On returning back home, Foonsky asked me about the trip.

"Great," I said. "Mosquitos, ticks, poison oak. Can hardly wait to go back."

"Sorry I missed out," he answered.

Mosquitos, No-See-Ums, Gnats and Horseflies

On a trip to Canada, Foonsky and I were fishing a small lake from the shore when suddenly a black horde of mosquitos could be seen moving across the lake toward us. It was like when the French Army looked across the Rhine and saw the Wehrmacht coming. There was a literal buzz in the air. We fought them off for a few minutes, then made a fast retreat to the truck and jumped in, content the buggers had been fooled. But somehow, still unknown to us, the mosquitos gained entry to the truck. In 10 minutes, we squished 15 of them while they attempted to plant their oil derricks in our skin. Just outside the truck, the black horde waited for us to make a tactical error, like roll down a window. It finally took a miraculous hailstorm to wipe out the attack.

When it comes to mosquitos, no-see-ums, gnats and horseflies, there are times when there is nothing you can do. However, in most situations you can muster a defense to repel the attack.

The first key with mosquitos is to wear clothing too heavy for them to drill through. Expose a minimum of skin, wear a hat and tie a bandanna around your neck, preferably one that has been sprayed with repellent. If you try to get by with just a cotton T-shirt, you will be declared a federal mosquito sanctuary.

So first your skin must be well covered, exposing only your hands and face. Second, you should have your companion spray your clothes with repellent. Third, you should dab liquid repellent directly on your skin.

Taking Vitamin B1 and eating garlic are reputed to act as natural insect repellents, but I've met a lot of mosquitos that are not convinced. A better bet is to examine the contents of the repellent in question. The key is the percentage of the ingredient called "non-diethyl-metatoluamide." That is the poison, and the percentage of it in the container must be listed and will indicate that brand's effectiveness. Inert ingredients are just excess fluids used to fill the bottles.

At night, the easiest way to get a good sleep without mosquitos buzzing in your ear is to sleep in a bug-proof tent. If the nights are warm and you want to see the stars, new tent models are available that have a skylight covered with mosquito netting. If you don't like tents on summer evenings, mosquito netting rigged with an air space at your head can solve the problem. Otherwise prepare to get bit, even with the use of mosquito repellent.

If your problems are with no-see-ums or biting horseflies, then you need a slightly different approach.

No-see-ums are tiny, black insects that look like nothing more than a sliver of dirt on your skin. Then you notice something stinging, and when you rub the area, you scratch up a little no-see-um. The results are similar to mosquito bites, making your skin itch, splotch and, when you get them bad, swell. In addition to using the techniques described to repel mosquitos, you should go one step further.

The problem is, no-see-ums are tricky little devils. Somehow they can actually get under your socks and around your ankles where they will bite to their heart's content all night long while you sleep, itch, sleep and itch some more. The best solution is to apply a liquid repellent to your ankles, then wear clean socks.

Horseflies are another story. They are rarely a problem, but when they get their dander up, they can cause trouble you'll never forget.

One such episode occurred when Foonsky and I were paddling a canoe along the shoreline of a large lake. This giant horsefly, about the size of a fingertip, started dive-bombing the canoe. After 20 minutes, it landed on his thigh. Foonsky immediately slammed it with an open hand, then let out a blood-curdling "yeeeee-ow" that practically sent ripples across the lake. When Foonsky whacked it, the horsefly had somehow turned around and bit him in the hand, leaving a huge, red welt.

In the next 10 minutes, that big fly strafed the canoe on more dive-bomb runs. I finally got my canoe paddle, swung it as if it was a baseball bat and nailed that horsefly like I'd hit a home run. It landed about 15 feet from the boat, still alive and buzzing in the water. While I was trying to figure what it would take to kill this bugger, a large rainbow trout surfaced and snatched it out of the water, finally avenging the assault.

If you have horsefly or yellowjacket problems, you'd best just leave the area. One, two or a few can be dealt with. More than that and your fun camping trip will be about as fun as being roped to a tree and stung by an electric shock rod.

On most trips, you will spend time doing everything possible to keep from getting bit by mosquitos or no-see-ums. When that fails, you must know what to do next, and fast, if you are among those ill-fated campers who get big, red lumps from a bite inflicted from even a microscopic-sized mosquito.

A fluid called After Bite™ or a dab of ammonia should be applied immediately to the bite. To start the healing process, apply a first-aid gel, not a liquid, such as Campho-Phenique™.

Ticks

Ticks are nasty little vermin that will wait in ambush, jump on unsuspecting prey, and then crawl to a prime location before filling their bodies with their victim's blood.

I call them Dracula Bugs, but by any name they can be a terrible camp pest. Ticks rest on grass and low plants and attach themselves to those who brush against the vegetation (dogs are particularly vulnerable). Typically, they are no more than 18 inches above ground, and if you stay on the trails, you can usually avoid them.

There are two common species of ticks. The common coastal tick is larger, brownish in color, and prefers to crawl around prior to putting its clamps on you. The latter habit can give you the creeps, but when you feel it crawling, you can just pick it off and dispatch it. The coastal tick's preferred destination is usually the back of your neck, just where the hairline starts. The other species, a wood tick, is small and black, and when he puts his clamps in, it's immediately painful. When a wood tick gets into a dog for a few days, it can cause a large, red welt. In either case, ticks should be removed as soon as possible.

If you have hiked in areas infested with ticks, it is advisable to shower as soon as possible, washing your clothes immediately. If you just leave your clothes in a heap, a tick can crawl from your clothes and invade your home. They like warmth, and one way or another, they can end up in your bed. Waking up in the middle of the night with a tick crawling across you chest can really give you the creeps.

Once a tick has its clampers on you, you must decide how long it has been there. If it has been a short time, the most painless and effective method for removal is to take a pair of sharp tweezers and grasp the little devil, making certain to isolate the mouth area, then pull him out. Reader Johvin Perry sent in the suggestion to coat the tick with Vaseline, which will cut off its oxygen supply, after which it may voluntarily give up the hunt.

If the tick has been in longer, you may wish to have a doctor extract it. Some people will burn a tick with a cigarette, or poison it with lighter fluid, but this is not advisable. No matter how you do it, you must take care to remove all of it, especially its claw-like mouth.

The wound, however small, should then be cleansed and dressed. This is done by applying liquid peroxide, which cleans and sterilizes, and then applying a dressing coated with a first-aid gel such as First-Aid Cream™, Campho-Phenique™, or Neosporin™.

Lyme disease, which can be transmitted by the bite of the deer tick, is rare but common enough to warrant some attention. To prevent tick bites, some people tuck their pant legs into their hiking socks and spray tick repellent, called Permamone™, on their pants.

The first symptom of Lyme disease is that the bite area will develop a bright red, splotchy rash. Other early symptoms sometimes include headache, nausaea, fever and/or a stiff neck. If this happens, or if you have any doubts, you should see your doctor immediately. If you do get Lyme disease, don't panic. Doctors say it is easily treated in the early stages with simple antibiotics. If you are nervous about getting Lyme disease, carry a small plastic bag with you when you hike. If a tick manages to get his clampers into you, put it in the plastic bag after you pull it out. Then give it to your doctor for analysis, to see if the tick is a carrier of the disease.

During the course of my hiking and camping career, I have removed ticks from my skin hundreds of times without any problems. However, if you are really worried about ticks, you can purchase a tick removal kit from any outdoors store. These kits allow you to remove ticks in such a way that their toxins are guaranteed not to enter your bloodstream.

Poison Oak

After a nice afternoon hike, about a five-miler, I was concerned about possible exposure to poison oak, so I immediately showered and put on clean clothes. Then I settled into a chair with my favorite foamy elixir to watch the end of a baseball game. The game went 18 innings and meanwhile, my dog, tired from the hike, went to sleep on my bare ankles.

A few days later I had a case of poison oak. My feet looked like they had been on fire and put out with an ice pick. The lesson? Don't always trust your dog, give him a bath as well, and beware of extra-inning ball games.

You can get poison oak only from direct contact with the oil residue from the leaves. It can be passed in a variety of ways, as direct as skin to leaf contact or as indirect as leaf to dog, dog to sofa, sofa to skin. Once you have it, there is little you can do but itch yourself to death. Applying Caladryl™ lotion or its equivalent can help because it contains antihistamines, which attack and dry the itch.

A tip that may sound crazy but seems to work is advised by my pal Furniss. You should expose the afflicted area to the hottest water you can stand, then suddenly immerse it in cold water. The hot water opens the skin pores and gets the "itch" out, and the cold water then quickly seals the pores.

In any case, you're a lot better off if you don't get poison oak to begin with. Remember the old Boy Scout saying: "Leaves of three, let them be." Also remember that poison oak can disguise itself. In the spring, it is green, then it gradually turns reddish in the summer. By fall, it becomes a bloody, ugly-looking red. In the winter, it loses its leaves altogether and appears to be nothing more than barren, brown sticks of small plant. However, at any time and in any form, skin contact can cause quick infection.

Some people are more easily afflicted than others, but if you are one of the lucky few who aren't, don't cheer too loudly. While some people can be exposed to the oil residue of poison oak with little or no effect, the body's resistance can gradually be worn down with repeated exposures. At one time, I could practically play in the stuff and the only symptom would be a few little bumps on the inside of my wrist. Now, some 15 years later, my resistance has broken down. If I merely rub against poison oak now, in a few days the exposed area can look like it was used for a track meet.

So regardless if you consider yourself vulnerable or not, you should take heed to reduce your exposure. That can be done by staying on trails when you hike and making sure your dog does the same. Remember, the worst stands of poison oak are usually brush-infested areas just off the trail. Protect yourself also by dressing so your skin is completely covered, wearing long-sleeve shirts, long pants and boots. If you suspect you've been exposed, immediately wash your clothes, then wash yourself with aloe vera, rinsing with a cool shower.

And don't forget to give your dog a bath as well.

Sunburn

The most common injury suffered on camping trips is sunburn, yet some people wear it as a badge of honor, believing that it somehow enhances their virility. Well, it doesn't. Neither do suntans. And too much sun can lead to serious burns or sunstroke.

It is easy enough to avoid. Use a high-level sunscreen on your skin, chapstick on your lips, and wear sunglasses and a hat. If any area gets burned, apply first-aid cream, which will soothe and provide moisture for your parched, burned skin.

The best advice is not to get even a suntan. Those who do are involved in a practice that can be eventually ruinous to their skins.

A Word About Giardia

You have just hiked in to your backwoods spot, you're thirsty and a bit tired, but you smile as you consider the prospects. Everything seems perfect—there's not a stranger in sight, and you have nothing to do but relax with your pals.

You toss down your gear, grab your cup and dip it into the stream, and take a long drink of that ice-cold mountain water. It seems crystal pure and sweeter than anything you've ever tasted. It's not till later that you find out that it can be just like drinking a cup of poison.

Whether you camp in the wilderness or not, if you hike, you're going to get thirsty. And if your canteen runs dry, you'll start eyeing any water source. Stop! Do not pass Go. Do not drink.

By drinking what appears to be pure mountain water without first treating it, you can ingest a microscopic protozoan called *Giardia lamblia.* The pain of the ensuing abdominal cramps can make you feel like your stomach and intestinal tract are in a knot, ready to explode. With that comes long-term diarrhea that is worse than even a bear could imagine.

Doctors call the disease giardiasis, or Giardia for short, but it is difficult to diagnose. One friend of mine who contracted Giardia was told he might have stomach cancer before the proper diagnosis was made.

Drinking directly from a stream or lake does not mean you will get Giardia, but you are taking a giant chance. There is no reason to take such a risk, potentially ruining your trip and enduring weeks of misery.

A lot of people are taking that risk. I made a personal survey of campers in the Yosemite National Park wilderness, and found that roughly only one in 20 were equipped with some kind of water-purification system. The result, according to the Public Health Service, is that an average of 4 percent of all backpackers and campers suffer giardiasis. According to the Parasitic Diseases Division of the Center for Infectious Diseases, the rates range from 1 percent to 20 percent across the country.

But if you get Giardia, you are not going to care about the statistics. "When I got Giardia, I just about wanted to die," said Henry McCarthy, a California camper. "For about 10 days, it was the most terrible thing I have ever experienced. And through the whole thing, I kept thinking, 'I shouldn't have drunk that water, but it seemed all right at the time.'"

That is the mistake most campers make. The stream might be running free, gurgling over boulders in the high country, tumbling into deep, oxygenated pools. It looks pure. Then the next day, the problems suddenly start. Drinking untreated water from mountain streams is a lot like playing Russian roulette. Sooner or later, the gun goes off.

Anyone venturing into the outdoors should be acquainted with the several solutions to the water-purification problem. I have tested them all. Here are my findings:

• **Katadyn Water Filter:** This is the best system for screening out Giardia, as well as other microscopic bacteria more commonly found in stream and lake water that can cause stomach problems.

To work the filter, place the nozzle in the water, then pump the water directly from a spout at the top of the pump into a canteen. This can require fairly rigorous pumping, especially as the filter becomes plugged. On the average, it takes a few minutes to fill a canteen.

The best advantages are that the device has a highly advanced screening system (a ceramic element), and it can be cleaned repeatedly with a small brush.

The drawbacks are that the filter is expensive, it can easily break when dropped because its body is made of porcelain, and if you pack very light, its weight (about two pounds) may be a factor. But those are good trade-offs when you can drink ice-cold stream water without risk.

• **First-Need or Sweetwater Water Purifiers:** These are the most cost-effective water-purification systems for a variety of reasons.

They are far less expensive than the Katadyn, yet provide much better protection than anything cheaper. They are small and lightweight, so they don't add much weight to your pack. And if you use some care to pump water from sediment-free sources, the purifiers will easily last a week, the length of most outdoor trips.

These devices consist of a plastic pump and a hose that connects to a separate filter canister. They pump faster and with less effort than the Katadyn, mainly because the filter is not as fine-screened.

The big drawback is that if you pump water from a mucky lake, the filter can clog in a few days. Therein lies the weakness. Once plugged up, it is useless and you have to replace it or take your chances.

One trick to extend the filter life is to fill your cook pot with water, let the sediment settle, then pump from there. As an added insurance policy, always have a spare filter canister on hand.

• **Boiling water:** Except for water filtration, this is the only treatment that you can use with complete confidence. According to the federal Parasitic Diseases Division, it takes a few minutes at a rolling boil to be certain you've killed *Giardia lamblia.* At high elevations, boil for three to five minutes. A side benefit is that you'll also kill other dangerous bacteria that live undetected in natural waters.

But to be honest, boiling water is a thorn for most people on backcountry trips. For one thing, if you boil water on an open fire, what should taste like crystal-pure mountain water tastes instead like a mouthful of warm ashes. If you don't have a campfire, it wastes stove fuel. And if you are thirsty *now,* forget it. The water takes hours to cool.

The only time boiling always makes sense, however, is when you are preparing dinner. The ash taste will disappear in whatever freeze-dried dinner, soup, or hot drink you make.

• **Water-purification pills:** Pills are the preference for most backcountry campers, and this can get them in trouble. At just $3 to $8 per bottle, which can figure up to just a few cents per canteen, they do come cheap. In addition, they kill most of the bacteria, regardless of whether you use iodine crystals or potable aqua iodine tablets.

The problem is they just don't always kill *Giardia lamblia,* and that is the one critter worth worrying about on your trip. That makes water-treatment pills unreliable and dangerous.

Another key element is the time factor. Depending on the water's temperature, organic content, and pH level, these pills can take a long time to do the job. A minimum wait of 20 minutes is advised. Most people don't like waiting that long, especially when they're hot and thirsty after a hike and thinking, "What the heck, the water looks fine."

And then there is the taste. On one trip, my water filter clogged and we had to use the iodine pills instead. It doesn't take long to get tired of the iodine-tinged taste of the water. Mountain water should be one of the greatest tasting beverages of the world, but the iodine kills that.

• **No treatment:** This is your last resort and, using extreme care, can be executed with success. One of my best hiking buddies, Michael Furniss, is a nationally-renowned hydrologist, and on wilderness trips he has showed me the difference between "safe" and "dangerous" water sources.

Long ago, people believed that just finding water running over a rock used to be a guarantee of its purity. Imagine that. What we've learned is that the safe water sources are almost always small creeks or springs located in high, craggy mountain areas. The key is making sure no one has been upstream from where you drink.

Furniss mentioned that another potential problem in bypassing water treatment is that even in settings free of Giardia, you can still ingest other bacteria that can cause stomach problems.

The only sure way to beat the problem is to filter or boil your water before drinking, eating, or brushing your teeth. And the best way to prevent the spread of Giardia is to bury your waste products at least eight inches deep and 100 feet away from natural waters.

Hypothermia

No matter how well planned your trip might be, a sudden change in weather can turn it into a puzzle for which there are few answers. Bad weather or an accident can set in motion a dangerous chain of events.

Such a chain of episodes occurred for my brother, Rambob, and me on a fishing trip one fall day just below the snow line. The weather had suddenly turned very cold and ice was forming along the shore of the lake. Suddenly, the canoe became terribly imbalanced and just that quick, it flipped. The little life vest seat cushions were useless, and using the canoe as a paddle board, we tried to kick our way back to shore where my dad was going crazy at the thought of his two sons drowning before his eyes.

It took 17 minutes in that 38-degree water, but we finally made it to the shore. When they pulled me out of the water, my legs were dead, not strong enough even to hold up my weight. In fact, I didn't feel so much cold as tired, and I just wanted to lay down and go to sleep.

I closed my eyes, and my brother-in-law, Lloyd Angal, slapped me in the face several times, then got me on my feet and pushed and pulled me about.

In the celebration over making it to shore, only Lloyd had realized that hypothermia was setting in. Hypothermia is the condition in which the temperature of the body is lowered to the point that it causes poor reasoning, apathy and collapse. It can look like the afflicted person is just tired and needs to sleep, but that sleep can be the first step to a coma.

Ultimately, my brother and I shared what little dry clothing remained. Then we began hiking around to get muscle movement, creating internal warmth. We ate whatever munchies were available because the body produces heat by digestion. But most important, we got our heads as dry as possible. More body heat is lost through wet hair than any other single factor.

A few hours later, we were in a pizza parlor replaying the incident, talking about how only a life vest can do the job of a life vest. We decided never again to rely on those little flotation seat cushions that disappear when the boat flips.

Almost by instinct we had done everything right to prevent hypothermia: Don't go to sleep, start a physical activity, induce shivering, put dry clothes on, dry your head and eat something. That's how you fight hypothermia. In a dangerous situation, whether you fall in a lake or a stream or get caught unprepared in a storm, that's how you can stay alive.

After being in that ice-bordered lake for almost 20 minutes and then finally pulling ourselves to the shoreline, we discovered a strange thing. My canoe was flipped right-side up, and almost all of its contents were lost: tackle box, floatation cushions and cooler. But remaining was one paddle and one fishing rod, the trout rod my grandfather had given me for my 12th birthday.

Lloyd gave me a smile. "This means that you are meant to paddle and fish again," he said with a laugh.

Getting Unlost

You could not have been more lost. But there I was, a guy who is supposed to know about these things, transfixed by confusion, snow and hoof prints from a big deer.

I discovered it is actually quite easy to get lost. If you don't get your bearings, getting found is the difficult part. This occurred on a wilderness trip where I'd hiked in to a remote lake and then set up a base camp for a deer hunt.

"There are some giant bucks up on that rim," confided Mr. Furnai, who lives near the area. "But it takes a mountain man to even get close to them."

That was a challenge I answered. After four-wheeling it to the trailhead, I tromped off with pack and rifle, gut-thumped it up 100 switchbacks over the rim, then followed a creek drainage up to a small but beautiful lake. The area was stark and nearly treeless, with bald granite broken only by large boulders. To keep from getting lost, I marked my route with piles of small rocks to act as directional signs for the return trip.

But at daybreak the next day, I stuck my head out of my tent and found eight inches of snow on the ground. I looked up into a gray sky filled by huge, cascading snowflakes. Visibility was about 50 yards, with fog on the mountain rim. "I better get out of here and get back to my truck," I said to myself. "If my truck gets buried at the trailhead, I'll never get out."

After packing quickly, I started down the mountain. But after 20 minutes, I began to get disoriented. You see, all the little piles of rocks I'd stacked to mark the way were now buried in snow, and I had only a smooth white blanket of snow to guide me. Everything looked the same, and it was snowing even harder now.

Five minutes later I started chewing on some jerky to keep warm, then suddenly stopped. Where was I? Where was the creek drainage? Isn't this where I was supposed to cross over a creek and start the switchbacks down the mountain?

Right then I looked down and saw the tracks of a huge deer, the kind Mr. Furnai had talked about. What a predicament: I was lost and snowed in, and seeing big hoof prints in the snow. Part of me wanted to abandon all safety and go after that deer, but a little voice in the back of my head won out. "Treat this as an emergency," it said.

The first step in any predicament is to secure your present situation, that is, to make sure it does not get any worse. I unloaded my rifle (too easy to slip, fall and have a misfire), took stock of my food (three days worth), camp fuel (plenty), and clothes (rain gear keeping me dry). Then I wondered, "Where the hell am I?"

I took out my map, compass and altimeter, then opened the map and laid it on the snow. It immediately began collecting snowflakes. I set the compass atop the map and oriented it to north. Because of the fog, there was no way to spot landmarks, such as prominent mountain tops, to verify my position. Then I checked the altimeter, which read 4,900 feet. Well, the elevation at my lake was 5,320 feet. That was critical information.

I scanned the elevation lines on the map and was able trace the approximate area of my position, somewhere downstream from the lake, yet close to a 4,900-foot elevation. "Right here," I said, point to a spot on the map with a finger. "I should pick up the switchback trail down the mountain somewhere off to the left, maybe just 40 or 50 yards away."

Slowly and deliberately, I pushed through the light, powdered snow. In five minutes, I suddenly stopped. To the left, across a 10-foot depression in the snow, appeared a flat spot that veered off to the right. "That's it! That's the crossing."

In minutes, I was working down the switchbacks, on my way, no longer lost. I thought of the hoof prints I had seen, and now that I knew my position, I wanted to head back and spend the day hunting.

Then I looked up at the sky, saw it filled with falling snowflakes, and envisioned my truck buried deep in snow. Alas, this time logic won out over dreams.

In a few hours, now trudging through more than a foot of snow, I was at my truck at a spot called Doe Flat, and next to it was a giant, all-terrain Forest Service vehicle and two rangers.

"Need any help?" I asked them.

They just laughed. "We're here to help you," one answered. "It's a good thing you filed a trip plan with our district office in Gasquet. We wouldn't have known you were out here."

"Winter has arrived," said the other. "If we don't get your truck out now, it will be stuck here until next spring. If we hadn't found you, you might have been here until the end of time."

They connected a chain from the rear axle of their giant rig to the front axle of my truck and started towing me out, back to civilization. On the way to pavement, I figured I had gotten some of the more important lessons of my life. Always file a trip plan, have plenty of food, fuel and a camp stove you can rely on. Make sure your clothes, weather gear, sleeping bag and tent will keep you dry and warm. Always carry a compass, altimeter and map with elevation lines, and know how to use them, practicing in good weather to get the feel of it.

And if you get lost and see the hoofprints of a giant deer, well, there are times when it is best to pass them by.

CATCHING FISH, AVOIDING BEARS & HAVING FUN

Feet tired and hot, stomachs hungry, we stopped our hike for lunch beside a beautiful little river pool that was catching the flows from a long but gentle waterfall. My brother, Rambob, passed me a piece of jerky. I took my boots off, then slowly dunked my feet into the cool, foaming water.

I was gazing at a towering peak across a canyon, when suddenly, Wham! There was a quick jolt at the heel of my right foot. I pulled my foot out of the water and incredibly, a trout had bitten it.

My brother looked at me like I had antlers growing out of my head. "Wow!" he exclaimed. "That trout almost caught himself an outdoors writer!"

It's true that in remote areas trout sometimes bite on almost anything, even feet. On one high-country trip, I have caught limits of trout using nothing but a bare hook. The only problem is that the fish will often hit the splitshot sinker instead of the hook. Of course, fishing isn't usually that easy. But it gives you an idea of what is possible.

America's wildlands are home for a remarkable abundance of fish and wildlife. Deer browse with little fear of man, bears keep an eye out for your food, and little critters like squirrels and chipmunks are daily companions. Add in the fishing and you've got yourself a camping trip.

Your camping adventures will evolve into premium outdoor experiences if you can work in a few good fishing trips, avoid bear problems, and occasionally add a little offbeat fun with some camp games.

Trout and Bass

He creeps up on the stream as quiet as an Indian scout, keeping his shadow off the water. With his little spinning rod, he'll zip his lure within an inch or two of its desired mark, probing along rocks, the edges of riffles, pocket water or wherever he can find a change in river habitat. It's my brother, Rambob, trout fishing, and he's a master at it.

In most cases, he'll catch a trout on his first or second cast. After that it's time to move up the river, giving no spot much more than five minutes due. Stick and move, stick and move, stalking the stream like a bobcat zeroing in on an unsuspecting rabbit. He might keep a few trout for dinner, but mostly he releases what he catches. Rambob doesn't necessarily fish for food. It's the feeling that comes with it.

Fishing can give you a sense of exhilaration, like taking a hot shower after being coated with dust. On your walk back to camp, the steps come easy. You suddenly understand what John Muir meant when he talked of developing a oneness with nature, because you have it. That's what fishing can provide.

You don't need a million dollars worth of fancy gear to catch fish. What you need is the right outlook, and that can be learned. That goes regardless of whether you are fishing for trout or bass, the two most popular fisheries in America. Your fishing tackle selection should be as simple and as clutter-free as possible.

At home, I've got every piece of fishing tackle you might imagine, more than 30 rods and many tackle boxes, racks and cabinets filled with all kinds of stuff. I've got one lure that looks like a chipmunk and another that resembles a miniature can of beer with hooks. If I hear of something new, I want to try it, and usually do. It's a result of my lifelong fascination with the sport.

But if you just want to catch fish, there's an easier way to go. And when I go fishing, I take that path. I don't try to bring everything. It would be impossible. Instead, I bring a relatively small amount of gear. At home I will scan my tackle boxes for equipment and lures, make my selections and bring just the essentials. Rod, reel and tackle will fit into a side pocket of my backpack or a small carrying bag.

So what kind of rod should be used on an outdoor trip? For most camper/anglers, I suggest the use of a light, multi-piece spinning rod that will break down to a small size. One of the best deals on the fishing market is the six-piece Daiwa 6.5-foot pack rod, No. 6752. It retails for as low as $30, yet is made of a graphite/glass composite that gives it the quality of a much more expensive model. And it comes in a hard plastic carrying tube for protection. Other major rod manufacturers, such as Fenwick, offer similar premium rods. It's tough to miss with any of them.

The use of graphite/glass composites in fishing rods has made them lighter and more sensitive, yet stronger. The only downside to graphite as a rod material is that it can be brittle. If you rap your rod against something, it can crack or cause a weak spot. That weak spot can eventually snap when under even light pressure, like setting a hook or casting. Of course, a bit of care will prevent that from ever occurring.

If you haven't bought a fishing reel in some time, you will be surprised at the quality and price of micro spinning reels on the market. The reels come tiny and strong, with rear-control drag systems. Sigma, Shimano, Cardinal, Abu and others all make premium reels. They're worth it. With your purchase, you've just bought a reel that will last for years and years.

The one downside to spinning reels is that after long-term use, the bail spring will weaken. The result is that after casting and beginning to reel, the bail will sometimes not flip over and allow the reel to retrieve the line. Then you have to do it by hand. This can be incredibly frustrating, particularly when stream fishing, where instant line pickup is essential. The solution is to have a new bail spring installed every few years. This is a cheap, quick operation for a tackle expert.

You might own a giant tackle box filled with lures, but on your fishing trip you are better off to fit just the essentials into a small container. One of the best ways to do that is to use the Plano Micro-Magnum 3414, a tiny two-sided tackle box for trout fishermen that fits into a shirt pocket. In mine, I can fit 20 lures in one side of the box and 20 flies, splitshot and snap swivels in the other. For bass lures, which are larger, you need a slightly larger box, but the same principle applies.

There are more fishing lures on the market than you can imagine, but a few special ones can do the job. I make sure these are in my box on every trip. For trout, I carry a small black Panther Martin spinner with yellow spots, a small gold Kastmaster, a yellow Roostertail, a gold Z-Ray with red spots, a Super Duper, and a Mepps Lightning spinner.

You can take it a step further using insider's wisdom. My old pal Ed the Dunk showed me his trick of taking a tiny Dardevle spoon, then spray painting it flat black and dabbing five tiny red dots on it. It's a real killer, particularly in tiny streams where the trout are spooky.

The best trout catcher I've ever used on rivers is a small metal lure called a Met-L Fly. On days when nothing else works, it can be like going to a shooting gallery. The problem is that the lure is near impossible to find. Rambob and I consider the few we have remaining so valuable that if the lure is snagged on a rock, a cold swim is deemed mandatory for its retrieval. These lures are as hard to find in tackle shops as trout can be to catch without one.

For bass, you can also fit all you need into a small plastic tackle box. I have fished with many bass pros and all of them actually use just a few lures: a white spinner bait, a small jig called a Gits-It, a surface plug called a Zara Spook, and plastic worms. At times, like when the bass move into shoreline areas during the spring, shad minnow imitations like those made by Rebel or Rapala can be dynamite. My favorite is the one-inch blue-silver Rapala. Every spring, as the lakes begin to warm and the fish snap out of their winter doldrums, I like to float and paddle around in my small raft. I'll cast that little Rapala along the shoreline and catch and release hundreds of bass, bluegill and sunfish. The fish are usually sitting close to the shoreline, awaiting my offering.

Fishing Tips

There's an old angler's joke about how you need to "think like a fish." But if you're the one getting zilched, you may not think it's so funny.

The irony is that it is your mental approach, what you see and what you miss, that often determines your fishing luck. Some people will spend a lot of money on tackle, lures and fishing clothes, and that done, just saunter up to a stream or lake, cast out and wonder why they are not catching fish. The answer is their mental outlook. They are not attuning themselves to their surroundings.

You must live on nature's level, not your own. Try this and you will become aware of things you never believed even existed. Soon you will see things that will allow you to catch fish. You can get a head start by reading about fishing, but to get your degree in fishing, you must attend the University of Nature.

On every fishing trip, regardless what you fish for, try to follow three hard-and-fast rules:

1—Always approach the fishing spot so you will be undetected.

2—Present your lure, fly or bait in a manner so it appears completely natural, as if no line was attached.

3—Stick and move, hitting one spot, working it the best you can, then move to the next.

Here's a more detailed explanation.

1—Approach: No one can just walk up to a stream or lake, cast out and start catching fish as if someone had waved a magic wand. Instead, give the fish credit for being smart. After all, they live there.

Your approach must be completely undetected by the fish. Fish can sense your presence through sight and sound, though this is misinterpreted by most people. By sight, this rarely means the fish actually see you, but more likely, they will see your shadow on the water, or the movement of your arm or rod while casting. By sound, it doesn't mean they hear you talking, but that they will detect the vibrations of your footsteps along the shore, kicking a rock, or the unnatural plunking sound of a heavy cast hitting the water. Any of these elements can spook them off the bite. In order to fish undetected, you must walk softly, keep your shadow off the water, and keep your casting motion low. All of these keys become easier at sunrise or sunset, when shadows are on the water. At midday, a high sun causes a high level of light penetration in the water, which can make the fish skittish to any foreign presence.

Like hunting, you must stalk the spots. When my brother Rambob sneaks up on a fishing spot, he is like a burglar sneaking through an unlocked window.

2—Presentation: Your lure, fly or bait must appear in the water as if no line was attached, so it appears as natural as possible. My pal Mo Furniss has skin-dived in rivers to watch what the fish see when somebody is fishing.

"You wouldn't believe it," he said. "When the lure hits the water, every trout within 40 feet, like 15, 20 trout, will do a little zigzag. They all see the lure and are aware something is going on. Meanwhile, onshore the guy casting doesn't get a bite and thinks there aren't any fish in the river."

If your offering is aimed at fooling a fish into striking, it must appear as part of its natural habitat, as if it is an insect just hatched or a small fish looking for a spot to hide. That's where you come in.

After you have snuck up on a fishing spot, you should zip your cast upstream, then start your retrieve as soon as it hits the water. If you let the lure sink to the bottom, then start the retrieve, you have no chance. A minnow, for instance, does not sink to the bottom then start swimming. On rivers, the retrieve should be more of a drift, as if the "minnow" was in trouble and the current was sweeping it downstream.

When fishing on trout streams, always hike and cast up river, then retrieve as the offering drifts downstream in the current. This is effective because trout will sit almost motionless, pointed upstream, finning against the current. This way they can see anything coming their direction, and if a potential food morsel arrives, all they need to do is move over a few inches, open their mouths, and they've got an easy lunch. Thus you must cast upstream.

Conversely, if you cast downstream, your retrieve will bring the lure from behind the fish, where he cannot see it approaching. And I've never seen a trout that had eyes in its tail. In addition, when retrieving a downstream lure, the river current will tend to sweep your lure inshore to the rocks.

3—Finding spots: A lot of fishermen don't catch fish and a lot of hikers never see any wildlife. The key is where they are looking.

The rule of the wild is that fish and wildlife will congregate wherever there is a distinct change in the habitat. This is where you should begin your search. To find deer, for instance, forget probing a thick forest, but look for when it breaks into a meadow, or a clear-cut has splayed a stand of trees. That's where the deer will be.

In a river, it can be where a riffle pours into a small pool, a rapid that plunges into a deep hole and flattens, a big boulder in the middle of a long riffle, a shoreline point, a rock pile, a submerged tree. Look for the changes. Conversely, long straight stretches of shoreline will not hold fish—the habitat is lousy.

On rivers, the most productive areas are often where short riffles tumble into small oxygenated pools. After sneaking up from the downstream side and staying low, you should zip your cast so the lure plops gently in the white water just above the pool. Starting your retrieve instantly, the lure will drift downstream and plunk into the pool. Bang! That's where the trout will hit. Take a few more casts, then head upstream to the next spot.

With a careful approach and lure presentation, and by fishing in the right spots, you have the ticket to many exciting days on the water.

Of Bears and Food

The first time you come nose-to-nose with a bear, it can make your skin quiver.

Even the sight of mild-mannered black bears, the most common bear in America, can send shock waves through your body. They range from 250 to 400 pounds and have large claws and teeth that are made to scare campers. When they bound, the muscles on their shoulders roll like ocean breakers.

Bears in camping areas are accustomed to sharing the mountains with hikers and campers. They have become specialists in the food-raiding business. As a result, you must be able to make a bear-proof food hang, or be able to scare the fellow off. Many campgrounds provide bear- and raccoon-proof food lockers. You can also stash your food in your vehicle, but that limits the range of your trip.

If you are staying at one of the easy backpack sites listed in this book, there will be no food lockers available. (The exceptions are the High Sierra camps in Yosemite National Park, where rangers have placed high wires for food hangs, the next best thing to food lockers.) Your car will not be there, either. The solution is to make a bear-proof food hang, suspending all of your food wrapped in a plastic garbage bag from a rope in midair, 10 feet from the trunk of a tree and 20 feet off the ground. (Counter-balancing two bags with a rope thrown over a tree limb is very effective, but finding an appropriate limb can be difficult.)

This is accomplished by tying a rock to a rope, then throwing it over a high but sturdy tree limb. Next, tie your food bag to the rope, and hoist it up in the air. When you are satisfied with the position of the food bag, tie off the end of the rope to another tree. In an area frequented by bears, a good food bag is a necessity—nothing else will do.

I've been there. On one trip, my pal Foonsky and my brother Rambob had left to fish, and I was stoking up an evening campfire when I felt the eyes of an intruder on my back. I turned around and this big bear was heading straight for our camp. In the next half hour, I scared the bear off twice, but then he got a whiff of something sweet in my brother's pack.

The bear rolled into camp like a semi truck, grabbed my brother's pack, ripped it open, and plucked out the Tang and the Swiss Miss. The 350-pounder then sat astride a nearby log and lapped at the goodies like a thirsty dog drinking water.

Once a bear gets his mitts on your gear, he considers it his. I took two steps toward the pack and that bear jumped off the log and galloped across the camp right at me. Scientists say a man can't outrun a bear, but they've never seen how fast I can go up a granite block with a bear on my tail.

Shortly thereafter, Foonsky returned to find me perched on top of the rock, and demanded to know how I could let a bear get our Tang. It took all three of us, Foonsky, Rambob, and myself, charging at once and shouting like madmen, to clear the bear out of the camp and send him off over the ridge. We learned never to let food sit unattended.

The Grizzly

When it comes to grizzlies, well, my friends, you need what we call an "attitude adjustment." Or that big ol' bear may just decide to adjust your attitude for you, making your stay at the park a short one.

Grizzlies are nothing like black bears. They are bigger, stronger, have little fear and take what they want. Some people believe there are many different species of this critter, like Alaskan brown, silvertip, cinnamon and Kodiak, but the truth is they are all grizzlies. Any difference in appearance has to do with diet, habitat and life habits, not speciation. By any name, they all come big.

The first thing you must do is determine if there are grizzlies in the area where you are camping. That can usually be done by asking local rangers. If you are heading into Yellowstone or Glacier National Park, or the Bob Marshall Wilderness of Montana, well, you don't have to ask. They're out there, and they're the biggest and potentially most dangerous critters you could run into.

One general way to figure the size of a bear is from his footprint. Take the width of the footprint in inches, add one to it—and you'll have an estimated length of the bear in feet. For instance, a nine-inch footprint equals a 10-foot bear. Any bear that big is a grizzly, my friends. In fact, most grizzly footprints average about nine to ten inches across, and black bears (though they may be brown in color) tend to have footprints only four-and-a-half to six inches across.

If you are hiking in a wilderness area that may have grizzlies, then it becomes a necessity to wear bells on your pack. That way, the bear will hear you coming and likely get out of your way. Keep talking, singing or maybe even debating the country's foreign policy, but whatever, do not fall into a silent hiking vigil. And if a breeze is blowing in your face, you must make even more noise (a good excuse to rant and rave about the government's domestic affairs). Noise is important, because your smell will not be carried in the direction you are hiking. As a result, the bear will not smell you coming.

If a bear can hear you and smell you, it will tend to get out of the way and let you pass without your knowing it was even close by. The exception is if you are carrying fish or lots of sweets in your pack, or if you are wearing heavy, sweet deodorants or makeup. All three are bear attractants.

Most encounters with grizzlies occur when hikers fall into a silent march in the wilderness with the wind in their faces, and they walk around a corner and right into a big, unsuspecting grizzly. If you do this, and see a big hump just behind its neck, well, don't think twice: It's a grizzly.

And then what should you do? Get up a tree, that's what. Grizzlies are so big that their claws cannot support their immense weight, and thus they cannot climb trees. And although their young can climb, they rarely want to get their mitts on you.

If you do get grabbed, every instinct in your body will tell you to fight back. Don't believe it. Play dead. Go limp. Let the bear throw you around a little, because after awhile you become unexciting play material, and the bear will get bored. My grandmother was grabbed by a grizzly in Glacier National Park and after a few tosses and hugs, was finally left alone to escape.

Some say it's a good idea to tuck your head under his chin, since that way, the bear will be unable to bite your head. I'll take a pass on that one. If you are taking action, any action, it's a signal that you are a force to be reckoned with, and he'll likely respond with more aggression. And bears don't lose many wrestling matches.

What grizzlies really like to do, believe it or not, is to pile a lot of sticks and leaves on you. Just let them, and keep perfectly still. Don't fight them; don't run. And when you have a 100-percent chance (not 98 or 99) to dash up a nearby tree, that's when you let fly. Once safely in a tree, then you can hurl down insults and let your aggression out.

In a wilderness camp, there are special precautions you should take. Always hang your food at least 100 yards downwind of your camp and get it high, 30 feet is reasonable. In addition, circle your camp with rope, and hang the bells from your pack on it. Thus, if a bear walks into your camp, he'll run into your rope, the bells will ring, and everybody will have a chance to get up a tree before ol' griz figures out what's going on. Often, the unexpected ringing of bells is enough to send him off in search of a quieter environment.

You see, more often than not, grizzlies tend to clear the way for campers and hikers. So, be smart, don't act like bear bait, and always have a plan if you are confronted by one.

My pal Foonsky had such a plan during a wilderness expedition in Montana's northern Rockies. On our second day of hiking, we started seeing scratch marks on the trees, 13 to 14 feet off the ground.

"Mr. Griz made those," Foonsky said. "With spring here, the grizzlies are coming out of hibernation and using the trees like a cat uses a scratch board to stretch the muscles."

The next day, I noticed Foonsky had a pair of track shoes tied to the back of his pack. I just laughed.

"You're not going to outrun a griz," I said. "In fact, there's hardly any animals out here in the wilderness that man can outrun."

Foonsky just smiled.

"I don't have to outrun a griz," he said. "I just have to outrun you!"

Fun and Games

"Now what are we supposed to do?" the young boy asked his dad.

"Yeah, Dad, think of something," said another son.

Well, Dad thought hard. This was one of the first camping trips he'd taken with his sons and one of the first lessons he received was that kids don't appreciate the philosophic release of mountain quiet. They want action, and lots of it. With a glint in his eye, Dad searched around the camp and picked up 15 twigs, breaking them so each was four inches long. He laid them in three separate rows, three twigs in one row, five twigs in another, and seven in the other.

"OK, this game is called 3-5-7," said dad. "You each take turns picking up sticks. You are allowed to remove all or as few as one twig from a row, but here's the catch: You can only pick from one row per turn. Whoever picks up the last stick left is the loser."

I remember this episode well because those two little boys were my brother Bobby, as in Rambobby, and me. And to this day, we still play 3-5-7 on campouts, with the winner getting to watch the loser clean the dishes. What I have learned in the span of time since that original episode is that it does not matter what your age is: Campers need options for camp fun.

Some evenings, after a long hike or ride, you are likely to feel too worn-out to take on a serious romp downstream to fish, or a climb up to a ridge for a view. That is especially true if you have been in the outback for a week or more. At that point a lot of campers will spend their time resting and gazing at a map of the area, dreaming of the next day's adventure, or just take a seat against a rock, watching the colors of the sky and mountain panorama change minute-by-minute. But kids in the push-button video era, and a lot of adults too, want more. After all, "I'm on vacation; I want some fun."

There are several options, like the 3-5-7 twig game, and they should be just as much a part of your pre-trip planning as arranging your gear.

For kids, plan on games, the more physically challenging the competition, the better. One of the best games is to throw a chunk of wood into a lake, then challenge the kids to hit it by throwing rocks. It wreaks havoc on the fishing, but it can keep kids totally absorbed for some time. Target practice with a wrist-rocket slingshot is also all-consuming for kids, firing rocks away at small targets like pine cones set on a log.

You can also set kids off on little missions near camp, like looking for the footprints of wildlife, searching out good places to have a "snipe hunt," picking up twigs to get the evening fire started, or having them take the water purifier to a stream to pump some drinking water into a canteen. The latter is an easy, fun, yet important task that will allow kids to feel a sense of equality they often don't get at home.

For adults, the appeal should be more to the intellect. A good example is star and planet identification, and while you are staring into space, you're bound to spot a few asteroids, or shooting stars. A star chart can make it easy to locate and identify many distinctive stars and constellations, such as Pleiades (the Seven Sisters), Orion and others from the zodiac, depending on the time of year. With a little research, this can add a unique perspective to your trip. You could point to Polaris, one of the most easily identified of all stars, and note that navigators in the 1400s used it to find their way. Polaris, of course, is the "North Star," and is at the end of the handle of the Little Dipper. Pinpointing Polaris is quite easy. First find the Big Dipper, then locate the outside stars of the ladle of the Big Dipper. They are called the "Pointer Stars" because they point right at Polaris.

A tree identification book can teach you a few things about your surroundings. It is also a good idea for one member of the party to research the history of the area you have chosen and another to research the geology. With shared knowledge, you end up with a deeper love of wild places.

Another way to add some recreation into your trip is to bring a board game, a number of which have been miniaturized for campers. The most popular are chess, checkers and cribbage. The latter comes with an equally miniature set of playing cards. And if you bring those little cards, that opens a vast set of other possibilities. With kids along, for instance, just take the Queen of Clubs out of the deck and you can instantly play Old Maid.

But there are more serious card games and they come with high stakes. Such occurred on one high country trip where Foonsky, Rambob and myself sat down for a late afternoon game of poker. In a game of seven-card stud, I caught a straight on the sixth card and felt like a dog licking on a T-bone. Already, I had bet several Skittles and peanut M&Ms on this promising hand.

Then I examined the cards Foonsky had face up. He was showing three sevens, and acting as happy as a grizzly with a pork chop, like he had a full house. He matched my bet of two peanut M&Ms, then raised me three SweetTarts, one Starburst and one sour apple Jolly Rancher. Rambob folded, but I matched Foonsky's bet and hoped for the best as the seventh and final card was dealt.

Just after Foonsky glanced at that last card, I saw him sneak a look at my grape stick and beef jerky stash.

"I raise you a grape stick," he said.

Rambob and I both gasped. It was the highest bet ever made, equivalent to a million dollars laid down in Las Vegas. Cannons were going off in my chest. I looked hard at my cards. They looked good, but were they good enough?

Even with a great hand like I had, a grape stick was too much to gamble, my last one with 10 days of trail ahead of us. I shook my head and folded my cards. Foonsky smiled at his victory.

But I still had my grape stick.

Old Tricks Don't Always Work

Most people are born honest, but after a few camping trips, they usually get over it.

I remember some advice I got from Rambob, normally an honest soul, on one camping trip. A giant mosquito had landed on my arm and he alerted me to some expert advice.

"Flex your arm muscles," he commanded, watching the mosquito fill with my blood. "He'll get stuck in your arm, then he'll explode."

For some unknown reason, I believed him. We both proceeded to watch the mosquito drill countless holes in my arm.

Alas, the unknowing face sabotage from their most trusted companions on camping trips. It can arise at any time, usually in the form of advice from a friendly, honest-looking face, as if to say, "What? How can you doubt me?" After that mosquito episode, I was a little more skeptical of my dear old brother. Then, the next day, when another mosquito was nailing me in the back of the neck, out came this gem:

"Hold your breath," he commanded. I instinctively obeyed. "That will freeze the mosquito," he said, "then you can squish him."

But in the time I wasted holding my breath, the little bugger was able to fly off without my having the satisfaction of squishing him. When he got home, he probably told his family, "What a dummy I got to drill today!"

Over the years, I have been duped numerous times with dubious advice:

On a grizzly bear attack: "If he grabs you, tuck your head under the grizzly's chin, then he won't be able to bite you in the head." This made sense to me until the first time I looked face-to-face with a nine-foot grizzly, 40 yards away. In seconds, I was at the top of a tree, which suddenly seemed to make the most sense.

On coping with animal bites: "If a bear bites you in the arm, don't try to jerk it away. That will just rip up your arm. Instead force your arm deeper into his mouth. He'll lose his grip and will have to open it to get a firmer hold, and right then you can get away." I was told this in the Boy Scouts, and when I was 14, I had a chance to try it out when a friend's dog bit me when I tried to pet it. What happened? When I shoved my arm deeper into his mouth, he bit me about three extra times.

On cooking breakfast: "The bacon will curl up every time in a camp frying pan. So make sure you have a bacon stretcher to keep it flat." As a 12-year-old Tenderfoot, I spent two hours looking for the bacon stretcher until I figured out the camp leader had forgotten it. It wasn't for several years until I learned that there is no such thing.

On preventing sore muscles: "If you haven't hiked for a long time and you are facing a rough climb, you can keep from getting sore muscles in your legs, back and shoulders by practicing the 'Dead Man's Walk.' Simply let your entire body go slack, and then take slow, wobbling steps. This will clear your muscles of lactic acid, which causes them to be so sore after a rough hike." Foonsky pulled this one on me. Rambob and I both bought it, then tried it while we were hiking up Mount Whitney, which requires a 6,000-foot elevation gain in six miles. In one 45-minute period, about 30 other hikers passed us and looked at us as if we were suffering from some rare form of mental aberration.

Fish won't bite? No problem: "If the fish are not feeding or will not bite, persistent anglers can still catch dinner with little problem. Keep casting across the current, and eventually, as they hover in the stream, the line will feed across their open mouths. Keep reeling and you will hook the fish right in the side of the mouth. This technique is called 'lining.' Never worry if the fish will not bite, because you can always line 'em." Of course, heh, heh, heh, that explains why so many fish get hooked in the side of the mouth.

How to keep bears away: "To keep bears away, urinate around the borders of your campground. If there are a lot of bears in the area, it is advisable to go right on your sleeping bag." Yeah, surrrrrre.

What to do with trash: "Don't worry about packing out trash. Just bury it. It will regenerate into the earth and add valuable minerals." Bears, raccoons, skunks and other critters will dig up your trash as soon as you depart, leaving one huge mess for the next camper. Always pack out everything.

Often the advice comes without warning. That was the case after a fishing trip with a female companion, when she outcaught me two-to-one, the third such trip in a row. I explained this to a shopkeeper, and he nodded, then explained why.

"The male fish are able to detect the female scent on the lure, and thus become aroused into striking."

Of course! That explains everything!

Getting Revenge

I was just a lad when Foonsky pulled the old snipe-hunt trick on me. It's taken 30 years to get revenge.

You probably know about snipe hunting. That is where the victim is led out at night in the woods by a group, then is left holding a bag.

"Stay perfectly still and quiet," Foonsky explained. "You don't want to scare the snipe. The rest of us will go back to camp and let the woods settle down. Then when the snipe are least expecting it, we'll form a line and charge through the forest with sticks, beating bushes and trees, and we'll flush the snipe out right to you. Be ready with the bag. When we flush the snipe out, bag it. But until we start our charge, make sure you don't move or make a sound or you will spook the snipe and ruin everything."

I sat out there in the woods with my bag for hours, waiting for the charge. I waited, waited and waited. Nothing happened. No charge, no snipe. It wasn't until well past midnight that I figured something was wrong. When I finally returned to camp, everybody was sleeping.

Well, I tell ya, don't get mad at your pals for the tricks they pull on you. Get revenge. Some 25 years later, on the last day of a camping trip, the time finally came.

"Let's break camp early," Foonsky suggested to Mr. Furnai and me. "Get up before dawn, eat breakfast, pack up, then be on the ridge to watch the sun come up. It will be a fantastic way to end the trip."

"Sounds great to me," I replied. But when Foonsky wasn't looking, I turned his alarm clock ahead three hours. So when the alarm sounded at the appointed 4:30 a.m. wakeup time, Mr. Furnai and I knew it was actually only 1:30 a.m.

Foonsky clambered out of his sleeping bag and whistled with a grin. "Time to break camp."

"You go ahead," I answered. "I'll skip breakfast so I can get a little more sleep. At the first sign of dawn, wake me up, and I'll break camp."

"Me too," said Mr. Furnai.

Foonsky then proceeded to make coffee, cook a breakfast and eat it, sitting on a log in the black darkness of the forest, waiting for the sun to come up. An hour later, with still no sign of dawn, he checked his clock. It now read 5:30 a.m. "Any minute now we should start seeing some light," he said.

He made another cup of coffee, packed his gear and sat there in the middle of the night, looking up at the stars, waiting for dawn. "Anytime now," he said. He ended up sitting there all night long.

Revenge is sweet. Prior to a fishing trip at a lake, I took Foonsky aside and explained that the third member of the party, Jimbobo, was hard of hearing and very sensitive about it. "Don't mention it to him," I advised. "Just talk real loud."

Meanwhile, I had already told Jimbobo the same thing. "Foonsky just can't hear very good."

We had fished less than 20 minutes when Foonsky got a nibble.

"GET A BITE?" shouted Jimbobo.

"YEAH!" yelled back Foonsky, smiling. "BUT I DIDN'T HOOK HIM!"

"MAYBE NEXT TIME!" shouted Jimbobo with a friendly grin.

Well, they spent the entire day yelling at each other from the distance of a few feet. They never did figure it out. Heh, heh, heh.

That is, I thought so, until we made a trip salmon fishing. I got a strike that almost knocked my fishing rod out of the boat. When I grabbed the rod, it felt like Moby Dick was on the other end. "At least a 25-pounder," I said. "Maybe bigger."

The fish dove, ripped off line and then bulldogged. "It's acting like a 40-pounder," I announced, "Huge, just huge. It's going deep. That's how the big ones fight."

Some 15 minutes later, I finally got the "salmon" to the surface. It turned out to be a coffee can that Foonsky had clipped on the line with a snap swivel. By maneuvering the boat, he made the coffee can fight like a big fish.

This all started with a little old snipe hunt years ago. You never know what your pals will try next. Don't get mad. Get revenge!

CAMPING OPTIONS

Boat-in Seclusion

Most campers would never think of trading in their car, pickup truck or motor home for a boat, but people who go by boat on a camping trip have a virtual guarantee of seclusion and top-quality outdoor experiences.

Camping with a boat is a do-it-yourself venture in living in primitive circumstances. Yet at the same time you can bring along any luxury item you wish, from giant coolers, stoves and lanterns to portable gasoline generators. Weight is almost never an issue.

In California, many outstanding boat-in campgrounds are available in many beautiful areas. The best are on the shores of lakes accessible by canoe or skiff, and at offshore islands reached by saltwater cruisers. Several boat-in camps are detailed in this book.

If you want to take the adventure a step further and create your own boat-in camp, perhaps near a special fishing spot, this is a go-for-it deal that provides the best way possible to establish your own secret campsite. But most people who set out free-lance style forget three critical items for boat-in camping: a shovel, a sunshade and an ax. Here is why these three items can make a key difference in your trip:

1—A shovel: Many lakes and virtually all reservoirs have steep, sloping banks. At reservoirs subject to drawdowns, what was lake bottom in the spring can be a prospective campsite in late summer. If you want a flat area for a tent site, the only answer is to dig one out yourself. A shovel gives you that option.

2—A sunshade: The flattest spots to camp along lakes often have a tendency to support only sparse tree growth. As a result, a natural shield from sun and rain is rarely available. What? Rain in the summer? Oh yeah, don't get me started. A light tarp, set up with poles and staked ropes, solves the problem.

3—An ax: Unless you bring your own firewood, which is necessary at some sparsely wooded reservoirs, there is no substitute for a good, sharp ax. With an ax, you can almost always find dry firewood, since the interior of an otherwise wet log will be dry. When the weather turns bad is precisely when you will most want a fire. You may need an ax to get one going.

In the search to create your own personal boat-in campsite, you will find that the flattest areas are usually the tips of peninsulas and points, while the protected back ends of coves are often steeply sloped. At reservoirs, the flattest areas are usually near the mouths of the feeder streams, and the points are quite steep. On rivers, there are usually sand bars on the inside of tight bends that make for ideal campsites.

At boat-in campsites developed by government agencies, virtually all are free of charge, but you are on your own. Only in extremely rare cases is piped water available.

Any way you go, by canoe, skiff or power cruiser, you end up with a one-in-a-million campsite you can call your own.

Desert Outings

It was a cold, snowy day in Missouri when 10-year-old Rusty Ballinger started dreaming about the vast deserts of the West.

"My dad was reading aloud from a Zane Grey book called *Riders of the Purple Sage*," Ballinger said. "He would get animated when he got to the passages about the desert. It wasn't long before I started to have the same feelings."

That was in 1947. Ballinger, now in his 50s, has spent a good part of his life exploring the West, camping along the way. "The deserts are the best part. There's something about the uniqueness of each little area you see," Ballinger said. "You're constantly surprised. Just the time of day and the way the sun casts a different color. It's like the lady you care about. One time she smiles, the next time she's pensive. The desert is like that. If you love nature, you can love the desert. After awhile, you can't help but love it."

A desert adventure is not just an antidote for a case of cabin fever in the winter. Whether you go by motor home, pickup truck, car or on foot, it provides its own special qualities.

If you go camping in the desert, your approach has to be as unique as the setting. For starters, don't plan on any campfires, but bring a camp stove instead. And unlike in the mountains, do not camp near a water hole. The reason is an animal, like a badger, coyote or desert bighorn might be desperate for water, and if you set up camp in the animal's way, you may be forcing a confrontation.

In some areas, there is a danger of flash floods. An intense rain can fall in one area, collect in a pool, then suddenly burst through a narrow canyon. If you are in its path, you could be injured or drowned. The lesson? Never camp in a gully.

"Some people might wonder, 'What good is this place?'" Ballinger said. "The answer is that it is good for looking at. It is one of the world's unique places."

GETTING ALONG

The most important thing about a camping, fishing or hunting trip is not where you go, how many fish you catch or how many shots you fire. It often has little to do with how beautiful the view is, how easy the campfire lights, or how sunny the days are.

Oh yeah? Then what is the most important factor? The answer: The people you are with. It is that simple.

Who would you rather camp with? Your enemy at work or your dream mate in a good mood? Heh, heh. You get the idea. A camping trip is a fairly close-knit experience, and you can make lifetime friends or lifelong enemies in the process. That is why your choice of companions is so important. Your own behavior is equally consequential.

Yet most people spend more time putting together their camping gear than considering why they enjoy or hate the company of their chosen companions. Here are rules of behavior for good camping mates:

1—No whining: Nothing is more irritating than being around a whiner. It goes right to the heart of adventure, since often the only difference between a hardship and an escapade is simply whether or not an individual has the spirit for it. The people who do can turn a rugged day in the outdoors into a cherished memory. Those who don't can ruin it with their incessant sniveling.

2—Activities must be agreed upon: Always have a meeting of the minds with your companions over the general game plan. Then everybody will possess an equal stake in the outcome of the trip. This is absolutely critical. Otherwise they will feel like merely an addendum to your trip, not an equal participant, and a whiner will be born (see No. 1).

3—Nobody's in charge: It is impossible to be genuine friends if one person is always telling another what to do, especially if the orders involve simple camp tasks. You need to share the space on the same emotional plane, and the only way to do that is to have a semblance of equality, regardless of differences in experience. Just try ordering your mate around at home for a few days. You'll quickly see the results, and they aren't nice.

4—Equal chances at the fun stuff: It's fun to build the fire, fun to get the first cast at the best fishing spot, and fun to hoist the bagged food for a bear-proof food hang. It is not fun to clean the dishes, collect firewood, or cook every night. So obviously, there must be an equal distribution of the fun stuff and the not-fun stuff, and everybody on the trip must get a shot at the good and the bad.

5—No heroes: No awards are bestowed for achievement in the outdoors, yet some guys treat mountain peaks, big fish and big game as if they are a trophy competition. Actually, nobody cares how wonderful you are, which is always a surprise to trophy chasers. What people care about is the heart of the adventure, the gut-level stuff.

6—Agree on a wakeup time: It is a good idea to agree on a general wakeup time before closing your eyes for the night, and that goes regardless of whether you want to sleep in late or get up at dawn. Then you can proceed on course regardless of what time you crawl out of your sleeping bag in the morning, without the risk of whining (see No. 1).

7—Think of the other guy: Be self-aware instead of self-absorbed. A good test is to count the number of times you say, "What do you think?" A lot of potential problems can be solved quickly by actually listening to the answer.

8—Solo responsibilities: There are a number of essential camp duties on all trips, and while they should be shared equally, most should be completed solo. That means that when it is time for you to cook, you don't have to worry about me changing the recipe on you. It means that when it is my turn to make the fire, you keep your mitts out of it.

9—Don't let money get in the way: Of course everybody should share equally in trip expenses, such as the cost of food, and it should be split up before you head out yonder. Don't let somebody pay extra, because that person will likely try to control the trip. Conversely, don't let somebody weasel out of paying a fair share.

10—Accordance on the food plan: Always have complete agreement on what you plan to eat each day. Don't figure that just because you like Steamboat's Sludge, everybody else will, too, especially youngsters. Always, always, always check for food allergies such as nuts, onions, or cheese, and make sure each person brings their own personal coffee brand. Some people drink only decaffeinated; others might gag on anything but Burma monkey beans.

Obviously, it is difficult to find companions who will agree on all of these elements. This is why many campers say that the best camping buddy they'll ever have is their mate, someone who knows all about them and likes them anyway.

Outdoors With Kids

How do you get a boy or girl excited about the outdoors? How do you compete with the television and remote control? How do you prove to a kid that success comes from persistence, spirit and logic, which the outdoors teaches, and not from pushing buttons?

The answer is in the Ten Camping Commandments for Kids. These are lessons that will get youngsters excited about the outdoors, and will make sure adults help the process along, not kill it. Some are obvious, some are not, but all are important:

1—Trips with children should be to places where there is a guarantee of action. A good example is camping in a park where large numbers of wildlife can be viewed, such as squirrels, chipmunks, deer and even bear. Other good choices are fishing at a small pond loaded with bluegill, or hunting in a spot where a kid can shoot a .22 at pine cones all day. Boys and girls want action, not solitude.

2—Enthusiasm is contagious. If you aren't excited about an adventure, you can't expect a child to be. Show a genuine zest for life in the outdoors, and point out everything as if it is the first time you have ever seen it.

3—Always, always, always be seated when talking to someone small. This allows the adult and child to be on the same level. That is why fishing in a small boat is perfect for adults and kids. Nothing is worse for youngsters than having a big person look down at them and give them orders. What fun is that?

4—Always show how to do something, whether it is gathering sticks for a campfire, cleaning a trout or tying a knot. Never tell— always show. A button usually clicks to "off" when a kid is lectured. But they can learn behavior patterns and outdoor skills by watching adults, even when the adults are not aware they are being watched.

5—Let kids be kids. Let the adventure happen, rather than trying to force it within some preconceived plan. If they get sidetracked watching pollywogs, chasing butterflies or sneaking up on chipmunks, let them be. A youngster can have more fun turning over rocks and looking at different kinds of bugs that sitting in one spot, waiting for a fish to bite.

6—Expect young peoples' attention spans to be short. Instead of getting frustrated about it, use it to your advantage. How? By bringing along a bag of candy and snacks. Where there is a lull in the camp activity, out comes the bag. Don't let them know what goodies await, so each one becomes a surprise.

7—Make absolutely certain the child's sleeping bag is clean, dry and warm. Nothing is worse than discomfort when trying to sleep, but a refreshing sleep makes for a positive attitude the next day. In addition, kids can become quite scared of animals at night. The parent should not wait for any signs of this, but always play the part of the outdoor guardian, the one who will "take care of everything."

8—Kids quickly relate to outdoor ethics. They will enjoy eating everything they kill, building a safe campfire and picking up all their litter, and they will develop a sense of pride that goes with it. A good idea is to bring extra plastic garbage bags to pick up any trash you come across. Kids long remember when they do something right that somebody else has done wrong.

9—If you want youngsters hooked on the outdoors for life, take a close-up photograph of them holding up fish they have caught, blowing on the campfire or completing other camp tasks. Young children can forget how much fun they had, but they never forget if they have a picture of it.

10—The least important word you can ever say to a kid is "I." Keep track of how often you are saying "Thank you" and "What do you think?" If you don't say them very often, you'll lose out. Finally, the most important words of all are: "I am proud of you."

PREDICTING WEATHER

Foonsky climbed out of his sleeping bag, glanced at the nearby meadow and scowled hard.

"It doesn't look good," he said. "Doesn't look good at all."

I looked at my companion of 20 years of adventures, noted his discontent, and then I looked at the meadow and immediately understood why: *"When the grass is dry at morning light, look for rain before the night."*

"How bad you figure?" I asked him.

"We'll know soon enough, I reckon," Foonsky answered. "Short notice, soon to pass. Long notice, long it will last."

When you are out in the wild, spending your days fishing and your nights camping, you learn to rely on yourself for weather predictions. It can make or break you. If a storm hits the unprepared, it can quash the trip and possibly endanger the participants. If you are ready for it, what could be a hardship ends up as an added adventure.

You can't rely on TV weather forecasters either, people who don't even know that when all the cows on a hill are pointed north, it will rain that night for sure. God forbid if the cows are all sitting. But what do you expect from TV's talking heads?

Foonsky made a campfire, started boiling some water for coffee and soup, and we started to plan the day. In the process, I noticed the smoke of the campfire: It was sluggish, drifting and hovering.

"You notice the smoke?" I asked, chewing on a piece of home-made jerky.

"Not good," Foonsky said. "Not good." He knew that sluggish, hovering smoke indicates rain.

"You'd think we'd have been smart enough to know last night that this was coming," Foonsky said. "Did you take a look at the moon or the clouds?"

"I didn't look at either," I answered. "Too busy eating the trout we caught." You see, if the moon is clear and white, the weather will be good the next day. But if there is a ring around the moon, you can count the number of stars inside the ring, and that is how many days until the next rain. As for clouds, the high, thin clouds called cirrus indicate a change in the weather.

We were quiet for a while, planning our strategy, but while we did so, some terrible things happened: A chipmunk scattered past with his tail high, a small flock of geese flew by very low, and a little sparrow perched on a tree limb quite close to the trunk.

"We're in for trouble," I told Foonsky.

"I know, I know," he answered. "I saw 'em, too. And come to think of it, no crickets were chirping last night either."

"Damn, that's right!"

These are all signs of an approaching storm. Foonsky pointed at the smoke of the campfire and shook his head as if he had just been condemned. Sure enough, now the smoke was blowing towards the north, a sign of a south wind. *"When the wind is from the south, the rain is in its mouth."*

"We'd best stay hunkered down until it passes," Foonsky said.

I nodded. "Let's gather as much firewood now as we can, get our gear covered up, then plan our meals."

"Then we'll get a poker game going."

As we accomplished these camp tasks, the sky clouded up, then darkened. Within an hour, we had gathered enough firewood to make a large pile, enough wood to keep a fire going no matter how hard it rained. The day's meals had been separated out of the food bag, so it wouldn't have to be retrieved during the storm. We buttoned two ponchos together, staked two of the corners with ropes to the ground, and tied the other two with ropes to different tree limbs to create a slanted roof/shelter.

As the first raindrop fell with that magic sound on our poncho roof, Foonsky was just starting to shuffle the cards.

"Cut for deal," he said.

Just as I did so, it started to rain a bit harder. I pulled out another piece of beef jerky and started chewing on it. It was just another day in paradise…

Weather lore can be valuable. Small signs provided by nature and wildlife can be translated to provide a variety of weather information. Here is the list I have compiled over the years:

When the grass is dry at morning light,
Look for rain before the night.

Short notice, soon to pass.
Long notice, long it will last.

When the wind is from the east,
'Tis fit for neither man nor beast.
When the wind is from the south,
The rain is in its mouth.
When the wind is from the west,
Then it is the very best.

Red sky at night, sailors' delight.
Red sky in the morning, sailors take warning.

When all the cows are pointed north,
Within a day rain will come forth.

Onion skins very thin, mild winter coming in.
Onion skins very tough, winter's going to be very rough.

When your boots make the squeak of snow,
Then very cold temperatures will surely show.

If a goose flies high, fair weather ahead.
If a goose flies low, foul weather will come instead.

A thick coat on a woolly caterpillar means a big, early snow is coming.

Chipmunks will run with their tails up before a rain.

Bees always stay near their hives before a rainstorm.

When the birds are perched on large limbs near tree trunks, an intense but short storm will arrive.

On the coast, if groups of seabirds are flying a mile inland, look for major winds.

If crickets are chirping very loud during the evening, the next day will be clear and warm.

If the smoke of a campfire at night rises in a thin spiral, good weather is assured for the next day.
If the smoke of a campfire at night is sluggish, drifting and hovering, it will rain the next day.

If there is a ring around the moon, count the number of stars inside the ring, and that is how many days until the next rain.
If the moon is clear and white, the weather will be good the next day.

The high, thin clouds called cirrus indicate a change in the weather.
The oval-shaped clouds called lenticular indicate high winds.

Two different levels of clouds moving in different directions indicate changing weather soon.

Huge, dark billowing clouds called cumulonimbus, suddenly forming on warm afternoons in the mountains, mean that a short but intense thunderstorm with lightning can be expected.

When squirrels are busy gathering food for extended periods, it means good weather is ahead in the short term, but a hard winter is ahead in the long term.

And God forbid if all the cows are sitting down...

Keep It Wild

"Enjoy America's country and leave no trace." That is the motto of the Leave No Trace organization, and we strongly support it. The following list was developed from the policies of Leave No Trace, with their input and support for its publication. For a free, pocket-sized, weatherproof card printed with these policies, as well as information that details how to minimize human impact on wild areas, phone (800) 332-4100.

Plan ahead and prepare

1. Learn about the regulations and issues that apply to the area you are visiting.
2. Avoid heavy-use areas.
3. Obtain all maps and permits.
4. Bring extra garbage bags to pack out any refuse you come across.

Keep the wilderness wild

1. Let nature's sound prevail. Avoid loud voices and noises.
2. Leave radios and tape players at home. At drive-in camping sites, never open car doors with music playing.
3. Careful guidance is necessary when choosing any games to bring for children. Most toys, especially any kind of gun toys with which children simulate shooting at each other, should not be allowed on a camping trip.
4. Control pets at all times, or leave them with a sitter at home.
5. Treat natural heritage with respect. Leave plants, rocks and historical artifacts where you find them.

Respect other users

1. Horseback riders have priority over hikers. Step to the downhill side of the trail and talk softly when encountering horseback riders.
2. Hikers and horseback riders have priority over mountain bikers. When mountain bikers encounter other users, even on wide trails, they should pass at an extremely slow speed. On very narrow trails, they should dismount and get off to the side, so the hiker or horseback rider can pass without having their trip disrupted.
3. Mountain bikes are not permitted on most single-track trails and are expressly prohibited on all portions of the Pacific Crest Trail, in designated wilderness areas and on most state park trails. Mountain

bikers breaking these rules should be confronted, told to dismount and walk their bikes until they reach a legal area.

4. It is illegal for horseback riders to break off branches that may lay in the path of wilderness trails.
5. Horseback riders on overnight trips are prohibited from camping in many areas, and are usually required to keep stock animals in specific areas where they can do no damage to the landscape.

Travel lightly

1. Visit the backcountry in small groups.
2. Below tree line, always stay on designated trails.
3. Do not cut across switchbacks.
4. When traveling cross-country where no trails are available, follow animal trails or spread out with your group so no new routes are created.
5. Read your map and orient yourself with landmarks, a compass and altimeter. Avoid marking trails with rock cairns, tree scars or ribbons.

Camp with care

1. Choose a preexisting, legal site. Restrict activities to areas where vegetation is compacted or absent.
2. Camp at least 75 steps (200 feet) from lakes, streams and trails.
3. Always choose sites that will not be damaged by your stay.
4. Preserve the feeling of solitude by selecting camps that are out of view when possible.
5. Do not construct structures or furniture or dig trenches.

Campfires

1. Fire use can scar the backcountry. If a fire ring is not available, use a lightweight stove for cooking.
2. Where fires are permitted, use existing fire rings, away from large rocks or overhangs.
3. Do not char rocks by building new rings.
4. Gather sticks from the ground that are no larger than the diameter of your wrist.
5. Do not snap branches of live, dead or downed trees, which can cause personal injury and also scar the natural setting.
6. Put the fire "dead out" and make sure it is cold before departing. Remove all trash from the fire ring.
7. Remember that some forest fires can be started by a campfire that appears to be out. Hot embers burning deep in the pit can cause tree

roots to catch on fire and burn underground. If you ever see smoke rising from the ground, seemingly from nowhere, dig down and put the fire out.

Sanitation

If no refuse facility is available:

1. Deposit human waste in "cat holes" dug six to eight inches deep. Cover and disguise the cat hole when finished.
2. Deposit human waste at least 75 paces (200 feet) from any water source or camp.
3. Use toilet paper sparingly. When finished, carefully burn it in the cat hole, then bury it.
4. If no appropriate burial locations are available, such as in popular wilderness camps above tree line in hard granite settings—Devil's Punchbowl in the Siskiyou Wilderness is such an example—then all human refuse should be double-bagged and packed out.
5. At boat-in campsites, chemical toilets are required. Chemical toilets can also solve the problem of larger groups camping or long stays at one location where no facilities are available.
6. To wash dishes or your body, carry water away from the source and use small amounts of biodegradable soap. Scatter dishwater after all food particles have been removed.
7. Scour your campsites for even the tiniest piece of trash and any other evidence of your stay. Pack out all the trash you can, even if it's not yours. Finding cigarette butts, for instance, provides special irritation for most campers. Pick them up and discard them properly.
8. Never litter. Never. Or you become the enemy of all others.

RESOURCE GUIDE

Now you're ready to join the Five Percent Club, that is, the five percent of campers who know the secret spots where they can camp, fish and hike and have the time of their lives doing it.

To aid in that pursuit, there are a number of contacts, map sources and reservation systems available for your use. These include contacts for national forests, state parks, national parks, the Bureau of Land Management and motor home parks. The state and federal agencies listed can provide detailed maps at low cost and any additional information you might require.

National Forests

The Forest Service provides many secluded camps and permits camping anywhere except where it is specifically prohibited. If you ever want to clear the cobwebs and get away from it all, this is the way to go.

Many Forest Service campgrounds are quite remote and have no developed water. You don't need to check in, you don't need reservations and there is no fee. At many Forest Service campgrounds that provide piped water, the camp fee is often only a few dollars, with payment made on the honor system. Because most of these camps are in mountain areas, they are subject to closure for snow or mud during the winter.

Dogs are permitted in national forests at no extra charge and with no hassle. They must be on leashes in the campgrounds. Conversely, in state and national parks, dogs are not allowed on trails.

Some of the more popular camps in national forests can be reserved in advance. The phone number to make a reservation at these camps is (800) 280-2267 (CAMP). The fee to make a reservation is usually $7.50 to $7.75 for single sites.

Maps for national forests are among the best you can get. They detail all backcountry streams, lakes, hiking trails and logging roads for access. They cost $3 (although wilderness maps cost between $1 and $6) and can be obtained by writing to USDA-Forest Service/ National Park Service, Henry Jackson Federal Building, 915 Second Avenue Room 442, Seattle, WA 98174. They can be reached by phone at (206) 220-7450. Or write to Office of Information, U.S. Forest Service, 333 Southwest First Avenue, Portland, OR 97208, or phone (503) 326-2877.

We've found the Forest Service personnel to be the most helpful of the government agencies when obtaining camping or hiking trail information. Unless you are buying a map, it is advisable to phone, not write, to get the best service. For specific information on a National Forest, write or phone the following:

WASHINGTON
Gifford Pinchot National Forest: write to 6926 East 4th Plain Boulevard, Vancouver, WA 98668-8944 or phone (360)750-5000.

Olympic National Forest: write to 1835 Black Lake Boulevard SW, Olympia, WA 98512 or phone (360)956-2300.

Mount Baker-Snoqualmie National Forest: write to 21905 64th Avenue West, Mountlake Terrace, WA 98043, or phone (206) 775-9702.

Colville National Forest: write to 765 South Main Street, Colville, WA 99114 or phone (509)684-3711.

Wenatchee National Forest: write to 301 Yakima Street, Wenatchee, WA 98807-0811 or phone (509)662-4335.

Okanogan National Forest: write to 1240 Second Avenue South, Okanogan, WA 98840 or phone (509)826-3275.

OREGON
Deschutes National Forest: write to 1645 Highway 20 East, Bend, OR 97701 or phone (541)388-2715.

Fremont National Forest: write to 524 North G Street, Lakeview, OR 97630 or phone (541)947-2151.

Malheur National Forest: write to 139 NE Dayton Street, John Day, OR 97845 or phone (541)575-1731.

Mount Hood National Forest: write to 2955 NW Division Street, Gresham, OR 97030 or phone (503)666-0700.

Ochoco National Forest: write to 3000 East Third Street, Prineville, OR 97754 or phone (541)416-6500.

Rogue River National Forest: write to 333 West 8th Street, Medford, OR 97501 or phone (541)776-3600.

Siskiyou National Forest: write to 200 NE Greenfield Road, Grants Pass, OR 97526 or phone (541)471-6500.

Siuslaw National Forest: write to 4077 Research Way, Corvallis, OR 97333 or phone (541)750-7000.

Umatilla National Forest: write to 2517 SW Hailey Avenue, Pendleton, OR 97801 or phone (541)278-3716.

Umpqua National Forest: write to 2900 NW Stewart Parkway, Roseburg, OR 97470 or phone (541)672-6601.

Wallowa-Whitman National Forest: write to 1550 Dewey

Avenue, Baker City, OR 97814 or phone (541)523-6391 or (541) 426-4978.

Willamette National Forest: write to 211 East 7th Avenue, Eugene, OR 97401 or phone (541)465-6522.

Winema National Forest: write to 2819 Dahlia Street, Klamath Falls, OR 97601 or phone (541)883-6714.

State Parks

The Washington and Oregon State Parks systems provide many popular camping spots. Reservations are often a necessity during the summer months. The camps include drive-in, numbered sites, tent spaces, picnic tables, with showers and bathrooms provided nearby. Although some parks are well-known, there are still some little-known gems in the State Parks systems where campers can get seclusion, even in the summer months.

Washington and Oregon have joined in sponsoring a new central reservation system. Effective January 1996, reservations can be made for 34 Washington and 26 Oregon state parks through Reservations Northwest at (800) 452-5687. Campgrounds under the new system are clearly noted in the "reservations, fee" paragraph of their listings in this book. A nonrefundable reservation fee of $6 and the first night's fee will be required as an advance deposit, charged to a MasterCard or Visa credit card. Under the new system, reservations can be made throughout the year.

A new Washington state parks central information number is now available: (800) 233-0321. General information regarding Oregon state parks can be obtained from the Reservations Northwest switchboard at (800) 452-5687.

WASHINGTON

State Parks and Recreation Commission: write to Public Affairs Office, 7150 Cleanwater Lane, P.O. Box 42650, Olympia, WA 98504-2650 or phone (206)753-2027 or (206)753-5755.

Belfair State Park: write to NE 410 Beck Road, Belfair, WA 98528-9426 or phone (360)275-0668.

Birch Bay State Park: write to 5105 Helwig Road, Blaine, WA 98230-9625 or phone (360)371-2800.

Fort Canby State Park: write to P.O. Box 488, Ilwaco, WA 98624-0488 or phone (360)642-3078.

Fort Flagler State Park: write to 10541 Flagler Road, Norland, WA 98358-9699 or phone (360)385-1259.

Ike Kinswa State Park: write to 873 Harmony Road, Silver Creek, WA 98585-9706 or phone (360)983-3402.

Lake Chelan State Park: write to Route 1, Box 90, Chelan, WA 98816-9755 or phone (509)687-3710.

Moran State Park: write to Star Route, Box 22, Eastsound, WA 98245-9603 or phone (360)376-2326.

Lincoln Rock State Park: write to Route 3, Box 3137, East Wenatchee, WA 98801-9566 or phone (509)884-8702.

Pearrygin Lake State Park: write to Route 1, Box 300, Winthrop, WA 98862-9710 or phone (509)996-2370.

Steamboat Rock State Park: write to P.O. Box 370, Electric City, WA 99123-0370 or phone (509)633-1304.

Twin Harbors-Grayland Beach: write c/o Twin Harbors State Park, Westport, WA 98595-9801, or phone (360)268-9717.

OREGON

State Parks and Recreation Division: write to 1115 Commercial Street NE, Salem, OR 97310-1001 or phone (503)378-6305.

State Parks, Portland Office: write to 2501 Southwest First Avenue, Portland, OR 97266 or phone (503)731-3293 or (503) 731-3294.

State Parks, Coos Bay Office: write or phone Portland Office.

State Parks, Bend Office: write to Central Oregon Service Center, Empire Corporate Park, Suite B1, 20310 Empire Avenue, Bend, OR 97701 or phone (541)388-6211.

State Parks, LaGrande Office: write to 2034 Auburn, Baker City, OR 97814 or phone (541)523-2499.

National Parks

The National Parks in Washington and Oregon are natural wonders, ranging from the spectacular Mount Rainer National Park to the lava-strewn Mount St. Helens National Monument to the often fog-bound Olympic National Park.

For information on each of the national parks in Washington and Oregon, you should contact the parks directly at the following numbers or addresses.

WASHINGTON

Olympic National Park: write to 600 East Park Avenue, Port Angeles, WA 98362 or phone (360)452-4501.

Mount St. Helens National Volcanic Monument: write to 42218 NE Yale Bridge Road, Amboy, WA 98601 or phone (360) 247-5473.

Mount Rainier National Park: write to Tahoma Woods, Star Route, Ashford, WA 98304 or phone (360)569-2211.

North Cascades National Park: write to Ross Lake and Lake Chelan National Recreation Areas, 2105 Highway 20, Sedro Woolley, WA 98284 or phone (206)856-5700.

Coulee Dam National Recreation Area: write to P.O. Box 37, Coulee Dam, WA 99116 or phone (509)633-9441.

OREGON

Crater Lake National Park: write to P.O.Box 7, Crater Lake, OR 97604 or phone (541)594-2211.

Fort Clatsop National Memorial: write to Route 3, Box 604-FC, Astoria, OR 97103 or phone (503)861-2471.

John Day Fossil Beds National Monument: write to 420 West Main Street, St. John Day, OR 97845 or phone (541)987-2333.

Oregon Caves National Monument: write to 19000 Caves Highway, Cave Junction, OR 97523 or phone (541)592-2100.

DEPARTMENT OF NATURAL RESOURCES

The Department of Natural Resources manages about five million acres of public land in Washington. All of it is managed under the concept of "multiple use," designed to provide the greatest recreational opportunities while still protecting natural resources.

The campgrounds in these areas are among the most primitive, remote and least known of the camps listed in this book. The cost is usually free and you are asked to remove all litter and trash from the area, leaving only your footprints behind.

In addition to maps of the area it manages, the Department of Natural Resources also has U.S. Geological Survey maps and U.S. Army Corps of Engineer maps. For information, write or phone: **Department of Natural Resources,** Photo and Map Sales, P.O. Box 47031, Olympia, WA 98504-7031; (360)902-1234 or (360)902-1000 or (800)527-3305.

BUREAU OF LAND MANAGEMENT

Oregon/Washington State Office: write to P.O. Box 2965, Portland, OR 97208 or phone (503)280-7001.

Burns District: write to HC74-12533 Highway 20 West,Hines, OR 97738 or phone (503)573-5241.

Coos Bay District: write to 1300 Airport Lane, North Bend, OR 97459-2000 or phone (503)756-0100.

Eugene District: write to 2890 Chad Drive, Eugene, OR 97440 or phone (541)683-6600.

Lakeview District: write to 1000 South Ninth Street, Lakeview, OR 97630 or phone (541)947-2177.

Medford District: write to 3040 Biddle Road, Medford, OR 97501 or phone (541)770-2200.

Prineville District: write to 185 East 4th Street, Prineville, OR 97754 or phone (541)447-4115.

Roseburg District: write to 777 NW Garden Valley Boulevard, Roseburg, OR 97470 or phone (541)440-4930.

Salem District: write to 1717 Fabry Road SE, Salem, OR 97306 or phone (503)375-5646.

Vale District: write to 100 Oregon Street, Vale, OR 97918 or phone (541)473-3144.

Camping Gear Checklist

• **Cooking Gear**

Matches bagged in zip-lock bags
Fire-starter cubes or candle
Camp stove
Camp fuel
Pot, pan, cup
Pot grabber
Knife, fork
Dish soap and scrubber
Salt, pepper, spices
Itemized food
Plastic spade

Optional Cooking Gear:

Ax or hatchet
Wood or charcoal for barbecue
Ice chest
Spatula
Grill
Tin foil
Dust pan
Tablecloth
Whisk broom
Clothespins
Can opener

• **Camping Clothes**

Polypropylene underwear
Cotton shirt
Long sleeve cotton/wool shirt
Cotton/canvas pants
Vest
Parka
Rain jacket, pants or poncho
Hat
Sunglasses
Chapstick

Optional Clothing:

Seam Lock™
Shorts
Swimming suit
Gloves
Ski cap

• **Hiking Gear**

Quality hiking boots
Backup lightweight shoes
Polypropylene socks
Thick cotton socks
80% wool socks
Strong boot laces
Innersole or foot cushion
Moleskin and medical tape
Gaiters
Water-repellent boot treatment

• **Sleeping Gear**

Sleeping bag
Insulite™ or Therm-a-Rest™ pad
Ground tarp
Tent

Optional Sleeping Gear:

Air pillow
Mosquito netting
Foam pad for truck bed
Windshield light screen for RV
Catalytic heater

• First Aid

Band-Aids
Sterile gauze pads
Roller gauze
Athletic tape
Moleskin
Thermometer
Aspirin
Ace bandage
Mosquito repellent
After-Bite™ or ammonia
Campho-Phenique™ gel
First-Aid Cream™
Sunscreen
Neosporin™
Caladryl™
Biodegradable soap
Towelette
Tweezers

Optional First Aid:

Water purification system
Coins for emergency phoning
Extra set of matches
Mirror for signaling

• Fishing/Recreational Gear

Fishing rod
Fishing reel with fresh line
Small tackle box with lures,
    splitshot, snap swivels
Pliers
Knife

Optional Recreation Gear:

Stargazing chart
Tree identification handbook
Deck of cards
Backpacking cribbage board
Knapsack for each person

• Miscellaneous

Maps
Flashlight
Lantern and fuel
Nylon rope for food hang
Handkerchief
Camera and film
Plastic garbage bags
Toilet paper
Toothbrush and toothpaste
Compass
Watch
Feminine hygiene products

Optional Miscellaneous:

Binoculars
Notebook and pen
Towel

WASHINGTON

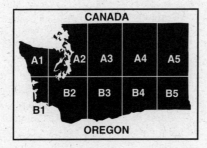

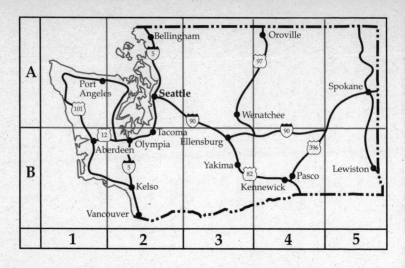

Map A1—48 listings pages 92-111
Featuring: Neah Bay, Olympic National Park, Clallam Bay, Lake Ozette, Strait of Juan de Fuca, Lyre River, Bear Creek, Soleduck River, Lake Crescent, Elwha River, Port Angeles, Hoh River, Bogachiel River, Bogachiel State Park, Bert Cole State Forest, Clearwater River, Quinault Lake, Queets River, Humptulips River, Olympic National Forest, Wynoochee Lake, Skokomish River

Map A2—131 listings pages 112-165
Featuring: Point Roberts, Birch Bay, Nooksack River, Mount Baker-Snoqualmie National Forest, San Juan Islands, Patos Island State Park, Orcas Island, Bellingham, Roche Harbor, Moran State Park, Spencer Spit State Park, Padilla Bay, Samish Bay, Larrabee State Park, Skagit River, Anacortes, Washington Park, Puget Sound, Fort Worden State Park, Lake Goodwin, Fort Casey State Park, Dungeness River, Sequim Bay, Stillaguamish River, Blue Mountain, Olympic National Park, Olympic National Forest, Gray Wolf River, Hood Canal, Kitsap Memorial State Park, Quilcene River, Dosewallips River, Silver Lake, Blackman's Lake, Duckabush River, Seattle, Hamma Hamma River, Bert Cole State Forest, Tahuya State Forest, Lake Sammamish State Park, Cascade Mountains, Snoqualmie River, Tacoma, Stuck River

Map A3—122 listings pages 166-215
Featuring: Nooksack River , Mount Baker-Snoqualmie National Forest, Ross Lake National Recreation Area, Baker Lake, Diablo Lake, Okanogan National Forest, Pasayten Wilderness, Chewack River, Skagit River, North Cascades National Park, Cascade River, Methow River, Twisp River, Pearrygin Lake, Twin Lakes, Sauk River, Suiattle River, Glacier Peak Wilderness, Wenatchee National Forest, Stillaguamish River, Lake Chelan, Ashland Lakes, Chiwawa River, Entiat River, Bald Mountain, Greider Lakes, Skykomish River, Wenatchee River, White River, Alpine Lakes Wilderness, Beckler River, Mad River, Columbia River, Icicle Creek, Cle Elum Lake, Kachess Lake, Keechelus Lake, Teanaway River, Cle Elum River

Map A4—62 listings pages 216-243
Featuring: Cold Creek, Toats Coulee Creek, Chopaka Lake, Wannacut Lake, Palmer Lake, Osoyoos Lake State Park, Okanogan National Forest, Spectacle Lake, Beaver Lake,

Beth Lake, Tiffany Lake, Okanogan River, Bonaparte Lake, Conconully Lake, Curlew Lake, Lyman Lake, Ferry Lake, Long Lake, Swan Lake, Colville National Forest, Leader Lake, Rock Lake, Okanogan River, Sanpoil River, Columbia River, Alta Lake, Crawfish Lake, Banks Lake, Lake Chelan, Franklin Roosevelt Lake, Coulee Dam National Recreation Area, Rufus Woods Lake, Bridgeport State Park, Blue Lake, Grand Coulee Dam, Sun Lakes State Recreation Park, Banks Lake, Park Lake

Map A5—73 listings pages 244-273
Featuring: Colville National Forest, Pierre Lake, Sheep Creek, Sullivan Lake, Columbia River, Franklin Roosevelt Lake, Coulee Dam National Recreation Area, Williams Lake, Pend Oreille River, Lake Leo, Big Meadow Lake, Lake Ellen, Rocky Lake, Deep Lake, Twin Lakes, Lake Thomas, Lake Gillette, Skookum Lake, Browns Lake, Waitts Lake, Jump Off Joe Lake, Box Canyon Reservoir, Eloika Lake, Loon Lake, Spokane River, Spokane, Mount Spokane, Medical Lake, Silver Lake, Turnbull National Wildlife Refuge, Clear Lake, Sprague Lake, Williams Lake

Map B1—48 listings pages 274-293
Featuring: Copalis Beach, Humptulips River, Satsop River, Westport, Ocean City State Park, Lake Sylvia, Twin Harbors, Leadbetter Point State Park, Willapa Bay, Grays Harbor, Willapa River, Long Beach, Fort Canby State Park, Columbia River, Fort Columbia State Park, Chinook

Map B2—89 listings pages 294-329
Featuring: Squaxin Island, Puget Sound, Tacoma, Hartstene Island, Puyallup River, Green River, Capitol Forest, Black Lake, Olympia, Long Lake, Tanwax Lake, Carbon River,

Mount Baker-Snoqualmie National Forest, Mount Rainier National Park, Deep Lake, Offut Lake, Mima Falls, Chehalis River, Alder Lake, Centralia, Lewis and Clark State Park, Cowlitz River, Mayfield Lake, Toutle River, Riffe Lake, Gifford Pinchot National Forest, Silver Lake, Cispus River, Coweeman River, Mount St. Helens, Columbia River, Lewis River, Kalama River, Pacific Crest Trail, Yale Lake, Wind River, Indian Heaven Wilderness, Meadow Lake, Paradise Point State Park, Battle Ground Lake, Mosquito Lakes, Washougal River

Map B3—75 listings pages 330-361
Featuring: Lake Easton, Teanaway River, Yakima River, Wenatchee National Forest, Mount Baker-Snoqualmie National Forest, Bumping River, American River, Naches River, White River, Mount Rainier National Park, Bumping Lake, Gifford Pinchot National Forest, Ohanapecosh River, Clear Lake, Dog Lake, Leech Lake, Rimrock Lake, Tieton River, Goat Rocks Wilderness, Yakima, Takhlakh Lake, Horseshoe Lake, Olallie Lake, Council Lake, Cispus River, Mount Adams, Walupt Lake, Trout Lake, Brooks Memorial State Park, Dalles Dam, Mount Adams Wilderness, White Salmon River, Columbia River

Map B4—19 listings pages 362-371
Featuring: Soap Lake, Moses Lake State Park, Columbia River, Frenchman Hills Lakes, Potholes Reservoir, Ginkgo-Wanapum State Park, Yakima River, Snake River, Sacajawea Lake, Pasco

Map B5—14 listings pages 372-378
Featuring: Ritzville, Snake River, Palouse River, Umatilla National Forest, Lewis and Clark Trail, Fort Walla Walla Park, Wenaha-Tucannon Wilderness, Puffer Butte, Fields Spring State Park

MAP A1

WASHINGTON MAP .... see page 90
Adjoining Maps

48 LISTINGS
PAGES 92-111

NORTH .... no map
EAST (A2) .... see page 112
SOUTH (B1) .... see page 274
WEST .... no map

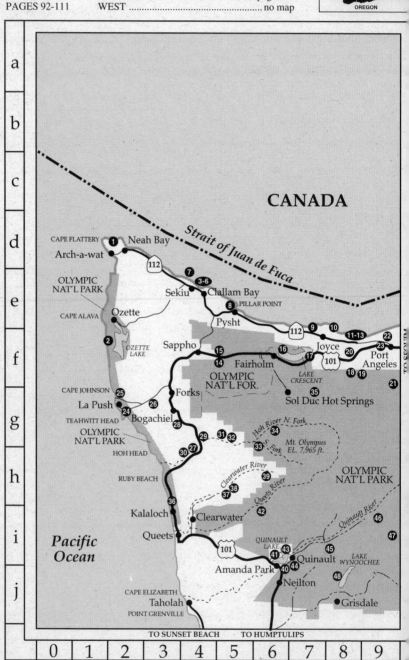

Washington Map A1 featuring: Neah Bay, Olympic National Park, Clallam Bay, Lake Ozette, Strait of Juan de Fuca, Lyre River, Bear Creek, Soleduck River, Lake Crescent, Elwha River, Port Angeles, Hoh River, Bogachiel River, Bogachiel State Park, Bert Cole State Forest, Clearwater River, Quinault Lake, Queets River, Humptulips River, Olympic National Forest, Wynoochee Lake, Skokomish River

---

1.   TYEE MOTEL AND RV PARK   RV

Reference: **In Neah Bay; map A1, grid d2.**

Campsites, facilities: There are 20 pull-through sites for trailers or RVs of any length. Electricity, piped water and sewer hookups are provided. Bottled gas, sanitary services, toilets, laundry and ice are available. A store and a cafe are located within one mile. Showers are available for an extra fee. Pets and motorbikes are permitted. Boat docks, launching facilities and rentals are nearby.

Reservations, fee: Reservations accepted; $15 fee per night; MasterCard and Visa accepted. Open all year.

Who to contact: Phone the park at (360) 645-2223 or write to P.O. Box 193, Neah Bay, WA 98357.

Location: From Interstate 5 at Olympia, turn north on US 101 and drive 127 miles (five miles past the town of Port Angeles). Turn west on Highway 112 and drive 63 miles to the town of Neah Bay. The campground is located just off the highway in the middle of town.

Trip note: For RVs and trailers only, this private, developed campground is located near the northwestern tip of the Olympic Peninsula. It's a fairly plain-looking park, with two long strips of spaces, but a few sites have ocean views. Fishing is excellent in this area. Recreation options include the world-renowned Makah Museum, which details the history of the Makah Indian tribe, and the half-mile hike to Cape Flattery, the northwestern tip of North America. Cape Flattery offers many hiking trails and opportunities for viewing whales, seals and walrus. Nearby Makah Bay has a beautiful beach and is a popular spot for surfing.

---

2.   OZETTE   RV

Reference: **On Lake Ozette, in Olympic National Park; map A1, grid e2.**

Campsites, facilities: There are 14 sites for tents or RVs up to 21 feet long. Piped water, picnic tables, vault toilets and fire grills are available. Leashed pets are permitted.

Reservations, fee: No reservations; no fee. Open all year.

Who to contact: Phone the Olympic National Park at (360) 452-4501 or write to 600 East Park Avenue, Port Angeles, WA 98362.

Location: From Interstate 5 at Olympia, turn north on US 101 and drive 127 miles (five miles past the town of Port Angeles). Turn west on Highway 112 and drive to the town of Ozette. Turn on Hoko-Ozette Road and drive about 21 miles to the ranger station. The camp parking lot is a short distance on the right.

Trip note: Very few people visit this site, set on the shore of Lake Ozette just a few miles from the Pacific Ocean. This is a boater's delight. Access is limited to boaters and backpackers. The camp is remote and private with an isolated, mysterious feel to it.

3.   VAN RIPERS' RESORT HOTEL   RV.

Reference: **On Clallam Bay; map A1, grid e4.**

Campsites, facilities: There are 60 drive-through sites for trailers or RVs of any
length. Electricity, piped water and picnic tables are provided. Sanitary
services, toilets, showers and ice are available. Bottled gas, a store, a cafe and
laundry are located within one mile. Sewer hookups and firewood are available
for an extra fee. Pets and motorbikes are permitted. Boat docks, launching
facilities and rentals are available.

Reservations, fee: No reservations; $11-$15 fee per night; MasterCard and Visa
accepted. Open April to late September.

Who to contact: Phone the park at (360) 963-2334 or write to P.O. Box 246, Sekiu,
WA 98381.

Location: From Interstate 5 at Olympia, turn north on US 101 and drive 127 miles
(five miles past the town of Port Angeles). Turn west on Highway 112 and
drive 53 miles to Sekiu. The campground is located off Highway 112, at the
north end of Front Street.

Trip note: This urban park is for RVs and trailers only. Part of the campground
is on the waterfront and the other part is on a hill overlooking the Strait of Juan
de Fuca. The sites are graveled, many with ocean views. Hiking, fishing and
boating are among your options here. The beaches in the area are a mixture of
sand and gravel, and rockhounding for agates and fossils is popular.

4.   SAM'S TRAILER AND RV PARK   RV.

Reference: **On Clallam Bay; map A1, grid e4.**

Campsites, facilities: There are 10 tent sites and 20 drive-through sites for trailers
or RVs of any length. Electricity, piped water, sewer hookups and picnic tables
are provided. Sanitary services, toilets, showers, cable TV and laundry are
available. Bottled gas, a store, a cafe and ice are located within one mile. Pets
and motorbikes are permitted. Boat docks, launching facilities and rentals are
nearby.

Reservations, fee: Reservations accepted; $8-$13 fee per night. Open all year.

Who to contact: Phone the park at (360) 963-2402 or write to P.O. Box 45,
Clallam Bay, WA 98326.

Location: From Interstate 5 at Olympia, turn north on US 101 and drive 127 miles
(five miles past the town of Port Angeles). Turn west on Highway 112 and
drive 43 miles to the town of Clallam Bay. The campground is on the right just
as you come into town.

Trip note: This is an option to Coho Resort and Trailer Park, Surfside Resort,
Olson's Resort and Van Ripers' Resort Hotel on Clallam Bay. It's a family-
oriented park, with grassy sites and many recreation options nearby. Beaches
and shopping are within walking distance. This is a good central location for
those wanting to visit Cape Flattery, Hoh Rain Forest or Port Angeles.

5.   OLSON'S RESORT   RV.

Reference: **In Sekiu; map A1, grid e4.**

Campsites, facilities: There are 30 tent sites and 100 sites for trailers or RVs of
any length, 45 with full and 10 with electrical hookups. Picnic tables, piped
water, sanitary services, toilets, showers, a laundry, a store and ice are
available. A cafe, boat docks, launching facilities and boat rentals are located
within one mile. Leashed pets and motorbikes are permitted.

Reservations, fee: No reservations; $10-$14 fee per night; MasterCard and Visa accepted. Open all year.

Who to contact: Phone the park at (360) 963-2311 or write to P.O. Box 216, Sekiu, WA 98381.

Location: From Interstate 5 at Olympia, turn north on US 101 and drive 127 miles (five miles past the town of Port Angeles). Turn west on Highway 112 and drive 53 miles to Sekiu. The campground is located off Highway 112, at the north end of Front Street.

Trip note: This large, private camp is developed with full-services. The marina nearby is salmon fishing headquarters. In fact, the resort caters to anglers, offering all-day salmon fishing trips and boat moorage. Chartered trips are available by reservation. A tackle shop, cabins and a motel are also available. See the trip note for Van Ripers' for details on the Sekiu area.

---

6. SURFSIDE RESORT   RV

Reference: **In Sekiu; map A1, grid e4.**

Campsites, facilities: There are 20 tent sites and 10 drive-through sites for trailers or RVs of any length. Electricity, piped water, sewer hookups and picnic tables are provided. Sanitary services, cable TV, toilets and showers are available. Bottled gas, a store, a cafe, laundry and ice are located within one mile. Leashed pets and motorbikes are permitted. Boat docks, launching facilities and rentals are nearby.

Reservations, fee: Reservations accepted; $10-$15 fee per night. Open May to September.

Who to contact: Phone the park at (360) 963-2723 or write to P.O. Box 39, Sekiu, WA 98381.

Location: From Interstate 5 at Olympia, turn north on US 101 and drive 127 miles (five miles past the town of Port Angeles). Turn west on Highway 112 and drive 43 miles to the town of Clallam Bay. Continue about one mile west; the campground is located halfway between Sekiu and Clallam Bay.

Trip note: This park is smaller, less-crowded and more secluded than many in the area. Campers can enjoy the park's private beach and panoramic views of the Strait of Juan de Fuca and Vancouver Island to the north. Nearby recreation options include marked hiking and bike trails, beachcombing, a full-service marina and the finest fishing for miles.

---

7. COHO RESORT AND TRAILER PARK   RV

Reference: **Near Sekiu; map A1, grid e4.**

Campsites, facilities: There are 200 sites for tents, trailers or RVs of any length. Electricity, piped water, sewer hookups and cable TV are provided. Sanitary services, toilets, a cafe, laundry and ice are available. Bottled gas and a store are located within one mile. Showers are available for an extra fee. Boat docks, launching facilities and rentals are available. Pets and motorbikes are permitted.

Reservations, fee: No reservations; $10-$14 fee per night. Open April through September.

Who to contact: Phone the park at (360) 963-2333 or write to HCR 61, P.O. Box 15, Sekiu, WA 98381.

Location: From Interstate 5 at Olympia, turn north on US 101 and drive 127 miles (five miles past the town of Port Angeles). Turn west on Highway 112 and drive 44 miles. The campground is located about three-quarters of a mile east of Sekiu between mileposts 15 and 16.

Trip note: This is one of several camps in the immediate area. A full-service marina nearby provides boating access. See trip notes for Van Ripers', Olson's and Surfside resorts for information on the area.

---

8.   PILLAR POINT RECREATION AREA   RV

Reference: **Near the Strait of Juan de Fuca; map A1, grid e5.**

Campsites, facilities: There are 20 tent sites and 18 sites for trailers or RVs up to 24 feet long. Sewer hookups and picnic tables are provided. Toilets are available. A store is located within one mile. Firewood can be purchased. There is **no piped water,** so bring your own. Pets and motorbikes are permitted. Boat launching facilities are nearby.

Reservations, fee: No reservations; $6-$8 fee per night. Open mid-May to mid-September.

Who to contact: Phone the park at (360) 963-2301 or write to Star Route 2, P.O. Box 8, Clallam Bay, WA 98326.

Location: From Interstate 5 at Olympia, turn north on US 101 and drive 127 miles (five miles past the town of Port Angeles). Turn west on Highway 112 and drive 29 miles. Turn right on Pillar Point Road and drive one-half mile north to the campground.

Trip note: This camp is set on the northwestern edge of the Olympic Peninsula, near the mouth of the Strait of Juan de Fuca. Fishermen can launch here and try to intercept migrating salmon. The spaces are graveled and set close together, and the campground is set in a wooded area. Most sites have beautiful views of the water.

---

9.   WHISKEY CREEK BEACH   RV

Reference: **On Strait of Juan de Fuca; map A1, grid e7.**

Campsites, facilities: There are 50 tent sites and 11 sites for trailers or RVs of any length. There are also five cabins on the beach. Piped water and picnic tables are provided. Sanitary services, a laundry and some sewer hookups are available. Pets are permitted. Boat launching facilities are nearby.

Reservations, fee: Reservations accepted; $10 fee per night; $50 cabin fee per night. Open May to late October.

Who to contact: Phone the park at (360) 928-3489 or write to P.O. Box 60, Joyce, WA 98343.

Location: From Interstate 5 at Olympia, turn north on US 101 and drive 127 miles (five miles past the town of Port Angeles). Turn west on Highway 112 and drive 13 miles west. Turn north on Whiskey Creek Beach Road and continue 1.5 miles to the campground.

Trip note: Set on the beach along Strait of Juan de Fuca, this campground covers 400 acres, with Agate Beach nearby. The campground is in a rustic setting, with one mile of beach access and five miles of hiking trails nearby. Five miles away is Olympic National Park, which offers numerous recreation options. This camp is a good option if the national park camps are full.

---

10.   CAROL'S CRESCENT BEACH   RV

Reference: **On the Strait of Juan de Fuca; map A1, grid e8.**

Campsites, facilities: There are 60 sites for tents, trailers or motors homes. Restrooms, showers, a private phone, a recreation field and a laundromat are available. The facilities are **wheelchair accessible.** Pets are permitted on leashes.

Reservations, fee: Reservations recommended; $16 fee per night. The day-use fee is $3 per person. Open from May 15 to September 15.

Who to contact: Phone (360) 928-3344 or write to 2860 Crescent Beach Road, Port Angeles, WA 98362.

Location: From Interstate 5 at Olympia, turn north on US 101 and drive 127 miles (five miles past the town of Port Angeles). Turn west on Highway 112 and drive 10 miles to Camp Hayden Road (between mileposts 53 and 54). Drive northwest on Camp Hayden Park Road for four miles. The campground is located on the left.

Trip note: Set on a half-mile stretch of sandy beach, this campground makes a perfect weekend spot. Recreation options include swimming, fishing and beachcombing. Numerous attractions and recreation options are available in Port Angeles.

---

11. LYRE RIVER

Reference: **On Lyre River; map A1, grid e8.**

Campsites, facilities: There are 11 primitive tent sites. Picnic tables, fire grills, tent pads, vault toilets and piped water are provided. A roofed group shelter with fireplace is available. Leashed pets are permitted.

Reservations, fee: No reservations, no fee. Open all year.

Who to contact: Phone the Department of Natural Resources at (360) 374-6131 or write to Department of Natural Resources, Olympic Region, 411 Tillicum Lane, Forks, WA 98331-9797.

Location: From Interstate 5 at Olympia, turn north on US 101 and drive 127 miles (five miles past the town of Port Angeles). Turn west on Highway 112 and drive to milepost 46. Look to the right for a paved road between mileposts 46 and 47, then turn north and drive one-half mile. The camp is on the left.

Trip note: One of the rare free campgrounds on the Olympic Peninsula, this campground is a prime spot. It is quite primitive, but it does offer piped water and an even more precious commodity in these parts—privacy. It is set along the Lyre River and is just a short distance from the ocean.

---

12. LYRE RIVER RV PARK   RV.

Reference: **Near Lyre River; map A1, grid e8.**

Campsites, facilities: There are 15 tent sites and 60 drive-through sites for trailers or RVs of any length. Electricity, piped water, sewer hookups and picnic tables are provided. Bottled gas, sanitary services, toilets, a store, laundry and ice are available. Showers and firewood are available for an extra fee. Pets and motorbikes are permitted.

Reservations, fee: Reservations accepted; $15-$22 fee per night. Group reservations are welcome with advance deposit. Open all year.

Who to contact: Phone the park at (360) 928-3436 or write to 596 West Lyre River Road, Port Angeles, WA 98362.

Location: From Interstate 5 at Olympia, turn north on US 101 and drive 127 miles (five miles past the town of Port Angeles). Turn west on Highway 112 and drive 15 miles. Turn right on Lyre River Road and drive one-half mile to the park.

Trip note: This beautiful 80-acre camp is in a wooded area tucked between the Strait of Juan de Fuca and the Lyre River. Freshwater and saltwater beaches are available, giving the park a unique flavor. For kids, there is a pond stocked with trout, and for adult anglers there is excellent fishing in the Lyre River and the strait. Tubing down the river is popular here, and bike trails and hiking trails are available nearby.

13. SALT CREEK RECREATION AREA RV

Reference: **Near Strait of Juan de Fuca; map A1, grid e8.**

Campsites, facilities: There are 41 tent sites and 39 sites for trailers or RVs of any length. Picnic tables are provided. Sanitary services, toilets, showers, a playground are available. Firewood is available for an extra fee. Pets are permitted.

Reservations, fee: No reservations; $6-$8 fee per night. Open all year.

Who to contact: Phone the park at (360) 928-3441 or write to 3506 Camp Hayden Road, Port Angeles, WA 98362.

Location: From Interstate 5 at Olympia, turn north on US 101 and drive 127 miles (five miles past the town of Port Angeles). Turn west Highway 112 and drive 10 miles to Camp Hayden Road. Turn north and drive four miles to the campground.

Trip note: This 192-acre park overlooks the Strait of Juan de Fuca. Nearby recreation options include marked hiking trails. Other possible activities are swimming, fishing, horseshoes and field sports. It's a good layover spot if you're planning to take the ferry out of Port Angeles to Victoria, British Columbia.

14. BEAR CREEK MOTEL AND RV PARK RV

Reference: **On Bear Creek; map A1, grid f5.**

Campsites, facilities: There are eight tent sites and 20 drive-through sites for trailers or RVs of any length. Electricity, piped water, sewer hookups and picnic tables are provided. Bottled gas, sanitary services, toilets, showers, a cafe, a laundry and firewood are available. Pets are permitted. Boat launching facilities are nearby.

Reservations, fee: No reservations; $8-$15 fee per night. Discover, MasterCard and Visa accepted. Open all year.

Who to contact: Phone the park at (360) 327-3660 or write to P.O. Box 213, Beaver, WA 98305.

Location: From Interstate 5 at Olympia, turn north on US 101 and drive about 163 miles north and west to the campground (located 15 miles northeast of Forks at milepost 205).

Trip note: This quiet little spot is set where Bear Creek empties into the Soleduck River. It's private and developed, with a choice of sunny or shaded sites in a wooded setting. There are many recreation options in the area, including fishing, hunting and nature and hiking trails leading to the ocean. Soleduck Hot Springs is 25 miles north and well worth the trip. A restaurant next to the camp serves family-style meals.

15. KLAHOWYA RV

Reference: **On Soleduck River in Olympic National Forest; map A1, grid f5.**

Campsites, facilities: There are 25 tent sites and 30 sites for trailers or RVs up to 30 feet long. Picnic tables are provided. Piped water, vault and flush toilets are available. Leashed pets are permitted. **Wheelchair accessible** restrooms are available. A boat ramp is nearby.

Reservations, fee: Reserve some sites by calling (800) 280-CAMP ($7.50 reservation fee); $7-$10 fee per night. Open May to mid-October with full service. Limited service in the off-season.

Who to contact: Phone Olympic National Forest at (360) 374-6522 or write to Soleduck Ranger District, Star Route 1, P.O. Box 5750, Forks, WA 98331.

Location: From Interstate 5 at Olympia, turn north on US 101 and drive approximately 158 miles north and west to the campground, located 20 miles northeast of Forks.

Trip note: This is a good choice if you don't want to venture far from US 101, yet want to retain the feel of Olympic National Forest. The camp is 32 acres and set along the headwaters of the Soleduck River. It is pretty and wooded, with hiking trails in the area. Due to its close proximity to the highway, this is an extremely popular camp and fills up quickly in the summer.

16. FAIRHOLM   RV

Reference: **On Lake Crescent in Olympic National Park; map A1, grid f6.**

Campsites, facilities: There are 87 sites for tents, trailers or RVs up to 21 feet long. Picnic tables and fire grills are provided. A sanitary disposal station, restrooms, drinking water and **wheelchair facilities** are available. A store and a cafe are within one mile. Leashed pets are permitted. Boat launching facilities are nearby on Lake Crescent.

Reservations, fee: No reservations; $10 fee per night. Open all year, weather permitting.

Who to contact: Phone the Olympic National Park at (360) 452-4501 or write to 600 East Park Avenue, Port Angeles, WA 98362.

Location: From Interstate 5 at Olympia, turn north on US 101 and drive approximately 122 miles to Port Angeles. Continue 26 miles west on US 101, then turn right and drive one mile to the camp on North Shore Road.

Trip note: This camp is set on the shore of Lake Crescent, a pretty lake situated within boundaries of Olympic National Park. It is less than a mile off US 101 and gets heavy use during tourist months. A naturalist program is available in summer months. The elevation is 580 feet.

17. LOG CABIN RESORT   RV

Reference: **On Lake Crescent in Olympic National Park; map A1, grid f7.**

Campsites, facilities: There are 40 sites for trailers or RVs of any length. Electricity, piped water, sewer hookups and picnic tables are provided. Sanitary services, toilets, a store, a cafe, laundry, ice and a playground are available. Showers and firewood are available for an extra fee. Pets are permitted at specified sites. Boat docks, launching facilities and rentals are located at Lake Crescent.

Reservations, fee: Reservations accepted; $22 fee per night; MasterCard and Visa accepted. Open May to October.

Who to contact: Phone the resort at (360) 928-3325 or write to 3183 East Beach Road, Port Angeles, WA 98362.

Location: From Interstate 5 at Olympia, turn north on US 101 and drive 122 miles to Port Angeles. Continue 18 miles northwest on US 101, then turn right on East Beach Road and drive three miles to the camp at Log Cabin Resort.

Trip note: This pretty spot lies along the shore of Lake Crescent and is a good spot for boaters. There are many sites on the lake shore with excellent views. Fishing and swimming are two options at this family-oriented resort. A marked hiking trail traces the lake's shoreline.

---

18.   ALTAIRE   **RV**

Reference: **On Elwha River in Olympic National Park; map A1, grid f8.**

Campsites, facilities: There are 30 sites for tents, trailers or RVs up to 21 feet long. Picnic tables and fire grills are provided. Restrooms and drinking water are available. Leashed pets are permitted. Some facilities are **wheelchair accessible.**

Reservations, fee: No reservations; $10 fee per night. Open June to September.

Who to contact: Phone the Olympic National Park at (360) 452-4501 or write to 600 East Park Avenue, Port Angeles, WA 98362.

Location: From Interstate 5 at Olympia, turn north on US 101 and drive approximately 122 miles to Port Angeles. Continue nine miles west on US 101, then turn left at the signed entrance road and drive four miles south along Elwha River.

Trip note: This camp is set on the Elwha River about a mile from Lake Mills. It's a pretty camp, well-treed with easy highway access. It's a nice layover spot for a one-nighter before taking the ferry boat at Port Angeles to Victoria, British Columbia.

---

19.   ELWHA   **RV**

Reference: **On Elwha River in Olympic National Park; map A1, grid f8.**

Campsites, facilities: There are 41 sites for tents, trailers or RVs up to 21 feet long. Picnic tables and fire grills are provided. Restrooms and drinking water are available. Leashed pets are permitted. Some facilities are **wheelchair accessible.**

Reservations, fee: No reservations; $10 fee per night. Open all year.

Who to contact: Phone the Olympic National Park at (360) 452-4501 or write to 600 East Park, Port Angeles, WA 98362.

Location: From Interstate 5 at Olympia, turn north on US 101 and drive approximately 122 miles to Port Angeles. Continue nine miles west on US 101, then turn right at the signed entrance road and drive three miles south along Elwha River.

Trip note: This camp is set along the Elwha River and gets regular use. There are some excellent hiking trails in the park; check at one of the visitor centers for maps and backcountry information. See also the trip note for nearby Altaire.

---

20.   ELWHA RESORT AND CAMPGROUND   **RV**

Reference: **On Elwha River; map A1, grid f8.**

Campsites, facilities: There are nine tent sites and four sites for trailers or RVs up to 32 feet long. Electricity, piped water, sewer hookups and picnic tables are provided. Bottled gas, toilets, a store, a cafe, ice and a playground are available. Sanitary services and laundry are located within ten miles. Showers and firewood are available for an extra fee. Pets and motorbikes are permitted. Boat docks, launching facilities and cabin rentals are nearby at the Elwha River.

Reservations, fee: Reservations accepted; $8-$15 fee per night; MasterCard and Visa accepted. Open all year.

Who to contact: Phone the park at (360) 457-7011 or write to 239521 Highway

101 West, Port Angeles, WA 98362.

Location: From Interstate 5 at Olympia, turn north on US 101 and drive 130 miles (eight miles past the town of Port Angeles) to the park at 239521 Highway 101 West.

Trip note: This small, private campground, set at sea level next to the Elwha River, offers more seclusion than nearby sites. It has spacious, wooded sites in a pretty setting. Nearby recreation options include marked hiking trails, Lake Adwell and Olympic National Park.

21. HEART O' THE HILLS **RV**

Reference: **In Olympic National Park; map A1, grid f9.**

Campsites, facilities: There are 105 sites for tents, trailers or RVs to 21 feet long. Picnic tables are provided. Restrooms and drinking water are available. Leashed pets are permitted. **Wheelchair accessible** facilities are available.

Reservations, fee: No reservations; $10 fee per night. Open all year, weather permitting. (Access roads can be impassable in severe weather.)

Who to contact: Phone the Olympic National Park at (360) 452-4501 or write to 600 East Park Avenue, Port Angeles, WA 98362.

Location: From Interstate 5 at Olympia, turn north on US 101 and drive approximately 122 miles to Port Angeles. Drive five miles south on Hurricane Ridge Road to the camp on the left.

Trip note: This camp is set on the northern edge of Olympic National Park. You can drive deeper into the interior of the park on Hurricane Ridge Road and take one of numerous hiking trails. This camp is set at 1,807 feet. Evening naturalist programs are available in the summer.

22. PEABODY CREEK RV PARK **RV**

Reference: **In Port Angeles; map A1, grid f9.**

Campsites, facilities: There are 42 sites for trailers or RVs of any length. Electricity, piped water and sewer hookups are provided. Bottled gas, sanitary services, toilets, ice and laundry are available. A store and a cafe are within one mile. Showers are available for an extra fee. Leashed pets are permitted. Boat docks, launching facilities and rentals are nearby.

Reservations, fee: Reservations accepted; $19 fee per night. Open all year.

Who to contact: Phone the park at (360) 457-7092 or write to 127 South Lincoln, Port Angeles, WA 98362.

Location: From Interstate 5 at Olympia, turn north on US 101 and drive 122 miles to Port Angeles. Turn east at the intersection of Lincoln and Second Streets and drive 75 feet on Lincoln Street to the park.

Trip note: This three-acre RV park is right in the middle of town, but offers a wooded streamside setting. Nearby recreation options include salmon fishing, an 18-hole golf course, marked biking trails, a full-service marina and tennis courts. The park is within walking distance to shopping and ferry services.

23. WELCOME INN TRAILER AND RV PARK **RV**

Reference: **Near Port Angeles; map A1, grid f9.**

Campsites, facilities: There are 100 sites for tents, trailers or RVs of any length. Electricity, piped water, sewer hookups, dump stations and picnic tables are provided. Bottled gas, sanitary services, toilets and laundry are available. A store, a cafe and ice are within one mile. Showers are available for an extra fee.

Pets and motorbikes are permitted. Boat docks and launching facilities are nearby.

Reservations, fee: Reservations accepted; $12-$18 fee per night. Open all year.

Who to contact: Phone the park at (360) 457-1553 or write to 112 Highway 101 West, Port Angeles, WA 98362.

Location: From Interstate 5 at Olympia, turn north on US 101 and drive 122 miles to Port Angeles. Drive another 1.5 miles west on US 101 to the park.

Trip note: A privately-developed campground for RVs and tent campers, it's an eight-acre camp set in the woods. Nearby recreation options include an 18-hole golf course, marked hiking trails, a full-service marina and tennis courts. The park caters to tourists, offering arrangements for Victoria, British Columbia tours and fishing charters.

---

24. MORA

Reference: **Near the Pacific Ocean in Olympic National Park; map A1, grid g2.**

Campsites, facilities: There are 94 sites for tents or RVs up to 21 feet long. Picnic tables and fire grills are provided. Drinking water, a sanitary disposal station and restrooms are available. Leashed pets are permitted. **Wheelchair facilities** are available.

Reservations, fee: No reservations; $10 fee per night. Open all year.

Who to contact: Phone the Olympic National Park at (360) 452-4501 or write to 600 East Park Avenue, Port Angeles, WA 98362.

Location: From Interstate 5 at Olympia, turn north on US 101 and drive approximately 175 miles to La Push Highway (two miles north of Forks). Turn west and drive 12 miles to the campground, making sure to follow the Mora campground signs.

Trip note: This is a good out-of-the-way choice set near the Pacific Ocean and the Olympic Coast Marine Sanctuary at an elevation of 50 feet. Soleduck River feeds into the ocean near here. In summer months, a naturalist program is available.

---

25. SHORELINE RESORT AND OCEAN PARK

Reference: **On the Pacific Ocean; map A1, grid g2.**

Campsites, facilities: There are 62 drive-through sites for trailers or RVs of any length. Electricity, piped water and sewer hookups are provided. Bottled gas, sanitary services, toilets, a store and laundry are available. A cafe and ice are located within one mile. Showers are available for an extra fee. Pets are permitted. Boat docks and launching facilities are nearby.

Reservations, fee: No reservations; $12-$13 fee per night; MasterCard and Visa accepted. Open all year.

Who to contact: Phone the park at (360) 374-6488 or write to P.O. Box 26, La Push, WA 98350.

Location: From Interstate 5 at Olympia, turn north on US 101 and drive approximately 178 miles to Forks. Turn west on La Push Road and drive 14 miles to the campground on the left.

Trip note: This private, developed park is set along the Pacific Ocean and the coastal Dungeness National Wildlife Refuge. It offers numerous recreation options such as fishing, beachcombing, boating, whale-watching and sunbathing.

26.   THREE RIVERS RESORT   RV

Reference: **On Soleduck River; map A1, grid g3.**

Campsites, facilities: There are 10 sites for tents, trailers or RVs of any length and five rental cabins. Picnic tables are provided. Bottled gas, toilets, a store, a cafe, laundry and ice are available. Electricity, piped water, sewer hookups, showers and firewood can be purchased for an extra fee. Leashed pets are permitted.

Reservations, fee: Reservations accepted; $8-$12 fee per night; cabins are $35-$45 per night. MasterCard and Visa accepted. Open all year.

Who to contact: Phone the park at (360) 374-5300 or write to HC 79, P.O. Box 280, Forks, WA 98331.

Location: From Interstate 5 at Olympia, turn north on US 101 and drive approximately 178 miles to Forks. Turn west on La Push Road and drive nine miles to the campground.

Trip note: This small, private camp is set on the Soleduck River. It's a pretty park with wooded, spacious sites. Beachcombing, hiking and fishing are options here. The coastal Dungeness National Wildlife Refuge and Pacific Ocean are a short drive to the west. Hoh Rain Forest is about 45 minutes away and a worthwhile sidetrip.

27.   HOH RIVER RESORT   RV

Reference: **On Hoh River; map A1, grid g4.**

Campsites, facilities: There are 23 sites for tents, trailers or RVs of any length. Electricity, piped water, sewer hookups and picnic tables are provided. Toilets, a store, laundry and ice are available. Showers and firewood are available for an extra fee. Pets and motorbikes are permitted.

Reservations, fee: Reservations accepted; $8-$13 fee per night. Open all year.

Who to contact: Phone the park at (360) 374-5566 or write to HC 80, P.O. Box 750, Forks, WA 98331.

Location: From Interstate 5 at Olympia, turn north on US 101 and drive 178 miles to Forks. Continue 15 miles south on US 101 to the campground.

Trip note: This is a nice camp along US 101 with a choice of grassy or graveled shady sites. Marked hiking trails are in the area. It's a pleasant little park, with steelhead and salmon fishing available and elk hunting in season. Horseshoe pits and a recreation field are provided for campers.

28.   BOGACHIEL STATE PARK   RV

Reference: **On Bogachiel River; map A1, grid g4.**

Campsites, facilities: There are two primitive tent sites, 34 developed tent sites, and six hookup sites for trailers or RVs up to 35 feet long. Picnic tables and fire grills are provided. A sanitary disposal station, restrooms, coin-operated showers and drinking water are available. A store and ice are located within one mile. A boat ramp is nearby. Leashed pets are permitted.

Reservations, fee: No reservations; $10-$15 fee per night. Open all year.

Who to contact: Phone the Washington State Parks Information Center at (800) 233-0321 or contact the park at (360) 374-6356 or HC 80, P.O. Box 500, Forks, WA 98331.

Location: From Interstate 5 at Olympia, turn north on US 101 and drive approximately 169 miles to the park on the left. It is located about six miles south of Forks.

Trip note: This is a good base camp for salmon or steelhead fishing trips. This 119-acre park is set on the Bogachiel River. There are marked hiking trails in the area. It can be noisy at times; there is a logging mill located directly across the river from the campground. Hunting is popular in the adjacent national forest.

29.　　　　　　HOH OXBOW

Reference: **On Hoh River; map A1, grid g4.**

Campsites, facilities: There are seven sites for tents or small trailers. Picnic tables, fire grills and tent pads are provided. Vault toilets and a hand boat launch are available. There is one **wheelchair accessible** site. Firearms are prohibited. **No piped water** is available. Pets on leashes are permitted.

Reservations, fee: No reservations; no fee. Open all year.

Who to contact: Phone the Department of Natural Resources at (360) 374-6131 or write to Department of Natural Resources, Olympic Region, 411 Tillicum Lane, Forks, WA 98331-9797.

Location: From Interstate 5 at Olympia, turn north on US 101 and drive approximately 175 miles to Forks. Continue south on US 101 for four miles and camp east of the highway next to the river.

Trip note: This is the most populated of the five camps on the Hoh River. It is primitive, close to the highway and the price is right. The adjacent boat launch makes this a popular camp with anglers.

30.　　　　　　COTTONWOOD

Reference: **On Hoh River; map A1, grid g4.**

Campsites, facilities: There are nine sites for tents or small trailers. Picnic tables, fire grills and tent pads are provided. Vault toilets, piped water and a boat launch are available. Pets on leashes are permitted.

Reservations, fee: No reservations; no fee. Open all year.

Who to contact: Phone the Department of Natural Resources at (360) 374-6131 or write to Department of Natural Resources, Olympic Region, 411 Tillicum Lane, Forks, WA 98331-9797.

Location: From Interstate 5 at Olympia, turn north on US 101 and drive approximately 175 miles to Forks. Continue 15 miles south on US 101, and then turn west on Oil City Road and drive 2.3 miles. Turn left on Road H 4060 (gravel) and drive one mile to the camp.

Trip note: An option to Willoughby Creek, Minnie Peterson and Hoh Oxbow, this primitive camp is also set along Hoh River. Like Hoh Oxbow, this camp offers the bonus of a boat launch. Being set some distance from the highway, almost insures fewer people.

31.　　　　　　WILLOUGHBY CREEK

Reference: **In Bert Cole State Forest; map A1, grid g5.**

Campsites, facilities: There are three campsites for tents or small trailers. Picnic tables, fire grills and tent pads are provided. Vault toilets are available, but there is **no piped water.** Pets on leashes are permitted.

Reservations, fee: No reservations; no fee. Open all year.

Who to contact: Phone the Department of Natural Resources at (360) 374-6131 or write to Department of Natural Resources, Olympic Region, 411 Tillicum Lane, Forks, WA 98331-9797.

Location: From Interstate 5 at Olympia, go north on US 101 and drive approximately 175 miles to Forks. Continue 14 miles south on US 101 and turn east on Hoh Rain Forest Road. Drive 3.5 miles to the camp on the right.

Trip note: This is a little-known, tiny and rustic camp set along Willoughby Creek and the Hoh River. The area gets heavy rainfall. There is good fishing in the area. Other campground options in the area are Hoh Oxbow, Minnie Peterson and Cottonwood.

32.   MINNIE PETERSON

Reference: **On Hoh River; map A1, grid g5.**

Campsites, facilities: There are eight campsites for tents or small trailers. Picnic tables, fire grills and tent pads are provided. Vault toilets and piped water are available. Firearms are prohibited. Pets on leashes are permitted.

Reservations, fee: No reservations; no fee. Open all year.

Who to contact: Phone the Department of Natural Resources at (360) 374-6131 or write to Department of Natural Resources, Olympic Region, 411 Tillicum Lane, Forks, WA 98331-9797.

Location: From Interstate 5 at Olympia, turn north on US 101 and drive approximately 175 miles to Forks. Continue 14 miles south on US 101 and turn east on Hoh Rain Forest Road. Drive 4.5 miles to the camp on the left.

Trip note: This is a primitive camp, set on the Hoh River on the edge of the Hoh Rain Forest. Bring your rain gear. Not many folks know about this spot. It is quite pretty and forested, with nice riverside sites.

33.   SOUTH FORK HOH

Reference: **In Bert Cole State Forest; map A1, grid g6.**

Campsites, facilities: There are three campsites for tents or small trailers. Picnic tables, fire grills and tent pads are provided. Vault toilets are available. There is **no piped water,** so bring your own. Pets on leashes are permitted.

Reservations, fee: No reservations; no fee. Open all year.

Who to contact: Phone the Department of Natural Resources at (360) 374-6131 or write to Department of Natural Resources, Olympic Region, 411 Tillicum Lane, Forks, WA 98331-9797.

Location: From Interstate 5 at Olympia, turn north on US 101 and drive approximately 175 miles to Forks. Continue 15 miles south on US 101, then turn east on Hoh Mainline Road and drive 6.5 miles. Turn left on Road H1000 and drive 7.5 miles to the camp on the right.

Trip note: This one is way out there. It's a rarely used camp set along the South Fork of Hoh River. Not many folks know about it. It is tiny and primitive, but offers a guarantee of peace and quiet, something many US 101 cruisers would cheerfully give a limb for after a few days of fighting crowds.

34.   HOH RAIN FOREST   **RV**

Reference: **In Olympic National Park; map A1, grid g6.**

Campsites, facilities: There are 89 sites for tents or RVs up to 21 feet long. Picnic tables and fire grills are provided. A sanitary disposal station, restrooms and drinking water are available. Leashed pets are permitted. Facilities are **wheelchair accessible.**

Reservations, fee: No reservations; $10 fee per night. Open all year.

Who to contact: Phone the Olympic National Park at (360) 452-4501 or write to 600 East Park Avenue, Port Angeles, WA 98362.

Location: From Interstate 5 at Olympia, turn north on US 101 and drive approximately 178 miles to Forks. Continue 14 miles south on US 101, then 19 miles east along the Hoh River until you arrive at the campground.

Trip note: This camp is at a trailhead leading into the interior of Olympic National Park and is located in the heart of a temperate, old growth rain forest. Willoughby Creek, Minnie Peterson, Cottonwood and Hoh Oxbow are nearby campgrounds, set downstream on the Hoh River, outside national park boundaries. In the summer, there are evening naturalist programs, and there is a visitor center nearby. This is one of the most popular camps in the park

---

35. SOL DUC RV

Reference: On Soleduck River in Olympic National Park; map A1, grid g7.

Campsites, facilities: There are 80 sites for tents or RVs up to 21 feet long. Picnic tables and fire grills are provided. A sanitary disposal station, restrooms, drinking water and **wheelchair facilities** are available. A store and a cafe are within one mile. Leashed pets are permitted.

Reservations, fee: No reservations; $10 fee per night. Open May to late October with limited winter facilities.

Who to contact: Phone the Olympic National Park at (360) 452-4501 or write to 600 East Park Avenue, Port Angeles, WA 98362.

Location: From Interstate 5 at Olympia, turn north on US 101 and drive approximately 122 miles to Port Angeles. Continue drive 27 miles west on US 101, then turn left at the Sol Duc turnoff and drive 12 miles to the camp.

Trip note: This site is a nice hideaway, with Soleduck Hot Springs a highlight. The problem is that it's quite popular. The camp fills up quickly on weekends, and a fee is charged to use the hot springs, which have been fully-developed since the early 1900s. The camp is set at 1,680 feet along Soleduck River. A naturalist program is available in summer months.

---

36. KALALOCH RV

Reference: Near the Pacific Ocean in Olympic National Park; map A1, grid h3.

Campsites, facilities: There are 177 sites for tents or RVs up to 21 feet long. Picnic tables and fire grills are provided. Restrooms, drinking water, **wheelchair facilities** and a trailer sanitary station are available. A store and a restaurant are within one mile. Pets on leashes are permitted in the campground.

Reservations, fee: No reservations; $10 fee per night. Open all year.

Who to contact: Phone the Olympic National Park at (360) 452-4501 or write to 600 East Park Avenue, Port Angeles, WA 98362.

Location: From Interstate 5 at Olympia, turn north on US 101 and drive approximately 178 miles to Forks. Continue 25 miles south on US 101.

Trip note: This camp is located on a bluff above the beach and some sites have ocean views. Like other camps set on the coast of the Olympic Peninsula, heavy rain in winter and spring is common. It's often foggy in summer. A naturalist program is offered in summer months. There are several good hiking trails in the park; see the visitor center for maps and information.

---

37. COPPERMINE BOTTOM

Reference: On Clearwater River; map A1, grid h5.

Campsites, facilities: There are nine campsites for tents or small trailers. Picnic tables, fire grills and tent pads are provided. Vault toilets, a group shelter and a hand boat launch are available. There is **no piped water** available. Pets on leashes are permitted.

Reservations, fee: No reservations; no fee. Open all year.

Who to contact: Phone the Department of Natural Resources at (360) 374-6131 or write to Department of Natural Resources, Olympic Region, 411 Tillicum Lane, Forks, WA 98331-9797.

Location: From Interstate 5 at Olympia, turn north on US 101 and drive approximately 175 miles to Forks. Continue south on US 101 to milepost 147, then turn north on Hoh Clearwater Mainline Road and drive 12.5 miles. Turn right on C1010 (a graveled one-lane road) and drive 1.5 miles. The camp is on the left.

Trip note: Few tourists ever visit this primitive, hidden campground with river dory launching facilities. It's set on Clearwater River, a tributary to the Queets River, which runs to the ocean. The boat launch is a bonus, and makes this a perfect camp for anglers who want to avoid the usual Highway 101 crowds.

38.   UPPER CLEARWATER

Reference: **On Clearwater River; map A1, grid h5.**

Campsites, facilities: There are nine sites for tents or small trailers. Picnic tables, fire grills and tent pads are provided. Vault toilets, piped water and a hand boat launch are available. Pets on leashes are permitted.

Reservations, fee: No reservations; no fee. Open all year.

Who to contact: Phone the Department of Natural Resources at (360) 374-6131 or write to Department of Natural Resources, Olympic Region, 411 Tillicum Lane, Forks, WA 98331-9797.

Location: From Interstate 5 at Olympia, turn north on US 101 and drive approximately 175 miles to Forks. Continue south on US 101 to milepost 147, then turn north on Hoh Clearwater Mainline Road. Drive 13 miles, then turn right on C3000 (a gravel one-lane road) and drive 3.3 miles. The camp entrance is on the right.

Trip note: This is one of the three primitive camps set along the Clearwater River. It has river dory launching facilities. This is a great camp—it's pretty, unused by most tourists, has a boat ramp, piped water and all other amenities, and best of all, it's free.

39.   YAHOO LAKE

Reference: **Hike-in only in Bert Cole State Forest; map A1, grid h6.**

Campsites, facilities: There are four tent sites at this primitive hike-in camp. Pit toilets, a group shelter with a fireplace and a boat dock are available. There is **no piped water,** so bring your own. Pets on leashes are permitted.

Reservations, fee: No reservations; no fee. Open all year, weather permitting.

Who to contact: Phone the Department of Natural Resources at (360) 374-6131 or write to Department of Natural Resources, Olympic Region, 411 Tillicum Lane, Forks, WA 98331-9797.

Location: From Interstate 5 at Olympia, turn north on US 101 and drive approximately 175 miles to Forks. Continue south on US 101 to milepost 147, then turn north on Hoh Clearwater Mainline Road. Drive 13 miles, then turn right on C3000 (a graveled one-lane road) and drive four miles. Turn right on C 3100 (a graveled two-lane road), keep left and continue on C 3100 another three-quarters of a mile to the trailhead. Hike in 500 feet to the camp.

Trip note: This camp is set at about 2,000 feet on the edge of tiny Yahoo Lake. It's an idyllic setting that few people take advantage of. There are hiking trails in the area and fishing in the lake. If you're willing to take a little time to get here, this can be the camper's ideal getaway.

40. WILLABY   **RV**

Reference: **On Quinault Lake in Olympic National Forest; map A1, grid i6.**

Campsites, facilities: There are 22 sites for tents, trailers or RVs up to 16 feet long. Picnic tables are provided. Piped water, flush toilets and electricity in the bathrooms are available. Leashed pets are permitted. Boat docks, launching facilities and rentals are available at nearby Quinault Lake.

Reservations, fee: No reservations; $12.50 fee per night. Open mid-April to mid-November.

Who to contact: Phone the Quinault Ranger District at (360) 288-2525 or write to Quinault Ranger District, P.O. Box 9, Quinault, WA 98575.

Location: From Interstate 5 north of Olympia, take exit 104 and drive west on Highway 8 for 27 miles to Elma (where Highway 8 becomes US 12). Continue 25 miles on US 12 to US 101. Drive north on US 101 for 45 miles to Quinault. Turn northeast on County Road 5 and drive 1.5 miles to the camp.

Trip note: This 14-acre camp is set on the shore of Quinault Lake at 200 feet. The Quinault Rain Forest Nature Trail and the Quinault Loop National Recreation Trail are nearby. Quinault Lake covers about six square miles. This camp is concessionaire-operated.

41. JULY CREEK

Reference: **On Quinault Lake, walk-in only in Olympic National Park; map A1, grid i6.**

Campsites, facilities: There are 29 walk-in tent sites. Picnic tables and fire grills are provided. Toilets and drinking water are available. Pets are permitted on leashes.

Reservations, fee: No reservations; no fee. Open all year.

Who to contact: Phone the Olympic National Park at (360) 452-4501 or write to 600 East Park Avenue, Port Angeles, WA 98362.

Location: From Interstate 5 south of Olympia, take exit 88 and turn west on US 12. Drive 46 miles, then turn north on US 101 and drive 46 miles to the town of Amanda Park. Continue two miles north on US 101, then turn right and drive for two miles along north shore of Quinault Lake to the camp.

Trip note: This primitive alternative is on the north shore of Quinault Lake. The camp is set where July Creek empties into the lake. Full supplies are available on the southern shoreline of the lake, which has a marina. This is a good choice for hikers looking to avoid crowds.

42. QUEETS

Reference: **On Queets River in Olympic National Park; map A1, grid i6.**

Campsites, facilities: There are 20 primitive tent sites. Picnic tables and fire grills are provided. Toilets are available, but there is **no piped water**. Pets are permitted. Restrooms are **wheelchair accessible.**

Reservations, fee: No reservations; no fee. Open year-round.

Who to contact: Phone the Olympic National Park at (360) 452-4501 or write to 600 East Park Avenue, Port Angeles, WA 98362.

Location: From Interstate 5 south of Olympia, take exit 88 and turn west on US 12. Drive 46 miles, then turn north on US 101 and drive 46 miles to the town of Amanda Park. Continue 19 miles north, then turn northeast on an unpaved road (there is a sign indicating the campground) and drive 14 miles along Queets River. The campground is at the end of the road.

Trip note: This is a gem of a find if you don't mind bringing your own water or purifying river water. The camp is primitive and set on the shore of the Queets River. Being so close to the highway, it gets a fair amount of use, so it is advisable to arrive as early in the day as possible. A trailhead is available for hikes into the interior of Olympic National Park.

43. GATTON CREEK **RV**

Reference: **On Quinault Lake in Olympic National Forest; map A1, grid i7.**

Campsites, facilities: There are five tent sites and eight overflow RV sites (in a parking area). Picnic tables are provided. Vault toilets, **wheelchair-accessible** restrooms and firewood are available. Leashed pets are permitted.

Reservations, fee: No reservations; $7 fee per night. There is no charge for picnicking. Open May to October.

Who to contact: Phone the Quinault Ranger District at (360) 288-2525 or write to Quinault Ranger District, P.O. Box 9, Quinault, WA 98575.

Location: From Interstate 5 south of Olympia, take exit 88 and turn west on US 12. Drive 46 miles, then turn north on US 101 and drive 45 miles to the South Shore Lake Quinault turnoff (County Road 5). Turn northeast and drive 3.5 miles to the camp on the shore of Quinault Lake.

Trip note: This three-acre camp is set on the shore of Quinault Lake at a 200-foot elevation where Gatton Creek empties into it. The Quinault Rain Forest Nature Trail and the Quinault Loop National Recreation Trail are nearby. Quinault Lake covers about six square miles. This camp, like the others on Quinault Lake, is concessionaire-operated.

44. FALLS CREEK **RV**

Reference: **On Quinault Lake in Olympic National Forest; map A1, grid i7.**

Campsites, facilities: There are 11 tent sites and 20 sites for trailers or RVs up to 16 feet long. Picnic tables are provided. Piped water, flush toilets, and electricity in the bathrooms are available. Pets on leashes are permitted. Boat docks, launching facilities and rentals are available at nearby Quinault Lake. **Wheelchair-accessible** restrooms are available.

Reservations, fee: No reservations; $12.50 fee per night. Open Memorial Day through Labor Day.

Who to contact: Phone the Quinault Ranger District, Olympic National Forest at (360) 288-2525 or write to Quinault Ranger District, P.O. Box 9, Quinault, WA 98575.

Location: From Interstate 5 south of Olympia, take exit 88 and turn west on US 12. Drive 46 miles, then turn north on US 101 and drive 45 miles to the Quinault turnoff (County Road 5). Turn northeast and drive three miles to the camp on the shore of Quinault Lake.

Trip note: This scenic five-acre camp is set at 200 feet, where Falls Creek empties into Quinault Lake. The Quinault Rain Forest Nature Trail and Quinault Loop National Recreation Trail are nearby. The camp is located adjacent to the Quinault Ranger Station and historic Lake Quinault Lodge.

45.   CAMPBELL TREE GROVE   RV

Reference: **On Humptulips River in Olympic National Forest; map A1, grid i8.**

Campsites, facilities: There are eight tent sites and three sites for trailers or RVs up to 16 feet long. Picnic tables are provided. Vault toilets and well water are available. Leashed pets are permitted.

Reservations, fee: No reservations; no fee. Open year-round.

Who to contact: Phone the Quinault Ranger District, Olympic National Forest at (360) 288-2525 or write to Quinault Ranger District, P.O. Box 9, Quinault, WA 98575.

Location: From Interstate 5 south of Olympia, take exit 88 and turn west on US 12. Drive 46 miles, then turn north on US 101 and drive 22 miles to Humptulips. Turn north on Forest Service Road 22 and drive eight miles, then turn north on Forest Service Road 2204 and continue about 14 miles to the campground.

Trip note: This 14-acre camp is set at 1,100 feet. Trails leading into the Colonel Bob Wilderness are nearby; see a Forest Service map for locations. The West Fork of the Humptulips River runs near the camp. It's a prime base camp for a wilderness expedition. Fishing is an option here as well.

46.   GRAVES CREEK   RV

Reference: **Near Quinault River in Olympic National Park; map A1, grid i9.**

Campsites, facilities: There are 30 sites for tents or RVs up to 21 feet long. Picnic tables, fire grills, drinking water and restrooms are available. The facilities are **wheelchair accessible.** Leashed pets are permitted.

Reservations, fee: No reservations; no fee. Open all year with limited winter facilities.

Who to contact: Phone the Olympic National Park at (360) 452-4501 or write to 600 East Park Avenue, Port Angeles, WA 98362.

Location: From Interstate 5 south of Olympia, take exit 88 and turn west on US 12. Drive 46 miles, then turn north on US 101 and drive approximately 45 miles to the Quinault turnoff. Turn east and drive 15 miles. The campground and Graves Creek Ranger District are located at road's end.

Trip note: This camp is set at 540 feet and set a short distance from a trailhead leading into many areas in the backcountry of Olympic National Park. See an Olympic Forest Service National Park map for details. The upper Quinault River is nearby, but there are lakes in the area.

47.   STAIRCASE   RV

Reference: **On North Fork Skokomish River in Olympic National Park; map A1, grid i9.**

Campsites, facilities: There are 59 sites for tents or RVs up to 21 feet long. Picnic tables and fire grills are provided. Restrooms, drinking water and **wheelchair facilities** are available. Leashed pets are permitted in camp.

Reservations, fee: No reservations; $8 fee per night. Open all year.

Who to contact: Phone the Olympic National Park at (360) 452-4501 or write to 600 East Park Avenue, Port Angeles, WA 98362.

Location: From Interstate 5 at Olympia, turn north on US 101 and drive 37 miles to the town of Hoodsport. Turn west on Lake Cushman Road and drive 17 miles to the camp.

Trip note: This camp is located on the Staircase Rapids of the North Fork of the Skokomish River, about one mile from where it empties into Lake Cushman.

It is a take-your-pick spot. A major trailhead at the camp leads to many areas in the backcountry of Olympic National Park. See an Olympic National Park and Forest Service maps for details. A beautiful two-mile loop trail runs along the river.

---

48. COHO   RV

Reference: **On Wynoochee Lake in Olympic National Forest; map A1, grid j8.**

Campsites, facilities: There are 58 sites for tents, trailers or RVs up to 36 feet long. Picnic tables are provided. Flush toilets, piped water and **wheelchair-accessible** restrooms are available. Leashed pets are permitted. Boat docks and launching facilities are available at Wynoochee Lake.

Reservations, fee: No reservations; $5-$7 fee per night. Open May to mid-November.

Who to contact: Phone the Hood Canal Ranger District at (360) 877-5254 or write to Hood Canal Ranger District at P.O. Box 68, Hoodsport, WA 98548.

Location: From Interstate 5 south of Olympia, take exit 88 and turn west on US 8, which becomes US 12 in 15 miles. Drive 36 miles to Montesano. Turn north on Wynoochee Valley Road, one mile west of Montesano, and drive 12 miles, then continue north for another 22 miles on Forest Service Road 22 to the camp on the west shore of Wynoochee Lake. A Forest Service map is essential.

Trip note: This eight-acre camp is set on the shore of Wynoochee Lake at 900 feet. Points of interest include a working forest nature trail, Wynoochee Dam Viewpoint and a 12-mile national recreation trail that goes around the lake. This is one of the most idyllic drive-to settings you could hope to find.

WASHINGTON MAP .... see page 90
Adjoining Maps
NORTH .... no map
EAST (A3) .... see page 166
SOUTH (B2) .... see page 294
WEST (A1) .... see page 92

131 LISTINGS
PAGES 112-165

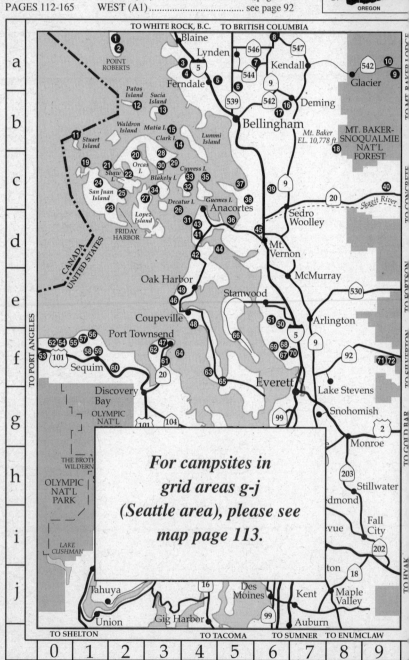

For campsites in
grid areas g-j
(Seattle area), please see
map page 113.

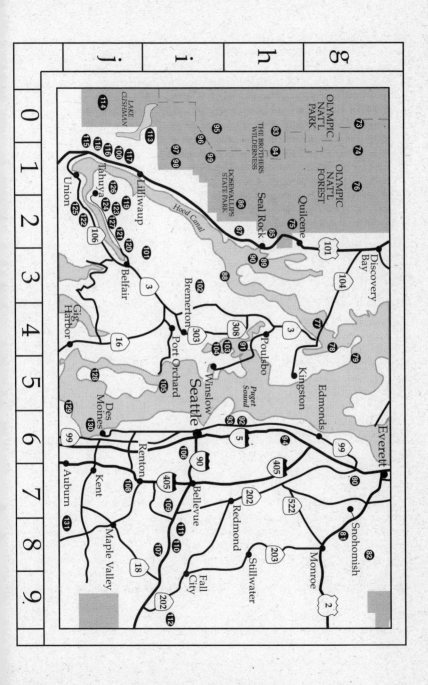

Washington Map A2 featuring: Point Roberts, Birch Bay, Nooksack River, Mount Baker-Snoqualmie National Forest, San Juan Islands, Patos Island State Park, Orcas Island, Bellingham, Roche Harbor, Moran State Park, Spencer Spit State Park, Padilla Bay, Samish Bay, Larrabee State Park, Skagit River, Anacortes, Washington Park, Puget Sound, Fort Worden State Park, Lake Goodwin, Fort Casey State Park, Dungeness River, Sequim Bay, Stillaguamish River, Blue Mountain, Olympic National Park, Olympic National Forest, Gray Wolf River, Hood Canal, Kitsap Memorial State Park, Quilcene River, Dosewallips River, Silver Lake, Blackman's Lake, Duckabush River, Seattle, Hamma Hamma River, Bert Cole State Forest, Tahuya State Forest, Lake Sammamish State Park, Cascade Mountains, Snoqualmie River, Tacoma, Stuck River

---

1.   SUNNY POINT RESORT   RV

Reference: **On Point Roberts; map A2, grid a2.**

Campsites, facilities: There are approximately 25 spaces for tents and 50 sites for trailers or RVs. Restrooms, showers, a public phone and a recreation field is available. Pets are permitted on leashes.

Reservations, fee: Reservations recommended; $10-$17 fee per night. Open year round.

Who to contact: Phone the park at (360) 945-1986 or write to 1408 Gulf Road, Point Roberts, WA 98281.

Location: The park is located on Point Roberts. From Bellingham, take Interstate 5 north through Blaine and the border customs to Highway 99N (British Columbia). Follow the signs for the Victoria Ferry to Highway 17. Turn south on Highway 17 through Twassen. Cross the U.S./Canada border (where Highway 17 becomes Tyee Road). Continue on Tyee Road, turning right on Gulf Road and drive one-half mile to the park on the right.

Trip note: This park is set on remote Point Roberts, a beautiful spot. It is a pretty camp, suitable for both trailers and tents and a bit smaller and more private than Whalen's RV Park. The campground is located only 2.5 blocks from the ocean and just one-half mile from Lighthouse Park. A golf course is nearby.

---

2.   WHALEN'S RV PARK   RV

Reference: **On Point Roberts; map A2, grid a2.**

Campsites, facilities: There are 100 sites for tents and 65 sites for trailers or RVs of any length. Electricity, piped water and picnic tables are provided. Flush toilets, sanitary services, firewood and showers are available. A store, a cafe, a laundromat and ice are located within one mile. Pets are permitted. Boat docks, launching facilities and rentals are nearby.

Reservations, fee: Reservations accepted; $15-$18 fee per night. Open May to late October.

Who to contact: Phone (360) 945-2874 or write to P.O. Box 985, Point Roberts, WA 98281.

Location: From Bellingham, take Interstate 5 north through Blaine and border customs to Highway 99N (British Columbia). Drive 11 miles north on BC 99, then turn west on BC 10 and drive to Benson Road. Turn left and drive to

Boundary Bay Road. Turn left and drive to Bay View Road. Turn left again and drive one-half mile to the park on the left.

Trip note: This little spot, a mix of woods and water, is known to few. It requires a roundabout drive into Canada to reach, and therefore is missed by most tourists. The park has grassy sites and lots of trees. A recreation field is provided for campers. Nearby recreational options include an 18-hole golf course, a full-service marina and tennis courts.

---

3.   BIRCH BAY TRAILER PARK   RV

Reference: **On Birch Bay; map A2, grid a4.**

Campsites, facilities: There are 64 drive-through sites for trailers or RVs of any length (40 are full hookup sites). Electricity, piped water, sewer hookups and picnic tables are provided. Flush toilets, bottled gas, sanitary services, showers, a recreation hall, satellite TV and a laundromat are available. A store, a cafe and ice are located within one mile. Pets and motorbikes are permitted. Boat launching facilities are nearby.

Reservations, fee: Reservations accepted; $17-$20 fee per night. MasterCard and Visa accepted. Open all year.

Who to contact: Phone (360) 371-7922 or write to 8080 Harbor View, Blaine, WA 98230.

Location: From Interstate 5 south of Blaine, take exit 270 and drive four miles west on Birch Bay-Lynden Road, then 300 feet south on Harbor View to the park.

Trip note: This private campground provides good ocean access on Birch Bay. This camp is actually a large mobile home park with a few spaces for campers. Nearby recreational options include a full-service marina and tennis courts.

---

4.   BIRCH BAY STATE PARK   RV

Reference: **On Birch Bay; map A2, grid a4.**

Campsites, facilities: There are 147 sites for tents or self-contained RVs, and 20 partial-hookup (water and electric) sites for trailers or RVs of any length. Picnic tables and fire grills are provided. Flush toilets, coin-operated showers, firewood and a sanitary disposal station are available. A store, a restaurant, a laundromat and ice are located within one mile. Some facilities are **wheelchair accessible**. Leashed pets are permitted.

Reservations, fee: Contact Reservations Northwest at (800) 452-5687 ($6 reservation fee); $10-$16 fee per night, $5 per extra vehicle per night. Open all year.

Who to contact: Phone (800) 233-0321 or (360) 371-2800 or write to 5105 Helwig Road, Blaine, WA 98230.

Location: From Interstate 5 at Blaine, drive 10 miles south and take the Grandview exit (Exit 266). Turn right on Grandview Road and follow the signs for about seven miles. Turn right on Jackson Road and drive one-quarter mile to Helwig Road. Turn left into the park.

Trip note: This park covers 193 acres and includes a mile-long beach. More than 100 different species of birds, many of which are migrating on the Pacific Flyway, can be seen here. Recreation options here include fishing and clam digging. Be sure to check out the Terrell Marsh Interpretive Trail. Several 18-hole golf courses are available nearby.

5. FERNDALE CAMPGROUND RV

Reference: **In Ferndale; map A2, grid a5.**

Campsites, facilities: There are 127 sites for tents, trailers or RVs of any length. Electricity, piped water and sewer hookups are provided. Flush toilets, showers, bottled gas, a laundromat, a playground, a small store and ice are available. Small pets are permitted.

Reservations, fee: Reservations accepted; $18-$20 fee per night. Open all year.

Who to contact: Phone (360) 384-2622 or write to 6335 Portal Way, Ferndale, WA 98248.

Location: From Interstate 5 at Ferndale, take exit 263 and drive one mile north on Portal Way.

Trip note: An option to KOA Lynden and Windmill Inn, this campground provides more direct access from Interstate 5. It's a nice, clean camp with spacious sites and trees. A fishing pond, horseshoe pits, a game room and a recreation field provide possible activities for campers. A golf course and riding stable provide nearby options.

---

6. WINDMILL INN RV

Reference: **Near Nooksack River; map A2, grid a5.**

Campsites, facilities: There are eight sites for trailers or RVs of any length. Electricity, piped water, sewer, cable TV and phone hookups, a park and picnic tables are provided. Flush toilets, showers, bottled gas, a store, a cafe, a laundromat and ice are available within one mile. Pets are permitted. Boat launching facilities are nearby.

Reservations, fee: Reservations accepted; $15 fee per night; MasterCard, Visa, American Express and Discovery accepted. Open all year.

Who to contact: Phone (360) 354-3424 or write to 8022 Guide Meridian Road, Lynden, WA 98264.

Location: From Interstate 5 at Bellingham, take exit 256 and drive 10 miles north on Highway 539.

Trip note: This nice little spot is set near the Nooksack River and Wiser Lake. This camp is used primarily as a layover for people heading up to Canada; it's the last stop before the border. It is quiet and pretty, with lots of trees and flowers. Area attractions include Mount Baker, the quaint little shops of Lynden and the nearby Birch Bay area, which offers numerous recreation options.

---

7. KOA LYNDEN RV

Reference: **In Lynden; map A2, grid a6.**

Campsites, facilities: There are 80 tent sites and 100 sites (25 drive-through) for trailers or RVs of any length. There are also 12 cabins. Electricity, piped water, sewer hookups and picnic tables are provided. Flush toilets, bottled gas, sanitary services, showers, firewood, a recreation hall, store, a cafe, a laundromat, ice, a playground, mini-golf and a swimming pool are available. Pets are permitted. Boat rentals are available.

Reservations, fee: Reservations accepted; $15-$25 fee per night. Cabins are $33 per night. MasterCard and Visa accepted. Open all year.

Who to contact: Phone (360) 354-4772 or write to 8717 Line Road, Lynden, WA 98264.

Location: From Interstate 5 at Bellingham, take exit 256 and drive 12 miles north on Highway 539, then turn east on Highway 546 (Badger Road) and drive three miles. Turn south on Line Road and drive one block to the campground.

Trip note: This campground is a holdover spot for vacationers heading north to Canada via Highways 539 and 546. It is exceptionally clean and in a lovely setting, with pretty grassy sites and lots of trees. There is a pond where campers can fish for trout. Tackle and boat rentals are available. Nearby recreational options include an 18-hole golf course and tennis courts.

8. SUMAS RV PARK

Reference: **In Sumas; map A2, grid a7.**

Campsites, facilities: There are six tent sites and 30 sites (five drive-through) for trailers or RVs of any length. Electricity, piped water and picnic tables are provided. Flush toilets, sanitary services, showers, firewood and a ballpark are available. Bottled gas, a store, a cafe, a laundromat and ice are located within one mile. Pets and motorbikes are permitted.

Reservations, fee: Reservations accepted; $10-$15 fee per night. Open all year.

Who to contact: Phone (360) 988-8875 or write to 9600 Easterbrook Road, Sumas, WA 98295.

Location: From Interstate 5 at Bellingham, take exit 256 and drive 12 miles, then turn north on Highway 546 (Badger Road) and drive 14 miles to Sumas. At the junction of Highway 9 and Cherry Street, turn south on Cherry Street and drive two blocks to the park on the left.

Trip note: Set on the edge of the U.S./Canada border, this campground is a holdover spot to spend American dollars before heading into British Columbia. It has graveled sites and a few trees, set in the grassy flatlands. Nearby recreation options include an 18-hole golf course and tennis courts.

9. EXCELSIOR GROUP CAMP

Reference: **Near Nooksack River in Mount Baker-Snoqualmie National Forest; map A2, grid a9.**

Campsites, facilities: There are two group sites only. Picnic tables, vault toilets and fire grills are provided, but there is **no piped water**. Leashed pets are permitted.

Reservations, fee: Reservations required for all groups; call (800) 280-CAMP for current fee. Open May to October.

Who to contact: Phone the Mount Baker-Snoqualmie National Forest at (360) 599-2714 or write to Mt. Baker Ranger District, 2105 State Route 20, Sedro Woolley, WA 98284.

Location: From Interstate 5 at Bellingham, turn east on Highway 542 and drive 31 miles to Glacier. Continue 6.5 miles east on Highway 542 to the camp.

Trip note: This campground is set near the Nooksack River less than a mile from Nooksack Falls and 1.5 miles from the site of the Excelsior Mine. There are numerous hiking trails available in the Mount Baker Wilderness, located to the east and south. Remember to bring your own water.

10. DOUGLAS FIR

Reference: **On Nooksack River in Mount Baker-Snoqualmie National Forest; map A2, grid a9.**

Campsites, facilities: There are 30 sites for tents, trailers or RVs up to 31 feet long. Picnic tables and fire grills are provided. Well water and vault toilets are available. A store, a cafe, a laundromat and ice are located within five miles. Leashed pets are permitted.

Reservations, fee: Reserve sites by calling (800) 280-CAMP ($7.50 reservation fee); $8 fee per night. Open May to October with self-service access the remainder of the year.

Who to contact: Phone the Mount Baker-Snoqualmie National Forest at (360) 599-2714 or write to Mt. Baker Ranger District, 2105 State Route 20, Sedro Woolley, WA 98284.

Location: From Interstate 5 at Bellingham, turn east on Highway 542 and drive 31 miles to Glacier. Continue two miles northeast on Highway 542 to the campground.

Trip note: Set along the Nooksack River, this camp is an option to Silver Fir, Excelsior Group Camp, Douglas Fir and Larrabee State Park. Fishing is available on the river, and there are hiking trails in the area. See the trip notes for above camps for more information on the area.

11.   STUART ISLAND MARINE STATE PARK

Reference: **Near San Juan Island, boat-in only; map A2, grid b1.**

Campsites, facilities: There are 19 primitive campsites. Picnic tables and piped water are provided. Pit toilets are available. Twenty-two buoys and floats are available for overnight moorage.

Reservations, fee: No reservations; $5-$11 fee per night. Open May 1 through Labor Day.

Who to contact: Phone (800) 233-0321, (360) 902-8563 or (360) 378-2044 or write to 6158 Lighthouse Road, Friday Harbor, WA 98250.

Location: The park is on the north side of Stuart Island and is accessible only by boat. Stuart Island is located northwest of San Juan Island.

Trip note: This is really stalking the unknown. It's a remote little island on the edge of Canadian waters that covers 153 acres and has excellent harbors for mooring. It is the western-most of the marine parks and is a jumpoff point for Limekiln, Sucia Island, Orcas Island and San Juan Island parks. There is good fishing at nearby Reed and Provost harbors. This park is very quiet and primitive, receiving little use even in the summer months.

12.   PATOS ISLAND STATE PARK

Reference: **Near Sucia Island, boat-in only; map A2, grid b2.**

Campsites, facilities: There are seven primitive campsites. Vault and pit toilets are available, but there is **no piped water**. Boat buoys are available for overnight moorage.

Reservations, fee: No reservations; $5 fee per night. Open all year.

Who to contact: Phone (800) 233-0321, (360) 902-8563 or (360) 378-2044 or write to 6158 Lighthouse Road, Friday Harbor, WA 98250.

Location: The park is on the east side of Patos Island, which is 2.5 miles northwest of Sucia Island and five miles northwest of Orcas Island. It is accessible only by boat and is the northernmost of the coastal islands.

Trip note: If you are going to get stranded on an island, this is not a bad choice, providing you like your companion. There are good hiking trails and excellent fishing opportunities here. It is tiny, primitive and used by few.

13.   SUCIA ISLAND MARINE STATE PARK

Reference: **Near Orcas Island, boat-in only; map A2, grid b3.**

Campsites, facilities: There are 55 primitive campsites. Picnic tables are provided and vault and composting toilets are available. Campers are asked to pack out their garbage. Boat buoys and floats are available for overnight moorage.

Reservations, fee: No reservations; $11 fee per night. Open May 1 through September.

Who to contact: Phone (800) 233-0321, (360) 902-8563 or (360) 378-2044 or write to 6158 Lighthouse Road, Friday Harbor, WA 98250.

Location: The park is on the north side of Sucia Island, which is located 2.5 miles north of Orcas Island. It is accessible only by boat.

Trip note: A classic spot, with rocky outcrops for lookout points and good beach and fishing areas. This island covers 562 acres, and provides opportunities for hiking, clamming, crabbing, canoeing and scuba diving. Though primitive, the campground is beautiful and well worth the trip.

14.   CLARK ISLAND STATE PARK

Reference: **Near Orcas Island, boat-in only; map A2, grid b3.**

Campsites, facilities: There are eight primitive campsites. Vault toilets are available, but there is **no piped water**. Boat buoys are available for overnight moorage. No trash services are provided, so you must pack out your garbage.

Reservations, fee: No reservations; $5 fee per night. Open all year.

Who to contact: Phone (800) 233-0321, (360) 902-8563 or (360) 378-2044 or write to 6158 Lighthouse Road, Friday Harbor, WA 98250.

Location: The campground is on tiny Clark Island, located northeast of Orcas Island. It is accessible only by boat.

Trip note: This island state park offers beautiful beaches with opportunities for scuba diving. Beachcombing and sunbathing are two other popular options. For just $5 a night, you can pretend you're on a deserted Caribbean island. Well, almost. There are excellent views of the other nearby islands from the campground.

15.   MATIA ISLAND STATE PARK

Reference: **Near Orcas Island, boat-in only; map A2, grid b3.**

Campsites, facilities: There are six primitive campsites. Composting toilets are available. There is a boat dock, and buoys and floats are available for overnight moorage.

Reservations, fee: No reservations; $5-$11 fee per night. Open May 1 through September.

Who to contact: Phone (800) 233-0321, (360) 902-8563 or (360) 378-2044 or write to 6158 Lighthouse Road, Friday Harbor, WA 98250.

Location: The campground is located on the northeast side of Matia Island, which is 2.5 miles northeast of Orcas Island. It is accessible only by boat.

Trip note: The campsites are located just a short walk from the docking facilities. Many of the other island campgrounds don't have docks. Good fishing and beachcombing are among the highlights. Scuba diving is also popular here.

16.　　　　　　LILY LAKE

Reference: **Near Bellingham, hike-in only; map A2, grid b7.**

Campsites, facilities: There are six primitive tent sites. Leashed pets are allowed.

Reservations, fee: No reservations; no fee. Open all year.

Who to contact: Phone the Department of Natural Resources at (360) 856-3500 or write to Department of Natural Resources, Northwest Region, 919 North Township Street, Sedro Woolley, WA 98284-9395.

Location: From Interstate 5 south of Bellingham, take exit 240 and drive one-half mile north on Samish Lake Road. Turn left on Barrel Springs Road and drive one mile, then turn right on Road SW-C-1000 and drive 1.5 miles to the Blanchard Hill Trailhead. Hike 2.7 miles, then veer right and continue one-half mile to the campground.

Trip note: This tiny, remote campground is one of those that few people ever go to or even know about. Set on little Lily Lake, it is completely secluded and very primitive; you will have to pack in everything you need and pack out everything that's left. This is a prime area for hiking, and the nearby trails are used by hikers and horse-packers alike.

17.　　　　　　LIZARD LAKE

Reference: **Near Bellingham, hike-in only; map A2, grid b7.**

Campsites, facilities: There are three primitive tent sites. Picnic tables, tent pads, fire grills and vault toilets are available, but there is **no piped water**. Leashed pets are permitted.

Reservations, fee: No reservations; no fee. Open all year.

Who to contact: Phone the Department of Natural Resources at (360) 856-3500 or write to Department of Natural Resources, Northwest Region, 919 North Township Street, Sedro Woolley, WA 98284-9395.

Location: From Interstate 5 south of Bellingham, take exit 240 and drive one-half mile north on Samish Lake Road. Turn left on Barrel Springs Road and drive one mile, then turn right on Road SW-C-1000 and drive 1.5 miles to the Blanchard Hill Trailhead. Hike 2.7 miles, then veer right and continue three-quarters of a mile to the campground.

Trip note: Set just two-tenths of a mile down the trail from Lily Lake Campground, this campground is even smaller and more isolated. It is set on Lizard Lake in a pretty, forested area. See the trip note for Lily Lake.

18.　　　　　　HUTCHINSON CREEK

Reference: **Near South Fork in Nooksack River; map A2, grid b8.**

Campsites, facilities: There are 11 sites for tents or small trailers. Picnic tables, fire grills vault toilets and tent pads are provided, but there is **no piped water**. A store is located within one mile. Leashed pets are permitted.

Reservations, fee: No reservations; no fee. Open all year.

Who to contact: Phone the Department of Natural Resources at (360) 856-3500 or write to Department of Natural Resources, Northwest Region, 919 North Township Street, Sedro Woolley, WA 98284-9395.

Location: From Interstate 5 at Burlington, turn east on Highway 20 and drive seven miles. Turn north on Highway 9 and drive 16 miles to Acme, just north of the Nooksack River Bridge. Turn east on Mosquito Lake Road and drive 2.5 miles, then turn right on a gravel road and continue for one-half mile to the campground.

Trip note: This campground is set in the forest along Hutchinson Creek near the South Fork of the Nooksack River. Managed by the Department of Natural Resources, it's rustic, beautiful, primitive and unknown to out-of-towners.

19.   POSEY ISLAND STATE PARK

Reference: **Near Roche Harbor, boat-in only; map A2, grid c1.**

Campsites, facilities: There is one primitive campsite. Fire rings and composting toilets are provided.

Reservations, fee: No reservations; $5 fee per night. Open all year.

Who to contact: Phone (800) 233-0321, (360) 902-8563 or (360) 378-2044 or write to 6158 Lighthouse Road, Friday Harbor, WA 98250.

Location: This little island is just north of Roche Harbor (on San Juan Island) and is accessible only by small boat.

Trip note: If you want a beautiful little spot all to yourself, this is it, the smallest campground in Washington. It is difficult to get here, however. The best way is by skiff, a short cruise from San Juan Island.

20.   WEST BEACH RESORT   **RV**

Reference: **On Orcas Island; map A2, grid c2.**

Campsites, facilities: There are 62 sites for tents, trailers or RVs. Restrooms, showers, a sanitary dump, a public phone, a laundromat, ice, a playground and LP gas bottles are available. There is also a boat ramp, dock, marina and rentals available. Pets are permitted on leashes; there is a small charge.

Reservations, fee: Reservations recommended; $14-$20 fee per night. Visa and MasterCard accepted. Open year round.

Who to contact: Phone the resort at (360) 376-2240 or write to Route 1, P.O. Box 510, Eastsound, WA 98245.

Location: From Bellingham, drive south on Interstate 5 past Mount Vernon and follow the signs to the San Juan Islands Ferry Terminals (about 45 minutes). Take the ferry from Anacortes to Orcas Island. From the ferry landing, turn left and drive for 11 miles on Horseshoe Highway to the entrance of town. There is a green sign that directs you toward Moran State Park (left). The West Beach Resort is a quarter mile further on the left, there is a sign for the resort but the road is not named.

Trip note: Right on the beach, this resort offers salmon fishing, boating and swimming. It is an excellent alternative to the often-full Moran State Park and offers all the same recreation opportunities. The beaches at Orcas Island are prime spots for whale watching and sunset viewing.

21.   JONES ISLAND MARINE STATE PARK

Reference: **Near Orcas Island, boat-in only; map A2, grid c1.**

Campsites, facilities: There are 21 primitive campsites. Picnic tables are provided and vault, composting and pit toilets are available. Boat buoys and floats are available for overnight moorage.

Reservations, fee: No reservations; $5-$11 fee per night. Open May through September.

Who to contact: Phone (360) 753-2027 or write to 6158 Lighthouse Road, Friday Harbor, WA 98250.

Location: The campground is on tiny Jones Island, located one mile off the southwest tip of Orcas Island. It is accessible only by boat.

Trip note: This little island is another hidden spot that gets little use. The campground is near the beach, so you don't have to carry your gear very far. The area provides good fishing and scuba diving. A note of caution: Raccoons have become pests and campers are advised to keep food well-contained.

22.　　BLIND ISLAND STATE PARK

Reference: **Near Shaw Island, boat-in only; map A2, grid c2.**

Campsites, facilities: There are four primitive campsites. Composting and pit toilets are available, but there is **no piped water**. Boat buoys are available for overnight moorage.

Reservations, fee: No reservations; $5 fee per night. Open all year.

Who to contact: Phone (800) 233-0321, (360) 902-8563 or (360) 378-2044 or write to 6158 Lighthouse Road, Friday Harbor, WA 98250.

Location: The campground is located just west of the Shaw Island ferry dock on little Blind Island, which is just north of Shaw Island. It is accessible only by boat.

Trip note: This island has few trees and is known for its rocky shoreline. It is dangerous and ill-advised to try beaching cruiser-style boats. Bring a life raft to paddle ashore. This park is a designated natural area and is committed to conserving a natural environment in a minimally-developed state. This is not a place to tromp around or throw big barbecues.

23.　　GRIFFIN BAY

Reference: **On San Juan Island, boat-in only; map A2, grid c2.**

Campsites, facilities: There is one primitive campsite and three picnic sites. Piped water and picnic tables are provided. Pit toilets are available. Two boat buoys are available for overnight moorage.

Reservations, fee: No reservations; no fee. Open all year.

Who to contact: Phone the Department of Natural Resources at (360) 856-3500 or write to Department of Natural Resources, Northwest Region, 919 North Township Street, Sedro Woolley, WA 98284-9395.

Location: Griffin Bay is on the southeast side of San Juan Island, south of Friday Harbor. It is accessible only by boat.

Trip note: This is a tiny, remote camp that receives almost no use at all, yet is located on one of the prettiest islands in the area. If you're one of the smart few who are willing to take the time to travel there, you are practically guaranteed a beautiful little spot all to yourself. The camp is within a few miles of the San Juan National Historic Park, a day-use area. There are several other state parks on the island as well.

24.　　LAKEDALE CAMPGROUND　　**RV**

Reference: **On San Juan Island; map A2, grid c2.**

Campsites, facilities: There are 84 tent sites and 12 drive-through sites for trailers or RVs up to 34 feet long. Electricity, piped water and picnic tables are provided. Toilets, a store and ice are available. Showers and firewood are available for an extra fee. Pets and motorbikes are permitted. Boat docks and boat rentals are nearby.

Reservations, fee: Reservations accepted; $9-$18 fee per night for car and RV campers; $4.50 for bicyclists. MasterCard and Visa accepted. Open April to late September.

Who to contact: Phone (360) 378-2350 or write to 2627 Roche Harbor, Friday Harbor, WA 98250.

Location: From Interstate 5 at Burlington, turn west on Highway 20 and drive 12 miles, then turn north at the sign for Anacortes and drive to town. Take the ferry to Friday Harbor on San Juan Island. From the ferry landing, proceed two blocks on Spring Street, then turn northwest on Second Street and drive one-half mile to Tucker Avenue (Roche Harbor Road). Turn north and continue 4.5 miles to the campground on the left.

Trip note: This is a nice spot for visitors who want the solitude of an island camp, yet all the amenities of a privately-run campground. Fishing, swimming and boating are available at the Lakedale Lakes. Horseshoe pits and a grassy sports field are also available.

25. TURN ISLAND STATE PARK

Reference: **Near Friday Harbor, boat-in only; map A2, grid c2.**

Campsites, facilities: There are 12 primitive campsites. Picnic tables are provided and vault and pit toilets are available. There is **no piped water**. Boat buoys are available for overnight moorage.

Reservations, fee: No reservations; $5 fee per night. Open all year.

Who to contact: Phone (800) 233-0321, (360) 902-8563 or (360) 378-2044 or write to 6158 Lighthouse Road, Friday Harbor, WA 98250.

Location: Turn Island is located just east of Friday Harbor and San Juan Island. It is accessible only by boat.

Trip note: This is one of about 30 campgrounds we detail in the area that can be reached only by boat. Quiet, primitive and beautiful, this spot offers good hiking trails and year-round rockfishing. There are pretty beaches for shell collectors. No cars are allowed, unless they float.

26. JAMES ISLAND STATE PARK

Reference: **Near Decatur Island, boat-in only; map A2, grid c3.**

Campsites, facilities: There are 13 primitive campsites. Pit toilets are available. Boat floats and buoys are available for moorage off the east side of the island. A moorage dock on the west side of the island is open from May through September.

Reservations, fee: No reservations; $5-$11 fee per night from May 1 through Labor Day. Open all year.

Who to contact: Phone (800) 233-0321, (360) 902-8563 or (360) 378-2044 or write to 6158 Lighthouse Road, Friday Harbor, WA 98250.

Location: This island is east of Decatur Island on Rosario Strait and is only accessible by boat. The campground is on the east side of the island.

Trip note: This small, hidden island provides good opportunities for hiking, fishing and scuba diving. It's quiet and primitive, with lots of trees and a pretty beach for walking or sunbathing.

27. SPENCER SPIT STATE PARK   **RV**

Reference: **On Lopez Island; map A2, grid c3.**

Campsites, facilities: There are 10 walk-in sites and 35 sites for tents or self-contained RVs up to 20 feet long. There are no hookups available. Picnic tables and fire grills are provided. A sanitary disposal station and flush toilets are available. Boat docks are nearby. Leashed pets are permitted. Some facilities are **wheelchair accessible**.

Reservations, fee: Contact Reservations Northwest at (800) 452-5687 ($6 reservation fee); $10-$11 fee per night. Open March through October.

Who to contact: Phone (800) 233-0321, (360) 902-8563 or (360) 378-2044 or write to Route 2, P.O. Box 3600, Lopez, WA 98261.

Location: From Interstate 5 south of Bellingham, take the Highway 20 exit and drive west through Anacortes to the ferry terminal. Take the ferry to the eastern shore of Lopez Island. You can then drive or walk in to the campground.

Trip note: Spencer Spit State Park offers one of the few island campgrounds accessible to cars via a ferry boat ride. A long sliver of sand extends far into the water and provides good access to prime clamming areas. Picnicking, beachcombing and sunbathing are some pleasant activities for campers looking for relaxation.

---

28. MORAN STATE PARK **RV**

Reference: **On Orcas Island; map A2, grid c3.**

Campsites, facilities: There are 15 primitive tent sites and 151 developed sites for tents or RVs up to 45 feet long. No hookups are available. Picnic tables and fire grills are provided. Flush toilets, showers and firewood are available. Some facilities are **wheelchair accessible**. Leashed pets are permitted. Boat docks, fishing supplies, launching facilities and boat rentals are located at the concession stand in the park.

Reservations, fee: Contact Reservations Northwest at (800) 452-5687 ($6 reservation fee); $5-$11 fee per night. Open all year.

Who to contact: Phone (800) 233-0321 or (360) 376-2326 or write to Star Route, Box 22, Eastsound, WA 98245.

Location: From Interstate 5 at Burlington, turn west (Exit 230) onto Highway 20 and drive through Anacortes to the ferry terminal. Take the ferry from Anacortes to Orcas Island. From the ferry landing, turn left and drive 13 miles on Horseshoe Highway to Moran State Park. Proceed to the campground registration booth and you will receive directions to your site.

Trip note: This is a big park (5,175 acres) that offers hiking trails and lake fishing. There are actually four separate campgrounds plus a primitive area. If you drive to the top of Mount Constitution, you will have a view of Vancouver, Mount Baker and the San Juan Islands. No RVs are allowed on this winding road. Nearby recreation options include a nine-hole golf course.

---

29. DOE ISLAND STATE PARK

Reference: **Near Orcas Island, boat-in only; map A2, grid c3.**

Campsites, facilities: There are five primitive campsites. Vault toilets are available. Boat floats are available for moorage.

Reservations, fee: No reservations; $5-$11 fee per night. Open all year.

Who to contact: Phone (800) 233-0321 or (360) 902-8563 or write to 6158 Lighthouse Road, Friday Harbor, WA 98250.

Location: This small, secluded island is just southeast of Orcas Island. It is accessible only by boat.

Trip note: This island has a rocky shoreline, which makes for an ideal fish habitat. The scuba diving and fishing are exceptional. Doe Island State Park is a tiny, primitive park that receives little use.

30. OBSTRUCTION PASS

Reference: **On Orcas Island, hike-in only; map A2, grid c3.**

Campsites, facilities: There are nine primitive campsites. Picnic tables are provided and vault toilets are available. There is **no piped water**. Boat buoys are available for overnight moorage.

Reservations, fee: No reservations; no fee. Open all year.

Who to contact: Phone the Department of Natural Resources at (360) 856-3500 or write to Department of Natural Resources, Northwest Region, 919 North Township Street, Sedro Woolley, WA 98284-9395.

Location: On Orcas Island at the town of Olga, travel east on Doe Bay Road for one-half mile, then take a right on Obstruction Pass Road and drive two-thirds of a mile. Keep right for one-third mile, then proceed straight for less than a mile to the parking area. Hike one-half mile to the campground.

Trip note: It takes a ferry boat ride, a tricky drive and then a short walk to reach this campground, but that helps set it apart from others—you'll find a unique, primitive spot set in a forested area near the shore of Orcas Island with good hiking. Moran State Park is a more developed alternative on this island, with many recreation options.

31. SCIMITAR RIDGE RANCH **RV**

Reference: **On Fidalgo Island, in the San Juan Islands; map A2, grid c4.**

Campsites, facilities: There are 91 sites for tents and RVs. There are also 24 covered wagons available. Cable TV, restrooms, showers, a public phone and a laundromat are provided. A recreation hall, game room, a playground and a recreation field are available. If RV camping, pets are permitted.

Reservations, fee: Reservations recommended, two-night minimum, Visa and MasterCard accepted. $23-$35 fee per night; covered wagon fees are $25-$30. Open all year.

Who to contact: Phone (800) 798-5355 or (360) 293-5355 or write to the ranch at 527 Miller Road, Anacortes, WA 98221.

Location: From Seattle, drive north on Interstate 5. Take exit 230 and travel west on Highway 20 for 12 miles. At the traffic signal, turn left (still Highway 20) and drive a half mile to Miller Road, turn west. The ranch is located on Miller Road a quarter of a mile down on the right side. It is approximately 65 miles from Seattle.

Trip note: This site offers resort camping in the beautiful San Juan Islands. Tall trees, breathtaking views, cascading waterfalls and country hospitality can all be found here. Side trips include nearby Deception Pass State Park (eight minutes away) and ferries to Victoria, British Columbia. Activities include horseback riding, horseshoes, wagon rides, a free 18-hole golf course, relaxing spas and lake fishing.

32. CYPRESS HEAD

Reference: **On Cypress Island, boat-in only; map A2, grid c4.**

Campsites, facilities: There are five primitive campsites. Picnic tables and vault toilets are available. There is **no piped water**. Five boat buoys are available for overnight moorage.

Reservations, fee: No reservations; no fee. Open all year.

Who to contact: Phone the Department of Natural Resources at (360) 856-3500 or write to Department of Natural Resources, Northwest Region, 919 North Township Street, Sedro Woolley, WA 98284-9395.

Location: This camp is set on the east shore of Cypress Island and is accessible only by boat. It is just south of Pelican Beach Campground.

Trip note: This is an option to Pelican Beach Campground. The camp is primitive but pretty, in a forested setting right on Puget Sound.

33.   PELICAN BEACH

Reference: **On Cypress Island, boat-in only; map A2, grid c4.**

Campsites, facilities: There are four primitive campsites. Picnic tables, a group shelter and vault toilets are available. There is **no piped water** available. Six buoys are available for overnight moorage.

Reservations, fee: No reservations; no fee. Open all year.

Who to contact: Phone the Department of Natural Resources at (360) 856-3500 or write to Department of Natural Resources, Northwest Region, 919 North Township Street, Sedro Woolley, WA 98284-9395.

Location: This camp is set on the east shore of Cypress Island and is accessible only by boat. It is just north of Cypress Head Campground.

Trip note: This forested island campground offers a group shelter, beach access and hiking trails. The 1.2-mile trail to Eagle Cliff is a must. Like Cypress Head, this camp is set on the oceanfront in a well-treed area, and is quite scenic.

34.   STRAWBERRY ISLAND

Reference: **Near Cypress Island, boat-in only; map A2, grid c3.**

Campsites, facilities: There are three primitive campsites. Picnic tables are provided and vault toilets are available. There is **no piped water**.

Reservations, fee: No reservations; no fee. Open all year.

Who to contact: Phone the Department of Natural Resources at (360) 856-3500 or write to Department of Natural Resources, Northwest Region, 919 North Township Street, Sedro Woolley, WA 98284-9395.

Location: This island is off the west coast of Cypress Island and is accessible only by small boat. Note: The Department of Natural Resources cautions that strong currents and submerged rocks can make landing difficult. They recommend anchoring your boat, then proceeding in a skiff or kayak.

Trip note: This campground is rarely used because of the hazards of landing here. If you can manage to land, however, you will be rewarded with a pretty, forested camp and complete privacy.

35.   SADDLEBAG ISLAND STATE PARK

Reference: **Near Guemes Island, boat-in only; map A2, grid c4.**

Campsites, facilities: There are five primitive campsites. Vault and pit toilets are available, but there is **no piped water**.

Reservations, fee: No reservations: $5 fee per night. Open all year.

Who to contact: Phone (800) 233-0321 or (360) 902-8563 or write to 6158 Lighthouse Road, Friday Harbor, WA 98250.

Location: From Interstate 5 at Burlington, turn west on Highway 20 and proceed to Anacortes. Launch your boat and head north to Saddlebag Island. It is two miles northeast of Anacortes and east of Guemes Island. The camp is accessible only by boat.

Trip note: This is a good cruise from Anacortes. The island is quiet and primitive. There's a nice beach nearby for beachcombing and good crabbing in the bay.

36. BAY VIEW STATE PARK RV

Reference: **On Padilla Bay; map A2, grid c5.**

Campsites, facilities: There are three primitive sites, 67 sites for tents or self-contained RVs and nine sites with full hookups for RVs up to 40 feet long. There is also one group tent camp for a maximum of 64 people. Picnic tables are provided. Flush toilets, piped water, a dump station and coin-operated showers are available. A store and a laundromat are eight miles away in Burlington. Leashed pets are permitted.

Reservations, fee: No reservations for family camping; $10-$11 fee per night. Reservation required for group camp ($25 reservation fee); $1 fee per group camper per night. Open all year.

Who to contact: Phone (800) 233-0321 or (360) 757-0227 or write to 1093 Bay View-Edison Road, Brighton, WA 98273.

Location: From Interstate 5 at Burlington, take the Highway 20 exit (exit 230) and drive seven miles west toward Anacortes. Turn right (north) on Bayview-Edison Road and drive four miles to the park on the right.

Trip note: This is a good family campground with a large, grassy play area for kids. It's set on Padilla Bay. A good day trip is to take the ferry at Anacortes to Lopez Island (there are several campgrounds there as well).

37. LARRABEE STATE PARK RV

Reference: **On Samish Bay; map A2, grid c5.**

Campsites, facilities: There are three primitive tent sites, 60 developed tent sites, and 26 sites for trailers or RVs up to 60 feet. Picnic tables and fire grills are provided. Flush toilets, sanitary disposal station, piped water, sewer hookups, showers and firewood are available. Leashed pets are permitted. Boat launching facilities are available nearby.

Reservations, fee: No reservations; $7-$16 fee per night. Open all year.

Who to contact: Phone (800) 233-0321 or (360) 676-2093 or write to 245 Chuckanut, Bellingham, WA 98225.

Location: From Bellingham, drive seven miles south on Chuckanut Drive (Highway 11) to the park on the right.

Trip note: This 2,683-acre state park is on Samish Bay in Puget Sound. It offers tide pools and nine miles of hiking trails, including two that go to small lakes. The park lies on a beautiful stretch of coastline and offers prime spots for wildlife viewing. A relatively short drive south will take you to Anacortes, where you can catch a ferry to Lopez Island.

38. TIMBERLINE RV PARK RV

Reference: **Map A2, grid c5.**

Campsites, facilities: There are 20 tent sites and 39 sites for trailers or RVs. Cable TV, restrooms, showers, a private phone, a laundromat, ice, LP gas bottles, a store and a barbecue are available. There are also horseshoe pits, a recreation hall, a playground and a recreation field. Facilities are **wheelchair accessible**. Pets are permitted on leashes.

Reservations, fee: No reservations necessary; $12-$15 fee per night.

Who to contact: Phone the park at (360) 826-3131.

Location: From Bellingham, drive south on Interstate 5 for approximately 20 miles to exit 232 (Cook Road). Follow the road up and over the highway to the flashing light. Turn left on Cook Road. Drive four miles and turn left onto Highway 20 at the light. Follow the winding Highway 20 for 19 miles to Russell Road, turn left. Just past mile marker 82 there is a sign for the campsite. The camp is a quarter mile further up the hill on the left.

Trip note: This is a rural RV park just far enough off the main highway to be overlooked by most tourists. It is clean with large sites. Nearby attractions include Larrabee and Bay View state parks. Both provide beach access and hiking opportunities.

---

39. BURLINGTON KOA **RV**

Reference: **Map A2, grid c6.**

Campsites, facilities: There are 45 tent sites and 45 sites for trailers or RVs. Restrooms, showers, a sanitary dump, water, electricity and sewer hookups, a public phone, a laundromat, limited groceries, ice, LP gas and a barbecue are available. There is also a heated pool, a spa, horseshoes, a recreation hall, a game room, a playground and a recreation field. The facilities are **wheelchair accessible**. Pets are permitted on leashes.

Reservations, fee: No reservations necessary; $15.50-$21.50 fee per night. Visa and MasterCard accepted.

Who to contact: Phone the park at (360) 724-5511 or write to 646 North Green Road, Burlington, WA 98233.

Location: From Bellingham, drive south on Interstate 5 for approximately 20 miles to exit 232. Turn east and cross over the highway to the flashing light, turn left on Cook Road. Then turn left on Old Highway 99, the campground is about 3.5 miles further on the right.

Trip note: This is a typical KOA campground, complete with all the amenities. The sites are spacious and comfortable. It is an option to Creekside Camp, with this one a little closer to the highway. Stream fishing is possible nearby.

---

40. CREEKSIDE CAMPGROUND **RV**

Reference: **Near Skagit River; map A2, grid c9.**

Campsites, facilities: There are 27 sites for tents, trailers or RVs of any length. Electricity, piped water, sewer hookups and picnic tables are provided. Flush toilets, sanitary services, a store, a laundromat, ice, a playground and showers are available. A cafe is located within one mile. Pets and motorbikes are permitted.

Reservations, fee: Reservations recommended; $10-$16 fee per night. Open all year.

Who to contact: Phone (360) 826-3566 or write to 761 Baker Lake Road, Concrete, WA 98237.

Location: From Interstate 5 south of Bellingham, take exit 232. Drive 4.4 miles on Cook Road, then turn left at the junction of Highway 20 and Cook Road and follow it for about 17 miles. Turn left on Baker Lake Road and drive one-quarter mile to the camp.

Trip note: This pretty, wooded campground is centrally located to nearby recreational opportunities at Baker Lake and the Skagit River. Trout fishing is excellent here. Tackle is available nearby. Horseshoe pits and a recreation hall provide recreation options.

41.   ANACORTES RV PARK

Reference: **In Anacortes; map A2, grid d4.**

Campsites, facilities: There are 14 sites for tents and 16 sites for trailers or RVs of any length. Electricity, piped water, sewer hookups and picnic tables are provided. Bottled gas, sanitary services, toilets, showers, a recreation hall, a laundromat and a playground are available. A store and a cafe are located within one mile. Firewood can be purchased. Pets and motorbikes are permitted.

Reservations, fee: Reservations accepted; $12-$17 fee per night. Open all year.

Who to contact: Phone (360) 293-3700 or write to 1255 Highway 20, Anacortes, WA 98221.

Location: From Interstate 5 at Burlington, turn west on Highway 20 and drive 12 miles to the Whidbey Island junction. At the Oak Harbor turnoff, continue 100 yards south on Highway 20 to the park on the left.

Trip note: This wooded park covers six acres and is set near the shoreline. It is not particularly scenic, but close to numerous recreation attractions. It's a small park and a decent layover spot for tourists planning on taking the ferry to San Juan Island.

---

42.   DECEPTION PASS STATE PARK

Reference: **On Whidbey and Fidalgo Islands; Map A2, grid d4.**

Campsites, facilities: There are five primitive tent sites and 246 sites for tents, trailers or self-contained RVs up to 50 feet. Picnic tables, fire pits, piped water, showers, flush toilets and a sanitary disposal station are provided. A concession stand, a boat launch, boat rentals, buoys and floats are available. The facilities are **wheelchair accessible**. Leashed pets are permitted.

Reservations, fee: No reservations; $5-$10 fee per night. Open all year with limited winter services.

Who to contact: Phone (800) 233-0321 or the park at (360) 675-2417 or write to 5175 North State Highway 20, Oak Harbor, WA 98277.

Location: From Interstate 5 at Burlington, turn west on Highway 20 and drive 12 miles. Take Highway 20 South and drive six miles, across the bridge at Deception Pass, to the park on the right.

Trip note: This state park is located on beautiful Deception Pass on the west side of Whidbey Island. Recreation options include fishing and swimming at Pass Lake, a freshwater lake within the park. Fly fishing for trout is a unique bonus for anglers. Scuba diving is also popular. There are several historic Civilian Conservation Corps buildings near the campground.

---

43.   WASHINGTON PARK

Reference: **In Washington Park; map A2, grid d4.**

Campsites, facilities: There are 70 sites for tents and RVs available. Piped water, restrooms, showers, a public phone, a playground, a recreation field and a laundromat are available. A day-use area is provided. A boat launch is also available. Pets are permitted on leashes.

Reservations, fee: No reservations, except for city of Anacortes residents (April 15-September 15); $8-$12 fee per night.

Who to contact: Phone the park at (360) 293-1927 or write to P.O. Box 547, Anacortes, WA 98221.

Location: From Bellingham, drive south on Interstate 5 for 30 miles. Take the

Highway 20 exit west (Anacortes/San Juan Islands exit). Follow this road until it dead ends, approximately 20 miles. Turn right on Commercial Avenue. Turn left on 12th Street and follow it until it dead ends into the park (12th Street changes names several times, keep following it).

Trip note: Set in the woods, this city park has many hiking trails in addition to a 2.3-mile paved trail for hikers and bicyclists. Picnic areas are also provided. The Washington State Ferry Terminals are located one-half mile away, providing access to the San Juan Islands. This is a very popular camp, and it's a good idea to arrive early to claim your spot.

44.   HOPE ISLAND STATE PARK

Reference: **In Skagit Bay, boat-in only; map A2, grid d5.**

Campsites, facilities: There are five primitive campsites. **No piped water** is available. There are two mooring buoys.

Reservations, fee: No reservations; $5 fee per night.

Who to contact: Phone (800) 233-0321 or (360) 675-2417 or write to 5175 Northstate Highway 20, Oak Harbor, WA 98277.

Location: This little island is in Skagit Bay, two miles north of the entrance to Swinomish Bay. It is accessible only by private boat.

Trip note: This site on the north side of the island is a primitive alternative to the nearby and more developed Anacortes RV Park. The only catch is you must have a boat to reach it. It offers solitude, but has little to offer in the way of recreation besides beach access, where campers can sunbathe, walk or scout for shells.

45.   RIVERBEND PARK   **RV**

Reference: **On Skagit River; map A2, grid d6.**

Campsites, facilities: There are 25 tent sites and 95 drive-through sites for trailers or RVs of any length. Electricity, piped water, sewer and cable TV hookups and picnic tables are provided. Flush toilets, sanitary services, showers, a laundromat and a playground are available. Bottled gas, a store, a cafe, ice and a swimming pool are located within one mile. Pets are permitted.

Reservations, fee: Reservations accepted; $12-$17 fee per night. MasterCard and Visa accepted. Open all year.

Who to contact: Phone (360) 428-4044 or write to 305 West Stewart Road, Mount Vernon, WA 98273.

Location: From Interstate 5 at Mount Vernon, take the College Way exit and drive one block west to Freeway Drive, then turn north and go one-half mile to the park.

Trip note: This is a pleasant layover spot for Interstate 5 travelers. While not particularly scenic, this park is clean and spacious. Access to the Skagit River here is a high point. Nearby recreational options include a casino, an 18-hole golf course, marked bike trails and tennis courts.

46.   FORT EBEY STATE PARK   **RV**

Reference: **On Whidbey Island; map A2, grid e3.**

Campsites, facilities: There are three primitive tents sites and 50 developed campsites for tents or self-contained RVs up to 70 feet long. Picnic tables and fire grills are provided. Sanitary disposal service, flush toilets and coin-operated showers are available. Leashed pets are permitted. Some facilities are

wheelchair accessible.

Reservations, fee: No reservations; $5-$10 fee per night. Open April through September.

Who to contact: Phone (800) 233-0321 or (360) 678-4636 or write to 395 North Fort Ebey Road, Coupeville, WA 98239.

Location: From Interstate 5 at Burlington, take the Highway 20 exit and turn west. Drive approximately 23 miles southwest on Highway 20 to the park entrance on the right.

Trip note: This park, located on the west side of Whidbey Island at Point Partridge, covers 228 acres and has access to a beach that is rocky and good for hiking. Other options here include fishing and wildlife viewing. Fort Ebey is the site of an historic World War II bunker. There is also a freshwater lake.

---

47. FORT WORDEN STATE PARK 🔳RV

Reference: **Near Puget Sound, map A2, grid f3.**

Campsites, facilities: There are three primitive, hike-in/bike-in tent sites and 80 sites for trailers or RVs up to 50 feet long. Picnic tables and fire grills are provided. Toilets, laundromat, a store, a dinner restaurant and conference facilities are available. Electricity, piped water, sewer hookups, showers and firewood are available for an extra fee. Leashed pets are permitted. Boat docks, buoys, floats and launching facilities are nearby. **Wheelchair-accessible** facilities are available.

Reservations, fee: Contact Reservations Northwest at (800) 452-5687 ($6 reservation fee); $5-$16 fee per night. Open all year.

Who to contact: Phone (800) 233-0321 or (360) 385-4730 or write to 200 Battery Way, Port Townsend, WA 98638.

Location: This park is set on the northeastern tip of the Olympic Peninsula, at the northern end of Port Townsend. From Interstate 5 at Olympia, turn north on US 101 and drive approximately 86 miles. Turn north on Highway 20 and drive about 13 miles to Port Townsend.

Trip note: The highlights here are the great lookouts over the Strait of Juan de Fuca as it feeds into Puget Sound. This 339-acre park is at historic Fort Worden and includes buildings from the turn of the century. Nearby recreation options include marked hiking trails, marked bike trails and tennis courts. A ferry at Port Townsend will take you across the strait to Whidbey Island.

---

48. FORT CASEY STATE PARK 🔳RV

Reference: **On Whidbey Island; map A2, grid e4.**

Campsites, facilities: There are three primitive tent sites and 35 developed campsites for tents or self-contained RVs up to 40 feet long. Picnic tables and fire grills are provided. Flush toilets and coin-operated showers are available. Some facilities are **wheelchair accessible**. Pets are permitted. Boat launching facilities are located in the park.

Reservations, fee: No reservations; $5-$10 fee per night. Open all year.

Who to contact: Phone (800) 233-0321 or (360) 678-4519 or write to 1280 Fort Casey, Coupeville, WA 98239.

Location: From Interstate 5 at Burlington, take the Highway 20 exit and turn west. Drive approximately 35 miles to Coupeville. Continue south on Highway 20 for three miles to the park entrance on the right.

Trip note: This is a good spot to set up a base camp for a fishing trip. There is excellent rockfishing year-round and good salmon and steelhead fishing in season. This park covers 137 acres and is the site of a historic U.S. Defense Post. There is also an underwater park for divers. You can also take a ferry from here to Fort Townsend on the Olympic Peninsula.

49.   OAK HARBOR CITY BEACH PARK   **RV**

Reference: **In Oak Harbor; map A2, grid e4.**

Campsites, facilities: There are 55 sites for trailers or RVs of any length. Electricity, piped water and picnic tables are provided. Sewer hookups, sanitary services, toilets, coin-operated showers and a playground are available. Bottled gas, a store, a cafe, a laundromat and ice are located within one mile. Leashed pets are permitted. Boat launching facilities are at nearby Oak Harbor.

Reservations, fee: No reservations; $15 fee per night. Open all year.

Who to contact: Phone (360) 679-5551 or write to 3075-300 Avenue West, Oak Harbor, WA 98277.

Location: From Interstate 5 at Burlington, turn west on State Route 20 and drive 28 miles to the intersection of State Route 20 and Pioneer Way in the town of Oak Harbor, where State Route 20 becomes 80th SW Road. Continue on 80th SW Road about one block to the park on the left.

Trip note: Fishing, swimming, boating and sunbathing are all options here. Nearby recreation options include an 18-hole golf course, a full-service marina and tennis courts. Fort Ebey and Fort Casey state parks are both within a short drive and are excellent side trips.

50.   CEDAR GROVE SHORES   **RV**

Reference: **On Lake Goodwin; map A2, grid e6.**

Campsites, facilities: There are 48 sites for trailers or RVs. No tents are allowed. Electricity, piped water, sewer hookups and picnic tables are provided. Flush toilets, showers, a laundromat and firewood are available. Bottled gas, sanitary services, a store, a cafe and ice are located within one mile. Boat docks, launching facilities and rentals are nearby on Lake Goodwin.

Reservations, fee: Reservations accepted; $20-$24 fee per night. Open all year.

Who to contact: Phone (360) 652-7083 or write to 16529 52nd Avenue NW, Stanwood, WA 98292.

Location: From Interstate 5 north of Everett, take exit 206 (Smokey Point) and drive five miles west to West Lake Goodwin Road and drive one-half mile to park.

Trip note: This wooded resort is set on the shore of Lake Goodwin near Wenberg State Park. Trout fishing and swimming are the highlights. Tenters should try Lake Goodwin Resort. An 18-hole golf course is nearby.

51.   JIM MARION'S LAKE MARTHA RESORT   **RV**

Reference: **Near Lake Goodwin; map A2, grid e6.**

Campsites, facilities: There are seven tent sites and 24 drive-through sites for trailers or RVs of any length. Electricity, piped water, sewer hookups and picnic tables are provided. Flush toilets, sanitary services, showers and a laundromat are available. A store and ice are located within one mile. Boat docks and launching facilities are nearby on Lake Martha.

Reservations, fee: Reservations accepted; $15-$25 fee per night. Open all year.

Who to contact: Phone (360) 652-8412 or write to 8105 Lakewood Road, Stanwood, WA 98292.

Location: From Interstate 5 north of Everett, take exit 206 (Smokey Point), then drive seven miles west and bear left at fork in the road. Follow the signs for one-half mile to the resort.

Trip note: This is a small, family-oriented campground, especially good for tent campers. Camping here is an option to the nearby and slightly larger Lake Goodwin. It's a good summer spot for fishing and swimming. An 18-hole golf course is nearby.

---

52. KOA PORT ANGELES-SEQUIM   RV

Reference: **Near Port Angeles; map A2, grid f0.**

Campsites, facilities: There are 88 sites (45 drive-through) for tents, trailers or RVs of any length. Picnic tables are provided. There are also 12 cabins available. Bottled gas, sanitary services, toilets, showers, a store, laundry, ice, a playground, a recreation room and a swimming pool are available. A cafe is located within two miles. Electricity, piped water, sewer hookups and firewood are available for an extra fee. Some facilities are **wheelchair accessible**. Pets and motorbikes are permitted.

Reservations, fee: Reservations accepted; $19-$25 fee per night; $35-$40 cabin fee. MasterCard and Visa accepted. Open April through October.

Who to contact: Phone the park at (360) 457-5916 or write to 2065 Highway 101 East, Port Angeles, WA 98362.

Location: From Interstate 5 at Olympia, turn north on US 101 and drive 116 miles to O'Brien Road (located six miles southeast of Port Angeles). Turn left at O'Brien Road and drive one-half block to the campground on the right.

Trip note: This private, developed camp covers 41 acres and is in a country setting. It's a pleasant park, a typical KOA complete with pool, recreation hall and playground. Horseshoe pits and a sports field are also available. Mini-golf, two 18-hole golf courses, marked hiking trails and tennis courts are recreation options.

---

53. ELMER'S TRAVEL TRAILER PARK   RV

Reference: **Near the Pacific Ocean; map A2, grid f0.**

Campsites, facilities: There are 12 sites for trailers or RVs up to 31 feet long. Electricity, piped water and sewer hookups are provided. Sanitary services, flush toilets and laundry are available. Bottled gas, a store, a cafe and ice are within one mile. Showers are available for an extra fee. Small pets are permitted.

Reservations, fee: No reservations; $14 fee per night. Open all year.

Who to contact: Phone (360) 457-4392 or write to 2442 East Highway 101, Port Angeles, CA 98362.

Location: From Interstate 5 at Olympia, turn north on US 101 and drive 120 miles to the park, located two miles east of Port Angeles.

Trip note: Located at about 1,000 feet, this 10-acre camp is near the ocean, yet in an urban setting. It is hardly scenic, but will do as a layover for US 101 travelers. Nearby recreation options include an 18-hole golf course, marked hiking trails and a full-service marina.

54.   AL'S RV TRAILER PARK   RV

Reference: **Near Port Angeles; map A2, grid f0.**

Campsites, facilities: There are 31 sites for trailers or RVs up to 35 feet long. Electricity, piped water and sewer hookups are provided. Bottled gas, toilets, showers and laundry are available. A store, a cafe and ice are within one mile. Boat docks and launching facilities are nearby.

Reservations, fee: No reservations; $16-$20 fee per night. Open all year.

Who to contact: Phone the park at (360) 457-9844 or write to 521 North Lees Creek Road, Port Angeles, WA 98362.

Location: From Interstate 5 at Olympia, turn north on US 101 and drive 122 miles to Port Angeles. Continue two miles west on US 101, then turn left on Lees Creek Road and drive one-half mile to park.

Trip note: This is a good choice for motor home owners. It is set in the country at about 1,000 feet, yet not far from the Strait of Juan de Fuca. Nearby recreation options include an 18-hole golf course and a full-service marina. Olympic National Park and the Victoria ferry are a short drive away.

---

55.   DUNGENESS RECREATION AREA   RV

Reference: **Near Strait of Juan de Fuca; map A2, grid f1.**

Campsites, facilities: There are 65 sites (six pull-through) for tents, trailers or RVs of any length. Picnic tables are provided. Sanitary services, toilets and a playground are available. Showers and firewood are available for an extra fee. Leashed pets are permitted.

Reservations, fee: No reservations; $8-$10 fee per night. Open February to October with facilities limited to day use in winter.

Who to contact: Phone the park at (360) 683-5847 or write to 223 East Fourth, Port Angeles, WA 98362.

Location: From Interstate 5 at Olympia, turn north on US 101 and drive 105 miles to Sequim. Continue 10 miles west on US 101, then turn right on Kitchen Dick Road and drive four miles to the park.

Trip note: This park overlooks the Strait of Juan de Fuca, and is set near the Dungeness National Wildlife Refuge. Nearby recreation options include marked hiking trails, fishing and swimming. The toll ferry at Port Angeles can take you to Victoria, British Columbia.

---

56.   RAINBOW'S END   RV

Reference: **On Sequim Bay; map A2, grid f1.**

Campsites, facilities: There are 10 tent sites and 37 sites for trailers or RVs of any length. Electricity, piped water, sewer hookups and cable TV are provided. Sanitary services, toilets, showers, bottled gas and laundry are available. A store, a cafe and ice are located within one mile. Firewood is available for an extra fee. Leashed pets and motorbikes are permitted.

Reservations, fee: Reservations accepted; $15-$19 fee per night. Open year-round.

Who to contact: Phone the park at (360) 683-3863 or write to 261831 Highway 101, Sequim, WA 98382.

Location: From Interstate 5 at Olympia, turn north on US 101 and drive 105 miles to Sequim. At Sequim Avenue, drive two miles west on US 101 to the park on the right.

Trip note: Of the several camps on Sequim Bay, this is one of the nicest. The park is pretty and clean with shaded, spacious sites. There is a pond and a trout stream. Nearby recreation options include an 18-hole golf course, marked bike trails, a full-service marina and tennis courts.

57. SUNSHINE RV PARK   RV

Reference: **Near Sequim; map A2, grid f1.**

Campsites, facilities: There are 45 sites for tents, trailers or RVs of any length. Electricity, piped water, sewer hookups and picnic tables are provided. Toilets, showers, a recreation hall and laundry are available. Sanitary services, a store and a cafe are located within one mile. Pets and motorbikes are permitted.

Reservations, fee: Reservations accepted; $15-$17 fee per night. Open all year.

Who to contact: Phone the park at (360) 683-4769 or write to 259790 Highway 101 West, Sequim, WA 98382.

Location: From Interstate 5 at Olympia, turn north on US 101 and drive 105 miles to Sequim. At Sequim Avenue, drive four miles west on US 101 to park.

Trip note: This six-acre, private camp is set at about 1,000 feet in a wooded area outside of Sequim. It is primarily an RV park, although tents are permitted. It has paved, shaded sites, horseshoe pits and a recreation hall. Nearby recreation options include an 18-hole golf course and a full-service marina at Sequim Bay.

58. SEQUIM WEST RV PARK   RV

Reference: **Near Dungeness River; map A2, grid f1.**

Campsites, facilities: There are 29 drive-through sites for trailers or RVs of any length. No tents are allowed. Electricity, piped water, sewer hookups and picnic tables are provided. Toilets, showers, laundry and ice are available. Bottled gas, sanitary services, a store, a cafe are located within one mile. Pets are permitted.

Reservations, fee: Reservations accepted; $12-$18 fee per night. American Express, MasterCard, Visa, Discover and Diner's Club accepted. Open all year.

Who to contact: Phone the park at (360) 683-4144 or (800) 528-4527 or write to 740 West Washington, Sequim, WA 98382.

Location: From Interstate 5 at Olympia, turn north on US 101 and drive 105 miles to Sequim. At Sequim Avenue, continue three-quarters of a mile west on US 101 (Washington Avenue) to the park on the right.

Trip note: This two-acre camp is near the Dungeness River within 10 miles of Dungeness Spit State Park. The camp is pleasant, with full facilities and an urban setting. Nearby recreation options include an 18-hole golf course and a full-service marina at Sequim Bay.

59. SEQUIM BAY RESORT   RV

Reference: **On Sequim Bay; map A2, grid f2.**

Campsites, facilities: There are 43 sites (34 pull-through) for trailers or RVs of any length. Electricity, piped water and sewer and cable TV hookups are provided. Flush toilets and a laundry are available. Showers are available for an extra fee. Pets are permitted if on leashes. Boat docks and launching facilities are nearby.

Reservations, fee: No reservations; $15 fee per night. Open all year.

Who to contact: Phone the park at (360) 681-3853 or write to 2634 West Sequim

Bay Road, Sequim, WA 98382.

Location: From Interstate 5 at Olympia, turn north on US 101 and drive 102 miles to Whitefeather Way (located between mileposts 267 and 268, 2.5 miles east of Sequim). Turn north and drive one-half mile to West Sequim Bay Road. Turn west and drive one block to the park on the left.

Trip note: This is the headquarters on Sequim Bay for salmon fishermen. It is set in a wooded, hilly area, close to many activity centers. Nearby recreation options include an 18-hole golf course.

---

60. SEQUIM BAY STATE PARK RV

Reference: **On Sequim Bay; map A2, grid f2.**

Campsites, facilities: There are three primitive tent sites, 60 developed sites for tents or self-contained RVs, and 26 sites with full hookups for trailers or RVs up to 30 feet long. Picnic tables and fire grills are provided. Sanitary disposal station, toilets, drinking water, showers and a playground are available. Leashed pets are permitted. Boat docks, launching facilities and moorage camping are available. Facilities are **wheelchair accessible**.

Reservations, fee: Contact Reservations Northwest at (800) 452-5687; $5-$15 fee per night. Open all year.

Who to contact: Phone (800) 233-0321 or (360) 683-4235 or write to 269035 Highway 101, Sequim, WA 98382.

Location: From Interstate 5 at Olympia, turn north on US 101 and drive approximately 100 miles north to the park on the right. Then entrance is located four miles southeast of the town of Sequim.

Trip note: This 90-acre camp is on Sequim Bay. Nearby recreation options include marked hiking trails and tennis courts. Because of its unique location, it gets far less rain than other areas on the Olympic Peninsula, which makes it popular with campers. There is an underwater park for scuba divers.

---

61. OLD FORT TOWNSEND STATE PARK RV

Reference: **Near Quilcene; map A2, grid f3.**

Campsites, facilities: There are three primitive tent sites and 40 sites for tents or RVs up to 40 feet long. Picnic tables and fire grills are provided. Flush toilets, coin-operated showers, a playground and boat buoys are available. Firewood and showers are available for an extra fee. Leashed pets are permitted.

Reservations, fee: No reservations; $5-$10 fee per night. Open all year with limited winter facilities.

Who to contact: Phone (800) 233-0321 or (360) 385-3595 or write to Route 1, Port Townsend, WA 98368.

Location: From Interstate 5 at Olympia, turn north on US 101 and drive approximately 86 miles. Turn north on Highway 20 and drive 10 miles to the park on the right, located three miles south of Port Townsend.

Trip note: This fort was built in 1859, one of the oldest remaining in the state. The campground has access to a good clamming beach and there is a self-guided walking tour available. Hiking and fishing are among other options here.

---

62. POINT HUDSON RESORT RV

Reference: **In Port Townsend; map A2, grid f3.**

Campsites, facilities: There are 20 drive-through sites for trailers or RVs of any length (with full hookups). No tents are allowed. Flush toilets, a store, a cafe, laundromat and ice are available. Showers are available for an extra fee. A boat dock and launching ramp is nearby.

Reservations, fee: Reservations accepted; $15-$18 fee per night. Open all year.

Who to contact: Phone (360) 385-2828 or write to Point Hudson Harbor, Port Townsend, WA 98368.

Location: From Interstate 5 at Olympia, turn north on US 101 and drive 86 miles. Turn north on Highway 20 and drive 13 miles to Port Townsend. Turn north on Water Street and drive one-half mile, then turn west on Monroe Street and drive two blocks. Turn north on Jefferson Street and drive two blocks to the campground on the right.

Trip note: This park is set in the suburbs of Port Townsend, in a wooded, hilly area. Fishing and boating are popular here. Nearby recreation options include an 18-hole golf course, a full-service marina, Old Fort Townsend State Park, Fort Flagler State Park and Fort Worden State Park.

---

63.   SOUTH WHIDBEY STATE PARK   RV

Reference: **On Whidbey Island; map A2, grid f4.**

Campsites, facilities: There are six primitive tent sites and 54 developed campsites for tents or self-contained RVs up to 45 feet long. Picnic tables and fire grills are provided. Sanitary disposal services, coin-operated showers and toilets are available. Firewood can be obtained for an extra fee. Some facilities are **wheelchair accessible**. Leashed pets are permitted.

Reservations, fee: No reservations; $5-$10 fee per night. Open February 24 through October.

Who to contact: Phone (800) 233-0321 or (360) 321-4559 or write to 4128 Smugglers Cove Road, Freeland, WA 98429.

Location: From Interstate 5 at Burlington, take the Highway 20 exit and turn west. Drive approximately 28 miles, pass Coupeville, to the Highway 525 cutoff. Turn south on Highway 525 and drive eight miles (through Greenbank) to the park on the right.

Trip note: This wooded park is located on the southwest end of Whidbey Island. It covers 85 acres and provides opportunities for hiking, scuba diving, picnicking and beachcombing along a sandy beach. There are spectacular views of the Puget Sound and the Olympic Mountains.

---

64.   FORT FLAGLER STATE PARK   RV

Reference: **Near Port Townsend; map A2, grid f4.**

Campsites, facilities: There are 102 tent sites and 14 partial hookup (water and electric) sites for trailers or RVs up to 50 feet long. Picnic tables and fire grills are provided. Flush toilets, coin-operated showers, a sanitary dump station, a store, a cafe, boat buoys, floats and a launch are available. Facilities are **wheelchair-accessible**. Leashed pets are permitted.

Reservations, fee: Contact Reservations Northwest at (800) 452-5687 ($6 reservation fee); $10-$16 fee per night.

Who to contact: Phone (800) 233-0321 or (360) 385-1259 or write to 10541 Flagler Road, Nordland, WA 98358.

Location: From Interstate 5 at Olympia, take the US 101 exit and turn north. Drive 86 miles north on US 101 then turn right on Highway 20 and drive about seven miles. Turn right on Highway 19 and drive five miles. Turn left on Highway 116 and drive 14 miles to the park at the end of the road. The park is eight miles northeast of Hadlock.

Trip note: This is a pretty, unique state park, set on an island east of Port Townsend. The campgrounds are right on the beach. It's a good place for fishermen, with year-round rockfish and salmon fishing. Crabbing and clamming are good in season. The park offers an underwater park and is popular with scuba divers. Tours are available for Fort Flagler, which was built in 1898. There is a youth hostel in the park.

---

65.   MUTINY BAY RESORT   RV

Reference: **On Whidbey Island; map A2, grid f5.**

Campsites, facilities: There are 30 sites for trailers or RVs up to 28 feet long. No tents are allowed. Electricity, piped water, sewer hookups and picnic tables are provided. Toilets, showers and ice are available. Bottled gas, a store, a cafe and a laundromat are located within one mile. Boat docks and launching facilities are nearby.

Reservations, fee: Reservations accepted; $15-$20 fee per night; MasterCard and Visa accepted. Open all year.

Who to contact: Phone (360) 321-4500 or write to P.O. Box 249, Freeland, WA 98249.

Location: From Interstate 5 south of Everett, take exit 189 and drive west on Highway 526 to Mukilteo. Take the ferry north to Whidbey Island. At the ferry landing, turn north on Highway 525 and drive 10 miles, then turn west on Fish Road and drive one mile. Turn north on Mutiny Bay Road and continue 50 yards to the campground on the left. Note: If you want to avoid the ferry, you may access the camp via Interstate 5 and Highway 20 to the north.

Trip note: This privately-operated park provides an option to the nearby South Whidbey State Park. This resort caters to RVs, with swimming, salmon fishing and boating among the available activities. Horseshoe pits and shuffleboard are offered as well.

---

66.   CAMANO ISLAND STATE PARK   RV

Reference: **Near Stanwood; map A2, grid f5.**

Campsites, facilities: There is one primitive tent site and 87 developed campsites for tents or self-contained RVs up to 30 feet long. There is also one group camp for a maximum of 200 people. Picnic tables and fire grills are provided. Sanitary disposal service, flush toilets, coin-operated showers and a playground are available. Firewood can be obtained for an extra fee. Leashed pets are permitted. Boat launching facilities are located in the park.

Reservations, fee: No reservations for family camping; $5-$10 fee per night; $5 fee per extra vehicle per night. Reservation required for group camp, phone (360) 387-3031; group camp base fee is $25 plus $1 per person per night. Open all year.

Who to contact: Phone (800) 233-0321 or (360) 387-3031 or write to 2269 South Lowell Point Road, Stanwood, WA 98292.

Location: From Interstate 5 north of Everett, take exit 212 and drive west on Highway 532 to Stanwood. Continue 14 miles southeast to the park.

Trip note: The campsites are quiet and private in this wooded park. Good inshore rockfishing is available year-round and salmon fishing is also good in season. Clamming is excellent during low tides in June. An underwater park is provided for divers. There is also a self-guided nature trail.

67.　　　WENBERG STATE PARK　　　RV

Reference: **On Lake Goodwin; map A2, grid f6.**

Campsites, facilities: There are 65 developed tent sites, and 10 sites for trailers or RVs up to 50 feet long. Picnic tables are provided. A sanitary disposal station, flush toilets, piped water, coin-operated showers, a store and a playground are available. Leashed pets are permitted. Boat launching facilities are located on Lake Goodwin.

Reservations, fee: Contact Reservations Northwest at (800) 452-5687 ($6 reservation fee); $11-$16 fee per night. Open all year.

Who to contact: Phone (800) 233-0321 or (360) 652-7417 or write to 15430 East Lake Goodwin Road, Stanwood, WA 98292.

Location: From Everett on Interstate 5, drive 12 miles north to exit 206 (Smokey Point), then west on Highway 531 for seven miles to the park on the right.

Trip note: This state park is set along the shore of Lake Goodwin, where the trout fishing can be great. Power boats are allowed and there is a seasonal concession stand that provides food and fishing supplies. Lifeguards are on duty in the summer.

68.　　　LAKE GOODWIN RESORT　　　RV

Reference: **On Lake Goodwin; map A2, grid f6.**

Campsites, facilities: There are 20 tent sites and 85 sites (eight drive-through) for trailers or RVs of any length. There is also one fully-equipped cabin available. Electricity, piped water, sewer hookups and picnic tables are provided. Flush toilets, bottled gas, sanitary services, a recreation hall, a store, a cafe, a laundromat, ice, a playground, showers and firewood are available. Boat docks, launching facilities and rentals are nearby on Lake Goodwin.

Reservations, fee: Reservations accepted; $15-$25 fee per night; cabin fee is $50 per night. American Express, MasterCard and Visa accepted. Open all year.

Who to contact: Phone (360) 652-8169 or write to 4726 176th NW, Stanwood, WA 98292.

Location: From Interstate 5 north of Everett, take exit 206 (Smokey Point), then drive west for 5.5 miles to the park (follow the signs for Seven Lakes Area).

Trip note: This private campground is set on Lake Goodwin, a lake known for good trout fishing. Motorboats are permitted on the lake and there is an 18-hole golf course nearby. Swimming is allowed, and horseshoe pits, shuffleboard and a recreation field provide other recreation possibilities.

69.　　　KAYAK POINT COUNTY PARK　　　RV

Reference: **On Puget Sound; map A2, grid f6.**

Campsites, facilities: There are nine tent sites and 23 drive-through sites for trailers or RVs up to 25 feet long. Piped water and picnic tables are provided. Flush toilets, firewood and a playground are available. Leashed pets are permitted. Boat docks and launching facilities are nearby on Puget Sound.

Reservations, fee: No reservations; $10-$14 fee per night. Open May to late September.

Who to contact: Phone (360) 339-1208 or (360) 652-7992.

Location: From Everett, drive north on Interstate 5, then take exit 199 (Tulalip) at Marysville. The road winds for 14 miles through the Tulalip Indian Reservation, then you'll see the park entrance on your left.

Trip note: This large, wooded county park is set on the shore of the Puget Sound. Nearby recreation options include an 18-hole golf course.

---

70.   SMOKEY POINT RV PARK   RV

Reference: **Near Lake Goodwin; map A2, grid f7.**

Campsites, facilities: There are 104 sites (38 drive-through) for trailers or RVs of any length with full hookups. Piped water and picnic tables are provided. Flush toilets, sanitary services, showers, a recreation hall, a laundromat, a playground, electricity, bottled gas, ice and sewer and cable TV hookups are available. Firewood, a store and a cafe are located within one mile. Pets are permitted.

Reservations, fee: Reserve by calling (800) 662-7275; $18-$25 fee per night; MasterCard and Visa accepted. Open all year.

Who to contact: Phone (360) 652-7300 or write to 17019 28th Drive NE, Arlington, WA 98223.

Location: From Interstate 5 north of Everett, take exit 206 (Smokey Point). Drive west for one-half block on 172nd Street and you'll see the park on the southwest corner.

Trip note: This is an ideal stopover for motor home cruisers heading up Interstate 5 and looking for a place to spend the night. It is located just off the freeway and is only five miles from the state park and resorts on Lake Goodwin. The park is pleasant and clean, with full facilities and spacious, shady sites. Nearby recreation options include marked bike trails. Use of a nearby athletic club with swimming pool, sauna and jacuzzi is complimentary to park guests.

---

71.   TURLO   RV

Reference: **On the South Fork of Stillaguamish River in Mount Baker-Snoqualmie National Forest; map A2, grid f9.**

Campsites, facilities: There are 19 sites for tents or RVs up to 31 feet long. Picnic tables are provided. Vault toilets, piped water and firewood are available. Some facilities are **wheelchair accessible**. A store, a cafe and ice are located one mile away in Robe. Pets are permitted on a six-foot leash.

Reservations, fee: Reserve sites by calling (800) 280-CAMP ($7.75 reservation fee); $10 fee per night; $4 additional vehicle. Open mid-May to late September.

Who to contact: Phone the Mount Baker-Snoqualmie National Forest at (360) 436-1155 or write to Darrington Ranger District, 1405 Emmens Street, Darrington, WA 98241.

Location: From Interstate 5 at Everett, turn east on Highway 92 and drive approximately 15 miles to the town of Granite Falls. Continue 10.6 miles east on Highway 92 and you'll see the campground entrance on the right.

Trip note: This campground is set at 900 feet along the South Fork of the Stillaguamish River, the most westerly of the camps located on this stretch of Highway 92. A Forest Service Public Information Center is nearby. Riverside campsites are available, and the fishing can be good here. There are a few hiking trails in the area; see a Forest Service map or consult the nearby information center for locations.

72. VERLOT   📷

Reference: On the South Fork of Stillaguamish River in Mount Baker-Snoqualmie National Forest; map A2, grid f9.

Campsites, facilities: There are 26 sites for tents, trailers or RVs up to 31 feet long. Picnic tables are provided. Flush toilets, firewood and piped water are available. A store, a cafe and ice are located within one mile. Pets are permitted on a six-foot leash.

Reservations, fee: Reserve sites by calling (800) 280-CAMP ($7.75 reservation fee); $10 fee per night; $4 additional vehicle fee. Open mid-May to late September.

Who to contact: Phone the Mount Baker-Snoqualmie National Forest at (360) 436-1155 or write to Darrington Ranger District, 1405 Emmens Street, Darrington, WA 98241.

Location: From Interstate 5 at Everett, turn east on Highway 92 and drive approximately 15 miles to the town of Granite Falls. Continue 11 miles east on Highway 92 and you'll see the campground entrance on the right.

Trip note: This campground is set along the South Fork of the Stillaguamish River, a short distance from the Lake Twenty-Two Research Natural Area and the Maid of the Woods Trail. A Forest Service map details back roads and hiking trails. Fishing is another recreation option. Campsites with river views are available.

---

73. DEER PARK

Reference: Near Blue Mountain in Olympic National Park; map A2, grid g0.

Campsites, facilities: There are 18 tent sites. Picnic tables and fire grills are provided. Restrooms and drinking water are available. Leashed pets are permitted.

Reservations, fee: No reservations; no fee. Open mid-June to late September with limited winter facilities.

Who to contact: Phone the Olympic National Park at (360) 452-4501 or write to 600 East Park Avenue, Port Angeles, WA 98362.

Location: From Interstate 5 at Olympia, turn north on US 101 and drive approximately 114 miles to Deer Park Road (about six miles southeast of Port Angeles). Turn left and drive 18 miles south to the campground.

Trip note: This camp is set in the Olympic Peninsula's high country at 5,400 feet, just below 6,000-foot Blue Mountain. There are numerous trails in the area, including a major trailhead into the backcountry of Olympic National Park and the Buckhorn Wilderness.

---

74. DUNGENESS FORKS

Reference: On Dungeness and Gray Wolf rivers in Olympic National Forest; map A2, grid g1.

Campsites, facilities: There are 10 tent sites. Picnic tables are provided. Well water and vault toilets are available. Leashed pets are permitted.

Reservations, fee: No reservations; $7 fee per night. Open late May to early September.

Who to contact: Phone the Quilcene Ranger District, Olympic National Forest at (360) 765-3368 or write to Quilcene Ranger District, P.O. Box 280, Quilcene, WA 98376.

Location: From Interstate 5 at Olympia, turn north on US 101 and drive approximately 100 miles to Palo Alto Road (located three miles southeast of Sequim). Turn south and drive seven miles, then turn west on Forest Service Road 2880 and drive one mile to the campground. A Forest Service map is essential.

Trip note: This pretty, wooded spot is set at the confluence of Dungeness and Gray Wolf rivers. It offers seclusion, yet easy access from the highway. If you want quiet, you'll find it here.

75.   FALLS VIEW   RV

Reference: **On Big Quilcene River in Olympic National Forest; map A2, grid h2.**

Campsites, facilities: There are 30 sites for tents, trailers or RVs up to 21 feet long. Picnic tables are provided. Piped water and flush toilets are available. Leashed pets are permitted. **Wheelchair-accessible** restrooms are available.

Reservations, fee: No reservations; $5 fee per night. Open mid-May to mid-September.

Who to contact: Phone the Quilcene Ranger District, Olympic National Forest at (360) 765-3368 or write to Quilcene Ranger District, P.O. Box 280, Quilcene, WA 98376.

Location: From Interstate 5 at Olympia, turn north on US 101 and drive approximately 70 miles to the campground entrance (located about four miles south of Quilcene).

Trip note: In spite of the rustic setting, this spot on the edge of the Olympic National Forest has many facilities available and is very popular.

76.   EAST CROSSING

Reference: **In Olympic National Forest; map A2, grid g2.**

Campsites, facilities: There are 10 sites for tents only. Picnic tables are provided. Well water and vault toilets are available. Leashed pets are permitted.

Reservations, fee: No reservations; $4 fee per night. Open year-round.

Who to contact: Phone the Quilcene Ranger District, Olympic National Forest at (360) 765-3368 or write to Quilcene Ranger District, P.O. Box 280, Quilcene, WA 98376.

Location: From Interstate 5 at Olympia, turn north on US 101 and drive approximately 100 miles to Palo Alto Road (located three miles southeast of Sequim). Turn south and drive eight miles, then turn south on Forest Service Road 2860 and drive two miles to the campground. A Forest Service map is essential.

Trip note: A nearby option to Dungeness Forks, this seven-acre camp is set at about 1,200 feet. It offers some improvements, but it is still for individuals seeking an out-of-the-way spot.

77.   KITSAP MEMORIAL STATE PARK   RV

Reference: **On Hood Canal; map A2, grid g4.**

Campsites, facilities: There are 51 sites for tents or self-contained RVs to 30 feet long. Picnic tables and fire grills are provided. A sanitary disposal service, toilets and a playground are available. Showers and firewood can be obtained for an extra fee. Leashed pets are permitted. Boat buoys are available.

Reservations, fee: No reservations; $10 fee per night. Open all year.

Who to contact: Phone (800) 233-0321 or (360) 779-3205 or write to 202 NE Park Street, Poulsbo, WA 98370.

Location: From Interstate 5 at Tacoma, turn north on Highway 16 and drive 44 miles. Continue north on Highway 3 for about eight miles to the park on the left. The entrance is located three miles south of Hood Canal Bridge.

Trip note: This is a nice spot for tent campers along the Hood Canal. Nearby recreation options include an 18-hole golf course and swimming, fishing and hiking at nearby Anderson Lake Recreation Area. A short drive north will take you to historic Old Fort Townsend, an excellent day trip.

---

78.   POINT NO POINT BEACH RESORT   RV

Reference: **In Hansville; map A2, grid g5.**

Campsites, facilities: There are four tent sites and 38 drive-through sites for trailers or RVs up to 32 feet long. Electricity, piped water and sewer hookups are provided. Bottled gas, toilets, showers, a cafe, a laundromat and ice are available. A store is located within one mile. Boat docks and boat rentals are nearby.

Reservations, fee: Reservations accepted; $9-$15 fee per night. Open mid-May to mid-October.

Who to contact: Phone (360) 638-2233 or write to 8708 NE Point No Point Road, Hansville, WA 98340.

Location: From Interstate 5 at Tacoma, turn north on Highway 16 and drive about 42 miles. Highway 16 turns into Highway 3; continue north for 11 miles to Port Gamble. Turn southeast toward Kingston. About three miles northwest of Kingston you'll see the turnoff for Hansville. Turn north and drive eight miles. Once in Hansville, turn east and follow the signs to the lighthouse and Point No Point.

Trip note: This is a summer resort with beach access on the northern tip of Bremerton Island. It's a bit of a roundabout trip to get here, but this is the easiest way to go with the constant road construction on Highway 3. And it's well worth your trip, with beautiful panoramic ocean views in a pretty, remote setting. Some nearby recreation options include the old lighthouse and the Old Man House near Kingston. Kitsap Memorial State Park is not far and provides a camping option.

---

79.   CAPTAIN'S LANDING   RV

Reference: **In Hansville; map A2, grid g5.**

Campsites, facilities: There are 22 drive-through sites for trailers or RVs of any length. Electricity, piped water, sewer hookups and picnic tables are provided. Flush toilets, showers, a store and ice are available. Pets are permitted. Boat docks, launching facilities and boat rentals are nearby.

Reservations, fee: Reservations accepted; $18-$20 fee per night. Open all year.

Who to contact: Phone (360) 638-2257 or write to P.O. Box 113, Hansville, WA 98340.

Location: From Interstate 5 at Tacoma, turn north on Highway 16 and drive about 42 miles. Highway 16 turns into Highway 3; continue north for 11 miles to Port Gamble. Turn southeast toward Kingston. About three miles northwest of Kingston you'll see the turnoff for Hansville. Turn north and drive eight miles. The park is located in town.

Trip note: This campground provides an option to Point No Point Beach Resort for tent campers. The sites are grassy and open. Nearby recreation options include an 18-hole golf course and a full-service marina. See the trip note for Point No Point for additional recreation information.

80. SILVER SHORES RV PARK 🚐

Reference: **On Silver Lake; map A2, grid g7.**

Campsites, facilities: There are 10 tent sites and 50 sites for trailers or RVs. Electricity, piped water and picnic tables are provided. Flush toilets, sanitary services, showers and a laundromat are available. Firewood, a store, a cafe and ice are located within one mile.

Reservations, fee: Reservations accepted; $20-$25 fee per night. Open all year.

Who to contact: Phone (360) 337-8741 or write to 11621 West Silver Lake Road, Everett, WA 98208.

Location: From Interstate 5 at Everett, take exit 186 and head east to the intersection of 128th Street and Bothell-Everett Highway (also called Highway 527 or 19th Avenue SW). Turn left on 19th Avenue and drive to the first stop light. Turn left on Silver Lake Road and drive about one-half mile to the park on the right.

Trip note: This is a good layover for travelers heading up Interstate 5. This wooded park is set along the shore of Silver Lake, a quiet lake with an eight miles per hour speed limit, good trout fishing and swimming opportunities. The park is quiet, pretty and centrally located, close to shopping and Seattle. There are tennis courts nearby.

81. FERGUSON PARK 🚐

Reference: **On Blackman's Lake; map A2, grid g8.**

Campsites, facilities: There are about seven sites for tents and 11 sites for trailers or RVs. Restrooms, showers, a sanitary dump, a public phone, limited groceries, a recreation hall and a barbecue are available. A boat ramp is provided. No pets are allowed.

Reservations, fee: No reservations; $10-$15 fee per night. Open year round.

Who to contact: Phone City Hall at (360) 568-3115 or write to 116 Union Avenue, Snohomish, WA 98290.

Location: From Everett, drive east on Highway 2 for about 15 miles toward Monroe. Take the Snohomish Historical Society exit (Bickford Avenue). This turns into Avenue D. Take the first left after the blinking light into Ferguson Park. The turn is immediately before the shopping center.

Trip note: This is a pretty city park set next to a small lake. Grassy, shaded sites are available. Recreational activities on Blackman's Lake includes swimming, boating (electric motors only) and trout fishing. There is a picnic and swimming park located directly across the river from camp.

82. FLOWING LAKE COUNTY PARK 🚐

Reference: **Near Snohomish; map A2, grid g8.**

Campsites, facilities: There are 10 tent sites and 32 drive-through sites for trailers or RVs up to 25 feet long. Electricity, piped water, sewer hookups and picnic tables are provided. Flush toilets, sanitary services, firewood and a playground are available. Leashed pets are permitted. Boat docks and launching facilities are nearby.

Reservations, fee: No reservations; $10-$14 fee per night. Open mid-May to late

September.

Who to contact: Phone (360) 339-1208 or write to 303 3000 Rockefeller Avenue, Everett, WA 98201.

Location: From Interstate 5 at Everett, turn east on US 2 and drive to milepost 10. At the sign for 100th Street and Westwick Road turn left. Drive five miles on 171st Street SE, then turn right on 48th Street SE and drive about one-half mile into the park at the end of the road.

Trip note: This campground has a little something for everyone. The recreational possibilities include swimming, power boating, waterskiing and good fishing at the lake.

83.   DOSEWALLIPS

Reference: **On Dosewallips River in Olympic National Park; map A2, grid h0.**

Campsites, facilities: There are 30 tent sites. Picnic tables and fire grills are provided. Restrooms, drinking water and **wheelchair facilities** are available. Leashed pets are permitted.

Reservations, fee: No reservations; $8 fee per night. Open from June to late September.

Who to contact: Phone the Olympic National Park at (360) 452-4501 or write to 600 East Park Avenue, Port Angeles, WA 98362.

Location: From Interstate 5 at Olympia, turn north on US 101 and drive approximately 61 miles to a signed turnoff (located about one mile south of Brinnon). Turn west and drive 15 miles along the Dosewallips River.

Trip note: This offers a more remote option to Elkhorn and Collins. This camp is set on the Dosewallips River at 1,540 feet. It provides a major trailhead into the backcountry of Olympic National Park. The trail follows Dosewallips River over Anderson Pass then along Quinault River and ultimately reaches Quinault Lake.

84.   ELKHORN   **RV**

Reference: **On Dosewallips River in Olympic National Forest; map A2, grid h1.**

Campsites, facilities: There are 20 sites for tents, trailers or RVs up to 21 feet long. Picnic tables are provided. Well water and vault toilets are available. Leashed pets are permitted.

Reservations, fee: No reservations; $6-$8 fee per night. Open May to September.

Who to contact: Phone the Quilcene Ranger District, Olympic National Forest at (360) 765-3368 or write to Quilcene Ranger District, P.O. Box 280, Quilcene, WA 98376.

Location: From Interstate 5 at Olympia, turn north on US 101 and drive 62 miles to Brinnon. Continue one mile north on US 101, then turn left and drive 10 miles west on Dosewallips Road and Forest Service Road 2610 (same road). The camp is on the left.

Trip note: This eight-acre camp is set on the Dosewallips River at 600 feet. It is wooded, with river and fishing access available. It is not far from Olympic National Park, a good side trip.

85.   RAINBOW

Reference: **Near Quilcene in Olympic National Forest; map A2, grid h2.**

Campsites, facilities: There are nine tent sites. Picnic tables and fire grills are provided. There is **no piped water.** Vault toilets are available. A store, a cafe, laundromat and ice are within five miles. Leashed pets are permitted.

Reservations, fee: For reservation and fee information call (360) 796-4886.

Who to contact: Phone the Quilcene Ranger District, Olympic National Forest at (360) 765-3368 or write to Quilcene Ranger District, P.O. Box 280, Quilcene, WA 98376.

Location: From Interstate 5 at Olympia, turn north on US 101 and drive approximately 69 miles to the campground.

Trip note: This is a rugged, primitive setting on edge of Olympic National Forest, with backcountry access provided on Forest Service roads. This is an excellent layover spot for US 101 cruisers. Olympic National Park is just a short drive away. It's advisable to obtain Forest Service map.

86.　　　　　COLLINS　　　　RV

Reference: **On Duckabush River in Olympic National Forest; map A2, grid h2.**

Campsites, facilities: There are six tent sites and 10 sites for trailers or RVs up to 21 feet long. Picnic tables are provided. Well water and vault toilets are available. Leashed pets are permitted.

Reservations, fee: No reservations; no fee. Open mid-May to October.

Who to contact: Phone the Hood Canal Ranger District, Olympic National Forest at (360) 877-5254 or write to Hood Canal Ranger District, P.O. Box 68, Hoodsport, WA 98548.

Location: From Interstate 5 at Olympia, turn north on US 101 and drive approximately 59 miles. Turn left on Forest Service Road 2510 and drive five miles west. The camp is on the left.

Trip note: Most tourists cruising US 101 don't have a clue about this spot, yet it's not far from the highway. This four-acre camp is set on the Duckabush River at 200 feet. It has small, shaded spots and river access nearby. Fishing and hiking are two options. Dosewallips State Park and Olympic National Park provide two side trips within easy driving distance.

87.　　　DOSEWALLIPS STATE PARK　　RV

Reference: **On Dosewallips Creek; map A2, grid h2.**

Campsites, facilities: There are 88 sites for tents, trailers or RVs up to 60 feet long. Fire grills are provided. Showers, flush toilets, picnic tables, stoves and drinking water are available. A recreation hall, a store, a cafe and laundry are within one mile. Electricity and sewer hookups are available for an extra fee. Leashed pets are permitted. Facilities are **wheelchair accessible**.

Reservations, fee: Contact Reservations Northwest at (800) 452-5687 ($6 reservation fee); $5-$16 fee per night. Open all year.

Who to contact: Phone (800) 233-0321 or (360) 796-4415 or write to P.O. Drawer K, Brinnon, WA 98320.

Location: From Interstate 5 at Olympia, turn north on US 101 and drive 61 miles to the park. The entrance is located one mile south of Brinnon.

Trip note: This 425-acre park is set on the shore of Hood Canal at the mouth of Dosewallips Creek, which gets a fair run of steelhead in winter months. In Hood Canal, rockfish and salmon fishing is popular. Beachcombers might consider clamming, but check with the Department of Health prior to harvesting any shellfish, due to seasonal and local conditions. This is a popular camp because it's set right off a major highway, so it's advisable to arrive early to insure a space.

88. SCENIC BEACH STATE PARK RV

Reference: **On Hood Canal; map A2, grid h3.**

Campsites, facilities: There are two primitive tent sites and 50 sites for tents, trailers or self-contained RVs up to 40 feet long. Picnic tables, piped water, fire grills, showers, a sanitary disposal station and flush toilets are provided. Leashed pets are permitted. The facilities are **wheelchair-accessible**.

Reservations, fee: Contact Reservations Northwest at (800) 452-5687 ($6 reservation fee); $5-$11 fee per night. Open April to Mid-November.

Who to contact: Phone (800) 233-0321 or (360) 830-5079 or write to P.O. Box 7, Seabeck, WA 98380.

Location: From Interstate 5 at Tacoma, turn north on Highway 16 and drive 30 miles to Bremerton. Continue north on Highway 3 for about nine miles and take the first Silverdale exit (Newberry Hill Road). Turn left and drive approximately three miles to the end of the road, then turn right on Seabeck Highway and follow it to Seabeck. Once in town, take the only road that follows the bay west, then turn right at the first street after the grade school. Continue 1.5 miles on the winding road to the park.

Trip note: This is an exceptionally beautiful state park, with beach access and superb views of the Olympic Mountains. Beachcombing, oyster hunting and salmon fishing are among your options. A public boat launch is available one mile north at Misery Point. **Wheelchair accessible** nature trails are available at the park.

---

89. COVE TRAILER PARK RV

Reference: **Near Dabob Bay; map A2, grid h3.**

Campsites, facilities: There are 35 sites (one pull-through) for trailers or RVs up to 30 feet long. Electricity, piped water, sewer hookups and picnic tables are provided. Bottled gas, sanitary services, toilets, a store, laundry and ice are available. Showers are available for an extra fee. Pets are permitted. Boat docks and launching facilities are nearby on the Hood Canal.

Reservations, fee: Reservations accepted; $12.50 fee per night. Open all year.

Who to contact: Phone the park at (360) 796-4723 or write to 28453 Highway 101, Brinnon, WA 98320.

Location: From Interstate 5 at Olympia, turn north on US 101 and drive 62 miles to Brinnon. Continue three miles north on US 101. The camp is located between mileposts 303 and 304.

Trip note: This five-acre, private camp is in a rural setting, yet it is fully developed. It is near the shore of Dabob Bay at sea level. It has grassy and graveled sites and a few trees. Dosewallips State Park is a short drive away and a possible side trip.

---

90. SEAL ROCK RV

Reference: **On Dabob Bay in Olympic National Forest; map A2, grid h3.**

Campsites, facilities: There are 40 sites for tents, trailers or RVs up to 21 feet long. Picnic tables are provided. Piped water, flush toilets and **wheelchair facilities** are available. Leashed pets are permitted. Boat docks and launching facilities are nearby on the Hood Canal and in Dabob Bay.

Reservations, fee: For reservation information call (360) 796-4886; $8-$12 fee per night. Open mid-April to November.

Who to contact: Phone the Olympic National Forest at (360) 765-3368 or write to Quilcene Ranger District, P.O. Box 280, Quilcene, WA 98376.

Location: From Interstate 5 at Olympia, turn north on US 101 and drive 62 miles to Brinnon. Continue two miles north on US 101. The camp is on the shore at Seal Rock.

Trip note: This 30-acre camp is set along the shore near the mouth of Dabob Bay. The modern, developed setting provides a good spot for boat owners. This camp gets extremely crowded in the summer months, so reserve your site early.

---

91.   FAY BAINBRIDGE STATE PARK   RV

Reference: **On Bainbridge Island; map A2, grid h5.**

Campsites, facilities: There are 10 primitive tent sites and 26 sites for tents or self grid contained RVs up to 30 feet long. Picnic tables and fire grills are provided. Sanitary disposal service, piped water, coin-operated showers, toilets and a playground are available. A store and a cafe are located within one mile. Firewood can be obtained for an extra fee. Some facilities are **wheelchair accessible**. Leashed pets are permitted. Boat docks and launching facilities are nearby.

Reservations, fee: No reservations; $11 fee per night. Open April through August.

Who to contact: Phone (800) 233-0321 or (206) 842-3931 or write to 15546 Sunrise, Bainbridge Island, WA 98110.

Location: From Interstate 5 at Tacoma, turn north on Highway 16 and drive 30 miles to the junction with Highway 3. Continue north on Highway 3 for about 18 miles, then turn south on Highway 305 and continue to the park at the southeast end of Bainbridge Island.

Trip note: Set on the edge of Puget Sound, this park provides all the recreation possibilities of a typical beach park. The primitive walk-in sites are heavily wooded, and the developed sites have great views of Puget Sound. Clamming, diving, picnicking, beachcombing and kite flying are popular pastimes here. On clear days, campers can enjoys views of Mt. Rainier and Mt. Baker to the east, and at night the park provides beautiful vistas of the lights of Seattle. In the winter months, there is excellent salmon fishing just offshore of the park.

---

92.   ORCHARD TRAILER PARK   RV

Reference: **In Seattle; map A2, grid h6.**

Campsites, facilities: There are 10 sites for trailers or RVs of any length. Electricity, piped water and sewer hookups are provided. A laundromat is available. Bottled gas, a store, a cafe and ice are located within one mile. Pets are not permitted.

Reservations, fee: No reservations; $16 fee per night. Open all year.

Who to contact: Phone (206) 243-1210 or write to 4011 South 146th Street, Seattle, WA 98168.

Location: From Interstate 5 in Seattle, take exit 154 (Burien) and drive one mile west to Highway 99. Continue north for three-quarters of a mile to South 146th Street, turn east (right) and drive to trailer park.

Trip note: This is the smallest and most intimate of the motor home parks in the Seattle area. It is in an urban setting and makes a decent layover spot. Nearby recreation options include an 18-hole golf course.

93. HOLIDAY PARK RESORT
RV

Reference: **In Seattle; map A2, grid h6.**

Campsites, facilities: There are 22 sites for trailers or RVs up to 32 feet long. Electricity, piped water, sewer hookups and picnic tables are provided. Flush toilets, showers, a cafe and a laundromat are available. Bottled gas, sanitary services, a store and ice are located within one mile.

Reservations, fee: Reservations accepted; $16 fee per night. Open all year.

Who to contact: Phone (206) 542-2760 or write to 19250 Aurora Avenue North, Seattle, WA 98133.

Location: From Interstate 5 in Seattle, take the 176th Avenue exit and drive west to Aurora Avenue. Turn north and drive to 19250 Aurora Avenue North.

Trip note: Be sure to reserve in advance; this camp is usually full. The downtown sights of Seattle are just a short drive away. Nearby recreation options include an 18-hole golf course, marked bike trails and tennis courts.

94. LAKE PLEASANT RV PARK
RV

Reference: **On Lake Pleasant; map A2, grid h6.**

Campsites, facilities: There are 11 tent sites and 196 sites for trailers or RVs. Cable TV, restrooms, showers, a sanitary dump, a public phone, a laundromat, a playground and LP gas are available. Facilities are **wheelchair accessible**. Pets are permitted on leashes.

Reservations, fee: Reservations recommended; $18 per night. Visa and MasterCard accepted. Open all year.

Who to contact: Phone the park at 487-1785 or (800) 742-0386 or write to 24025 Bothell Highway, SE, Bothell, WA 98021.

Location: From Seattle, take Interstate 405 north for about 20 miles to exit 26. Follow Bothell/Everett Highway over the freeway for about a mile. The park is marked by a large sign on the left side of the road.

Trip note: Set on Lake Pleasant, this large, developed camp is geared primarily toward RVs. It's a pretty setting, with lakeside sites and plenty of trees. It's a very popular camp, right off the highway, so expect lots of company. This is a good spot for a little trout fishing.

95. LENA LAKE

Reference: **Near Hamma Hamma River, walk-in only in Olympic National Forest; map A2, grid i0.**

Campsites, facilities: There are 29 primitive sites at this hike-in campground. Vault toilets are available. Leashed pets are permitted.

Reservations, fee: No reservations; no fee. Open all year, weather permitting.

Who to contact: Phone the Hood Canal Ranger District, Olympic National Forest at (360) 877-5254 or write to Hood Canal Ranger District, P.O. Box 68, Hoodsport, WA 98548.

Location: From Interstate 5 at Olympia, turn north on US 101 and drive 37 miles to Hoodsport. Continue 14 miles north on US 101, then head west for eight miles on Forest Service Road 25 to Lena Creek. Hike 2.5 miles to Lena Lake. Campsites are scattered around the lake.

Trip note: You can't beat the price—free. This 135-acre camp is set on Lena Lake and is popular in the summer. The hike in from Lena Creek to the campground is suitable for the entire family, and well worth it. The majority of weekend campers would rather not deal with the hassle, so this spot is rarely crowded. It's a lovely setting, too, with a pleasantly mild climate in summer.

96. LENA CREEK   **RV**

Reference: **On Hamma Hamma River in Olympic National Forest; map A2, grid i0.**

Campsites, facilities: There are 14 sites for tents, trailers or RVs up to 21 feet long. Picnic tables are provided. Well water and vault toilets are available. Leashed pets are permitted. **Wheelchair-accessible** restrooms are available.

Reservations, fee: No reservations; $7 fee per night. Open mid-May to September.

Who to contact: Phone the Hood Canal Ranger District, Olympic National Forest at (360) 877-5254 or write to Hood Canal Ranger District, P.O. Box 68, Hoodsport, WA 98548.

Location: From Interstate 5 at Olympia, turn north on US 101 and drive 37 miles to Hoodsport. Continue 14 miles north on US 101, then turn left on Forest Service Road 25 and drive eight miles to the camp on the left.

Trip note: This seven-acre camp is set where Lena Creek empties into the Hamma Hamma River. A trail from the camp leads three miles to Lena Lake and seven miles to Upper Lena Lake. A map of the Olympic National Forest details the trail and road system. The camp is rustic with some improvements. If this camp is full, try the hike in to Lena Lake—with a little extra effort, you can camp for free.

97. LILLIWAUP CREEK

Reference: **On Lilliwaup Creek in Bert Cole State Forest; map A2, grid i1.**

Campsites, facilities: There are 13 campsites for tents or small trailers. Picnic tables, fire grills and tent pads are provided. Vault toilets and piped water are available. Leashed pets are permitted.

Reservations, fee: No reservations; no fee. Open all year.

Who to contact: Phone the Department of Natural Resources at (360) 825-1631 or write to Department of Natural Resources, South Puget Sound Region, P.O. Box 68, Enumclaw, WA 98022-0068.

Location: From Interstate 5 at Olympia, turn north on US 101 and drive 41 miles to Lilliwaup (four miles north of Hoodsport). Continue seven miles north on US 101, then turn left on Jorsted Creek Road (Forest Service Road 24) and drive 6.5 miles west to the camp. It is on the right of Lilliwaup Creek.

Trip note: An alternative to Melbourne, this is also a primitive, quiet setting, but has piped water provided. Lilliwaup Creek makes for a nice backdrop. Fishing is a recreation alternative.

98. MELBOURNE

Reference: **On Melbourne Lake in Bert Cole State Forest; map A2, grid i1.**

Campsites, facilities: There are five campsites for tents or small trailers. Picnic tables, fire grills and tent pads are provided. Vault toilets are available. There is **no piped water**, so bring your own. Firearms are prohibited. Leashed pets are permitted.

Reservations, fee: No reservations; no fee. Open all year.

Who to contact: Phone the Department of Natural Resources at (360) 825-1631 or write to Department of Natural Resources, South Puget Sound Region, P.O. Box 68, Enumclaw, WA 98022-0068.

Location: From Interstate 5 at Olympia, turn north on US 101 and drive 41 miles to Lilliwaup (four miles north of Hoodsport). Continue seven miles north on US 101, then turn left on Jorsted Creek Road (Forest Service Road 24) and drive 5.5 miles. Turn left and travel on a gravel road for 1.7 miles, then bear left and drive three quarters of a mile to the camp which is on Melbourne Lake.

Trip note: This primitive camp is on Melbourne Lake at about 1,000 feet in a little-known, rustic setting. If you want quiet, and don't mind a lack of facilities, this is a good drive-to option. An option is Lilliwaup Creek, which has piped water.

---

99. HAMMA HAMMA RV

Reference: **On Hamma Hamma River in Olympic National Forest; map A2, grid i1.**

Campsites, facilities: There are three tent sites and 12 sites for trailers or RVs up to 21 feet long. Picnic tables are provided. Well water and vault toilets are available. Leashed pets are permitted. Some facilities are **wheelchair accessible**.

Reservations, fee: No reservations; $7 fee per night. Open May to mid-November.

Who to contact: Phone the Hood Canal Ranger District, Olympic National Forest at (360) 877-5254 or write to Hood Canal Ranger District, P.O. Box 68, Hoodsport, WA 98548.

Location: From Interstate 5 at Olympia, turn north on US 101 and drive 37 miles to Hoodsport. Continue 14 miles north on US 101, then turn left on Forest Service Road 25 and drive 6.5 miles west to the camp on the left side of the road.

Trip note: Good holdover for vacationers cruising US 101. This camp is set on the Hamma Hamma River at about 600 feet. It is small and primitive, but can be preferable to the expensive developed camps on the US 101 circuit.

---

100. MINERVA BEACH MOBILE VILLAGE RV
AND RV RESORT

Reference: **On Pacific Ocean; map A2, grid j1.**

Campsites, facilities: There are 20 tent sites and 23 sites for trailers or RVs. Cable TV, restrooms, a public phone, a laundromat, limited groceries, ice, RV supplies and LP gas are available. There are also horseshoe pits, a driving range, a gift shop and a recreation hall. Facilities are **wheelchair accessible**. Pets are permitted on leashes.

Reservations, fee: Reservations recommended; $14-$18 fee per night. Visa and MasterCard accepted. Open all year.

Who to contact: Phone the park at (360) 877-5145 or write to North 21110 Highway 101, Shelton, WA 98584.

Location: From Olympia, drive on Highway 104 west toward Aberdeen. Take the Shelton/Port Angeles exit. Turn right on Highway 101 north. Drive about 20 miles and pass Potlatch State Park. Minerva Beach Mobile Village and RV Resort is just past Potlatch on both sides. Access to the resort office is by the driveway on the left.

Trip note: Located on the ocean, this is a perfect layover spot if you're cruising up or down US 101. Recreational opportunities at this park include swimming and salmon fishing. A good side trip is nearby Potlatch State Park.

101.   TOONERVILLE

Reference: **In Tahuya State Forest; map A2, grid i2.**

Campsites, facilities: There are four campsites for tents or small trailers. Picnic tables, fire grills and tent pads are provided. Vault toilets are available, but there is **no piped water**. Motorbikes are permitted. Pets on leashes are permitted.

Reservations, fee: No reservations; no fee. Open all year.

Who to contact: Phone the Department of Natural Resources at (360) 825-1631 or write to Department of Natural Resources, South Puget Sound Region, P.O. Box 68, Enumclaw, WA 98022-0068.

Location: From Interstate 5 at Tacoma, turn north on Highway 16 and drive 30 miles to Bremerton. Turn south on Highway 3 and drive nine miles southwest to the town of Belfair. From Belfair, take Highway 300 west for one-third mile, then bear left and continue for another 3.3 miles. Turn right on Belfair-Tahuya Road and drive one-half mile, then turn right on Elfendahl Pass Road for 2.5 miles (past the Tahuya four-wheel-drive trailhead). Continue straight through the intersection with Goat Ranch Road and drive 3.3 miles to the camp, which is on the left.

Trip note: Primitive and rustic, this campground is managed by the Department of Natural Resources and has trails for use by hikers, horses and motorbikes. It is pretty, forested, and little-used. Be sure to bring your own water, because there is none to be found near here.

102.   GREEN MOUNTAIN CAMP

Reference: **In Tahuya State Forest, hike-in only; map A2, grid i3.**

Campsites, facilities: There are 13 hike-in campsites for tents only. Picnic tables, fire grills and tent pads are provided. Vault toilets, hand-pumped water and facilities for horses are available.

Reservations, fee: No reservations; no fee. Open all year.

Who to contact: Phone the Department of Natural Resources at (360) 825-1631 or write to Department of Natural Resources, South Puget Sound Region, P.O. Box 68, Enumclaw, WA 98022-0068.

Location: From Silverdale on State Route 3, turn west on Newberry Hill Road and drive three miles. Turn left on Seabeck Highway and drive two miles, then turn right on Holly Road and travel four miles. Turn left on Tahuya Lake Road and drive one mile. At Green Mountain Road, the Department of Natural Resources provides a parking lot where your four-mile hike-in will begin.

Trip note: A prime spot, primitive yet with hand-pumped water provided, this campground is operated by the Department of Natural Resources and is located in Tahuya State Forest. There are facilities for horses here and trails for motor biking, hiking and horseback riding.

103.   ILLAHEE STATE PARK   **RV**

Reference: **Near Bremerton; map A2, grid i4.**

Campsites, facilities: There are eight primitive tent sites and 25 sites for tents or self-contained RVs up to 30 feet long. Picnic tables and fire grills are provided. A sanitary disposal service, toilets and a playground are available. Showers and firewood can be obtained for an extra fee. A laundromat and ice are located within one mile. Some facilities are **wheelchair accessible**. Leashed pets are permitted. Boat docks and launching facilities are available.

Reservations, fee: No reservations; $5-$10 fee per night. Open all year.

Who to contact: Phone (800) 233-0321 or (360) 478-6460 or write to 3540 Bahia Vista, Bremerton, WA 98310.

Location: From Interstate 5 at Tacoma, turn north on Highway 16 and drive 30 miles to Bremerton. Turn east on Highway 303 and continue three miles northeast, then take the east turnoff to the park on the right.

Trip note: This 75-acre park is just three miles from civilization in Bremerton, yet virtually unknown to out-of-towners touring the area. The campsites are set in a pretty, forested area, some with open grassy areas. The park has a ball field and a playground as well as beach access. The shoreline is fairly rocky, though there is a small sandy area available for sunbathers. Clamming is popular here also. A fishing pier and a moorage float are available for anglers.

---

104. MANCHESTER STATE PARK ▨▨

Reference: **On Puget Sound; map A2, grid i4.**

Campsites, facilities: There are 53 sites for tents or self-contained RVs up to 42 feet long. Picnic tables and fire grills are provided. Piped water, sanitary disposal station and toilets are available. Showers and firewood can be obtained for an extra fee. Some facilities are **wheelchair accessible**. Leashed pets are permitted.

Reservations, fee: Contact Reservations Northwest at (800) 452-5687 ($6 reservation fee); $5-$10 fee per night. Open all year with limited winter facilities.

Who to contact: Phone (800) 233-0321 or (360) 871-4065 or write to P.O. Box 36, Manchester, WA 98353.

Location: From Interstate 5 at Tacoma, take the Highway 16 exit and head north to Bremerton. Take the Sedgwick exit off Highway 16 and follow the signs that direct you to the park.

Trip note: Set on the edge of Point Orchard, this campground has excellent lookouts across Puget Sound. There are many good hiking trails in the park. Fishing and clamming are other options. This campground gets relatively little use, especially in the off-season, so you're almost always guaranteed a spot. Group and day-use reservations are available.

---

105. BLAKE ISLAND STATE PARK

Reference: **Near Seattle, boat-in only; map A2, grid i5.**

Campsites, facilities: There are 54 primitive tent sites. Picnic tables and fire grills are provided. Piped water, portable toilets, showers, firewood and a unique restaurant are available. Some facilities are **wheelchair accessible**. Leashed pets are permitted. Boat buoys and floats are available.

Reservations, fee: No reservations; $5-$10 fee per night. Open all year.

Who to contact: Phone (800) 233-0321 or (360) 731-0770 or write to P.O. Box 277, Manchester, WA 98353.

Location: This little island is three miles west of Seattle. It is accessible only by boat.

Trip note: Set right in the middle of the massive Seattle metropolitan area on a small island, this camp offers a combination of primitive settings and developed facilities. Tillicum Village offers unique northwest Indian dining. There is good bottom fishing off the reef. A three-quarter-mile nature trail and 15 miles of hiking trails are available.

106. SEATTLE SOUTH KOA **RV**

Reference: **Map A2, grid i6.**

Campsites, facilities: There are 10 tent sites and 131 sites for trailers or RVs. Facilities include restrooms, showers, water, electricity and sewer hookups, a sanitary dump, a public phone, a laundromat, limited groceries, ice and RV supplies. A large playground, a game room, a heated swimming pool, a recreation hall and horseshoes are also available. Facilities are **wheelchair accessible**. Pets are permitted on leashes.

Reservations, fee: Reservations recommended; $18-$25 fee per night. Visa, MasterCard and Discover accepted. Open year round.

Who to contact: Phone the park at (206) 872-8652 or write to 5801 South 212th Street, Kent, WA 98032.

Location: From Seattle, drive south on Interstate 5 to 188th Street (exit 152), drive 50 feet on 188th Street. Turn east on Orillia Road and drive 2.5 miles to the campground on the right.

Trip note: This is a popular urban campground, not far from the highway yet in a pleasant setting. The sites are spacious, with several pull-throughs to accommodate large RVs. A public golf course is located nearby. During the summer, a tour of Seattle can be taken from the campground.

107. BLUE SKY RV PARK **RV**

Reference: **Map A2, grid i8.**

Campsites, facilities: There are 51 sites for trailers or RVs. Cable TV, electricity, sewer hookups, restrooms, showers, a public phone and a laundromat are available. Facilities are **wheelchair accessible**. Pets are permitted on leashes.

Reservations, fee: Reservations recommended; $18.50 fee per night. Open year-round.

Who to contact: Phone the park at (206) 222-7910 or write to 9002 302nd Street SE, Issaquah, WA 98027.

Location: From Seattle, take Interstate 5 east to Highway 90. Turn east on Highway 90 and drive about 13 miles to exit 22 (Preston/Falls City exit). Turn right on Southeast 82nd Street and at the first stop sign, turn left on 302nd Avenue SE. Drive a short distance on 302nd Avenue SE to the campground entrance at the end of the road.

Trip note: This park is in an urban setting just outside of Seattle. It is a good off-the-beaten-path alternative to the crowded camps in the metro area, yet still only a short drive from the main attractions in the city. Nearby Lake Sammamish State Park provides more rustic recreation opportunities, including hiking and fishing.

108. AQUA BARN RANCH **RV**

Reference: **Map A2, grid i7.**

Campsites, facilities: There are approximately 40 tent sites and 200 sites for trailers or RVs. Restrooms, showers, a sanitary dump, a public phone, a laundromat, ice, restaurant and LP gas are available. Recreational facilities include horseshoe pits, a game room, a spa, an indoor heated swimming pool, horseback riding and a playground. Some of the facilities are **wheelchair accessible**. Pets are permitted on leashes.

Reservations, fee: Reservations recommended; $15-$23 fee per night. Visa and MasterCard accepted.

Who to contact: Phone (800) 284-2227 or (206) 255-4618 or write to 15227 SE Renton-Maple Valley Highway, Renton, WA 98058.

Location: From Seattle, drive south on Interstate 5 for about 10 miles. Turn north on Highway 405 and take the Enumclaw/Maple Valley exit, turning right on Service Road 169/Maple Road. Drive about three miles to the campground on the right.

Trip note: This is an ideal layover spot for campers who want to avoid the metro-area crowds. It is a large park and offers spacious sites (grassy for tent campers) and all the amenities, including a pool and hot tub. Numerous recreation options are available in the Seattle area, just 20 minutes north.

109. TRAILER INNS RV PARK & RECREATION CENTER

Reference: **Near Lake Sammamish State Park; map A2, grid i7.**

Campsites, facilities: There are 115 drive-through sites for trailers or RVs of any length. Electricity, piped water, sewer hookups and picnic tables are provided. Flush toilets, bottled gas, showers, a recreation hall, a swimming pool, a laundromat, ice and a playground are available. Sanitary services, a store and a cafe are available within one mile. Pets and motorbikes are permitted.

Reservations, fee: Reservations accepted; $23-$29 fee per night; MasterCard and Visa accepted. Open all year.

Who to contact: Phone (206) 747-9181 or write to 15531 Interstate 90, Bellevue, WA 98006.

Location: From the junction of Interstate 405 and Interstate 90 in Bellevue, go east on Interstate 90 for two miles to exit 11A, then go south on the frontage road to the park.

Trip note: This park is a haven for motor home travelers, with all the amenities provided. Nearby Lake Sammamish State Park is a highlight. Nearby recreation options include an 18-hole golf course, hiking trails, marked bike trails and tennis courts.

110. ISSAQUAH VILLAGE RV PARK

Reference: **Near Cascade Mountains; map A2, grid i8.**

Campsites, facilities: There are 112 sites for trailers or RVs of any length. No tents are allowed. Cable TV, water, electricity and sewer hookups, restrooms, showers, a sanitary dump, a public phone, a laundromat and LP gas are available. Picnic areas, a playground and a recreation field are also provided. The facilities are **wheelchair accessible**. Pets are permitted on leashes.

Reservations, fee: Reservations recommended; $24.50 fee per night. Visa and MasterCard accepted. Open year round.

Who to contact: Phone the park at (206) 392-9233 or (800) 258-9233 or write to 50 First Avenue NE, Issaquah, WA 98027.

Location: From Seattle, take Interstate 90 east for 17 miles to exit 17. Turn left and go under the freeway. Take the first right for a very short distance and keep bearing right. You will end up paralleling the freeway. The park is on the left in about a quarter of a mile.

Trip note: This park doesn't allow tents, but is set in a beautiful environment, ringed by the Cascade Mountains. It is a more scenic alternative to Blue Sky RV Park. Recreation opportunities are available at Lake Sammamish State Park, just a few miles north.

111. VASA PARK RESORT

Reference: **On Lake Sammamish; map A2, grid i8.**

Campsites, facilities: There are 16 tent sites and five sites for trailers or RVs of any length. Piped water, sewer hookups and picnic tables are provided. Flush toilets, sanitary services, a playground, electricity and showers are available. Bottled gas, firewood, a store, a cafe and a laundromat are located within one mile. Pets and motorbikes are permitted. Boat launching facilities are nearby on Lake Sammamish.

Reservations, fee: Reservations accepted; $10-$20 fee per night. Open mid-May to October.

Who to contact: Phone (206) 746-3260 or write to 3560 West Lake Sammamish, Bellevue, WA 98008.

Location: From Interstate 90 in Bellevue, take exit 13 and drive one mile north. The campground is on the west side of Lake Sammamish.

Trip note: This is the most rustic of the parks in the immediate Seattle area, The resort is on Lake Sammamish. The state park is at the south end of the lake. Nearby recreation options include an 18-hole golf course, hiking trails, marked bike trails and a riding stable.

112. SNOQUALMIE RIVER CAMPGROUND

Reference: **On Snoqualmie River; map A2, grid i9.**

Campsites, facilities: There are 110 tent sites and 80 sites for trailers or RVs of any length. Piped water and picnic tables are provided. Flush toilets, sanitary services, showers and a playground are available. Electricity and firewood can be obtained for an extra fee. Bottled gas, a store, a cafe and ice are located within one mile. Pets and motorbikes are permitted. Boat launching facilities are nearby.

Reservations, fee: Reservations accepted; $18 fee per night. Open April to late October and some off-season weekends.

Who to contact: Phone (206) 222-5545 or write to P.O. Box 16, Fall City, WA 98024.

Location: From Interstate 5 at Seattle, turn east on Interstate 90 and drive 26 miles to exit 22 (Preston-Fall City). Turn north on Preston-Fall City Road and drive 4.5 miles, then turn east on SE 44th Place and drive one-half mile to the campground at the end of the road.

Trip note: If you're in the Seattle area and stuck for a place for the night, this pretty 10-acre park set along the Snoqualmie River may be a welcome option. Among the recreation options are fishing, swimming, hiking, biking and rafting. Nearby recreation options include several 9-hole golf courses. A worthwhile 3.5-mile side trip is beautiful Snoqualmie Falls in the famed "Twin Peaks" country.

113. LAKE CUSHMAN STATE PARK

Reference: **On Lake Cushman; map A2, grid i0.**

Campsites, facilities: There are 50 tent sites, 30 sites with full hookups for trailers or RVs up to 60 feet long and two primitive sites. Picnic tables and fire grills are provided. Sanitary disposal services, piped water, restrooms, showers and **wheelchair facilities** are available. A store, restaurant and ice are available within one mile. Firewood is available for an extra fee. Leashed pets are permitted. Boat docks and launching facilities are available at nearby Lake Cushman.

Reservations, fee: Contact Reservations Northwest at (800) 452-5687 ($6 reservation fee); $10-$15 fee per night. Open April through October.

Who to contact: Phone (800) 233-0321 or (360) 877-5491 or write to P.O. Box 128, Hoodsport, WA 98548.

Location: From Interstate 5 at Olympia, take the US 101 exit and drive 37 miles north to Hoodsport. Turn west (left) on Highway 119 (Staircase Road) and continue seven miles to the park on the left.

Trip note: This 603-acre camp is set at on the shore of Lake Cushman and has beach access and good trout fishing. Lake Cushman is a 10-mile-long lake that is surrounded by the Olympic Mountains. Nearby recreation options include an 18-hole golf course and marked hiking trails.

114.　　　　　　BROWN CREEK　　　　　　RV

Reference: **On Brown Creek in Olympic National Forest; map A2 grid j0.**

Campsites, facilities: There are seven tent sites and 12 sites for trailers or RVs up to 25 feet long. Picnic tables are provided. Well water and vault toilets are available. Leashed pets are permitted.

Reservations, fee: No reservations; $7 fee per night. Open all year.

Who to contact: Phone (800) 233-0321 or the Hood Canal Ranger District at (360) 877-5254 or write to Hood Canal Ranger District, P.O. Box 68, Hoodsport, WA 94548.

Location: From Interstate 5 at Olympia, take Exit 104 onto State Route 8 and drive for six miles. Drive north on US 101 for 23 miles. Turn left on Skokomish Valley Road and drive five miles. Turn on Forest Service Road 23 and drive nine miles. Turn at Forest Service Road 2353 and drive for three-quarters of a mile. Turn onto Forest Service Road 2340 into the campground. A Forest Service map is essential.

Trip note: This camp is virtually unknown to outsiders. It is accessible to two-wheel-drive vehicles, but the road connects to a network of primitive, back-country Forest Service roads. The camp is small, just six acres, but is within the vast Olympic National Forest, which offers a plethora of opportunities for outdoors enthusiasts. Obtain a Forest Service map to expand your trip.

115.　　　　POTLATCH STATE PARK　　　　RV

Reference: **On Hood Canal; map A2, grid j1.**

Campsites, facilities: There are two primitive tent sites, 17 developed tent sites, and 18 drive-through sites with full hookups for trailers or RVs up to 60 feet long. Picnic tables, fire grills and drinking water are provided. Sanitary disposal services and restrooms with showers are available. Firewood is available for an extra fee. Leashed pets are permitted. A boat launch is available at the park, and boat docks are available at nearby Hood Canal.

Reservations, fee: No reservations; $5-$16 fee per night. Open late March through October.

Who to contact: Phone (800) 233-0321 or (360) 877-5361 or write to P.O. Box D, Hoodsport, WA 98548.

Location: From Interstate 5 at Olympia, turn north on US 101 and drive 22 miles to Shelton. Continue north on US 101 for 12 miles to the park, located along the shoreline of Hood Canal.

Trip note: This is a good camp for vacationers towing boats because the drive-through sites provide plenty of space. This 57-acre park is set along Hood Canal which offers opportunities for fishing, clamming, crabbing and scuba diving. Nearby recreation options include marked hiking trails.

116. REST A WHILE

Reference: **On Hood Canal; map A2, grid j1.**

Campsites, facilities: There are five tent sites and 92 sites (36 pull-through) for trailers or RVs of any length. Electricity, piped water, sewer and cable TV hookups are provided. Bottled gas, toilets, firewood, a recreation hall, a store, laundry and ice are available. A cafe is less than a mile from the park. Showers are available for an extra fee. Leashed pets and motorbikes are permitted. Boat docks, launching facilities, boat rentals and a private clamming beach are available.

Reservations, fee: Reservations accepted; $17-$18 fee per night. Open all year.

Who to contact: Phone the park at (360) 877-9474 or write to N 27001 Highway 101, Hoodsport, WA 98548.

Location: From Interstate 5 at Olympia, turn north on US 101 and drive 37 miles to Hoodsport. Continue 2.5 miles north on US 101 to the camp.

Trip note: This seven-acre park, located at sea level, is on Hood Canal. It offers waterfront sites and a private beach for clamming and oysters. There are numerous opportunities to fish, boat and scuba dive. It's an alternative to Potlatch State Park and Glen Ayr RV Park.

117. BIG CREEK

Reference: **Near Lake Cushman in Olympic National Forest; map A2, grid j1.**

Campsites, facilities: There are 23 sites for tents or RVs up to 30 feet long. Sheltered picnic tables are provided. Well water, firewood (summer months), vault toilets and **wheelchair-accessible** restrooms are available. Leashed pets are permitted. A boat dock and ramp are located at nearby Lake Cushman.

Reservations, fee: No reservations; $5 fee per night. Open from May through mid-November.

Who to contact: Phone the Hood Canal Ranger District at (360) 877-5254 or write to P.O. Box 68, Hoodsport, WA 94548.

Location: From Interstate 5 at Olympia, turn north on US 101 and drive 37 miles to Hoodsport. Turn northwest on State Route 119 and drive nine miles to the T intersection. Turn left and the campground is on the right.

Trip note: This camp is a good alternative to Staircase (see Chapter A1) on the North Fork Skokomish River and Lake Cushman State Park on Lake Cushman, both of which get heavier use. The sites are large and well-spaced over 30 acres.

118. GLEN AYR RV PARK

Reference: **On Hood Canal; map A2, grid j1.**

Campsites, facilities: There are 45 sites (nine pull-through) for trailers or RVs of any length. Electricity, piped water, sewer hookups and picnic tables are provided. Bottled gas, toilets, showers, cable TV, a recreation hall and laundry are available. A store, a cafe and ice are within one mile. A boat dock is nearby. Pets are permitted.

Reservations, fee: Reservations accepted but not required; $19 fee per night;

MasterCard, Discover and Visa accepted. Open all year.

Who to contact: Phone the park at (360) 877-9522 or write to N 25381 Highway 101, Hoodsport, WA 98548.

Location: From Interstate 5 at Olympia, turn north on US 101 and drive 37 miles to Hoodsport. Continue one mile north on US 101 to the park on the left.

Trip note: This adult-oriented, fully-developed, nine-acre park is located at sea level on Hood Canal, where there are opportunities to fish and scuba dive. Salmon fishing is especially excellent. Swimming and boating are two other options. The park provides a spa, a full-service marina, horseshoe pits and a recreation field. There is also a hotel in the park.

---

119. ALDRICH LAKE

Reference: **On Aldrich Lake, Tahuya State Forest; map A2, grid j1.**

Campsites, facilities: There are four primitive campsites for tents or small trailers. Picnic tables, fire grills and tent pads are provided. Vault toilets and piped water are available. A hand launch for small boats is located at the lake. Pets on leashes are permitted.

Reservations, fee: No reservations; no fee. Open April 5 to October 5.

Who to contact: Phone the Department of Natural Resources at (360) 825-1631 or write to Department of Natural Resources, South Puget Sound Region, P.O. Box 68, Enumclaw, WA 98022-0068.

Location: From Interstate 5 at Tacoma, turn north on Highway 16 and drive 30 miles to Bremerton. Turn west on Highway 3 and drive nine miles to Belfair, then turn west on Highway 300 and proceed approximately 12 miles to the town of Tahuya. Turn north on Belfair-Tahuya Road and drive four miles, then turn left on Dewatto Road and drive two miles. Turn left again on Hobaj Lane and drive one-half mile, then turn right and drive two-thirds of a mile. Turn right again and drive 200 yards to the campsites.

Trip note: This campground is on Aldrich Lake and is managed by the Department of Natural Resources. Robbins Lake is nearby and has day-use facilities and a hand launch for small boats. To reach Robbins Lake, follow the directions above—except that after turning left on Hobaj Lane and driving one-half mile, you make another left and drive one mile to the lake.

---

120. SNOOZE JUNCTION RV PARK 🅁🆅

Reference: **Near Belfair; map A2, grid j2.**

Campsites, facilities: There are 36 sites (12 drive-through) for trailers or motor homes of any length. Electricity, piped water, sewer hookups and picnic tables are provided. Bottled gas, sanitary services, toilets, showers and a recreation hall are available. A store, a cafe, a laundromat and ice are located within one mile. Pets and motorbikes are permitted. Boat docks and launching facilities are nearby.

Reservations, fee: Reservations accepted; $16 fee per night. Open all year.

Who to contact: Phone (360) 275-2381 or write to P.O. Box 880, Belfair, WA 98528.

Location: From Interstate 5 at Olympia, turn north on US 101 and drive 22 miles to Shelton. Turn north on Highway 3 and drive approximately 24 miles northeast to Gladwin Beach Road (located between mileposts 1 and 2). Drive one-half mile southwest to the campground on the left.

Trip note: This is a good holdover spot for motor home campers preparing to head north. It's a pleasant park, with ocean access and spacious sites. Recreation options include fishing, swimming, an 18-hole golf course and marked bike trails.

121. BELFAIR STATE PARK RV

Reference: **On Hood Canal; map A2, grid j2.**

Campsites, facilities: There are 184 sites for tents, trailers or RVs up to 75 feet long. Picnic tables and fire grills are provided. Sanitary disposal station, flush toilets, coin-operated showers and a playground are available. A store and a restaurant are located within one mile. Electricity, piped water and sewer hookups can be obtained for an extra fee. Some facilities are **wheelchair accessible**. Leashed pets are permitted.

Reservations, fee: Contact Reservations Northwest at (800) 45205687 ($6 reservation fee); $10 fee per night. Open all year.

Who to contact: Phone (800) 233-0321 or (360) 275-0668 or write to NE 410 Beck Road, Belfair, WA 98528.

Location: From Interstate 5 at Tacoma, take the Highway 16 exit and drive northwest for 30 miles to Bremerton. Turn south on Highway 3 and continue nine miles to Belfair. Turn west and drive three miles on Highway 300 to the park on the left.

Trip note: Tent campers will consider this a good alternative to Snooze Junction RV Park. Set along edge of the Hood Canal, this park offers an unguarded saltwater swimming area, a sports area and a few wooded campsites. Nearby recreation options include the town of Shelton, which boasts the Forest Festival in May and the Oysterfest in October, and the Puget Sound Naval Shipyard in Bremerton. Big Mission Creek and Little Mission Creek, both located in the park, are habitat for chum salmon during spawning season in the fall.

122. TWANOH STATE PARK RV

Reference: **Near Union; map A2, grid j2.**

Campsites, facilities: There are 38 tent sites and nine sites for trailers or RVs up to 35 feet long. Picnic tables and fire grills are provided. Flush toilets, a store and a playground are available. Electricity, piped water, sewer hookups, showers and firewood can be obtained for an extra fee. Some facilities are **wheelchair accessible**. Leashed pets are permitted.

Reservations, fee: No reservations; $5-$16 fee per night. Open all year with limited winter facilities.

Who to contact: Phone (800) 233-0321 or (360) 275-2222 or write to P.O. Box 2520, Belfair, WA 98528.

Location: From Interstate 5 at Olympia, turn north on US 101 and drive 32 miles. Turn east on Highway 106 and drive 10 miles (through the town of Union) to the park.

Trip note: If you are cruising US 101, this camp is only a short drive east off Highway 106. It is often bypassed by visitors touring Washington. It's a prime recreation area, with opportunities for swimming, waterskiing, fishing and boating on beautiful Hood Canal. The water here is warmer because it is saltwater from the sound. There is a tennis court, horseshoe pits and a concession stand.

123.   TAHUYA RIVER HORSE CAMP

Reference: **On Tahuya River, Tahuya State Forest; map A2, grid j2.**

Campsites, facilities: There are nine primitive campsites for tents or small trailers. Picnic tables, fire grills and tent pads are provided. Vault toilets, piped water and equestrian facilities are available. Motorbikes are permitted. Pets on leashes are also permitted.

Reservations, fee: No reservations; no fee. Open all year.

Who to contact: Phone the Department of Natural Resources at (360) 825-1631 or write to Department of Natural Resources, South Puget Sound Region, P.O. Box 68, Enumclaw, WA 98022-0068.

Location: From Interstate 5 at Tacoma, turn north on Highway 16 and drive 30 miles to Bremerton. Turn south on Highway 3 and drive eight miles southwest to the town of Belfair. From Belfair, take Highway 300 west for one-third mile, then bear left and follow it for 3.3 miles. Turn right on Belfair-Tahuya Road and drive 1.7 miles, then turn right on Spillman Road and drive two miles. Turn left and drive three-quarters of a mile to the campground.

Trip note: This camp is set along the Tahuya River and is a good base camp for trips into the Tahuya State Forest. The nearby trails can be used by hikers, horses or motorbikes. Fishing is another recreation option here.

124.   HOWELL LAKE

Reference: **In Tahuya State Forest; map A2, grid j2.**

Campsites, facilities: There are six campsites for tents or small trailers. Picnic tables, fire grills and tent pads are provided. Vault toilets and piped water are available. A boat launch for small craft is located at Howell Lake. Motorbikes are permitted. Pets on leashes are also allowed.

Reservations, fee: No reservations; no fee. Open all year.

Who to contact: Phone the Department of Natural Resources at (360) 825-1631 or write to Department of Natural Resources, South Puget Sound Region, P.O. Box 68, Enumclaw, WA 98022-0068.

Location: From Interstate 5 at Tacoma, turn north on Highway 16 and drive 30 miles to Bremerton. Turn south on Highway 3 and drive eight miles southwest to the town of Belfair. From Belfair, take Highway 300 for one-third mile and then follow it left for another 3.3 miles. Turn right on Belfair-Tahuya Road and continue 4.5 miles.

Trip note: This pretty spot doesn't get a lot of use. The campground is managed by the Department of Natural Resources and set along Lake Howell. There are trails for use by hikers, horses or motorbikes. It's a great deal, with water, scenery, a boat launch and very few people.

125.   ROBIN HOOD VILLAGE   **RV**

Reference: **Near Hood Canal; map A2, grid j2.**

Campsites, facilities: There are 18 sites for trailers or RVs of any length. Electricity, piped water, sewer and cable TV hookups and picnic tables are provided. Toilets, showers, a restaurant, a liquor store and a laundromat are available. Bottled gas, sanitary services, a store and ice are available within one mile. Pets are permitted. Boat docks and launching facilities are nearby.

Reservations, fee: Reservations accepted; $16 fee per night; MasterCard and Visa accepted. Open all year.

Who to contact: Phone (360) 898-2163 or write to East 6780 Highway 106, Union, WA 98592.

Location: From Interstate 5 at Tacoma, turn north on Highway 16 and drive 30 miles to the junction with Highway 3. Turn southwest and drive eight miles to Belfair, then continue southwest on Highway 106 for 13 miles to East 6780 Highway 106.

Trip note: This wooded park, an option to Toonerville Multiple Use Area and Howell Lake, has access to the Hood Canal. Nearby recreation options include an 18-hole golf course and a full-service marina.

---

126.   TWIN LAKES

Reference: **In Tahuya State Forest; map A2, grid j2.**

Campsites, facilities: There are six primitive campsites for tents or small trailers. Picnic tables, fire grills and tent pads are provided. Vault toilets are available, but there is **no piped water**. A hand launch for small boats is available at the lake. Pets on leashes are permitted.

Reservations, fee: No reservations; no fee. Open all year.

Who to contact: Phone the Department of Natural Resources at (360) 825-1631 or write to Department of Natural Resources, South Puget Sound Region, P.O. Box 68, Enumclaw, WA 98022-0068.

Location: From Interstate 5 at Tacoma, turn north on Highway 16 and drive 30 miles to Bremerton. Turn south on Highway 3 and drive nine miles to the town of Belfair. From Belfair, drive one-third mile on Highway 300, continue to follow it left for 3.3 miles, then turn right on Belfair-Tahuya Road. Drive one-half mile, then turn right on Elfendahl Pass Road and drive 2.5 miles. At Twin Lakes Road turn left and drive 1.7 miles, then turn right and drive one-half mile to the camp.

Trip note: Little known, free and quiet, this wooded campground is in Tahuya State Forest and is managed by the Department of Natural Resources. The fishing can be decent here. You get privacy, shady sites, lake views and even a boat ramp. Don't forget to bring water.

---

127.   -   CAMP SPILLMAN

Reference: **On Tahuya River in Tahuya State Forest; map A2, grid j2.**

Campsites, facilities: There are six primitive campsites for tents or small trailers. Picnic tables, fire grills and tent pads are provided. Vault toilets and piped water are available. Motorbikes are permitted. Pets on leashes are also permitted.

Reservations, fee: No reservations; no fee. Open all year.

Who to contact: Phone the Department of Natural Resources at (360) 825-1631 or write to Department of Natural Resources, South Puget Sound Region, P.O. Box 68, Enumclaw, WA 98022-0068.

Location: From Interstate 5 at Tacoma, turn north on Highway 16 and drive 30 miles to Bremerton. Turn south on Highway 3 and drive nine miles to the town of Belfair. From Belfair, drive one-third mile on Highway 300, continue to follow it left for 3.3 miles, then turn right on Belfair-Tahuya Road. Drive one-half mile, then turn right on Elfendahl Pass Road and drive 2.5 miles. At Twin Lakes Road turn left and drive two-thirds of a mile to the camp.

Trip note: This is one of four campgrounds (Howell Lake, Tahuya River Horse Camp, Camp Spillman and Twin Lakes) set in the immediate vicinity of the

Tahuya State Forest. This one sits along the Tahuya River, with wooded riverside sites and trails for hikers, horses and motorbikes.

---

128.   GIG HARBOR RV RESORT   RV

Reference: **Near Tacoma; map A2, grid j4.**

Campsites, facilities: There are 102 drive-through sites for trailers or RVs of any length. Electricity, piped water, sewer hookups and picnic tables are provided. Bottled gas, cable TV, sanitary services, toilets, showers, a recreation hall, a store, a cafe, a laundromat, ice, a playground, a sports field and a heated swimming pool are available. Pets and motorbikes are permitted.

Reservations, fee: Reservations recommended in the summer; $19-$22 fee per night; MasterCard and Visa accepted. Open all year.

Who to contact: Phone (206) 858-8138 or (800) 526-8311 or write to 9515 Burnham Drive NW, Gig Harbor, WA 98332.

Location: From Interstate 5 in Tacoma, turn west on Highway 16 and drive 12 miles northwest. Take the North Rosedale Truck Route. At the stop sign, take a right on Burnham Drive and proceed 1.5 miles to the campground on the left.

Trip note: This is a popular layover spot for folks heading up to Bremerton. It's a pleasant spot, clean and friendly and just a short jaunt off the highway. Nearby recreation options include an 18-hole golf course, a full-service marina and tennis courts. There's a great view of Mt. Rainier from the end of the harbor.

---

129.   DASH POINT STATE PARK   RV

Reference: **Near Tacoma; map A2, grid j5.**

Campsites, facilities: There are 110 tent sites and 28 sites for trailers or RVs up to 35 feet long. Water and electrical hookups are available. Picnic tables are provided. Flush toilets, sanitary disposal station, a playground, electricity, piped water, showers and firewood are available. Leashed pets are permitted.

Reservations, fee: Contact Reservations Northwest at (800) 452-5687 ($6 reservation fee); $5-$15 fee per night. Open all year.

Who to contact: Phone (800) 233-0321 or (206) 593-2206 or write to 5700 West Dash Point Road, Federal Way, WA 98003.

Location: From Interstate 5 at Tacoma, drive five miles northeast on Highway 509 to the park on the right.

Trip note: This urban state park has beach access. Nearby recreation options include an 18-hole golf course and marked hiking trails. Tacoma offers a variety of activities and attractions, including the Tacoma Art Museum with a children's gallery, the Washington State Historical Society Museum, the Seymour Botanical Conservatory at Wrights Park, Point Defiance Park, Zoo and Aquarium, the Western Washington Forest Industries Museum and the Fort Lewis Military Museum. The Old Town area along the waterfront has been renovated and there are two public fishing piers there.

---

130.   SALTWATER STATE PARK   RV

Reference: **Near Seattle; map A2, grid j6.**

Campsites, facilities: There are 52 sites for tents or self-contained RVs up to 50 feet long. Picnic tables and fire grills are provided. Flush toilets, a sanitary disposal station, showers, a playground and firewood are available. A store, a restaurant and ice are located within one mile. Some facilities are **wheelchair accessible**. Leashed pets are permitted. Boat buoys are nearby on Puget Sound.

Reservations, fee: No reservations; $10 fee per night. Open late March through early September.

Who to contact: Phone (800) 233-0321 or (206) 764-4128 or write to 25205 8th Place South, Des Moines, WA 98198.

Location: From Interstate 5 at Seattle, drive eight miles south to Des Moines, then turn south on Highway 509 and drive two miles to the park on the left.

Trip note: This is a nice state park for tent or motor home campers, set on the edge of Seattle and beautiful Puget Sound. Beaches offer clamming and picnic facilities. There are also foot trails that lead through Kent Smith Canyon. McSorely Creek runs through the park. Scuba diving is popular here.

131. THE GAME FARM WILDERNESS PARK RV

Reference: **On the Stuck River in Auburn; map A2, grid j7.**

Campsites, facilities: There are six group camp sites for tents, trailers and RVs, each with water and power hookups, a fire ring and picnic table. There are four sleeping units per site. Campers also have access to an open-air shelter during their stay. A dump station and restrooms are located on site.

Reservations, fee: Reservations are required; $25 per night, per group site. Reservations may be made up to one year in advance. Open March through October.

Who to contact: Write the City of Auburn Parks and Recreation Department at 25 West Main, Auburn, WA 98001 or call (206) 931-3043.

Location: From Seattle, go south to Highway 18. Go east on Highway 18, take the Auburn/Enumclaw exit. At the light, turn left onto Auburn Way South. Travel south approximately one mile to Howard Road. Exit to the right onto Howard Road. At the stop sign take a right onto R Street. Continue on R Street for approximately 1.5 miles to Stuck River Drive SE (just over the river). Turn left on Stuck River Drive SE. The camp is a quarter of a mile up-river on the left.

Trip note: The Game Farm Wilderness Park is just minutes from downtown Auburn. Located along the scenic Stuck River, this park was designed with group outings in mind. Mt. Rainier, the Seattle Waterfront and the Cascade Mountains are all within a short drive.

LEAVE NO TRACE TIPS

Plan ahead and prepare.

• Learn about the regulations and special concerns
of the area you are visiting.

• Visit the backcountry in small groups.

• Avoid popular areas during peak-use periods.

• Choose equipment and clothing in subdued colors.

• Pack food in reusable containers.

MAP A3

WASHINGTON MAP .... see page 90
Adjoining Maps
NORTH .... no map
EAST (A4) .... see page 216
SOUTH (B3) .... see page 330
WEST (A2) .... see page 112

122 LISTINGS
PAGES 166-215

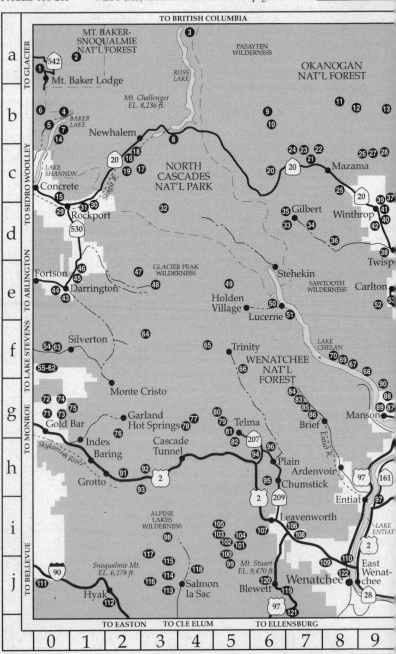

Washington Map A3 featuring: Nooksack River, Mount Baker-Snoqualmie National Forest, Ross Lake National Recreation Area, Baker Lake, Diablo Lake, Okanogan National Forest, Pasayten Wilderness, Chewuck River, Skagit River, North Cascades National Park, Cascade River, Methow River, Twisp River, Pearrygin Lake, Twin Lakes, Sauk River, Suiattle River, Glacier Peak Wilderness, Wenatchee National Forest, Stillaguamish River, Lake Chelan, Ashland Lakes, Chiwawa River, Entiat River, Bald Mountain, Greider Lakes, Skykomish River, Wenatchee River, White River, Alpine Lakes Wilderness, Beckler River, Mad River, Columbia River, Icicle Creek, Cle Elum Lake, Kachess Lake, Keechelus Lake, Teanaway River, Cle Elum River

---

1. SILVER FIR · RV

Reference: On the North Fork of Nooksack River in Mount Baker-Snoqualmie National Forest; map A3, grid a0.

Campsites, facilities: There are 20 sites for tents, trailers or RVs up to 21 feet long. Picnic tables and barbecue grills are provided. Well water, vault toilets and a group picnic shelter are available. Leashed pets are permitted.

Reservations, fee: Reserve some sites by calling (800) 280-CAMP ($7.75 reservation fee); $10 fee per night. Open May through September.

Who to contact: Phone the Mount Baker-Snoqualmie National Forest at (360) 599-2714, (360) 856-5700 or (360) 599-2714 or write to Mt. Baker Ranger District, 2105 State Route 20, Sedro Wooley, WA 98284.

Location: From Interstate 5 at Bellingham, turn east on Highway 542 and drive 31 miles to Glacier. Continue on Highway 542 for 12.5 miles east to the campground on the right.

Trip note: This campground is set on the North Fork of the Nooksack River, just a short distance from the North Fork Nooksack Research Natural Area. Fishing is available nearby, and in the winter, the area becomes a cross-country ski area. You are strongly advised to obtain a Forest Service map in order take maximum advantage of the recreational opportunities in the area.

---

2. HANNEGAN

Reference: **On Ruth Creek in Mount Baker-Snoqualmie National Forest; map A3, grid a1.**

Campsites, facilities: This is a primitive area with no designated campsites and **no piped water** provided. There is one pit toilet. Leashed pets are permitted.

Reservations, fee: No reservations; no fee. Open all year, weather permitting.

Who to contact: Phone the Mount Baker-Snoqualmie National Forest at (360) 599-2714, (360) 856-5700 or (360) 599-2714 or write to Mt. Baker Ranger District, 2105 State Route 20, Sedro Wooley, WA 98284.

Location: From Interstate 5 at Bellingham, turn east (left) on Highway 542 and drive 31 miles to Glacier. Continue 12.5 miles east on Highway 542, then turn east on Forest Service Road 32 and drive four miles to the campground at the end of the road. A Forest Service map is essential.

Trip note: This quiet, rustic spot is set on Ruth Creek on the border of the Mount Baker Wilderness and is at the trailhead that leads into the Mount Baker Wilderness across Hannegan Pass. The trail extends into North Cascades

National Park, where a permit is required for overnight stays. The free permit can be obtained at the Glacier Ranger Station. This is a perfect base camp for a wilderness backpacking expedition, and is used primarily as such.

3. HOZOMEEN RV

Reference: **On Ross Lake in Ross Lake National Recreation Area; map A3, grid a4.**

Campsites, facilities: There are 122 campsites for tents or RVs up to 22 feet long. Picnic tables and fireplaces are provided. Pit toilets, piped water and a boat launch on Ross Lake are available. Leashed pets are permitted.

Reservations, fee: No reservations; no fee. Open from late May to late October.

Who to contact: Phone the North Cascades National Park at (360) 856-5700 or write to them at 2105 State Route 20, Sedro Woolley, WA 98284.

Location: This campground is accessible only through Canada. From the town of Hope, British Columbia, drive 38 miles south on Silver Skagit Road to the campground at the north end of Ross Lake. Much of it is a rough dirt road.

Trip note: This camp is set just inside the U.S./Canada border at the north end of Ross Lake. It takes quite an effort to get here, which tends to weed out all but the most stalwart campers. This is good news for those few, for they will find a quiet, uncrowded camp in a beautiful setting.

4. PARK CREEK

Reference: **Near Baker Lake in Mount Baker-Snoqualmie National Forest; map A3, grid b0.**

Campsites, facilities: There are two group sites only. Picnic tables are provided. Vault toilets are available, but there is **no piped water**. Leashed pets are permitted. Boat docks, launching facilities and rentals are nearby on Baker Lake.

Reservations, fee: Reservations required; call (800) 280-CAMP ($15 reservation fee). Call for current fees. Open mid-May to mid-September.

Who to contact: Phone the Mount Baker-Snoqualmie National Forest at (360) 856-5700 or write to Mount Baker Ranger District, 2105 State Route 20, Sedro Woolley, WA 98284.

Location: From Interstate 5 at Burlington, turn east on State Route 20 and drive approximately 24 miles to milepost 82. Turn north on Baker Lake Highway and drive about 18 miles, then take Forest Service Road 1144 about 200 yards northwest and you're there. A Forest Service map is essential.

Trip note: This campground is set on Park Creek a short distance from the north shore of Baker Lake. It is primitive and small, but still gets its fair share of use. It is a pretty camp, set at 800 feet amidst a heavily wooded area.

5. PANORAMA POINT RV

Reference: **On Baker Lake in Mount Baker-Snoqualmie National Forest; map A3, grid b0.**

Campsites, facilities: There are 16 sites for tents, trailers or RVs up to 21 feet long. Picnic tables are provided. Well water and vault toilets are available. A store and ice are located within one mile. Leashed pets are permitted. A boat ramp is adjacent to camp. Boat docks and rentals are nearby.

Reservations, fee: Reserve some sites by calling (800) 280-CAMP ($7.75 reservation fee); $10 fee per night. Open May to October.

Who to contact: Phone the Mount Baker-Snoqualmie National Forest at (360) 856-5700 or write to Mount Baker Ranger District, 2105 State Route 20, Sedro Woolley, WA 98284.

Location: From Interstate 5 at Burlington, turn east on Highway 20 and drive approximately 24 miles to milepost 82. Turn north on Baker Lake Highway and drive about 17 miles to the campground entrance on the right.

Trip note: This well-maintained campground is on the northwest shore of Baker Lake. The reservoir is one of the better fishing lakes in the area. The camp is true to its name, with incredible scenic views. Hiking trails are nearby.

---

6.   BOULDER CREEK

Reference: **Near Baker Lake in Mount Baker-Snoqualmie National Forest; map A3, grid b0.**

Campsites, facilities: There are eight tent sites and two group sites. Picnic tables and fire grills are provided. Pit toilets are available, but there is **no piped water**. Leashed pets are permitted. Boat docks and launching facilities are nearby on Baker Lake.

Reservations, fee: For reservation and fee information, phone (360) 856-5700. Open mid-May to mid-September.

Who to contact: Phone the Mount Baker-Snoqualmie National Forest at (360) 856-5700 or write to Mount Baker Ranger District, 2105 State Route 20, Sedro Woolley, WA 98284.

Location: From Interstate 5 at Burlington, turn east on Highway 20 and drive approximately 24 miles to milepost 82. Turn north on Baker Lake Highway and drive about 13 miles. The campground is on the right.

Trip note: The campground is an alternative to Horseshoe Cove, set on Boulder Creek about one mile from the shore of Baker Lake. A boat launch is located at Panorama Point. In season, wild berries are available in the area. This campground offers prime views of Mount Baker.

---

7.   MAPLE GROVE

Reference: **On Baker Lake, walk-in or boat-in, in Mount Baker-Snoqualmie National Forest; map A3, grid b0.**

Campsites, facilities: There are five primitive tent sites which are only accessible by boat or on foot. Picnic tables are provided. There is **no piped water**. Leashed pets are permitted. Boat launching facilities are located nearby on Baker Lake.

Reservations, fee: No reservations; no fee. Open all year.

Who to contact: Phone the Mount Baker-Snoqualmie National Forest at (360) 856-5700 or write to Mount Baker Ranger District, 2105 State Route 20, Sedro Woolley, WA 98284.

Location: From Interstate 5 at Burlington, turn east on Highway 20 and drive approximately 24 miles to milepost 82. Turn north on Baker Lake Highway and drive about 13 miles. Turn east (right) on Forest Service Road 1106 and drive across Baker Dam, where Forest Service Road 1106 becomes Forest Service Road 1107. Continue one-half mile to the parking area and the trailhead on the left. Launch your boat here and proceed northeast across Baker Lake to the campground or take trail 610 and walk-in four miles to the camp. A Forest Service map is recommended.

Trip note: You want a quiet spot on the edge of a lake? Okay, here it is. This rustic campground is on the shore of Baker Lake and is hike-in or boat-in only. You get privacy and great mountain views, and it's all free.

8.   COLONIAL CREEK CAMPGROUND   RV

Reference: **On Diablo Lake in Ross Lake National Recreation Area; map A3, grid b3.**

Campsites, facilities: There are 164 campsites for tents or RVs up to 22 feet long. Picnic tables and fireplaces are provided. Flush toilets, piped water, a sanitary dump station and a boat ramp are available. Some facilities are **wheelchair accessible**. Leashed pets are permitted.

Reservations, fee: No reservations; $10 fee per night. Open from mid-April to mid-October.

Who to contact: Phone North Cascades Headquarters at (360) 856-5700 or write to them at 2105 State Route 20, Sedro Woolley, WA 98284.

Location: From Interstate 5 at Burlington, take Exit 230 and turn east on State Route 20. Drive 58 miles to Marblemount. Continue east on State Route 20 for 24 miles to the campground entrance.

Trip note: This campground is located at 1,200 feet in elevation along the shore of Diablo Lake in the Ross Lake National Recreation Area. The lake is five miles long and offers numerous hiking and fishing possibilities. A naturalist program is available in summer months.

9.   HARTS PASS

Reference: **Near Pasayten Wilderness in Okanogan National Forest; map A3, grid b6.**

Campsites, facilities: There are five tent sites. Picnic tables and fire grills are provided. Vault toilets are available, but there is **no piped water**. No garbage service is provided, so trash must be packed out. Leashed pets are permitted.

Reservations, fee: No reservations; no fee. Open mid-July to late September.

Who to contact: Phone the Okanogan National Forest at (509) 996-2266 or write to Methow Valley Ranger District, Winthrop Office, P.O. Box 579, Winthrop, WA 98862.

Location: From Interstate 5 south of Bellingham, turn east on Highway 20 and drive approximately 120 miles to County Road 1163 (located 13 miles west of Winthrop). Turn left and drive northwest for seven miles, then drive 12.5 miles northwest on Forest Service Road 5400 and you'll arrive at the campground. Be aware that this last stretch of road is closed to trailers and RVs.

Trip note: This pretty little campground is set near the Pasayten Wilderness, which offers 500 miles of trails to alpine meadows, glacier-fed lakes and streams, and along ridges to spectacular mountain heights. Contact the district ranger for details. The Pacific Crest Trail passes near camp, and nearby Slate Peak, at 7,500 feet, offers a great view of the northern Cascade Range.

10.   MEADOWS

Reference: **Near Pacific Crest Trail in Okanogan National Forest; map A3, grid b6.**

Campsites, facilities: There are 14 tent sites. Picnic tables and fire grills are provided. Vault toilets are available, but there is **no piped water**. No garbage service is provided, so trash must be packed out. Leashed pets are permitted.

Reservations, fee: No reservations; no fee. Open mid-July to late September.

Who to contact: Phone the Okanogan National Forest at (509) 996-2266 or write to Methow Valley Ranger District, Winthrop Office, P.O. Box 579, Winthrop, WA 98862.

Location: From Interstate 5 south of Bellingham, turn east on Highway 20 and drive approximately 120 miles to County Road 1163 (located 13 miles west of Winthrop). Turn left and drive northwest for seven miles, then drive 12.5 miles northwest on Forest Service Road 5400. Turn south on Forest Service Road 500 and drive one mile to the campground.

Trip note: This campground is about one mile from Harts Pass and offers the same opportunities. See that trip note. The camp is adjacent to the Pacific Crest Trail.

11.   HONEYMOON   🚐

Reference: **On Eightmile Creek in Okanogan National Forest; map A3, grid b8.**

Campsites, facilities: There are five sites for tents, trailers or RVs. Picnic tables and fire grills are provided. Vault toilets are available, but there is **no piped water**. Garbage service is not provided, so trash must be packed out. Leashed pets are permitted.

Reservations, fee: No reservations; no fee. Open June to late September.

Who to contact: Phone the Okanogan National Forest at (509) 996-2266 or write to Methow Valley Ranger District, Winthrop Office, P.O. Box 579, Winthrop, WA 98862.

Location: From Interstate 5 south of Bellingham, turn east on Highway 20 and drive approximately 134 miles to Winthrop. Turn north on County Road 1213 and drive 6.5 miles, then continue north on Forest Service Road 51 for 2.5 miles. Turn northwest on Forest Service Road 5130 and drive nine miles to the campground.

Trip note: This campground is set at 3,300 feet along Eightmile Creek. If you continue north seven miles to the end of Forest Service Road 5130, you will reach a trailhead that provides access to the Pasayten Wilderness. See a Forest Service map for details. Why is it named Honeymoon? Well, seems a forest ranger and his bride chose that very spot to spend their wedding night.

12.   CHEWUCK

Reference: **On Chewuck River in Okanogan National Forest; map A3, grid b9.**

Campsites, facilities: There are four tent sites. Picnic tables and fire grills are provided. Vault toilets are available. There is **no piped water**. No garbage service is provided, so trash must be packed out. Leashed pets are permitted.

Reservations, fee: No reservations; no fee. Open June to late September.

Who to contact: Phone the Okanogan National Forest at (509) 996-2266 or write to Methow Valley Ranger District, Winthrop Office, P.O. Box 579, Winthrop, WA 98862.

Location: From Interstate 5 south of Bellingham, turn east on Highway 20 and drive approximately 134 miles to Winthrop. Turn north on County Road 1213 and drive 6.5 miles, then continue northeast on Forest Service Roads 51 and 5160 for 8.5 miles to the campground.

Trip note: This campground is set along the Chewuck River. It's a more primitive option to nearby Falls Creek. Fishing is one of your recreation options, and by traveling north, you can access trailheads that lead into the Pasayten Wilderness. See a Forest Service map for specific locations.

13.   CAMP 4

Reference: **On Chewuck River in Okanogan National Forest; map A3, grid b9.**

Campsites, facilities: There are five tent sites. Picnic tables and fire grills are provided. Vault toilets are available. There is **no piped water**. No garbage service is provided, so trash must be packed out. Leashed pets are permitted.

Reservations, fee: No reservations; no fee. Open June to late September.

Who to contact: Phone the Okanogan National Forest at (509) 996-2266 or write to Methow Valley Ranger District, Winthrop Office, P.O. Box 579, Winthrop, WA 98862.

Location: From Interstate 5 south of Bellingham, turn east on Highway 20 and drive approximately 134 miles to Winthrop. Turn north on County Road 1213 and drive 6.5 miles, then continue northeast on Forest Service Roads 51 and 5160 for 11 miles to the campground.

Trip note: This campground is set along the Chewuck River, the smallest and most primitive of three camps on the river. There are two trailheads five miles north of camp: one is at Lake Creek and the other at Andrews Creek. They both have corrals, hitching rails, truck docks and water for the stock. Trails leading into the Pasayten Wilderness leave from both locations. Contact the Forest Service for details.

---

14. HORSESHOE COVE 🚐

Reference: **On Baker Lake in Mount Baker-Snoqualmie National Forest; map A3, grid c0.**

Campsites, facilities: There are eight sites for tents only and 34 sites for tents, trailers or RVs up to 25 feet long. Picnic tables are provided. Piped water and vault toilets are available. Leashed pets are permitted. A boat ramp is adjacent to camp.

Reservations, fee: Reserve some sites by calling (800) 280-CAMP ($7.75 reservation fee); $10 fee per night. Open May through September.

Who to contact: Phone the Mount Baker-Snoqualmie National Forest at (360) 856-5700 or write to Mount Baker Ranger District, 2105 State Route 20, Sedro Woolley, WA 98284.

Location: From Interstate 5 at Burlington, turn east on Highway 20 and drive approximately 24 miles to milepost 82. Turn north on Baker Lake Highway and drive about 13 miles. Take Forest Service Road 1118 east for two miles to the campground. A Forest Service map is recommended.

Trip note: This campground is set on the shore of 5,000-acre Baker Lake, a good fishing lake for rainbow trout, kokanee salmon, cutthroat trout and Dolly Varden trout. There is swimming access from this campground, and the boat ramp is a bonus for anglers. Some hiking trails are nearby.

---

15. ROCKPORT STATE PARK 🚐

Reference: **Near Skagit River; map A3, grid c0.**

Campsites, facilities: There are three primitive tent sites, eight developed, walk-in tent sites, and 50 sites for trailers or RVs up to 60 feet long. There is also one group tent site. Picnic tables and fire grills are provided. Flush toilets, sanitary disposal station, electricity, piped water, sewer hookups, showers and firewood are available. Some facilities are **wheelchair accessible**. A store, gas and ice are located within one mile. Leashed pets are permitted.

Reservations, fee: No reservations for family sites; $5-$15 fee per night. For group site reservation, call contact number below; $25 base group site fee plus $1 per person per night. Open April to late October.

Who to contact: Phone (360) 853-8461 or write to 5051 Highway 20, Concrete, WA 98237.

Location: From Interstate 5 at Burlington, turn east on Highway 20 and drive 40 miles to Rockport. Continue one mile west on Highway 20 to the park.

Trip note: This state park covers 457 acres and offers five miles of hiking trails and four adirondack (three-sided, roofed) shelters. The campground is set among old-growth Douglas firs and is near the Skagit River, a good steelhead stream.

16. GOODELL CREEK CAMPGROUND RV

Reference: **On Goodell Creek and Skagit River in Ross Lake National Recreation Area; map A3, grid c2.**

Campsites, facilities: There are 21 campsites for tents or RVs up to 22 feet long. Picnic tables and fireplaces are provided. Pit toilets, piped water and group sites are available. Leashed pets are permitted.

Reservations, fee: No reservations for family camping; $7 fee per night. Call (360) 873-4590, extension 1516 for group site reservation and fee information. Open all year, but there are no services in winter (and also no fee).

Who to contact: Phone North Cascades Headquarters at (360) 856-5700 or write to them at 2105 State Route 20, Sedro Woolley, WA 98284.

Location: From Interstate 5 at Burlington, take Exit 230 and turn east on State Route 20 and drive 58 miles to Marblemount. Continue 13 miles east on State Route 20 to the campground entrance.

Trip note: This campground is an alternative to the nearby and larger Newhalem Creek Campground. This one is set where Goodell Creek pours into the Skagit River in the Ross Lake National Recreation Area. It's a popular put-in for raft trips down river.

17. MARBLE CREEK RV

Reference: **On Marble Creek in Mount Baker-Snoqualmie National Forest; map A3, grid c2.**

Campsites, facilities: There are 24 sites for tents, trailers or RVs up to 32 feet long. Picnic tables and fire grills are provided. Vault toilets are available, but there is **no piped water**. Leashed pets are permitted.

Reservations, fee: Call for current status on reservations and fees. Open mid-May to mid-September.

Who to contact: Phone the Mount Baker-Snoqualmie National Forest at (360) 856-5700 or write to Mount Baker Ranger District, 2105 State Route 20, Sedro Wooley, WA 98284.

Location: From Interstate 5 at Burlington, take Exit 230 and turn east on Highway 20 and drive 48 miles to Marblemount. Turn east on County Road 3528 (Cascade River Road) and drive eight miles, then turn south on Forest Service Road 1530 and drive one mile to the campground on the right. A Forest Service map is recommended.

Trip note: This primitive campground is set on Marble Creek. Continuing on Forest Service Road 1530 will take you up to Bush Lake. A trailhead to Hidden Lake just inside the boundary of North Cascades National Park can be found about five miles from camp at the end of Forest Service Road 1540. See a Forest Service map for details.

18.   NEWHALEM CREEK CAMPGROUND   RV

Reference: **Near Skagit River in Ross Lake National Recreation Area; map A3, grid c2.**

Campsites, facilities: There are 128 sites for tents or RVs. Picnic tables and fireplaces are provided. Flush toilets, piped water and a sanitary dump station are available. Some facilities are **wheelchair accessible**. Leashed pets are permitted.

Reservations, fee: No reservations; $10 fee per night. Open from mid-May to late September.

Who to contact: Phone North Cascades Headquarters at (360) 856-5700 or write to them at 2105 State Route 20, Sedro Woolley, WA 98284.

Location: From Interstate 5 at Burlington, take Exit 230 and turn east on State Route 20 and drive 58 miles to Marblemount. Continue 14 miles east on State Route 20 to the camp.

Trip note: One of the newer camps set in the Ross Lake National Recreation Area, this spot is set along the Skagit River below Newhalem. There are good hiking possibilities in the immediate area. Be sure to visit the North Cascades Visitor Center.

---

19.   ALPINE RV PARK AND CAMPGROUND   RV

Reference: **Near Skagit River; map A3, grid c2.**

Campsites, facilities: There are 15 tent sites and 30 drive-through sites for trailers or RVs of any length. Electricity, piped water, sewer hookups and picnic tables are provided. Flush toilets, firewood, a laundromat, showers and a playground are available. Bottled gas, a store, a cafe and ice are located within one mile. Pets and motorbikes are permitted.

Reservations, fee: Reservations accepted; $5-$10 fee per night. MasterCard and Visa accepted. Open all year.

Who to contact: Phone (360) 873-4142 or write to P.O. Box 148, Marblemount, WA 98267.

Location: From Interstate 5 at Burlington, turn east on Highway 20 and drive 48 miles to Marblemount. Continue 1.5 miles past town and you'll see the campground.

Trip note: This campground has access to the Skagit River. A trail from the nearby National Park Service ranger station ascends to Helen Buttes.

---

20.   LONE FIR   RV

Reference: **On Early Winters Creek in Okanogan National Forest; map A3, grid c6.**

Campsites, facilities: There are 27 sites for tents, trailers or RVs up to 21 feet long. Piped water, fire grills and picnic tables are provided. Vault toilets are available. Leashed pets are permitted.

Reservations, fee: No reservations; $6-$8 fee per night. Open June to late September.

Who to contact: Phone the Okanogan National Forest at (509) 996-2266 or write to Methow Valley Ranger District, Winthrop Office, P.O. Box 579, Winthrop, WA 98862

Location: From Interstate 5 south of Bellingham, turn east on Highway 20 and drive approximately 107 miles to the campground (it is located about 11 miles west of Mazama).

Trip note: This campground is set at 3,800 feet along the banks of Early Winters Creek. To the south is Washington Pass Overlook, which offers a spectacular view. There is fishing in the creek, and many hiking trails in the area. A Forest Service map will provide details. See trip note for Early Winters for other area information.

21.　　　　　　　EARLY WINTERS　　　　　　RV

Reference: **On Early Winters Creek in Okanogan National Forest; map A3, grid c7.**

Campsites, facilities: There are seven tent sites and six sites for tents, trailers or RVs up to 16 feet long. Piped water, fire grills and picnic tables are provided. Vault toilets are available. Leashed pets are permitted.

Reservations, fee: No reservations; $6-$8 fee per night. Open June to late September.

Who to contact: Phone the Okanogan National Forest at (509) 996-2266 or write to Methow Valley Ranger District, Winthrop Office, P.O. Box 579, Winthrop, WA 98862.

Location: From Interstate 5 south of Bellingham, turn east on Highway 20 and drive approximately 118 miles to the campground (located about one mile west of Mazama).

Trip note: This campground is set at the confluence of Early Winters Creek and the Methow River. There are several hiking trails in the area, including one that leads south to Cedar Falls. Other possible side trips are Goat Wall to the north and the town of Winthrop to the south, which boasts a historical museum, a state fish hatchery and Pearrygin Lake State Park. Early Winters Information Center is adjacent to the camp and can provide detailed information.

22.　　　　　　　BALLARD

Reference: **Near Methow River in Okanogan National Forest; map A3, grid c7.**

Campsites, facilities: There are seven tent sites. **No piped water** is available. No garbage service is provided, so trash must be packed out. Picnic tables and fire grills are provided. Vault toilets are available and leashed pets are permitted.

Reservations, fee: No reservations; no fee. Open June to late September.

Who to contact: Phone the Okanogan National Forest at (509) 996-2266 or write to Methow Valley Ranger District, Winthrop Office, P.O. Box 579, Winthrop, WA 98862.

Location: From Interstate 5 south of Bellingham, turn east on Highway 20 and drive approximately 120 miles to County Road 1163. Turn left and drive northwest for seven miles, then travel two miles northwest on Forest Service Road 5400 until you see the campground.

Trip note: This campground is set at 2,600 feet, about one-half mile from River Bend. Facilities for horse packing, including a hitch rail, truck dock and water, are available at a primitive camp less than a mile northeast of Ballard. There are numerous hiking trails in the area, including one that heads west and eventually hooks up with the Pacific Crest Trail. See trip note for Early Winters for area information.

23.　　　　　　　RIVER BEND　　　　　**RV**

Reference: **On Methow River in Okanogan National Forest; map A3, grid c7.**

Campsites, facilities: There are five sites for tents, trailers or RVs. Picnic tables and fire grills are provided, but there is **no piped water**. Vault toilets are available and leashed pets are permitted.

Reservations, fee: No reservations; no fee. Open June to late September.

Who to contact: Phone the Okanogan National Forest at (509) 996-2266 or write to Methow Valley Ranger District, Winthrop Office, P.O. Box 579, Winthrop, WA 98862.

Location: From Interstate 5 south of Bellingham, turn east on Highway 20 and drive approximately 120 miles to County Road 1163. Turn left and drive northwest for seven miles, then travel 2.5 miles northwest on Forest Service Road 5400. Turn west on Forest Service Road 54060 and drive one-half mile to the campground.

Trip note: This campground is set along the Methow River about two miles from the boundary of the Pasayten Wilderness. There are several trails near camp that provide access to the wilderness, as well as one that follows the Methow River west for about eight miles before hooking up with the Pacific Crest Trail near Azurite Peak; a Forest Service map will show you the options. If you are interested in traveling with pack animals or horses there is a Forest Service camp nearby that provides facilities. See the trip note for Ballard for further details.

24.　　　　　　　KLIPCHUCK　　　　　**RV**

Reference: **On Early Winters Creek in Okanogan National Forest; map A3, grid c7.**

Campsites, facilities: There are six tent sites and 40 sites for tents, trailers or RVs up to 32 feet long. Piped water and picnic tables are provided. Flush and vault toilets are available. Leashed pets are permitted.

Reservations, fee: No reservations; $6-$8 fee per night. Open June to late September.

Who to contact: Phone the Okanogan National Forest at (509) 996-2266 or write to Methow Valley Ranger District, Winthrop Office, P.O. Box 579, Winthrop, WA 98862.

Location: From Interstate 5 south of Bellingham, turn east on Highway 20 and drive approximately 115 miles to Forest Service Road 300. Turn left and drive one mile northwest to the campground.

Trip note: This campground is set along Early Winters Creek at 3,000 feet. A trail from the camp leads about five miles up and over Delancy Ridge to the Methow River. Another trail starts nearby on Forest Service Road 200 (Sandy Butte-Cedar Creek Road) and goes two miles up Cedar Creek to lovely Cedar Creek Falls. See trip note for Early Winters camp for other information.

25.　　　ROCKING HORSE RANCH　　　**RV**

Reference: **In Methow River Valley; map A3, grid c8.**

Campsites, facilities: There are 25 tent sites and 10 drive-through sites for trailers or RVs of any length. Electricity, piped water, sewer hookups and picnic tables are provided. Flush toilets, sanitary services, showers, firewood and a recreation hall are available. Some facilities are **wheelchair accessible**. Pets and motorbikes are permitted.

Reservations, fee: Reservations accepted; $12-$15 fee per night. Open April to late October.

Who to contact: Phone (509) 996-2768 or write to Star Route, P.O. Box 35, Winthrop, WA 98862.

Location: From Interstate 5 at Burlington, turn east on Highway 20 and drive 123 miles to the campground, located nine miles northwest of Winthrop.

Trip note: This ranch is set in the lovely Methow River Valley, which is flanked on both sides by national forest. There are numerous trails nearby and a horse stable at the ranch. Owen Wister, who wrote the novel, *The Virginian*, lived in the nearby town of Winthrop at the turn of the century. Portions of the novel were based on his experiences in this area.

---

26.   NICE

Reference: On Eightmile Creek in Okanogan National Forest; map A3, grid c9.

Campsites, facilities: There are four tent sites. Picnic tables and fire grills are provided. Vault toilets are available, but there is **no piped water**. No garbage service is provided, so trash must be packed out. Leashed pets are permitted.

Reservations, fee: No reservations; no fee. Open June to late September.

Who to contact: Phone the Okanogan National Forest at (509) 996-2266 or write to Methow Valley Ranger District, Winthrop Office, P.O. Box 579, Winthrop, WA 98862.

Location: From Interstate 5 south of Bellingham, turn east on Highway 20 and drive approximately 134 miles to Winthrop. Turn north on County Road 1213 and drive 6.5 miles, then continue north on Forest Service Road 51 for three miles. Turn northwest on Forest Service Road 5130 and drive four miles to the campground.

Trip note: This campground is set along Eightmile Creek about four miles from Buck Lake. At the end of Forest Service Road 5130 there is a trail that leads into the Pasayten Wilderness. Pearrygin Lake State Park is just a few miles to the south, near Winthrop.

---

27.   FLAT   **RV**

Reference: On Eightmile Creek in Okanogan National Forest; map A3, grid c9.

Campsites, facilities: There are 12 sites for tents, trailers or RVs up to 15 feet long. Picnic tables and fire grills are provided, but there is **no piped water**. Vault toilets are available and leashed pets are permitted.

Reservations, fee: No reservations; no fee. Open June to late September.

Who to contact: Phone the Okanogan National Forest at (509) 996-2266 or write to Methow Valley Ranger District, Winthrop Office, P.O. Box 579, Winthrop, WA 98862.

Location: From Interstate 5 south of Bellingham, turn east on Highway 20 and drive approximately 134 miles to Winthrop. Turn north on County Road 1213 and drive 6.5 miles, then continue three miles north on Forest Service Road 51. Turn northwest on Forest Service Road 5130 and proceed for two miles to the campground.

Trip note: This campground is set along Eightmile Creek two miles from where it empties to the Chewuck River. Buck Lake is about three miles away. This is the closest of six camps to County Road 1213. Being the closest to the main road, it gets some of the heaviest use. Other options are Nice, Falls Creek and Honeymoon.

28.   FALLS CREEK   RV

Reference: **On Chewuck River in Okanogan National Forest; map A3, grid c9.**

Campsites, facilities: There are seven sites for tents, trailers or RVs up to 15 feet long. Piped water and picnic tables are provided. Vault toilets are available. Leashed pets are permitted.

Reservations, fee: No reservations; $6-$8 fee per night. Open June to late September.

Who to contact: Phone the Okanogan National Forest at (509) 996-2266 or write to Methow Valley Ranger District, Winthrop Office, P.O. Box 579, Winthrop, WA 98862.

Location: From Interstate 5 south of Bellingham, turn east on Highway 20 and drive approximately 134 miles to Winthrop. Turn north on County Road 1213 and drive 6.5 miles, then continue north on Forest Service Roads 51 and 5160 for five miles to the campground.

Trip note: This campground is set at the confluence of Falls Creek and the Chewuck River, a quiet and pretty spot that is about a 20-minute drive out of Winthrop. Nearby Chewuck camp and Camp 4 do not have piped water, but this camp does. There is fishing access from the campground.

29.   HOWARD MILLER STEELHEAD   RV

Reference: **On Skagit River; map A3, grid d0.**

Campsites, facilities: There are 40 tent sites and 60 sites (11 pull-through) for trailers or RVs of any length. Electricity, piped water and picnic tables are provided. Flush toilets, sanitary services, showers and a playground are available. Bottled gas, a store, a cafe and ice are located within one mile. Pets and motorbikes are permitted. Boat launching facilities are nearby on Skagit River.

Reservations, fee: No reservations; $10-$12 fee per night. Open all year.

Who to contact: Phone (360) 853-8808 or write to P.O. Box 97, Rockport, WA 98283.

Location: From Interstate 5 south of Bellingham, turn east on Highway 20 and drive 44 miles to Rockport. At the junction of Highway 20 and Rockport-Darrington Road (Highway 530), then turn south and drive three blocks to the camp.

Trip note: This grassy city park has access to the Skagit River, which has been designated a Wild and Scenic river. There is good steelhead fishing in season. This is a pretty spot, with sunny, spacious sites.

30.   WILDERNESS VILLAGE AND RV PARK   RV

Reference: **Near Skagit River; map A3, grid d1.**

Campsites, facilities: There are 20 tent sites and 32 drive-through sites for trailers or RVs of any length. Electricity, piped water, sewer hookups and picnic tables are provided. Flush toilets, sanitary services, showers, a recreation hall and a laundromat are available. A cafe and ice are located within one mile. Pets are permitted.

Reservations, fee: Reservations accepted; $9-$15 fee per night. Open all year.

Who to contact: Phone (360) 873-2571 or write to 5550 Highway 20, Rockport, WA 98283.

Location: From Interstate 5 south of Bellingham, turn east on Highway 20 and drive 44 miles to Rockport. Continue five miles east on Highway 20. The park is between mileposts 102 and 103 on the right.

Trip note: This park is near the Skagit River. It's cool and wooded, with nice grassy sites and nearby access to the river and fishing. Horseshoe pits and a recreation field offer recreation alternatives. Rockport State Park and hiking trails are nearby.

---

31.   CLARK'S SKAGIT RIVER CABINS AND RVS   RV

Reference: **On the Skagit River; map A3, grid d1.**

Campsites, facilities: There are 48 sites for tents, trailers and RVs. There are also 23 cabins available. Restrooms, showers, a sanitary dump, a public phone, a laundromat and a restaurant are available. Recreational facilities include horseshoes and a recreation field for volleyball, croquet and badminton. Leashed pets are permitted. There is a charge for pets.

Reservations, fee: Reservations recommended; $7-$15 fee per night. Cabins range from $47-$97. Visa, MasterCard and Discover are accepted. Open year round.

Who to contact: Phone the park at (360) 873-2250 or (800) 273-2606 or write to 5675 Highway 20, Rockport, WA 98283.

Location: From Bellingham, take Interstate 5 south for about 20 miles. Take exit 232 and follow the road up and over the highway. At the light, turn left onto Cook Road. Drive for four miles and turn left (east) onto Highway 20. Continue on Highway 20 for about 45 miles past Concrete and Rockport. The camp-ground is located on the left between mileposts 103 and 104.

Trip note: This beautiful camp is set in the trees along the Skagit River. Activities include trout fishing and river walks. Some side trips include nearby hiking trails among glaciers and waterfalls. There are also three hydroelectric plants nearby that offer tours.

---

32.   MINERAL PARK

Reference: **On Cascade River in Mount Baker-Snoqualmie National Forest; map A3, grid d3.**

Campsites, facilities: There are four tent sites. Picnic tables, fire rings and vault toilets are provided, but there is **no piped water**. Leashed pets are permitted.

Reservations, fee: No reservation necessary; no fee. Call ahead for availability; usually open mid-May to mid-September.

Who to contact: Phone the Mount Baker-Snoqualmie National Forest at (360) 856-5700 or write to Mount Baker Ranger District, 2105 State Route 20, Sedro Woolley, WA 98284.

Location: From Interstate 5 south of Bellingham, turn east on Highway 20 and drive 48 miles to Marblemount. Turn east on County Road 3528 (Cascade River Road) and drive 15 miles to the campground.

Trip note: Here's another classic, primitive, unknown camping area that can provide a jumpoff for many adventures. This rustic site is set on the Cascade River and is near numerous trails leading into Glacier Peak Wilderness. Fishing is available in the river and can be quite good at times.

33.   SOUTH CREEK

Reference: **On Twisp River in Okanogan National Forest; map A3, grid d7.**

Campsites, facilities: There are four sites for tents or small trailers. **No piped water** is available. Picnic tables and fire grills are provided. Vault toilets are available. No garbage service is provided, so trash must be packed out. Leashed pets are permitted.

Reservations, fee: No reservations; no fee. Open late May to early September.

Who to contact: Phone the Okanogan National Forest at (509) 997-2131 or write to Methow Valley Ranger District, Twisp Office, P.O. Box 188, Twisp, WA 98856.

Location: From Interstate 5 south of Bellingham, turn east on Highway 20 and drive approximately 145 miles to Twisp. Turn west on County Road 9114 and drive 11 miles, then continue west on Forest Service Roads 44 and 4440 for 11 miles to the campground.

Trip note: This site is small, quiet and little-known, yet with good recreation options. It is set at the confluence of the Twisp River and South Creek at a major trailhead that accesses Lake Chelan-Sawtooth Wilderness. See a Forest Service map for details. South Creek campground also has horse facilities.

34.   POPLAR FLAT   · RV.

Reference: **On Twisp River in Okanogan National Forest; map A3, grid d7.**

Campsites, facilities: There are 16 sites for tents, trailers or RVs up to 21 feet long. Piped water, fire grills and picnic tables are provided. Vault toilets are available. Some facilities are **wheelchair accessible**. Pets are permitted.

Reservations, fee: No reservations; $5 fee per night. Open May to September.

Who to contact: Phone the Okanogan National Forest at (509) 997-2131 or write to Methow Valley Ranger District, Twisp Office, P.O. Box 188, Twisp, WA 98856.

Location: From Interstate 5 south of Bellingham, turn east on Highway 20 and drive approximately 145 miles to Twisp. Turn west on County Road 9114 and drive 11 miles, then continue west on Forest Service Roads 44 and 4440 for 9.5 miles to the campground.

Trip note: This campground is set at 2,900 feet along the Twisp River. There are many trails in the area that follow streams, in some cases providing access to Lake Chelan-Sawtooth Wilderness. South Creek campground, about two miles northwest of this campground, has horse facilities.

35.   ROADS END

Reference: **On Twisp River in Okanogan National Forest; map A3, grid d7.**

Campsites, facilities: There are four sites for tents or small trailers. **No piped water** is available. Picnic tables and fire grills are provided. Vault toilets and firewood are available. No garbage service is provided, so trash must be packed out. Leashed pets are permitted.

Reservations, fee: No reservations; no fee. Open late May to early September.

Who to contact: Phone the Okanogan National Forest at (509) 997-2131 or write to Methow Valley Ranger District, Twisp Office, P.O. Box 188, Twisp, WA 98856.

Location: From Interstate 5 south of Bellingham, turn east on Highway 20 and drive approximately 145 miles to Twisp. Turn west on County Road 9114 and drive 11 miles, then continue west on Forest Service Roads 44 and 4440 for

13.5 miles to the campground.

Trip note: This campground is set along the Twisp River at a major trailhead that provides access to Lake Chelan-Sawtooth Wilderness. The trail intersects with the Pacific Crest Trail about nine miles from the camp. A Forest Service map is essential.

---

36. WAR CREEK   RV

Reference: **On Twisp River in Okanogan National Forest; map A3, grid d8.**

Campsites, facilities: There are 12 sites for tents, trailers or RVs up to 21 feet long. Piped water, fire grills and picnic tables are provided. Vault toilets and firewood are available. Leashed pets are permitted.

Reservations, fee: No reservations; $5-$7 fee per night. Open May to September.

Who to contact: Phone the Okanogan National Forest at (509) 997-2131 or write to Methow Valley Ranger District, Twisp Office, P.O. Box 188, Twisp, WA 98856.

Location: From Interstate 5 south of Bellingham, turn east on Highway 20 and drive approximately 145 miles to Twisp. Turn west on County Road 9114 and drive 11 miles, then continue west on Forest Service Road 44 for 3.5 miles to the campground.

Trip note: This campground is set along the Twisp River near the trailhead for trail 408, which provides access to the Lake Chelan-Sawtooth Wilderness. Backpackers can take this path down into the Lake Chelan National Recreation Area, finishing the trip at the shore of Lake Chelan and the National Park Service outpost. It's a 15-mile trek, so contact the Forest Service for details.

---

37. PEARRYGIN LAKE STATE PARK   RV

Reference: **On Pearrygin Lake; map A3, grid d9.**

Campsites, facilities: There are 26 tent sites and 57 sites for tents or RVs of any length (30 full and 27 water-only hookups). Picnic tables and fire grills are provided. Flush toilets and sanitary services, electricity, piped water, sewer hookups, showers and firewood are available. A store, a cafe and ice are located within one mile. Some facilities are **wheelchair accessible**. Leashed pets are permitted. Boat launching facilities are available.

Reservations, fee: Contact Reservations Northwest at (800) 452-5687 ($6 reservation fee); $11-$16 fee per night. Open April through October.

Who to contact: Phone (800) 233-0321 or (509) 996-2370 or write to Route 1, P.O. Box 300, Winthrop, WA 98862.

Location: From Interstate 5 south of Bellingham, turn east on Highway 20 and drive approximately 134 miles to Winthrop. Turn north on County Road 1631 and drive about four miles to the park on the right.

Trip note: This 578-acre park is located in the beautiful Methow Valley, ringed by the North Cascade Mountains. The area is ideal for wildflower and wildlife viewing in the spring. The campground has access to a sandy beach and facilities for swimming, boating, fishing and hiking. The sites are set close together and don't offer much privacy, but they are spacious and a variety of recreation options make it worth the crunch. In the winter there are opportunities for snowmobiling, cross-country skiing and ice fishing. A nine-hole golf course is nearby.

38.   RIVER BEND TRAILER PARK   RV

Reference: **Near Methow River; map A3, grid d9.**

Campsites, facilities: There are 10 tent sites and 86 sites (12 drive-through) for trailers or RVs of any length. Picnic tables are provided. Flush toilets, sanitary services, firewood, a store, a laundromat, ice, a playground, electricity, piped water, sewer hookups and showers are available. Pets and motorbikes are permitted.

Reservations, fee: Reservations accepted; $14-$18 fee per night. MasterCard and Visa accepted. Open all year.

Who to contact: Phone (509) 997-3500 or write to Route 2, P.O. Box 30, Twisp, WA 98856.

Location: From Interstate 5 south of Bellingham, turn east on Highway 20 and drive approximately 140 miles to the campground (two miles west of Twisp).

Trip note: This campground is set along the shore of the Methow River. Trout fishing, river rafting and swimming are two options. There is a nice separate area for tent campers set right along the river. The trip note for KOA Methow River details the recreation possibilities available within 10 miles.

39.   DERRY'S RESORT   RV

Reference: **On Pearrygin Lake; map A3, grid d9.**

Campsites, facilities: There are 90 tent sites and 64 drive-through sites for trailers or RVs of any length. Electricity, piped water, sewer hookups and picnic tables are provided. Flush toilets, bottled gas, showers, firewood, sanitary services, a store, a laundromat, ice and a playground are available. A cafe is located within three miles. Pets and motorbikes are permitted. Boat docks, launching facilities and rentals are available on Pearrygin Lake.

Reservations, fee: Reservations accepted; $14-$17 fee per night. Open mid-April to November.

Who to contact: Phone (509) 996-2322 or write to Route 1, P.O. Box 307, Winthrop, WA 98862.

Location: From Interstate 5 south of Bellingham, turn east on Highway 20 and drive approximately 134 miles to Winthrop. Turn north on Riverside Avenue and drive one-tenth of a mile, then turn northeast on Bluff Street and drive 1.5 miles. Turn east on Pearrygin Lake Road and continue one mile to the resort on the right.

Trip note: This campground is also set along the shore of Pearrygin Lake. It is exceptionally clean and pretty, with comfortable shady sites and fishing, swimming and boating access a short distance away. Other nearby recreation options include an 18-hole golf course, hiking trails and a riding stable. See the trip note for KOA Methow River for details on the area.

40.   KOA METHOW RIVER-WINTHROP   RV

Reference: **On Methow River; map A3, grid d9.**

Campsites, facilities: There are 110 sites (76 drive-through) for tents, trailers or RVs of any length. Piped water and picnic tables are provided. Flush toilets, electricity, firewood, sewer hookups, sanitary services, showers, a recreation hall, bike and video rentals, a store, a laundromat, ice, a playground and swimming pool are available. Bottled gas and a cafe are located within one mile. Pets and motorbikes are permitted.

Reservations, fee: Reservations accepted; $18-$23 fee per night. MasterCard and Visa accepted. Open mid-April to November.

Who to contact: Phone (509) 996-2258 or write to P.O. Box 305, Winthrop, WA 98862.

Location: From Interstate 5 south of Bellingham, turn east on Highway 20 and drive approximately 134 miles to Winthrop. Continue one mile east on Highway 20. The camp is on the left, between mileposts 194 and 195.

Trip note: This campground is set along the Methow River, which offers opportunities for fishing, boating, swimming and rafting. The park has a free shuttle into Winthrop, an interesting town with many restored, turn-of-the-century buildings lining the main street, including the Shafer Museum, which displays lots of old items from that era. If you would like to observe wildlife, take a short, two-mile drive southeast out of Winthrop on County Road 9129, on the east side of the Methow River. Turn east on County Road 1631 into Davis Lake, and follow the signs to the Methow River Habitat Management Area Headquarters. Depending upon the time of year, you may see mule deer, porcupine, bobcat, mountain lion, snowshoe hare, black bear, red squirrel and many species of birds. However, if you are looking for something tamer, other nearby recreation options include an 18-hole golf course and tennis courts.

---

41.   PINE-NEAR TRAILER PARK   [RV]

Reference: **On Methow River; map A3, grid d9.**

Campsites, facilities: There are 40 tent sites and 28 sites (14 drive-through) for trailers or RVs of any length. Electricity, piped water, sewer hookups and picnic tables are provided. Flush toilets, sanitary services, showers and a laundromat are available. A store and a cafe are located within one mile. Pets and motorbikes are permitted.

Reservations, fee: Reservations accepted; $8-$12 fee per night. Open all year.

Who to contact: Phone (509) 996-2391 or write to Route 1, P.O. Box 400-32, Winthrop, WA 98862.

Location: From Interstate 5 south of Bellingham, turn east on Highway 20 and drive approximately 134 miles to Winthrop. One block north of Riverside Drive, turn east on Castle Avenue and drive three blocks to the park on the left.

Trip note: This campground is set not far from the Methow River. It is an adequate layover spot for Highway 20 cruisers and a good alternative camp to the more crowded sites at Pearrygin Lake. See the trip note for KOA Methow River for information on the various activities available in the Winthrop area.

---

42.   BIG TWIN LAKE CAMPGROUND   [RV]

Reference: **On Twin Lakes; map A3, grid d9.**

Campsites, facilities: There are 35 tent sites and 68 sites for trailers or RVs of any length (18 drive-through). Electricity, piped water, sewer hookups and picnic tables are provided. Flush toilets, sanitary services, showers, firewood, a laundromat, ice and a playground are available. Pets and motorbikes are permitted. Boat docks, launching facilities and rentals can be obtained on Big Twin Lake.

Reservations, fee: Reservations accepted; $10-$16 fee per night. Open April to late October.

Who to contact: Phone (509) 996-2650 or write to Big Twin Lake Road, Winthrop, WA 98862.

Location: From Interstate 5 south of Bellingham, turn east on Highway 20 and drive approximately 134 miles to Winthrop. Continue three miles east on Highway 20, then turn west on Big Twin Lake Road and drive two miles to the campground.

Trip note: This campground is set along the shore of Twin Lakes. See the trip note for KOA Methow River for information on the various activities available in the Winthrop area.

43.   CLEAR CREEK   RV

Reference: **On Clear Creek and Sauk River in Mount Baker-Snoqualmie National Forest; map A3, grid e0.**

Campsites, facilities: There are 12 sites for tents, trailers or RVs up to 21 feet long. Picnic tables and fire grills are provided. Vault toilets and firewood are available. There is **no piped water**. Some facilities are **wheelchair accessible**. A store, a cafe, a laundromat and ice are located within four miles. Leashed pets are permitted.

Reservations, fee: No reservations; no fee. Open late May to early September.

Who to contact: Phone the Mount Baker-Snoqualmie National Forest at (360) 436-1155 or write to Darrington Ranger District, 1405 Emmens Street, Darrington, WA 98241.

Location: From Interstate 5 south of Bellingham, take exit 208 and head east on Highway 530. Drive 32 miles to Darrington, then drive 2.5 miles south on Forest Service Road 20 to the campground entrance on the left.

Trip note: This nice, secluded spot does not get heavy use. This campground is set at the confluence of Clear Creek and the Sauk River, a designated Wild and Scenic river. A trail from camp leads about one mile up to Frog Lake.

44.   SQUIRE CREEK COUNTY PARK   RV

Reference: **On Squire Creek; map A3, grid e0.**

Campsites, facilities: There are 30 drive-through sites for trailers or RVs up to 25 feet long. Piped water, sewer hookups and picnic tables are provided. Flush toilets, sanitary services and firewood are available. Leashed pets are permitted. A store is located nearby in Darrington.

Reservations, fee: No reservations; $10-$14 fee per night. Open mid-May to mid-September.

Who to contact: Phone (206) 339-1208 or write to 303 3000 Rockefeller Avenue, Everett, WA 98201.

Location: From Interstate 5 south of Bellingham, take exit 208 and head east on Highway 530. Drive 32 miles to Darrington, then drive three miles west on Highway 530 and you'll see the park on the left.

Trip note: This wooded park is set along Squire Creek about three miles from the boundaries of the Boulder River Wilderness. It's a low-cost motor home park set near the outback.

45. CASCADE KAMLOOPS TROUT FARM / RV PARK   RV

Reference: **In Darrington; map A3, grid e1.**

Campsites, facilities: There are four tent sites and 32 sites for trailers or RVs of any length. Electricity, piped water, sewer hookups and picnic tables are provided. Flush toilets, sanitary services, showers, firewood and a recreation hall are available. Bottled gas, a store, a cafe, a laundromat and ice are located within one mile. Pets and motorbikes are permitted.

Reservations, fee: Reservations accepted; $10-$15 fee per night. Open all year.

Who to contact: Phone (360) 436-1003 or write to P.O. Box 1205, Darrington, WA 98241.

Location: From Interstate 5 south of Bellingham, take exit 208 and drive east on Highway 530 for about 30 miles to Darrington. In Darrington, turn right on Madison Street and drive about six blocks to Darrington Street. Turn right and drive two blocks to the park.

Trip note: This campground offers a little bit of both worlds—a rustic quietness with all facilities available. A bonus is a nearby trout pond, which is stocked in season. No boats are allowed. Nearby recreation options include marked hiking trails and tennis courts. Management changed in 1995.

46.   WILLIAM C. DEARINGER

Reference: **On Sauk River; map A3, grid e1.**

Campsites, facilities: There are 12 sites for tents or small trailers. Picnic tables, fire grills and tent pads are provided. Vault toilets and firewood are available, but there is **no piped water**. Leashed pets are permitted.

Reservations, fee: No reservations; no fee. Open all year.

Who to contact: Phone the Department of Natural Resources at (360) 856-3500 or write to Department of Natural Resources, Northwest Region, 411 Tillicum Lane, Forks, WA 98331-9797.

Location: From Interstate 5, take exit 208 and turn east on Highway 530. Drive 35 miles to Darrington. Continue one-third mile northeast on Highway 530, then drive east on Mountain Loop Road for one-half mile. Continue straight for five miles, then turn left and drive two-thirds of a mile on East Sauk Prairie Road. Stay right on Road SWD 5000 and drive 2.6 miles, then bear right for one mile. Turn left on Road SWD 5400 and drive about 400 yards to the campground.

Trip note: This secluded campground is on the Sauk River and is managed by the Department of Natural Resources. It may be a little difficult to get there, but that's why you'll probably be the only one there. It's pretty, with lots of trees and sites overlooking the river.

47.   BUCK CREEK   ■RV▪

Reference: **Near Suiattle River in Mount Baker-Snoqualmie National Forest; map A3, grid e2.**

Campsites, facilities: There are 29 tent sites and 10 sites for trailers or RVs up to 30 feet long. Picnic tables are provided. Vault toilets and firewood are available, but **no piped water** is available. Leashed pets are permitted.

Reservations, fee: No reservations; no fee. Open late May to early September.

Who to contact: Phone the Mount Baker-Snoqualmie National Forest at (360) 436-1155 or write to Darrington Ranger District, 1405 Emmens Street, Darrington, WA 98241.

Location: From Interstate 5 south of Bellingham, take exit 208 and head east on Highway 530. Drive 32 miles to Darrington, then continue 7.5 miles north on Highway 530 and turn right (southeast) on Forest Service Road 26. Drive 15.2 miles to the campground. A Forest Service map is essential. Note: In the past, Forest Service Road 26 has been closed due to flooding; it's a good idea to phone ahead for current condition.

Trip note: This primitive campground is set along Buck Creek near its confluence with the Suiattle River in the Glacier Peak Wilderness. There's a large (18 by 18 foot) adirondack shelter by the creek and stands of old growth timber. It's quiet and remote. A zigzagging trail routed into the Glacier Peak Wilderness is accessible about one mile west of camp. See a Forest Service map for specifics. Suiattle Forest Station is located a mile east.

48. SULPHUR CREEK 〖RV〗

Reference: On Suiattle River in Mount Baker-Snoqualmie National Forest; map A3, grid e3.

Campsites, facilities: There are 20 sites for tents, trailers or RVs up to 15 feet long. Picnic tables and fire grills are provided. Downed wood is available to gather and use for firewood. Vault toilets are available. There is **no piped water**. Leashed pets are permitted.

Reservations, fee: No reservations; no fee is required, but donations are accepted. Open June to early September.

Who to contact: Phone the Mount Baker-Snoqualmie National Forest at (360) 436-1155 or write to Darrington Ranger District, 1405 Emmens Street, Darrington, WA 98252.

Location: From Interstate 5 south of Bellingham, take exit 208 and head east on Highway 530. Drive 32 miles to Darrington, then continue 7.5 miles north on Highway 530. Turn right on Forest Service Road 26 and drive 30 miles southeast to the campground on the right. A Forest Service map is advisable. Note: In the past, Forest Service Road 26 has been closed due to flooding; it's a good idea to phone ahead for current condition.

Trip note: This campground is set along the Suiattle River near the border of Glacier Peak Wilderness. There is fishing access to the river across the road. It is a good base camp for a wilderness expedition. A horse ramp and a trailhead leading deep into the backcountry can be found about a mile south of the campground. The trail hooks up with the Pacific Crest Trail.

49. HOLDEN BALLPARK

Reference: Near Glacier Peak Wilderness, boat-in or ferry only, in Wenatchee National Forest; map A3, grid e5.

Campsites, facilities: There are two primitive tent sites that are accessible only by boat or ferry. Picnic tables and fire rings are provided. One Wallowa (non-enclosed, platform) pit toilet is available, but there is **no piped water**.

Reservations, fee: No reservations; no fee. Open mid-June to late September.

Who to contact: Phone Wenatchee National Forest at (509) 682-2576 or write to Chelan Ranger District, 428 West Woodin Avenue, Chelan, WA 98816.

Location: From Interstate 5 at Everett, turn east on US 2 and drive approximately 120 miles. Turn north on US 97 and continue about 40 miles to Chelan. Take the ferry from there (another ferry is available at Fields Point Landing, a few miles northwest of Chelan) and proceed to Lucerne, 41 miles northwest of the town of Chelan. (This spectacular voyage costs about $20 for a roundtrip, depending on your destination. For more information call (509) 682-2224). From Lucerne, take the bus 12 miles west to Holden Village. The campground is at the end of the road.

Trip note: Getting there is half the fun, with a ferry boat and bus rides. Ferry rides are provided by the Lake Chelan Boat Company, who emphasize fun and education along with transportation. Several trails to lakes in the Glacier Peak Wilderness are accessible from a trail next to the campground, which is set along Railroad Creek. Since this area is along the eastern slope of the Cascade Range, it is drier than the western slopes and not as heavily forested. However, there is no shortage of glacier-fed streams and lakes in the area. See a Forest Service map for details. Less than a mile from the campground is the Holden Mine site, which was Washington's largest gold, copper and zinc mine until it closed in 1957. Many of the buildings from the mining town have been preserved and Holden Village offers housing and meals for travelers as space allows.

50. DOMKE LAKE

Reference: **Near Glacier Peak Wilderness, boat-in, ferry or float plane only, in Wenatchee National Forest; map A3, grid e6.**

Campsites, facilities: There are six tent sites accessible only by boat. Picnic tables are provided. Pit toilets are available, but there is **no piped water**. Boat docks and rentals are nearby.

Reservations, fee: No reservations; no fee. Open May to late October.

Who to contact: Phone Wenatchee National Forest at (509) 682-2576 or write to Chelan Ranger District, 428 West Woodin Avenue, Chelan, WA, 98816.

Location: From Interstate 5 at Everett, turn east on US 2 and drive approximately 120 miles. Turn north on US 97 and continue about 40 miles to Chelan. Take the ferry from there (another ferry is available at Fields Point Landing, a few miles northwest of Chelan) and proceed to Lucerne, 41 miles northwest of the town of Chelan. (This spectacular voyage costs about $20 for a roundtrip, depending on your destination. For more information call (509) 682-2224). From Lucerne, hike, bike or motorbike 2.5 miles on Trail #1280 to Domke Lake and the campground. The campground is also directly accessible by float plane. Call Chelan Airways at (509) 682-5555 for more information.

Trip note: Little-known and little-used, this is a perfect jumpoff for a wilderness backpacking trip. Domke Lake is about one mile long and one-half mile wide, offering good fishing by boat. A national recreation trail continues past the lake into Glacier Peak Wilderness. See a Forest Service map for details.

51. LUCERNE

Reference: **On Lake Chelan, boat-in, ferry or float plane only, in Wenatchee National Forest; map A3, grid e7.**

Campsites, facilities: There are two boat-in tent sites. Piped water, fire grills and picnic tables are provided. Pit toilets are available. Boat docks are nearby.

Reservations, fee: No reservations; no fee. Open May to late October.

Who to contact: Phone Wenatchee National Forest at (509) 682-2576 or write to Chelan Ranger District, 428 West Woodin Avenue, Chelan, WA, 98816.

Location: From Interstate 5 at Everett, turn east on US 2 and drive approximately 120 miles. Turn north on US 97 and continue about 40 miles to Chelan. Take the ferry from there (another ferry is available at Fields Point Landing, a few miles northwest of Chelan) and proceed to Lucerne, 41 miles northwest of the town of Chelan. (This spectacular voyage costs about $20 for a roundtrip, depending on your destination. For more information call (509) 682-2224). The camp is in Lucerne. The campground is also directly accessible by float plane. Call Chelan Airways at (509) 682-5555 for more information.

Trip note: This campground is set along the shore of Lake Chelan, a 55-mile long lake. It's the second deepest lake in North America, with a depth of 1,500 feet. Mountains reaching to 8,000 feet flank each side of the lake. This is the only national forest camp in the vicinity that offers piped water. Fishing, hiking and boating are among your options here. See the trip note for Holden camp for information on the Holden Mine and Village.

52. FOGGY DEW RV.

Reference: **On Foggy Dew Creek in Okanogan National Forest; map A3, grid e9.**

Campsites, facilities: There are 13 sites for tents, trailers or RVs. Picnic tables and fire grills are provided. Vault toilets and firewood are available, but there is **no piped water**. No garbage service is provided, so trash must be packed out. Leashed pets are permitted.

Reservations, fee: No reservations; no fee. Open late May to early September.

Who to contact: Phone the Okanogan National Forest at (509) 997-2131 or write to Methow Valley Ranger District, Twisp Office, P.O. Box 188, Twisp, WA 98856.

Location: From Interstate 5 south of Bellingham, turn east on Highway 20 and drive approximately 145 miles to Twisp. Continue three miles east on Highway 20, then turn south on Highway 153 and drive 12 miles to County Road 1029. Turn south and drive one mile, then turn west on Forest Service Road 4340 and drive four miles to the campground.

Trip note: This private, remote campground is set at the confluence of Foggy Dew Creek and the North Fork of Gold Creek. There are several trails nearby that provide access to various backcountry lakes and streams. To get to the trailheads, just follow the Forest Service Roads near camp. Bicycles are allowed on Trails 417, 429 and 431. In the winter the area is open for both cross-country skiing and snowmobiling. See a Forest Service map for options.

53. CARLTON RESTAURANT AND RV PARK RV.

Reference: **On Methow River; map A3, grid e9.**

Campsites, facilities: There are 10 tent sites and 12 sites for trailers or RVs of any length. Electricity, piped water and sewer hookups are provided. Flush toilets, sanitary services and showers are available. Bottled gas, a store, a laundromat and ice are located within one mile. Motorbikes are permitted. Boat launching facilities are nearby.

Reservations, fee: Reservations accepted; $10-$15 fee per night. MasterCard and Visa accepted. Open April to late November.

Who to contact: Phone (509) 997-0833 or write to P.O. Box 57, Carlton, WA 98814.

Location: From Interstate 5 south of Bellingham, turn east on Highway 20 and drive approximately 145 miles to Twisp. Continue three miles east on Highway 20, then turn south on Highway 153 and drive eight miles to Carlton. The campground is located in town on the left.

Trip note: This nice, little out-of-the-way place for RVs is set along the Methow River. A good side trip is to explore westward up Libby Creek, a tributary to the Methow. Be sure to check out the yearly Bluegrass Festival in nearby Winthrop.

54. GOLD BASIN RV

Reference: **On the South Fork of Stillaguamish River in Mount Baker-Snoqualmie National Forest; map A3, grid f0.**

Campsites, facilities: There are 10 tent sites and 83 sites for tents, trailers or RVs up to 60 feet long. There is an overflow area available for group camping with three sites, each accommodating a maximum of 25 people. Picnic tables are provided. Vault toilets, piped water and firewood are available. A store, a cafe and ice are located within 2.5 miles. Some facilities are **wheelchair accessible**. Pets are permitted on a six-foot leash.

Reservations, fee: Reserve some sites by calling (800) 280-CAMP ($7.75 reservation fee); $10 fee per night; group camp fee is $50 per night. Open mid-May to early September.

Who to contact: Phone the Mount Baker-Snoqualmie National Forest at (360) 436-1155 or write to Darrington Ranger District, 1405 Emmens Street, Darrington, WA 98241.

Location: From Interstate 5 at Everett, turn east on Highway 92 and drive about 15 miles to the town of Granite Falls. Continue 13.5 miles east on Highway 92 to the campground entrance on the left.

Trip note: This is the largest campground in Mount Baker-Snoqualmie National Forest. With all facilities available this site is preferable for most motor home campers. It is set at 1,100 feet along the South Fork of the Stillaguamish River, with riverside sites, easy access and a **wheelchair-accessible** interpretive trail. Fishing and hiking are two options.

55. BEAVER PLANT LAKE

Reference: **On Beaver Plant Lake, hike-in only; map A3, grid f0.**

Campsites, facilities: There are six tent sites at this primitive, hike-in campground. Picnic tables, fire grills and tent pads are provided. Portable vault toilets and firewood are available. There is **no piped water**. Leashed pets are permitted.

Reservations, fee: No reservations; no fee. Open mid-June through October.

Who to contact: Phone the Department of Natural Resources at (360) 856-3500 or write to Department of Natural Resources, Northwest Region, 919 North Township Street, Sedro Woolley, WA 98284-9395.

Location: From Interstate 5 at Everett, turn east on Highway 92 and drive northeast to the town of Granite Falls. Turn north on Mountain Loop Highway and drive 15 miles. Turn south on Forest Service Road 4020 and drive 2.5 miles, then turn right on Forest Service Road 4021 and drive two miles to the Ashland Lakes Trailhead. From Ashland Lakes Trailhead, hike two miles to the campground.

Trip note: This campground is on Beaver Plant Lake, one of four campgrounds (Beaver Plant Lake, Upper Ashland Lake, Lower Ashland Lake and Twin Falls Lake) highlighted in the area. There are some excellent hiking trails in the area.

56. UPPER ASHLAND LAKE

Reference: **Near Upper Ashland Lake, hike-in only; map A3, grid f0.**

Campsites, facilities: There are six tent sites at this primitive, hike-in campground. Picnic tables, fire grills and tent pads are provided. Portable vault toilets and firewood are available, but there is **no piped water**. Leashed pets are permitted.

Reservations, fee: No reservations; no fee. Open mid-June through October.

Who to contact: Phone the Department of Natural Resources at (360) 856-3500 or write to Department of Natural Resources, Northwest Region, 919 North Township Street, Sedro Woolley, WA 98284-9395.

Location: From Interstate 5 at Everett, turn east on Highway 92 and drive northeast to the town of Granite Falls. Turn north on Mountain Loop Highway and drive 15 miles. Turn south on Forest Service Road 4020 and drive 2.5 miles, then turn right on Forest Service Road 4021 and drive two miles to the Ashland Lakes Trailhead. From Ashland Lakes Trailhead, hike 2.5 miles to the campsite.

Trip note: The lake is just a short hike away and well worth the effort. It's very primitive, but also very beautiful, and the site is little-known, so you can expect quiet and privacy. There are several good hiking trails near camp. Get a map from the Department of Natural Resources.

57.   LOWER ASHLAND LAKE

Reference: **On Lower Ashland Lake, hike-in only; map A3, grid f0.**

Campsites, facilities: There are six tent sites at this primitive, hike-in campground. Picnic tables, fire grills and tent pads are provided. Portable vault toilets and firewood are available. There is **no piped water**. Leashed pets are permitted.

Reservations, fee: No reservations; no fee. Open mid-June through October.

Who to contact: Phone the Department of Natural Resources at (360) 856-3500 or write to Department of Natural Resources, Northwest Region, 919 North Township Street, Sedro Woolley, WA 98284-9395.

Location: From Interstate 5 at Everett, turn east on Highway 92 and drive northeast to the town of Granite Falls. Turn north on Mountain Loop Highway and drive 15 miles. Turn south on Forest Service Road 4020 and drive 2.5 miles, then turn right on Forest Service Road 4021 and drive two miles to the Ashland Lakes Trailhead. From Ashland Lakes Trailhead, hike three miles to the campsite.

Trip note: This campground is on Lower Ashland Lake, set adjacent to Upper Ashland Lake. See above trip note for details.

58.   ESSWINE GROUP CAMP

Reference: **In Mount Baker-Snoqualmie National Forest; map A3, grid f0.**

Campsites, facilities: This a specially-designated group campground with four tent sites. Picnic tables are provided. Vault toilets and firewood are available, but there is **no piped water**. Pets are permitted on a six-foot leash. A store, a cafe and ice are located within four miles.

Reservations, fee: Reservations required; $40 first night fee and $30 fee per night thereafter. Open mid-May to early September.

Who to contact: Phone the Mount Baker-Snoqualmie National Forest at (360) 436-1155 or write to Darrington Ranger District, 1405 Emmens Street, Darrington, WA 98241.

Location: From Interstate 5 at Everett, turn east on Highway 92 and drive about 15 miles to the town of Granite Falls. Continue 16 miles east on Highway 92 and you'll see the campground entrance on the left.

Trip note: This is a small, quiet camp, a great place for a restful group getaway. The lack of piped water is the only drawback. This is one of the few Forest

Service campgrounds in the area that requires (or even accepts) reservations; get yours in early. Fishing access is available nearby. The Boulder River Wilderness is located to the north; see a Forest Service map for trailhead locations.

59.   BOARDMAN CREEK   **RV**

Reference: **On the South Fork of Stillaguamish River in Mount Baker-Snoqualmie National Forest; map A3, grid f0.**

Campsites, facilities: There are eight tent sites and two sites for tents, trailers or RVs of any length. Picnic tables are provided. Vault toilets and firewood are available, but there is **no piped water**. Leashed pets are permitted.

Reservations, fee: No reservations; no fee. Open year-round.

Who to contact: Phone the Mount Baker-Snoqualmie National Forest at (360) 436-1155 or write to Darrington Ranger District, 1405 Emmens Street, Darrington, WA 98241.

Location: From Interstate 5 at Everett, turn east on Highway 92 and drive about 15 miles to the town of Granite Falls. Continue 16.5 miles east on Highway 92 and you'll see the campground entrance on the left.

Trip note: This is a pretty riverside camp with roomy sites and river access. The fishing is rumored to be excellent near here. Nearby Forest Service roads will take you to several backcountry lakes, including Boardman Lake, Lake Evan, Clear Lake and Ashland Lakes. Get a Forest Service map, set up your camp and go for it.

60.   COAL CREEK BAR GROUP CAMP   **RV**

Reference: **On the South Fork of Stillaguamish River in Mount Baker-Snoqualmie National Forest; map A3, grid f0.**

Campsites, facilities: There are two tent sites and two trailer sites. Picnic tables and fire grills are provided. Vault toilets and firewood are available. There is **no piped water**. Pets are permitted.

Reservations, fee: Reservations required; $40 fee per night for the entire camp. Open mid-May to late September.

Who to contact: Phone the Mount Baker-Snoqualmie National Forest at (360) 436-1155 or write to Darrington Ranger District, 1405 Emmens Street, Darrington, WA 98241.

Location: From Interstate 5 at Everett, turn east on Highway 92 and drive about 15 miles to the town of Granite Falls. Continue 23.5 miles east on Highway 92 and you'll see the campground entrance.

Trip note: This campground is set along the South Fork of the Stillaguamish River near Coal Creek. Fishing access is available. Nearby Forest Service roads lead to Coal Lake and a trailhead that takes you to other backcountry lakes. A Forest Service map will unlock this beautiful country for you.

61.   TULALIP MILLSITE GROUP CAMP

Reference: **On the South Fork of Stillaguamish River in Mount Baker-Snoqualmie National Forest; map A3, grid f0.**

Campsites, facilities: This is a specially-designated group camp and will accommodate up to 80 people. Picnic tables and fire grills are provided. Vault toilets are available, but **no piped water** is available. Pets are permitted.

Reservations, fee: Reservations required; $50 fee per night. Open mid-May to late September.

Who to contact: Phone the Mount Baker-Snoqualmie National Forest at (360) 436-1155 or write to Darrington Ranger District, 1405 Emmens Street, Darrington, WA 98241.

Location: From Interstate 5 at Everett, turn east on Highway 92 and drive about 15 miles to the town of Granite Falls. Continue 18.5 miles east on Highway 92 and you'll see the campground entrance on the right.

Trip note: Like Turlo, Verlot, Gold Basin, Esswine, Boardman Creek, Red Bridge and Coal Creek Bar, this campground is set along the South Fork of the Stillaguamish River. A trailhead about one mile east of camp leads north into the Boulder River Wilderness. There are numerous creeks and streams that crisscross this area, providing good fishing prospects.

---

62. RED BRIDGE 🚐

Reference: **On the South Fork of Stillaguamish River in Mount Baker-Snoqualmie National Forest; map A3, grid f0.**

Campsites, facilities: There are two tent sites and 14 sites for tents, trailers or RVs up to 31 feet long. Picnic tables are provided. Vault toilets are available, but there is **no piped water**. Some facilities are **wheelchair accessible**. Pets are permitted.

Reservations, fee: No reservations; no fee, but donations are accepted. Open late May to early September.

Who to contact: Phone the Mount Baker-Snoqualmie National Forest at (360) 436-1155 or write to Darrington Ranger District, 1405 Emmens Street, Darrington, WA 98241.

Location: From Interstate 5 at Everett, turn east on Highway 92 and drive about 15 miles to the town of Granite Falls. Continue 18 miles east on Highway 92 and you'll see the campground entrance.

Trip note: This is another classic spot, one of several in the vicinity. This campground is set at 1,300 feet on the South Fork of the Stillaguamish River near Mahardy Creek. It has pretty, riverside sites. A trailhead two miles east of camp leads to Granite Pass in the Boulder River Wilderness. It makes a good base camp for a backpacking expedition.

---

63. TWIN FALLS LAKE

Reference: **On Twin Falls Lake, hike-in only; map A3, grid f0.**

Campsites, facilities: There are five tent sites at this primitive hike-in campground. Picnic tables are provided. Portable vault toilets and firewood are available. There is **no piped water**. Leashed pets are permitted.

Reservations, fee: No reservations; no fee. Open mid-June through October.

Who to contact: Phone the Department of Natural Resources at (360) 856-3500 or write to Department of Natural Resources, Northwest Region, 919 North Township Street, Sedro Woolley, WA 98284-9395.

Location: From Interstate 5 at Everett, turn east on Highway 92 and drive northeast to the town of Granite Falls. Turn north on Mountain Loop Highway and drive 15 miles. Turn south on Forest Service Road 4020 and drive 2.5 miles, then turn right on Forest Service Road 4021 and drive two miles to the Ashland Lakes Trailhead. From Ashland Lakes Trailhead, hike in 4.5 miles.

Trip note: There is good hiking, backpacking and trout fishing at this site for people willing to grunt a little. It's a beautiful and secluded area, yet it's not a long drive from Seattle.

64.   BEDAL   **RV**

Reference: **On Sauk River in Mount Baker-Snoqualmie National Forest; map A3, grid f2.**

Campsites, facilities: There are 19 sites for tents, trailers or RVs up to 21 feet long. Picnic tables and a picnic shelter are provided. Vault toilets are available, but there is **no piped water**. Some facilities are **wheelchair accessible**. A Forest Service district office is nearby.

Reservations, fee: No reservations; no fee, but donations area accepted. Open June to early September.

Who to contact: Phone the Mount Baker-Snoqualmie National Forest at (360) 436-1155 or write to Darrington Ranger District, 1405 Emmens Street, Darrington, WA 98241.

Location: (Note: Due to flooding, access is no longer possible from Granite Falls.) *Alternate directions:* From Interstate 5 at Everett, turn right (east) on Highway 530 and drive 33 miles to the junction of Highway 530 and Mountain Loop Highway (Forest Service Road 20) in Darrington. Turn right (south) on Forest Service Road 20 and drive 22 miles to the campground on the right. A Forest Service map is essential.

Trip note: This campground is set at the confluence of the North and South Forks of the Sauk River. It offers shaded sites, river views and good fishing. It's a bit primitive, but you can't beat the price. North Fork Falls is about a mile up the North Fork of the Sauk from camp and worth the trip.

---

65.   PHELPS CREEK

Reference: **On Chiwawa River in Wenatchee National Forest; map A3, grid f5.**

Campsites, facilities: There are seven tent sites. Picnic tables and fire grills are provided. Pit toilets are available, but there is **no piped water**. Horse facilities are nearby. Leashed pets are permitted.

Reservations, fee: No reservations; no fee. Open mid-June to mid-October.

Who to contact: Phone (509) 763-3103 or write to Lake Wenatchee Ranger District, 22976 Highway 207, Leavenworth, WA 98826.

Location: From Interstate 5 at Everett, turn east on US 2 and drive approximately 87 miles. Turn north on Highway 207 and drive four miles, then turn east on Chiwawa Loop Road and drive 1.4 miles. Head north on Chiwawa Valley Road and Forest Service Road 6200 for 23.6 miles to the campground.

Trip note: This campground is set at the confluence of Phelps Creek and the Chiwawa River. There's a key trailhead for backpackers and horseback riders nearby that provides access to Glacier Peak Wilderness. It's advisable to obtain a Forest Service map.

---

66.   COTTONWOOD   **RV**

Reference: **On Entiat River in Wenatchee National Forest; map A3, grid f6.**

Campsites, facilities: There are 25 tent sites and two additional sites for tents or small RVs. Hand-pumped water, fire grills and picnic tables are provided. Pit toilets are available. Leashed pets are permitted.

Reservations, fee: No reservations; $4 fee per night. Open early June to mid-October.

Who to contact: Phone Wenatchee National Forest at (509) 784-1511 or write to Entiat Ranger District, P.O. Box 476, Entiat, WA 98822.

Location: From Interstate 5 at Everett, turn east on US 2 and drive approximately 120 miles. Turn north on US 97-A and drive 15.5 miles to County Road 371 (Entiat River Road). Turn northwest and drive 25 miles. Turn northwest on Forest Service Road 5100 and drive 13 miles to the campground.

Trip note: At 3,100 feet, this campground is at a major trailhead leading into the Glacier Peak Wilderness. It is set along the Entiat River. A Forest Service map details the back country. A bonus is good berry picking in season. Fishing is another alternative.

---

67.   DEER POINT

Reference: **On Lake Chelan, boat-in, ferry or float plane only in Wenatchee National Forest; map A3, grid f8.**

Campsites, facilities: There are five tent sites accessible only by boat. Picnic tables and fire rings are provided. Pit toilets are available, but there is **no piped water**. A floating dock can accommodate about eight boats.

Reservations, fee: No reservations; no fee. Open May to late October.

Who to contact: Phone Wenatchee National Forest at (509) 682-2576 or write to Chelan Ranger District, 428 West Woodin Avenue, Chelan, WA 98816.

Location: From Interstate 5 at Everett, turn east on US 2 and drive approximately 120 miles. Turn north on US 97 and continue about 40 miles to Chelan. Take the ferry from there (another ferry is available at Fields Point Landing, a few miles northwest of Chelan) and proceed to Deer Point, 22 miles from Chelan. (This spectacular voyage costs about $20 for a roundtrip, depending on your destination. For more information call (509) 682-2224). The campground is also directly accessible by float plane. Call Chelan Airways at (509) 682-5555 for more information.

Trip note: Another little-known spot set along the shore of Lake Chelan. If you want to camp on the remote east shore, this is one of three camps. The others are Prince Creek and Mitchell Creek. This is a good camp for anglers, because there isn't much to do at this spot but wait for the fish to bite.

---

68.   TWENTY-FIVE MILE CREEK STATE PARK   RV

Reference: **Near Lake Chelan; map A3, grid f8.**

Campsites, facilities: There are 63 standard campsites and 23 utility sites for trailers or RVs up to 30 feet long. Picnic tables are provided. A boat dock, restrooms, piped water, electricity and sewer hookups are available.

Reservations, fee: Contact Reservations Northwest at (800) 452-5687 ($6 reservation fee); $11-$16 fee per night. Open early April to late October.

Who to contact: Phone (800) 233-0321 or (509) 687-3710 or write Route 1, P.O. Box 142A, Chelan, WA 98816.

Location: From Interstate 5 at Everett, turn east on US 2 and drive approximately 120 miles. Turn north on US 97 and continue about 40 miles to Chelan. Turn north on South Shore Road and drive 18 miles to the park at the end of the road.

Trip note: This campground is located on Twenty-Five Mile Creek near where it empties into Lake Chelan. There is nearby fishing access, and fishing supplies, a dock and boat moorage are available. There is also a small wading area for kids. Forest Service Road 5900, which heads west from the park, accesses several trailheads leading into the Forest Service lands of the Chelan Mountains. Obtain a Wenatchee National Forest Service map for details.

69.   GRAHAM HARBOR

Reference: **On Lake Chelan, boat-in, ferry or float plane only, in Wenatchee National Forest; map A3, grid f8.**

Campsites, facilities: There are five tent sites accessible only by boat. Picnic tables and fire rings are provided. Pit toilets are available, but there is **no piped water**. A floating dock can accommodate about 10 boats.

Reservations, fee: No reservations; no fee. Open all year.

Who to contact: Phone Wenatchee National Forest at (509) 682-2576 or write to Chelan Ranger District, 428 West Woodin Avenue, Chelan, WA 98816.

Location: From Interstate 5 at Everett, turn east on US 2 and drive approximately 120 miles. Turn north on US 97 and continue about 40 miles to Chelan. Take the ferry from there (another ferry is available at Fields Point Landing, a few miles northwest of Chelan) and proceed to Graham Harbor Creek, 31 miles from Chelan. (This spectacular voyage costs about $20 for a roundtrip, depending on your destination. For more information call (509) 682-2224). Take the 8:30 a.m. ferry from Chelan, Manson or Fields Point Landing and get off at Graham Harbor Creek, 31 miles from Chelan. See Holden for additional ferry information. The campground is also directly accessible by float plane. Call Chelan Airways at (509) 682-5555 for more information.

Trip note: This campground is set along Lake Chelan at the mouth of Graham Harbor Creek. It is one of the more remote and primitive campgrounds on giant Chelan. Fishing and boating are the main recreation attractions here.

70.   PRINCE CREEK

Reference: **On Lake Chelan, boat-in, ferry or float plane only, in Wenatchee National Forest; map A3, grid f8.**

Campsites, facilities: There are six tent sites accessible only by boat. Picnic tables and fire rings are provided. Pit toilets are available, but there is **no piped water**. A floating dock can accommodate about three boats.

Reservations, fee: No reservations; no fee. Open May to mid-November.

Who to contact: Phone Wenatchee National Forest at (509) 682-2576 or write to Chelan Ranger District, 428 West Woodin Avenue, Chelan, WA 98816.

Location: From Interstate 5 at Everett, turn east on US 2 and drive approximately 120 miles. Turn north on US 97 and continue about 40 miles to Chelan. Take the ferry from there (another ferry is available at Fields Point Landing, a few miles northwest of Chelan) and proceed to Prince Creek, 35 miles from Chelan. (This spectacular voyage costs about $20 for a roundtrip, depending on your destination. For more information call (509) 682-2224). The campground is also directly accessible by float plane. Call Chelan Airways at (509) 682-5555 for more information.

Trip note: This camp is set along the shore of Lake Chelan at the mouth of Prince Creek. A trail from camp follows Prince Creek into the Lake Chelan-Sawtooth Wilderness, and then connects to a network of other trails—all of which lead to various lakes and streams. A Forest Service map shows details.

71.   WALLACE FALLS STATE PARK

Reference: **Near Gold Bar; map A3, grid g0.**

Campsites, facilities: There are six tent sites. Picnic tables and fire grills are provided. Flush toilets and piped water are available. Leashed pets are permitted. Some facilities are **wheelchair accessible**.

Reservations, fee: No reservations; $10 fee per night, $5 per extra vehicle per night. Open all year.

Who to contact: Phone (800) 233-0321 or (360) 793-0420 or write to P.O. Box 106, Gold Bar, WA 98251.

Location: From Interstate 5 at Everett, turn east on US 2 and drive about 28 miles to the town of Gold Bar. Turn northeast at the sign for Wallace Falls State Park and proceed two miles to the park.

Trip note: This beautiful, tiny spot is nestled in the forest near the scenic Wallace Falls. The campground is located in a heavily treed area at the trailhead to the falls. The trail leads along the Wallace River and is a beautiful hike. Seattle is loaded with people, but very few of them know of this jewel.

---

72.   CUTTHROAT LAKES

Reference: On Bald Mountain, hike-in only; map A3, grid g0.

Campsites, facilities: There are 10 tent sites at this primitive, hike-in campground. Picnic tables, fire grills and tent pads are provided. Portable vault toilets are available, but there is **no piped water**. Leashed pets are permitted.

Reservations, fee: No reservations; no fee. Open mid-June through October.

Who to contact: Phone the Department of Natural Resources at (360) 856-3500 or write to Department of Natural Resources, Northwest Region, 919 North Township Street, Sedro Woolley, WA 98284-9395.

Location: From Interstate 5 at Everett, turn east on Highway 92 and drive about 15 miles to the town of Granite Falls. Continue 18 miles east on Highway 92 to Forest Service Road 4030. Turn south and drive for three miles to Forest Service Road 4032. Follow Road 4032 all the way to the end where the trailhead begins. The hike to Cutthroat Lakes is about four miles.

Trip note: To reach this spot requires following difficult directions, but it is worth the effort. You'll find beautiful lakeside camps, trout fishing, hiking and few other campers. The "lakes" are actually small ponds, but very pretty.

---

73.   BIG GREIDER LAKE

Reference: On Big Greider Lake, hike-in only; map A3, grid g1.

Campsites, facilities: There are five tent sites at this primitive hike-in campground. Picnic tables, fire grills and tent pads are provided. Portable vault toilets and firewood are available, but there is **no piped water**. Leashed pets are permitted.

Reservations, fee: No reservations; no fee. Open mid-June through October.

Who to contact: Phone the Department of Natural Resources at (360) 856-3500 or write to Department of Natural Resources, Northwest Region, 919 North Township Street, Sedro Woolley, WA 98284-9395.

Location: From Interstate 5 at Everett, turn east on US 2 and drive 24 miles to Sultan. Continue one-half mile east, then turn north on Sultan Basin Road and drive 13.6 miles. Take the middle road (Road SLS 4000) for about 8.5 miles to the Greider Lake Trailhead. From Greider Lake Trailhead, hike three miles to the campsite.

Trip note: This primitive campground is on Big Greider Lake. It's an alternative to Little Greider Lake Campground, adjacent to Little Greider Lake. Hiking trails are available nearby.

74.   LITTLE GREIDER LAKE

Reference: **On Little Greider Lake, hike-in only; map A3, grid g1.**

Campsites, facilities: There are nine tent sites at this primitive hike-in campground. Picnic tables, fire grills and tent pads are provided. Portable vault toilets and firewood are available. There is **no piped water**. Leashed pets are permitted.

Reservations, fee: No reservations; no fee. Open mid-June through October.

Who to contact: Phone the Department of Natural Resources at (360) 856-3500 or write to Department of Natural Resources, Northwest Region, 919 North Township Street, Sedro Woolley, WA 98284-9395.

Location: From Interstate 5 at Everett, turn east on US 2 and drive 24 miles to Sultan. Continue one-half mile east, then turn north on Sultan Basin Road and drive 13.6 miles. Take the middle road (Road SLS 4000) for about 8.5 miles to the Greider Lake Trailhead. From Greider Lake Trailhead, hike 2.5 miles to the campsite.

Trip note: This is prime country for hiking, backpacking and trout fishing. The primitive, wooded campground is on Little Greider Lake.

75.   BOULDER LAKE

Reference: **On Boulder Lake, hike-in only; map A3, grid g1.**

Campsites, facilities: There are nine campsites for tents at this primitive hike-in campground. Picnic tables, fire grills and tent pads are provided. Portable vault toilets and firewood are available. There is **no piped water**. Leashed pets are permitted.

Reservations, fee: No reservations; no fee. Open mid-June through October.

Who to contact: Phone the Department of Natural Resources at (360) 856-3500 or write to Department of Natural Resources, Northwest Region, 919 North Township Street, Sedro Woolley, WA 98284-9395.

Location: From Interstate 5 at Everett, turn east on US 2 and drive 24 miles to Sultan. Continue one-half mile east, then turn north on Sultan Basin Road and drive 13.6 miles. Take the middle road (Road SLS 4000) for about 8.5 miles to the Greider Lake Trailhead. Stay right on Road SLS 7000 and drive one mile to the Boulder Lake Trailhead. From the Boulder Lake Trailhead hike 3.5 miles to campsite.

Trip note: This primitive hike-in campground is on Boulder Lake. It's one of three hike-in camps in the immediate area; Little Greider Lake and Big Greider Lake are the other two. Hiking and fishing are two options.

76.   TROUBLESOME CREEK   **RV**

Reference: **On the North Fork of Skykomish River in Mount Baker-Snoqualmie National Forest; map A3, grid g2.**

Campsites, facilities: There are 24 sites for tents, trailers or RVs up to 21 feet long and six walk-in tent sites. Picnic tables are provided. Vault toilets are available, but there is **no piped water**. Leashed pets are permitted. Some facilities are **wheelchair accessible**.

Reservations, fee: Some sites, including three that are **wheelchair-accessible,** may be reserved by phoning (800) 280-CAMP ($7.75 reservation fee); $6.50-$10 fee per night. Open Memorial Day through Labor Day.

Who to contact: Phone the Mount Baker-Snoqualmie National Forest at (360)

677-2414 or write to Skykomish Ranger District, P.O. Box 305, Skykomish, WA 98288.

Location: From Interstate 5 at Everett, turn east on US 2 and drive 36 miles to the town of Index. From there, drive 12 miles northeast on Forest Service Road 63 (Index-Galena Road) to the campground on the right.

Trip note: Here's another one I bet you've never heard of. This campground is set along the North Fork of the Skykomish River. There is a nature trail adjacent to camp. There is good fishing in the North Fork Skykomish River.

77. SODA SPRINGS

Reference: **On Little Wenatchee River in Wenatchee National Forest; map A3, grid g4.**

Campsites, facilities: There are five tent sites. Picnic tables and fire grills are provided. Pit toilets are available, but there is **no piped water**.

Reservations, fee: No reservations; no fee. Open May to late October.

Who to contact: Phone Wenatchee National Forest at (509) 763-3103 or write to Lake Wenatchee Ranger District, 22976 Highway 207, Leavenworth, WA 98826.

Location: From Interstate 5 at Everett, turn east on US 2 and drive approximately 87 miles to Highway 207. Turn north and drive 10.5 miles, then turn west and drive 1.5 miles. Continue west on Forest Service Road 6500 and drive 6.4 miles to the campground.

Trip note: This campground is set along the Wenatchee River. It's a small, quiet closer-to-civilization option to Tumwater, without piped water. There are some excellent hiking trails nearby.

78. LAKE CREEK

Reference: **On Little Wenatchee River in Wenatchee National Forest; map A3, grid g4.**

Campsites, facilities: There are eight tent sites. Picnic tables and fire grills are provided, but **no piped water** is available. Pit toilets are available.

Reservations, fee: No reservations; no fee. Open May to early November.

Who to contact: Phone Wenatchee National Forest at (509) 763-3103 or write to Lake Wenatchee Ranger District, 22976 Highway 207, Leavenworth, WA 98826.

Location: From Interstate 5 at Everett, turn east on US 2 and drive approximately 87 miles. Turn north on Highway 207 and drive 10.5 miles. Turn west and drive 1.5 miles, then continue west on Forest Service Road 6500 for nine miles to the campground.

Trip note: This camp is set along the Wenatchee River, in a remote and primitive spot. Fishing in this area can be excellent. Berry picking is a bonus in late summer.

79. NAPEEQUA CROSSING   **RV**

Reference: **On White River in Wenatchee National Forest; map A3, grid g5.**

Campsites, facilities: There are five sites for tents, trailers or RVs up to 31 feet long. Picnic tables and fire grills are provided. Pit toilets are available, but there is **no piped water**. Leashed pets are permitted.

Reservations, fee: No reservations; no fee. Open mid-May to late October.

Who to contact: Phone Wenatchee National Forest at (509) 763-3103 or write to

Lake Wenatchee Ranger District, 22796 Highway 207, Leavenworth, WA 98826.

Location: From Interstate 5 at Everett, turn east on US 2 and drive approximately 87 miles. Turn north on Highway 207 and drive 10.5 miles. Head northwest on White River Road and Forest Service Road 6400 for 6.2 miles to the campground.

Trip note: This campground is set along the White River. A trail from camp heads east for about two miles to Twin Lakes in Glacier Peak Wilderness. It's definitely worth the hike, with scenic views and marvelous wildlife and vegetation as your reward. Fishing access is available near camp.

80.   WHITE RIVER FALLS

Reference: **On White River in Wenatchee National Forest; map A3, grid g5.**

Campsites, facilities: There are five tent sites. Picnic tables and fire grills are provided. Pit toilets are available, but there is **no piped water**. Leashed pets are permitted.

Reservations, fee: No reservations; no fee. Open June to mid-October.

Who to contact: Phone Wenatchee National Forest at (509) 763-3103 or write to Lake Wenatchee Ranger District, 22976 Highway 207, Leavenworth, WA 98826.

Location: From Interstate 5 at Everett, turn east on US 2 and drive approximately 87 miles. Turn north on Highway 207 and drive 10.5 miles. Head northwest on White River Road and Forest Service Road 6400 for nine miles to the campground.

Trip note: This campground is set close to the White River Falls on the White River. It is located at a major trailhead that connects to a network of hiking trails into the Glacier Peak Wilderness. Though very primitive, it is quiet and beautiful, a perfect spot for those seeking solitude in the wilderness.

81.   LAKE WENATCHEE STATE PARK   RV

Reference: **On Lake Wenatchee; map A3, grid g5.**

Campsites, facilities: There are two primitive tent sites and 197 developed sites for tents or self-contained RVs. Piped water, fire grills and picnic tables are provided. Flush toilets, sanitary disposal station, a store, ice, showers, firewood, a restaurant, a playground and horse rentals are available. Some facilities are **wheelchair accessible**. Boat docks, launching facilities and rentals are nearby. Leashed pets are permitted.

Reservations, fee: No reservations; $5-$10 fee per night. Open all year.

Who to contact: Phone (800) 233-0321 or (509) 763-3101 or write to Highway 207, Leavenworth, WA 98826.

Location: From Interstate 5 at Everett, turn east on US 2 and drive approximately 100 miles to Leavenworth. Turn north on Highway 207 and drive 22 miles to the park entrance.

Trip note: This park is set in a nice spot and the drive-in sites are spaced just right, so you can expect plenty of company. The secluded campsites are near the Wenatchee River, which offers plenty of recreation opportunities including groomed cross-country ski trails in winter.

82.   GLACIER VIEW   RV

Reference: **On Lake Wenatchee in Wenatchee National Forest; map A3, grid g5.**

Campsites, facilities: There are 16 tent sites and four sites for trailers or RVs up to 30 feet long. Piped water, fire grills and picnic tables are provided. Pit toilets and a boat launch are available. Leashed pets are permitted.

Reservations, fee: No reservations; $7 fee per night. Open May to October.

Who to contact: Phone Wenatchee National Forest at (509) 763-3103 or write to Lake Wenatchee Ranger District, 22976 Highway 207, Leavenworth, WA 98826.

Location: From Interstate 5 at Everett, turn east on US 2 and drive approximately 87 miles. Turn north on Highway 207 and drive 3.5 miles. Turn west on County Road 413 (Cedar Brae Road) and drive four miles, then continue west on Forest Service Road 6750 for 1.5 miles to the campground.

Trip note: This campground is on the southwestern shore of Lake Wenatchee, one of the quieter camps on the lake. It's a popular spot for boating, swimming, fishing and waterskiing. There are some good hiking trails in the area.

83.   SILVER FALLS   RV

Reference: **On Entiat River in Wenatchee National Forest; map A3, grid g7.**

Campsites, facilities: There are 30 sites for tents, trailers or RVs up to 21 feet long. Hand-pumped water, fire grills and picnic tables are provided. Vault toilets are available. Some facilities are **wheelchair accessible**. Pets are permitted.

Reservations, fee: Reservations necessary for groups only; $5-$7 fee per night for single sites; $30 for groups. Open mid-May to mid-November.

Who to contact: Phone Wenatchee National Forest at (509) 784-1511 or write to Entiat Ranger District, P.O. Box 476, Entiat, WA 98822.

Location: From Interstate 5 at Everett, turn east on US 2 and drive approximately 120 miles. Turn north on US 97-A and drive 15.5 miles to County Road 371 (Entiat River Road). Turn northwest and drive 25 miles. Turn on Forest Service Road 5100 and drive 5.5 miles to the campground.

Trip note: This campground, an enchanted spot, is set at the confluence of Silver Creek and the Entiat River. A trail from camp leads one-half mile to the base of beautiful Silver Falls. Fishing access is available in Silver Creek.

84.   NORTH FORK

Reference: **On Entiat River in Wenatchee National Forest; map A3, grid g7.**

Campsites, facilities: There are eight tent sites and one site for a small motor home. Hand-pumped water, fire grills and picnic tables are provided. Pit toilets are available. Leashed pets are permitted.

Reservations, fee: No reservations; $3 fee per night. Open mid-May to mid-November.

Who to contact: Phone Wenatchee National Forest at (509) 784-1511 or write to Entiat Ranger District, P.O. Box 476, Entiat, WA 98822.

Location: From Interstate 5 at Everett, turn east on US 2 and drive approximately 120 miles. Turn north on US 97-A and drive 15.5 miles to County Road 371 (Entiat River Road). Turn northwest and drive 25 miles. Turn on Forest Service Road 1500 and drive 8.5 miles to the campground.

Trip note: This is one of the seven campgrounds nestled along the Entiat River.

This one is set near the confluence of the Entiat and the North Fork of the Entiat River. It is pretty and shaded, with river fishing access. Entiat Falls is nearby.

85.   LAKE CREEK

Reference: **On Entiat River in Wenatchee National Forest; map A3, grid g7.**

Campsites, facilities: There are 18 tent sites. Hand-pumped water, picnic tables and fire grills are provided. Vault toilets are available. Leashed pets are permitted.

Reservations, fee: No reservations; $4 fee per night. Open May to late October.

Who to contact: Phone Wenatchee National Forest at (509) 784-1511 or write to Entiat Ranger District, P.O. Box 476, Entiat, WA 98822.

Location: From Interstate 5 at Everett, turn east on US 2 and drive approximately 120 miles. Turn north on US 97-A and drive 15.5 miles to County Road 371 (Entiat River Road). Turn northwest and drive 25 miles. Turn on Forest Service Road 1500 and drive three miles to the campground.

Trip note: This camp is set at the confluence of Lake Creek and the Entiat River. It is at a trail crossroads. One heads northeast up to Lake Creek Basin in the Chelan Mountains, and several others head south and west into the Entiat Mountains. See a Forest Service map for details. Fox Creek is a nearby spot with well water.

86.   FOX CREEK

Reference: **On Entiat River in Wenatchee National Forest; map A3, grid g7.**

Campsites, facilities: There are 16 tent sites. Hand-pumped water, fire grills and picnic tables are provided. Vault toilets are available. Leashed pets are permitted.

Reservations, fee: No reservations; $4-$6 fee per night. Open May to early November.

Who to contact: Phone Wenatchee National Forest at (509) 784-1511 or write to Entiat Ranger District, P.O. Box 476, Entiat, WA 98822.

Location: From Interstate 5 at Everett, turn east on US 2 and drive approximately 120 miles. Turn north on US 97-A and drive 15.5 miles to County Road 371 (Entiat River Road). Turn northwest and drive 27 miles to the campground on the left.

Trip note: This camp is set along the Entiat River near Fox Creek. It is a good alternative to Lake Creek but without the traffic. There is fishing access. During the winter, some of the snow-covered logging roads in the area are open for use by snowmobiles and cross-country skiers. Contact the Forest Service for details.

87.   LAKE CHELAN STATE PARK   **RV**

Reference: **On Lake Chelan; map A3, grid g9.**

Campsites, facilities: There are two primitive tent sites, 127 developed tent sites, and 17 sites for trailers or RVs up to 30 feet with full hookups. Picnic tables are provided. Flush toilets, sanitary disposal station, a store, a restaurant, ice, a playground, electricity, piped water, sewer hookups, showers, a boat dock and launching facilities are available. Some facilities are **wheelchair accessible**.

Reservations, fee: Contact Reservations Northwest at (800) 453-5687 ($6 reservation fee); $11-$16 fee per night. Open April through October.

Who to contact: Phone (800) 233-0321 or (509) 687-3710 or write to Route 1, P.O.

Box 90, Chelan, WA 98816.

Location: From Interstate 5 at Everett, turn east on US 2 and drive approximately 120 miles. Turn north on US 97 and continue toward the town of Chelan for about 35 miles. At the sign for Lake Chelan State Park, turn left and proceed northwest to the park, which is nine miles west of Chelan.

Trip note: This is the recreation headquarters for Lake Chelan. The park provides boat docks and concession stands on the shore of the 55-mile lake. See the trip notes for Holden, Lucerne, Domke Lake, Prince Creek, Graham Harbor Creek, Deer Point and Big Creek for some of the options available. Water sports include fishing, swimming, scuba diving and waterskiing.

---

88.   KAMEI RESORT   RV

Reference: **On Lake Wapato; map A3, grid g9.**

Campsites, facilities: There are 40 sites for tents, trailers or RVs of any length. Electricity, piped water, sewer hookups and picnic tables are provided. Flush toilets, showers and ice are available. Pets and motorbikes are permitted. Boat docks, launching facilities and rentals are nearby.

Reservations, fee: Reservations accepted; $11-$12 fee per night. Open late April through July.

Who to contact: Phone (509) 687-3690 or write to Route 1, P.O. Box 238, Manson, WA 98831.

Location: From Interstate 5 at Everett, turn east on US 2 and drive approximately 120 miles. Turn north on US 97 and continue 40 miles to the town of Chelan. Turn west on Highway 150 and drive seven miles, then turn north on Wapato Lake Road and drive three miles to the resort.

Trip note: This resort is on Lake Wapato, about two miles from Lake Chelan. Note that this is a seasonal lake and closes midsummer. If you have an extra day, take the ferry boat ride on Lake Chelan, which is detailed in Holden. It's an adventure in itself.

---

89.   LAKEVIEW PARK   RV

Reference: **On Lake Chelan; map A3, grid g9.**

Campsites, facilities: There are 50 sites for trailers or RVs of any length. The sites will also accommodate tents, but only families are permitted to tent camp. Electricity, piped water and sewer hookups are provided. Flush toilets, sanitary services, showers, a playground, bottled gas, a store, a cafe, a laundromat and ice are available. Pets are permitted. Boat docks and launching facilities are nearby.

Reservations, fee: Reservations accepted; $10-$15 fee per night. Open April to November.

Who to contact: Phone (509) 687-3612 or write to P.O. Box 324, Manson, WA 98831.

Location: From Interstate 5 at Everett, turn east on US 2 and drive approximately 120 miles. Turn north on US 97 and continue 40 miles to the town of Chelan. Turn west on Highway 150 and drive 5.2 miles northwest to the park on the right.

Trip note: This developed park for RVs and trailers is set along the shore of Lake Chelan. It is a more commercial option to the primitive Forest Service campgrounds scattered around the lake. This resort has an interesting quirk: they will accept tent campers, but only families with children. No couples or singles. Their reason? To discourage noise and parties, they say. No such restrictions for RVers, though.

---

90. MITCHELL CREEK

Reference: **On Lake Chelan, boat-in, ferry or float plane only in Wenatchee National Forest; map A3, grid g9.**

Campsites, facilities: There are six tent sites accessible only by boat. Picnic tables and fire rings are provided. Pit toilets are available, but there is **no piped water**. Boat docks are nearby.

Reservations, fee: No reservations; no fee. Open May to late October.

Who to contact: Phone Wenatchee National Forest at (509) 682-2576 or write to Chelan Ranger District, 428 West Woodin Avenue, Chelan, WA 98816.

Location: From Interstate 5 at Everett, turn east on US 2 and drive approximately 120 miles. Turn north on US 97 and continue about 40 miles to Chelan. Take the ferry from there (another ferry is available at Fields Point Landing, a few miles northwest of Chelan) and proceed to Mitchell Creek, 15 miles from Chelan. (This spectacular voyage costs about $20 for a roundtrip, depending on your destination. For more information call (509) 682-2224). The campground is also directly accessible by float plane. Call Chelan Airways at (509) 682-5555.

Trip note: This campground is set along the shore of Lake Chelan. It is primitive and remote. Fishing, swimming, boating, hiking and waterskiing are all options here.

---

91. MONEY CREEK CAMPGROUND   RV

Reference: **On the Skykomish River in Mount Baker-Snoqualmie National Forest; Map A3, grid h2.**

Campsites, facilities: There are 24 sites for tents, trailers or RVs up to 21 feet long. Picnic tables are provided. Vault toilets and piped water are available. A store, cafe and ice are located within three miles. Some sites are wheelchair accessible. Leashed pets are permitted.

Reservations, fee: Some sites can be reserved by phoning (800) 280-CAMP ($7.75 reservation fee); $10 fee per night; $6.50 each additional vehicle. Open Memorial Day through Labor Day.

Who to contact: Phone the Skykomish Ranger District at (360) 677-2414 or write to P.O. Box 305, Skykomish, WA 98288.

Location: From Interstate 5 at Everett, turn east on US 2 and drive about 46 miles. Turn south on Old Cascade Highway and drive across the bridge to the campground.

Trip note: This campground is set on the Skykomish River in an old-growth stand. There are hiking trails within a moderate driving distance of the camp. Railroad buffs will be interested in the fact that the Burlington Northern rail runs along the western boundary of the campground.

---

92. BECKLER RIVER   RV

Reference: **On Beckler River in Mount Baker-Snoqualmie National Forest; map A3, grid h2.**

Campsites, facilities: There are 27 sites for tents, trailers or RVs up to 21 feet long. Picnic tables and fire grills are provided. Vault toilets and piped water are available. A store, a cafe, and ice are located within two miles. Leashed pets are permitted. Some sites and facilities are **wheelchair accessible**.

Reservations, fee: Reserve some sites by calling (800) 280-CAMP ($7.75 reservation fee); $10 fee per night. Open Memorial Day through Labor Day.

Who to contact: Phone the Mount Baker-Snoqualmie National Forest at (360) 677-2414 or write to Skykomish Ranger District, P.O. Box 305, Skykomish, WA 98288.

Location: From Interstate 5 at Everett, turn east on US 2 and drive approximately 49 miles to Skykomish. Drive one-half mile east on US 2, then 1.6 miles north on Forest Service Road 65 on the left.

Trip note: This spot is on the Beckler River, set at 900 feet. It has scenic sites on the riverside, and good fishing prospects. Skykomish Ranger Station is just a couple of miles away, and they will be happy to provide you with maps and answer any questions.

---

93.   MILLER RIVER GROUP CAMP   RV

Reference: **Near Alpine Lakes Wilderness in Mount Baker-Snoqualmie National Forest; map A3, grid h2.**

Campsites, facilities: This is a group camp with 18 sites for tents, trailers or RVs. Picnic tables and fire grills are provided. Vault toilets, piped water, a group barbecue and a 24-foot group table are available. A store, cafe, and ice are within five miles. Leashed pets are permitted.

Reservations, fee: Reserve by calling (800) 280-CAMP ($15 reservation fee); $50 fee. Open mid-May to mid-September.

Who to contact: Phone the Mount Baker-Snoqualmie National Forest at (360) 677-2414 or write to Skykomish Ranger District, P.O. Box 305, Skykomish, WA 98288.

Location: From Interstate 5 at Everett, turn east on US 2 and drive approximately 46 miles to Old Cascade Highway (about three miles west of Skykomish). Turn south and drive one mile, then turn on Forest Service Road 6410 and go two miles south.

Trip note: This campground is set along the Miller River a short distance from the boundary of the Alpine Lakes Wilderness. It is prime mountain territory. If you continue another seven miles on Forest Service Road 6410 you will get to a trailhead leading to Lake Dorothy and many other backcountry lakes. Be aware that there is a group limit of 12 people in wilderness areas. A Forest Service map is essential.

---

94.   NASON CREEK   RV

Reference: **Near Lake Wenatchee in Wenatchee National Forest; map A3, grid h6.**

Campsites, facilities: There are 29 tent sites and 41 sites for tents, trailers or RVs up to 31 feet long. Piped water, fire grills, picnic tables and flush toilets are provided. Boat launching facilities are nearby.

Reservations, fee: No reservations; $8 fee per night. Open May to late October.

Who to contact: Phone Wenatchee National Forest at (509) 763-3103 or write to Lake Wenatchee Ranger District, 22976 Highway 207, Leavenworth, WA 98826.

Location: From Interstate 5 at Everett, turn east on US 2 and drive approximately 87 miles to Highway 207 (one mile west of Winton). Turn north and drive 3.5 miles, then head west on Cedar Brae Road (County Road 413) for 100 yards to the campground.

Trip note: This campground is on Nason Creek near Lake Wenatchee. Recreation activities include swimming, fishing and waterskiing. Boat rentals, horseback riding and golfing are nearby.

95. TUMWATER   RV

Reference: **Near Alpine Lakes Wilderness in Wenatchee National Forest; map A3, grid h6.**

Campsites, facilities: There are 84 sites for tents, trailers or RVs up to 30 feet long. Piped water, fire grills and picnic tables are provided. Flush toilets are available. Leashed pets are permitted.

Reservations, fee: Reserve by phoning (800) 380-2267; $8 fee per night for single sites; $50 for group sites. Open May to mid-October.

Who to contact: Phone Wenatchee National Forest at (509) 782-1413 or write to Leavenworth Ranger District, 600 Sherbourne, Leavenworth, WA 98826.

Location: From Interstate 5 at Everett, turn east on US 2 and drive approximately 93 miles to the campground, located 10 miles west of Leavenworth.

Trip note: This large, popular camp provides a little bit of both worlds. It is a good layover for campers cruising US 2. But there are also two Forest Service roads nearby, each less than a mile long, which end at trailheads that provide access to the Alpine Lakes Wilderness. If you don't like to hike, no problem. The camp is on the Wenatchee River in the Tumwater Canyon.

96. MIDWAY VILLAGE GROCERY & RV PARK   RV

Reference: **On Wenatchee River; map A3, grid h6.**

Campsites, facilities: There are 18 sites for trailers or RVs of any length. Electricity, piped water, sewer hookups and picnic tables are provided. A store, showers, firewood, a cafe, a laundromat, ice and a playground are available. Leashed pets and motorbikes are permitted. Boat docks, launching facilities and rentals are nearby.

Reservations, fee: Reservations accepted; $12 fee per night. Open all year.

Who to contact: Phone (509) 763-3344 or write to 14193 Chiwawa Loop Road, Leavenworth, WA 98826.

Location: From Interstate 5 at Everett, turn east on US 2 and drive approximately 88 miles to Highway 207 (one mile west of Winton). Turn north and drive four miles to the bridge over the Wenatchee River. Continue east for one mile and you'll see the park.

Trip note: This private campground is a short distance from Lake Wenatchee State Park and is set along the Wenatchee River. Nearby recreation options include waterskiing, swimming, boating, fishing, hiking and bike riding.

97. ENTIAT CITY PARK   RV

Reference: **On Columbia River; map A3, grid h9.**

Campsites, facilities: There are 50 tent sites and 31 sites for trailers or RVs. Electricity, piped water and picnic tables are provided. Flush toilets, sanitary services, showers, a playground, bottled gas, a store, a cafe, a laundromat and ice are available. Motorbikes are permitted. Boat docks and launching facilities are nearby.

Reservations, fee: Reservations accepted; $13-$16 fee per night. Open April to mid-September.

Who to contact: Phone (509) 784-1500 or write to P.O. Box 228, Entiat, WA 98822.

Location: From Interstate 5 at Everett, turn east on US 2 and drive approximately 120 miles to Wenatchee. Turn north on US 97 and drive 16 miles to Entiat. The park is set along the shore of Lake Entiat.

Trip note: Lake Entiat is actually a dammed portion of the Columbia River. Rocky Reach Dam, located 10 miles south, is the closest to this campground. This is a good camping spot for boaters because of the launching facilities nearby.

---

98. FISH LAKE

Reference: **On Tucquala Lake in Wenatchee National Forest; map A3, grid i3.**

Campsites, facilities: There are 15 tent sites. Picnic tables and fire grills are provided. Vault toilets are available, but there is **no piped water**. Leashed pets are permitted.

Reservations, fee: No reservations; no fee. Open July to October.

Who to contact: Phone Wenatchee National Forest at (509) 674-4411 or write to Cle Elum Ranger District, West Second Street, Cle Elum, WA 98922.

Location: From Interstate 5 at Seattle, turn east on Interstate 90 and drive approximately 78 miles to Exit 80 (two miles before Cle Elum). Turn north on Bullfrog Road and drive four miles. Continue north on Highway 903 and drive about 20 miles to Forest Service Road 4330. Turn northeast and drive 11 miles to the campground. The access road is rough; no trailers are allowed.

Trip note: This campground is way out there, just a short jaunt to the Alpine Lakes Wilderness. There are numerous opportunities to access trails into the backcountry. This camp is nestled along the shore of tiny Tucquala Lake, a jewel near the headwaters of the Cle Elum River.

---

99. EIGHTMILE   RV

Reference: **Near Alpine Lakes Wilderness in Wenatchee National Forest; map A3, grid i5.**

Campsites, facilities: There are 45 sites for tents, trailers or RVs up to 21 feet long. Hand-pumped water, fire grills and picnic tables are provided. Vault toilets are available. Leashed pets are permitted.

Reservations, fee: Reserve group sites only by phoning (800) 274-6104; $8 fee per night for single sites; $50 group fee. Open mid-April to late October.

Who to contact: Phone Wenatchee National Forest at (509) 782-1413 or write to Leavenworth Ranger District, 600 Sherbourne, Leavenworth, WA 98826.

Location: From Interstate 5 at Everett, turn east on US 2 and drive approximately 103 miles to Leavenworth. Turn south on County Road 76 (Icicle River Road) and drive three miles. Turn west on Forest Service Road 7600 and drive four miles to the campground.

Trip note: This campground is set along Icicle Creek and Eightmile Creek. A key trailhead for backpackers is located here that provides access to many lakes and streams in the Alpine Lakes Wilderness.

---

100. BRIDGE CREEK

Reference: **On Icicle Creek in Wenatchee National Forest; map A3, grid i5.**

Campsites, facilities: There are six tent sites. Hand-pumped water, fire grills and picnic tables are provided. Vault toilets and firewood are available. Leashed pets are permitted.

Reservations, fee: Reservations required for groups only, phone (800) 274-6104; $7-$8 fee per night; $50 group fee. Open mid-April to late October.

Who to contact: Phone Wenatchee National Forest at (509) 782-1413 or write to Leavenworth Ranger District, 600 Sherbourne, Leavenworth, WA 98826.

Location: From Interstate 5 at Everett, turn east on US 2 and drive approximately 103 miles to Leavenworth. Turn south on County Road 76 (Icicle River Road) and drive three miles. Turn northwest on Forest Service Road 7600 and drive 5.5 miles to campground.

Trip note: This is a small, quiet spot set along Icicle Creek and Bridge Creek. About one mile south of the camp at Eightmile Creek is a trail that accesses the Alpine Lakes Wilderness. See a Forest Service map for details.

101.　　　　　JOHNNY CREEK　　　　　RV

Reference: **On Icicle Creek in Wenatchee National Forest; map A3, grid i5.**

Campsites, facilities: There are 65 sites for tents, trailers or RVs up to 30 feet long. Hand-pumped water, fire grills and picnic tables are provided. Vault toilets are available. Leashed pets are permitted.

Reservations, fee: No reservations; $7-$8 fee per night. Open May to late October.

Who to contact: Phone Wenatchee National Forest at (509) 782-1413 or write to Leavenworth Ranger District, 600 Sherbourne, Leavenworth, WA 98826.

Location: From Interstate 5 at Everett, turn east on US 2 and drive approximately 103 miles to Leavenworth. Turn south on County Road 76 and drive three miles. Turn northwest on Forest Service Road 7600 and drive eight miles to campground.

Trip note: This campground is set along Icicle Creek and Johnny Creek.

102.　　　　　CHATTER CREEK　　　　　RV

Reference: **Near Alpine Lakes Wilderness in Wenatchee National Forest; map A3, grid i5.**

Campsites, facilities: There are nine tent sites and three sites for tents, trailers or RVs up to 21 feet long. Hand-pumped water, fire grills and picnic tables are provided. Vault toilets are available. Leashed pets are permitted.

Reservations, fee: Reservations required for group sites only; $7 fee per night for single sites; $50 fee per night for group sites. Open May to late October.

Who to contact: Phone Wenatchee National Forest at (509) 782-1413 or write to Leavenworth Ranger District, 600 Sherbourne, Leavenworth, WA 98826.

Location: From Interstate 5 at Everett, turn east on US 2 and drive approximately 103 miles to Leavenworth. Turn south on County Road 76 (Icicle River Road) and drive three miles. Turn northwest on Forest Service Road 7600 and drive 12.5 miles to the campground.

Trip note: This campground is set along Icicle Creek and Chatter Creek. Trails lead out in several directions from the camp into the Alpine Lakes Wilderness.

103.　　　　　ROCK ISLAND　　　　　RV

Reference: **Near Alpine Lakes Wilderness in Wenatchee National Forest; map A3, grid i5.**

Campsites, facilities: There are 12 tent sites and 10 sites for tents, trailers or RVs up to 21 feet long. Hand-pumped water, fire grills and picnic tables are provided. Vault toilets are available. Leashed pets are permitted.

Reservations, fee: No reservations; $7 fee per night. Open May to late October.

Who to contact: Phone Wenatchee National Forest at (509) 782-1413 or write to Leavenworth Ranger District, 600 Sherbourne, Leavenworth, WA 98826.

Location: From Interstate 5 at Everett, turn east on US 2 and drive approximately 103 miles to Leavenworth. Turn south on County Road 76 (Icicle River Road) and drive three miles. Turn northwest on Forest Service Road 7600 and drive 14 miles to the campground.

Trip note: This campground is one of several in the immediate area, set along Icicle Creek about a mile from the trailhead that accesses the Alpine Lakes Wilderness. This is a pretty spot, with good fishing access.

---

104.   IDA CREEK   RV.

Reference: **On Icicle Creek in Wenatchee National Forest; map A3, grid i5.**

Campsites, facilities: There are five tent sites and five sites for tents, trailers or RVs up to 21 feet long. Hand-pumped water, fire grills and picnic tables are provided. Vault toilets are available. Leashed pets are permitted.

Reservations, fee: No reservations; $7 fee per night. Open May to late October.

Who to contact: Phone Wenatchee National Forest at (509) 782-1413 or write to Leavenworth Ranger District, 600 Sherbourne, Leavenworth, WA 98826.

Location: From Interstate 5 at Everett, turn east on US 2 and drive approximately 103 miles to Leavenworth. Turn south on County Road 76 (Icicle River Road) and drive three miles. Turn northwest on Forest Service Road 7600 and drive 10 miles to campground.

Trip note: This campground is one of several small, quiet campgrounds set along Icicle Creek and Ida Creek, with similar recreation options to Chatter Creek and Rock Island.

---

105.   BLACKPINE CREEK HORSE CAMP   RV.

Reference: **Near Alpine Lakes Wilderness in Wenatchee National Forest; map A3, grid i5.**

Campsites, facilities: There are 14 sites for tents, trailers or RVs up to 21 feet long. Hand-pumped water, fire grills and picnic tables are provided. Vault toilets, firewood and riding facilities are available. Leashed pets are permitted.

Reservations, fee: No reservations; $6 fee per night. Open mid-May to late October.

Who to contact: Phone Wenatchee National Forest at (509) 782-1413 or write to Leavenworth Ranger District, 600 Sherbourne, Leavenworth, WA 98826.

Location: From Interstate 5 at Everett, turn east on US 2 and drive approximately 103 miles to Leavenworth. Turn south on County Road 76 (Icicle River Road) and drive three miles. Turn northwest on Forest Service Road 7600 and drive 15 miles to the campground.

Trip note: This campground is set on Black Pine Creek near Icicle Creek, at a major trailhead leading into the Alpine Lakes Wilderness. It is one of seven rustic camp spots on the creek, with the distinction of being the only camp with facilities for horses. For that reason, it is often used as a base camp for horse pack trips.

106. PINE VILLAGE RESORT/ KOA LEAVENWORTH **RV**

Reference: **Near Wenatchee River; map A3, grid i6.**

Campsites, facilities: There are 40 tent sites and 60 sites (22 drive-through) for trailers or RVs of any length. Picnic tables are provided. Flush toilets, sanitary services, showers, firewood, a recreation hall, cable TV, a store, a laundromat, ice, a playground, a spa, a heated swimming pool, electricity, piped water and sewer hookups are available. Bottled gas and a cafe are located within one mile. Pets and motorbikes are permitted.

Reservations, fee: Reservations accepted; $23-$29 fee per night. American Express, MasterCard, Visa and Discover accepted. Open April to November.

Who to contact: Phone (509) 548-7709 or write to 11401 River Bend Drive, Leavenworth, WA 98826.

Location: From Interstate 5 at Everett, turn east on US 2 and drive approximately 103 miles to Leavenworth. Continue one-quarter mile east on US 2 to River Bend Drive, then drive north one-half mile to the campground on the right.

Trip note: This resort is lovely, set near the quaint "Bavarian Village" of Leavenworth, to which the park provides a free shuttle in the summer. The area is spectacularly scenic, surrounded by the Cascade Mountains and set among Ponderosa pines. The camp has access to the Wenatchee River and many luxurious extras, including a hot tub and heated pool. The park allows campfires and has firewood available. Nearby recreation options include an 18-hole golf course and hiking trails. Make a point to spend a day in Leavenworth if possible; it offers authentic German food and architecture along with music and art shows in the summer.

107. ICICLE RIVER RV PARK **RV**

Reference: **On Icicle Creek; map A3, grid i6.**

Campsites, facilities: There are 30 tent sites and 58 sites (14 drive-through) for trailers or RVs of any length. Electricity, piped water, sewer hookups and picnic tables are provided. Flush toilets and bottled gas are available. Showers and firewood are available for an extra fee. Pets and motorbikes are permitted.

Reservations, fee: Reservations accepted; $20-$25 fee per night. Open April to late October.

Who to contact: Phone (509) 548-5420 or write to 7305 Icicle Road, Leavenworth, WA 98826.

Location: From Interstate 5 at Everett, turn east on US 2 and drive approximately 103 miles to Leavenworth. Take the Icicle Road exit and drive three miles southwest to the park on the left.

Trip note: This is one of three campgrounds in the immediate area. The others are Pine Village Resort and Chalet Trailer Park. This pretty, wooded spot is set along Icicle River, where fishing and swimming are available. The park is exceptionally clean and scenic, and even has its own putting green. An 18-hole golf course and hiking trails are nearby.

108. CHALET TRAILER PARK **RV**

Reference: **On Wenatchee River; map A3, grid i6.**

Campsites, facilities: There are 29 sites for trailers or RVs of any length. Electricity, piped water, sewer and cable TV hookups and picnic tables are provided. Flush toilets, sanitary services, propane and showers are available. Bottled gas, a store, a cafe, a laundromat and ice are available within one mile. Pets and motorbikes are permitted.

Reservations, fee: Reservations recommended; $18-$22 fee per night. Open all year.

Who to contact: Phone (800) 477-2697 or (509) 548-4578 or write to P.O. Box 293, Leavenworth, WA 98826.

Location: From Interstate 5 at Everett, turn east on US 2 and drive approximately 100 miles to Leavenworth. Turn south on Duncan Road and drive 150 feet to the campground on the right.

Trip note: This park is set along the Wenatchee River near the Leavenworth. It is within walking distance to the quaint Bavarian Village shops and restaurants. A pleasant grassy area is provided for tents. Nearby recreation options include an 18-hole golf course.

109.   WENATCHEE RIVER COUNTY PARK   **RV**

Reference: **On Wenatchee River in Chelan County; map A3, grid i7.**

Campsites, facilities: There are 15 tent sites and 64 sites (24 drive-through) for trailers or RVs of any length. Electricity, piped water, sewer hookups and picnic tables are provided. Flush toilets, showers, sanitary services and a playground are available. A store and ice are available within one mile. Leashed pets and motorbikes are permitted. Boat launching facilities are available nearby (within three miles).

Reservations, fee: No reservations; $12.50-$16 per night. Open April to late October.

Who to contact: Phone (509) 662-2525 or write to P.O. Box 254, Monitor, WA 98836.

Location: From Interstate 5 at Everett, turn east on US 2 and drive approximately 116 miles to Monitor. The camp is just off the highway on the right.

Trip note: This municipal park is set along the Wenatchee River, with access nearby. This is an excellent spot for fishing. It's the only option for tent campers in the immediate area.

110.   LINCOLN ROCK STATE PARK   **RV**

Reference: **On Lake Entiat; map A3, grid i8.**

Campsites, facilities: There are 27 sites for tents or self-contained RVs, and 67 sites with full hookups for trailers or RVs up to 65 feet. Picnic tables and fire grills are provided. Flush toilets, a sanitary disposal station, a playground, showers and firewood are available. Some facilities are **wheelchair accessible**. Boat docks and launching facilities are located on Lake Entiat. Leashed pets are permitted.

Reservations, fee: Contact Reservations Northwest at (800) 452-5687 ($6 reservation fee); $5-$14 fee per night. Open all year.

Who to contact: Phone (800) 233-0321 or (509) 884-8702 or write to Route 3, P.O. Box 3137, East Wenatchee, WA 98801.

Location: From Interstate 5 at Everett, turn east on US 2 and drive approximately 125 miles to the park. It is located seven miles north of Wenatchee on the east side of the highway.

Trip note: An option to nearby Entiat City Park, this park is ideal for families with RVs or trailers. It's set adjacent to the Rocky Reach Hydro Electric Dam along the shore of Lake Entiat. Water sports include swimming, boating and waterskiing.

---

111.   TINKHAM   RV

Reference: **On Snoqualmie River in Mount Baker-Snoqualmie National Forest; map A3, grid j0.**

Campsites, facilities: There are 47 sites for tents, trailers or RVs up to 21 feet long. Picnic tables are provided. Vault toilets, firewood and hand-pumped water are available. Some facilities are **wheelchair accessible**. Pets are permitted.

Reservations, fee: Reserve some sites by calling (800) 280-CAMP ($7.75 reservation fee); $10 fee per night. Open mid-May to mid-September.

Who to contact: Phone the Mount Baker-Snoqualmie National Forest at (206) 888-1421 or write to North Bend Ranger District, 42404 SE North Bend Way, North Bend, WA 98045.

Location: From Interstate 5 at Seattle, turn east on Interstate 90 and take Exit 42. Turn right on Forest Service Road 55 and drive 1.5 miles southeast to the campground. A Forest Service map is advisable.

Trip note: This campground is set along the Snoqualmie River, and is a good layover for the night for travelers heading west to Seattle. Not far north is the Alpine Lakes Wilderness, a spectacularly beautiful area. See a Forest Service map for trail locations. There are several ski areas to the east. Franklin Falls, a side trip worth taking, is also nearby.

---

112.   CRYSTAL SPRINGS   RV

Reference: **Near Kachess and Keechelus lakes in Wenatchee National Forest; map A3, grid j2.**

Campsites, facilities: There are 20 tent sites and six sites for tents, trailers or RVs up to 21 feet long. Piped water, fire grills and picnic tables are provided. Pit toilets and firewood are available. Boat docks and rentals are nearby. Leashed pets are permitted.

Reservations, fee: No reservations; $5-$7 fee per night. Open mid-May to mid-September.

Who to contact: Phone Wenatchee National Forest at (509) 674-4411 or write to Cle Elum Ranger District, West Second Street, Cle Elum, WA 98922.

Location: From Seattle, turn east on Interstate 90 and drive approximately 60.5 miles. Take Exit 62 to Forest Service Road 54 (about 8.5 miles west of Easton). Turn southwest and drive one-half mile to the campground.

Trip note: This campground is just off Interstate 90 and a short drive from Kachess Lake and Keechelus Lake. There are boat ramps at both lakes. For winter sports, there are also several sno-parks in the area, which provide parking and access to Forest Service roads and open areas which are available for snowmobiling and cross-country skiing. The Pacific West Ski Area is at the north end of Keechelus Lake.

---

113.   WISH POOSH   RV

Reference: **On Cle Elum Lake in Wenatchee National Forest; map A3, grid j3.**

Campsites, facilities: There are 17 tent sites and 22 sites for tents, trailers or RVs up to 21 feet long. Piped water, fire grills and picnic tables are provided. Flush toilets, firewood, a restaurant and ice are available. Boat docks and launching facilities are located on Cle Elum Lake. Leashed pets are permitted.

Reservations, fee: No reservations; $8-$10 fee per night. Open mid-May to mid-November.

Who to contact: Phone Wenatchee National Forest at (509) 674-4411 or write to Cle Elum Ranger District, West Second Street, Cle Elum, WA 98922.

Location: From Seattle, turn east on Interstate 90 and drive approximately 78 miles to Exit 80 (two miles before Cle Elum). Turn north on Bullfrog Road and drive four miles. Continue on Highway 903 and drive about nine miles to the campground.

Trip note: This campground is set along the shore of Cle Elum Lake, where waterskiing, sailing, fishing and swimming are among recreation possibilities. In the winter months, this is a popular area for sports such as cross-country skiing and snowshoeing.

---

114. RED MOUNTAIN

Reference: **On Cle Elum River in Wenatchee National Forest; map A3, grid j3.**

Campsites, facilities: There are 11 sites for tents. Picnic tables and fire grills are provided. Pit toilets and firewood are available, but there is **no piped water**. Leashed pets are permitted.

Reservations, fee: Reserve some sites by phoning (800) 280-CAMP ($7.75 reservation fee); no fee. Open mid-May to mid-November.

Who to contact: Phone Wenatchee National Forest at (509) 674-4411 or write to Cle Elum Ranger District, West Second Street, Cle Elum, WA 98922.

Location: From Seattle, turn east on Interstate 90 and drive approximately 78 miles to Exit 80 (two miles before Cle Elum). Turn north on Bullfrog Road and drive four miles. Continue north on Highway 903 and drive about 13 miles to the campground.

Trip note: This option to nearby Wish Poosh has two big differences. This site has **no piped water** and is not on Cle Elum Lake. It is also free. The campground is set along the Cle Elum River a mile from the lake, just above where the river feeds into it. It has the same wintertime options as Wish Poosh.

---

115. SALMON LA SAC **RV**

Reference: **On Cle Elum River in Wenatchee National Forest; map A3, grid j3.**

Campsites, facilities: There are 30 tent sites and 96 sites for tents, trailers or RVs up to 21 feet long. A horse-use camp is also available. Piped water, fire grills and picnic tables are provided. Flush toilets are available. Some facilities are **wheelchair accessible**. Leashed pets are permitted.

Reservations, fee: Reserve some sites by calling (800) 280-CAMP ($7.75 reservation fee); $8-$10 fee per night; $50 group fee. Open late May to late October.

Who to contact: Phone Wenatchee National Forest at (509) 674-4411 or write to Cle Elum Ranger District, West Second Street, Cle Elum, WA 98922.

Location: From Seattle, turn east on Interstate 90 and drive approximately 78 miles to Exit 80 (two miles before Cle Elum). Turn north on Bullfrog Road and drive four miles. Continue north on Highway 903 and drive about 21 miles to the campground.

Trip note: This is one of the most developed camps in the area, an ideal base camp for backpackers and day hikers. The camp is set along the Cle Elum River at a major trailhead. Hikers can follow creeks heading off in several directions, including into the Alpine Lakes Wilderness. Campground hosts will answer all your questions.

---

116. KACHESS RV

Reference: **On Kachess Lake in Wenatchee National Forest; map A3, grid j3.**

Campsites, facilities: There are 133 tent sites and 50 sites for trailers or RVs up to 32 feet long. A group site is also available. Piped water, fire grills and picnic tables are provided. Restrooms and a sanitary disposal stations are located at Kachess Lake. Some facilities are **wheelchair accessible**. Leashed pets are permitted but are not allowed in swimming areas.

Reservations, fee: Reserve some sites by calling (800) 280-CAMP ($7.75 reservation fee); $8-$10 campsite fee per night. Open late May to mid-September.

Who to contact: Phone Wenatchee National Forest at (509) 674-4411 or write to Cle Elum Ranger District, West Second Street, Cle Elum, WA 98922.

Location: From Seattle, turn east on Interstate 90 and drive approximately 59 miles to exit 62 on Forest Service Road 49. Turn northeast and drive five miles to the campground.

Trip note: This is the only campground on the shore of Kachess Lake and it is a winner. Recreation opportunities include waterskiing, fishing, hiking and bicycling. A trail from camp heads north into the Alpine Lakes Wilderness. See a Forest Service map for details. A self-guided interpretive trail is also available. The Kachess Sno-Park is about a mile south of the campground, which provides parking and access to Forest Service Roads and open areas which are ideal for snowmobiling and cross-country skiing.

---

117. OWHI

Reference: **On Cooper Lake in Wenatchee National Forest, walk-in only; map A3, grid j3.**

Campsites, facilities: There are 28 tent sites. Picnic tables and fire grills are provided. Pit toilets are available, but there is **no piped water**. Boat docks and launching facilities are nearby. Leashed pets are permitted.

Reservations, fee: No reservations; no fee. Open mid-June to mid-October.

Who to contact: Phone Wenatchee National Forest at (509) 674-4411 or write to Cle Elum Ranger District, West Second Street, Cle Elum, WA 98922.

Location: From Seattle, turn east on Interstate 90 and drive approximately 78 miles to Exit 80 (two miles before Cle Elum). Turn north on Bullfrog Road and drive four miles. Continue north on Highway 903 for 19 miles. Turn west on Forest Service Road 46. Proceed five miles to Forest Service Road 4616 and follow it for almost one mile. Turn left onto Spur Road 113 and drive about 300 yards to the campground.

Trip note: This spot has everything. Well, everything but piped water. It is located on the shore of Cooper Lake, near the boundary of Alpine Lakes Wilderness. A nearby trailhead provides access to several lakes in the wilderness and extends to the Pacific Crest Trail. See a Forest Service map for details. Fishing, swimming and canoeing or non-motorized boating are all popular at Cooper Lake.

## 118.	BEVERLY	RV

Reference: On the North Fork of Teanaway River in Wenatchee National Forest; map A3, grid j4.

Campsites, facilities: There are 13 tent sites and three sites for trailers or RVs up to 21 feet long. Picnic tables and fire grills are provided. Pit toilets are available, but there is **no piped water**. Leashed pets are permitted.

Reservations, fee: No reservations; no fee. Open June to mid-November.

Who to contact: Phone Wenatchee National Forest at (509) 674-4411 or write to Cle Elum Ranger District, West Second Street, Cle Elum, WA 98922.

Location: From Seattle, turn east on Interstate 90 and drive approximately 80 miles to Cle Elum. Take exit 86 to County Road 970. Drive east for eight miles. Turn north on Teanaway River Road and drive 13 miles to the end of the paved road. Continue north on Forest Service Road 9737 and drive four miles to campground.

Trip note: This primitive campground is set along the North Fork of the Teanaway River, which has good fishing. This is primarily a hiker's camp, though, with several trails near camp leading up nearby creeks and into the Alpine Lakes Wilderness. Self-issued permits are required for wilderness hiking.

## 119.	BONANZA	RV

Reference: On Tronsen Creek in Wenatchee National Forest; map A3, grid j6.

Campsites, facilities: There are four tent sites and one site for tents, trailers or RVs up to 15 feet long. Hand-pumped water, fire grills and picnic tables are provided. Vault toilets are available. Leashed pets are permitted.

Reservations, fee: No reservations; no fee. Open mid-April to late November.

Who to contact: Phone Wenatchee National Forest at (509) 782-1413 or write to Leavenworth Ranger District, 600 Sherbourne, Leavenworth, WA 98826.

Location: From Interstate 5 at Everett, turn east on US 2 and drive approximately 103 miles to Leavenworth. Continue 4.5 miles southeast on US 2, then turn south on US 97 and drive 13 miles to the campground.

Trip note: This campground is just off US 97 and is set along Tronsen Creek. It is used primarily as a layover spot, with few recreation options in the immediate area. Though it doesn't seem to have much to offer, it can become quite crowded, so plan to arrive early if you want to guarantee a spot.

## 120.	BLU SHASTIN RV PARK	RV

Reference: Near Penshastin Creek; map A3, grid j6.

Campsites, facilities: There are 20 tent sites and 50 sites (10 drive-through) for trailers or RVs of any length. Electricity, piped water, sewer hookups and picnic tables are provided. Flush toilets, sanitary services, showers, a recreation hall, firewood, a laundromat, ice, a playground and a swimming pool are available. Bottled gas, a store and a cafe are located within one mile. Pets and motorbikes are permitted.

Reservations, fee: Reservations accepted; $14-$18 fee per night; MasterCard and Visa accepted. Open all year.

Who to contact: Phone (509) 548-4184 or write to 3300 Highway 97, Leavenworth, WA 98826.

Location: From Interstate 5 at Everett, turn east on US 2 and drive approximately

103 miles to Leavenworth. Continue three miles southeast on US 2 to the junction with US 97, then turn south and drive seven miles to the park on the right.

Trip note: This park is set in a mountainous area near Penshastin Creek. It has sites on the river bank and plenty of shade trees. A heated pool, a recreation field and horseshoe pits provide possible activities in the park. Nearby recreation options include hiking trails and marked bike trails.

121. SWAUK **RV**

Reference: **On Swauk Creek in Wenatchee National Forest; map A3, grid j6.**

Campsites, facilities: There are 23 sites for tents, trailers or RVs. Fire grills and picnic tables are provided. Pit toilets and firewood are available, but there is **no piped water**. Leashed pets are permitted.

Reservations, fee: No reservations; no fee. Open mid-April to late November.

Who to contact: Phone Wenatchee National Forest at (509) 674-4411 or write to Cle Elum Ranger District, West Second Street, Cle Elum, WA 98922.

Location: From Seattle, turn east on Interstate 90 and drive approximately 80 miles to Cle Elum. Take Exit 86 to County Road 970 and drive east 12 miles. Turn north on US 97 and drive 10 miles to the campground.

Trip note: This campground is set along Swauk Creek, with good fishing and some decent hiking trails. It is a prime spot, particularly during winter months. About three miles east of the campground is Swauk Sno-Park, which provides a parking area and access to Forest Service Roads and open areas for snowmobiling and cross-country skiing. Also near the Sno-Park on Forest Service Road 9716 is the Swauk Forest Discovery Trail. This interpretive trail is three miles long and explains how logging affects forest service management of the landscape.

122. WENATCHEE CONFLUENCE STATE PARK **RV**

Reference: **On Columbia River; map A3, grid j8.**

Campsites, facilities: There are eight developed tent sites and 51 hookup sites for trailers or RVs up to 65 feet long. Picnic tables, stoves, piped water, showers, flush toilets and a sanitary disposal station are provided. A boat launch is available. The facilities are **wheelchair accessible**. Leashed pets are permitted.

Reservations, fee: Contact Reservations Northwest at (800) 452-5687 ($6 reservation fee); $11-$16 fee per night. Open all year.

Who to contact: Phone (800) 233-0321 or (509) 664-6373 or write to 333 Old Station Road, Wenatchee, WA 98801.

Location: From Interstate 5 at Everett, turn east on US 2 and drive approximately 121 miles to Wenatchee. The park is located at the north end of Wenatchee on Old Station Road.

Trip note: This state park, set just outside of Wenatchee on the Columbia River, provides a relaxing atmosphere and many activities. Recreation possibilities include fishing, swimming, boating and waterskiing. Interpretive hiking trails are also available. Sports enthusiasts are provided with playing fields, tennis and basketball courts. Daroga State Park and Lake Chelan to the north offer side trip possibilities.

MAP A4

WASHINGTON MAP .... see page 90
Adjoining Maps
NORTH .... no map
EAST (A5) .... see page 244
SOUTH (B4) .... see page 362
WEST (A3) .... see page 166

62 LISTINGS
PAGES 216-243

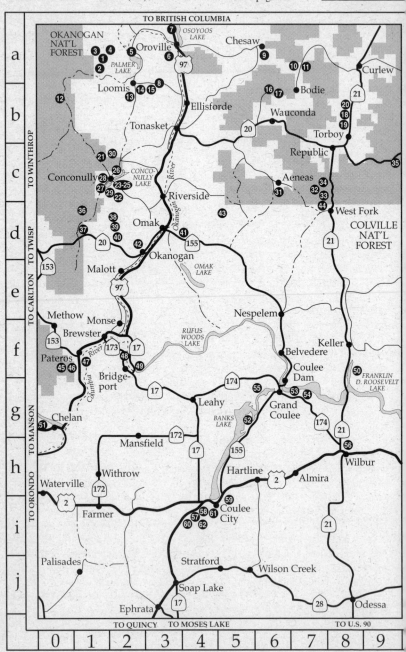

Washington Map A4 featuring: Cold Creek, Toats Coulee Creek, Chopaka Lake, Wannacut Lake, Palmer Lake, Osoyoos Lake State Park, Okanogan National Forest, Spectacle Lake, Beaver Lake, Beth Lake, Tiffany Lake, Okanogan River, Bonaparte Lake, Conconully Lake, Curlew Lake, Lyman Lake, Ferry Lake, Long Lake, Swan Lake, Colville National Forest, Leader Lake, Rock Lake, Okanogan River, Sanpoil River, Columbia River, Alta Lake, Crawfish Lake, Banks Lake, Lake Chelan, Franklin Roosevelt Lake, Coulee Dam National Recreation Area, Rufus Woods Lake, Bridgeport State Park, Blue Lake, Grand Coulee Dam, Sun Lakes State Recreation Park, Banks Lake, Park Lake

---

1.   TOATS COULEE

Reference: **On Toats Coulee Creek; map A4, grid a1.**

Campsites, facilities: There are nine campsites for tents or small trailers. Picnic tables, fire grills and tent pads are provided. Vault toilets are available. There is **no piped water**. Leashed pets are permitted.

Reservations, fee: No reservations; no fee. Open all year.

Who to contact: Phone the Department of Natural Resources at (360) 902-1234 or (509) 684-7474 or write to Department of Natural Resources, Northeast Region, P.O. Box 190, Colville, WA 99114-0190.

Location: From Interstate 5 at Everett, turn east on US 2 and drive 106 miles to the junction with US 97. Turn north and drive 120 miles to Tonasket. Turn north on County Road 9437 an drive five miles, then head west to Loomis on County Road 9425. From Loomis, continue north on County Road 9425 for two miles, then turn left on Toats Coulee Road. Travel 5.5 miles to the lower camp. Continue 100 yards to the upper camp at the junction of Roads OMT 2000 and OMT 1000.

Trip note: This wooded camp is set along Toats Coulee Creek. Some moose are in the area. A road for snowmobile use follows the South Fork of Toats Coulee Creek swinging south, then heading east along Cecil Creek. Contact the Department of Natural Resources for details. This is one of three little-known camps in the vicinity.

---

2.   COLD SPRINGS

Reference: **Near Cold Creek; map A4, grid a1.**

Campsites, facilities: There are nine campsites for tents or small trailers. Picnic tables, fire grills and tent pads are provided. Vault toilets and piped water are available. Horse stalls and feeder boxes are also available. Leashed pets are permitted.

Reservations, fee: No reservations; no fee. Open all year.

Who to contact: Phone the Department of Natural Resources at (360) 902-1234 or (509) 684-7474 or write to Department of Natural Resources, Northeast Region, P.O. Box 190, Colville, WA 99114-0190.

Location: From Interstate 5 at Everett, turn east on US 2 and drive 106 miles to the junction with US 97. Turn north and drive 120 miles to Tonasket. Turn north on County Road 9437 an drive five miles, then head west to Loomis on County Road 9425. From Loomis, continue north on County Road 9425 for two miles, then turn left on Toats Coulee Road. Travel 5.5 miles to the lower

---

camp. Continue 100 yards to the upper camp at the junction of Roads OMT 2000 and OMT 1000. Take OMT-1000 Road for two miles to Cold Creek Road (gravel) and turn right. Travel one-half mile, keep right and continue for two miles. Then keep left and continue two miles to the picnic area or three miles to the campground.

Trip note: It's quite a drive to get here, but you'll be happy you made the effort. It's pretty and forested, with sites set near a small stream. There are trails here for horseback riding, hiking and snowmobiling. Because it is little known and remote, it is advisable to obtain a map of the area to aid directions. Some moose tromp around these parts.

---

3.   NORTH FORK NINE MILE

Reference: **On the North Fork of Touts Coulee Creek; map A4, grid a1.**

Campsites, facilities: There are 11 campsites for tents or small trailers. Picnic tables, fire grills and tent pads are provided. Vault toilets and piped water are available. Leashed pets are permitted.

Reservations, fee: No reservations; no fee. Open all year.

Who to contact: Phone the Department of Natural Resources at (360) 902-1234 or (509) 684-7474 or write to Department of Natural Resources, Northeast Region, P.O. Box 190, Colville, WA 99114-0190.

Location: From Interstate 5 at Everett, turn east on US 2 and drive 106 miles to the junction with US 97. Turn north and drive 120 miles to Tonasket. Turn north on County Road 9437 an drive five miles, then head west to Loomis on County Road 9425. From Loomis, continue north on County Road 9425 for two miles, then turn left on Toats Coulee Road. Travel 5.5 miles to the lower camp. Continue 100 yards to the upper camp at the junction of Roads OMT 2000 and OMT 1000. Take OMT-1000 Road for 2.5 miles to the campground.

Trip note: This campground is set in the forest along the North Fork of Toats Coulee Creek and Nine Mile Creek. This area is frequented by the northwestern moose. It is advisable to obtain a map that details the area from the Department of Natural Resources.

---

4.   CHOPAKA LAKE

Reference: **On Chopaka Lake; map A4, grid a2.**

Campsites, facilities: There are 15 campsites for tents or small trailers. Picnic tables, fire grills and tent pads are provided. Vault toilets, piped water and boat launching facilities are available. Leashed pets are permitted.

Reservations, fee: No reservations; no fee. Open all year.

Who to contact: Phone the Department of Natural Resources at (360) 902-1234 or (509) 684-7474 or write to Department of Natural Resources, Northeast Region, P.O. Box 190, Colville, WA 99114-0190.

Location: From Interstate 5 at Everett, turn east on US 2 and drive 106 miles to the junction with US 97. Turn north and drive 120 miles to Tonasket. Turn north on County Road 9437 an drive five miles, then head west to Loomis on County Road 9425. From Loomis, continue north on County Road 9425 for two miles, then turn left on Toats Coulee Road. Travel 1.5 miles. Turn right onto a steep, one lane road and drive 3.5 miles, keep left and drive 1.5 miles, then turn right and drive two miles to the campground.

Trip note: This campground is set along the western shore of Chopaka Lake. The lake is stocked with Atlantic salmon and only catch and release fly fishing with barbless hooks is allowed. It's a classic setting for the expert angler.

5.   PALMER LAKE

Reference: **On Palmer Lake; map A4, grid a2.**

Campsites, facilities: There are six campsites for tents or small trailers. Picnic tables, fire grills and tent pads are provided. Vault toilets are available, but there is **no piped water**. Leashed pets are permitted.

Reservations, fee: No reservations; no fee. Open all year.

Who to contact: Phone the Department of Natural Resources at (360) 902-1234 or (509) 684-7474 or write to Department of Natural Resources, Northeast Region, P.O. Box 190, Colville, WA 99114-0190.

Location: From Interstate 5 at Everett, turn east on US 2 and drive 106 miles to the junction with US 97. Turn north and drive 120 miles to Tonasket. Turn north on County Road 9437 an drive five miles, then head west to Loomis on County Road 9425. From Loomis, continue north on County Road 9425 for 8.5 miles, keep right, and you'll find the campground at the north end of the lake.

Trip note: This campground is set along the shore of Palmer Lake, the only camp at the lake. The winter range of the deer is in the Sinlahekin Valley to the south of Palmer Lake. There are numerous migration routes in the area. Wildlife (not for hunting) include the endangered Bighorn sheep, cougar, bald and golden eagles, black and brown bear and grouse. See Chopaka Lake Campground for information on fishing for Atlantic salmon in nearby Chopaka Lake.

6.   SUN COVE RESORT   **RV**

Reference: **On Wannacut Lake; map A4, grid a3.**

Campsites, facilities: There are 22 tent sites and 28 drive-through sites for trailers or RVs of any length. Electricity, piped water, sewer hookups and picnic tables are provided. Flush toilets, sanitary services, a recreation hall, a store, a cafe, a laundromat, ice, a playground and swimming pool are available. Showers are available for an extra fee. Pets and motorbikes are permitted. Boat docks, launching facilities and rentals are available.

Reservations, fee: Reservations accepted; $18-$20 fee per night. MasterCard and Visa accepted. Open late April to November.

Who to contact: Phone (509) 476-2223 or write to Route 2, P.O. Box 1294, Oroville, WA 98844.

Location: From Interstate 5 at Burlington, turn east on Highway 20 and drive 174 miles. Turn north on US 97 and proceed 37 miles to Ellisford. Turn west on Loomis Highway and drive seven miles to Wannacut Lake Road. Turn north and drive five miles to the resort at the end of the road.

Trip note: This resort is a nice little spot that doesn't get much traffic. It's a beautiful resort, surrounded by trees and hills and set along the shore of Wannacut Lake. Fishing, swimming, boating and hiking are all summertime options. The park provides full facilities, including a heated pool and a playground and recreation hall for kids.

7.   OSOYOOS LAKE STATE PARK   **RV**

Reference: **On Osoyoos Lake; map A4, grid a3.**

Campsites, facilities: There are six primitive tent sites and 80 sites for tents or self-contained RVs up to 45 feet long. Picnic tables and fire grills are provided. Flush toilets, piped water, sanitary services, a store, a cafe, showers, firewood and a playground are available. A laundromat and ice are located within one mile. Leashed pets are permitted. Boat launching facilities are nearby.

Reservations, fee: Contact Reservations Northwest at (800) 452-5687 ($6 reservation fee); $5-$11 fee per night. Open all year.

Who to contact: Phone (800) 233-0321 or (509) 476-3321 or write to Route 1, P.O. Box 102 A, Oroville, WA 98844.

Location: From Interstate 5 at Burlington, turn east on Highway 20 and drive 174 miles. Turn north on US 97 and proceed 48 miles to Oroville. Continue one mile north on US 97 to the park. Note: In the winter, sections of Highway 20 are closed; take an alternate route to US 97.

Trip note: This is a beautiful park set near the Canadian border. Many years ago, this area was the site of the annual Okanogan, which means "rendezvous," of the Washington and British Columbia Indians. They would gather and share supplies of fish and game for the year. The park is set along the shore of Osoyoos Lake, where swimming, waterskiing and fishing for trout and spiny-rays are all possibilities. Osoyoos Lake is a winter nesting area for geese. Nearby recreation options include an 18-hole golf course. Fishing gear and concessions are available at the park.

---

8. SPECTACLE LAKE RESORT 🚐

Reference: **On Spectacle Lake; map A4, grid a3.**

Campsites, facilities: There are 40 drive-through sites for tents, trailers or RVs of any length. Electricity, piped water, sewer hookups and picnic tables are provided. Flush toilets, bottled gas, sanitary services, showers, a store, a laundromat, ice, a playground and swimming pool are available. Pets and motorbikes are permitted. Boat docks, launching facilities and rentals are also available.

Reservations, fee: Reservations accepted; $12-$14 fee per night. Open mid-April to late October.

Who to contact: Phone (509) 223-3433 or write to 10 McCammon Road, Tonasket, WA 98855.

Location: From Interstate 5 at Burlington, turn east on Highway 20 and drive 174 miles. Turn north on US 97 and drive 37 miles to Ellisford. Turn west on Loomis Highway and drive 7.7 miles. Turn south on Holmes Road and drive one-half mile to McCammon Road, then turn west and drive one block to the park at the end of the road.

Trip note: This resort is set along the shore of long, narrow Spectacle Lake. It's a pleasant campground with grassy, shaded sites. Nearby recreation options include swimming, fishing, hunting and horseback riding. A riding stable is nearby.

---

9. BETH LAKE 🚐

Reference: **On Beth Lake in Okanogan National Forest; map A4, grid a6.**

Campsites, facilities: There are 17 sites for tents, trailers or RVs up to 31 feet long. Piped water and picnic tables are provided. Vault toilets are available, and pets are permitted. Boat launching facilities are available.

Reservations, fee: For reservation and fee information, phone (509) 486-2186. Open mid-May to mid-September.

Who to contact: Phone the Okanogan National Forest at (509) 486-2186 or write to Tonasket Ranger District, P.O. Box 466, Tonasket, WA 98855.

Location: From Interstate 5 south of Bellingham, turn east on Highway 20 and drive approximately 200 miles east and north to Tonasket. Continue 20 miles east on Highway 20 to County Road 4953, then drive north to Forest Service Road 32. Turn north and drive five miles. From there, drive northwest on County Road 9480 to the campground.

Trip note: This campground is set along little Beth Lake, which is adjacent to Beaver Lake. Side trip options in the area include Lost Lake, Bonaparte Lake and several hiking trails, one of which leads up to the Mount Bonaparte Lookout.

---

10.   LOST LAKE   RV

Reference: **On Lost Lake in Okanogan National Forest; map A4, grid a6.**

Campsites, facilities: There are 20 sites for tents, trailers or RVs up to 31 feet long. Piped water and picnic tables are provided. Vault toilets are available and leashed pets are permitted. Boat docks and launching facilities are nearby.

Reservations, fee: For reservation and fee information, phone (509) 486-2186. Open mid-May to mid-September.

Who to contact: Phone the Okanogan National Forest at (509) 486-2186 or write to Tonasket Ranger District, P.O. Box 466, Tonasket, WA 98855.

Location: From Interstate 5 south of Bellingham, turn east on Highway 20 and drive approximately 200 miles east and north to Tonasket. Continue 20 miles east on Highway 20 to County Road 4953, then drive north to Forest Service Road 32. Turn north and drive three miles, then turn northwest on Forest Service Road 33 and drive 6.5 miles to the campground.

Trip note: This site is set along the shore of Lost Lake where fishing, swimming, hiking, hunting and horseback riding are some of the possibilities. It is about a mile from the Big Tree Botanical Area.

---

11.   BEAVER LAKE   RV

Reference: **On Beaver Lake in Okanogan National Forest; map A4, grid a6.**

Campsites, facilities: There are four sites for tents, trailers or RVs up to 21 feet long. Piped water and picnic tables are provided. Vault toilets are available. Leashed pets are permitted.

Reservations, fee: For reservation and fee information, phone (509) 486-2186. Open mid-May to mid-September.

Who to contact: Phone the Okanogan National Forest at (509) 486-2186, write to Tonasket Ranger District, P.O. Box 466, Tonasket, WA 98855.

Location: From Interstate 5 south of Bellingham, turn east on Highway 20 and drive approximately 200 miles east and north to Tonasket. Continue 20 miles east on Highway 20 to County Road 4953, then drive north to Forest Service Road 32. Turn north and drive five miles to the campground.

Trip note: This campground is set along the southeastern shore of long, narrow Beaver Lake, one of several lakes in this area. Fishing, swimming, hunting and hiking are all possibilities here. See the trip notes for Bonaparte Lake and Lost Lake for information on the other lakes.

---

12.   TIFFANY SPRING   RV

Reference: **Near Tiffany Lake in Okanogan National Forest; map A4, grid b0.**

Campsites, facilities: There are six tent sites for trailers or RVs up to 15 feet long. Picnic tables are provided. Vault toilets are available, but there is **no piped water**. No garbage service is provided, so trash must be packed out. Leashed pets are permitted.

Reservations, fee: No reservations; no fee. Open July to late September.

Who to contact: Phone the Okanogan National Forest at (509) 486-2186 or write to Tonasket Ranger District, P.O. Box 466, Tonasket, WA 98855.

Location: From Interstate 5 south of Bellingham, turn east on Highway 20 and drive approximately 180 miles east and north to Okanogan. Turn north on County Road 9229 and drive about 17.5 miles northwest to Conconully. Turn left on County Road 2017 and drive 1.5 miles southwest, then turn northwest on Forest Service Road 37 and drive 21 miles. Turn northeast on Forest Service Road 39 and proceed 7.5 miles to the campground.

Trip note: This campground is set at 6,800 feet and is less than a mile hike from Tiffany Lake. Tiffany Mountain rises 8,200 feet in the distance. There are some good hiking trails in the area. No other campgrounds are in the vicinity, and it is advisable to obtain a Forest Service map of the area.

---

13.   STAGE STOP AT SULL'S RV   🚐

Reference: **Near Chopaka Lake; map A4, grid b2.**

Campsites, facilities: There are 10 tent sites and 20 drive-through sites for trailers or RVs. Electricity, piped water, sewer hookups and picnic tables are provided. Bottled gas, a store, a cafe, ice and a playground are available. Pets and motorbikes are permitted.

Reservations, fee: Reservations accepted; $8-$10 fee per night. Open all year.

Who to contact: Phone (509) 223-3275 or write to P.O. Box 5, Loomis, WA 98826.

Location: From Interstate 5 at Burlington, turn east on Highway 20 and drive 174 miles. Turn north on US 97 and proceed 30 miles to Tonasket. Turn northwest on Loomis Highway and drive 20 miles to Loomis. The park is in town on the right side of Palmer Road.

Trip note: This campground is in rural Loomis, less than five miles from Chopaka Lake, Palmer Lake and Spectacle Lake. It's a pretty camp with comfortable sites. Nearby recreation options include hiking trails, a riding stable, a full-service marina and tennis courts.

---

14.   RAINBOW RESORT   🚐

Reference: **On Spectacle Lake; map A4, grid b3.**

Campsites, facilities: There are 10 tent sites and 40 drive-through sites for trailers or RVs of any length. Electricity, piped water, sewer hookups and picnic tables are provided. Flush toilets, showers, firewood and ice are available. Pets and motorbikes are permitted. Boat docks, launching facilities and rentals are nearby.

Reservations, fee: Reservations accepted; $13 fee per night. Open April through October.

Who to contact: Phone (509) 223-3700 or write to 761 Loomis Highway, Tonasket, WA 98855.

Location: From Interstate 5 at Burlington, turn east on Highway 20 and drive 174 miles. Turn north on US 97 and proceed 37 miles to Ellisford. Turn west on Loomis Highway and drive 9.5 miles to the resort on the left.

Trip note: This resort is set along the shore of Spectacle Lake. It is an option to Spectacle Lake Resort, with pretty lake views and full facilities. Nearby recreation options include swimming, fishing, hunting and tennis.

15.   SPECTACLE FALLS RESORT   RV

Reference: **On Spectacle Lake; map A4, grid b3.**

Campsites, facilities: There are 10 tent sites and 28 drive-through sites for trailers or RVs of any length. Electricity, piped water, sewer hookups and picnic tables are provided. Flush toilets, sanitary services, showers and ice are available. Pets and motorbikes are permitted. Boat docks, launching facilities and rentals are nearby.

Reservations, fee: Reservations accepted; $14 fee per night. Open mid-April to late July.

Who to contact: Phone (509) 223-4141 or write to 879 Loomis Highway, Tonasket, WA 98855.

Location: From Interstate 5 at Burlington, turn east on Highway 20 and drive 174 miles. Turn north on US 97 and drive 30 miles to Tonasket. Turn northwest on Loomis Highway and drive 15 miles to the resort.

Trip note: This resort is set along the shore of Spectacle Lake. It is open only as long as fishing on the lake is allowed, which means an early closing in July. Be sure to phone ahead of time to verify whether they're open. Nearby recreation options include hiking, swimming, fishing, horseback riding and tennis. A riding stable is nearby.

16.   BONAPARTE LAKE   RV

Reference: **On Bonaparte Lake in Okanogan National Forest; map A4, grid b6.**

Campsites, facilities: There are 27 sites for tents, trailers or RVs up to 31 feet long. Piped water, vault toilets, fire grills and picnic tables are provided. Sanitary services, a store, a cafe, and ice are available within one mile. Leashed pets are permitted. Boat docks and launching facilities are also available.

Reservations, fee: For reservation and fee information, phone (509) 486-2186. Open mid-May to mid-September.

Who to contact: Phone the Okanogan National Forest at (509) 486-2186 or write to Tonasket Ranger District, P.O. Box 466, Tonasket, WA 98855.

Location: From Interstate 5 south of Bellingham, turn east on Highway 20 and drive approximately 200 miles east and north to Tonasket. Continue 20 miles east on Highway 20 to County Road 4953, then drive north to Forest Service Road 32. Turn north and drive 5.5 miles to the campground.

Trip note: This campground is set along the southern shore of Bonaparte Lake. See the trip note for Bonaparte Lake Resort for lake recreation information. There are several trails nearby that provide access to Mount Bonaparte Lookout. See a Forest Service map for details.

17.   BONAPARTE LAKE RESORT   RV

Reference: **On Bonaparte Lake; map A4, grid b6.**

Campsites, facilities: There are 10 tent sites and 35 drive-through sites for trailers or RVs of any length. Electricity, piped water, sewer hookups and picnic tables are provided. Flush toilets, bottled gas, sanitary services, showers, firewood, a recreation hall, a store, a cafe, a laundromat, ice and a playground are available. Leashed pets and motorbikes are permitted. Boat docks, launching facilities and rentals are also available.

Reservations, fee: Reservations accepted; $7-$11 fee per night; MasterCard and Visa accepted. Open April through October.

Who to contact: Phone (509) 486-2828 or write to 695 Bonaparte, Tonasket, WA 98855.

Location: From Interstate 5 at Burlington, turn east on Highway 20 and drive 174 miles. Turn north on US 97 and proceed 30 miles to Tonasket. Continue 20 miles east on Highway 20 to Bonaparte Road. Turn north and drive six miles to the resort on the left.

Trip note: This resort is set along the southeast shore of Bonaparte Lake, where fishing is popular. Nearby recreation options include hiking and hunting in the nearby Forest Service lands. In the winter, the area is open for snowmobiling and cross-country skiing.

18.   CURLEW LAKE STATE PARK   RV

Reference: On Curlew Lake; map A4, grid b8.

Campsites, facilities: There are five primitive tent sites, 57 developed tent sites, and 25 sites for trailers or RVs up to 30 feet long. Picnic tables are provided. Flush toilets, sanitary services, electricity, piped water, sewer hookups, showers and firewood are available. Leashed pets are permitted. Boat launching facilities are also available.

Reservations, fee: No reservations; $10-$16 fee per night. Open April to late October.

Who to contact: Phone (800) 233-0321 or (509) 775-3592 or write to 974 Curlew Lake Street, Republic, WA 99166.

Location: From Interstate 90 at Spokane, turn north on US 395 and drive 87 miles. Turn west on Highway 20 and continue 34 miles to Highway 21 (two miles east of Republic). Turn north and drive 6.5 miles to the park entrance on the left.

Trip note: This park is set along the eastern shore of Curlew Lake. There is beach access, swimming, waterskiing and hiking. There is also excellent fishing for trout and bass. Nearby recreation options include an 18-hole golf course, and in the winter, snowmobiling. The park is located in the heart of an historic goldmining district, so you may want to bring along a pan a give it a whirl.

19.   TIFFANY'S RESORT   RV

Reference: On Curlew Lake; map A4, grid b8.

Campsites, facilities: There are four tent sites and 15 sites for trailers or RVs of any length. Electricity, piped water, sewer hookups and picnic tables are provided. Flush toilets, showers, firewood, a store, a laundromat, ice and a playground are available. Pets and motorbikes are permitted. Boat docks, launching facilities and rentals are nearby.

Reservations, fee: Reservations accepted; $15 fee per night. Open April to late October.

Who to contact: Phone (509) 775-3152 or write to 1026 Tiffany Road, Republic, WA 99166.

Location: From Interstate 90 at Spokane, turn north on US 395 and drive 87 miles. Turn west on Highway 20 and drive 34 miles to Highway 21 (two miles east of Republic). Turn north and drive 10 miles, then turn north on West Curlew Lake Road and drive five miles to the resort.

Trip note: This resort is set along the western shore of Curlew Lake, where fishing can be good. It's a pretty setting, with lake access and spacious, wooded sites. This is a smaller, more private alternative to Black's Beach Resort.

20. BLACK'S BEACH RESORT   **RV**

Reference: **On Curlew Lake; map A4, grid b8.**

Campsites, facilities: There are 120 sites for trailers or RVs of any length (60 are drive-through). Electricity, piped water, sewer hookups and picnic tables are provided. Flush toilets, bottled gas, sanitary services, showers, firewood, recreation hall, a store, a cafe, a laundromat, ice and a playground are available. Pets and motorbikes are permitted. Boat docks, launching facilities and rentals are located nearby.

Reservations, fee: Reservations accepted; $15-$17 fee per night. Open all year.

Who to contact: Phone (509) 775-3989 or write to 848 Blacks Beach Road, Republic, WA 99166.

Location: From Interstate 90 at Spokane, turn north on US 395 and drive 87 miles. Turn west on Highway 20 and continue 34 miles to Highway 21 (two miles east of Republic). Turn north and drive ten miles, then turn north on West Curlew Lake Road and continue to the resort on the lake.

Trip note: This is another resort set along Curlew Lake. It is much larger, with beautiful waterfront sites available and full facilities. Waterskiing, swimming and fishing are all options here.

21. KERR   **RV**

Reference: **On Salmon Creek in Okanogan National Forest; map A4, grid c1.**

Campsites, facilities: There are nine sites for tents, trailers or RVs up to 21 feet long. Picnic tables and fire grills are provided. Vault toilets are available, but there is **no piped water**. No garbage service is provided, so trash must be packed out. Leashed pets are permitted.

Reservations, fee: No reservations; no fee. Open mid-May to mid-September.

Who to contact: Phone the Okanogan National Forest at (509) 486-2186 or write to Tonasket Ranger District, P.O. Box 466, Tonasket, WA 98855.

Location: From Interstate 5 south of Bellingham, turn east on Highway 20 and drive approximately 180 miles east and north to Okanogan. Turn north on County Road 9229 and drive about 17.5 miles northwest to Conconully. Turn northwest on County Road 2361 and drive two miles, then continue northwest on Forest Service Road 38 for two miles to the campground.

Trip note: This campground is set at 3,100 feet along Salmon Creek, about four miles north of Conconully Lake. It's one of the many campgrounds located near the lake. Fishing prospects can be decent here, and there are numerous recreation options available at Conconully Lake.

22. JACK'S RV PARK AND MOTEL   **RV**

Reference: **Near Conconully Lake; map A4, grid c2.**

Campsites, facilities: There are 10 tent sites and 63 sites (30 drive-through) for trailers or RVs of any length. Electricity, piped water, sewer hookups and picnic tables are provided. Flush toilets, bottled gas, sanitary services, showers, firewood, a laundromat and a swimming pool are available. Sanitary services, a store, a cafe and ice are located within one mile. Pets and motorbikes are permitted. Boat docks, launching facilities and rentals are nearby.

Reservations, fee: Reservations accepted; $12-$14 fee per night; MasterCard and Visa accepted. Open all year.

Who to contact: Phone (509) 826-0132 or write to P.O. Box 98, Conconully, WA 98819.

Location: From Interstate 5 south of Bellingham, turn east on Highway 20 and drive approximately 180 miles east and north to Okanogan. Turn north on Conconully Highway and drive about 17.5 miles northwest to Conconully. Turn east on Broadway Street and drive one block, then turn north on A Avenue and drive less than one block to the park on the right.

Trip note: This park is in town, not far from Conconully Lake. There is a pool and horseshoe pits in the park, and nearby recreation options include hiking trails and water sports at the lake.

23.　　　　LAZY DAYS RV PARK　　　　RV

Reference: **Near Conconully Lake; map A4, grid c2.**

Campsites, facilities: There are 43 drive-through sites for trailers or RVs of any length. Electricity, piped water, sewer hookups and picnic tables are provided. Flush toilets, firewood, showers, a laundromat, cable TV, ice and a swimming pool are available. Bottled gas, sanitary services, a store, a cafe and ice are located within one mile. Leashed pets are permitted. Boat docks, launching facilities and rentals are nearby.

Reservations, fee: Reservations accepted; $14 fee per night. Open April to mid-November, weather permitting.

Who to contact: Phone (509) 826-0326 or write to P.O. Box 67, Conconully, WA 98819.

Location: From Interstate 5 south of Bellingham, turn east on Highway 20 and drive approximately 180 miles east and north to Okanogan. Turn north on Conconully Highway and drive about 17.5 miles northwest to Conconully. Turn east on Silver Street and drive one block, then turn south on A Avenue and drive about 50 feet to the park on the right.

Trip note: This park is in downtown Conconully, a short distance from the lake. The park is geared specifically toward RVs, with shaded grassy sites. Nearby recreation options include hiking trails and fishing, swimming and boating at the lake.

24.　　　MAPLE FLATS RV PARK AND RESORT　　　RV

Reference: **On Conconully Lake; map A4, grid c2.**

Campsites, facilities: There are six tent sites and 23 sites for trailers or RVs of any length (13 are drive-through). Electricity, piped water, sewer hookups and picnic tables are provided. Flush toilets, showers, a laundromat, cable TV and a gazebo are available. Bottled gas, sanitary services, a store, a cafe, a laundromat and ice are located within one mile. Pets and motorbikes are permitted. Boat docks, launching facilities and rentals are nearby.

Reservations, fee: Reservations accepted; $10-$14 fee per night. Open all year.

Who to contact: Phone (509) 826-4231 or write to 310 A Avenue, Conconully, WA 98819.

Location: From Interstate 5 south of Bellingham, turn east on Highway 20 and drive approximately 180 miles east and north to Okanogan. Turn north on Conconully Highway and drive about 17.5 miles northwest to Conconully. Turn east on Loomis Road and drive one block, then turn east on "A" Avenue and drive to the park on the right.

Trip note: This campground is set along the shore of Conconully Lake. It is beautiful, surrounded by pine trees and mountains, with panoramic views. Nearby recreation options include hiking and biking on the many nature trails in the area, an 18-hole golf course (15 miles away), trout fishing in the well-stocked upper and lower Conconully lakes and, in the winter, snowmobiling and cross-country skiing.

25. KOZY KABINS AND RV PARK RV

Reference: Near Conconully Lake; map A4, grid c2.

Campsites, facilities: There are six tent sites and 12 drive-through sites for trailers or RVs of any length. Electricity, piped water, sewer hookups and picnic tables are provided. Flush toilets, showers and firewood are available. Bottled gas, sanitary services, a store, a cafe, a laundromat and ice are located within one mile. Pets and motorbikes are permitted. Cabin rentals, boat docks, launching facilities and rentals are nearby.

Reservations, fee: Reservations accepted; $7-$10 fee per night. Cabins are $25 per night. Open all year.

Who to contact: Phone (509) 826-6780 or write to P.O. Box 38, Conconully, WA 98819.

Location: From Interstate 5 south of Bellingham, turn east on Highway 20 and drive approximately 180 miles east and north to Okanogan. Turn north on Conconully Highway and drive about 17.5 miles northwest to Conconully. The park is at the junction of "A" Avenue and Broadway.

Trip note: This park is in Conconully not far from the lake. It's quiet, private and secluded, with a small creek running through and plenty of greenery. Nearby recreation options include a full-service marina. If you continue northeast of town on County Road 4015, the road will get a bit narrow for awhile, but it will widen again when you enter the Sinlahekin Habitat Management Area, which is managed by the Department of Fish and Game. There are some primitive campsites in this valley, especially along the shores of the lakes in the area.

26. CONCONULLY LAKE RESORT RV

Reference: On Upper Conconully Lake; map A4, grid c2.

Campsites, facilities: There are 11 sites for trailers or RVs of any length. Electricity, piped water, sewer hookups and picnic tables are provided. Flush toilets, showers and ice are available. Bottled gas, sanitary services, a store, a cafe and a laundromat are available within one mile. Pets and motorbikes are permitted. Boat docks, launching facilities and rentals are available.

Reservations, fee: Reservations accepted; $12-$15 fee per night. Open late-April to late October.

Who to contact: Phone (509) 826-0813 or write to P.O. Box 131, Conconully, WA 98819.

Location: From Interstate 5 south of Bellingham, turn east on Highway 20 and drive approximately 180 miles east and north to Okanogan. Turn north on Conconully Highway and drive about 17.5 miles northwest to Conconully. Turn east on Sinlahekin Road and continue one mile to the park on the right.

Trip note: This resort is one of several in Conconully, set along the shore of Conconully Lake. No tents are permitted, but this is a prime vacation destination for RVers. Trout fishing, swimming and boating are all options here.

27.　　　　LIAR'S COVE RESORT　　　　RV

Reference: **On Conconully Lake; map A4, grid c1.**

Campsites, facilities: There are 30 sites (20 drive-through) for trailers or RVs up to 50 feet long. Electricity, piped water, sewer hookups and picnic tables are provided. Flush toilets, showers and ice are available. Bottled gas, sanitary services, a store and a cafe are located within one mile. Pets and motorbikes are permitted. Boat docks, launching facilities and rentals are nearby.

Reservations, fee: Reservations accepted; $14-$15 fee per night. MasterCard and Visa accepted. Open April to early November.

Who to contact: Phone (509) 826-1288 or (800) 830-1288 or write to P.O. Box 72, Conconully, WA 98819.

Location: From Interstate 5 south of Bellingham, turn east on Highway 20 and drive approximately 180 miles east and north to Okanogan. Turn north on Conconully Highway and drive about 16.5 miles northwest to the park on the left. It is located about one-quarter mile south of Conconully.

Trip note: This park is set along the shore of the Conconully Lake. It has roomy sites for RVs and tents are allowed. Nearby recreation options include fishing, swimming, boating and hiking.

28.　　　　SHADY PINES RESORT　　　　RV

Reference: **On Conconully Lake; map A4, grid c2.**

Campsites, facilities: There are 23 sites for trailers or RVs of any length (21 full hookups). Electricity, piped water, sewer hookups and picnic tables are provided. Flush toilets, ice, showers and firewood are available. Bottled gas, sanitary services, a store, a cafe and a laundromat are located within one mile. Pets and motorbikes are permitted. Boat launching facilities and rentals are nearby.

Reservations, fee: Reservations accepted; $17-$18 fee per night. MasterCard and Visa accepted. Open mid-April to late October.

Who to contact: Phone (509) 826-2287 or (800) 552-2287 or write to P.O. Box 44, Conconully, WA 98819.

Location: From Interstate 5 south of Bellingham, turn east on Highway 20 and drive approximately 180 miles east and north to Okanogan. Turn north on Conconully Highway and drive about 17.5 miles northwest to Conconully. Turn west on Broadway Street and drive one mile. The park is on the west shore of the lake.

Trip note: This campground is set along Conconully Lake, near Conconully State Park. This is an option if the state park campground is full, which occurs often in the summertime. See the trip notes for Conconully State Park and Kozy Kabins RV Park for area information.

29.　　　　CONCONULLY STATE PARK　　　　RV

Reference: **On Conconully Lake; map A4, grid c2.**

Campsites, facilities: There are six primitive tent sites and 75 sites for tents or self-contained RVs up to 60 feet long. Piped water, fire grills and picnic tables are provided. Flush toilets, sanitary disposal station, showers, firewood and a playground are available. A store, a cafe, a laundromat and ice are located within one mile. Leashed pets are permitted. Boat launching facilities are nearby.

Reservations, fee: No reservations; $5-$16 fee per night. Open all year with limited winter facilities.

Who to contact: Phone (800) 233-0321 or (509) 826-7408 or write to P.O. Box 95, Conconully, WA 98819.

Location: From Interstate 5 south of Bellingham, turn east on Highway 20 and drive approximately 185 miles east and north to Omak. Take the north Omak exit. At the base of the hill, turn right and proceed two miles until you reach the Conconully Highway. Take another right and continue about 17 miles north to the park entrance.

Trip note: This park is set along Conconully Reservoir, where there is a boat launch, beach access and swimming and fishing opportunities. There is a nice half-mile nature trail to explore. Of special interest is the Sinlahekin Habitat Management Area which is accessible via County Road 4015. This route heads northeast along the shore of Conconully Lake on the other side of US 97. The road is narrow at first, but then becomes wider as you enter the Habitat Management Area.

---

30. SUGARLOAF 📷

Reference: **On Sugarloaf Lake in Okanogan National Forest; map A4, grid c2.**

Campsites, facilities: There are four tent sites and one site for a tent, trailer or RVs up to 21 feet long. Picnic tables are provided, but there is **no piped water**. No garbage service is provided, so trash must be packed out. Vault toilets and firewood are available. Leashed pets are permitted. Boat launching facilities are available nearby.

Reservations, fee: No reservations; no fee. Open mid-May to mid-September.

Who to contact: Phone the Okanogan National Forest at (509) 486-2186 or write to Tonasket Ranger District, P.O. Box 466, Tonasket, WA 98855.

Location: From Interstate 5 south of Bellingham, turn east on Highway 20 and drive approximately 180 miles east and north to Okanogan. Turn north on County Road 9229 and drive about 17.5 miles northwest to Conconully. Turn northwest on County Road 4015 and drive 4.5 miles to the campground.

Trip note: At 2,400 feet, this campground is set along the shore of Sugarloaf Lake. This is the smallest, most private of the camps on the lake, and one of the least-used. Conconully State Park and information center are nearby.

---

31. LYMAN LAKE 📷

Reference: **On Lyman Lake in Okanogan National Forest; map A4, grid c6.**

Campsites, facilities: There are six sites for tents, trailers or RVs up to 31 feet long. Picnic tables and fire grills are provided. Vault toilets are available, but there is **no piped water**. No garbage service is provided, so trash must be packed out. Leashed pets are permitted.

Reservations, fee: No reservations; no fee. Open mid-May to mid-September.

Who to contact: Phone the Okanogan National Forest at (509) 486-2186 or write to Tonasket Ranger District, P.O. Box 466, Tonasket, WA 98855.

Location: From Interstate 5 south of Bellingham, turn east on Highway 20 and drive approximately 200 miles east and north to Tonasket. Continue 12.5 miles east on Highway 20, then turn southeast on County Road 9455 and drive 13 miles. Turn south on County Road 3785 and proceed 2.5 miles to the campground entrance.

Trip note: This campground is set along the shore of little Lyman Lake. Little-known and little-used, it is an idyllic setting for those wanting solitude and quiet. The lake is quite small, but fishing is an option for patient anglers.

---

32. SWAN LAKE   RV

Reference: **On Swan Lake in Colville National Forest; map A4, grid c7.**

Campsites, facilities: There are 25 sites for tents, trailers or RVs up to 31 feet long. Piped water, fire grills and picnic tables are provided. Vault toilets and firewood are available. Leashed pets are permitted. Boat docks and launching facilities are available. Internal combustion engines are prohibited on the lake.

Reservations, fee: No reservations; $6 fee per night. Open May to September.

Who to contact: Phone the Colville National Forest at (509) 775-3305 or write to Republic Ranger District, Republic, WA 99166.

Location: From Spokane on Interstate 90, turn north on US 395 and drive approximately 84 miles. Turn west on Highway 20 and drive 40 miles to Republic. Turn south on Highway 21 and drive seven miles, then turn southwest on Forest Service Road 53 (Scatter Creek Road) and proceed eight miles to the campground.

Trip note: This campground is set along the shore of Swan Lake, elevation 3,700 feet. This is a very pretty area, with scenic views on the drive in as well as in the campground. Also, a beautiful hiking trail circles the lake. Swimming, boating, fishing, mountain biking and hiking are some of the possibilities here. It's a good out-of-the-way spot for motor home cruisers seeking a rustic setting.

---

33. LONG LAKE   RV

Reference: **On Long Lake in Colville National Forest; map A4, grid c7.**

Campsites, facilities: There are 12 sites for tents, trailers or RVs up to 21 feet long. Piped water, fire grills and picnic tables are provided. Vault toilets and firewood are available. Leashed pets are permitted. Launching facilities are nearby.

Reservations, fee: No reservations; $5 fee per night. Open May to September.

Who to contact: Phone the Colville National Forest at (509) 775-3305 or write to Republic Ranger District, Republic, WA 99166.

Location: From Spokane on Interstate 90, turn north on US 395 and drive approximately 84 miles. Turn west on Highway 20 and drive 40 miles to Republic. From Republic, drive seven miles south on Highway 21, then turn southwest on Forest Service Road 53 (Scatter Creek Road) and continue eight miles. Turn south on Forest Service Road 400 and drive 1.5 miles to the camp.

Trip note: This is the third and smallest of the three lakes in this area. No internal combustion engines are allowed on the lake and fishing is restricted (fly fishing only). Expert fishermen can get a quality angling experience here. There is a nice hiking trail that circles the lake. The drive on Highway 21 south of Republic is particularly beautiful, with views of the Sanpoil River.

---

34. FERRY LAKE   RV

Reference: **On Ferry Lake in Colville National Forest; map A4, grid c7.**

Campsites, facilities: There are nine sites for tents, trailers or RVs up to 20 feet long. There is **no piped water**. Fire grills and picnic tables are provided. Vault toilets and firewood are available. Leashed pets are permitted. Launching facilities are nearby. Internal combustion engines are prohibited on the lake.

Reservations, fee: No reservations; no fee. Open May to September.

Who to contact: Phone the Colville National Forest at (509) 775-3305 or write to Republic Ranger District, Republic, WA 99166.

Location: From Spokane on Interstate 90, turn north on US 395 and drive approximately 84 miles. Turn west on Highway 20 and drive 40 miles to Republic. From Republic, drive seven miles south on Highway 21, then turn southwest on Forest Service Road 53 (Scatter Creek Road) and go six miles. Turn north on Forest Service Road 5330 and drive one mile, then continue north on Forest Service Road 100 for 500 yards to the campground.

Trip note: This is one of three fishing lakes within a four-square-mile area. The others are Swan Lake and Long Lake. See trip notes for those camps for area information.

35.   SHERMAN PASS OVERLOOK   RV

Reference: **At Sherman Pass in Colville National Forest; map A4, grid c9.**
Campsites, facilities: There are nine sites for tents, trailers or RVs up to 24 feet long. Hand-pumped water, fire grills and picnic tables are provided. Vault toilets are available. Leashed pets are permitted.
Reservations, fee: No reservations; no fee. Open mid-May to late September.
Who to contact: Phone the Colville National Forest at (509) 738-6111 or write to Kettle Falls Ranger District, 255 West 11th Street, Kettle Falls, WA 99141.
Location: From Spokane on Interstate 90, turn north on US 395 and drive approximately 84 miles. Turn west on Highway 20 and drive 19.5 miles to the campground.
Trip note: This roadside campground is located near Sherman Pass (5,575 feet), the highest pass in the state of Washington. Sherman Pass Scenic Byway routed by there. Several trails pass through camp that provide access to various peaks and vistas in the area. No other campgrounds are in the immediate vicinity.

36.   LOUP LOUP   RV

Reference: **Near Loup Loup Ski Area in Okanogan National Forest; map A4, grid d1.**
Campsites, facilities: There are 25 sites for tents, trailers or RVs up to 21 feet long. Piped water and picnic tables are provided. Vault toilets are available. Leashed pets are permitted.
Reservations, fee: For reservation and fee information, phone (509) 997-2131. Open May to September.
Who to contact: Phone the Okanogan National Forest at (509) 997-2131 or write to Methow Valley Ranger District, Twisp Office, P.O. Box 188, Twisp, WA 98856.
Location: From Interstate 5 south of Bellingham, turn east on Highway 20 and drive approximately 145 miles to Twisp. Continue 13 miles east on Highway 20, then turn north on Forest Service Road 42 and drive one mile to the campground.
Trip note: At 4,200 feet, this campground is set next to the Loup Loup ski area, which has facilities for both downhill and cross-country skiing. It's just far enough off Highway 20 to be missed by many out-of-towners.

37.   J. R.   RV

Reference: **On Frazier Creek in Okanogan National Forest; map A4, grid d1.**
Campsites, facilities: There are six sites for tents, trailers or RVs up to 16 feet long.

Piped water and picnic tables are provided. Vault toilets are available. Leashed pets are permitted.

Reservations, fee: For reservation and fee information, phone (509) 997-2131. Open late May to early September.

Who to contact: Phone the Okanogan National Forest at (509) 997-2131 or write to Methow Valley Ranger District, Twisp Office, P.O. Box 188, Twisp, WA 98856.

Location: From Interstate 5 south of Bellingham, turn east on Highway 20 and drive approximately 145 miles to Twisp. Continue 12 miles east on Highway 20 to the campground.

Trip note: This campground is set along Frazier Creek near the Loup Loup summit and ski area. Some of the recreation options in the surrounding area include fishing, hunting, cross-country skiing, snowmobiling, hiking and bicycling. This is a good layover for travelers looking for a spot on Highway 20.

38. ROCK LAKES

Reference: **On Rock Lake; map A4, grid d2.**

Campsites, facilities: There are eight campsites for tents or small trailers. Picnic tables, fire grills and tent pads are provided. Vault toilets are available, but there is **no piped water**. Leashed pets are permitted.

Reservations, fee: No reservations; no fee. Open all year.

Who to contact: Phone the Department of Natural Resources at (509) 684-7474 or write to Department of Natural Resources, Northeast Region, P.O. Box 190, Colville, WA 99114-0190.

Location: From Interstate 5 at Burlington, turn east on Highway 20 and drive 164 miles to Loup Loup Canyon Road (10 miles west of Okanogan). Turn right and drive five miles. Turn left on Rock Lakes Road and drive six miles, then turn left and drive 300 yards to the campground.

Trip note: This campground is set in a forested area along the shore of Rock Lake. Trout fishing can be good. There are some hiking trails in the area. A good bet is to combine a trip here with nearby Leader Lake. Highway 20 east of Interstate 5 is a designated scenic route.

39. ROCK CREEK

Reference: **On Rock Creek and Loup Loup Creek; map A4, grid d2.**

Campsites, facilities: There are six campsites for tents or small trailers. Picnic tables, fire grills and tent pads are provided. Vault toilets and piped water are available. Leashed pets are permitted.

Reservations, fee: No reservations; no fee. Open all year.

Who to contact: Phone the Department of Natural Resources at (509) 684-7474 or write to Department of Natural Resources, Northeast Region, P.O. Box 190, Colville, WA 99114-0190.

Location: From Interstate 5 at Burlington, turn east on Highway 20 and drive 164 miles to Loup Loup Canyon Road (10 miles west of Okanogan). Turn right and drive four miles to the camp on the left.

Trip note: This wooded campground is at the confluence of Rock Creek and Loup Loup Creek. A group shelter is available. It's advisable to obtain a map detailing the area from the Department of Natural Resources.

40.   LEADER LAKE

Reference: **On Leader Lake; map A4, grid d2.**

Campsites, facilities: There are 16 campsites for tents or small trailers. Picnic tables, fire grills and tent pads are provided. Pit toilets are available, but there is **no piped water**. Boat launching facilities are nearby. Leashed pets are permitted.

Reservations, fee: No reservations; no fee. Open all year.

Who to contact: Phone the Department of Natural Resources at (509) 684-7474 or write to Department of Natural Resources, Northeast Region, P.O. Box 190, Colville, WA 99114-0190.

Location: From Interstate 5 at Burlington, turn east on Highway 20 and drive 166 miles to Leader Lake Road (eight miles west of Okanogan). Turn right and drive 400 yards to the campground.

Trip note: This campground is set along the shore of Leader Lake, where trout fishing can be good in season. It gets missed by many because it is just far enough off the beaten path. It's quite primitive, but pretty, and the boat ramp is an added bonus.

---

41.   EASTSIDE PARK AND CAMPGROUND   **RV**

Reference: **On Okanogan River; map A4, grid d3.**

Campsites, facilities: There are 50 tent sites and 76 drive-through sites for trailers or RVs of any length. Electricity, piped water, sewer hookups and picnic tables are provided. Flush toilets, sanitary services, showers, swimming pool and a playground are available. A store, a cafe, a laundromat and ice are located within one mile. Pets are permitted. Boat launching facilities are nearby.

Reservations, fee: No reservations; $10-$12 fee per night. Open April to late October.

Who to contact: Phone (509) 826-1170 or write to P.O. Box 72, Omak, WA 98841.

Location: From Interstate 5 south of Bellingham, turn east on Highway 20 and drive approximately 180 miles east and north to Okanogan. Turn north on US 97 and drive six miles to Omak. Turn east on Highway 155 and drive three-tenths of a mile to the campground.

Trip note: This city park is in town, along the shore of the Okanogan River. Trout fishing is excellent here, and there is a boat ramp near the campground. Nearby recreation options include an 18-hole golf course, a pool and a recreation field.

---

42.   AMERICAN LEGION PARK   **RV**

Reference: **On Okanogan River; map A4, grid d3.**

Campsites, facilities: There are 35 sites for trailers or RVs of any length. Piped water and picnic tables are provided. Flush toilets and showers are available. A store, a cafe, a laundromat and ice are located within one mile.

Reservations, fee: No reservations; $5-$7 fee per night. Open all year.

Who to contact: Phone (509) 422-3600 or write to Okanogan City Hall, Okanogan, WA 98840.

Location: From Interstate 5 south of Bellingham, turn east on Highway 20 and drive approximately 180 miles east and north to Okanogan. Turn north on Highway 215 and drive one mile to the campground.

Trip note: This city park is set along the shore of the Okanogan River in an urban setting. The sites are graveled and sunny. Anglers may want to try their hand at the excellent bass fishing here. There is a historical museum in town.

43.   CRAWFISH LAKE   RV

Reference: On Crawfish Lake in Okanogan National Forest; map A4, grid d5.

Campsites, facilities: There are 27 sites for tents, trailers or RVs up to 31 feet long. Picnic tables and fire grills are provided. Vault toilets are available, but there is **no piped water**. No garbage service is provided, so trash must be packed out. Leashed pets are permitted. Boat launching facilities are located on the lake.

Reservations, fee: No reservations; no fee. Open mid-May to mid-September.

Who to contact: Phone the Okanogan National Forest at (509) 486-2186 or write to Tonasket Ranger District, P.O. Box 466, Tonasket, WA 98855.

Location: From Interstate 5 south of Bellingham, turn east on Highway 20 and drive approximately 185 miles to Riverside. Turn east on County Road 9320 and drive 17.5 miles, then head south on Forest Service Road 30 for 1.5 miles. Next, turn southeast on Forest Service Road 30100 and drive 400 yards to the campground.

Trip note: This campground is pretty, remote and primitive, set at 4,500 feet along the shore of Crawfish Lake. Fishing and crawdad hunting are popular. For the latter, just put a small piece of chicken on a hook and wait 'til the little critters get their pinchers on it.

44.   TEN MILE   RV

Reference: On Sanpoil River in Colville National Forest; map A4, grid d7.

Campsites, facilities: There are 13 sites for tents, trailers or RVs up to 21 feet long. Picnic tables, vault toilets and firewood are available. There is **no piped water**. Leashed pets are permitted.

Reservations, fee: No reservations; no fee. Open mid-May to mid-October.

Who to contact: Phone the Colville National Forest at (509) 775-3305 or write to Republic Ranger District, Republic, WA 99166.

Location: From Spokane on Interstate 90, turn north on US 395 and drive approximately 84 miles. Turn west on Highway 20 and drive 40 miles to Republic. From Republic, drive 10 miles south on Highway 21 and you'll see the campground entrance.

Trip note: This campground is set along the Sanpoil River. It is about nine miles from Swan Lake, Ferry Lake and Long Lake. A good choice is a multi-day trip, visiting each of the lakes. There is fishing in the Sanpoil River and a hiking trail that leads west from camp for about 2.5 miles.

45.   WHISTLIN' PINE RESORT   RV

Reference: On Alta Lake; map A4, grid f0.

Campsites, facilities: There are 30 tent sites and nine sites for trailers or RVs up to 30 feet long. Cabins are also available for rental. Electricity, piped water and picnic tables are provided. Flush toilets, showers, firewood and ice are available. Sanitary services are available within one mile. Pets and motorbikes are permitted. Boat docks, launching facilities and rentals are nearby.

Reservations, fee: Reservations accepted; $13-$18 fee per night. Cabins are $40 per night. Open April to October.

Who to contact: Phone (509) 923-2548 or write to P.O. Box 284, Pateros, WA 98846.

Location: From Interstate 5 at Everett, turn east on US 2 and drive 121 miles, then turn north on US 97 and drive about 46 miles to Highway 153 (just south of Pateros). Drive two miles northwest on Highway 153 to Alta Lake Road, turn southwest on Alta Lake Road and drive three miles to the resort.

Trip note: This campground is set along the shore of Alta Lake and offers horseback riding and a nearby 18-hole golf course at the lake. See the trip note for Alta Lake State Park for listing of additional activities.

---

46.   ALTA LAKE STATE PARK   RV

Reference: On Alta Lake; map A4, grid f0.

Campsites, facilities: There are 11 primitive tent sites, 158 developed tent sites, and 31 sites for trailers or RVs up to 40 feet long. Picnic tables and fireplaces are provided. Flush toilets, piped water, showers, electricity, firewood and sanitary services are available. A store, a cafe and ice are available within one mile. Some facilities are **wheelchair accessible**. Pets are permitted. Boat launching facilities are nearby.

Reservations, fee: No reservations; $5-$16 fee per night. Open all year.

Who to contact: Phone (800) 233-0321 or (509) 923-2473 or write to Star Route 40, Pateros, WA 98846.

Location: From Interstate 5 at Everett, turn east on US 2 and drive 121 miles, then turn north on US 97 and drive approximately 46 miles to Highway 153 (just south of Pateros). Drive two miles northwest on Highway 153 to Alta Lake Road, turn southwest on Alta Lake Road and drive three miles to the park.

Trip note: This state park is set among the pines along the shore of Alta Lake, where a half-mile long swimming beach and boat launch are available. Nearby recreation options include an 18-hole golf course and a riding stable. There is a nice one-mile hiking trail that leads up to a scenic lookout.

---

47.   SUPERSTOP RV PARK AND MARINA   RV

Reference: On Columbia River; map A4, grid f1.

Campsites, facilities: There are three tent sites and 12 sites for trailers or RVs of any length. Electricity, piped water and sewer and cable TV hookups are provided. Flush toilets, bottled gas, sanitary services, a store, a restaurant, a laundromat and ice are available. Pets and motorbikes are permitted. Boat docks and launching facilities are nearby.

Reservations, fee: Reservations accepted; $10-$16 fee per night; MasterCard and Visa accepted. Open all year.

Who to contact: Phone (509) 923-2200 or write to P.O. Box 147, Pateros, WA 98846.

Location: From Interstate 5 at Everett, turn east on US 2 and drive 121 miles, then turn north on US 97 and drive about 47 miles to Pateros. This park is at the south end of town on the right.

Trip note: This park and marina is set along the shore of the Columbia River. Nearby recreation options include an 18-hole golf course, hiking trails, a riding stable and tennis courts. Special note for RV campers: a full hookup gets you 10 percent off anything in the restaurant.

48. ROCK GARDEN RV PARK   RV

Reference: **Map A4, grid f2.**

Campsites, facilities: There are approximately 100 tent sites and 22 sites for trailers or RVs. Piped water, restrooms, showers, a sanitary dump, a private phone, a playground and a laundromat are provided. The facilities are **wheelchair accessible**. Pets are permitted on leashes.

Reservations, fee: No reservations necessary; $5-$10 fee per night.

Who to contact: Phone the park at (509) 686-5343 or write to P.O. Box 322, Bridgeport, WA 98813.

Location: From Interstate 5 south of Bellingham, turn east on Highway 20 and drive approximately 174 miles east. At Okanogan, turn south on US 97 and drive 27 miles to Brewster. Turn southeast on Highway 173; the campground is located on Highway 173 between Bridgeport and Brewster on the left. The turnoff is well-signed.

Trip note: This large campground is a good alternative if nearby Bridgeport State Park is full. It is rarely crowded here even in the busy summer months. The sites are open and grassy, surrounded by trees. Nearby side trip options include Alta Lake State Park and Lake Chelan to the south.

49. BRIDGEPORT STATE PARK   RV

Reference: **On Rufus Woods Lake; map A4, grid f2.**

Campsites, facilities: There are 14 sites for tents or self-contained RVs, and 20 sites with water and electrical hookups for trailers or RVs up to 45 feet. Eight group campsites are also available. Piped water, fire grills and picnic tables are provided. Flush toilets, showers, firewood and a sanitary disposal station are available. A store, a cafe and ice are located within one mile. Leashed pets are permitted. Boat docks and launching facilities are nearby on both the upper and lower portions of the reservoir.

Reservations, fee: No reservations; $10-$16 fee per night. Open April to late October.

Who to contact: Phone (800) 233-0321 or (509) 686-7231 or write to P.O. Box 846, Bridgeport, WA 98813.

Location: From Interstate 5 south of Bellingham, turn east on Highway 20 and drive approximately 174 miles east. At Okanogan, turn south on US 97 and drive 21 miles, then turn south on Highway 17 and drive eight miles southeast to the park entrance.

Trip note: This park is set along the shore of Rufus Woods Lake, a reservoir on the Columbia River above the Chief Joseph Dam. There is beach access and a boat launch. There are also hiking trails, but the parks department warns that there are rattlesnakes in certain areas. Nearby recreation options include an 18-hole golf course.

50. KELLER FERRY   RV

Reference: **On Franklin Roosevelt Lake in Coulee Dam National Recreation Area; map A4, grid f8.**

Campsites, facilities: There are 50 sites for tents, trailers or RVs up to 16 feet long. Piped water, fire grills and picnic tables are provided. Flush toilets, sanitary services, ice and a playground are available. A cafe is located within one mile. Leashed pets are permitted. Boat docks, launching facilities, fuel and marine dump station are also available.

Reservations, fee: No reservations; $10 fee per night, May through August; $6 launch fee. Open all year, weather permitting.

Who to contact: Phone the Coulee Dam National Recreation Area at (509) 633-9441 or write to 1008 Crest Drive, Coulee Dam, WA 99116.

Location: From Interstate 90 at the town of Moses Lake, turn north on Highway 17 and drive 45 miles, then turn east on US 2 and travel 34 miles to Wilbur. Turn north on Highway 21 and drive 14 miles to the campground.

Trip note: This campground is set along the shore of Franklin Roosevelt Lake, a large reservoir created by the Grand Coulee Dam, about 15 miles west of camp. Waterskiing, fishing and swimming are all options here.

51. LAKESHORE TRAILER PARK & MARINA 🚐

Reference: **On Lake Chelan; map A4, grid g0.**

Campsites, facilities: There are 160 sites for trailers or RVs of any length. Electricity, piped water, sewer hookups and picnic tables are provided. Flush toilets, sanitary services, showers, a store, a cafe, a laundromat, ice, a playground, bottled gas are available within one mile. Boat docks and launching facilities are nearby.

Reservations, fee: Reservations accepted; $11-$24.50 fee per night. Open March to November.

Who to contact: Phone (509) 682-8024 or write to P.O. Box 1669, Chelan, WA 98816.

Location: From Interstate 5 at Everett, turn east on US 2 and drive 106 miles to the junction with US 97. Turn north on US 97 and drive 40 miles to Chelan. Turn north on Highway 150 (Manson Road) and drive one-half mile to the park on the left.

Trip note: This municipal park and marina on Lake Chelan serves all members of the family, with fishing, swimming, boating and hiking among the available activities. Nearby recreation options include an 18-hole golf course, a miniature golf course and lighted tennis courts. A visitor center is nearby. A trip worth taking is the ferry ride to one of several landings on the lake.

52. STEAMBOAT ROCK STATE PARK 🚐

Reference: **On Banks Lake; map A4, grid g5.**

Campsites, facilities: There are two primitive tent sites, five sites for tents or self-contained RVs and 100 sites with full hookups for trailers or RVs up to 60 feet. 13 boat-in campsites are available as well. Picnic tables and fire grills are provided. Flush toilets, a cafe and a playground are available. Electricity, piped water, sewer hookups and showers can be obtained for an extra fee. Some facilities are **wheelchair accessible.** Pets are permitted. Boat launching facilities are nearby.

Reservations, fee: Contact Reservations Northwest at (800) 452-5687 ($6 reservation fee); $5-$16 fee per night; Open all year with limited winter facilities.

Who to contact: Phone (800) 233-0321 or (509) 633-1304 or write to P.O. Box 352, Electric City, WA 99123.

Location: From Seattle on Interstate 90, drive about 200 miles east to the town of Moses Lake. Turn north on Highway 17 and drive 45 miles. Turn east on US 2 and drive five miles, then turn north on Highway 155 and drive 18 miles to the park on the left.

Trip note: This state park is set along the shores of Banks Lake, a reservoir a few miles down from the Grand Coulee Dam. There is a swimming beach, and fishing and waterskiing are popular. Horse trails are available in nearby Northrup Canyon. During the winter, the park is used by snowmobilers, cross-country skiers and ice fishermen.

53.   SPRING CANYON   RV

Reference: **On Franklin Roosevelt Lake in Coulee Dam National Recreation Area; map A4, grid g6.**

Campsites, facilities: There are 87 sites for tents, trailers or self-contained RVs up to 26 feet long. Piped water, fire grills and picnic tables are provided. Flush toilets, sanitary services, a cafe and a playground are available. Some facilities are **wheelchair accessible**. Leashed pets are permitted. Boat docks and launching facilities are available.

Reservations, fee: No reservations; $10 fee per night, May through August; $6 launch fee. Open all year, weather permitting.

Who to contact: Phone the Coulee Dam National Recreation Area at (509) 633-9441 or write to 1008 Crest Drive, Coulee Dam, WA 99116.

Location: From Seattle on Interstate 90, drive about 200 miles east to the town of Moses Lake. Turn north on Highway 17 and drive 45 miles. Turn east on US 2 and drive five miles, then turn north on Highway 155 and continue 26 miles to Grand Coulee. Turn east on Highway 174 and drive three miles to the campground entrance.

Trip note: This is a large, developed campground that is a popular vacation destination. Fishing for bass, walleye, trout and sunfish are popular at the Franklin Roosevelt Lake. And, if you don't like to fish, try waterskiing. The campground is not far from the Grand Coulee Dam. Coulee Dam National Recreation Area offers numerous recreation options, such as programs conducted by rangers that include guided canoe trips, historical tours, campfire talks and guided hikes. All programs are free of charge. This lake is known as a prime location to view bald eagles, especially in the winter months. Side trip options include visiting the Colville Tribal Museum in the town of Coulee Dam and touring the Grand Coulee Dam Visitor Center.

54.   LAKEVIEW TERRACE MOBILE PARK   RV

Reference: **Near Franklin Roosevelt Lake; map A4, grid g6.**

Campsites, facilities: There are 20 tent sites and 15 drive-through sites for trailers or RVs of any length. Electricity, piped water, sewer hookups and picnic tables are provided. Flush toilets, showers, a laundromat and a playground are available. Pets and motorbikes are permitted. Boat docks, launching facilities and rentals are nearby.

Reservations, fee: Reservations accepted; $10-$15 fee per night. Open all year.

Who to contact: Phone (509) 633-2169 or write to Highway 174, Grand Coulee, WA 99133.

Location: From Seattle on Interstate 90, drive about 200 miles east to the town of Moses Lake. Turn north on Highway 17 and drive 45 miles. Turn east on US 2 and drive five miles, then turn north on Highway 155 and continue 26 miles to Grand Coulee. Turn east on Highway 174 and drive 3.5 miles east to the park entrance.

Trip note: This pleasant resort is set near Franklin Roosevelt Lake, which is created by the Grand Coulee Dam. It is a slightly less crowded option to the national park camps in the vicinity. See the trip note for Spring Canyon for water recreation options. A full-service marina and tennis courts are nearby.

55. COULEE PLAYLAND RESORT & RV PARK 🚐

Reference: **Near Grand Coulee Dam; map A4, grid g6.**

Campsites, facilities: There are 65 sites for tents, trailers or RVs of any length. Electricity, piped water, sewer hookups and picnic tables are provided. Flush toilets, sanitary services, a store, a laundromat, showers, firewood, ice, a playground and a bait and tackle store are available. Bottled gas and a cafe are located within one mile. Pets and motorbikes are permitted. Boat docks, launching facilities and rentals are nearby.

Reservations, fee: Reservations accepted; $14-$18 fee per night; MasterCard, Visa, American Express and Discover accepted. Open all year.

Who to contact: Phone (509) 633-2671 or write to P.O. Box 457, Electric City, WA 99123.

Location: From Seattle on Interstate 90, drive about 200 miles east to the town of Moses Lake. Turn north on Highway 17 and drive 45 miles, then turn east on US 2 and drive five miles. Turn north on Highway 155 and drive 26 miles to Grand Coulee. Continue five miles north on Highway 155 to Electric City. The campground is just off the highway.

Trip note: This park is set on North Banks Lake, south of Grand Coulee Dam. It's a pretty park, well-treed with spacious sites for both tents and RVs. The Grand Coulee Laser Light Show is just two miles away and well worth a visit. Nearby recreation options include hiking trails, marked bike trails, a full-service marina and tennis courts.

56. RIVER RUE RV PARK 🚐

Reference: **Near Columbia River; map A4, grid j8.**

Campsites, facilities: There are 60 sites for tents, trailers or RVs. Restrooms, showers, a sanitary dump, a private phone, limited groceries, ice, snacks, RV supplies, fishing tackle and LP gas are available. Recreational facilities include a playground, a recreation field and horseshoe pits. The facilities are **wheelchair accessible**. Pets are permitted on leashes.

Reservations, fee: Reservations recommended; $11-$16 fee per night. Visa and MasterCard are accepted. Open from April through October.

Who to contact: Phone the park at (509) 647-2647 or write to HCR 11, Box 20, Wilbur, WA 99185.

Location: From Spokane, drive west on Highway 2 for about 66 miles (one mile past Wilbur). Turn north on Highway 174 and drive one-quarter mile. Turn north on Highway 21 and drive 13 miles to the park on the right at mile marker 81.

Trip note: This camp is set in high desert terrain, but surrounded by lots of trees. Several hiking trails are available from the campground. It is one mile from the Columbia River, where you can fish, swim, waterski or rent a houseboat. Another nearby side trip is the Grand Coulee Dam.

57. BLUE LAKE RESORT 🚐

Reference: **On Blue Lake; map A4, grid i4.**

Campsites, facilities: There are 30 tent sites and 56 sites (10 drive-through) for trailers or RVs of any length. Electricity, piped water, sewer hookups and picnic tables are provided. Flush toilets, sanitary services, firewood, showers, a store, ice and a playground are available. Pets and motorbikes are permitted. Boat docks, launching facilities and rentals are nearby.

Reservations, fee: Reservations accepted; $12.50 fee per night. Open April to October.

Who to contact: Phone (509) 632-5364 or write to 31199 Highway 17 North, Coulee City, WA 99115.

Location: From Seattle on Interstate 90, drive about 200 miles east to the town of Moses Lake. Turn north on Highway 17 and drive approximately 34 miles to the park on the right.

Trip note: This park is set in a desert-like area along the shore of Blue Lake between Sun Lakes State Park and Lake Lenore Caves State Park. Both offer excellent side trip options. Activities at Blue Lake include trout fishing, swimming and boating. Tackle and boat rentals are available at the resort.

58. SUN LAKES STATE PARK RV

Reference: **On Park Lake; map A4, grid i4.**

Campsites, facilities: There are 174 sites for tents or self-contained RVs, 10 group campsites and 18 sites with full hookups for trailers or RVs up to 50 feet long. Picnic tables are provided. Flush toilets, sanitary disposal station, a cafe, a laundromat, ice, a swimming pool, electricity, piped water, sewer hookups, showers and firewood are available. A store is located within one mile. Some facilities are **wheelchair accessible**. Pets are permitted. Boat docks, launching facilities and rentals are nearby.

Reservations, fee: Contact Reservations Northwest at (800)452-5687 ($6 reservation fee); $11-$16 fee per night. Open all year.

Who to contact: Phone (800) 233-0321 or (509)632-5583 or write to Star Route 1, P.O. Box 136, Coulee City, WA 99115.

Location: From Seattle on Interstate 90, drive about 200 miles east to the town of Moses Lake. Turn north on Highway 17 and drive 38 miles to the park on your right.

Trip note: Sun Lakes State Park is set along the shore of Park Lake, which is used primarily by boaters and waterskiers. The Lake Lenore Caves can be reached by a trail at the north end of the lake. Dry Falls and the interpretive center are also within the park boundaries. Nearby recreation options include an 18-hole golf course, hiking trails and a riding stable.

59. COULEE CITY PARK RV

Reference: **On Banks Lake; map A4, grid i5.**

Campsites, facilities: There are 60 tent sites and 60 sites (nine drive-through) for trailers or RVs up to 35 feet long. Electricity, piped water, sewer hookups and picnic tables are provided. Flush toilets, sanitary services, showers and a playground are available. Bottled gas, firewood, a store, a cafe, a laundromat and ice are located within one mile. Boat docks and launching facilities are nearby.

Reservations, fee: No reservations; $8-$10 fee per night. Open mid-April to October.

Who to contact: Phone (509) 632-5331 or write to P.O. Box 398, Coulee City, WA 99115.

Location: From Seattle on Interstate 90, drive about 200 miles east to the town of Moses Lake. Turn north on Highway 17 and drive 45 miles, then turn east on US 2 and drive two miles to Coulee City. Continue one mile east on US 2 to the park.

Trip note: This park is set along the south shore of 30-mile-long Banks Lake, where boating, fishing and waterskiing are popular. Nearby recreation options include an 18-hole golf course.

---

60. SUN VILLAGE RESORT RV

Reference: **On Blue Lake; map A4, grid i4.**

Campsites, facilities: There are six tent sites and 100 sites (65 drive-through) for trailers or RVs of any length. Electricity, piped water, sewer hookups and picnic tables are provided. Flush toilets, bottled gas, sanitary services, a store, a cafe, a laundromat, ice and a playground are available. Showers and firewood can be obtained for an extra fee. Pets and motorbikes are permitted. Boat docks, launching facilities and rentals are nearby.

Reservations, fee: Reservations accepted; $12-$16 fee per night. MasterCard and Visa accepted. Open mid-April to October.

Who to contact: Phone (509) 632-5664 or write to 33575 Park Lake Road NE, Coulee City, WA 99115.

Location: From Seattle on Interstate 90, drive about 200 miles east to the town of Moses Lake. Turn north on Highway 17 and drive 36 miles to Blue Lake. Turn east on Park Lake Road (the south entrance) and drive one-half mile to the resort on the right.

Trip note: Like Blue Lake Resort, this campground is set along the shore of Blue Lake. This is a hot desert setting, perfect for swimming and fishing. See the trip note for Sun Lakes State Park for information on the nearby state parks and other recreation options.

---

61. SUN LAKES PARK RESORT RV

Reference: **Sun Lakes State Recreation Park; map A4, grid i4.**

Campsites, facilities: There are 110 sites (64 drive-through) for trailers or RVs of any length. Electricity, piped water, sewer hookups and picnic tables are provided. Flush toilets, bottled gas, sanitary services, a store, showers, firewood, a cafe, a laundromat, ice, a playground and a swimming pool are available. Pets are permitted. Boat docks, launching facilities and rentals are nearby.

Reservations, fee: Reservations accepted; $14-$16 fee per night; MasterCard and Visa accepted. Open mid-April to November.

Who to contact: Phone (509) 632-5291 or write to 34228 Park Lake Road NE, Coulee City, WA 99115.

Location: From Seattle on Interstate 90, drive about 200 miles east to the town of Moses Lake. Turn north on Highway 17 and drive 40 miles. At Park Lake Road (within Sun Lakes State Park) take a right and drive one mile east to the park.

Trip note: This is the concession that operates within Sun Lakes State Park. It offers full facilities and is slightly more developed option to the state campground. See the trip note for Sun Lakes State Park.

62.   COULEE LODGE RESORT   RV

Reference: **On Blue Lake; map A4, grid i4.**

Campsites, facilities: There are 14 tent sites and 28 sites (14 drive-through) for trailers or RVs up to 35 feet. Electricity, piped water, sewer hookups and picnic tables are provided. Flush toilets, bottled gas, sanitary services, a store, showers, firewood, a laundromat and ice are available. A cafe is located within one mile. Some facilities are **wheelchair accessible**. Pets and motorbikes are permitted. Boat docks, launching facilities and rentals are nearby.

Reservations, fee: Reservations accepted; $12-$15 fee per night. MasterCard and Visa accepted. Open mid-April to October.

Who to contact: Phone (509) 632-5565 or write to HCR-1, P.O. Box 156, Coulee City, WA 99115.

Location: From Seattle on Interstate 90, drive about 200 miles east to the town of Moses Lake. Turn north on Highway 17 and drive 39 miles to the park on the right.

Trip note: This is one of five camps in the general area and one of three in the immediate vicinity. Blue Lake offers plenty of summertime recreation options. See the trip note for Sun Lakes State Park for details.

LEAVE NO TRACE TIPS

Travel and camp with care.

On the trail:

• Stay on designated trails.
Walk single file in the middle of the path.

• Do not take shortcuts on switchbacks.

• When traveling cross-country where there are no trails,
follow animal trails or spread out your group so no new routes are created.
Walk along the most durable surfaces available,
such as rock, gravel, dry grasses, or snow.

• Use a map and compass to eliminate the need for
rock cairns, tree scars, or ribbons.

• If you encounter pack animals, step to the downhill side
of the trail and speak softly to avoid startling them.

At camp:

• Choose an established, legal site that will not be damaged by your stay.

• Restrict activities to areas where vegetation is compacted or absent.

• Control pets at all times, or leave them at home
with a sitter. Remove dog feces.

MAP A5

WASHINGTON MAP .... see page 90
Adjoining Maps

73 LISTINGS
PAGES 244-273

NORTH .... no map
EAST .... no map
SOUTH (B5) .... see page 372
WEST (A4) .... see page 216

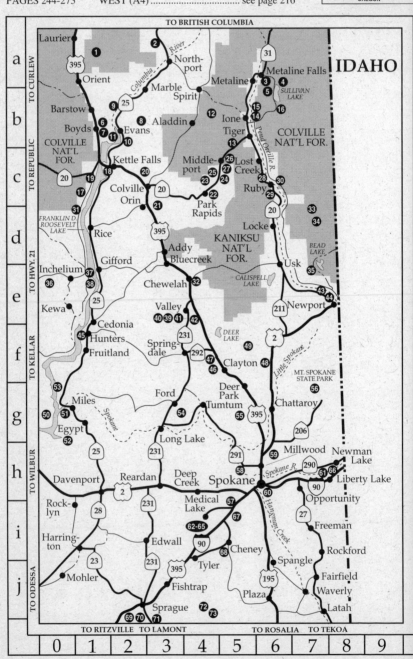

TO BRITISH COLUMBIA

IDAHO

a
Laurier
① ②
Orient
② North-port
③1

b
Barstow
⑨ ②5
⑥
Boyds
⑦
⑪ Evans
⑩
⑧ Aladdin
Marble Spirit
Metaline
Metaline Falls
④
⑤
SULLIVAN LAKE
⑫ Ione
⑮ ⑯
⑭
Tiger
COLVILLE NAT'L FOR.

c
COLVILLE NAT'L FOR.
Kettle Falls
⑳
②0 Colville
Orin
②0
②1 ②2
Park Rapids
Middle-port
②6 Lost Creek
②5 ②7
②3 ②4
Ruby
②8 ③0
②9
②0
③3
③4

d
②0
⑰
③1
FRANKLIN D. ROOSEVELT LAKE
Rice
Gifford
③95
Addy
Bluecreek
KANIKSU NAT'L FOR.
Locke
Usk
BEAD LAKE
③5

e
Inchelium
③7
③6
③8
②5
Kewa
Chewelah
③2
CALISPELL LAKE
Valley
④0 ③9 ④1 ④2
②31
Newport
②11
④3
④4

f
Cedonia
⑤3
Hunters
Fruitland
④5
Spring-dale
②92 ④7
④6
Clayton
④8
DEER LAKE
④9
Little Spokane

g
Miles
⑤0 ⑤1
Egypt
⑤2
Spokane
Ford
⑤4
Deer Park
Tumtum
⑤5
③95
Chattaroy
MT. SPOKANE STATE PARK
⑤6
②06

h
Davenport
②5
Reardan
②
Long Lake
②31
Deep Creek
②91
⑤8
Spokane
⑤9 Millwood
②90
⑥1 ⑥6
Newman Lake
Liberty Lake
⑥0
Opportunity
⑨0

i
Rock-lyn
②8
Harring-ton
②3
Edwall
②31
Medical Lake
⑤7
⑥7
⑥2-65
⑨0
Cheney
⑥8
②7
Freeman
Rockford
Spangle
Hangman Creek

j
Mohler
Tyler
③95
Fishtrap
Sprague
⑥9 ⑦0 ⑦1
⑦2 ⑦3
Plaza
①95
Fairfield
Waverly
Latah

TO CURLEW
TO REPUBLIC
TO HWY. 21
TO KELLAR
TO WILBUR
TO ODESSA

TO RITZVILLE   TO LAMONT   TO ROSALIA   TO TEKOA

0 1 2 3 4 5 6 7 8 9

Washington Map A5 featuring: Colville National Forest, Pierre Lake, Sheep Creek, Sullivan Lake, Columbia River, Franklin Roosevelt Lake, Coulee Dam National Recreation Area, Williams Lake, Pend Oreille River, Lake Leo, Big Meadow Lake, Lake Ellen, Rocky Lake, Deep Lake, Twin Lakes, Lake Thomas, Lake Gillette, Skookum Lake, Browns Lake, Waitts Lake, Jump Off Joe Lake, Box Canyon Reservoir, Eloika Lake, Loon Lake, Spokane River, Spokane, Mount Spokane, Medical Lake, Silver Lake, Turnbull National Wildlife Refuge, Clear Lake, Sprague Lake, Williams Lake

---

1.　　　　　　　　PIERRE LAKE　　　　　　　　　RV.

Reference: **On Pierre Lake in Colville National Forest; map A5, grid a1.**

Campsites, facilities: There are 15 sites for tents, trailers or RVs up to 24 feet long. Hand-pumped water, fire grills and picnic tables are provided. Vault toilets, boat docks and launching facilities are available. A store and ice are located within seven miles. Leashed pets are permitted.

Reservations, fee: No reservations; no fee. Open mid-April to mid-October.

Who to contact: Phone the Colville National Forest at (509) 738-6111 or write to Kettle Falls Ranger District, Kettle Falls, WA 99141.

Location: From Spokane, turn north on US 395 and drive 74 miles to Colville. Continue for about 25 miles north on US 395 to Barstow. Turn north on County Road 4013 and drive nine miles to the campground.

Trip note: This campground is set along the shore of Pierre Lake, a quiet, little-known jewel near the Canadian border. It is only a short drive from US 395, yet the campground gets relatively little use. Boating, fishing and hiking are some of your recreation options here.

2.　　　　　　　　SHEEP CREEK

Reference: **On Sheep Creek; map A5, grid a3.**

Campsites, facilities: There are 11 campsites for tents or small trailers. Picnic tables, fire grills and tent pads are provided. Vault toilets, piped water and a group shelter are available. Leashed pets are permitted.

Reservations, fee: No reservations; no fee. Open all year.

Who to contact: Phone the Department of Natural Resources at (509) 684-7474 or write to Department of Natural Resources, Northeast Region, P.O. Box 190, Colville, WA 99114-0190.

Location: From Spokane, turn north on US 395 and drive 84 miles to Kettle Falls. Turn north on Highway 25 and drive 33 miles to Northport. Continue one mile north on Highway 25, then turn left on Sheep Creek Road and travel four miles. Turn right into the campground.

Trip note: This campground is set in a forested area along Sheep Creek, about four miles from the Columbia River, and very close to the Canadian border. It's a primitive camp, yet it has piped water. The fishing can be good nearby.

3.　　　　　　　　MILL POND　　　　　　　　　RV.

Reference: **Near Sullivan Lake in Colville National Forest; map A5, grid a6.**

Campsites, facilities: There are 10 sites for tents, trailers or RVs up to 21 feet long. Piped water, fire grills and picnic tables are provided. Vault toilets are available. A trailer dump station is located within one mile. Leashed pets are permitted. A small boat launch is available.

Reservations, fee: For reservation and fee information, phone Sullivan Lake Ranger District at (509) 446-7500. Open late May to early September.

Who to contact: Phone the Colville National Forest at (509) 446-7500 or write to Sullivan Lake Ranger District, 12641 Sullivan Lake Road, Metaline Falls, WA 99153.

Location: From Spokane on Interstate 90, turn north on US 2 and drive 48 miles to the junction with Highway 20 at the Washington/Idaho border. Turn west on Highway 20 and drive 48 miles northwest to Tiger, then turn north on Highway 31 and drive 15 miles to the town of Metaline Falls. Turn east on County Road 9345 and drive 3.5 miles to the campground.

Trip note: This campground is set along the shore of a small reservoir just north of Sullivan Lake. This is a good base camp for backpackers. A trail starts across the road and takes off into the backcountry. A **wheelchair-accessible** historical interpretive trail is located at the opposite end of the lake. There's also a pretty waterfall with a great view. All amenities are a few minutes drive away in Metaline Falls. See trip note for Sullivan Lake for other information about the area.

---

4. EAST SULLIVAN   RV

Reference: **On Sullivan Lake in Colville National Forest; map A5, grid a6.**

Campsites, facilities: There are 38 sites for tents, trailers or RVs up to 50 feet long. Piped water, fire grills and picnic tables are provided. Vault toilets and a trailer dump station are available. Some facilities are **wheelchair accessible**. Leashed pets are permitted. Boat docks and launching facilities are nearby.

Reservations, fee: For reservation and fee information, phone Sullivan Lake Ranger District at (509) 446-7500. Open late May to September.

Who to contact: Phone the Colville National Forest at (509) 446-7500 or write to Sullivan Lake Ranger District, 12641 Sullivan Lake Road, Metaline Falls, WA 99153.

Location: From Spokane on Interstate 90, turn north on US 2 and drive 48 miles to the junction with Highway 20 at the Washington/Idaho border. Turn west on Highway 20 and drive 48 miles northwest to Tiger, then turn north on Highway 31 and drive 15 miles to the town of Metaline Falls. Turn east on County Road 9345 and drive five miles. Turn east on Forest Service Road 22 and drive two-tenths of a mile to the campground.

Trip note: This campground is set along the north shore of Sullivan Lake. This is a popular vacation destination, with boating, fishing, swimming, sailing, waterskiing and hiking trails among the activities available. The beautiful Salmo-Priest Wilderness is located just three miles to the east. It gets light use, which means quiet, private trails. This is a prime place to view wildlife, including the rare Woodland caribou and Rocky Mountain bighorn sheep. A nearby grass airstrip provides an opportunity for fly-in camping.

---

5. WEST SULLIVAN   RV

Reference: **On Sullivan Lake in Colville National Forest; map A5, grid a6.**

Campsites, facilities: There are six sites for tents, trailers or RVs up to 30 feet long. Piped water, fire grills and picnic tables are provided. Vault toilets are available. A trailer dump station is located within one mile. Some facilities are wheelchair accessible. Leashed pets are permitted.

Reservations, fee: Some sites may be reserved by calling (800) 280-CAMP. Contact the Sullivan Lake Ranger District for fees. Open late May through August.

Who to contact: Phone the Colville National Forest at (509) 446-7500 or write to Sullivan Lake Ranger District, 12641 Sullivan Lake Road, Metaline Falls, WA 99153.

Trip note: This campground is set along the northwestern shore of Sullivan Lake and is a popular destination for boating, fishing, swimming, sailing, waterskiing and hiking. A nearby grass airstrip provides the opportunity for fly-in camping.

---

6. WHISPERING PINES RV PARK ℝV

Reference: **On Columbia River; map A5, grid b1.**

Campsites, facilities: There are 15 tent sites and 42 sites for trailers or RVs of any length (40 are drive-through). Electricity, sewer hookups and picnic tables are provided. Flush toilets, sanitary services, a laundromat, a playground, piped water, showers and firewood are available. Leashed pets are permitted.

Reservations, fee: Reservations accepted; $14 fee per night. Open all year.

Who to contact: Phone (509) 738-2593 or write to P.O. Box 778, Kettle Falls, WA 99141.

Location: From Spokane on Interstate 90, turn north on US 395 and drive 84 miles to the town of Kettle Falls. Continue 6.5 miles north on US 395. Turn east at the sign for the campground and drive 300 yards to the entrance.

Trip note: This campground is a good layover for US 395 motor home cruisers. It is set along the shore of the Columbia River. Nearby recreation options include marked bike trails, a full-service marina and tennis courts. A good side trip is to Colville National Forest East Portal Interpretive Area, which is less than 10 miles away. To reach it, drive south to the junction of Highway 20 and go southwest for about six miles. There's a nature trail and the Bangs Mountain Auto Tour, a five-mile drive that takes you through old-growth forest to Bangs Mountain Vista, which overlooks the Columbia River-Kettle Falls area.

---

7. KAMLOOPS

Reference: **On Franklin Roosevelt Lake, Coulee Dam National Recreation Area; map A5, grid b1.**

Campsites, facilities: There are 14 tent sites. Picnic tables and fire grills are provided. Pit toilets are available, but there is **no piped water**. Leashed pets are permitted. Boat docks are nearby.

Reservations, fee: No reservations; no fee. Open all year, weather permitting.

Who to contact: Phone the Coulee Dam National Recreation Area at (509) 633-9441 or write to 1008 Crest Drive, Coulee Dam, WA 99116.

Location: From Spokane on Interstate 90, turn north on US 395 and drive 84 miles to the town of Kettle Falls. Continue seven miles west and then north on US 395 to the campground.

Trip note: This is one of the more primitive campsites located along Franklin Roosevelt Lake. It is set at Kamloops Island, an optimum area for waterskiing and fishing.

8.   WILLIAMS LAKE

Reference: **On Williams Lake; map A5, grid b2.**

Campsites, facilities: There are eight sites for tents or small trailers. Picnic tables, fire grills and tent pads are provided. Vault toilets, piped water and a boat launch are available. Leashed pets are permitted.

Reservations, fee: No reservations; no fee. Open all year.

Who to contact: Phone the Department of Natural Resources at (509) 684-7474 or write to Department of Natural Resources, Northeast Region, P.O. Box 190, Colville, WA 99114-0190.

Location: From Spokane, turn north on US 395 and drive 74 miles to Colville. Continue 1.5 miles north, then head north on Williams Lake Road and drive 15.2 miles. Turn left and then immediately left again.

Trip note: With a plethora of camps set on nearby Franklin Roosevelt Lake, this secluded spot provides a less crowded alternative. It is set along the shore of Williams Lake, where the trout fishing is good. In winter, ice fishing is an option. It's a pretty, forested setting.

9.   NORTH GORGE   RV

Reference: **On Franklin Roosevelt Lake in Coulee Dam National Recreation Area; map A5, grid b2.**

Campsites, facilities: There are 10 sites for tents, trailers or RVs. Piped water, fire grills and picnic tables are provided. Pit toilets, boat docks and launching facilities are available. Leashed pets are permitted.

Reservations, fee: No reservations; $10 fee per night; $6 launch fee. Open all year.

Who to contact: Phone the Coulee Dam National Recreation Area at (509) 633-9441 or write to 1008 Crest Drive, Coulee Dam, WA 99116.

Location: From Spokane on Interstate 90, turn north on US 395 and drive 84 miles to the town of Kettle Falls. Turn north on Highway 25 and drive approximately 20 miles to the campground entrance.

Trip note: This is the first of many campgrounds we discovered along the shore of 130-mile-long Franklin Roosevelt Lake, which was formed by damming the Columbia River at Coulee. Recreation options include waterskiing and swimming. There is also fishing for walleye, trout, bass and sunfish. During winter, the lake level is drawn down and a unique trip is to walk along the barren lake's edge. See Kamloops camp for further recreation information.

10.   EVANS   RV

Reference: **On Franklin Roosevelt Lake in Coulee Dam National Recreation Area; map A5, grid b2.**

Campsites, facilities: There are 46 sites for tents, trailers or RVs up to 26 feet long. Piped water, fire grills and picnic tables are provided. Flush toilets, a sanitary disposal station, a store, boat docks, launching facilities and a playground are available. Leashed pets are permitted. Some facilities are **wheelchair accessible**.

Reservations, fee: No reservations; $10 fee per night; $6 launch fee. Open year-round with limited facilities in winter.

Who to contact: Phone the Coulee Dam National Recreation Area at (509) 633-9441 or write to 1008 Crest Drive, Coulee Dam, WA 99116.

Location: From Spokane on Interstate 90, turn north on US 395 and drive 84 miles to the town of Kettle Falls. Turn north on Highway 25 and drive eight miles to the campground entrance.

Trip note: Like North Gorge, this campground is set along the shore of Franklin Roosevelt Lake. Fishing, swimming and waterskiing are all options here. See Kamloops for more information.

11.　　　　MARCUS ISLAND　　　　RV.

Reference: **On Franklin Roosevelt Lake in Coulee Dam National Recreation Area; map A5, grid b2.**

Campsites, facilities: There are 20 sites for tents, trailers or RVs up to 20 feet long. Piped water, fire grills and picnic tables are provided. Pit toilets and a boat dock are available. A store is located within one mile. Leashed pets are permitted.

Reservations, fee: No reservations; $10 fee per night. Open all year, weather permitting.

Who to contact: Phone the Coulee Dam National Recreation Area at (509) 633-9441 or write to 1008 Crest Drive, Coulee Dam, WA 99116.

Location: From Spokane on Interstate 90, turn north on US 395 and drive 84 miles to the town of Kettle Falls. Turn north on Highway 25 and continue four miles to the campground.

Trip note: This campground is set just south of Evans and is quite similar to that camp, including being nestled along the lake's edge. Waterskiing, fishing and swimming are the primary recreation options. See the trip note for Kamloops for information about the park and side trip options in the area.

12.　　　　BIG MEADOW LAKE　　　　RV.

Reference: **On Big Meadow Lake in Colville National Forest; map A5, grid b4.**

Campsites, facilities: There are 16 sites for tents, trailers or RVs up to 32 feet long. Fire grills, picnic tables and vault toilets are provided, but there is **no piped water**. A boat launch, restrooms and a **wheelchair-accessible** nature trail are available. Leashed pets are permitted.

Reservations, fee: No reservations; no fee. Open May to October.

Who to contact: Phone the Colville National Forest at (509) 684-7010 or write to Colville Ranger District, 755 South Main, Colville, WA 99114.

Location: From Spokane on Interstate 90, turn north on US 395 and drive 74 miles to Colville. Turn east on Highway 20 and drive one mile, then turn north on the Aladdin Highway and drive 20 miles to Meadow Creek Road. Turn east and travel six miles to the campground. Note: The road surface may be soft and/or rough, depending on the season.

Trip note: Big Meadow Lake is at 3,400 feet with 71 surface acres. This is a quiet, remote camp that is relatively unknown. It is in a beautiful scenic area, and the Forest Service has provided a wildlife viewing platform and an environmental education lab near the campground.

13.　　　　LAKE LEO　　　　RV.

Reference: **On Lake Leo in Colville National Forest; map A5, grid b5.**

Campsites, facilities: There are eight sites for tents, trailers or RVs up to 15 feet long. Hand-pumped water and picnic tables are provided. Pit toilets and firewood are available. Leashed pets are permitted. Boat docks, launching facilities and rentals are nearby.

Reservations, fee: No reservations; $5 fee per night. Open mid-May to mid-September.

Who to contact: Phone the Colville National Forest at (509) 684-7010 or write to Colville Ranger District, 755 South Main, Colville, WA 99114.

Location: From Spokane on Interstate 90, turn north on US 395 and drive 74 miles to Colville. Turn east on Highway 20 and drive 23 miles to the campground.

Trip note: Lake Leo is the northernmost camp on the chain of lakes. This is the quietest of the camps in the immediate vicinity. Frater and Nile lakes, both quite small, are set a mile north. In winter, there is a nordic ski trail that starts adjacent to the camp. Fishing and boating are two options here.

14.   IONE RV PARK AND MOTEL   RV

Reference: **On Pend Oreille River; map A5, grid b5.**

Campsites, facilities: There are seven tent sites and 17 sites for trailers or RVs of any length. Electricity, piped water, sewer hookups and picnic tables are provided. Flush toilets, sanitary services, showers, a laundromat and a playground are available. A store, a cafe and ice are located within one mile. Leashed pets and motorbikes are permitted. Boat docks and launching facilities are nearby.

Reservations, fee: Reservations accepted; $10-$12 fee per night. Open all year.

Who to contact: Phone (509) 442-3213 or write to P.O. Box 730, Ione, WA 99139.

Location: From Spokane on Interstate 90, turn north on US 395 and drive 74 miles to Colville. Turn east on Highway 20 and drive 36 miles, then turn north on Highway 31 and drive four miles to Ione. The campground is located at the end of a bridge off Highway 31, two blocks south of Main Street.

Trip note: This is a good layover for campers with RVs or trailers who want to stay in town. The park is set along the shore of the Pend Oreille River, which offers pan fishing, swimming and boating. There are several bike trails in the area as well.

15.   EDGEWATER   RV

Reference: **On Pend Oreille River in Colville National Forest; map A5, grid b5.**

Campsites, facilities: There are 23 sites for tents, trailers or RVs up to 20 feet long. Piped water, fire grills and picnic tables are provided. Pit toilets are available and leash pets are permitted. A boat launch is nearby.

Reservations, fee: No reservations; no fee. Open late May to early September.

Who to contact: Phone the Colville National Forest at (509) 446-7500 or write to Sullivan Lake Ranger District, 12641 Sullivan Lake Road, Metaline Falls, WA 99153.

Location: From Spokane on Interstate 90, turn north on US 2 and drive 48 miles to the junction with Highway 20 at the Washington/Idaho border. Turn west on Highway 20 and drive 48 miles northwest to Tiger. Turn north on Highway 31 and drive three miles to County Road 9345 (one mile south of Ione). Turn east and drive 300 yards, then turn north on County Road 3669 and drive two miles. Turn west and proceed to the campground.

Trip note: This campground is set along the shore of the Pend Oreille River, about two miles upstream from the Box Canyon Dam. The camp is not far out of Ione, yet it has a rustic feel to it. Waterskiing and fishing are two popular activities.

16. NOISY CREEK ▣

Reference: **On Sullivan Lake in Colville National Forest; map A5, grid b6.**

Campsites, facilities: There are 19 sites for trailers or RVs up to 35 feet long. Piped water, fire grills and picnic tables are provided. Vault toilets are available. Leashed pets are permitted. Boat launching facilities are nearby.

Reservations, fee: For reservation and fee information, contact Sullivan Lake Ranger District at (509) 446-7500. Open late May to early September.

Who to contact: Phone the Colville National Forest at (509) 446-7500 or write to Sullivan Lake Ranger District, 12641 Sullivan Lake Road, Metaline Falls, WA 99153.

Location: From Spokane on Interstate 90, turn north on US 2 and drive 48 miles to the junction with Highway 20 at the Washington/Idaho border. Turn west on Highway 20 and drive 48 miles northwest to Tiger. Turn north on Highway 31 and drive three miles to County Road 9345 (one mile south of Ione). Turn east and drive nine miles to the campground.

Trip note: This campground is situated in an idyllic setting, adjacent to where Noisy Creek pours into Sullivan Lake. Sullivan Lake is about 3.5 miles long and waterskiing is allowed. There is a trail from camp that heads east along Noisy Creek and then north up to Hall Mountain (elevation 6,323 feet), which is bighorn sheep country.

17. LAKE ELLEN ▣

Reference: **On Lake Ellen in Colville National Forest; map A5, grid c1.**

Campsites, facilities: There are 11 sites for tents, trailers or RVs up to 22 feet long. Hand-pumped water and picnic tables are provided. Vault toilets and boat docks are available. Some facilities **are wheelchair accessible.** Leashed pets are permitted.

Reservations, fee: No reservations; no fee. Open mid-April to mid-October.

Who to contact: Phone the Colville National Forest at (509) 738-6111 or write to Kettle Falls Ranger District, 255 West 11th Street, Kettle Falls, WA 99141.

Location: From Spokane, turn north on US 395 and drive approximately 87 miles. Head west on Highway 20 four miles to County Road 3. Turn left and drive south for 4.5 miles, then turn right on County Road 412 and drive five miles to the campground.

Trip note: Fishing and swimming are permitted on this good-sized lake, located about three miles west of the Columbia River and the Coulee Dam National Recreation Area. There are some good hiking trails to the west. See a Forest Service map for details.

18. KETTLE FALLS ▣

Reference: **On Franklin Roosevelt Lake in Coulee Dam National Recreation Area; map A5, grid c1.**

Campsites, facilities: There are 77 sites for tents, trailers or RVs up to 26 feet long. Piped water, fire grills and picnic tables are provided. Flush toilets, a sanitary disposal station, firewood, a cafe and a playground are available. A store is available within one mile. Some facilities are **wheelchair accessible**. Leashed pets are permitted. Boat docks, fuel and launching facilities are available.

Reservations, fee: No reservations; $10 fee per night; $6 launch fee. Open year-round with limited facilities in the winter.

Who to contact: Phone the Coulee Dam National Recreation Area at (509) 633-9441 or write to 1008 Crest Drive, Coulee Dam, WA 99116.

Location: From Spokane on Interstate 90, turn north on US 395 and drive 84 miles to the town of Kettle Falls. Continue two miles west on US 395 to the campground entrance.

Trip note: This is a modern, developed campground that attracts fairly heavy use in the summer months. It is set along the shore of Franklin Roosevelt Lake, where waterskiing, swimming and fishing are all options. In the summer, the rangers offer campfire programs in the evenings.

---

19. CANYON CREEK   RV

Reference: **Near East Portal Historical Site in Colville National Forest; map A5, grid c1.**

Campsites, facilities: There are 12 sites for tents, trailers or RVs up to 30 feet long. Hand-pumped water, fire grills and picnic tables are provided. Vault toilets are available. Some facilities are **wheelchair accessible.** Pets are permitted.

Reservations, fee: No reservations; no fee. Open mid-April to late October.

Who to contact: Phone the Colville National Forest at (509) 738-6111 or write to Kettle Falls Ranger District, 255 West 11th Street, Kettle Falls, WA 99141.

Location: From Spokane, turn north on US 395 and drive approximately 87 miles. Head west on Highway 20 for 11 miles, then turn left and drive south on Forest Road 136 for one-third mile to the campground.

Trip note: This roadside campground is located near Bangs Mountain Driving Tour and within hiking distance of the East Portal Historical Site. It is a very pretty area that is not far from the Columbia River, which offers a myriad of recreation options.

---

20. DOUGLAS FALLS

Reference: **On Mill Creek; map A5, grid c2.**

Campsites, facilities: There are 10 campsites for tents or small trailers. Picnic tables, fire grills and tent pads are provided. Vault toilets and piped water are available. A baseball field is nearby. Leashed pets are permitted.

Reservations, fee: No reservations; no fee. Open April through November.

Who to contact: Phone the Department of Natural Resources at (509) 684-7474 or write to Department of Natural Resources, Northeast Region, P.O. Box 190, Colville, WA 99114-0190.

Location: From Spokane, turn north on US 395 and drive 74 miles to Colville. Turn east on Highway 20, then take Aladdin Road north. Drive two miles, then continue straight for five miles. You'll see the parking area on the left.

Trip note: This campground is set in a wooded area along Mill Creek near Douglas Falls, just outside of town. It is one of the best deals in the state—it has piped water, a beautiful setting, easy access, a waterfall nearby, and even a baseball field—all for free. It is a great camp for families or groups.

---

21. ROCKY LAKE

Reference: **On Rocky Lake; map A5, grid c3.**

Campsites, facilities: There are seven sites for tents or small trailers. Picnic tables, fire grills and tent pads are provided. Vault toilets, piped water and a boat launch are available. Leashed pets are permitted.

Reservations, fee: No reservations; no fee. Open all year.

Who to contact: Phone the Department of Natural Resources at (509) 684-7474 or write to Department of Natural Resources, Northeast Region, P.O. Box 190, Colville, WA 99114-0190.

Location: From Spokane, turn north on US 395 and drive 74 miles to Colville. Turn east on Highway 20 and drive six miles east, then turn right on Rocky Lake Road and continue three miles. Turn right again onto a one-lane gravel road and drive about 100 yards. Stay to the left and continue another 300 yards to the campground.

Trip note: This is not exactly paradise, but it has remarkable recreational diversity nearby. The campground is set on Rocky Lake, a shallow, weedy pond lined with a lot of rocks. But if you backtrack a bit on Rocky Lake Road you'll see the entrance signs for the nearby Little Pend Oreille Habitat Management Area. This is a premium area for hiking, fishing, hunting and photographing wildlife.

22.　　　　FLODELLE CREEK

Reference: On Flodelle Creek; map A5, grid c4.

Campsites, facilities: There are eight campsites for tents or small trailers. Picnic tables, fire grills and tent pads are provided. Vault toilets and piped water are available. Motorbikes are permitted. Leashed pets are permitted.

Reservations, fee: No reservations; no fee. Open all year.

Who to contact: Phone the Department of Natural Resources at (509) 684-7474 or write to Department of Natural Resources, Northeast Region, P.O. Box 190, Colville, WA 99114-0190.

Location: From Spokane, turn north on US 395 and drive 74 miles to Colville. Turn east on Highway 20 and drive 20 miles. Turn right on a two-lane gravel road and travel 300 yards, then turn left and drive 100 yards to the campground entrance.

Trip note: This little-known campground is set along the banks of Flodelle Creek, where hiking, hunting and fishing are quite good. It is advisable to obtain a detailed map of the area from the Department of Natural Resources. Motorbike trails are also available at this camp and are often used, so don't count on a particularly quiet spot.

23.　　　　LITTLE TWIN LAKES　　　RV

Reference: On Little Twin Lakes in Colville National Forest; map A5, grid c4.

Campsites, facilities: There are 20 sites for tents, trailers or RVs up to 16 feet long. Fire grills and picnic tables are provided. There is **no piped water.** Pit toilets and firewood are available. Leashed pets are permitted. Boat docks and launching facilities are located nearby.

Reservations, fee: No reservations; no fee. Open mid-May to late September.

Who to contact: Phone the Colville National Forest at (509) 684-7010 or write to Colville Ranger District, 755 South Main, Colville, WA 99114.

Location: From Spokane, turn north on US 395 and drive 74 miles to Colville. Turn east on Highway 20 and drive 12.5 miles, then turn northeast on County Road 4915 and drive 1.5 miles. Turn north on Forest Service Road 4939 and drive 4.5 miles to the campground.

Trip note: This campground is set along the shore of Little Twin Lakes. It's a pretty, wooded camp with lake views. It's rare to find a pretty lakeside camp with water that's free. See the trip note for North Gorge for more information.

24. GILLETTE ᴿⱽ

Reference: **Near Lake Gillette in Colville National Forest; map A5, grid c5.**

Campsites, facilities: There are 14 sites for tents, trailers or RVs up to 31 feet long. Piped water, fire grills and picnic tables are provided. Vault toilets and sanitary services are available. A store and ice are located within one mile. Some facilities are **wheelchair accessible**. Leashed pets are permitted. Boat docks, launching facilities and rentals are nearby.

Reservations, fee: Some sites may be reserved by calling (800) 280-CAMP ($7.50 reservation fee); $5-$10 fee per night. Open mid-May to late September.

Who to contact: Phone the Colville National Forest at (509) 684-7010 or write to Colville Ranger District, 755 South Main, Colville, WA 99114.

Location: From Spokane on Interstate 90, turn north on US 395 and drive 74 miles to Colville. Turn east on Highway 20 and drive 20 miles. Continue east on County Road 200 for one-half mile to the campground on the right.

Trip note: This campground is near Lake Gillette, just south of Beaver Lodge Resort and Lake Thomas and part of the chain of lakes. This is a beautiful and extremely popular campground; reserve early in the season. There are a few hiking trails in the area. See the trip note for Beaver Lodge Resort for other recreation information.

25. LAKE GILLETTE ᴿⱽ

Reference: **On Lake Gillette in Coleville National Forest; map A5, grid c5.**

Campsites, facilities: There are 30 sites for tents, trailers or RVs up to 31 feet long. Piped water, fire grills and picnic tables are provided. Vault toilets and sanitary services are available. A store and ice are located within once mile. Some facilities are **wheelchair accessible.** Boat docks, launching facilities and rentals are nearby. Leashed pets are permitted.

Reservations, fee: Some sites may be reserved by calling (800) 280-CAMP ($7.50 reservation fee); $5-$10 fee per night. Open mid-May to late September.

Who to contact: Phone the Colville National Forest at (509) 684-7010 or write to Colville Ranger District, 755 South Main, Colville, WA 99114.

Location: From Spokane on Interstate 90, turn north on US 395 and drive 74 miles to Colville. Turn east on Highway 20 and drive 20 miles. Continue east on County Road 200 for one-half mile to the campground on the left.

Trip note: This beautiful and popular campground is right on the shores of Lake Gillette and like neighboring Gillette campground, it fills up fast in the summer. Make reservations early. The camp is popular with ORV users.

26. LAKE THOMAS

Reference: **On Lake Thomas in Colville National Forest; map A5, grid c5.**

Campsites, facilities: There are 15 tent sites. Piped water, fire grills and picnic tables are provided. Vault toilets and firewood are available. Sanitary services are located within one mile. Leashed pets are permitted. Boat docks, launching facilities and rentals are nearby.

Reservations, fee: No reservations; $5 fee per night. Open mid-May to late September.

Who to contact: Phone the Colville National Forest at (509) 684-7010 or write to Colville Ranger District, 755 South Main, Colville, WA 99114.

Location: From Spokane on Interstate 90, turn north on US 395 and drive 74 miles to Colville. Turn east on Highway 20 and drive 20 miles. Continue east on County Road 200 for one mile to the campground.

Trip note: This campground is set along the shore of Lake Thomas. It is a less crowded option to East Gillette camp. See the trip notes for Gillette and Beaver Lodge Resort for recreation information.

27.　　　BEAVER LODGE RESORT　　

Reference: **On Lake Thomas; map A5, grid c5.**

Campsites, facilities: There are 35 sites for trailers or RVs of any length. Several cabins are also available. Electricity, piped water, sewer hookups and picnic tables are provided. Flush toilets, bottled gas, showers, firewood, a recreation hall, a store, a cafe, ice and a playground are available. Sanitary services are located within one mile. Pets and motorbikes are permitted. Boat docks, launching facilities and rentals are nearby.

Reservations, fee: Reservations accepted; $8-$14 fee per night; $40 cabin fee. MasterCard and Visa accepted. Open all year.

Who to contact: Phone (509) 684-5657 or write to 2430 Highway 20 East, Colville, WA 99114.

Location: From Spokane on Interstate 90, turn north on US 395 and drive 74 miles to Colville. Turn east on Highway 20 and drive 25 miles to the lodge on the right.

Trip note: This developed camp is set along the shore of Lake Thomas, one in a chain of seven lakes. Information is available at Little Pend Oreille at the southern end of the chain. At the northern end of the lake chain, at Lake Leo, there is a nordic ski trail during the winter. Nearby recreation options include hiking trails and marked bike trails.

28.　　　BLUESIDE RESORT　　

Reference: **On Pend Oreille River; map A5, grid c6.**

Campsites, facilities: There are 20 tent sites and 46 drive-through sites for trailers or RVs of any length. There are also five cabins available. Electricity, piped water, sewer hookups and picnic tables are provided. Flush toilets, sanitary services, showers, a recreation hall, several recreation fields, a store, a laundromat, ice, firewood, a playground and a swimming pool are available. Pets and motorbikes are permitted. Boat docks, launching facilities, boat fuel and rentals are available.

Reservations, fee: Reservations accepted; $12-$16 fee per night. Open all year with limited winter facilities.

Who to contact: Phone (509) 445-1327 or write to 400041 Highway 20, Cusick, WA 99119.

Location: From Spokane on Interstate 90, turn north on US 2 and drive 48 miles to the junction with Highway 20 at the Washington/Idaho border. Turn west on Highway 20 and drive 37 miles to the park, located at milepost 400 on the right.

Trip note: This resort is set along the shore of the Pend Oreille River, where trout fishing is excellent. The resort offers full facilities for anglers, including tackle, boat rentals and a marina. The park is lovely, with grassy shaded sites. Nearby recreation options include marked bike trails. The only other campground in the vicinity is The Outpost Resort.

29. THE OUTPOST RESORT **RV**

Reference: **On Pend Oreille River; map A5, grid c6.**

Campsites, facilities: There are 30 tent sites and 20 drive-through sites for trailers or RVs of any length. Picnic tables are provided. Flush toilets, sanitary services, a store, a cafe, ice, electricity, piped water, sewer hookups and showers are available. Pets and motorbikes are permitted. Boat docks and launching facilities are nearby.

Reservations, fee: Reservations accepted; $10-$15 fee per night. Open all year with limited winter facilities.

Who to contact: Phone (509) 445-1317 or write to 405351 Highway 20, Cusick, WA 99119.

Location: From Spokane on Interstate 90, turn north on US 2 and drive 48 miles to the junction with Highway 20 at the Washington/Idaho border. Turn west on Highway 20 and drive 33 miles. The resort is between mileage markers 305 and 306.

Trip note: This is a comfortable campground set along the shore of the Pend Oreille River. It has fairly spacious sites and a pretty setting. If you are cruising Highway 20, Blueside Resort is located about five miles north, the nearest alternative if this camp is full.

---

30. PANHANDLE **RV**

Reference: **On Pend Oreille River in Colville National Forest; map A5, grid c6.**

Campsites, facilities: There are 11 sites for tents, trailers or RVs up to 30 feet long. Piped water and picnic tables are provided. Vault toilets are available. Leashed pets are permitted.

Reservations, fee: No reservations; $8 fee per night. Open late May to late September.

Who to contact: Phone the Colville National Forest at (509) 447-7300 or write to Newport Ranger District, 315 North Warren Avenue, Newport, WA 99156.

Location: From Spokane on Interstate 90, turn north on US 2 and drive 48 miles to Newport. Turn west on Highway 20 and drive six miles northwest to the town of Usk. Cross the Pend Oreille River and drive 15 miles north on LeClerc Road. The campground is on the left side.

Trip note: Here is a scenic setting along the shore of the Pend Oreille River. It is a good base camp for a fishing or waterskiing trip. The campground is located directly across the river from The Outpost Resort. A network of hiking trails can be accessed by taking Forest Service roads to the east. See a Forest Service map for details.

---

31. HAAG COVE **RV**

Reference: **On Franklin Roosevelt Lake in Coulee Dam National Recreation Area; map A5, grid d1.**

Campsites, facilities: There are 18 sites for tents, trailers or RVs up to 26 feet long. Piped water, fire grills and picnic tables are provided. Pit toilets and boat docks are available. Leashed pets are permitted.

Reservations, fee: No reservations; $10 fee per night. Open all year, weather permitting.

Who to contact: Phone the Coulee Dam National Recreation Area at (509) 633-9441 or write to 1008 Crest Drive, Coulee Dam, WA 99116.

Location: From Spokane on Interstate 90, turn north on US 395 and drive 84 miles to the town of Kettle Falls. Turn west on Highway 20 and drive 12 miles to County Road 3. Turn south and drive five miles to the campground.

Trip note: This campground is tucked away in a cove along the shore of Franklin Roosevelt Lake (Columbia River). A good side trip is to the Sherman Creek Habitat Management Area, located just north of camp. It is rugged and steep, but a good place to see and photograph wildlife.

---

32. THE NEW 49er MOTEL AND RV PARK 🚐

Reference: **Near Chewelah; map A5, grid d4.**

Campsites, facilities: There are 15 tent sites and 25 sites (three drive-through) for trailers or RVs up to 30 feet long. Electricity, piped water, sewer hookups and picnic tables are provided. Flush toilets, sanitary services, showers, a spa, a recreation hall, ice and a swimming pool are available. Bottled gas, a store, a cafe and a laundromat are located within one mile. Pets are permitted.

Reservations, fee: Reservations accepted; $8-$15 fee per night; MasterCard and Visa accepted. Open all year.

Who to contact: Phone (800) 821-4856 or (509) 935-8613 or write to P.O. Box 124, Chewelah, WA 99109.

Location: From Spokane on Interstate 90, turn north on US 395 and drive 44 miles to Chewelah. The park is on the south edge of town (follow the signs).

Trip note: This is in the heart of mining country. The park is in a wooded, hilly setting next to a motel, with grassy sites. Nearby recreation options include an 18-hole golf course, hiking trails and marked bike trails. This is a good deal for motor home cruisers, a rustic setting in town.

---

33. BROWNS LAKE 🚐

Reference: **On Browns Lake in Colville National Forest; map A5, grid d7.**

Campsites, facilities: There are 18 sites for tents, trailers or RVs up to 21 feet long. Hand-pumped water and picnic tables are provided. Vault toilets are available. Leashed pets are permitted. A primitive boat launch is available for small boats such as canoes, row boats and inflatables.

Reservations, fee: No reservations; $8 fee per night; $4 per extra vehicle. Open late May to late September.

Who to contact: Phone the Colville National Forest at (509) 447-7300 or write to Newport Ranger District, 315 North Warren Avenue, Newport, WA 99156.

Location: From Spokane, turn north on US 2 and drive for 30 miles to the Metaline cutoff (Highway 211). Take Highway 211 for 15 miles to the junction of Highway 20. Cross Highway 20 to the town of Usk. From Usk, continue on Highway 20 across the Pend Oreille River. Turn east on County Road 3389 and drive for 6.5 miles, then turn north on Forest Service Road 5030 and continue three miles to the campground.

Trip note: This campground is set along the shore of Browns Lake about five miles from South Skookum Lake. No motorized boats are permitted on the lake, and only flyfishing is allowed. A hiking trail leaves the campground and ties into a **wheelchair-accessible** interpretive trail with beautiful views along way.

34. SOUTH SKOOKUM LAKE **RV**

Reference: **On South Skookum Lake in Colville National Forest; map A5, grid d7.**

Campsites, facilities: There are 24 sites for tents, trailers or RVs up to 30 feet long. Hand-pumped water and picnic tables are provided. Vault toilets are available. Leashed pets are permitted. A boat launch for small boats and a **wheelchair accessible** dock for fishing are available.

Reservations, fee: No reservations; $8 fee per night; $4 per extra vehicle. Open late May to late September.

Who to contact: Phone the Colville National Forest at (509) 447-7300 or write to Newport Ranger District, 315 North Warren Avenue, Newport, WA 99156.

Location: From Spokane, turn north on US 2 and drive for 30 miles to the Metaline cutoff (Highway 211). Take Highway 211 for 15 miles to the junction of Highway 20. Cross Highway 20 to the town of Usk. From Usk, proceed across the Pend Oreille River and continue east on County Road 3389 for 7.5 miles to the campground.

Trip note: This campground is set along the western shore of South Skookum Lake, at the foot of Kings Mountain (4,383 feet). There is a 1.3-mile-long hiking trail around the lake. A spur trail has an overlook of the lake and a view of Kings Mountain.

---

35. SKOOKUM CREEK

Reference: **Near Pend Oreille River; map A5, grid d7.**

Campsites, facilities: There are 10 sites for tents or small trailers. Picnic tables, fire grills and tent pads are provided. Vault toilets and piped water are available. Leashed pets are permitted.

Reservations, fee: No reservations; no fee. Open all year.

Who to contact: Phone the Department of Natural Resources at (509) 684-7474 or write to Department of Natural Resources, Northeast Region, P.O. Box 190, Colville, WA 99114-0190.

Location: From Spokane, turn north on US 2 and drive 48 miles to Newport. Turn west on Highway 20 and drive 16 miles northwest to the town of Usk. Continue east across the bridge and turn right on LeClerc Road. Drive 2.5 miles, then turn left and drive about 400 yards to the campground on the left.

Trip note: This campground is in a wooded area along Skookum Creek, about 1.5 miles from where it empties into the Pend Oreille River. It's a good canoeing spot, has piped water and gets little attention. You can't beat the price of admission.

---

36. RAINBOW BEACH RESORT **RV**

Reference: **On Twin Lakes Reservoir; map A5, grid e0.**

Campsites, facilities: There are three tent sites and 14 sites for trailers or RVs of any length (five drive-through). Electricity, piped water, sewer hookups and picnic tables are provided. Flush toilets, bottled gas, sanitary services, a shower, firewood, a recreation hall, a store, a laundromat, ice and a playground are available. Pets are permitted. Boat docks, launching facilities and rentals are nearby.

Reservations, fee: Reservations required; $8.50-$14 fee per night; MasterCard and Visa accepted. Open all year.

Who to contact: Phone (509) 722-5901 or write to HC 1, Box 146, Inchelium, WA 99138.

Location: From Spokane on Interstate 90, turn north on US 395 and drive 84 miles to the town of Kettle Falls. Turn east on Highway 20 and drive about five miles to the turnoff for Inchelium. Turn south and drive about 20 miles to Inchelium, then turn west on Bridge Creek-Twin Lakes County Road and drive two miles to Stranger Creek Road. Turn left and drive one-quarter mile to the resort on the right.

Trip note: This resort is set along the shore of Twin Lakes Reservoir. Nearby recreation options include hiking trails, marked bike trails, a full-service marina and tennis courts. You get a unique chance at a quality campground set in the Colville Indian Reservation.

---

37. CLOVER LEAF

Reference: **On Franklin Roosevelt Lake in Coulee Dam National Recreation Area; map A5, grid e1.**

Campsites, facilities: There are eight tent sites. Piped water, fire grills and picnic tables are provided. Pit toilets are available. Leashed pets are permitted. A boat dock is available.

Reservations, fee: No reservations; $10 fee per night from May through August; $6 launch fee. Open all year with limited winter facilities.

Who to contact: Phone the Coulee Dam National Recreation Area at (509) 633-9441 or write to 1008 Crest Drive, Coulee Dam, WA 99116.

Location: From Spokane on Interstate 90, turn west on US 2 and drive 34 miles, then turn north on Highway 25 and drive 61 miles. The campground is located about two miles south of Gifford.

Trip note: This camp is small and quite primitive. In this particular area of Roosevelt Lake, waterskiing is not advised, but fishing is. See the trip notes for North Gorge and Kamloops for recreation details.

---

38. GIFFORD   **RV**

Reference: **On Franklin Roosevelt Lake in Coulee Dam National Recreation Area; map A5, grid e1.**

Campsites, facilities: There are 47 sites for tents, trailers or RVs up to 20 feet long. Piped water, fire grills and picnic tables are provided. Pit toilets are available. Leashed pets are permitted. Boat docks and launching facilities are nearby.

Reservations, fee: No reservations; $10 fee per night from May through August; $6 launch fee. Open all year with limited winter facilities.

Who to contact: Phone the Coulee Dam National Recreation Area at (509) 633-9441 or write to 1008 Crest Drive, Coulee Dam, WA 99116.

Location: From Spokane on Interstate 90, turn west on US 2 and drive 34 miles, then turn north on Highway 25 and drive 60 miles. The campground is located about three miles south of Gifford.

Trip note: This campground is set along the shore of Franklin Roosevelt Lake (Columbia River). Fishing and waterskiing are two of the recreation options here. For a more detailed description of Roosevelt Lake, see the trip notes for North Gorge and Kamloops.

39. WINONA BEACH RESORT & RV PARK

Reference: **On Waitts Lake; map A5, grid e3.**

Campsites, facilities: There are 17 tent sites and 38 drive-through sites for trailers or RVs of any length. Electricity, piped water, sewer hookups and picnic tables are provided. Flush toilets, showers, sanitary services, firewood, a recreation hall, a general store, a cafe, an antique store and ice are available. Pets and motorbikes are permitted. Boat docks, launching facilities and rentals are available on-site.

Reservations, fee: Reservations accepted; $12-$16 fee per night. Open April through October.

Who to contact: Phone (509) 937-2231 or write to Route 1, P.O. Box 38, Valley, WA 99181.

Location: From Spokane on Interstate 90, turn north on US 395 and drive 42 miles. Turn west at Valley exit 1 on Waitts Lake Road and and drive five miles to the resort.

Trip note: This resort is set along the shore of Waitts Lake. It is beautiful and comfortable, with spacious sites and friendly folks. In the spring, the fishing for brown trout and rainbow trout can be quite good. In summer, the trout head to deeper water, and bluegills and perch are easier to catch.

40. SILVER BEACH RESORT

Reference: **On Waitts Lake; map A5, grid e3.**

Campsites, facilities: There are 53 sites (two drive-through) for trailers or RVs of any length. Electricity, piped water, sewer hookups and picnic tables are provided. Flush toilets, bottled gas, sanitary services, a recreation hall, a store, showers, a restaurant, a laundromat, ice and a playground are available. Pets are permitted. Boat docks, launching facilities and rentals are available.

Reservations, fee: Reservations accepted; $13-$16 fee per night. Open late April to late October.

Who to contact: Phone (509) 937-2811 or write to 3323 Waitts Lake Road, Valley, WA 99181.

Location: From Spokane on Interstate 90, turn north on US 395 and drive 38 miles north to the Valley exit, then head west for six miles until you get to Waitts Lake. The resort is on the lake.

Trip note: This resort offers grassy sites set along the shore of Waitts Lake where fishing and waterskiing are popular. See the trip note for Winona Beach Resort and RV Park for information about the lake.

41. TEAL'S WAITTS LAKE

Reference: **On Waitts Lake; map A5, grid e3.**

Campsites, facilities: There are 15 tent sites and 15 sites for trailers or RVs of any length. Electricity, piped water and picnic tables are provided. Flush toilets, bottled gas, sanitary services, showers, a store, firewood, a cafe and ice are available. Boat docks, launching facilities and rentals are nearby.

Reservations, fee: Reservations required; $13.50 fee per night. MasterCard, Visa and Discover accepted. Open early April to late October.

Who to contact: Phone (509) 937-2400 or write to Route 1, P.O. Box 50, Valley, WA 99181.

Location: From Spokane on Interstate 90, turn north on US 395 and drive 42 miles. Then turn north on Highway 232 and drive 1.5 miles and then head west on Highway 231 to Waitts Lake.

Trip note: This resort is set along the shore of Waitts Lake. It is clean and comfortable, with lake views available. See the trip note for Winona Beach Resort and RV Park for information about the lake.

42.   JUMP OFF JOE MOBILE PARK & RESORT   RV

Reference: **On Jump Off Joe Lake; map A5, grid e4.**

Campsites, facilities: There are 10 sites for tents and 19 sites for trailers or RVs. Restrooms, showers, a private phone, horseshoe pits, a recreation field and a barbecue are available. The camp also rents boats and has a boat ramp and dock. The facilities are **wheelchair accessible**. Pets are permitted on leashes.

Reservations, fee: Reservations recommended; $12-$15 fee per night. Open from April through October.

Who to contact: Phone the resort at (509) 937-2133 or write to 3290 East Jump Off Joe Road, Valley, WA 99181.

Location: From Spokane on Interstate 90, turn north on US 395. Take the Jump Off Joe Road exit (three miles south of the town of Valley) and drive west on Jump Off Joe Road for 1.2 miles to the campground on the right.

Trip note: This camp is set on the edge of Jump Off Joe Lake. The campground is wooded, with lake views and easy boating access. Recreational activities include boating, fishing and swimming. Spokane and the Grand Coulee Dam are both within a short drive and provide excellent side trip options.

43.   PIONEER PARK   RV

Reference: **On Pend Oreille River in Colville National Forest; map A5, grid e8.**

Campsites, facilities: There are 14 sites for tents, trailers or RVs up to 24 feet long. Piped water and picnic tables are provided. Vault toilets are available. Leashed pets are permitted. Boat docks, launching facilities and rentals are nearby.

Reservations, fee: No reservations; $8 fee per night. Open late May to late September.

Who to contact: Phone the Colville National Forest at (509) 447-7300 or write to Newport Ranger District, 315 North Warren Avenue, Newport, WA 99156.

Location: From Spokane, turn north on US 2 and drive 41 miles to Newport. Continue across the Pend Oreille River and take an immediate left onto LeClerc Road. Travel two miles to the campground.

Trip note: This campground is set along the shore of Box Canyon Reservoir on the Pend Oreille River near Newport. The launch and adjoining parking area are suitable for larger boats. Waterskiing and water sports are popular here. There is a **wheelchair accessible** interpretive trail with a boardwalk and beautiful views of the river. Signs along the way explain the history of Native Americans who once inhabited the area.

44.   OLD AMERICAN KAMPGROUND   RV

Reference: **Near Pend Oreille River; map A5, grid e8.**

Campsites, facilities: There are 25 tent sites and 50 sites for trailers or RVs of any length. Electricity, piped water, sewer hookups and picnic tables are provided. Flush toilets, sanitary services and showers are available. Bottled gas and a laundromat are available. Boat docks, launching facilities, cable TV and propane gas are available. Pets and motorbikes are permitted.

Reservations, fee: Reservations accepted; $10-$25 fee per night. Open all year.

Who to contact: Phone (509) 447-3663 or write to 701 North Newport Avenue, Newport, WA 99156.

Location: From Spokane at Interstate 90, turn north on US 2 and drive 48 miles to Newport. Turn north on Newport Avenue and drive one block to the campground at the end of the road.

Trip note: This campground is near the Pend Oreille River, right in Newport at the Washington/Idaho border. It is a major junction for this part of the country, where US 2 and Highway 41 intersect. The park is pretty, with river frontage and full facilities for boating and fishing. If you want a more secluded spot, Pioneer Park is about a 15-minute drive away, on the east side of the river.

---

45. HUNTERS RV

Reference: **On Franklin Roosevelt Lake in Coulee Dam National Recreation Area; map A5, grid f1.**

Campsites, facilities: There are 42 sites for tents, trailers or RVs up to 26 feet long. Piped water, fire grills and picnic tables are provided. Flush toilets, a store and ice are available within one mile. Leashed pets are permitted. Boat docks and launching facilities are nearby.

Reservations, fee: No reservations; $10 fee per night from May through August; $6 launch fee. Open all year with limited winter facilities.

Who to contact: Phone the Coulee Dam National Recreation Area at (509) 633-9441 or write to 1008 Crest Drive, Coulee Dam, WA 99116.

Location: From Spokane on Interstate 90, turn west on US 2 and drive 34 miles, then turn north on Highway 25 and drive 47 miles to Hunter. Turn west on the signed access road and proceed to the campground.

Trip note: This campground is set on a shoreline point along Roosevelt Lake (Columbia River). It's a good spot for swimming, fishing or waterskiing. See the trip notes for North Gorge (camp number 9) and Kamloops (camp number 7) for further information on the area.

---

46. SHORE ACRES RV

Reference: **On Loon Lake; map A5, grid f4.**

Campsites, facilities: There are 33 sites for trailers or RVs up to 30 feet long. Electricity, piped water, sewer hookups and picnic tables are provided. Flush toilets, sanitary services, a store, showers, firewood, ice and a playground are available. Motorbikes are permitted. Boat docks, launching facilities and rentals are available.

Reservations, fee: Reservations accepted; $16.50 fee per night. Visa and MasterCard accepted. Open mid-April to late October.

Who to contact: Phone (509) 233-2474 or (800) 900-2474 or write to 401987 Shore Acres Road, Loon Lake, WA 99148.

Location: From Spokane on Interstate 90, turn north on US 395 and drive 30 miles. Then turn west on Highway 292 and drive 1.5 miles to Shore Acres Road. Turn left and drive 1.5 miles to the park.

Trip note: Set along the shore of Loon Lake, this campground offers a long expanse of beach and is an option to Granite Point Rock across the lake. Note: If you're planning on visiting this park on a weekend, be aware of their policy of full-weekend reservations. You can't stay just a Friday or Saturday night — you have to reserve for the whole weekend. See the trip note for Granite Point Rock for details about the fishing.

47.   GRANITE POINT ROCK   🚐

Reference: **On Loon Lake; map A5, grid f4.**

Campsites, facilities: There are 68 sites for trailers or RVs of any length. Electricity, piped water, sewer hookups and picnic tables are provided. Flush toilets, showers, a recreation hall, a store, a cafe, a laundromat, ice and a playground are available. Bottled gas is located within one mile. Pets are not permitted. Boat docks, launching facilities and rentals are nearby.

Reservations, fee: Reservations accepted; $15-$20 fee per night. Open mid-April to mid-September.

Who to contact: Phone (509) 233-2100 or write to 41000 Granite Point Road, Loon Lake, WA 99148.

Location: From Spokane on Interstate 90, turn north on US 395 and drive a total of 26 miles (eight miles past the town of Deer Park) to the campground.

Trip note: This campground is set along the shore of Loon Lake, a clear, clean spring-fed lake. In the spring, the Mackinaw trout range from 4 to 30 pounds and can be taken by deep water trolling, downriggers suggested. Easier to catch are the Kokanee salmon and rainbow trout in the 12- to 14-inch class. A sprinkling of perch, sunfish and bass come out of their hiding places when the weather heats up.

48.   JERRY'S LANDING   🚐

Reference: **On Eloika Lake; map A5, grid f6.**

Campsites, facilities: There are five tent sites and 20 drive-through sites for trailers or RVs of any length. Picnic tables are provided. Flush toilets, sanitary services, a store, ice, electricity, piped water, sewer hookups, showers and firewood are available. Bottled gas is available within one mile. Pets and motorbikes are permitted. Boat docks, launching facilities and rentals are nearby.

Reservations, fee: Reservations accepted; $10-$15 fee per night. Open April to November.

Who to contact: Phone (509) 292-2337 or write to North 41114 Lakeshore Drive, Elk, WA 99009.

Location: From Spokane on Interstate 90, turn north on US 2 and drive 23 miles, then head west on Oregon Road for one mile to the campground.

Trip note: This campground is set along the shore of Eloika Lake. It's a lovely setting, wooded with abundant wildlife. Trout fishing can be excellent as soon as the ice is off the lake in spring. During the hot days of summer, crappie fishing is good.

49.   PEND OREILLE PARK   🚐

Reference: **Map A5, grid f5.**

Campsites, facilities: There are 34 sites for tents and two sites for RVs or trailers. Restrooms, showers and a barbecue are provided. Pets are permitted on leashes.

Reservations, fee: Reservations accepted; $8 fee per night. Open Memorial Day to Labor Day.

Who to contact: Phone the park at (509) 447-4821.

Location: From Spokane on Interstate 90, turn north on US 2 and drive about 30 miles. After you cross the border between Spokane County and Pend Oreille County look for signs for the state park entrance on the left. You'll see the park.

Trip note: This is the only campground around, and it's not a bad choice if you're looking for a layover spot. It's a good alternative to the often-crowded Mount Spokane State Park. There are many hiking trails and nature hikes available on the grounds, and other nearby activities include fishing and hunting.

50.   SEVEN BAYS RESORT AND MARINA   RV

Reference: **On Franklin Roosevelt Lake; map A5, grid g0.**

Campsites, facilities: There are 20 tent sites and 26 sites for trailers or RVs of any length (26 with full hookups, one drive-through). Electricity, piped water, sewer hookups and picnic tables are provided. Flush toilets, bottled gas, sanitary services, showers, a store, a cafe, a laundromat and ice are available. Pets are permitted. Boat docks and launching facilities are nearby.

Reservations, fee: Reservations accepted; $10-$15 fee per night. Senior discounts. Open March to October.

Who to contact: Phone (509) 725-1676 or write to Route 1, P.O. Box 62L, Davenport, WA 99122.

Location: From Spokane on Interstate 90, turn west on US 2 and drive 34 miles to Davenport. Turn north on Highway 25 and continue 23 miles to Miles, then turn south on Creston Road and drive five miles to the resort.

Trip note: This resort is set along the shore of Roosevelt Lake, and is an option to Fort Spokane and Hawk Creek campgrounds. Lakeside sites are the highlight here, along with friendly folks. A full-service marina sets this spot apart from the others.

51.   FORT SPOKANE   RV

Reference: **On Franklin Roosevelt Lake in Coulee Dam National Recreation Area; map A5, grid g0.**

Campsites, facilities: There are 67 sites for tents, trailers or RVs up to 26 feet long. Piped water, picnic tables and fire grills are provided. Flush toilets, sanitary services and a playground are available. A store and ice are located within one mile. Some facilities are **wheelchair accessible**. Leashed pets are permitted. Boat docks, launching facilities and a marine dump station are nearby.

Reservations, fee: No reservations; $10 fee per night from May through August; $6 launch fee. Open all year with limited winter facilities.

Who to contact: Phone the Coulee Dam National Recreation Area at (509) 633-9441 or write to 1008 Crest Drive, Coulee Dam, WA 99116.

Location: From Spokane on Interstate 90, turn west on US 2 and drive 34 miles, then turn north on Highway 25 and drive 26 miles to the campground.

Trip note: This modern campground is set along the shore of Roosevelt Lake. Rangers offer evening campfire programs and guided daytime activities. This is one of 16 campgrounds on 130-mile-long Roosevelt Lake.

52.   HAWK CREEK   RV

Reference: **On Franklin Roosevelt Lake in Coulee Dam National Recreation Area; map A5, grid g0.**

Campsites, facilities: There are 25 sites for tents or trailers and RVs up to 16 feet long. Picnic tables, fire grills and piped water are provided. Pit toilets are available. Leashed pets are permitted. Boat docks and launching facilities are nearby.

Reservations, fee: No reservations; $10 fee per night from May through August; $6 launch fee. Open all year with limited winter facilities.

Who to contact: Phone the Coulee Dam National Recreation Area at (509) 633-9441 or write to 1008 Crest Drive, Coulee Dam, WA 99116.

Location: From Spokane on Interstate 90, turn west on US 2 and drive 34 miles, then turn north on Highway 25 and drive 23 miles to Miles. Turn west on Creston Road and drive 10 miles to the campground at the mouth of Hawk Creek.

Trip note: This is a pleasant camping spot set along the shore of Roosevelt Lake (Columbia River), adjacent to the mouth of Hawk Creek. The bay is a popular fishing spot.

---

53.   PORCUPINE BAY   RV

Reference: **On Franklin Roosevelt Lake in Coulee Dam National Recreation Area; map A5, grid g0.**

Campsites, facilities: There are 31 sites for tents, trailers or RVs up to 20 feet long. Piped water, picnic tables and fire grills are provided. Flush toilets and a playground are available. Leashed pets are permitted. Boat docks and launching facilities are nearby. Some facilities are **wheelchair accessible**.

Reservations, fee: No reservations; $10 fee per night from May through August; $6 launch fee. Open all year, weather permitting.

Who to contact: Phone the Coulee Dam National Recreation Area at (509) 633-9441 or write to 1008 Crest Drive, Coulee Dam, WA 99116.

Location: From Spokane on Interstate 90, turn west on US 2 and drive 34 miles, then turn north on Highway 25 and drive 20 miles. At the sign for the Coulee Dam National Recreation Area, head north on the county road and you'll see the campground.

Trip note: This is a good spot for campers with boats because of its proximity to a nearby dock and launch. A swimming beach is adjacent to the campground.

---

54.   LONG LAKE CAMP AND PICNIC AREA

Reference: **On Spokane River; map A5, grid g3.**

Campsites, facilities: There are seven campsites for tents or small trailers. Picnic tables, fire grills and tent pads are provided. Vault toilets and piped water are available.

Reservations, fee: No reservations; no fee. Open April through September.

Who to contact: Phone the Department of Natural Resources at (509) 684-7474 or write to Department of Natural Resources, Northeast Region, P.O. Box 190 Colville, WA 99114-0190.

Location: From Spokane, turn north on US 2 and drive 21 miles to Reardan. Drive north on Highway 231 for 14 miles, then turn right on Long Lake Dam Road. Drive five miles and turn right into the campground.

Trip note: This is a secret spot that Spokaners should take advantage of. It's about a 45-minute drive out of Spokane and you get a small, quiet spot set along the Spokane River. It has picnic facilities, drinking water, a scenic river view, and it is free. It is slightly more well-known than many of the Department of Natural Resources camps, but still uncrowded.

55.　　　　DRAGOON CREEK

Reference: **Near Little Spokane River; map A5, grid g5.**

Campsites, facilities: There are 22 sites for tents or small trailers. Picnic tables, fire grills and tent pads are provided. Vault toilets and piped water are available. Leashed pets are permitted.

Reservations, fee: No reservations; no fee. Open April through September.

Who to contact: Phone the Department of Natural Resources at (509) 684-7474 or write to Department of Natural Resources, Northeast Region, P.O. Box 190, Colville, WA 99114-0190.

Location: From Spokane, drive north on US 395 for 16 miles. Turn left on Dragoon Creek Road and drive one-half mile to the campground entrance.

Trip note: This spot is not far from US 395, but it's quiet, rustic and set along Dragoon Creek, a tributary to the Little Spokane River. The Department of Natural Resources offers a map that details the area. The area is forested and the camp has shaded sites.

56.　　　MOUNT SPOKANE STATE PARK　　RV

Reference: **On Mount Spokane; map A5, grid g7.**

Campsites, facilities: There are two primitive tent sites and 12 sites for tents or self-contained RVs up to 30 feet long. Piped water, fire grills and picnic tables are provided. Flush toilets and a cafe are available. A laundromat is located within one mile. Pets are permitted.

Reservations, fee: No reservations; $5-$10 fee per night. Open all year with limited winter facilities.

Who to contact: Phone (509) 456-4169 or write to Route 1, P.O. Box 336, Mead, WA 99021.

Location: From Interstate 90 at Spokane, turn east on US 2 and drive about six miles northeast. Turn northeast on Highway 206 and drive 24 miles north to the park.

Trip note: This is a prime hideaway on the slopes of Mount Spokane (5,878 feet). Mount Kit Carson (5,180 feet) sits alongside, its little brother. Nearby recreation options include marked hiking trails, an equestrian trail and tennis courts. In the winter Mount Spokane Ski Resort operates here. There is a wonderful restaurant, Vista House, which offers fantastic views. This is one of the better short trips available out of Spokane.

57.　　　　OVERLAND STATION　　RV

Reference: **Near Eloika Lake; map A5, grid h5.**

Campsites, facilities: There are 40 tent sites and 32 sites (18 drive-through) for trailers or RVs of any length. Electricity, piped water, sewer hookups and picnic tables are provided. Flush toilets, showers, a store, a laundromat, ice and a playground are available. Pets and motorbikes are permitted.

Reservations, fee: No reservations; $15-$18 fee per night. Open all year.

Who to contact: Phone (509) 747-1703 or write to 10711 West Geiger Boulevard, Spokane, WA 99204.

Location: From Interstate 90 in Spokane, take exit 272. Drive one block east to the park on the right.

Trip note: This is one of seven campgrounds located in the immediate Spokane area. A number of side trips are available to learn the history of the area, including the Cheney Cowles Memorial Museum and the Museum of Native American Cultures. Riverfront Park is the site of the 1974 World Exposition, and it now offers a science center and planetarium, opera house, Japanese garden, gondola ride, carousel, ice-skating rink and five-screen theater. The closest lake with good fishing is Eloika Lake, described in the trip note for Jerry's Landing, camp number 48.

---

58.   RIVERSIDE STATE PARK   RV

Reference: **Near Spokane; map A5, grid h5.**

Campsites, facilities: There are two primitive tent sites and 101 sites for tents or self-contained RVs up to 45 feet long. Picnic tables and fire grills are provided. Flush toilets, showers and firewood are available. A store, a restaurant and ice are available within three miles. Leashed pets are permitted. Boat launching facilities are located on the Spokane River about seven miles away at the reservoir.

Reservations, fee: No reservations; $7-$11 fee per night. Open all year.

Who to contact: Phone (800) 233-0321 or (509) 456-3964 or write to Riverside State Park, North 4427 Aubrey L. White Parkway, Spokane, WA 99205.

Location: From Spokane on Interstate 90, drive north on Division Street. Turn left on Mission Street. (Mission Street will become Maxwell Street and then Petett Drive). The park entrance is on Petett Drive and the campground is two miles inside the park on the left. The park is five miles from Interstate 90.

Trip note: This is a good option for people looking for a more rural alternative to the camps set on the outskirts of Spokane. This large state park provides an interpretive center, riding stable and trails for hiking, horseback riding and off-road vehicles. Nearby recreation options include an 18-hole golf course. A local point of interest is the unique Bowl and Pitcher Lava Formation in the river.

---

59.   SHADOWS MOTEL AND TRAILER PARK   RV

Reference: **In Spokane; map A5, grid h6.**

Campsites, facilities: There are 10 tent sites and 25 drive-through sites for trailers or RVs of any length. Electricity, piped water and sewer hookups are provided. Flush toilets, sanitary services, showers and a laundromat are available. Bottled gas, a store, a cafe and ice are located within one mile. Pets and motorbikes are permitted.

Reservations, fee: Reservations accepted; $10-$20 fee per night. MasterCard and Visa accepted. Open all year, with limited winter facilities.

Who to contact: Phone (509) 467-6951 or write to N 9025 Division, Spokane, WA 99208.

Location: From Interstate 90 in Spokane, take the Division Street exit (exit 281) and drive six miles to N 9025 Division Street. The campground is located at the junction of US 2 and US 395.

Trip note: This park is primarily a pit stop for highway cruisers. Nearby recreation options include an 18-hole golf course, hiking trails, marked bike trails and tennis courts. See the trip note for Overland Station for information on attractions in Spokane.

60.　　　TRAILER INNS RV PARK　　　RV

Reference: **In Spokane; map A5, grid h6.**

Campsites, facilities: There are 99 sites for trailers or RVs of any length (39 drive-through). Electricity, piped water, sewer hookups and picnic tables are provided. Flush toilets, bottled gas, showers, color TV, a laundromat, ice and a playground are available. Sanitary services, a store and a cafe are within one mile. Pets and motorbikes are permitted.

Reservations, fee: Reservations accepted; $18-$25 fee per night; MasterCard and Visa accepted. Open all year.

Who to contact: Phone (509) 535-1811 or write to 6021 East Fourth Avenue, Spokane, WA 99212.

Location: From eastbound, take exit 285 (Sprague Avenue/Eastern Road) off Interstate 90 in Spokane and drive one-tenth of a mile on Eastern Road. Then turn west on Fourth Avenue and drive one mile to the campground. From westbound, take exit 284 (Havana Street) and drive one block south on Havana Street. Turn east on Fourth Avenue and drive one mile.

Trip note: This is a large RV park that is perfect for a layover on the way to Idaho. It's as close to a hotel as an RV park can get. Nearby recreation options include an 18-hole golf course, a racquet club and tennis courts. See the trip note for Overland Station for information on attractions in Spokane.

61.　　　　　KOA SPOKANE　　　　　RV

Reference: **On Spokane River; map A5, grid h7.**

Campsites, facilities: There are 50 tent sites and 150 sites (109 drive-through) for trailers or RVs of any length. Electricity and sewer hookups are available. Piped water and picnic tables are provided. Flush toilets, sanitary services, showers, a recreation hall, a store, a laundromat, ice, a playground and a swimming pool are available. A cafe is located within one mile. Pets are permitted.

Reservations, fee: Reservations accepted; $15-$25 fee per night. MasterCard and Visa accepted. Open March to late October.

Who to contact: Phone (509) 924-4722 or write to 3025 North Barker, Otis Orchards, WA 99027.

Location: From Spokane, drive 13 miles east on Interstate 90 and take exit 293. Drive north on Barker Road for 1.25 miles to the campground.

Trip note: This campground is set along the shore of the Spokane River. Nearby recreation options include an 18-hole golf course and tennis courts. See the trip note for Overland Station for information on attractions in Spokane.

62.　　PICNIC PINES ON SILVER LAKE　　RV

Reference: **On Silver Lake; map A5, grid i4.**

Campsites, facilities: There are 10 tent sites and 29 drive-through sites for trailers or RVs of any length. Electricity, piped water, sewer hookups and picnic tables are provided. Flush toilets, a recreation hall, a store, a cafe, ice and a playground are available. Bottled gas and a laundromat are located within two miles. Pets and motorbikes are permitted. Boat docks, launching facilities and rentals are available.

Reservations, fee: Reservations accepted; $8-$10 fee per night; MasterCard and Visa accepted. Open all year.

Who to contact: Phone (509) 299-3223 or write to South 9212 Silver Lake Road, Medical Lake, WA 99022.

Location: From Interstate 90 west of Spokane, take exit 270 and drive three miles west on Medical Lake Road to Silver Lake Road. Turn left and drive one-half mile to the park.

Trip note: This resort is set along the shore of Medical Lake. It caters primarily to RVs, although tent campers are welcome. Fishing can be excellent in Silver Lake. Nearby recreation options include marked bike trails, a full-service marina and tennis courts. See the trip note for West Medical Lake Resort for further details.

---

63. WEST MEDICAL LAKE RESORT RV

Reference: **On West Medical Lake; map A5, grid i4.**

Campsites, facilities: There are 20 tent sites and 18 sites for trailers or RVs. Picnic tables are provided. Flush toilets, showers, a cafe and ice are available. Electricity, piped water and sewer hookups can be obtained for an extra fee. Pets and motorbikes are permitted. Boat docks, launching facilities and rentals are nearby.

Reservations, fee: Reservations required; $8-$12 fee per night. Open mid-April to July.

Who to contact: Phone (509) 299-3921 or write to P.O. Box 216, Medical Lake, WA 99022.

Location: Take exit 264 off Highway 90 near Medical Lake and drive 4.5 miles north on Salnave Road, then turn west on Fancher and travel one-half mile to the resort.

Trip note: This family-operated resort is set along the shore of Medical Lake, one of five campgrounds on the lake. It is a popular spot for Spokane locals making the half-hour drive. There are actually two lakes. West Medical is the larger of the two and also has the better fishing, with boat rentals available. Medical Lake is just a quarter-mile wide and a half-mile long, and boating is restricted to rowboats, canoes, kayaks and sailboats. The lakes got their names from the wondrous medical powers once attributed to these waters.

---

64. BARBER'S RESORT RV

Reference: **On Medical Lake; map A5, grid i4.**

Campsites, facilities: There are 35 tent sites and 50 drive-through sites for trailers or RVs of any length. Electricity, piped water and picnic tables are provided. Flush toilets, bottled gas, sanitary services, showers, a cafe, ice and a playground are available. Pets and motorbikes are permitted. Boat docks, launching facilities and rentals are nearby.

Reservations, fee: Reservations accepted; $12 fee per night. Open mid-April to late September.

Who to contact: Phone (509) 299-3830 or write to Route 1, P.O. Box 64, Cheney, WA 99004.

Location: From Interstate 90 west of Spokane, take exit 264 and drive two miles west on Salnave Road. Follow the signs to the resort.

Trip note: This resort is set along the shore of Medical Lake. Nearby recreation options include marked bike trails, a riding stable and tennis courts. See the trip note for West Medical Lake Resort.

65.   RAINBOW COVE CAMPGROUND   RV

Reference: **On Clear Lake; map A5, grid i4.**

Campsites, facilities: There are five tent sites and 16 sites for trailers or RVs of any length. Electricity, piped water, sewer hookups and picnic tables are provided. Showers, flush toilets, a cafe and ice are available. Pets are permitted. Boat docks, launching facilities and rentals are nearby.

Reservations, fee: Reservations accepted; $12 fee per night. Open mid-April to late September.

Who to contact: Phone (509) 299-3717 or write to South 12514 Clear Lake Road, Medical Lake, WA 99022.

Location: From Interstate 90 west of Spokane, take exit 264 and drive 300 feet west on Salnave Road, then turn north on Clear Lake Road and follow the signs to the campground.

Trip note: This resort is set along the shore of Medical Lake. It is pretty and wooded, with lake access. Nearby recreation options include marked bike trails and tennis courts. See the trip note for West Medical Lake Resort for more details about the lake.

66.   ALPINE MOTEL-RV   RV
AND TENT PARK OF SPOKANE

Reference: **Map A5, grid h8.**

Campsites, facilities: There are 110 sites for tents, trailers or RVs. Restrooms, showers, a public phone, a laundromat, a heated swimming pool and ice are available. The facilities are **wheelchair accessible**. Pets are permitted on leashes.

Reservations, fee: Reservations recommended; $16-$20 fee per night. Visa and MasterCard accepted. Open year round.

Who to contact: Phone the park at (509) 928-2700 or write to P.O. Box 363, Greenacres, WA 99016.

Location: From Spokane, drive east on Interstate 90 for about 12 miles to Barker Road/Green Acres (exit 293). Travel north one-half block on Barker Road to the campground on the left.

Trip note: This is an urban campground set just outside of Spokane. It is primarily a layover camp, but could be a good base point for those planning on visiting the Spokane area for a while. Recreational activities include basketball, croquet, badminton, volleyball and swimming.

67.   PONDEROSA HILL RV PARK   RV

Reference: **In Spokane; map A5, grid i5.**

Campsites, facilities: There are 50 tent sites and 100 sites for trailers or RVs up to 30 feet long (35 drive-through). Electricity, piped water, sewer and cable TV hookups are provided. Flush toilets, sanitary services, showers, firewood, propane, a laundromat and a playground are available. Electricity, piped water and sewer hookups can be obtained for an extra fee. Pets and motorbikes are permitted.

Reservations, fee: Reservations accepted; $14-$23 fee per night. Open all year. Triple A and Good Sam member.

Who to contact: Phone (800)494-7275, extension 801 or write to P.O. Box 363, 7520 South Thomas Mallen Road, Spokane, WA 99204.

Location: From Interstate 90 in Spokane, take exit 272 and drive one mile east on Hallet Road. Turn south on Thomas Mallen Road and drive one-half mile to the campground on the right.

Trip note: This park is in a wooded, rural area, yet just a short jaunt from downtown Spokane. The park is large and grassy, with pretty hiking trails and an 18-hole golf course next door. See the trip note for Overland Station camp for details on the Spokane area.

---

68. PEACEFUL PINES CAMPGROUND RV

Reference: **Near Turnbull National Wildlife Refuge; map A5, grid i5.**

Campsites, facilities: There are 20 tent sites and 18 sites for trailers or RVs of any length. Electricity, piped water, sewer hookups and picnic tables are provided. Flush toilets, sanitary services and showers are available. A store, a cafe, a laundromat and ice are located within one mile. Pets and motorbikes are permitted.

Reservations, fee: Reservations accepted; $9.50-$12 fee per night. Open all year.

Who to contact: Phone (509) 235-4966 or write to West 13314-SR904, Cheney, WA 99004.

Location: From Interstate 90 southwest of Spokane, take the Highway 904 exit to Cheney. Drive six miles south to Cheney on Highway 904, then continue one mile to the campground.

Trip note: This campground is a little-known, remote site located just a short distance from Turnbull National Wildlife Refuge, an expanse of marsh and pine that is a significant stopover point for migratory birds on the Pacific Flyway. You can pick up a map and bird checklist at the refuge headquarters. This is a prime spot, only a 45-minute drive out of Spokane, yet relatively unknown.

---

69. SPRAGUE LAKE RESORT RV

Reference: **On Sprague Lake; map A5, grid j2.**

Campsites, facilities: There are 50 tent sites and 30 drive-through sites for trailers or RVs of any length. Electricity, piped water, sewer hookups and picnic tables are provided. Flush toilets, sanitary services, a store, a laundromat, showers, ice and a playground are available. Pets are permitted. Boat docks, launching facilities and rentals are nearby.

Reservations, fee: Reservations accepted; $11-$15 fee per night. Open April to mid-October.

Who to contact: Phone (509) 257-2864 or write to Route 1, P.O. Box 5, Sprague, WA 99032.

Location: From Interstate 90 west of Spokane, take the Sprague Business Center exit. Follow the signs and drive two miles to the resort.

Trip note: This developed campground is set along the shore of Sprague Lake, about 35 miles from Spokane. It's a pleasant setting, clean and grassy.

---

70. FOUR SEASONS CAMPGROUND RV

Reference: **On Sprague Lake; map A5, grid j2.**

Campsites, facilities: There are 25 tent sites and 30 drive-through sites for trailers or RVs. Electricity, piped water, sewer hookups and picnic tables are provided. Flush toilets, sanitary services, showers, firewood, ice, a playground and a swimming pool are available. Pets and motorbikes are permitted. Boat docks, launching facilities and rentals are nearby.

Reservations, fee: Reservations accepted; $12-$14 fee per night. Open mid-April to October.

Who to contact: Phone (509) 257-2332 or write to Route 1, P.O. Box 41, Sprague, WA 99032.

Location: From Interstate 90 west of Spokane, take exit 231 in Sprague. Head east on Keystone and follow the signs to the lake and the campground.

Trip note: This campground is set along the shore of Sprague Lake. The sites are spacious, with plenty of vegetation. The fishing for rainbow trout is best in May and June, with some bass in spring and fall. Because there is an abundance of natural feed in the lake, the fish reach larger sizes here than in neighboring lakes. In late July through August, a fair algae bloom is a turnoff for swimmers and waterskiers.

---

71. LAST ROUNDUP MOTEL, RV PARK AND CAMPGROUND RV

Reference: **Near Sprague Lake; map A5, grid j3.**

Campsites, facilities: There are 13 sites for trailers or RVs up to 40 feet long. There is also a grass area for tents. Electricity, piped water and sewer hookups are provided. Flush toilets, showers, a laundromat and ice are available. Bottled gas, sanitary services, a store and a cafe are located within one mile. Pets and motorbikes are permitted.

Reservations, fee: Reservations accepted; $8-$15 fee per night. MasterCard and Visa accepted. Open April to November.

Who to contact: Phone (509) 257-2583 or write to 312 East First Street, Sprague, WA 99032.

Location: From Spokane, drive west on Interstate 90 for 35 miles to Sprague. Take exit 245 and drive one-half mile south on Highway 23 to Fourth Street. Turn west and drive one block to B Street. Turn north and drive three blocks to First Street. Turn east on First Street and drive one block to the park on the right.

Trip note: The camp is set just on the outskirts of Sprague. It's in a meadow-like, flat area with a rural feel. The sites are sunny and grassy. The best game in town is at nearby Sprague Lake.

---

72. WILLIAMS LAKE RESORT RV

Reference: **On Williams Lake; map A5, grid j4.**

Campsites, facilities: There are 15 tent sites and 60 sites for trailers or RVs of any length (seven drive-through) . Electricity, piped water and picnic tables are provided. Flush toilets, bottled gas, sanitary services, firewood, a store, a cafe, a restaurant, showers, ice and a playground are available. Pets and motorbikes are permitted. Boat docks, launching facilities and rentals are available.

Reservations, fee: Reservations accepted; $12-$15 fee per night. Open mid-April to October.

Who to contact: Phone (800) 274-1540 or (509) 235-2391 or write to West 18617 Williams Lake Road, Cheney, WA 99004.

Location: From Spokane, drive west on Interstate 90 for 10 miles to exit 270, turn south on Highway 904 and drive six miles to Cheney. Turn south on Cheney Plaza Road and drive 11.2 miles to Williams Lake Road. Turn west and drive 3.5 miles to the campground on the left.

Trip note: This resort is set along the shore of Williams Lake. The lake is just under three miles long and is popular for swimming and waterskiing. It is also one of the top fishing lakes in the region for rainbow and cutthroat trout. The lake is bordered in some areas by rocky cliffs. See the trip note for Peaceful Pines Campground for information on nearby Turnbull National Wildlife Refuge.

73.　　　　　　BUNKERS RESORT　　　　　　RV

Reference: **On Williams Lake; map A5, grid j4.**

Campsites, facilities: There are 10 drive-through sites for trailers or RVs of any length. Electricity, piped water and picnic tables are provided. Flush toilets, bottled gas, sanitary services, recreation hall, cabins, a restaurant, a store, a cafe and ice are available. Pets are permitted. Boat docks, fishing docks, launching facilities and rentals are nearby.

Reservations, fee: Reservations accepted; $10.50-$17.50 fee per night. MasterCard and Visa accepted. Open mid-April to October.

Who to contact: Phone (509) 235-5212 or write to S36402 Bunker Landing Road, Cheney, WA 99004.

Location: From Interstate 90 west of Spokane, take the Cheney exit and drive six miles south to Cheney. Turn south on Mullinex Road and drive 12 miles to the resort.

Trip note: This campground is set along the shore of Williams Lake. See the trip note for Williams Lake Resort for information on the lake, and the trip note for Peaceful Pines Campground for information on nearby Turnbull National Wildlife Refuge.

MAP B1

WASHINGTON MAP .... see page 90

Adjoining Maps

NORTH (A1) .... see page 92
EAST (B2) .... see page 294
SOUTH .... Oregon
WEST .... no map

48 LISTINGS
PAGES 274-293

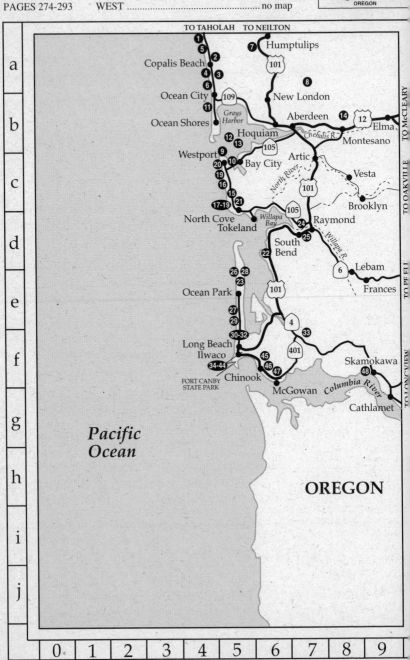

Pacific Ocean

OREGON

Washington Map B1 featuring: Copalis Beach, Humptulips River, Satsop River, Westport, Ocean City State Park, Lake Sylvia, Twin Harbors, Leadbetter Point State Park, Willapa Bay, Grays Harbor, Willapa River, Long Beach, Fort Canby State Park, Columbia River, Fort Columbia State Park, Chinook

---

1. PACIFIC BEACH STATE PARK **RV**

Reference: **On the Pacific Ocean; map B1, grid a4.**

Campsites, facilities: There are 31 tent sites and 33 sites for trailers or RVs up to 45 feet long. Picnic tables are provided. A sanitary disposal station, coin-operated showers and toilets are available. Electricity and piped water are available for an extra fee. Some facilities are **wheelchair-accessible.** Leashed pets are permitted.

Reservations, fee: Contact Reservations Northwest at (800) 452-5687 ($6 reservation fee); $10-$15 fee per night. Open all year.

Who to contact: Phone (800) 233-0321 or the state park at (360) 289-3553 or write to 148 State Route 115, Hoquiam, WA 98550.

Location: From Interstate 5 south of Olympia, take exit 88 and turn west on State Route 12. Drive 46 miles, then turn west on Highway 109 and drive 27 miles to Pacific Beach. The park is in town.

Trip note: This nine-acre, in-town campground is on the beach, but it tends to get crowded since there are no other coastal camps in the immediate vicinity. Your recreation options here include clamming, beachcombing and surf fishing.

---

2. TIDELANDS ON THE BEACH **RV**

Reference: **Near Copalis Beach; map B1, grid a4.**

Campsites, facilities: There are 100 tent sites and 55 sites (25 drive-through) for trailers or RVs of any length. There are also three two-bedroom cabins available. Electricity, piped water, sewer hookups and picnic tables are provided. Sanitary services, toilets, firewood, coin-operated showers and a playground are available. Bottled gas, a store, a cafe and ice are located within one mile. Pets are permitted.

Reservations, fee: Reservations accepted; $10-$15 fee per night; $75 cabin fee. Open all year.

Who to contact: Phone (360) 289-8963 or write to P.O. Box 36, Copalis Beach, WA 98535.

Location: From Olympia, drive south on Interstate 5 to exit 88. Turn west on State Route 12 and drive 46 miles. Turn west on Highway 109 and drive about 16 miles to the campground. It is located about one mile south of Copalis Beach between mileposts 20 and 21.

Trip note: This wooded park covers 47 acres and has beach access. It's primarily an RV park, but it has pleasant, grassy sites. Horseshoe pits and recreation field offer recreation possibilities. This a more remote option than the other sites in the area.

---

3. ROD'S BEACH RESORT **RV**

Reference: **Near Copalis Beach; map B1, grid a4.**

Campsites, facilities: There are 80 sites (25 drive-through) for trailers or RVs of any length. No tents are allowed. Electricity, piped water, sewer hookups and cable TV are provided. There is also a motel at the site. Sanitary services, toilets, showers, a recreation hall, a store, a cafe, ice and a playground are available. Bottled gas is located within one mile. A swimming pool is available for an extra fee. Leashed pets are permitted.

Reservations, fee: Reservations accepted; $12-$16 fee per night. MasterCard and Visa accepted. Open February to late November.

Who to contact: Phone the park at (360) 289-2222 or write to Rod's Beach Resort, Copalis Beach, WA 98535.

Location: From Interstate 5 south of Olympia, take exit 88 and turn west on State Route 12. Drive 46 miles, then turn west on Highway 109 and drive approximately 15.5 miles to the campground. It is located about 1.5 miles south of Copalis Beach at milepost 20.

Trip note: This park covers 10 acres and has a beach, plus nice sunsets. It's a well-maintained park with large, grassy sites and access to the ocean and fishing. This is a prime spot for RVers.

4.　　　DRIFTWOOD ACRES OCEAN CAMP　　🅡🆅

Reference: **Near Copalis Beach; map B1, grid a4.**

Campsites, facilities: There are 50 tent sites and 50 sites for trailers or RVs of any length. Piped water, sewer hookups, fire pits and picnic tables are provided. Electricity, cable TV, showers, sanitary services, toilets and firewood are available. Bottled gas, a store, a cafe and ice are located within one mile. Pets are permitted on leashes.

Reservations, fee: Reservations accepted; call ahead for fees. Open April to late October.

Who to contact: Phone (360) 289-3484 or write to P.O. Box 216, Copalis Beach, WA 98535.

Location: From Interstate 5 south of Olympia, take exit 88 and turn west on State Route 12. Drive 46 miles, then turn west on Highway 109 and drive 14 miles to the town of Copalis Beach. Continue one-quarter mile south to the campground. Park at milepost 21.5.

Trip note: This wooded campground covers 150 acres and has beach access and marked hiking trails. Additional facilities found within five miles of the campground include an 18-hole golf course and a riding stable.

5.　　　　COPALIS BEACH RV PARK　　🅡🆅

Reference: **In Copalis Beach; map B1, grid a4.**

Campsites, facilities: There are five tent sites and 44 sites (20 drive-through) for trailers or RVs of any length. Electricity, piped water, sewer hookups, cable TV hookups and picnic tables are provided. Sanitary services, a laundry, toilets, showers, a cafe and ice are available. Bottled gas and a store are located within one mile. Pets are permitted.

Reservations, fee: Reservations accepted; $12-$20 fee per night; MasterCard and Visa accepted. Open all year.

Who to contact: Phone (360) 289-2707 or write to P.O. Box 208, Copalis Beach, WA 98535.

Location: From Olympia, drive south on Interstate 5 to exit 88. Turn west on State Route 12 and drive 46 miles. Turn west on Highway 109 and drive about 17 miles. Turn west on Copalis Beach Road and drive two-tenths of a mile to the campground.

Trip note: This park covers five acres and has beach access. It's a decent layover for a motor home vacation. This is not a particularly scenic park, but it will do the job if you're tired and ready to get off US 101. The surrounding terrain is flat and grassy.

6. RIVERSIDE RV RESORT   RV

Reference: **Near Copalis Beach; map B1, grid a4.**

Campsites, facilities: There are 15 tent sites and 53 sites (20 drive-through) for trailers or RVs of any length. Electricity, piped water, sewer hookups and picnic tables are provided. Bottled gas, sanitary services, toilets, showers, hot tub, firewood and a recreation hall are available. A store, a cafe and ice are located within one mile. Leashed pets and motorbikes are permitted.

Reservations, fee: Reservations accepted; $12-$15 fee per night; MasterCard and Visa accepted. Open all year.

Who to contact: Phone (360) 289-2111 or write to P.O. Box 307, Copalis Beach, WA 98535.

Location: From Interstate 5 south of Olympia, take exit 88 and turn west on State Route 12. Drive 46 miles, then turn west on Highway 109 and drive approximately 20 miles to the town of Copalis Beach. The park is off the highway on the left.

Trip note: This park covers three acres and has river access. Salmon fishing is said to be excellent in the Copalis River and a boat ramp is available nearby for anglers. Swimming and beachcombing are two other options. This is a nice and exceptionally clean park.

7. RIVERVIEW RECREATION AREA   RV

Reference: **On Humptulips River; map B1, grid a6.**

Campsites, facilities: There are eight tent sites and 12 drive-through sites for trailers or RVs of any length. Picnic tables are provided. Sanitary services, toilets, coin-operated showers and firewood are available. A store, a cafe and ice are within one mile. Electricity, piped water and sewer hookups are available for an extra fee. Pets and motorbikes are permitted. Boat launching facilities are available at the nearby Humptulips River.

Reservations, fee: No reservations; $6-$15 fee per night. Open all year.

Who to contact: Phone the park at (360) 987-2216 or write to P.O. Box 97, Humptulips, WA 98552.

Location: From Interstate 5 south of Olympia, take exit 88 and turn west on State Route 12. Drive 46 miles, then turn north on US 101 and drive 22 miles to Humptulips. Continue one-quarter mile west on Beach Cutoff Road to the park.

Trip note: This five-acre camp is set at about 1,000 feet along the Humptulips River. It's a beautiful spot, with boating and fishing access not far from camp. It's a good layover if you're cruising US 101. It is also a popular layover, so plan on arriving early.

8. SCHAFER STATE PARK   RV

Reference: **On Satsop River; map B1, grid a7.**

Campsites, facilities: There are two primitive tent sites, 47 developed tent sites, and six sites with water and electric hookups for trailers or RVs up to 40 feet long. Picnic tables and fire grills are provided. Sanitary disposal station, toilets and a playground are available. Water, showers and firewood are an additional charge. Some facilities are **wheelchair accessible**. Leashed pets are permitted.

Reservations, fee: No reservations; $5-$14 fee per night. Open all year with limited winter facilities.

Who to contact: Phone (360) 482-3852 or write to Route 1, P.O. Box 87, Elma, WA 98541.

Location: From Interstate 5 south of Olympia, take exit 88 and turn west on State Route 12. Drive 32 miles to East Satsop Road (four miles east of Montesano). Turn north and drive eight miles to the park.

Trip note: This heavily-wooded, rural camp covers 119 acres and is on the East Fork of the Satsop River. There are good canoeing and kayaking spots, some with Class II and Class III rapids, along the Middle and West Forks of the Satsop River. At one time this park was the Schafer Logging Company Park and was used by the employees and their families.

---

9.   JOLLY ROGERS RV PARK   **RV**

Reference: **Near Westport Harbor; map B1, grid c5.**

Campsites, facilities: There are 25 sites with full hookups for trailers or RVs of any length. Sanitary services, toilets, coin-operated showers and boat docks are available. Bottled gas, a store, a cafe and laundry are available within one mile. Pets and motorbikes are permitted.

Reservations, fee: Reservations accepted; $14 fee per night. Open all year.

Who to contact: Phone the park at (360) 268-0265 or write to P.O. Box 342, Westport, WA 98595.

Location: From Olympia, drive south on Interstate 5 to exit 88. Turn west on State Route 12 and drive 46 miles. Turn south on Highway 105 and drive 22 miles southwest to Westport. Drive north to Point Chehalis on Neddie Rose Drive. The park is at the Westport Docks.

Trip note: This park covers one acre and is near Westport Harbor. It is your typical beachside RV park, with concrete sites and nearby beach access. This is a prime spot to watch ocean sunsets. Westport Light and Westhaven state parks are nearby and offer day-use facilities along the ocean.

---

10.   COHO RV PARK   **RV**

Reference: **Near Westport Harbor; map B1, grid b5.**

Campsites, facilities: There are 76 sites with full hookups for trailers or RVs of any length (six drive-through). No tents are permitted. Sanitary services, cable TV, toilets, showers, laundry, a meeting hall and ice are available. Bottled gas, a store and a cafe are within one mile. Pets are permitted. Boat docks, launching facilities and fishing charters are located one block from this park.

Reservations, fee: Reservations accepted; $14-$18 fee per night. Open all year.

Who to contact: Phone (360) 268-0111 or write to P.O. Box 1087, Westport, WA 98595.

Location: From Olympia, drive south on Interstate 5 and take exit 88. Turn west on State Route 12 and drive 46 miles. Turn south on Highway 105 and drive 22 miles southwest to Westport. Turn northeast on Montesano Street (just south of town) and drive 3.5 miles to Nyhus Street. Turn northwest and drive 2.5 blocks to the campground on the left.

Trip note: This park covers two acres and is one of 10 camping options in the immediate area. Both Westhaven and Westport Light state parks are nearby. They are popular parks for rockhounds, scuba divers and surf fishermen. A full-service marina is within five miles of the campground.

11.   OCEAN CITY STATE PARK   **RV**

Reference: **Near Hoquiam; map B1, grid b5.**

Campsites, facilities: There are three primitive tent sites, 149 developed tent sites, and 29 sites with full hookups for trailers or RVs up to 55 feet long. Picnic tables are provided, and sanitary services and toilets are available. Showers and firewood (in the summer) are available for an extra fee. Some facilities are **wheelchair accessible**. Pets are permitted.

Reservations, fee: Contact Reservations Northwest at (800) 452-5687 ($6 reservation fee); $10-$15 fee per night. Open all year.

Who to contact: Phone (800) 233-0321 or the the state park at (360) 289-3553 or write to 148 State Route 115, Hoquiam, WA 98550.

Location: From Interstate 5 south of Olympia, take exit 88 and turn west on State Route 12. Drive 46 miles, then turn northwest on Highway 109 and drive 20 miles. Turn left on Highway 115 and drive 1.5 miles south to the park.

Trip note: This is one of the choice spots in the area for tent campers. The camp is on the ocean and covers 131 acres. It is near many interesting shops and restaurants in town, and a short drive from an 18-hole golf course. Beachcombing, clamming and fishing are possibilities at this park.

---

12.   TOTEM RV AND TRAILER PARK   **RV**

Reference: **In Westport; map B1, grid c5.**

Campsites, facilities: There are 10 tent sites and 76 sites (55 drive-through) for trailers or RVs of any length. Electricity, piped water, sewer hookups and picnic tables are provided. Sanitary services, toilets, showers, a store, laundry and ice are available. Bottled gas and a cafe are located within one mile. Pets and motorbikes are permitted. Boat docks, launching facilities and fishing charters are nearby.

Reservations, fee: Reservations accepted; $12-$13 fee per night. Open all year.

Who to contact: Phone (360) 268-0025 or write to P.O. Box 1166, Westport, WA 98595.

Location: From Olympia, drive south on Interstate 5 to exit 88. Turn west on State Route 12 and drive 46 miles. Turn south on Highway 105 and drive 18 miles southwest to the turnoff for Westport. Drive north on the Highway 105 spur for four miles. Turn east on Dock Avenue and drive one block. Turn north on Nyhus Street and drive two blocks to the park on the left.

Trip note: This park covers two acres and has large, graveled sites. It is near Westhaven State Park which offers day-use facilities. Additional facilities within five miles of the campground include marked bike trails, a full-service marina and tennis courts.

---

13.   HOLAND CENTER   **RV**

Reference: **In Westport; map B1, grid c5.**

Campsites, facilities: There are 80 sites with full hookups for trailers or RVs up to 30 feet long. Picnic tables are provided. Toilets, a laundry and showers are available. Bottled gas, a store, a cafe, laundry and ice are located within one mile. Pets are permitted. Boat docks and launching facilities are nearby.

Reservations, fee: Reservations accepted; $10-$13 fee per night. Open all year.

Who to contact: Phone (360) 268-9582 or write to P.O. Box 1752, Westport, WA 98595.

Location: From Olympia, drive south on Interstate 5 to exit 88. Turn west on State Route 12 and drive 46 miles to Highway 105. Turn south and drive 22 miles to Westport. The park is at the corner of Highway 105 and Wilson Street.

Trip note: This camp covers 18 acres. It is a pleasant RV park, one of several in the immediate area. The sites are graveled and have ample space. There is no beach access from the park, but full recreation facilities are nearby.

14. LAKE SYLVIA STATE PARK   RV

Reference: **On Lake Sylvia; map B1, grid b8.**

Campsites, facilities: There are two primitive tent sites and 35 sites for tents or self-contained RVs up to 30 feet long. Picnic tables, fire grills are provided. Piped water, sanitary disposal station, toilets, a store, fishing supplies, a car-top boat launch, boat rentals and a playground are available. Showers and firewood are available for an extra fee. Laundry and ice are located within one mile. Some facilities are **wheelchair accessible**. Leashed pets are permitted.

Reservations, fee: No reservations; $10-$14 fee per night. Open all year.

Who to contact: Phone (800) 233-0321 or (360) 249-3621 or write to P.O. Box 701, Montesano, WA 98563.

Location: From Interstate 5 south of Olympia, take exit 88 and turn west on State Route 12. Drive 36 miles to Montesano. Turn north at the sign for Lake Sylvia State Park and drive one mile.

Trip note: This camp is on the shore of Lake Sylvia and covers 234 acres. There are numerous marked hiking trails. Additional recreation options include trout fishing and swimming. If Lake Sylvia is full, nearby camps are Big Creek, East Crossing (see Chapter A2) and Rainbow Cove (see Chapter A5).

15. TWIN HARBORS STATE PARK   RV

Reference: **On the Pacific Ocean; map B1, grid c5.**

Campsites, facilities: There are 224 sites for trailers or RVs up to 35 feet long (49 with full hookups). Picnic tables and fire grills are provided. Piped water, a sanitary disposal station, toilets and a playground are available. A store, a cafe and ice are available within one mile. Firewood is available for an extra fee. Some facilities are **wheelchair accessible**. Leashed pets are permitted.

Reservations, fee: Contact Reservations Northwest at (800) 452-5687 ($6 reservation fee); $10 fee per night. Open all year.

Who to contact: Phone (800) 233-0321 or (360) 268-9717 or write to Twin Harbors State Park, Westport, WA 98595.

Location: From Interstate 5 south of Olympia, take exit 88 and turn west on State Route 12. Drive 46 miles to the turnoff for Highway 105. Turn left and continue southwest for approximately 20 miles to the park entrance. The park is located three miles south of Westport.

Trip note: This park covers 1,881 acres, and has beach access and marked hiking trails, including the Shifting Sands Nature Trail. Nearby in Westport there are fishing boats to charter. This is one of the largest campgrounds on the coast, and therefore quite popular. The sites are very close together and often crammed to capacity in the summer months.

16. PACIFIC MOTEL AND RV PARK   RV

Reference: **Near Twin Harbors; map B1, grid c5.**

Campsites, facilities: There are 20 tent sites and 80 sites (32 drive-through) for trailers or RVs of any length. Electricity, piped water and sewer hookups are provided. Sanitary services, toilets, a recreation hall with kitchen, cable TV, public phone and fax, coin-operated showers and a swimming pool are available. Bottled gas, a store, a cafe, laundry and ice are located within one mile. Pets and motorbikes are permitted. Boat docks and launching facilities are nearby.

Reservations, fee: Reservations accepted; $11-$16 fee per night; MasterCard and Visa accepted. Open all year.

Who to contact: Phone (360) 268-9325 or write to 330 South Forrest, Westport, WA 98595.

Location: From Interstate 5 south of Olympia, take exit 88 and turn west on State Route 12. Drive 46 miles, then turn south on Highway 105 and drive 18 miles southwest. At the Highway 105 spur road turnoff to Westport, turn north and continue 1.7 miles to the park.

Trip note: This park covers five acres and has grassy, shaded sites in a wooded setting. It is near Twin Harbors and Westport Light state parks, both of which have beach access. Additional facilities found within five miles of the campground include a full-service marina.

---

17. GRAYLAND BEACH STATE PARK ▆RV

Reference: On the Pacific Ocean; map B1, grid c5.

Campsites, facilities: There are three primitive tent sites and 60 full hookup sites for trailers or RVs up to 40 feet long. Picnic tables, toilets and fire grills are provided. Showers are available for an extra fee. Some facilities are **wheelchair accessible**.

Reservations, fee: Contact Reservations Northwest at (800) 452-5687 ($6 reservation fee); $10 fee per night. Open all year.

Who to contact: Phone (800) 233-0321 or (360) 268-9717 or write to Grayland Beach State Park, c/o Twin Harbors State Park, Westport, WA 98595.

Location: From Interstate 5 south of Olympia, take exit 88 and turn west on State Route 12. Drive 46 miles to the turnoff for Highway 105. Turn left and continue southwest for approximately 22 miles to the park entrance. The park is just south of the town of Grayland.

Trip note: This oceanfront park covers 200 acres and has nearly 4,000 feet of excellent beach access, including a self-guided interpretive trail. It's one of the best parks in the immediate area and quite popular with out-of-towners, especially in the summer season. Recreation options include fishing, beachcombing and kite flying. The sites are relatively spacious for a state park, but not especially private.

---

18. OCEAN GATE RESORT ▆RV

Reference: In Grayland; map B1, grid c5.

Campsites, facilities: There are 20 tent sites and 24 drive-through sites for trailers or RVs of any length. There are also six cabins available. Electricity, piped water, sewer hookups and picnic tables are provided. Toilets, showers and a playground are available, and firewood is available for an extra fee. Bottled gas, a store, a cafe, a laundry and ice are found within one mile. Pets and motorbikes are permitted.

Reservations, fee: Reservations accepted; $10-$14 fee per night; $35-$45 cabin fee per night for two people ($8 each additional person per night).

Who to contact: Phone (800) 473-1956 or (360) 267-1956 or write to P.O. Box 67, Grayland, WA 98547.

Location: From Olympia, drive south on Interstate 5 to exit 88. Turn west on State Route 12 and drive 46 miles. Turn south on Highway 105 and drive about 21 miles to the Y in the road. Take Highway 105 left toward Grayland. The park is in Grayland between mileposts 26 and 27.

Trip note: This is a privately-run park that provides an option to the publicly run Grayland Beach State Park. The park covers seven acres and has beach access. Fishing and beachcombing are two options.

19. HAMMOND TRAILER PARK   RV

Reference: In Westport; map B1, grid c5.

Campsites, facilities: There are 18 sites with full hookups for trailers or RVs of any length. Sanitary services, toilets, showers and laundry are available. Bottled gas, a store, a cafe and ice are within one mile. Leashed pets are permitted. Boat docks, launching facilities and boat rentals are nearby.

Reservations, fee: Reservations accepted; $12 fee per night. Open all year.

Who to contact: Phone (360) 268-9645 or write to P.O. Box 1648, Westport, WA 98595.

Location: From Olympia, drive south on Interstate 5 to exit 88. Turn west on State Route 12 and drive 46 miles. Turn south on Highway 105 and drive 22 miles to Westport. Turn south on Montesano Street and drive one-quarter mile to the park on the left.

Trip note: This park covers five acres and has nearby beach access. It is a good option for tent campers, as many of the parks in the area cater to RVs. A full-service marina is within five miles of the camp.

20. ISLANDER RV PARK   RV

Reference: On Grays Harbor; map B1, grid c5.

Campsites, facilities: There are 60 sites (30 drive-through) with full hookups for trailers or RVs up to 40 feet long. Toilets, showers, a cafe, laundry, ice, a swimming pool and boat docks are available. Bottled gas, sanitary services and a store are located within one mile. Pets and motorbikes are permitted.

Reservations, fee: Reservations accepted; $15-$20 fee per night; credit cards accepted. Open all year.

Who to contact: Phone (800) 322-1740 or (360) 268-9166 or write to P.O. Box 488, Westport, WA 98595.

Location: From Olympia, drive south on Interstate 5 to exit 88. Turn west on State Route 12 and drive 46 miles. Turn south on Highway 105 and drive 22 miles to Westport. Turn east on Dock Avenue and drive three blocks. Turn north on Westhaven Drive and drive one-third mile. Turn east on Neddie Rose Avenue and drive one block to the park.

Trip note: This park covers three acres and is on Grays Harbor, not far from Westport Light and Westhaven state parks, which offer oceanfront, day-use facilities. The park has a restaurant, motel, live music, dancing and even fishing charters available. A full-service marina is within five miles of the camp.

21. BEST WESTERN SHORES MOTEL & RV PARK   RV

Reference: In Grayland; map B1, grid c5.

Campsites, facilities: There are 30 drive-through sites for trailers or RVs of any length. Electricity, piped water, sewer hookups and picnic tables are provided. Bottled gas, toilets, ice and a playground are available. Showers are available for an extra fee. Sanitary services, firewood, a store and a cafe are located within one mile. Pets and motorbikes are permitted.

Reservations, fee: Reservations accepted; $12.50 fee per night; MasterCard and Visa accepted. Open all year.

Who to contact: Phone (360) 267-6115 or write to P.O. Box 689, Grayland, WA 98547.

Location: From Interstate 5 south of Olympia, take exit 88 and turn west on State Route 12. Drive 46 miles to the turnoff for Highway 105. Turn south and continue 22 miles southwest to Grayland. The camp is located in town.

Trip note: This is a small, private park designed for families. Beach access is not far, and Twin Harbors and Grayland Beach state parks are just a few minutes away. This is an excellent layover for tourists who want to get off US 101.

22. KOA HAPPY TRAILS-BAY CENTER 🆁🆅

Reference: **On Willapa Bay; map B1, grid d6.**

Campsites, facilities: There are 10 tent sites and 32 sites (14 drive-through) for trailers or RVs of any length. Piped water and picnic tables are provided. Bottled gas, sanitary services, toilets, showers, a recreation hall, a store, laundry and ice are available. Electricity, sewer hookups and firewood can be purchased for an extra fee. There is a cafe nearby. Pets and motorbikes are permitted. Boat docks and launching facilities are about three miles from camp on Willapa Bay.

Reservations, fee: Reservations accepted; $15-$20 fee per night. MasterCard and Visa accepted. Open March through October.

Who to contact: Phone (360) 875-6344 or write to P.O. Box 315, Bay Center, WA 98527.

Location: From Interstate 5 at Kelso, turn west on Highway 4 and drive 63 miles. Then turn north and drive about 10 miles, then take the Bay Center exit and drive one mile south to the campground.

Trip note: This camp covers 11 acres and is on the shore of Willapa Bay. A trail from the campground leads to the beach. The campsites are graveled and shady.

23. EVERGREEN COURT 🆁🆅

Reference: **Near Leadbetter Point State Park; map B1, grid e5.**

Campsites, facilities: There are eight tent sites and 34 sites for trailers or RVs of any length. Electricity, piped water, sewer hookups, cable TV and picnic tables are provided. Sanitary services, toilets, showers, firewood and a playground are available. A store, a cafe and laundry are within two miles. Pets and motorbikes are permitted.

Reservations, fee: Reservations accepted; $9-$11 fee per night; MasterCard and Visa accepted. Open all year.

Who to contact: Phone the park at (360) 665-6351 or write to P.O. Box 488, Ocean Park, WA 98640.

Location: From Interstate 5 at Longview, turn west on Highway 4 and drive 63 miles. Turn south on US 101 and drive 13 miles to the junction with Highway 103. Turn north on Highway 103 and drive nine miles to the campground.

Trip note: This wooded campground covers five acres and has beach access. Nearby is Leadbetter Point State Park, a day-use park and natural area that adjoins a wildlife refuge. The trails at Leadbetter Point State Park lead through the dunes and woods and provide opportunities for seeing both marine birds and waterfowl, especially in the spring and fall. There is also a boat launch. Within five miles of the campground are two nine-hole golf courses.

---

24. TIMBERLAND RV PARK

Reference: **Near Willapa River; map B1, grid d7.**

Campsites, facilities: There are six tent sites and 24 drive-through sites for trailers or RVs of any length. Electricity, piped water, sewer hookups, cable TV and picnic tables are provided. Toilets and showers are available. Bottled gas, sanitary services, a store, a cafe, laundry and ice are located within one mile. Pets and motorbikes are permitted. Boat docks are nearby where the Willapa River empties into Willapa Bay.

Reservations, fee: Reservations accepted; $9-$15 fee per night. Open mid-March to November.

Who to contact: Phone (360) 942-3325 or write to 850 Crescent, Raymond, WA 98577.

Location: From Olympia, drive south on Interstate 5 to exit 88. Turn west on State Route 12 and drive 46 miles to Hoquiam. Turn south on US 101 and drive 21 miles to Raymond. At the junction of Highway 105 and US 101, turn west on Highway 105 and drive six blocks. Turn south on Crescent Street and drive two blocks to the park at the end of the street.

Trip note: This park covers three acres on the Willapa River, a popular river during salmon or steelhead runs. It is in a wooded setting with fishing, hunting, clamming and golfing among the nearby recreation options.

---

25. SOUTHBEND MOBILE AND RV PARK

Reference: **On Willapa River; map B1, grid d7.**

Campsites, facilities: There are two tent sites and 12 drive-through sites for trailers or RVs of any length. Electricity, piped water and sewer hookups are provided. Toilets, showers, a recreation hall and laundry are available. Bottled gas, a store, a cafe and ice are within one mile. Pets and motorbikes are permitted. Boat docks and launching facilities are nearby where the Willapa River empties into Willapa Bay.

Reservations, fee: Reservations accepted; $15 fee per night. Open all year.

Who to contact: Phone (360) 875-5165 or write to P.O. Box 4, South Bend, WA 98586.

Location: From Interstate 5 at Longview, turn west on Highway 4 and drive 63 miles, then turn north and drive about 20 miles to South Bend. Turn south on Central and proceed to the campground in town.

Trip note: This small, wooded park covers two acres near the Willapa River. It makes a decent layover for tourists traveling US 101. Additional facilities within five miles of the campground include an 18-hole golf course.

---

26. OCEAN PARK RESORT

Reference: **On Willapa Bay; map B1, grid e5.**

Campsites, facilities: There are six tent sites and 70 sites (34 drive-through) for trailers or RVs of any length. Electricity, piped water, sewer hookups and picnic tables are provided. Bottled gas, toilets, a recreation hall, laundry, ice, a playground, firewood, a hot tub and a swimming pool are available. Showers are available for an extra fee. A store and a cafe can be found within one mile.

Pets and motorbikes are permitted. Boat docks and launching facilities are located nearby on Willapa Bay.

Reservations, fee: Reservations accepted; $17 fee per night; MasterCard, Discover and Visa accepted. Open all year.

Who to contact: Phone the park at (800) 835-4634 or (360) 665-4585 or write to P.O. Box 339, Ocean Park, WA 98640.

Location: From Interstate 5 at Portland, turn northwest on Highway 30 and drive approximately 100 miles to Longview, turn west on Highway 4 and drive 63 miles, then turn south on US 101 and drive 13 miles to the junction with Highway 103. Turn north on Highway 103 and drive 11 miles to the town of Ocean Park, then turn east on 259th Street and drive two blocks to the park at the end of the road.

Trip note: This wooded campground covers 10 acres and has access to the shoreline of Willapa Bay. It's primarily for RVs. The sites are grassy and shaded. Leadbetter Point State Park to the north provides a side trip option.

27.　WESTGATE MOTOR & TRAILER COURT　RV

Reference: **Near Long Beach; map B1, grid e5.**

Campsites, facilities: There are 39 sites for trailers or RVs of any length (15 drive-through). Electricity, piped water and sewer hookups are provided. Restrooms, showers, a recreation hall and ice are available. A store, a cafe and laundry can be found within two miles. Pets are permitted. Boat docks and launching facilities are located nearby on Willapa Bay.

Reservations, fee: Reservations accepted; $16-$17 fee per night; MasterCard and Visa accepted. Open all year.

Who to contact: Phone the park at (360) 665-4211 or write to 20803 Pacific Highway, Ocean Park, WA 98640.

Location: From Interstate 5 at Longview, turn west on Highway 4 and drive 63 miles, then turn south on US 101 and drive 13 miles to the junction with Highway 103. Turn north on Highway 103 and drive 7.5 miles to the campground on the south edge of the town of Ocean Park.

Trip note: This camp covers four acres and has beach access. It's a very pretty, very clean park, with oceanfront sites and all the amenities. Full-facility cabins are available for rental. Additional facilities within five miles of the campground include an 18-hole golf course.

28.　OCEAN AIRE　RV

Reference: **Near Willapa Bay; map B1, grid e5.**

Campsites, facilities: There are 46 drive-through sites for trailers or RVs of any length. No tents are allowed. Electricity, piped water, sewer hookups and picnic tables are provided. Bottled gas, sanitary services, toilets, showers, laundry and ice are available. A store and a cafe can be found within one mile. Pets are permitted. Boat rentals are nearby on Willapa Bay.

Reservations, fee: Reservations accepted; $10-$15 fee per night. Open all year.

Who to contact: Phone (360) 665-4027 or write to P.O. Box 155, Ocean Park, WA 98640.

Location: From Interstate 5 at Portland, turn northwest on Highway 30 and drive approximately 100 miles to Astoria. Turn north on Highway 101 into Washington state. Continue north for about 10 miles to the junction with Highway 103. Turn north on Highway 103 and drive 11 miles to the town of Ocean Park, then turn east on 259th Street. Drive two blocks to the camp.

Trip note: This camp covers two acres and has access to the shoreline of Willapa Bay. Additional facilities found within five miles of the campground include tennis courts. About eight miles north of this campground is Leadbetter Point State Park which is open for day use and provides footpaths for walking through the state-designated natural area and wildlife refuge.

29.   PEGG'S OCEANSIDE TRAILER PARK   **RV**

Reference: **Near Long Beach; map B1, grid e5.**

Campsites, facilities: There are six tent sites and 30 sites for trailers or RVs of any length. Electricity, piped water, sewer hookups and picnic tables are provided. Sanitary services, toilets, a recreation hall and ice are available. Showers are available for an extra fee. Bottled gas, a store, a cafe and laundry can be found within one mile. Pets and motorbikes are permitted.

Reservations, fee: Reservations accepted; $11-$15 fee per night. Open mid-April to mid-September.

Who to contact: Phone (360) 642-2451 or write to Route 1, P.O. Box 460, Long Beach, WA 98631.

Location: From Interstate 5 at Portland, turn northwest on Highway 30 and drive approximately 100 miles to Astoria. Turn north on Highway 101 into Washington state. Continue north for about 10 miles to the junction with Highway 103. Turn north on Highway 103 and drive 5.5 miles to the campground.

Trip note: This wooded campground covers three acres and has beach access. Pan fishing and beachcombing are two possible activities. Additional facilities within five miles of the campground include an 18-hole golf course.

30.   PACIFIC PARK TRAILER PARK   **RV**

Reference: **Near Long Beach; map B1, grid e5.**

Campsites, facilities: There are 53 sites for trailers or RVs of any length. Electricity, piped water, sewer hookups and picnic tables are provided. Toilets, laundry and ice are available, and showers are available for an extra fee. Bottled gas, a store and a cafe can be found within one mile. Pets are permitted.

Reservations, fee: Reservations accepted; $14 fee per night. Open all year.

Who to contact: Phone (360) 642-3253 or write to Route 1, P.O. Box 543, Long Beach, WA 98631.

Location: From Interstate 5 at Portland, turn northwest on Highway 30 and drive approximately 100 miles to Astoria. Turn north on Highway 101 into Washington state. Continue north for about 10 miles to the junction with Highway 103. Turn north on Highway 103 and drive four miles to the campground.

Trip note: This park covers two acres and has beach access. No tents are permitted. The sites are concrete, spacious and near the beach. Additional facilities found within five miles of the campground include an 18-hole golf course, marked bike trails and a riding stable.

31.   CRANBERRY TRAILER PARK   **RV**

Reference: **Near Long Beach; map B1, grid e5.**

Campsites, facilities: There are 20 sites (one drive-through) for trailers or RVs of any length in this adult-only campground. No tents are allowed. Electricity, piped water, sewer hookups and picnic tables are provided. Sanitary services, toilets, showers and ice are available. Bottled gas, a store, a cafe and laundry can be found within one mile. Pets are permitted.

Reservations, fee: Reservations accepted; $10-$12 fee per night. Open all year.
Who to contact: Phone (360) 642-2027 or write to Route 1, P.O. Box 522B, Long Beach, WA 98631.
Location: From Interstate 5 at Portland, turn northwest on Highway 30 and drive approximately 100 miles to Astoria. Turn north on Highway 101 into Washington state. Continue north for about 10 miles to the junction with Highway 103. Turn north on Highway 103 and drive 4.5 miles to Cranberry Road, then turn east and continue one-quarter mile to the campground.
Trip note: This park covers two acres and has beach access. Additional facilities found within five miles of the campground include an 18-hole golf course, marked bike trails and a riding stable.

32. ANDERSEN'S RV PARK ON THE OCEAN   🆁🆅

Reference: **Near Long Beach; map B1, grid e5.**
Campsites, facilities: There are 15 tent sites and 59 sites for trailers or RVs of any length. Electricity, piped water, sewer hookups, cable TV and picnic tables are provided. Sanitary services, toilets, showers, a hall, laundry, ice, propane, bottled gas, a fax machine, a horseshoe pit and a playground are available. A store and cafe can be found within two miles. Pets are permitted.
Reservations, fee: Reservations accepted; $12-$16 fee per night. MasterCard and Visa accepted. Open all year.
Who to contact: Phone (360) 642-2231 or (800) 645-6795, or write to Route 1, P.O. Box 480, Long Beach, WA 98631.
Location: From Interstate 5 at Longview, turn west on Highway 4 and drive 63 miles, then turn south on US 101 and drive 13 miles to the junction with Highway 103. Turn north on Highway 103 and drive five miles to the park.
Trip note: This camp covers five acres and has quick beach access on a path through the dunes. It is set in a flat, sandy area with graveled sites. Recreation options include beach bonfires, beachcombing, surf fishing and clamming (seasonal). Additional facilities found within five miles of the campground include a nine-hole golf course, a riding stable and tennis courts.

33. WESTERN LAKES

Reference: **Near Naselle; map B1, grid e7.**
Campsites, facilities: There are three primitive tent sites. Picnic tables, fire grills, tent pads and vault toilets are provided, but there is **no piped water**. Pets are permitted.
Reservations, fee: No reservations; no fee. Open all year.
Who to contact: Phone the Department of Natural Resources at (360) 748-2383 or write to Department of Natural Resources, Central Region, 1405 Rush Road, Chehalis, WA 98532-8763.
Location: From Interstate 5 at Longview, turn west on Highway 4 and drive approximately 60 miles to milepost 3, just past Naselle. Turn north on C-Line Road and drive one mile (take the right fork to Naselle Youth Camp). Turn right on Road C-4000 and drive 1.4 miles, then turn left on Road C-2600 and drive one mile. Turn right on Road WA-WT-8520 and drive one-third mile to the campground.
Trip note: You want quiet and solitude? You found it. This tiny, primitive campground is a jewel, set in a wooded area near Western Lakes, just outside of Naselle. It is a prime camp for travelers heading to the coast who want a day

or two of privacy before they hit the crowds. There are some good hiking trails nearby.

34.   THE BEACON-CHARTERS RV PARK   RV

Reference: **Near Fort Canby State Park; map B1, grid f5.**

Campsites, facilities: There are 60 sites for trailers or RVs of any length. Electricity, piped water and sewer hookups are provided. Toilets and ice are available. Showers can be obtained for an extra fee. Bottled gas, a store, a cafe and laundry are located within one mile. Pets are permitted. Boat docks and launching facilities are nearby.

Reservations, fee: Reservations accepted; $14-$16 fee per night. Open all year.

Who to contact: Phone (360) 642-2138 or write to P.O. Box 74, Ilwaco, WA 98624.

Location: From Interstate 5 at Longview, turn west on Highway 4 and drive 63 miles, then turn south on US 101 and drive 15 miles to Ilwaco. The park is on the corner of Howerton and Elizabeth at the Port of Ilwaco

Trip note: This park is located at the Port of Ilwaco docks, covers two acres and has riverside access and a view of the Columbia River. The park features fishing charters during the season (roughly from mid-May through late September). Fort Canby State Park is nearby. It offers numerous hiking trails and an interpretive center on maritime and military history. Additional facilities within five miles of the campground include an 18-hole golf course.

35.   COVE RV AND TRAILER PARK   RV

Reference: **Near Fort Canby State Park; map B1, grid f5.**

Campsites, facilities: There are 43 sites for trailers or RVs of any length. Electricity, piped water, sewer and cable TV hookups are provided. Sanitary services, toilets, coin-operated showers and laundry are available. Bottled gas, a store and a cafe are located within one mile. Pets are permitted. Boat docks, launching facilities and rentals are nearby.

Reservations, fee: Reservations accepted; $12-$15 fee per night. Open all year.

Who to contact: Phone (360) 642-3689 or write to P.O. Box 38, Ilwaco, WA 98624.

Location: From Interstate 5 at Longview, turn west on Highway 4 and drive 63 miles, then turn south on US 101 and drive 15 miles to Ilwaco. At the junction of Spruce Street SW and First Street, turn west on Spruce Street and drive one block, then turn south on Second Avenue SW and drive four blocks south to the campground.

Trip note: This park is located where the Pacific Ocean and the Columbia River meet. The park covers five acres and has beach and fishing access nearby. Fish and clam cleaning facilities are available in the park. Additional facilities found within five miles of the campground include a maritime museum, hiking trails, a full-service marina and a riding stable.

36.   WILDWOOD RV PARK & CAMPGROUND   RV

Reference: **Near Fort Canby State Park; map B1, grid f5.**

Campsites, facilities: There are 25 tent sites and 30 sites for trailers or RVs of any length. Electricity, piped water, sewer hookups and picnic tables are provided. Sanitary services and toilets are available. Showers can be obtained for an extra fee. Bottled gas, firewood, a store, a cafe, laundry and ice are located within one mile. Pets are permitted.

Reservations, fee: Reservations accepted; $12-$17 fee per night. Open April through October.

Who to contact: Phone the park at (360) 642-2131 or write to Route 1, P.O. Box 76, Long Beach, WA 98631.

Location: From Interstate 5 at Portland, turn northwest on Highway 30 and drive approximately 100 miles to Astoria. Turn north on Highway 101 into Washington state. Continue north for about 10 miles to Sandridge Road (located one-half mile east of the junction with Highway 103). Turn north and drive three-quarters of a mile to the park.

Trip note: This pretty wooded park, for citizens of age 50 and over, covers five acres and has beach access, pan fishing and its own little pond. Additional facilities found within five miles of the campground include an 18-hole golf course, a full-service marina and tennis courts. See The Beacon-Charters RV Park for attractions at nearby Fort Canby State Park.

---

37.   KOA ILWACO   RV

Reference: **Near Fort Canby State Park; map B1, grid f5.**

Campsites, facilities: There are 50 tent sites and 114 drive-through sites for trailers or RVs of any length. Two cabins are also available. Electricity, piped water, sewer and cable TV hookups are provided. Bottled gas, sanitary services, toilets, showers, firewood, a recreation hall, a store, laundry, ice and a playground are available. Electricity, piped water and sewer hookups can be obtained for an extra fee. Pets are permitted.

Reservations, fee: Reservations accepted; $18-$25 fee per night; for cabin reservation and fee information phone contact number below. MasterCard and Visa accepted. Open mid-May to mid-October.

Who to contact: Phone the park at (360) 642-3292, (800) 562-3258 or write to P.O. Box 549, Ilwaco, WA 98624.

Location: From Interstate 5 at Longview, turn west on Highway 4 and drive 63 miles, then turn south on US 101 and drive nine miles to Ilwaco. The campground is at the junction of US 101 South and US 101 Alternate.

Trip note: This campground covers 17 acres and is about nine miles from the beach. Pan fishing, horseshoe pits and a recreation room provide possible activities. Additional facilities found within five miles of the campground include a maritime museum, hiking trails and a nine-hole golf course.

---

38.   SOU'WESTER LODGE & TRAILER PARK   RV

Reference: **In Long Beach; map B1, grid f5.**

Campsites, facilities: There are 10 tent sites and 60 sites for trailers or RVs of any length (five drive-through). Electricity, piped water and sewer hookups are provided. Toilets, showers, cable TV and laundry are available. Bottled gas, sanitary services, a store, a cafe and ice are located within one mile. Pets and motorbikes are permitted. Boat launching facilities are nearby.

Reservations, fee: Reservations accepted; $13.50-$20 fee per night.

Who to contact: Phone the park at (360) 642-2542 or write to P.O. Box 102, Seaview, WA 98644.

Location: From Interstate 5 at Portland, turn northwest on Highway 30 and drive approximately 100 miles to Astoria. Turn north on Highway 101 into Washington state. Continue north for about 10 miles to the junction with Highway

103. Continue one block south on US 101, then one block west on 38th Place (Beach Access Road) to the campground.

Trip note: This is one of the few sites in immediate area that provides spots for tent camping. It covers three acres and has beach access. Fishing is a recreation option. Additional facilities found within five miles of the campground include an 18-hole golf course, a full-service marina and a riding stable.

39.   FORT CANBY STATE PARK   [RV]

Reference: **On the Pacific Ocean; map B1, grid f5.**

Campsites, facilities: There are four primitive tent sites, 183 developed tent sites and 60 sites with full hookups for trailers or RVs up to 45 feet long. Picnic tables and fire grills are provided. A sanitary disposal station and toilets are available. Showers can be obtained for an extra fee. A store and a restaurant are located within one mile. Pets are permitted. Boat launching facilities are nearby.

Reservations, fee: Contact Reservations Northwest at (800) 452-5687 ($6 reservation fee); $11-$16 fee per night. Open all year.

Who to contact: Phone (800) 233-0321 or (360) 642-3078 or write to P.O. Box 488, Ilwaco, WA 98624.

Location: Drive to the small town of Ilwaco on US 101. At the traffic light in town, turn west and drive three miles on the main road to the park entrance. Follow the signs to the campground areas.

Trip note: This is the choice spot of the area for tent campers. There are two spots to camp: a general camping area and the Lake O'Neil area, which offers sites right on the water. This park covers 1,881 acres and provides hiking trails and opportunities for surf, jetty and ocean fishing. There is an interpretive center that highlights the Lewis and Clark expedition, maritime and military history.

40.   OCEANIC RV PARK   [RV]

Reference: **In Long Beach; map B1, grid f5.**

Campsites, facilities: There are 20 drive-through sites for trailers or RVs of any length. No tents are allowed. Electricity, piped water and sewer hookups are provided. Toilets and showers are available. Bottled gas, sanitary services, a store, a cafe, laundry and ice are located within one mile. Pets are permitted. Boat docks, launching facilities and rentals are nearby.

Reservations, fee: Reservations accepted; $10-$14 fee per night; MasterCard and Visa accepted. Open all year.

Who to contact: Phone (360) 642-3836 or write to Route 1, P.O. Box 169E, Long Beach, WA 98631.

Location: From Interstate 5 at Portland, turn northwest on Highway 30 and drive approximately 100 miles to Astoria. Turn north on Highway 101 into Washington state. Continue north for about 10 miles to the junction with Highway 103. Turn north on Highway 103 and drive two miles to Long Beach. The campground is at the south junction of Pacific Highway and Fifth Avenue.

Trip note: This camp covers two acres. Additional facilities within five miles of the campground include an 18-hole golf course, marked bike trails and a full-service marina.

41.   SAND-LO MOTEL AND RV PARK   [RV]

Reference: **Near Long Beach; map B1, grid f5.**

Campsites, facilities: There are 15 sites for trailers or RVs of any length.

Electricity, piped water, cable TV and sewer hookups are provided. Sanitary services, toilets, showers and laundry are available. Bottled gas, a store, a cafe and ice are available within one mile. Pets and motorbikes are permitted.

Reservations, fee: Reservations accepted; $16 fee per night; MasterCard, Visa, American Express and Discover accepted. Open all year.

Who to contact: Phone (360) 642-2600 or write to P.O. Box 736, Long Beach, WA 98631.

Location: From Interstate 5 at Longview, turn west on Highway 4 and drive 63 miles, then turn south on US 101 and drive 13 miles to the junction with Highway 103. Turn north on Highway 103 and drive three miles to the park.

Trip note: This tiny park covers three acres and has beach access. Additional facilities found within five miles of the campground include an 18-hole golf course, a full-service marina and a riding stable.

42. DRIFTWOOD RV PARK AND CABINS RV

Reference: **Near Long Beach; map B1, grid f5.**

Campsites, facilities: There are 60 sites (26 drive-through) for trailers or RVs of any length. Electricity, piped water, sewer hookups and picnic tables are provided. Toilets, showers, a laundry and cable TV are available. Bottled gas, a store, a cafe and laundry can be found within one mile. Pets are permitted.

Reservations, fee: Reservations accepted; $16 fee per night. Open all year.

Who to contact: Phone (360) 642-2711 or write to P.O. Box 296, 1512 North Pacific Highway, Long Beach, WA 98631.

Location: From Interstate 5 at Portland, turn northwest on Highway 30 and drive approximately 100 miles to Astoria. Turn north on Highway 101 into Washington state. Continue north for about 10 miles to the junction with Highway 103. Turn north on Highway 103 and drive two miles to the park on the right.

Trip note: This park covers two acres and has beach access. The sites are grassy and shaded. Additional facilities within five miles of the campground include an 18-hole golf course and a full-service marina.

43. ANTHONY'S HOME COURT RV PARK RV

Reference: **In Long Beach; map B1, grid f5.**

Campsites, facilities: There are 25 sites for trailers or RVs. Electricity, piped water, sewer hookups and picnic tables are provided. Toilets, laundry, ice, cable TV and a playground are available. Showers are available for an extra fee. Bottled gas, sanitary services, a store and a cafe are located within one mile. Pets are permitted.

Reservations, fee: Reservations accepted; $11-$15 fee per night; MasterCard, Visa and Discover accepted. Open all year.

Who to contact: Phone (360) 642-2802 or write to P.O. Box 1276, Long Beach, WA 98631.

Location: From Interstate 5 at Portland, turn northwest on Highway 30 and drive approximately 100 miles to Astoria. Turn north on Highway 101 into Washington state. Continue north for about 10 miles to the junction with Highway 103. Turn north on Highway 103 and drive two miles to the park on the right.

Trip note: This park covers two acres and has beach access. It is an option to Driftwood RV Park, which is just down the street. Additional facilities found within five miles of the campground include an 18-hole golf course, marked bike trails and a riding stable.

44.   SAND CASTLE RV PARK   RV

Reference: **In Long Beach; map B1, grid f5.**

Campsites, facilities: There are 10 tent sites and 38 sites for trailers or RVs of any length. Electricity, piped water, sewer hookups and picnic tables are provided. Sanitary services, toilets, laundry and ice are available. Showers are available for an extra fee. Bottled gas, a store and a cafe can be found within one mile. Pets and motorbikes are permitted. Boat docks, launching facilities and rentals are nearby.

Reservations, fee: Reservations accepted; $15-$20 fee per night. Open all year.

Who to contact: Phone (360) 642-2174 or write to Route 1, P.O. Box 614, Long Beach, WA 98631.

Location: From Interstate 5 at Portland, turn northwest on Highway 30 and drive approximately 100 miles to Astoria. Turn north on Highway 101 into Washington state. Continue north for about 10 miles to the junction with Highway 103. Turn north and drive two miles to the park on the right.

Trip note: This park covers two acres, has beach access and is one of several in the immediate area. No tents are permitted here. It is a very clean park, although not particularly scenic. Additional facilities found within five miles of the campground include an 18-hole golf course, marked bike trails, a full-service marina and a riding stable.

45.   CHRIS' CAMPGROUND & RV PARK   RV

Reference: **In Chinook; map B1, grid f6.**

Campsites, facilities: There are 40 tent sites and 65 sites for trailers or RVs. Electricity and piped water are provided. A laundromat, a sanitary dump station, toilets, a store and ice are available. Showers can be obtained for an extra fee. Bottled gas and a cafe are located within one mile. Pets are permitted. Boat docks and launching facilities are available nearby on the Columbia River.

Reservations, fee: Reservations accepted; $10-$12 fee per night. Open April to late October.

Who to contact: Phone (360) 777-8475 or write to P.O. Box 204, Chinook, WA 98614.

Location: From Longview, turn west on Highway 4 and drive 63 miles, then turn south on US 101 and drive 20 miles to Chinook. This park is in Chinook.

Trip note: This camp covers seven acres and has river access. Additional facilities found within five miles of the campground include a full-service marina. This park caters to fishermen; a complete bait and tackle shop is located on the premises, and in the months of April and May, the owner offers samples of free sturgeon bait and special discounts to all of his fishing customers. Nice folks.

46.   RIVER'S END CAMPGROUND & RV PARK   RV

Reference: **Near Fort Columbia State Park; map B1, grid f6.**

Campsites, facilities: There are 40 tent sites and 60 sites (seven drive-through) for trailers or RVs of any length. Electricity, piped water, sewer hookups, cable TV and picnic tables are provided. Sanitary services, toilets, a recreation hall, laundry, ice and a playground are available. Showers and firewood can be obtained for an extra fee. Bottled gas, a store and a cafe are located within one mile. Pets and motorbikes are permitted. Boat docks, launching facilities and rentals are nearby on the Columbia River.

Reservations, fee: Reservations accepted; $12-$16 fee per night. Open April to late October.

Who to contact: Phone (360) 777-8317 or write to P.O. Box 280, Chinook, WA 98614.

Location: From Interstate 5 at Kelso, turn west on Highway 4 and drive 63 miles, then turn south on US 101 and drive 20 miles to Chinook. The campground is at the north edge of town.

Trip note: This wooded campground covers five acres and has riverside access. Salmon and fishing are available here. Additional facilities found within five miles of the campground include marked bike trails and a full-service marina. Also nearby is Fort Columbia State Park which has an interpretive center featuring the history of coastal artillery.

47.　　　　　MAUCH'S SUNDOWN RV PARK　　　RV

Reference: Near Fort Columbia State Park; map B1, grid f6.

Campsites, facilities: There are 10 tent sites and 50 sites for trailers or RVs of any length. Electricity, piped water, sewer hookups and picnic tables are provided. Sanitary services, cable TV, toilets, firewood, laundry and ice are available. Showers can be obtained for an extra fee. Bottled gas, a store and a cafe are located within one mile. Motorbikes are permitted. Boat docks and launching facilities are nearby on the Columbia River.

Reservations, fee: Reservations accepted; $8-$15 fee per night. Open all year.

Who to contact: Phone (360) 777-8713 or write to P.O. Box 129, Chinook, WA 98614.

Location: From Astoria, Oregon, on Highway 30, drive north into Washington state for approximately eight miles to Chinook. The park is in town near the Astoria Bridge.

Trip note: Mauch's, an adults-only park, covers four acres, has riverside access and is in a wooded, hilly setting with grassy sites. It is near Fort Columbia State Park which has a newly renovated interpretive center featuring the history of coastal artillery.

48.　　　　　SKAMOKAWA VISTA PARK　　　RV

Reference: Near Columbia River; map B1, grid f9.

Campsites, facilities: There are four tent sites and 30 sites for trailers or RVs of any length. Electricity, piped water and picnic tables are provided. Six of the 21 motor home sites offer direct water hookups. Sanitary services, toilets, showers, firewood and a playground are available. Bottled gas, a store, a cafe and ice are located within one mile. Pets and motorbikes are permitted. Boat docks and launching facilities are nearby.

Reservations, fee: Reservations accepted; $8-$12 fee per night. Open all year.

Who to contact: Phone the park at (360) 795-8605 or write to P.O. Box 220, Skamokawa, WA 98647.

Location: From Interstate 5 at Kelso, turn west on Highway 4 and drive 35 miles to Skamokawa. Continue one-half mile west on Highway 4 to the campground.

Trip note: This camp covers 30 acres and has access to the Columbia River, where fishing, swimming and boating are all options. Additional facilities found within five miles of the campground include a full-service marina and tennis courts.

MAP B2

WASHINGTON MAP .... see page 90
Adjoining Maps
NORTH (A2) .... see page 112
EAST (B3) .... see page 330
SOUTH .... Oregon
WEST (B1) .... see page 274

89 LISTINGS
PAGES 294-329

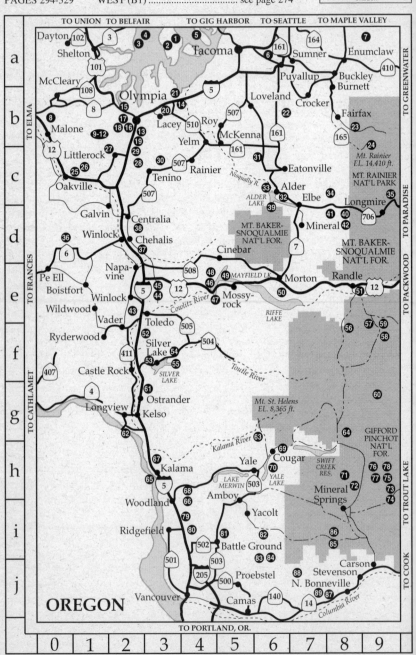

Washington Map B2 featuring: Squaxin Island, Puget Sound, Tacoma, Hartstene Island, Puyallup River, Green River, Capitol Forest, Black Lake, Olympia, Long Lake, Tanwax Lake, Carbon River, Mount Baker-Snoqualmie National Forest, Mount Rainier National Park, Deep Lake, Offut Lake, Mima Falls, Chehalis River, Alder Lake, Centralia, Lewis and Clark State Park, Cowlitz River, Mayfield Lake, Toutle River, Riffe Lake, Gifford Pinchot National Forest, Silver Lake, Cispus River, Coweeman River, Mount St. Helens, Columbia River, Lewis River, Kalama River, Pacific Crest Trail, Yale Lake, Wind River, Indian Heaven Wilderness, Meadow Lake, Paradise Point State Park, Battle Ground Lake, Mosquito Lakes, Washougal River

---

1.   PENROSE POINT STATE PARK   🚐

Reference: **On Puget Sound; map B2, grid a3.**

Campsites, facilities: There is one primitive tent site and 83 developed sites for tents or self-contained RVs up to 35 feet long. Picnic tables and fire grills are provided. A sanitary disposal station, coin-operated showers and toilets are available. Some facilities are **wheelchair accessible**. Leashed pets are permitted. Boat docks are nearby and are available for overnight moorage for a fee.

Reservations, fee: Contact Reservations Northwest at (800) 452-5687 ($6 reservation fee); $5-$11 fee per night. Open all year.

Who to contact: Phone (800) 233-0321 or (206) 884-2514 or write to 321-158th Avenue KPS, Lakebay, WA 98439.

Location: From Interstate 5 at Tacoma, turn north on Highway 16 and drive 10 miles. Then turn west on Highway 302 and drive 5.25 miles. Turn south on Key Peninsula Highway for 9.2 miles, through the towns of Key Center and Home. Turn left at Cornwall Road KPS and drive 1.25 miles. Turn left on 158th Avenue KPS and drive into the park.

Trip note: This park is set on Carr Inlet in Puget Sound, overlooking Lake Bay. It has a remote feel, but it's actually not far from Tacoma. Because of the circular driving route it takes to get here, a lot of people bypass it. This park is known for its excellent fishing, clamming and oysters.

---

2.   JOEMMA BEACH STATE PARK   🚐

Reference: **On Puget Sound; map B2, grid a3.**

Campsites, facilities: There are 23 sites for tents, trailers or RVs up to 35 feet long. Picnic tables, fire grills and tent pads are provided. Vault toilets, piped water, boat launching facilities and a dock are available. Pets are permitted on leashes.

Reservations, fee: No reservations; $10 fee per night; $3 launch fee. Open Memorial Day through Labor Day.

Who to contact: Phone (800) 233-0321 or (206) 265-3606 or write to 11101 56th Street NW, Gig Harbor, WA 98332.

Location: From Tacoma drive 10 miles northwest on Highway 16, then continue west for about 15 miles on Highway 302 to the town of Home. From the bridge in Home, follow Longbranch Road south for 1.3 miles, turn right on Whiteman Road and drive 2.3 miles, then turn right on Bay Road and drive one mile to the camp on the right.

Trip note: This beautiful camp is set along the shore of the peninsula. It is a less crowded alternative to Penrose Point State Park. Piped water and boating facilities make it a winner.

3.   JARRELL COVE STATE PARK   RV

Reference: **On Harstine Island; map B2, grid a3.**

Campsites, facilities: There are 20 sites for tents or self-contained RVs up to 30 feet long. Picnic tables and fire grills are provided. Flush toilets and coin-operated showers are available. Some facilities are **wheelchair accessible**. Leashed pets are permitted. Boat docks are available for overnight moorage for a fee.

Reservations, fee: No reservations; $10 fee per night; $8-$11 moorage fee. Open April through October.

Who to contact: Phone (800) 233-0321 or (360) 426-9226 or write to East 391 Wingert Road, Shelton, WA 98584.

Location: From Interstate 5 at Olympia, turn north on US 101 and drive 22 miles to Shelton. Turn north on Highway 3 and drive about eight miles. Turn right on Spencer Lake Road and continue to the Harstine Bridge. Cross the bridge to Harstine Island and turn left at the stop sign. Continue four miles to the park on the left.

Trip note: This wooded park is rarely crowded and offers a protected cove for boating and docking facilities. A private marina is nearby. Fishing here is excellent and there is a nice beach for sunbathing or beachcombing.

---

4.   JARRELL COVE MARINA   RV

Reference: **Near Shelton; map B2, grid a3.**

Campsites, facilities: There are four drive-through sites for trailers or RVs up to 27 feet long. Piped water, electricity and picnic tables are provided. Bottled gas, toilets, showers, sanitary services, a store, a laundromat and ice are available. Pets are permitted. Boat docks and boat rentals are available.

Reservations, fee: Reservations accepted; $20 fee per night; MasterCard and Visa accepted. Open all year.

Who to contact: Phone (360) 426-8823 or write to East 220 Wilson Road, Shelton, WA 98584.

Location: From Olympia, turn north on Interstate 5, then north on US 101, and drive 22 miles to Shelton. Turn east on Highway 3 and drive about eight miles northeast. Turn right on Pickering Road and drive to Hartstene Bridge. Cross the bridge and continue north on North Island Drive. Turn west on Haskell Hill Road and drive one mile to the marina.

Trip note: Marina and boat rentals are the big bonus here. The drive-through sites are ideal for pickup campers towing boats on trailers.

---

5.   KOPACHUCK STATE PARK   RV

Reference: **On Puget Sound; map B2, grid a4.**

Campsites, facilities: There are two primitive tent sites and 41 developed campsites for tents or self-contained RVs up to 35 feet long. Picnic tables and fire grills are provided. A sanitary disposal station, coin-operated showers and toilets are available. Some facilities are **wheelchair accessible**. Leashed pets are permitted. Boat buoys are available.

Reservations, fee: No reservations; $7-$10 fee per night. Open March through October.

Who to contact: Phone (800) 233-0321 or (206) 265-3606 or write to 11101 56th Street NW, Gig Harbor, WA 98332.

Location: From Interstate 5 at Tacoma, turn north on Highway 16 and drive seven miles. At the sign for Kopachuck State Park, turn west and drive five miles to the camp.

Trip note: This park is on Henderson Bay in Puget Sound, near Tacoma. It's a nice, developed park with full facilities for tent campers. There is a large beach area for clamming or lounging. Fishing access is available by boat only. A boat launch is located not far from camp.

---

6. MAJESTIC MANOR RV PARK [RV]

Reference: **On Puyallup River; map B2, grid a6.**

Campsites, facilities: There are 12 tent sites and 118 sites for trailers or RVs of any length. Electricity, piped water and sewer hookups are provided. Flush toilets, bottled gas, sanitary services, showers, a recreation hall, a store, a laundromat, ice and a swimming pool are available. A cafe is located within one mile. Pets and motorbikes are permitted.

Reservations, fee: Reservations accepted; $13-$17 fee per night. Open all year.

Who to contact: Phone (800) 348-3144 or (206) 845-3144 or write to 7022 River Road, Puyallup, WA 98371.

Location: From Interstate 5 near Tacoma, take exit 135 and drive four miles east on Highway 167 (River Road) to the park on the right.

Trip note: This park is set along the Puyallup River. It's a clean, pretty park that caters to RVs. Nearby recreation options include an 18-hole golf course, a full-service marina and tennis courts. For information on the attractions in Tacoma, see the trip note for Dash Point State Park.

---

7. KANASKAT-PALMER STATE PARK [RV]

Reference: **On Green River; map B2, grid a9.**

Campsites, facilities: There are 31 tent sites and 19 drive-through sites for trailers or RVs up to 35 feet long. Picnic tables are provided. Electricity, flush toilets, showers and sanitary services are available. Some facilities are **wheelchair accessible**. Leashed pets are permitted. Boat rentals are available on the Green River nearby.

Reservations, fee: No reservations; $10-$15 fee per night. Open all year with limited facilities in the winter.

Who to contact: Phone (800) 233-0321 or (360) 886-0148 or write to 23700 Flaming Geyser, Auburn, WA 98002.

Location: From Interstate 5 at Tacoma, turn east on Highway 410 and drive about 25 miles to Enumclaw. Turn northeast on Farman Road and drive 11 miles to the park on the left.

Trip note: This wooded campground offers private campsites set along the Green River. In summer, the river is ideal for rafting and kayaking. In winter, it attracts a nice run of steelhead. You can explore the area's hiking trails year-round.

---

8. PORTER CREEK

Reference: **On Porter Creek in Capitol Forest; map B2, grid b0.**

Campsites, facilities: There are 14 primitive campsites for tents or small trailers. Picnic tables, fire grills and tent pads are provided. **No piped water.** Vault toilets and horse-loading ramps are available. Motorbikes and leashed pets are permitted.

Reservations, fee: No reservations; no fee. Open all year.

Who to contact: Phone the Department of Natural Resources at (360) 748-2383 or write to Department of Natural Resources, Central Region, 1405 Rush Road, Chehalis, WA 98532-8763.

Location: From Interstate 5 south of Olympia, turn west on State Route 12 and drive 21 miles to Porter. Travel northeast on Porter Creek Road for three miles, then continue straight for another one-half mile. The campground is on the left.

Trip note: This primitive, rustic campground is less than 20 miles from Olympia. It is in Capitol Forest and is managed by the Department of Natural Resources. Set along the shore of Porter Creek, it offers trails for hiking, horseback riding or motorbiking.

9.   MIDDLE WADDELL

Reference: **On Waddell Creek in Capitol Forest; map B2, grid b1.**

Campsites, facilities: There are three primitive campsites for tents or small trailers. Picnic tables, fire grills and tent pads are provided. Vault toilets are available, but there is **no piped water**. Motorbikes and pets on leashes are permitted.

Reservations, fee: No reservations; no fee. Open all year.

Who to contact: Phone the Department of Natural Resources at (360) 748-2383 or write to Department of Natural Resources, Central Region, 1405 Rush Road, Chehalis, WA 98532-8763.

Location: From Interstate 5 south of Olympia, take exit 95 and turn west on Highway 121. Drive four miles to Littlerock. Continue west for one mile and turn right on Waddell Creek Road. Drive three miles, turn left and continue 100 yards to the campsite on your left.

Trip note: This wooded campground is set along Waddell Creek in the Capitol Forest. The trails are used primarily for motorbikes, making for a rather noisy campground. Remember, **no piped water** is available here.

10.   MOUNT MOLLY

Reference: **Near Waddell Creek in Capitol Forest; map B2, grid b1.**

Campsites, facilities: There are 10 primitive campsites for tents or small trailers. Picnic tables, fire grills and tent pads are provided. Vault toilets are available, but there is **no piped water**. Motorbikes are permitted.

Reservations, fee: No reservations; no fee. Open all year.

Who to contact: Phone the Department of Natural Resources at (360) 748-2383 or write to Department of Natural Resources, Central Region, 1405 Rush Road, Chehalis, WA 98532-8763.

Location: From Interstate 5 at Olympia, turn north on US 101 and drive four miles. Take the Mud Bay exit and drive south on Delphi Road for six miles. Drive straight on Waddell Creek Road for three miles, then turn right and continue 1.5 miles. Take the left fork and drive one mile to the campground on the left.

Trip note: This campground is set in the forest. The nearby trails are used primarily for motorbiking. Weekdays are often quiet, but weekends are filled with the hum of motorcycles, so if you're looking for peace and quiet this is probably not your camp.

11.   FALL CREEK

Reference: **On Fall Creek in Capitol Forest; map B2, grid b1.**

Campsites, facilities: There are eight primitive campsites for tents or small trailers. Picnic tables, fire grills and tent pads are provided. Vault toilets, piped water and a horse-loading ramp are available, but there is **no piped water.** Leashed pets are permitted.

Reservations, fee: No reservations; no fee. Open all year.

Who to contact: Phone the Department of Natural Resources at (360) 748-2383 or write to Department of Natural Resources, Central Region, 1405 Rush Road, Chehalis, WA 98532-8763.

Location: From Interstate 5 at Olympia, turn north on US 101 and drive four miles. Take the Mud Bay exit and drive south on Delphi Road for six miles. Continue straight on Waddell Creek Road for three miles, turn right and go 1.5 miles. Take the left fork and drive two miles on C-Line Road and then turn left onto Road C 4000 and drive 2.5 miles. Turn right and proceed 200 yards to the campground.

Trip note: This camp is a good option to Middle Waddell and Mount Molly campgrounds, since the trails here are for hikers and horseback riders only. This means no motorbikes and a more peaceful setting. The campground is wooded and set along Fall Creek in Capitol Forest.

12.   MARGARET McKENNY

Reference: **In Capitol Forest; map B2, grid b2.**

Campsites, facilities: There are 12 primitive campsites for tents or small trailers. Picnic tables, fire grills and tent pads are provided. Pit toilets, a campfire circle and a horse-loading ramp are available, but there is **no piped water**. Leashed pets are permitted.

Reservations, fee: No reservations; no fee. Open all year.

Who to contact: Phone the Department of Natural Resources at (360) 748-2383 or write to Department of Natural Resources, Central Region, 1405 Rush Road, Chehalis, WA 98532-8763.

Location: From Interstate 5 south of Olympia, take exit 95 and turn west on Highway 121. Drive four miles to Littlerock. Continue west for one mile and turn right on Waddell Creek Road. Drive 2.5 miles, then turn left and drive about 200 yards to the campground.

Trip note: This streamside campground is in the Capitol Forest and managed by the Department of Natural Resources. There are trails nearby that can be used by hikers or horseback riders. This is a cool, scenic camp.

13.   OLYMPIA CAMPGROUND   RV

Reference: **Near Olympia; map B2, grid b2.**

Campsites, facilities: There are 105 sites (40 drive-through) for tents, trailers or RVs of any length. Two cabins are also available. Piped water and picnic tables are provided. Flush toilets, bottled gas, sanitary services, showers, a recreation hall, TV hookups, a store, a laundromat, ice, a playground, a heated swimming pool in the summer, electricity, sewer hookups and firewood are available. A cafe is located within one mile. Pets and motorbikes are permitted.

Reservations, fee: Reservations accepted; $17-$23 fee per night for two people; ($3 fee per night for each additional person); $30 cabin fee per night for four people. MasterCard, Visa, American Express, Discover, Diners Club and Texaco accepted. Open all year.

Who to contact: Phone (360) 352-2551 or write to 1441 83rd Avenue SW, Olympia, WA 98512.

Location: From Olympia on Interstate 5, take exit 101 and drive east for one-quarter mile on Airdustrial Way. Turn right on Center Street; drive one mile. Turn right on 83rd Avenue and drive one-eighth of a mile to the park on the left.

Trip note: This wooded campground has all the comforts. Nearby recreation options include an 18-hole golf course, hiking trails, marked bike trails and tennis courts. It is one of two sites (Pleasant Acres Resort is the other) in the immediate area.

14. MARTIN WAY MOTORHOME & RV PARK [RV]

Reference: In Olympia; map B2, grid b4.

Campsites, facilities: There are 18 sites for trailers or RVs of any length (seven drive-through) in this adult-oriented campground. Electricity, piped water, sewer and cable TV hookups are provided. Flush toilets, showers and a laundromat are available. Bottled gas, sanitary services, a store, a cafe and ice are located within one mile.

Reservations, fee: Reservations accepted; $13-$20 fee per night. Open all year.

Who to contact: Phone (360) 491-6840 or write to 8103 Martin Way SE, Lacey, WA 98506.

Location: From Interstate 5 in Olympia, take exit 111 and drive three-quarters of a mile south to Martin Way, turn west and drive one-quarter mile to the park.

Trip note: This park, oriented to ages 55 and over, is set in urban Olympia. Nearby recreation options include an 18-hole golf course, a full-service marina, tennis courts and the Nisqually National Wildlife Refuge. The refuge offers seven miles of foot trails along which you may view a great variety of plant and animal life.

15. COACH POST TRAILER PARK [RV]

Reference: Near Olympia; map B2, grid b2.

Campsites, facilities: There are 20 drive-through sites for trailers or RVs of any length. Electricity, piped water, sewer hookups and picnic tables are provided. Flush toilets, showers and a laundromat are available. Bottled gas, a store, a cafe and ice are located within one mile. Pets are permitted.

Reservations, fee: Reservations accepted; $20 fee per night. Open all year.

Who to contact: Phone (360) 754-7580 or write to 3633 Seventh Avenue SW, Olympia, WA 98512.

Location: From US 101 in Olympia, take the Black Lake exit and turn left at the fourth stop light. Drive one mile on Seventh Avenue SW to the campground.

Trip note: This wooded park is in a rural area just west of Olympia. Nearby recreation options include an 18-hole golf course, a full-service marina, a riding stable and tennis courts.

16. BLACK LAKE RV PARK [RV]

Reference: On Black Lake; map B2, grid b2.

Campsites, facilities: There are 10 tent sites and 21 sites (seven drive-through) for trailers or RVs of any length. Electricity, piped water, sewer hookups and picnic tables are provided. Flush toilets, bottled gas, sanitary services, a recreation hall, a store, ice, showers and firewood are available. A cafe is located within one mile. Pets are permitted. Boat docks, launching facilities and rentals are nearby.

Reservations, fee: Reservations accepted; $8-$15 fee per night. Open all year.

Who to contact: Phone (360) 357-6775 or write to 4325 Black Lake-Belmore Road, Olympia, WA 98502.

Location: If you are northbound on Interstate 5, take exit 102 (Tumwater-Black Lake) in Tumwater and take Trosper Road to Black Lake. Follow the signs to the park. Heading south on Interstate 5, take the Black Lake Boulevard exit and follow the signs to the park.

Trip note: Here's a good spot for campers traveling Interstate 5 who don't want to get stuck in a hotel for the night. This campground is set along the shore of Black Lake, with trout fishing, swimming and boating among your options. Nearby options include an 18-hole golf course (within five miles) and a full-service marina.

17.　　　　COLUMBUS PARK　　　　RV

Reference: **On Black Lake; map B2, grid b2.**

Campsites, facilities: There are 31 sites for trailers or RVs of any length. Electricity, piped water and picnic tables are provided. Flush toilets, sanitary services, a store, a laundromat, ice, showers, firewood and a playground are available. Bottled gas and a cafe are located within one mile. Leashed pets are permitted. Boat docks and launching facilities are available.

Reservations, fee: Reservations recommended; $15 fee per night. Open all year.

Who to contact: Phone (360) 786-9460 or write to 5700 Black Lake Boulevard, Olympia, WA 98502.

Location: From Interstate 5 in Olympia, take the US 101 exit and drive northwest on US 101 for 1.7 miles, then continue south on Black Lake Boulevard for 3.5 miles to park on the left.

Trip note: This spot is an option to Black Lake RV Park and Salmon Shores Resort. It is a wooded area set along the shore of Black Lake. Nearby recreation options include an 18-hole golf course and a full-service marina.

18.　　　SALMON SHORES RESORT　　　RV

Reference: **On Black Lake; map B2, grid b2.**

Campsites, facilities: There are 20 tent sites and 45 sites for trailers or RVs of any length. Electricity, piped water, sewer hookups and picnic tables are provided. Flush toilets, bottled gas, sanitary services, showers, a store, a laundromat, ice, firewood and a playground are available. A cafe is located within one mile. Boat docks, launching facilities and rentals are nearby on Black Lake.

Reservations, fee: Reservations accepted; $10-$14 fee per night; MasterCard and Visa accepted. Open all year.

Who to contact: Phone (360) 357-8618 or write to 5446 Black Lake Boulevard, Olympia, WA 98512.

Location: From Interstate 5 in Olympia, take the US 101 exit and drive 1.7 miles northwest. Turn south on Black Lake Boulevard and drive 3.5 miles to the resort.

Trip note: This resort is set along the shore of Black Lake. It is a large, popular campground that comfortably accommodates tents and RVs alike. Sites are near the lakeshore. Nearby recreation options include an 18-hole golf course, a full-service marina and a riding stable. This is one of three camps in the immediate vicinity.

19.　　AMERICAN HERITAGE CAMPGROUND　　RV

Reference: **Near Olympia; map B2, grid b2.**

Campsites, facilities: There are 33 tent sites and 72 sites for trailers or RVs of any length. Piped water and picnic tables are provided. Flush toilets, bottled gas, sanitary services, showers, a recreation hall, recreation programs, a store, a cafe, a laundromat, ice, a playground, a heated swimming pool, electricity and sewer hookups and firewood are available. Pets and motorbikes are permitted.

Reservations, fee: Reservations accepted; $17-$25 fee per night for two people; ($3.50 per night for each additional person). MasterCard and Visa accepted. Open Memorial Day through Labor Day weekend.

Who to contact: Phone (360) 943-8778 or write to 9610 Kimmie Street SW, Olympia, WA 98512.

Location: From Olympia, drive five miles south on Interstate 5 to exit 99 and drive one-half mile east. Turn south on Kimmie Street and drive one-quarter mile to the campground on the left.

Trip note: This spacious, wooded campground is set just off the highway and is near several recreation options, including an 18-hole golf course, hiking trails, marked bike trails and tennis courts. The park features novelty bike rentals, free wagon rides and free nightly movies. It is exceptionally clean and very pretty, making for a pleasant layover on your way up or down Interstate 5.

20.　　　　　　LAKESIDE RV PARK　　　　　RV

Reference: **On Long Lake; map B2, grid b3.**

Campsites, facilities: There are 20 tent sites and 60 drive-through sites for trailers or RVs of any length. Electricity, piped water, sewer hookups and picnic tables are provided. Flush toilets, sanitary services, showers, a recreation hall, a store, a cafe and a laundromat are available. Firewood is available for an extra fee. Bottled gas and ice are available within one mile. Pets and motorbikes are permitted. Boat docks, launching facilities and rentals are available nearby.

Reservations, fee: Reservations accepted; $11 fee per night. Open all year.

Who to contact: Phone (360) 491-3660 or write to 7225 14th Avenue SE, Lacey, WA 98503.

Location: From Interstate 5 in Olympia, take exit 109 and drive one mile east on Martin Way, then turn south and go 1.5 miles on Carpenter Road. Turn east on 14th Avenue and drive to the resort.

Trip note: A nice layover spot for Interstate 5 travelers, this wooded park is set along the shore of Long Lake, a narrow 4.5-mile long lake. The best fishing is at either end of the lake. Nearby recreation options include an 18-hole golf course, hiking trails, marked bike trails and a full-service marina.

21.　　　　NISQUALLY PLAZA RV PARK　　　RV

Reference: **Near McAlister Creek; map B2, grid b3.**

Campsites, facilities: There are 48 sites (eight drive-through) for trailers or RVs of any length. Electricity, piped water, sewer hookups, telephone, cable TV and picnic tables are provided. Flush toilets, bottled gas, sanitary services, a store, a cafe, a laundromat, ice, a playground and a swimming pool are available. Showers and firewood can be obtained for an extra fee. Pets are permitted. Boat launching facilities are nearby.

Reservations, fee: Reservations accepted; $8-$17 fee per night. Open all year.

Who to contact: Phone (360) 491-3831 or write to 10220 Martin Way East, Olympia, WA 98503.

Location: Heading north on Interstate 5 in Olympia, take exit 114 and turn right. Drive 200 feet, turn right onto Martin Way, and you'll see the campground.

Trip note: This campground is located on McAlister Creek, where salmon fishing and boating are popular. Nearby recreation options include an 18-hole golf course and Nisqually National Wildlife Refuge, which offers seven miles of foot trails, along which you may view a great variety of flora and fauna.

---

22.   RAINBOW RESORT   RV

Reference: **On Tanwax Lake; map B2, grid b6.**

Campsites, facilities: There are seven tent sites and about 50 sites for trailers or RVs up to 30 feet long. Electricity, piped water, sewer hookups and picnic tables are provided. Flush toilets, bottled gas, firewood, a recreation hall, showers, a store, a laundromat, a hot tub, ice, cable TV and a playground are available. A cafe is located within one mile. Boat docks, launching facilities and rentals are nearby.

Reservations, fee: Reservations accepted; $7-$14 fee per night. Open all year.

Who to contact: Phone (360) 879-5115 or write to 34217 Tanwax Lake Court East, Eatonville, WA 98328.

Location: From Interstate 5 at Tacoma, drive 27 miles south on Highway 7, then turn east to Eatonville on Highway 161 and drive seven miles north to Tanwax Drive. Turn and drive east to the resort on Lake Tanwax.

Trip note: This wooded park is set along the shore of Tanwax Lake. The sites are spacious and shady, with especially pretty tent sites. There is good fishing on the lake and a seasonal fish pond on site. Nearby recreation options include a riding stable.

---

23.   EVANS CREEK

Reference: **On Evans Creek in Mount Baker-Snoqualmie National Forest; map B2, grid b8.**

Campsites, facilities: There are 27 tent sites. Picnic tables, hand-pumped water and fire grills are provided. Vault toilets, hand-pumped water and firewood are available. Leashed pets are permitted.

Reservations, fee: No reservations; no fee. Open mid-June to late September.

Who to contact: Phone Mount Baker-Snoqualmie National Forest at (360) 825-6585 or write to the White River Ranger District, 857 Roosevelt Avenue East, Enumclaw, WA 98022.

Location: From Tacoma on Interstate 5, turn east on Highway 167 and drive nine miles, then continue 11 miles east on Highway 410 to Buckley. Drive 11 miles south on Highway 165 and turn left on Forest Service Road 7920. Drive 1.5 miles to the campground on the right.

Trip note: This primitive campground is set near Evans Creek in an off-road-vehicle area near the northwestern corner of Mount Rainier National Park. If you're looking for a quiet, secluded spot, this is not your place. The two nearby roads that lead into the park are secondary or gravel roads and provide access to several other primitive campgrounds and backcountry trails in the park. A national forest map details the back roads and hiking trails.

---

24.   IPSUT CREEK   RV

Reference: **Near Carbon River in Mount Rainier National Park; map B2, grid b9.**

Campsites, facilities: There are 29 sites for tents or RVs up to 20 feet long, and one group camp is also available. Picnic tables are provided. Pit toilets and piped water are available. Leashed pets are permitted.

Reservations, fee: No reservations; $6 fee per night. Open Memorial Day to Labor Day.

Who to contact: Phone Mount Rainier National Park at (360) 569-2211 or write to Mount Rainier National Park, Tahoma Woods, Ashford, WA 98304.

Location: From Interstate 5 at Tacoma, turn east on Highway 512 and drive 12 miles. Turn right (east) on Highwway 167 and drive for one mile. Turn east on Highway 410 and drive 13 miles to Buckley. Turn southeast on Highway 165 and drive about 13 miles to the Carbon River Park entrance. The campground is five miles into the park.

Trip note: This camp is at the end of Carbon River Road and at the beginning of several trails that lead into the backcountry of Mount Rainier National Park, past lakes, glaciers, waterfalls and many other wonders. Obtain a map from the National Park Service for details, and get a permit if you plan to do some overnight backpacking.

25.   NORTH CREEK

Reference: **On Cedar Creek; map B2, grid c1.**

Campsites, facilities: There are five primitive sites for tents or small trailers. Picnic tables, fire grills and tent pads are provided. Vault toilets and piped water are available. Leashed pets are permitted.

Reservations, fee: No reservations; no fee. Open April through October.

Who to contact: Phone the Department of Natural Resources at (360) 748-2383 or write to Department of Natural Resources, Central Region, 1405 Rush Road, Chehalis, WA 98532-8763.

Location: From Interstate 5 south of Olympia, turn west on State Route 12 and drive 12 miles to Oakville. Continue 2.5 miles west on US 12 to D-Line Road, then head east for two miles. Take the right fork and drive three miles. You'll see the camp on your right.

Trip note: This little-known, wooded campground is set along Cedar Creek and is managed by the Department of Natural Resources. There are trails for hikers only. An option is visiting Chehalis River, a short drive to the west. A canoe launch off US 12 is available north of Oakville.

26.   SHERMAN VALLEY

Reference: **On Cedar Creek in Capitol Forest; map B2, grid c1.**

Campsites, facilities: There are five primitive sites for tents or small trailers. Picnic tables, fire grills and tent pads are provided. Vault toilets and piped water are available. Leashed pets are permitted.

Reservations, fee: No reservations; no fee. Open April through October.

Who to contact: Phone the Department of Natural Resources at (360) 748-2383 or write to Department of Natural Resources, Central Region, 1405 Rush Road, Chehalis, WA 98532-8763.

Location: From Interstate 5 south of Olympia, turn west on US 12 and drive 12 miles to Oakville. Continue 2.5 miles west on US 12 to D-Line Road, then head east for 1.6 miles and take the fork on the right. Continue 4.5 miles to the campground on the right.

Trip note: This is one of nine secluded camp spots set in the Capitol Forest, which is managed by the Department of Natural Resources. It is set along the shore of Porter Creek and there are hiking trails nearby. It is shady, with nice streamside sites.

---

27.   MIMA FALLS TRAILHEAD

Reference: **Near Mima Falls; map B2, grid c1.**

Campsites, facilities: There are five primitive sites for tents or small trailers. Picnic tables, fire grills and tent pads are provided. Vault toilets, piped water and a horse-loading ramp are available. Leashed pets are permitted.

Reservations, fee: No reservations; no fee. Open all year.

Who to contact: Phone the Department of Natural Resources at (360) 748-2383 or write to Department of Natural Resources, Central Region, 1405 Rush Road, Chehalis, WA 98532-8763.

Location: From Interstate 5 south of Olympia, take the Highway 121 exit off and drive four miles west to Littlerock. Continue west for one mile, then turn left on Mima Road and drive 1.5 miles. Turn right on Bordeaux Road and drive one-half mile. At Marksman Road, turn right and continue two-thirds of a mile. Turn left and the campground is about 200 yards away.

Trip note: A highlight here is the trail that leads to Mima Falls. It is excellent for hikers or horseback riders. The campground is very quiet and pretty, which, when combined with the piped water and free admission, makes it a first-rate choice.

---

28.   MILLERSYLVANIA STATE PARK   RV

Reference: **On Deep Lake; map B2, grid c2.**

Campsites, facilities: There are four primitive tent sites, 135 developed tent sites, and 52 sites for trailers or RVs up to 45 feet long. Picnic tables and fire grills are provided. Flush toilets, a sanitary disposal station, a playground, electricity, piped water, showers and firewood are available. A store, a restaurant and ice are located within one mile. Some facilities are **wheelchair accessible**. Leashed pets are permitted. Boat docks and launching facilities are nearby on Deep Lake.

Reservations, fee: No reservations; $5-$14 fee per night. Open all year.

Who to contact: Phone (800) 233-0321 or (360) 753-1519 or write to 1224 Tilley Road South, Olympia, WA 98502.

Location: From Interstate 5 south of Olympia, take exit 95 and drive east on Maytown Road. Turn north on Tilley Road and continue one-half mile to the park.

Trip note: This is a popular park, not too far from Olympia. It offers many choices, including swimming, trout fishing and hiking. There are even a few gut-thumping fitness trails. The park is set along the shore of Deep Lake. Historic highlights are the groves of old growth trees and old Civilian Conservation Corps buildings.

29.   DEEP LAKE RESORT   RV

Reference: **Near Deep Lake; map B2, grid c2.**

Campsites, facilities: There are seven tent sites and 43 sites for trailers or RVs up to 35 feet long. Electricity, piped water, sewer hookups and picnic tables are provided. Flush toilets, sanitary services, a recreation hall, a store, a cafe, a laundromat, ice, bicycle rentals, a playground, showers and firewood are available. Pets and motorbikes are permitted. Boat docks, launching facilities and rentals are nearby at the resort.

Reservations, fee: Reservations accepted; $15-$19 fee per night. MasterCard and Visa accepted. Open mid-April to late September.

Who to contact: Phone (360) 352-7388 or write to 12405 Tilley Road South, Olympia, WA 98512.

Location: From Olympia, drive south on Interstate 5 to exit 95. Turn east on Maytown Road and drive for 2.5 miles. Turn north on Tilley Road and drive one-half mile to the park.

Trip note: This beautiful, wooded, well-maintained campground is set along the shore of Deep Lake near Millersylvania State Park. It offers swimming, fishing and boating opportunities along with spectacular scenery. Other nearby recreation options include an 18-hole golf course and marked bike trails.

---

30.   OFFUT LAKE RV RESORT   RV

Reference: **On Offut Lake; map B2, grid c3.**

Campsites, facilities: There are nine tent sites and 51 sites (35 with full hookups) for trailers or RVs of any length. There are also two cabins available. Electricity, piped water, sewer hookups and picnic tables are provided. Flush toilets, bottled gas, sanitary services, firewood, a recreation hall, a store, a cafe, a laundromat, ice, coin-operated showers, boat docks, boat rentals and a playground are available. Showers can be obtained for an extra fee. Pets and motorbikes are permitted.

Reservations, fee: Reservations accepted; $12-$17 fee per night; MasterCard and Visa accepted. Open year-round.

Who to contact: Phone (360) 264-2438 or write to 4005 120th SE, Tenino, WA 98589.

Location: From Olympia, drive south on Interstate 5 for about 16 miles. Turn east on Highway 507 and drive eight miles to exit 88A (Tenino). Turn north on Old Highway 99 and drive four miles. Turn east on Offut Lake Road and drive 1.5 miles to the resort.

Trip note: This wooded campground is on Offut Lake, just enough off the beaten track to provide a bit of seclusion. This is a lovely campground, with opportunities for fishing, swimming and boating. Everything you'll need for fishing, including tackle and boat rentals, can be obtained at the resort.

31.   HENLEY'S SILVER LAKE RESORT   RV

Reference: **Map B2, grid c6.**

Campsites, facilities: There is an unlimited number of sites for tents and 30 sites for trailers or RVs (20 are full hookups). There are also six cabins available. Restrooms, a sanitary dump, a public phone and snacks are available. Boat rentals, a boat ramp and dock are available. Pets are permitted on leashes.

Reservations, fee: Reservations for cabins and full-hookup RV sites only; $8-$11 per night; $55 cabin fee. Open from opening day of fishing season in April through October.

Who to contact: Phone the resort at (360) 832-3580 or write to 40718 South Silver Lake Road East, Eatonville, WA 98328.

Location: From Tacoma, drive south on Interstate 5 to Highway 7. Turn south on Highway 7 and drive about 20 miles to the yellow blinking light. Drive about 4.5 miles and you will see a sign for Silver Lake Recreation Area. Bear right and drive one-quarter mile to the resort on the left.

Trip note: This is a full-facility resort that is a perfect family vacation destination. It is one of the rare private resorts that caters to tent campers and motor home cruisers. Silver Lake is beautiful and provides opportunities for boating and trout fishing. Featured are a 250-foot boat dock and 50 rental rowboats.

---

32.   ALDER LAKE PARK   RV

Reference: **On Alder Lake; map B2, grid c6.**

Campsites, facilities: There are 20 tent sites and 15 sites for trailers or RVs of any length. Electricity and piped water are provided. Vault toilets are available. Boat docks and launching facilities are located on Alder Lake.

Reservations, fee: No reservations; $8-$12 fee per night. Open all year with limited facilities in the winter.

Who to contact: Phone (360) 569-2778 or write 50324 School Road, Eatonville WA 98330.

Location: From Interstate 5 at Tacoma, drive 35 miles south on Highway 7 to Alder Lake. Turn left and proceed to the park.

Trip note: This municipal park is set along the shore of Alder Lake. It's pretty, with sites near the lake's shore and lots of trees and shrubbery. It's a very decent spot to spend a weekend, especially if you want to get off the highway and enjoy some peace and quiet. Of the two campgrounds on the lake, it is the only one that allows tents. The Mount Rainier Scenic Railroad leaves from Elbe regularly and makes its way through the forests to Mineral Lake. It features open deck cars, live music and restored passenger cars.

---

33.   EAGLE'S NEST ALDER LAKE   RV

Reference: **On Alder Lake; map B2, grid c6.**

Campsites, facilities: There are eight sites for trailers or RVs up to 25 feet long. Electricity, piped water and sewer hookups are provided. Sanitary services are available. Boat launching facilities are located on Alder Lake.

Reservations, fee: Reservations accepted; $15 fee per night; MasterCard and Visa accepted. Open all year.

Who to contact: Phone (360) 569-2533 or write to 52120 Mountain Highway East, Eatonville, WA 98328.

Location: From Interstate 5 at Tacoma, drive 29 miles south on Highway 7 and you'll see the turnoff for the park.

Trip note: This wooded RV park, overlooking Alder Lake, is a cozy, little spot with all amenities. It's a smaller, more secluded option for RVs, yet still close to Tacoma. The Mount Rainier Scenic Railroad leaves from Elbe regularly and makes its way through the forests to Mineral Lake. It features open deck cars, live music and restored passenger cars.

34. ELBE HILLS

Reference: **Near Elbe; map B2, grid c8.**

Campsites, facilities: There are three primitive campsites for tents or small trailers. Picnic tables, fire grills and tent pads are provided. Pit toilets and a group shelter are available, but there is **no piped water**. Leashed pets are permitted.

Reservations, fee: No reservations; no fee. Open all year.

Who to contact: Phone the Department of Natural Resources at (360) 825-1631 or write to Department of Natural Resources, South Puget Sound Region, P.O. Box 68, Enumclaw, WA 98022-0068.

Location: From Interstate 5 south of Olympia, take exit 68 and turn east on US 12. Drive 30 miles, then turn north on Highway 7 and drive 17 miles to Elbe. Turn east on Highway 706 and drive six miles, then turn left on a dead end road and continue three miles. Keep right and continue one-half mile, then turn left and drive about 100 yards to the four-wheel drive trailhead.

Trip note: Here's a spot for four-wheel drive cowboys. The Department of Natural Resources manages this wooded campground and provides eight miles of trails for short wheelbase four-wheel drive vehicles. Beware: Trucks often get stuck here or can't make it up the hills when it is wet and slippery.

35. COUGAR ROCK 📮

Reference: **In Mount Rainier National Park; map B2, grid c9.**

Campsites, facilities: There are 200 sites for tents or RVs up to 30 feet long. A group camp is also available. Picnic tables are provided. Flush toilets, piped water, a camp store (two miles away) and a sanitary disposal station are available. Some facilities are **wheelchair accessible**. Leashed pets are permitted.

Reservations, fee: No reservations; $8 fee per night. Open mid-May to mid-October.

Who to contact: Phone Mount Rainier National Park at (360) 569-2211 or write to Mount Rainier National Park, Tahoma Woods, Ashford, WA 98304.

Location: From Interstate 5 south of Olympia, take exit 68 and turn east on US 12. Drive 30 miles, then turn north on Highway 7 and drive 17 miles to Elbe. Turn east on Highway 706 and drive about 12 miles to the park entrance, then 11 miles to the campground entrance on the left about two miles past the Longmire developed area.

Trip note: This camp is set at 3,180 feet. The park provides a recreation program, and trout fishing is allowed without a permit. See Gateway Inn and RV Park (camp number 40) for information on the nearby park sights and visitor centers.

36. RAINBOW FALLS STATE PARK 📮

Reference: **On Chehalis River; map B2, grid d0.**

Campsites, facilities: There are three primitive tent sites and 47 sites for tents or self-contained RVs up to 32 feet long. Picnic tables are provided. Flush toilets, piped water, a sanitary disposal station, showers, firewood and a playground are available. Pets are permitted.

Reservations, fee: No reservations; $5-$10 fee per night. Open all year.

Who to contact: Phone (800) 233-0321 or (360) 291-3767 or write to 4008 Highway 6, Chehalis, WA 98532.

Location: From Interstate 5 at Chehalis, take exit 77 and travel 17 miles west on

Highway 6 to the park entrance.

Trip note: Although this campground is only about a 20-minute drive from Interstate 5, out-of-towners pass it every time. It's a nice spot, with a swinging bridge (built in 1934) over the Chehalis River. There's a pool at the base of Rainbow Falls for swimming, trout fishing opportunities and 6.5 miles of hiking trails, including a self-guided nature trail through the old growth forest. There is also a playground for kids.

---

37. STAN HEDWALL PARK 🚐

Reference: **On Chehalis River; map B2, grid d2.**

Campsites, facilities: There are 29 sites for trailers or RVs of any length. Electricity, piped water and picnic tables are provided. Flush toilets, showers, sanitary services and a playground are available. Bottled gas, a store, a cafe and a laundromat are available within one mile. Pets are permitted.

Reservations, fee: Reservations accepted; $10-$15 fee per night. Open March to November.

Who to contact: Phone (360) 748-0271 or write to P.O. Box 871, Chehalis, WA 98532.

Location: Take exit 76 off Interstate 5, near Chehalis, and drive one-eighth mile south on Rice Road.

Trip note: This park, set along the Chehalis River, is a possible layover for Interstate 5 travelers. Access for fishing and swimming is provided. A playground and recreation field offer other activities. Nearby recreation options include an 18-hole golf course and hiking trails.

---

38. PEPPERTREE WEST RV PARK 🚐

Reference: **In Centralia; map B2, grid d2.**

Campsites, facilities: There are 20 tent sites and 42 sites (28 drive-through) for trailers or RVs of any length. Electricity, piped water and sewer hookups are provided. Flush toilets, sanitary services, showers, a recreation hall, a laundromat, ice, bottled gas, a store and a cafe are available. Pets and motorbikes are permitted. Boat launching facilities are available nearby.

Reservations, fee: Reservations accepted; $14-$18 fee per night; MasterCard and Visa accepted. Open all year.

Who to contact: Phone (360) 736-1124 or write to 1208 Alder Street, Centralia, WA 98531.

Location: From Olympia, drive south on Interstate 5 about 23 miles to exit 81 in Centralia. Drive west on Melon Street, taking the first left, and drive to the park. The park is in the southeast corner of Centralia.

Trip note: If you're driving Interstate 5 and looking for a stopover, this spot, along with Trailer Village, offers a good layover for tent campers or RVs. Surrounded by Chehalis Valley farmland, this campground is near an 18-hole golf course, hiking trails and tennis courts.

---

39. ALDER LAKE

Reference: **On Alder Lake; map B2, grid d6.**

Campsites, facilities: There are 27 sites for tents or small trailers. Picnic tables, fire grills and tent pads are provided. Vault toilets, piped water, a group shelter and a boat launch are available. Leashed pets are permitted.

Reservations, fee: No reservations; no fee. Open all year.

Who to contact: Phone the Department of Natural Resources at (360) 748-2383 or write to Department of Natural Resources, Central Region, 1405 Rush Road, Chehalis, WA 98532-8763.

Location: From Interstate 5 south of Olympia, take exit 68 and turn east on US 12. Drive 30 miles, then turn north on Highway 7 and drive 15 miles to Pleasant Valley Road (two miles south of Elbe). Turn right and drive 3.5 miles. Bear left on a paved, one-lane road for 100 yards and you'll see the campground on your right.

Trip note: This campground is set along the shore of Alder Lake in an area managed by the Department of Natural Resources. It's a nice, forested camp with good fishing nearby. Another recreation option is the Mount Rainier Scenic Railroad excursion that travels from Elbe through the forests to Mineral Lake.

---

40. GATEWAY INN AND RV PARK RV

Reference: Near Mount Rainier National Park; map B2, grid d8.

Campsites, facilities: There are 16 sites for trailers or RVs of any length (eight full hookups). There are also nine cabins. Electricity, piped water and picnic tables are provided. A restaurant and lounge are available. Pets are permitted.

Reservations, fee: Reservations accepted; $12-$15 fee per night; $59 cabin fee for two people, $10 each additional person. MasterCard, Visa and American Express accepted. Open all year.

Who to contact: Phone (360) 569-2506 or write to 38820 SR 706 East, Ashford, WA 98304.

Location: From Interstate 5 south of Olympia, take exit 68 and turn east on US 12. Drive 30 miles, then turn north on Highway 7 and drive 17 miles to Elbe. Turn east on Highway 706 and continue for 12 miles to the campground on the right. This park is located near the southwestern entrance to Mount Rainier National Park.

Trip note: This wooded park is very close to Mount Rainier, one of the most spectacular mountains in the hemisphere. After entering at the Nisqually (southwestern) entrance to the park and driving on Nisqually Paradise Road, you will find the Longmire Visitor Center about five miles into the park. It offers general park information and exhibits on the plants and geology of the area. Continuing into the park for 10 more miles, you will arrive at the Paradise Visitor Center, which has more exhibits and an observation deck. This is the only road into the park that is open all year.

---

41. MOUNTHAVEN AT CEDAR PARK RV

Reference: Near Mount Rainier National Park; map B2, grid d8.

Campsites, facilities: There are 20 sites for trailers or RVs of any length. Electricity, piped water and sewer hookups are provided. Flush toilets, showers, a laundromat, firewood, ice and a playground are available. A cafe, a bakery and a store are within one mile. Pets are permitted.

Reservations, fee: Reservations accepted; $20 fee per night. MasterCard and Visa accepted. Open all year.

Who to contact: Phone (360) 569-2594 or write to 38210 Highway 706 East, Ashford, WA 98304.

Location: From Interstate 5 south of Olympia, take exit 68 and turn east on US 12. Drive 30 miles, then turn north on Highway 7 and drive 17 miles to Elbe. Turn east on Highway 706 and continue for 11 miles. This park is located near the southwestern entrance to Mount Rainier National Park.

Trip note: Two creeks run through this wooded campground which is near the Nisqually entrance to Mount Raïnier National Park. See the trip note for Gateway Inn and RV Park for information about sights at the national park.

42.　　　　SUNSHINE POINT　　　　RV

Reference: **In Mount Rainier National Park; map B2, grid d8.**

Campsites, facilities: There are 18 sites for tents or RVs up to 25 feet long. Picnic tables are provided. Piped water and pit toilets are available. Some facilities are **wheelchair accessible**. Leashed pets are permitted.

Reservations, fee: No reservations; $6 fee per night. Open all year.

Who to contact: Phone Mount Rainier National Park at (360) 569-2211 or write to Mount Rainier National Park, Tahoma Woods, Ashford, WA 98304.

Location: From Interstate 5 south of Olympia, take exit 68 and turn east on US 12. Drive 30 miles, then turn north on Highway 7 and drive 17 miles to Elbe. Turn east on Highway 706 and continue for 12 miles. The campground is just inside the park entrance.

Trip note: This is one of five campgrounds in Mount Rainier National Park, set near the Nisqually entrance. Cougar Rock, Ipsut, White River (see Chapter B3) and Ohanapecosh (see Chapter B3) are also located within the park. This campground is the only one open year-round. See the trip note for Gateway Inn and RV Park for information about nearby sights and facilities.

43.　　　　RIVER OAKS CAMPGROUND　　　　RV

Reference: **On Cowlitz River; map B2, grid e2.**

Campsites, facilities: There are 50 tent sites and 24 sites for trailers or RVs of any length. Piped water and picnic tables are provided. Flush toilets, electricity, showers, sanitary services, ice, and a lighted boat launch are available. Bottled gas, a store, a cafe and a laundromat are located within one mile. Pets and motorbikes are permitted. Boat launching facilities are nearby.

Reservations, fee: Reservations accepted; $12-$20 fee per night. Open all year.

Who to contact: Phone (360) 864-2895 or write to 491 Highway 506, Toledo, WA 98591.

Location: From Interstate 5 near Castle Rock, take exit 59 and drive west on Highway 506 for one-half mile to the campground.

Trip note: This camp is set right on the Cowlitz River, with opportunities for swimming, boating and fishing. Every spring the river is the site of a big smelt run. They come thick. Using a dip net, you can fill a five-gallon bucket with just a couple of dips.

44.　　　　FROST ROAD TRAILER PARK　　　　RV

Reference: **Near Lewis and Clark State Park; map B2, grid e3.**

Campsites, facilities: There are 15 tent sites and 20 drive-through sites for trailers or RVs of any length. Electricity, piped water, sewer hookups and picnic tables are provided. Flush toilets, bottled gas, sanitary services, showers and a recreation hall are available. Pets are permitted.

Reservations, fee: Reservations accepted; $9-$13 fee per night. Open all year.

Who to contact: Phone (360) 785-3616 or write to 762 Frost Road, Winlock, WA 98596.

Location: From Olympia, drive south on Interstate 5 about 40 miles to exit 63 (near Winlock). Turn east on Highway 505 and drive about 3.5 miles to Henriot Road. Turn left and drive about one-quarter mile to a T where Henriot Road ends at Frost Road. Turn left on Frost Road and drive to the park at 762 Frost Road.

Trip note: This is an excellent option to the campground at nearby Lewis and Clark State Park, which is often crowded to capacity. The campsites are wooded and quiet. See the trip note for Lewis and Clark State Park for recreation options.

45. LEWIS & CLARK STATE PARK RV

Reference: **Near Chehalis; map B2, grid e3.**

Campsites, facilities: There are 25 sites for tents or self-contained RVs. Picnic tables and fire grills are provided. Flush toilets, piped water, firewood and a playground are available. Leashed pets are permitted.

Reservations, fee: No reservations; $10 fee per night. Open all year.

Who to contact: Phone (800) 233-0321 or (360) 864-2643 or write to 4583 Jackson Highway, Winlock, WA 98596.

Location: From Chehalis on Interstate 5, drive 12 miles southeast on Jackson Highway 99 and you'll see the park.

Trip note: The highlight at this state park is the immense old-growth forest, which contains some good hiking trails and a 1.5-mile nature trail. There is an interpretive center for Mount St. Helens. There is also a kids' fishing pond stocked with trout.

46. MAYFIELD LAKE COUNTY PARK RV

Reference: **On Mayfield Lake; map B2, grid e4.**

Campsites, facilities: There are 54 sites for tents, trailers or self-contained RVs. Restrooms, showers, a sanitary dump, a public phone, snacks and a barbecue are available. Facilities are **wheelchair accessible**. Pets are allowed on leashes.

Reservations, fee: Reservations recommended; $5-$11 fee per night.

Who to contact: Phone the park at (360) 985-2364 or write to 180 H Road, Mossyrock, WA 98564.

Location: Drive 14 miles south of Centralia on Interstate 5 to the junction with US 12, then drive east for 11 miles. You will see signs for the campground on the left.

Trip note: This popular park is set on the edge of Mayfield Lake, a less-developed option to Mayfield Lake Marina. The campground has a relaxing atmosphere and comfortable, wooded sites. Recreational activities include waterskiing, fishing, swimming and boating. A good side trip is touring nearby Mount St. Helens.

47. MAYFIELD LAKE MARINA RESORT RV

Reference: **On Mayfield Lake; map B2, grid e4.**

Campsites, facilities: There are 35 tent sites, 10 full hookup sites and 37 with electricity only for trailers or RVs of any length. Picnic tables are provided. Flush toilets, sanitary services, showers, a recreation hall, firewood, a store and ice are available. A laundromat is located within seven miles. Leashed pets are permitted. Boat docks and launching facilities are available.

Reservations, fee: Reservations accepted; $11-$17 fee per night. Open all year.

Who to contact: Phone (360) 985-2357 or write to 350 Hadaller Road, Mossyrock, WA 98564.

Location: From Centralia, drive south on Interstate 5 for 14 miles to the exit for US 12. Drive east on US 12 for 15 miles to Winston Creek Road. Turn south and drive two miles to Hadaller Road. Turn right and drive one mile to the resort.

Trip note: This resort is on the shore of Mayfield Reservoir. Nearby recreation options include fishing, swimming and boating.

---

48.   HARMONY LAKESIDE RV PARK   RV

Reference: **Near Mayfield Lake; map B2, grid e4.**

Campsites, facilities: There are 80 sites for trailers or RVs of any length (48 are full hookup sites, the rest have water and electricity only). Flush toilets, sanitary services, showers, firewood and ice are available. Pets and motorbikes are permitted. Boat docks and launching facilities are available.

Reservations, fee: Reservations accepted; $15-$17 fee per night. Open all year.

Who to contact: Phone (360) 983-3804 or write to 563 State Route 122, Silver Lake, WA 98585.

Location: From Centralia, drive south on Interstate 5 for 14 miles to the exit for US 12. Drive 18 miles east on US 12 to State Route 122. Turn north and drive 2.5 miles to the park.

Trip note: This park is set on Mayfield Lake. Mayfield Lake Marina Resort and Ike Kinswa State Park provide nearby options. Mayfield Lake offers numerous recreation options, including fishing, swimming and boating.

---

49.   IKE KINSWA STATE PARK   RV

Reference: **At Mayfield Lake; map B2, grid e5.**

Campsites, facilities: There are two primitive tent sites, 60 developed tent sites, and 41 sites for trailers or RVs up to 60 feet long. Picnic tables and fire grills are provided. Flush toilets, a sanitary disposal station, a store, a cafe, a playground, piped water, showers and firewood are available. Some facilities are **wheelchair accessible**. Leashed pets are permitted. Boat docks and launching facilities are nearby.

Reservations, fee: Contact Reservations Northwest at (800) 452-5687 ($6 reservation fee); $5-$14 fee per night. MasterCard and Visa accepted. Open all year.

Who to contact: Phone (800) 233-0321 or (360) 983-3402 or write to 873 Harmony Road, Silver Lake, WA 98585.

Location: From Interstate 5 south of Olympia, turn east on US 12 and drive 18 miles to the entrance road on the left.

Trip note: This campground covers 454 acres on the shore of Mayfield Reservoir. This site provides more amenities. Nearby recreation options include hiking trails, driftwood collecting, swimming, waterskiing and boating. Fishing for rainbow and silver trout is a year-round affair here, and can be quite good. Two fish hatcheries are located nearby. A spectacular view of Mount St. Helens is available at a vista point 11 miles east. This is a very popular campground and space is rarely available on summer weekends. Be sure to reserve at least a month in advance.

50.   REDMON'S RV PARK   **RV**

Reference: **Near Riffe Lake; map B2, grid e6.**

Campsites, facilities: There are six drive-through sites for trailers or RVs of any length. Electricity, piped water and sewer hookups are provided. Flush toilets, bottled gas, sanitary services, a cafe, a store and ice are available. Leashed pets are permitted.

Reservations, fee: Reservations accepted; $10-$15 fee per night. Open all year.

Who to contact: Phone (360) 498-5425 or write to 8136 Highway 12, Glenoma, WA 98336.

Location: From Centralia, drive south on Interstate 5 for 14 miles to the exit for US 12. Drive east on US 12 for 50 miles to Glenoma. The park is in town, on US 12.

Trip note: This is a clean, comfortable campground in a beautiful setting. Recreation options include visiting huge Riffe Lake to the southeast, or driving up Strawberry Mountain or to the edge of Mount St. Helens National Park— from Randle, drive south on Highway 26.

51. MAPLE GROVE CAMPGROUND & RV PARK   **RV**

Reference: **On Cowlitz River; map B2, grid e8.**

Campsites, facilities: There are 10 tent sites and about 64 drive-through sites for trailers or RVs of any length. Electricity, piped water and picnic tables are provided. Flush toilets, sanitary services, firewood, a recreation hall, a store, a cafe, a laundromat, showers, bottled gas, ice and a playground are available. Pets are permitted.

Reservations, fee: Reservations accepted; $10-$15 fee per night. Open year-round with limited winter facilities.

Who to contact: Phone (360) 497-2741 or write to P.O. Box 205, Randle, WA 98377.

Location: From Interstate 5 south of Olympia, turn east on US 12 and drive 48 miles to Randle. The park is in town on the highway.

Trip note: This RV park is set along the shore of the Cowlitz River. Nearby recreation options include hiking trails. One excellent drive is along winding Highway 26, which starts at Randle and heads up to Strawberry Mountain (5,464 feet). It's a good lookout point towards Mount St. Helens to the west.

52.   FOX STORE AND RV PARK   **RV**

Reference: **Near Toutle River; map B2, grid f2.**

Campsites, facilities: There are 37 sites for trailers or RVs of any length. Electricity, piped water, sewer hookups and picnic tables are provided. Flush toilets, showers, firewood, a store and ice are available. Pets and motorbikes are permitted. Boat launching facilities are nearby.

Reservations, fee: Reservations accepted; $10-$15 fee per night. Open all year.

Who to contact: Phone (360) 274-6785 or write to 112 Burma Road, Castle Rock, WA 98611.

Location: From Interstate 5 at Castle Rock, take exit 52 and drive 100 yards east to the park.

Trip note: This wooded park is about 400 yards from the Toutle River and one-half mile from the Cowlitz River. Take your pick. Seaquest State Park and Silver Lake to the east provide two excellent side trip options with many activities available.

53.   MOUNT SAINT HELENS RV PARK   **RV**

Reference: **Near Silver Lake; map B2, grid f2.**

Campsites, facilities: There are approximately 90 sites for tents, trailers or RVs. Cable TV, restrooms, showers, a laundromat, a sanitary dump, a public phone and ice are available. Horseshoes, a recreation hall and a playground are also provided. The facilities are **wheelchair accessible**. Pets are permitted on leashes.

Reservations, fee: No reservations necessary, $9-$14 fee per night. Visa and MasterCard are accepted. Open all year.

Who to contact: For reservations, phone (360) 274-8522 or write to 167 Schaffran, Castle Rock, WA 98611.

Location: From Interstate 5 at Castle Rock, take exit 49. Turn east on Highway 504 and drive two miles to a sign on the right indicating the park to the left. Turn left at the sign onto Schaffran Road and drive to the park at the top of the hill.

Trip note: This is a cozy park just outside of Castle Rock. Though close to the highway, it has a secluded feel. Fishing and boating are available nearby on Silver Lake. A good side trip is touring Mount St. Helens. The park is located only three miles from the Mount St. Helens Visitor Center.

54.   SEAQUEST STATE PARK   **RV**

Reference: **Near Silver Lake; map B2, grid f3.**

Campsites, facilities: There are four primitive tent sites and 92 sites for tents and self-contained RVs (16 with full hookups). Piped water and picnic tables are provided. Flush toilets, playground, six horseshoe pits, a ball field, a sanitary disposal station, showers and firewood are available. A store is available within one mile. Some facilities are **wheelchair accessible**.

Reservations, fee: Contact Reservations Northwest at (800)452-5687 ($6 reservation fee); $5-$16 fee per night. Open all year.

Who to contact: Phone (800) 233-0321 or (360) 274-8633 or write to P.O. Box 3030, Spirit Lake Highway, Castle Rock, WA 98611.

Location: From Interstate 5, take exit 49 and drive seven miles east on Highway 504 to the park.

Trip note: This state park is located across from Silver Lake which is considered to be one of western Washington's premier bass, trout and salmon fishing lakes. There are eight miles of hiking trails and the Mount St. Helens Interpretive Center, provided by the Forest Service, is located within the park. This is a popular park for day use as well as camping; it is advisable to arrive early to claim a spot.

55.   SILVER LAKE MOTEL AND RESORT   **RV**

Reference: **On Silver Lake; map B2, grid f3.**

Campsites, facilities: There are 13 tent sites and 22 sites for trailers or RVs of any length. Electricity, piped water, sewer hookups and picnic tables are provided. Flush toilets, a store, showers, ice and playground are available. Sanitary services and a cafe are located within one mile. Pets and motorbikes are permitted. Boat docks, launching facilities and rentals are nearby.

Reservations, fee: Reservations accepted; $9-$13 fee per night. MasterCard and Visa accepted. Open all year.

Who to contact: Phone (360) 274-6141 or write to 3201 Spirit Lake Highway,

Silver Lake, WA 98645.

Location: From Interstate 5, take exit 49 and drive 6.5 miles east on Highway 504 to the park on the right.

Trip note: This park is set along the shore of Silver Lake, one of Washington's better bass fishing lakes. It is an excellent option to the more crowded campground at Seaquest State Park.

56. IRON CREEK   RV

Reference: **On Cispus River in Gifford Pinchot National Forest; map B2, grid f8.**

Campsites, facilities: There are 98 sites for tents, trailers or RVs. Piped water and picnic tables are provided. Vault toilets and firewood are available. Leashed pets are permitted. Some facilities are **wheelchair accessible**.

Reservations, fee: Reserve some sites by calling (800) 280-CAMP ($7.50 reservation fee); $10 fee per night for a single site, $20 fee per night for a double site; $5 each additional vehicle. Open mid-May to late October.

Who to contact: Phone Gifford Pinchot National Forest at (360) 497-7565 or write to Randle Ranger District, P.O. Box 670, Randle, WA 98377.

Location: From Interstate 5 south of Olympia, take exit 68 and head east on Highway 12. Drive 48 miles to Randle and take State Route 131 south. Drive one mile, then continue south for nine miles on Forest Service Road 25 to the campground entrance.

Trip note: This is one of the more popular Forest Service campgrounds. This spot is set along the Cispus River near its confluence with Iron Creek. A Forest Service Visitor Center which provides information about the Mount St. Helens-Mount Adams area is nearby. The camp is located along the access route to the best eastside viewing areas for Mount St. Helens.

57. TOWER ROCK   RV

Reference: **On Cispus River in Gifford Pinchot National Forest; map B2, grid f9.**

Campsites, facilities: There are 22 sites for tents, trailers or RVs up to 21 feet long. Piped water and picnic tables are provided. Vault toilets and firewood are available. Leashed pets are permitted.

Reservations, fee: No reservations; $9 fee per night; $18 double site fee; $5 each additional vehicle. Open mid-May to late September.

Who to contact: Phone Gifford Pinchot National Forest at (360) 497-7565 or write to Randle Ranger District, P.O. Box 670, Randle, WA 98377.

Location: From Interstate 5 south of Olympia, take exit 68 and head east on Highway 12. Drive 48 miles to Randle and take State Route 131 south. Drive one mile, then continue south on Forest Service Road 23 for 6.5 miles. Turn south on Forest Service Road 28 and drive 1.5 miles, then proceed two miles west on Forest Service Road 76 to the campground. A Forest Service map is essential.

Trip note: This campground is set along the Cispus River, an option to nearby Iron Creek and North Fork. It has shaded and sunny sites to choose from, with lots of trees and plenty of room. Fishing is popular here.

58.   BLUE LAKE CREEK   RV

Reference: **Near Blue Lake in Gifford Pinchot National Forest; map B2 grid f9.**

Campsites, facilities: There are 11 sites for tents, trailers or RVs up to 31 feet long. Picnic tables are provided. Vault toilets and hand-pumped water are available. Firewood can be gathered outside of the campground area. Leashed pets are permitted.

Reservations, fee: No reservations; $8 fee per night. Open mid-May to late October.

Who to contact: Phone Gifford Pinchot National Forest at (360) 497-7565 or write to Randle Ranger District, P.O. Box 670, Randle, WA 98377.

Location: From Interstate 5 south of Olympia, take exit 68 and head east on Highway 12. Drive 48 miles to Randle and take State Route 131 south. Drive one mile, then continue south on Forest Service Road 23 for 15 miles to the campground.

Trip note: This is a classic Washington hideaway. The campground is set along Blue Lake Creek, a good base camp for the 3.5-mile hike to Blue Lake. The trailhead is about one-half mile from the camp. Mountain biking is another option here.

---

59.   NORTH FORK   RV

Reference: **On Cispus River in Gifford Pinchot National Forest; map B2, grid f9.**

Campsites, facilities: There are 33 sites for tents, trailers or RVs up to 31 feet long. Piped water and picnic tables are provided. Vault toilets and firewood are available. Leashed pets are permitted.

Reservations, fee: No reservations; $9 fee per night; $18 double site fee; $5 each additional vehicle. Open mid-May to late September.

Who to contact: Phone Gifford Pinchot National Forest at (360) 497-7565 or write to Randle Ranger District, P.O. Box 670, Randle, WA 98377.

Location: From Interstate 5 south of Olympia, take exit 68 and head east on Highway 12. Drive 48 miles to Randle and take State Route 131 south. Drive one mile, then continue south for 11 miles on Forest Service Road 23 to the campground.

Trip note: This campground is set along the North Cispus River. In addition to fishing, there are nature trails and bike paths. There is also a scenic viewing area. A national forest map details the backcountry.

---

60.   POLE PATCH

Reference: **Near French Butte in Gifford Pinchot National Forest; map B2, grid g9.**

Campsites, facilities: There are 12 tent sites. Picnic tables are provided. Pit toilets are available, but there is **no piped water**. Firewood can be gathered outside of the campground. Leashed pets are permitted.

Reservations, fee: No reservations; no fee. Open July to mid-September.

Who to contact: Phone Gifford Pinchot National Forest at (360) 497-7565 or write to Randle Ranger District, P.O. Box 670, Randle, WA 98377.

Location: From Interstate 5 south of Olympia, take exit 68 and head east on Highway 12. Drive 48 miles to Randle and take State Route 131 south. Drive one mile, then continue south on Forest Service Road 25 for 10 miles. Turn east on Forest Service Road 76 and drive three miles. Turn south on Forest Service

Road 77 and continue 16 miles to the campground. A Forest Service map is essential.

Trip note: This primitive camp is at 4,400 feet and is in an isolated alpine area near French Butte. This campground is no longer maintained by the Forest Service and is being allowed to return to its original state. Before taking your first step, you should obtain a map of the Gifford Pinchot National Forest, which details all backcountry roads, trails, lakes and streams. In season, there is good berry picking in the area.

61.　　　　　CEDARS RV PARK　　　　　RV

Reference: **Near Coweeman River; map B2, grid g2.**

Campsites, facilities: There are seven tent sites and 25 sites (two drive-through) for trailers or RVs of any length. Electricity, sewer and cable TV hookups, piped water and picnic tables are provided. Flush toilets, showers, sanitary services and a laundromat are available. There is a mini-mart 1.5 miles away. Pets and motorbikes are permitted.

Reservations, fee: Reservations accepted; $11-$15 fee per night. Open all year.

Who to contact: Phone (360) 274-5136 or write to 115 Beauvais Road, Kelso, WA 98626.

Location: Take exit 46 off Interstate 5 and drive 100 feet east on Headquarters Road. Turn north on Bond Road and drive one-third mile, then turn east on Beauvais Road and continue 50 feet to the park on the right.

Trip note: This private park provides a good stopover for Interstate 5 travelers looking for a spot near Kelso. Campsites are graveled and shady. The nearby Coweeman River is a highlight, along with the park's natural setting.

62.　　　OAKS TRAILER AND RV PARK　　　RV

Reference: **In Commerce; map B2, grid g2.**

Campsites, facilities: There are 62 drive-through sites for trailers or RVs up to 30 feet long. Electricity, piped water and sewer hookups are provided. Flush toilets, sanitary services, showers and a laundromat are available. Bottled gas, a store and a cafe are located within one mile. Pets are permitted.

Reservations, fee: Reservations accepted; $13.45 fee per night. Open all year.

Who to contact: Phone (360) 425-2708 or write to 636 California Way, Longview, WA 98632.

Location: From Interstate 5 near Longview, take exit 36 and drive west on Highway 432 for 3.5 miles to Commerce. Drive one block south and then turn southeast to the park.

Trip note: This park is in an urban area near Longview. It is a good layover spot if you're heading south on Interstate 5 to Oregon or west on Highway 4 to the coast. Nearby recreation options include an 18-hole golf course and a full-service marina.

63.　　　　　LAKE MERRILL

Reference: **Near Mount St. Helens; map B2, grid g6.**

Campsites, facilities: There are 11 campsites for tents or small trailers. Picnic tables, fire grills and tent pads are provided. Vault toilets, firewood and piped water are available. Boat launching facilities are located on Lake Merrill. Leashed pets are permitted.

Reservations, fee: No reservations; no fee. Open May to September.

Who to contact: Phone the Department of Natural Resources at (360) 577-2025 or write to Department of Natural Resources, Southwest Region, P.O. Box 280, Castle Rock, WA 98611-0280.

Location: From Interstate 5 at Woodland, take exit 21 and drive 29 miles east on Highway 503 to Cougar. Drive north on Cougar Road for 5.5 miles, then turn left on Forest Service Road 81 and drive 4.5 miles. Turn left on the access road and continue to the campground.

Trip note: This is the best choice in the area for campers seeking a quiet setting. This wooded campground is nestled on the shore of Lake Merrill, very near Mount St. Helens. It is a less expensive and often less-crowded alternative to the more developed parks in the area.

---

64.   LOWER LEWIS RIVER FALLS   RV

Reference: **On Lewis River in Gifford Pinchot National Forest; map B2, grid g8.**

Campsites, facilities: There are 42 sites for tents, trailers or RVs up to 70 feet long. Composting toilets and hand-pumped water are available. Leashed pets are permitted.

Reservations, fee: No reservations; $9 fee per night; $18 double site fee; $5 each additional vehicle. Open May to October.

Who to contact: Phone Gifford Pinchot National Forest at (360) 750-3900 or write to Mount St. Helens National Volcanic Monument, 42218 Yale Bridge Road, Amboy, WA 98601-0369.

Location: From Interstate 5 at Woodland, take exit 21 and drive east on Highway 503 to Cougar. Drive east on Forest Service Road 90 for 28 miles to the campground.

Trip note: This is one of the great spots in the Pacific Northwest. The camp is set in the primary viewing area for three major waterfalls on the Lewis River. The spectacular Lewis River Trail is available for hiking or horseback riding, and there is a **wheelchair-accessible** loop. There are several other hiking trails in the area that branch off along backcountry streams. See a Forest Service map for details. The elevation is 1,400 feet.

---

65.   LOUIS RASMUSSEN RV PARK   RV

Reference: **On Columbia River; map B2, grid h3.**

Campsites, facilities: There are five tent sites and 22 sites for trailers or RVs of any length. Electricity, piped water and sewer hookups are provided. Flush toilets, showers and sanitary services are available. Bottled gas, a store, a cafe, a laundromat and ice are located within one mile. Pets and motorbikes are permitted. Boat docks and launching facilities are nearby.

Reservations, fee: Reservations accepted; $7-$12 fee per night. Open all year.

Who to contact: Phone (360) 673-2626 or write to P.O. Box 70, Kalama, WA 98625.

Location: From Interstate 5 near Kalama, take exit 30 and drive 100 feet west to Hendrickson Road. Turn south and drive one-half mile to the park.

Trip note: This park is in an urban area along the shore of the Columbia River. This is a perfect layover spot for Interstate 5 cruisers heading for Portland. Nearby recreation options include a full-service marina and tennis courts.

66.　　　　　　WOODLAND

Reference: **Near Woodland; map B2, grid h3.**

Campsites, facilities: There are 10 campsites for tents or small trailers. Picnic tables, fire grills and tent pads are provided. Vault toilets, piped water, firewood and a children's playground are available. Some facilities are **wheelchair accessible**. Leashed pets are permitted.

Reservations, fee: No reservations; no fee. Open May to September.

Who to contact: Phone the Department of Natural Resources at (360) 577-2025 or write to Department of Natural Resources, Southwest Region, P.O. Box 280, Castle Rock, WA 98611-0280.

Location: From Interstate 5 at Woodland, take exit 21 and drive 100 yards east on Highway 503. Turn right to East CC Street and proceed to just south of the bridge. Turn right on County Road 1 and drive 300 yards, then turn left on County Road 38 and drive 2.5 miles to the campground on the left.

Trip note: This is an optimum spot for people who are touring Washington on Interstate 5 but want a quiet setting along the way. This campground is nestled in a forest area that is managed by the Department of Natural Resources. It's private and wooded, yet near the main highway and has playground equipment for the kids.

67.　　　　CAMP KALAMA CAMPGROUND　　　**RV**

Reference: **On Kalama River; map B2, grid h3.**

Campsites, facilities: There are 30 tent sites and 120 sites (17 drive-through) for trailers or RVs of any length. Electricity, piped water, sewer hookups and picnic tables are provided. Flush toilets, bottled gas, sanitary services, a store, showers, firewood, a laundromat, ice and playground are available. Pets and motorbikes are permitted. Boat launching facilities are located nearby.

Reservations, fee: Reservations accepted; $21 fee per night; MasterCard, Visa and Discover accepted. Open all year.

Who to contact: Phone (360) 673-2456, (800) 750-2456 or write to 5055 North Meeker Drive, Kalama, WA 98625.

Location: From Interstate 5 near Kalama, take exit 32 and drive one block south on the frontage road to the campground.

Trip note: This is an option to Louis Rasmussen RV Park with a more rustic setting and some accommodations for tent campers. It is set along the Kalama River, where fishing is popular. A full-service marina is nearby.

68.　　　　LEWIS RIVER RV PARK　　　**RV**

Reference: **On Lewis River; map B2, grid h3.**

Campsites, facilities: There are 90 sites for tents, trailers or RVs of any length (five drive-through). Electricity, piped water, sewer hookups and picnic tables are provided. Flush toilets, bottled gas, firewood, sanitary services, showers, bathhouse, a store, a laundromat, ice and a swimming pool are available. Pets are permitted. Boat docks and launching facilities are nearby on the Lewis River.

Reservations, fee: Reservations accepted; $16-$18 per night; MasterCard and Visa accepted. Open all year.

Who to contact: Phone (360) 225-9556 or write to 3125 Lewis River Road, Woodland, WA 98674.

Location: From Castle Rock, drive about 38 miles south on Interstate 5 to exit 21 in Woodland. Drive four miles east on Highway 503/Lewis River Road to the park.

Trip note: This park is set along the Lewis River, where the salmon and the steelhead can run thick in season. It's a pleasant camp, with a choice of graveled or grassy shaded sites. There is an 18-hole golf course nearby.

---

69. LONE FIR RESORT   **RV**

Reference: **Near Yale Lake; map B2, grid h6.**

Campsites, facilities: There are 13 tent sites and 17 sites for trailers or RVs of any length. Electricity, piped water, sewer hookups and picnic tables are provided. Flush toilets, a laundromat, a restaurant, showers, ice and a swimming pool are available. Bottled gas, sanitary services, a store and a cafe are located within one mile. Pets and motorbikes are permitted. Boat docks and launching facilities are nearby.

Reservations, fee: Reservations accepted; $13-$16 fee per night; MasterCard and Visa accepted. Open all year.

Who to contact: Phone (360) 238-5210 or write to 16806 Lewis River Road, Cougar, WA 98616.

Location: From Castle Rock, drive about 38 miles south on Interstate 5 to exit 21 in Woodland. Drive 29 miles east on Highway 503/Lewis River Road to the resort. (You can see it from the highway.)

Trip note: This campground is near Yale Lake, the smallest of four lakes in the area. This private camp is designed primarily for motor home use, with grassy sites and plenty of shade trees. Mount St. Helens is a side trip option.

---

70. VOLCANO VIEW CAMPGROUND   **RV**

Reference: **Near Mount St. Helens; map B2, grid h6.**

Campsites, facilities: There are 47 sites for trailers or RVs of any length. Electricity, piped water, sewer hookups and picnic tables are provided. Flush toilets, sanitary services, showers, firewood, a store and ice are available. Pets are permitted.

Reservations, fee: Reservations accepted; $10-$12 fee per night. Open all year.

Who to contact: Phone (360) 231-4329 or write to 438 Yale Bridge Road, Ariel, WA 98603.

Location: From Interstate 5 in Woodland, take exit 21 and drive 23 miles east to Jack's Restaurant, then turn south and go one mile to campground.

Trip note: This campground is close to Mount St. Helens and along the edge of Yale Lake. Lake Merrill and Swift Creek Reservoir are nearby.

---

71. PARADISE CREEK   **RV**

Reference: **On Paradise Creek and Wind River in Gifford Pinchot National Forest; map B2, grid h8.**

Campsites, facilities: There are 42 sites for tents, trailers or RVs up to 25 feet long. Hand-pumped well water, fire grills and picnic tables are provided. Pit toilets are available. One toilet is **wheelchair accessible**. Leashed pets are permitted.

Reservations, fee: Some sites may be reserved by calling (800) 280-CAMP ($7.75 reservation fee); $9-$18 fee per night; $5 each additional vehicle. Open mid-May to mid-November.

Who to contact: Phone Gifford Pinchot National Forest at (509) 427-3200 or write to Wind River Ranger District, 1262 Hemlock Road, Carson, WA 98610.

Location: From Interstate 5 at Vancouver, turn east on Highway 14 and drive approximately 50 miles to Carson. Turn north on the Wind River Highway and drive 20 miles to the camp.

Trip note: This is an option to Beaver; this campground is set deeper in the Gifford Pinchot National Forest. It's located at the confluence of Paradise Creek and the Wind River. Lava Butte is a short distance from the camp and accessible by trail.

72.   FALLS CREEK-CREST HORSE CAMP   RV

Reference: **Near Pacific Crest Trail in Gifford Pinchot National Forest; map B2, grid h8.**

Campsites, facilities: There are six sites for tents, trailers or RVs up to 15 feet long. Picnic tables and fire grills are provided. Pit toilets are available, but there is **no piped water**. Leashed pets are permitted.

Reservations, fee: No reservations; no fee. Open mid-June to late September.

Who to contact: Phone Gifford Pinchot National Forest at (509) 427-3200 or write to Wind River Ranger District, Carson, WA 98610.

Location: From Interstate 5 at Vancouver, turn east on Highway 14 and drive approximately 50 miles to Carson. Turn north on the Wind River Highway and drive six miles, then continue 15 miles north on Forest Service Road 65 to the campground.

Trip note: This camp is set along the Race Track Trail and adjacent to the Indian Heaven Wilderness.

73.   SMOKEY CREEK   RV

Reference: **Near Indian Heaven Wilderness in Gifford Pinchot National Forest; map B2, grid h9.**

Campsites, facilities: There are three sites for trailers or RVs up to 22 feet long. Picnic tables are provided. Pit toilets are available, but there is **no piped water**. Leashed pets are permitted.

Reservations, fee: No reservations; no fee. Open June to late September.

Who to contact: Phone Gifford Pinchot National Forest at (509) 395-3400 or write to Mount Adams Ranger District, 2455 Highway 141, Trout Lake, WA 98650.

Location: From Interstate 5 at Vancouver, turn east on Highway 14 and drive 66 miles. Turn north on Highway 141 and drive 25.5 miles to Forest Service Road 24 (5.5 miles southwest of the town of Trout Lake). Turn northwest and drive seven miles to the campground.

Trip note: This primitive, little-used campground is set along Smokey Creek. A trail leading into the Indian Heaven Wilderness passes near the camp. Berry picking can be good here in season. See the trip notes for Walupt Lake Horse Camp (see Chapter B3), Morrison Creek (see Chapter B3), Saddle and Tillicum for details of the recreation options of the immediate area.

74.   GOOSE LAKE   RV

Reference: **On Goose Lake in Gifford Pinchot National Forest; map B2, grid h9.**

Campsites, facilities: There are 25 tent sites and one site for trailers or RVs up to 18 feet long. Picnic tables and fire rings are provided. Vault toilets are available, but there is **no piped water**. A boat ramp is nearby. Leashed pets are permitted.

Reservations, fee: No reservations; $6 fee per night; $4 each additional vehicle.

Open mid-June to late September.

Who to contact: Phone Gifford Pinchot National Forest at (509) 395-3400 or write to Mount Adams Ranger District, 2455 Highway 141, Trout Lake, WA 98650.

Location: From Interstate 5 at Vancouver, turn east on Highway 14 and drive 66 miles. Turn north on Highway 141 and drive 25.5 miles to Forest Service Road 24 (5.5 miles southwest of the town of Trout Lake). Continue on Forest Service Road 24 west to Forest Service Road 60. Continue west for five more miles.

Trip note: This campground is set at an elevation of 3,200 feet along the shore of Goose Lake. Fishing and berry picking are two summertime options here. The northern edge of Big Lava Bed and nearby crater are adjacent to camp. See the trip note for Falls Creek-Crest Horse Camp for details.

---

75. CULTUS CREEK   RV

Reference: **Near Indian Heaven Wilderness in Gifford Pinchot National Forest; map B2, grid h9.**

Campsites, facilities: There are 51 sites for tents, trailers or RVs up to 32 feet long. Piped water, picnic tables and fire rings are provided. Vault toilets and firewood are available. Some facilities are **wheelchair accessible**. Leashed pets are permitted.

Reservations, fee: No reservations; $9 fee per night; $18 double site fee; $5 each additional vehicle. Open June to September.

Who to contact: Phone Gifford Pinchot National Forest at (509) 395-3400 or write to Mount Adams Ranger District, 2455 Highway 141, Trout Lake, WA 98650.

Location: From Interstate 5 at Vancouver, turn east on Highway 14 and drive 66 miles. Turn north on Highway 141 and drive 25.5 miles to Forest Service Road 24 (5.5 miles southwest of the town of Trout Lake). Continue 2.5 miles, then turn northwest and drive 12.5 miles to the campground.

Trip note: This campground is set at an elevation of 4,000 feet along Cultus Creek and on the edge of Indian Heaven Wilderness. Nearby trails will take you into this backcountry area, which has numerous small meadows and lakes among the stands of firs and pines. Horse trails are available as well. The Pacific Crest Trail runs nearby. Evening programs are offered by the campground hosts for campers.

---

76. TILLICUM   RV

Reference: **Near Meadow Lake in Gifford Pinchot National Forest; map B2, grid h9.**

Campsites, facilities: There are eight sites for tents only and 37 sites for tents, trailers or RVs up to 18 feet long. Piped water, picnic tables and fire rings are provided. Pit toilets and firewood are available. Leashed pets are permitted.

Reservations, fee: No reservations; no fee. Open mid-June to late September.

Who to contact: Phone Gifford Pinchot National Forest at (509) 395-3400 or write to Mount Adams Ranger District, 2455 Highway 141, Trout Lake, WA 98650.

Location: From Interstate 5 at Vancouver, turn east on Highway 14 and drive 66 miles. Turn north on Highway 141 and drive 25.5 miles to Forest Service Road 24 (5.5 miles southwest of the town of Trout Lake). Turn northwest and drive 19 miles to the campground.

Trip note: This is a pretty camp, primitive but well-forested and within walking distance of a number of recreation options. A trail from the camp leads southwest past little Meadow Lake to Squaw Butte, then over to Big Creek.

Give it a try; it's a nice hike, as well as an excellent ride for mountain bikers. This is a premium area for picking huckleberries in August and early September. The Lone Butte Wildlife Emphasis Area to the south provides a great side trip opportunity.

77.   LITTLE GOOSE   RV

Reference: **On Little Goose Creek in Gifford Pinchot National Forest; map B2, grid h9.**

Campsites, facilities: There are 28 sites for tents, trailers or RVs up to 18 feet long. Piped water, picnic tables and fire rings are provided. Pit toilets are available. Leashed pets are permitted.

Reservations, fee: No reservations; no fee. Open June to late September.

Who to contact: Phone Gifford Pinchot National Forest at (509) 395-3400 or write to Mount Adams Ranger District, 2455 Highway 141, Trout Lake, WA 98650.

Location: From Interstate 5 at Vancouver, turn east on Highway 14 and drive 66 miles. Turn north on Highway 141 and drive 25.5 miles to Forest Service Road 24 (5.5 miles south of the town of Trout Lake). Turn northwest and drive 10 miles to the campground.

Trip note: This campground is near Little Goose Creek and the backcountry of the Indian Heaven Wilderness. See Walupt Lake Horse Camp (see Chapter B3), Morrison Creek (see Chapter B3), Saddle and Tillicum for details of the area. Since this camp has piped water available, it gets heavier use than most of the others in the immediate vicinity. Huckleberry picking is quite good in August and early September in the area.

78.   SADDLE

Reference: **Near Mosquito Lakes in Gifford Pinchot National Forest; map B2, grid h9.**

Campsites, facilities: There are 12 tent sites. Picnic tables and fire rings are provided. Pit toilets and firewood are available, but there is **no piped water**. Leashed pets are permitted.

Reservations, fee: No reservations; no fee. Open mid-June to late September.

Who to contact: Phone Gifford Pinchot National Forest at (509) 395-3400 or write to Mount Adams Ranger District, 2455 Highway 141, Trout Lake, WA 98650.

Location: From Interstate 5 at Vancouver, turn east on Highway 14 and drive 66 miles. Turn north on Highway 141 and drive 25.5 miles to Forest Service Road 24 (5.5 miles south of the town of Trout Lake). Turn northwest and drive 19 miles. Take Forest Service Road 2480 north for one mile to the campground.

Trip note: This is a rustic site that receives relatively little use. There are two lakes nearby called Big and Little Mosquito lakes which are fed by Mosquito Creek. So, while we're on the subject, mosquito attacks in late spring and early summer can be like squadrons of World War II bombers moving in. The Pacific Crest Trail passes right by camp. The area is known for premium huckleberry picking in August and early September.

79.   PARADISE POINT STATE PARK   RV

Reference: **On the East Fork of Lewis River; map B2, grid i3.**

Campsites, facilities: There are nine primitive tent sites and 70 sites for tents or self-contained RVs up to 45 feet long. Piped water, fire grills and picnic tables are provided. Flush toilets, sanitary services, firewood and showers are available. Leashed pets are permitted. Boat launching facilities are located nearby on the East Fork of the Lewis River.

Reservations, fee: Contact Reservations Northwest at (800) 452-5687 ($6 reservation fee); $5-$10 fee per night. Open all year.

Who to contact: Phone (800) 233-0321 or (360) 263-2350 or write to Route 1, P.O. Box 33914, Ridgefield, WA 98642.

Location: From Vancouver, Washington, drive 15 miles north. Take the Paradise Point State Park exit and follow the signs to the campground.

Trip note: This campground is set along the East Fork of the Lewis River, which offers good fishing. Nearby recreation options include an 18-hole golf course and a two-mile hiking trail. This is a good motor home layover spot for I-5 travelers, but it does fill up quickly, so plan on arriving early in the day.

---

80. BIG FIR CAMPGROUND RV

Reference: **Near Paradise Point State Park; map B2, grid i4.**

Campsites, facilities: There are 33 tent sites and 37 sites (three drive-through) for trailers or RVs of any length. Electricity, piped water, sewer hookups and picnic tables are provided. Flush toilets, sanitary services, showers, a store and ice are available. Pets and motorbikes are permitted. Boat launching facilities are located nearby.

Reservations, fee: Reservations accepted; $10-$18 fee per night. MasterCard, Visa and Discover accepted. Open all year.

Who to contact: Phone (360) 887-8970, (800) 532-4397 or write to 5515 NE 259th Street, Ridgefield, WA 98642.

Location: Take the Ridgefield exit 14 off Interstate 5 and drive four miles east to the campground on the right.

Trip note: This wooded campground is in a rural area not far from Paradise Point State Park. It is set in a wooded, hilly area with shaded gravel sites. See the trip note for Paradise Point State Park for details on the area.

---

81. BATTLE GROUND LAKE STATE PARK RV

Reference: **On Battle Ground Lake; map B2, grid i4.**

Campsites, facilities: There are 15 primitive tent sites and 35 sites for tents or self-contained RVs up to 50 feet long. Piped water, fire grills and picnic tables are provided. Flush toilets, sanitary disposal station, showers, a store, firewood, a restaurant and playground are available. Some facilities are **wheelchair accessible**. Leashed pets are permitted. Boat launching facilities and rentals are nearby.

Reservations, fee: Contact Reservations Northwest at (800) 452-5687 ($6 reservation fee); $5-$10 fee per night. Open all year.

Who to contact: Phone (800) 233-0321 or (360) 687-4621 or write to 17612 NE Palmer Road, Battleground, WA 98604.

Location: From Vancouver, Washington, turn north on Highway 503 and drive approximately 15 miles until you get to the Battle Ground crossroads. Head east for three miles, then turn north and continue 1.5 miles to the lake.

Trip note: This state park has horseback riding trails and some primitive campsites that will accommodate campers with horses. It is a good lake for swimming as well as fishing and it has a nice beach area. No motorized boats are allowed. If you are traveling on Interstate 5 and looking for a layover, this is ideal and only about a 15-minute drive from the highway. In July and August, there are several local fairs and celebrations. Like many of the easy-access state parks on Interstate 5, it fills up quickly on weekends.

82. SUNSET   RV

Reference: **On the East Fork of Lewis River in Gifford Pinchot National Forest; map B2, grid i6.**

Campsites, facilities: There are six walk-in sites and 10 sites for tents, trailers or RVs up to 22 feet long. Well water and picnic tables are provided. Pit toilets and firewood are available. Leashed pets are permitted.

Reservations, fee: No reservations; $9 fee per night; $5 each additiional vehicle. Open year-round.

Who to contact: Phone Gifford Pinchot National Forest at (360) 750-3900 or write to Mount St. Helens National Volcanic Monument, 42218 NE Yale Bridge Road, Amboy, WA 98601.

Location: From Interstate 5 at Vancouver, turn north on Highway 503 and travel approximately 20 miles to County Road 12 (near the town of Yacolt). Turn east and drive 13 miles to the campground.

Trip note: This campground is set at 1,000 feet along the East Fork of the Lewis River. There are a number of trails in the area for fishing, huckleberry picking and mushroom hunting.

83. COLD CREEK

Reference: **On Cedar Creek; map B2, grid i6.**

Campsites, facilities: There are six campsites for tents or small trailers. Picnic tables, fire grills and tent pads are provided. Vault toilets and hand-pumped water are available. Leashed pets are permitted.

Reservations, fee: No reservations; no fee. Open May to September.

Who to contact: Phone the Department of Natural Resources at (360) 577-2025 or write to Department of Natural Resources, Southwest Region, P.O. Box 280, Castle Rock, WA 98611-0280.

Location: From Interstate 5 north of Vancouver, Washingtón, take exit 9 and drive east on NE 179th Street for 5.5 miles. Turn right on Highway 503 and drive 1.5 miles. Turn left on NE 159th Street and drive three miles, then turn right on 182nd Avenue. From there drive one mile, then turn left on NE 139th (Road L 1400) and continue eight miles. Turn left on Road L 1000 and drive three miles. Make another left and continue about one mile to the campground.

Trip note: Okay, the directions are complicated, but few things worth remembering come easy, right? This campground is set in a forested area along Cold Creek. There are trails nearby for hiking and horseback riding. It gets minimal use although it has piped water. A large shelter is available for groups, and makes this an ideal camp for family trips.

84. ROCK CREEK

Reference: **On Rock Creek; map B2, grid i6.**

Campsites, facilities: There are 19 campsites for tents or small trailers. Picnic tables, fire grills and tent pads are provided. Vault toilets and piped water are available. A horse loading ramp is on-site. Some facilities are **wheelchair accessible**. There is a campground host on-site. Leashed pets are permitted.

Reservations, fee: No reservations; no fee. Open all year.

Who to contact: Phone the Department of Natural Resources at (360) 577-2025 or write to Department of Natural Resources, Southwest Region, P.O. Box 280, Castle Rock, WA 98611-0280.

Location: From Interstate 5 north of Vancouver, Washington, take exit 9 and drive east on NE 179th Street for 5.5 miles. Turn right on Highway 503 and drive 1.5 miles. Turn left on NE 159th Street and drive three miles, then turn right on 182nd Avenue and drive one mile. Turn left on NE 139th (Road L 1400) and drive eight miles, then turn left on Road L 1000 and drive 3.5 miles. (You'll pass Cold Creek campground after three miles.) Turn left on Road L 1200 and proceed about 200 yards to the campground, which will be on your right.

Trip note: A nearby option to Cold Creek, also managed by the Department of Natural Resources. This camp is set in a wooded area along Rock Creek. Nearby trails are for use by hikers and horseback riders. For equestrians, this camp has the added bonus of facilities for horses.

---

85. PANTHER CREEK   RV

Reference: **On Panther Creek in Gifford Pinchot National Forest; map B2, grid i7.**

Campsites, facilities: There are 33 sites for tents, trailers or RVs up to 25 feet long. Hand-pumped well water and picnic tables are provided. Pit toilets are available. Leashed pets are permitted.

Reservations, fee: Reserve some sites by calling (800) 280-CAMP ($7.50 reservation fee); $9-$18 fee per night. Open mid-May to mid-October.

Who to contact: Phone Gifford Pinchot National Forest at (509) 427-3200 or write to Wind River Ranger District, Carson, WA 98610.

Location: From Interstate 5 at Vancouver, turn east on Highway 14 and drive approximately 50 miles to Carson. Turn north on the Wind River Highway and drive nine miles, then turn east on Forest Service Road 6517 and travel 1.5 miles. Turn south on Forest Service Road 65 and drive 100 yards to the campground.

Trip note: This campground is set along Panther Creek, several miles from the Wind River Ranger Station. Just west of the ranger station is the Wind River Nursery, a tree nursery that has the capacity to produce 27 million seedlings per year. Tours are available. Fishing is an option here, as well as hiking or horseback riding.

---

86. BEAVER   RV

Reference: **On Wind River in Gifford Pinchot National Forest; map B2, grid i7.**

Campsites, facilities: There are 26 sites for tents, trailers or RVs up to 25 feet long. Piped water, fire grills, and picnic tables are provided. Pit toilets are available. Two campsites are **wheelchair accessible**. Group camping facilities are also available. Leashed pets permitted.

Reservations, fee: Reserve some sites by calling (800) 280-CAMP ($7.75 reservation fee); $9-$18 fee per night; $45 group fee. Open mid-April to late September.

Who to contact: Phone Gifford Pinchot National Forest at (509) 427-3200 or write to Wind River Ranger District, Carson, WA 98610.

Location: From Interstate 5 at Vancouver, turn east on Highway 14 and drive approximately 50 miles to Carson. Turn north on the Wind River Highway and drive 12 miles to the campground entrance.

Trip note: This campground is set along Wind River. It's a nice spot, with fishing access and pretty, shaded sites. It is small and remote, yet it has piped water—the perfect combination.

87.   BEACON ROCK STATE PARK   🚐

Reference: **On Columbia River; map B2, grid j7.**

Campsites, facilities: There are 33 developed sites for tents or self-contained RVs up to 50 feet long. Picnic tables and fire grills are provided. Flush toilets, sanitary disposal station, coin-operated showers and a playground are available. Firewood is available for an extra fee. Some facilities are **wheelchair accessible**. Boat docks, launching facilities and rentals are nearby.

Reservations, fee: No reservations; $10 fee per night; $4 launch fee. Open all year with limited winter facilities.

Who to contact: Phone (800) 233-0321 or (509) 427-8265 or write to 34841 State Route 14, Skamania, WA 98648.

Location: From Interstate 5 at Vancouver, Washington, turn east on Highway 14 and drive 35 miles. The park straddles the highway; follow the signs to the campground.

Trip note: This state park is set along the Columbia River with 14 miles of hiking trails heading inland. One trail leads to Beacon Rock, the second largest monolith in the world, which overlooks the Columbia River Gorge. If you like to fish, sturgeon are plentiful in the Columbia. Remember, there is a six-foot maximum size limit for Mr. Sturgeon.

88.   DOUGAN CREEK

Reference: **Near Washougal River; map B2, grid j7.**

Campsites, facilities: There are seven campsites for tents or small trailers. Picnic tables, fire grills and tent pads are provided. Vault toilets and piped water are available. Leashed pets are permitted.

Reservations, fee: No reservations; no fee. Open mid-May to mid-September.

Who to contact: Phone the Department of Natural Resources at (360) 577-2025 or write to Department of Natural Resources, Southwest Region, P.O. Box 280, Castle Rock, WA 98611-0280.

Location: From Interstate 5 at Vancouver, Washington, turn east on Highway 14 and drive 20 miles, then turn north on Highway 140 and drive five miles to Washougal River Road. Turn right on Washougal River Road and drive about seven miles until you see the campground on your right.

Trip note: This campground is set along Dougan Creek where it empties into the Washougal River. It's small, remote, but has piped water and an on-site host. The camp is heavily forested and has pretty sites with river views.

89.   BEACON ROCK TRAILER PARK   🚐

Reference: **On Columbia River; map B2, grid j7.**

Campsites, facilities: There are 20 sites for trailers or RVs of any length (three drive-through). Electricity, piped water, sewer hookups and picnic tables are provided. Flush toilets, bottled gas, sanitary services, showers, firewood, a store, a recreation hall, a laundromat and ice are available. Pets are permitted. Boat launching facilities are located nearby on the Columbia River.

Reservations, fee: Reservations accepted with deposit; $8-$14 fee per night. MasterCard, Visa and Discover accepted. Open all year.

Who to contact: Phone (509) 427-8473 or write to 62 Moorage Road, Skamania, WA 98648.

Location: From Interstate 5 at Vancouver, Washington, turn east on Highway 14 and drive 34 miles. The park is in Skamania at the corner of Highway 14 and Moorage Road.

Trip note: This trailer park is set along the Columbia River, a short distance from Beacon Rock State Park. See the trip note for Beacon Rock State Park for details. Nearby recreation options include an 18-hole golf course.

MAP B3

WASHINGTON MAP .... see page 90
Adjoining Maps
NORTH (A3) .... see page 166
EAST (B4) .... see page 362
SOUTH .... Oregon
WEST (B2) .... see page 294

75 LISTINGS
PAGES 330-361

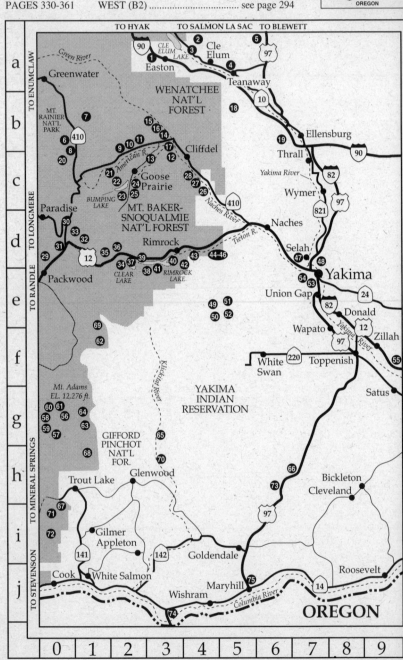

Washington Map B3 featuring: Lake Easton, Teanaway River, Yakima River, Wenatchee National Forest, Mount Baker-Snoqualmie National Forest, Bumping River, American River, Naches River, White River, Mount Rainier National Park, Bumping Lake, Gifford Pinchot National Forest, Ohanapecosh River, Clear Lake, Dog Lake, Leech Lake, Rimrock Lake, Tieton River, Goat Rocks Wilderness, Yakima, Takhlakh Lake, Horseshoe Lake, Olallie Lake, Council Lake, Cispus River, Mount Adams, Walupt Lake, Trout Lake, Brooks Memorial State Park, Dalles Dam, Mount Adams Wilderness, White Salmon River, Columbia River

---

1. LAKE EASTON STATE PARK RV

Reference: **On Lake Easton; map B3, grid a3.**
Campsites, facilities: There are two primitive tent sites, 92 developed tent sites, and 45 sites for trailers or RVs up to 60 feet long. Picnic tables and fire grills are provided. Flush toilets, sanitary disposal station, a playground, electricity, piped water, sewer hookups, showers and firewood are available. A cafe and ice are located within one mile. Some facilities are **wheelchair accessible**. Leashed pets are permitted. Boat launching facilities and floats are located on Lake Easton.
Reservations, fee: Contact Reservations Northwest at (800) 452-5687 ($6 reservation fee); $7-$16 fee per night. Open April 19-October 16.
Who to contact: Phone (800) 233-0321 or (509) 656-2586 or write to P.O. Box 26, Easton, WA 98925.
Location: From Interstate 5 at Seattle, turn east on Interstate 90 and drive approximately 68 miles to the park entrance (located one mile west of the town of Easton).
Trip note: This campground offers a multitude of recreational opportunities. For starters, it is set along the shore of Lake Easton, with Kachess Lake and Keechelus Lake just a short drive away. The park provides opportunities for both summer and winter recreation, including swimming, fishing, boating, cross-country skiing and snowmobiling. Nearby recreation options include an 18-hole golf course and hiking trails.

---

2. INDIAN CAMP

Reference: **On the Middle Fork of Teanaway River; map B3, grid a4.**
Campsites, facilities: There are nine campsites for tents or small trailers. Picnic tables, fire grills and tent pads are provided. Pit toilets are available, but there is **no piped water**. Leashed pets are permitted.
Reservations, fee: No reservations; no fee. Open all year.
Who to contact: Phone the Department of Natural Resources at (509) 925-6131 or write to Department of Natural Resources, Southeast Region, 2211 Airport Road, Ellensburg, WA 98926-9341.
Location: From Seattle, turn east on Interstate 90 and drive 80 miles to Cle Elum, take exit 85 and drive east on Highway 970 for seven miles. Turn left on Teanaway Road and drive 7.5 miles, then turn left on West Fork Teanaway Road and drive one-half mile. Turn right on Middle Fork Teanaway Road and drive four miles to the campground, which will be on your left.
Trip note: This campground is set along the Middle Fork Teanaway River. It is

a very primitive setting, with sunny, open sites along the river. Be sure to bring your own drinking water. This is a little-used camp offering quiet and solitude.

---

3. McKEAN'S TRAILER PARK ⟨RV⟩

Reference: **Near Yakima River; map B3, grid a4.**

Campsites, facilities: There are 15 sites for trailers or RVs. Electricity, piped water, sewer hookups and picnic tables are provided. A cafe is available. Bottled gas, sanitary services, a store, a laundromat and ice are located within one mile. Pets are permitted.

Reservations, fee: Reservations recommended; $10-$12 fee per night. Open March to late December.

Who to contact: Phone (509) 674-2254 or write to 327 Lincoln Street, Cle Elum, WA 98922.

Location: From Interstate 5 at Seattle, turn east on Interstate 90 and drive approximately 80 miles to Cle Elum. The park is in Cle Elum at 1011 East 1st Street.

Trip note: You can rent rafts and canoes in Cle Elum and take a 16-mile raft trip down the Yakima River to Thorp, where they offer to pick you up and bring you back to Cle Elum. Cle Elum is the Indian word for "swift water". The Cle Elum Historical Telephone Museum is also in town. Lake Easton State Park and Trailer Corral are also set near the Yakima River.

---

4. TRAILER CORRAL ⟨RV⟩

Reference: **On Yakima River; map B3, grid a5.**

Campsites, facilities: There are five tent sites and 24 sites for trailers or RVs of any length. There are also six cabins available. Electricity, piped water, sewer and cable TV hookups and picnic tables are provided. Flush toilets, sanitary services, showers, firewood, a laundromat and ice are available. A store and a laundromat are located within one mile. Pets are permitted. Boat launching facilities are nearby.

Reservations, fee: Reservations accepted; $12-$16 fee per night. Open all year.

Who to contact: Phone (509) 674-2433 or write to 2781 Highway 970, Cle Elum, WA 98922.

Location: From Interstate 5 at Seattle, turn east on Interstate 90 and drive approximately 80 miles to Cle Elum. Continue one mile east on Interstate 90 to exit 85, then head east on Highway 970 for one mile to the park on the left.

Trip note: This wooded campground is set along the Yakima River, with a choice of grassy or graveled sites. See the trip note for McKean's Trailer Park for river rafting information. Nearby recreation options include an 18-hole golf course, marked hiking trails and tennis courts.

---

5. MINERAL SPRINGS ⟨RV⟩

Reference: **On Medicine Creek in Wenatchee National Forest; map B3, grid a6.**

Campsites, facilities: There are five tent sites and seven sites for tents, trailers or RVs up to 21 feet long. Piped water and picnic tables are provided. Flush toilets, showers, a store, a restaurant, and gas for snowmobiles are available.

Reservations, fee: No reservations; $8 fee per night. Open mid-April to late November.

Who to contact: Phone Wenatchee National Forest at (509) 674-4411 or write to Cle Elum Ranger District, 830 West Second Street, Cle Elum, WA 98922.

Location: From Interstate 5 at Seattle, turn east on Interstate 90 and drive approximately 80 miles to Cle Elum. Take exit 86 to County Road 970 and drive east 12 miles, then turn northeast on US 97 and drive about seven miles to the campground.

Trip note: This campground is set at the confluence of Medicine Creek and Swauk Creek. It is one of five campgrounds along US 97. Fishing, berry picking and hunting are good in season in this area. In the winter, cross-country skiing and snowshoeing are two options.

---

6. SILVER SPRINGS

Reference: **In Mount Baker-Snoqualmie National Forest; map B3, grid b0.**

Campsites, facilities: There are 16 tent sites and 40 sites for tents, trailers or RVs up to 21 feet long. Picnic tables and fire grills are provided. Vault toilets, piped water and firewood are available. Leashed pets are permitted.

Reservations, fee: Reserve some sites by calling (800) 280-CAMP ($7.75 reservation fee); $8-$10 fee per night. Open mid-May to late September.

Who to contact: Phone Mount Baker-Snoqualmie National Forest at (360) 825-6585, or write to White River Ranger District, 857 Roosevelt Avenue East, Enumclaw, WA 98022.

Location: From Interstate 5 south of Tacoma, take exit 127 and turn east on Highway 512. Drive northeast until you hit Highway 167, then turn east and continue a short distance to Highway 410. Turn east and drive 15 miles to Enumclaw. From there, continue 31 miles southeast on Highway 410 and you'll see the campground entrance on your right.

Trip note: This campground is set along the White River on the northeastern border of Mount Rainier National Park. This is a good option to the more crowded camps in the park. It is set in a beautiful section of old-growth forest and is particularly scenic. There are numerous recreation options in the area, including hiking, fishing and picnicking. A Forest Service information center is nearby.

---

7. CORRAL PASS

Reference: **In Mount Baker-Snoqualmie National Forest; map B3, grid b1.**

Campsites, facilities: There are 20 tent sites. Picnic tables and fire grills are provided. Vault toilets, a horse-loading ramp and firewood are available, but there is **no piped water**. Leashed pets are permitted.

Reservations, fee: No reservations; no fee. Open July to late September.

Who to contact: Phone Mount Baker-Snoqualmie National Forest at (360) 825-6585 or write to White River Ranger District, 857 Roosevelt Avenue East, Enumclaw, WA 98022.

Location: From Interstate 5 south of Tacoma, take exit 127 and turn east on Highway 512. Drive northeast until you hit Highway 167, then turn east and continue a short distance to Highway 410. Turn east and drive 15 miles to Enumclaw. From there, continue 31 miles southeast on Highway 410, then six miles east on Forest Service Road 7174. It is a winding, dirt road and not suitable for trailers or RVs.

Trip note: This is the most remote of the campgrounds in the area. Primitive, quiet and an ideal base camp for a hiking trip, this campground is at 5,600 feet. It is also commonly used by groups of horse-packers heading into the adjacent Norse Peak Wilderness. There are several trails near camp that lead to backcountry fishing lakes and streams. See a Forest Service map for details. In late summer and fall, visitors can find wild berries in the area.

---

8. THE DALLES · RV

Reference: **In Mount Baker-Snoqualmie National Forest; map B3, grid b1.**

Campsites, facilities: There are 19 tent sites and 26 sites for tents, trailers or RVs up to 21 feet long. Picnic tables, fire grills, vault toilets and piped water are provided. Firewood is available. Leashed pets are permitted. There is a large shaded picnic area available for day use.

Reservations, fee: Reserve some sites by calling (800) 280-CAMP ($7.75 reservation fee); $8-$10 fee per night. Open mid-May to late September.

Who to contact: Phone Mount Baker-Snoqualmie National Forest at (360) 825-6585, or write to White River Ranger District, 857 Roosevelt Avenue East, Enumclaw, WA 98022.

Location: From Interstate 5 south of Tacoma, take exit 127 and turn east on Highway 512. Drive northeast until you hit Highway 167, then turn east and continue a short distance to Highway 410. Turn east and drive 15 miles to Enumclaw. From there, continue 25.5 miles southeast on Highway 410 and you'll see the campground on your right.

Trip note: This campground is set along the White River. There is a nature trail nearby, and the White River entrance to Mount Rainier National Park is about 14 miles south on Highway 410. The camp is set amidst a grove of old-growth trees, and a particular point of interest is a huge old Douglas fir tree, over nine feet in diameter and 235 feet tall. This is one of the prettiest camps in the area.

---

9. PLEASANT VALLEY · RV

Reference: **On American River in Wenatchee National Forest; map B3, grid b2.**

Campsites, facilities: There are 26 sites for tents, trailers or RVs up to 30 feet long. Picnic tables and fire grills are provided. Hand-pumped water and pit toilets are available. Firewood is not provided but may be gathered. Leashed pets are permitted.

Reservations, fee: No reservations; $9 fee per night; $17 double site fee; $5 each additional vehicle. Open mid-June to late November.

Who to contact: Phone Wenatchee National Forest at (360) 653-2205 or write to Naches Ranger District, 10061 Highway 12, Naches, WA 98937.

Location: From Yakima on Interstate 82, drive 13 miles northwest on State Route 12 to Naches. From there, continue 4.5 miles west on State Route 12, then drive 37 miles northwest on Highway 410 to the campground on the left.

Trip note: This campground is set along the American River and is a good base camp for a hiking trip. A trail from the camp follows Kettle Creek up to the American Ridge and Kettle Lake in the William O. Douglas Wilderness. It joins another trail there that follows the ridge and then drops down to Bumping Lake. A Forest Service map is essential. In the winter, the area is popular with cross-country skiers.

---

10. PINE NEEDLE GROUP CAMP · RV

Reference: **On American River in Wenatchee National Forest; map B3, grid b2.**

Campsites, facilities: There are six sites for tents, trailers or RVs up to 21 feet long. Picnic tables are provided. Pit toilets are available, but there is **no piped water**. Firewood is not provided but may be gathered. Leashed pets are permitted.

Reservations, fee: Reservations required; $40 fee per night. Open late April to mid-September.

Who to contact: Phone Wenatchee National Forest at (509) 653-2205 or write to Naches Ranger District, 10061 Highway 12, Naches, WA 98937.

Location: From Yakima on Interstate 82, drive 13 miles northwest on State Route 12 to Naches. From there, drive 4.5 miles west on State Route 12, then 30.5 miles northwest on Highway 410 to the campground on the left.

Trip note: This campground is a reservations-only group site and is set on the edge of the William O. Douglas Wilderness, along the American River. There are trails leading south into the backcountry at nearby camps; see a Forest Service map. The camp is easy to reach, rustic and beautiful. Fishing access is available. A side trip option is to visit Bumping Lake to the south, where boating, fishing and swimming are among your options.

---

11. HELLS CROSSING   RV

Reference: On American River in Wenatchee National Forest; map B3, grid b2.

Campsites, facilities: There are 18 sites for tents, trailers or RVs up to 16 feet long. Piped water and picnic tables are provided. Pit toilets are available. Firewood is not provided but may be gathered. Leashed pets are permitted.

Reservations, fee: No reservations; $9 fee per night; $17 double site fee; $5 each additional vehicle. Open late May to late November.

Who to contact: Phone Wenatchee National Forest at (509) 653-2205 or write to Naches Ranger District, 10061 Highway 12, Naches, WA 98937.

Location: From Yakima on Interstate 82, drive 13 miles northwest on State Route 12 to Naches. From there, drive 4.5 miles west on State Route 12, then drive 33.5 miles northwest on Highway 410 to the campground on the right.

Trip note: This campground is set along the American River. A steep trail from the camp leads up to Goat Peak and follows the American Ridge in the William O. Douglas Wilderness. Other trails join the ridgetop trail and connect with lakes and streams. A Forest Service map details the backcountry.

---

12. SAWMILL FLAT   RV

Reference: On Naches River in Wenatchee National Forest; map B3, grid c3.

Campsites, facilities: There are 27 sites for tents, trailers or RVs up to 21 feet long. Hand-pumped water and picnic tables are provided. Pit toilets, an adirondack group shelter and firewood are available. Some facilities are **wheelchair accessible**. Pets are permitted.

Reservations, fee: No reservations; $9 fee per night; $17 double site fee; $5 each additional vehicle. Open April to December.

Who to contact: Phone Wenatchee National Forest at (509)653-2205 or write to Naches Ranger District, 10061 Highway 12, Naches, WA 98937.

Location: From Yakima on Interstate 82, drive 13 miles northwest on State Route 12 to Naches. From there, drive 4.5 miles west on State Route 12, then 23.5 miles northwest on Highway 410 to the campground on the left.

Trip note: This campground is set on the Naches River near Halfway Flat. Fishing access is available. There is a hiking trail that leads west from Halfway Flat for several miles into the backcountry. Another trailhead is located at Boulder Cave to the south. See a Forest Service map.

13.   CEDAR SPRINGS   ⛺

Reference: **On Bumping River in Wenatchee National Forest; map B3, grid c3.**

Campsites, facilities: There are 15 sites for tents, trailers or RVs up to 21 feet long. Hand-pumped water is available. Picnic tables are provided. Pit toilets and firewood are available. Pets are permitted.

Reservations, fee: No reservations; $9 fee per night; $17 double site fee; $5 each additional vehicle. Open late May to late November.

Who to contact: Phone Wenatchee National Forest at (509)653-2205 or write to Naches Ranger District, 10061 Highway 12, Naches, WA 98937.

Location: From Yakima on Interstate 82, drive 13 miles northwest on State Route 12 to Naches. From there, drive 4.5 miles west on State Route 12, then turn northwest on Highway 410 and drive 28.5 miles. Turn southwest on Forest Service Road 2000 and proceed one-half mile to the campground on the left.

Trip note: This campground is set along the Bumping River. If you continue driving southwest for 11 miles on Forest Service Road 174, you will get to Bumping Lake, where recreation options abound.

14.   LITTLE NACHES   ⛺

Reference: **On Little Naches River in Wenatchee National Forest; map B3, grid b3.**

Campsites, facilities: There are 21 sites for tents, trailers or RVs up to 15 feet long. Hand-pumped water, picnic tables and fire grills are provided. Pit toilets and firewood are available. Leashed pets are permitted.

Reservations, fee: No reservations; $9 fee per night; $17 double site fee; $5 each additional vehicle. Open late May to late November.

Who to contact: Phone Wenatchee National Forest at (509) 653-2205 or write to Naches Ranger District, 10061 Highway 12, Naches, WA 98937.

Location: From Yakima on Interstate 82, drive 13 miles northwest on State Route 12 to Naches. From there, drive 4.5 miles west on State Route 12, then turn northwest on Highway 410 and drive 25 miles. Turn and drive 100 yards northwest on Forest Service Road 1900 to the campground on the left.

Trip note: This campground is set on the Little Naches River near the American River. It is set just one-tenth of a mile off the road, making the easy access a major attraction for highway cruisers. Fishing access is available from camp.

15.   CROW CREEK   ⛺

Reference: **On Naches River in Wenatchee National Forest; map B3, grid b3.**

Campsites, facilities: There are 15 sites for tents, trailers or RVs up to 16 feet long. Picnic tables and fire grills are provided. Pit toilets are available, but there is **no piped water**. Firewood is not provided but may be gathered. Leashed pets are permitted.

Reservations, fee: No reservations; no fee. Open mid-April to late November.

Who to contact: Phone Wenatchee National Forest at (509) 653-2205 or write to Naches Ranger District, 10061 Highway 12, Naches, WA 98937.

Location: From Yakima on Interstate 82, drive 13 miles northwest on State Route 12 to Naches. From there, drive 4.5 miles west on State Route 12, then turn northwest on Highway 410 and drive 24.5 miles. Turn northwest on Forest Service Road 1900 and continue 2.5 miles, then turn west on Forest Service Road 1902 and proceed one-half mile to the campground on the right.

Trip note: This campground is set along the Naches River and is popular with OHVers. A trail from the campground leads into the backcountry and then forks in several directions. One way leads to the American River, another follows West Quartz Creek and another goes along Fife's Ridge into the Norse Peak Wilderness. See a Forest Service map for details. There is good hunting and fishing in season in this area.

16.   KANER FLAT   **RV**

Reference: **Near Naches River in Wenatchee National Forest; map B3, grid b3.**
Campsites, facilities: There are 49 sites for tents, trailers or RVs up to 30 feet long. Piped water and picnic tables are provided. Pit, composting and flush toilets and firewood are available. Leashed pets are permitted.
Reservations, fee: No reservations; $8-$10 fee per night; $5 each additional vehicle. Open mid-April to late November.
Who to contact: Phone Wenatchee National Forest at (509) 653-2205 or write to Naches Ranger District, 10061 Highway 12, Naches, WA 98937.
Location: From Yakima on Interstate 82, drive 13 miles northwest on State Route 12 to Naches. From there, drive 4.5 miles west on State Route 12, then turn northwest on Highway 410 and drive 25 miles. Turn northwest on Forest Service Road 1900 and drive 2.5 miles to the campground on the right.
Trip note: This campground is on the site of an old wagon trail campsite on the Old Naches Trail, a route used in the 1800s by wagon trains, Native Americans and the U.S. Cavalry on their way to west side markets. The Naches Trail is now used by motorcyclists and narrow clearance four-wheel-drive enthusiasts. It is set near the Naches River.

17.   INDIAN FLAT GROUP CAMP   **RV**

Reference: **On American River in Wenatchee National Forest; map B3, grid b3.**
Campsites, facilities: There are 11 sites for tents, trailers or RVs up to 16 feet long. Piped water and picnic tables are provided. Pit toilets and firewood are available. Leashed pets are permitted.
Reservations, fee: Reservations required; $40 fee per night. Open late May to mid-September.
Who to contact: Phone Wenatchee National Forest at (509) 653-2205 or write to Naches Ranger District, 10061 Highway 12, Naches, WA 98937.
Location: From Yakima on Interstate 82, drive 13 miles northwest on State Route 12 to Naches. From there, drive 4.5 miles west on State Route 12, then drive 27 miles northwest on Highway 410 to the campground on the left.
Trip note: This campground is a reservations-only group site set along the American River. Fishing access is available. A trail from the camp leads into the backcountry, west along Fife's Ridge and further north to the West Quartz Creek drainage. A Forest Service map details the adventure possibilities.

18.   TANEUM   **RV**

Reference: **On Taneum Creek in Wenatchee National Forest; map B3, grid b5.**
Campsites, facilities: There are 14 sites for trailers or RVs up to 21 feet long. Picnic tables are provided. Piped water and firewood are available. Some facilities are **wheelchair accessible**. Leashed pets are permitted.
Reservations, fee: No reservations; $9 fee per night; $17 double site; $5 each additional vehicle. Open May to late November.

Who to contact: Phone Wenatchee National Forest at (509) 674-4411 or write to Cle Elum Ranger District, West Second Street, Cle Elum, WA 98922.

Location: From Interstate 5 at Seattle, turn east on Interstate 90 and drive approximately 80 miles to Cle Elum. Continue nine miles southeast on Interstate 90 to exit 93. Cross the freeway and drive south on Thorp Prairie Road for four miles. Cross back over the freeway to Taneum Road. Turn right and drive west for three miles to Forest Service Road 33. Continue west six miles to the campground on the left.

Trip note: This rustic spot, set along Taneum Creek, has been getting increased use in recent years due to off-road-vehicle displacement in other areas. Fishing is popular here in the summer, and in the winter months snowshoeing and cross-country skiing trails are available.

---

19. KOA ELLENSBURG ■RV■

Reference: **On Yakima River; map B3, grid b6.**

Campsites, facilities: There are 50 tent sites and 100 sites for trailers or RVs of any length (48 drive-through). There are also three teepees available. Piped water and picnic tables are provided. Flush toilets, sanitary services, showers, a recreation hall, a store, a laundromat, ice, a playground, nightly movies, a wading pool and a swimming pool are available. Electricity and sewer hookups can be obtained for an extra fee. Bottled gas and a cafe are located within one mile. Pets and motorbikes are permitted.

Reservations, fee: Reservations accepted; $10-$25 fee per night; $20 teepee fee for two people. MasterCard and Visa accepted. Open April to mid-October.

Who to contact: Phone (509) 925-9319 or write to 32 Thorp Highway South, Ellensburg, WA 98926.

Location: From Seattle, drive about 106 miles on Interstate 90 to exit 106 near Ellensburg. You will see the campground as you exit.

Trip note: This is the only campground in a 25-mile radius, and it is exceptionally clean and scenic. It offers well-maintained, shaded campsites set along the Yakima River. The Kittitas County Historical Museum is in town at Third and Pine streets and then there's the town-sponsored Ellensburg Roundup every weekend during the summer. Nearby recreation options include an 18-hole golf course and tennis courts.

---

20. WHITE RIVER ■RV■

Reference: **On White River in Mount Rainier National Park; map B3, grid c0.**

Campsites, facilities: There are 117 sites for tents or RVs up to 20 feet long. Picnic tables and fire grills are provided. Flush toilets and piped water are available. Some facilities are **wheelchair accessible**. Leashed pets are permitted.

Reservations, fee: No reservations; $8 fee per night. Open mid-June to mid-September.

Who to contact: Phone Mount Rainier National Park at (360) 569-2211 or write to Mount Rainier National Park, Tahoma Woods, Ashford, WA 98304.

Location: From Interstate 5 at Tacoma, turn east on Highway 512 and drive 12 miles. Turn east on Highway 167 for one mile to the junction with Highway 410. Turn east on Highway 410 and drive to Enumclaw. Continue 27 miles southeast on Highway 410 to the White River entrance into the park. Take White River Road to the right and drive about seven miles to the campground.

Trip note: This campground is set on the White River at 4,400 feet. A trail near camp leads a short distance (but vertically, it's a rise of 2200 feet) to the Sunrise Visitor Center. (Local rangers recommend that trailers be left at White River Campground and the 11-mile road trip to Sunrise be made by car.) From there, you can take several trails that lead to backcountry lakes and glaciers. This camp is often used by climbers planning to summit Mount Rainier.

21. LODGE POLE   RV

Reference: **On American River in Wenatchee National Forest; map B3, grid c2.**

Campsites, facilities: There are 32 sites for tents, trailers or RVs up to 21 feet long. Piped water and picnic tables are provided. Pit toilets and firewood are available. Leashed pets are permitted.

Reservations, fee: No reservations; $9 fee per night; $17 double site fee; $5 each additional vehicle. Open mid-June to mid-September.

Who to contact: Phone Wenatchee National Forest at (509) 653-2205 or write to Naches Ranger District, 10061 Highway 12, Naches, WA 98937.

Location: From Yakima on Interstate 82, drive 13 miles northwest on State Route 12 to Naches. From there, drive 4.5 miles on State Route 12, then turn northwest on Highway 410 and drive 40.5 miles to the campground on the right.

Trip note: This campground is set along the American River about seven miles west of the western boundary of Mount Rainier National Park. See the trip note for Gateway Inn and RV Park (Chapter B2) for information on Mount Rainier. Fishing access is available nearby.

22. BUMPING CROSSING   RV

Reference: **On Bumping River in Wenatchee National Forest; map B3, grid c2.**

Campsites, facilities: There are seven sites for tents, trailers or RVs up to 15 feet long. Picnic tables are provided. Pit toilets and firewood are available, but there is **no piped water**. A store, a cafe and ice are located within one mile. Leashed pets are permitted. Boat docks, launching facilities and rentals are nearby on Bumping Lake.

Reservations, fee: No reservations; no fee. Open late May to late November.

Who to contact: Phone Wenatchee National Forest at (509) 653-2205 or write to Naches Ranger District, 10061 Highway 12, Naches, WA 98937.

Location: From Yakima on Interstate 82, drive 13 miles northwest on State Route 12 to Naches. From there, drive 4.5 miles west on State Route 12, then turn northwest on Highway 410 and drive 28.5 miles. Turn southwest on Forest Service Road 2000 and drive 10 miles to the campground on the right.

Trip note: This campground is set along the Bumping River about a mile from the boat landing at Bumping Lake. It is a more primitive option to Bumping Lake and Boat Landing. It's a very good spot for a weekend trip, but remember to bring your own drinking water.

23. BUMPING LAKE AND BOAT LANDING   RV

Reference: **On Bumping Lake in Wenatchee National Forest; map B3, grid c2.**

Campsites, facilities: There are 50 sites for tents, trailers or RVs up to 21 feet long. Hand-pumped water and picnic tables are provided. Pit toilets and firewood are available. Pets are permitted. Boat docks, launching facilities and rentals are nearby.

Reservations, fee: No reservations; $9 fee per night; $17 double site fee; $5 each additional vehicle. Open mid-May to late November.

Who to contact: Phone Wenatchee National Forest at (509) 653-2205 or write to Naches Ranger District, 10061 Highway 12, Naches, WA 98937.

Location: From Yakima on Interstate 82, drive 13 miles northwest on State Route 12 to Naches. From there, drive 4.5 miles west on State Route 12, then turn northwest on Highway 410 and drive 28.5 miles. Turn southwest on Forest Service Road 2000 and continue 11 miles to the campground on the right.

Trip note: Woods and water, this spot has them both. A variety of water activities are allowed at Bumping Lake, including waterskiing, fishing and swimming. There are also several hiking trails that go into the wilderness area surrounding the lake. This is one of the more developed camps in the area, with the added bonus of a boat ramp.

---

24.   SODA SPRINGS   🆁🆅

Reference: **On Bumping River in Wenatchee National Forest; map B3, grid c3.**

Campsites, facilities: There are 26 sites for tents, trailers or RVs. Piped water and picnic tables are provided. Pit toilets and firewood are available. Some **wheelchair-accessible** facilities are available. Pets are permitted. A picnic shelter with a fireplace is available.

Reservations, fee: No reservations; $9 fee per night; $17 double site fee; $5 each additional vehicle. Open May to late November.

Who to contact: Phone Wenatchee National Forest at (509) 653-2205 or write to Naches Ranger District, 10061 Highway 12, Naches, WA 98937.

Location: From Yakima on Interstate 82, drive 13 miles northwest on State Route 12 to Naches. From there, drive 4.5 miles west on State Route 12, then turn northwest on Highway 410 and drive 28.5 miles. Turn southwest on Forest Service Road 2000 and continue five miles to the campground on the left.

Trip note: This campground is set along Bumping Creek and offers natural mineral springs and a nature trail. Fishing access is available. A sheltered picnic area is provided.

---

25.   COUGAR FLAT   🆁🆅

Reference: **On Bumping River in Wenatchee National Forest; map B3, grid c3.**

Campsites, facilities: There are nine sites for tents, trailers or RVs up to 16 feet long. Hand-pumped water and picnic tables are provided. Pit toilets and firewood are available. Leashed pets are permitted.

Reservations, fee: No reservations; $9 fee per night; $17 double site fee; $5 each additional vehicle. Open late May to mid-September.

Who to contact: Phone Wenatchee National Forest at (509) 653-2205 or write to Naches Ranger District, 10061 Highway 12, Naches, WA 98937.

Location: From Yakima on Interstate 82, drive 13 miles northwest on State Route 12 to Naches. From there, drive 4.5 miles west on State Route 12, then turn northwest on Highway 410 and drive 28.5 miles. Turn southwest on Forest Service Road 2000 and continue six miles to the campground on the left.

Trip note: This campground is set along the Bumping River, with good fishing in the area. A trail from the camp follows the river and then heads up the tributaries. It is one of several camps in the immediate vicinity. See the Chapter B3 map for details.

26.   SQUAW ROCK RESORT   🚐

Reference: **Near the Naches River; map B3, grid c4.**

Campsites, facilities: There are 25 tent sites and 65 sites for trailers or RVs of any length. Electricity, piped water and picnic tables are provided. Flush toilets, bottled gas, sanitary services, showers, a recreation hall, a store, a cafe, ice, a playground and a swimming pool are available. Sewer hookups are available at some sites. Pets and motorbikes are permitted.

Reservations, fee: Reservations accepted; $18 fee per night; MasterCard and Visa accepted. Open all year.

Who to contact: Phone (509) 658-2926 or write to 15070 State Route 410, Naches, WA 98937.

Location: From Yakima on Interstate 82, turn northwest on State Route 12 and drive 13 miles to Naches. Drive five miles west on State Route 12, then turn north on State Route 410 and drive 15 miles northwest to the campground on the left.

Trip note: This park is near the Naches River. Nearby recreation options include trout fishing, hiking trails, marked bike trails and a riding stable. The park provides a pool and hot tub. The nearby town of Naches, located southeast of the campground on Highway 410, offers all services.

27.   COTTONWOOD   🚐

Reference: **On Naches River in Wenatchee National Forest; map B3, grid c4.**

Campsites, facilities: There are 17 sites for tents, trailers or RVs up to 21 feet long. Piped water is available. Picnic tables are provided. Pit toilets, firewood, sanitary disposal station, a store, a cafe and ice are available nearby. Some facilities are **wheelchair accessible.** Leashed pets are permitted.

Reservations, fee: No reservations; $9 fee per night; $17 double site fee; $5 each additional vehicle. Open April to December.

Who to contact: Phone Wenatchee National Forest at (509) 653-2205 or write to Naches Ranger District, 10061 Highway 12, Naches, WA 98937.

Location: From Yakima on Interstate 82, drive 13 miles northwest on State Route 12 to Naches. From there, drive 4.5 miles west on State Route 12, then turn northwest on Highway 410 drive 17.5 miles to the campground on the left.

Trip note: This campground is set along the Naches River. Halfway Flat, Sawmill Flat, Crow Creek, Kaner Flat and Little Naches provide nearby options if this one doesn't grab your fancy. It very well may, though, with pretty, shaded sites and river views.

28.   HALFWAY FLAT   🚐

Reference: **On Naches River in Wenatchee National Forest; map B3, grid c4.**

Campsites, facilities: There are 12 sites for tents, trailers or RVs up to 27 feet long. Picnic tables are provided. Pit toilets and firewood are available, but there is **no piped water**. Leashed pets are permitted.

Reservations, fee: No reservations; no fee. Open April to late November.

Who to contact: Phone Wenatchee National Forest at (509) 653-2205 or write to Naches Ranger District, 10061 Highway 12, Naches, WA 98937.

Location: From Yakima on Interstate 82, drive 13 miles northwest on State Route 12 to Naches. From there, drive 4.5 miles west on State Route 12, then turn northwest on Highway 410 and drive 21 miles. Turn northwest on Forest

Service Road 1704 and drive three miles to the campground on the left.

Trip note: This campground is set along the Naches River. A trail leads from the campground into the backcountry of the William O. Douglas Wilderness, which can also be reached by car. Try hoofing it.

29. PACKWOOD TRAILER AND RV PARK RV

Reference: **In Packwood; map B3, grid d0.**

Campsites, facilities: There are 15 tent sites and 57 sites for trailers or RVs of any length. Electricity, piped water, sewer hookups and picnic tables are provided. Flush toilets, sanitary services, showers, bottled gas, a store, a cafe, a laundromat and ice are available. Pets and motorbikes are permitted.

Reservations, fee: Reservations accepted; $12-$17 fee per night; MasterCard and Visa accepted. Open all year.

Who to contact: Phone (360) 494-5145 or write to P.O. Box 309, Packwood, WA 98361.

Location: From Interstate 5 south of Olympia, turn east on State Route 12 and drive 65 miles to Packwood. The park is on the left side of the highway in town.

Trip note: This is a pleasant campground suitable for both tent and motor home campers and groups are welcome. Mount Rainier National Park is just 25 miles north, and this camp is a good alternative if the park is full. Nearby recreation options include a riding stable and tennis courts.

30. OHANAPECOSH RV

Reference: **On Ohanapecosh River in Mount Rainier National Park; map B3, grid d0.**

Campsites, facilities: There are 205 sites for tents or RVs up to 30 feet long. Picnic tables are provided. Flush toilets, piped water and a sanitary disposal station are available. Some facilities are **wheelchair accessible**. Pets are permitted.

Reservations, fee: No reservations; $10 fee per night. Open mid-May to October.

Who to contact: Phone Mount Rainier National Park at (360) 569-2211 or write to Mount Rainier National Park, Tahoma Woods, Ashford, WA 98304.

Location: From Interstate 5 south of Olympia, turn east on State Route 12 and drive 65 miles to Packwood. Continue seven miles northeast on State Route 12, then turn north on Highway 123 and drive five miles to the Ohanapecosh entrance to the park. The camp is next to the visitor center as you enter the park.

Trip note: This campground is set along the Ohanapecosh River. The nearby visitor center provides exhibits on the history of the forest and visitor information. Highway 706, heading west, and Highway 123 heading north, are closed by snowfall in winter.

31. LA WIS WIS RV

Reference: **On Cowlitz River in Gifford Pinchot National Forest; map B3, grid d0.**

Campsites, facilities: There are 100 sites for tents, trailers or RVs up to 38 feet long. Picnic tables are provided. Flush and vault toilets, piped water and firewood are available. Leashed pets are permitted.

Reservations, fee: No reservations; $9-$15 fee per night; maximum stay is 14 days. Open early May to late September.

Who to contact: Phone Gifford Pinchot National Forest Ranger Station at (360) 494-5515 or write to Packwood Ranger District, Packwood, WA 98361.

Location: From Interstate 5 south of Olympia, take exit 68 and turn east on State Route 12. Drive 65 miles to Packwood. Continue seven miles east on State Route 12, then drive one-half mile west on Forest Service Road 1272.

Trip note: This campground is set on the Cowlitz River, near the Ohanapecosh River in an old growth forest and offers nature trails. It is about seven miles south of the entrance to Mount Rainier National Park and the Ohanapecosh Hot Springs. The camp is ideally located for day trips to Mount Rainier and Mount St. Helens.

32.   SODA SPRINGS

Reference: **On Summit Creek in Gifford Pinchot National Forest; map B3, grid d1.**

Campsites, facilities: There are eight primitive tent sites. Picnic tables are provided. Pit toilets are available, but there is **no piped water**. Pets are permitted.

Reservations, fee: No reservations; no fee. Open mid-June to early September.

Who to contact: Phone Gifford Pinchot National Forest at (360) 494-5515 or write to Packwood Ranger District, Packwood, WA 98361.

Location: From Interstate 5 south of Olympia, take exit 68 and turn east on State Route 12. Drive 65 miles to Packwood. Continue 10 miles northeast on State Route 12, then turn north on Forest Service Road 45 and continue to Forest Service Road 4510. Drive seven miles to the end of the road.

Trip note: This campground is set along Summit Creek, a good base camp for a backpacking expedition or daily hiking trips in the Cascade Range. There are many trails and lakes to choose from as destinations. Obtain a Forest Service map for details.

33.   SUMMIT CREEK

Reference: **On Summit Creek in Gifford Pinchot National Forest; map B3, grid d1.**

Campsites, facilities: There are seven primitive tent sites. Picnic tables are provided. Pit toilets are available, but there is **no piped water**. Leashed pets are permitted.

Reservations, fee: No reservations; no fee. Open mid-June to early September.

Who to contact: Phone Gifford Pinchot National Forest at (360) 494-5515 or write to Packwood Ranger District, Packwood, WA 98361.

Location: From Interstate 5 south of Olympia, take exit 68 and turn east on State Route 12. Drive 65 miles to Packwood. Continue 10 miles northeast on State Route 12, then turn north on Forest Service Road 45 and continue to Road 4510. Turn and drive about three miles to the campground.

Trip note: Set along Summit Creek, this campground is another good base camp for trips into the Cascade Range backcountry. See the trip note for Soda Springs.

34.   CLEAR LAKE NORTH   RV

Reference: **On Clear Lake in Wenatchee National Forest; map B3, grid d2.**

Campsites, facilities: There are 35 sites for tents, trailers or RVs up to 22 feet long. Picnic tables are provided. Vault toilets and firewood are available, but there is **no piped water**. Leashed pets are permitted. Boat docks, launching facilities and rentals are nearby.

Reservations, fee: No reservations; $5 fee per night. Open mid-April to late November.

Who to contact: Phone Wenatchee National Forest at (509) 653-2205 or write to Naches Ranger District, 10061 Highway 12, Naches, WA 98937.

Location: From Yakima on Interstate 82, drive 13 miles northwest on State Route 12 to Naches. Continue 35.5 miles west on State Route 12, then drive one mile south on County Road 1200. Continue one-half mile south on Forest Service Road 1200-840.

Trip note: This campground is set at 3,100 feet elevation along the shore of Clear Lake, which is the forebay for Rimrock Lake. No swimming is allowed, only fishing. This camp is primitive and gets relatively little use. With no charge, few people and lake views, you get a great deal.

---

35.   WHITE PASS LAKE   RV

Reference: On Leech Lake in Wenatchee National Forest; map B3, grid d2.

Campsites, facilities: There are 16 sites for tents, trailers or RVs up to 20 feet long. Picnic tables are provided. Vault toilets and firewood are available, but there is **no piped water**. A store, a cafe, a laundromat and ice are located within one mile. Leashed pets are permitted. Boat docks and launching facilities are nearby. No motorized boats are permitted.

Reservations, fee: No reservations; no fee. Open June to late November.

Who to contact: Phone Wenatchee National Forest at (509) 653-2205 or write to Naches Ranger District, 10061 Highway 12, Naches, WA 98937.

Location: From Interstate 5 south of Olympia, take exit 68 and turn east on State Route 12. Drive approximately 65 miles to Packwood, then continue 19 miles northeast on State Route 12. Turn north on the entrance road and drive 200 yards to Leech Lake.

Trip note: This campground is on the shore of Leech Lake at 4,500 feet elevation. Nearby trails lead into the Goat Rocks Wilderness to the south and the William O. Douglas Wilderness to the north. The trailhead to the Pacific Crest Trail is nearby. This is a beautiful and popular fly fishing area. White Pass Ski Area is located across the highway.

---

36.   DOG LAKE   RV

Reference: On Dog Lake in Wenatchee National Forest; map B3, grid d2.

Campsites, facilities: There are 11 sites for tents, trailers or RVs up to 20 feet long. Picnic tables are provided. Vault toilets and firewood are available, but there is **no piped water**. Leashed pets are permitted. No horses permitted on the campgrounds. Boat docks and launching facilities are nearby.

Reservations, fee: No reservations; no fee. Open late May to late November.

Who to contact: Phone Wenatchee National Forest at (509) 653-2205 or write to Naches Ranger District, 10061 Highway 12, Naches, WA 98937.

Location: From Interstate 5 south of Olympia, take exit 68 and turn east on State Route 12. Drive approximately 65 miles to Packwood. Continue 22 miles northeast on State Route 12 to the campground.

Trip note: This campground is on the shore of Dog Lake at 3,400 feet in elevation. Nearby trails lead into the William O. Douglas Wilderness. See a Forest Service map for details. Boating and fishing are two options here.

37. CLEAR LAKE SOUTH RV

Reference: **In Wenatchee National Forest; map B3, grid d2.**

Campsites, facilities: There are 23 sites for tents, trailers or RVs up to 22 feet long. Piped water is provided. Hand-pumped water, picnic tables and vault toilets are available. Firewood is not provided but may be gathered. Leashed pets are permitted. Boat docks, launching facilities and rentals are nearby.

Reservations, fee: No reservations; $5 fee per night. Open mid-April to late November.

Who to contact: Phone Wenatchee National Forest at (509) 653-2205 or write to Naches Ranger District, 10061 Highway 12, Naches, WA 98937.

Location: From Yakima on Interstate 82, drive 13 miles northwest on State Route 12 to Naches. From Naches, continue 35.5 miles west on State Route 12, then drive one mile south on County Road 1200 to the campground.

Trip note: This campground is located near the east shore of Clear Lake at 3,100 feet elevation, which is the forebay for Rimrock Lake. Only fishing is allowed, no swimming. For winter travelers, there are several sno-parks in the area which offer snowmobiling and cross-country skiing. There are many hiking trails to the north; see a Forest Service map.

38. SILVER BEACH RESORT RV

Reference: **On Rimrock Lake; map B3, grid d3.**

Campsites, facilities: There are 65 tent sites and 30 sites for trailers or RVs. Electricity, piped water, sewer hookups and picnic tables are provided. A cafe, ice, boat docks, launching facilities and boat rentals are available. A store and bottled gas are available within one mile. Pets and motorbikes are permitted.

Reservations, fee: Reservations accepted; $9-$15 fee per night. Open all year with limited winter facilities.

Who to contact: Phone (509) 672-2500 or write to 40350 Highway 12, Rimrock, WA 98937.

Location: From Interstate 82 at Yakima, turn west on State Route 12 and drive 40 miles to the resort on Rimrock Lake.

Trip note: This resort is set along the shore of Rimrock Lake and is one of several camps in the immediate area. It is very scenic, with beautiful lakefront sites available. Nearby recreation options include hiking trails, marked bike trails, a full-service marina and a riding stable.

39. INDIAN CREEK RV

Reference: **On Rimrock Lake in Wenatchee National Forest; map B3, grid d3.**

Campsites, facilities: There are 39 sites for tents, trailers or RVs up to 32 feet long. Piped water and picnic tables are provided. Vault toilets, a cafe, a store and ice are available. Firewood is not provided but may be gathered. Leashed pets are permitted. Boat docks, launching facilities and rentals are available nearby.

Reservations, fee: No reservations; $8 fee per night. Open late May to mid-September.

Who to contact: Phone Wenatchee National Forest at (509) 653-2205 or write to Naches Ranger District, 10061 Highway 12, Naches, WA 98937.

Location: From Yakima on Interstate 82, drive 13 miles northwest on State Route 12 to Naches. Continue 31.5 miles west on State Route 12 and you'll see the entrance.

Trip note: This campground is set along the shore of Rimrock Lake at 3,000 feet elevation. Fishing, swimming and waterskiing are allowed. The camp is adjacent to Rimrock Lake Marina. There are many excellent hiking trails to the north that are routed into the William O. Douglas Wilderness.

40. SOUTH FORK   RV

Reference: On South Fork Tieton River in Wenatchee National Forest; map B3, grid d3.

Campsites, facilities: There are 15 sites for tents, trailers or RVs up to 16 feet long. Picnic tables are provided. Vault toilets and firewood are available, but there is **no piped water**. Leashed pets are permitted. Boat docks are nearby.

Reservations, fee: No reservations; no fee. Open late May to mid-September.

Who to contact: Phone Wenatchee National Forest at (509) 653-2205 or write to Naches Ranger District, 10061 Highway 12, Naches, WA 98937.

Location: From Yakima on Interstate 82, drive 13 miles northwest on State Route 12 to Naches. Continue 22.5 miles west on State Route 12, then drive four miles south on County Road 1200. Turn south on Forest Service Road 1203 and drive one-half mile to the campground.

Trip note: This campground is set at 5,000 feet elevation along the South Fork of the Tieton River, less than a mile from where it empties into Rimrock Lake. This is often a good spot for trout fishing and swimming. By traveling a bit farther south on Tieton River Road, you can see the huge Blue Slide, an enormous prehistoric rock and earth slide that has a curious blue tinge to it.

41. PENINSULA   RV

Reference: On Rimrock Lake in Wenatchee National Forest; map B3, grid d3.

Campsites, facilities: There are 19 sites for tents, trailers or RVs up to 20 feet long. Picnic tables are provided. Vault toilets and firewood are available, but there is **no piped water**. Leashed pets are permitted. Boat docks and launching facilities are nearby.

Reservations, fee: No reservations; no fee. Open mid-April to late November.

Who to contact: Phone Wenatchee National Forest at (509) 653-2205 or write to Naches Ranger District, 510 Highway 12, Naches, WA 98937.

Location: From Yakima on Interstate 82, drive 13 miles northwest on State Route 12 to Naches. Continue 22.5 miles west on State Route 12, then drive three miles south on County Road 1200. At Forest Service Road 1382, turn west and drive one more mile.

Trip note: This campground is set along the shore of Rimrock Lake at 3,000 feet elevation. It is one of several on the lake. Swimming, fishing and waterskiing are all allowed. A sno-park is nearby and offers many wintertime recreation options, including cross-country skiing and snowmobiling.

42. RIVER BEND GROUP CAMP   RV

Reference: On Tieton River in Wenatchee National Forest; map B3, grid d4.

Campsites, facilities: There is one group camp which can accommodate up to 30 people and 10 vehicles. Piped water and picnic tables are provided. Vault toilets and firewood are available. Leashed pets are permitted. Boat docks, launching facilities and rentals are located on Rimrock Lake.

Reservations, fee: Reservations recommended; $35 fee per night. Open April to mid-September.

Who to contact: Phone Wenatchee National Forest at (509) 653-2205 or write to Naches Ranger District, 10061 Highway 12, Naches, WA 98937.

Location: From Yakima on Interstate 82, drive 13 miles northwest on State Route 12 to Naches. Continue 22 miles southwest of Naches on State Route 12 to the campground.

Trip note: This campground is a reservations-only group campsite located near Hause Creek at 2,500 feet elevation. It is set on the Tieton River about five miles from Rimrock Lake. It has easy highway access and nice riverside sites. A sno-park is nearby.

43. WILDROSE

Reference: **On Tieton River in Wenatchee National Forest; map B3, grid d4.**

Campsites, facilities: There are eight sites for tents, trailers or RVs up to 22 feet long. Picnic tables are provided. Vault toilets and firewood are available, but there is **no piped water**. Leashed pets are permitted.

Reservations, fee: No reservations; no fee. Open April to late November.

Who to contact: Phone Wenatchee National Forest at (509) 653-2205 or write to Naches Ranger District, 10061 Highway 12, Naches, WA 98937.

Location: From Yakima on Interstate 82, drive 13 miles northwest on State Route 12 to Naches. Continue 20.5 miles southwest on State Route 12 to the campground.

Trip note: This campground is set along the Tieton River at 2,400 feet elevation. It's an option to Hause Creek, River Bend, Willows, South Fork and Windy Point. It is quite primitive and used slightly less than the others. If you're willing to do without the luxuries, it can serve as a good layover camp, with easy highway access.

44. WILLOWS

Reference: **On Tieton River in Wenatchee National Forest; map B3, grid d4.**

Campsites, facilities: There are 16 sites for tents, trailers or RVs up to 20 feet long. Picnic tables are provided. Hand-pumped water, vault toilets, sanitary disposal service and firewood are available. Leashed pets are permitted.

Reservations, fee: No reservations; $7 fee per night. Open April to late November.

Who to contact: Phone Wenatchee National Forest at (509)653-2205 or write to Naches Ranger District, 10061 Highway 12, Naches, WA 98937.

Location: From Yakima on Interstate 82, drive 13 miles northwest on State Route 12 to Naches. Continue 20 miles southwest on State Route 12 to the campground.

Trip note: This campground is set along the Tieton River at 2,400 feet elevation. The site is primitive, beautiful and has easy access. Rimrock Lake to the west provides many recreation options, and there are hiking trails leading into the William O. Douglas Wilderness within driving distance.

45. HAUSE CREEK

Reference: **On Tieton River in Wenatchee National Forest; map B3, grid d4.**

Campsites, facilities: There are 42 sites for tents, trailers or RVs up to 30 feet long. Piped water and picnic tables are provided. Flush toilets and firewood are available. Some facilities are **wheelchair accessible**. Leashed pets are permitted. Boat docks, launching facilities and rentals are located on Rimrock Lake.

Reservations, fee: No reservations; $8 fee per night. Open late May to late November.

Who to contact: Phone Wenatchee National Forest at (509) 653-2205 or write to Naches Ranger District, 10061 Highway 12, Naches, WA 98937.

Location: From Yakima on Interstate 82, drive 13 miles northwest on State Route 12 to Naches. Continue 22 miles southwest on State Route 12 to the campground.

Trip note: This campground is set at 2,500 feet elevation, along the Tieton River, where several creeks converge. The Tieton Dam, which creates Rimrock Lake, is just upstream. This is one of the larger, more developed camps in the area. Primitive options include River Bend, Wild Rose and Willows.

---

46. WINDY POINT   **RV**

Reference: **On Tieton River in Wenatchee National Forest; map B3, grid d5.**

Campsites, facilities: There are 15 sites for tents, trailers or RVs up to 22 feet long. Hand-pumped water and picnic tables are provided. Vault toilets, sanitary disposal service and firewood are available. Leashed pets are permitted.

Reservations, fee: No reservations; $8 fee per night. Open April to late November.

Who to contact: Phone Wenatchee National Forest at (509) 653-2205 or write to Naches Ranger District, 10061 Highway 12, Naches, WA 98937.

Location: From Yakima on Interstate 82, drive 13 miles northwest on State Route 12 to Naches. Continue 13 miles west on State Route 12 to the campground.

Trip note: This campground, set along the Tieton River at 2,000 feet elevation, is more isolated than the camps set westward toward Rimrock Lake. Piped water is a bonus. Fishing access is available.

---

47. YAKIMA SPORTSMAN STATE PARK   **RV**

Reference: **On Yakima River; map B3, grid d7.**

Campsites, facilities: There are two primitive tent sites, 28 sites for tents or self-contained RVs, and 36 drive-through sites with full hookups for trailers or RVs of any length. Picnic tables and fire grills are provided. Flush toilets, sanitary services and a playground are available. Showers and firewood can be obtained for an extra fee. A store and ice are available within one mile. Leashed pets are permitted.

Reservations, fee: No reservations; $7-$16 fee per night. Open all year.

Who to contact: Phone (800) 233-0321 or (509) 575-2774 or write to Route 9, P.O. Box 498, Yakima, WA 98901.

Location: From Yakima on Interstate 82, drive one mile east to the park.

Trip note: This park is set along the Yakima River where kayaking and rafting are options, but no swimming is allowed. There is also a pond in the park for children to fish in (no anglers over age 15 allowed). Nearby recreation options include an 18-hole golf course and hiking trails. See the trip note for KOA Yakima for information on other points of interest in Yakima.

---

48. KOA YAKIMA   **RV**

Reference: **On Yakima River; map B3, grid d7.**

Campsites, facilities: There are 50 tent sites and 90 drive-through sites for trailers or RVs of any length. There are also cabins available. Picnic tables are provided. Flush toilets, bottled gas, sanitary services, showers, a recreation hall, A store, a laundromat, ice, a playground, electricity, piped water, sewer hookups and firewood are available. A cafe is located within one mile. Pets and motorbikes are permitted. Boat rentals, including paddle boats, are available.

Reservations, fee: Reservations accepted; $18-$22 fee per night. Open all year.

Who to contact: Phone (509) 248-5882, (800) 562-5773 or write to 1500 Keyes Road, Yakima, WA 98901.

Location: From Interstate 82 at Yakima, take the Highway 24 exit and drive one-half mile east. Turn north on Keyes Road and drive 300 yards to the campground.

Trip note: This campground offers well-maintained, shaded sites. It is set along the Yakima River, with fishing access available. Some points of interest in Yakima are the Yakima Valley Museum and the Yakima Trolley Lines which offer rides on restored trolley cars originally built in 1906. Indian Rock Paintings State Park is five miles west of Yakima on State Route 12. Nearby recreation options include an 18-hole golf course, hiking trails, marked bike trails and tennis courts.

---

49. CLOVER FLATS

Reference: **Near Goat Rocks Wilderness; map B3, grid e4.**

Campsites, facilities: There are nine campsites for tents or small trailers. Picnic tables, fire grills and tent pads are provided. Pit toilets and piped water are available. Leashed pets are permitted.

Reservations, fee: No reservations; no fee. Open all year.

Who to contact: Phone the Department of Natural Resources at (509) 925-6131 or write to Department of Natural Resources, Southeast Region, 2211 Airport Road, Ellensburg, WA 98926-9341.

Location: From Interstate 82 at Yakima, drive two miles south to Union Gap. Turn west on Ahtanum Road and drive to Tampico, then continue west on Road A 2000 (Middle Fork Road) for 18.5 miles to the campground. Note: The last few miles of Road A 2000 are very steep, with a 12 to 13 percent grade.

Trip note: This campground is in the subalpine zone on the slope of Darland Mountain, which peaks at 6,982 feet. There are trails that connect this area with Goat Rocks Wilderness, six miles to the west. Contact the Department of Natural Resources or Wenatchee National Forest for details. See the trip note for Ahtanum Camp for information on winter snowmobiling.

---

50. TREE PHONES

Reference: **On Middle Fork Ahtanum Creek; map B3, grid e4.**

Campsites, facilities: There are 14 campsites for tents or small trailers. Picnic tables, fire grills and tent pads are provided. Pit toilets are available, but there is **no piped water**. Motorbikes are permitted. Saddlestock facilities are also available. Leashed pets are permitted.

Reservations, fee: No reservations; no fee. Open all year.

Who to contact: Phone the Department of Natural Resources at (509) 925-6131 or write to Department of Natural Resources, Southeast Region, 2211 Airport Road, Ellensburg, WA 98926-9341.

Location: From Interstate 82 at Yakima, drive two miles south to Union Gap. Turn west on Ahtanum Road and drive to Tampico, then continue west on Road A 2000 (Middle Fork Road) for 15 miles, then turn left and drive 100 yards to the campground.

Trip note: This forested campground is set along the Middle Fork of Ahtanum

Creek. The nearby trails are used by motorbike riders, hikers and horseback riders. A shelter with a wood stove is available year-round for picnics. During summer months, there are beautiful wildflower displays. See the trip note for Ahtanum Camp for snowmobiling information.

51.   SNOW CABIN

Reference: **On the North Fork of Ahtanum Creek; map B3, grid e5.**

Campsites, facilities: There are eight campsites for tents or small trailers. Picnic tables, fire grills and tent pads are provided. Pit toilets are available, but there is **no piped water**. Saddlestock facilities are available. Leashed pets are permitted.

Reservations, fee: This campground flooded in 1996 and will probably remain closed until 1998. Please phone the Department of Natural Resources for further information.

Who to contact: Phone the Department of Natural Resources at (509) 925-6131 or write to Department of Natural Resources, Southeast Region, 2211 Airport Road, Ellensburg, WA 98926-9341.

Location: From Interstate 82 at Yakima, drive two miles south to Union Gap. Turn west on Ahtanum Road and drive to Tampico, then continue west on Road A 2000 (Middle Fork Road) for 9.5 miles to Ahtanum Camp. From there, take the North Fork Ahtanum Road (A 3000) and drive 4.5 miles. Keep left and drive 2.5 miles to the campground, which will be on your left.

Special note: This campground is temporarily closed. Please phone the Department of Natural Resources for further information.

52.   AHTANUM CAMP

Reference: **On Ahtanum Creek; map B3, grid e5.**

Campsites, facilities: There are 11 campsites for tents or small trailers. Picnic tables, fire grills and tent pads are provided. Pit toilets and piped water are available. Leashed pets are permitted.

Reservations, fee: This campground flooded in 1996 and will probably remain closed until 1997. Phone the Department of Natural Resources for current information.

Who to contact: Phone the Department of Natural Resources at (509) 925-6131 or write to Department of Natural Resources, Southeast Region, 2211 Airport Road, Ellensburg, WA 98926-9341.

Location: From Interstate 82 at Yakima, drive two miles south to Union Gap. Turn west on Ahtanum Road and drive to Tampico, then continue west on Road A 2000 (Middle Fork Road) for 9.5 miles to the campground, which will be on the left.

Trip note: This campground is set along Ahtanum Creek, one of four primitive campsites in a 10-mile vicinity. A good side trip is to continue driving on Road A 2000 for 14 miles, where you will reach the Darland Mountain viewpoint at 6,900 feet. The road gets very steep near the lookout and is not suitable for RVs or trailers. In the winter, this area offers 60 miles of groomed trails for snowmobilers. A snow shelter with firewood is provided at Tree Phones. Contact the Department of Natural Resources for a map.

53.   CIRCLE H RV RANCH   RV.

Reference: In Yakima; map B3, grid e7.

Campsites, facilities: There are 25 tent sites and 51 sites (nine drive-through) for trailers or RVs of any length. Electricity, piped water, sewer hookups and picnic tables are provided. Flush toilets, showers, a recreation hall, a laundromat, a playground, and a swimming pool are available. Bottled gas, sanitary services, a store, a cafe and ice are located within one mile. Pets and motorbikes are permitted.

Reservations, fee: Reservations accepted; $17-$20 fee per night; MasterCard and Visa accepted. Open all year.

Who to contact: Phone (509) 457-3683 or write to 1107 South 18th Street, Yakima, WA 98901.

Location: From Interstate 82 in Yakima, take exit 34 and drive one block to South 18th Street. Turn north and drive one-quarter mile to the campground on the right.

Trip note: This is a pleasant, clean park with a western flavor. The sites are comfortable and spacious. Nearby recreation options include an 18-hole golf course, hiking trails, marked bike trails and a riding stable. See the trip note for KOA Yakima for information on points of interest in Yakima.

54.   TRAILER INNS RV PARK   RV.

Reference: In Yakima; map B3, grid e7.

Campsites, facilities: There are 152 sites for trailers or RVs of any length (30 drive-through) . Electricity, piped water, sewer hookups and picnic tables are provided. Flush toilets, bottled gas, sanitary services, showers, a recreation hall, a laundromat, ice, a swimming pool, a whirlpool, a sauna, a TV room with 52-inch screen, a dog walk, an enclosed barbecue and a playground are available. A store and a cafe are located within one mile. Pets are permitted.

Reservations, fee: Reservations accepted; $17-$21 fee per night; MasterCard and Visa accepted. Open all year.

Who to contact: Phone (509) 452-9561 or write to 1610 North First Street, Yakima, WA 98901.

Location: From Interstate 82 in Yakima, take exit 32 and drive three blocks south on North First Street to the park on the west side of the road.

Trip note: Like the Trailer Inns RV Park in Spokane, this has many of the luxuries you'd find in a hotel, including a pool, hot tub, sauna, on-site security and large-screen TV. Nearby recreation options include an 18-hole golf course, hiking trails, marked bike trails and tennis courts. See the trip note for KOA Yakima (camp number 48) for information on some of the points of interest in Yakima.

55.   GRANGER RV PARK   RV.

Reference: Near Yakima River; map B3, grid f9.

Campsites, facilities: There are 45 tent sites and 25 drive-through sites for trailers or RVs of any length. Electricity, piped water and sewer hookups are provided. Flush toilets, sanitary services, showers and a laundromat are available. Bottled gas, a store, a cafe and ice are located within one mile. Pets are permitted.

Reservations, fee: Reservations accepted; $11-$13 fee per night. Open all year.

Who to contact: Phone (509) 854-1300 or write to P.O. Box 695, Granger, WA ·98932.

Location: From Yakima on Interstate 82, drive 25 miles south to Granger. Take the Highway 223 exit in Granger and you'll see the park.

Trip note: This park is near the Yakima River. It has nice grassy sites with lots of shade. Granger is known as "Washington's Fruit Basket" and tourists can pick their own fruits and vegetables from local farmers. There are several wineries in the area which offer tours. A unique side trip can be made to the Toppenish Wildlife Refuge, which is particularly good for birdwatching. It is 15 miles away, south of Toppenish on US 97. Call for information at (509) 865-2405.

---

56. HORSESHOE LAKE **RV**

Reference: **On Horseshoe Lake in Gifford Pinchot National Forest; map B3, grid g0.**

Campsites, facilities: There are 11 sites for tents, trailers or RVs up to 16 feet long. Picnic tables are provided. Pit toilets are available, but there is **no piped water**. Firewood may be gathered outside the campground area. Primitive launching facilities are located on the lake, but all gasoline motors are prohibited on the lake. Leashed pets are permitted.

Reservations, fee: No reservations; no fee. Open mid-June to late September.

Who to contact: Phone Gifford Pinchot National Forest at (360) 497-7565 or write to Randle Ranger District, P.O. Box 670, Randle, WA 98377.

Location: From Interstate 5 south of Olympia, take exit 68 and turn east on State Route 12. Drive 48 miles to Randle and take State Route 131 south. Drive one mile, then turn southeast on Forest Service Road 23 and continue 30 miles. Turn northeast on Forest Service Road 2329 and drive seven miles, then turn west and travel 1.5 miles on Forest Service Road 78.

Trip note: This campground is set along the shore of Horseshoe Lake. A trail from the camp goes up nearby Green Mountain (elevation 5,000 feet). Another trail heads up the north flank of Mount Adams. See a Forest Service map for details. Berry picking is an option in the late summer months, and fishing and horseback riding are other available activities.

---

57. TAKHLAKH **RV**

Reference: **On Takhlakh Lake in Gifford Pinchot National Forest; map B3, grid g0.**

Campsites, facilities: There are 54 sites for tents, trailers or RVs up to 21 feet long. Piped water and picnic tables are provided. Vault toilets are available. Firewood may be gathered outside the campground area. Boat launching facilities are available in the day-use area, but all gasoline motors are prohibited on the lake. Leashed pets are permitted. Some facilities are **wheelchair accessible**.

Reservations, fee: No reservations; $9 fee per night; $5 each additional vehicle. Open mid-June to late September.

Who to contact: Phone Gifford Pinchot National Forest at (360) 497-7565 or write to Randle Ranger District, P.O. Box 670, Randle, WA 98377.

Location: From Interstate 5 south of Olympia, take exit 68 and turn east on State Route 12. Drive 48 miles to Randle and take State Route 131 south. Drive one mile, then turn southeast on Forest Service Road 23 and continue 30 miles. Turn northeast on Forest Service Road 2329 and drive two miles to the camp.

Trip note: This campground is set along the shore of Takhlakh Lake. This is one of five lakes in the area, all accessible by car. It is a beautiful place, but alas, mosquitoes abound until late July. There is a viewing area available for visitors, and berry picking, fishing and hiking for the more adventurous.

58. OLALLIE LAKE   RV

Reference: **On Olallie Lake in Gifford Pinchot National Forest; map B3, grid g0.**

Campsites, facilities: There are five sites for tents, trailers or RVs up to 21 feet long. Picnic tables are provided. Pit toilets are available, but there is **no piped water**. Firewood may be gathered outside the campground area. Boat launching facilities are available nearby, but all gasoline motors are prohibited on the lake. Leashed pets are permitted.

Reservations, fee: No reservations; $6 fee per night; $4 each additional vehicle. Open July to late September.

Who to contact: Phone Gifford Pinchot National Forest at (360) 497-7565 or write to Randle Ranger District, P.O. Box 670, Randle, WA 98377.

Location: From Interstate 5 south of Olympia, take exit 68 and turn east on State Route 12. Drive 48 miles to Randle and take State Route 131 south. Drive one mile, then turn southeast on Forest Service Road 23 and continue 30 miles. Turn northeast on Forest Service Road 2329 and drive one mile, then continue north on Forest Service Road 5601 for one-half mile to the campground. A Forest Service map is essential.

Trip note: This campground is set along the shore of Olallie Lake at 4,000 feet. This small alpine lake is one of several in the area fed by streams coming off the glaciers on nearby Mount Adams (elevation 12,326 feet). A word to the wise: Mosquitoes can be a problem in the spring and early summer. See the chapter about protection against insects.

59. COUNCIL LAKE   RV

Reference: **On Council Lake in Gifford Pinchot National Forest; map B3, grid g0.**

Campsites, facilities: There are nine sites for tents, trailers or RVs up to 15 feet long. Picnic tables are provided. Pit toilets are available, but there is **no piped water**. Firewood may be gathered outside the campground area. Boat launching facilities are available, but all gasoline motors are prohibited. Leashed pets are permitted.

Reservations, fee: No reservations; $6 fee per night; $4 each additional vehicle. Open July to mid-September.

Who to contact: Phone Gifford Pinchot National Forest at (360) 497-7565 or write to Randle Ranger District, P.O. Box 670, Randle, WA 98377.

Location: From Interstate 5 south of Olympia, take exit 68 and turn east on State Route 12. Drive 48 miles to Randle and take State Route 131 south. Drive one mile, then turn southeast on Forest Service Road 23 and continue 31 miles. Turn west on Forest Service Road 2334 and drive one mile to the campground.

Trip note: This campground is set along the shore of Council Lake on the northwest flank of Mount Adams at about 4,000 feet. It is one of three lakeside campgrounds in the area (the others are Olallie Lake and Takhlakh). This one offers access to trails for hikers, bikers and equestrians, although horses are not allowed in the campground.

60. ADAMS FORK   **RV**

Reference: On Cispus River in Gifford Pinchot National Forest; map B3, grid g0.

Campsites, facilities: There are 24 sites for tents, trailers or RVs up to 21 feet long. Hand-pumped water and picnic tables are provided. Vault toilets are available. Firewood may be gathered outside the campground area. Leashed pets are permitted.

Reservations, fee: No reservations; $9 fee per night; $11-$22 group fee; $5 each additional vehicle. Open May to late October.

Who to contact: Phone Gifford Pinchot National Forest at (360) 497-7565 or write to Randle Ranger District, P. O. Box 670, Randle, WA 98377.

Location: From Interstate 5 south of Olympia, take exit 68 and turn east on State Route 12. Drive 48 miles to Randle and take State Route 131 south. Drive one mile, then turn southeast on Forest Service Road 23 and continue 18 miles. Turn southeast on Forest Service Road 21 and drive five miles, then turn east and proceed 200 yards on Forest Service Road 56 to the campground.

Trip note: This campground is set along the upper Cispus River near Adams Creek and at the foot of Mount Adams (2,600 feet). A nearby trail leads north to Blue Lake, about a half-mile walk from the camp.

61. CAT CREEK   **RV**

Reference: On Cat Creek and Cispus River in Gifford Pinchot National Forest; map B3, grid g0.

Campsites, facilities: There are five sites for tents, trailers or RVs up to 15 feet long. Picnic tables and fire grills are provided. Pit toilets and firewood are available, but there is **no piped water**. Firewood may be gathered outside the campground area. Leashed pets are permitted.

Reservations, fee: No reservations; $6 fee per night; $4 each additional vehicle. Open mid-May to late October.

Who to contact: Phone Gifford Pinchot National Forest at (360) 497-7565 or write to Randle Ranger District, P.O. Box 670, Randle, WA 98377.

Location: From Interstate 5 south of Olympia, take exit 68 and turn east on State Route 12. Drive 48 miles to Randle and take State Route 131 south. Drive one mile, then turn southeast on Forest Service Road 23 and continue 18 miles. Turn east on Forest Service Road 21 and drive six miles to the campground.

Trip note: A pretty spot, this campground is set along Cat Creek at its confluence with the Cispus River about 10 miles from the summit of Mount Adams. A trail starts less than a mile from the camp and leads up along Blue Lake Ridge to Blue Lake. See a Forest Service map for details.

62. WALUPT HORSE CAMP   **RV**

Reference: Near Goat Rocks Wilderness in Gifford Pinchot National Forest; map B3, grid g1.

Campsites, facilities: There are six sites for tents, trailers or RVs up to 18 feet long. Picnic tables and piped water are provided. Pit toilets and firewood are available.

Reservations, fee: No reservations; $9 fee per night; $5 each additional vehicle. Open June to September.

Who to contact: Phone Gifford Pinchot National Forest at (360) 494-5515 or write to Packwood Ranger District, Packwood, WA 98361.

Location: From Interstate 5 south of Olympia, take exit 68 and turn east on State Route 12. Drive 62.5 miles to Forest Service Road 2100 (2.5 miles southwest of Packwood), then drive southeast on Forest Service Road 2100 for 16.5 miles. Head east on Forest Service Road 2160 for 3.5 miles to the campground.

Trip note: Walupt Lake is just a mile away from the camp, where you can fish. Several trails lead from Walupt Lake into the backcountry of southern Goat Rocks Wilderness, which has 85 miles of trails that can be used by horses. If you have planned a multi-day horse packing trip, you need to bring in your own feed for the horses. Feed must be pellets or processed grain only.

---

53. KILLEN CREEK RV

Reference: Near Mount Adams in Gifford Pinchot National Forest; map B3, grid g1.

Campsites, facilities: There are eight sites for tents, trailers or RVs up to 21 feet long. Picnic tables are provided. Pit toilets are available, but there is **no piped water**. Firewood may be gathered outside the campground area. Leashed pets are permitted.

Reservations, fee: No reservations; no fee. Open July to late September.

Who to contact: Phone Gifford Pinchot National Forest at (360) 497-7565 or write to Randle Ranger District, P.O. Box 670, Randle, WA 98377.

Location: From Interstate 5 south of Olympia, take exit 68 and turn east on State Route 12. Drive 48 miles to Randle and take State Route 131 south. Drive one mile, then turn southeast on Forest Service Road 23 and continue 30 miles. Turn southeast on Forest Service Road 2329 and drive six miles, then continue 200 yards west on Forest Service Road 073.

Trip note: This campground is set along Killen Creek at the foot of Mount Adams (elevation 12,326 feet). A trail from the camp leads up the mountain and connects with the Pacific Crest Trail, about a three-mile hike. It's worth the effort. Berry picking and horseback riding are two other summertime options.

54. KEENE'S HORSE CAMP RV

Reference: On the South Fork of Spring Creek in Gifford Pinchot National Forest; map B3, grid g1.

Campsites, facilities: There are 13 sites for tents, trailers or RVs up to 21 feet long. Picnic tables and fire grills are provided. Pit toilets and horse corrals are available, but there is **no piped water**. Firewood may be gathered outside the campground area. Leashed pets are permitted.

Reservations, fee: No reservations; no fee. Open July to late September.

Who to contact: Phone Gifford Pinchot National Forest at (360) 497-7565 or write to Randle Ranger District, P.O. Box 670, Randle, WA 98377.

Location: From Interstate 5 south of Olympia, take exit 68 and turn east on State Route 12. Drive 48 miles to Randle and take State Route 131 south. Drive one mile, then turn southeast on Forest Service Road 23 and continue 30 miles. Turn northeast on Forest Service Road 2329 and drive eight miles, then turn west on Forest Service Road 82 and drive 100 yards to the campground. A Forest Service map is essential.

Trip note: This campground is set at 4,200 feet along the South Fork of Spring Creek on the northwest flank of Mount Adams (elevation 12,276 feet). The Pacific Crest Trail passes within a couple of miles of the camp. There are a

number of trails from the camp leading into the backcountry and to severa
alpine meadows. The meadows are fragile, so walk along their outer edges.

65. ISLAND CAMP

Reference: **On Bird Creek; map B3, grid g3.**

Campsites, facilities: There are six campsites for tents or small trailers. Picnic
tables, fire grills and tent pads are provided. Pit toilets are available, but there
is **no piped water**. Leashed pets are permitted.

Reservations, fee: No reservations; no fee. Open all year.

Who to contact: Phone the Department of Natural Resources at (509) 925-613
or write to Department of Natural Resources, Southeast Region, 2211 Airpor
Road, Ellensburg, WA 98926-9341.

Location: From Interstate 82 at Yakima, turn south and drive 20 miles. Turn south
on US 97 and drive 53 miles to Goldendale. Turn west and drive 34 miles to
Glenwood. From the post office in Glenwood, drive 300 yards west, then turn
right on Bird Creek Road and drive one mile. Turn left, then right on a dirt road
and drive one mile. Stay left on Road K 3000 and drive 300 yards, cross a grave
road, stay right for the next two miles, go past the Bird Creek camp entrance
and continue on Road K 3000 for 1.5 miles. Stay right for 1.5 miles then turn
right into the campground.

Trip note: This campground is set in a forested area along Bird Creek. There are
lava tubes and blow holes nearby. In the winter the roads are used for
snowmobiling. A snowmobile shelter with a wood stove is available year
round for picnics. See the trip note for Maryhill State Park (camp number 75
for information on the nearby Klickitat Habitat Management Area.

66. BROOKS MEMORIAL STATE PARK [RV]

Reference: **Near Goldendale Observatory; map B3, grid g7.**

Campsites, facilities: There are two primitive tent sites, 22 developed sites for
tents or self-contained RVs and 23 sites with water and electrical hookups for
trailers or RVs up to 50 feet long. Picnic tables and fire grills are provided
Flush toilets, sanitary services and a playground are available. Electricity
piped water, sewer hookups and showers can be obtained for an extra fee. A
store is located within one mile. Leashed pets are permitted.

Reservations, fee: No reservations; $7-$16 fee per night. Open all year with
limited winter facilities.

Who to contact: Phone (800) 233-0321 or (509) 773-5382 or write to 2465
Highway 97, Goldendale, WA 98620.

Location: From Interstate 5 at Vancouver, Washington, turn east on Highway 1
and drive approximately 106 miles. Turn north on US 97 and drive 11 miles to
Goldendale. Continue northeast on US 97 for 15 miles to the park.

Trip note: There is only one other campground (Maryhill State Park) within 2
miles. This forested park is set at nearly 3,000 feet. There are several miles of
hiking trails and a 1.5-mile-long nature trail. There is excellent fishing for trout
in the nearby Klickitat River. A unique side trip is birdwatching at Toppenish
National Wildlife Refuge, 28 miles north of the park on US 97; phone the
refuge at (509) 865-2405 for details. If you like star gazing, the Goldendale
Observatory is located just one mile north of Goldendale. It houses one of the
largest telescopes in the world that is available for public use; phone (509) 773
3141 for hours of operation.

67.   PETERSON PRAIRIE   **RV**

Reference: **Near town of Trout Lake in Gifford Pinchot National Forest; map B3, grid h0.**

Campsites, facilities: There are 30 sites for tents, trailers or RVs up to 32 feet long, and one group site. Piped water, picnic tables and fire rings are provided. Vault toilets are available. Some facilities are **wheelchair accessible**.

Reservations, fee: Reservations necessary for group site only; $9 fee per night; $22-$32 group site fee. Open May to late September.

Who to contact: Phone Gifford Pinchot National Forest at (509) 395-3400 or write to Mount Adams Ranger District, 2455 Highway 141, Trout Lake, WA 98650.

Location: From Interstate 5 at Vancouver, turn east on Highway 14 and drive 66 miles. Turn north on Highway 141 and drive 25.5 miles to Forest Service Road 24 (5.5 miles southwest of the town of Trout Lake). Continue west on Forest Service Road 24 for 2.5 miles to the campground.

Trip note: A good base camp if you want to have a short ride to town as well as access to the nearby wilderness areas. This is a prime spot for huckleberry picking, too. The nearby sno-park area provides winter recreation, including snowmobiling and cross-country skiing trails.

68.   MORRISON CREEK

Reference: **On Morrison Creek in Gifford Pinchot National Forest; map B3, grid h1.**

Campsites, facilities: There are 12 tent sites. Picnic tables and fire rings are provided in some sites. Pit toilets are available, but there is **no piped water**. Leashed pets are permitted.

Reservations, fee: No reservations; no fee. Open July to late September.

Who to contact: Phone Gifford Pinchot National Forest at (509) 395-3400 or write to Mount Adams Ranger District, 2455 Highway 141, Trout Lake, WA 98650.

Location: From Interstate 5 at Vancouver, turn east on Highway 14 and drive 66 miles. Turn north on Highway 141 and drive 25 miles to County Road 17 (just 200 yards east of the town of Trout Lake). Turn north and drive two miles, then continue north on Forest Service Road 80 for 3.5 miles. Proceed six miles north on Forest Service Road 8040.

Trip note: Here is a prime, yet little-known spot. It is set along Morrison Creek at an elevation of 4,600 feet near the southern slopes of Mount Adams, the second highest mountain in Washington (Rainier is higher). Nearby trails will take you to the snow fields and alpine meadows of the Mount Adams Wilderness.

69.   WALUPT LAKE   **RV**

Reference: **On Walupt Lake in Gifford Pinchot National Forest; map B3, grid g1.**

Campsites, facilities: There are 44 sites for tents, trailers or RVs up to 21 feet long. Picnic tables are provided. Piped water, pit and vault toilets are available. Boat docks are located nearby on Walupt Lake. Leashed pets are permitted.

Reservations, fee: No reservations; $9 fee per night; $5 each additional vehicle. Open mid-June to early September.

Who to contact: Phone Gifford Pinchot National Forest at (360) 494-5515 or write to Packwood Ranger District, Packwood, WA 98361.

Location: From Interstate 5 south of Olympia, take exit 68 and turn east on State Route 12. Drive 62.5 miles to Forest Service Road 21 (2.5 miles southwest of Packwood). Turn right and drive 16.5 miles southeast, then head east on Forest Service Road 2160 for 4.5 miles to the campground.

Trip note: This is a good base-camp for a multi-day vacation. For starters, the camp is set along the shore of Walupt Lake. In addition, several nearby trails lead into the backcountry and other smaller alpine lakes. See a Forest Service map for details.

---

70.   BIRD CREEK

Reference: **Near Mount Adams Wilderness; map B3, grid h3.**

Campsites, facilities: There are eight campsites for tents or small trailers. Picnic tables, fire grills and tent pads are provided. Pit toilets are available, but there is **no piped water**, so bring your own. Leashed pets are permitted.

Reservations, fee: No reservations; no fee. Open all year.

Who to contact: Phone the Department of Natural Resources at (360) 902-1000 or (509) 925-6131 or write to Department of Natural Resources, Southeast Region, 2211 Airport Road, Ellensburg, WA 98926-9341

Location: From Interstate 82 at Yakima, turn south and drive 20 miles. Turn south on US 97 and drive 53 miles to Goldendale. Turn west and drive 34 miles to Glenwood. From the post office in Glenwood, drive 300 yards west, then turn right on Bird Creek Road and drive one mile. Turn left, then right on a dirt road and drive one mile. Stay left on Road K 3000 and drive 300 yards, cross a gravel road, stay right for the next two miles, and then turn right into the campground.

Trip note: This campground is set in a forested area along Bird Creek, one of two camps in the immediate area. (The other is Island Camp, also a primitive site.) This spot is just east of the Mount Adams Wilderness area and is within three miles of Island Camp, where there are snowmobile trails. See the trip note for Maryhill State Park (camp number 75) for information on the nearby Klickitat Habitat Management Area.

---

71.   OKLAHOMA   RV.

Reference: **On White Salmon River in Gifford Pinchot National Forest; map B3, grid i0.**

Campsites, facilities: There are 23 sites for tents, trailers or RVs up to 22 feet long. Piped water, fire rings and picnic tables are provided. Vault toilets are available. Some facilities are **wheelchair accessible**. Pets are permitted.

Reservations, fee: No reservations; $9 fee per night; $5 each additional vehicle. Open mid-May to mid-October.

Who to contact: Phone Gifford Pinchot National Forest at (509) 395-3400 or write to Mount Adams Ranger District, 2455 Highway 141, Trout Lake, WA 98650.

Location: From Interstate 5 at Vancouver, turn east on Highway 14 and drive approximately 50 miles to Cook. Turn north on County Road 1800 and drive 14 miles to the campground entrance.

Trip note: This campground is set along the little White Salmon River. Fishing can be excellent in this area. As to why they named this camp "Oklahoma," who knows? Guess they had to name it something.

72.   MOSS CREEK   RV.

Reference: **On White Salmon River in Gifford Pinchot National Forest; map B3, grid i0.**

Campsites, facilities: There are 18 sites for tents, trailers or RVs up to 32 feet long. Piped water, fire rings and picnic tables are provided. Vault toilets are available. Some facilities are **wheelchair accessible**. Pets are permitted.

Reservations, fee: No reservations; $9 fee per night; $5 each additional vehicle. Open mid-May to late September.

Who to contact: Phone Gifford Pinchot National Forest at (509) 395-2501 or write to Mount Adams Ranger District, 2455 Highway 141, Trout Lake, WA 98650.

Location: From Interstate 5 at Vancouver, turn east on Highway 14 and drive approximately 50 miles to Cook. Turn north on County Road 1800 and drive eight miles to the campground.

Trip note: This campground is set along the Little White Salmon River, a short distance from Willard and Big Cedars County Park. Good fishing prospects here, and usually not many people. You get all the amenities, including nice, shaded sites.

73.   PINE SPRINGS RESORT   RV.

Reference: **Near Brooks Memorial State Park; map B3, grid i5.**

Campsites, facilities: There are 11 tent sites and 21 sites for trailers or RVs. Air conditioning, cable TV, water, electricity and sewer hookups, a public phone, limited groceries, ice, snacks, RV supplies and LP gas are available. Horseshoe pits are also provided. Pets are permitted on leashes.

Reservations, fee: Reservations recommended; $5-$12 fee per night.

Who to contact: Phone the park at (509) 773-4434 or write to 2471 Highway 99, Goldendale, WA 98620.

Location: From Interstate 5 at Vancouver, turn east on Highway 14 and drive approximately 100 miles, then turn north on US 97 and drive 11 miles to Goldendale. Continue north on US 97 for 11.5 miles. The park is next to Brooks Memorial State Park, between mileposts 24 and 25. The resort is located on the left.

Trip note: This is an alternative to the state campground at Brooks Memorial. It is a small, wooded camp with a stream running close by. Side trips include adjacent Brooks Memorial State Park, Goldendale Observatory State Park and the Columbia River.

74.   HORSETHIEF LAKE STATE PARK   RV.

Reference: **Near Dalles Dam; map B3, grid j3.**

Campsites, facilities: There are two primitive tent sites and 12 sites for tents or self-contained RVs up to 30 feet long. Piped water, fire grills and picnic tables are provided. Flush toilets, firewood and sanitary services are available. A store and a cafe are located within one mile. Pets are permitted. Boat launching facilities are located on both the lake and the river.

Reservations, fee: No reservations; $5-$10 fee per night. Open April to late October.

Who to contact: Phone (800) 233-0321 or (509) 767-1159 or write to 50 Highway 97, Goldendale, WA 98620.

Location: From Interstate 5 at Vancouver, Washington, turn east on Highway 14 and drive approximately 90 miles to the park entrance on the right.

Trip note: This is a good spot to camp if you are driving along the Columbia River Highway. This state park is set along the shore of Horsethief Lake adjacent to the Dalles Dam. There are hiking trails and access both to the lake and the Columbia River. Only non-powered boats are allowed, and fishing is for trout and bass. See the trip note for Maryhill State Park for information on other recreation options in the area.

---

75. MARYHILL STATE PARK   RV

Reference: **On Columbia River; map B3, grid j5.**

Campsites, facilities: There are 23 tent sites (three primitive) and 50 sites with full hookups for trailers or RVs up to 50 feet long. Picnic tables are provided. Flush toilets, sanitary services, a store and a cafe are available. Electricity, piped water, sewer hookups, showers and firewood can be obtained for an extra fee. Some facilities are **wheelchair accessible**. Leashed pets are permitted. Boat docks and launching facilities are nearby.

Reservations, fee: Contact Reservations Northwest at (800) 452-5687 ($6 reservation fee); $11-$16 fee per night. Call for group camping information. Open all year.

Who to contact: Phone (800) 233-0321 or (509) 773-5007 or write to 50 Highway 97, Goldendale, WA 98620.

Location: From Interstate 5 at Vancouver, Washington, turn east on Highway 14 and drive approximately 106 miles. The park is one mile north on US 97.

Trip note: This park is set along the Columbia River and the recreation opportunities include fishing, waterskiing and windsurfing. The climate here is very pleasant from March through mid-November. There are two interesting spots near Maryhill, one is a replica of Stonehenge, which is located on a bluff overlooking the Columbia River, and the other is the Maryhill Museum—phone (509) 773-3733 for details. A great side trip, 30 miles northwest, is the Klickitat Habitat Management Area. It is run by the Department of Game and has some primitive camping spots and a boat launch along the Klickitat River, where you can enjoy boating, fishing, hunting or observing wildlife. To get there drive 11 miles west of Goldendale on Highway 142, then continue northwest on Glendale Road for five miles and look for the headquarters on your left. The public areas beyond the wildlife refuge headquarters are easier to get to. Another treat at the refuge is Stinson Flat, a good steelhead spot.

LEAVE NO TRACE TIPS

Pack it in and pack it out.

• Take everything you bring into the wild back out with you.

• Protect wildlife and your food by storing rations securely. Pick up all spilled foods.

• Use toilet paper or wipes sparingly; pack them out.

• Inspect your campsite for trash and any evidence of your stay. Pack out all trash—even if it's not yours!

MAP B4

19 LISTINGS
PAGES 362-371

WASHINGTON MAP .... see page 90
Adjoining Maps
NORTH (A4) .... see page 216
EAST (B5) .... see page 372
SOUTH .... Oregon
WEST (B3) .... see page 330

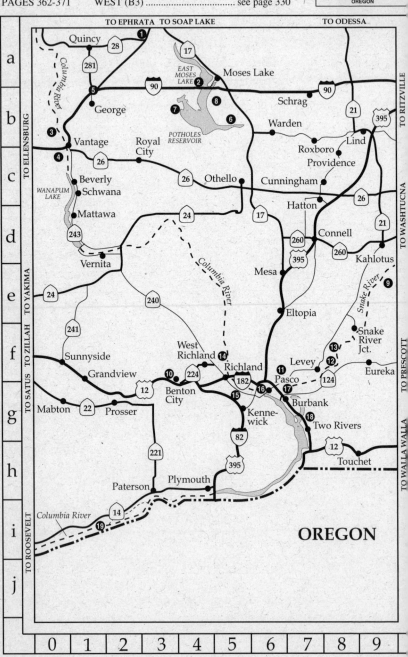

Washington Map B4 featuring: Soap Lake, Moses Lake State Park, Columbia River, Frenchman Hills Lakes, Potholes Reservoir, Ginkgo-Wanapum State Park, Yakima River, Snake River, Sacajawea Lake, Pasco

1.　　　　　　　OASIS PARK RESORT　　　　　　　RV

Reference: **Near Soap Lake; map B4, grid a3.**

Campsites, facilities: There are 38 tent sites and 68 sites (10 drive-through) for trailers or RVs of any length. Picnic tables, flush toilets, a golf course, bottled gas, sanitary services, a store, propane gas, a laundromat, ice, a swimming pool, and a fishing pond for children are provided. Electricity, piped water, sewer hookups and showers are available. A cafe is located within one mile. Pets and motorbikes are permitted.

Reservations, fee: Reservations requested; $9-$15 fee per night; MasterCard and Visa accepted. Open all year.

Who to contact: Phone (509) 754-5102 or write to 2541 Basin Street SW, Ephrata, WA 98823.

Location: From Seattle, drive about 180 miles east on Interstate 90 to Moses Lake. Turn north on Highway 17 and drive 25 miles to Highway 28. Turn west and drive five miles to Ephrata. Drive another 1.5 miles southwest on Highway 28 to the park.

Trip note: This can be a warm, arid area in the summer, but fortunately, this park offers shaded sites. There are two fishing ponds: one has bass and crappie, while the other is for kids. Nearby recreation options include an 18-hole golf course. There are mineral baths a few miles north of this park.

2.　　　　　　　　BIG SUN RESORT　　　　　　　　RV

Reference: **Near Moses Lake State Park; map B4, grid a4.**

Campsites, facilities: There are 10 tent sites and 50 sites (19 drive-through) for trailers or RVs of any length. Electricity, piped water, sewer hookups and picnic tables are provided. Flush toilets, a recreation hall, a laundromat, ice and a playground are available. Showers can be obtained for an extra fee. Bottled gas, sanitary services, a store and a cafe are located within one mile. Pets and motorbikes are permitted. Boat docks, launching facilities and rentals are nearby.

Reservations, fee: Reservations accepted; $10-$14 fee per night. Open all year.

Who to contact: Phone (509) 765-8294 or write to 2300 West Marina, Moses Lake, WA 98837.

Location: From Seattle, drive about 170 miles east on Interstate 90 to exit 176. Drive one-half mile on Broadway to Burress Avenue. Turn west on Burress Avenue and drive one block, straight into the park.

Trip note: This park is a short distance from Moses Lake State Park, which is open for day-use only. You will find shady picnic spots with tables and fire grills, beach access and moorage floats. Waterskiing is allowed on the lake.

3.　　　　　　　　　KOA VANTAGE　　　　　　　　　RV

Reference: **On Columbia River; map B4, grid b0.**

Campsites, facilities: There are 50 tent sites and 50 sites for trailers or RVs of any length. Piped water and picnic tables are provided. Electricity, sewer hookups, flush toilets, bottled gas, sanitary services, showers, a recreation hall, a laundromat, ice, a playground and a swimming pool are available. A store and a cafe are located within one mile. Pets and motorbikes are permitted. Boat docks and launching facilities are nearby.

Reservations, fee: Reservations accepted; $15-$20 fee per night. MasterCard and Visa accepted. Open all year.

Who to contact: Phone (509) 856-2230 or write to P.O. Box 1101, Vantage, WA 98950.

Location: Drive 29 miles east of Ellensburg on Interstate 90 to Vantage, then take exit 136 and drive north for one-half mile to the park.

Trip note: This campground offers pleasant, grassy sites overlooking the Columbia River, a short distance from the state park (see Ginkgo-Wanapum State Park). This is the only campground in the immediate area that provides space for tent camping. The next closest is 12 miles away at Shady Tree RV Park in George.

4. GINKGO-WANAPUM STATE PARK   RV

Reference: **On Columbia River and Wanapum Lake; map B4, grid c0.**

Campsites, facilities: There are 50 sites with full hookups for trailers or RVs up to 60 feet. Picnic tables and fire grills are provided. Flush toilets are provided and electricity, piped water, sewer hookups, showers and firewood are available for an extra fee. Pets are permitted. Boat docks and launching facilities are nearby.

Reservations, fee: No reservations; $16 fee per night. Open April through October.

Who to contact: Phone (800) 233-0321 or (509) 856-2700, or write to Ginkgo-Wanapum State Park, Vantage, WA 98950.

Location: From Interstate 5 at Seattle, turn east on Interstate 90 and drive 108 miles to Ellensburg. Continue east on Interstate 90 for 29 miles, then take the Vantage exit and drive three miles south to the park on the right.

Trip note: There are actually two separate parks here, Ginkgo State Park and Wanapum State Recreation Area. Camping is permitted only at Wanapum, which is a seven miles south of the main entrance at Ginkgo. The recreation highlights are at Ginkgo, which is set along Wanapum Lake and the Columbia River. It is the site of an ancient petrified forest and there is an interpretive center and trail. Options include hiking, swimming, boating, waterskiing and fishing. The campground at Wanapum is set up primarily for RVs, with full hookups, restrooms and showers.

5. SHADY TREE RV PARK   RV

Reference: **Near Frenchman Hills Lakes; map B4, grid b1.**

Campsites, facilities: There are five tent sites and 44 drive-through sites for trailers or RVs of any length. Electricity, piped water, sewer hookups and picnic tables are provided. Flush toilets, showers and a laundromat are available. Sanitary services are located within one mile. Pets and motorbikes are permitted.

Reservations, fee: No reservations; $10-$15 fee per night. Open all year.

Who to contact: Phone (509) 785-2851 or write to P.O. Box 5306, George, WA 98824.

Location: From Interstate 5 at Seattle, turn east on Interstate 90 and drive 108 miles to Ellensburg. Continue 41 miles east on Interstate 90 to George. Proceed to the intersection of Highways 281 and 283 and you'll see the park.

Trip note: This is an oasis in a desert-like area, with shade trees and grassy sites. A good side trip is to Frenchman Hills Lakes, bordered by sand dunes. Another option is Moses Lake State Park, which offers boating, swimming and fishing.

6. MAR-DON RESORT   🚐

Reference: **Near Potholes Reservoir; map B4, grid b5.**

Campsites, facilities: There are 300 sites (seven drive-through) for tents, trailers or RVs of any length. Electricity, piped water, sewer hookups and picnic tables are provided. Flush toilets, bottled gas, sanitary services, showers, a game room, a store, a laundromat, ice and a playground are available. Pets and motorbikes are permitted. Boat docks, rentals and launching facilities are available.

Reservations, fee: Reservations recommended; $13-$18 fee per night. Discover, MasterCard and Visa accepted. Open all year.

Who to contact: Phone (800) 416-2736 or (509) 346-2651 or write to 8198 Highway 262 East, Othello, WA 99344.

Location: From Seattle, drive about 180 miles east on Interstate 90 to exit 179 in the town of Moses Lake. Turn south on Highway 17 and drive 1.5 miles to Road M. Turn west and drive seven miles to Highway 262. Turn west and drive seven miles to the resort.

Trip note: This park is located on Potholes Reservoir with opportunities for fishing, swimming and boating. A marina, tackle and boat rentals are all available. Nearby recreation options include hiking trails and marked bike trails. There is also a 25-unit motel at the resort.

7. POTHOLES STATE PARK   🚐

Reference: **On Potholes Reservoir; map B4, grid b4.**

Campsites, facilities: There are 126 sites for tents, trailers or RVs up to 50 feet long (60 with full hookups). Picnic tables and fire grills are provided. Flush toilets, sanitary services, a store and a playground are available. Electricity, piped water, sewer hookups, showers and firewood can be obtained for an extra fee. Leashed pets are permitted. Boat launching facilities and rentals are nearby.

Reservations, fee: Contact Reservations Northwest at (800) 452-5687 ($6 reservation fee); $5-$16 fee per night. Open April through October.

Who to contact: Phone (800) 233-0321 or (509) 765-7271 or write to 6762 Highway 262 East, Othello, WA 99344.

Location: From the town of Moses Lake on Interstate 90, take exit 179 and turn south on Highway 17. Drive about nine miles to the sign for the park, then turn right and continue ten more miles to the park. The road is well-signed.

Trip note: This park is set along Potholes Reservoir, where fishing is the highlight. Trout, walleye, crappie and perch are among the species taken here. Waterskiing and hiking are two other options. There is a nice beach near the campground. A side trip to the Columbia Wildlife Refuge is recommended.

8. WILLOWS TRAILER VILLAGE   🚐

Reference: **Near Moses Lake State Park; map B4, grid b5.**

Campsites, facilities: There are 20 tent sites and 65 drive-through sites for trailers or RVs of any length. Electricity, piped water, sewer hookups and picnic tables are provided. Flush toilets, bottled gas, showers, a store, a laundromat and ice are available. Pets and motorbikes are permitted.

Reservations, fee: No reservations; $10-$15 fee per night. Open all year.

Who to contact: Phone (509) 765-7531 or write to 1347 Road M South East, Moses Lake, WA 98837.

Location: From Seattle, drive about 180 miles east on Interstate 90 to exit 179 in the town of Moses Lake. Drive 2.5 miles south on Highway 17 to Road M. Turn southwest and drive 300 years to the park.

Trip note: This is one of four campgrounds set in the area. This one has grassy, shaded sites along with horseshoe pits, barbecues and a recreation field. See the trip note for Big Sun Resort for information on recreation spots in this area.

---

9. WINDUST   RV

Reference: **On Sacajawea Lake; map B4, grid e9.**

Campsites, facilities: There is space for 30 tents, trailers or RVs in open camping areas at both ends of the park. Piped water, picnic tables and fire grills are provided. Flush toilets and a playground are available. Leashed pets and motorbikes are permitted. Some facilities are **wheelchair accessible**. Boat docks and launching facilities are nearby.

Reservations, fee: No reservations; $6 fee per night. Open all year.

Who to contact: Phone the Army Corps of Engineers at (509) 547-7781 or write to Route 6, Box 393, Pasco, WA 99301.

Location: Take exit 102 off Interstate 82 and drive 12 miles east to Pasco. Drive five miles southeast on US 12. Turn east on the Pasco/Kaholtus Highway and drive 28 miles to Burr Canyon Road. Turn right on Burr Canyon Road and drive six miles to the park.

Trip note: This is the only game in town, with no other campgrounds within a 20-mile radius. This campground is set along the shore of Sacajawea Lake near the Lower Monumental Dam on the Snake River. Swimming and fishing are popular. The Lower Monumental Dam Visitor Center is nearby, open April to October, providing a chance to view migrating salmon and steelhead.

---

10. BEACH RV PARK   RV

Reference: **On Yakima River; map B4, grid f3.**

Campsites, facilities: There are 36 sites for trailers or RVs of any length (five drive through). Electricity, piped water, sewer hookups and cable TV are provided. Flush toilets, showers, a laundromat and ice are available. Bottled gas, sanitary services, a store and a cafe are located within one mile. Pets and motorbikes are permitted. Boat launching facilities are nearby.

Reservations, fee: Reservations accepted; $18 per night. Open all year.

Who to contact: Phone (509) 588-5959 or write to Route 3, P.O. Box 2094 C, Benton City, WA 99320.

Location: From Interstate 82 west of Richland, take the Benton City exit and drive one block north, then turn west on Abby Street to the park at 113 Abby.

Trip note: If you are heading west on Interstate 182 and it is getting late, you'd best stop here. There is nowhere else to stop for a long stretch. This park is set along the shore of the Yakima River. It is a pleasant spot, with spacious RV sites and a large grassy area for tents. Nearby recreation options include an 18-hole golf course, a full-service marina and tennis courts.

11.   ARROWHEAD RV PARK   📮

Reference: **Near Columbia River; map B4, grid f6.**

Campsites, facilities: There are 80 tent sites and 35 sites (27 drive-through) for trailers or RVs of any length. Electricity, piped water, sewer hookups and picnic tables are provided. Flush toilets, showers, a laundromat and ice are available. A store and a cafe are located within one mile. Small pets and motorbikes are permitted.

Reservations, fee: Reservations accepted; $20 fee per night for two people. Open all year.

Who to contact: Phone (509) 545-8206 or write to 3120 Commercial Avenue, Pasco, WA 99301.

Location: Take exit 113 off Interstate 82 and drive nine miles to Pasco. This park is located on the eastern edge of Pasco at 3120 Commercial Street.

Trip note: This is a decent layover spot in Pasco. Nearby recreation options include an 18-hole golf course, a full-service marina and tennis courts.

---

12.   CHARBONNEAU PARK   📮

Reference: **On Snake River; map B4, grid f8.**

Campsites, facilities: There are 55 sites (17 drive-through) for tents, trailers or RVs of any length. Picnic tables and fire grills are provided. Flush toilets, sanitary services, showers, a playground, electricity, piped water and sewer hookups are available. Some facilities are **wheelchair accessible**. Leashed pets are permitted. A marina with boat docks, launching facilities and a marine dump station are nearby. An overflow camping area is available.

Reservations, fee: No reservations; $12-$14 fee per night. Open April 1 to October 31 with full facilities; there are limited facilities the rest of the year.

Who to contact: Phone the Army Corps of Engineers at (509) 547-7781 or write to Route 6, Box 693, Pasco, WA 99301-9165.

Location: Take exit 102 off Interstate 82 and drive 12 miles to Pasco. Drive six miles southeast of Pasco on US 12, then drive eight miles northeast on Highway 124. Turn north on Sun Harbor Road and drive two miles to the park.

Trip note: This campground is set along the shore of the Snake River, just above Ice Harbor Dam. Fishing, boating, swimming and waterskiing are options here. The dam's visitor center (open daily April to October) features exhibits and a fish-viewing room.

---

13.   FISHHOOK PARK   📮

Reference: **On Snake River; map B4, grid f8.**

Campsites, facilities: There are 20 tent-only sites and 40 sites (eight drive-through) for tents, trailers or RVs of any length. Picnic tables and fire grills are provided. Piped water, electricity, flush toilets, sanitary services, showers, telephone service and a playground are available. Some facilities are **wheelchair accessible**. Leashed pets are permitted. Boat docks and launching facilities are nearby.

Reservations, fee: No reservations; $9-$12.50 fee per night. Open April 1 to September 30. Park gates are locked from 10 p.m. to 6 a.m.

Who to contact: Phone U.S. Army Corp of Engineers at (509) 547-7781 or write to Route 6, Box 693, Pasco, WA 99301-9165.

Location: Take exit 102 off Interstate 82 and drive 12 miles to Pasco. Drive six miles southeast of Pasco on US 12, then drive 16 miles northeast on Highway 124. Turn left on Fishhook Park Road and drive four miles to the park.

Trip note: If you are driving along Highway 124 and you need a spot for the night, make the turn on Fishhook Park Road and check out this park. It is set along the Snake River, is wooded with some lawn area and provides a swim area as well as opportunities for fishing and waterskiing.

---

14. LLOYD'S DESERT GOLD RV PARK RV

Reference: **Near Columbia River; map B4, grid f5.**

Campsites, facilities: There are 69 sites (18 drive-through) for trailers or RVs of any length. Electricity, piped water, sewer hookups and picnic tables are provided. Flush toilets, showers, bottled gas, sanitary services, a store, a laundromat, ice and a swimming pool are available. A cafe is located within one mile. Pets are permitted. Boat docks and launching facilities are nearby on the Columbia River.

Reservations, fee: Reservations accepted; $17 fee per night. MasterCard and Visa accepted. Open all year.

Who to contact: Phone (800) 788-GOLD or (509) 627-1000 or write to 611 SE Columbia Drive, Richland, WA 99352.

Location: Take exit 102 off Interstate 82 and drive six miles to Richland. Take Columbia Drive west for one-quarter mile to 611 Columbia Drive SE.

Trip note: This is a nice motor home park set about a mile from the Columbia River. Nearby recreation options include an 18-hole golf course, hiking trails, a full-service marina, tennis courts or a visit to the Department of Energy public information center at the Hanford Science Center. The park also has a pool and spa if you just want to relax without going anywhere.

---

15. COLUMBIA PARK CAMPGROUND RV

Reference: **On Columbia River; map B4, grid g5.**

Campsites, facilities: There are 22 tent sites and 100 sites (26 drive-through) for trailers or RVs. Electricity, piped water and picnic tables are provided. Flush toilets, sanitary services, ice and a playground are available. Showers and firewood can be obtained for an extra fee. A store and a cafe are located within one mile. Pets and motorbikes are permitted. Boat docks and launching facilities are nearby.

Reservations, fee: Reservations accepted; $6-$12 fee per night. Open mid-April to mid-October.

Who to contact: Phone (509) 783-3711 or write to 6601 SE Columbia, Richland, WA 99352.

Location: From the junction of Highway 14 and US 12, drive four miles west on US 12 to Columbia Center Boulevard. Turn north and drive one-half mile to Columbia Drive, then turn east and continue one mile to the park.

Trip note: The campground is in a suburban, grassy area, set on the Columbia River, adjacent to Columbia Park. Nearby recreation options include waterskiing on the Columbia River, an 18-hole golf course, hiking trails, marked bike trails and tennis courts. The sun can feel like a branding iron during the summer.

16. GREENTREE RV PARK RV

Reference: In Pasco; map B4, grid g6.

Campsites, facilities: There are 40 sites for trailers or RVs of any length. Electricity, piped water and sewer hookups are provided. A laundromat and showers are available. Bottled gas, a store, a cafe and ice are located within one mile. Pets and motorbikes are permitted. Boat docks, launching facilities and rentals are nearby.

Reservations, fee: Reservations accepted; $12-$14 fee per night. Open all year.

Who to contact: Phone (509) 547-6220 or write to 2103 North Fifth Avenue #69, Pasco, WA 99301.

Location: Take exit 102 off Interstate 82 and drive 12 miles east to Pasco. Take exit 13 off Interstate 182 and you'll see it on the southwest corner.

Trip note: This park is in urban Pasco. Nearby recreation options include an 18-hole golf course, hiking trails, a full-service marina and tennis courts. The Franklin County Historical Museum, which is located in town, and the Sacajawea State Park Museum and Interpretive Center, located three miles southeast of town, both offer extensive collections of Native American artifacts.

---

17. HOOD PARK RV

Reference: On Columbia River; map B4, grid g6.

Campsites, facilities: There are 68 sites for tents, trailers or RVs of any length. Piped water, fire grills and picnic tables are provided. Flush toilets, sanitary services, showers, electricity and a playground are available. A restaurant and convenience store is located within two miles. Some facilities are **wheelchair accessible**. Leashed pets are permitted. Boat docks and launching facilities are nearby. A primitive overflow camping area is available.

Reservations, fee: No reservations; $12 fee per night; $7 per night in overflow area. Open April 1 to September 30. Gates are locked from 10 p.m. to 6 a.m.

Who to contact: Phone the Army Corps of Engineers at (509) 547-7781 or write to Route 6, Box 693, Pasco, WA 99301-9165.

Location: Take exit 102 off Interstate 82 and drive 12 miles east to Pasco. Drive six miles southeast of Pasco on US 12, then head east on Highway 124 to the campground.

Trip note: A more developed, nearby alternative to Columbia Park Campground, this park has river access for swimming and boating. Other recreation options include basketball and horseshoes. McNary Wildlife Refuge and Sacajawea State Park are nearby.

---

18. McNARY HABITAT MANAGEMENT AREA RV

Reference: Near Columbia River; map B4, grid g7.

Campsites, facilities: There are 24 primitive sites for tents, trailers or RVs. **No piped water** is available. Boat launching facilities are nearby.

Reservations, fee: No reservations; no fee. Open all year.

Who to contact: Phone Department of Fish and Game at (509) 456-4082 or write to North 8702 Division Street, Spokane, WA 99218.

Location: Take exit 102 off Interstate 82 and drive 12 miles east to Pasco. Continue 10 miles southeast on US 12. The area is located between the Snake and the Walla Walla rivers.

Trip note: This premium spot is only a 10-minute drive from Pasco. Though primitive, it is an ideal getaway or layover spot for those wanting to avoid the highway crowds. This area adjoins the McNary National Wildlife Refuge, accessible by foot or horseback. Seven miles of stream frontage along the Columbia River is accessible. Fishing on the adjacent wildlife refuge is good for bass, bluegill, bullhead and carp. Some hunting is allowed in season.

19.   CROW BUTTE STATE PARK   RV

Reference: **On Columbia River; map B4, grid i1.**

Campsites, facilities: There are two primitive tent sites and 50 sites with full hookups for trailers or RVs up to 60 feet long. Fire grills and picnic tables are provided. Flush toilets, showers and sanitary disposal station are available. Some facilities are **wheelchair accessible**. Boat launching facilities are nearby. Leashed pets are permitted.

Reservations, fee: No reservations; $5-$16 fee per night. Open all year with limited winter facilities.

Who to contact: Phone (800) 233-0321 or (509) 875-2644 or write to P.O. Box 217, Paterson, WA 99345.

Location: From Interstate 5 at Vancouver, Washington, turn east on Highway 14 and drive approximately 156 miles to the park on the right side of the highway.

Trip note: This state park is set along the Columbia River, the only campground in a 25-mile radius. Recreation options include waterskiing, fishing, swimming and hiking. The Umatilla National Wildlife Refuge is adjacent to the park and allows fishing and hunting in specified areas.

LEAVE NO TRACE TIPS

Properly dispose of what you can't pack out.

• If no refuse facility is available, deposit human waste in catholes dug six to eight inches deep at least 200 feet from water, camps, or trails. Cover and disguise the cathole when you're finished.

• To wash yourself or your dishes, carry the water 200 feet from streams or lakes and use small amounts of biodegradable soap. Scatter the strained dishwater.

WASHINGTON MAP .... see page 90
Adjoining Maps
NORTH (A5) .... see page 244
EAST .... no map
SOUTH .... Oregon
WEST (B4) .... see page 362

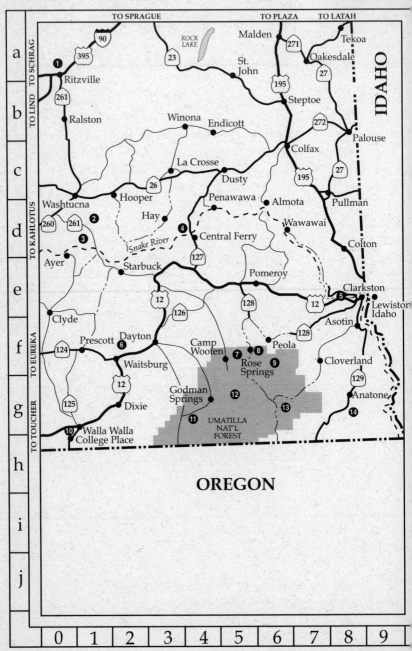

Washington Map B5 featuring: Ritzville, Snake River, Palouse River, Umatilla National Forest, Lewis and Clark Trail, Fort Walla Walla Park, Wenaha-Tucannon Wilderness, Puffer Butte, Fields Spring State Park

1.　　HERITAGE INN MOTEL AND RV PARK　　**RV**

Reference: In Ritzville; map B5, grid a0.

Campsites, facilities: There are 30 drive-through sites for tents, trailers or RVs of any length. Electricity, piped water, sewer hookups and picnic tables are provided. Flush toilets, sanitary services, showers, a laundromat, ice, a playground and a swimming pool are available. Bottled gas, a store and a cafe are located within one mile. Pets and motorbikes are permitted.

Reservations, fee: Reservations accepted; $20-$25 fee per night. MasterCard and Visa accepted. Open mid-April to mid-October.

Who to contact: Phone (509) 659-1007 or write to 1405 Smitty's Boulevard, Ritzville, WA 99169.

Location: From Interstate 90 at Spokane, turn west and drive 55 miles to Ritzville. Take exit 221 and you'll see the motel one-half block off the freeway.

Trip note: If all you have is a tent, well, this is the only site within a radius of 25 miles. The nearest fishing is at Sprague Lake, 30 miles north on Highway 395. Burroughs Historical Museum is a possible side trip in town. Nearby recreation options include an 18-hole golf course and tennis courts.

2.　　PALOUSE FALLS STATE PARK　　**RV**

Reference: On Snake and Palouse rivers; map B5, grid d1.

Campsites, facilities: There are 10 primitive campsites and 10 sites for tents, self-contained trailers or RVs up to 40 feet long. Picnic tables and fire grills are provided. Pit toilets are available. Some facilities are **wheelchair-accessible**. Leashed pets are permitted.

Reservations, fee: No reservations; $7 fee per night. Open April to late September, weather permitting.

Who to contact: Phone (800) 233-0321 or (509) 646-3252 or write to P.O. Box 157, Starbuck, WA 99359.

Location: From Spokane, turn south on US 195 and drive 59 miles. Turn east on Highway 26 and drive 17 miles southwest, then turn south on Highway 127 and continue southwest for 28 miles. Turn west on State Route 12 and drive nine miles, then turn west again on Highway 261 and drive eight miles to Starbuck. Continue 14 miles northwest on Highway 261 to the park entrance (located seven miles northwest of Lyons Ferry).

Trip note: You have to navigate a roundabout circuit of highways to get here, but it's well worth the trip. This remote state park is set at the confluence of the Snake and Palouse rivers. It is almost unknown and gets relatively little use even in the summer months. Spectacular 190-foot Palouse Falls is a sight not to miss. In recent years, a handicapped-accessible trail has been completed. The park is very scenic, with nice shaded picnic facilities and an abundance of wildlife for animal lovers.

3.　　LYON'S FERRY STATE PARK　　**RV**

Reference: On Snake River; map B5, grid d1.

Campsites, facilities: There are two primitive tent sites and 50 sites for tents or self-contained trailers or RVs. Picnic tables and fire grills are provided. Flush toilets, sanitary services and showers are available. Some facilities are **wheel-chair-accessible**. Pets are permitted. Boat docks and launching facilities are nearby.

Reservations, fee: No reservations; $10 fee per night. Open April to September.

Who to contact: Phone (800) 233-0321 or (509) 646-3252 or write to P.O. Box 157, Starbuck, WA 99359.

Location: From Spokane, turn south on US 195 and drive 59 miles. Turn east on Highway 26 and drive 17 miles southwest, then turn south on Highway 127 and continue southwest for 28 miles. Turn west on State Route 12 and drive nine miles, then turn west again on Highway 261 and drive eight miles to Starbuck. Continue eight miles northwest on Highway 261 to the park on the right.

Trip note: This state park is set at the confluence of the Snake and Palouse rivers. Fishing, hiking, swimming, waterskiing and boating are all options here. A good side trip is a visit to beautiful Palouse Falls, located seven miles north.

4.   CENTRAL FERRY STATE PARK   **RV**

Reference: On Snake River; map B5, grid d4.

Campsites, facilities: There are eight primitive tent sites and 60 sites with full hookups for trailers or RVs up to 45 feet long. There is also one group camp accommodating up to 100 people. Picnic tables and fire grills are provided. Flush toilets, a sanitary service station, electricity, piped water, sewer hookups, a group fire ring, three horseshoe pit areas and showers are available. A store and a restaurant are within two miles. Some facilities are **wheelchair accessible**. Leashed pets are permitted. Boat docks, launching facilities and a fishing pier are within the park.

Reservations, fee: Contact Reservations Northwest at (800) 452-5687 ($6 reservation fee); $15 fee per night. For group camp reservations, phone (509) 549-3551; $25 base group camp fee per night plus $1 per night per tent and $10 per night per RV. Open mid-March to mid-November.

Who to contact: Phone (800) 233-0321 or (509) 549-3551 or write to Route 3, P.O. Box 99, Pomeroy, WA 99347.

Location: From Spokane, turn south on US 195 and drive 59 miles. Turn east on Highway 26 and drive 17 miles southwest, then turn south on Highway 127 and continue southwest for 17 miles to the park entrance on the right.

Trip note: This is the only campground within a 20-mile radius. It is set along the shore of the Snake River and has a beach. Waterskiing, sailing, boating, swimming and fishing for bass and catfish are all options here.

5.   CHIEF TIMOTHY STATE PARK   **RV**

Reference: On Snake River; map B5, grid e8.

Campsites, facilities: There are two primitive tent sites and 60 sites with water and electrical hookups for trailers or RVs of any length. Picnic tables and fire grills are provided. Flush toilets, sanitary services and a playground are available. Electricity, piped water, sewer hookups, showers and firewood can be obtained for an extra fee. Some facilities are **wheelchair accessible**. Pets are permitted. Boat docks and launching facilities are nearby.

Reservations, fee: No reservations; $7-$16 fee per night. Open all year.

Who to contact: Phone (800) 233-0321 or (509)758-9580 or write to Highway 12, Clarkston, WA 99403.

Location: From Spokane, turn south on US 195 and drive approximately 95 miles to the Washington/Idaho border. Turn south on Highway 128 and drive a short distance to State Route 12, then turn west and drive to Clarkston. Turn north at the sign for the park and proceed about eight miles.

Trip note: This unique state park is set on a bridged island in the Snake River, yet is accessible to cars. It offers all water sports, including fishing, swimming, boating, waterskiing and sailing. There are docks for boating campers, a beach area and an interpretive center on the Lewis and Clark Expedition. There are outfitters in Clarkston that will take you sightseeing up the Grand Canyon of the Snake River. Call the Chamber of Commerce at (509) 758-7712 for details.

6.   LEWIS AND CLARK TRAIL STATE PARK

Reference: **On Lewis and Clark Trail; map B5, grid f2.**

Campsites, facilities: There are 16 primitive tent sites and 30 sites for tents or self-enclosed trailers or RVs up to 28 feet long. Picnic tables and fire grills are provided. Flush toilets, showers, firewood and sanitary services are available. A store, a cafe and ice are located within one mile. Pets are permitted.

Reservations, fee: No reservations; $7-$16 fee per night. Open all year.

Who to contact: Phone (800) 233-0321 or (509) 337-6457 or write to Route 1, P.O. Box 90, Dayton, WA 99328.

Location: From Walla Walla on State Route 12, turn east on State Route 12 and drive 24 miles to the park entrance.

Trip note: If it's getting late and you need a spot, you'd better pick this one. There are no other campgrounds within 20 miles. It is not a bad choice, since it's set along the original Lewis and Clark Trail. During the summer, the rangers offer campfire programs where they share the details of this site's history. The campground is set in a forested, "prairie country" environment.

7.   TUCANNON   RV

Reference: **In Umatilla National Forest; map B5, grid f5.**

Campsites, facilities: There are 13 sites for tents, trailers or RVs up to 15 feet long. Picnic tables and fire grills are provided. Vault toilets are available, but there is **no piped water**. Leashed pets are permitted.

Reservations, fee: No reservations; no fee. Open May to late November.

Who to contact: Phone Umatilla National Forest at (509)843-1891 or write to Pomeroy Ranger District, Route 1, Box 53-F, Pomeroy, WA 99347.

Location: From Spokane, turn south on US 195 and drive 59 miles. Turn west on Highway 26 and drive 17 miles to Dusty, then turn south on Highway 127 and continue 28 miles to Dodge. Turn east on State Route 12 and proceed 13 miles to Pomeroy. Turn south on County Road 101 and drive 17 miles, then head southwest on Forest Service Road 47 for four miles. Turn south on Forest Service Road 160 and drive 200 yards to the campground on the left.

Trip note: For people willing to rough it, this backcountry camp in Umatilla National Forest is the place. There is plenty of hiking, fishing and hunting all in a rugged setting. The camp is not far from the Tucannon River, which offers a myriad of options for vacationers.

8.   ALDER THICKET   RV

Reference: **In Umatilla National Forest; map B5, grid f5.**

Campsites, facilities: There are six sites for tents, trailers or RVs up to 15 feet long. Picnic tables and fire grills are provided. Vault toilets are available, but there is **no piped water**. Leashed pets are permitted.

Reservations, fee: No reservations; no fee. Open mid-May to mid-November.

Who to contact: Phone Umatilla National Forest at (509) 843-1891 or write to Pomeroy Ranger District, Route 1, Box 53-F, Pomeroy, WA 99347.

Location: From Spokane, turn south on US 195 and drive 59 miles. Turn west on Highway 26 and drive 17 miles to Dusty, then turn south on Highway 127 and continue 28 miles to Dodge. Turn east on State Route 12 and proceed 13 miles to Pomeroy. Turn south on Highway 128 and drive 10 miles south. At the fork continue straight to Forest Service Road 40 and continue 3.5 miles to the campground on the right.

Trip note: This is probably the first time you've heard of this spot. Hardly anybody knows about it, including people who live relatively nearby in Walla Walla. It is a prime base camp for a backcountry hiking adventure in summer or a jumpoff point for a hunting trip in the fall. This is a very primitive camp, but great if you're looking for quiet and solitude.

9.   BIG SPRINGS

Reference: **In Umatilla National Forest; map B5, grid f6.**

Campsites, facilities: There are 15 tent sites. Picnic tables are provided. Vault toilets are available, but there is **no piped water**. Leashed pets are permitted.

Reservations, fee: No reservations; no fee. Open mid-May to mid-November.

Who to contact: Phone Umatilla National Forest at (509) 843-1891 or write to Pomeroy Ranger District, Route 1, Box 53-F, Pomeroy, WA 99347.

Location: From Spokane, turn south on US 195 and drive 59 miles. Turn west on Highway 26 and drive 17 miles to Dusty, then turn south on Highway 127 and continue 28 miles to Dodge. Turn east on State Route 12 and proceed 13 miles to Pomeroy. Turn south on Highway 128 and drive ten miles to the "Y," then continue straight to mountain Road 40. Pass the national forest boundary and continue nine miles to the Clearwater lookout tower. Turn left on Road 42 and continue for three miles, then turn left on Road 4225 to the campground on the left. From Clarkston, drive on County Road 128 for 20 miles, then turn left on Iron Springs Road (County Road 42). Continue for about five miles, turning right on Forest Service Road 4225 to the campground on the right.

Trip note: In the fall, this site is used primarily by hunters. In the summer, it is a possible base camp for a backpacking trip. It's quite primitive, with little in the way of activity options, but a perfect spot to get away from it all. This is a nice, cool spot in the summer. It's advisable to obtain a Forest Service map.

10.   WALLA WALLA CAMPGROUND   🆁🆅

Reference: **In Fort Walla Walla Park; map B5, grid g0.**

Campsites, facilities: There are 50 tent sites and 76 sites for trailers or RVs up to 35 feet. An overflow area is provided as well. Restrooms, showers, water and electricity hookups, a phone and sanitary dump station are available. Leashed pets are permitted.

Reservations, fee: Reservations accepted; $8.50-$11 fee per night. Open year-round with limited winter services.

Who to contact: Phone the park at (509) 527-3770 or write to Dalles Military Road, Route 8, P.O. Box 36B, Walla Walla, WA 99362.

Location: From State Route 12 in Walla Walla, take the Highway 125 exit and drive approximately 2.5 miles south. Turn right on Dalles Military Road and continue one-half mile to the campground.

Trip note: This 300-acre park is set within Walla Walla city limits, yet provides a rustic feel. The campground is wooded, with grassy sites. The park is divided by Garrison Creek, with the campground on one side and a picnic area, playground and historical museum on the other. In May, the Balloon Stampede, a well-known hot air balloon festival, brings tourists in hordes, as does July's Mountain Man Rendezvous. Also in July, the drama department from the city college performs musicals at the park's amphitheater. This is the only campground we've found for miles, and it's a prime choice.

11. GODMAN 🚐

Reference: **Near Wenaha-Tucannon Wilderness in Umatilla National Forest; map B5, grid g4.**

Campsites, facilities: There are eight sites for tents, trailers or RVs up to 15 feet long. There is also one cabin which can accommodate up to four people. Picnic tables and fire grills are provided. Vault toilets are available, but there is **no piped water**. Leashed pets are permitted. Facilities are available for horses, including hitching rails, feed mangers and a spring.

Reservations, fee: No reservations; no fee for sites; $25 base cabin fee per night plus $5 each person. Open mid-June to late October.

Who to contact: Phone Umatilla National Forest at (509) 843-1891 or write to Pomeroy Ranger District, Route 1, Box 53-F, Pomeroy, WA 99347.

Location: From Spokane, turn south on US 195 and drive 59 miles. Turn west on Highway 26 and drive 17 miles to Dusty, then turn south on Highway 127 and continue 28 miles to Dodge. Turn west on State Route 12 and drive 24 miles to Dayton. Turn right on County Road 118 and drive 14 miles southeast, then head south on Forest Service Road 46 (Kendall Skyline Road) for 11 miles to the campground on the right.

Trip note: This tiny, little-known spot borders a wilderness area. It is primarily used as a base camp for wilderness expeditions. There is a trailhead that provide access to the Wenaha-Tucannon Wilderness for both hikers and horseback riders. Horse facilities are available at the trailhead. In the winter the trails and roads are used for snowmobiling.

12. TEAL SPRING 🚐

Reference: **In Umatilla National Forest; map B5, grid g5.**

Campsites, facilities: There are 10 sites for tents, trailers or RVs up to 15 feet long. **No piped water** is available. Picnic tables and fire grills are provided. Vault toilets are available. Leashed pets are permitted.

Reservations, fee: No reservations; no fee. Open June to mid-November.

Who to contact: Phone Umatilla National Forest at (509) 843-1891 or write to Pomeroy Ranger District, Route 1, Box 53-F, Pomeroy, WA 99347.

Location: From Spokane, turn south on US 195 and drive 59 miles. Turn west on Highway 26 and drive 17 miles to Dusty, then turn south on Highway 127 and continue 28 miles to Dodge. Turn east on Highway 12 and drive 13 miles to Pomeroy, then drive 10 miles south on Highway 128. At the "Y," continue straight to mountain Road 40 and enter the national forest boundary. Drive nine miles to the Clearwater lookout tower; the campground turnoff is about a half-mile past the tower on the right.

Trip note: This is one of several small, primitive camps in the area. A national forest map details the backcountry roads, trails and streams. Hunting is popular in the fall, and a snow shelter is available for winter use.

13. WICKIUP ᴿⱽ

Reference: **In Umatilla National Forest; map B5, grid g6.**

Campsites, facilities: There are five sites for tents, trailers or RVs up to 15 feet long. Picnic tables and fire grills are provided. Vault toilets are available, but there is **no piped water**. A cold water spring is available 100 yards from the campground. Leashed pets are permitted.

Reservations, fee: No reservations; no fee. Open mid-June to late October.

Who to contact: Phone Umatilla National Forest at (509) 843-1891 or write to Pomeroy Ranger District, Route 1, Box 53-F, Pomeroy, WA 99347.

Location: From Spokane, turn south on US 195 and drive 59 miles. Turn west on Highway 26 and drive 17 miles to Dusty, then turn south on Highway 127 and continue 28 miles to Dodge. Turn east on Highway 12 and drive 13 miles to Pomeroy, then drive 10 miles south on Highway 128. At the "Y," continue straight to mountain Road 40. At Troy Junction, about 17 miles, follow Road 44 for three miles. Wickiup is at the intersection of Roads 44 and 43. From Asotin, take road leading west through Cloverland and onto Forest Road 43. Continue to the intersection at Road 44, where the camp is located.

Trip note: This is a primitive Forest Service campground that gets very little camping pressure. Most people have no idea it is even here; one forest ranger describes it as "little more than a wide spot in the road." However, it offers plenty of peace and quiet and is a good jumpoff for summer backpacking trips or a fall hunting trip. A Forest Service map details backcountry roads and trails.

---

14. FIELDS SPRING STATE PARK ᴿⱽ

Reference: **Near Puffer Butte; map B5, grid g8.**

Campsites, facilities: There are two primitive tent sites and 20 sites for tents or self-contained RVs up to 30 feet long. Piped water, picnic tables and fire grills are provided. Flush toilets, a sanitary disposal station and a playground are available. Showers and firewood can be obtained for an extra fee. A store, a restaurant and ice are located within one mile. Some facilities are **wheelchair accessible**. Pets are permitted.

Reservations, fee: No reservations; $5-$10 fee per night. Open all year, with limited winter facilities.

Who to contact: Phone (800) 233-0321 or (509) 256-3332 or write to P.O. Box 86, Anatone, WA 99401.

Location: From Spokane, turn south on US 195 and drive approximately 95 miles to the Washington/Idaho border. Turn south on Highway 128 and drive a short distance to State Route 12, then turn west and drive to Clarkston. Turn south on Highway 129 and drive 28.5 miles to the park entrance.

Trip note: Just about nobody knows about this spot, and it's a good one. Tucked away in the southeast corner of the state, it is a designated environmental learning center. This park is noted for its variety of bird life and wildflowers. A hiking trail leads up to Puffer Butte at 4,500 feet, which offers a panoramic view of the Snake River Canyon, the Wallowa Mountains and Idaho, Oregon and Washington. Two day-use areas with boat launches, managed by the Department of Fish and Game, are within about 25 miles of the park. One is called the Snake River Access, 22.5 miles south of Asotin on Snake River Road; the other is the Grande Ronde River Access, 24 miles south of Asotin on the same road. During the winter, this state park is open for snowmobiling and cross-country skiing.

OREGON

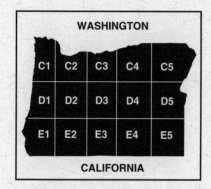

WASHINGTON

C1	C2	C3	C4	C5
D1	D2	D3	D4	D5
E1	E2	E3	E4	E5

CALIFORNIA

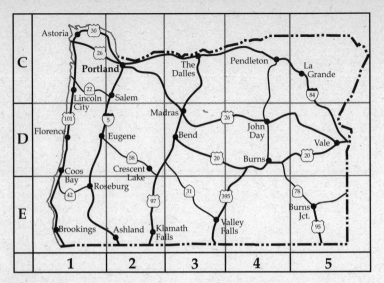

Map C1—43 listings pages 382-399
Featuring: Columbia River, Fort
Stevens State Park, Necanicum River,
Neawanna River, Saddle Mountain,
Ecola State Park, Netarts Bay,
Garibaldi, Tillamook River, Tillamook
Bay, Three Rivers, Nestucca River,
Hebo Lake, Siuslaw National Forest,
South Yamhill River, Siletz River,
Salmon River, Devil's Lake State
Park, Depoe Bay State Park, Siletz Bay

Map C2—80 listings pages 400-433
Featuring: Columbia River, Sandy
River, Cascade Locks, Columbia
Wilderness, Mount Hood National
Forest, Pacific Crest Trail, Sandy
River, Willamette River, Portland,
Hood River, Molalla River, Clackamas
River, Collawash River, Promontory
Lake, Zigzag River, Salmon River,
Rock Lakes Basin, Trillium Lake,
White River, Roaring River, Crater
Lake, Timothy Lake, Santiam River,
Salem, Summit Lake, Willamette Na-
tional Forest, Clackamas Lake, Bull of
the Woods Wilderness, Breitenbush
River, Olallie Lake, Round Lake,
Breitenbush Lake

Map C3—21 listings pages 434-443
Featuring: Hood River, Columbia
River Gorge, Columbia River,
Deschutes River, Badger Lake, Mount
Hood National Forest, Pine Hollow
Reservoir, Warm Springs Indian Res-
ervation, Fossil

Map C4—32 listings pages 444-457
Featuring: Columbia River, Umatilla
River, McKay Creek National
Wildlife Refuge, Langdon Lake,
Umatilla National Forest, Umatilla
Indian Reservation, Grande Ronde
River, Wallowa-Whitman National
Forest, John Day River, Bull Prairie
Lake, Grande Ronde Lake, Anthony
Lake, Mud Lake

Map C5—32 listings pages 458-471
Featuring: Jubilee Lake, Umatilla
National Forest, Touchet River, Walla
Walla River, Wallowa-Whitman
National Forest, Grande Ronde River,
Wallowa Lake, Hot Lake, Eagle Cap
Wilderness, Buckhorn Lake, Hells
Canyon Wilderness, Lostine River,
Twin Lakes, Imnaha River, Fish Lake

Map D1—69 listings pages 472-499
Featuring: Yaquina Bay, Alsea Bay,
Corvallis, Seal Rock State Park,
Siuslaw National Forest, South Beach
State Park, Alsea River, Willamette
River, Cape Perpetua, Cape Creek ,
Alder Lake, Siuslaw River, Florence,
Sutton Lake, Woahink Lake, Mercer
Lake, Fern Ridge Reservoir, Siltcoos
River, Siltcoos Lake, Cleowax Lake,
Oregon Dunes National Recreation

Area, Carter Lake, Eugene, Tahkenitch Lake, Umpqua River, Winchester Bay, Tenmile Lake, Eel Lake, Eel River, Loon Lake, Coos Bay, Bluebill Lake, Cottage Grove Reservoir, Sunset Bay, Cape Arago State Park

Map D2—161 listings pages 500-561
Featuring: Santiam River, Detroit Lake, Willamette National Forest, Mount Jefferson Wilderness, Willamette River, Deschutes National Forest, McKenzie River, Scott Lake, Smith Reservoir, Carmen Reservoir, Trailbridge Reservoir, Clear Lake, Scout Lake, Suttle Lake, Big Lake, Pacific Crest Trail, Cougar Lake, Blue River Reservoir, Sparks Lake, Todd Lake, Devil's Lake, Lookout Point Reservoir, Dorena Lake, Umpqua National Forest, Three Sisters Wilderness, Elk Lake, Blair Lake, Chucksney Mountain, Hosmer Lake, Cultus Lake, Crane Prairie Reservoir, Lava Lake, Deschutes River, Fall River, Odell Lake, Waldo Lake Gold Lake, Crescent Lake, Davis Lake, South Twin Lake, Wickiup Reservoir, Umpqua River, Toketee Lake, Timpanogas Lake, Lemolo Lake

Map D3—46 listings pages 562-579
Featuring: Lake Billy Chinook, Deschutes National Forest, Metolius River, Haystack Reservoir, Ochoco National Forest, Ochoco Lake State Park, Smith Rock State Park, Branchwater Lake, McKenzie River, Sisters, Antelope Flat Reservoir, Crooked River, Walton Lake, Deschutes River, Bend, Prineville Reservoir, Three Creeks Lake, Paulina Lake, Arnold Ice Caves, East Lake

Map D4—39 listings pages 580-595
Featuring: Olive Lake, Umatilla National Forest, Wallowa-Whitman National Forest, Unity Reservoir, John Day River, Burnt River, Malheur National Forest, Magone Lake, Starr Ridge, Ochoco National Forest, Strawberry Mountain Wilderness, Canyon Meadows Reservoir, Malheur River, Prairie City, Divine Canyon, Yellowjacket Lake, Delintment Lake

Map D5—12 listings pages 596-601
Featuring: Wallowa-Whitman National Forest, Phillips Lake, Vale, Snake River, Juntura, Owyhee Lake, Malheur River

Map E1—86 listings pages 602-635
Featuring: Coquille River, Bandon State Park, Umpqua River, Roseburg, Elk River, Sixes River, Siskiyou National Forest, Laird Lake, Gold Beach, Glendale, Rogue River, Squaw Lake, Grants Pass, Oregon Caves National Monument, Chetco River, Illinois River, Lake Selmac, Applegate River, Winchuck River, Rogue River National Forest, Bolan Lake

Map E2—84 listings pages 636-669
Featuring: Little River, Umpqua National Forest, Umpqua River, Lake of the Woods, Hemlock Lake, Big Twin Lake, Lemolo Lake, Rogue River National Forest, Rogue River, Diamond Lake, Clearwater River, Miller Lake, Winema National Forest, Rogue River Trail, Crater Lake National Park, Crater Lake Pinnacles, Sky Lakes Wilderness, Lost Creek Lake, Pacific Crest Trail, Williamson River, Wood River, Collier Memorial State Park, Snowshoe Butte, Parker River, Willow Lake, Fish Lake, Klamath Lake, Fourmile Lake, Sprague River, Hyatt Lake, Howard Prairie Lake, Ashland, Emigrant Lake, Tingley Lake

Map E3—22 listings pages 670-679
Featuring: Fremont National Forest, Thompson Reservoir, Sprague River, Chewaucan River, Gearhart Mountain Wilderness, Campbell Lake, Deadhorse Lake, Gerber Reservoir, Lofton Lake, Cottonwood Meadow Lake, Adel, Goose Lake, Junipers Reservoir, Dog Lake, Lakeview

Map E4—5 listings pages 680-683
Featuring: Fish Lake, Malheur National Wildlife Refuge, Blitzen River, Adel

Map E5—1 listing pages 684-685
Featuring: Owyhee Lake

OREGON MAP .... see page 380

Adjoining Maps

NORTH .... Washington

EAST (C2) .... see page 400

SOUTH (D1) .... see page 472

WEST .... no map

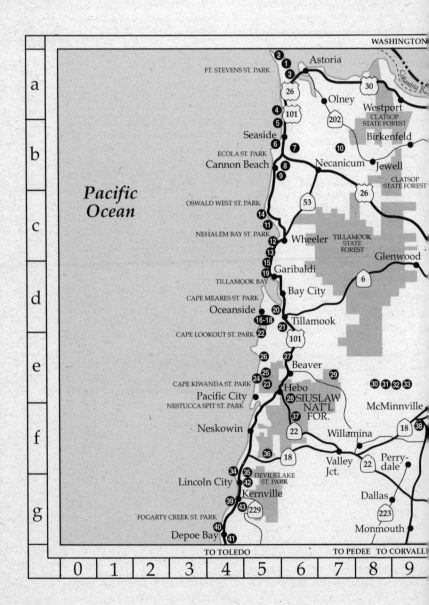

Oregon Map C1 featuring: Columbia River, Fort Stevens State Park, Necanicum River, Neawanna River, Saddle Mountain, Ecola State Park, Netarts Bay, Garibaldi, Tillamook River, Tillamook Bay, Three Rivers, Nestucca River, Hebo Lake, Siuslaw National Forest, South Yamhill River, Siletz River, Salmon River, Devil's Lake State Park, Depoe Bay State Park, Siletz Bay

1. ASTORIA/WARRENTON SEASIDE KOA RV

Reference: **Map C1, grid a6.**

Campsites, facilities: There are 82 sites for tents, trailers or RVs up to 55 feet. Cable TV, restrooms, showers, security, a public phone, a laundromat, limited groceries, ice, snacks, RV supplies, LP gas and a barbecue are available. Recreational facilities include a playground, a game room, a recreation field, horseshoes, a spa and a heated swimming pool. Some facilities are **wheelchair accessible**.

Reservations, fee: Reservations recommended; $21-$30 fee per night. Visa and MasterCard accepted.

Who to contact: Phone the park at (503) 861-2606 or write to 1100 Ridge Road, Hammond, OR 97121.

Location: From Portland, turn west on US 26 and drive 73 miles to the junction with US 101. Turn north and drive approximately 15 miles. One-quarter mile past the Camp Rilea Army Base, turn west at the sign for Fort Stevens State Park and follow the signs to Ridge Road. Turn on Ridge Road and drive to the campground, located directly across from the state park.

Trip note: This campground is set in a wooded area adjacent to Fort Stevens State Park and tours of that historical military site are available. It is an excellent option if the state park campground is full. Numerous recreation options are available in the immediate area, including bicycling, hiking, deep sea fishing and beachcombing. See the trip note for Fort Stevens State Park for further details about the area.

2. FORT STEVENS STATE PARK RV

Reference: **At the mouth of Columbia River; map C1, grid a6.**

Campsites, facilities: There are 262 tent sites, 343 sites with full or partial hookups for trailers or RVs of any length and a special camping area for hikers and bicyclists. Picnic tables and fire grills are provided. Flush toilets, a sanitary disposal station, showers, firewood and a playground are available. Some facilities are **wheelchair accessible**. Leashed pets are permitted. Boat docks and launching facilities are nearby.

Reservations, fee: Contact Reservations Northwest at (800) 452-5687 ($6 reservation fee); $14-$19 fee per night; $4 for hikers/bikers. Open all year.

Who to contact: Phone (503) 861-1671 or (800) 452-5687 or write to Hammond, OR 97121.

Location: From Portland, turn west on US 26 and drive 73 miles to the junction with US 101. Turn north and drive approximately 15 miles. One-quarter mile past the Camp Rilea Army Base, turn west at the sign for Fort Stevens State Park and continue to the park.

Trip note: This is a classic spot, set at the northern tip of Oregon, right where the Columbia River enters the Pacific Ocean. This large state park offers five miles of ocean frontage, three miles of Columbia River frontage and several small lakes. Fishing is best out at the point, swimming is best in the small lakes. There is an 8.5-mile bike trail and nine miles of hiking trails. The trailhead for the Oregon Coast Trail is here as well. For history buffs, there is a museum, tours of the fort and artillery batteries, and the remains of the Peter Iredale shipwreck.

3.　　　KAMPERS WEST CAMPGROUND　　RV

Reference: **Near Fort Stevens State Park; map C1, grid a6.**

Campsites, facilities: There are 10 tent sites and 210 drive-through sites for trailers or RVs of any length. Electricity, piped water and picnic tables are provided. Flush toilets, bottled gas, sanitary services, showers, a laundromat and ice are available. A store and a cafe are within one mile. Pets and motorbikes are permitted.

Reservations, fee: Reservations accepted; $15-$20 fee per night. Open all year.

Who to contact: Phone (503) 861-1814 or write to 1140 NW Warrenton Drive, Warrenton, OR 97146.

Location: From Portland, turn west on US 30 and drive 105 miles north and west to Astoria. Turn south on US 101 and drive 6.5 miles to the Warrenton/ Hammond Junction. Turn west and drive one mile. Turn west on Warrenton and drive 1.5 miles to the campground on the right.

Trip note: Located just four miles from Fort Stevens State Park, this privately-run site offers full RV services. Nearby recreation options include an 18-hole golf course, hiking trails, marked bike trails and a riding stable.

4.　　　　　　BUD'S CAMPGROUND　　　RV

Reference: **On the Pacific Ocean; map C1, grid a6.**

Campsites, facilities: There are eight sites for tents and 24 sites for trailers or RVs of any length. Electricity, piped water, sewer hookups and picnic tables are provided. Flush toilets, showers, a store, a laundromat, bottled gas and ice are available. A cafe is located within one mile. Pets and motorbikes are permitted. Boat docks, launching facilities and rentals are nearby.

Reservations, fee: Reservations accepted; $12-$17 fee per night. Open all year.

Who to contact: Phone (503) 738-6855 or (800) 730-6855 or write to 4412 Highway 101 North, Gearhart, OR 97138.

Location: From Interstate 5 at Portland, turn west on US 26 and drive 73 miles. Turn north on US 101 and drive about six miles to Gearhart. Continue one mile north on US 101 to the campground entrance on the left.

Trip note: This private campground is set along the ocean, about three miles north of Seaside (see the trip notes for Pine Cove RV Park and Venice RV Park). Nearby recreation options include an 18-hole golf course, hiking trails and a riding stable.

5.　　　　　PINE COVE RV PARK　　　RV

Reference: **Near the Pacific Ocean; map C1, grid b6.**

Campsites, facilities: There are 25 sites for trailers or RVs of any length. No tent camping. Electricity, piped water and sewer hookups are provided. Flush toilets, showers, a laundromat and firewood are available. A store, a cafe and ice are located within one mile. Leashed pets are permitted.

Reservations, fee: Reservations accepted; $15 fee per night. Open all year.

Who to contact: Phone (503) 738-5243 or write to 2481 Highway 101 North,

Seaside, OR 97138.

Location: From Interstate 5 at Portland, turn west on US 26 and drive 73 miles to the junction with US 101, then turn north on US 101 and drive four miles to Seaside. Continue north about one mile. The park is located at 2481 Highway 101 North.

Trip note: This park and motel is set among the pines about a mile from Seaside. It is a good spot for fishing, both in the ocean and in the two rivers that run through town, where you can fish from the bridges. Crabbing in the ocean is good on calm spring days. Nearby recreation options include an 18-hole golf course and hiking trails. See the trip note for Venice RV Park for more information about Seaside.

---

6. VENICE RV PARK   RV

Reference: **On Neawanna River; map C1, grid b6.**

Campsites, facilities: There are 26 drive-through sites for trailers or RVs of any length. Electricity, piped water, sewer hookups and picnic tables are provided. Flush toilets, showers, a laundromat and ice are available. A store and a cafe are located within one mile. Leashed pets are permitted.

Reservations, fee: Reservations accepted; $16-$18 fee per night. Open all year.

Who to contact: Phone (503) 738-8851 or write to 1032 24th Avenue, Seaside, OR 97138.

Location: From Interstate 5 at Portland, turn west on US 26 and drive 73 miles to the junction with US 101, then turn north on US 101 and drive four miles to Seaside. Drive to the north end of town, turn west on 24th Avenue and drive to the campground at 1032 24th Avenue.

Trip note: This park is set along the Neawanna River, one of two rivers that run through Seaside. The park is less than a mile from the beach. Seaside offers beautiful ocean beaches for fishing and surfing, moped and bike rentals, shops and a theater. The city provides swings and volleyball nets on the beach. An 18-hole golf course is available nearby.

---

7. SAM'S RESORT   RV

Reference: **On Necanicum River; map C1, grid b6.**

Campsites, facilities: There are 25 tent sites and 33 sites for trailers or RVs of any length (14 drive-through). Electricity, piped water, sewer hookups and picnic tables are provided. Flush toilets, showers, firewood, a laundromat and ice are available. Bottled gas, sanitary services, a store and a cafe are located within one mile. Pets and motorbikes are permitted. Boat launching facilities are nearby.

Reservations, fee: Reservations accepted; $13-$19 fee per night. A 20 percent discount is offered in the winter. Open all year.

Who to contact: Phone (503) 738-6779 or write to Hamlet Route, Box 255, Seaside, OR 97138.

Location: From Interstate 5 at Portland, turn west on US 26 and drive 73 miles to the junction with US 101, then turn north on US 101 and drive just under one mile to the park.

Trip note: This park is set along the shore of the Necanicum River, which attracts a steelhead run every winter. The river is low during the summer but still provides many pools for swimming. Boating is allowed on the river. There is a small scenic lake in the campground that attracts wildlife. No swimming or boating is allowed on the campground lake, but it is stocked with trout, a practice that began in 1988. Nearby recreation options include an 18-hole golf course and a riding stable.

---

8.   SEA RANCH RESORT   **RV**

Reference: **Near the Pacific Ocean; map C1, grid b6.**

Campsites, facilities: There are 71 sites for tents, trailers and RVs. Restrooms, showers, a sanitary dump and a public phone are available.

Reservations, fees: Reservations recommended; $14-$18 fee per night. Open all year.

Who to contact: Phone the resort at (503) 436-2815 or write to P.O. Box 214, Cannon Beach, OR 97110.

Location: From Interstate 5 at Portland, turn west on US 26 and drive 73 miles to the junction with US 101, then turn south and drive three miles to the Cannon Beach exit. The resort is south three-tenths of a mile on the left.

Trip note: This resort is in a wooded setting with nearby access to the beach. Activities at the camp include stream fishing, swimming and hunting. The beach and the town of Cannon Beach are within walking distance of the resort. There is horseback riding available on the beach.

---

9.   RV RESORT AT CANNON BEACH   **RV**

Reference: **Near Ecola State Park; map C1, grid b6.**

Campsites, facilities: There are 100 sites (11 drive-through) for trailers or RVs of any length. Electricity, piped water, sewer hookups and picnic tables are provided. Flush toilets, bottled gas, showers, firewood, a recreation hall, a store, a cafe, a laundromat, ice, a playground and a swimming pool are available. Leashed pets are permitted.

Reservations, fee: Reservations accepted; $22-$33 fee per night; American Express, MasterCard, Discover and Visa accepted. Open all year.

Who to contact: Phone (503) 436-2231 or write to P.O. Box 219, Cannon Beach, OR 97110.

Location: From Interstate 5 at Portland, turn west on US 26 and drive 73 miles to the junction with US 101, then turn south on US 101 and drive four miles to the Cannon Beach exit at milepost 29.5. Turn east and drive 200 feet to the campground.

Trip note: This private resort is located about seven blocks from one of the nicest beaches in the region. From the town of Cannon Beach you can walk for miles in either direction. Ecola State Park is just two miles north. Nearby recreation options include marked bike trails, a riding stable and tennis courts.

---

10.   SADDLE MOUNTAIN STATE PARK

Reference: **On Saddle Mountain; map C1, grid b7.**

Campsites, facilities: There are nine primitive tent sites. Picnic tables and fire grills are provided. Flush toilets and firewood are available. Leashed pets are permitted.

Reservations, fee: No reservations; $10 fee per night. Open mid-April to late October.

Who to contact: Phone (503) 861-1671 or (800) 452-5687 or write to Saddle Mountain State Park, Cannon Beach, OR 97110.

Location: From Portland, turn west on US 26 and drive about 63 miles to

Necanicum Junction. Turn north on the park entrance road and continue eight miles.

Trip note: This is a good alternative to the many beachfront parks to the south. A 2.5-mile trail climbs to the top of Saddle Mountain, a great lookout on clear days. This park is a real find for the naturalist interested in rare and unusual varieties of plants, many of which have established themselves along the slopes of this isolated mountain.

---

11.   NEHALEM BAY STATE PARK   RV

Reference: **On the Pacific Ocean; map C1, grid c5.**

Campsites, facilities: There are 291 sites for trailers or RVs of any length and a special camping area for hikers and bicyclists. Electricity, piped water, picnic tables and fire grills are provided. Flush toilets, a sanitary disposal station, showers and firewood are available. Some facilities are **wheelchair accessible**. Leashed pets are permitted. Boat launching facilities are located nearby on Nehalem Bay.

Reservations, fee: Contact Reservations Northwest at (800) 452-5687 ($6 reservation fee); $17 fee per night; $4 for hikers/bikers. Open year-round.

Who to contact: Phone (503) 368-5943 or write to 8300-R Third Street Necarney, Nehalem, OR 97131.

Location: From Portland, turn west on US 26 and drive 73 miles, then turn south on US 101 and drive 21 miles to Nehalem, then head west on the entrance road for 1.5 miles to the park.

Trip note: This state park is located on a sandy point that separates the Pacific Ocean and Nehalem Bay. It offers six miles of beach frontage. The Oregon Coast Trail passes through the park. A horse camp with corrals and a 7.5-mile equestrian trail are available. There is also a 1.5-mile bike trail. An airport is adjacent to the park.

---

12.   JETTY FISHERY RV PARK   RV

Reference: **On Nehalem Bay; map C1, grid c5.**

Campsites, facilities: There are 10 tent sites and 30 drive-through sites for trailers or RVs of any length. Electricity, piped water and picnic tables are provided. Flush toilets, bottled gas, firewood, a store, showers, a cafe and ice are available. Leashed pets are permitted. Boat docks, launching facilities and rentals are available.

Reservations, fee: Reservations accepted; $17 fee per night; MasterCard and Visa accepted. Open all year.

Who to contact: Phone (503) 368-5746 or write to 27550 Highway 101 North, Rockaway, OR 97136.

Location: From Interstate 5 at Portland, turn west on US 26 and drive 73 miles to the junction with US 101, then turn south on US 101 and drive 27 miles to the park entrance.

Trip note: This small park is located at the base of a mile-long jetty, which extends out into Nehalem Bay and the ocean. Fishing and crabbing are good off the jetty, but sometimes the snags bite good, too. There is a small beach on the bay side of the jetty, a popular spot for kids. For boaters, a full-service marina is nearby.

13. SHOREWOOD TRAVEL TRAILER VILLAGE 🚐

Reference: **On the Pacific Ocean; map C1, grid c5.**

Campsites, facilities: There are 12 sites for trailers or RVs of any length. No tents are allowed. Electricity, piped water, and picnic tables are provided. Flush toilets, sanitary services, cable TV, showers, firewood, a laundromat, ice and a playground are available. A store and a cafe are located within one mile. Leashed pets are permitted.

Reservations, fee: Reservations accepted; $17-$19 fee per night. Open all year.

Who to contact: Phone (503) 355-2278 or write to 17600 Ocean Boulevard, Rockaway Beach, OR 97136.

Location: From Interstate 5 at Portland, turn west on US 26 and drive 73 miles to the junction with US 101, then turn south on US 101 and drive 30 miles to the town of Rockaway Beach. Drive one mile south of town to the Shorewood sign, then turn west and drive three blocks to the park.

Trip note: This park is set along a beach that is ideal for surf fishing for perch or beachcombing during low tides. The 1.5-mile hike to Tillamook Bay jetty is a good side trip. An 18-hole golf course is located a short drive from the park.

14. OSWALD WEST STATE PARK

Reference: **On the Pacific Ocean, walk-in only; map C1, grid c5.**

Campsites, facilities: There are 36 primitive walk-in tent sites. Wheelbarrows are available for campers to transport their supplies. Picnic tables and fire grills are provided. Piped water, flush toilets and firewood are available. Leashed pets are permitted.

Reservations, fee: No reservations; $13 fee per night. Open mid-March to late October.

Who to contact: Phone (800) 452-5687 or (503) 368-5943 or write to 8300-R Third Street Necarney, Nehalem, OR 97130.

Location: From Portland, turn west on US 26 and drive 73 miles, then turn south on US 101 and travel four miles to Cannon Beach. Continue 10 miles south on US 101 to the parking area. Walk one-quarter mile to the campground.

Trip note: This state park is set along a dramatic section of the Oregon coast with rugged cliffs rising high above the ocean. This is not beach-walking territory, but the park does offer 15 miles of hiking trails, including the Oregon Coast Trail and a trail to the point of Cape Falcon, where campers can enjoy scenic views. A small beach and several fishing streams are nearby. The park is in a beautiful rain forest setting, with gigantic spruce and cedar trees.

15. BARVIEW JETTY COUNTY PARK 🚐

Reference: **Near Garibaldi; map C1, grid d5.**

Campsites, facilities: There are 200 tent sites and 40 drive-through sites for trailers or RVs of any length. Electricity, piped water, sewer hookups and picnic tables are provided. Flush toilets, sanitary services, showers and a playground are available. Bottled gas, a store, a cafe and ice are located within one mile. Leashed pets are permitted.

Reservations, fee: Reservations accepted; $10-$12 fee per night. Open all year.

Who to contact: Phone (503) 322-3477 or write to P.O. Box 633, Garibaldi, OR 97118.

Location: From Interstate 5 at Portland, turn west on US 26 and drive 73 miles to the junction with US 101, then turn south on US 101 and drive approximately 32 miles to Cedar Street (two miles north of Garibaldi). Turn west and drive one-quarter mile to campground.

Trip note: This park is near the beach, yet set in a wooded area. The sites are set on grassy hills. Nearby recreation options include an 18-hole golf course, hiking trails, bike trails and a full-service marina.

16. HAPPY CAMP RESORT RV

Reference: On Netarts Bay; map C1, grid d5.

Campsites, facilities: There are 42 sites for trailers or RVs of any length. Electricity, piped water and picnic tables are provided. Flush toilets, sanitary services, showers, sewer hookups, cable TV are available. A store, a cafe, a laundromat, bottled gas, ice and firewood are available within one mile. Leashed pets are permitted. Boat docks, launching facilities and rentals are nearby.

Reservations, fee: Reservations accepted; $20 fee per night. Open all year.

Who to contact: Phone (503) 842-4012 or write to P.O. Box 82, Netarts, OR 97143.

Location: From Portland, turn west on Highway 26 and drive 24 miles. Turn west on Highway 6 and drive 44 miles to Tillamook. Turn west on Netart Highway and drive seven miles to the campground entrance.

Trip note: Netarts Bay offers sheltered waters, perfect for small boaters to take advantage of the excellent crabbing. Shoreliners can discover good crabbing and fair perch fishing. Crabbing gear, boat rentals and crab cooking gear are available. The camp is set along the shore of Netarts Bay, a short drive from Cape Lookout State Park, Cape Meares State Park and the national wildlife refuge.

17. BIG SPRUCE TRAILER PARK RV

Reference: On Netarts Bay; map C1, grid d5.

Campsites, facilities: There are 23 sites for trailers or RVs of any length (seven drive through). Electricity, piped water, sewer hookups and picnic tables are provided. Flush toilets, bottled gas, cable TV, showers and a laundromat are available. A store, a cafe and ice are located within one mile. Leashed pets are permitted. Boat docks and launching facilities are nearby.

Reservations, fee: Reservations accepted; $17 fee per night. Open all year.

Who to contact: Phone (503) 842-7443 or write to 4850 Netarts Highway West, Tillamook, OR 97141.

Location: From Portland, turn west on Highway 26 and drive 24 miles. Turn west on Highway 6 and drive 44 miles to Tillamook. From Tillamook, drive 6.5 miles west on Netarts Highway to the campground.

Trip note: This trailer park is one block from the boat launch on Netarts Bay. See the trip note for Happy Camp Resort for details on the fishing here.

18. BAY SHORE RV PARK RV

Reference: On Netarts Bay; map C1, grid d5.

Campsites, facilities: There are 53 sites for trailers or RVs of any length (11 drive-through). Electricity, piped water, sewer hookups and picnic tables are provided. Flush toilets, bottled gas, showers, firewood, a recreation hall, a laundromat and ice are available. A store and a cafe are located within one mile.

Leashed pets are permitted. Boat docks, launching facilities and rentals are nearby.

Reservations, fee: Reservations accepted; $17 fee per night; MasterCard and Visa accepted. Open all year.

Who to contact: Phone (503) 842-7774 or write to P.O. Box 218, Netarts, OR 97413.

Location: From Portland, turn west on Highway 26 and drive 24 miles. Turn west on Highway 6 and drive for 44 miles to Tillamook. Turn west on Netarts Highway and drive six miles to the park entrance.

Trip note: This is one of three camps set on the east shore of Netarts Bay. See the trip note for Happy Camp Resort for more information about the fishing here.

---

19.   BIAK-BY-THE-SEA TRAILER COURT   RV

Reference: On Tillamook Bay; map C1, grid d5.

Campsites, facilities: There are 45 drive-through sites for trailers or RVs of any length. Electricity, piped water, sewer hookups, cable TV are provided. Flush toilets, showers and a laundromat are available. Bottled gas, a store, a cafe and ice are located within one mile. Pets and motorbikes are permitted. Boat docks, launching facilities and rentals are nearby.

Reservations, fee: Reservations accepted; $16 fee per night. Open all year.

Who to contact: Phone (503) 322-0111 or write to P.O. Box 916, Garibaldi, OR 97118.

Location: From Portland, turn west on Highway 26 and drive 24 miles. Turn west on Highway 6 and drive 44 miles to Tillamook. Turn north on US 101 and drive 10 miles. Turn left on 10th Street and drive to the park on the left (just over the tracks).

Trip note: This park is set along the shore of Tillamook Bay. The deep sea fishing, crabbing, clamming, surf fishing, scuba diving and beachcombing make it a prime retreat. The nearby town of Tillamook offers a cheese factory and a historical museum. A good side trip is Cape Meares State Park, where you can hike through the national wildlife preserve and see where the seabirds nest along the cliffs.

---

20.   PACIFIC CAMPGROUND   RV

Reference: On Tillamook Bay; map C1, grid d5.

Campsites, facilities: There are 20 tent sites and 29 drive-through sites for trailers or RVs of any length. Electricity, piped water, sewer hookups and picnic tables are provided. Flush toilets, cable TV, showers, firewood and ice are available. A store and a cafe are located within one mile. Leashed pets and motorbikes are permitted.

Reservations, fee: Reservations accepted; $9-$17 fee per night for two people; $1 each additional person. Open all year.

Who to contact: Phone (503) 842-5201 or write to 1950 Suppress Road North, Tillamook, OR 97141.

Location: From Portland, turn west on Highway 26 and drive 24 miles. Turn west on Highway 6 and drive for 44 miles to Tillamook. Turn north on US 101 and drive 2.5 miles. The campground entrance is across from the Tillamook Cheese Factory.

Trip note: This campground is set at the southern end of Tillamook Bay, not far from the Wilson River. The Tillamook Cheese Factory is just south of the park (they offer mouth-watering tours), and an 18-hole golf course is also nearby. See the trip note for Biak-By-The-Sea Trailer Court for more information about the area.

21.   PLEASANT VALLEY RV PARK   RV

Reference: **On Tillamook River; map C1, grid d6.**

Campsites, facilities: There are 12 tent sites and 71 sites for trailers or RVs of any length. There is also one cabin. Piped water and picnic tables are provided. Flush toilets, bottled gas, sanitary services, showers, firewood, a recreation hall, electricity, sewer hookups, cable TV, a store, a Mexican restaurant in summer, a laundromat, ice and a playground are available. Leashed pets are permitted. Boat launching facilities are available nearby.

Reservations, fee: Reservations accepted; $14-$19.50 fee per night; $25 cabin fee. MasterCard and Visa accepted. Open all year.

Who to contact: Phone (503) 842-4779 or write to 11880 Highway 101 South, Tillamook, OR 97141.

Location: From Portland, turn west on Highway 26 and drive 24 miles. Turn west on Highway 6 and drive 44 miles to Tillamook. Turn south on Highway 101 and drive six miles to the campground entrance on the right.

Trip note: This campground is set along the Tillamook River. It is very clean, with many recreation options in the immediate area.

22.   CAPE LOOKOUT STATE PARK   RV

Reference: **Near Netarts Bay; map C1, grid e5.**

Campsites, facilities: There are 197 tent sites, 53 sites with full hookups for trailers or RVs up to 60 feet long, and a special camping area for hikers and bicyclists. Picnic tables and fire grills are provided. Flush toilets, sanitary services, showers and firewood are available. A restaurant is located within one mile. Some facilities are **wheelchair accessible**. Leashed pets are permitted.

Reservations, fee: Contact Reservations Northwest at (800) 452-5687 ($6 reservation fee); $15-$18 fee per night; $4 for hikers/bikers. Open all year.

Who to contact: Phone (503) 842-4981 or or (800) 452-5687 write to 13000 Whiskey Creek Road West, Tillamook, OR 97141.

Location: From Portland, turn west on Highway 26 and drive 24 miles. Turn west on Highway 6 for 44 miles to Tillamook. Turn southwest on Netarts Road and drive 11 miles to the park entrance.

Trip note: This unique park offers an assortment of walks. One trail leads out along a ridge to headlands high above the ocean. Another walk will take you out through a variety of estuarine habitats along the five-mile sand spit that extends between the ocean and Netarts Bay. This is a paradise for birdwatchers, with 154 species to view. Fishing is another option here.

23.   WEBB PARK   RV

Reference: **Near Pacific Ocean; map C1, grid e5.**

Campsites, facilities: There are 30 sites for tents, trailers or RVs. Toilets, piped water, a sanitary dump and a boat ramp are provided. Leashed pets are permitted.

Reservations, fee: No reservations; $8 fee per night. Open all year.

Who to contact: Phone the park at (503) 322-3477.

Location: From Portland, turn west on Highway 26 and drive 24 miles. Turn west on Highway 6 and drive 44 miles to Tillamook. Turn south on Highway 101 and drive approximately 25 miles to the Pacific City exit. From Pacific City, turn north on Highway 30 and drive one mile to Cape Kiwanda. The camp is located on the right.

Trip note: This public campground is an excellent alternative to the more crowded commercial RV parks off US 101. It is not as developed, but offers a quiet, private setting and access to the ocean. Fishing and swimming are among your options here.

---

24. CAPE KIWANDA RV PARK   🚐

Reference: **On the Pacific Ocean; map C1, grid e5.**

Campsites, facilities: There are 12 tent sites and 130 sites for trailers or RVs of any length. Electricity, piped water, sewer hookups and picnic tables are provided. Flush toilets, sanitary services, showers, firewood, a recreation hall, a laundromat and a playground are available. Bottled gas, a store, a cafe and ice are located within one mile. Pets and motorbikes are permitted. Boat docks, launching facilities and rentals are nearby.

Reservations, fee: Reservations accepted; $9-$14.50 fee per night. Open all year.

Who to contact: Phone (503) 965-6230 or write to P.O. Box 129, Pacific City, OR 97135.

Location: From Portland, turn west on Highway 26 and drive 24 miles. Turn west on Highway 6 and drive 44 miles to Tillamook. Turn south on US 101 and drive 25 miles to Pacific City. Drive three miles west on Pacific City Loop Road, then cross the bridge and travel one mile north and you'll see the park entrance.

Trip note: This park is set along the ocean, a short distance from Cape Kiwanda State Park, which is open for day-use only. There is a boat launch there and hiking trails that lead out to the cape. A recreation option is four miles south at Nestucca Spit, where there is another day-use park. The point extends about three miles and is a good spot for birdwatching.

---

25. RAINES RESORT AND RV PARK   🚐

Reference: **On Nestucca River; map C1, grid e5.**

Campsites, facilities: There are 12 sites for trailers or RVs of any length. Electricity, piped water, sewer hookups and picnic tables are provided. Flush toilets, sanitary services, showers, a store and a laundromat are available. Bottled gas, a cafe and ice are located within one mile. Boat docks, launching facilities and rentals are nearby.

Reservations, fee: Reservations accepted; $12-$15 fee per night. Open all year.

Who to contact: Phone (503) 965-6371 or write to P.O. Box 777, Pacific City, OR 97135.

Location: From Portland, turn west on Highway 26 and drive 24 miles. Turn west on Highway 6 for 44 miles to Tillamook. Turn south on US 101 and drive 25 miles to Pacific City. Turn north on Brooten Road and drive 1.5 miles to Woods Bridge and drive one block west to the park.

Trip note: This campground is set along the Nestucca River, which attracts a king salmon run from late August through Thanksgiving. Nearby recreation options include a full-service marina. Note: Tent campers and owners of small RVs may want to consider the free primitive BLM campgrounds up the river. See trip notes for Alder Glen, Elk Bend, Fan Creek and Dovre (camp numbers 30 to 33).

26. SAND BEACH 🚐

Reference: **In Siuslaw National Forest; map C1, grid e5.**

Campsites, facilities: There are 101 sites for tents, trailers or RVs up to 30 feet long. (If filled, the east and west parking lots provide additional sites for trailers or RVs.) Picnic tables and fire pits are provided. Piped water and flush toilets are available. Leashed pets are permitted.

Reservations, fee: Reserve some sites by calling (800) 280-CAMP ($7.50 reservation fee); $10 fee per night. Open mid-May to early September.

Who to contact: Phone at (503) 392-3161 or write to Siuslaw National Forest, Hebo Ranger District, Hebo, OR 97122.

Location: On US 101 southwest of Portland, drive to the little town of Pacific City. At the blinking red light, turn west and drive over the bridge. Make a sharp right, pass Cape Kiwanda and drive about nine miles to the Sand Lake store. Turn left on Gallaway Road and drive to the campground at the end of the road.

Trip note: This area is known for its large sand dunes, which are open to off-road vehicles. The campground is set along the shore of Sand Lake, which is actually more like an estuary since the ocean is just around the bend. This is the only coastal Forest Service campground for many miles, and it's quite popular. If you're planning a trip for midsummer, be sure to reserve far in advance. Entry permits are required for three-day weekends in summer.

27. CAMPER COVE PARK 🚐

Reference: **On Beaver Creek; map C1, grid e6.**

Campsites, facilities: There are two tent sites and 15 drive-through sites for trailers or RVs up to 31 feet long. Electricity, piped water, sewer hookups and picnic tables are provided. Flush toilets, bottled gas, sanitary services, showers, firewood, a recreation hall, a laundromat and ice are available. Leashed pets are permitted.

Reservations, fee: Reservations accepted; $9.50-$12.50 fee per night. Open year-round.

Who to contact: Phone (503) 398-5334 or write to P.O. Box 42, Beaver, OR 97108.

Location: From Portland, turn west on Highway 26 and drive 24 miles. Turn west on Highway 6 and drive 44 miles to Tillamook. Turn south on US 101 and drive 11.5 miles to the park entrance (2.5 miles north of Beaver).

Trip note: This small, wooded campground is set along Beaver Creek, just far enough off the highway to provide quiet. The park can be used as a base camp for fishermen, with steelhead and salmon fishing in season in the nearby Nestucca River. It gets crowded here, especially in the summer months, so be sure to make a reservation whenever possible.

28. HEBO LAKE 🚐

Reference: **On Hebo Lake in Siuslaw National Forest; map C1, grid e6.**

Campsites, facilities: There are 16 sites for tents, trailers or RVs up to 18 feet long. Picnic tables and fire pits are provided. Piped water and vault toilets are available. Leashed pets are permitted. Boats without motors are permitted on the lake.

Reservations, fee: No reservations; $6 fee per night. Open May to mid-October.

Who to contact: Phone the Siuslaw National Forest at (503) 392-3161 or write to

Hebo Ranger District, Hebo, OR 97122.

Location: On US 101 southwest of Portland, drive to the town of Hebo. Turn east on Highway 22 and drive one-quarter mile to Forest Service Road 14. Turn left (east) and drive for five miles to the campground.

Trip note: This Forest Service campground is set along the shore of Hebo Lake. This is a secluded campground where the campsites are nestled under trees. The trailhead for the eight-mile-long Pioneer-Indian Trail is located in the campground. The trail around the lake is barrier-free.

29.　　　　ROCKY BEND

Reference: **On Nestucca River in Siuslaw National Forest; map C1 grid e7.**

Campsites, facilities: There are six tent sites. **No piped water** is available. Picnic tables and fire pits are provided. Vault toilets are available. Leashed pets are permitted. No garbage service is provided; you must pack it out.

Reservations, fee: No reservations; no fee. Open all year.

Who to contact: Phone the Siuslaw National Forest at (503) 392-3161 or write to Hebo Ranger District, Hebo, OR 97122.

Location: On US 101 southwest of Portland, drive to the tiny town of Beaver. Turn east on Blaine Road (keep right; Blaine Road turns into Nestucca Access Road) and drive 15.5 miles to the campground.

Trip note: This campground is set along the Nestucca River, a little-known, secluded spot that provides guaranteed peace and quiet. There isn't much in the way of recreational activities out here, but hiking, fishing, clamming and swimming are available along the coast, a relatively short drive away.

30.　　　　ALDER GLEN　　　　**RV**

Reference: **On Nestucca River; map C1, grid e8.**

Campsites, facilities: There are 11 sites for tents, trailers or RVs up to 30 feet. Fire grills, vault toilets and hand-pumped water are provided. Leashed pets are permitted.

Reservations, fee: No reservations; $6 fee per night; 14-day limit. Open all year with limited winter facilities.

Who to contact: Phone the Bureau of Land Management at (503) 842-7546 or write to 4610 Third Street, Tillamook, OR 97141.

Location: On US 101 southwest of Portland, drive to the tiny town of Beaver. Turn east on Blaine Road (keep right; Blaine Road turns into Nestucca Access Road) and drive 18 miles to the campground.

Trip note: Set in a wooded area along the beautiful Nestucca River, this campground is one of five on the scenic Nestucca River Backcountry Byway. This area is exceptionally lovely, with a wide variety of wildflowers and lush vegetation. Fishing is an option here, too.

31.　　　　ELK BEND

Reference: **On Nestucca River; map C1, grid e8.**

Campsites, facilities: There are three walk-in tent sites. Picnic tables, fire grills, pit toilets and hand-pumped water are provided. Leashed pets are permitted.

Reservations, fee: No reservations; no fee; 14-day limit. Open all year with limited winter facilities.

Who to contact: Phone the Bureau of Land Management at (503) 842-7546 or write to 4610 Third Street, Tillamook, OR 97141.

Location: On US 101 southwest of Portland, drive to the tiny town of Beaver. Turn east on Blaine Road (keep right; Blaine Road turns into Nestucca Access Road) and drive 21 miles. Park in the lot and walk into the campground.

Trip note: This camp is set just a few miles up the road from Alder Glen camp. It offers the same facilities and attractions, but gets less use, presumably because campers must walk into it instead of driving (the sites are actually just below the parking lot). It doubles as a day-use picnic area. Insider tip: The best campsite is set apart from the others—it is located about 100 yards down the river and is private and secluded.

---

32.   FAN CREEK   RV.

Reference: **On Nestucca River; map C1, grid e9.**

Campsites, facilities: There are 11 sites for tents, trailers or RVs up to 16 feet. Fire grills, pit toilets and hand-pumped water are provided. Leashed pets are permitted.

Reservations, fee: No reservations; $6 fee per night; 14-day limit. Open all year with limited winter facilities.

Who to contact: Phone the Bureau of Land Management at (503) 842-7546 or write to 4610 Third Street, Tillamook, OR 97141.

Location: On US 101 southwest of Portland, drive to the tiny town of Beaver. Turn east on Blaine Road (keep right; Blaine Road turns into Nestucca Access Road) and drive 24 miles to the campground.

Trip note: The largest in the series of primitive camps along the Nestucca River, this site is popular with anglers. When fishing season comes around, the pools and falls along the Nestucca are choice spots for Coho salmon, Chinook salmon, steelhead and trout. It is set in the trees with easy river access.

---

33.   DOVRE   RV.

Reference: **On Nestucca River; map C1, grid e9.**

Campsites, facilities: There are six tent sites and four sites for tents, trailers or RVs up to 30 feet. Fire grills, vault toilets and hand-pumped water are provided. Leashed pets are permitted.

Reservations, fee: No reservations; $6 fee per night; 14-day limit. Open all year with limited winter facilities.

Who to contact: Phone the Bureau of Land Management at (503) 842-7546 or write to 4610 Third Street, Tillamook, OR 97141.

Location: On US 101 southwest of Portland, drive to the tiny town of Beaver. Turn east on Blaine Road (keep right; Blaine Road turns into Nestucca Access Road) and drive 26.5 miles to the campground.

Trip note: This is the last campground you'll come across on the Nestucca River Scenic Backcountry Byway. This site is set amidst tall Douglas fir trees, wildflowers and lush ground vegetation. In late summer and fall, visitors are treated to a show of brilliant red vine maple. This camp provides easy river access and is used heavily by anglers in the spring.

---

34.   TREE N' SEA TRAILER PARK   RV.

Reference: **On the Pacific Ocean; map C1, grid f4.**

Campsites, facilities: There are seven sites for trailers or RVs of any length. Electricity, piped water and sewer hookups are provided. Flush toilets and showers are available. A store, a cafe and a laundromat are available within one mile. Leashed pets are permitted.

Reservations, fee: Reservations recommended; $22 fee per night. Open all year.

Who to contact: Phone (503) 996-3801 or write to 1015 Southwest 51st Street, Lincoln City, OR 97367.

Location: From Portland, turn south on Highway 99 West and drive southwest to Highway 18. Turn west on Highway 18 and drive 47 miles to US 101. Turn south and drive five miles to Lincoln City. Turn west onto Southwest 51st Street and drive one block to the park.

Trip note: This park is set along the ocean in Lincoln City. It is a pleasant motor home park that makes an adequate layover spot. See the trip notes for KOA Lincoln City and Devil's Lake State Park for recreation options.

---

35.   KOA LINCOLN CITY

Reference: **On the Pacific Ocean; map C1, grid f5.**

Campsites, facilities: There are 18 tent sites and 55 sites for trailers or RVs of any length (13 are drive-through). Picnic tables are provided. Flush toilets, bottled gas, sanitary services, showers, firewood, a recreation hall, a store, a cafe, a laundromat, ice and a playground are available. Electricity, piped water, sewer, and cable TV hookups are located for an extra fee. Leashed pets and motorbikes are permitted. Boat launching facilities are nearby.

Reservations, fee: Reservations accepted; $17-$21 fee per night; MasterCard and Visa accepted. Open all year.

Who to contact: Phone (503) 994-2961 or write to 5298 NE Park Lane, Otis, OR 97368.

Location: From Portland, turn south on Highway 99W and drive southwest to Highway 18. Turn west on Highway 18 and drive 47 miles. Turn south on US 101 and drive five miles to Lincoln City. From Lincoln City, drive another 1.2 miles north on US 101. Turn east on East Devil's Lake Road and drive one mile to the park.

Trip note: This area offers opportunity for beachcombing, tidepooling and fishing along a seven-mile stretch of beach. Two stops to consider if you're going into Lincoln City for supplies: the Premier Market, which has smoked salmon, and the Colonial Bakery, which carries the best pastries west of Paris. Nearby recreation options include an 18-hole golf course and tennis courts.

---

36.   LEE'S EVERGREEN PARK

Reference: **On Salmon River; map C1, grid f5.**

Campsites, facilities: There are 25 sites for tents, trailers and RVs. Restrooms, showers, a sanitary dump, a public phone, a laundromat, limited groceries, ice, RV supplies and LP gas are available. Recreational facilities include a recreation hall and horseshoes. Small pets are permitted on leashes.

Reservations, fee: No reservations; $12-$14.50 fee per night. Open all year.

Who to contact: Phone (503) 994-3116 or write to 6029 Salmon River Highway, Otis, OR 97368.

Location: From Salem, drive west on Highway 22 for 25 miles to Highway 18. Drive west on Highway 18 for about 25 miles toward Otis. Turn right at milepost 6. The camp is located on the right.

Trip note: This wooded camp is set on the Salmon River, with opportunities for trout fishing. Nearby side trip options include H. B. Van Ouzer Forest Wayside and Devil's Lake State Park. Beach access is just a short drive west.

37. CASTLE ROCK

Reference: **On Three Rivers in Siuslaw National Forest; map C1 grid f6.**

Campsites, facilities: There are four tent sites. Piped water, picnic tables and vault toilets are provided. Leashed pets are permitted.

Reservations, fee: No reservations; no fee. Open all year.

Who to contact: Phone the Siuslaw National Forest at (503) 392-3161 or write to Hebo Ranger District, Hebo, OR 97122.

Location: On US 101 southwest of Portland, drive to the tiny town of Hebo. Turn east on Highway 22 and drive five miles to the campground.

Trip note: This tiny spot provides an alternative for tent campers to the large beachfront RV parks popular on the Oregon coast. It is set along Three Rivers. Fishing can be good here. Though primitive, this is a well-used camp and can fill up quickly.

38. MULKEY RV PARK   RV

Reference: **Near South Yamhill River; map C1, grid f9.**

Campsites, facilities: There are 70 sites for tents, trailers or RVs of any length. Electricity, piped water, sewer hookups and picnic tables are provided. Flush toilets, showers, a store, bottled gas and a laundromat are available. Pets and motorbikes are permitted.

Reservations, fee: Reservations recommended; $14-$18 fee per night. Open all year.

Who to contact: Phone (503) 472-2475 or write to 14325 SW Highway 18, McMinnville, OR 97128.

Location: From Portland, turn south on Highway 99 and drive about 31 miles to McMinnville. Take Highway 18 southwest for 3.5 miles to the park entrance.

Trip note: If you are in the area and looking for a camping spot, you had best stop here—there are no other campgrounds within 30 miles. This wooded park is set near the South Yamhill River. Nearby recreation options include an 18-hole golf course, tennis courts and the Western Deer Park and Arboretum, which has a playground.

39. SEA AND SAND RV PARK   RV

Reference: **Near Siletz Bay; map C1, grid g4.**

Campsites, facilities: There are 85 sites for trailers or RVs up to 35 feet long. Electricity, piped water, sewer hookups and picnic tables are provided. Flush toilets, showers, sanitary services, firewood and a laundromat are available. A store, a cafe and ice are located within one mile. Leashed pets are permitted.

Reservations, fee: Reservations accepted; $15-$20 fee per night. Open all year.

Who to contact: Phone (503) 764-2313 or write to 4985 Highway 101 North, Depoe Bay, OR 97341.

Location: From Portland, turn south on Highway 99 West and drive southwest to Highway 18. Turn west on Highway 18 and drive 47 miles to US 101. Turn south and drive five miles to Lincoln City. Drive another nine miles south to the campground entrance.

Trip note: Beachcombing for fossils and agates is popular at this park, set on the ocean near Gleneden Beach on Siletz Bay. The sites have ocean views and pleasant terraces. The Siletz River and numerous small creeks are in the area.

40.   HOLIDAY RV PARK & SURF LODGE   RV

Reference: **Near Depoe Bay State Park; map C1, grid g4.**

Campsites, facilities: There are 110 sites for trailers or RVs of any length. Electricity, piped water, sewer hookups and picnic tables are provided. Flush toilets, bottled gas, showers, a recreation hall, a store, a laundromat, ice, a playground and swimming pool are available. Pets are permitted.

Reservations, fee: Reservations accepted; $15-$28 fee per night. MasterCard, Discover and Visa accepted. Open all year.

Who to contact: Phone (503) 765-2302 or write to P.O. Box 9, Depoe Bay, OR 97341.

Location: From Portland, turn south on Highway 99 West and drive southwest to Highway 18. Turn west on Highway 18 and drive 47 miles to US 101. Turn south and drive five miles to Lincoln City. Drive 13 miles south. This park is located on US 101 at the north edge of the town of Depoe Bay.

Trip note: Set on rock cliffs overlooking the ocean, this park has everything an ocean-camper could want. Prime oceanfront sites are available, and this is an excellent spot for whale watching (best in August, when they migrate north, and in January and February, when they return south). This is a scenic stretch of coastline and some of the prime side trips include Depoe Bay State Park and Depoe Creek. Nearby recreation options include an 18-hole golf course, tennis courts and a public aquarium.

---

41.   BEVERLY BEACH STATE PARK   RV

Reference: **On the Pacific Ocean; map C1, grid g4.**

Campsites, facilities: There are 152 tent sites, 127 sites with full or partial hookups for trailers or RVs of any length and a special camping area for hikers and bicyclists, as well as a reserved group area. Picnic tables and fire grills are provided. Piped water, flush toilets, showers and a sanitary disposal station are available. Some facilities are **wheelchair accessible**. Pets are permitted.

Reservations, fee: Contact Reservations Northwest at (800) 452-5687 ($6 reservation fee); $16-$19 fee per night; $4 for hikers/bikers. Open all year.

Who to contact: Phone (503) 265-9278 or (800) 452-5687, or write to 198 NE 123rd Street, Newport, OR 97365.

Location: From Interstate 5 at Albany, turn west on US 20 and drive 66 miles to Newport. Turn north on US 101 and drive seven miles to the park entrance.

Trip note: This beautiful campground is set in a wooded, grassy area on the east side of US 101. Like magic, you walk through a tunnel under the roadway and emerge on the beach. A one-mile hiking trail is available. Just a mile to the north is a small, day-use state park called Devil's Punchbowl, named because of the unusual bowl-shaped rock formation which has caverns under it where the waves rumble about. For some great ocean views, head north one more mile to the Otter Crest Wayside.

---

42.   DEVIL'S LAKE STATE PARK   RV

Reference: **On Devil's Lake; map C1, grid g5.**

Campsites, facilities: There are 68 tent sites and 32 sites with full hookups for trailers or RVs of any length. A separate area for hikers and bikers is available. Picnic tables and fire grills are provided. Flush toilets, showers and firewood are available. Some facilities are **wheelchair accessible**. Leashed pets are permitted. Boat docks and launching facilities are nearby.

Reservations, fee: Contact Reservations Northwest at (800) 452-5687 ($6 reservation fee); $16-$19 fee per night; $4 for hikers/bikers. Open mid-April to late October.

Who to contact: Phone (503) 994-2002 or (800) 452-5687, or write to 1452 NE Sixth Street, Lincoln City, OR 97367.

Location: From Portland, turn south on Highway 99 West and drive southwest to Highway 18. Turn west on Highway 18 and continue 47 miles to US 101. Turn south and continue five miles to Lincoln City. Follow the signs to the park; it is in town.

Trip note: This is a take-your-pick deal. At Devil's Lake, you can boat, fish or waterski. An alternative is to head west and explore the seven miles of beaches. Lincoln City also has a number of art and craft galleries in town. Devil's Lake State Park is two miles east and offers facilities for day-use only.

---

43.   SPORTSMAN'S LANDING RV PARK   ⚃

Reference: **On Siletz River; map C1, grid g5.**

Campsites, facilities: There are 30 sites for trailers or RVs of any length. Electricity, piped water and sewer hookups are provided. Flush toilets, bottled gas, sanitary services, showers, a store, a cafe, a laundromat, ice and a playground are available. Leashed pets are permitted. Boat launching and moorage facilities and a fishing dock are available.

Reservations, fee: Reservations accepted; $15 fee per night. MasterCard and Visa accepted. Open all year.

Who to contact: Phone (503) 996-4225 or write to 3804 Siletz Highway, Lincoln City, OR 97367.

Location: From Portland, turn south on Highway 99 West and drive southwest to Highway 18. Turn west on Highway 18 and continue 47 miles to US 101. Turn south and continue five miles to Lincoln City. Continue six miles south on US 101, then drive four miles east on Highway 229 to the park entrance.

Trip note: This park is set along the shore of the Siletz River, with full boating facilities and a restaurant that is world-famous for its Belgian waffles and crepes. If you head farther east on Highway 229, you will discover several Forest Service roads that lead into the Siuslaw National Forest and provide access to a number of creeks. See a Forest Service map for details.

MAP C2

80 LISTINGS
PAGES 400-433

OREGON MAP .... see page 380
Adjoining Maps
NORTH .... Washington
EAST (C3) .... see page 434
SOUTH (D2) .... see page 500
WEST (C1) .... see page 382

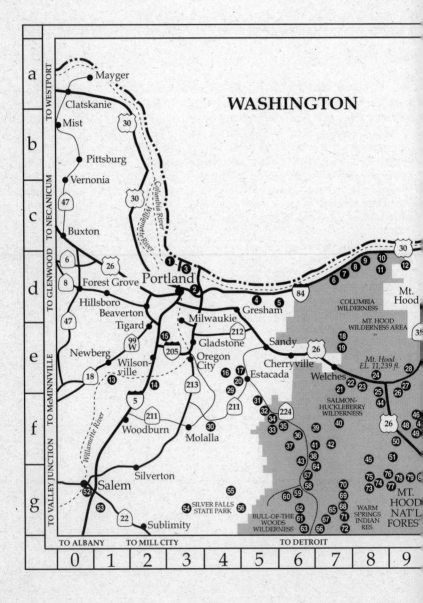

Oregon Map C2 featuring: Columbia River, Sandy River, Cascade Locks, Columbia Wilderness, Mount Hood National Forest, Pacific Crest Trail, Sandy River, Willamette River, Portland, Hood River, Molalla River, Clackamas River, Collawash River, Promontory Lake, Zigzag River, Salmon River, Rock Lakes Basin, Trillium Lake, White River, Roaring River, Crater Lake, Timothy Lake, Santiam River, Salem, Summit Lake, Willamette National Forest, Clackamas Lake, Bull of the Woods Wilderness, Breitenbush River, Olallie Lake, Round Lake, Breitenbush Lake

---

1.   JANTZEN BEACH RV PARK   **RV**

Reference: **Near Columbia River; map C2, grid d3.**

Campsites, facilities: There are 169 sites for trailers or RVs of any length. Electricity, piped water, sewer hookups and picnic tables are provided. Flush toilets, showers, a recreation hall, a laundromat, ice, a playground and a swimming pool are available. Bottled gas, a store and a cafe are within one mile. Pets are permitted. Boat docks, launching facilities and rentals are nearby.

Reservations, fee: Reservations accepted; $20-$22 fee per night; MasterCard and Visa accepted. Open all year.

Who to contact: Phone (503) 289-7626 or write to 1503 North Hayden Island Drive, Portland, OR 97217.

Location: Take Interstate 5 about four miles north of Portland and look for the Jantzen Beach exit (exit 308), then drive one-half mile west on Hayden Island Drive to the park on the right.

Trip note: This motor home campground is set near the banks of the Columbia River on the outskirts of Portland. Though it is close to the highway, it has a rural feel, with nice shady sites. Nearby recreation options include an 18-hole golf course, a riding stable and tennis courts.

2.   PORTLAND MEADOWS RV PARK   **RV**

Reference: **Near Columbia River; map C2, grid d3.**

Campsites, facilities: There are 100 sites for trailers or RVs of any length. Electricity, piped water and sewer hookups are provided. Flush toilets, bottled gas, sanitary services, showers, a store, a cafe, a laundromat and ice are available. Leashed pets are permitted.

Reservations, fee: Reservations accepted; $20 fee per night. Open all year.

Who to contact: Phone (503) 285-1617 or write to 222 NE Gertz Road, Portland, OR 97211.

Location: Take the Columbia Boulevard exit off Interstate 5 in Portland. Drive one-half mile east, then turn north on Martin Luther King Boulevard (Union Avenue) and continue another half-mile. Turn east on Gertz Road and proceed to the campground.

Trip note: Many recreation opportunities are available in the Portland area. Numerous marinas on the Willamette and Columbia rivers offer boat trips and rentals, and the city parks and nearby state parks—call (503) 238-7488 for more information—offer hiking, bicycling and horseback riding possibilities. The Columbia River Highway (US 30) is a scenic drive. If golf is your game, Portland has 18 public golf courses. The winter ski areas at Mount Hood are within an hour.

3. FIR GROVE RV & TRAILER PARK

Reference: **Near Columbia River; map C2, grid d3.**

Campsites, facilities: There six sites for trailers or RVs of any length. Electricity, piped water and sewer hookups are provided. Flush toilets and showers are available. Bottled gas, sanitary services, a store, a cafe and a playground are located within one mile. Pets and motorbikes are permitted.

Reservations, fee: Reservations accepted; $15 fee per night. Open all year.

Who to contact: Phone (503) 252-9993 or write to 5541 Northeast 72nd, Portland, OR 97218.

Location: In Portland off Interstate 205, take exit 236 and drive about 400 yards northeast on Columbia Boulevard, then one mile west on Northeast Killingsworth and you'll see the park entrance.

Trip note: This park is set near the banks of the Columbia River in the outskirts of Portland. See the trip note for Portland Meadows RV Park for information about the nearby recreation opportunities.

4. CROWN POINT RV PARK

Reference: **Near Columbia River; map C2, grid d5.**

Campsites, facilities: There are 10 tent sites and 21 sites for trailers or RVs of any length. Electricity, piped water and picnic tables are provided. Flush toilets, bottled gas, sanitary services, showers and a laundromat are available. There is a store and ice within one mile. Leashed pets are permitted.

Reservations, fee: Reservations accepted, phone (800) 291-4520; $17-$20 fee per night. Open all year.

Who to contact: Phone (503) 695-5207 or write to 37000 East Historic Columbia River Highway, Corbett, OR 97019.

Location: From Portland, drive east on Interstate 84 to exit 22, near Troutdale. Drive about 400 yards southeast on US 30 (Crown Point Highway) to the park. (Note: This route includes a 10% grade. To avoid it, take the following route: From Portland, drive east on Interstate 84 to exit 18/Lewis and Clark State Park exit. Drive through the park for 7.3 miles on the Historic Columbia River Highway to the park on the right.)

Trip note: This little park is located near the Columbia River along scenic US 30. Crown Point State Park is nearby and is open during the day. It offers views of the Columbia River Gorge and the historical Vista House, a memorial built in 1918 to honor Oregon's pioneers. Multnomah Falls offers another possible side trip.

5. OXBOW COUNTY CAMPGROUND

Reference: **On Sandy River; map C2, grid d6.**

Campsites, facilities: There are 45 sites for tents, trailers or RVs up to 35 feet long. Picnic tables are provided. Piped water, pit toilets, firewood and a playground are available. Boat launching facilities are nearby.

Reservations, fee: No reservations; $10-$12 fee per night. Open all year, but subject to flooding, so please call to confirm status.

Who to contact: Phone (503) 663-4708 or write to 3010 Southeast Oxbow Parkway, Gresham, OR 97030.

Location: From Portland, take US 26 to Gresham, then take Southeast Division four miles east. Continue east four miles on Oxbow Parkway to the park.

Trip note: This 1,000-acre park is set along the Sandy River, a short distance from the Columbia River Gorge and has been designated a natural preservation area. Fishing, swimming and non-motorized boating are permitted here.

---

6. AINSWORTH STATE PARK   RV

Reference: **In Columbia River Gorge; map C2, grid d7.**

Campsites, facilities: There are 45 sites with full hookups for trailers or RVs of any length. Picnic tables and fire grills are provided. Flush toilets, showers, firewood and a laundromat are available. Leashed pets are permitted.

Reservations, fee: No reservations; $17 fee per night. Open mid-April to late October (or later, weather permitting).

Who to contact: Phone (503) 695-2361 or (800) 452-5687 or write to Columbia River Gorge District, P.O. Box 100, Corbett, OR 97019.

Location: From Portland, turn east on Interstate 84 and drive 35 miles. Take the US 30 exit and turn southwest; continue a short distance to the park. An alternate route is to take US 30, a designated scenic highway, all the way from Portland (37 miles).

Trip note: This state park is set along the scenic Columbia River Gorge. A two-mile section of the Columbia River Gorge Trail connects this park with John Yeon State Park, which is open during the day. Fishermen should check out the Bonneville Fish Hatchery, where there is a giant sturgeon that's a unique sight.

---

7. EAGLE CREEK   RV

Reference: **Near Columbia Wilderness in Mount Hood National Forest; map C2, grid d7.**

Campsites, facilities: There are 19 sites for tents, trailers or RVs up to 20 feet long. Picnic tables and fire grills are provided. Piped water and flush toilets are available. Leashed pets are permitted. Boat docks and launching facilities are nearby on the Columbia River.

Reservations, fee: No reservations; $8 fee per night. Open mid-May to October. Reservations are required for groups.

Who to contact: Phone (541) 386-2333, or write to Columbia River Gorge National Scenic Area, 902 Wasco Avenue, Suite 200, Hood River, OR 97031.

Location: From Portland, turn east at exit 41 on Interstate 84 and drive approximately 43 miles to the campground. It is located two miles east of Bonneville.

Trip note: This is a good base camp for a hiking trip. The Eagle Creek Trail leaves the campground and goes 13 miles to Wahtum Lake, where it intersects with the Pacific Crest Trail. There is a primitive campground at the 7.5-mile point. The upper seven miles of the trail pass through the Columbia Wilderness.

---

8. CASCADE LOCKS MARINE PARK   RV

Reference: **In Cascade Locks; map C2, grid d8.**

Campsites, facilities: There are 10 tent sites and 30 drive-through sites for trailers or RVs of any length. Picnic tables are provided. Flush toilets, sanitary services, showers and a playground are available. Bottled gas, a store, a cafe, a laundromat and ice are located within one mile. Pets and motorbikes are permitted. Boat docks and launching facilities are nearby.

Reservations, fee: No reservations; $10 fee per night. Open all year, with limited winter facilities.

Who to contact: Phone (503) 374-8619 or write to P.O. Box 307, Cascade Locks, OR 97014.

Location: From Portland, turn east on Interstate 84 and drive approximately 46 miles to Cascade Locks. Take exit 44 and drive one mile east on Wanapa Street to the sign for the park on the left. Follow the signs to the park.

Trip note: This public riverfront park covers 200 acres and offers a museum and boat rides. The salmon fishing is excellent here. Nearby recreation options include hiking trails and tennis courts.

---

9. HERMAN HORSE CAMP **RV**

Reference: **Near Pacific Crest Trail in Mount Hood National Forest; map C2, grid d8.**

Campsites, facilities: There are seven sites for tents, trailers or RVs up to 24 feet long. Piped water, fire grills and picnic tables are provided. Stock handling facilities are available. Sanitary services, showers, a store, a cafe, a laundromat and ice are nearby. Leashed pets are permitted.

Reservations, fee: No reservations; $6 fee per night. Open mid-May to October.

Who to contact: Phone (503) 386-2333, or write to Columbia River Gorge National Scenic Area, 902 Wasco Avenue, Suite 200, Hood River, OR 97031.

Location: From Portland, turn east on Interstate 84 and drive about 45 miles to the town of Cascade Locks. Continue east for 1.5 more miles to the campground entrance.

Trip note: This campground is located about one-half mile from Herman Creek, not far from the Pacific Crest Trail. This is a particularly beautiful area, separated from Washington by the Columbia River. There are many recreation options here, including biking, hiking, fishing and boat trips.

---

10. WYETH **RV**

Reference: **On Gordon Creek in Mount Hood National Forest; map C2, grid d8.**

Campsites, facilities: There are 17 sites for tents, trailers or RVs up to 32 feet long. Fire grills and picnic tables are provided. Piped water and flush toilets are available. Leashed pets are permitted.

Reservations, fee: No reservations; $8 fee per night. Open mid-May to October.

Who to contact: Phone (503) 386-2333, or write to Columbia River Gorge National Scenic Area, 902 Wasco Avenue, Suite 200, Hood River, OR 97031.

Location: From Portland, turn east at exit 51 on Interstate 84 and drive about 45 miles to the town of Cascade Locks. Continue seven miles east to the Wyeth exit, then drive one-half mile on a county road (you'll see a sign) to the campground entrance.

Trip note: This is a good layover spot for Columbia River corridor cruisers. It is set along Gordon Creek, near the Columbia. See trip note for Herman Horse Camp for recreation details.

---

11. KOA CASCADE LOCKS **RV**

Reference: **Near Columbia River; map C2, grid d8.**

Campsites, facilities: There are 25 sites for tents and 74 sites for trailers or RVs of any length. There are also nine cabins available. Electricity, piped water, sewer hookups and picnic tables are provided. Flush toilets, bottled gas, sanitary services, showers, firewood, hot tub, cable TV hookups, a recreation hall, a store, a laundromat, ice, a playground and a heated swimming pool are available. The indoor heated pool is open May 20 through October 15; the hot tub from April through September. A cafe is located within one mile. Pets and motorbikes are permitted.

Reservations, fee: Reservations accepted; $16-$21 fee per night; $28-$33 cabin fee for two people. MasterCard and Visa accepted. Open mid-March to mid-October.

Who to contact: Phone (503) 374-8668 or write to Star Route, Box 660, Cascade Locks, OR 97014.

Location: From Portland, turn east on Interstate 84 and drive about 45 miles to the town of Cascade Locks. Take exit 44 and travel two miles east on Forest Lane to the campground.

Trip note: This is a good layover for motor home campers touring the Columbia River corridor. It offers level, shaded RV sites and grassy tent sites. Nearby recreation options include bike trails, hiking trails and tennis courts. The 200-acre Cascade Locks and Marine Park is nearby and offers everything from museums to boat trips.

12. VIENTO STATE PARK 🚐

Reference: **In Columbia River Gorge; map C2, grid d9.**

Campsites, facilities: There are 18 tent sites and 58 sites with water and electrical hookups for trailers or RVs up to 30 feet long. Picnic tables and fire grills are provided. Flush toilets, showers, firewood and a laundromat are available. Leashed pets are permitted.

Reservations, fee: Reservations accepted; $13-$14 fee per night. Open mid-April to late October (or later, weather permitting).

Who to contact: Phone (541) 374-8811 or (800) 452- 5687 or write to Columbia River Gorge District, P.O. Box 100, Corbett, OR 97019.

Location: From Portland, turn east on Interstate 84 and drive approximately 57 miles to the park entrance. It is located eight miles west of the town of Hood River.

Trip note: This park is set along the Columbia River Gorge and offers scenic hiking trails. Take the picturesque drive along old US 30, which skirts the Columbia River. There are three other day-use state parks along Interstate 84 just west of Viento: Wygant, Vinzenz Lausmann and Seneca Fouts. All are accessible by eastbound traffic only and offer quality hiking trails and scenic views.

13. CHAMPOEG STATE PARK 🚐

Reference: **On Willamette River; map C2, grid e1.**

Campsites, facilities: There are six tent sites and 48 sites with water and electrical hookups for trailers or RVs up to 50 feet long. There are also three group areas which accommodate a maximum of 25 tents each and an RV group site with 25 sites. Picnic tables and fire grills are provided. Flush toilets, sanitary disposal station, showers, a group recreation hall for up to 60 people and firewood are available. Some facilities are **wheelchair accessible**. Leashed pets are permitted. Boat docking facilities are nearby.

Reservations, fee: Contact Reservations Northwest at (800) 452-5687 ($6 reservation fee); $14-$18 fee per night. Open all year with limited winter facilities.

Who to contact: Phone (503) 633-8170 or (800) 452-5687 or write to 7679 Champoeg Road NE, Saint Paul, OR 97137.

Location: From Interstate 5 between Salem and Portland, take the Donald/Aurora exit and follow the signs for eight miles west to the park.

Trip note: This state park is set along the banks of the Willamette River and offers an interpretive center, a botanical garden featuring native plants, and hiking and bike trails. In July, an historical pageant reenacting the early history of the area is staged Thursday through Sunday evenings. There is also a log cabin museum and the historic Newell House.

14. ISBERG RV PARK RV

Reference: **Near Aurora; map C2, grid e2.**

Campsites, facilities: There are 84 sites for trailers or RVs of any length. Electricity, piped water and sewer hookups are provided. Flush toilets, bottled gas, sanitary services, showers, a recreation hall, a store, a swimming pool, a laundromat and ice are available. Leashed pets are permitted.

Reservations, fee: Reservations accepted; $18-$20 fee per night; MasterCard and Visa accepted. Open all year.

Who to contact: Phone (503) 678-2646 or write to 21599 Dolores Way Northeast, Aurora, OR 97002.

Location: Take Interstate 5 north for about seven miles from Woodburn, then take exit 278 at Aurora and drive east about 200 yards to the park.

Trip note: This motor home campground is in a rural area just off the main highway and offers a recreation room, a jogging trail and a pitch-and-putt golf course. The setting is very pretty, surrounded by lots of evergreen trees and sheltered from the highway. Portland and Salem are just 20 minutes away.

15. TRAILER PARK OF PORTLAND RV

Reference: **In Tualatin; map C2, grid e3.**

Campsites, facilities: There are 100 drive-through sites for trailers or RVs of any length. Electricity, piped water, sewer hookups and picnic tables are provided. Flush toilets, sanitary services, showers, a laundromat and a playground are available. Bottled gas, a store, a cafe and ice are located within one mile. Pets and motorbikes are permitted.

Reservations, fee: Reservations accepted; $22 fee per night. MasterCard and Visa accepted. Open all year.

Who to contact: Phone (503) 692-0225 or write to 6645 Southwest Nyberg Road, Tualatin, OR 97062.

Location: Take Interstate 5 south from Portland to Tualatin, then take exit 289 and follow Highway 212 east for about one-quarter mile to the park.

Trip note: This park is set just south of Portland in a wooded setting. The sites are spacious and all have access to lawn areas. See the trip note for Portland Meadows RV Park for information about recreation possibilities in the area.

16. BARTON PARK RV

Reference: **On Clackamas River; map C2, grid e4.**

Campsites, facilities: There are a total of 58 sites for tents, trailers and RVs. Restrooms, showers, a sanitary dump, a public phone and a barbecue are available. Recreational facilities include horseshoe pits, a playground and a boat ramp. Pets are permitted on leashes.

Reservations, fee: Reservations recommended; $10-$14 fee per night. Open from May 1 through September.

Who to contact: Phone the Clackamas County Parks Department at (503) 655-8521 or write to 902 Abernathy Road, Oregon City, OR 97045.

Location: From Portland, drive south on Interstate 205 for about 20 miles to the Clackamas/Estacada exit (Highway 212). Continue on Highway 212 to the Carver Road exit. Turn right and cross the bridge over the Clackamas River. Turn left on Springwater Road to the town of Springwater. Just outside of town, turn right on Barton Park Road and drive one-quarter mile to the park straight ahead.

Trip note: Getting here is a bit of a maze, but the trip is well worth it. This camp, set on the Clackamas River, is surrounded by woods and tall trees. There is a fishing and swimming area in the creek. The nearby Clackamas River provides good salmon fishing.

17.　　　MILO McIVER STATE PARK　　RV

Reference: **On Collawash River; map C2, grid e5.**

Campsites, facilities: There are four primitive tent sites and 49 sites with water and electrical hookups for trailers or RVs of any length. Picnic tables and fire grills are provided. Flush toilets, sanitary services, showers and firewood are available. Facilities are **wheelchair accessible**. Leashed pets are permitted. Boat launching facilities are nearby. Group facilities are available.

Reservations, fee: Contact Reservations Northwest at (800) 452-5687 ($6 reservation fee); $ 9-$16 fee per night. Open mid-March to mid-November.

Who to contact: Phone (503) 630-7150, (503) 731-3411 or (800) 452-5687 or write to 24101 South Entrance Road, Estacada, OR 97023.

Location: From Portland, turn east on US 26 and drive approximately 25 miles, then turn south on Highway 211 and continue seven miles to the park.

Trip note: This park is not far from the Portland area, yet it is far enough off the beaten track to provide a feeling of separation from the metropolitan area. It is set along the banks of the Collawash River and has a boat ramp. Trails for hiking are available, and a 4.5-mile equestrian trail is also accessible. A fish hatchery is a nearby point of interest.

18.　　　　　　McNEIL　　　　　　RV

Reference: **On the Clear Fork of Sandy River in Mount Hood National Forest; map C2, grid e7.**

Campsites, facilities: There are 34 sites for tents, trailers or RVs up to 22 feet long. Picnic tables and vault toilets are provided. There is **no piped water**. Leashed pets are permitted.

Reservations, fee: No reservations; $7 fee per night. Open May to late September.

Who to contact: Phone the Zigzag Ranger District at (503) 666-0704 or write to Mount Hood National Forest, 70220 East Highway 26, Zigzag, OR 97049.

Location: From Portland, turn east on US 26 and drive 40 miles to Zigzag. Turn northeast on County Road 18 and drive 4.5 miles, then three-quarters of a mile northeast on Forest Service Road 1825.

Trip note: This campground is set along the Clear Fork of the Sandy River. Several trails nearby provide access to the wilderness backcountry. See a Forest Service map for details.

19.　　　RILEY HORSE CAMP　　RV

Reference: **Near the Clear Fork of Sandy River in Mount Hood National Forest; map C2, grid e7.**

Campsites, facilities: There are 14 sites for tents, trailers or RVs up to 16 feet long.

Piped water, fire grills, vault toilets and picnic tables are provided. Facilities for horses are available. Leashed pets are permitted.

Reservations, fee: Reserve some sites by calling (800) 280-CAMP ($7.75 reservation fee); $9 fee per night. Open May to late September.

Who to contact: Phone the Zigzag Ranger District at (503) 666-0704 or write to Mount Hood National Forest, 70220 East Highway 26, Zigzag, OR 97049.

Location: From Portland, turn east on US 26 and drive 40 miles to Zigzag. Turn northeast on County Road 18 and drive four miles, then proceed one mile east on Forest Service Road 1825. The campground is about 100 yards south on Forest Service Road 382.

Trip note: This campground is near McNeil and offers the same opportunities, except this camp provides stock handling facilities. This is a popular base camp for horse packing trips into nearby old-growth forest.

---

20.   LOST CREEK   RV

Reference: **On Lost Creek in Mount Hood National Forest; map C2, grid e7.**

Campsites, facilities: There are five walk-in sites for tents and nine sites for trailers or RVs up to 22 feet long. Facilities are **wheelchair accessible.** Well water, fire grills, vault toilets and picnic tables are provided. Leashed pets are permitted.

Reservations, fee: Reserve some sites by calling (800) 280-CAMP ($7.75 reservation fee); $9 fee per night; $18 double-site fee. Open May to late September.

Who to contact: Phone the Zigzag Ranger District at (503) 666-0704 or write to Mount Hood National Forest, 70220 East Highway 26, Zigzag, OR 97049.

Location: From Portland, drive east on US 26 for 40 miles to Zigzag. Turn north on County Road 18/East Lolo Pass Road and drive 4.5 miles. Turn right on Forest Service Road 1825 and drive two miles to the campground on the right, just past the entrance to Riley Horse Camp.

Trip note: This campground is near McNeil and Riley camps and offers some of the same opportunities. It is barrier-free and offers an interpretative nature trail about one-mile long and a **wheelchair accessible** fishing pier.

---

21.   GREEN CANYON   RV

Reference: **On Salmon River in Mount Hood National Forest; map C2, grid e7.**

Campsites, facilities: There are 15 sites for tents, trailers or RVs up to 22 feet long. Picnic tables, well water and fire grills are provided. Pit toilets are available. A store, a cafe and ice are located within five miles. Some facilities are **wheelchair accessible**. Leashed pets are permitted.

Reservations, fee: No reservations; $9-$11 fee per night. Open May to late September.

Who to contact: Phone the Zigzag Ranger District at (503) 666-0704 or write to Mount Hood National Forest, 70220 East Highway 26, Zigzag, OR 97049.

Location: From Portland, turn east on US 26 and drive about 39 miles to Forest Service Road 2618 (just north of Zigzag). Turn right and drive 4.5 miles south to the campground.

Trip note: This winner is one that few out-of-towners know about. The locals do, however, and it is well-used in the summer. It is set along the banks of the Salmon River. There is a long trail that passes through camp and parallels the Salmon River, passing through a magnificent old-growth forest. See a Forest Service map for details.

22. TOLL GATE RV

Reference: **On Zigzag River in Mount Hood National Forest; map C2, grid e7.**

Campsites, facilities: There are 15 tent sites and nine sites for trailers or RVs up to 16 feet long. Picnic tables and fire grills are provided. Piped water and pit toilets are available. Leashed pets are permitted.

Reservations, fee: Reserve some sites by calling (800) 280-CAMP ($7.75 reservation fee); $9-$11 fee per night. Open late May to late September.

Who to contact: Phone the Zigzag Ranger District at (503) 666-0704 or write to Mount Hood National Forest, 70220 East Highway 26, Zigzag, OR 97049.

Location: From Portland, turn east on US 26 and drive 40 miles to Zigzag. Continue 2.5 miles southeast on US 26 to the campground entrance.

Trip note: This campground is set along the banks of the Zigzag River near Rhododendron. This camp is extremely popular and finding a site on a summer weekend can be next to impossible. Luckily, you can get a reservation. There are numerous hiking trails in the area. The nearest one to this campground leads east for several miles along the river.

23. CAMP CREEK RV

Reference: **Near Zigzag River in Mount Hood National Forest; map C2, grid e8.**

Campsites, facilities: There are 24 sites for tents, trailers or RVs up to 22 feet long. Piped water, fire grills and picnic tables are provided. Vault toilets are available. Leashed pets are permitted.

Reservations, fee: Reserve some sites by calling (800) 280-CAMP ($7.75 reservation fee); $9-$18 fee per night; $18 double site fee. Open late May to late September.

Who to contact: Phone the Zigzag Ranger District at (503) 666-0704 or write to Mount Hood National Forest, 70220 East Highway 26, Zigzag, OR 97049.

Location: From Portland, turn east on US 26 and drive 40 miles to Zigzag. Continue southeast on US 26 for about four miles to camp.

Trip note: This campground is set along Camp Creek, not far from the Zigzag River. A hiking trail runs through camp and along the Zigzag River, and another leads south to Still Creek. This campground, along with Toll Gate to the west, is very popular and you'll probably need a reservation.

24. ALPINE

Reference: **Near Pacific Crest Trail in Mount Hood National Forest; map C2, grid e8.**

Campsites, facilities: There are 16 tent sites. Piped water, fire grills, vault toilets and picnic tables are provided. Leashed pets are permitted.

Reservations, fee: No reservations; $7 fee per night. Open July to late September.

Who to contact: Phone the Zigzag Ranger District at (503) 666-0704 or write to Mount Hood National Forest, 70220 East Highway 26, Zigzag, OR 97049.

Location: From Portland, turn east on US 26 and drive 55 miles to the small town of Government Camp. Continue east a short distance to Timberline Lodge Road (Forest Service Road 173), turn north and proceed 4.5 miles to the campground.

Trip note: This small campground is one mile from the Timberline Ski Area lodge on the south slopes of Mount Hood. It can get quite crowded here on weekends. The camp is managed by the same folks who run the lifts in winter. The Pacific

Crest Trail can be accessed from the Timberline Lodge. Be sure to come prepared for very cold nights.

25. STILL CREEK   **RV**

Reference: **On Still Creek in Mount Hood National Forest; map C2, grid e8.**

Campsites, facilities: There are 27 sites for tents, trailers or RVs up to 27 feet long. Picnic tables and fire grills are provided. Pit toilets and piped water are available. Leashed pets are permitted.

Reservations, fee: Reserve some sites by calling (800) 280-CAMP ($7.75 reservation fee); $9 fee per night. Open mid-June to late September.

Who to contact: Phone the Zigzag Ranger District at (503) 666-0704 or write to Mount Hood National Forest, 70220 East Highway 26, Zigzag, OR 97049.

Location: From Portland, turn east on US 26 and drive 55 miles to the small town of Government Camp. Continue one mile east on US 26, then 500 yards south on Forest Service Road 2650.

Trip note: This primitive camp is set near the junction of US 26 and Highway 35, located along Still Creek where it pours off the south slope of Mount Hood. Anglers should bring along their poles: the fishing in Still Creek can be excellent.

26. GRINDSTONE

Reference: **Near Barlow Creek in Mount Hood National Forest; map C2, grid e9.**

Campsites, facilities: There are two primitive sites for tents. Picnic tables and fire grills are provided. Vault toilets are available, but there is **no piped water**. Leashed pets are permitted.

Reservations, fee: No reservations; no fee. Open May to October.

Who to contact: Phone the Bear Springs Ranger District at (503) 328-6211 or write to Mount Hood National Forest, Route 1, P.O. Box 222, Maupin, OR 97037.

Location: From Portland, turn east on US 26 and drive 55 miles to the small town of Government Camp. Continue two miles east on US 26, then drive 4.5 miles east on Highway 35. From there, turn right and travel two miles southeast on Forest Service Road 3530 to the campground on the right.

Trip note: This tiny campground is set on Barlow Creek, on Old Barlow Road. It's a little-known and little-used spot. You won't find much out here but wind, water and trees, but sometimes that's all you need.

27. DEVIL'S HALF ACRE MEADOW   **RV**

Reference: **On Barlow Creek in Mount Hood National Forest; map C2, grid e9.**

Campsites, facilities: There are five sites for tents, trailers or RVs up to 16 feet long. Picnic tables and fire grills are provided. Firewood and pit toilets are available. There is **no piped water**. Leashed pets are permitted.

Reservations, fee: No reservations; no fee. Open May to October.

Who to contact: Phone the Bear Springs Ranger District at (503) 328-6211 or write to Mount Hood National Forest, Route 1, P.O. Box 222, Maupin, OR 97037.

Location: From Portland, turn east on US 26 and drive 55 miles to the small town of Government Camp. Continue two miles east on US 26, then drive 4.5 miles east on Highway 35. From there, go one mile southeast on Forest Service Road 3530.

Trip note: This campground is set a few miles upstream on Barlow Creek from Grindstone. Several hiking trails are nearby, including the Pacific Crest Trail, which provide access to some small lakes in the area. There are many historic points of interest in the vicinity.

---

28. ROBINHOOD

Reference: **On the East Fork of Hood River in Mount Hood National Forest; map C2, grid e9.**

Campsites, facilities: There are 24 sites for tents or trailers up to 18 feet long. Piped water and picnic tables are provided. Leashed pets are permitted.

Reservations, fee: No reservations; $8 fee per night. Open mid-May to early September.

Who to contact: Phone the Hood River Ranger District at (503) 352-6002 or write to Hood River Ranger District, 6780 Highway 35, Mount Hood, OR 97041.

Location: From Portland, turn east on Interstate 84 and drive 65 miles to the town of Hood River. Turn south on Highway 35 (exit 64) and drive 28 miles to the campground on the right.

Trip note: This campground is set along the East Fork of the Hood River at the base of Mount Hood. A trail from the camp follows the river north for about four miles to Sherwood campground. From there, it joins a network of trails that provide access to the Mount Hood Wilderness. Fishing is another option here.

---

29. METZLER PARK   **RV**

Reference: **On Clear Creek; map C2, grid f4.**

Campsites, facilities: There are 70 sites for tents, trailers and RVs. Restrooms, showers, a sanitary dump, a public phone, a playground and a recreation field are available. Leashed pets are permitted.

Reservations, fee: Reservations recommended; $10-$14 fee per night. Open May through September.

Who to contact: Phone the park at (503) 630-4743. For reservations, phone the Clackamas County Parks Department at (503) 655-8521 or write to 902 Abernathy Road, Oregon City, OR 97045.

Location: From Portland, drive south on Highway 205 for about 20 miles to the Clackamas/Estacada exit (Highway 212). Drive on Highway 212 to the Carver Road exit. Turn right and cross the bridge over the Clackamas River. Turn left on Springwater Road to the town of Springwater. Just outside of town, turn right on Metzler Park Road and drive three-quarters of a mile to the campground.

Trip note: This county campground is set on a small stream not far from the Clackamas River. Fishing, swimming and picnicking are among your options here. This park is very popular so be sure to make your reservation early.

---

30. FEYRER MEMORIAL PARK   **RV**

Reference: **On Molalla River; map C2, grid f4.**

Campsites, facilities: There are 60 sites for tents, trailers and RVs. Restrooms, showers, a sanitary dump and a public phone are provided. There is also a playground and recreation field. Some facilities are **wheelchair accessible**. Pets are permitted on leashes.

Reservations, fee: Reservations recommended; $10-$14 fee per night. Open year-round.

Who to contact: For reservations, phone (503) 655-8521; ask for the county parks department. To reach the park, phone (503) 829-6621. For information, write to Clackamas County Parks, 902 Abernathy Road, Oregon City, OR 97045.

Location: From Interstate 5 at Salem, drive north on Highway 213 for about 30 miles to Molalla. From Molalla, drive east on Highway 212 for three miles to the campground on the right.

Trip note: Located on the scenic Molalla River, this county park offers swimming and excellent salmon fishing. This is a superb option for weary Interstate 5 cruisers; the park is only 30 minutes off the highway and provides a peaceful, serene environment.

---

31. PROMONTORY   RV

Reference: **On North Fork Reservoir; map C2, grid f5.**

Campsites, facilities: There are 58 sites for tents, trailers or RVs up to 35 feet. There are no hookup sites. Restrooms, showers, limited groceries, ice and snacks are provided. A playground, horseshoes, a boat ramp, dock and rentals are available. Pets are permitted on leashes.

Reservations, fee: Reservations recommended; $10 fee per night. Visa and MasterCard are accepted. Open from May 15 to November 1.

Who to contact: Phone the park at (503) 630-5152 or write to P.O. Box 984, Estacada, OR 97023.

Location: From Portland, drive south on Highway 205 for about 20 miles to the Clackamas/Estacada exit (Highway 212). Travel on Highway 212 to Highway 224 and take the Carver/Estacada exit. From the town of Estacada, travel southeast for seven miles on Highway 224 to the campground on the right. There are prominent signs along the road indicating the directions to the camp.

Trip note: Set on North Fork Reservoir, this camp is part of a large recreation area and park. The lake provides excellent trout fishing and boating. This reservoir is actually a dammed-up overflow of the Clackamas River. The water is calm and ideal for boating.

---

32. LAZY BEND   RV

Reference: **On Clackamas River in Mount Hood National Forest; map C2, grid f5.**

Campsites, facilities: There are 21 sites for tents, trailers or RVs up to 16 feet long. Picnic tables and fireplaces are provided. Piped water and flush toilets are available. Leashed pets are permitted.

Reservations, fee: Reserve some sites by calling (800) 280-CAMP ($7.75 reservation fee); $8 fee per night. Open late April through Labor Day.

Who to contact: Phone the Estacada Ranger District at (503) 630-6861 or write to Mount Hood National Forest, 595 NW Industrial Way, Estacada, OR 97023.

Location: From Interstate 5 south of Portland, take exit 288 and head east on Interstate 205 for 12 miles to Gladstone. Turn east on Highway 224 and drive 15 miles to Estacada. Continue 10.5 miles southeast on Highway 224 to the campground.

Trip note: This campground is set along the banks of the Clackamas River, near the large North Fork Reservoir. It is far enough off the highway to provide a secluded, primitive feeling, though it get its fair share of use on the weekends. The Clackamas River Trail starts at camp and leads east along the river, with some excellent fishing spots.

33. FISH CREEK 🚐

Reference: **On Clackamas River in Mount Hood National Forest; map C2, grid f5.**

Campsites, facilities: There are 24 sites for tents, trailers or RVs up to 16 feet long. Picnic tables and fire grills are provided. Vault toilets and hand-pumped water are available. Leashed pets are permitted.

Reservations, fee: Reserve some sites by calling (800) 280-CAMP ($7.75 reservation fee); $8 fee per night. Open late May to early September.

Who to contact: Phone the Estacada Ranger District at (503) 630-6861 or write to Mount Hood National Forest, 595 NW Industrial Way, Estacada, OR 97023.

Location: From Interstate 5 south of Portland, take exit 288 and head east on Interstate 205 for 12 miles to Gladstone. Turn east on Highway 224 and drive 15 miles to Estacada. Continue 15.5 miles southeast on Highway 224 to the campground.

Trip note: This campground is set along the banks of the Clackamas River, not far from the Clackamas River Trail and North Fork Reservoir. There is an amphitheater near the camp. Fishing is good in the Clackamas River as well as Fish Creek, which runs along the road south of camp.

34. ARMSTRONG 🚐

Reference: **On Clackamas River in Mount Hood National Forest; map C2, grid f5.**

Campsites, facilities: There are 12 sites for tents, trailers or RVs up to 16 feet long. Picnic tables and fire rings are provided. Vault toilets and hand-pumped water are available. Some facilities are **wheelchair accessible**. Leashed pets are permitted.

Reservations, fee: Reserve some sites by calling (800) 280-CAMP ($7.75 reservation fee); $8 fee per night. Open late May to early September.

Who to contact: Phone the Estacada Ranger District at (503) 630-6861 or write to Mount Hood National Forest, 595 NW Industrial Way, Estacada, OR 97023.

Location: From Interstate 5 south of Portland, take exit 288 and head east on Interstate 205 for 12 miles to Gladstone. Turn east on Highway 224 and drive 15 miles to Estacada. Continue 15 miles southeast on Highway 224 to the campground.

Trip note: This campground is set along the banks of the Clackamas River and offers good fishing access. See Fish Creek Camp for more details on the area.

35. LOCKABY 🚐

Reference: **On Clackamas River in Mount Hood National Forest; map C2, grid f6.**

Campsites, facilities: There are 30 sites for tents, trailers or RVs up to 16 feet long. Picnic tables, fireplaces, hand-pumped water and vault toilets are available. Leashed pets are permitted.

Reservations, fee: Reserve some sites by calling (800) 280-CAMP ($7.75 reservation fee); $9 fee per night. Open late May to early September.

Who to contact: Phone the Estacada Ranger District at (503) 630-6861 or write to Mount Hood National Forest, 595 NW Industrial Way, Estacada, OR 97023.

Location: From Interstate 5 south of Portland, take exit 288 and head east on Interstate 205 for 12 miles to Gladstone. Turn east on Highway 224 and drive

15 miles to Estacada. Continue 15 more miles southeast on Highway 224 to the campground.

Trip note: This campground is set along the banks of the Clackamas River. It is set next to Armstrong and Fish Creek camps, and gets heavy use from fishermen. Get there early to insure a choice spot.

---

36.   ROARING RIVER   **RV**

Reference: **On Roaring River in Mount Hood National Forest; map C2, grid f6.**

Campsites, facilities: There are 19 sites for tents, trailers or RVs up to 16 feet long. Picnic tables, fireplaces, hand-pumped water and vault toilets are available. Leashed pets are permitted.

Reservations, fee: Reserve some sites by calling (800) 280-CAMP ($7.75 reservation fee); $9 fee per night. Open mid-May to mid-September.

Who to contact: Phone the Estacada Ranger District at (503) 630-6861 or write to Mount Hood National Forest, 595 NW Industrial Way, Estacada, OR 97023.

Location: From Interstate 5 south of Portland, take exit 288 and head east on Interstate 205 for 12 miles to Gladstone. Turn east on Highway 224 and drive 15 miles to Estacada. Continue 18 miles south on Highway 224 to the campground.

Trip note: This campground is set at the confluence of the Roaring River and the Clackamas River. The sites have river views and you get access to the Dry Ridge Trail and several other trails into the adjacent roadless area. See a Forest Service map for details.

---

37.   SUNSTRIP   **RV**

Reference: **On Clackamas River in Mount Hood National Forest; map C2, grid f6.**

Campsites, facilities: There are nine sites for tents, trailers or RVs up to 15 feet long. Picnic tables, fireplaces, hand-pumped water and vault toilets, are available. Leashed pets are permitted.

Reservations, fee: Reserve some sites by calling (800) 280-CAMP ($7.75 reservation fee); $9 fee per night. Open late May to early September.

Who to contact: Phone the Estacada Ranger District at (503) 630-6861 or write to Mount Hood National Forest, 595 NW Industrial Way, Estacada, OR 97023.

Location: From Interstate 5 south of Portland, take exit 288 and head east on Interstate 205 for 12 miles to Gladstone. Turn east on Highway 224 and drive 15 miles to Estacada. Continue southeast about 19 miles on Highway 224 to the campground.

Trip note: This campground is set along the banks of the Clackamas River and offers fishing and rafting access. It is one of several campgrounds set along the Highway 224 corridor. This camp is popular, especially with rafting enthusiasts, and can fill up quickly on weekends.

---

38.   ALDER FLAT

Reference: **On Clackamas River, hike-in only in Mount Hood National Forest; map C2, grid f6.**

Campsites, facilities: There are six tent sites at this hike-in campground. Picnic tables and fire grills are provided. Vault toilets are available. There is **no piped water**. Pets are permitted.

Reservations, fee: No reservations; no fee. Open late April to late September.

Who to contact: Phone the Clackamas Ranger District at (503) 630-4256 or write to Mount Hood National Forest, 61431 East Highway 224, Estacada, OR 97023.

Location: From Interstate 5 south of Portland, take exit 288 and head east on Interstate 205 for 12 miles to Gladstone. Turn east on Highway 224 and drive 15 miles to Estacada. Continue southeast for 26 miles to the Ripplebrook Ranger Station. Parking for the camp is about one-half mile west of the ranger station. Hike one mile to the campground.

Trip note: This secluded hike-in campground is set along the banks of the Clackamas River. If you want peace and quiet and don't mind the short walk to get it, this is the spot. Be sure to pack out whatever you bring in.

---

39.   HIDEAWAY LAKE

Reference: **Near Rock Lakes Basin in Mount Hood National Forest; map C2, grid f7.**

Campsites, facilities: There are nine sites for tents, small trailers or camper vans. Picnic tables and fire grills are provided. Pit toilets are available. There is **no piped water**. Leashed pets are permitted.

Reservations, fee: No reservations; no fee. Open mid-June to late September.

Who to contact: Phone the Clackamas Ranger District at (503) 630-4256 or write to Mount Hood National Forest, 61431 East Highway 224, Estacada, OR 97023.

Location: From Interstate 5 south of Portland, take exit 288 and head east on Interstate 205 for 12 miles to Gladstone. Turn east on Highway 224 and drive 15 miles to Estacada. Continue southeast on Highway 224 for 27 miles, then 7.5 miles east on Forest Service Road 57. From there, take Forest Service Road 58, and travel three miles north to Forest Service Road 5830, turn northwest and drive 5.5 miles to the campground.

Trip note: This is a jewel of a spot, a small, deep lake set at 3,800 feet. The campsites are separate and set around the lake. At the north end of the lake there is an 8.5-mile loop trail that goes past a number of lakes in the Rock Lakes Basin, all of which support populations of rainbow and brook trout. If you don't want to make the whole trip in a day, you can camp overnight at Serene Lake. See a Forest Service map for information.

---

40.   HIGH ROCK SPRINGS

Reference: **Near Rock Lakes Basin in Mount Hood National Forest; map C2, grid f7.**

Campsites, facilities: There are seven tent sites. Picnic tables and fire grills are provided. Pit toilets are available. There is **no piped water**. Leashed pets are permitted.

Reservations, fee: No reservations; no fee. Open mid-June to late September.

Who to contact: Phone the Clackamas Ranger District at (503) 630-4256 or write to Mount Hood National Forest, 61431 East Highway 224, Estacada, OR 97023.

Location: From Interstate 5 south of Portland, take exit 288 and head east on Interstate 205 for 12 miles to Gladstone. Turn east on Highway 224 and drive 15 miles to Estacada. Continue southeast on Highway 224 for 27 miles, then drive 7.5 miles east on Forest Service Road 57. Turn northeast on Forest Service Road 58 and travel 10.5 miles to the campground.

Trip note: This small, remote campground is adjacent to High Rock. A half-mile climb offers a tremendous view of the surrounding area, including Mount Hood. About four miles east of the camp are trails that lead to some of the fishing lakes in Rock Lakes Basin. In August and September, ripe huckleberries are available in the area.

41. INDIAN HENRY   **RV**

Reference: **On Clackamas River in Mount Hood National Forest; map C2, grid f7.**

Campsites, facilities: There are 86 sites for tents, trailers or RVs up to 22 feet long. Picnic tables and fire grills are provided. Flush toilets, a sanitary dump station and piped water are available. Some facilities are **wheelchair accessible**. Leashed pets are permitted.

Reservations, fee: Reserve some sites by calling (800) 280-CAMP ($7.75 reservation fee); $10 fee per night. Open late May to early September.

Who to contact: Phone the Estacada Ranger District at (503) 630-6861 or write to Mount Hood Ranger District at 595 NW Industrial Way, Estacada, OR 97023.

Location: From Interstate 5 south of Portland, take exit 288 and head east on Interstate 205 for 12 miles to Gladstone. Turn east on Highway 224 and drive 15 miles to Estacada. Continue southeast on Highway 224 for 23 miles, then drive one-half mile southeast on Forest Service Road 4620.

Trip note: This campground is set along the banks of the Clackamas River and offers a trail that can be traveled on by wheelchair. Group campsites and an amphitheater are available. The Clackamas River Trail is nearby, with fishing access. This is one of the most popular campgrounds in the Estacada Ranger District.

42. LAKE HARRIET   **RV**

Reference: **In Mount Hood National Forest; map C2, grid f7.**

Campsites, facilities: There are 13 sites for tents, trailers or RVs up to 20 feet long. Picnic tables and fire grills are provided. Piped water and vault toilets are available. Some facilities are **wheelchair accessible**. Leashed pets are permitted. Boat docks and launching facilities are located on the lake. No horses are allowed in the campground.

Reservations, fee: Reserve some sites by calling (800) 280-CAMP ($7.75 reservation fee); $9 fee per night. Open late April to late September.

Who to contact: Phone the Clackamas Ranger District at (503) 630-4256 or write to Mount Hood National Forest, 61431 East Highway 224, Estacada, OR 97023.

Location: From Portland, turn east on US 26 and drive 55 miles to the small town of Government Camp. Continue 15 miles southeast on US 26, then eight miles south on Forest Service Road 42. Turn west on Forest Service Road 57 and drive 15 miles to Forest Service Road 58. Drive one mile south on Forest Service Road 58, then west on Forest Service Road 4630 for two miles to the campground.

Trip note: This little lake has been formed by a dam on the Oak Grove Fork of the Clackamas River and is a popular spot during the summer. Rowboats and boats with small motors are permitted. The lake can provide good fishing for a variety of trout, including brown, brook, rainbow and cutthroat.

43. RIPPLEBROOK

RV

Reference: On the Oak Grove Fork of Clackamas River in Mount Hood National Forest; map C2, grid f7.

Campsites, facilities: There are 13 sites for trailers or RVs up to 16 feet long. Picnic tables and fire grills are provided. Vault toilets are available, but there is **no piped water**. Leashed pets are permitted; horses are not allowed in the campground.

Reservations, fee: Reserve some sites by calling (800) 280-CAMP ($7.75 reservation fee); $9 fee per night. Open late April to late September.

Who to contact: Phone the Clackamas Ranger District at (503) 630-4256 or write to Mount Hood National Forest, 61431 East Highway 224, Estacada, OR 97023.

Location: From Interstate 5 south of Portland, take exit 288 and head east on Interstate 205 for 12 miles to Gladstone. Turn east on Highway 224 and drive 15 miles to Estacada. Continue 26.5 miles southeast on Highway 224 to the campground entrance.

Trip note: This campground is set along the banks of the Oak Grove Fork of the Clackamas River, offering shaded sites with river views. There is a four-mile foot trail from the camp that follows the river south to Riverside Campground, a nice walk in beautiful country. This is one of the more popular camps in the area.

---

44. TRILLIUM LAKE

RV

Reference: On Trillium Lake in Mount Hood National Forest; map C2, grid f8.

Campsites, facilities: There are 55 sites for tents, trailers or RVs up to 40 feet long. Picnic tables and fire grills are provided. Pit toilets and piped water are available. Leashed pets are permitted. All sites are **wheelchair accessible**. Boat docks and launching facilities are available on the lake, but no motors are permitted.

Reservations, fee: Reserve some sites by calling (800) 280-CAMP ($7.75 reservation fee); $10-$12 fee per night; $20 multi-family site fee. Open late May to late September.

Who to contact: Phone the Zigzag Ranger District at (503) 666-0704 or write to Mount Hood National Forest, 70220 East Highway 26, Zigzag, OR 97049.

Location: From Portland, turn east on US 26 and drive 55 miles to the small town of Government Camp. Continue two miles southeast on US 26, then drive south on Forest Service Road 2656 for 1.3 miles to the campground.

Trip note: This campground is set along the shores of Trillium Lake, which is about one-half mile long and one-quarter mile wide. There is good fishing in the evening here, and the nearby boat ramp makes this an ideal camp for anglers. It is a good lake for canoes and rafts as well as small rowboats. This camp is an extremely popular vacation destination, so expect plenty of company. Reservations are highly recommended.

---

45. MEDITATION POINT

Reference: On Timothy Lake, boat-in or walk-in only in Mount Hood National Forest; map C2, grid f8.

Campsites, facilities: There are four boat-in or walk-in tent sites accessible. Picnic tables and fire grills are provided. Pit toilets are available. There is **no piped water**. Pets are permitted. Boat docks and launching facilities are nearby.

Reservations, fee: No reservations; no fee. Open late May to mid-September.

Who to contact: Phone the Bear Springs Ranger District at (503) 328-6211 or write to Mount Hood National Forest, Route 1, P.O. Box 222, Maupin, OR 97037.

Location: From Portland, turn east on US 26 and drive 55 miles to the small town of Government Camp. Continue southeast on US 26 for 15 miles, then drive eight miles south on Forest Service Road 42. Park at Pine Point Campground, located five miles west on Forest Service Road 57, and hike one mile or take a boat to the north shore of the lake.

Trip note: Accessible only by foot or boat, this camp offers a more secluded location along Timothy Lake than Gone Creek, Hoodview, Oak Fork and Pine Point. It's the only campground on the north shore of the lake, which means you'll get a quieter, less crowded environment, though you'll have to bring your own water. See the trip notes for Gone Creek and Hoodview for details about the lake.

46.   BARLOW CREEK

Reference: On Barlow Creek in Mount Hood National Forest; map C2, grid f9.

Campsites, facilities: There are five sites for tents. Picnic tables and fire grills are provided. Vault toilets are available, but there is **no piped water**. Leashed pets are permitted.

Reservations, fee: No reservations; no fee. Open May through September.

Who to contact: Phone the Bear Springs Ranger District at (503) 328-6211 or write to Mount Hood National Forest, Route 1, P.O. Box 222, Maupin, OR 97037.

Location: From Portland, turn east on US 26 and drive 55 miles to the small town of Government Camp. Drive another 12 miles east on Highway 26. Turn north (left) on Forest Service Road 43 and drive five miles. Turn north (left) on Highway 35/30 and drive 1.5 miles to the campground on the right.

Trip note: This campground is set along Barlow Creek on Old Barlow Road, which was the wagon trail for early settlers in this area. This is one of several primitive Forest Service camps in the immediate vicinity. There may not be much to do in these parts, but you sure can't beat the price.

47.   BARLOW CROSSING

Reference: On Barlow Creek in Mount Hood National Forest; map C2, grid f9.

Campsites, facilities: There are five sites for tents. Picnic tables and fire grills are provided. Pit toilets are available. There is **no piped water**. Leashed pets are permitted.

Reservations, fee: No reservations; no fee. Open mid-May to September.

Who to contact: Phone the Bear Springs Ranger District at (503) 328-6211 or write to Mount Hood National Forest, Route 1, P.O. Box 222, Maupin, OR 97037.

Location: From Portland, turn east on US 26 and drive 55 miles to the small town of Government Camp. Drive another 12 miles east on Highway 26. Turn north (left) on Forest Service Road 43 and drive five miles. Turn north (left) on Highway 35/30 and drive one-half mile to the campground on the right.

Trip note: This small roadside campground is set where Barlow Creek meets the White River. It's quiet, remote, little-used and an excellent fishing spot.

48.   FROG LAKE   RV

Reference: **Near Pacific Crest Trail in Mount Hood National Forest; map C2, grid f9.**

Campsites, facilities: There are 33 sites for tents, trailers or RVs up to 22 feet long. Hand-pumped water and picnic tables are provided. Vault toilets and firewood are available. Leashed pets are permitted. Boat launching facilities are nearby. No motorized boats allowed.

Reservations, fee: Some sites may be reserved by calling (800) 280-CAMP ($7.75 reservation fee); $10-$12 fee per night; $5 each additional vehicle. Open mid-June to mid-September.

Who to contact: Phone the Bear Springs Ranger District at (503) 328-6211 or write to Mount Hood National Forest, Route 1, P.O. Box 222, Maupin, OR 97037.

Location: From Portland, turn east on US 26 and drive 55 miles to the small town of Government Camp. Continue seven miles southeast on US 26, then one mile southeast on Forest Service Road 2610. The camp is about 500 yards south on Forest Service Road 230.

Trip note: This classic spot in the Cascade Range is set on the shore of little Frog Lake, a short distance from the Pacific Crest Trail. Several other trails lead to nearby lakes. A possible day trip is Clear Lake to the south, which offers several recreation options.

49.   WHITE RIVER STATION

Reference: **On White River in Mount Hood National Forest; map C2, grid f9.**

Campsites, facilities: There are five sites for tents and RVs to 16 feet. Picnic tables and fire grills are provided. Vault toilets are available, but there is **no piped water**. Leashed pets are permitted.

Reservations, fee: No reservations; no fee. Open May through September.

Who to contact: Phone the Bear Springs Ranger District at (503) 328-6211 or write to Mount Hood National Forest, Route 1, P.O. Box 222, Maupin, OR 97037.

Location: From Portland, turn east on US 26 and drive 55 miles to the small town of Government Camp. Continue two miles east on US 26, then drive two miles east on Highway 35. Turn south on Forest Service Road 48 and travel nine miles southeast, then turn east and drive one mile to Forest Service Road 3530. Turn south and drive one mile to the campground on the left.

Trip note: This tiny campground is set along the White River on Old Barlow Road, an original wagon trail used by early settlers. This is one of several small, secluded camps in the area. This camp is quiet and private, with good fishing prospects.

50.   CLEAR LAKE   RV

Reference: **Near Pacific Crest Trail in Mount Hood National Forest; map C2, grid f9.**

Campsites, facilities: There are 28 sites for tents, trailers or RVs up to 32 feet long. Picnic tables, fire grills, hand-pumped water, firewood and vault toilets are available. Leashed pets are permitted. Boat launching facilities are nearby. Motorboats are allowed and there is 10 mile-per-hour speed limit.

Reservations, fee: Some sites may be reserved by calling (800) 280-CAMP ($7.75

reservation fee); $10-$12 fee per night; $5 each additional vehicle. Open late May to early September.

Who to contact: Phone the Bear Springs Ranger District at (503) 328-6221 or write to Mount Hood National Forest, Route 1, P.O. Box 222, Maupin, OR 97037.

Location: From Portland, turn east on US 26 and drive 55 miles to the small town of Government Camp. Continue nine miles southeast on US 26, then drive one mile south on Forest Service Road 2630 to the campground on the right.

Trip note: This campground is set along the shore of Clear Lake, a spot favored by fishermen, swimmers and windsurfers. The camp is wooded, with shady sites. A nearby trail heads north from the lake and provides access to the Pacific Crest Trail and Frog Lake.

---

51.   LITTLE CRATER   RV

Reference: On Crater Lake in Mount Hood National Forest; map C2, grid f9.

Campsites, facilities: There are 16 sites for tents, trailers or RVs up to 22 feet long. Picnic tables and fire grills are provided. Vault toilets, firewood and hand-pumped water are available. Leashed pets are permitted.

Reservations, fee: Some sites may be reserved by calling (800) 280-CAMP; $7.75 reservation fee; $9 fee per night; $5 each additional vehicle. Open June to mid-September.

Who to contact: Phone the Bear Springs Ranger District at (503) 328-6211 or write to Mount Hood National Forest, Route 1, P.O. Box 222, Maupin, OR 97037.

Location: From Portland, turn east on US 26 and drive 55 miles to the small town of Government Camp. Continue 15 miles southeast on US 26, then drive six miles south on Forest Service Road 42. From there, proceed 2.5 miles northwest on Forest Service Road 58 to the campground.

Trip note: This camp is next to Crater Creek and scenic, Little Crater Lake. It offers options for hikers and anglers alike; it is adjacent to the Pacific Crest Trail, about a mile from Timothy Lake. See the trip note for Gone Creek for more information about Timothy Lake.

---

52.   SALEM TRAILER PARK VILLAGE   RV

Reference: Near Willamette River; map C2, grid g0.

Campsites, facilities: There are 38 sites for trailers or RVs of any length. Electricity, piped water and sewer hookups are provided. Flush toilets, showers and a laundromat are available. Bottled gas, a store, a cafe and ice are located within one mile. Pets are not permitted.

Reservations, fee: Reservations accepted; $15 fee per night. Open all year.

Who to contact: Phone (503) 393-7424 or write to 4733 Portland Road Northeast, Salem, OR 97305.

Location: From Interstate 5 at Salem, take Highway 99E one-half mile east to the park.

Trip note: This park is set in the city of Salem, Oregon's capital. Several museums and parks are located in town, and the Willamette River flows nearby. Other recreation options include an 18-hole golf course, marked bike trails and a full-service marina.

53. SALEM CAMPGROUND AND RVS   RV.

Reference: **In Salem; map C2, grid g1.**

Campsites, facilities: There are 30 tent sites and 190 drive-through sites for trailers or RVs of any length. Picnic tables are provided. Flush toilets, bottled gas, sanitary services, showers, a recreation hall, a store, a laundromat, ice, a playground, electricity, piped water and sewer hookups are available. A cafe is located within one mile. Pets and motorbikes are permitted.

Reservations, fee: Reservations accepted; $12-$18 fee per night; MasterCard, Discover and Visa accepted. Open all year.

Who to contact: Phone (800) 826-9605 or (503) 581-6736 or write to 3700 Hagers Grove Road Southeast, Salem, OR 97301.

Location: From Salem, take exit 253 off Highway 22 and drive to Lancaster Drive. Turn south and drive to 1595 Lancaster Drive.

Trip note: This park is just off Interstate 5 in Salem, with shaded sites. A picnic area and a lake for swimming are available within walking distance. Nearby recreation options include a nine-hole golf course, hiking trails, a riding stable and tennis courts.

54. SILVER FALLS STATE PARK   RV.

Reference: **Near Salem; map C2, grid g3.**

Campsites, facilities: There are 51 tent sites and 53 sites with water and electrical hookups for trailers or RVs up to 60 feet long. Picnic tables and fire grills are provided. Flush toilets, sanitary services, showers, firewood and a playground are available. Some facilities are **wheelchair accessible**. Leashed pets are permitted.

Reservations, fee: Reservations accepted; $16-$18 fee per night. Open mid-April to late October.

Who to contact: Phone (503) 873-8681 or (800) 452-5687 or write to 20024 Silver Falls Highway SE, Sublimity, OR 97385.

Location: From Interstate 5 at Salem, turn east on Highway 22 and drive five miles, then turn east Highway 214 and drive 15 miles to the park.

Trip note: This is Oregon's largest state park, covering more than 8,000 acres. Numerous trails are available here, including a seven-mile jaunt that meanders past 10 waterfalls over 100 feet high, in the moist forest of Silver Creek Canyon. A horse camp and a 14-mile equestrian trail are available in the park. Fitness-conscious campers can check out the three-mile jogging trail or the four-mile bike trail. There is also a rustic nature lodge and group lodging facilities.

55. SHADY COVE

Reference: **North Santiam River in Willamette National Forest; map C2, grid g4.**

Campsites, facilities: There are 12 tent sites. Picnic tables, fire grills and vault toilets are available. There is **no piped water**. Leashed pets are permitted.

Reservations, fee: No reservations; $5-$10 fee per night. Open mid-May to late September.

Who to contact: Phone the Detroit Ranger District at (503) 854-3366, or write Willamette National Forest, HC 73, P.O. Box 320, Mill City, OR 97360.

Location: From Interstate 5 at Salem, take exit 253 and turn east on Highway 22.

Drive 23 miles to Mehama, then turn left on Little North Santiam Road and drive 19 miles northeast to the campground.

Trip note: This campground is set on the little North Santiam River. This camp is located in the midst of a heavily mined area. There are some quality hiking trails located off Forest Service roads to the south and east.

---

56. ELKHORN VALLEY RV

Reference: **On Little North Santiam River; map C2, grid g4.**

Campsites, facilities: There are 23 sites for tents, trailers or RVs up to 18 feet long. Picnic tables, fire grills, vault toilets and piped water are available. Leashed pets are permitted.

Reservations, fee: No reservations; $8 fee per night; 14-day limit. Open mid-May to late September.

Who to contact: Phone (503) 375-5646 or write to Bureau of Land Management, 1717 Fabry Road SE, Salem, OR 97306.

Location: From Interstate 5 at Salem, take exit 253 and turn east on Highway 22. Drive 25 miles east, then turn northeast on North Fork Road and drive nine miles to the campground.

Trip note: This campground is set along the Little North Santiam River, not far from the North Fork of the Santiam River. It is pretty, with easy access and only a short drive to a major metropolitan area. This is an option to Shady Cove camp, which is located about 10 miles to the east.

---

57. RIVERSIDE RV

Reference: **On Clackamas River in Mount Hood National Forest; map C2, grid g6.**

Campsites, facilities: There are 16 sites for tents, trailers or RVs up to 22 feet long. Picnic tables and fire grills are provided. Vault toilets and piped water are available. Leashed pets are permitted; no horses are allowed in the campground.

Reservations, fee: Some sites may be reserved by calling (800) 280-CAMP ($7.75 reservation fee); $9 fee per night. Open mid-May to late September.

Who to contact: Phone the Clackamas Ranger District at (503) 854-3366 or write to Mount Hood National Forest, 61431 East Highway 224, Estacada, OR 97023.

Location: From Interstate 5 south of Portland, take exit 288 and head east on Interstate 205 for 12 miles to Gladstone. Turn east on Highway 224 and drive 15 miles to Estacada. Continue southeast on Highway 224 for 27 miles, then drive 2.5 miles south on Forest Service Road 46 to the campground.

Trip note: This campground is set along the banks of the Clackamas River. A trail worth hiking leaves the camp and follows the river for four miles north. Fishing is another option here. There are several old Forest Service roads in the vicinity that make excellent mountain biking trails.

---

58. RIVERFORD

Reference: **On Clackamas and Collawash rivers in Mount Hood National Forest; map C2, grid g6.**

Campsites, facilities: There are 10 sites for tents. Picnic tables and fire grills are provided. Vault toilets are available. There is **no piped water** at the campground; water is available at nearby Two Rivers Picnic Area. Leashed pets are permitted.

Reservations, fee: No reservations; $7 fee per night. Open late April to late September.

Who to contact: Phone the Clackamas Ranger District at (503) 630-4256 or write to Mount Hood National Forest, 61431 East Highway 224, Estacada, OR 97023.

Location: From Interstate 5 south of Portland, take exit 288 and head east on Interstate 205 for 12 miles to Gladstone. Turn east on Highway 224 and drive 15 miles to Estacada. Continue 27 miles southeast on Highway 224, then drive 3.5 miles south on Forest Service Road 46 to the campground.

Trip note: This campground is set at the confluence of the Clackamas and the Collawash rivers. Some nice swimming spots are available, but use care, some areas are rocky, swift and treacherous. The fishing in this area can be good.

59.　　　　　　　　　　RAAB　　　　　　　　　RV

Reference: **On Collawash River in Mount Hood National Forest; map C2, grid g6.**

Campsites, facilities: There are 27 sites for tents, trailers or RVs up to 22 feet long. Picnic tables and fire grills are provided. Pit toilets are available. There is **no piped water** in the campground; water is available one mile away at Two Rivers Picnic Area. Leashed pets are permitted.

Reservations, fee: Some sites may be reserved by calling (800) 280-CAMP ($7.75 reservation fee); $6 fee per night. Open late May to early September.

Who to contact: Phone the Clackamas Ranger District at (503) 630-4256 or write to Mount Hood National Forest, 61431 East Highway 224, Estacada, OR 97023.

Location: From Interstate 5 south of Portland, take exit 288 and head east on Interstate 205 for 12 miles to Gladstone. Turn east on Highway 224 and drive 15 miles to Estacada. Continue southeast on Highway 224 for 27 miles, then drive four miles south on Forest Service Road 46 to the campground.

Trip note: This campground is set along the banks of the Collawash River, about a mile from its confluence with the Clackamas River. This camp gets moderate use, but it's usually quiet and has a nice secluded atmosphere. Swimming and fishing are two recreation options here.

60.　　　　　　　　KINGFISHER　　　　　　　RV

Reference: **On the Hot Springs Fork of Collawash River in Mount Hood National Forest; map C2, grid g6.**

Campsites, facilities: There are 23 sites for tents, trailers or RVs up to 16 feet long. Picnic tables and fireplaces provided. Vault toilets and hand-pumped water are available. Leashed pets are permitted.

Reservations, fee: Some sites may be reserved by calling (800) 280-CAMP ($7.75 reservation fee); $9 fee per night. Open late May to early September.

Who to contact: Phone the Estacada Ranger District at (503) 630-6861 or write to Mount Hood National Forest, 595 NR Industrial Way, Estacada, OR 97023.

Location: From Interstate 5 south of Portland, take exit 288 and head east on Interstate 205 for 12 miles to Gladstone. Turn east on Highway 224 and drive 15 miles to Estacada. Continue 26 miles southeast on Highway 224 to Forest Service Road 46. Turn right and drive 3.5 miles south on Forest Service Road 46, then three miles south on Forest Service Road 63. Turn west on Forest Service Road 70 and drive one mile to the campground.

Trip note: This pretty campground is set along the banks of the Hot Springs Fork of the Collawash River, about three miles from Bagby Hot Springs, a Forest Service day-use area. It is an easy 1.5-mile hike to the hot springs from the day-use area. There is fishing access near the campground.

61. HUMBUG 🆁🆅

Reference: **On Breitenbush River in Willamette National Forest; map C2, grid g6.**

Campsites, facilities: There are 21 sites for tents, trailers or RVs up to 22 feet long. Picnic tables, fire grills, piped water and vault toilets are available. Leashed pets are permitted.

Reservations, fee: No reservations; $8 fee per night. Open mid-April to late September.

Who to contact: Phone the Detroit Ranger District at (503) 854-3366, or write Willamette National Forest, HC 73, P.O. Box 320, Mill City, OR 97360.

Location: From Interstate 5 at Salem, take exit 253 and turn east on Highway 22. Drive 52 miles to Detroit, then turn left on Forest Service Road 46 (Breitenbush Road) and travel five miles northeast to the campground.

Trip note: This campground is set along the bank of Breitenbush River about four miles from where it empties into Detroit Lake. Fishing and hiking are popular here. Nearby Detroit Lake offers many other recreation opportunities.

62. ELK LAKE

Reference: **Near Bull of the Woods Wilderness in Willamette National Forest; map C2, grid g6.**

Campsites, facilities: There are 14 primitive tent sites. Picnic tables, fire grills and pit toilets are available. There is **no piped water**. Leashed pets are permitted. Primitive launching facilities are available.

Reservations, fee: No reservations; no fee. Open July to mid-September.

Who to contact: Phone the Detroit Ranger District at (503) 854-3366 or write to Willamette National Forest, HC 73, P.O. Box 320, Mill City, OR 97360.

Location: From Interstate 5 at Salem, take exit 253 and turn east on Highway 22. Drive 52 miles to Detroit, then turn left on Forest Service Road 46 (Breitenbush Road) and travel 4.5 miles. Continue 10 miles north on Forest Service Road 4696 (Elk Lake Road) to the campground. The road is extremely rough for the last two miles. High-clearance vehicles are recommended.

Trip note: This remote campground is set along the shore of Elk Lake, where boating, fishing and swimming can be quite good in summer. Several trails are nearby that provide access to the Bull of the Woods Wilderness. Please pack out your garbage.

63. BREITENBUSH LAKE

Reference: **On Breitenbush Lake in Mount Hood National Forest; map C2, grid g6.**

Campsites, facilities: There are 20 sites for tents or trailers. Picnic tables and fire grills are provided. Vault toilets are available. There is **no piped water**. A store and ice are located within five miles. Leashed pets are permitted. Boat docks, launching facilities and rentals are nearby.

Reservations, fee: No reservations; no fee. Open mid-June to late September.

Who to contact: Phone the Clackamas Ranger District at (503) 630-4256 or write to Mount Hood National Forest, 61431 East Highway 224, Estacada, OR 97023.

Location: From Interstate 5 south of Portland, take exit 288 and head east on Interstate 205 for 12 miles to Gladstone. Turn east on Highway 224 and drive 15 miles to Estacada. Continue 27 miles southeast on Highway 224, then drive 28.5 miles south on Forest Service Road 46. Turn east on Forest Service Road 4220 and drive 8.5 miles to the lake. Be aware that the access road to the lake is not maintained and can be pretty rough. Only high-clearance vehicles are recommended.

Trip note: This lakeside campground is set at 5,500 feet on the western border of the Warm Springs Indian Reservation. Breitenbush is a large lake, which borders on the Mount Jefferson Wilderness Area. Numerous trails provide access to other lakes in the area, and horses are allowed in areas specified by the Forest Service. The Pacific Crest Trail skirts the camp to the west. Ripe huckleberries can be found in the area in late August and September.

64.   RAINBOW   RV.

Reference: **On the Oak Grove Fork of Clackamas River in Mount Hood National Forest; map C2, grid g7.**

Campsites, facilities: There are 17 sites for tents, trailers or RVs up to 16 feet long. There is **no piped water.** Fire grills and picnic tables are provided. Vault toilets are available. Leashed pets are permitted.

Reservations, fee: Some sites may be reserved by calling (800) 280-CAMP ($7.75 reservation fee); $9 fee per night. Open late April to late September.

Who to contact: Phone the Clackamas Ranger District at (503) 630-4256 or write to Mount Hood National Forest, 61431 East Highway 224, Estacada, OR 97023.

Location: From Interstate 5 south of Portland, take exit 288 and head east on Interstate 205 for 12 miles to Gladstone. Turn east on Highway 224 and drive 15 miles to Estacada. Continue 27 miles southeast on Highway 224 to Forest Service Road 46. The camp is about 100 yards south on Forest Service Road 46.

Trip note: This campground is set along the banks of the Oak Grove Fork of the Clackamas River not far from where it empties into the Clackamas River. Nearby Ripplebrook Campground provides an option. See that trip note for area details.

---

65.   ROUND LAKE

Reference: **On Round Lake, walk-in only in Mount Hood National Forest; map C2, grid g7.**

Campsites, facilities: There are six tent sites at this hike-in campground. Picnic tables and fire grills are provided. Pit toilets are available. There is **no piped water**. Leashed pets are permitted.

Reservations, fee: No reservations; no fee. Open mid-June to late September.

Who to contact: Phone the Clackamas Ranger District at (503) 630-4256 or write to Mount Hood National Forest, 61431 East Highway 224, Estacada, OR 97023.

Location: From Interstate 5 south of Portland, take exit 288 and head east on Interstate 205 for 12 miles to Gladstone. Turn east on Highway 224 and drive 15 miles to Estacada. Continue 27 miles southeast on Highway 224, then 3.5 miles south on Forest Service Road 46. Turn on Forest Service Road 63 and travel southeast for 12.5 miles, then continue southeast on Forest Service Road 6370 for 6.7 miles until you get to the campground parking area. Walk one-half mile to the campground.

Trip note: This is an idyllic spot, beautiful and secluded, set at the edge of Round Lake. It's well worth figuring out the maze of Forest Service roads and then making the half-mile hike. The walk-in stipulation keeps out die-hard car campers, so it's possible to have this lovely site all to yourself.

---

66.   BREITENBUSH   RV

Reference: **On Breitenbush River in Willamette National Forest; map C2, grid g7.**

Campsites, facilities: There are 29 sites for tents, trailers or RVs up to 22 feet long (longer trailers may have difficulty parking and turning). Picnic tables and fire grills are provided. Piped water and vault toilets are available. Leashed pets are permitted.

Reservations, fee: No reservations; $8-$16 fee per night. Open mid-April to late September.

Who to contact: Phone the Detroit Ranger District at (503) 854-3366 or write to Willamette National Forest, HC 73 Box 320, Mill City, OR 97360.

Location: From Interstate 5 at Salem, take exit 253 and turn east on Highway 22. Drive 50 miles to Detroit. From Detroit, travel ten miles northeast on Forest Service Road 46 (Breitenbush Road) to the campground.

Trip note: This campground is set along the Breitenbush River and has fishing access available. South Breitenbush Gorge National Recreation Trail is three miles away. It is detailed on a map of Willamette National Forest. Breitenbush Hot Springs is just over a mile away. If this campground is crowded, try nearby Cleator Bend camp.

---

67.   CLEATER BEND   RV

Reference: **Near Breitenbush River in Willamette National Forest; map C2, grid g7.**

Campsites, facilities: There are nine sites for tents, trailers or RVs up to 16 feet long. Picnic tables, fire grills, piped water and vault toilets are available. Leashed pets are permitted.

Reservations, fee: No reservations; $8 fee per night. Open mid-May to late September.

Who to contact: Phone the Detroit Ranger District at (503) 854-3366 or write to Willamette National Forest, HC 73, P.O. Box 320, Mill City, OR 97360.

Location: From Interstate 5 at Salem, take exit 253 and turn east on Highway 22. Drive 50 miles to Detroit. From Detroit, travel nine miles northeast on Forest Service Road 46 (Breitenbush Road) to the campground.

Trip note: This camp is set on the banks of the Breitenbush River, with pretty, shaded sites, many with creek views. It's not far from Breitenbush Campground; see that trip note for area details.

---

68.   CAMP TEN   RV

Reference: **On Olallie Lake in Mount Hood National Forest; map C2, grid g7.**

Campsites, facilities: There are seven sites for tents, trailers or RVs up to 16 feet long. Picnic tables and fire grills are provided. Pit toilets are available. There is **no piped water**. Leashed pets are permitted. A store that sells fishing tackle and other supplies is nearby. Boat docks, launching facilities and rentals are nearby.

Reservations, fee: No reservations; $6 fee per night. Open mid-June to late September.

Who to contact: Phone the Clackamas Ranger District at (503) 630-4256 or write to Mount Hood National Forest, 61431 East Highway 224, Estacada, OR 97023.

Location: From Interstate 5 south of Portland, take exit 288 and head east on Interstate 205 for 12 miles to Gladstone. Turn east on Highway 224 and drive 15 miles to Estacada. Continue southeast on Highway 224 for 27 miles, then drive south on Forest Service Road 46 for about 22 miles. From there, travel on Forest Service Road 4690 southeast for 8.2 miles. When you reach Forest Service Road 4220, head south for six miles to the campground.

Trip note: This is one of several campgrounds set along the shore of Olallie Lake, a popular area. This one is on the western shore. Boats without motors, such as canoes, kayaks and rafts, are permitted on the lake. This camp is set in the midst of the Olallie Lake Scenic Area, which is home to a number of pristine mountain lakes and a network of hiking trails. See a Forest Service map for trail locations.

---

69.   LOWER LAKE

Reference: Near Olallie Lake in Mount Hood National Forest; map C2, grid g7.

Campsites, facilities: There are nine tent sites. Picnic tables and fire grills are provided. Pit toilets are available. There is **no piped water**. Leashed pets are permitted. Boat docks, launching facilities and rentals are nearby at Olallie Lake.

Reservations, fee: No reservations; no fee. Open mid-June to late September.

Who to contact: Phone the Clackamas Ranger District at (503) 630-4256 or write to Mount Hood National Forest, 61431 East Highway 224, Estacada, OR 97023.

Location: From Interstate 5 south of Portland, take exit 288 and head east on Interstate 205 for 12 miles to Gladstone. Turn east on Highway 224 and drive 15 miles to Estacada. Continue southeast on Highway 224 for 27 miles, then drive south on Forest Service Road 46 for about 22 miles. From there, travel on Forest Service Road 4690 southeast for 8.5 miles. When you reach Forest Service Road 4220, head south for 4.5 miles to the parking area. Hike one-half mile to the campground.

Trip note: This sunny, open campground is set along the shore of Lower Lake, a small, deep lake that's perfect for fishing and swimming. It is a short distance from Olallie Lake and near a network of trails that provide access to other nearby lakes. We advise you to obtain a Forest Service map that details the backcountry roads and trails.

---

70.   OLALLIE MEADOWS   [RV]

Reference: Near Olallie Lake in Mount Hood National Forest; map C2, grid g7.

Campsites, facilities: There are five sites for tents, trailers or RVs up to 16 feet long. Picnic tables and fire grills are provided. Pit toilets are available. There is **no piped water**. Leashed pets are permitted. Boat docks, launching facilities and rentals are located about three miles away on Olallie Lake.

Reservations, fee: No reservations; no fee. Open mid-June to late September.

Who to contact: Phone the Clackamas Ranger District at (503) 630-4256 or write to Mount Hood National Forest, 61431 East Highway 224, Estacada, OR 97023.

Location: From Interstate 5 south of Portland, take exit 288 and head east on Interstate 205 for 12 miles to Gladstone. Turn east on Highway 224 and drive 15 miles to Estacada. Continue southeast on Highway 224 for 27 miles, then drive south on Forest Service Road 46 for about 22 miles. From there, travel on Forest Service Road 4690 southeast for 8.2 miles. When you reach Forest Service Road 4220, head south for 1.5 miles to the campground.

Trip note: This campground is set at 4,500 feet in a large, peaceful meadow about three miles from Olallie Lake. The Pacific Crest Trail passes very close to camp. Horses are permitted only at specified campsites. See the trip note for Camp Ten for area details.

---

71. PAUL DENNIS

Reference: On Olallie Lake in Mount Hood National Forest; map C2, grid g7.

Campsites, facilities: There are 15 sites for tents or small campers (trailers are not recommended) and three hike-in tent sites. Picnic tables and fire grills are provided. Pit toilets are available. There is **no piped water.** A store and ice are nearby. Leashed pets are permitted. Boat docks, launching facilities and rentals are located on Olallie Lake.

Reservations, fee: No reservations; $6 fee per night. Open mid-June to late September.

Who to contact: Phone the Clackamas Ranger District at (503) 630-4256 or write to Mount Hood National Forest, 61431 East Highway 224, Estacada, OR 97023.

Location: From Interstate 5 south of Portland, take exit 288 and head east on Interstate 205 for 12 miles to Gladstone. Turn east on Highway 224 and drive 15 miles to Estacada. Continue southeast on Highway 224 for 27 miles, then drive south on Forest Service Road 46 for about 22 miles. From there, travel on Forest Service Road 4690 southeast for 8.2 miles. When you reach Forest Service Road 4220, head south for 6.2 miles to the campground.

Trip note: This campground is set along the north shore of Olallie Lake. From here, you can see the reflection of Mount Jefferson (10,497 feet). Boats with motors are not permitted on the lake. A trail from camp leads to Nep-Te-Pa Lake, Monon Lake and Long Lake, which lies just east of the border of the Warm Springs Indian Reservation. It's advisable to obtain a Forest Service map.

---

72. PENINSULA   RV

Reference: On Olallie Lake in Mount Hood National Forest; map C2, grid g7.

Campsites, facilities: There are 35 sites for tents, trailers or RVs up to 22 feet long, and six walk-in tent sites. Picnic tables and fire grills are provided. Vault toilets are available. There is **no piped water.** Some facilities are **wheelchair accessible**. Leashed pets are permitted. Boat docks, launching facilities and rentals are nearby.

Reservations, fee: No reservations; $6 fee per night. Open mid-June to late September.

Who to contact: Phone the Clackamas Ranger District at (503) 630-4256 or write to Mount Hood National Forest, 61431 East Highway 224, Estacada, OR 97023.

Location: From Interstate 5 south of Portland, take exit 288 and head east on Interstate 205 for 12 miles to Gladstone. Turn east on Highway 224 and drive 15 miles to Estacada. Continue southeast on Highway 224 for 27 miles, then drive south on Forest Service Road 46 for about 22 miles. From there, travel on Forest Service Road 4690 southeast for 8.2 miles. When you reach Forest Service Road 4220, head south for 6.5 miles to the campground.

Trip note: This is the largest of several campgrounds set along the shore of Olallie Lake. This one is on the south shore. The amphitheater is near camp, and, during the summer, rangers present campfire programs. Boats without motors are permitted on the lake. Numerous smaller lakes in the area can be reached from trails nearby. See trip note for Camp Ten for details.

---

73. SHELLROCK CREEK RV

Reference: **On Shellrock Creek in Mount Hood National Forest; map C2, grid g8.**

Campsites, facilities: There are five sites for tents, trailers or RVs up to 16 feet long. Picnic tables and fire grills are provided. Vault toilets are available. There is **no piped water**. Leashed pets are permitted.

Reservations, fee: No reservations; $7 fee per night. Open mid-June to early September.

Who to contact: Phone the Clackamas Ranger District at (503) 630-4256 or write to Mount Hood National Forest, 61431 East Highway 224, Estacada, OR 97023.

Location: From Portland, turn east on US 26 and drive 55 miles to the small town of Government Camp. Continue 15 miles southeast on US 26, then eight miles south on Forest Service Road 42. Turn west on Forest Service Road 57 and drive 15 miles to Forest Service Road 58. The campground is one mile south on Forest Service Road 58.

Trip note: This quiet little campground is at a nice spot on Shellrock Creek, good for "sneak fishing" for trout. It's advisable to obtain a Forest Service map that details the backcountry roads and trails.

---

74. OAK FORK RV

Reference: **On Timothy Lake in Mount Hood National Forest; map C2, grid g8.**

Campsites, facilities: There are 47 sites for tents, trailers or RVs up to 32 feet long. Picnic tables and fire grills are provided. Hand-pumped water, firewood and vault toilets are available. Leashed pets are permitted. A boat ramp and launching facilities are nearby.

Reservations, fee: Some sites may be reserved by calling (800) 280-CAMP ($7.75 reservation fee); $10-$12 fee per night. Open June through mid-September.

Who to contact: Phone the Bear Springs Ranger District at (503) 328-6211 or write to Mount Hood National Forest, Route 1, P.O. Box 222, Maupin, OR 97037.

Location: From Portland, turn east on US 26 and drive 55 miles to the small town of Government Camp. Continue southeast on US 26 for 15 miles, then drive eight miles south on Forest Service Road 42. Turn right on Forest Service Road 57 and drive three miles to the park on the right.

Trip note: This camp is set along the south shore of Timothy Lake, just east of Gone Creek and Hoodview campgrounds. See those trip notes for details.

75.   PINE POINT   RV

Reference: On Timothy Lake in Mount Hood National Forest; map C2, grid g8.

Campsites, facilities: There are 25 sites for tents, trailers or RVs up to 31 feet long: 10 single sites, 10 double sites and five group campsites. Picnic tables and fire grills are provided. Piped water, firewood , a **wheelchair accessible** fishing pier and vault toilets are available. Leashed pets are permitted. A boat ramp and launching facilities are nearby.

Reservations, fee: Some sites may be reserved by calling (800) 280-CAMP ($7.75 reservation fee); $10-$35 fee per night depending on type of campsite; $5 each additional vehicle. Open late May to mid-September.

Who to contact: Phone the Bear Springs Ranger District at (503) 328-6211 or write to Mount Hood National Forest, Route 1, P.O. Box 222, Maupin, OR 97037.

Location: From Portland, turn east on US 26 and drive 55 miles to the small town of Government Camp. Continue southeast on US 26 for 15 miles, then drive eight miles south on Forest Service Road 42. Turn right on Forest Service Road 57 and drive four miles to the campground on the right.

Trip note: This is one of five camps on Timothy Lake. This one is located on the southwest shore, and has lake access. The trail that leads around the lake and to the Pacific Crest Trail is just outside of camp. See the trip note for Gone Creek camp for boating and fishing details.

76.   HOODVIEW   RV

Reference: On Timothy Lake in Mount Hood National Forest; map C2, grid g9.

Campsites, facilities: There are 43 sites for tents, trailers or RVs up to 31 feet long. Picnic tables and fire grills are provided. Piped water, firewood and vault toilets are available. Leashed pets are permitted. A boat ramp is nearby.

Reservations, fee: Some sites may be reserved by calling (800) 280-CAMP ($7.75 reservation fee); $10-$12 fee per night; $5 each additional vehicle. Open mid-May to mid-September.

Who to contact: Phone the Bear Springs Ranger District at (503) 328-6211 or write to Mount Hood National Forest, Route 1, P.O. Box 222, Maupin, OR 97037.

Location: From Portland, turn east on US 26 and drive 55 miles to the small town of Government Camp. Continue southeast on US 26 for 15 miles, then drive eight miles south on Forest Service Road 42. Turn right on Forest Service Road 57 and continue three miles to the campground on the right.

Trip note: This site is also set along the south shore of Timothy Lake. A trail out of camp branches south for a few miles, and if followed to the east, eventually leads to the Pacific Crest Trail. See the trip note for Gone Creek for boating and fishing details.

77.   SUMMIT LAKE

Reference: On Summit Lake in Mount Hood National Forest; map C2, grid g9.

Campsites, facilities: There are six tent sites. Fire grills and picnic tables are provided. Vault toilets and piped water are available. There is **no piped water**. Leashed pets are permitted. No motorboats are allowed.

Reservations, fee: No reservations; no fee. Open late May through September.

Who to contact: Phone the Bear Springs Ranger District at (503) 328-6211 or write to Mount Hood National Forest, Route 1, P.O. Box 222, Maupin, OR 97037.

Location: From Portland, turn east on US 26 and drive 55 miles to the small town of Government Camp. Continue southeast on US 26 for 15 miles, then drive 12 miles south on Forest Service Road 42. Head west on Forest Service Road 141 (a dirt road) for one mile to the campground on the left.

Trip note: This is an idyllic setting in a remote area along the western slopes of the Cascade Range. The camp is located on the shore of little Summit Lake. It's primitive, but it's a jewel. It's perfect alternative to the more crowded camps at Timothy Lake, but you can access all the same recreation options by driving just a short distance north.

78. GONE CREEK RV.

Reference: **On Timothy Lake in Mount Hood National Forest; map C2, grid g9.**

Campsites, facilities: There are 45 sites for tents, trailers or RVs up to 31 feet long. Piped water, fire grills and picnic tables are provided. Vault toilets and firewood are available. Leashed pets are permitted. A boat ramp is nearby.

Reservations, fee: Some sites may be reserved by calling (800) 280-CAMP ($7.75 reservation fee); $10-$12 fee per night; $5 each additional vehicle. Open mid-May to mid-September.

Who to contact: Phone the Bear Springs Ranger District at (503) 328-6211 or write to Mount Hood National Forest, Route 1, P.O. Box 222, Maupin, OR 97037.

Location: From Portland, turn east on US 26 and drive 55 miles to the small town of Government Camp. Continue southeast on US 26 for 15 miles, then drive eight miles south on Forest Service Road 42. Turn right on Forest Service Road 57 and drive one mile west to the campground on the right.

Trip note: This campground is set along the south shore of Timothy Lake at 3,200 feet. It is one of four camps at the lake. Timothy Lake provides good fishing for brook trout, cutthroat trout, rainbow trout and Kokanee salmon. Boats with motors are allowed, but a 10 miles per hour speed limit keeps it quiet. Several trails are in the area, including the Pacific Crest Trail, which provide access to several small mountain lakes.

79. JOE GRAHAM HORSE CAMP RV.

Reference: **Near Clackamas Lake in Mount Hood National Forest; map C2, grid g9.**

Campsites, facilities: There are 14 sites for tents, trailers, horse trailers or RVs up to 28 feet long (nine with corrals). Picnic tables, hitching posts and fire grills are provided. Piped water, vault toilets and firewood are available. Leashed pets are permitted.

Reservations, fee: Some sites may be reserved by calling (800) 280-CAMP ($7.75 reservation fee); $9 fee per night; $5 each additional vehicle. Open mid-May to mid-September.

Who to contact: Phone the Bear Springs Ranger District at (503) 328-6211 or write to Mount Hood National Forest, Route 1, P.O. Box 222, Maupin, OR 97037.

Location: From Portland, turn east on US 26 and drive 55 miles to the small town of Government Camp. Continue southeast on US 26 for 15 miles, then drive eight miles south on Forest Service Road 42 to the campground on the left.

Trip note: This campground, named for a forest ranger, is set just north of tiny Clackamas Lake and is one of two campgrounds in the area that allows horses. See the trip note for Clackamas Lake for additional information. Timothy Lake (Gone Creek, Hoodview, Oak Fork, Pine Point and Meditation Point) provides a nearby alternative to the northwest. The Pacific Crest Trail is located just east of camp.

80. CLACKAMAS LAKE ⛺

Reference: **Near Clackamas River in Mount Hood National Forest; map C2, grid g9.**

Campsites, facilities: There are 46 sites for tents, trailers, horse trailers or RVs up to 16 feet long (19 with corrals). Piped water, fire grills and picnic tables are provided. Vault toilets and firewood are available. Leashed pets are permitted. Boat docks and launching facilities are nearby at Timothy Lake.

Reservations, fee: Some sites may be reserved by calling (800) 280-CAMP ($7.75 reservation fee); $9 fee per night; $5 each additional vehicle. Open June to mid-September.

Who to contact: Phone the Bear Springs Ranger District at (503) 328-6211 or write to Mount Hood National Forest, Route 1, P.O. Box 222, Maupin, OR 97037.

Location: From Portland, turn east on US 26 and drive 55 miles to the small town of Government Camp. Continue southeast on US 26 for 15 miles, then drive eight miles south on Forest Service Road 42/Skyline Road, about 500 feet past the Clackamas Lake Historic Ranger Station. Turn east (left) on Forest Service Road 4270 and drive one-half mile to the campground on the left.

Trip note: Clackamas Lake is small and shallow, but not far from the Clackamas River. The Pacific Crest Trail passes nearby and Timothy Lake is little more than a one-mile hike from camp. See the trip note for Gone Creek for information on Timothy Lake.

LEAVE NO TRACE TIPS

Keep the wilderness wild.

• Treat our natural heritage with respect.
Leave plants, rocks, and historical artifacts as you found them.

• Good campsites are found, not made. Do not alter a campsite.

• Let nature's sounds prevail; keep loud voices and noises to a minimum.

• Do not build structures or furniture or dig trenches.

OREGON MAP .... see page 380
Adjoining Maps
NORTH .... Washington
EAST (C4) .... see page 444
SOUTH (D3) .... see page 562
WEST (C2) .... see page 400

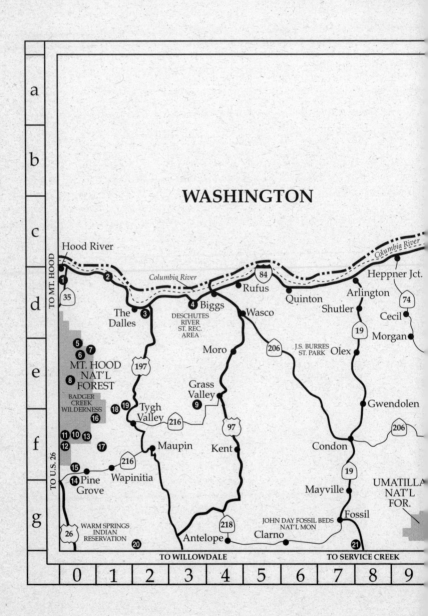

Oregon Map C3 featuring: Hood River, Columbia River Gorge, Columbia River, Deschutes River, Badger Lake, Mount Hood National Forest, Pine Hollow Reservoir, Warm Springs Indian Reservation

1. TUCKER PARK

Reference: **On Hood River; map C3, grid d0.**

Campsites, facilities: There are five tent sites and 29 sites for tents, trailers or RVs of any length. Picnic tables are provided. Electricity, piped water, flush toilets, showers, firewood and a playground are available. A store, a cafe, laundromat and ice are located within one mile. Leashed pets and motorbikes are permitted.

Reservations, fee: No reservations; $10-$15 fee per night. Open April to November.

Who to contact: Phone (541) 386-6323 or write to 2440 Dee Highway, Hood River, OR 97031.

Location: From Portland, turn east on Interstate 84 and drive about 65 miles to the town of Hood River, then travel four miles south on Highway 281 to the park.

Trip note: This county park is set along the banks of the Hood River. It's just far enough out of the way to be missed by most of the tourist traffic. Recreation options include trout fishing and swimming.

---

2. MEMALOOSE STATE PARK

Reference: **In Columbia River Gorge; map C3, grid d1.**

Campsites, facilities: There are 67 tent sites and 43 sites with full hookups for trailers or RVs of any length. Picnic tables and fire grills are provided. Flush toilets, sanitary services, showers and firewood are available. Some facilities are **wheelchair accessible**. Pets and motorbikes are permitted.

Reservations, fee: Contact Reservations Northwest at (800) 452-5687 ($6 reservation fee); $13-$19 fee per night. Open mid-April to late October.

Who to contact: Phone (541) 478-3008 or (800) 452-5687 or write to Columbia River Gorge District, P.O. Box 100, Corbett, OR 97019.

Location: This park is accessible only to westbound traffic on Interstate 84. From The Dalles, drive 11 miles west on Interstate 84 to the signed turnoff. It is located about 75 miles east of Portland.

Trip note: This park borrows its name from ancient Native Americans, who used a nearby offshore island as a sacred burial ground. It is set along the scenic Columbia River Gorge and makes a prime layover spot for campers cruising the Oregon-Washington border. This is a popular camp which receives a good deal of traffic, so plan on arriving early to claim a spot.

---

3. LONE PINE TRAVEL PARK

Reference: **Near Columbia River; map C3, grid d2.**

Campsites, facilities: There are 22 drive-through sites for trailers or RVs of any length. Electricity, piped water and sewer hookups are provided. Flush toilets, showers, a cafe, a laundromat, ice and a playground are available. Bottled gas and sanitary services are located within one mile. Leashed pets are permitted. Boat docks and launching facilities are nearby.

Reservations, fee: Reservations accepted; $20 fee per night. MasterCard and Visa accepted. Open mid-April through September.

Who to contact: Phone (541) 296-9133 or write to 335 US 197, The Dalles, OR 97058.

Location: From Portland, turn east on Interstate 84 and drive approximately 90

miles to The Dalles. Take exit 87 to US 197 and follow it to the park.

Trip note: This private park is set not far from the Columbia River, where fishing, boating and swimming are options. This area gets hot weather and occasional winds shooting through the river canyon during summer months. Nearby recreation options include an 18-hole golf course and tennis courts.

4. DESCHUTES RIVER STATE PARK 🚐

Reference: **On Deschutes River; map C3, grid d3.**

Campsites, facilities: There are 34 primitive sites for tents, trailers or self-contained RVs up to 30 feet long. Picnic tables and fire grills are provided. Piped water and flush toilets are available. Leashed pets are permitted.

Reservations, fee: No reservations; $11 fee per night. Open mid-April to late October.

Who to contact: Phone (541) 739-2322 or (800) 452-5687 or write to 89600 Biggs-Rufus Highway, Wasco, OR 97065.

Location: From Portland, turn east on Interstate 84 and drive approximately 90 miles to The Dalles. Continue 12 miles east on Interstate 84, then take exit 97 at Celilo and turn south on Highway 206. Drive five miles to the park.

Trip note: This park is set along the Deschutes River near where it enters the Columbia River. It offers bicycling and hiking trails and good steelhead fishing in season. There's a small day-use state park called Heritage Landing across the river, which has a boat ramp and restroom facilities. The Army Corps of Engineers offers a free train ride and tour of the dam at The Dalles during the summer. Good rafting is a bonus here. For 25 miles upstream, the river is mostly inaccessible by car.

5. KNEBAL SPRINGS 🚐

Reference: **Near Knebal Springs in Mount Hood National Forest; map C3, grid e0.**

Campsites, facilities: There are five sites for tents and small trailers or RVs. Piped water, picnic tables and fire grills are provided. Pit toilets are available. Horse loading and tending facilities are available. Leashed pets are permitted.

Reservations, fee: No reservations; no fee. Open June to early October.

Who to contact: Phone (541) 352-6002 or write to the Hood River Ranger District, 6780 Highway 35 South, Mount Hood-Parkdale, OR 97041.

Location: From Portland, turn east on Interstate 84 and drive approximately 90 miles. Take exit 87 and turn south on US 197. Drive 13 miles south to Dufur, then turn right on Dufur Valley Road and drive 12 miles west. Continue on Forest Service Road 44 and continue west to Forest Service Road 4430. Turn north and travel four miles, then drive southwest on Forest Service Road 1720 for one mile to the campground.

Trip note: This is in a semi-primitive area near Knebal Springs, an ephemeral water source. A trail from the camp provides access to a network of other trails in the area. A Forest Service map is advised.

6. EIGHTMILE CROSSING 🚐

Reference: **On Eightmile Creek in Mount Hood National Forest; map C3, grid e0.**

Campsites, facilities: There are 24 sites for tents, trailers or RVs up to 30 feet long. **No piped water** is available. Picnic tables and fire grills are provided. Pit toilets are available. Leashed pets are permitted.

Reservations, fee: No reservations; no fee. Open June to mid-October.

Who to contact: Phone (541) 352-6002 or write to the Hood River Ranger District, 6780 Highway 35 South, Mount Hood-Parkdale, OR 97041.

Location: From Portland, turn east on Interstate 84 and drive approximately 90 miles. Take exit 87 and turn south on US 197. Drive 13 miles south to Dufur, then turn right on Dufur Valley Road and drive 12 miles west. Continue on Forest Service Road 44 and continue west to Forest Service Road 4430. Turn north and travel one-half mile to the campground.

Trip note: This campground is set along Eightmile Creek and gets relatively little camping pressure. It's pretty and shaded, with sites along the creek. From the day-use area, you can access a nice hiking trail that runs along Eightmile Creek. The fishing can be good here.

---

7. PEBBLE FORD

Reference: **In Mount Hood National Forest; map C3, grid e0.**

Campsites, facilities: There are three sites for tents, trailers or RVs up to 15 feet long. Picnic tables and fire grills provided. Pit toilets are available. There is **no piped water**. Leashed pets are permitted.

Reservations, fee: No reservations; no fee. Open June to early October.

Who to contact: Phone (541) 352-6002 or write to the Hood River Ranger District, 6780 Highway 35 South, Mount Hood-Parkdale, OR 97041.

Location: From Portland, turn east on Interstate 84 and drive approximately 90 miles. Take exit 87 and turn south on US 197. Drive 13 miles south to Dufur, then turn right on Dufur Valley Road and drive 12 miles west. Continue on Forest Service Road 44 and drive five miles west. Turn south on Forest Service Road 130 and travel one-half mile to the campground.

Trip note: This is just a little camping spot by the side of the gravel Forest Service road. It is primitive and quiet, an alternative to the better-known Eightmile Crossing. There are some quality hiking trails in the area if you're willing to travel a bit to the trailheads.

---

8. BADGER LAKE

Reference: **On Badger Lake in Mount Hood National Forest; map C3, grid e0.**

Campsites, facilities: There are four sites for tents only, accessible only by high-clearance vehicles. Picnic tables and fire grills are provided. Pit toilets are available. There is **no piped water**. Leashed pets are permitted.

Reservations, fee: No reservations; no fee. Open July to early October.

Who to contact: Phone the Barlow Ranger District at (541) 467-2291 or write to Mount Hood National Forest, P.O. Box 67, Dufur, OR 97021.

Location: From Portland, turn east on Interstate 84 and drive 65 miles to the town of Hood River. Turn south on Highway 35 (exit 64) and drive 37 miles, then turn left onto Forest Service Road 48 and drive 16 miles to Forest Service Road 4860. Turn north and drive eight miles to Forest Service Road 140 and drive four miles to the lake. The last two miles on this primitive road require a high-clearance vehicle. Got that?

Trip note: This high-country campground is set along the shore of Badger Lake. Boating is permitted, if you can manage to get a boat in here. No trailers are allowed on campground roads. It is adjacent to the Badger Creek Wilderness area and numerous trails provide access to the backcountry. The nearest trail heads out of camp northeast along Badger Creek for several miles.

---

9. BEAVERTAIL   RV

Reference: **On Deschutes River; map C3, grid e3.**

Campsites, facilities: There are 21 sites for tents, trailers or RVs up to 30 feet long. Picnic tables and fire grills are provided. Vault toilets are available. There is **no piped water**. Leashed pets are permitted. Boat launching facilities are nearby.

Reservations, fee: No reservations; $3 fee per night; 14-day limit. Open all year.

Who to contact: Phone (541) 447-4115, or write to Bureau of Land Management, P.O. Box 550, Prineville, OR 97754.

Location: From Portland, turn east on US 26 and drive approximately 68 miles. Turn east on Highway 216 and drive 26 miles, then turn south on US 197 and drive three miles to Maupin. Turn north on Deschutes River Road and drive 17 miles northeast to the campground.

Trip note: This isolated campground is set along the banks of the Deschutes River on BLM land with fishing and rafting options. The Deschutes is one of the classic trout streams in the Pacific Northwest. It's a small, pretty spot, with roomy sites, lots of trees and river views.

10. BONNEY MEADOWS   RV

Reference: **In Mount Hood National Forest; map C3, grid f0.**

Campsites, facilities: There are five sites for tents or small trailers or RVs. Picnic tables and fire grills are provided. Pit toilets are available. There is **no piped water**. Leashed pets are permitted.

Reservations, fee: No reservations; no fee. Open July to early October.

Who to contact: Phone the Barlow Ranger District at (541) 467-2291 or write to Mount Hood National Forest, P.O. Box 67, Dufur, OR 97021.

Location: From Portland, turn east on Interstate 84 and drive 91 miles. Take exit 87 and turn south on US 197. Drive 31 miles to Tygh Valley, then turn west and head toward Wamic. From Wamic, drive six miles west on County Road 226, then continue south and west on Forest Service Road 48 for 14 miles. Next, drive two miles north on Forest Service Road 4890, then continue four miles north on Forest Service Road 4891 to the campground.

Trip note: This high-elevation, primitive campground is located on the east side of the Cascade Range. As a result, there is little water in the area. There are also very few people, so you're liable to have the place all to yourself. Several trails are available, one of which travels 1.5 miles up to a group of small lakes. See a Forest Service map for details.

11. KEEPS MILL

Reference: **On Clear Creek in Mount Hood National Forest; map C3, grid f0.**

Campsites, facilities: There are five sites for tents. The road to the campground is not good for trailers. Picnic tables and fire grills are provided. Vault toilets are available. There is **no piped water**. Leashed pets are permitted.

Reservations, fee: No reservations; no fee. Open May through September.

Who to contact: Phone the Bear Springs Ranger District at (541) 328-6211 or write to Mount Hood National Forest, Route 1, P.O. Box 222, Maupin, OR 97037.

Location: From Portland, turn east on US 26 and drive 55 miles to Government Camp. Continue east for 25 miles, then turn east on Highway 216. Travel three miles and turn north on Forest Service Road 2120. Travel three miles to the end of the road and the campground.

Trip note: This small, pretty campground is located at the confluence of Clear Creek and the White River. Many hiking trails are in the area. A map of Mount Hood National Forest details the back roads and trails and is strongly advised.

12. CLEAR CREEK CROSSING

Reference: On Clear Creek in Mount Hood National Forest; map C3, grid f0.

Campsites, facilities: There are five sites for tents. Picnic tables and fire grills are provided. Vault toilets are available. There is **no piped water**. Leashed pets are permitted.

Reservations, fee: No reservations; no fee. Open May through September.

Who to contact: Phone the Bear Springs Ranger District at (541) 328-6211 or write to Mount Hood National Forest, Route 1, P.O. Box 222, Maupin, OR 97037.

Location: From Portland, turn east on US 26 and drive 55 miles to the small town of Government Camp. Take Highway 26 east and drive 25 miles to the Highway 216. Turn east (left) on Highway 216 and drive three miles. Turn north on Forest Service Road 2130 and drive another three miles. Turn east on Forest Service Road 260 and drive one-half mile directly into the campground.

Trip note: This campground is set along the banks of Clear Creek. It's a secluded, little-known camp in Mount Hood National Forest. Fishing and hiking are two recreation options here.

13. ROCK CREEK RESERVOIR   **RV**

Reference: On Rock Creek Reservoir in Mount Hood National Forest; map C3, grid f0.

Campsites, facilities: There are 33 sites for tents, trailers or RVs up to 22 feet long. Picnic tables and fire grills are provided. Pit toilets, piped water and firewood are available. Some facilities are **wheelchair accessible**. Leashed pets are permitted. There are boat docks nearby but no motorboats are allowed on the reservoir.

Reservations, fee: Some sites may be reserved by calling (800) 280-CAMP ($7.75 reservation fee); $9-$11 fee per night. Open mid-April to early October.

Who to contact: Phone the Barlow Ranger District at (541) 467-2291 or write to Mount Hood National Forest, P.O. Box 67, Dufur, OR 97021.

Location: From Portland, turn east on Interstate 84 and drive 91 miles. Take exit 87 and turn south on US 197. Drive 31 miles to Tygh Valley, then turn west and head toward Wamic. From Wamic, drive six miles west on County Road 226, then continue west on Forest Service Road 48 for one mile. The campground is located about 200 yards west on Forest Service Road 4820.

Trip note: This campground is set along the shore of Rock Creek Reservoir. Fishing is excellent here, with a perfect environment for canoes or rafts. There are no hiking trails in the immediate vicinity, but there are many old Forest Service roads that are ideal for walking or mountain biking.

14. BEAR SPRINGS   **RV**

Reference: On Indian Creek in Mount Hood National Forest; map C3, grid f0.

Campsites, facilities: There are 21 sites for tents, trailers or RVs up to 32 feet long. Piped water, fire grills and picnic tables are provided. Vault toilets and firewood are available. Leashed pets are permitted.

Reservations, fee: Some sites may be reserved by calling (800) 280-CAMP ($7.75

reservation fee); $8 fee per night; $5 each additional vehicle. Open June through September.

Who to contact: Phone the Bear Springs Ranger District at (541) 328-6211 or write to Mount Hood National Forest, Route 1, P.O. Box 222, Maupin, OR 97037.

Location: From Portland, turn east on US 26 and drive 55 miles to the small town of Government Camp. Continue southeast on US 26 for 25 miles, then turn east on Highway 216 and drive five miles. Turn east (right) on Reservation Road and look for the campground on the right.

Trip note: This campground is set along the banks of Indian Creek on the border of the Warm Springs Indian Reservation. The Bear Springs Ranger District is located near the camp, where rangers will be happy to supply maps and answer your questions about the area. There are a few good hiking trails nearby along US 26; see a Forest Service map for details.

---

15. McCUBBINS GULCH **RV.**

Reference: In Mount Hood National Forest; map C3, grid f0.

Campsites, facilities: There are five sites for tents and RVs. Picnic tables and fire grills are provided. Pit toilets available. There is **no piped water**. Leashed pets are permitted.

Reservations, fee: No reservations; no fee. Open May through September.

Who to contact: Phone the Bear Springs Ranger District at (541) 328-6211 or write to Mount Hood National Forest, Route 1, P.O. Box 222, Maupin, OR 97037.

Location: From Portland, turn east on US 26 and drive 55 miles to the small town of Government Camp. Continue southeast on US 26 for 25 miles, then turn east on Highway 216. Continue on Highway 216 for six miles, then make a sharp left onto Forest Service Road 2110 and continue for 1.5 miles. Look for the campground entrance on the right side.

Trip note: This is a small, primitive camp set along a small creek that offers decent fishing and OHV recreation. Though it's out of the way, it is heavily used, so claim a spot early in the day. To the south is the Warm Springs Indian Reservation. A nearby option is Bear Springs Campground.

---

16. FOREST CREEK **RV.**

Reference: On Forest Creek in Mount Hood National Forest; map C3, grid f1.

Campsites, facilities: There are eight sites for tents, trailers or RVs up to 16 feet long. **No piped water** is available. Picnic tables and fire grills are provided. Pit toilets are available. Leashed pets are permitted.

Reservations, fee: No reservations; no fee. Open June to early October.

Who to contact: Phone the Barlow Ranger District at (541) 467-2291 or write to Mount Hood National Forest, P.O. Box 67, Dufur, OR 97021.

Location: From Portland, turn east on Interstate 84 and drive 91 miles. Take exit 87 and turn south on US 197. Drive 31 miles to Tygh Valley, then turn west and head toward Wamic. From Wamic, drive six miles west on County Road 226, then continue south and west on Forest Service Road 48 for 12.5 miles. From there drive one mile southeast on Forest Service Road 4885, then south for one-quarter mile on Forest Service Road 3530 to the campground.

Trip note: This is a very old camp set along Forest Creek on the original Barlow Trail. Early settlers used to camp here. You cross a small bridge to reach the camp. By venturing a few miles north on the network of Forest Service roads, you can access a number of trails that lead into the Badger Creek Wilderness Area. See a Forest Service map for specific roads and trails.

---

17.   BONNEY CROSSING   RV

Reference: **On Badger Creek in Mount Hood National Forest; map C3, grid f1.**

Campsites, facilities: There are eight sites for tents, trailers or RVs up to 16 feet long. Picnic tables and fire grills are provided. Pit toilets are available. There is **no piped water**. Leashed pets are permitted.

Reservations, fee: No reservations; $5 fee per night. Open mid-April to mid-October.

Who to contact: Phone the Barlow Ranger District at (541) 467-2291 or write to Mount Hood National Forest, P.O. Box 67, Dufur, OR 97021.

Location: From Portland, turn east on Interstate 84 and drive 91 miles. Take exit 87 and turn south on US 197. Drive 31 miles to Tygh Valley, then turn west and head toward Wamic. From Wamic, drive six miles west on County Road 226, then continue west on Forest Service Road 48 for one mile. From there, drive 200 yards west on Forest Service Road 4810 to the campground.

Trip note: This campground is set along Badger Creek and is the trailhead for the Badger Creek Trail, which provides access to the Badger Creek Wilderness. The camp gets fairly light use and is usually very quiet. Fishing is available in the creek.

---

18.   PINE HOLLOW LAKESIDE RESORT   RV

Reference: **On Pine Hollow Reservoir; map C3, grid f1.**

Campsites, facilities: There are 35 tent sites and 75 sites for trailers or RVs. Electricity, piped water, sewer hookups and picnic tables are provided. Flush toilets, bottled gas, sanitary services, showers, firewood, a store, a cafe, a laundromat and ice are available. Pets and motorbikes are permitted. Boat docks, launching facilities and rentals are nearby.

Reservations, fee: Reservations accepted; $15 fee per night; MasterCard and Visa accepted. Open all year.

Who to contact: Phone (541) 544-2271 or write to 34 North Mariposa Drive, Wamic, OR 97063.

Location: From Portland, turn east on Interstate 84 and drive 91 miles. Take exit 87 and turn south on US 197. Drive south to the Tygh Valley Road exit, then drive 4.5 miles west on Wamic Market Road to Ross Road and follow it north 3.5 miles.

Trip note: This resort is set along the shore of Pine Hollow Reservoir. It's the best game in town for motor home campers, with shaded lakefront sites available. Year-round fishing, boating, swimming and waterskiing are some recreation options here.

---

19.   WASCO COUNTY FAIRGROUNDS   RV

Reference: **On Badger Creek; map C3, grid f1.**

Campsites, facilities: There are 50 tent sites and 150 drive-through sites for trailers or RVs of any length. Electricity, piped water and picnic tables are provided. Flush toilets, a dump station, sanitary services and showers are available. A store, a cafe and ice are located within one mile. Leashed pets are permitted.

Reservations, fee: Reservations accepted; $10 fee per night. Open all year.

Who to contact: Phone (541) 483-2288 or write to 81849 Fairground Road, Tygh Valley, OR 97063.

Location: From Portland, turn east on Interstate 84 and drive 91 miles. Take exit 87 and turn south on US 197. Drive south to the Tygh Valley Road exit, then drive northwest for about two miles. The campground is located on Fairgrounds Road.

Trip note: This county campground is set near the confluence of Badger Creek and Tygh Creek. Nearby recreation options include hiking trails, marked bike trails and tennis courts.

20. KAH-NEE-TA RESORT

Reference: **On Warm Springs Indian Reservation; map C3, grid g2.**

Campsites, facilities: There are 90 drive-through sites for tents, trailers or RVs of any length. Electricity, piped water and sewer hookups are provided. Flush toilets, bottled gas, sanitary services, showers, a cafe, a laundromat, ice, a playground and a swimming pool are available. Some **wheelchair accessible** facilities. Pets and motorbikes are permitted, but some areas are restricted.

Reservations, fee: Reservations accepted; $15-$26 fee per night; American Express, MasterCard and Visa accepted. Open all year.

Who to contact: Phone (541) 553-1112 or write to P.O. Box K, Warm Springs, OR 97761.

Location: From Portland, turn east on US 26 and drive approximately 105 miles to Warm Springs. Drive 11 miles northeast on Highway 3 to Kah-Nee-Ta to the resort on the right.

Trip note: This is the only public camp on the east side of the Warm Springs Indian Reservation; there are no other camps within 30 miles. The Warm Springs River runs nearby, with opportunities for fishing. Nearby recreation options include an 18-hole golf course, mini-golf, biking and hiking trails, a riding stable and tennis courts.

21. SHELTON STATE PARK

Reference: **Near Fossil; map C3, grid g8.**

Campsites, facilities: There are 36 primitive sites for tents, trailers or RVs up to 30 feet long. Picnic tables and fire grills are provided. Piped water, firewood and vault toilets are available. Pets are permitted.

Reservations, fee: No reservations; $7 fee per night. Open mid-April to late October.

Who to contact: Phone (541) 575-2773 or (800) 452-5687 or write to Clyde Holliday State Park at P.O. Box 9, Canyon City, OR 97820.

Location: From Interstate 84 at Biggs, take exit 104 and turn south on US 97. Drive 57 miles, then turn east on Highway 218 and drive 44 miles to Fossil. Turn southeast on Highway 19 and drive 10 miles to the park on the right.

Trip note: This is a good layover if you are stuck in the area with no place to camp for the night; there are no campgrounds on major roadways for an hour's drive in any direction. The closest options are primitive sites (Bull Prairie and Fairview, see Chapter C4), accessible by Forest Service roads. There is a nice two-mile hiking trail at the park.

LEAVE NO TRACE TIPS

Minimize use and impact of fires.

• Campfires can have a lasting impact on the backcountry. Always carry a lightweight stove for cooking, and use a candle lantern instead of building a fire whenever possible.

• Where fires are permitted, use established fire rings only. Do not scar large rocks or overhangs.

• Gather sticks for your campfire that are no larger than the diameter of your wrist. Do not scar the natural setting by snapping the branches off live, dead, or downed trees.

• Completely extinguish your campfire and make sure it is cold before departing. Remove all unburned trash from the fire ring and scatter the cold ashes over a large area well away from any camp.

MAP C4

32 LISTINGS
PAGES 444-457

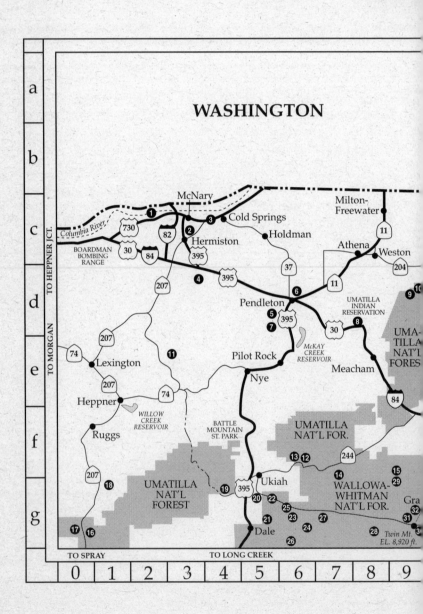

Oregon Map C4 featuring: Columbia River, Umatilla River, McKay Creek National Wildlife Refuge, Langdon Lake, Umatilla National Forest, Umatilla Indian Reservation, Grande Ronde River, Wallowa-Whitman National Forest, John Day River, Bull Prairie Lake, Grande Ronde Lake, Anthony Lake, Mud Lake

1. SHADY REST MOBILE HOME PARK [RV]

Reference: **On Columbia River; map C4, grid c2.**

Campsites, facilities: There are 26 drive-through sites for trailers or RVs of any length. Electricity, piped water and sewer hookups are provided. Flush toilets, showers, a laundromat and a swimming pool are available. A store, a cafe and ice are located within one mile. Leashed pets are permitted. Boat docks and launching facilities are nearby.

Reservations, fee: Reservations accepted; $12-$15 fee per night. Open all year.

Who to contact: Phone (541) 922-5041 or write to Route 1, P.O. Box 240, Umatilla, OR 97882.

Location: From Interstate 84 west of Pendleton, take exit 188 and drive six miles north on US 395 to Hermiston. Continue five miles northwest on US 395 to the junction with Interstate 82 and drive to Umatilla. Turn west on US 730 and drive one-half mile to the park on the right at milepost 182.

Trip note: This campground is set along the Columbia River, in a grassy area surrounded by trees. Nearby recreation options include a golf course, a marina and tennis courts.

2. DUN-ROLLIN TRAILER PARK [RV]

Reference: **Near the Columbia River; map C4, grid c3.**

Campsites, facilities: There are 15 sites for trailers or RVs of any length. Electricity, piped water and sewer hookups are provided. Flush toilets, sanitary disposal services, showers, a laundromat and a playground are available. Bottled gas, a store, a cafe and ice are located within one mile. Pets and motorbikes are permitted.

Reservations, fee: Reservations accepted; $12 fee per night. Open all year.

Who to contact: Phone (541) 567-6918 or write to 445 East Jennie, Hermiston, OR 97838.

Location: From Interstate 84 west of Pendleton, take exit 188 and drive six miles north on US 395 to Hermiston. Continue one-quarter mile north on US 395 to Jennie, then drive one-half mile east to the park on the left.

Trip note: This motor home park is not far from the Columbia River and Cold Springs National Wildlife Refuge. Nearby recreation options include a golf course, bike paths, a marina and tennis courts.

3. HAT ROCK CAMPGROUND [RV]

Reference: **Near Columbia River; map C4, grid c4.**

Campsites, facilities: There are 40 tent sites and 30 drive-through sites for trailers or RVs of any length. Electricity, piped water, sewer hookups and picnic tables are provided. Flush toilets, sanitary disposal services, showers, a store, a cafe, a laundromat and ice are available. Pets are permitted. Boat docks and launching facilities are nearby.

Reservations, fee: Reservations accepted; $14 minimum fee per night. Open all year.

Who to contact: Phone (541) 567-4188 or write to Route 3, P.O. Box 3780, Hermiston, OR 97838.

Location: From Interstate 84 west of Pendleton, take exit 188 and drive six miles north on US 395 to Hermiston. Turn northeast on Highway 207 and drive seven miles, then turn east on Highway 730 and drive one mile. Turn north on the state park access road and continue one-half mile to the park on the left.

Trip note: This campground is not far from Hat Rock State Park, a day-use area with a boat launch along the banks of the Columbia River. The campground itself is very pretty, with lots of trees and close access to the river and fishing.

---

4.   FORT HENRIETTA RV PARK   RV

Reference: **On Umatilla River; map C4, grid d3.**

Campsites, facilities: There are seven sites for tents, trailers or RVs. Restrooms, showers and a sanitary dump are provided. Some of the facilities are **wheelchair accessible**. The camp is within walking distance of two restaurants.

Reservations, fee: No reservations; $12 fee per night. Open all year.

Who to contact: Phone the park at (541) 376-8411 or write to P.O. Box 9, Echo, OR 97826.

Location: From Interstate 84 west of Pendleton, take exit 188 and drive one mile southeast on Echo Highway. Cross the railroad tracks, turn south on Dupont Street and drive three-tenths of a mile to Main Street. The park is west one block on Main Street on the left side.

Trip note: The park is located in the historical community of Echo, along the Umatilla River. The river provides some good trout fishing. This is a quiet, pleasant layover spot for travelers cruising Interstate 84.

---

5.   SHADEVIEW MOBILE HOME PARK   RV

Reference: **Near Umatilla River; map C4, grid d5.**

Campsites, facilities: There are eight drive-through sites for trailers or RVs of any length. Electricity, piped water and sewer hookups are provided. Flush toilets and showers are available. Bottled gas, sanitary disposal services, a store, a cafe, a laundromat and ice are located within one mile. Pets are permitted.

Reservations, fee: Reservations accepted; $13 fee per night. Open all year.

Who to contact: Phone (541) 276-0688 or write to 1417 Southwest 37th Street, Pendleton, OR 97801.

Location: From Pendleton on Interstate 84, turn south on US 395 and drive one mile, then one-quarter mile west on Southgate Place. The park is one block north on 37th Street.

Trip note: This park is set near the Umatilla River. A levee along the river offers walking and fishing opportunities. Nearby recreation options include marked bike trails and tennis courts. The Cold Springs National Wildlife Refuge is eight miles east of Hermiston and offers a large variety of waterfowl.

---

6.   BROOKE RV   RV

Reference: **Near McKay Creek National Wildlife Refuge; map C4, grid d6.**

Campsites, facilities: There are 28 sites for trailers or RVs of any length. Electricity, piped water, sewer hookups and picnic tables are provided. Flush toilets, cable TV, showers, a laundromat and ice are available. Bottled gas, sanitary disposal services, a store and a cafe are located within one mile. Leashed pets are permitted.

Reservations, fee: Reservations accepted; $17 fee per night. Open all year.

Who to contact: Phone (541) 276-5353 or write to 5 Northeast Eighth Street, Pendleton, OR 97801.

Location: From Pendleton on Interstate 84, take exit 213 and drive 2.3 miles. Turn right on Northeast Eighth Street and drive two blocks past the bridge to where the road deadends at the park.

Trip note: This suburban park is a pleasant, riverside site in Pendleton. It is also on the historic Oregon Trail. Waterfowl can be observed at the National Wildlife Refuge seven miles south of Pendleton. The Pendleton Mills and outlet are in town. Other nearby recreation options include a golf course, bike paths and tennis courts.

7. BROOKE RV-WEST   **RV**

Reference: **Near McKay Creek National Wildlife Refuge; map C4, grid d6.**

Campsites, facilities: There are 50 sites for trailers or RVs up to 60 feet long. Electricity, piped water, sewer hookups and picnic tables are provided. Flush toilets, cable TV, showers, a laundromat and ice are available. Bottled gas, sanitary disposal services, a store and a cafe are within one mile. Leashed pets are permitted.

Reservations, fee: Reservations accepted; $17 fee per night. Open all year.

Who to contact: Phone (541) 276-5353 or write to 5 Northeast Eighth Street, Pendleton, OR 97801.

Location: From Pendleton on Interstate 84, take exit 207 and turn left into the park.

Trip note: See trip note for Brooke RV.

8. EMIGRANT SPRINGS STATE PARK   **RV**

Reference: **Near Umatilla Indian Reservation; map C4, grid d8.**

Campsites, facilities: There are 33 tent sites and 18 sites with full hookups for trailers or RVs of any length. There is also a totem bunkhouse available for rent. Picnic tables and fire grills are provided. Flush toilets, showers, firewood, a laundromat, some horse facilities, a community building with kitchen and a playground are available. Leashed pets are permitted.

Reservations, fee: Contact Reservations Northwest at (800) 452-5687 ($6 reservation fee); $13-$20 per night; $20 totem bunkhouse fee. Open May through October.

Who to contact: Phone (541) 983-2277 or write to P.O. Box 85, Meacham, OR 97859.

Location: From Pendleton, drive 26 miles southeast on Interstate 84 to the park on the right.

Trip note: This wooded state park offers group camping and a display about the Oregon Trail. This is a good layover for people driving Interstate 84. It's set just south of the Umatilla Indian Reservation.

9. UMATILLA FORKS   **RV**

Reference: **Near Umatilla River in Umatilla National Forest; map C4, grid d9.**

Campsites, facilities: There are seven tent sites and eight sites that can accommodate tents, trailers or RVs. Piped water, picnic tables, fire grills and vault toilets are provided. Leashed pets are permitted.

Reservations, fee: No reservations; no fee. Open April to October.

Who to contact: Phone Umatilla National Forest at (509) 525-6290, or write to Walla Walla Ranger District, 1415 West Rose Avenue, Walla Walla, WA 99362.

Location: From Pendleton, drive 33 miles east on Umatilla River Road. Umatilla River Road eventually becomes Forest Service Road 32.

Trip note: This camp is located between the South and North Forks of the Umatilla River, set at 2,400 feet. Recreation opportunities include hiking and fishing. It provides the rare combination of piped water with no fee, and has an added bonus of being relatively unknown. A prime spot.

---

10. WOODWARD

Reference: **Near Langdon Lake in Umatilla National Forest; map C4, grid d9.**

Campsites, facilities: There are 18 sites for tents, trailers or RVs. Piped water, picnic tables, fire grills and vault toilets are provided. A large sheltered picnic area is available for reservation. Leashed pets are permitted.

Reservations, fee: No reservations; $4 fee per night. Open mid-June to mid-September.

Who to contact: Phone Umatilla National Forest at (509) 525-6290, or write to Walla Walla Ranger District, 1415 West Rose Avenue, Walla Walla, WA 99362.

Location: From Pendleton on Interstate 84, turn north on Highway 11 and drive approximately 27 miles to Weston. Turn east on Highway 204 and drive 17 miles. The campground is located just off the highway, near Langdon Lake.

Trip note: This campground is located near Langdon Lake, which is privately owned. A pretty hiking trail circles the campground. This is one of the few campgrounds in the area that charges a fee, but it offers all the comforts of a developed campground in exchange.

---

11. CUTSFORTH COUNTY PARK

Reference: **Map C4, grid e3.**

Campsites, facilities: There are 35 sites for tents, trailers or RVs up to 30 feet. Restrooms, showers, horseshoes and a playground are provided. Some facilities are **wheelchair accessible**.

Reservations, fee: No reservations; $5-$9 fee per night. Open from May 15 to November 20.

Who to contact: Phone the Morrow County Courthouse at (541) 676-9061 or write to Morrow County Parks, P.O. Box 453, Lexington, OR 97839.

Location: From Interstate 84 west of Pendleton, exit on Highway 207 and drive 30 miles to Lexington. Turn left on Highway 74 and drive 10.5 miles. Turn left on Willow Creek Road and drive for 26.5 miles to the park.

Trip note: This park is just a short jaunt from the interstate, yet it is secluded and private. It is set on a handicapped-accessible, small pond in a quiet, wooded area. Trout fishing is available in the pond. See the trip note for Anson Wright County Park for details on the area.

---

12. LANE CREEK

Reference: **On Camus Creek in Umatilla National Forest; map C4, grid f6.**

Campsites, facilities: There are eight sites for tents, trailers or RVs up to 45 feet long. **No piped water** is available. Picnic tables and fire grills are provided. Vault toilets are available. Leashed pets are permitted.

Reservations, fee: No reservations; no fee. Open June 1 through October.

Who to contact: Phone the North Fork John Day Ranger District at (541) 427-3231 or write to Umatilla National Forest, P.O. Box 158, Ukiah, OR 97880.

Location: From Pendleton on Interstate 84, turn south on US 395 and drive 50 miles to Ukiah. Turn east on Highway 244 and travel nine miles to the campground.

Trip note: This campground is set at 3,850 feet along Camus Creek. It is set just inside the forest boundary, with easy access to all the amenities of town. There is a nearby hot springs and good hunting and fishing in the area. A Forest Service map details the back roads.

13.   BEAR WALLOW CREEK   RV.

Reference: **On Bear Wallow Creek in Umatilla National Forest; map C4, grid f6.**

Campsites, facilities: There are eight sites for tents, trailers or RVs up to 30 feet long. **No piped water** is available. Picnic tables and fire grills are provided. Vault toilets are available. Leashed pets are permitted.

Reservations, fee: No reservations; no fee; 14-day limit. Open June through October.

Who to contact: Phone the North Fork John Day Ranger District at (541) 427-3231 or write to Umatilla National Forest, P.O. Box 158, Ukiah, OR 97880.

Location: From Pendleton on Interstate 84, turn south on US 395 and drive 50 miles to Ukiah. Turn east on Highway 244 and drive 10 miles to the camp.

Trip note: This campground is set near the confluence of Bear Wallow Creek and Camus Creek at 3,900 feet elevation. This is one of three camps off Highway 244. The others are Lane Creek and Frazier. Bear Wallow Creek Camp is primarily used in the fall by hunters. It is quiet, primitive and free. A three-quarter-mile interpretive trail meanders next to Bear Wallow Creek, highlighting steelhead habitat. The trail is **wheelchair-accessible.**

14.   FRAZIER   RV.

Reference: **On Frazier Creek in Umatilla National Forest; map C4, grid f7.**

Campsites, facilities: There are 21 sites for tents, trailers or RVs up to 30 feet long. Picnic tables, fire grills and vault toilets are available. There is **no piped water**. Leashed pets are permitted. Some facilities are **wheelchair accessible**. An all-terrain-vehicle loading ramp is available.

Reservations, fee: No reservations; no fee. Open year-round.

Who to contact: Phone the North Fork John Day Ranger District at (541) 427-3231 or write to Umatilla National Forest, P.O. Box 158, Ukiah, OR 97880.

Location: From Pendleton on Interstate 84, turn south on US 395 and drive 50 miles to Ukiah. Turn east on Highway 244 and drive 16 miles, then one half mile south on Forest Service Road 5226.

Trip note: This campground is set at 4,300 feet along the banks of Frazier Creek. This is a popular hunting area that also has some fishing. It's advisable to obtain a map of Umatilla National Forest. There are nearly 100 miles of all-terrain-vehicle and motorcycle trails at the nearby Winom-Frazier Off-Highway-Vehicle Complex. Lehman Hot Springs provides a nearby side trip option.

15.　　　　　　　　SPOOL CART　　　　　　　　🚐

Reference: **On Grande Ronde River in Wallowa-Whitman National Forest; map C4, grid f9.**

Campsites, facilities: There are 16 sites for tents, trailers or RVs up to 22 feet long. Picnic tables and fire grills are provided. Firewood and vault toilets are available. There is **no piped water**. Leashed pets are permitted.

Reservations, fee: No reservations; no fee. Open late May to late November.

Who to contact: Phone the LaGrande Ranger District at (541) 963-7186 or write to Wallowa-Whitman National Forest, P.O. Box 907, Baker City, OR 97814.

Location: From LaGrande, drive nine miles northwest on Interstate 84, then 13 miles southwest on Highway 244. Turn south and drive seven miles on Forest Service Road 51 to the campground on the right.

Trip note: This campground is set on the banks of the Grande Ronde River and gets its name from the large cable spools that were left on a cart at the site for some years. Hilgard Junction State Park to the north provides numerous recreation options, and the Oregon Trail Interpretive Park is nearby. It is advisable to obtain a map of Wallowa-Whitman National Forest that details the back roads and other side-trips available.

16.　　　　　　　　BULL PRAIRIE　　　　　　　　🚐

Reference: **On Bull Prairie Lake in Umatilla National Forest; map C4, grid g0.**

Campsites, facilities: There are 25 sites for tents, trailers or RVs up to 31 feet long. Picnic tables and fire grills are provided. Piped water, sanitary disposal services, firewood and vault toilets are available. Pets are permitted. Boat docks and launching facilities are on site.

Reservations, fee: No reservations; $6 fee per night. Open May to October.

Who to contact: Phone the Heppner Ranger District at (541) 676-9187 or write to Umatilla National Forest, P.O. Box 7, Heppner, OR 97836.

Location: From Interstate 5 at Albany, turn east on US 20 and drive 100 miles to Sisters. Turn east on Highway 126 and drive 39 miles to Prineville, then continue east on US 26 for 48 miles to the Highway 207 turnoff. Drive north on Highway 207 approximately 50 miles to Forest Service Road 2039 (paved). Turn right and drive three miles northeast.

Trip note: This campground is set along the shore of Bull Prairie Lake. Boating (no motors permitted), swimming, fishing and hunting are some of the options here. This spot attracts little attention from out-of-towners, yet offers plenty of recreation opportunities, making it an ideal vacation destination for many.

17.　　　　　　　　FAIRVIEW　　　　　　　　🚐

Reference: **Near Bull Prairie Lake in Umatilla National Forest; map C4, grid g0.**

Campsites, facilities: There are five sites for trailers or RVs up to 16 feet long. Picnic tables and fire grills are provided. Firewood and vault toilets are available. There is **no piped water**. Pets are permitted. Boat docks and launching facilities are nearby at Bull Prairie Lake.

Reservations, fee: No reservations; no fee. Open May to late October.

Who to contact: Phone the Heppner Ranger District at (541) 676-9187 or write to Umatilla National Forest, P.O. Box 7, Heppner, OR 97836.

Location: From Interstate 5 at Albany, turn east on US 20 and drive 100 miles to Sisters. Turn east on Highway 126 and drive 39 miles to Prineville, then continue east on US 26 for 48 miles to the Highway 207 turnoff. Drive north on Highway 207 approximately 49 miles. Turn west on Forest Service Road 400 and drive 500 yards.

Trip note: This campground is set adjacent to Fairview Springs near Mahogany Butte. It's a small, primitive site known by very few people. Set in a remote area at 4,300 feet, it is primarily used as a base camp by hunters.

18.   ANSON WRIGHT COUNTY PARK   RV

Reference: **Map C4, grid g1.**

Campsites, facilities: There are 30 sites for tents, trailers or RVs up to 30 feet. Restrooms, showers, a barbecue and a playground are provided. Some facilities are **wheelchair accessible**.

Reservations, fee: No reservations; $5-$8 fee per night. Open from May 16 to November 16.

Who to contact: Phone the Morrow County Courthouse at (541) 676-9061 or write to Morrow County Parks, P.O. Box 453, Lexington, OR 97839.

Location: From Interstate 84 west of Pendleton, take exit 182. Turn southwest on Highway 207 and drive 46 miles to the park access road (signed). Continue south for 21 miles to the park.

Trip note: Set within wooded hills on a small stream, this county park offers visitors prime trout fishing and hiking opportunities. There is a handicapped-accessible fishing pond. Attractions in the area include the Pendleton Mills, Emigrant Springs State Park, Hardman Ghost Town (24 miles away) and the Columbia River.

19.   DIVIDE WELL   RV

Reference: **In Umatilla National Forest; map C4, grid g4.**

Campsites, facilities: There are five primitive tent sites. Picnic tables and a vault toilet are provided, but there is **no piped water**. Leashed pets are permitted.

Reservations, fee: No reservations; no fee. Open year-round.

Who to contact: Phone North Fork John Day Ranger District at (541) 427-3231, or write to Umatilla National Forest, P.O. Box 158, Ukiah, OR 97880.

Location: From Pendleton on Interstate 84, turn south on US 395 and drive 50 miles to Ukiah. Turn west on Forest Service Road 53 and drive 10 miles, then turn left on Forest Service Road 5312 and drive six miles. Turn right on Forest Service Road 5320 and travel one mile, then turn right on Forest Service Road 5327 and continue one-half mile to the campground. A Forest Service map is recommended.

Trip note: This is a primitive, remote campground set at 4,700 feet. It can serve as a good base camp for a hunting trip. Mule deer and Rocky Mountain elk are abundant in the surrounding pine forest. Potamus Point Scenic Overlook, offering a spectacular view of the John Day River drainage, is 11 miles south of the camp on Forest Service Road 5316.

20.   UKIAH-DALE FOREST STATE PARK   RV

Reference: **On North Fork John Day River; map C4, grid g5.**

Campsites, facilities: There are 25 primitive sites for tents, trailers or self-contained RVs up to 40 feet long. Picnic tables and fire grills are provided.

Piped water, firewood and vault toilets are available. Pets are permitted.

Reservations, fee: No reservations; $10 fee per night. Open mid-April to late October.

Who to contact: Phone (541) 983-2277 or (800) 452-5687 or write to c/o P.O. Box 85, Meacham, OR 97859.

Location: From Pendleton on Interstate 84, turn south on US 395 and drive 48 miles to Ukiah. Continue three miles south on US 395 to the park.

Trip note: This campground is set near the banks of the North Fork of the John Day River. Fishing is an option here. It's a good layover for visitors cruising US 395 looking for a spot for the night. Emigrant Springs State Park near Pendleton is a possible side trip.

21.   TOLLBRIDGE   **RV**

Reference: **On the North Fork John Day River in Umatilla National Forest; map C4, grid g5.**

Campsites, facilities: There are seven sites for tents, trailers or RVs up to 31 feet long. Picnic tables and fire grills are provided. Piped water and a vault toilet are available. Leashed pets are permitted.

Reservations, fee: No reservations; no fee; 14-day limit. Open June through October.

Who to contact: Phone the North Fork John Day Ranger District at (541) 427-3231 or write to Umatilla National Forest, P.O. Box 158, Ukiah, OR 97880.

Location: From Pendleton on Interstate 84, turn south on US 395 and drive 62 miles to Forest Service Road 55 (one mile north of Dale). Turn left and drive one half mile southeast, then 100 yards on Forest Service Road 10.

Trip note: This campground is set at the confluence of Desolation Creek and the North Fork of the John Day River, and is adjacent to the Bridge Creek Wildlife Area. It's small and secluded. Hunting and fishing are two options here. The elevation is 3,800 feet.

22.   DRIFT FENCE   **RV**

Reference: **Near Ross Springs in Umatilla National Forest; map C4, grid g5.**

Campsites, facilities: There are five sites for tents, trailers or RVs up to 16 feet long. There is **no piped water**. A vault toilet and picnic tables are available. Leashed pets are permitted.

Reservations, fee: No reservations; no fee. Open year-round.

Who to contact: Phone the North Fork John Day Ranger District at (541) 427-3231 or write to Umatilla National Forest, P.O. Box 158, Ukiah, OR 97880.

Location: From Pendleton on Interstate 84, turn south on US 395 and drive 50 miles to Ukiah. Turn east on Forest Service Road 52 and drive seven miles to the campground.

Trip note: This campground is set at 4,200 feet. This is a good area for elk and deer, and the camp is popular with hunters. The camp is adjacent to Blue Mountain National Forest Scenic Byway. Bridge Creek Interpretive Trail, located three miles northwest of the campground off Forest Service Road 52, leads to a viewpoint where elk may be seen roaming in the Bridge Creek area.

23.   GOLD DREDGE CAMP   RV

Reference: **On North Fork John Day River in Umatilla National Forest; map C4, grid g6.**

Campsites, facilities: There are eight sites for trailers or RVs. **No piped water** or fire grills are provided, but vault toilets and picnic tables are available. Leashed pets are permitted.

Reservations, fee: No reservations; no fee. Open year-round.

Who to contact: Phone the North Fork John Day Ranger District at (541) 427-3231 or write to Umatilla National Forest, P.O. Box 158, Ukiah, OR 97880.

Location: From Pendleton on Interstate 84, turn south on US 395 and drive 62 miles to Forest Service Road 55 (one mile north of Dale). Turn left and drive six miles to the crossroads. Continue east on Forest Service Road 5506 for 2.5 miles to the campground.

Trip note: This campground is set along the banks of the North Fork of the John Day River, a federally certified Wild and Scenic river. Hunting and fishing are two of the options here. By traveling to the end of Forest Service Road 5506, you can access a trail that heads into the adjacent North Fork John Day Wilderness.

24.   ORIENTAL CREEK

Reference: **On North Fork John Day River in Umatilla National Forest; map C4, grid g6.**

Campsites, facilities: There are seven primitive tent sites. Pit toilets and picnic tables are available, but there is **no piped water**. One toilet is **wheelchair accessible**. Leashed pets are permitted.

Reservations, fee: No reservations; no fee. Open year-round.

Who to contact: Phone the North Fork John Day Ranger District at (541) 427-3231 or write to Umatilla National Forest, P.O. Box 158, Ukiah, OR 97880.

Location: From Pendleton on Interstate 84, turn south on US 395 and drive 62 miles to Forest Service Road 55 (one mile north of Dale). Turn left and drive six miles to the crossroads. Continue east on Forest Service Road 5506 for six miles to the campground. This road is not recommended for trailers.

Trip note: This campground is set at 3,500 feet along the banks of the North Fork of the John Day River. Nearby trails provide access to the North Fork John Day Wilderness. Hunting and fishing are two of the options here. No motorbikes are permitted in the wilderness area.

25.   DRIFTWOOD

Reference: **On the North Fork John Day River in Umatilla National Forest; map C4, grid g6.**

Campsites, facilities: There are seven sites for tents and trailers. A vault toilet and picnic tables are provided, but there is **no piped water**. Leashed pets are permitted.

Reservations, fee: No reservations; no fee. Open year-round.

Who to contact: Phone North Fork John Day Ranger District at (541) 427-3231, or write to Umatilla National Forest, P.O. Box 158, Ukiah, OR 97880.

Location: From Pendleton on Interstate 84, turn south on US 395 and drive 62 miles to Forest Service Road 55 (one mile north of Dale). Turn left and drive six miles to the crossroads. Continue east on Forest Service Road 5506 for one mile.

Trip note: This tiny campground is located on the banks of the North Fork John Day River at 2,500 feet in elevation. Recreational opportunities include hunting, fishing, swimming, rafting and float tubing.

---

26. WELCH CREEK

Reference: **On Desolation Creek in Umatilla National Forest; map C4, grid g6.**

Campsites, facilities: There are five primitive tent sites. Picnic tables and a vault toilet are provided, but there is **no piped water**.

Reservations, fee: No reservations; no fee. Open April to October.

Who to contact: Phone North Fork John Day Ranger District at (541) 427-3231, or write to Umatilla National Forest, P.O. Box 158, Ukiah, OR 97880.

Location: From Pendleton on Interstate 84, turn south on US 395 and drive 62 miles to Forest Service Road 55 (one mile north of Dale). Turn left and drive one mile, then turn right on Forest Service Road 10 and continue 13 miles to the campground.

Trip note: This primitive camp, located on the banks of Desolation Creek, is remote and out of the way. Hunting and fishing are popular here.

---

27. BIG CREEK MEADOWS

Reference: **On Big Creek in Umatilla National Forest; map C4, grid g7.**

Campsites, facilities: There are four primitive tent sites. A picnic table and a vault toilet are provided, but there is **no piped water**. Leashed pets are permitted.

Reservations, fee: No reservations; no fee. Open year-round.

Who to contact: Phone North Fork John Day Ranger District at (541) 427-3231, or write to Umatilla National Forest, P.O. Box 158, Ukiah, OR 97880.

Location: From Pendleton on Interstate 84, turn south on US 395 and drive 50 miles to Ukiah. Turn east on Forest Service Road 52 and drive 22 miles. Turn right on Forest Service Road 5225 and travel a short distance, then turn right on Forest Service Road 5225-020 and continue one-half mile to the camp.

Trip note: This primitive campground is located on the banks of Big Creek. The North Fork John Day Wilderness is located about one-quarter mile away. Fishing and hunting are among the activities available here. The elevation is 5,100 feet.

---

28. NORTH FORK JOHN DAY　　　　　　　**RV**

Reference: **On the North Fork John Day River in Umatilla National Forest; map C4, grid g8.**

Campsites, facilities: There are eight sites for tents, trailers or RVs up to 22 feet long. Picnic tables and fire grills are provided. Vault toilets are available. There is **no piped water**. Leashed pets are permitted.

Reservations, fee: No reservations; no fee; 14-day limit. Open June through October.

Who to contact: Phone the North Fork John Day Ranger District at (541) 427-3231 or write to Umatilla National Forest, P.O. Box 158, Ukiah, OR 97880.

Location: From Pendleton on Interstate 84, turn south on US 395 and drive 50 miles to Ukiah. Turn east on Forest Service Road 52 and travel 36 miles to the campground.

Trip note: This campground is set along the banks of the North Fork John Day

River. This is an ideal base camp for a wilderness backpacking trip. A horse-handling area is also available for wilderness users. Trails from camp lead into the North Fork John Day Wilderness. The camp is located at the intersection of Elkhorn and Blue Mountain National Forest Scenic Byway. No motorbikes are permitted in the wilderness.

29.   RIVER

Reference: **On Grande Ronde River in Wallowa-Whitman National Forest; map C4, grid g9.**

Campsites, facilities: There are six sites for tents or trailers. Picnic tables and fire grills are provided. Firewood and vault toilets are available. There is **no piped water**. Leashed pets are permitted.

Reservations, fee: No reservations; no fee. Open late May to late November.

Who to contact: Phone the LaGrande Ranger District at (541) 963-7186 or write to Wallowa-Whitman National Forest, P.O. Box 907, Baker City, OR 97814.

Location: From LaGrande, drive nine miles northwest on Interstate 84, then 13 miles southwest on Highway 244. From there, continue 11 miles south on Forest Service Road 51.

Trip note: This campground is set along the banks of the Grande Ronde River. This is one of four small, primitive camps along Forest Service Road 51 and adjoining Road 5125. See the trip note for Spool Cart (camp number 15).

30.   ANTHONY LAKE   RV

Reference: **On Anthony Lake in Wallowa-Whitman National Forest; map C4, grid g9.**

Campsites, facilities: There are 37 sites for tents, trailers or RVs up to 22 feet long. Piped water, fire grills and picnic tables are provided. Vault toilets are available. Some facilities are **wheelchair accessible**. Leashed pets are permitted. Boat launching facilities are nearby.

Reservations, fee: No reservations; $5 fee per night. Open July to late September.

Who to contact: Phone the Baker Ranger District at (541) 523-1932 or write to Wallowa-Whitman National Forest, P.O. Box 907, Baker City, OR 97814.

Location: From Interstate 84 at Baker City, turn north on US 30 and drive 13 miles to Haines. Drive 17 miles northwest on County Road 1146, then nine miles west on Forest Service Road 73.

Trip note: This campground is set adjacent to Anthony Lake, where boating without motors is permitted. Several smaller lakes are within two miles by car or trail. These are ideal for trout fishing from a raft, float tube or canoe. The trailhead for the Elkhorn Crest Trail is near here.

31.   GRANDE RONDE LAKE   RV

Reference: **On Grande Ronde Lake in Wallowa-Whitman National Forest; map C4, grid g9.**

Campsites, facilities: There are eight sites for tents, trailers or RVs up to 16 feet long. Picnic tables and fire grills are provided. Piped water and vault toilets are available. Leashed pets are permitted. Boat docks and launching facilities are nearby.

Reservations, fee: No reservations; $3 fee per night. Open July to mid-September.

Who to contact: Phone the Baker Ranger District at (541) 523-1932 or write to Wallowa-Whitman National Forest, P.O. Box 907, Baker City, OR 97814.

Location: From Interstate 84 at Baker City, turn north on US 30 and drive 13 miles to Haines. Drive 17 miles northwest on County Road 1146, then 9.5 miles west on Forest Service Road 73. The camp is one-half mile northwest on Forest Service Road 43.

Trip note: This campground is set at 7,200 feet, along the shore of Grande Ronde Lake, a small lake where the trout fishing can be good. Several other trails are south near Anthony Lake. A map of Wallowa-Whitman National Forest details the possibilities.

---

32.   MUD LAKE   RV

Reference: **On Mud Lake in Wallowa-Whitman National Forest; map C4, grid g9.**

Campsites, facilities: There are three tent sites and five sites for trailers or RVs up to 16 feet long. Picnic tables and fire grills are provided. Piped water, firewood and vault toilets are available. Leashed pets are permitted. Boat docks and launching facilities are nearby at Anthony Lake.

Reservations, fee: No reservations; $3 fee per night. Open July to mid-September.

Who to contact: Phone the Baker Ranger District at (541) 523-1932 or write to Wallowa-Whitman National Forest, P.O. Box 907, Baker City, OR 97814.

Location: From Interstate 84 at Baker City, turn north on US 30 and drive 13 miles to Haines. Drive 17 miles northwest on County Road 1146, then nine miles west on Forest Service Road 73.

Trip note: This campground is set along the shore of Mud Lake. It's a small lake and the trout fishing can be fairly good here. The campground is tiny and pleasant, with lots of vegetation and relatively little use. Bring your mosquito repellent.

LEAVE NO TRACE TIPS

Plan ahead and prepare.

• Learn about the regulations and special concerns of the area you are visiting.

• Visit the backcountry in small groups.

• Avoid popular areas during peak-use periods.

• Choose equipment and clothing in subdued colors.

• Pack food in reusable containers.

MAP C5

OREGON MAP .... see page 380

Adjoining Maps

32 LISTINGS
PAGES 458-471

NORTH .... Washington
EAST .... no map
SOUTH (D5) .... see page 596
WEST (C4) .... see page 444

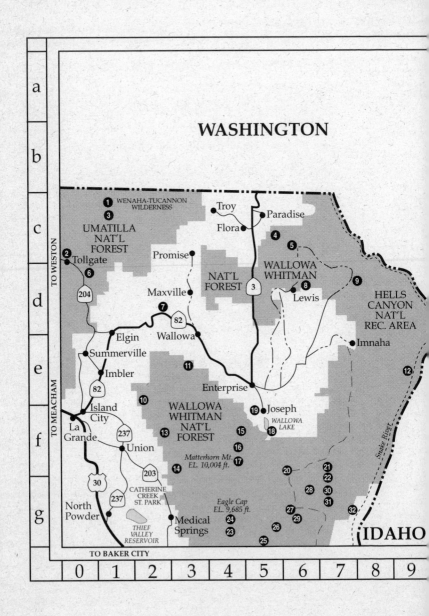

Oregon Map C5 featuring: Jubilee Lake, Umatilla National Forest, Touchet River, Walla Walla River, Wallowa-Whitman National Forest, Grande Ronde River, Wallowa Lake, Hot Lake, Eagle Cap Wilderness, Buckhorn Lake, Hells Canyon Wilderness, Lostine River, Twin Lakes, Imnaha River, Fish Lake

---

1. MOTTET

Reference: **Near the South Fork of Touchet River in Umatilla National Forest; map C5, grid b2.**

Campsites, facilities: There are seven sites for tents. Picnic tables and fire grills are provided. Spring water and vault toilets are available. Leashed pets are permitted. Trash must be packed out; no garbage facilities are provided.

Reservations, fee: No reservations; no fee. Open July to mid-October.

Who to contact: Phone the Walla Walla Ranger District at (509) 522-6290 or write to Umatilla National Forest, 1415 West Rose Avenue, Walla Walla, WA 99362.

Location: From Pendleton on Interstate 84, turn north on Highway 11 and drive approximately 27 miles to Weston. Turn east on Highway 204 and drive 17.5 miles to Forest Service Road 64. Turn left and drive four miles northeast. Continue for 12 miles on Forest Service Road 6403. High-clearance vehicles are recommended.

Trip note: This campground is set at 5,200 feet, adjacent to a trailhead which leads down to the South Fork of the Walla Walla River. It's a nice spot, located far from the beaten path. It's quite primitive and relatively unknown, so you're almost guaranteed privacy.

---

2. TARGET MEADOWS
RV.

Reference: **Near South Fork Walla Walla River in Umatilla National Forest; map C5, grid c0.**

Campsites, facilities: There are 20 sites for tents, trailers or RVs. Piped water, picnic tables, fire grills and vault toilets are provided. Leashed pets are permitted.

Reservations, fee: No reservations; $5 fee per night. Open mid-June to mid-September.

Who to contact: Phone Umatilla National Forest at (509) 522-6290, or write to Walla Walla Ranger District, 1415 West Rose Avenue, Walla Walla, WA 99362.

Location: From Pendleton on Interstate 84, turn north on Highway 11 and drive approximately 27 miles to Weston. Turn east on Highway 204 and drive 17.5 miles to Forest Service Road 64. Turn left and drive one-half mile. Continue for two miles on Forest Service Road 6401. The camp is located about 1,000 yards north on spur road 050.

Trip note: This campground is set at 4,800 feet, adjacent to the Burnt Cabin Trailhead which leads to the South Fork Walla Walla River. This is a popular camp with hunters in the fall months.

---

3. JUBILEE LAKE
RV.

Reference: **On Jubilee Lake in Umatilla National Forest; map C5, grid c1.**

Campsites, facilities: There are 51 sites for tents, trailers or RVs up to 22 feet long. Picnic tables and fire grills are provided. Piped water, firewood and flush toilets are available. Some facilities are **wheelchair accessible**. Leashed pets are permitted. Boat docks and launching facilities are nearby.

Reservations, fee: No reservations; $10 fee per night. Open June to September.

Who to contact: Phone the Walla Walla Ranger District at (509) 522-6290 or write to Umatilla National Forest, 1415 West Rose Avenue, Walla Walla, WA 99362.

Location: From Pendleton on Interstate 84, turn north on Highway 11 and drive approximately 27 miles to Weston. Turn east on Highway 204 and drive 17.5 miles to Forest Service Road 64. Turn left and drive 12 miles northeast. The camp is 700 yards south on Forest Service Road 250.

Trip note: This campground is set along the shore of Jubilee Lake at 4,800 feet. It's a good area for swimming, fishing, hiking and hunting. Boats are permitted, but electric motors only. A 2.5-mile trail loops around the lake and is designated to provide different levels of handicapped accessibility. Fishing access is available along the trail.

4.　　　　　　　COYOTE　　　　　　　RV

Reference: **Near Coyote Springs in Wallowa-Whitman National Forest; map C5, grid c5.**

Campsites, facilities: There are 29 sites for tents, trailers or RVs up to 22 feet long. Picnic tables and fire grills are provided. Firewood and vault toilets are available, but there is **no piped water**. Inside note: A spring is located within one-quarter mile. Leashed pets are permitted.

Reservations, fee: No reservations; no fee. Open mid-May to December.

Who to contact: Phone the Wallowa Valley Ranger District at (541) 426-4978 or write to Wallowa Mountains Visitor Center, 88401 Highway 82, Enterprise, OR 97828.

Location: From LaGrande on Interstate 84, turn north on Highway 82 and drive 62 miles north and east to Enterprise. Turn north on Highway 3 and drive 15 miles, then 25 miles northeast on Forest Service Road 46 to the campground.

Trip note: This campground is set at 4,800 feet, adjacent to Coyote Springs. It is the largest camp of the three primitive camps in the vicinity, offering open sites and privacy.

5.　　　　　　　DOUGHERTY　　　　　　　RV

Reference: **Near Dougherty Springs in Wallowa-Whitman National Forest; map C5, grid c6.**

Campsites, facilities: There are 12 sites for tents, trailers or RVs up to 22 feet long. Picnic tables and fire grills are provided. Vault toilets are available, but there is **no piped water**. Leashed pets are permitted.

Reservations, fee: No reservations; no fee. Open June to late November.

Who to contact: Phone the Hells Canyon National Recreation Area at (541) 426-4978 or write to Wallowa Mountains Visitor Center, 88401 Highway 82, Enterprise, OR 97828.

Location: From LaGrande on Interstate 84, turn north on Highway 82 and drive 62 miles north and east to Enterprise. Turn north on Highway 3 and drive 15 miles, then 30 miles northeast on Forest Service Road 46.

Trip note: This campground is set at 5,000 feet adjacent to Dougherty Springs. It is one in a series of remote camps set near natural springs, wooded and primitive. Hells Canyon National Recreation Area to the east provides many recreation options.

6. WOODLAND

Reference: **In Umatilla National Forest; map C5, grid d0.**

Campsites, facilities: There are seven sites for tents, trailers or RVs. Picnic tables, fire grills, and vault toilets are provided, but there is **no piped water**. Leashed pets are permitted. No garbage facilities are provided, so campers must pack out their own trash.

Reservations, fee: No reservations; no fee. Open mid-June to mid-September.

Who to contact: Phone Umatilla National Forest at (509) 522-6290, or write to Walla Walla Ranger District, 1415 West Rose Avenue, Walla Walla, WA 99362.

Location: From Pendleton on Interstate 84, turn north on Highway 11 and drive approximately 27 miles to Weston. Turn east on Highway 204 and drive 23 miles. The campground is located just off the highway.

Trip note: This is a primitive camp with easy highway access. It is mainly used as a base camp for hunters in the fall, and it doesn't offer much in the way of activities. However, it can be a perfect spot for Interstate 84 cruisers looking for a short detour. See a Forest Service map for details about the recreation options within driving distance.

7. MINAM STATE PARK

Reference: **Near Grande Ronde River; map C5, grid d2.**

Campsites, facilities: There are 12 primitive sites for tents, trailers or self-contained RVs of any length. Picnic tables and fire grills are provided. Piped water and pit toilets are available. Leashed pets are permitted.

Reservations, fee: No reservations; $11 fee per night; weekly rates available from October through mid-May. Open mid-April to late October.

Who to contact: Phone (541) 432-8855 or (800) 452-5687, or write to c/o 72214 Marina Lane, Joseph, OR 97846.

Location: From Pendleton on Interstate 84, turn east and drive approximately 54 miles to LaGrande. Take exit 261 and turn north on Highway 82. Drive 16 miles to Elgin, then continue 15 miles northeast on Highway 82. Turn north on the park entrance road and drive one-half mile to the park.

Trip note: This campground is set along the banks of the Minam River. Morning and evening trout fishing can be decent. This is a good launch point to float the Wild and Scenic Grande Ronde River. This is a small but pretty state park, and well worth the detour off Interstate 84.

8. VIGNE

Reference: **On Chesnimnus Creek in Wallowa-Whitman National Forest; map C5, grid d6.**

Campsites, facilities: There are seven sites for tents, trailers or RVs up to 22 feet long. Picnic tables and fire grills are provided. Piped water, firewood and vault toilets are available. Leashed pets are permitted.

Reservations, fee: No reservations; no fee. Open mid-April to late November.

Who to contact: Phone the Wallowa Valley Ranger District at (541) 426-4978 or write to Wallowa Mountains Visitor Center, 88401 Highway 82, Enterprise, OR 97828.

Location: From LaGrande on Interstate 84, turn north on Highway 82 and drive 62 miles north and east to Enterprise. Turn north on Highway 3 and drive 15 miles, then 10 miles northeast on Forest Road 46. Turn east on Forest Road 4625 and continue 10 miles to the campground.

Trip note: This campground is set along the banks of Chesnimnus Creek, with pretty, shaded riverside sites. Fishing is a recreation possibility here, along with exploring a few of the many hiking trails in the area. See a Forest Service map for details. This is the only Forest Service camp in the area that has piped water available.

---

9.   BUCKHORN

Reference: **Near Buckhorn Lookout in Wallowa-Whitman National Forest; map C5, grid d7.**

Campsites, facilities: There are six sites for tents or trailers. Picnic tables and fire grills are provided. Firewood and vault toilets are available, but there is **no piped water**. Leashed pets are permitted.

Reservations, fee: No reservations; no fee. Open June to late November.

Who to contact: Phone the Hells Canyon National Recreation Area at (541) 426-4978 or write to Wallowa Mountains Visitor Center, 88401 Highway 82, Enterprise, OR 97828.

Location: From LaGrande on Interstate 84, turn north on Highway 82 and drive 62 miles north and east to Enterprise. Continue three miles south on Highway 82, then drive 32 miles northeast on County Road 772. Continue 10 miles northeast on Forest Road 46.

Trip note: This campground is set at 5,200 feet adjacent to Buckhorn Springs. It's a small, primitive and obscure camp that gets little use. The elevation offers a spectacular view of the Imnaha River drainage.

---

10.   HOT LAKE RV RESORT   RV

Reference: **On Hot Lake; map C5, grid e2.**

Campsites, facilities: There are 100 sites for tents, trailers or RVs. Restrooms, showers, a laundromat, groceries, a sanitary dump, a public phone, a swimming pool, a hot spa, ice and RV supplies are available. Some facilities are **wheelchair accessible**.

Reservations, fee: Reservations recommended; $20 fee per night. Open May to October.

Who to contact: Phone the park at (541) 963-5253 or write to 65182 Hot Lake Lane, LaGrande, OR 97850.

Location: From the south end of LaGrande, at the junction of Interstate 84 and Highway 203, take exit 265. Drive southeast on Highway 203 for five miles to Foothill Road. The resort is on Foothill Road, west three-tenths of a mile on the left side of the road.

Trip note: This camp is located on the shore of Hot Lake, where fishing, boating and swimming are options. The camp is also on the historic Old Oregon Trail. Attractions in the area include Hilgard Junction State Park and Wallowa-Whitman National Forest.

---

11.   BOUNDARY

Reference: **Near Eagle Cap Wilderness in Wallowa-Whitman National Forest; map C5, grid e3.**

Campsites, facilities: There are eight primitive campsites. Leashed pets are permitted.

Reservations, fee: No reservations; no fee. Open mid-June to November.

Who to contact: Phone the Eagle Cap Ranger District at (541) 426-4978 or write to Wallowa Mountains Visitor Center, 88401 Highway 82, Enterprise, OR 97828.

Location: From LaGrande on Interstate 84, turn north on Highway 82 and drive 46 miles to Wallowa. Turn south on Forest Service Road 8250 and drive eight miles, then three-quarters of a mile south on Forest Service Road 8250-040.

Trip note: This campground is set along the banks of Bear Creek, pretty and private. Nearby trails provide access to the Eagle Cap Wilderness. This is another in a series of little-known primitive sites in the area.

---

12.   SADDLE CREEK

Reference: **Near Hells Canyon Wilderness in Wallowa-Whitman National Forest; map C5, grid e9.**

Campsites, facilities: There are seven sites for tents. Picnic tables and fire grills are provided. Firewood and vault toilets are available, but there is **no piped water**. Leashed pets are permitted. Note: RVs and trailers are not recommended on the access road.

Reservations, fee: No reservations; no fee. Open July to mid-November.

Who to contact: Phone the Hells Canyon National Recreation Area at (541) 426-4978 or write to Wallowa Mountains Visitor Center, 88401 Highway 82, Enterprise, OR 97828.

Location: From LaGrande on Interstate 84, turn north on Highway 82 and drive 62 miles to Enterprise. Continue south on Interstate 84 for six miles to Joseph. Turn east on Highway 350 toward the small town of Imnaha. Turn southeast on Forest Service Road 4240 and drive 24 miles to the campground.

Trip note: This campground is set at 6,900 feet in a wooded environment. Trails are nearby that provide access to Saddle Creek and the Hells Canyon National Recreation Area.

---

13.   MOSS SPRINGS

Reference: **Near Eagle Cap Wilderness in Wallowa-Whitman National Forest; map C5, grid f2.**

Campsites, facilities: There are 11 tent sites. Picnic tables and fire grills are provided. Horse facilities and vault toilets are available. Leashed pets are permitted.

Reservations, fee: No reservations; no fee. Open June to mid-October.

Who to contact: Phone the LaGrande Ranger District at (541) 963-7186 or write to Wallowa-Whitman National Forest, P.O. Box 907, Baker City, OR 97814.

Location: From Interstate 84 at LaGrande, turn east on Highway 237 and drive 15 miles to Cove. Drive 1.5 miles southeast of Cove on County Road 237, then eight miles east on Forest Service Road 6220 to the camp entrance at the end of the road.

Trip note: This campground is set at a trailhead that provides access to the Eagle Cap Wilderness, a good jumpoff point for a multi-day backpacking trip. It is advisable to obtain a map of Wallowa-Whitman National Forest. This camp is also a popular spot with horse-packers. A loading ramp is provided.

14.　NORTH FORK CATHERINE TRAILHEAD

Reference: **Near Eagle Cap Wilderness in Wallowa-Whitman National Forest; map C5, grid f3.**

Campsites, facilities: There are six sites for tents or trailers. Picnic tables and fire grills are provided. Vault toilets are available. There is **no piped water**. Leashed pets are permitted.

Reservations, fee: No reservations; no fee. Open June to late October.

Who to contact: Phone the LaGrande Ranger District at (541) 963-7186 or write to Wallowa-Whitman National Forest, P.O. Box 907, Baker City, OR 97813.

Location: From LaGrande on Interstate 84, travel 14 miles southeast on Highway 203 to Union. Drive 10 miles southeast of Union on Highway 203, then four miles east on Forest Service Road 7785. The camp is 3.5 miles northeast on Forest Service Road 7785.

Trip note: This campground is set along the North Fork of Catherine Creek at a trailhead that provides access to various lakes and streams in the Eagle Cap Wilderness. It's a good jumpoff point for a hiking trip. A national forest map details the possibilities.

15.　　　　　HURRICANE CREEK

Reference: **Near Eagle Cap Wilderness in Wallowa-Whitman National Forest; map C5, grid f4.**

Campsites, facilities: There are eight tent sites. Picnic tables and fire grills are provided. Firewood and vault toilets are available, but there is **no piped water**. Leashed pets are permitted.

Reservations, fee: No reservations; no fee. Open mid-June to late October.

Who to contact: Phone the Eagle Cap Ranger District at (541) 426-4978 or write to Wallowa Mountains Visitor Center, 88401 Highway 82, Enterprise, OR 97828.

Location: From Interstate 84 at LaGrande, turn north on Highway 82 and drive 62 miles to Enterprise. Continue six miles south to Joseph. The campground is located 3.5 miles southwest of Joseph on Forest Service Road 8205.

Trip note: This campground is set at along Hurricane Creek at the edge of the Eagle Cap Wilderness. It's a good jumpoff point for a wilderness backpacking trip. There is no access for RVs, providing more of a wilderness environment. It's essential to obtain maps of the area from the ranger district.

16.　　　　　　　SHADY　　　　　　　　　RV.

Reference: **On Lostine River in Wallowa-Whitman National Forest; map C5, grid f4.**

Campsites, facilities: There are 12 sites for tents, trailers or RVs up to 16 feet long. **No piped water** is available. Picnic tables and fire grills are provided. Vault toilets are available. Leashed pets are permitted.

Reservations, fee: No reservations; no fee. Open mid-June to November.

Who to contact: Phone the Eagle Cap Ranger District at (541) 426-4978 or write to Wallowa Mountains Visitor Center, 88401 Highway 82, Enterprise, OR 97828.

Location: From Interstate 84 at LaGrande, turn north on Highway 82 and drive 52 miles to Lostine. Drive 15 miles south of Lostine on Forest Service Road 8210.

Trip note: This campground is set along the banks of the Lostine River. Nearby trails provide access to the Eagle Cap Wilderness, a beautiful and pristine area that is perfect for an extended backpacking trip.

17. TWO PAN

Reference: **On Lostine River in Wallowa-Whitman National Forest; map C5, grid f4.**

Campsites, facilities: There are eight tent or trailer sites. **No piped water** is available. Picnic tables and fire grills are provided. Vault toilets are available. Leashed pets are permitted.

Reservations, fee: No reservations; no fee. Open mid-June to November.

Who to contact: Phone the Eagle Cap Ranger District at (541) 426-4978 or write to Wallowa Mountains Visitor Center, 88401 Highway 82, Enterprise, OR 97828.

Location: From Interstate 84 at LaGrande, turn north on Highway 82 and drive 52 miles to Lostine. Drive 17 miles south of Lostine on Forest Service Road 8210.

Trip note: This campground is set at the end of the Forest Service road on the banks of the Lostine River. Adjacent trails provide access to numerous lakes and streams in the Eagle Cap Wilderness. At 5,600 feet, this is a prime jumpoff spot for a multi-day wilderness adventure.

18. WALLOWA LAKE STATE PARK **RV**

Reference: **On Wallowa Lake; map C5, grid f5.**

Campsites, facilities: There are 89 tent sites and 121 full-hookup sites for trailers or RVs of any length. Group campsites are available. Electricity, piped water, sewer hookups and picnic tables are provided. Flush toilets, sanitary disposal services, showers and firewood are available. A store, a cafe and ice are located within one mile. Some facilities are **wheelchair accessible**. Leashed pets are permitted. Boat docks, launching facilities and rentals are nearby.

Reservations, fee: Contact Reservations Northwest at (800) 452-5687 ($6 reservation fee); $16-$19 fee per night. Open mid-April to late October.

Who to contact: Phone (541) 432-8855 or (800) 452-5687, or write to 72214 Marina Lane, Joseph, OR 97846.

Location: From Pendleton on Interstate 84, turn east and drive approximately 54 miles to LaGrande. Take exit 261 and turn north on Highway 82. Drive 68 miles to Joseph, then continue six miles south on Highway 82 to the south shore of the lake.

Trip note: This campground is set along the shore of scenic Wallowa Lake. There is a pretty one-mile nature trail, and trailheads that provide access into Eagle Cap Wilderness. A marina is nearby for boaters and anglers. Picnicking, swimming and wildlife viewing are a few of the other activities available to visitors.

19. MOUNTAIN VIEW MOTEL & TRAILER PARK **RV**

Reference: **Near Wallowa Lake; map C5, grid f5.**

Campsites, facilities: There are 20 tent sites and 25 drive-through sites for trailers or RVs of any length. Electricity, piped water, sewer hookups and picnic tables are provided. Flush toilets, sanitary disposal services and showers are available. Bottled gas, a store, a cafe and a laundromat are located within one mile. Leashed pets are permitted.

Reservations, fee: Reservations accepted; $8-$13 fee per night; MasterCard and Visa accepted. Open all year.

Who to contact: Phone (541) 432-2982 or write to 91094 Joseph Highway, Joseph, OR 97846.

Location: From LaGrande on Interstate 84, turn north on Highway 82 and drive 62 miles to Enterprise. Continue seven miles southeast on Highway 82 to the campground, located one mile southwest of Joseph.

Trip note: This park is not far from Wallowa Lake. Nearby recreation options include a golf course, hiking trails, bike paths and a riding stable.

---

20.   LICK CREEK   RV.

Reference: **On Lick Creek in Wallowa-Whitman National Forest; map C5, grid f6.**

Campsites, facilities: There are seven tent sites and five sites for trailers or RVs up to 30 feet long. Picnic tables and fire grills are provided. Piped water, firewood and vault toilets are available. Leashed pets are permitted.

Reservations, fee: No reservations; $4 fee per night. Open mid-June to late November.

Who to contact: Phone the Hells Canyon National Recreation Area at (541) 426-4978 or write to Wallowa Mountains Visitor Center, 88401 Highway 82, Enterprise, OR 97828.

Location: From Interstate 84 at LaGrande, turn north on Highway 82 and drive 62 miles to Enterprise. Continue six miles south to Joseph, then drive 7.5 miles east on Highway 350. Turn south on Forest Service Road 39 and continue 15 miles.

Trip note: This campground is set along the banks of Lick Creek, in Hells Canyon National Recreation Area. The camp is secluded and pretty.

---

21.   BLACKHORSE   RV.

Reference: **On Imnaha River in Wallowa-Whitman National Forest; map C5, grid f7.**

Campsites, facilities: There are 16 sites for tents, trailers or RVs up to 30 feet long. Picnic tables and fire grills are provided. Piped water, firewood and vault toilets are available. Leashed pets are permitted.

Reservations, fee: No reservations; $4 fee per night. Open June to late November.

Who to contact: Phone the Hells Canyon National Recreation Area at (541) 426-4978 or write to Wallowa Mountains Visitor Center, 88401 Highway 82, Enterprise, OR 97828.

Location: From Interstate 84 at LaGrande, turn north on Highway 82 and drive 62 miles to Enterprise. Continue six miles south to Joseph, then drive 7.5 miles east on Highway 350. Turn south on Forest Service Road 39 and continue 29 miles.

Trip note: This campground is set along the banks of the Imnaha River in Hells Canyon National Recreation Area. It's a secluded spot in Wallowa-Whitman National Forest at an elevation of 4,000 feet.

---

22.   OLLOKOT   RV.

Reference: **On Imnaha River in Wallowa-Whitman National Forest; map C5, grid f7.**

Campsites, facilities: There are 12 sites for tents, trailers or RVs up to 30 feet long. Picnic tables and fire grills are provided. Piped water and vault toilets are available. Leashed pets are permitted.

Reservations, fee: No reservations; $4 fee per night. Open June to late November.

Who to contact: Phone the Hells Canyon National Recreation Area at (541) 426-4978 or write to Wallowa Mountains Visitor Center, 88401 Highway 82, Enterprise, OR 97828.

Location: From Interstate 84 at LaGrande, turn north on Highway 82 and drive 62 miles to Enterprise. Continue six miles south to Joseph, then drive 7.5 miles east on Highway 350. Turn south on Forest Service Road 39 and continue 30 miles.

Trip note: This campground is set along the banks of the Imnaha River in Hells Canyon National Recreation Area at 4,000 feet elevation. It is a primitive option to the other camps in the immediate area.

---

23. TAMARACK RV

Reference: **On Eagle Creek in Wallowa-Whitman National Forest; map C5, grid g4.**

Campsites, facilities: There are 12 tent sites and 12 sites for trailers or RVs up to 22 feet long. Picnic tables and fire grills are provided. Piped water, firewood and vault toilets are available. Leashed pets are permitted.

Reservations, fee: No reservations; no fee. Open June to late October.

Who to contact: Phone the Pine Ranger District at (541) 742-7511 or write to General Delivery, Halfway, OR 97834.

Location: From Interstate 84 at Baker City, drive 23 miles northeast on Highway 203 to the town of Medical Springs. From Medical Springs, travel 15.5 miles southeast on Forest Service Road 67 to the bridge across Eagle Creek. The camp is 300 yards east on Forest Service Road 77.

Trip note: This campground is set along the banks of Eagle Creek, a beautiful area with lush vegetation and abundant wildlife. This is a good spot for a fishing and hiking trip in a remote setting.

---

24. TWO COLOR RV

Reference: **On Eagle Creek in Wallowa-Whitman National Forest; map C5, grid g4.**

Campsites, facilities: There are 14 sites for tents and six sites for trailers or RVs up to 22 feet long. Picnic tables and fire grills are provided. Piped water and vault toilets are available. Leashed pets are permitted.

Reservations, fee: No reservations; no fee. Open mid-June to late October.

Who to contact: Phone the LaGrande Ranger District at (541) 963-7186 or write to Wallowa-Whitman National Forest, P.O. Box 907, Baker City, OR 97814.

Location: From Interstate 84 at Baker City, drive 23 miles northeast via Interstate 84 and Highway 203 to the town of Medical Springs. From Medical Springs, go 15.5 miles southeast on Forest Service Road 6700, then 1.5 miles northeast on Forest Service Road 7755 to the park entrance on the right.

Trip note: This campground is set along the banks of Eagle Creek, about a mile north of Tamarack Campground. See that trip note for ideas.

---

25. EAGLE FORKS RV

Reference: **On Eagle Creek in Wallowa-Whitman National Forest; map C5, grid g5.**

Campsites, facilities: There are seven tent sites and five sites for trailers or RVs up to 21 feet long. Picnic tables and fire grills are provided. Firewood, piped water and vault toilets are available. Leashed pets are permitted.

Reservations, fee: No reservations; no fee. Open June to late October.

Who to contact: Phone the Pine Ranger District at (541) 742-7511 or write to General Delivery, Halfway, OR 97834.

Location: From Interstate 84 at Baker City, drive four miles north, then turn east on Highway 86 and drive 36 miles to Richland. From Richland, travel north to New Bridge 11 miles via a county road and Forest Service Road 7735.

Trip note: This campground is set at the confluence of Little Eagle Creek and Eagle Creek. A trail leaves camp and follows the creek northwest for five miles. It's a prime day-hike, yet the spot attracts few people. It's quite pretty as well, and is a perfect spot for a weekend getaway or an extended layover.

---

26. McBRIDE   RV

Reference: **On Brooks Ditch in Wallowa-Whitman National Forest; map C5, grid g5.**

Campsites, facilities: There are 11 tent sites and eight sites for trailers or RVs up to 16 feet long. Picnic tables and fire grills are provided. Piped water and vault toilets are available. Leashed pets are permitted.

Reservations, fee: No reservations; no fee. Open mid-May to late October.

Who to contact: Phone the Pine Ranger District at (541) 742-7511 or write to General Delivery, Halfway, OR 97834.

Location: From Interstate 84 at Baker City, drive four miles north, then turn east on Highway 86 and drive 52 miles to Halfway. Continue six miles northwest of Halfway on Highway 413, then drive 2.5 miles west on Forest Service Road 7710.

Trip note: This campground is set along the banks of Brooks Ditch. It's a little-used, primitive and obscure camp. It is not particularly scenic, but it will work as a quick, free layover spot.

---

27. TWIN LAKES

Reference: **Near Twin Lakes in Wallowa-Whitman National Forest; map C5, grid g6.**

Campsites, facilities: There are six tent sites. Picnic tables and fire grills are provided. Firewood and vault toilets are available, but there is **no piped water**. Leashed pets are permitted.

Reservations, fee: No reservations; no fee. Open July to mid-September.

Who to contact: Phone the Pine Ranger District at (541) 742-7511 or write to General Delivery, Halfway, OR 97834.

Location: From Interstate 84 at Baker City, drive four miles north, then turn east on Highway 86 and drive 52 miles to Halfway. From Halfway, drive five miles north on County Road 733, then 24 miles north Forest Service Road 66.

Trip note: This campground is set between the little Twin Lakes, both of which offer excellent fishing. Nearby trails provide access to backcountry lakes and streams. See a Forest Service map for details.

---

28. HIDDEN

Reference: **On Imnaha River in Wallowa-Whitman National Forest; map C5, grid g6.**

Campsites, facilities: There are 10 tent sites. Picnic tables and fire grills are provided. Piped water, firewood and vault toilets are available. Leashed pets are permitted.

Reservations, fee: No reservations; $4 fee per night. Open June to late November.

Who to contact: Phone the Hells Canyon National Recreation Area at (541) 426-4978 or write to Wallowa Mountains Visitor Center, 88401 Highway 82, Enterprise, OR 97828.

Location: From Interstate 84 at LaGrande, turn north on Highway 82 and drive 62 miles to Enterprise. Continue six miles south to Joseph, then drive 7.5 miles east on Highway 350. Turn south on Forest Service Road 39 and continue 29 miles, then proceed seven miles southwest on Forest Service Road 3960.

Trip note: This campground is set along the banks of the Imnaha River, in the Hells Canyon National Recreation Area. This is an exceptionally pretty spot, with river views and spacious sites. It is essential to obtain a map of Wallowa-Whitman National Forest that details back roads and hiking trails.

---

29.   FISH LAKE   RV

Reference: **On Fish Lake in Wallowa-Whitman National Forest; map C5, grid g6.**

Campsites, facilities: There are 10 tent sites and five sites for trailers or RVs up to 22 feet long. Picnic tables and fire grills are provided. Spring water, firewood and vault toilets are available. Leashed pets are permitted. Boat launching facilities are nearby.

Reservations, fee: No reservations; no fee. Open mid-June to late October.

Who to contact: Phone the Pine Ranger District at (541) 742-7511 or write to General Delivery, Halfway, OR 97834.

Location: From Interstate 84 at Baker City, drive four miles north, then turn east on Highway 86 and drive 52 miles to Halfway. From Halfway, drive five miles north on County Route 733, then 18.5 miles north on Forest Service Road 66.

Trip note: This campground is set along the shore of Fish Lake, a good base camp for a fishing trip. This is a pretty camp, well-forested with comfortable sites. Side trip options include hiking out on nearby trails that lead to mountain streams.

---

30.   EVERGREEN   RV

Reference: **On Imnaha River in Wallowa-Whitman National Forest; map C5, grid g7.**

Campsites, facilities: This is a group campsites for tents, trailers or RVs up to 31 feet long. **No piped water** is available. Picnic tables and fire grills are provided. Vault toilets are available. Leashed pets are permitted.

Reservations, fee: No reservations; no fee. Open June to late November.

Who to contact: Phone the Hells Canyon National Recreation Area at (541) 426-4978 or write to Wallowa Mountains Visitor Center, 88401 Highway 82, Enterprise, OR 97828.

Location: From Interstate 84 at LaGrande, turn north on Highway 82 and drive 62 miles to Enterprise. Continue six miles south to Joseph. Take Highway 350 east from Joseph for 7.5 miles, then continue 29 miles south on Forest Service Road 39. The camp is eight miles southwest on Forest Service Road 3960 at the end of the road.

Trip note: This campground is set along the banks of the Imnaha River in Hells Canyon National Recreation Area. It's one of seven camps in the vicinity.

31.　　　　INDIAN CROSSING　　　　RV

Reference: **On Imnaha River in Wallowa-Whitman National Forest; map C5, grid g7.**

Campsites, facilities: There are 14 sites for tents, trailers or RVs up to 30 feet long. Piped water, picnic tables and fire grills are provided. Firewood and vault toilets are available. Leashed pets are permitted. Horse facilities are available.

Reservations, fee: No reservations; $4 fee per night. Open June to late November.

Who to contact: Phone the Hells Canyon National Recreation Area at (541) 426-4978, or to write to Wallowa Mountains Visitor Center, 88401 Highway 82, Enterprise, OR 97828.

Location: From Interstate 84 at LaGrande, turn north on Highway 82 and drive 62 miles to Enterprise. Continue six miles south to Joseph. From Joseph, drive 7.5 miles east on Highway 350, then 29 miles south on Forest Service Road 39. The campground is nine miles southwest on Forest Service Road 3960 on the left.

Trip note: The trailhead for the Eagle Cap Wilderness is nearby. Obtain a Forest Service map for side trip possibilities.

32.　　　　LAKE FORK　　　　RV

Reference: **On Lake Fork Creek in Wallowa-Whitman National Forest; map C5, grid g7.**

Campsites, facilities: There are 10 sites for tents, trailers or RVs up to 22 feet long. Picnic tables and fire grills are provided. Piped water and vault toilets are available. Leashed pets are permitted.

Reservations, fee: No reservations; $4 fee per night. Open June to late November.

Who to contact: Phone the Hells Canyon National Recreation Area at (541) 426-4978 or write to Wallowa Mountains Visitor Center, 88401 Highway 82, Enterprise, OR 97828.

Location: From Baker City on Interstate 84, drive four miles north, then turn east on Highway 86 and travel 62 miles. Proceed eight miles north on Forest Service Road 39, then turn left and continue one-half mile to the campground.

Trip note: This campground is set along the banks of Lake Fork Creek, an ideal jumpoff point for a backpacking trip. A trail from camp follows the creek west for about 10 miles to Fish Lake. It continues beyond Fish Lake to several smaller lakes.

LEAVE NO TRACE TIPS

Travel and camp with care.

On the trail:

• Stay on designated trails.
Walk single file in the middle of the path.

• Do not take shortcuts on switchbacks.

• When traveling cross-country where there are no trails,
follow animal trails or spread out your group so no new routes are created.
Walk along the most durable surfaces available,
such as rock, gravel, dry grasses, or snow.

• Use a map and compass to eliminate the need for
rock cairns, tree scars, or ribbons.

• If you encounter pack animals, step to the downhill side
of the trail and speak softly to avoid startling them.

At camp:

• Choose an established, legal site that will not be damaged by your stay.

• Restrict activities to areas where vegetation is compacted or absent.

• Control pets at all times, or leave them at home
with a sitter. Remove dog feces.

MAP D1

OREGON MAP .... see page 380
Adjoining Maps

69 LISTINGS
PAGES 472-499

NORTH (C1) .... see page 382
EAST (D2) .... see page 500
SOUTH (E1) .... see page 602
WEST .... no map

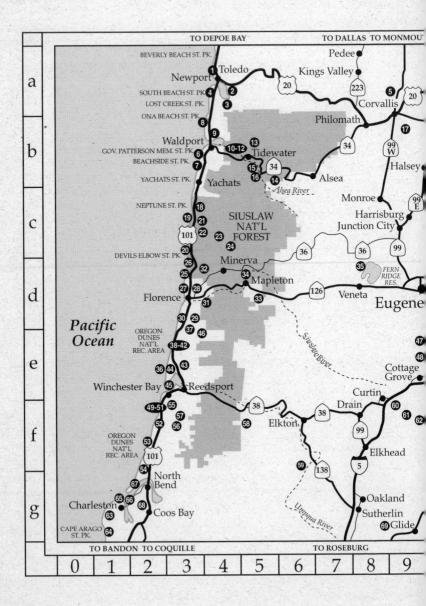

Oregon Map D1 featuring: Yaquina Bay, Alsea Bay, Corvallis, Seal Rock State Park, Siuslaw National Forest, South Beach State Park, Alsea River, Willamette River, Cape Perpetua, Cape Creek , Alder Lake, Siuslaw River, Florence, Sutton Lake, Woahink Lake, Mercer Lake, Fern Ridge Reservoir, Siltcoos River, Siltcoos Lake, Cleowax Lake, Oregon Dunes National Recreation Area, Carter Lake, Eugene, Tahkenitch Lake, Umpqua River, Winchester Bay, Tenmile Lake, Eel Lake, Eel River, Loon Lake, Coos Bay, Bluebill Lake, Cottage Grove Reservoir, Sunset Bay, Cape Arago State Park

1. AGATE BEACH RV PARK   **RV**

Reference: **Near the Pacific Ocean; map D1, grid a4.**
Campsites, facilities: There are 32 sites for trailers or RVs of any length. Electricity, piped water, sewer hookups and picnic tables are provided. Flush toilets, sanitary services, showers and a laundromat are available. A store and ice are located within one mile. Leashed pets are permitted.
Reservations, fee: Reservations accepted; $15-$18 fee per night. Open all year.
Who to contact: Phone (541) 265-7670 or write to 6138 North Coast Highway, Newport, OR 97365.
Location: From Interstate 5 at Albany, turn west on US 20 and drive 66 miles to Newport. Turn north on US 101 and drive three miles to the park on the north end of town.
Trip note: This park is a short distance from Agate Beach Wayside, a small state park with beach access. Agate hunting can be good. Sometimes the agates are covered by a layer of sand and you have to dig a bit. But other times, wave action will clear the sand, unveiling the agates at low tides.

2. HARBOR VILLAGE RV PARK   **RV**

Reference: **On Yaquina Bay; map D1, grid a4.**
Campsites, facilities: There are 140 sites for trailers or RVs of any length. Electricity, piped water, sewer hookups and picnic tables are provided. Flush toilets, showers and a laundromat are available. Bottled gas, a store and a cafe are located within one mile. Boat docks, launching facilities and rentals are nearby.
Reservations, fee: Reservations accepted; $15 fee (two people) per night; MasterCard, Visa and Discover accepted. Open all year.
Who to contact: Phone (541) 265-5088 or write to 923 Southeast Bay Boulevard, P.O. Box 6, Newport, OR 97365.
Location: From Interstate 5 at Albany, turn west on US 20 and drive 65.5 miles. Turn south on John Moore Road and drive one-half mile to the bay. Turn left on Bay Boulevard and you'll see the entrance to the trailer park on the left.
Trip note: This park is set near the shore of Yaquina Bay in a wooded area. See the trip note for Newport Marina and RV Park for information on attractions in Newport. Nearby recreation options include clamming, crabbing, deep sea fishing, an 18-hole golf course, hiking trails and a full-service marina.

3. NEWPORT MARINA AND RV PARK   **RV**

Reference: **On Yaquina Bay; map D1, grid a4.**
Campsites, facilities: There are 120 sites for trailers or RVs. Electricity, piped

water and sewer hookups are provided. Flush toilets, showers, cable TV, a store, a laundromat, ice and are available. Leashed pets are permitted. A marina with boat docks and launching facilities are nearby.

Reservations, fee: Reservations accepted; $17 fee per night; MasterCard, Visa and Discover accepted. Open all year.

Who to contact: Phone (541) 867-3321 or write to 600 SE Bay Boulevard, Newport, OR 97365.

Location: From Interstate 5 at Albany, turn west on US 20 and drive 66 miles to Newport. Turn south on US 101 and travel one-quarter mile, then one-half mile east on Marine Science Drive and you'll see the park entrance on the left.

Trip note: This park is set along the shore of Yaquina Bay, near Newport, a resort town which offers a variety of attractions. Among them are ocean fishing, a museum and aquarium at the nearby Hatfield Marine Science Center, the Undersea Garden, the Waxworks, Ripley's Believe It or Not and the Lincoln County Historical Society Museum. Nearby recreation options include an 18-hole golf course, hiking trails, a full-service marina and tennis courts.

4. SOUTH BEACH STATE PARK RV

Reference: **On the Pacific Ocean; map D1, grid a4.**

Campsites, facilities: There are 244 sites for trailers or RVs of any length, and a special primitive camping area for hikers and bicyclists. There are also three group sites and 10 yurts. Electricity and water hookups, fire grills and picnic tables are provided. Flush toilets, a sanitary disposal station, showers and firewood are available. Some facilities are **wheelchair accessible**. Leashed pets are permitted.

Reservations, fee: Contact Reservations Northwest at (800) 452-5687 ($6 reservation fee); $15-$19 fee per night; $25 yurt fee; $50 group fee; $4 for hikers/bikers. Open all year.

Who to contact: Phone (541) 867-4715 or (800) 452-5687 or write to 5580 South Coast Highway, South Beach, OR 97366.

Location: From Interstate 5 at Albany, turn west on US 20 and drive 66 miles to Newport. Turn south on US 101 and drive two miles to the park entrance on the right.

Trip note: This park is set along the beach and offers opportunities for hiking, beachcombing and fishing. The Oregon Coast Trail goes through the park and there is a primitive hike-in campground available. See the trip note for Newport Marina and RV Park for information on attractions in Newport.

5. CORVALLIS MOTORHOME PARK RV

Reference: **In Corvallis; map D1, grid a9.**

Campsites, facilities: There are 27 sites for trailers or RVs. Electricity, piped water and sewer hookups are provided. Flush toilets, showers, a store, a cafe, a laundromat and ice are available. Bottled gas and sanitary services are located within one mile. Pets are permitted.

Reservations, fee: Reservations accepted; $15 fee per night. Open all year.

Who to contact: Phone (541) 752-2334 or write to 200 Northwest 53rd Street, Corvallis, OR 97330.

Location: From US 20 at Corvallis, continue 2.5 miles west on US 20, then turn north on 53rd Street and travel 1.3 miles to the park on the right.

Trip note: This is a decent layover spot on your way to and from the coast. Nearby recreation options include an 18-hole golf course, hiking trails and a riding stable.

6.   BEACHSIDE STATE PARK   RV

Reference: **Near Alsea Bay; map D1, grid b3.**

Campsites, facilities: There are 50 sites for tents, 32 sites with water and electrical hookups for trailers or RVs up to 30 feet long, and a special camping area for hikers and bicyclists. Picnic tables and fire grills are provided. Flush toilets, showers and firewood are available. Some facilities are **wheelchair accessible**. Leashed pets are permitted.

Reservations, fee: Contact Reservations Northwest at (800) 452-5687 ($6 reservation fee); $16-$19 fee per night; $4-$5 hikers/bikers. Open all year.

Who to contact: Phone (541) 563-3220 or write to P.O. Box 693, Waldport, OR 97394.

Location: From Interstate 5 at Albany, turn west on US 20 and drive 66 miles to Newport. Turn south on US 101 and drive 16 miles to Waldport. Continue four miles south on US 101 to the park entrance at milepost 158.

Trip note: This state park offers about nine miles of beach and is not far from Alsea Bay and the Alsea River. See the trip notes for Alsea Bay Trailer Park and Kozy Kove Marina for more information on the fishing opportunities in the area.

7.   TILLICUM BEACH   RV

Reference: **On the Pacific Ocean in Siuslaw National Forest; map D1, grid b3.**

Campsites, facilities: There are 61 sites for tents, trailers or RVs up to 32 feet long. Picnic tables and fire grills are provided. Flush toilets and piped water are available. Leashed pets are permitted.

Reservations, fee: No reservations; $10 fee per night. Open all year.

Who to contact: Phone (541) 563-3211 or write to Siuslaw National Forest, Waldport Ranger District, P.O. Box 400, Waldport, OR 97394.

Location: From Interstate 5 at Albany, turn west on US 20 and drive 66 miles to Newport. Turn south on US 101 and drive 14 miles to Waldport. Continue 4.5 miles south on US 101 to the campground entrance on your right.

Trip note: You get ocean view campsites, and that may be just what you're looking for. This campground is set along the ocean, just south of Beachside State Park. Nearby Forest Service roads provide access to streams in the mountains east of the beach area. A Forest Service map details the possibilities. Since it is just off the highway, this camp fills up very quickly in the summer; expect crowds.

8.   SEAL ROCK TRAILER COVE   RV

Reference: **Near Seal Rock State Park; map D1, grid b4.**

Campsites, facilities: There are 26 drive-through sites for trailers or RVs of any length. Electricity, piped water, sewer hookups and picnic tables are provided. Flush toilets, sanitary services and showers are available. Firewood, a store, a cafe and ice are located within one mile.

Reservations, fee: No reservations; $14-$16 fee per night. Open all year.

Who to contact: Phone (541) 563-3955 or write to P.O. Box 71, Seal Rock, OR 97376.

Location: From Interstate 5 at Albany, turn west on US 20 and drive 66 miles to Newport. Turn south on US 101 and drive 10 miles to the town of Seal Rock. Continue one-quarter mile south on US 101 to the park entrance on the right.

Trip note: This trailer park is set along the rugged coastline near Seal Rock State Park, which is open for day-use only. There you can see seals, sea lions and a variety of birds.

9.   ALSEA BAY TRAILER PARK   `RV`

Reference: **On Alsea Bay; map D1, grid b4.**

Campsites, facilities: There are 75 sites for trailers or RVs of any length. Electricity, piped water and sewer hookups are provided. Flush toilets, showers and a recreation hall are available. Bottled gas, sanitary services, a store, a cafe, a laundromat and ice are located within one mile. Leashed pets are permitted. Boat docks, launching facilities and rentals are nearby.

Reservations, fee: Reservations accepted; $12-$26 fee per night. Open all year.

Who to contact: Phone (541) 563-2250 or write to P.O. Box 397, Waldport, OR 97394.

Location: From Interstate 5 at Albany, turn west on US 20 and drive 66 miles to Newport. Turn south on US 101 and drive to milepost 155 at the north end of the Alsea Bay Bridge. The park is located on the west side of the bridge.

Trip note: This is a pretty park, set amidst pine trees and within walking distance to the beach, the bay, and downtown Waldport. Beautiful ocean views can be seen from the campsites. This area is a favorite for fishermen because Alsea Bay has sandy and rocky shorelines. The crabbing and clamming can also be quite good. Ona Beach State Park is about five miles north on US 101 and offers additional fishing opportunities and a boat ramp along Beaver Creek. It is open for day-use only. Other nearby recreation options include hiking trails, marked bike trails, the Oregon Coast Aquarium and a marina.

---

10.   DRIFT CREEK LANDING   `RV`

Reference: **On Alsea River; map D1, grid b4.**

Campsites, facilities: There are 60 drive-through sites for trailers or RVs of any length. Electricity, piped water and sewer hookups are provided. Flush toilets, private telephone service, cable TV, bottled gas, showers, a recreation hall, store, a cafe and a laundromat are available. Leashed pets are permitted. Boat docks, launching facilities and rentals are nearby.

Reservations, fee: Reservations accepted; $13-$18 fee per night. Open all year.

Who to contact: Phone (541) 563-3610 or write to 3850 Highway 34, Waldport, OR 97394.

Location: From Interstate 5 at Albany, turn west on US 20 and drive 66 miles to Newport. Turn south on US 101 and drive 14 miles to Waldport. Then turn east on Highway 34 and travel 3.5 miles to the campground.

Trip note: This campground is set along the shore of the Alsea River. The area is heavily treed and mountainous. The Oregon Coast Aquarium is 15 miles away and an 18-hole golf course is located nearby. For more information on the area, see the trip note for Alsea Bay Trailer Park.

---

11.   FISHIN' HOLE TRAILER PARK   `RV`

Reference: **On Alsea River; map D1, grid b4.**

Campsites, facilities: There are 16 tent sites and 33 sites for trailers or RVs of any length. Electricity, piped water, sewer hookups and picnic tables are provided. Flush toilets, showers, a store, a cafe and a laundromat are available. Bottled gas is located within one block. Leashed pets are permitted. Boat docks, launching facilities and rentals are nearby.

Reservations, fee: Reservations accepted; $13 fee per night. Open all year.

Who to contact: Phone (541) 563-3401 or write to 3911 Highway 34, Waldport, OR 97394.

Location: From Interstate 5 at Albany, turn west on US 20 and drive 66 miles to Newport. Turn south on US 101 and drive 14 miles to Waldport. Turn east on Highway 34 and drive four miles to the entrance on the left.

Trip note: This is one of several campgrounds set along the shore of the Alsea River here. For information on the area, see the trip note for Alsea Bay Trailer Park.

12. CHINOOK TRAILER PARK

Reference: **On Alsea River; map D1, grid b5.**

Campsites, facilities: There are 22 sites for trailers or RVs of any length. Electricity, piped water and sewer hookups are provided. Flush toilets, showers and a laundromat are available. Bottled gas, a store, a cafe and ice are located within one mile. Pets and motorbikes are permitted. Boat docks are nearby.

Reservations, fee: Reservations accepted; $16 fee per night. Open all year.

Who to contact: Phone (541) 563-3485 or write to 3299 Highway 34, Waldport, OR 97394.

Location: From Interstate 5 at Albany, turn west on US 20 and drive 66 miles to Newport. Turn south on US 101 and drive 14 miles to Waldport. Turn east on Highway 34 and drive 3.5 miles to the entrance.

Trip note: This trailer park is set along the shore of the Alsea River. For more information on the area, see the trip note for Alsea Bay Trailer Park.

13. TAYLOR'S LANDING

Reference: **On Alsea River; map D1, grid b5.**

Campsites, facilities: There are six tent sites and 28 sites for trailers or RVs of any length. Electricity, piped water, sewer hookups and picnic tables are provided. Flush toilets, bottled gas, showers, a cafe and a laundromat are available. Pets and motorbikes are permitted. Boat docks, launching facilities and rentals are nearby.

Reservations, fee: Reservations accepted; $15 fee per night. MasterCard and Visa accepted. Open all year.

Who to contact: Phone (541) 528-3388 or write to 4250 Highway 34, Waldport, OR 97394.

Location: From Interstate 5 at Albany, turn west on US 20 and drive 66 miles to Newport. Turn south on US 101 and drive 14 miles to Waldport. Turn east on Highway 34 and drive seven miles to the entrance on the right.

Trip note: This campground is set along the Alsea River. For more information on the area, see the trip notes for Alsea Bay Trailer Park and Kozy Kove Marina.

14. KOZY KOVE MARINA

Reference: **On Alsea River; map D1, grid b5.**

Campsites, facilities: There are 10 sites for tents and 25 sites for trailers or RVs of any length. Cable TV, electricity, piped water, sewer hookups and picnic tables are provided. Flush toilets, bottled gas, sanitary services, showers, a store, a cafe, a laundromat and ice are available. Pets and motorbikes are permitted. Boat docks, launching facilities and rentals are nearby. There are boat ramps on-site.

Reservations, fee: Reservations accepted; $10-$15 fee per night; MasterCard and Visa accepted. Open all year.

Who to contact: Phone (541) 528-3251 or write to 9464 Alsea Highway, Tightwater, OR 97394.

Location: From Interstate 5 at Albany, turn west on US 20 and drive 66 miles to Newport. Turn south on US 101 and drive 14 miles to Waldport. Turn east on Highway 34 and drive 9.5 miles to the entrance on the left.

Trip note: This campground is set along the Alsea River about 10 miles east of Waldport. Nearby Forest Service roads provide access to the various creeks and streams in the surrounding mountains. Consult a Siuslaw National Forest map for details.

15.　　　　　CANAL CREEK　　　　RV

Reference: **On Canal Creek in Siuslaw National Forest; map D1, grid b5.**

Campsites, facilities: There are seven sites for tents only and 10 sites for tents or small RVs. Picnic tables and fire grills are provided. Piped water and vault toilets are available. A picnic shelter and a play area are also available.

Reservations, fee: No reservations; $5 fee per night. Open all year.

Who to contact: Phone (541) 563-3211 or write to Siuslaw National Forest, Waldport Ranger District, Waldport, OR 97394.

Location: From Interstate 5 at Albany, turn west on US 20 and drive 15 miles to Philomath. Turn south on Highway 34 and drive 52 miles to Forest Service Road 3462, then turn south and drive four miles to the campground.

Trip note: This pleasant little campground is just off the beaten path in a large, wooded, open area along Canal Creek. It feels remote, yet has easy access and is close to the coast and all the amenities. The climate here is relatively mild, with 13 degrees Fahrenheit being the coldest winter temperature recorded in recent years. On the other hand, there is the rain—lots of it.

16.　　　　　BLACKBERRY　　　　RV

Reference: **On Alsea River in Siuslaw National Forest; map D1, grid b5.**

Campsites, facilities: There are 32 sites for tents, trailers or RVs. Picnic tables and fire grills are provided. Piped water and flush toilets are available. There is no firewood. A boat ramp is on the site.

Reservations, fee: No reservations; $7 fee per night. Open May through October. Note: Phone ahead to make sure this site is open; it may close without notice.

Who to contact: Phone (541) 563-3211 or write to Siuslaw National Forest, Waldport Ranger District, P.O. Box 400, Waldport, OR 97394.

Location: From Interstate 5 at Albany, turn west on US 20 and drive 15 miles to Philomath. Turn south on Highway 34 just past Philomath, and drive 41 miles to the campground entrance.

Trip note: This is a good base camp for a fishing trip on the Alsea River. The Forest Service provides boat launches and picnic areas at several spots along this stretch of river. Often there will be a "camp host," who can give you inside information on nearby recreational opportunities. Note: Phone ahead to make sure this site is open; it may close without notice.

17.   WILLAMETTE CITY PARK   RV

Reference: **On Willamette River; map D1, grid b9.**

Campsites, facilities: There are 10 sites for tents, trailers or RVs of any length. Vault toilets, piped water, a covered outdoor kitchen area, picnic tables and a small playground are available. Bottled gas, a store, a cafe, a laundromat and ice are within one mile. There is a dump station in the center of town, three miles away. Leashed pets are permitted. Boat docks and launching facilities are located two miles away.

Reservations, fee: No reservations; $7 fee per night. Open April to late October.

Who to contact: Phone (541) 757-6918 or write to Corvallis Department of Parks and Recreation, P.O. Box 1083, Corvallis, OR 97339.

Location: From US 20 at Corvallis, drive one mile south on Highway 99W, then proceed one-half mile east on SE Goodnight Road to the park.

Trip note: This 40-acre city park is set along the banks of the Willamette River, just outside Corvallis. The camping area is actually a large clearing near the entrance to the park, which has been left in its natural state. There are trails leading down to the river, and the birdwatching is good here.

18.   CAPE PERPETUA   RV

Reference: **On Cape Creek in Siuslaw National Forest; map D1, grid c3.**

Campsites, facilities: There are 37 sites for tents, trailers or RVs up to 22 feet long. Picnic tables and fire grills are provided. Flush toilets, piped water and sanitary services are available. Leashed pets are permitted.

Reservations, fee: No reservations; $10 fee per night. Open mid-May to late September.

Who to contact: Phone Siuslaw National Forest at (541) 563-3211 or write to Waldport Ranger District, Waldport, OR 97394.

Location: From Interstate 5 at Albany, turn west on US 20 and drive 66 miles to Newport. Turn south on US 101 and drive 23 miles to Yachats. Continue three miles south on US 101 to the entrance on the left.

Trip note: This Forest Service campground is set along Cape Creek in the Cape Perpetua Scenic Area. The visitor information center provides hiking and driving maps to guide you through this spectacular area. A movie is available for viewing which explains this unique area. Maps also highlight the tidepool and picnic areas. The coastal cliffs are perfect for whale watching from December through March. Neptune State Park is just south and offers additional rugged coastline vistas.

19.   SEA PERCH   RV

Reference: **Near Cape Perpetua; map D1, grid c3.**

Campsites, facilities: There are 10 drive-through sites for tents, trailers or RVs of any length. Electricity, piped water, sewer hookups and picnic tables are provided. Flush toilets, bottled gas, sanitary services, showers, firewood, a recreation hall, a store, a cafe, a laundromat, ice and a playground are available. Pets and motorbikes are permitted.

Reservations, fee: Reservations accepted; $16-$22.50 fee per night. MasterCard and Visa accepted. Open all year.

Who to contact: Phone (541) 547-3505 or write to 95480 Highway 101, Yachats, OR 97498.

Location: From Interstate 5 at Albany, turn west on US 20 and drive 66 miles to Newport. Turn south on US 101 and drive 6.5 miles to the campground at milepost 171 on the right.

Trip note: This is one of the most scenic areas on the Oregon coast, and Sea Perch is right in the middle of it. This private camp is set just south of Cape Perpetua, offering sites on the beach and lawn areas. The campground has its own shell museum. For more information on the area, see the trip note for Cape Perpetua.

---

20.   CARL G. WASHBURNE STATE PARK   RV

Reference: **On the Pacific Ocean; map D1, grid c3.**

Campsites, facilities: There are six primitive walk-in sites, two tent sites and 58 sites with full hookups for trailers or RVs up to 45 feet long. A special area is available for hikers and bicyclists. Picnic tables are provided. Flush toilets, showers and firewood are available. Leashed pets are permitted.

Reservations, fee: No reservations; $15-$19 fee per night; $4 for hikers/bikers. Open all year.

Who to contact: Phone (541) 547-3416 or (800) 452-5687, or write to Carl G. Washburne State Park, Florence, OR 97439.

Location: From Interstate 5 at Eugene, turn west on Highway 126 and drive 61 miles to Florence. Turn north on US 101 and drive 12.5 miles, then one-quarter mile west on the park entrance road.

Trip note: This park is located in a unique area with a variety of exciting trips. Short hikes lead from the campground to a two-mile-long beach, extensive tidepools along the base of the cliffs and the opportunity to tour the lighthouse. The inland sections of this park are frequented by elk, which are commonly spotted by campers. Just three miles south of the park are the Sea Lion Caves, where there is an elevator to take visitors down into the cavern, providing an insider's view of the life of a sea lion.

---

21.   ROCK CREEK   RV

Reference: **On Rock Creek in Siuslaw National Forest; map D1, grid c4.**

Campsites, facilities: There are 17 sites for tents, trailers or RVs up to 22 feet long. Fire grills and picnic tables are provided. Flush toilets and piped water are available. Leashed pets are permitted.

Reservations, fee: No reservations; $10 fee per night. Open late May to mid-September.

Who to contact: Phone (541) 563-3211 or write to Siuslaw National Forest, Waldport Ranger District, Waldport, OR 97394.

Location: From Interstate 5 at Albany, turn west on US 20 and drive 66 miles to Newport. Turn south on US 101 and drive 23 miles to Yachats. Continue south on US 101 for 10 miles to the campground entrance on your left.

Trip note: This little out-of-the-way campground is set along Rock Creek, just one-quarter of a mile from the ocean. It's a premium spot for coastal-highway travelers, although it can get packed very quickly. An excellent side trip is Cape Perpetua, a designated scenic area located a few miles up the coast. The cape offers beautiful ocean views and a visitor center which will supply you with information on nature trails, picnic spots, tidepools and the best viewpoints in the area.

22.   LANHAM BIKE CAMP

Reference: **Hike-in in Siuslaw National Forest; map D1, grid c4.**

Campsites, facilities: There are 10 primitive hike-in/bike-in tent sites. Picnic tables and fire grills are provided. Vault toilets are available. There is **no piped water**.

Reservations, fee: No reservations; no fee. Open all year.

Who to contact: Phone (541) 563-3211 or write to Siuslaw National Forest, Waldport Ranger District, Waldport, OR 97394.

Location: From Interstate 5 at Albany, turn west on US 20 and drive 66 miles to Newport. Turn south and drive 23 miles to Yachats. Continue south on US 101 for 10 miles, pass Rock Creek Campground and hike in from there.

Trip note: This is a good layover spot for bikers working their way along the coast highway. And you can't beat the price. See the trip note for Rock Creek for area information.

23.   TENMILE CREEK   **RV**

Reference: **Near Cummins Creek and Rock Creek in Siuslaw National Forest; map D1, grid c4.**

Campsites, facilities: There are four sites for tents, small trailers or RVs. Fire grills and picnic tables are provided. Vault toilets are available, but there is **no piped water**.

Reservations, fee: No reservations; no fee. Open all year.

Who to contact: Phone (541) 563-3211 or write to Siuslaw National Forest, Waldport Ranger District, Waldport, OR 97394.

Location: From Interstate 5 at Eugene, turn west on Highway 126 and drive 61 miles to Florence. Turn north on US 101, drive for about 20 miles, then turn east on Forest Service Road 56 and drive 5.5 miles to the campground entrance.

Trip note: This small, secluded spot is only 15 or 20 minutes from the highway, yet it remains a virtual secret. A map of Siuslaw National Forest details the surrounding backcountry. Bring your own drinking water or a water filter. If you're going to stick around for a while, plan on spending a day at Cape Perpetua. It's spectacularly scenic, with great hiking trails and perfect viewpoints for whale watching.

24.   NORTH FORK SIUSLAW

Reference: **On the North Fork of Siuslaw River in Siuslaw National Forest; map D1, grid c4.**

Campsites, facilities: There are five tent sites. Picnic tables and fire grills are provided. Pit toilets are available, but there is **no piped water**. Leashed pets are permitted.

Reservations, fee: No reservations; no fee in winter; $5 fee per night in summer. Open all year.

Who to contact: Phone (541) 268-4473 or write to Siuslaw National Forest, Mapleton Ranger District, Mapleton, OR 97453.

Location: From Interstate 5 at Eugene, turn west on Highway 126 and drive 50 miles to County Road 5070/North Fork (located one mile east of Florence). Turn right and drive 12 miles northeast to the campground.

Trip note: Little-known and little-used, this camp is the ideal hideaway. It is set along the North Fork of the Siuslaw River. A dirt road opposite the camp follows Wilhelm Creek for about two miles. A newly constructed trail through old growth forest is nearby. See a Forest Service map for other side trip possibilities.

25. ALDER DUNE

RV

Reference: **Near Alder Lake in Siuslaw National Forest; map D1, grid d3.**

Campsites, facilities: There are 39 sites for tents, trailers or RVs up to 30 feet long. Picnic tables and fire grills are provided. Flush toilets and piped water are available. Leashed pets are permitted.

Reservations, fee: No reservations; $10 fee per night. Open mid-May to mid-September.

Who to contact: Phone (541) 268-4473 or write to Mapleton Ranger District, Mapleton, OR 97453.

Location: From Interstate 5 at Eugene, turn west on Highway 126 and drive 61 miles to Florence. Turn north on US 101 and drive seven miles to the campground on the left.

Trip note: This campground is set near four lakes, Alder Lake, Sutton Lake, Dune Lake and Mercer Lake (largest). A boat launch is available at Sutton Lake. An option is exploring the expansive sand dunes in the area by foot. There is no off-road-vehicle access here. See the trip note for Lane County Harbor Vista Park for other information on the area.

26. SUTTON

RV

Reference: **Near Sutton Lake in Siuslaw National Forest; map D1, grid d3.**

Campsites, facilities: There are 80 sites for tents, trailers or RVs up to 30 feet long. Picnic tables and fire grills are provided. Flush toilets and piped water are available. Leashed pets are permitted. Group sites are also available. A boat ramp is nearby.

Reservations, fee: Reservations necessary for group sites only; $10 fee per night for single sites; $40-$100 for group sites. Open all year.

Who to contact: Phone (541) 268-4473 or write to Mapleton Ranger District, Mapleton, OR 97453.

Location: From Interstate 5 at Eugene, turn west on Highway 126 and drive 61 miles to Florence. Turn north on US 101 and drive six miles, then 1.5 miles northwest on Forest Service Road 794. From there, proceed one-quarter mile northeast on Forest Service Road 793 and you'll see the campground entrance.

Trip note: This campground is located adjacent to Sutton Creek, not far from Sutton Lake. Holman Vista on Sutton Beach Road provides a beautiful view of the dunes and ocean. Wading and fishing are both popular. A hiking trail system leads from camp out to the dunes. There is no off-road-vehicle access here. An alternative camp is Alder Dune to the north.

27. LANE COUNTY HARBOR VISTA PARK

RV

Reference: **Near Florence; map D1, grid d3.**

Campsites, facilities: There are 27 sites for tents, trailers or RVs up to 32 feet long. Picnic tables are provided. Flush toilets, sanitary services, showers, piped water and a playground are available. Pets and motorbikes are permitted.

Reservations, fee: No reservations; $11-$15 fee per night. Open all year.

Who to contact: Phone (541) 997-5987 or write to P.O. Box 700, Florence, OR 97439.

Location: From Interstate 5 at Eugene, turn west on Highway 126 and drive 61 miles to Florence. From Florence, travel three miles north on Rhododendron Drive, then take Harbor Vista Road to 87658 Harbor Vista Road.

Trip note: This county park is set out among the dunes near the entrance to the harbor and offers a great lookout point from the observation deck. There are a number of side trips available, including Darlington State Park, Jessie M. Honeyman Memorial State Park (see the trip note for Jessie M. Honeyman) and the Indian Forest, just four miles north of Florence. Florence also has displays of Native American dwellings and crafts.

---

28.   B & E WAYSIDE MOBILE & RV PARK   🚐

Reference: Near Florence; map D1, grid d3.

Campsites, facilities: There are 24 sites for trailers or RVs of any length. Electricity, piped water, sewer hookups and picnic tables are provided. Flush toilets, sanitary services, showers and a laundromat are available. Bottled gas, a store, a cafe and ice are located within two miles. Leashed pets are permitted. Boat launching facilities are nearby.

Reservations, fee: Reservations accepted; $15 fee per night. Open all year.

Who to contact: Phone (541) 997-6451 or write to 3760 Highway 101 North, Florence, OR 97439.

Location: From Interstate 5 at Eugene, turn west on Highway 126 and drive 61 miles to Florence. Turn north on US 101 and drive 1.8 miles to the park on the right.

Trip note: This park is clean and quiet. See the trip notes for Lane County Harbor Vista Park and Port of Siuslaw RV and Marina side trip ideas. Nearby recreation options include two golf courses and a riding stable (two miles away).

---

29.   LAKESHORE TRAILER PARK   🚐

Reference: On Woahink Lake; map D1, grid d3.

Campsites, facilities: There are 25 sites for trailers or RVs of any length (six drive-throughs). Electricity, piped water and sewer hookups are provided. Flush toilets, cable TV, showers and a laundromat are available. A cafe is located within one mile. Leashed pets are permitted. Boat docks are nearby.

Reservations, fee: Reservations accepted; $18 fee per night. Open all year.

Who to contact: Phone (541) 997-2741 or write to 83763 Highway 101, Florence, OR 97439.

Location: From Interstate 5 at Eugene, turn west on Highway 126 and drive 61 miles to Florence. Turn south on US 101 and drive four miles to the park on the left at milepost 195.

Trip note: This is a prime area for vacationers. This park is set along the shore of Woahink Lake, a popular spot to fish for trout, perch, catfish, crappie, bluegill and bass. It is adjacent to Jessie M. Honeyman Memorial State Park and the Oregon Dunes National Recreation Area. Off-road-vehicle access to the dunes can be found four miles northeast of the park. Hiking trails through the dunes can be found at Honeyman Memorial State Park. If you set out across the dunes off the trail, note your path. People hiking off-trail commonly get lost here.

30. JESSIE M. HONEYMAN [RV]
MEMORIAL STATE PARK

Reference: **Near Cleowax Lake; map D1, grid d3.**

Campsites, facilities: There are 380 sites for tents, trailers or RVs up to 60 feet long, and a special camping area for hikers and bicyclists. Picnic tables and fire grills are provided. Flush toilets, sanitary services, showers and firewood are available. Some facilities are **wheelchair accessible**. Leashed pets are permitted. Boat docks and launching facilities are nearby.

Reservations, fee: Contact Reservations Northwest at (800) 452-5687 ($6 reservation fee); $14-$18 fee per night; $4 for hikers/bikers. Open all year.

Who to contact: Phone (541) 563-3220 or write to 84505 Highway 101, Florence, OR 97439.

Location: From Interstate 5 at Eugene, turn west on Highway 126 and drive 61 miles to Florence. Turn south on US 101 and drive three miles to the park entrance.

Trip note: This is a popular state park set along the shore of Cleowax Lake and adjacent to the dunes of the Oregon Dunes National Recreation Area. The dunes here are quite impressive, with some reaching to 500 feet. The three lakes in the park offer facilities for boating, fishing and swimming. A one-mile hiking trail with access to the dunes is available in the park.

31. PORT OF SIUSLAW RV AND MARINA [RV]

Reference: **On Siuslaw River; map D1, grid d4.**

Campsites, facilities: There are 84 sites for tents, trailers or RVs of any length. Electricity, piped water, sewer hookups and picnic tables are provided. Flush toilets, cable TV, bottled gas, sanitary services, showers, a store, a laundromat and ice are available. A cafe is located within one mile. Leashed pets are permitted. Boat docks and launching facilities are nearby.

Reservations, fee: Reservations accepted; $13-$16 fee per night. Open all year.

Who to contact: Phone (541) 997-3040 or write to P.O. Box 1638, Florence, OR 97439.

Location: From Interstate 5 at Eugene, turn west on Highway 126 and drive 61 miles to Florence. In Florence, turn off US 101 and drive about one-half mile east on First Street to Harbor Street and the marina.

Trip note: This public resort is set along the Siuslaw River in a grassy, urban setting. Fishermen with boats will find the Highway 101 bridge support pilings make good spots for crabbing and fishing for perch and flounder.

32. MERCER LAKE RESORT [RV]

Reference: **On Mercer Lake; map D1, grid d4.**

Campsites, facilities: There are 15 drive-through sites for trailers or RVs of any length. Electricity, piped water, sewer hookups and picnic tables are provided. Flush toilets, bottled gas, sanitary services, showers, a store, a laundromat, ice and a playground are available. Leashed pets are permitted. Boat docks, launching facilities and rentals are nearby.

Reservations, fee: Reservations accepted; $15-$19 fee per night. MasterCard and Visa accepted. Open all year.

Who to contact: Phone (541) 997-3633 or write to 88875 Bay Berry, Florence, OR 97439.

Location: From Interstate 5 at Eugene, turn west on Highway 126 and drive 61 miles to Florence. Turn north on US 101 and drive five miles, then one mile east on Mercer Lake Road. Turn north onto Resort Road to the campground.

Trip note: This resort is set along the shore of Mercer Lake, one of a number of lakes that have formed among the ancient dunes in this area.

33. ARCHIE KNOWLES **RV**

Reference: **On Knowles Creek in Siuslaw National Forest; map D1, grid d5.**

Campsites, facilities: There are nine sites for tents, trailers or RVs up to 16 feet long. Picnic tables and fire grills are provided. Flush toilets and piped water are available. Leashed pets are permitted.

Reservations, fee: No reservations; $8 fee per night. Open May to early September.

Who to contact: Phone (541) 268-4473 or write to Siuslaw National Forest, Mapleton Ranger District, Mapleton, OR 97453.

Location: From Interstate 5 at Eugene, turn west on Highway 126 and drive 44 miles to the campground entrance (it's located three miles east of Mapleton).

Trip note: This little campground is set along Knowles Creek about three miles east of Mapleton. This is a rustic camp, but in close proximity to the highway. There is a ranger station in Mapleton that can provide maps and information and answer any questions.

34. MAPLE LAKE TRAILER PARK-MARINA **RV**

Reference: **On Siuslaw River; map D1, grid d5.**

Campsites, facilities: There are two tent sites and 46 sites for tents, trailers or RVs of any length. Electricity, piped water and sewer hookups are provided. Flush toilets, bottled gas, sanitary services and showers are available. A store, a cafe and ice are located within one mile. Tackle and bait shop is open during the fishing season. Small pets (under 15 pounds) are permitted. Boat docks and launching facilities are on-site.

Reservations, fee: Reservations accepted; $6-$13 fee per night. Open all year.

Who to contact: Phone (541) 268-4822 or write to 10730 Highway 126, Mapleton, OR 97453.

Location: From Interstate 5 at Eugene, turn west on Highway 126 and drive 47 miles to Mapleton. The park is located on Highway 126 behind the Forest Service station.

Trip note: This park is set along the shore of the Siuslaw River in Mapleton. There are boat rentals and hiking trails nearby. The general area is surrounded by Siuslaw National Forest land. A Forest Service map details nearby backcountry side trip options.

35. FERN RIDGE SHORES **RV**

Reference: **On Fern Ridge Reservoir; map D1, grid d8.**

Campsites, facilities: There are 61 sites for tents, trailers and RVs up to 28 feet. Restrooms, showers, a sanitary dump, security, a public phone and ice are available. Recreational facilities include horseshoes, a recreation field, a boat ramp, dock and rentals. Some facilities are **wheelchair accessible**.

Reservations, fee: Reservations recommended; $16-$20 fee per night. Open all year.

Who to contact: Phone the park at (541) 935-2335 or write to 29652 Jeans Road, Veneta, OR 97487.

Location: From Interstate 5 at Eugene, drive 10 miles west on Highway 126 to Veneta. From the junction of Highway 126 (West 11th Street) and Beltline Road, drive west for 7.6 miles on Highway 126 to Ellmaker Road. Turn north on Ellmaker Road and continue 1.1 miles to Jeans Road. Then turn east and continue for 1.3 miles to the park on the right.

Trip note: This camp is set in a wooded area along the shore of Fern Ridge Reservoir. Activities on the reservoir include swimming, boating and bass fishing. This is a friendly, family-oriented park that makes a great vacation destination, as well as an excellent layover spot for travelers cruising Interstate 5.

---

36. CARTER LAKE **RV**

Reference: **On Carter Lake in Oregon Dunes National Recreation Area; map D1, grid e2.**

Campsites, facilities: There are 32 sites for tents, trailers or RVs up to 22 feet long. Picnic tables and fire grills are provided. Piped water and flush toilets are available. Leashed pets are permitted.

Reservations, fee: No reservations; $10 fee per night. Open all year.

Who to contact: Phone (541) 271-3611 or write to Oregon Dunes National Recreation Area, 855 Highway Avenue, Reedsport, OR 97467.

Location: From Interstate 5 at Eugene, turn west on Highway 126 and drive 61 miles to Florence. Turn south on US 101 and drive 8.5 miles. Then turn west on Forest Service Road 1084 and drive 200 yards to the campground.

Trip note: This campground is set along the north shore of Carter Lake. Boating, swimming and fishing are permitted on this long, narrow lake, which is set among dunes overgrown with vegetation. Nearby Taylor Dunes Trail is an easy half-mile **wheelchair-accessible** trail to the dunes past Taylor Lake. Hiking is allowed in the dunes, but there is no off-road-vehicle access here. If you want ORV access, then head north one mile to Siltcoos Road, turn west and drive 1.3 miles to Driftwood II.

---

37. WOAHINK LAKE RV RESORT **RV**

Reference: **On Woahink Lake; map D1, grid e3.**

Campsites, facilities: There are 38 sites for trailers or RVs of any length. There is no tent camping permitted. Restrooms, showers, cable TV, a public phone and a laundromat are available. Recreational facilities include horseshoe pits, a recreation hall, a game room and a boat dock.

Reservations, fee: Reservations recommended; $18 fee per night. Open all year.

Who to contact: Phone the park at (541) 997-6454 or write to 83570 Highway 101 South, Florence, OR 97439.

Location: From Interstate 5 at Eugene, turn west on Highway 126 and drive 61 miles to Florence. Turn south on US 101 and drive 5.1 miles to the camp on the right.

Trip note: This camp is located on Woahink Lake, where trout fishing is an option. It is one of several RV parks in the Florence area. Nearby Oregon Dunes National Recreation Area provides a good side trip.

---

38. SILTCOOS LAKE RESORT MOTEL **RV**

Reference: **On Siltcoos River; map D1, grid e3.**

Campsites, facilities: There are 12 drive-through sites for trailers or RVs up to 32 feet long. There is also an 8-unit motel on the resort. Electricity, piped water, cable TV, sewer hookups are provided. Flush toilets, showers, and a playground are available. A store is located within one mile. Pets and motorbikes are permitted. Boat docks, launching facilities and rentals are nearby.

Reservations, fee: Reservations accepted; $18-$20 fee per night; $55 per night motel fee. MasterCard and Visa accepted. Open all year.

Who to contact: Phone (541) 997-3741 or write to P.O. Box 36, Westlake, OR 97493.

Location: From Interstate 5 at Eugene, turn west on Highway 126 and drive 61 miles to Florence. Turn south on US 101 and drive six miles, then one-quarter mile east on Westlake turnoff to the motel on the right.

Trip note: This resort is set along the Siltcoos River adjacent to Siltcoos Lake, which is a large lake with many inlets, ideal for fishing. Just across the highway, you will find off-road vehicle and hiking access to the Oregon Dunes National Recreation Area.

---

39. DRIFTWOOD II   **RV**

Reference: Near Siltcoos Lake in Oregon Dunes National Recreation Area; map D1, grid e3.

Campsites, facilities: There are 69 sites for tents, trailers or RVs up to 55 feet long. Picnic tables and fire grills are provided. Piped water, flush and vault toilets are available. A sanitary disposal station is available within five miles. Some facilities are **wheelchair accessible**. Leashed pets are permitted. Boat docks, launching facilities and rentals are located about four miles away on Siltcoos Lake.

Reservations, fee: Some sites may be reserved by calling (800) 280-CAMP ($7.75 reservation fee); $10 fee per night. Open all year.

Who to contact: Phone (541) 271-3611 or write to Oregon Dunes National Recreation Area, 855 Highway Avenue, Reedsport, OR 97467.

Location: From Interstate 5 at Eugene, turn west on Highway 126 and drive 61 miles to Florence. Turn south on US 101 and drive seven miles, then 1.5 miles west on Siltcoos Beach Road to the campground.

Trip note: This is primarily a campground for off-road vehicles. It is set near the ocean in the Oregon Dunes National Recreation Area and has off-road-vehicle access. Several small lakes, the Siltcoos River and Siltcoos Lake are nearby.

---

40. LAGOON   **RV**

Reference: Near Siltcoos Lake in Oregon Dunes National Recreation Area; map D1, grid e3.

Campsites, facilities: There are 39 sites for tents, trailers or RVs up to 22 feet long. Picnic tables and fire grills are provided. Piped water and flush and pit toilets are available. A telephone and sanitary services are located within five miles. Leashed pets are permitted. Boat docks, launching facilities and rentals are nearby on Siltcoos Lake.

Reservations, fee: No reservations; $10 fee per night. Open late May through September.

Who to contact: Phone (541) 271-3611 or write to Oregon Dunes National Recreation Area, 855 Highway Avenue, Reedsport, OR 97467.

Location: From Interstate 5 at Eugene, turn west on Highway 126 and drive 61 miles to Florence. Turn south on US 101 and drive seven miles, then 1.3 miles west on Siltcoos Beach Road and you're there.

Trip note: This is one of several campgrounds in this area. Catch the interpretive programs on weekends during the summer. This one is set along the lagoon about one mile from Siltcoos Lake. There is wildlife viewing along the Lagoon Trail.

---

41. TYEE RV

Reference: **On Siltcoos River in Oregon Dunes National Recreation Area; map D1, grid e3.**

Campsites, facilities: There are 14 sites for tents, trailers or RVs up to 22 feet long. Picnic tables and fire grills are provided. Piped water, vault toilets and a nearby store are available. Leashed pets are permitted. Boat docks, launching facilities and rentals are nearby.

Reservations, fee: No reservations; $10 fee per night. Open May through October.

Who to contact: Phone (541) 271-3611 or write to Oregon Dunes National Recreation Area, 855 Highway Avenue, Reedsport, OR 97467.

Location: From Interstate 5 at Eugene, turn west on Highway 126 and drive 61 miles to Florence. Turn south on US 101 and drive six miles to the Westlake turnoff and you'll see the campground.

Trip note: This campground is set along the shore of Siltcoos River, an option to nearby Driftwood II and Lagoon campgrounds. Swimming, fishing and waterskiing are permitted at the nearby lake. Off-road-vehicle access to the dunes is available from Driftwood II and there are hiking trails nearby.

---

42. WAXMYRTLE RV

Reference: **Near Siltcoos Lake in Oregon Dunes National Recreation Area; map D1, grid e3.**

Campsites, facilities: There are 55 sites for tents, trailers or RVs up to 22 feet long. Picnic tables and fire grills are provided. Piped water and flush toilets are available. Leashed pets are permitted. Boat docks, launching facilities and rentals are nearby on Siltcoos Lake.

Reservations, fee: No reservations; $10 fee per night. Open late May to late September.

Who to contact: Phone (541) 271-3611 or write to Oregon Dunes National Recreation Area, 855 Highway Avenue, Reedsport, OR 97467.

Location: From Interstate 5 at Eugene, turn west on Highway 126 and drive 61 miles to Florence. Turn south on US 101 and drive seven miles, then drive 1.3 miles west on Siltcoos Beach Road to the campground on your left.

Trip note: This is one of three camps in the immediate vicinity. It is set adjacent to Lagoon and less than a mile from Driftwood II. The campground is near the Siltcoos River, a couple of miles from Siltcoos Lake, a good-sized lake with boating facilities where waterskiing, fishing and swimming are permitted. There are also hiking trails in the area.

---

43. TAHKENITCH LANDING RV

Reference: **Near Tahkenitch Lake in Oregon Dunes National Recreation Area; map D1, grid e3.**

Campsites, facilities: There are 26 sites for tents, trailers or RVs up to 22 feet long. Picnic tables are provided and vault toilets are available. There is **no piped water**. Leashed pets are permitted. Boat launching facilities and a floating dock are available.

Reservations, fee: No reservations; $8 fee per night. Open all year.

Who to contact: Phone (541) 271-3611 or write to Oregon Dunes National Recreation Area, 855 Highway Avenue, Reedsport, OR 97467.

Location: From Interstate 5 at Eugene, turn west on Highway 126 and drive 61 miles to Florence. Turn south on US 101 and drive 14 miles to the campground on the east side of the road.

Trip note: This camp overlooks Tahkenitch Lake and has easy access for fishing or swimming. There is **no piped water** here, but there is water nearby at Tahkenitch Lake.

---

44. TAHKENITCH RV

Reference: **Near Tahkenitch Lake in Oregon Dunes National Recreation Area; map D1, grid e3.**

Campsites, facilities: There are 36 sites for tents, trailers or RVs up to 22 feet long. Picnic tables and fire grills are provided. Piped water and flush and pit toilets are available. Leashed pets are permitted. Boat docks and launching facilities are on the lake.

Reservations, fee: No reservations; $10 fee per night. Open all year.

Who to contact: Phone (541) 271-3611 or write to Oregon Dunes National Recreation Area, 855 Highway Avenue, Reedsport, OR 97467.

Location: From Interstate 5 at Eugene, turn west on Highway 126 and drive 61 miles to Florence. Turn south on US 101 and drive 14 miles. The campground entrance is on the right.

Trip note: This campground is set in a wooded area across the highway from Tahkenitch Lake, which offers numerous coves and backwater areas for fishing and swimming. There is a hiking trail nearby that goes through the dunes out to the beach, and also to Threemile Lake. If this camp is filled, Tahkenitch Landing provides nearby space.

---

45. SURFWOOD CAMPGROUND & RV PARK RV

Reference: **On Winchester Bay; map D1, grid e3.**

Campsites, facilities: There are 22 tent sites and 141 sites for trailers or RVs (64 drive-through). Electricity, piped water, sewer hookups and picnic tables are provided. Flush toilets, sanitary services, showers, firewood, a store, a cafe, a laundromat, ice, a playground and a seasonal swimming pool are available. Pets and motorbikes are permitted. Boat docks and launching facilities are nearby.

Reservations, fee: Reservations accepted; $12-$16 fee per night. Open all year.

Who to contact: Phone (541) 271-4020 or write to 75381 US Highway 101, Reedsport, OR 97467.

Location: From Interstate 5 south of Eugene, take exit 162 and turn west on Highway 38. Drive 57 miles to Reedsport, then turn south on US 101 and drive 2.5 miles to the park, located one-half mile north of Winchester Bay.

Trip note: The pull-through sites are separated by shrubs, which creates privacy. This park is a half-mile drive from the marina at Winchester Bay. Fishing is the focal point, but there are other possibilities in the area. There are many trails nearby, leading west across the dunes to the ocean and east to lakes in wooded areas. Some 10 miles east, an elk preserve is located adjacent to Highway 38.

46.　　　　DARLINGS RESORT　　　　🚐

Reference: **On Siltcoos Lake; map D1, grid e4.**

Campsites, facilities: There are 35 sites for trailers or RVs of any length. Electricity, piped water, sewer hookups and picnic tables are provided. Flush toilets, showers, firewood, a store, a cafe and a laundromat are available. Leashed pets are permitted. Boat docks, launching facilities and rentals are nearby.

Reservations, fee: Reservations accepted; $18 fee per night. Open all year.

Who to contact: Phone (541) 997-2841 or write to 4879 Darling Loop, Florence, OR 97439.

Location: From Interstate 5 at Eugene, turn west on Highway 126 and drive 61 miles to Florence. Turn south on US 101 and drive five miles, then one-half mile east on North Beach Road to the resort.

Trip note: This park is set in a rural area along the north shore of Siltcoos Lake, adjacent to the extensive Oregon Dunes National Recreation Area. An access point to the dunes for hikers and off-road vehicles is just across the highway. There is a full-service marina at the lake.

47.　　　　KOA SHERWOOD FOREST　　　　🚐

Reference: **Near Eugene; map D1, grid e9.**

Campsites, facilities: There are 20 tent sites and 100 sites for trailers or RVs of any length. Electricity, piped water, sewer hookups and picnic tables are provided. Flush toilets, sanitary services, showers, a recreation hall, a store, a laundromat, ice, a playground and a swimming pool are available. Bottled gas and a cafe are within one mile. Pets and motorbikes are permitted.

Reservations, fee: Reservations accepted; $15-$21 fee per night; MasterCard, Visa, American Express and Discover accepted. Open all year.

Who to contact: Phone (541) 895-4110 or write to 298 East Oregon Avenue, Creswell, OR 97426.

Location: From Interstate 5 south of Eugene, take the Creswell exit and drive west on Oregon Avenue for one-half block to the campground at 298 East Oregon Avenue.

Trip note: This is a fairly good layover spot for motor home travelers heading north on Interstate 5. It is 10 miles south of Eugene. Nearby recreation options include a golf course and tennis courts.

48.　　　　TAYLOR'S TRAVEL PARK　　　　🚐

Reference: **Near Willamette River; map D1, grid e9.**

Campsites, facilities: There are 10 tent sites and 20 sites for trailers or RVs of any length. Electricity, piped water, sewer hookups and picnic tables are provided, in the summer months. Flush toilets, sanitary services, showers and a playground are available. Bottled gas, a store, a cafe, a laundromat and ice are within one mile. Pets and motorbikes are permitted.

Reservations, fee: Reservations accepted; $12 fee per night. Open all year, with limited winter facilities.

Who to contact: Phone (541) 895-4715 or write to 82149 Davisson Road, Creswell, OR 97426.

Location: From Interstate 5 south of Eugene, take the Creswell exit, then drive one-quarter mile west on Oregon Avenue and 1.2 miles south on Highway 99 to Davisson Road. From there, continue one-half mile south to the park.

Trip note: This is an option to nearby KOA Sherwood Forest. This campground is set near the coast fork of the Willamette River. Nearby recreation options include a golf course and a full-service marina (15 miles away).

49.   UMPQUA LIGHTHOUSE STATE PARK   **RV**

Reference: **On Umpqua River; map D1, grid f2.**

Campsites, facilities: There are 44 tent sites and 22 sites with full hookups for trailers or RVs up to 45 feet long. Piped water and picnic tables are provided. Flush toilets, showers and firewood are available. Leashed pets are permitted. Boat docks and launching facilities are on the Umpqua River.

Reservations, fee: Contact Reservations Northwest at (800) 452-5687 ($6 reservation fee); $9-$17 fee per night. Open all year.

Who to contact: Phone (541) 271-4118 or (800) 452-5687 or write to Umpqua Lighthouse State Park at 10965 Cape Arago Highway, Coos Bay, OR 97420.

Location: From Interstate 5 south of Eugene, take exit 162 and turn west on Highway 36. Drive 57 miles to Reedsport, then turn south on US 101 and drive six miles to the park entrance.

Trip note: This park is set near the mouth of the Umpqua River, a unique area where the dunes are as high as 500 feet. Hiking trails lead out from the park and south into Umpqua Dunes Scenic Area. The park offers over two miles of beach access on the ocean and one-half mile along the Umpqua River. The adjacent lighthouse is still in operation and provides a good side trip opportunity.

50.   DISCOVERY POINT RV PARK   **RV**

Reference: **On Winchester Bay; map D1, grid f2.**

Campsites, facilities: There are 15 tent sites and 50 drive-through sites for trailers or RVs of any length. Electricity, piped water, sewer hookups and picnic tables are provided. Flush toilets, showers, a store, a cafe, a laundromat and ice are available. Sanitary services and bottled gas are located within one mile. Pets and motorbikes are permitted. Boat docks and launching facilities are nearby.

Reservations, fee: Reservations accepted; $12.50-$18.50 fee per night; MasterCard, Visa and American Express accepted. Open all year.

Who to contact: Phone (541) 271-3443 or write to HC 81, P.O. Box 242, Reedsport, OR 97467.

Location: From Interstate 5 south of Eugene, take exit 162 and turn west on Highway 36. Drive 57 miles to Reedsport, then turn south on US 101 and drive to the Windy Cove exit near Winchester Bay. Continue 1.5 miles west to the resort.

Trip note: This resort is set on the shore of Winchester Bay in a fishing village near the mouth of the Umpqua River. For details on nearby recreation options, see the trip note for Surfwood Campground & RV Park (camp number 45).

51.   WINDY COVE COUNTY PARK   **RV**

Reference: **On the Pacific Ocean; map D1, grid f2.**

Campsites, facilities: There are 29 tent sites and 25 sites for trailers or RVs up to 30 feet long. Electricity, piped water, sewer hookups and picnic tables are provided. Flush toilets, showers and cable TV are available. Bottled gas, sanitary services, a store, a cafe, a laundromat and ice are located within one mile. Pets and motorbikes are permitted. Boat docks, launching facilities and rentals are nearby.

Reservations, fee: No reservations; $12.60 fee per night. Open all year.

Who to contact: Phone (541) 271-4138 for information. For tent sites, write to P.O. Box 265, Winchester Bay, OR 97467. For RV sites, write to P.O. Box 224, Winchester Bay, OR 97467.

Location: From Interstate 5 south of Eugene, take exit 162 and turn west on Highway 36. Drive 57 miles to Reedsport, then turn south on US 101 and drive five miles to Winchester Bay. Take the Windy Cove exit and proceed to the park on the left.

Trip note: This county park is actually two parks, Windy Cove "A" and "B." Set near ocean beaches and sand dunes, both offer other nearby recreation options including an 18-hole golf course and tennis courts.

52.　　　SEADRIFT MOTEL & RV PARK　　RV

Reference: **Near Tenmile Lake; map D1, grid f2.**

Campsites, facilities: There are 42 drive-through sites for trailers or RVs of any length. There is also a 10-unit motel in the park. Picnic tables are provided. Flush toilets, bottled gas, sanitary services, showers, a clubhouse, grounds security and cable TV are available. A store, a cafe and a laundromat are located within one mile. Leashed pets are permitted. Boat docks, launching facilities and rentals are nearby.

Reservations, fee: Reservations accepted; $12-$14 fee per night; $27-$45 motel fee per night for two people; $2 cable TV charge. MasterCard and Visa accepted. Senior discounts. Some weekly and monthly rates available. Open all year.

Who to contact: Phone (541) 759-3102 or write to Oregon Dunes National Recreation Area, 855 Highway Avenue, Reedsport, OR 97467.

Location: From Interstate 5 south of Eugene, take exit 162 and turn west on Highway 36. Drive 57 miles to Reedsport, then turn south on US 101 and drive 12 miles south. The campground entrance is on the right.

Trip note: This campground is set along Eel Creek, near both Eel Lake and Tenmile Lake and 12 miles north of Coos Bay. Waterskiing is allowed on Tenmile Lake but not on Eel Lake. There are hiking trails nearby that access the Umpqua Dunes Scenic Area. Access for off-road vehicles is available at Spinreel.

53.　　　　　　　SPINREEL　　　　　RV

Reference: **On Tenmile Creek in Oregon Dunes National Recreation Area; map D1, grid f2.**

Campsites, facilities: There are 37 sites for tents, trailers or RVs up to 32 feet long. Piped water and flush toilets are available. Picnic tables and fire grills are provided. Firewood, a store and a laundromat are nearby. Leashed pets are permitted. Boat docks, launching facilities and rentals are located on Tenmile Lake.

Reservations, fee: No reservations; $10 fee per night. Open all year.

Who to contact: Phone (541) 271-3611 or write to Oregon Dunes National Recreation Area, 855 Highway Avenue, North Bend, OR 97459.

Location: From Coos Bay on US 101, drive 10 miles north on US 101 and you'll see a sign directing you to Spinreel Campground. Drive one mile northwest to the campground.

Trip note: This campground is set at the outlet of Tenmile Lake in the Oregon Dunes National Recreation Area. A boat launch is located near the camp. There are hiking trails and off-road-vehicle access to the dunes. Off-road-vehicle rentals are available adjacent to the camp. This is primarily an off-road-vehicle campground.

---

54. BLUEBILL RV

Reference: **On Bluebill Lake in Oregon Dunes National Recreation Area; map D1, grid f2.**

Campsites, facilities: There are 19 sites for tents, trailers or RVs up to 22 feet long. Picnic tables and fire grills are provided. Flush toilets and piped water are available. Leashed pets are permitted.

Reservations, fee: No reservations; $10 fee per night. Open May through October.

Who to contact: Phone (541) 271-3611 or write to Oregon Dunes National Recreation Area, 855 Highway Avenue, Reedsport, OR 97467.

Location: From Coos Bay on US 101, drive 1.5 miles north on US 101, then a mile west on Horsfall Dunes and Beach Access Road. From there, drive two miles northwest on Horsfall Road and you'll see the campground entrance.

Trip note: This campground gets very little camping pressure. It is set next to little Bluebill Lake, which sometimes dries up during the summer. There is a one-mile trail around the lake bed. The camp is a short distance from Horsfall Lake, which is surrounded by private property. If you continue west on the Forest Service road you will come to a picnicking and parking area near the beach that has off-road-vehicle access to the dunes at Horsfall day-use area or Horsfall Beach.

---

55. WILLIAM M. TUGMAN STATE PARK RV

Reference: **On Eel Lake; map D1, grid f3.**

Campsites, facilities: There are 115 sites with water and electrical hookups for trailers or RVs up to 50 feet long, and a special camping area for hikers and bicyclists. Electricity, piped water and picnic tables are provided. Flush toilets, sanitary services, showers, firewood and a laundromat are available. Some facilities are **wheelchair accessible**. Leashed pets are permitted. Boat docks and launching facilities are nearby.

Reservations, fee: Contact Reservations Northwest at (800) 452-5687; $9-$17 fee per night; $4 for hikers/bikers. Open all year.

Who to contact: Phone (800) 233-0321 or Sunset Bay State Park at (541) 888-4902 or write to c/o 10965 Cape Arago Highway, Coos Bay, OR 97420.

Location: From Interstate 5 south of Eugene, take exit 162 and turn west on Highway 36. Drive 57 miles to Reedsport, then turn south on US 101 and drive eight miles to the park entrance on the left.

Trip note: This campground is set along the shore of Eel Lake, which offers almost five miles of shoreline for swimming and trout fishing. There is a boat ramp, but there is a 10-miles-per-hour speed limit for boats. Across the highway is the Oregon Dunes National Recreation Area. Hiking is available just a few miles north at Umpqua Lighthouse State Park.

---

56. NORTH LAKE RESORT & MARINA RV

Reference: **On Tenmile Lake; map D1, grid f3.**

Campsites, facilities: There are 100 sites for trailers or RVs of any length. Picnic tables are provided. Flush toilets, bottled gas, sanitary services, showers, firewood, a store, ice, a playground, electricity, piped water and sewer hookups are available. A cafe and a laundromat are located within one mile. Leashed pets are permitted. Boat docks, launching facilities and rentals are nearby.

Reservations, fee: Reservations accepted; $10-$15 fee per night. MasterCard accepted. Open all year.

Who to contact: Phone (541) 759-3515 or write to 2090 North Lake Avenue, Lakeside, OR 97449.

Location: From Interstate 5 south of Eugene, take exit 162 and turn west on Highway 36. Drive 57 miles to Reedsport, then turn south on US 101 and drive 11 miles. Take the Lakeside exit and drive three-quarters of a mile east to North Lake Avenue, then continue one-half mile east to the resort on the left.

Trip note: This resort is set along the shore of Tenmile Lake, which has a full-service marina. It is wooded and secluded, a perfect layover spot for US 101 travelers. Bass fishing in Tenmile Lake can be good.

57.   NORTH EEL CREEK   RV

Reference: **Near Eel Lake in Oregon Dunes National Recreation Area; map D1, grid f3.**

Campsites, facilities: There are 52 sites for tents, trailers or RVs up to 22 feet long. Picnic tables and fire grills are provided. Piped water, and flush and pit toilets are available. Leashed pets are permitted. Boat docks, launching facilities and rentals are nearby. An amphitheater is used for summer campground programs.

Reservations, fee: No reservations; $10 fee per night. Open all year.

Who to contact: Phone (541) 271-3611 or write to Oregon Dunes National Recreation Area, 855 Highway Avenue, Reedsport, OR 97467.

Location: From Interstate 5 at Eugene, turn west on Highway 126 and drive 61 miles to Florence. Turn south on US 101 and drive approximately 33 miles to the campground entrance on your right.

Trip note: This campground is set along Eel Creek, near both Eel Lake and Tenmile Lake. Waterskiing is allowed at Tenmile Lake, but not at Eel Lake. There are trails nearby that access the Umpqua Dunes Scenic Area with spectacular scenery in an area closed to off-road vehicles. Access for off-road vehicles is available at Spinreel.

58.   LOON LAKE LODGE RESORT   RV

Reference: **On Loon Lake; map D1, grid f5.**

Campsites, facilities: There are 24 sites for tents, trailers or RVs up to 32 feet. Facilities include a public phone, security, ice, an adult room, a game room and snacks. A boat ramp, dock, marina and rentals are also available. Pets are permitted on leashes.

Reservations, fee: Reservations recommended; $16 fee per night. Visa and MasterCard are accepted.

Who to contact: Phone the park at (541) 599-2244 or write to 9011 Loon Lake Road, Reedsport, OR 97467.

Location: From Interstate 5 south of Eugene, take exit 162. Drive west on Highway 99 for about six miles to Highway 38. Drive west on Highway 38 to the County Road 3 exit (milepost 13.5). Drive south on County Road 3 for 8.2 miles to the resort on the right.

Trip note: This resort is set among the trees on pretty Loon Lake. It is not a long drive from either US 101 or Interstate 5, making it an ideal layover spot for travelers eager to get off the highway. The lake offers good bass fishing, swimming and boating.

---

59.   TYEE   RV

Reference: On Umpqua River; map D1, grid f6.

Campsites, facilities: There are 15 sites for tents, trailers or RVs up to 25 feet long. Piped water, fire grills and picnic tables are provided. Vault toilets and firewood are available. A store is located within one mile. Leashed pets are permitted.

Reservations, fee: No reservations; $5 fee per night; $2 each additional vehicle. Open May 15 to October 5.

Who to contact: Phone (541) 440-4930 or write to Bureau of Land Management, 777 NW Garden Valley Boulevard, Roseburg, OR 97470.

Location: From Interstate 5 north of Roseburg, take exit 136 and turn west on Highway 138. Drive 11 miles northwest to the campground entrance.

Trip note: Here is a classic spot, set along the Umpqua River with great fishing in season, yet very few people know of it. It is not far from Interstate 5 and is the only campground in the immediate vicinity.

---

60.   PASS CREEK COUNTY PARK   RV

Reference: Near Roseburg, map D1, grid f9.

Campsites, facilities: There are 10 tent sites and 30 sites for trailers or RVs up to 30 feet long. Electricity, piped water, sewer hookups and picnic tables are provided. Flush toilets, showers and a playground are available. A store, a cafe, a laundromat and ice are within one mile. Pets are permitted.

Reservations, fee: No reservations; $9-$12 fee per night. Open all year.

Who to contact: Phone (541) 942-3281 or write to P.O. Box 81, Curtin, OR 97428.

Location: From Roseburg, travel 35 miles north on Interstate 5, then take exit 163 to the park entrance (well-signed).

Trip note: This is a decent layover spot for travelers on Interstate 5. It is set in a wooded, hilly area with many shaded sites. There are no other campgrounds in the immediate area, so if it's late and you need a place to stay, grab this one.

---

61.   PINE MEADOWS   RV

Reference: On Cottage Grove Reservoir; map D1, grid f9.

Campsites, facilities: There are 92 sites for tents, trailers or RVs of any length. Picnic tables and fire grills are provided. Flush toilets, sanitary services, showers and a playground are available. Pets and motorbikes are permitted. Boat docks and launching facilities are nearby.

Reservations, fee: No reservations; $10-$12 fee per night. Open May 17 to December 9.

Who to contact: Phone (541) 942-8657 or write to Army Corps of Engineers Recreation Information, Cottage Grove, OR 97424.

Location: From Interstate 5 south of Cottage Grove, take exit 170, then drive three miles south on London Road. Turn left on Reservoir Road and drive two miles to the park entrance.

Trip note: This campground is set near the banks of Cottage Grove Reservoir, where boating, fishing, waterskiing and swimming are among the recreation options. It's an easy hop from Interstate 5, but a lot of campers don't realize it.

62.   PRIMITIVE CAMPGROUND

Reference: **On Cottage Grove Reservoir; map D1, grid f9.**

Campsites, facilities: There are 15 sites for tents. Picnic tables, vault toilets, piped water, sanitary services and fire grills are available. Leashed pets and motorbikes permitted. Boat docks and launching facilities are nearby.

Reservations, fee: No reservations; $5-$6 fee per night. Open May 17 to December 9.

Who to contact: Phone (541) 942-8657 or write to Army Corps of Engineers, Recreation Information, Cottage Grove, OR 97424.

Location: From Interstate 5 south of Cottage Grove, take exit 170. Turn south on London Road and drive three miles. Turn left on Reservoir Road and drive two miles to the park entrance.

Trip note: This campground is set on the Cottage Grove Reservoir and offers boating, fishing, waterskiing and swimming. See trip note for neighboring Pine Meadows campground.

---

63.   SUNSET BAY STATE PARK   **RV**

Reference: **Near Sunset Bay; map D1, grid g1.**

Campsites, facilities: There are 108 sites for tents or self-contained RVs, 27 sites with full hookups for trailers or RVs up to 47 feet long, and a separate area for hikers and bicyclists. There are also four yurts available. Picnic tables and fire grills are provided. Flush toilets, showers and firewood are available. A restaurant is located within 2.5 miles. Some facilities are **wheelchair accessible**. Leashed pets are permitted.

Reservations, fee: Contact Reservations Northwest at (800) 452-5687 ($6 reservation fee); $15-$19 fee per night; $25 yurt fee for first five people, $5 each additional person; $2-$4 for hikers/bikers. Open May to September.

Who to contact: Phone (541) 888-4902 or write to 10965 Cape Arago Highway, Coos Bay, OR 97420.

Location: From Coos Bay on US 101, take the Charleston exit and proceed 12 miles southwest on the Cape Arago Highway to the park entrance on the left.

Trip note: This campground is set near Sunset Bay, which is a small, enclosed and well-protected bay with a nice beach for swimming. This is a very popular campground, offering easy access from US 101. Hiking, swimming and boating are just a few of your options here. Beautiful views of sandstone cliffs, expansive floral gardens and offshore reefs are available to visitors.

---

64.   BASTENDORFF BEACH PARK   **RV**

Reference: **Near Cape Arago State Park; map D1, grid g1.**

Campsites, facilities: There are 25 tents sites and 56 sites for trailers or RVs. Restrooms, showers, a sanitary dump, a public phone and a barbecue are provided. Horseshoe pits, a playground, basketball courts and a picnic area are also available. The facilities are **wheelchair accessible**. Pets are permitted on leashes.

Reservations, fee: No reservations; $13-$15 fee per night. Open year-round.

Who to contact: Phone the park at (541) 888-5353.

Location: From Coos Bay on US 101, take the Charleston exit and proceed to Charleston. Turn southwest on Cape Arago Highway and drive two miles, following the signs to the park.

Trip note: This campground provides access to the ocean and a small lake. Nearby activities include sand dune buggy riding, clamming, crabbing, fishing, swimming and boating. A nice side trip is to the Botanical Gardens, about 2.5 miles away.

65. CHARLESTON MARINA RV PARK   RV.

Reference: **On Coos Bay; map D1, grid g1.**

Campsites, facilities: There are 128 sites for tents, trailers or RVs of any length. Cable TV, restrooms, showers, a sanitary dump, a public phone, a laundromat and LP gas are available. A boat dock and ramp, a marina and a playground are provided. The facilities are **wheelchair accessible**. Pets are permitted on leashes.

Reservations, fee: Reservations recommended; $10-$14 fee per night. Open all year.

Who to contact: Phone the park at (541) 888-9512 or write to P.O. Box 5433, Charleston, OR 97420.

Location: From US 101 at Coos Bay, take the Charleston exit and turn west on the Cape Arago Highway. Drive nine miles and cross the Charleston/South Slough Bridge to Boat Basin Drive. Drive north on Boat Basin Drive for two blocks to Kingfisher Drive. Travel east for one block on Kingfisher Drive to the campground on the left.

Trip note: This campground is located near Charleston on the Pacific Ocean. It is a large, developed park and marina. Recreational activities in and near the campground include hiking, swimming, clamming, crabbing, boating, huckleberry and blackberry picking and fishing for tuna, salmon and halibut.

66. OCEANSIDE RV PARK   RV.

Reference: **Near Pacific Ocean; map D1, grid g1.**

Campsites, facilities: There are 10 tent sites and 20 sites for trailers or RVs. Restrooms, showers, a sanitary dump, a public phone and LP gas are available. The facilities are **wheelchair accessible**. Pets are permitted on leashes.

Reservations, fee: Reservations recommended; $8-$16 per night. Open year-round.

Who to contact: Phone the park at (541) 888-2598 or write to 9838 Cape Arago Highway, Charleston, OR 97420.

Location: From US 101 north of Coos Bay, take the Charleston Harbor exit and drive west on Charleston Harbor Highway for 8.5 miles to the west end of the Charleston Bridge. Turn west on Cape Arago Highway and drive 1.8 miles to the campground on the right.

Trip note: This is one of several private, developed parks in the Charleston area. The park is within walking distance of the Pacific Ocean, with opportunities for swimming, fishing, clamming, crabbing and boating. There is a marina 1.5 miles from the park.

67. HORSFALL   RV.

Reference: **In Oregon Dunes National Recreation Area; map D1, grid g2.**

Campsites, facilities: There are 70 sites for trailers or RVs of any length. Piped water, coin-operated showers and flush toilets are available. Leashed pets are permitted.

Reservations, fee: Some sites may be reserved by calling (800) 280-CAMP; $7.50

reservation fee; $10 fee per night. Open all year.

Who to contact: Phone (541) 271-3611 or write to Oregon Dunes National Recreation Area, 855 Highway Avenue, Reedsport, OR 97467.

Location: From Coos Bay on US 101, drive 1.5 miles north on US 101, then turn west on Horsfall Road and drive about one mile. Turn on the campground access road and drive one-half mile to the campground.

Trip note: This campground is actually a nice, large paved area for parking RVs. It is the staging area for off-road-vehicle access into the southern section of Oregon Dunes National Recreation Area.

---

68. KELLEY'S RV PARK RV

Reference: **Near Coos Bay; map D1, grid g2.**

Campsites, facilities: There are 38 drive-through sites for trailers or RVs of any length. Electricity, piped water, sewer hookups and picnic tables are provided. Flush toilets, sanitary services and a laundromat are available. Bottled gas, a store and a cafe are located within one mile. Leashed pets are permitted. Boat docks and launching facilities are nearby.

Reservations, fee: Reservations accepted; $10-$16 fee per night. Open all year.

Who to contact: Phone (541) 888-6531 or write to 555 South Empire Boulevard, Coos Bay, OR 97420.

Location: In Coos Bay, take the Charleston exit off US 101 and go 4.5 miles to 555 South Empire Boulevard.

Trip note: This RV park is in the town of Coos Bay, well-known for its salmon, deep sea fishing and lumber. Nearby recreation options include a full-service marina.

---

69. WHISTLER'S BEND RV

Reference: **On North Umpqua River; map D1, grid g8.**

Campsites, facilities: There are 24 sites for tents, trailers or RVs up to 30 feet long. Picnic tables and fire grills are provided. Piped water, flush toilets, showers and a playground are available. Leashed pets are permitted. Boat launching facilities are nearby.

Reservations, fee: No reservations; $7 fee per night; $3 each additional vehicle. Open all year.

Who to contact: Phone (541) 673-4863 or write to 2828 Whistlers Park Road, Roseburg, OR 97470.

Location: From Roseburg on Interstate 5, travel 15 miles east on Highway 138 to the signed cutoff to the park. Turn left and drive three miles to the end of the road and the park entrance.

Trip note: This county park is set along the bank of the North Umpqua River. It is an idyllic spot because it is just a 20-minute drive from Interstate 5, yet it gets little pressure from outsiders.

LEAVE NO TRACE TIPS

Pack it in and pack it out.

• Take everything you bring into the wild back out with you.

• Protect wildlife and your food by storing
rations securely. Pick up all spilled foods.

• Use toilet paper or wipes sparingly; pack them out.

• Inspect your campsite for trash and any evidence of your stay.
Pack out all trash—even if it's not yours!

MAP D2

161 LISTINGS
PAGES 500-561

OREGON MAP .... see page 380
Adjoining Maps
NORTH (C2) .... see page 400
EAST (D3) .... see page 562
SOUTH (E2) .... see page 636
WEST (D1) .... see page 472

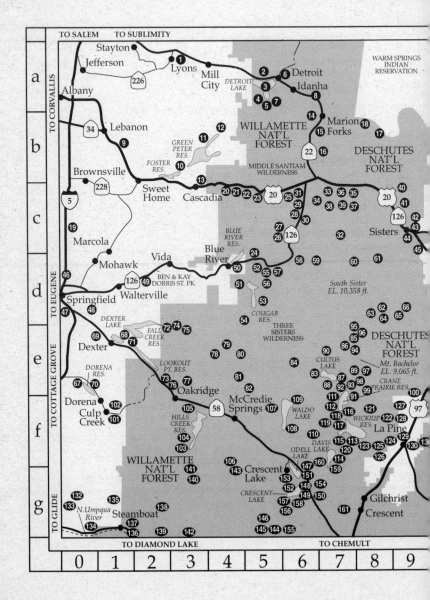

Oregon Map D2 featuring: Santiam River, Detroit Lake, Willamette National Forest, Mount Jefferson Wilderness, Willamette River, Deschutes National Forest, McKenzie River, Scott Lake, Smith Reservoir, Carmen Reservoir, Trailbridge Reservoir, Clear Lake, Scout Lake, Suttle Lake, Big Lake, Pacific Crest Trail, Cougar Lake, Blue River Reservoir, Sparks Lake, Todd Lake, Devil's Lake, Lookout Point Reservoir, Dorena Lake, Umpqua National Forest, Three Sisters Wilderness, Elk Lake, Blair Lake, Chucksney Mountain, Hosmer Lake, Cultus Lake, Cranc Prairie Reservoir, Lava Lake, Deschutes River, Fall River, Odell Lake, Waldo Lake Gold Lake, Crescent Lake, Davis Lake, South Twin Lake, Wickiup Reservoir, Umpqua River, Toketee Lake, Timpanogas Lake, Lemolo Lake

---

1.   JOHN NEAL MEMORIAL PARK   🆁🆅

Reference: **On North Santiam River; map D2, grid a3.**
Campsites, facilities: There are 40 sites for tents, trailers and self-contained RVs. Restrooms and piped water are provided. Recreational facilities include a boat ramp, a playground, horseshoes, a barbecue and a recreation field.
Reservations, fee: No reservations; $8 fee per night. Open May through October.
Who to contact: Phone the Linn County Parks Department at (541) 967-3917.
Location: From Interstate 5 at Salem, drive east on Highway 22 for about 20 miles to Lyons. From the junction of Highway 22 and Mehama-Lyons exit, drive south for one mile on Mehama-Lyons to Highway 226. Turn east and drive for 1.5 miles to 13th Street. Follow the signs to the campground.
Trip note: Set on the banks of the North Santiam River, this camp offers good boating and trout fishing possibilities. Other options include exploring lakes and trails in the adjacent national forest land or visiting Silver Falls State Park.

---

2.   DETROIT LAKE STATE PARK   🆁🆅

Reference: **On Detroit Lake; map D2, grid a5.**
Campsites, facilities: There are 134 tent sites and 177 sites with full or partial hookups for trailers or RVs up to 60 feet long. Fire grills and picnic tables are provided. Flush toilets, showers and firewood are available. Leashed pets are permitted. Boat docks and launching facilities are nearby.
Reservations, fee: Contact Reservations Northwest ($6 reservation fee); $12-$22 per night. Open March through November.
Who to contact: Phone (541) 851-3406 or (800) 452-5687, or write to P.O. Box 549, Detroit, OR 97342.
Location: From Interstate 5 at Salem, take exit 253 and turn east on Highway 22. Drive 50 miles to the park entrance, located two miles west of Detroit.
Trip note: This campground is set along the shore of Detroit Lake at 1,600 feet. Fishing, swimming and waterskiing are permitted. The park offers a fishing dock and a moorage area, and a boat ramp and bathhouse are available at nearby Mongold Day Use Area. The lake is very crowded on the opening day of trout season in late April because it is heavily stocked.

3.   PIETY ISLAND BOAT-IN

Reference: **On Detroit Lake, boat-in only in Willamette National Forest; map D2, grid a5.**

Campsites, facilities: There are 12 tent sites on this island campground which is accessible by boat only. Picnic tables and fire grills are provided. Pit toilets are available. Leashed pets are permitted. Boat docks, launching facilities and rentals are nearby.

Reservations, fee: No reservations; no fee. Open May to late September.

Who to contact: Phone the Detroit Ranger District at (503) 854-3366 or write to Willamette National Forest, HC 73, Box 320, Mill City, OR 97360.

Location: From Interstate 5 at Salem, take exit 253 and turn east on Highway 22. Drive about 45 miles to Detroit Lake. Continue east on Highway 22 along the north side of the lake. There is a boat ramp about three miles west of the town of Detroit. Launch your boat and head southeast to the island in the middle of the lake. The campground is located on the east side of the island.

Trip note: If you want to get away from the crowds at Detroit Lake State Park, this camp provides that possibility for boaters. Other campgrounds along the shore have piped water available. The Detroit Ranger Station, located on the north shore of the lake, can answer questions about the area and provide maps that detail nearby hiking trails.

---

4.   SOUTHSHORE   🆁🆅

Reference: **On Detroit Lake in Willamette National Forest; map D2, grid a5.**

Campsites, facilities: There are eight walk-in tent sites and 23 sites for tents, trailers or RVs up to 22 feet long. Fire grills and picnic tables are provided. Vault toilets and hand-pumped water are available. Leashed pets are permitted. Boat launching facilities are nearby at a day-use area.

Reservations, fee: No reservations; $8-$16 fee per night. Open mid-April to late September.

Who to contact: Phone the Detroit Ranger District at (503) 854-3366 or write to Willamette National Forest, HC 73, Box 320, Mill City, OR 97360.

Location: From Interstate 5 at Salem, take exit 253 and turn east on Highway 22. Drive 52 miles to Detroit. Continue 2.5 miles southeast on Highway 22, then four miles west on Forest Service Road 10 (Blow Out Road) to the camp.

Trip note: This campground is set along the south shore of Detroit Lake, where fishing, swimming and waterskiing are some of the recreation options. This is a popular place. The Stahlman Point Trailhead is about one-half mile from camp.

---

5.   HOOVER   🆁🆅

Reference: **On Detroit Lake in Willamette National Forest; map D2, grid a5.**

Campsites, facilities: There are 34 sites for tents, trailers or RVs up to 32 feet long. Some facilities are **wheelchair-accessible.** Picnic tables and fire grills are provided. Flush toilets and piped water are available. Leashed pets are permitted. Boat docks and launching facilities are nearby.

Reservations, fee: No reservations; $10-$20 fee per night. Open mid-April to mid-October.

Who to contact: Phone the Detroit Ranger District at (503) 854-3366 or write to Willamette National Forest, HC 73, Box 320, Mill City, OR 97360.

Location: From Interstate 5 at Salem, take exit 253 and turn east on Highway 22. Drive 52 miles to Detroit. Continue 2.5 miles southeast on Highway 22, then one mile northwest on Forest Service Road 10 (Blow Out Road) to the campground.

Trip note: This campground is along the eastern arm of Detroit Lake, near the mouth of the Santiam River. There is a **wheelchair-accessible** fishing area and nature trail. See the trip note for Southshore for other recreation options.

---

6. UPPER ARM

Reference: **On Detroit Lake in Willamette National Forest; map D2, grid a6.**

Campsites, facilities: There are five tent sites. Fire grills and picnic tables are provided. Pit toilets are available. There is **no piped water**. Leashed pets are permitted. Boat docks, launching facilities and rentals are nearby.

Reservations, fee: No reservations; no fee. Open mid-April to late October.

Who to contact: Phone the Detroit Ranger District at (503) 854-3366 or write to Willamette National Forest, HC 73, Box 320, Mill City, OR 97360.

Location: From Interstate 5 at Salem, take exit 253 and turn east on Highway 22. Drive 50 miles to Detroit, then turn left on Forest Service Road 46 (Breitenbush Road) and travel one mile northeast to the campground.

Trip note: This little campground is set along the shore of the narrow upper arm of Detroit Lake, close to where the Breitenbush River empties into it. It's the smallest and most primitive camp in the area, but also one of the most heavily used. Expect crowds and arrive as early as possible to claim a spot.

---

7. HOOVER GROUP CAMP   **RV**

Reference: **On Detroit Lake in Willamette National Forest; map D2, grid a6.**

Campsites, facilities: There are nine sites for tents, trailers or RVs up to 15 feet long. This is a group camp that will accommodate up to 70 people. Piped water and picnic tables are provided. Piped water, vault toilets and a group picnic shelter are available. Leashed pets are permitted. Boat docks, launching facilities and rentals are nearby.

Reservations, fee: Reservations required; call (800) 280-CAMP; $98 fee per night. Open mid-April to mid-October.

Who to contact: Phone the Detroit Ranger District at (503) 854-3366 or write to Willamette National Forest, HC 73, Box 320, Mill City, OR 97360.

Location: From Interstate 5 at Salem, take exit 253 and turn east on Highway 22. Drive 52 miles to Detroit. Continue 2.5 miles southeast on Highway 22, then one-half mile northwest on Forest Service Road 10 (Blow Out Road) to the campground.

Trip note: This is a perfect spot for a family reunion or club trip. Detroit Lake offers a myriad of activities: hiking, fishing, swimming and boating, just to name a few. The campground has nice, open sites and direct access to the lake.

---

8. WHISPERING FALLS   **RV**

Reference: **On Santiam River near Detroit Lake in Willamette National Forest; map D2, grid a6.**

Campsites, facilities: There are 16 sites for tents, trailers or RVs up to 22 feet long. Picnic tables and fire grills are provided. Piped water and flush toilets are available. A cafe is located within five miles. Leashed pets are permitted.

Reservations, fee: No reservations; $10 fee per night. Open mid-April to late September.

Who to contact: Phone the Detroit Ranger District at (503) 854-3366 or write to Willamette National Forest, HC 73, P.O. Box 320, Mill City, OR 97360.

Location: From Interstate 5 at Salem, take exit 253 and turn east on Highway 22. Drive 52 miles to Detroit. Continue eight miles east on Highway 22 to the campground.

Trip note: This popular campground is set along the banks of the Santiam River. If the campsites at Detroit Lake are crowded, this provides a more secluded option and it's only about a 10-minute drive from the lake. By driving 4.5 miles east on Forest Service Road 2243, you can access a good hiking trail that runs along Cheat Creek.

---

9. WATERLOO COUNTY CAMPGROUND RV

Reference: **On Santiam River; map D2, grid b1.**

Campsites, facilities: There are 60 sites for tents, trailers or RVs (50 partial hookups).

Reservations, fee: Reservations recommended for groups, phone (541) 967-3917; $12-$13 fee per night; $8 per person per night for group sites; $5 each additional vehicle. Senior discounts. Open April through October.

Who to contact: Phone the Linn County Parks Department at (541) 967-3917.

Location: From Interstate 5 at Albany, drive east on Highway 20 for about 20 miles, through Lebanon. Turn north at the Waterloo exit and drive approximately two miles to the camp on the right. The camp is on the south side of the Santiam River.

Trip note: There is over a mile of Santiam River frontage in this campground. Swimming, fishing, picnicking and field sports are options here.

---

10. SUNNYSIDE COUNTY PARK RV

Reference: **On Foster Lake; map D2, grid b3.**

Campsites, facilities: There ae 162 sites for tents, trailers or RVs. Electricity, flush toilets, showers and a sanitary dump station are provided. Picnic areas, volleyball courts, a boat ramp and moorage are available. Firewood is available for a fee.

Reservations, fee: Reservations recommended for groups, phone (541) 967-3917; $12-$13 per night; $8 per person per night for group sites; $5 each additional vehicle. Senior discounts. Open April through October.

Who to contact: Phone the Linn County Parks Department at (541) 967-3917.

Location: From Interstate 5 at Albany, take the Highway 20 exit and drive east about 35 miles, through Lebanon and Sweet Home, to the Quartzville Road exit; turn north and drive one mile on Quartzville Road to the campground on the right. The camp is on the south side of Foster Reservoir.

Trip note: This is Linn County's most popular park. Recreation options include boating, fishing, waterskiing and swimming.

---

11. WHITCOMB CREEK COUNTY PARK RV

Reference: **On Green Peter Reservoir; map D2, grid b3.**

Campsites, facilities: There are 39 tent, trailer or RV sites. Picnic tables are provided.

Reservations, fee: Reservations recommended for groups, phone (541) 967-

3917; $9 fee per night. Open April through October.

Who to contact: Phone the Linn County Parks Department at (541) 967-3917.

Location: From Interstate 5 at Albany, take the Highway 20 exit and drive east about 35 miles, through Lebanon and Sweet Home, to the Quartzville Road exit; turn northeast and drive 10 miles on Quartzville Road to the campground on the right. The camp is on the north shore of Green Peter Reservoir.

Trip note: Recreation options include swimming, hiking and picnicking.

---

12.   YELLOWBOTTOM   RV

Reference: On Quartzville Creek; map D2, grid b4.

Campsites, facilities: There are 22 tent sites and 10 drive-through sites for trailers or RVs up to 28 feet long. Picnic tables and fire grills are provided. Piped water and vault toilets are available. Leashed pets are permitted.

Reservations, fee: No reservations; $6 fee per night; 18-day stay limit. Open mid-May to late September.

Who to contact: Phone (503) 375-5646 or write to Bureau of Land Management, 1717 Fabry Road SE, Salem, OR 97306.

Location: From Interstate 5 at Albany, take exit 233 and turn east on US 20. Drive 26 miles to Sweet Home, then turn northeast on Quartzville Road and proceed 21 miles to the campground.

Trip note: This campground is set along the banks of Quartzville Creek and it is always missed by out-of-town visitors. It is located on the edge of Willamette National Forest and the Middle Santiam Wilderness. It is quite primitive, but perfect for a quiet getaway weekend.

---

13.   CASCADIA STATE PARK   RV

Reference: On Santiam River; map D2, grid b4.

Campsites, facilities: There are 26 primitive sites for tents, trailers or self-contained RVs up to 35 feet long. Picnic tables and fire grills are provided. Piped water, vault toilets and firewood are available. A store is located within one mile. Some facilities are **wheelchair accessible**. Pets are permitted.

Reservations, fee: No reservations; $9-$12 fee per night. Open March through October.

Who to contact: Phone (800) 452-5687 or (541) 851-3406 or write to P.O. Box 549, Detroit, OR 97542.

Location: From Interstate 5 at Albany, turn east on US 20 and drive 40 miles to the park on the left.

Trip note: This 258-acre park is set along the banks of the Santiam River. The highlight here is a scenic waterfall, with a two-mile hiking trail leading to it. Fishing is another alternative.

---

14.   RIVERSIDE   RV

Reference: On Santiam River in Willamette National Forest; map D2, grid b6.

Campsites, facilities: There are 37 sites for tents, trailers or RVs up to 21 feet long. Picnic tables and fire grills are provided. Piped water and pit toilets are available. Leashed pets are permitted.

Reservations, fee: No reservations; $8 fee per night. Open late April to late September.

Who to contact: Phone the Detroit Ranger District at (503) 854-3366 or write to Willamette National Forest, HC 73, Box 320, Mill City, OR 97360.

Location: From Interstate 5 at Salem, take exit 253 and turn east on Highway 22. Drive 50 miles to Detroit. Continue 14 miles southeast on Highway 22 to the campground.

Trip note: This campground is set along the banks of the Santiam River. The fishing can be good here. A point of interest is Marion Forks Hatchery, located just a few miles south. The Mount Jefferson Wilderness is located directly to the east in Willamette National Forest.

15. MARION FORKS   RV

Reference: **On Santiam River in Willamette National Forest; map D2, grid b7.**

Campsites, facilities: There are 15 sites for tents, trailers or RVs up to 22 feet long. Picnic tables and fire grills are provided. Pit toilets and piped water are available. Leashed pets are permitted.

Reservations, fee: No reservations; $8 fee per night. Open mid-May to mid-October.

Who to contact: Phone the Detroit Ranger District at (503) 854-3366 or write to Willamette National Forest, HC 73, Box 320, Mill City, OR 97360.

Location: From Interstate 5 at Salem, take exit 253 and turn east on Highway 22. Drive 50 miles to Detroit. Continue 16 miles southeast on Highway 22 to the campground.

Trip note: This campground is set along Marion Creek, adjacent to the Marion Forks Fish Hatchery. A Forest Service Guard Station and a restaurant are across Highway 22. There are some quality hiking trails in the area; see a Forest Service map for trailhead locations.

---

16. BIG MEADOWS   RV

Reference: **Near Mount Jefferson Wilderness in Willamette National Forest; map D2, grid b7.**

Campsites, facilities: There nine sites for tents, trailers or RVs. Picnic tables, fire grills and four horse corrals are provided at each site. Hand-pumped water and vault toilets are available.

Reservations, fees: No reservations; $7 fee per night.

Who to contact: Phone Detroit Ranger District at (503) 854-3366, or write Willamette National Forest, HC73, Box 320, Mill City, OR 97360.

Location: From Interstate 5 at Salem, take exit 253 and turn east on Highway 22. Drive 52 miles to Detroit. Continue southeast on Highway 22 for 27 miles to Big Meadows Road (Forest Service Road 2267). Turn left and drive one mile, then turn left again onto Forest Service Road 2257 and drive one-half mile to the campground.

Trip note: This is one of the newer and most popular campgrounds in the area. It was built by the Forest Service with the support of a horse club. It is used heavily by equestrians taking pack trips into Big Meadows and the adjacent Mount Jefferson Wilderness. If you're not a horse lover, you may want to stick with Marion Forks (camp number 15) or Riverside (camp number 14).

---

17. JACK CREEK   RV

Reference: **Near Mount Jefferson Wilderness in Deschutes National Forest; map D2, grid b8.**

Campsites, facilities: There are 16 sites for tents, trailers or RVs up to 40 feet long. Picnic tables and fire grills are provided. Vault toilets are available. There is **no**

piped water. Leashed pets are permitted.

Reservations, fee: No reservations; $5 fee per night. Open mid-April to mid-October.

Who to contact: Phone the Sisters Ranger District at (541) 549-2111 or write to Deschutes National Forest, P.O. Box 249, Sisters, OR 97759.

Location: From Interstate 5 at Albany, turn east on US 20 and drive approximately 87 miles. At the sign for Camp Sherman, turn north and drive about five miles. Continue northwest on Forest Service Roads 12 and 1230 to the campground.

Trip note: This campground is set along the banks of Jack Creek. No fishing is permitted here, to protect the bull trout habitat. A trail passes a mile east of camp heading nine miles south to Black Butte in one direction and northwest into the Mount Jefferson Wilderness in the other. This is a more primitive option to the other camps in the area.

---

18.   SHEEP SPRINGS HORSE CAMP   RV

Reference: **Near Mount Jefferson Wilderness in Deschutes National Forest; map D2, grid b8.**

Campsites, facilities: There are 11 sites for tents, trailers or RVs up to 15 feet long. Piped water and fire grills are provided. Vault toilets and box stalls for horses are available.

Reservations, fee: Reservations required; $5 fee per night. Open late May to mid-October.

Who to contact: Phone the Sisters Ranger District at (541) 549-2111 or write to Deschutes National Forest, P.O. Box 249, Sisters, OR 97759.

Location: From Interstate 5 at Albany, turn east on US 20 and drive approximately 87 miles. At the sign for Camp Sherman, turn north and drive about five miles. Travel four miles north of Camp Sherman on Forest Service Road 1420, then one mile north on Forest Service Road 12. From there, drive 1.5 miles northwest on Forest Service Road 1260 to the campground.

Trip note: This equestrian camp is located near the trailhead for the Metolius-Windigo Horse Trail, which heads northeast into the Mount Jefferson Wilderness and south to Black Butte. Contact the Forest Service for details and maps of the backcountry.

---

19.   DIAMOND HILL RV PARK   RV

Reference: **In Willamette Valley; map D2, grid c0.**

Campsites, facilities: There are 20 tent sites and 65 sites for trailers or RVs of any length. Electricity, piped water, sewer hookups and picnic tables are provided. Flush toilets, bottled gas, sanitary services, showers, firewood, a store, a laundromat, ice, a playground and a swimming pool are available. A cafe is located within one mile. Small pets and motorbikes are permitted.

Reservations, fee: Reservations accepted; $13-$17 fee per night; MasterCard and Visa accepted. Open all year.

Who to contact: Phone (541) 995-9279 or write to 32917 Diamond Hill Drive, Harrisburg, OR 97446.

Location: Drive 15 miles north of Eugene on Interstate 5, then take exit 209 and the campground is about one block away on the west side of the highway.

Trip note: This private campground is located in the center of the Willamette Valley, just off the highway. It is a great layover spot if you're cruising up or down Interstate 5. Eugene Kamping World is the closest camp, 10 miles south.

20. TROUT CREEK **RV**

Reference: **On Santiam River in Willamette National Forest; map D2, grid c4.**

Campsites, facilities: There are 24 sites for tents, trailers or RVs up to 22 feet long. Six of the sites will accommodate RVs up to 36 feet long. Picnic tables and fire grills are provided. Hand-pumped water and vault toilets are available. Leashed pets are permitted.

Reservations, fee: Some sites may be reserved by calling (800) 280-CAMP; $7.75 reservation fee; $8-$12 fee per night. Open May through September.

Who to contact: Phone the Sweet Home Ranger District at (541) 367-5168 or write to Willamette National Forest, Sweet Home, OR 97386.

Location: From Interstate 5 at Albany, take exit 233 and drive 26 miles east on US 20 to the town of Sweet Home. Continue 18.5 miles east on US 20 to the campground entrance on the right.

Trip note: This campground is set along the banks of the Santiam River, about seven miles east of Cascadia. Fishing and swimming are some of the possibilities here. The Trout Creek Trail, located just across the highway, is routed into the Menagerie Wilderness. The Walton Ranch Elk Viewing area is immediately west of the campground, and at the Trout Creek Trailhead you will also find a short trail leading to an elk-viewing platform.

21. YUKWAH **RV**

Reference: **On Santiam River in Willamette National Forest; map D2, grid c4.**

Campsites, facilities: There are 19 sites for tents, trailers or RVs up to 31 feet long. Picnic tables and fire grills are provided. Hand-pumped water and vault toilets are available. Leashed pets are permitted.

Reservations, fee: No reservations; $8-$12 fee per night from mid-May through September; no fee October 1 through May 15. Open all year with limited winter services.

Who to contact: Phone the Sweet Home Ranger District at (541) 367-5168 or write to Willamette National Forest, Sweet Home, OR 97386.

Location: From Interstate 5 at Albany, take exit 233 and drive 26 miles east on US 20 to the town of Sweet Home. Continue 19 miles east on US 20 to the campground.

Trip note: This campground is adjacent to Trout Creek Campground and offers the same recreation possibilities. See that trip note for details.

22. FERNVIEW **RV**

Reference: **On Santiam River in Willamette National Forest; map D2, grid c5.**

Campsites, facilities: There are 11 sites for tents, trailers or RVs up to 22 feet long. Picnic tables and fire grills are provided. Hand-pumped water and vault toilets are available. Leashed pets are permitted.

Reservations, fee: No reservations; $8 fee per night. Open May to September.

Who to contact: Phone the Sweet Home Ranger District at (541) 367-5168 or write to Willamette National Forest, Sweet Home, OR 97386.

Location: From Interstate 5 at Albany, take exit 233 and drive 26 miles east on US 20 to the town of Sweet Home. Continue 23 miles east on US 20 to the campground entrance on the right.

Trip note: This campground is set at the confluence of Boulder Creek and the Santiam River, just south of the Menagerie Wilderness. Just across US 20 lies the Rooster Rock Trail, which leads to—where else?—Rooster Rock, the site of an old lookout tower. Due to its close proximity to the highway, this camp gets its fair share of use in the summer months, so it's advisable to claim your spot early in the day.

23.　　　　HOUSE ROCK

Reference: **On Santiam River in Willamette National Forest; map D2, grid c5.**

Campsites, facilities: There are 17 tent sites. Picnic tables and fire grills are provided. Vault toilets and hand-pumped water are available. Leashed pets are permitted.

Reservations, fee: No reservations; $8-$12 fee per night, $10 for double site. Open May through September.

Who to contact: Phone the Sweet Home Ranger District at (541) 367-5168 or write to Willamette National Forest, Sweet Home, OR 97386.

Location: From Interstate 5 at Albany, take exit 233 and drive 26 miles east on US 20 to the town of Sweet Home. From Sweet Home, continue 26.5 miles east on US 20, then turn right on Forest Service Road 2044 and travel southeast for a short distance to the campground.

Trip note: This campground is set at the confluence of Sheep Creek and South Santiam River. Trout fishing can be good, particularly during summer evenings. The camp is located in the midst of an old-growth forest and is surrounded by huge, majestic evergreens. History buffs should explore the short loop trail out of camp, which passes by House Rock, an historic shelter for Native Americans, and continues to the Historic Old Santiam Wagon Road.

24.　　　　MONA　　　　RV

Reference: **Near Blue River Reservoir in Willamette National Forest; map D2, grid c5.**

Campsites, facilities: There are 23 sites for tents, trailers or RVs up to 21 feet long. Picnic tables and fire grills are provided. Piped water and flush toilets are available. Some facilities are **wheelchair accessible**. Leashed pets are permitted.

Reservations, fee: No reservations; $7-$14 fee per night. Open mid-May to late September.

Who to contact: Phone the Blue River Ranger District at (541) 822-3317 or write to P.O. Box 199, Blue River, OR 97413.

Location: From Interstate 5 at Springfield, turn east on Highway 126 and drive 37 miles to the town of Blue River. Continue east for three miles east on Highway 126, then head north on Forest Service Road 15 for three miles to the campground.

Trip note: This campground is set along the shore of Blue River Reservoir, close to where the Blue River joins it. There is a boat ramp across the river from the campground. After launching a boat, campers can ground it near the campsite. This camp is extremely popular when the reservoir is full.

25.　　　　LOST PRAIRIE　　　　RV

Reference: **On Hackleman Creek in Willamette National Forest; map D2, grid c6.**

Campsites, facilities: There are eight tent sites and two sites for trailers or RVs up to 22 feet long. Picnic tables and fire grills are provided. Hand-pumped water and vault toilets are available. Some facilities are **wheelchair accessible**. Leashed pets are permitted.

Reservations, fee: No reservations; $7-$10 fee per night. Open May through October.

Who to contact: Phone the Sweet Home Ranger District at (541) 367-5168 or write to Willamette National Forest, Sweet Home, OR 97386.

Location: From Interstate 5 at Albany, take exit 233 and drive 26 miles east on US 20 to the town of Sweet Home. Continue 40 miles east on US 20 to the camp on the right.

Trip note: This campground is set along the banks of Hackleman Creek at 3,300 feet. There are three excellent hiking trails within five miles of the camp: Hackleman Old Growth Grove, Cone Peak and Iron Mountain. The latter two offer spectacular wildflower viewing in the late spring and early summer. This camp is an alternative to nearby Fish Lake.

---

26. OLALLIE   🅁🅅

Reference: On McKenzie River in Willamette National Forest; map D2, grid c6.

Campsites, facilities: There are 17 sites for tents, trailers or RVs up to 30 feet long. Picnic tables and fire grills are provided. Vault toilets and hand-pumped water are available. Leashed pets are permitted.

Reservations, fee: No reservations; $6 fee per night; $3 each additional vehicle. Open late May to early September.

Who to contact: Phone the McKenzie Ranger District at (541) 822-3381 or write to Willamette National Forest, 57600 McKenzie Highway, McKenzie Bridge, OR 97413.

Location: From Interstate 5 at Eugene, turn east on Highway 126 and drive 47 miles to the town of McKenzie Bridge. Continue 11 miles northeast on Highway 126 to the campground.

Trip note: This campground is set along the banks of the McKenzie River and offers opportunities for boating, fishing and hiking. You get easy access from Highway 126 and a jump-off point into the Willamette National Forest. A Forest Service map details back roads and trails.

---

27. TRAILBRIDGE   🅁🅅

Reference: On Trailbridge Reservoir in Willamette National Forest; map D2, grid c6.

Campsites, facilities: There are 20 sites for tents and 21 sites for trailers or RVs. Picnic tables and fire grills are provided. Piped water, vault and flush toilets, and firewood are available. Leashed pets are permitted. Boat ramps are nearby.

Reservations, fee: No reservations; $5 fee per night; $2 each additional vehicle. Open late April to early September.

Who to contact: Phone the McKenzie Ranger District at (541) 822-3381 or write to Willamette National Forest, 57600 McKenzie Highway, McKenzie Bridge, OR 97413.

Location: From Interstate 5 near Springfield, take the Highway 126 exit and turn east. Drive 47 miles to the town of McKenzie Bridge. Continue northeast on Highway 126 for 13 miles, then turn southwest at the turnoff at the north end of Trailbridge Reservoir and continue 200 yards to the campground.

Trip note: This campground is set along the shore of Trailbridge Reservoir, where boating, fishing and hiking are recreation options. It's an exceptional spot for car campers. Highway 126 east of McKenzie Bridge is a designated scenic route, providing a pleasant trip in. A good side trip is to take the beautiful 40-minute drive east to the little town of Sisters. To the south you can see the Three Sisters Mountains (all over 10,000 feet), and you'll cross the Pacific Crest Trail as well. From this camp, there is access to the McKenzie River National Recreation Trail.

---

28.   LAKES END

Reference: **On Smith Reservoir, boat-in only in Willamette National Forest; map D2, grid c6.**

Campsites, facilities: There are 17 boat-in tent sites. Picnic tables and fire grills are provided. Pit toilets are available, but there is **no piped water**. Leashed pets are permitted. Boat docks are nearby.

Reservations, fee: No reservations; no fee. Open late May to early September.

Who to contact: Phone the McKenzie Ranger District at (541) 822-3381 or write to Willamette National Forest, 57600 McKenzie Highway, McKenzie Bridge, OR 97413.

Location: From Interstate 5 near Springfield, take the Highway 126 exit and turn east. Drive 47 miles to the town of McKenzie Bridge. Continue northeast on Highway 126 for 13 miles, then drive three miles north on Forest Service Road 1477 to the boat ramp. Travel by boat for another two miles to the north end of Smith Reservoir where the campground is located.

Trip note: This secluded boat-in campground is set along the shore of Smith Reservoir. It is one of the few boat-in campgrounds in the entire state. Here there are no cars, no traffic and most likely, no people. The trout fishing in this reservoir can be exceptionally good.

---

29.   ICE CAP   RV

Reference: **On Carmen Reservoir in Willamette National Forest; map D2, grid c6.**

Campsites, facilities: There are 11 tent sites and 11 sites for tents, trailers or RVs up to 16 feet long. Picnic tables and fire grills are provided. Piped water and flush toilets launching facilities and rentals are nearby.

Reservations, fee: No reservations; $8 fee per night; $2.50 each additional vehicle. Open late May to early September.

Who to contact: Phone the McKenzie Ranger District at (541) 822-3381 or write to Willamette National Forest, 57600 McKenzie Highway, McKenzie Bridge, OR 97413.

Location: From Interstate 5 near Springfield, take the Highway 126 exit and turn east. Drive 47 miles to the town of McKenzie Bridge. Continue northeast on Highway 126 for 19 miles, then drive 200 yards southwest on the entrance road to the campground.

Trip note: This campground is set on a hill above Carmen Reservoir, which was created by a dam on the McKenzie River. The McKenzie River National Recreation Trail passes by camp, and Koosah Falls and Sahalie Falls are nearby. Clear Lake, a popular local vacation destination, is a short drive away.

---

30.   COLDWATER COVE   RV

Reference: **On Clear Lake in Willamette National Forest; map D2, grid c6.**

Campsites, facilities: There are 35 sites for tents, trailers or RVs up to 30 feet long.

Picnic tables and fire grills are provided. Hand pumps for water and vault toilets are available. Leashed pets are permitted. Some facilities are **wheelchair accessible**. Boat docks, launching facilities, rowboats, a store, a cafe and cabin rentals are available nearby at Clear Lake Resort.

Reservations, fee: Reserve some sites by calling (800) 280-CAMP ($7.75 reservation fee); $9 fee per night; $4.50 each additional vehicle. Open late May to early September.

Who to contact: Phone the McKenzie Ranger District at (541) 822-3381 or write to Willamette National Forest, 57600 McKenzie Highway, McKenzie Bridge, OR 97413.

Location: From Interstate 5 near Springfield, take the Highway 126 exit and turn east. Drive 47 miles to the town of McKenzie Bridge. Continue northeast on Highway 126 for 14 miles, then turn east on Forest Service Road 1372 and continue to the campground.

Trip note: This campground is set along the south shore of Clear Lake. This spring-fed lake is formed by a natural lava dam and is the source of the McKenzie River. No motors are permitted on the lake, making it ideal for anglers in rowboats or canoes. The northern section of the McKenzie River National Recreation Trail passes by the camp.

---

31. FISH LAKE

Reference: **Near Clear Lake in Willamette National Forest; map D2, grid c6.**

Campsites, facilities: There are seven sites for tents, trailers or RVs up to 16 feet long. Picnic tables and fire grills are provided. Piped water and vault toilets are available. Leashed pets are permitted.

Reservations, fee: No reservations. $5 fee per night. Open late May to early September.

Who to contact: Phone the McKenzie Ranger District at (541) 822-3381 or write to Willamette National Forest, 57600 McKenzie Highway, McKenzie Bridge, OR 97413.

Location: From Interstate 5 near Springfield, take the Highway 126 exit and turn east. Drive 47 miles to the town of McKenzie Bridge. Continue northeast on Highway 126 for 23 miles, then drive 200 yards southwest on the entrance road to the campground.

Trip note: This campground is on the shore of Fish Lake. The "lake" usually dries up by the middle of the summer, however. An interpretive display is set up at the guard station nearby. Across the road is a trail that follows the Old Santiam Wagon Road and the northern trailhead for the McKenzie River National Recreation Trail. The Clear Lake picnic area is two miles south off Highway 126.

---

32. SCOTT LAKE

Reference: **On Scott Lake in Willamette National Forest; map D2, grid c7.**

Campsites, facilities: There are 12 tent sites. Picnic tables are provided. Pit toilets are available, but there is **no piped water**. Leashed pets are permitted.

Reservations, fee: No reservations; no fee. Open late June to early September.

Who to contact: Phone the McKenzie Ranger District at (541) 822-3381 or write to Willamette National Forest, 57600 McKenzie Highway, McKenzie Bridge, OR 97413.

Location: From Interstate 5 at Eugene, turn east on Highway 126 and drive 54 miles to the junction with Highway 242. Head east on Highway 242 (not recommended for trailers, speed limit is 35 miles-per-hour) for 14.5 miles to Forest Service Road 1532 and turn left to the campground.

Trip note: This campground offers hike-in sites set around Scott Lake. The elevation is 4,800 feet. Only non-motorized boats are allowed on the lake. There are trails leading out from camp that provide access to several small lakes in the Mount Washington Wilderness.

---

33.   BIG LAKE   **RV**

Reference: **On Big Lake in Willamette National Forest; map D2, grid c7.**

Campsites, facilities: There are 49 sites for tents, trailers or RVs up to 16 feet long. Picnic tables and fire grills are provided. Piped water, vault and flush toilets are available. Leashed pets are permitted. Boat ramps and launching facilities are nearby.

Reservations, fee: Reserve some sites by calling (800) 280-CAMP ($7.75 reservation fee); $9 fee per night; $4.50 each additional vehicle. Open late June to early September.

Who to contact: Phone the McKenzie Ranger District at (541) 822-3381 or write to Willamette National Forest, Sisters, OR 97759.

Location: From Interstate 5 at Albany, take exit 233 and turn east on US 20. Drive 74 miles to the convergence of Highways 20/126/22. Continue east on Highway 126 for five miles to Forest Service Road 2690, then turn south and continue for 3.5 miles to the campground.

Trip note: This jewel of a spot is set on the north shore of Big Lake at 4,650 feet. Fishing, swimming, waterskiing and hiking make it attractive. Big Lake has heavy motorized boat use. One of the better hikes is the five-mile wilderness loop trail that heads out from the south shore of the lake and cuts past a few small lakes before returning. It is quite heavily traveled, however, and requires a regulatory permit from the Forest Service to use.

---

34.   BIG LAKE WEST CAMPGROUND

Reference: **On Big Lake in Willamette National Forest; map D2, grid c7.**

Campsites, facilities: There are 11 walk-in sites. Fire pits and picnic tables are provided. Piped water and vault toilets are available. Leashed pets permitted.

Reservations, fee: Reserve some sites by calling (800) 280-CAMP ($7.75 reservation fee); $8 fee per night; $4 each additional vehicle. Open mid-June to early September.

Who to contact: Phone the McKenzie Ranger District at (541) 822-3381 or write to Willamette National Forest, Sisters, OR 97759.

Location: From Interstate 5 at Albany, take exit 233 and turn east on US 20. Drive 74 miles to the convergence of Highways 20/126/22. Continue east on Highway 126 for five miles to Forest Service Road 2690, then turn south and continue for 4.3 miles to the campground.

Trip note: This spot is west of Big Lake campground. While it has many of the same attractions, the walk-in sites offer some seclusion and quiet. The Mount Washington Wilderness and Patjens Lake access trails are accessible here. See Big Lake for some hiking options from the south shore of the lake.

---

35.   SCOUT LAKE   **RV**

Reference: **On Scout Lake in Deschutes National Forest; map D2, grid c7.**

Campsites, facilities: There are 13 sites for tents, trailers or RVs up to 40 feet long.

Picnic tables and fire grills are provided. Vault toilets and piped water are available. Leashed pets are permitted in the campground only (not in the day use area).

Reservations, fee: Reservations accepted; $12-$18 fee per night. Open mid-April to late September.

Who to contact: Phone the Sisters Ranger District at (541) 549-2111 or write Deschutes National Forest, P.O. Box 249, Sisters, OR 97759.

Location: From Interstate 5 at Albany, take exit 233 and turn east on US 20. Drive 74 miles to the convergence of highways 20, 126 and 22. Continue east on Highway 126 for 12 miles to Suttle Lake Forest Road, then head west. Turn south of Suttle Lake on Forest Service Road 2066 for a short distance to the campground.

Trip note: This campground is set about one-half mile from Suttle Lake. It is a good area for swimming and hiking. This campground is available for groups, but reservations need to be made in advance. Call the ranger district for details.

---

36.   BLUE LAKE RESORT   RV

Reference: On Blue Lake; map D2, grid c7.

Campsites, facilities: There are 40 sites for tents, trailers or RVs up to 34 feet long. Picnic tables and fire grills are provided. Electricity, piped water, sewer hookups, flush toilets, sanitary disposal station, showers, firewood, a store, a cafe, ice and a playground are available. Leashed pets are permitted. Horse rentals, boat docks, launching facilities and boat rentals are available.

Reservations, fee: Reservations accepted; $9-$17 fee per night for first two people; $0.50 each additional person; $5 pet fee. MasterCard and Visa accepted. Open all year.

Who to contact: Phone (541) 595-6671 or write to 13900 Blue Lake Drive, Sisters, OR 97759.

Location: From Interstate 5 at Albany, take exit 233 and turn east on US 20. Drive 74 miles to the convergence of Highways 20/126/22. Continue east on Highway 126 for 12 miles. Turn west on Suttle Lake Forest Road and drive 2.5 miles to the resort on the right.

Trip note: This 200-acre resort is set along the shore of Blue Lake. It is the only camp on the lake. Recreation options include fishing, boating (five mile-per-hour speed limit), swimming, hiking, bicycling and horseback riding.

---

37.   SOUTH SHORE   RV

Reference: On Suttle Lake in Deschutes National Forest; map D2, grid c7.

Campsites, facilities: There are 38 sites for tents, trailers or RVs up to 40 feet long. Picnic tables and fire grills are provided. Piped water and vault toilets are available. Leashed pets are permitted. Boat docks, launching facilities and rentals are nearby.

Reservations, fee: No reservations; $9 fee per night; $5 each additional vehicle. Open mid-April to late September.

Who to contact: Phone the Sisters Ranger District at (541) 549-2111 or write Deschutes National Forest, P.O. Box 249, Sisters, OR 97759.

Location: From Interstate 5 at Albany, take exit 233 and turn east on US 20. Drive 74 miles to the convergence of Highways 20/126/22. Continue east on Highway 126 for 12 miles to Suttle Lake Forest Road, then head west and proceed a short distance to the campground.

Trip note: This campground is located on the south shore of Suttle Lake, at 3,400 feet. Waterskiing is permitted on the lake. A hiking trail goes around the lake. A stable and horseback riding rentals are nearby. Fishing and windsurfing are other popular activities.

38.   LINK CREEK   RV

Reference: **On Suttle Lake in Deschutes National Forest; map D2, grid c7.**

Campsites, facilities: There are 33 sites for tents, trailers or RVs up to 40 feet long. Picnic tables and fire grills are provided. Piped water and vault toilets are available. Leashed pets are permitted. Boat docks, launching facilities and rentals are nearby.

Reservations, fee: No reservations; $9 fee per night; $5 each additional vehicle. Open mid-April to late September.

Who to contact: Phone the Sisters Ranger District at (541) 549-2111 or write Deschutes National Forest, P.O. Box 249, Sisters, OR 97759.

Location: From Interstate 5 at Albany, take exit 233 and turn east on US 20. Drive 74 miles to the convergence of Highways 20/126/22. Continue east on Highway 126 for 12 miles to Suttle Lake Forest Road, then head west. Continue a short distance to the campground.

Trip note: This campground is located at the west end of Suttle Lake. See the trip note for South Shore for recreation details.

39.   BLUE BAY   RV

Reference: **On Suttle Lake in Deschutes National Forest; map D2, grid c7.**

Campsites, facilities: There are 25 sites for tents, trailers or RVs up to 30 feet long. Picnic tables and fire grills are provided. Piped water and vault toilets are available. Leashed pets are permitted. Boat docks, launching facilities and rentals are nearby.

Reservations, fee: No reservations; $9 fee per night; $5 each additional vehicle. Open mid-April to late September.

Who to contact: Phone the Sisters Ranger District at (541) 549-2111 or write Deschutes National Forest, P.O. Box 249, Sisters, OR 97759.

Location: From Interstate 5 at Albany, take exit 233 and turn east on US 20. Drive 74 miles to the convergence of Highways 20/126/22. Continue east on Highway 126 for 12 miles to Suttle Lake Forest Road, then head west. Continue a short distance to the campground.

Trip note: This campground is set along the south shore of Suttle Lake. See the trip note for South Shore for recreation details.

40.   KOA SISTERS   RV

Reference: **On Branchwater Lake; map D2, grid c9.**

Campsites, facilities: There are 64 sites for tents, trailers or RVs. Air conditioning, electric heat, cable TV, restrooms, showers, a sanitary dump, security, a public phone, a laundromat, limited groceries, ice, snacks, RV supplies, LP gas and a barbecue are available. Recreational facilities include a recreation field, a playground, a game room, horseshoes, a spa and a heated swimming pool. Some facilities are **wheelchair accessible**.

Reservations, fee: Reservations recommended; $15-$20 fee per night. Visa and MasterCard are accepted.

Who to contact: Phone the park at (541) 549-3021 or write to 67667 Highway 20

West, Bend, OR 97701.

Location: From Interstate 5 at Albany, turn east on US 20 and drive 100 miles to Sisters. Continue approximately four miles southeast to the park on the right side of the highway.

Trip note: This park is located amidst wooded mountains outside of Sisters. The elevation is 3,200 feet. Branchwater Lake offers swimming and good trout fishing. See the trip note for Belknap Springs Lodge for information about the surrounding area.

41.   BELKNAP SPRINGS LODGE   **RV**

Reference: **On McKenzie River; map D2, grid c9.**

Campsites, facilities: There are seven sites for tents and 47 sites for trailers or RVs with electrical and water hookups. There is also a lodge with 10 rooms and four cabins available. Restrooms, showers, a sanitary dump and a public phone are provided. Recreational facilities include a heated swimming pool, a recreation field, horseshoes and a recreation hall. Some facilities are **wheelchair accessible**. Leashed pets are permitted, except in the lodge or the cabins.

Reservations, fee: Reservations recommended; $12-$18 fee per night; $60-$90 lodge fee; $35-$60 cabin fee. Visa and MasterCard accepted.

Who to contact: Phone the park at (541) 822-3512 or write to P.O. Box 2001, Blue River, OR 97413.

Location: From Interstate 5 at Albany, turn east on US 20 and drive 100 miles to Sisters. From the junction of Highway 242 and Highway 126 (in Sisters), drive east on Highway 126 for one mile to Belknap Springs Road. The lodge is north three-tenths of a mile on Belknap Springs Road. (Alternate route: From Hoodoo, on Interstate 126, drive west for 28 miles to the park).

Trip note: This beautiful park is located in a wooded, mountainous area and is set on the McKenzie River. Trout fishing can be excellent here. If you're looking for hiking opportunities, check out Three Sisters Wilderness Area and Mt. Washington Wilderness Area, both accessible by driving west of Sisters on Highway 242. These are exceptionally scenic and pristine expanses of forest and well worth exploring. The Pacific Crest Trail runs north and south through both wilderness areas.

42.   RIVERSIDE

Reference: **On Metolius River in Deschutes National Forest; map D2, grid c9.**

Campsites, facilities: There are 16 tent sites. Picnic tables and fire grills are provided. Vault toilets and piped water are available. Leashed pets are permitted.

Reservations, fee: No reservations; no fee. Open mid-April to mid-October.

Who to contact: Phone the Sisters Ranger District at (541) 549-2111 or write Deschutes National Forest, P.O. Box 249, Sisters, OR 97759.

Location: From Interstate 5 at Albany, turn east on US 20 and drive approximately 87 miles. At the sign for Camp Sherman, turn north and drive about five miles. From the store in Camp Sherman, drive two miles south on Forest Service Road 900 to the campground.

Trip note: This campground is set along the banks of the Metolius River, less than a mile from Metolius Springs at the base of Black Butte. It is just enough off the highway to be missed by most other people.

43.   INDIAN FORD   RV

Reference: **On Indian Ford Creek in Deschutes National Forest; map D2, grid c9.**

Campsites, facilities: There are 25 sites for tents, trailers or RVs up to 40 feet long. Picnic tables and fire grills are provided. Vault toilets and piped water are available. Leashed pets are permitted.

Reservations, fee: No reservations; $9 fee per night; $5 each additional vehicle. Open May to October.

Who to contact: Phone the Sisters Ranger District at (541) 549-2111 or write to Deschutes National Forest, P.O. Box 249, Sisters, OR 97759.

Location: From Interstate 5 at Albany, turn east on US 20 and drive 95 miles to the campground, located five miles northwest of Sisters.

Trip note: This campground is set along the banks of Indian Ford Creek. On the north side of nearby Black Butte is the spring which feeds the Metolius River, a good spot to fly fish for trout. Aspen trees provide great bird-watching opportunities.

44.   COLD SPRINGS   RV

Reference: **On Trout Creek in Deschutes National Forest; map D2, grid c9.**

Campsites, facilities: There are 23 sites for tents, trailers or RVs up to 40 feet long. Picnic tables and fire grills are provided. Vault toilets and piped water are available. Leashed pets are permitted.

Reservations, fee: No reservations; $9 fee per night; $5 each additional vehicle. Open May to October.

Who to contact: Phone the Sisters Ranger District at (541) 549-2111 or write to Deschutes National Forest, P.O. Box 249, Sisters, OR 97759.

Location: From Interstate 5 at Albany, turn east on US 20 and drive 100 miles to Sisters. Turn southwest on Highway 242 and drive five miles to the camp.

Trip note: This wooded campground is set at 3,400 feet at the source of little Trout Creek. A trail passes near camp and extends north and south for miles. It is just far enough off the main drag to be missed by many campers. Spring and early summer are the times for great birdwatching in the area's abundant aspen.

45.   CIRCLE 5 TRAILER PARK   RV

Reference: **Near Sisters; map D2, grid c9.**

Campsites, facilities: There are 10 tent sites and 22 drive-through sites for trailers or RVs of any length. Electricity, piped water, sewer hookups, cable TV and picnic tables are provided. Flush toilets, bottled gas, sanitary services, showers and a laundromat are available. A store, a cafe and ice are located within one mile. Leashed pets are permitted.

Reservations, fee: Reservations accepted; $10-$16 fee per night. Open all year.

Who to contact: Phone (541) 549-3861 or write to Box 1360, Sisters, OR 97759.

Location: From Interstate 5 at Albany, turn east on US 20 and drive 100 miles to Sisters. Continue one-half mile southeast on US 20 to the park entrance on the left.

Trip note: This motor home camp is just outside Sisters, within walking distance to the town. The sites are cool and shady. Nearby recreation options include a riding stable and tennis courts.

46. EUGENE KAMPING WORLD **RV**

Reference: **Near Willamette River; map D2, grid d0.**

Campsites, facilities: There are 30 tent sites and 114 drive-through sites for trailers or RVs of any length. Electricity, piped water, sewer hookups and picnic tables are provided. Flush toilets, bottled gas, sanitary services, showers, a recreation hall, cable TV, a miniature golf course, a store, a laundromat, ice and a playground are available. A cafe is located within one mile. Small, leashed pets are permitted.

Reservations, fee: Reservations accepted; $15-$20.50 fee per night; MasterCard and Visa accepted. Open all year.

Who to contact: Phone (800) 621-6628 or (541) 343-4832 or write to Route 2, P.O. Box 353, Eugene, OR 97401.

Location: Drive seven miles north of Eugene on Interstate 5. Take the Coburg exit (exit 199) and go 400 yards west to the campground access. Turn left and drive up the driveway.

Trip note: Eugene is one of Oregon's major cities, but it offers many riverside parks and hiking opportunities. Both the Willamette and McKenzie rivers run right through town. The McKenzie, in particular, provides good trout fishing. Nearby recreation options include a golf course and tennis courts.

---

47. EUGENE MOBILE VILLAGE **RV**

Reference: **Near Willamette River; map D2, grid d0.**

Campsites, facilities: There are 30 drive-through sites for trailers or RVs of any length. Electricity, piped water and sewer hookups are provided. Flush toilets, sanitary services, showers and a laundromat are available. Bottled gas, a store, a cafe and ice are located within one mile. Leashed pets are permitted.

Reservations, fee: Reservations accepted; $15-$17 fee per night; MasterCard and Visa accepted. Open all year.

Who to contact: Phone (541) 747-2257 or write to 4750 Franklin Boulevard, Eugene, OR 97403.

Location: In Eugene, take exit 189 off Interstate 5, then proceed one mile on Franklin Boulevard to the park on the left.

Trip note: This motor home park is in Eugene, one mile away from the Willamette River (see the trip note for Eugene Kamping World). The camp is wooded, but close to many attractions. Nearby recreation options include a golf course, bike paths, a full-service marina and tennis courts.

---

48. CHALET VILLAGE ANNEX **RV**

Reference: **Near Willamette and McKenzie rivers; map D2, grid d0.**

Campsites, facilities: There are 24 drive-through sites for trailers and 121 sites for RVs of any length. Electricity, piped water and sewer hookups are provided. Flush toilets, sanitary services, showers. A recreation hall and a swimming pool are available for RV campers only. Bottled gas, a store, a cafe, a laundromat and ice are within 100 yards. Small (15 pounds or less), leashed pets are permitted.

Reservations, fee: Reservations accepted; $15 fee per night; $70 per week and $234 per month; $1 pet fee. Open all year.

Who to contact: Phone (541) 747-8311 or write to 205 South 54th Street, Springfield, OR 97478.

Location: From Interstate 5 at Springfield, take exit 194 and drive seven miles on Highway 126, then turn west on Main Street and continue one block. Turn south on 54th Street and proceed one block to the park on the left.

Trip note: This is an urban RV park, a layover-only spot. Springfield is set on the outskirts of Eugene, close to the Willamette and McKenzie rivers. Highway 126 heading east borders the McKenzie River, known for good trout fishing and rafting opportunities.

---

49. VIDA-LEA MOBILE LODGE   RV

Reference: **On McKenzie River; map D2, grid d2.**

Campsites, facilities: There are 13 drive-through sites for trailers or RVs of any length in this adult only campground. Electricity, piped water and sewer hookups are provided. Flush toilets, sanitary services, showers and a laundromat are available. Leashed pets (one per unit) and motorbikes are permitted. Boat docks and launching facilities are nearby.

Reservations, fee: Reservations accepted; $16 fee per night. Open all year.

Who to contact: Phone (541) 896-3898 or write to 44221 McKenzie Highway, Leaburg, OR 97489.

Location: From Interstate 5 at Eugene, turn east on Highway 126 and drive 16 miles to Leaburg. Continue three miles east on Highway 126 to the park.

Trip note: This private resort is set along the banks of the scenic McKenzie River. Ben and Kay Dorris State Park, which is open for day use, is about six miles east of the campground on Highway 126 and is also set along the McKenzie River. Nearby recreation options include a golf course, hiking trails and bike paths.

---

50. LAZY DAYS   RV

Reference: **On McKenzie River; map D2, grid d4.**

Campsites, facilities: There are 24 drive-through sites for trailers or RVs of any length. Electricity, piped water, sewer hookups and picnic tables are provided. Flush toilets, bottled gas, telephones, storage lockers, showers, cable TV, firewood and a laundromat are available. Leashed pets are permitted. Boat launching facilities are nearby.

Reservations, fee: Reservations accepted; $15 fee per night for a maximum of four campers per site. Open all year.

Who to contact: Phone (541) 822-3889 or write to 52511 McKenzie, Blue River, OR 97413.

Location: From Interstate 5 at Eugene, turn east on Highway 126 and drive 37 miles to the town of Blue River. Continue 1.5 miles east on Highway 126 to the park on the left.

Trip note: This motor home park is set along the banks of the McKenzie River, not far from Blue River Reservoir. This lake covers about 1,400 acres and offers opportunities for fishing, swimming and waterskiing. A golf course and several restaurants are nearby.

---

51. PATIO RV PARK   RV

Reference: **Near South Fork of McKenzie River; map D2, grid d4.**

Campsites, facilities: There are 60 sites for trailers or RVs of any length in this adult-only campground. Electricity, piped water, sewer hookups and picnic tables are provided. Flush toilets, bottled gas, sanitary services, showers, firewood, a recreation hall and a laundromat are available. A store, a cafe and ice are within one mile. Leashed pets are permitted.

Reservations, fee: Reservations accepted; $18-$20 fee per night. Open all year, weather permitting.

Who to contact: Phone (541) 822-3596 or write to 55636 McKenzie, Blue River, OR 97413.

Location: From Interstate 5 at Springfield, turn east on Highway 126 and drive 37 miles to the town of Blue River. Continue east for six miles on Highway 126, then drive two miles east on McKenzie River Drive to the park on the right.

Trip note: This motor home park is set near the banks of the South Fork of the McKenzie River, not far from Cougar Lake, which offers opportunities for fishing, swimming and waterskiing. Nearby recreation options include a golf course, hiking trails and bike paths.

---

52.   DELTA   RV

Reference: **On McKenzie River in Willamette National Forest; map D2, grid d5.**

Campsites, facilities: There are 38 sites for tents, trailers or RVs up to 21 feet long. Picnic tables and fire grills are provided. Hand-pumped water and vault toilets are available. Some facilities are **wheelchair accessible**. Leashed pets are permitted.

Reservations, fee: No reservations; $14 fee per night. Open mid-May to late September.

Who to contact: Phone the Blue River Ranger District at (541) 822-3317 or write P.O. Box 199, Blue River, OR 97413.

Location: From Interstate 5 at Springfield, turn east on Highway 126 and drive 37 miles to the town of Blue River. Continue east on Highway 126 for another five miles. Turn south (right) on Forest Service Road 19 (Aufderheide Scenic Byway). Drive one-quarter of a mile, then turn right on Forest Service Road 400 and continue one mile to the campground.

Trip note: This popular campground is set along the banks of the McKenzie River in a stand of old-growth Douglas fir. The Delta Old Growth Nature Trail, a one-quarter-mile **wheelchair-accessible** interpretive trail, is routed through the campground. There is an amphitheater in the camp as well. Blue River Reservoir and Cougar Reservoir are nearby, both of which offer trout fishing, waterskiing and swimming.

---

53.   SLIDE CREEK   RV

Reference: **On Cougar Lake in Willamette National Forest; map D2, grid d5.**

Campsites, facilities: There are 16 sites for tents, trailers or RVs. Picnic tables and fire grills are provided. Hand-pumped water and vault toilets are available. Leashed pets are permitted. A boat ramp is available.

Reservations, fee: No reservations; $7-$14 fee per night. Open mid-May to mid-September.

Who to contact: Phone the Blue River Ranger District at (541) 822-3317 or write to P.O. Box 199, Blue River, OR 97413.

Location: From Interstate 5 at Springfield, turn east on Highway 126 and drive 37 miles to the town of Blue River. Continue east for five miles, then travel south on Forest Service Road 19 (Aufderheide Scenic Byway) for 11 miles. Take the

Eastside Road 500 for 1.5 miles along the east side of Cougar Reservoir to the campground.

Trip note: This campground is on the banks of Cougar Reservoir, which covers about 1,300 acres and offers opportunities for fishing and swimming. This is a pretty lakeside camp that is quite popular. Plan to arrive early on weekends.

---

54.   FRENCH PETE   🆁🆅

Reference: **On the South Fork of McKenzie River in Willamette National Forest; map D2, grid d5.**

Campsites, facilities: There are 17 sites for tents, trailers or RVs. Picnic tables and fire grills are provided. Hand-pumped water and vault toilets are available. Some facilities are **wheelchair accessible**. Leashed pets are permitted.

Reservations, fee: No reservations; $7-$14 fee per night. Open mid-May to mid-September.

Who to contact: Phone the Blue River Ranger District at (541) 822-3317 or write to P.O. Box 199, Blue River, OR 97413.

Location: From Interstate 5 near Springfield, take the Highway 126 exit and turn east. Drive 37 miles to the town of Blue River. Continue east for 5 miles on Highway 126, then turn south on Forest Service Road 19 (Aufderheide Drive) and travel 12 miles to the campground.

Trip note: This quiet, wooded campground is on the banks of the South Fork of the McKenzie River and French Pete Creek. There is a trail across the road from the campground that provides access to the Three Sisters Wilderness. Two more primitive camps (Homestead and Frissell Crossing) are a few miles southeast on the same road.

---

55.   McKENZIE BRIDGE   🆁🆅

Reference: **On McKenzie River in Willamette National Forest; map D2, grid d5.**

Campsites, facilities: There are 20 sites for tents, trailers or RVs up to 35 feet long. Picnic tables and fire grills are provided. Vault toilets and hand-pumps for water are available. Leashed pets are permitted.

Reservations, fee: Some sites may be reserved by calling (800) 280-CAMP ($7.75 reservation fee); $8 fee per night; $4 each additional vehicle. Open late May to early September.

Who to contact: Phone the McKenzie Ranger District at (541) 822-3381 or write to Willamette National Forest, 7600 McKenzie Highway, McKenzie Bridge, OR 97413.

Location: From Interstate 5 near Springfield, take the Highway 126 exit and turn east. Drive 46 miles to the campground, located one mile west of the town of McKenzie Bridge.

Trip note: This campground is set along the banks of the McKenzie River, near the town of McKenzie Bridge. There's good evening fly fishing for trout during summer on this stretch of river.

---

56.   HORSE CREEK GROUP CAMP   🆁🆅

Reference: **On Horse Creek in Willamette National Forest; map D2, grid d5.**

Campsites, facilities: There are eight tent sites and 13 sites for trailers or RVs up to 21 feet long. Picnic tables and fire grills are provided. Piped water, vault toilets and firewood are available. Leashed pets are permitted.

Reservations, fee: Reservations required. Call (800) 280-CAMP; $40-$60 fee per night. Open March through September.

Who to contact: Phone the McKenzie Ranger District at (541) 822-3381 or write to Willamette National Forest, 57600 McKenzie Highway, McKenzie Bridge, OR 97413.

Location: From Interstate 5 near Springfield, take the Highway 126 exit and turn east. Drive 47 miles to the town of McKenzie Bridge. Turn south on Horse Creek Road and drive three miles to the campground.

Trip note: This campground is reserved for groups. It is set along the banks of Horse Creek, near the town of McKenzie Bridge. Harris Wayside State Park is a possible side trip option, with hiking trails and wildlife viewing available. The park is available for day use only.

---

57. PARADISE   RV.

Reference: **On McKenzie River in Willamette National Forest; map D2, grid d6.**

Campsites, facilities: There are 64 sites for tents, trailers or RVs up to 40 feet long. Picnic tables and fire grills are provided. Flush toilets, piped water and firewood are available. Leashed pets are permitted.

Reservations, fee: Reserve some sites by calling (800) 280-CAMP ($7.75 reservation fee); $9 fee per night; $4.50 each additional vehicle. Open late May to early September.

Who to contact: Phone the McKenzie Ranger District at (541) 822-3381 or write to Willamette National Forest, 57600 McKenzie Highway, McKenzie Bridge, OR 97413.

Location: From Interstate 5 near Springfield, take the Highway 126 exit and turn east. Drive 47 miles to the town of McKenzie Bridge. Continue 3.5 miles east on Highway 126 to the campground.

Trip note: This campground is set along the banks of the McKenzie River. Here, you are right off the highway but in a rustic, streamside setting with access to the McKenzie River National Recreation Trail. Trout fishing can be good. See the trip note for McKenzie Bridge for other options.

---

58. LIMBERLOST

Reference: **On Lost Creek in Willamette National Forest; map D2, grid d6.**

Campsites, facilities: There are 12 sites for tents or small trailers (no longer than 35 feet). Picnic tables and fire grills are provided. Pit toilets are available, but there is **no piped water**. Leashed pets are permitted.

Reservations, fee: No reservations; $5.50 fee per night; $2.75 each additional vehicle. Open late May to early September.

Who to contact: Phone the McKenzie Ranger District at (541)822-3381 or write to Willamette National Forest, 57600 McKenzie Highway, McKenzie Bridge, OR 97413.

Location: From Interstate 5 near Springfield, take the Highway 126 exit and turn east. Drive 47 miles to the town of McKenzie Bridge. Continue four miles east on Highway 126, then drive 1.5 miles on Highway 242 to the camp. Note: Highway 242 is spectacularly scenic, but also very narrow, windy and steep. RVs and trailers are discouraged.

Trip note: This little campground is set along Lost Creek about two miles from where it empties into the McKenzie River. Hidden and secluded, it's a good base camp for a trout fishing trip.

59.   ALDER SPRINGS

Reference: **In Willamette National Forest; map D2, grid d6.**

Campsites, facilities: There are six tent sites. **No piped water** is available. Picnic tables and fire grills are provided. Pit toilets are available. Leashed pets are permitted.

Reservations, fee: No reservations; no fee. Open late May to early September.

Who to contact: Phone the McKenzie Ranger District at (541) 822-3381 or write to Willamette National Forest, McKenzie Bridge, OR 97413.

Location: From Interstate 5 near Springfield, take the Highway 126 exit and turn east. Drive 47 miles to the town of McKenzie Bridge. Continue east on Highway 126 for seven miles, then head east on Highway 242 for eight miles to the campground. Note: Highway 242 is spectacularly scenic, but also very narrow, windy and steep. RVs and trailers are discouraged.

Trip note: This remote campground is set at 3,600 feet and offers good hiking possibilities. A map of Willamette National Forest details the nearby back roads and trails. The Three Sisters Wilderness Area is located just south of the highway.

---

60.   LAVA CAMP LAKE   **RV**

Reference: **Near Pacific Crest Trail in Deschutes National Forest; map D2, grid d7.**

Campsites, facilities: There are 10 sites for tents, trailers or RVs up to 22 feet long. Picnic tables and fire grills are provided. Pit toilets are available. There is **no piped water**. Leashed pets are permitted.

Reservations, fee: No reservations; no fee. Open June to September, weather permitting.

Who to contact: Phone the Sisters Ranger District at (541) 549-2111 or write to Deschutes National Forest, P.O. Box 249, Sisters, OR 97759.

Location: From Interstate 5 at Albany, take exit 233 and turn east on US 20. Drive 100 miles to Sisters. Turn southwest on Highway 242 and drive 17 miles west to the campground.

Trip note: This wooded campground is set at 5,200 feet in the McKenzie Pass, not far from the Pacific Crest Trail. Other trails provide hiking possibilities as well. A map of Deschutes National Forest details back roads, trails and streams.

---

61.   WHISPERING PINE HORSE CAMP   **RV**

Reference: **Near Trout Creek Swamp in Deschutes National Forest; map D2, grid d8.**

Campsites, facilities: There are nine primitive sites for tents, trailers, or RVs. Picnic tables and fire grills are provided. Pit toilets are available. There is **no piped water**. Leashed pets are permitted.

Reservations, fee: No reservations; $5 fee per night; $3 each additional vehicle. Open June to September.

Who to contact: Phone the Sisters Ranger District at (541) 549-2111 or write to Deschutes National Forest, P.O. Box 249, Sisters, OR 97759.

Location: From Interstate 5 at Albany, take exit 233 and turn east on US 20. Drive 100 miles to Sisters. Turn southwest on Highway 242 and drive 11 miles on Highway 242 and Forest Service Road 1018 to the campground.

Trip note: This wooded campground is set at 4,400 feet near Trout Creek Swamp.

It is a pretty camp, isolated and private. Be sure to bring your own water. It is primarily set up as a horse camp with corrals. Although it is generally not crowded, groups of horse users fill up the camp occasionally.

62.   TODD LAKE

Reference: **On Todd Lake, hike-in only; in Deschutes National Forest; map D2, grid d8.**

Campsites, facilities: There are 11 tent sites. Picnic tables and fire grills are provided. Vault toilets are available. There is **no piped water**. Leashed pets are permitted.

Reservations, fee: No reservations; no fee. Open July to October.

Who to contact: Phone the Bend Ranger District at (541) 388-5664 or write to Deschutes National Forest, 1230 NE Third Street, Bend, OR 97701.

Location: From Interstate 5 at Albany, turn east on US 20 and drive 122 miles to Bend. Drive 25 miles west on Cascade Lakes Highway (Highway 46), then about one mile north on Forest Service Road 370. It is a one-half mile hike to the campground.

Trip note: This small campground is set along the shore of an alpine lake at 6,200 feet. It is popular for canoeing and offers great views. This is one of the numerous campsites in the area that offer a pristine mountain experience, yet can be reached by car.

63.   DEVIL'S LAKE

Reference: **On Devil's Lake, walk-in only; in Deschutes National Forest; map D2, grid d8.**

Campsites, facilities: There are nine walk-in tent sites. Picnic tables and fire grills are provided. Vault toilets are available. There is **no piped water**. Leashed pets are permitted.

Reservations, fee: No reservations; no fee. Open July to October.

Who to contact: Phone the Bend Ranger District at (541) 388-5664 or write to Deschutes National Forest, 1230 NE Third Street, Bend, OR 97701.

Location: From Interstate 5 at Albany, turn east on US 20 and drive 122 miles to Bend. From Bend, travel 27 miles west on Cascade Lakes Highway (Highway 46). Walk 200 yards to the campground.

Trip note: This walk-in campground is set along the shore of a scenic alpine lake with water that is an aqua-jade color. Devil's Lake is a popular rafting and canoeing spot, and there are several trailheads that lead from the lake into the wilderness.

64.   SODA CREEK   RV

Reference: **Near Sparks Lake in Deschutes National Forest; map D2, grid d8.**

Campsites, facilities: There are four tent sites and eight sites for tents, trailers or RVs up to 22 feet long. Picnic tables and fire grills are provided. Vault toilets are available. There is **no piped water**. Leashed pets are permitted.

Reservations, fee: No reservations; no fee. Open July to October.

Who to contact: Phone the Bend Ranger District at (541) 388-5664 or write to Deschutes National Forest, 1230 NE Third Street, Bend, OR 97701.

Location: From Interstate 5 at Albany, turn east on US 20 and drive 122 miles to Bend. From Bend, drive 25 miles west on Cascade Lakes Highway (Highway 46), then about 100 yards south on Forest Service Road 400.

Trip note: This campground is located on the road to Sparks Lake, nestled between two meadows in a pastoral setting. Boating, particularly canoeing,is ideal here. Only fly fishing is permitted.

65.　　THREE CREEKS LAKE　　RV

Reference: **On Three Creeks Lake in Deschutes National Forest; map D2, grid d9.**

Campsites, facilities: There are 10 sites for tents, trailers or RVs up to 16 feet long. Picnic tables and fire grills are provided. Vault toilets are available. There is **no piped water**. Leashed pets are permitted. Boat docks, launching facilities and rentals are nearby. Boats with motors are not permitted.

Reservations, fee: No reservations; $5 fee per night; $3 each additional vehicle. Open mid-June to mid-September, weather permitting.

Who to contact: Phone the Sisters Ranger District at (541) 549-2111 or write to Deschutes National Forest, P.O. Box 249, Sisters, OR 97759.

Location: From Interstate 5 at Albany, turn east on US 20 and drive 100 miles to Sisters. Turn south on Forest Service Road 16 and travel 18 miles to the campground.

Trip note: This wooded campground is set along the south shore of Three Creeks Lake in a pretty spot at 6,400 feet elevation. Fishing, swimming, hiking and non-motorized boating are the highlights. See also trip note for Driftwood.

66.　　DRIFTWOOD　　RV

Reference: **On Three Creeks Lake in Deschutes National Forest; map D2, grid d9.**

Campsites, facilities: There are 12 tent sites and five sites for tents, trailers or RVs up to 16 feet long. Picnic tables and fire grills are provided. Pit toilets are available. There is **no piped water**. Leashed pets are permitted. Boat docks, launching facilities and rentals are nearby. Motorboats are not permitted.

Reservations, fee: No reservations; $5 fee per night; $3 each additional vehicle. Open mid-June to mid-September, weather permitting.

Who to contact: Phone the Sisters Ranger District at (541) 549-2111 or write to Deschutes National Forest, P.O. Box 249, Sisters, OR 97759.

Location: From Interstate 5 at Albany, turn east on US 20 and drive 100 miles to Sisters. Turn south on Forest Service Road 16 and travel 18 miles to the camp.

Trip note: This wooded campground is set at an elevation of 6,400 feet, and snowdrifts often block the camp until July 4. Although it is on the lakeshore hidden from outsiders, the area can get very crowded. The campground is full most weekends from July 4 to Labor Day. Fishing, swimming, hiking and non-motorized boating are some of the recreation options.

67.　　SCHWARZ PARK　　RV

Reference: **On Dorena Lake; map D2, grid e0.**

Campsites, facilities: There are 80 sites for trailers or RVs of any length. Picnic tables and fire grills are provided. Flush toilets, sanitary services and showers are available. A store is within one mile. Pets and motorbikes are permitted, (but no off-road cycles without proof of insurance). Boat docks and launching facilities are nearby.

Reservations, fee: No reservations; $7-$10 fee per night. Open April to September.

Who to contact: Phone (541) 942-5631 or write to Army Corps of Engineers

Recreation Information, Cottage Grove, OR 97424.

Location: From Interstate 5 south of Eugene, take exit 174 in Cottage Grove, then drive four miles east on Row Road to the campground entrance.

Trip note: This large campground is set below the Dorena Lake on the Row River, where fishing, swimming, boating and waterskiing are among the recreation options.

---

68. DOLLY VARDEN   **RV**

Reference: **On Fall Creek in Willamette National Forest; map D2, grid e1.**

Campsites, facilities: There are three sites for tents and two sites for tents, trailers or RVs up to 16 feet long. Picnic tables and fire grills are provided. Vault toilets are available. There is **no piped water**. Leashed pets are permitted.

Reservations, fee: No reservations; $7 fee per night; $5 each additional vehicle. Open May to mid-September.

Who to contact: Phone the Lowell Ranger District at (541) 937-2129 or write to Willamette National Forest, 60 Pioneer Street, Lowell, OR 97452.

Location: From Interstate 5 south of Eugene, take exit 188 and turn east on Highway 58. Drive about 15 miles to Lowell, then drive two miles north on County Road 6220. Turn east on County Road 6240 and drive a short distance to Forest Service Road 18 (Fall Creek Road), then continue east to the campground. The total distance on the two roads is about 10 miles.

Trip note: This pretty campground is adjacent to Fall Creek and is at the lower trailhead for the scenic, 14-mile Fall Creek National Recreation Trail. This trail follows the creek and ranges between 960 and 1,385 feet in elevation.

---

69. DEXTER SHORES   **RV**
MOTORHOME & RV PARK

Reference: **Near Lookout Point Reservoir; map D2, grid e1.**

Campsites, facilities: There are 80 sites for trailers or RVs. Electricity, piped water, sewer-, cable TV- and telephone hookups and picnic tables are provided. Flush toilets, sanitary services, showers, firewood, a laundromat and a playground are available. Bottled gas, a cafe and ice are within one mile. Pets and motorbikes are permitted. Boat docks and launching facilities are nearby.

Reservations, fee: Reservations accepted; $18 fee per night. Open all year.

Who to contact: Phone (541) 937-3711 or write to P.O. Box 70, Dexter, OR 97431.

Location: From Interstate 5 south of Eugene, take exit 188 and turn east on Highway 58. Drive 11.5 miles, then turn south on Dexter Road and drive one block south to the park on the right.

Trip note: If you are traveling on Interstate 5, this motor home park is well worth the 15-minute drive out of Springfield. It is set across the street from Lookout Point Reservoir, where fishing and boating are permitted and within walking distance of Lookout Point. Swimming and waterskiing are allowed on nearby Dexter and Fall Creek lakes.

---

70. BAKER BAY COUNTY PARK   **RV**

Reference: **On Dorena Lake; map D2, grid e1.**

Campsites, facilities: There are 52 sites for tents, trailers or self-contained RVs up to 35 feet long. There are also two group sites. Picnic tables and fire grills are provided. Piped water and sanitary services are available. A store is located within two miles. Leashed pets are permitted. Boat docks and launching facilities are nearby.

Reservations, fee: Reservations for group sites only; $12 fee per night; $35 group site fee. Open late April to October.

Who to contact: Phone (541) 942-7669 or write to Lane County Recreation Department, Eugene, OR 97401.

Location: From Interstate 5 south of Eugene, take exit 174 (Dorena Lake exit) in Cottage Grove, then drive six miles east on Shore View Drive to the campground entrance on the left.

Trip note: This campground is set along the shore of Dorena Lake, a reservoir where fishing, waterskiing, canoeing, swimming and boating are among the recreation options here.

---

71.   WINBERRY   RV

Reference: On Winberry Creek in Willamette National Forest; map D2, grid e2.

Campsites, facilities: There are five sites for tents, and two sites for trailers or RVs up to 16 feet long. Picnic tables and fire grills are provided. Hand-pumped water and vault toilets are available. Leashed pets are permitted.

Reservations, fee: No reservations; $8-$10 fee per night; $4-$5 each additional vehicle. Open late May to mid-September.

Who to contact: Phone the Lowell Ranger District at (541) 937-2129 or write to Willamette National Forest, 60 Pioneer Street, Lowell, OR 97452.

Location: From Interstate 5 south of Eugene, take exit 188 and turn east on Highway 58. Drive about 15 miles to Lowell, then drive two miles north on County Road 6220. Turn on County Road 6245 (Winberry Road) and drive six miles southeast, then continue 3.5 miles on Forest Service Road 1802 to the campground.

Trip note: This campground is located on Winberry Creek. A little inside knowledge: On the map, Lookout Point Reservoir appears to be about three miles away, but to get there, you have to drive nine miles to Lowell, at the north end of the reservoir. The closest hiking option is just downstream from the campground on Forest Service Road 1802-150. Be cautious—there is poison oak at the top.

---

72.   BIG POOL   RV

Reference: On Fall Creek in Willamette National Forest; map D2, grid e2.

Campsites, facilities: There are three tent sites and two sites for tents, trailers or RVs up to 16 feet long. Picnic tables and fire grills are provided. Vault toilets are available. There is **no piped water**. Leashed pets are permitted.

Reservations, fee: No reservations; $7 fee per night; $5 each additional vehicle. Open May to mid-September.

Who to contact: Phone the Lowell Ranger District at (541) 937-2129 or write to Willamette National Forest, 60 Pioneer Street, Lowell, OR 97452.

Location: From Interstate 5 south of Eugene, take exit 188 and turn east on Highway 58. Drive about 15 miles to Lowell. Turn north on County Road 6220 and drive two miles, then 10 miles east on County Road 6240 and 1.5 miles on Forest Service Road 18 (Fall Creek Road) to the campground.

Trip note: This campground is set along Fall Creek at about 1,000 feet. It is quiet, secluded and primitive. The scenic Fall Creek National Recreation Trail passes camp on the other side of the creek. See the trip note for Dolly Varden.

73. BLACK CANYON RV

Reference: On the Middle Fork of Willamette River in Willamette National Forest; map D2, grid e2.

Campsites, facilities: There are 75 sites for tents, trailers or RVs up to 22 feet long. Picnic tables and fire grills are provided. Piped water, vault toilets and firewood are available. Sanitary services, a cafe and a laundromat are within five miles. Some of the facilities are **wheelchair accessible**. Leashed pets are permitted. Launching facilities are nearby at the south end of Lookout Point Lake.

Reservations, fee: No reservations; $9-$16 fee per night; $5 each additional vehicle. Open May to late October.

Who to contact: Phone the Lowell Ranger District at (541) 937-2129 or write to Willamette National Forest, 60 Pioneer Street, Lowell, OR 97452.

Location: From Interstate 5 south of Eugene, take exit 188 and drive 30 miles southeast on Highway 58. The camp is located six miles west of Oakridge.

Trip note: This campground is set along the banks of the Middle Fork of the Willamette River, not far from Lookout Point Reservoir, where fishing and boating are popular. The camp is pretty and wooded, with comfortable sites. Weekend programs are offered in the amphitheater in July and August.

---

74. BEDROCK RV

Reference: On Fall Creek in Willamette National Forest; map D2, grid e3.

Campsites, facilities: There are 20 sites for tents, trailers or RVs up to 22 feet long. Picnic tables and fire grills are provided. Vault toilets and hand-pumped water are available. Leashed pets are permitted.

Reservations, fee: No reservations; $9-$11 fee per night; $5 each additional vehicle. Open May to late October.

Who to contact: Phone the Lowell Ranger District at (541) 937-2129 or write to Willamette National Forest, 60 Pioneer Street, Lowell, OR 97452.

Location: From Interstate 5 south of Eugene, take exit 188 and turn east on Highway 58. Drive about 15 miles to Lowell. Turn north on County Road 6220 and drive two miles, then 10 miles east on County Road 6240 and six miles on Forest Service Road 18 (Fall Creek Road) to the campground.

Trip note: This campground is set along the banks of Fall Creek. It is one of the access points for the scenic Fall Creek National Recreation Trail. See the trip note for Dolly Varden for trail information. The campground is also adjacent to the Jones Trail, which heads north for about six miles before joining a forest service road.

---

75. PUMA CREEK RV

Reference: On Fall Creek in Willamette National Forest; map D2, grid e3.

Campsites, facilities: There are 11 sites for tents, trailers or RVs up to 16 feet long. Picnic tables and fire grills are provided. Vault toilets and hand-pumped water are available. Leashed pets are permitted.

Reservations, fee: No reservations; $9 fee per night; $3 each additional vehicle. Open May to late October.

Who to contact: Phone the Lowell Ranger District at (541) 937-2129 or write to Willamette National Forest, 60 Pioneer Street, Lowell, OR 97452.

Location: From Interstate 5 south of Eugene, take exit 188 and turn east on Highway 58. Drive about 15 miles to Lowell. Turn north on County Road 6220 and drive two miles, then 10 miles east on County Road 6240 and 6.5 miles east on Forest Service Road 18 (Fall Creek Road) to the campground.

Trip note: This campground is set along the banks of Fall Creek, across from the Fall Creek National Recreation Trail. It is one of four camps in the immediate area. See above trip notes.

76. SHADY DELL   RV

Reference: **On the Middle Fork of Willamette River in Willamette National Forest; map D2, grid e3.**

Campsites, facilities: There are nine sites for tents, trailers or RVs up to 15 feet long. Picnic tables and fire grills are provided. Hand-pumped water, vault toilets and firewood are available. Sanitary services, a cafe and a laundromat are available within five miles. Some of the facilities are **wheelchair accessible**. Leashed pets are permitted.

Reservations, fee: No reservations; $9 fee per night; $5 each additional vehicle. Open May to late October.

Who to contact: Phone the Lowell Ranger District at (541) 937-2129 or write to Willamette National Forest, 60 Pioneer Street, Lowell, OR 97452.

Location: From Interstate 5 south of Eugene, take exit 188 and drive 33 miles southeast on Highway 58. The camp is located five miles west of Oakridge.

Trip note: This campground is set along the banks of the Middle Fork of the Willamette River, across from Lookout Point Lake, a long narrow reservoir that sits adjacent to Highway 58. Noteworthy is a stand of old growth cedars.

77. SALMON CREEK FALLS   RV

Reference: **On Salmon Creek in Willamette National Forest; map D2, grid e3.**

Campsites, facilities: There are 14 sites for tents, trailers or RVs up to 24 feet long. Picnic tables and fire grills are provided. Hand-pumped water and vault toilets are available. A store, a cafe, a laundromat and ice are available within five miles. Leashed pets are permitted.

Reservations, fee: No reservations; $8-$10 fee per night; $4-$5 each additional vehicle. Open late April to mid-October.

Who to contact: Phone the Oakridge Ranger District at (541) 782-2291, or write Willamette National Forest, 46375 Highway 58, Westfir, OR 97492.

Location: From Interstate 5 south of Eugene, take exit 188 and drive 35 miles southeast on Highway 58 to Oakridge. Turn left and drive 3.5 miles northeast on Forest Service Road 24 (Salmon Creek Road) to the campground.

Trip note: This campground is set along the bank of Salmon Creek at an elevation of 1,500 feet. It is just far enough from Highway 58 to get missed by most campers. There are wild thimbleberries and hazelnuts to pick in the summer. It's pretty, with both sunny and shaded sites, and easy access. The camp is adjacent to the falls.

78. KIAHANIE   RV

Reference: **On the Middle Fork of Willamette River in Willamette National Forest; map D2, grid e4.**

Campsites, facilities: There are 19 sites for tents, trailers or RVs up to 24 feet long. Picnic tables and fire grills are provided. Hand-pumped water and vault toilets are available. Leashed pets are permitted.

Reservations, fee: No reservations; $8-$10 fee per night; $4-$5 each additional vehicle. Open late April through October.

Who to contact: Phone the Oakridge Ranger District at (541) 782-2291 or write to Willamette National Forest, 46375 Highway 58, Westfir, OR 97492.

Location: From Interstate 5 south of Eugene, take exit 188 and drive 35 miles southeast on Highway 58 to Oakridge. Continue two miles to Westfir. Head 19 miles northeast on Forest Service Road 19 (Aufderheide Scenic Byway) to the campground.

Trip note: We almost hate to reveal it, but this is one heck of a spot for fly fishing (the only kind allowed). This remote campground is set along the North Fork of the Middle Fork of the Willamette River, a designated Wild and Scenic river. You want beauty and quiet, you came to the right place. An even more remote campground is farther north on Forest Service Road 19 at Box Canyon Horse Camp.

---

79.   HOMESTEAD   **RV**

Reference: **On South Fork McKenzie River in Willamette National Forest; map D2, grid e4.**

Campsites, facilities: There are eight sites for tents, trailers or RVs. Picnic tables and fire grills are provided. Vault toilets and hand-pumped water are available. Leashed pets are permitted.

Reservations, fee: No reservations; no fee. Open mid-May to mid-September.

Who to contact: Phone the Blue River Ranger District at (541) 822-3317 or write to P.O. Box 199, Blue River, OR 97413.

Location: From Interstate 5 at Eugene, turn east on Highway 126 and drive 37 miles to the town of Blue River. Continue east for five miles, then drive south on Forest Service Road 19 (Aufderheide Drive) for 17 miles to the camp.

Trip note: This quiet little campground is set along the banks of the South Fork of the McKenzie River. It's primitive, little-known and free. Frissell Crossing is nearby and has water available from a hand pump.

---

80.   FRISSELL CROSSING   **RV**

Reference: **Near Three Sisters Wilderness in Willamette National Forest; map D2, grid e4.**

Campsites, facilities: There are 12 sites for tents, trailers or RVs. Picnic tables and fire grills are provided. Hand-pumped water and vault toilets are available. Leashed pets are permitted.

Reservations, fee: No reservations; $7-$14 fee per night. Open mid-May to mid-September.

Who to contact: Phone the Blue River Ranger District at (541) 822-3317 or write to P.O. Box 199, Blue River, OR 97413.

Location: From Interstate 5 at Eugene, turn east on Highway 126 and drive 37 miles to the town of Blue River. Continue east for five miles, then drive south on Forest Service Road 19 (Aufderheide Drive) for 23 miles to the camp.

Trip note: This campground is at 2,600 feet and is on the banks of the South Fork of the McKenzie River, adjacent to a trailhead that provides access to the backcountry of the Three Sisters Wilderness. This is the only camp in the immediate area that has drinking water. Homestead Camp provides free, primitive alternatives.

81.   BLAIR LAKE

Reference: **On Blair Lake in Willamette National Forest; map D2, grid e4.**

Campsites, facilities: There are seven walk-in tent sites. Picnic tables are provided. Hand-pumped water, fire rings and a pit toilet are available. Leashed pets are permitted.

Reservations, fee: No reservations; $8-$10 fee per night; $4-$5 each additional vehicle. Open June to mid-October.

Who to contact: Phone the Oakridge Ranger District at (541) 782-2291 or write to Willamette National Forest, 46375 Highway 58, Westfir, OR 97492.

Location: From Interstate 5 south of Eugene, take exit 188 and turn east on Highway 58. Drive 35 miles to the town Oakridge, then travel one mile east on County Road 149. Turn left on Forest Service Road 24 and drive eight miles northeast, then travel seven miles on Forest Service Road 1934. This is a gravel road that is not recommended for RVs or trailers.

Trip note: This campground is set at 4,800 feet along the shore of little Blair Lake and is popular with equestrians. The sites are pretty, well-shaded and close to the lake. There are wildflowers and huckleberries in season. Boats without motors are permitted and fishing is good.

82.   BOX CANYON HORSE CAMP

Reference: **Near Chucksney Mountain in Willamette National Forest; map D2, grid e5.**

Campsites, facilities: There are 12 sites that allow horse and rider to camp close together. Picnic tables, fire grills and corrals are provided. A manure disposal site and vault toilets are available. There is **no piped water**. Leashed pets are permitted.

Reservations, fee: No reservations; no fee. Open mid-May to mid-September.

Who to contact: Phone the Blue River Ranger District at (541) 822-3317 or write to P.O. Box 199, Blue River, OR 97413.

Location: From Interstate 5 at Eugene, turn east on Highway 126 and drive 37 miles to the town of Blue River. Continue east for five miles, then drive 30 miles south on Forest Service Road 19 (Aufderheide Forest Drive).

Trip note: Only 80 miles from Eugene, this unique and secluded campground offers trails into several wilderness areas, including the Chucksney Mountain Trail, Crossing-Way Trail and Grasshopper Trail. It's a good base camp for a backpacking trip.

83.   WEST CULTUS

Reference: **On Cultus Lake (boat-in or hike-in only) in Deschutes National Forest; map D2, grid e6.**

Campsites, facilities: There are 12 boat-in or hike-in tent sites. Picnic tables and fire grills are provided. Vault toilets are available. There is **no piped water**. Leashed pets are permitted. Boat docks and launching facilities are available on site; boat rentals are available at the adjacent Cultus Lake Resort.

Reservations, fee: No reservations; no fee. There is a $5 overnight parking fee. Open June to late September.

Who to contact: Phone High Lakes Contractors at (541) 382-9443 or write P.O. Box 989, Bend, OR 97709. Or phone the Bend Ranger District at (541) 388-5664 or write to Deschutes National Forest, 1230 NE Third, Bend, OR 97701.

Location: From Interstate 5 at Albany, turn east on US 20 and drive 122 miles to Bend. Turn southwest on Cascade Lakes Highway (Highway 46) and drive 45 miles. Turn west on Forest Service Road 4635 and travel 1.5 miles to the parking area, then travel by boat about three miles to the west shore of the lake or hike the trail around the lake.

Trip note: This campground is set at 4,700 feet along the west shore of Cultus Lake. It is accessible by boat or trail only. It's about three miles by trail from the parking area to the campground. This is a good spot for waterskiing, fishing and swimming. Trails branch out from the campground and provide access to numerous small backcountry lakes.

---

84. IRISH AND TAYLOR

Reference: **Near Pacific Crest Trail in Deschutes National Forest; map D2, grid e6.**

Campsites, facilities: There are six tent sites. Picnic tables and fire grills are provided. Pit toilets are available. There is **no piped water**. Leashed pets are permitted.

Reservations, fee: No reservations; no fee. Open mid-June to mid-September.

Who to contact: Phone the Bend Ranger District at (541) 388-5664 or write to Deschutes National Forest, 1230 NE Third, Bend, OR 97701.

Location: From Interstate 5 at Albany, turn east on US 20 and drive 122 miles to Bend. Turn southwest on Cascade Lakes Highway (Highway 46) and drive 43 miles, then 3.5 miles southwest on Forest Service Road 4630. The camp is 6.5 miles west on Forest Service Road 600. This is a rough road (high-clearance vehicles only), but it's worth the ride.

Trip note: This remote campground is set between two small lakes, about a mile from the Pacific Crest Trail. Other nearby trails provide access into the backcountry. This camp is little known, beautiful and free.

---

85. POINT 🚐

Reference: **On Elk Lake in Deschutes National Forest; map D2, grid e7.**

Campsites, facilities: There are eight sites for tents, trailers or RVs up to 22 feet long, but be advised the sites are uneven and difficult for RVs. Picnic tables and fire grills are provided. Vault toilets and piped water are available. Leashed pets are permitted. Boat docks and launching facilities are on-site. Boat rentals, a store, restaurant, gas and propane are available at Elk Lake Resort, one mile away.

Reservations, fee: No reservations; $9 fee per night. Open late May to late September.

Who to contact: Phone High Lakes Contractors at (541) 382-9443 or write P.O. Box 989, Bend, OR 97709. Or phone the Bend Ranger District at (541) 388-5664 or write to Deschutes National Forest, 1230 NE Third Street, Bend, OR 97701.

Location: From Interstate 5 at Albany, turn east on US 20 and drive 122 miles to Bend. Turn southwest on Cascade Lakes Highway (Highway 46) and drive 33 miles to the campground entrance.

Trip note: This hidden campground is set along the shore of Elk Lake. Fishing can be good here; the same goes for hiking. A map of the Deschutes National Forest details the trails.

86.　　　　　　　　ELK LAKE　　　　　　　　RV

Reference: **On Elk Lake in Deschutes National Forest; map D2, grid e7.**

Campsites, facilities: There are 23 sites for tents, trailers or RVs up to 22 feet long, but be advised the sites are uneven and difficult for RVs. Picnic tables and fire grills are provided. Vault toilets and piped water are available. Leashed pets are permitted. Boat docks and launching facilities are on-site. Boat rentals are available nearby.

Reservations, fee: No reservations; $9 fee per night. Open June to October.

Who to contact: Phone the Bend Ranger District at (541) 388-5664 or write to Deschutes National Forest, 1230 NE Third Street, Bend, OR 97701.

Location: From Interstate 5 at Albany, turn east on US 20 and drive 122 miles to Bend. Turn southwest on Cascade Lakes Highway (Highway 46) and drive 33 miles to Elk Lake. The campground is on the southwest side of the lake.

Trip note: This campground is set along the shore of Elk Lake, adjacent to a private resort (Elk Lake Resort). See the trip note for Point for recreation options.

87.　　　　　　　CULTUS LAKE

Reference: **On Cultus Lake (boat-in only) in Deschutes National Forest; map D2, grid e7.**

Campsites, facilities: There are 54 sites for tents. Picnic tables and fire grills are provided. Piped water and vault toilets are available. Leashed pets are permitted. Boat docks and launching facilities are on-site. Boat rentals are nearby.

Reservations, fee: No reservations; $9 fee per night. Open June to October.

Who to contact: Phone High Lakes Contractors at (541) 382-9443 or write P.O. Box 989, Bend, OR 97709. Or phone the Bend Ranger District at (541) 388-5664 or write to Deschutes National Forest, 1230 NE Third, Bend, OR 97701.

Location: From Interstate 5 at Albany, turn east on US 20 and drive 122 miles to Bend. Turn southwest on Cascade Lakes Highway (Highway 46) and drive 45 miles. Turn west on Forest Service Road 4635 and travel 1.5 miles.

Trip note: This campground is along the east shore of Cultus Lake, not far from a resort. It is a popular spot for windsurfing, waterskiing, swimming, fishing and hiking.

88.　　　　　　LITTLE CULTUS LAKE　　　　RV

Reference: **On Little Cultus Lake in Deschutes National Forest; map D2, grid e7.**

Campsites, facilities: There are 10 sites for tents, trailers or RVs up to 22 feet long. Picnic tables and fire grills are provided. Hand-pumped water and vault toilets are available. Leashed pets are permitted. A boat launch is available.

Reservations, fee: No reservations; $5 fee per night.
Open late May to late September.

Who to contact: Phone High Lakes Contractors at (541) 382-9443 or write P.O. Box 989, Bend, OR 97709. Or phone the Bend Ranger District at (541) 388-5664 or write to Deschutes National Forest, 1230 NE Third, Bend, OR 97701.

Location: From Interstate 5 at Albany, turn east on US 20 and drive 122 miles to Bend. Turn southwest on Cascade Lakes Highway (Highway 46) and drive 45 miles. Turn west on Forest Service Road 4635 and drive one-half mile to Forest Service Road 4630 and turn left. Drive 1.5 miles to Forest Service Road 600, then turn left and drive one mile to the campground.

Trip note: This campground is set along the shore of Little Cultus Lake. The campsites are not clearly marked. It's a popular spot for swimming, fishing, boating (speed restricted) and hiking. Nearby trails access numerous backcountry lakes, and the Pacific Crest Trail passes about six miles west of the camp.

---

89. LAVA LAKE RV

Reference: **On Lava Lake in Deschutes National Forest; map D2, grid e7.**

Campsites, facilities: There are 43 sites for tents, trailers or RVs up to 22 feet long. Picnic tables and fire grills are provided. Vault toilets, piped water, showers, a laundromat, fish cleaning station and sanitary disposal services are available. Leashed pets are permitted. Boat docks and launching facilities on-site. Boat rentals are nearby.

Reservations, fee: No reservations; $10 fee per night. Open April 20 through October, weather permitting.

Who to contact: Phone High Lakes Contractors at (541) 382-9443 or write P.O. Box 989, Bend, OR 97709. Or phone the Bend Ranger District at (541) 388-5664 or write to Deschutes National Forest, 1230 NE Third Street, Bend, OR 97701.

Location: From Interstate 5 at Albany, turn east on US 20 and drive 122 miles to Bend. Turn southwest on Cascade Lakes Highway (Highway 46) and drive 38 miles to the entrance to Lava Lake. The campground is on the lake.

Trip note: This well-designed campground is set along the shore of pretty Lava Lake. Mount Bachelor and the Three Sisters are in the background, making a classic picture. Boating and fishing are popular here.

---

90. CULTUS CORRAL HORSE CAMP RV

Reference: **Near Cultus Lake in Deschutes National Forest; map D2, grid e7.**

Campsites, facilities: There are 11 sites for tents, trailers or RVs of any length. Picnic tables, fire grills four-horse corrals are provided. Hand pumped water, vault toilets and a corral are available. Leashed pets are permitted.

Reservations, fee: No reservations; $5 fee per night. Open June to October.

Who to contact: Phone High Lakes Contractors at (541) 382-9443 or write P.O Box 989, Bend, OR 97709. Or phone the Bend Ranger District at (541) 388-5664 or write to Deschutes National Forest, 1230 NE Third, Bend, OR 97701

Location: From Interstate 5 at Albany, turn east on US 20 and drive 122 miles to Bend. Turn southwest on Cascade Lakes Highway (Highway 46) and drive 43 miles. Turn right on Forest Service Road 4630, travel one-quarter mile to the campground entrance.

Trip note: This campground is about one mile from Cultus Lake, near many trails that provide access to backcountry lakes. The Pacific Crest Trail passes about 10 miles from the camp, making this a good base camp for a backpacking trip

---

91. COW MEADOW RV

Reference: **On Deschutes River in Deschutes National Forest; map D2, grid e7**

Campsites, facilities: There are 20 sites for tents for tents, trailers or RVs up to 16 feet long. Picnic tables and fire grills are provided. Vault toilets are available There is **no piped water**. Leashed pets are permitted. Boat docks and a launch are nearby at Crane Prairie Campground.

Reservations, fee: No reservations; $5 fee per night. Open May to mid-October

Who to contact: Phone High Lakes Contractors at (541) 382-9443 or write P.O

Box 989, Bend, OR 97709. Or phone the Bend Ranger District at (541) 388-5664 or write to Deschutes National Forest, 1230 NE Third, Bend, OR 97701.
Location: From Interstate 5 at Albany, turn east on US 20 and drive 122 miles to Bend. Turn southwest on Cascade Lakes Highway (Highway 46) and drive 44 miles. Turn east on Forest Service Road 620 and drive to the end of the road, about two miles, to the campground. Note: The entrance road can be muddy.
Trip note: This campground is set along the Deschutes River, near the north end of Crane Prairie Reservoir. It's a pretty spot and the price is right.

92. CRANE PRAIRIE   RV.

Reference: **On Crane Prairie Reservoir in Deschutes National Forest; map D2, grid e7.**
Campsites, facilities: There are 146 sites for tents, trailers or RVs. Picnic tables and fire grills are provided. Piped water and vault toilets are available. Leashed pets are permitted. Boat docks, launching facilities and a fish cleaning station are available on-site. Boat rentals, showers, gas and laundry facilities are available nearby.
Reservations, fee: No reservations; $10 fee per night. Open April 20 through October, weather permitting.
Who to contact: Phone High Lakes Contractors at (541) 382-9443 or write P.O. Box 989, Bend, OR 97709. Or phone the Bend Ranger District at (541)388-5664 or write to Deschutes National Forest, 1230 NE Third, Bend, OR 97701.
Location: From Interstate 5 at Albany, turn east on US 20 and drive 122 miles to Bend. Turn south on US 97 and drive 20 miles to County Road 42. Turn west and drive 21 miles to Forest Service Road 4270. Turn north and drive 4.5 miles to the campground entrance.
Trip note: This campground is set along the north shore of Crane Prairie Reservoir. Recreational options include fishing, boating and hiking.

93. CRANE PRAIRIE RESORT   RV.

Reference: **On Crane Prairie Reservoir; map D2, grid e7.**
Campsites, facilities: There are 20 sites for trailers or RVs. Electricity, piped water, sewer hookups and picnic tables are provided. Bottled gas, firewood, a store and ice are available. Leashed pets are permitted. Boat docks, launching facilities and rentals are nearby.
Reservations, fee: Reservations accepted; $10-$15 fee per night. MasterCard and Visa accepted. Open late April to mid-October.
Who to contact: Phone (541) 385-2173 or write to P.O. Box 322, LaPine, OR 97739.
Location: From Interstate 5 at Albany, turn east on US 20 and drive 122 miles to Bend. From Bend, travel 48 miles southwest on Highway 46 (Cascade Lakes Highway). Turn on Forest Service Road 4270 and drive seven miles to the resort entrance.
Trip note: This resort is set along the north shore of popular Crane Prairie Reservoir, a good spot for canoeing and fishing. No waterskiing is permitted.

94. LITTLE FAWN GROUP CAMP   RV.

Reference: **On Elk Lake in Deschutes National Forest; map D2, grid e8.**
Campsites, facilities: There are 18 sites for tents, trailers or RVs up to 22 feet long. Picnic tables, hand pumped water and fire grills are provided. Vault toilets are

available. Leashed pets are permitted. Boat docks, launching facilities and rentals are nearby on the southwest shore of the lake.

Reservations, fee: Reservations required; $50 fee per night. Open June to October.

Who to contact: Phone High Lakes Contractors at (541) 382-9443 or write P.O. Box 989, Bend, OR 97709. Or phone the Bend Ranger District at (541) 382-9443 or write to Deschutes National Forest, 1230 NE Third Street, Bend, OR 97701.

Location: From Interstate 5 at Albany, turn east on US 20 and drive 122 miles to Bend. Turn southwest on Cascade Lakes Highway (Highway 46) and drive 31 miles, then two miles southeast on Forest Service Road 470. The campground is on the east side of Elk Lake.

Trip note: This campground is set along the eastern shore of Elk Lake. You can choose between sites on the lake's edge or nestled nearby in the forest. There is a play area for children at one of the lake's inlets. See the trip note for Point for recreation options.

---

95. MALLARD MARSH RV

Reference: **On Hosmer Lake in Deschutes National Forest; map D2, grid e8.**

Campsites, facilities: There are 15 sites for tents, trailers or RVs up to 22 feet long. Picnic tables and fire grills are provided. Vault toilets and hand pumped water are available. Leashed pets are permitted. Boat launching facilities are available nearby.

Reservations, fee: No reservations; $5 fee per night. Open late May to late September.

Who to contact: Phone High Lakes Contractors at (541) 382-9443 or write P.O. Box 989, Bend, OR 97709. Or phone the Bend Ranger District at (541) 388-5664 or write to Deschutes National Forest, 1230 NE Third Street, Bend, OR 97701.

Location: From Interstate 5 at Albany, turn east on US 20 and drive 122 miles to Bend. Turn southwest on Cascade Lakes Highway (Highway 46) and drive 31 miles, then two miles southeast on Forest Service Road 4625 to the camp.

Trip note: This campground is set along the shore of Hosmer Lake, which is stocked with brown trout and Atlantic salmon and reserved for catch-and-release, fly fishing only. It is a quiet campground and the lake is ideal for canoeing. You'll get a pristine, quality angling experience.

---

96. SOUTH RV

Reference: **On Hosmer Lake in Deschutes National Forest; map D2, grid e8.**

Campsites, facilities: There are 23 sites for tents, trailers or RVs up to 22 feet long. Picnic tables and fire grills are provided. Vault toilets and hand pumped water are available. Leashed pets are permitted. Boat launch facilities are available.

Reservations, fee: No reservations; $5 fee per night. Open late May to late September.

Who to contact: Phone High Lakes Contractors at (541) 382-9443 or write P.O. Box 989, Bend, OR 97709. Or phone the Bend Ranger District at (541) 388-5664 or write to Deschutes National Forest, 1230 NE Third Street, Bend, OR 97701.

Location: From Interstate 5 at Albany, turn east on US 20 and drive 122 miles to Bend. Turn southwest on Cascade Lakes Highway (Highway 46) and drive 31 miles, then three miles southeast on Forest Service Road 4625 to the camp.

Trip note: This campground is set along the shore of Hosmer Lake. See the trip note for Mallard Marsh for recreation details.

---

97.   LITTLE LAVA LAKE   RV

Reference: **Near Lava Lake in Deschutes National Forest; map D2, grid e8.**

Campsites, facilities: There are 10 sites for tents, trailers or RVs up to 22 feet long. Picnic tables and fire grills are provided. Vault toilets and piped water are available. Leashed pets are permitted. Boat docks and rentals are nearby. Launching facilities are on site.

Reservations, fee: No reservations; $5 fee per night. Open June to late September.

Who to contact: Phone High Lakes Contractors at (541) 382-9443 or write P.O. Box 989, Bend, OR 97709. Or phone the Bend Ranger District at (541) 388-5664 or write to Deschutes National Forest, 1230 NE Third Street, Bend, OR 97701.

Location: From Interstate 5 at Albany, turn east on US 20 and drive 122 miles to Bend. Turn southwest on Cascade Lakes Highway (Highway 46) and drive 38 miles to the entrance to Lava Lake. The campground is on Little Lava Lake.

Trip note: The campsites at this popular campground are not well marked, but the camping area is near the lakeshore. Boating, fishing, swimming and hiking are some of the recreation options.

---

98.   MILE   RV

Reference: **On Deschutes River in Deschutes National Forest; map D2, grid e8.**

Campsites, facilities: There are 10 sites for tents, trailers or RVs up to 22 feet long. Picnic tables and fire grills are provided. Vault toilets are available. There is **no piped water**. Leashed pets are permitted.

Reservations, fee: No reservations; no fee. Open late May to late September.

Who to contact: Phone the Bend Ranger District at (541) 388-5664 or write to Deschutes National Forest, 1230 NE Third, Bend, OR 97701.

Location: From Interstate 5 at Albany, turn east on US 20 and drive 122 miles to Bend. Turn southwest on Cascade Lakes Highway (Highway 46) and drive 40 miles to the campground.

Trip note: This quiet campground is set along the banks of the Deschutes River. It's a quiet, primitive spot. Fishing and hiking are among your options here. See a Forest Service map for trail locations.

---

99.   DESCHUTES BRIDGE   RV

Reference: **On Deschutes River in Deschutes National Forest; map D2, grid e8.**

Campsites, facilities: There are 12 sites for tents, trailers or RVs up to 22 feet long. Picnic tables and fire grills are provided. Piped water and vault toilets are available. Leashed pets are permitted.

Reservations, fee: Reservations required only for groups, phone (541) 382-9443; $7 fee per night; $50 group fee (up to 75 people). Open June to October.

Who to contact: Phone High Lakes Contractors at (541) 382-9443 or write P.O. Box 989, Bend, OR 97709. Or phone the Bend Ranger District at (541) 388-5664 or write to Deschutes National Forest, 1230 NE Third, Bend, OR 97701.

Location: From Interstate 5 at Albany, turn east on US 20 and drive 122 miles to Bend. Turn southwest on Cascade Lakes Highway (Highway 46) and drive 41 miles to the campground.

Trip note: This wooded campground is set along the banks of the Deschutes River. It's a beautiful spot, green and lush. It is slightly more developed than nearby Mile Campground.

100. BESSON CAMP

Reference: **On Deschutes River in Deschutes National Forest; map D2, grid e9.**

Campsites, facilities: There are five sites for tents, trailers or RVs up to 16 feet long. Picnic tables and fire grills are provided. A pit toilet is available. There is **no piped water**. Leashed pets are permitted. A boat launch is nearby.

Reservations, fee: No reservations; no fee. Open May to October.

Who to contact: Phone the Bend Ranger District at (541) 388-5664 or write to Deschutes National Forest, 1230 NE Third Street, Bend, OR 97701.

Location: From Interstate 5 at Albany, turn east on US 20 and drive 122 miles to Bend. From Bend, travel 14.5 miles south on US 97, then 4.5 miles west on Sun River-Spring River Road (Forest Service Road 40). The camp is one-half mile further north on Forest Service Road 41.

Trip note: This secluded and unknown little spot is set along the bank of the Deschutes River. It has a boat launch and good trout fishing.

101. SHARPS CREEK

Reference: **On Sharps Creek; map D2, grid f1.**

Campsites, facilities: There are 10 sites for tents, trailers or RVs up to 20 feet long. Picnic tables and fire grills are provided. Piped water, vault toilets and firewood are available. Leashed pets are permitted.

Reservations, fee: No reservations; $5 fee per night (14-day stay limit). Open mid-May to mid-October, weather permitting.

Who to contact: Phone (541) 683-6600 or write to Bureau of Land Management, P.O. Box 10266, Eugene, OR 97401.

Location: From Interstate 5 at Cottage Grove, take exit 174, then travel 18 miles east on Row River Road and four miles south on Sharps Creek Road.

Trip note: This campground is set along the bank of Sharps Creek. Like the nearby Rujada site, this is just far enough off the beaten path to be missed by most campers. It is quiet, primitive and remote. There are not many recreation options in the immediate area, but Cottage Grove Reservoir with swimming/fishing options is just a short drive away.

102. RUJADA

Reference: **On Layng Creek in Umpqua National Forest; map D2, grid f1.**

Campsites, facilities: There are 11 sites for tents, trailers or RVs up to 22 feet long. Picnic tables and fire pits are provided. Flush toilets and piped water are available. Some facilities are **wheelchair accessible**. Pets are permitted.

Reservations, fee: No reservations; $4 fee per night. Open late May to late September.

Who to contact: Phone the Cottage Grove Ranger District at (541) 942-5591 or write to Umpqua National Forest, 78405 Cedar Park Road, Cottage Grove, OR 97424.

Location: From Cottage Grove on Interstate 5, take exit 174 and head east on Row River Road for 19 miles. Turn left on Forest Service Road 17 (Layng Creek Road) and drive two miles to the campground on the right.

Trip note: This campground is set along the banks of Layng Creek, right at the national forest border. It's a good swimming spot about two miles upstream from its confluence with the Row River. There is fishing in the creek for those with time and patience. By continuing east on Forest Service Road 17, you can access a trailhead that leads one-half mile to beautiful Spirit Falls, a spectacular 60-foot waterfall. A bit farther east is another easy trail to Moon Falls, even more awe-inspiring at 125 feet.

103. SAND PRAIRIE RV

Reference: **On Willamette River in Willamette National Forest; map D2, grid f3.**
Campsites, facilities: There are 20 sites for tents, trailers or RVs up to 22 feet long. Picnic tables and fire grills are provided. Vault toilets and piped water are available. Some of the facilities are **wheelchair accessible**. Leashed pets are permitted. A boat launch is nearby on Hills Creek Reservoir.
Reservations, fee: No reservations; $8 fee per night; $4 each additional vehicle. Open mid-April to mid-November.
Who to contact: Phone the Rigdon Ranger District at (541) 782-2283 or write to Willamette National Forest, 49098 Salmon Creek Road, Oakridge, OR 97463.
Location: From Interstate 5 south of Eugene, drive 38 miles southeast on Highway 58 (two miles past Oakridge), then one-half mile on County Road 360. Then drive 11 miles south on Forest Service Road 21.
Trip note: This peaceful campground is set in a forest of old-growth trees along the Middle Fork of the Willamette River, just south of Hills Creek Lake. It is located at the Middle Fork Trail trailhead. This 30-mile trail is nearly complete.

104. PACKARD CREEK RV

Reference: **On Hills Creek Reservoir in Willamette National Forest; map D2, grid f3.**
Campsites, facilities: There are 33 sites for tents, trailers or RVs up to 30 feet long. Picnic tables and fire grills are provided. Piped water, vault toilets and firewood are available. Some facilities are **wheelchair accessible**. Leashed pets are permitted. Boat docks and launching facilities are nearby.
Reservations, fee: No reservations; $8 fee per night; $4 each additional vehicle. Open mid-May to mid-September.
Who to contact: Phone the Rigdon Ranger District at (541) 782-2283 or write to Willamette National Forest, 49098 Salmon Creek Road, Oakridge, OR 97463.
Location: From Interstate 5 south of Eugene, drive 38 miles southeast on Highway 58 two miles past Oakridge, then one-half mile southeast on County Road 360. The camp is five miles south on Forest Service Road 21.
Trip note: The campground is set at 1,600 feet along the west shore of Hills Creek Reservoir, a 2,900-acre reservoir where fishing and boating are popular. No boats with motors are permitted on the Larison Cove arm of the lake.

105. BLUE POOL RV

Reference: **On Salt Creek in Willamette National Forest; map D2, grid f3.**
Campsites, facilities: There are 24 sites for tents, trailers or RVs up to 18 feet long. Picnic tables and fire grills are provided. Piped water, vault and flush toilets are available. Leashed pets are permitted.
Reservations, fee: No reservations; $8-$10 fee per night: $4-$5 each additional vehicle. Open late April to mid-October.
Who to contact: Phone the Oakridge Ranger District at (541) 782-2291 or write

to Willamette National Forest, 46375 Highway 58, Westfir, OR 97492.

Location: From Interstate 5 south of Eugene, drive 45 miles southeast on Highway 58 to the campground.

Trip note: This campground is set along Salt Creek at 2,000 feet. With its close proximity to the highway and easy access to the creek, it's a decent layover spot. There is volleyball, a swimming hole and good fishing. McCredie Hot Springs is half a mile away.

106.   SACANDAGA   RV

Reference: **On Willamette River in Willamette National Forest; map D2, grid f4.**

Campsites, facilities: There are 20 sites for tents, trailers or RVs up to 21 feet long. Picnic tables and fire grills are provided and vault toilets and firewood are available. There is **no piped water**. Leashed pets are permitted.

Reservations, fee: No reservations; no fee. Open mid-April to mid-November.

Who to contact: Phone the Rigdon Ranger District at (541) 782-2283 or write to Willamette National Forest, 49098 Salmon Creek Road, Oakridge, OR 97463.

Location: From Interstate 5 south of Eugene, take exit 188 and turn east on Highway 58. Drive 38 miles southeast (two miles past Oakridge), then one-half mile on County Road 360. From there, continue 25 miles southeast on Forest Service Road 21. The camp is on the right.

Trip note: This primitive campground sits on a bluff overlooking the Willamette River. It's adjacent to historic Rigdon Meadows, the site of a stage coach station in pioneer days.

107.   SKOOKUM CREEK

Reference: **Near Three Sisters Wilderness in Willamette National Forest; map D2, grid f5.**

Campsites, facilities: There are eight walk-in tent sites, two of which are **wheelchair-accessible.** Picnic tables and fire grills are provided. Hand-pumped water, hitching rails and pit toilets are available. Leashed pets are permitted.

Reservations, fee: No reservations; $4 fee per night Open mid-May to mid-November.

Who to contact: Phone the Oakridge Ranger District at (541) 782-2291 or write to Willamette National Forest, 46375 Highway 58, Westfir, OR 97492.

Location: From Interstate 5 at Eugene, turn east on Highway 126 and drive 37 miles to the town of Blue River. Continue east for five miles to Forest Service Road 19 (Aufderheide Scenic Byway). Turn right and drive 30 miles south to Box Canyon. From there, drive south for three miles on Forest Service Road 1957 to the campground.

Trip note: This remote campground popular with equestrians is set near the border of the Three Sisters Wilderness. The Erma Bell Lakes trailhead at the camp provides access to numerous lakes and other trails in the backcountry. This is a primitive, little-known spot.

108.   SHADOW BAY   RV

Reference: **On Waldo Lake in Willamette National Forest; map D2, grid f6.**

Campsites, facilities: There are 92 sites for tents, trailers or RVs up to 30 feet long. Picnic tables and fire grills are provided. Piped water, flush toilets and pets are permitted. Boat launching facilities are nearby.

Reservations, fee: No reservations; $8-$12 fee per night; $4-$6 each additional vehicle. Open July through September, weather permitting.

Who to contact: Phone the Oakridge Ranger District at (541) 782-2291 or write to Willamette National Forest, 46375 Highway 58, Westfir, OR 97492.

Location: From Interstate 5 south of Eugene, take exit 188 and travel 59 miles southeast on Highway 58. Turn left and drive 5.5 miles north on Forest Service Road 5897, then two miles west on Forest Service Road 5896 to the camp.

Trip note: This camp is set at 5,400 feet, tucked away along the southeast shore of Waldo Lake. Waldo Lake has the special distinction of being one of the three purest lakes in the world. Trivia buffs note: Of those three lakes, two are in Oregon (the other is Crater Lake) and the third is in Siberia. For hikers, a trail circles the lake and intersects several other trails that provide access to the Waldo Lake Wilderness. The camps on this lake are in a great location and spectacularly lovely, but have one drawback—they are infested by mosquitos in June and July. Bring bug repellent and netting if you want a peaceful trip.

109. NORTH WALDO   **RV**

Reference: **On Waldo Lake in Willamette National Forest; map D2, grid f6.**

Campsites, facilities: There are 58 sites for tents, trailers or RVs up to 30 feet long. Picnic tables and fire grills are provided. Piped water and flush toilets are available. Pets are permitted. Boat launching facilities are available.

Reservations, fee: No reservations; $8-$10 fee per night; $4-$5 each additional vehicle. Open July through September, weather permitting.

Who to contact: Phone the Oakridge Ranger District at (541) 782-2291 or write to Willamette National Forest, 46375 Highway 58, Westfir, OR 97492.

Location: From Interstate 5 south of Eugene, take exit 188 and travel 59 miles southeast on Highway 58. Turn left and drive 10.5 miles north on Forest Service Road 5897, then two miles west on Forest Service Road 5898 to the entrance road to the campground.

Trip note: Mosquitos are especially bad news here in July. See the trip note for Shadow Bay for detailed information about Waldo Lake.

110. NORTH DAVIS CREEK   **RV**

Reference: **Near Wickiup Reservoir in Deschutes National Forest; map D2, grid f6.**

Campsites, facilities: There are 17 sites for tents, trailers or RVs up to 22 feet long. Picnic tables and fire grills are provided. Hand pumped water and vault toilets are available. Leashed pets are permitted. Boat docks and launching facilities are nearby.

Reservations, fee: No reservations; $7 fee per night. Open May to late October.

Who to contact: Phone the Bend Ranger District at (541) 388-5664 or write to Deschutes National Forest, 1230 NE Third, Bend, OR 97701.

Location: From Interstate 5 south of Eugene, take exit 188 and turn east on Highway 58. Drive 73 miles, then turn east on County Road 61. Drive three miles, then continue north on Cascade Lakes Highway (Highway 46) for about 13 miles to the campground.

Trip note: This campground is set along a western channel of Wickiup Reservoir. The area was logged in 1987 because of pine beetle infestation. In late summer, the reservoir level tends to drop. It is remote, secluded and receives little use.

111.   QUINN RIVER   RV

Reference: **On Crane Prairie Reservoir in Deschutes National Forest; map D2, grid f7.**

Campsites, facilities: There are 41 sites for tents, trailers or RVs up to 30 feet long. Picnic tables and fire grills are provided. Hand pumped water and vault toilets are available. Leashed pets are permitted. Boat launch facilities are available.

Reservations, fee: No reservations; $9 fee per night. Open late April to mid-October.

Who to contact: Phone High Lakes Contractors at (541) 382-9443 or write P.O. Box 989, Bend, OR 97709. Or phone the Bend Ranger District at (541) 388-5664 or write to Deschutes National Forest, 1230 NE Third, Bend, OR 97701.

Location: From Interstate 5 at Albany, turn east on US 20 and drive 122 miles to Bend. Turn south on US 97 and drive 20 miles to County Road 42. Turn west and drive 25 miles to Cascade Lakes Highway (Highway 46). Turn north and drive four miles to the campground.

Trip note: This campground is set along the western shore of Crane Prairie Reservoir, a popular spot for anglers. A large parking lot is available for boats and trailers.

112.   ROCK CREEK   RV

Reference: **On Crane Prairie Reservoir in Deschutes National Forest; map D2, grid f7.**

Campsites, facilities: There are 32 sites for tents, trailers or RVs up to 22 feet long. Picnic tables and fire grills are provided. Hand pumped water, a fish cleaning station and vault toilets are available. Leashed pets are permitted. Boat launching facilities are available on-site and boat docks are nearby.

Reservations, fee: No reservations; $9 fee per night. Open April 20 through October, weather permitting.

Who to contact: Phone High Lakes Contractors at (541) 382-9443 or write P.O. Box 989, Bend, OR 97709. Or phone the Bend Ranger District at (541) 388-5664 or write to Deschutes National Forest, 1230 NE Third, Bend, OR 97701.

Location: From Interstate 5 at Albany, turn east on US 20 and drive 122 miles to Bend. Turn south on US 97 and drive 20 miles to County Road 42. Turn west and drive 25 miles. Turn north on Cascade Lakes Highway (Highway 46) and drive three miles to the campground.

Trip note: This campground is set along the west shore of Crane Prairie Reservoir and is an option to the Quinn River camp.

113.   NORTH TWIN LAKE   RV

Reference: **On North Twin Lake in Deschutes National Forest; map D2, grid f7.**

Campsites, facilities: There are 10 sites for tents, trailers or RVs up to 22 feet long. Picnic tables and fire grills are provided. Vault toilets are available. There is **no piped water**. Leashed pets are permitted. Boat docks, launching facilities and rentals are nearby.

Reservations, fee: No reservations; $5 fee per night. Open June to late September.

Who to contact: Phone High Lakes Contractors at (541) 382-9443 or write P.O. Box 989, Bend, OR 97709. Or phone the Bend Ranger District at (541) 388-5664 or write to Deschutes National Forest, 1230 NE Third, Bend, OR 97701.

Location: From Interstate 5 at Eugene, take exit 188 and turn on Highway 58. Drive 73 miles, then turn east on County Road 61. Continue three miles. Turn north on Highway 46. Keep going for 18 miles and turn east on County Road 42. Travel five miles and turn south on Forest Service Road 4260 and drive one-half mile to the campground.

Trip note: This campground is set along the shore of North Twin Lake and is a popular weekend spot for families. It is small and fairly primitive, but has lake access and a pretty setting. Only non-motorized boats are permitted.

---

114.   LAVA FLOW   **RV**

Reference: **On Davis Lake in Deschutes National Forest; map D2, grid f7.**

Campsites, facilities: There are 12 sites for tents, trailers or RVs up to 22 feet long. Picnic tables and fire grills are provided. Vault toilets and firewood (to be gathered from surrounding area) are available. There is **no piped water**. Leashed pets are permitted. A boat launch is nearby.

Reservations, fee: No reservations; no fee. Open late May to late October, weather permitting.

Who to contact: Phone the Crescent Ranger District at (541) 433-2234 or write to Deschutes National Forest, P.O. Box 208, Crescent, OR 97733.

Location: From Interstate 5 south of Eugene, take exit 188 and turn east on Highway 58. Drive 86 miles, then turn east on County Road 61 and drive three miles, then continue nine miles north on Forest Service Road 46. The camp is located two miles north on Forest Service Road 850.

Trip note: This campground is set along the northeast shore of Davis Lake. It is a very shallow lake that provides good duck hunting during the fall. During early summer, there is decent fishing.

---

115.   WEST SOUTH TWIN   **RV**

Reference: **On Wickiup Reservoir in Deschutes National Forest; map D2, grid f7.**

Campsites, facilities: There are 24 sites for trailers or RVs up to 22 feet long. Picnic tables and fire grills are provided. Piped water and flush toilets are available. Leashed pets are permitted. Boat launching facilities are available on-site and boat rentals are nearby.

Reservations, fee: No reservations; $10 fee per night. Open mid-May to mid-October.

Who to contact: Phone High Lakes Contractors at (541) 382-9443 or write P.O. Box 989, Bend, OR 97709. Or phone the Bend Ranger District at (541) 388-5664 or write to Deschutes National Forest, 1230 NE Third, Bend, OR 97701.

Location: From Interstate 5 south of Eugene, take exit 188 and turn east on Highway 58. Drive 73 miles, then turn east on County Road 61. Continue three miles, then turn north on Cascade Lakes Highway (Highway 46). Travel another 18 miles to County Road 42. Turn east for five miles, then turn south for two miles on County Road 42 and 1.5 miles on Forest Service Road 4260.

Trip note: This campground is set on Wickiup Reservoir near the western shore of South Twin Lake, a major access point to the Wickiup Reservoir. It's a popular fishing spot with very good Kokanee salmon fishing.

116.   GULL POINT   **RV**

Reference: **On Wickiup Reservoir in Deschutes National Forest; map D2, grid f7.**

Campsites, facilities: There are 80 sites for tents, trailers or RVs up to 30 feet long. There are also two sites available for groups of up to 25 people. Picnic tables and fire grills are provided. Piped water, sanitary dump station, and flush and vault toilets are available. Leashed pets are permitted. Boat launching facilities are available on site.

Reservations, fee: No reservations except for group sites, phone (541) 382-9443; $10 fee per night; $40 group fee per site. Open mid-April through October.

Who to contact: Phone High Lakes Contractors at (541) 382-9443 or write P.O. Box 989, Bend, OR 97709. Or phone the Bend Ranger District at (541) 388-5664 or write to Deschutes National Forest, 1230 NE Third, Bend, OR 97701.

Location: From Interstate 5 south of Eugene, take exit 188 and turn east on Highway 58. Drive 73 miles to County Road 61. From here, turn east and drive three miles. Turn north on Cascade Lakes Highway (Highway 46). Continue 18 miles to County Road 42. Turn east and continue for five miles to Forest Service Road 4260, turn south and drive three miles to the campground.

Trip note: This campground is set along the north shore of Wickiup Reservoir. The setting is open, with sparse vegetation. You'll find good fishing for kokanee salmon here.

117.   TWIN LAKES RESORT   **RV**

Reference: **On Wickiup Reservoir; map D2, grid f7.**

Campsites, facilities: There are 120 sites for tents, trailers and RVs of any length (22 full hookups). There are also 14 cabins. Restrooms, showers, a sanitary dump, a private phone, a laundromat, limited groceries, a full-service restaurant, ice, snacks, RV supplies, LP gas and a barbecue are available. For boating, a ramp, rentals and a dock are provided.

Reservations, fee: Reservations recommended; $12-$18 fee per night; $62-$94 cabin fee. Visa and MasterCard accepted. Open from April 25 to October 15.

Who to contact: Phone the park at (541) 593-6526 or write to P.O. Box 3550, Sun River, OR 97707.

Location: From Interstate 5 south of Eugene, take exit 188 and turn east on Highway 58. Drive 86 miles, then turn north on US 97 and drive 26 miles to LaPine. Continue 2.5 miles northeast on US 97, then 11 miles west on County Road 43. Continue another four miles west on County Road 42 to the Twin Lakes Resort sign. Turn south and drive to the resort, two miles ahead.

Trip note: This resort is a popular family vacation destination, with a full-service marina and all the amenities, including beach areas. Recreational activities include hiking, fishing, swimming and boating on Wickiup Reservoir.

118.   SHEEP BRIDGE   **RV**

Reference: **Near Wickiup Reservoir in Deschutes National Forest; map D2, grid f7.**

Campsites, facilities: There are 18 sites for tents, trailers or RVs up to 22 feet long. Picnic tables and fire grills are provided. Hand pumped water and vault toilets are available. Leashed pets are permitted.

Reservations, fee: No reservations; $5 fee per night. Open April through October.

Who to contact: Phone High Lakes Contractors at (541) 382-9443 or write P.O. Box 989, Bend, OR 97709. Or phone the Bend Ranger District at (541) 388-5664 or write to Deschutes National Forest, 1230 NE Third, Bend, OR 97701.

Location: From Interstate 5 south of Eugene, take exit 188 and turn east on Highway 58. Drive 73 miles to County Road 61. From here, turn east and drive three miles. Turn north on Cascade Lakes Highway (Highway 46). Continue 18 miles to County Road 42. Turn east and continue for five miles to Forest Service Road 4260. From here, the camp is one-half mile down on the west side of the road.

Trip note: This campground is set along the channel north of Wickiup Reservoir. It is in an open, treeless area that has minimal privacy and is dusty in summer.

---

119. SOUTH TWIN LAKE   **RV**

Reference: On South Twin Lake in Deschutes National Forest; map D2, grid f7.

Campsites, facilities: There are 24 sites for tents, trailers or RVs up to 22 feet long. Picnic tables and fire grills are provided. Piped water and flush toilets are available. Leashed pets are permitted. Boat docks, launching facilities, boat rentals, showers and laundry facilities are available nearby.

Reservations, fee: No reservations; $10 fee per night. Open mid-April through October.

Who to contact: Phone High Lakes Contractors at (541) 382-9443 or write P.O. Box 989, Bend, OR 97709. Or phone the Bend Ranger District at (541) 388-5664 or write to Deschutes National Forest, 1230 NE Third, Bend, OR 97701.

Location: From Interstate 5 south of Eugene, take exit 188 and turn east on Highway 58. Drive 73 miles to County Road 61. From here, turn east and drive three miles. Turn north on Cascade Lakes Highway (Highway 46). Continue 18 miles to County Road 42. Turn east and continue for five miles to Forest Service Road 4260, then turn south and drive 1.5 miles to the campground.

Trip note: This campground is set along the shore of South Twin Lake, a popular spot for swimming, fishing and boating (non-motorized only).

---

120. RESERVOIR   **RV**

Reference: On Wickiup Reservoir in Deschutes National Forest; map D2, grid f7.

Campsites, facilities: There are 28 sites for tents, trailers or RVs up to 22 feet long. Picnic tables and fire grills are provided. Vault toilets are available, but there is **no piped water**. Boat launching facilities are available. Leashed pets are permitted.

Reservations, fee: No reservations; $5 fee per night. Open May to late October.

Who to contact: Phone the Bend Ranger District at (541) 388-5664 or write to Deschutes National Forest, 1230 NE Third, Bend, OR 97701.

Location: From Interstate 5 south of Eugene, take exit 188 and turn east on Highway 58. Drive 73 miles to County Road 61. Turn east and continue for three miles. Turn north on Cascade Lakes Highway (Highway 46). Drive 11 miles and turn east on Forest Service Road 44. Proceed 1.5 miles to the camp.

Trip note: This campground is set along the south shore of Wickiup Reservoir, where the kokanee salmon fishing is good. This camp is best in early summer, before the lake level drops. Because of pine beetle infestation, the area was logged in 1987.

121. FALL RIVER **RV**

Reference: **On Fall River in Deschutes National Forest; map D2, grid f8.**

Campsites, facilities: There are 12 sites for tents, trailers or RVs up to 22 feet long. Picnic tables and fire grills are provided. Vault toilets are available. There is **no piped water**. Leashed pets are permitted.

Reservations, fee: No reservations; $5 fee per night. Open mid-April through October.

Who to contact: Phone the Bend Ranger District at (541) 388-5664 or write to Deschutes National Forest, 1230 NE Third, Bend, OR 97701.

Location: From Interstate 5 at Albany, turn east on US 20 and drive 122 miles to Bend. From Bend, travel 16.5 miles south on US 97, then 15 miles southwest on County Road 42 to the campground.

Trip note: This campground is set along Fall River. Fishing is restricted to flyfishing only. Check the regulations for other restrictions. Open year round.

---

122. PRINGLE FALLS **RV**

Reference: **On Deschutes River in Deschutes National Forest; map D2, grid f8.**

Campsites, facilities: There are seven sites for tents, trailers or RVs up to 22 feet long. Picnic tables and fire grills are provided. Vault toilets are available. There is **no piped water**. Leashed pets are permitted.

Reservations, fee: No reservations; $5 fee per night. Open April to October.

Who to contact: Phone the Bend Ranger District at (541) 388-5664 or write to Deschutes National Forest, 1230 NE Third, Bend, OR 97701.

Location: From Interstate 5 at Albany, turn east on US 20 and drive 122 miles to Bend. Turn south on US 97 and drive 27.5 miles to County Road 43 (2.5 miles north of LaPine). Turn west and drive seven miles. The camp is about one-half mile northeast on Forest Service Road 4360.

Trip note: This pretty campground is set along the Deschutes River fairly close to Pringle Falls. It is a popular canoe launching point.

---

123. WICKIUP BUTTE **RV**

Reference: **On Wickiup Reservoir in Deschutes National Forest; map D2, grid f8.**

Campsites, facilities: There are 12 sites for tents, trailers or RVs up to 22 feet long. Picnic tables and fire grills are provided. Vault toilets are available. There is **no piped water**. Leashed pets are permitted. Boat launching facilities are nearby.

Reservations, fee: No reservations; $5 fee per night. Open May to late October

Who to contact: Phone the Bend Ranger District at (541) 388-5664 or write to Deschutes National Forest, 1230 NE Third, Bend, OR 97701.

Location: From Interstate 5 south of Eugene, take exit 188 and turn east on Highway 58. Drive 86 miles, then turn north on US 97 and drive 26 miles to LaPine. Continue 2.5 miles northeast on US 97, then seven miles west on County Road 43. The camp is located another seven miles west on Forest Service Road 44.

Trip note: This campground is set along the southeast shore of Wickiup Reservoir. Kokanee salmon fishing is good during early summer. See Reservoir Camp trip note for information on the lake environment.

124. RIVERVIEW TRAILER PARK   **RV**

Reference: **On Little Deschutes River; map D2, grid f8.**

Campsites, facilities: There are 15 tent sites and 19 sites for trailers or RVs of any length. Electricity, cable TV, piped water, sewer hookups and picnic tables are provided. Flush toilets, bottled gas, showers, a recreation hall and a laundromat are available. Small, leashed pets are permitted.

Reservations, fee: Reservations accepted; $10-$15 fee per night. Open all year.

Who to contact: Phone (541) 536-2382 or write to 52731 Huntington Road, LaPine, OR 97739.

Location: From Interstate 5 south of Eugene, take exit 188 and turn east on Highway 58. Drive 86 miles, then turn north on US 97 and drive 26 miles to LaPine. Continue 2.5 miles northeast on US 97, then one mile west on County Road 43. The camp is one mile north on Huntington Road on the left.

Trip note: This campground is set along the bank of the Little Deschutes River, which offers excellent trout fishing. It's missed by a lot of highway travelers; they just plain don't know about it.

---

125. HIDDEN PINES RV PARK   **RV**

Reference: **On Little Deschutes River; map D2, grid f8.**

Campsites, facilities: There are two tent sites and 18 drive-through sites for trailers or RVs of any length. Electricity, piped water, cable TV hookups, sewer hookups and picnic tables are provided. Flush toilets, sanitary services, showers, firewood, a laundromat and ice are available. Bottled gas, a store and a cafe are within one mile. Pets and motorbikes are permitted.

Reservations, fee: Reservations accepted; $9-$15 fee per night. Open April to mid-October.

Who to contact: Phone (541) 536-2265 or write to 52158 Elderberry Lane, LaPine, OR 97739.

Location: From Interstate 5 south of Eugene, take exit 188 and turn east on Highway 58. Drive 86 miles, then turn north on US 97 and drive 26 miles to LaPine. Continue 2.5 miles north on US 97, then 2.5 miles west at Wickiup Junction. The camp is one-half mile south on Pine Forest and 400 yards east on Wright Avenue.

Trip note: So you think you've come far enough, eh? If you want a spot in a privately-run motor home park near the bank of the Little Deschutes River, you've found it.

---

126. BULL BEND   **RV**

Reference: **On Deschutes River in Deschutes National Forest; map D2, grid f8.**

Campsites, facilities: There are 12 sites for tents, trailers or RVs. Picnic tables and fire grills are provided. Vault toilets are available. There is **no piped water**. Pets are permitted.

Reservations, fee: No reservations; $5 fee per night. Open April to October.

Who to contact: Phone the Bend Ranger District at (541) 388-5664 or write to Deschutes National Forest, 1230 NE Third Street, Bend, OR 97701.

Location: From Interstate 5 south of Eugene, take exit 188 and turn east on Highway 58. Drive 86 miles, then turn north on US 97 and drive 26 miles to LaPine. Continue 2.5 miles northeast on US 97, then eight miles west on County Road 43. The camp is 1.5 miles southwest on Forest Service Road 4370.

Trip note: This campground is set on the inside of a major bend in the Deschutes River. A mini float trip can be made by starting at the upstream end of camp, floating around the bend and then taking out at the downstream end of camp.

---

127. BIG RIVER [RV]

Reference: **On Deschutes River in Deschutes National Forest; map D2, grid f9.**

Campsites, facilities: There are five tent sites and eight sites for tents, trailers or RVs up to 22 feet long. Picnic tables and fire grills are provided. Vault toilets are available. There is **no piped water**. Leashed pets are permitted. Boat launching facilities are on-site.

Reservations, fee: No reservations; $5 fee per night. Open April to October.

Who to contact: Phone the Bend Ranger District at (541) 388-5664 or write to Deschutes National Forest, 1230 NE Third, Bend, OR 97701.

Location: From Interstate 5 at Albany, turn east on US 20 and drive 122 miles to Bend. From Bend, drive 16.5 miles south on US 97, then five miles southwest on County Road 42.

Trip note: This is a good spot along the banks of the Deschutes River in a nice location. Rafting, fishing and boating using motors are permitted. Access is easy.

---

128. LAPINE STATE PARK [RV]

Reference: **On Deschutes River; map D2, grid f9.**

Campsites, facilities: There are 145 sites with full or partial hookups for trailers or RVs of any length. Picnic tables are provided. Flush toilets, sanitary services, showers and firewood are available. Some facilities are **wheelchair accessible**. Leashed pets are permitted.

Reservations, fee: Contact Reservations Northwest at (800) 452-5687 ($6 reservation fee); $9-$16 fee per night. Open all year.

Who to contact: Phone (800) 233-0321 or (541) 388-6055 or write to c/o High Desert Management Unit, 62976 O.B. Riley Road, Bend, OR 97701.

Location: From Interstate 5 south of Eugene, take exit 188 and turn east on Highway 58. Drive 86 miles, then turn north on US 97 and drive 26 miles to LaPine. Continue eight miles north on US 97. Turn west on State Recreation Road and continue three miles.

Trip note: This state park is set along the banks of the Deschutes River, where trout fishing and canoeing are excellent. The park is the home of Oregon's appropriately named Big Tree, the largest ponderosa pine in the state. A half-mile hiking trail and cross-country skiing are also available.

---

129. HIGHLANDER MOTEL & TRAILER PARK [RV]

Reference: **Near Little Deschutes River; map D2, grid f9.**

Campsites, facilities: There are 30 sites for trailers or RVs up to 35 feet long (16 drive-through). Electricity, piped water and sewer hookups are provided. Flush toilets, bottled gas, sanitary services, showers, a store, a cafe and ice are available. A laundromat is located within one mile. Leashed pets are permitted.

Reservations, fee: Reservations accepted; $13 fee per night. MasterCard and Visa accepted. Open all year.

Who to contact: Phone (541) 536-2131 or write to P.O. Box 322, LaPine, OR 97739.

Location: From Interstate 5 south of Eugene, take exit 188 and turn east on

Highway 58. Drive 86 miles, then turn north on US 97 and drive 26 miles to LaPine. The campground is located at the north edge of town.

Trip note: This campground is near the Little Deschutes River. A golf course and tennis courts are nearby.

---

130.   PRAIRIE   RV

Reference: **On Paulina Creek in Deschutes National Forest; map D2, grid f9.**

Campsites, facilities: There are 16 sites for tents, trailers or RVs up to 30 feet long. Picnic tables and fire grills are provided. Piped water, firewood and vault toilets are available. Leashed pets are permitted.

Reservations, fee: No reservations; $7 fee per night. Open mid-May through October.

Who to contact: Phone Northwest Land Management at (541) 536-8344 or write P.O. Box 1917, Laping, OR 97739. Or phone the Fort Rock Ranger District at (541) 388-5664 or write Deschutes National Forest, 1230 NE Third Street, Bend, OR 97701.

Location: From Interstate 5 south of Eugene, take exit 188 and turn east on Highway 58. Drive 86 miles, then turn north on US 97 and drive 26 miles to LaPine. Continue five miles northeast on US 97, then three miles southeast on County Road 21 to the campground.

Trip note: This camp is set along the banks of Paulina Creek. Nearby is the trailhead for the Peter Skene Ogden National Recreation Trail.

---

131.   McKAY CROSSING   RV

Reference: **On Paulina Creek in Deschutes National Forest; map D2, grid f9.**

Campsites, facilities: There are ten sites for tents, trailers or RVs up to 22 feet long. Picnic tables and fire grills are provided. Vault toilets are available. There is **no piped water**. Leashed pets are permitted.

Reservations, fee: No reservations; no fee. Open June to late October.

Who to contact: Phone Northwest Land Management at (541) 536-8344 or write P.O. Box 1917, Laping, OR 97739. Or phone the Fort Rock Ranger District at (541) 388-5664 or write Deschutes National Forest, 1230 NE Third Street, Bend, OR 97701.

Location: From Interstate 5 south of Eugene, take exit 188 and turn east on Highway 58. Drive 86 miles, then turn north on US 97 and drive 26 miles to LaPine. Continue five miles northeast on US 97, then three miles southeast on County Road 21. The camp is two miles east on Forest Service Road 2120.

Trip note: This pleasant little campground is set along the bank of Paulina Creek. A nearby trail travels east for six miles to Paulina Lake (also reachable by car). See the trip note for Paulina Lake camps (Chapter D3) for recreation alternatives in the area.

---

132.   ROCK CREEK   RV

Reference: **On Rock Creek; map D2, grid g0.**

Campsites, facilities: There are 18 sites for tents, trailers or RVs up to 30 feet long. Picnic tables and fire grills are provided. Vault toilets, piped water and firewood are available. Leashed pets are permitted.

Reservations, fee: No reservations; $5 fee per night; 14-day limit. Open May 20 to mid-October.

Who to contact: Phone (541) 440-4930 or write to Bureau of Land Management,

777 NW Garden Valley Boulevard, Roseburg, OR 97470.

Location: From Interstate 5 at Roseburg, drive 18 miles east on Highway 138 to Glide. From Glide, travel 12 miles northeast on Rock Creek Road to the campground.

Trip note: This campground is set along the bank of Rock Creek in a relatively obscure spot. It is sparse and primitive but supplies all the necessities at a reasonable price. It is not well-known, either, so you're likely to have privacy as a bonus.

133. MILLPOND **RV**

Reference: **On Rock Creek; map D2, grid g0.**

Campsites, facilities: There are 12 sites for tents, trailers or RVs up to 30 feet long. Picnic tables and fire grills are provided. Flush and vault toilets, piped water, firewood, a playing field and a group shelter are available. Some facilities are **wheelchair accessible**. Leashed pets are permitted.

Reservations, fee: No reservations; $6 fee per night (14-day limit); $2 each additional vehicle. Open May through October.

Who to contact: Phone (541) 440-4930 or write to Bureau of Land Management, 777 NW Garden Valley Boulevard, Roseburg, OR 97470.

Location: From Interstate 5 at Roseburg, drive 18 miles east on Highway 138 to Glide. From Glide, travel 10 miles northeast on Rock Creek Road to the campground.

Trip note: This campground is set along the banks of Rock Creek. It is the first camp you will see along Rock Creek Road, which accounts for its relative popularity in this area. Like Rock Creek Campground, it is primitive and remote.

134. SUSAN CREEK **RV**

Reference: **On North Umpqua River; map D2, grid g0.**

Campsites, facilities: There are 31 sites for trailers or RVs up to 35 feet long. Picnic tables and fire grills are provided. Flush toilets, piped water, showers and firewood are available. Some facilities are **wheelchair accessible**. Leashed pets are permitted.

Reservations, fee: No reservations; $4 fee per night (14-day limit); $2 each additional vehicle. Open May 20 to October 5.

Who to contact: Phone (541) 440-4930 or write to Bureau of Land Management, 777 NW Garden Valley Boulevard, Roseburg, OR 97470.

Location: From Interstate 5 at Roseburg, travel 33 miles east on Highway 138 to the campground.

Trip note: This popular campground is set along the banks of the North Umpqua River. It's a good base camp for a fishing trip. It is in a pretty setting, with lots of trees and river access. There are some hiking trails in the area and opportunities for white water rafting and kayaking.

135. SCAREDMAN **RV**

Reference: **On Canton Creek; map D2, grid g1.**

Campsites, facilities: There are eight sites for tents, trailers or RVs up to 25 feet long. Picnic tables and fire grills are provided. Vault toilets are available. There is **no piped water**. Leashed pets are permitted.

Reservations, fee: No reservations; no fee; 14-day stay limit. Open all year.

Who to contact: Phone (541) 440-4930 or write to Bureau of Land Management, 777 NW Garden Valley Boulevard, Roseburg, OR 97470.

Location: From Interstate 5 at Roseburg, drive 39 miles east on Highway 138 to Steamboat. From Steamboat, drive three miles north on Canton Creek Road to the campground.

Trip note: This campground is set along the banks of Canton Creek. It's a small camp that is virtually unknown to out-of-towners. It is very primitive, offering little but cleared-out areas for tents, plus fishing and swimming; but it is also private and secluded.

---

136.   ISLAND   RV.

Reference: **On Umpqua River in Umpqua National Forest; map D2, grid g1.**

Campsites, facilities: There are seven sites for tents, trailers or RVs up to 24 feet long. Picnic tables and fire grills are provided. Vault toilets are available. There is **no piped water**. Leashed pets are permitted.

Reservations, fee: No reservations; no fee. Open year-round.

Who to contact: Phone the North Umpqua Ranger District at (541) 496-3532 or write to Umpqua National Forest, 18782 North Umpqua Highway, Glide, OR 97443.

Location: From Roseburg on Interstate 5, take exit 120 and drive 40 miles east on Highway 138. The campground is located on the right off the highway, just past a little settlement called Steamboat.

Trip note: This campground is set along the banks of the Umpqua River at a spot popular for both fishing and rafting. A hiking trail that leads east and west along the river is accessible by driving a short distance west. See a Forest Service map for details. A few miles east of Forest Service Road 38 is Steamboat Falls, a pretty waterfall where you can watch fish jump upstream. No fishing allowed, though.

---

137.   CANTON CREEK   RV.

Reference: **Near Umpqua River in Umpqua National Forest; map D2, grid g1.**

Campsites, facilities: There are five sites for tents, trailers or RVs up to 22 feet long. Picnic tables and fire grills are provided. Piped water and flush toilets are available. Leashed pets are permitted.

Reservations, fee: No reservations; $4 fee per night. Open mid-May to late October.

Who to contact: Phone the North Umpqua Ranger District at (541) 496-3532 or write to Umpqua National Forest, 18782 North Umpqua Highway, Glide, OR 97443.

Location: From Roseburg on Interstate 5, take exit 120 and drive about 39 miles east on Highway 138 to Steamboat. Turn left on Forest Service Road 38 and proceed about 400 yards to the campground.

Trip note: This campground is set at the confluence of Canton and Steamboat creeks, less than a mile from the North Umpqua River. This site gets little overnight use, but there are lots of day swimmers in July and August. No fishing is permitted on Steamboat or Canton creeks because they are spawning areas for steelhead and salmon. See the trip note for Island Campground for other area details.

138. STEAMBOAT FALLS   RV

Reference: **On Steamboat Creek in Umpqua National Forest; map D2, grid g2.**

Campsites, facilities: There are 10 sites for tents, trailers or RVs up to 24 feet long. Picnic tables, vault toilets and fire grills are provided. There is **no piped water**. Leashed pets are permitted.

Reservations, fee: No reservations; no fee. Open year-round.

Who to contact: Phone the North Umpqua Ranger District at (541) 496-3532 or write to Umpqua National Forest, 18782 North Umpqua Highway, Glide, OR 97443.

Location: From Roseburg on Interstate 5, take exit 120 and drive east on Highway 138 to Steamboat. Turn left and drive six miles northeast on Forest Service Road 38. The camp is one mile further on Forest Service Road 3810.

Trip note: This campground is set along the banks of Steamboat Creek, near beautiful Steamboat Falls, which features a fish ladder that provides passage for steelhead and salmon on their migratory, upstream journey. No fishing is permitted in Steamboat Creek. Other camping options are Canton Creek and Island.

139. BOULDER FLAT   RV

Reference: **On North Umpqua River in Umpqua National Forest; map D2, grid g2.**

Campsites, facilities: There are 11 sites for tents, trailers or RVs up to 24 feet long. Picnic tables and fire grills are provided. Vault toilets are available. There is **no piped water**. A store, propane and ice are located within five miles. Leashed pets are permitted. A raft launch is on-site.

Reservations, fee: No reservations; no fee. Open year-round.

Who to contact: Phone the North Umpqua Ranger District at (541) 496-3532 or write to Umpqua National Forest, 18782 North Umpqua Highway, Glide, OR 97443.

Location: From Roseburg on Interstate 5, take exit 120 and drive 54 miles east on Highway 138 to the campground.

Trip note: This campground is set along the banks of the North Umpqua River at the confluence of Boulder Creek. Across the river from the campground, a trail follows Boulder Creek north for 10.5 miles through the Boulder Creek Wilderness, a climb in elevation from 2,000 to 5,400 feet. Access to the trail is at Soda Springs Dam, two miles east of the camp. It's a good thumper for backpackers. A little over a mile to the east are some huge, dramatic pillars of volcanic rock, colored with lichen.

140. CAMPERS FLAT   RV

Reference: **On Willamette River in Willamette National Forest; map D2, grid g3.**

Campsites, facilities: There are five sites for tents, trailers or RVs up to 21 feet long. Picnic tables and fire grills are provided. Hand-pumped water, vault toilets and firewood are available. Leashed pets are permitted.

Reservations, fee: No reservations; $7 fee per night; $3 each additional vehicle. Open mid-May to mid-September.

Who to contact: Phone the Rigdon Ranger District at (541) 782-2283 or write to Willamette National Forest, 49098 Salmon Creek Road, Oakridge, OR 97463.

Location: From Interstate 5 south of Eugene, drive 38 miles southeast on Highway 58 (two miles past Oakridge), then one-half mile on County Road 360. Turn south onto Forest Service Road 21 and drive 20 miles to the camp.

Trip note: This campground is set along the Middle Fork of the Willamette River. Pretty and open, it is well-known and liked by the local people, so expect a lot of company.

---

141.   SECRET   RV

Reference: **On Willamette River in Willamette National Forest; map D2, grid g3.**

Campsites, facilities: There are six sites for tents, trailers or RVs up to 15 feet long. Picnic table and fire grills are provided. Vault toilets are available, but there is **no piped water**. Leashed pets are permitted.

Reservations, fee: No reservations; $5 fee per night; $3 each additional vehicle. Open mid-May to mid-September.

Who to contact: Phone the Rigdon Ranger District at (541) 782-2283 or write to Willamette National Forest, 49098 Salmon Creek Road, Oakridge, OR 97463.

Location: From Interstate 5 south of Eugene drive southeast on Highway 58 two miles past Oakridge, then one-half mile on County Road 360. Turn south onto Forest Service Road 21 and drive 18 miles to the camp.

Trip note: This campground is set along the Middle Fork of the Willamette River. Its nice setting attracts many of the local people, making it a very busy campground.

---

142.   TOKETEE LAKE   RV

Reference: **On Toketee Lake in Umpqua National Forest; map D2, grid g3.**

Campsites, facilities: There are 33 sites for tents, trailers or RVs up to 22 feet long. **No piped water** is available. Picnic tables and fire grills are provided. Vault toilets are available. Leashed pets are permitted. Boat docks and launching facilities are nearby.

Reservations, fee: No reservations; no fee. Open mid-April to late October.

Who to contact: Phone the Diamond Lake Ranger District at (541) 498-2531 or write to Umpqua National Forest, HC 60, Box 101, Idleyld Park, OR 97447.

Location: From Roseburg on Interstate 5, take exit 120 and drive about 60 miles east on Highway 138, then one mile on Forest Service Road 34, pass the lake, to the campground.

Trip note: This campground is set just north of Toketee Lake. The North Umpqua Trail passes near camp and continues north along the river for many miles. Die-hard hikers can also take it west, where it meanders for a while before heading north into the Boulder Creek Wilderness. Toketee Lake offers many recreation options, and a worthwhile point of interest is Toketee Falls, located just west of the lake turnoff. Another is Umpqua Hot Springs, a few miles northeast of the camp.

---

143.   INDIGO SPRINGS   RV

Reference: **Near Willamette River in Willamette National Forest; map D2, grid g4.**

Campsites, facilities: There are three sites for tents, trailers or RVs up to 16 feet long. Picnic tables and fire grills are provided. Vault toilets and firewood are available. There is **no piped water**. Leashed pets are permitted.

Reservations, fee: No reservations; no fee. Open mid-April to mid-November.

Who to contact: Phone the Rigdon Ranger District at (541) 782-2283 or write to Willamette National Forest, 49098 Salmon Creek Road, Oakridge, OR 97463.

Location: From Interstate 5 south of Eugene, take exit 188 and turn east on Highway 58. Drive 38 miles southeast (two miles past Oakridge), then one-half mile on County Road 360. From there, continue 29 miles southeast on Forest Service Road 21. The camp is on the left.

Trip note: This campground sits along the bank of Indigo Creek, not far from its confluence with the Middle Fork of the Willamette River. It gets it name from the several large springs in the area.

---

144.   EAST LEMOLO   RV

Reference: **On Lemolo Lake in Umpqua National Forest; map D2, grid g5.**

Campsites, facilities: There are no designated campsites, but one open area with room enough for about six cars or small RVs. **No piped water** is available. Picnic tables and fire grills are provided. Vault toilets are available. Leashed pets are permitted. Boat docks, launching facilities and rentals are nearby.

Reservations, fee: No reservations; no fee. Open mid-May to late October.

Who to contact: Phone the Diamond Lake Ranger District at (541) 498-2531 or write to Umpqua National Forest, HC 60, Box 101, Idleyld Park, OR 97447.

Location: From Roseburg on Interstate 5, take exit 120 and drive 74 miles east on Highway 138, then three miles north on Forest Service Road 2610. The campground is located about two miles east on Forest Service Road 2666.

Trip note: This campground is on the southeastern shore of Lemolo Lake, where boating and fishing are some of the recreation possibilities. Boats with motors are allowed. The North Umpqua River and adjacent trail are just beyond the north shore of the lake. If you hike for two miles northwest of the lake, you can reach spectacular Lemolo Falls.

---

145.   POOLE CREEK   RV

Reference: **On Lemolo Lake in Umpqua National Forest; map D2, grid g5.**

Campsites, facilities: There are 59 sites for tents, trailers or RVs up to 22 feet long. Picnic tables and fire grills are provided. Piped water and vault toilets are available. Leashed pets are permitted. Boat docks, launching facilities and rentals are nearby.

Reservations, fee: Reserve the group sites by calling (800) 280-CAMP ($7.75 reservation fee); $6-$8 fee per night. Open late April to late October.

Who to contact: Phone the Diamond Lake Ranger District at (541) 498-2531 or write to Umpqua National Forest, HC 60, Box 101, Idleyld Park, OR 97447.

Location: From Roseburg on Interstate 5, take exit 120 and drive 72 miles east on Highway 138, then four miles north on Forest Service Road 2610 to the campground.

Trip note: This campground is on the western shore of Lemolo Lake and not far from Lemolo Lake Resort which is open for recreation year-round. This is by far the most popular Forest Service camp at the lake. See the trip note for East Lemolo for more information.

---

146.   LEMOLO LAKE RESORT   RV

Reference: **On Lemolo Lake; map D2, grid g5.**

Campsites, facilities: There are five tent sites and 32 drive-through sites for trailers or RVs of any length. Electricity, piped water, sewer hookups and picnic tables are provided. Flush toilets, bottled gas, sanitary disposal services, showers, a store, a cafe, a laundromat and ice are available. Pets and motorbikes are permitted. Boat docks, launching facilities and rentals are available.

Reservations, fee: Reservations accepted; $10-$16 fee per night; MasterCard and Visa accepted. Open all year.

Who to contact: Phone (541) 793-3300 or write to HC 60, P.O. Box 79B, Idleyld Park, OR 97447.

Location: From Roseburg on Interstate 5, take exit 138 and drive approximately 80 miles east on Highway 138, then drive five miles north on Lemolo Lake Road (Bird's Point Road) to the resort.

Trip note: This resort is on the western shore of Lemolo Lake and offers recreation opportunities year-round. See the trip note for East Lemolo.

---

147.   TRAPPER CREEK   RV

Reference: **On Odell Lake in Deschutes National Forest; map D2, grid g6.**

Campsites, facilities: There are 32 sites for tents, trailers or RVs up to 22 feet long. Picnic tables and fire grills are provided. Piped water and vault toilets are available. Firewood may be gathered from the surrounding area. A store, a laundromat and ice are within one mile. Leashed pets are permitted.

Reservations, fee: No reservations; $9 fee per night. Open mid-May to late October.

Who to contact: Phone the Crescent Ranger District at (541) 433-2234 or write to Deschutes National Forest, P.O. Box 208, Crescent, OR 97733.

Location: From Interstate 5 south of Eugene, turn east on Highway 58 and drive approximately 61 miles to the turnoff for Odell Lake. Turn southwest on Forest Service Road 5810 and drive 1.25 miles to the campground.

Trip note: This campground is set along the west end of Odell Lake. Boat docks and rentals are nearby at the Shelter Cove Resort.

---

148.   SHELTER COVE RESORT   RV

Reference: **On Odell Lake; map D2, grid g6.**

Campsites, facilities: There are 11 tent sites and 58 drive-through sites for trailers or RVs up to 30 feet long. There are also eight cabins. Electricity and picnic tables are provided. Flush toilets, showers, a store, a cafe and ice are available. Leashed pets are permitted. Boat docks, launching facilities and rentals are nearby.

Reservations, fee: Reservations recommended; $9-$14 fee per night; $60-$130 cabin fee. MasterCard and Visa accepted. Open all year.

Who to contact: Phone (541) 433-2548 or write to West Odell Lake Road, Cascade Summit, OR 97425.

Location: From Interstate 5 south of Eugene, drive southeast on Highway 58 to Odell Lake. Take the West Odell Road turn off Highway 58 at the north end of Odell Lake, then drive 2.5 miles south on West Odell Road to the camp.

Trip note: This private resort is set along the north shore of Odell Lake. It offers opportunities for hiking, fishing and swimming. A general store and tackle shop are available.

149. SIMAX GROUP CAMP

Reference: On Crescent Lake in Deschutes National Forest; map D2, grid g6.

Campsites, facilities: There are three group camp sites for 25 to 50 campers each. Flush toilets, showers, picnic tables, fireplaces and a group shelter are available. Facilities are **wheelchair accessible.** Leashed pets are permitted.

Reservations, fee: Phone Crescent Ranger District for current reservation and fee information.

Who to contact: Phone the Crescent Ranger District at (541) 433-2234 or write to Deschutes National Forest, P.O. Box 208, Crescent, OR 97733.

Location: From Interstate 5 south of Eugene, take exit 188 and turn east on Highway 58. Drive about 70 miles to the town of Crescent Lake. Turn west on Forest Service Road 60 for one mile. Turn south on Forest Service Road 6005 for one more mile to the campground entrance.

Trip note: This is a new camp on Crescent Lake with trails to day-use beaches. See neighboring Contorta and Spring camps (camp numbers 157 and 158).

150. CRESCENT LAKE RV.

Reference: On Crescent Lake in Deschutes National Forest; map D2, grid g6.

Campsites, facilities: There are 47 sites for tents, trailers or RVs up to 21 feet long. Picnic tables and fire grills are provided. Piped water and vault toilets are available. Firewood may be gathered from the surrounding area. Leashed pets are permitted.

Reservations, fee: No reservations; $9 fee per night. Open mid-May to late October.

Who to contact: Phone the Crescent Ranger District at (541) 433-2234 or write to Deschutes National Forest, P.O. Box 208, Crescent, OR 97733.

Location: From Interstate 5 south of Eugene, drive approximately 70 miles southeast on Highway 58 to the town of Crescent Lake. From Crescent Lake, drive three miles southwest on Forest Service Road 60 to the campground.

Trip note: This campground is set along the north shore of Crescent Lake. Boat docks, launching facilities and rentals are nearby at Crescent Lake Resort, adjacent to the campground. A trail from the campground heads into the Diamond Peak Wilderness and also branches north to Odell Lake.

151. ODELL CREEK RV.

Reference: On Odell Lake in Deschutes National Forest; map D2, grid g6.

Campsites, facilities: There are 22 sites for tents, trailers or RVs up to 22 feet long. Picnic tables and fire grills are provided. Piped water and vault toilets are available. Firewood may be gathered from the surrounding area. Leashed pets are permitted.

Reservations, fee: No reservations; $9 fee per night. Open mid-May to late September.

Who to contact: Phone the Crescent Ranger District at (541) 433-2234 or write to Deschutes National Forest, P.O. Box 208, Crescent, OR 97733.

Location: From Interstate 5 south of Eugene, drive southeast on Highway 58 to Odell Lake. At the east end of the lake, take Forest Service Road 680 and drive 400 yards to the campground.

Trip note: This campground is set along the south shore of Odell Lake, where you can fish, swim and hike. A trail from nearby Crater Buttes trailhead heads southwest into the Diamond Peak Wilderness and provides access to several small lakes in the backcountry. Boat docks, launching facilities and rentals are nearby at the Odell Lake Lodge, adjacent to the campground.

152.　　　SUNSET COVE　　　RV

Reference: **On Odell Lake in Deschutes National Forest; map D2, grid g6.**

Campsites, facilities: There are 26 sites for tents, trailers or RVs up to 22 feet long. Picnic tables and fire grills are provided. Piped water and vault toilets are available. Firewood may be gathered from the surrounding area. Leashed pets are permitted. A boat launch and fish-cleaning facilities are available.

Reservations, fee: No reservations; $6 fee per night. Open mid-May to mid-October.

Who to contact: Phone the Crescent Ranger District at (541) 433-2234 or write to Deschutes National Forest, P.O. Box 208, Crescent, OR 97733.

Location: From Interstate 5 south of Eugene, turn southeast on Highway 58 and drive approximately 72 miles to the campground.

Trip note: This campground is set along the southeast shore of Odell Lake. Boat docks and rentals are available nearby at Odell Lake Lodge and Shelter Cove Resort.

153.　　　PRINCESS CREEK　　　RV

Reference: **On Odell Lake in Deschutes National Forest; map D2, grid g6.**

Campsites, facilities: There are 46 sites for tents, trailers or RVs up to 22 feet long. Picnic tables and fire grills are provided. Piped water and vault toilets are available. Firewood may be gathered from the surrounding area. Showers, a store, a laundromat and ice are available within five miles. Leashed pets are permitted.

Reservations, fee: No reservations; $9 fee per night. Open mid-May to late October.

Who to contact: Phone the Crescent Ranger District at (541) 433-2234 or write to Deschutes National Forest, P.O. Box 208, Crescent, OR 97733.

Location: From Interstate 5 south of Eugene, turn southeast on Highway 58 and drive approximately 68 miles to the campground.

Trip note: This campground is set along the northeast shore of Odell Lake. See the trip note for Odell Creek for recreation details. Boat docks and rentals are available nearby at Odell Lake Lodge and Shelter Cove Resort.

154.　　　GOLD LAKE　　　RV

Reference: **On Gold Lake in Willamette National Forest; map D2, grid g6.**

Campsites, facilities: There are 21 sites for tents, trailers or RVs up to 22 feet long. Picnic tables and fire grills are provided. Hand-pumped water, vault toilets and pets are permitted. Boat docks and launching facilities are nearby.

Reservations, fee: No reservations; $8-$10 fee per night; $4-$5 each additional vehicle. Open June through September.

Who to contact: Phone the Oakridge Ranger District at (541) 782-2291 or write to Willamette National Forest, 46375 Highway 58, Westfir, OR 97492.

Location: From Interstate 5 south of Eugene, take exit 188 and drive 61 miles southeast on Highway 58. Turn left on Forest Service Road 500 and drive two miles northeast to the campground.

Trip note: This campground is set along the shore of Gold Lake, where swimming and boating (for boats without motors) are permitted. Fishing is also permitted, but limited to fly fishing only. The campground is set along a trail that provides access to numerous small lakes to the west and Waldo Lake to the north. In summer, there are wildflowers and huckleberries.

---

155. INLET RV

Reference: On Lemolo Lake in Umpqua National Forest; map D2, grid g6.

Campsites, facilities: There are 13 sites for tents, trailers or RVs up to 22 feet long. **No piped water** is available. Picnic tables and fire grills are provided. Vault toilets are available. Leashed pets are permitted. Boat docks, launching facilities and rentals are nearby.

Reservations, fee: No reservations; no fee. Open mid-May to late October.

Who to contact: Phone the Diamond Lake Ranger District at (541) 498-2531 or write to Umpqua National Forest, HC 60, Box 101, Idleyld Park, OR 97447.

Location: From Roseburg on Interstate 5, take exit 120 and drive 74 miles east on Highway 138, then three miles north on Forest Service Road 2610. The camp is about three miles east on Forest Service Road 2666.

Trip note: This campground is set along the eastern inlet of Lemolo Lake. Just across the road is the Umpqua River Trail, which is routed east into the Oregon Cascades Recreation Area and the Mt. Thielsen Wilderness. See the trip note for East Lemolo, camp number 144, for recreation details.

---

156. TIMPANOGAS RV

Reference: On Timpanogas Lake in Willamette National Forest; map D2, grid g6.

Campsites, facilities: There are 10 sites for tents, trailers or RVs up to 21 feet long. Picnic tables and fire grills are provided. Hand-pumped water, vault toilets and firewood are available. Leashed pets are permitted. Boat docks are nearby. No boats with motors are permitted.

Reservations, fee: No reservations; $5 fee per night; $3 each additional vehicle. Open mid-June to mid-October.

Who to contact: Phone the Rigdon Ranger District at (541) 782-2283 or write to Willamette National Forest, 49098 Salmon Creek Road, Oakridge, OR 97463.

Location: From Interstate 5 south of Eugene, take exit 188 and turn east on Highway 58. Drive 38 miles southeast (two miles past Oakridge), then one-half mile on County Road 360. Turn southeast on Forest Service Road 21 and drive 38 miles to the campground.

Trip note: This remote campground is set along the shore of Timpanogas Lake in the Oregon Cascades Recreation Area. A trailhead adjacent to camp provides access into the backcountry. There is a hike-in campground about two miles away at Indigo Lake which has five primitive sites and pit toilets. It is accessible by trail from this camp.

---

157. SPRING RV

Reference: On Crescent Lake in Deschutes National Forest; map D2, grid g6.

Campsites, facilities: There are 68 sites for tents, trailers or RVs up to 22 feet long. Picnic tables and fire grills are provided. Piped water, vault toilets and firewood (to be gathered from the surrounding area) are available. Leashed pets are permitted.

Reservations, fee: No reservations; call for current fees. Open June to October.

Who to contact: Phone the Crescent Ranger District at (541) 433-2234 or write to Deschutes National Forest, P.O. Box 208, Crescent, OR 97733.

Location: From Interstate 5 south of Eugene, take exit 188 and turn east on Highway 58. Drive approximately 70 miles to the town of Crescent Lake. Drive eight miles west on Forest Service Road 60, then turn northeast on the entrance road to the campground.

Trip note: This campground is on the southern shore of Crescent Lake. See the trip note for Contorta Camp for more information.

---

158. CONTORTA   RV

Reference: **On Crescent Lake in Deschutes National Forest; map D2, grid g6.**

Campsites, facilities: There are 15 undeveloped sites for tents, trailers or RVs up to 22 feet long. There is **no piped water**. Picnic tables and vault toilets are provided. Leashed pets are permitted. Boat docks and launching facilities are located a mile away at the Spring Campground.

Reservations, fee: No reservations; no fee. Open June to late September.

Who to contact: Phone the Crescent Ranger District at (541) 433-2234 or write to Deschutes National Forest, P.O. Box 208, Crescent, OR 97733.

Location: From Interstate 5 south of Eugene, take exit 188 and turn east on Highway 58. Drive approximately 70 miles to the turnoff, which is just past Odell Lake at Crescent Lake Junction. Drive 11 miles southwest on Forest Service Road 60, then one mile on Forest Service Road 280.

Trip note: This campground is on the southern shore of Crescent Lake, where swimming, boating and waterskiing are among the summer pastimes. A number of trails from the nearby Windy-Oldenburg Trailhead provide access to lakes in the Diamond Peak Wilderness and Oregon Cascades Recreation Area. A parking area for snowmobiles and cross-country skiers is at the north end of the lake.

---

159. EAST DAVIS LAKE   RV

Reference: **On Davis Lake in Deschutes National Forest; map D2, grid g7.**

Campsites, facilities: There are 33 sites for tents, trailers or RVs up to 22 feet long. Picnic tables and fire grills are provided. Hand-pumped water and vault toilets are provided. Firewood may be gathered from the surrounding area. Leashed pets are permitted. Boat launching facilities are nearby at Lava Flow Campground.

Reservations, fee: No reservations; call for current fees. Open mid-May to late October.

Who to contact: Phone the Crescent Ranger District at (541) 433-2234 or write to Deschutes National Forest, P.O. Box 208, Crescent, OR 97733.

Location: From Interstate 5 south of Eugene, take exit 188 and turn east on Highway 58. Drive 73 miles, then turn east on County Road 61 and drive three miles, then continue 6.5 miles north on Forest Service Road 46. The camp is 1.5 miles west on Forest Service Road 46855.

Trip note: This campground is set along the south shore of Davis Lake in a wooded setting. Recreation options include fishing, boating and hiking.

---

160. WEST DAVIS LAKE   RV

Reference: **On Davis Lake in Deschutes National Forest; map D2, grid g7.**

Campsites, facilities: There are 25 sites for tents, trailers or RVs up to 22 feet long.

Picnic tables and fire grills are provided. Hand-pumped water, vault toilets and firewood (to be gathered from the surrounding area) are available. Leashed pets are permitted. Boat docks are nearby.

Reservations, fee: Some sites may be reserved by calling (800) 280-CAMP ($7.75 reservation fee); call for current fees. Open mid-May to late October.

Who to contact: Phone the Crescent Ranger District at (541) 433-2234 or write to Deschutes National Forest, P.O. Box 208, Crescent Lake, OR 97425.

Location: From Interstate 5 south of Eugene, take exit 188 and turn east on Highway 58. Drive 73 miles, then turn east on County Road 61. Drive three miles, then continue three miles north on Forest Service Road 46. Travel four miles on Forest Service Road 4660, then 1.5 miles on Forest Service Road 4669.

Trip note: This campground is set along the south shore of Davis Lake. It has spacious sites and easy access to the lake.

---

161.   CRESCENT CREEK   RV

Reference: **On Crescent Creek in Deschutes National Forest; map D2, grid g7.**

Campsites, facilities: There are 10 sites for tents, trailers or RVs up to 22 feet long. Picnic tables and fire g rills are provided. Hand-pumped water and vault toilets are available. Firewood may be gathered from the surrounding area. Leashed pets are permitted.

Reservations, fee: No reservations; call for current fees. Open May to late October.

Who to contact: Phone the Crescent Ranger District at (541) 433-2234 or write to Deschutes National Forest, P.O. Box 208, Crescent, OR 97733.

Location: From Interstate 5 at Eugene, take exit 188 and turn east on Highway 58. Drive 73 miles, then turn east on County Road 61 and drive 3.5 miles to the campground.

Trip note: This is one of the Cascade's classic hidden campgrounds. It is set along the banks of Crescent Creek at 4,500 feet. It's pretty, developed and private.

LEAVE NO TRACE TIPS

Properly dispose of what you can't pack out.

• If no refuse facility is available, deposit human waste in catholes dug six to eight inches deep at least 200 feet from water, camps, or trails. Cover and disguise the cathole when you're finished.

• To wash yourself or your dishes, carry the water 200 feet from streams or lakes and use small amounts of biodegradable soap. Scatter the strained dishwater.

MAP D3

46 LISTINGS
PAGES 562-579

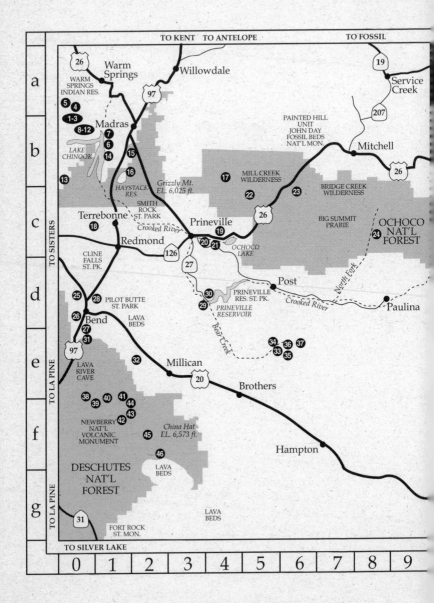

Oregon Map D3 featuring: Lake Billy Chinook, Deschutes National Forest, Metolius River, Haystack Reservoir, Ochoco National Forest, Ochoco Lake State Park, Smith Rock State Park, Branchwater Lake, McKenzie River, Sisters, Antelope Flat Reservoir, Crooked River, Walton Lake, Deschutes River, Bend, Prineville Reservoir, Three Creeks Lake, Paulina Lake, Arnold Ice Caves, East Lake

---

1. BLACK BUTTE MOTEL & RV PARK   🚐

Reference: **On Metolius River; map D3, grid a0.**

Campsites, facilities: There are 31 sites for trailers or RVs of any length. Electricity, piped water, sewer hookups and picnic tables are provided. Flush toilets, showers, firewood and a laundromat are available. Bottled gas, sanitary services, a store, a cafe and ice are located within one block. Pets and motorbikes are permitted.

Reservations, fee: Reservations accepted; $19 fee per night; MasterCard and Visa accepted. Open all year.

Who to contact: Phone (541) 595-6514 or write to HCR 97736, P.O. Box 1250, Camp Sherman, OR 97730.

Location: From Interstate 5 at Albany, turn east on US 20 and drive approximately 87 miles. At the sign for Camp Sherman, turn north and drive about five miles. Turn east on Forest Service Road 14 and drive one-quarter mile to the park on the right.

Trip note: This motor home park is set along the banks of the Metolius River. It has a choice of graveled or grassy sites in a clean, scenic environment. See the trip note for Camp Sherman, camp number 8.

---

2. COLD SPRINGS RESORT & RV PARK   🚐

Reference: **On Metolius River; map D3, grid a0.**

Campsites, facilities: There are 45 sites for trailers or RVs of any length with full hookups. Bottled gas, a store, a cafe, a laundromat and ice are located within one mile. Pets and motorbikes are permitted.

Reservations, fee: Reservations accepted; $18-$20 fee per night. Open all year.

Who to contact: Phone (541) 595-6271 or write to HCR, 1270 Cold Springs Resort Lane, Camp Sherman, OR 97730.

Location: From Interstate 5 at Albany, turn east on US 20 and drive approximately 87 miles. At the sign for Camp Sherman, turn north and drive about 5.5 miles to the park on the right.

Trip note: This pretty, wooded motor home park is fairly close to the Metolius River, world-famous for its fly fishing. Nearby recreation options include a golf course, hiking and biking trails, a riding stable and tennis courts.

---

3. ALLEN SPRINGS   🚐

Reference: **On Metolius River in Deschutes National Forest; map D3, grid a0.**

Campsites, facilities: There are four tent sites and 13 sites for tents, trailers or RVs up to 22 feet long. Picnic tables and fire grills are provided. Vault toilets and piped water are available. A store, a cafe, a laundromat and ice are located within five miles. Leashed pets are permitted.

Reservations, fee: No reservations; $10 fee per night; $5 each additional vehicle. May through September; free October through April (when **no water is available**).

Who to contact: Phone the Sisters Ranger District at (541) 549-2111 or write to Deschutes National Forest, P.O. Box 249, Sisters, OR 97759.

Location: From Interstate 5 at Albany, turn east on US 20 and drive approximately 87 miles. At the sign for Camp Sherman, turn north and drive about five miles. From Camp Sherman, travel five miles north on Forest Service Road 14 to the campground.

Trip note: This campground is set along the banks of the Metolius River, where fishing and hiking can be good. The Wizard Falls Fish Hatchery is about a mile away, a good side trip.

---

4.   PIONEER FORD   RV

Reference: On Metolius River in Deschutes National Forest; map D3, grid a0.

Campsites, facilities: There are two tent sites and 18 sites for tents, trailers or RVs up to 40 feet long. Piped water and fire grills are provided. Piped water, vault toilets and firewood are available. Leashed pets are permitted.

Reservations, fee: No reservations; $10 fee per night; $5 each additional vehicle. Open April through September.

Who to contact: Phone the Sisters Ranger District at (541) 549-2111 or write to Deschutes National Forest, P.O. Box 249, Sisters, OR 97759.

Location: From Interstate 5 at Albany, turn east on US 20 and drive approximately 87 miles. At the sign for Camp Sherman, turn north and drive about five miles. From Camp Sherman, travel seven miles north on Forest Service Road 14 to the campground.

Trip note: This campground is set along the banks of the Metolius River. See the trip note for Camp Sherman, camp number 8, for recreation options.

---

5.   LOWER BRIDGE   RV

Reference: On Metolius River in Deschutes National Forest; map D3, grid a0.

Campsites, facilities: There are 12 sites for tents, trailers or RVs up to 22 feet long. Picnic tables and fire grills are provided. Vault toilets and piped water are available. Leashed pets are permitted.

Reservations, fee: No reservations; $10 fee per night; $5 each additional vehicle. Open April through September.

Who to contact: Phone the Sisters Ranger District at (541) 549-2111 or write to Deschutes National Forest, P.O. Box 249, Sisters, OR 97759.

Location: From Interstate 5 at Albany, turn east on US 20 and drive approximately 87 miles. At the sign for Camp Sherman, turn north and drive about five miles. From Camp Sherman, travel nine miles north on Forest Service Road 14 to the entrance road to the campground.

Trip note: This campground is set along the banks of the Metolius River. See the trip note for Camp Sherman for details about the area.

---

6.   PERRY SOUTH   RV

Reference: On Lake Billy Chinook in Deschutes National Forest; map D3, grid b0.

Campsites, facilities: There are four tent sites and 59 sites for tents, trailers or RVs up to 40 feet long. Picnic tables and fire grills are provided. Piped water and vault toilets are available. Leashed pets are permitted. Boat docks and launching facilities are nearby.

Reservations, fee: No reservations; $9 fee per night; $5 each additional vehicle. Open May through September.

Who to contact: Phone the Sisters Ranger District at (541) 549-2111 or write to Deschutes National Forest, P.O. Box 249, Sisters, OR 97759.

Location: From Interstate 5 at Albany, turn east on US 20 and drive 100 miles to Sisters. Continue 20 miles east on Highway 126 to Redmond, then turn north on US 97 and drive about 10 miles to Culver. From Culver, drive 25 miles west and north on County Road 64 to the campground entrance.

Trip note: This campground is set near the shore of the Metolius arm of Lake Billy Chinook. See the trip note for Crooked River Ranch RV Park and KOA Madras for recreation details. This lake borders the Warm Springs Indian Reservation.

---

7. MONTY   RV

Reference: On Metolius River in Deschutes National Forest; map D3, grid b0.

Campsites, facilities: There are 20 sites for tents, trailers or RVs up to 22 feet long. Picnic tables and fire grills are provided. Firewood and vault toilets are available. There is **no piped water**. Leashed pets are permitted. Boat docks and launching facilities are nearby.

Reservations, fee: No reservations; no fee. Open May to October.

Who to contact: Phone the Sisters Ranger District at (541) 549-2111 or write to Deschutes National Forest, P.O. Box 248, Sisters, OR 97734.

Location: From Interstate 5 at Albany, turn east on US 20 and drive 100 miles to Sisters. Continue 20 miles east on Highway 126 to Redmond, then turn north on US 97 and drive about 10 miles to Culver. From Culver, drive 30 miles west and north on County Road 64 to the campground entrance.

Trip note: This remote campground is set along the banks of the Metolius River near where it empties into Lake Billy Chinook. Trout fishing can be good. It's located just outside Warm Springs Indian Reservation.

---

8. CAMP SHERMAN   RV

Reference: On Metolius River in Deschutes National Forest; map D3, grid b0.

Campsites, facilities: There are 15 sites for tents, trailers or RVs up to 40 feet long. Picnic tables and fire grills are provided. Vault toilets and piped water are available. Leashed pets are permitted.

Reservations, fee: No reservations; $10 fee per night; $5 each additional vehicle. Open May through September.

Who to contact: Phone the Sisters Ranger District at (541) 549-2111 or write to Deschutes National Forest, P.O. Box 249, Sisters, OR 97759.

Location: From Interstate 5 at Albany, turn east on US 20 and drive approximately 87 miles. At the sign for Camp Sherman, turn north and drive about five miles. From the store in Camp Sherman, travel one-half mile north on Forest Service Road 1419 to the campground.

Trip note: This campground is set along the banks of the Metolius River, where you can fish for wild trout. This place is for expert fly fishermen seeking a quality angling experience. It's advisable to obtain a map of the Deschutes National Forest that details back roads, trails and streams. This is one of five camps in the immediate area.

9. ALLINGHAM   RV

Reference: On Metolius River in Deschutes National Forest; map D3, grid b0.

Campsites, facilities: There are 10 sites for tents, trailers or RVs up to 40 feet long. Picnic tables and fire grills are provided. Vault toilets and piped water are available. Leashed pets are permitted.

Reservations, fee: No reservations; $10 fee per night; $5 each additional vehicle. Open April through September.

Who to contact: Phone the Sisters Ranger District at (541) 549-2111 or write to Deschutes National Forest, P.O. Box 249, Sisters, OR 97759.

Location: From Interstate 5 at Albany, turn east on US 20 and drive approximately 87 miles. At the sign for Camp Sherman, turn north and drive about five miles. From the store in Camp Sherman, travel one mile north to the campground.

Trip note: This campground is set along the banks of the Metolius River. It is one of five camps in the immediate area. See the trip note for Camp Sherman, camp number 8. Interpretive programs are offered in the Metolius Basin from July 4 through Labor Day. Included are evening programs and interpretive hikes.

---

10. SMILING RIVER   RV

Reference: On Metolius River in Deschutes National Forest; map D3, grid b0.

Campsites, facilities: There are 37 sites for tents, trailers or RVs up to 22 feet long. Picnic tables and fire grills are provided. Vault toilets and piped water are available. Leashed pets are permitted.

Reservations, fee: No reservations; $10 fee per night; $5 each additional vehicle. Open May through September.

Who to contact: Phone the Sisters Ranger District at (541) 549-2111 or write to Deschutes National Forest, P.O. Box 249, Sisters, OR 97759.

Location: From Interstate 5 at Albany, turn east on US 20 and drive approximately 87 miles. At the sign for Camp Sherman, turn north and drive about five miles. From the store in Camp Sherman, travel one mile north to the campground.

Trip note: This campground is set along the banks of the Metolius River. See the trip note for Camp Sherman, camp number 8.

---

11. PINE REST

Reference: On Metolius River in Deschutes National Forest; map D3, grid b0.

Campsites, facilities: There are eight tent sites. Picnic tables and fire grills are provided. Vault toilets and piped water are available. Leashed pets are permitted.

Reservations, fee: No reservations; $10 fee per night; $5 each additional vehicle. Open April through September.

Who to contact: Phone the Sisters Ranger District at (541) 549-2111 or write to Deschutes National Forest, P.O. Box 249, Sisters, OR 97759.

Location: From Interstate 5 at Albany, turn east on US 20 and drive approximately 87 miles. At the sign for Camp Sherman, turn north and drive about five miles. From the store in Camp Sherman, travel 1.5 miles north to the campground.

Trip note: This campground is set along the banks of the Metolius River. See the trip note for Camp Sherman, camp number 8.

12.   GORGE   **RV**

Reference: **On Metolius River in Deschutes National Forest; map D3, grid b0.**

Campsites, facilities: There are 18 sites for tents, trailers or RVs up to 22 feet long. Picnic tables and fire grills are provided. Vault toilets and piped water are available. Leashed pets are permitted.

Reservations, fee: No reservations; $10 fee per night; $5 each additional vehicle. Open April through September.

Who to contact: Phone the Sisters Ranger District at (541) 549-2111 or write to Deschutes National Forest, P.O. Box 249, Sisters, OR 97759.

Location: From Interstate 5 at Albany, turn east on US 20 and drive approximately 87 miles. At the sign for Camp Sherman, turn north and drive about five miles. From the store in Camp Sherman, travel two miles north to the camp.

Trip note: This campground is set along the banks of the Metolius River. See the trip note for Camp Sherman, camp number 8.

13.   BLACK PINE SPRING   **RV**

Reference: **Near Three Creeks Lake in Deschutes National Forest; map D3, grid b0.**

Campsites, facilities: There are four sites for tents, trailers or RVs up to 15 feet long. Picnic tables and fire grills are provided. Pit toilets are available. There is **no piped water**. Leashed pets are permitted.

Reservations, fee: No reservations; no fee. Open mid-June to mid-October.

Who to contact: Phone the Sisters Ranger District at (541) 549-2111 or write to Deschutes National Forest, P.O. Box 249, Sisters, OR 97759.

Location: From Interstate 5 at Albany, turn east on US 20 and drive 100 miles to Sisters. Turn north on Forest Service Road 16 and travel nine miles to the campground.

Trip note: This primitive, remote campground is set at 4,400 feet. Three Creeks Lake is about nine miles south on Forest Service Road 16.

14.   THE COVE PALISADES STATE PARK   **RV**

Reference: **On Lake Billy Chinook; map D3, grid b1.**

Campsites, facilities: There are 94 tent sites and 178 sites with full or partial hookups for trailers or RVs up to 60 feet long. Picnic tables and fire grills are provided. Flush toilets, sanitary services, showers, firewood, a store, a cafe and ice are available. Some facilities are **wheelchair accessible**. Leashed pets are permitted. Boat docks, launching facilities and rentals are nearby.

Reservations, fee: Contact Reservations Northwest at (800) 452-5687 ($6 reservation fee); $16-$20 per night. Open all year.

Who to contact: Phone (541) 546-3412 or (800) 452-5687, or write to Route 1, P.O. Box 60 CP, Culver, OR 97734.

Location: From Interstate 5 at Portland, turn east on US 26 and drive 118 miles southeast to Madras. Turn south on US 97 and drive nine miles to Culver, then head west on the entrance road for five miles.

Trip note: This park is a mile away from the shore of Lake Billy Chinook where some lakeshore cabins are available. Colorful rock formations rise from the canyon walls, and exceptional views are available from the park. Swimming, fishing, hiking and boating are just a few of your options here. Houseboats are available in the nearby marina.

15.   KOA MADRAS/CULVER   RV

Reference: **Near Lake Billy Chinook; map D3, grid b2.**

Campsites, facilities: There are 31 tent sites and 68 drive-through sites for trailers or RVs of any length. Electricity, piped water, sewer hookups and picnic tables are provided. Flush toilets, bottled gas, sanitary services, showers, firewood, a recreation hall, a store, a cafe, a laundromat, ice, a playground and a swimming pool are available. Pets and motorbikes are permitted. Boat docks and launching facilities are nearby.

Reservations, fee: Reservations accepted, phone (800) 563-1992; $17-$21 fee per night. MasterCard, Visa and American Express accepted. Open all year.

Who to contact: Phone (541) 546-3046 or write to 2435 Southwest Jericho Lane, Culver, OR 97734.

Location: From Portland, turn east on US 26 and drive 118 miles to Madras, then turn south on US 97 and drive nine miles. Continue one-half mile east on Jericho Lane to the campground.

Trip note: This campground is about three miles from Lake Billy Chinook, a steep-sided reservoir formed where the Crooked River, Metolius River, Deschutes River and Squaw Creek all merge. Like much of the country east of the Cascades, it is a high desert area.

16.   HAYSTACK LAKE   RV

Reference: **On Haystack Reservoir in Ochoco National Forest; map D3, grid b2.**

Campsites, facilities: There are 24 sites for tents, trailers or RVs up to 22 feet long. Picnic tables and fire grills are provided. Flush toilets and piped water are available. A store, a cafe and ice are located within five miles. Leashed pets are permitted. Boat docks, launching facilities and rentals are nearby.

Reservations, fee: No reservations; $6 fee per night. Open mid-May through September.

Who to contact: Phone the Crooked River National Grassland at (541) 416-6640 or write to P.O. Box 687, Prineville, OR 97754.

Location: From Interstate 5 at Portland, turn east on Interstate 84 and drive 91 miles. Turn south on US 97 and drive 90 miles to Madras. Continue south on US 97 for nine miles, then turn southeast on County Road 6 and drive three miles. Turn north on Forest Service Road 1275 and continue one-half mile to the campground.

Trip note: This campground is set along the shore of Haystack Reservoir, where waterskiing, swimming and fishing are some of the recreation options. The camping and fishing crowds are relatively light.

17.   WHISTLER SPRING

Reference: **In Ochoco National Forest; map D3, grid b4.**

Campsites, facilities: There is a large area for dispersed camping. A picnic table and a vault toilet are provided. There is **no piped water**. A horse corral is available. Leashed pets are permitted.

Reservations, fee: No reservations; no fee. Open late May to late October.

Who to contact: Phone the Prineville Ranger District at (541) 416-6500 or write to Ochoco National Forest, P.O. Box 490, Prineville, OR 97754.

Location: From Prineville on US 26, turn north on McKay Road and drive 12 miles, then drive 18 miles northeast on Forest Service Road 27. Turn south on Forest Service Road 2700-500 and drive one-quarter mile to the campground.

Trip note: This is a trailhead camp for a trail heading into the Mill Creek Wilderness. This area is extremely popular with rockhounds, who search for thundereggs, jasper and agates (digging is forbidden in wilderness areas, however.) Though primitive, this is a pretty camp and guarantees quiet and privacy.

18.   CROOKED RIVER RANCH RV PARK   RV

Reference: **Near Smith Rock State Park; map D3, grid c0.**

Campsites, facilities: There are 17 tent sites and 99 drive-through sites for trailers or RVs of any length. Electricity, piped water and sewer hookups are provided. Flush toilets, sanitary services, showers, a store, a cafe, a laundromat, ice, a playground and a swimming pool are available. Leashed pets are permitted.

Reservations, fee: Reservations accepted; $11-$16 fee per night. Good Sam member. Open April through October.

Who to contact: Phone (541) 923-1441 or write to P.O. Box 1448, Crooked River Ranch, OR 97760.

Location: From Interstate 5 at Albany, turn east on US 20 and drive approximately 100 miles to Sisters. Turn east on Highway 126 and continue 20 miles to Redmond. Turn north on US 97 and drive six miles, then turn west on Lower Bridge Road at Terrebonne and follow the signs for 7.5 miles.

Trip note: This campground is a short distance from Smith Rock State Park, which offers unique and colorful volcanic formations overlooking the Crooked River Canyon. To the north is Lake Billy Chinook, which offers waterskiing and fishing for bass and panfish. In the park there is a basketball court and a softball field; nearby recreation options include a golf course and tennis courts.

19.   CRYSTAL CORRAL RV PARK   RV

Reference: **Near Ochoco Lake State Park; map D3, grid c4.**

Campsites, facilities: There are 20 tent sites and 24 sites for trailers or RVs of any length. Electricity, piped water and sewer hookups are provided. Flush toilets, bottled gas, showers, a store, a cafe, a laundromat and ice are available. Pets (one per site) and motorbikes are permitted. Boat docks, launching facilities and rentals are nearby.

Reservations, fee: Reservations accepted; $8-$16 fee per night. Open all year.

Who to contact: Phone (541) 447-5932 or write to 226700 Crystal Corral, Prineville, OR 97754.

Location: From Interstate 5 at Portland, turn east on US 26 and drive approximately 147 miles to Prineville. Continue eight miles east on US 26 to the park on the left.

Trip note: This motor home park is not far from Ochoco Lake State Park, where recreation options include boating and fishing.

20.   OCHOCO LAKE STATE PARK   RV

Reference: **On Ochoco Lake; map D3, grid c4.**

Campsites, facilities: There are 22 primitive sites for tents, trailers or self-contained RVs up to 30 feet long, and a special area for hikers and bicyclists. Picnic tables and fire grills are provided. Piped water, firewood and flush toilets are available. Leashed pets are permitted. Boat launching facilities are nearby.

Reservations, fee: No reservations; $10 fee per night; $4 for hikers/bikers. Open all year.

Who to contact: Phone (541) 447-4363 or (800) 452-5687, or write to c/o Prineville Reservoir Route, 916777 Parkland Drive, Prineville, OR 97754.

Location: From Interstate 5 at Portland, turn east on US 26 and drive approximately 147 miles to Prineville. Continue seven miles east on US 26 to the park entrance.

Trip note: This is one of the nicer camps along Highway 26 in eastern Oregon. This state park is on the shore adjacent to Ochoco Lake, where boating and fishing are popular pastimes. There are some quality hiking trails available.

21.   LAKESHORE RV PARK & STORE   RV

Reference: On Ochoco Lake; map D3, grid c4.

Campsites, facilities: There are 43 sites for tents, trailers or RVs up to 45 feet. Air conditioning, electric heat, cable TV, restrooms, showers, a sanitary dump, a public phone, limited groceries, ice, RV supplies and LP gas are available. Recreational facilities include a recreation hall, a playground, a marina, a boat dock, ramp and rentals. Some facilities are **wheelchair accessible**.

Reservations, fee: Reservations recommended; $15 fee per night. Visa and MasterCard are accepted; Good Sam member. Open all year.

Who to contact: Phone the park at (541) 447-6059 or write to 226900 East Highway 26, Prineville, OR 97754.

Location: From Interstate 5 at Portland, turn east on US 26 and drive approximately 147 miles to Prineville. Continue eight miles east on US 26 to the park on the left.

Trip note: Set on grassy hills on beautiful Lake Ochoco, this park offers many recreational opportunities including hunting, trout fishing, swimming and boating. It is a more developed option to the nearby state park campground.

22.   WILDCAT   RV

Reference: On the East Fork of Mill Creek in Ochoco National Forest; map D3, grid c5.

Campsites, facilities: There are 17 sites for tents, trailers or RVs up to 30 feet long. Picnic tables and fire grills are provided. Piped water and vault toilets are available. Leashed pets are permitted.

Reservations, fee: No reservations; $6 fee per night. Open mid-April to late October.

Who to contact: Phone the Prineville Ranger District at (541) 416-6500 or write to Ochoco National Forest, P.O. Box 490, Prineville, OR 97754.

Location: From Interstate 5 at Albany, take exit 233 and turn east on US 20. Drive 74 miles, then turn east on Highway 126 and continue southeast for 65 miles to Prineville. Turn east on US 26 and drive nine miles, then turn northeast on Forest Service Road 33 and continue about 10.5 miles to the campground.

Trip note: This campground is set along the East Fork of Mill Creek near a trailhead that provides access into the Mill Creek Wilderness. Stein's Pillar and Twin Pillars, popular rock climbing spots, are nearby. Ochoco Lake and Ochoco Lake State Park to the south provide side trip possibilities.

23.   WALTON LAKE   RV

Reference: On Walton Lake in Ochoco National Forest; map D3, grid c6.

Campsites, facilities: There are 30 sites for tents, trailers or RVs up to 31 feet long. Picnic tables and fire grills are provided. Piped water and vault toilets are available. Leashed pets are permitted. Boat launching facilities are nearby.

Reservations, fee: No reservations; $6 fee per night. Open June to late September.

Who to contact: Phone Big Summit Ranger District at (541) 416-6645 or write to Ochoco National Forest, 348855 Ochoco Ranger District, Prineville, OR 97754-9612.

Location: From Interstate 5 at Albany, take exit 233 and turn east on US 20. Drive 74 miles, then turn east on Highway 126 and continue southeast for 65 miles to Prineville. Continue 16.5 miles east on US 26, then 14 miles northeast on County Route 123. Turn north on Forest Service Road 22 and proceed to the Ochoco Ranger Station. Continue seven miles to the campground.

Trip note: This campground is set along the shore of Walton Lake. Fishing and swimming are popular and boats without motors are allowed. Hikers can explore a nearby trail that leads south to Round Mountain.

---

24. DEEP CREEK ▥

Reference: **On the North Fork of Crooked River in Ochoco National Forest; map D3, grid c8.**

Campsites, facilities: There are six sites for tents, trailers or RVs up to 22 feet long. Picnic tables and fire grills are provided. Vault toilets are available, but there is **no piped water**. Leashed pets are permitted.

Reservations, fee: No reservations; no fee. Open June to mid-October.

Who to contact: Phone Big Summit Ranger District at (541) 416-6645 or write to 348855 Ochoco Ranger Station, Prineville, OR 97754.

Location: From Interstate 5 at Albany, take exit 233 and turn east on US 20. Drive 74 miles, then turn east on Highway 126 and continue southeast for 65 miles to Prineville. Continue 16.5 miles east on US 26, then 8.5 miles northeast on County Route 22. Turn southeast on Forest Service Road 42 and drive 23.5 miles to the campground.

Trip note: This camp is small and gets little use, but it is set at a nice spot—the confluence of Deep Creek and the North Fork of the Crooked River. It has pretty, shady sites and river access. Fishing is an option here.

---

25. TUMALO STATE PARK ▥

Reference: **On Deschutes River; map D3, grid d0.**

Campsites, facilities: There are 67 sites for tents, 21 sites with full hookups for trailers or RVs up to 44 feet long, and a special camping area for hikers and bicyclists. Electricity, piped water, sewer hookups, fire grills and picnic tables are provided. Flush toilets, showers, firewood, and a playground are available. A store, a cafe and ice are located within one mile. Leashed pets are permitted.

Reservations, fee: Contact Reservations Northwest at (800) 452-5687 ($6 reservation fee) ; $9-$19 fee per night; $4 for hikers/bikers. Open all year.

Who to contact: Phone (541) 388-6055 or (800) 452-5687, or write to High Desert Management Unit, 62976 O.B. Riley Road, Bend, OR 97701.

Location: From Interstate 5 at Albany, turn east on US 20 and drive approximately 117 miles to the park entrance (located five miles west of Bend). Drive one mile west to the campground on the left.

Trip note: This campground is set along the banks of the Deschutes River. Trout fishing can be good. The swimming area is safe and ideal for school children. Boating is also an option here. See the trip note for Bend Keystone RV Park, camp number 27, for more recreation information.

26.　　JOHN'S MOBILE AND RV PARK　　🚐

Reference: **Near the Deschutes River; map D3, grid d0.**

Campsites, facilities: There are 10 tent sites and 35 drive-through sites for trailers or RVs of any length. Electricity, piped water, picnic tables and sewer hookups are provided. Flush toilets, showers and a laundromat are available. Bottled gas, sanitary services, a store, a cafe and ice are located within one mile. Leashed pets are permitted.

Reservations, fee: Reservations accepted; $15 fee per night. Open all year.

Who to contact: Phone (541) 382-6206 or write to 61415 South US 97, Bend, OR 97701.

Location: From Interstate 5 at Albany, turn east on US 20 and drive 122 miles to Bend. Travel one-half mile south of Bend on US 97 and you'll see the trailer park entrance.

Trip note: This park is set near the Deschutes River. Nearby recreation options include a golf course, a stable, bike paths and tennis courts. See the trip note for Bend Keystone RV Park for additional recreation information.

27.　　　BEND KEYSTONE RV PARK　　🚐

Reference: **Near Deschutes River; map D3, grid d0.**

Campsites, facilities: There are 29 sites for trailers or RVs of any length. Electricity, cable TV, piped water and sewer hookups are provided. Flush toilets, showers and a laundromat are available. Bottled gas, sanitary services, a store, a cafe and ice are located within one mile. Cats are permitted.

Reservations, fee: Reservations accepted; $14 fee per night. Open all year.

Who to contact: Phone (541) 382-2335 or write to 305 Northeast Burnside, Bend, OR 97701.

Location: From Interstate 5 at Albany, turn east on US 20 and drive 122 miles to Bend. Turn south on US 97 and drive one-half mile to the turnoff for the park.

Trip note: Bend is a popular spot to use as a home base. The 100-mile Deschutes Forest Highway Loop connects here. Several state parks are within an hour's drive and several city-managed parks provide access to the Deschutes River. Good side trips include the Oregon High Desert Museum, just six miles south of Bend on US 97. Just a few miles further is the Lava River Cave and the Lava Butte Geological Area.

28.　　　　BEND KAMPGROUND　　🚐

Reference: **Near Bend; map D3, grid d1.**

Campsites, facilities: There are 40 tent sites and 74 drive-through sites for trailers or RVs of any length. Piped water and picnic tables are provided. Electricity, sewer hookups, flush toilets, showers, a laundromat, a store, a deli, ice, firewood, a playground, a swimming pool, recreation room, bottled gas and sanitary disposal station are available. Leashed pets are permitted.

Reservations, fee: Reservations accepted; $15-$20 fee per night; MasterCard and Visa accepted; Good Sam member. Open all year.

Who to contact: Phone (541) 382-7738 or write to 63615 North US 97, Bend, OR 97701.

Location: From Interstate 5 at Albany, turn east on US 20 and drive 122 miles to Bend. Travel two miles north of Bend on US 97 and you'll see the campground entrance.

Trip note: Nearby recreation options include a golf course, hiking trails, bike paths and tennis courts. See the trip note for Bend Keystone RV Park for additional recreation information.

29.   PRINEVILLE RESERVOIR RESORT   RV

Reference: **On Prineville Reservoir; map D3, grid d3.**

Campsites, facilities: There are 71 sites for trailers or RVs of any length (four drive through). Electricity, piped water, fire pits and picnic tables are provided. Flush toilets, bottled gas, sanitary disposal services, showers, firewood, a store, a cafe, a laundromat and ice are available. Pets are permitted. Boat docks, launching facilities and rentals are nearby.

Reservations, fee: Reservations accepted; $11-$17 fee per night. MasterCard, Visa and Discover accepted. Open mid-March to mid-October, weather permitting.

Who to contact: Phone to (541) 447-7468 or write to 1300 PLR, Prineville, OR 97754.

Location: From Interstate 5 at Albany, turn east on US 20 and drive 100 miles to Sisters. Turn east on Highway 126 and drive 39 mile to Prineville. Turn east on US 26 and drive one mile, then drive one mile south on Combs Flat Road. The camp is 18 miles south on Juniper Canyon Road.

Trip note: This resort is set along the shore of the Prineville Reservoir, a good spot for water sports and fishing. It has a combination of dirt and gravel sites, mostly shaded, with easy access to the reservoir.

30.   PRINEVILLE RESERVOIR STATE PARK   RV

Reference: **On Prineville Reservoir; map D3, grid d4.**

Campsites, facilities: There are 25 tent sites and 45 sites with partial hookups for trailers or RVs up to 40 feet long. Electricity, piped water, sewer hookups and picnic tables are provided. Flush toilets, showers and firewood are available. Pets are permitted. Boat docks and launching facilities are nearby.

Reservations, fee: Reservations accepted; $16-$20 fee per night. Open all year.

Who to contact: Phone to (541) 447-4363 or (800) 452-5687, or write to 916777 Parkland Drive, Prineville, OR 97754.

Location: From Interstate 5 at Portland, turn east on US 26 and drive approximately 147 miles to Prineville. Continue one mile east on US 26, then turn south on Combs Flat Road and drive one mile. Continue 16 miles southeast on Prineville Reservoir Road to the park.

Trip note: This state park is set along the shore of the Prineville Reservoir. Swimming, boating, fishing and waterskiing are among the options available here. The nearby boat docks and ramp are a bonus. This is one of two campgrounds on the lake; the other is Prineville Reservoir Resort (RVs only).

31.   CROWN VILLA RV PARK   RV

Reference: **Near Bend; map D3, grid e0.**

Campsites, facilities: There are 124 sites for trailers or RVs of any length (106 full hookups, 18 partial hookups). Electricity, piped water, sewer hookups and picnic tables are provided. Flush toilets, showers, cable TV, a laundromat, bottled gas, ice, sanitary disposal station and a playground are available. A store and a cafe are located within one mile. Leashed pets are permitted.

Reservations, fee: Reservations accepted; $17-$27 fee per night; MasterCard and

Visa accepted. Open all year.

Who to contact: Phone (541) 388-1131 or write to 60801 Brosterhous Road, Bend, OR 97702.

Location: From Interstate 5 at Albany, turn east on US 20 and drive 122 miles to Bend. Travel two miles south of Bend on US 97, then head east on Brosterhous Road to 60801 Brosterhous Road.

Trip note: This motor home park offers large, grassy sites. Nearby recreation options include horseback riding and golf. See the trip note for Bend Keystone RV Park for additional recreation information.

---

32.   SWAMP WELLS HORSE CAMP   RV

Reference: **Near Arnold Ice Caves in Deschutes National Forest; map D3, grid e2.**

Campsites, facilities: There are five primitive sites for tents, trailers or RVs up to 22 feet long. Picnic tables and fire grills are provided. There is **no piped water**. Leashed pets are permitted.

Reservations, fee: No reservations; no fee. Open April to late November.

Who to contact: Phone the Fort Rock Ranger District at (541) 388-5664 or write to Deschutes National Forest, 1230 NE Third Street, Bend, OR 97701.

Location: From Interstate 5 at Albany, turn east on US 20 and drive 122 miles to Bend. From Bend, travel 1.5 miles south on US 97, then six miles east on Forest Service Road 18. The camp is five miles south on Forest Service Road 1810, then three miles southeast on 1816. You'll be traveling on a dirt road, but a well-marked one.

Trip note: After looking at the map, this campground may appear to be quite remote, but it is actually in an area that has been heavily logged. It is a good place for horseback riding and the trails that go south reenter the forested areas. Nearby are the Arnold Ice Caves, a system of lava tubes that is fun to explore. A Forest Service map details trail options.

---

33.   ANTELOPE FLAT RESERVOIR   RV

Reference: **On Antelope Flat Reservoir in Ochoco National Forest; map D3, grid e5.**

Campsites, facilities: There are 24 sites for tents, trailers or RVs up to 30 feet long. Picnic tables and fire grills are provided. Hand-pumped water and vault toilets are available. Leashed pets are permitted. Boat launching facilities are nearby.

Reservations, fee: No reservations; $6 fee per night. Open early May to late October.

Who to contact: Phone the Prineville Ranger District at (541) 416-6500 or write to Ochoco National Forest, P.O. Box 490, Prineville, OR 97754.

Location: From Interstate 5 at Albany, take exit 233 and turn east on US 20. Drive 74 miles, then turn east on Highway 126 and continue southeast for 65 miles to Prineville. Turn south on County Road 380 and drive 30 miles southeast, then 11 miles south on Forest Service Road 17. The camp is 300 yards east on Forest Service Road 1700-600.

Trip note: This campground is set along the west shore of Antelope Flat Reservoir. Fishing can be good and boating with motors is permitted. This is also a good lake for canoes. This is a pretty spot, with wide sites and easy access to the lake.

34. PINE CREEK RV

Reference: **At the headwaters of Pine Creek in Ochoco National Forest; map D3, grid e5.**

Campsites, facilities: There are two primitive sites for tents, trailers or small RVs. Picnic tables, fire grills, a vault toilet and piped water are provided. Leashed pets are permitted.

Reservations, fee: No reservations; no fee. Open mid-May to late October.

Who to contact: Phone the Prineville Ranger District at (541) 416-6500 or write to Ochoco National Forest, P.O. Box 490, Prineville, OR 97754.

Location: From Interstate 5 at Albany, take exit 233 and turn east on US 20. Drive 74 miles, then turn east on Highway 126 and continue southeast for 65 miles to Prineville. Turn south on County Road 380 and drive 30 miles southeast, then turn south on Forest Service Road 17 and drive nine miles. Turn east on Forest Service Road 1750 and drive 100 yards, then turn into the campground on Forest Service Road 1750-450.

Trip note: This is a pretty, remote little camp set on Pine Creek. With only two primitive sites, this is about as close as you can get to having a campground all to yourself. Hiking trails are available in the area.

---

35. DOUBLE CABIN RV

Reference: **On Double Cabin Creek in Ochoco National Forest; map D3, grid e6.**

Campsites, facilities: There are five sites for tents, trailers or small RVs. Picnic tables, fire grills and a vault toilet are provided. There is **no piped water**. Leashed pets are permitted.

Reservations, fee: No reservations; no fee. Open mid-May to late October.

Who to contact: Phone the Prineville Ranger District at (541) 416-6500 or write to Ochoco National Forest, P.O. Box 490, Prineville, OR 97754.

Location: From Interstate 5 at Albany, take exit 233 and turn east on US 20. Drive 74 miles, then turn east on Highway 126 and continue southeast for 65 miles to Prineville. Turn south on County Road 380 and drive 30 miles southeast, then turn south on Forest Service Road 17 and drive ten miles. Turn east on Forest Service Road 16 and drive five miles, then turn north on Forest Service Road 1600-350 and drive one-quarter mile to the campground.

Trip note: This is an even more primitive option to Pine Creek Campground. For a nice side trip, go back to Forest Service Road 16 and travel one-quarter mile further up the road to beautiful little Double Cabin Pond. You will pass old beaver dams on Road 16. Hikers can enjoy breathtaking views by trudging up the ridge to the north of camp.

---

36. ELKHORN RV

Reference: **Near Drake Creek in Ochoco National Forest; map D3, grid e6.**

Campsites, facilities: There are four sites for tents, trailers or small RVs. Picnic tables, fire grills and a vault toilet are provided. There is **no piped water**. Leashed pets are permitted.

Reservations, fee: No reservations, no fee. Open mid-May to late October.

Who to contact: Phone the Prineville Ranger District at (541) 416-6500 or write to Ochoco National Forest, P.O. Box 490, Prineville, OR 97754.

Location: From Interstate 5 at Albany, take exit 233 and turn east on US 20. Drive

74 miles, then turn east on Highway 126 and continue southeast for 65 miles to Prineville. Turn south on County Road 380 and drive 34 miles, then five miles southeast on Forest Service Road 16 to the campground.

Trip note: Set near Drake Creek and Miller Lake, this wooded camp is an alternative to Wiley Flat Campground. This is a popular rockhounding area, with moss agates the most sought-after. A designated collecting area is three-quarters of a mile north on Forest Service Road 1690, about 1.5 miles west of Elkhorn Campground.

---

37.   WILEY FLAT   **RV**

Reference: **On Wiley Creek in Ochoco National Forest; map D3, grid e6.**

Campsites, facilities: There are five sites for tents, trailers or RVs up to 30 feet long. Picnic tables and fire grills are provided. Vault toilets are available, but there is **no piped water**. Leashed pets are permitted.

Reservations, fee: No reservations; no fee. Open mid-June to late October.

Who to contact: Phone the Prineville Ranger District at (541) 416-6500 or write to Ochoco National Forest, P.O. Box 490, Prineville, OR 97754.

Location: From Interstate 5 at Albany, take exit 233 and turn east on US 20. Drive 74 miles, then turn east on Highway 126 and continue southeast for 65 miles to Prineville. Turn south on County Road 380 and drive 34 miles, then ten miles southeast on Forest Service Road 16. The camp is one mile west on Forest Service Road 1600-400.

Trip note: This campground is set along Wiley Creek. It is a nice, hidden spot with minimal crowds. A map of Ochoco National Forest details nearby access roads. A good gut-thumping hike is the trip to Tower Point Lookout. It's one mile north of camp and a 1,000-foot climb straight up. Double Cabin Campground provides a nearby, but more primitive, alternative.

---

38.   PAULINA LAKE   **RV**

Reference: **On Paulina Lake in Deschutes National Forest; map D3, grid f1.**

Campsites, facilities: There are 69 sites for trailers or RVs up to 30 feet long. Picnic tables and fire grills are provided. Flush toilets, showers and a laundromat are located within five miles. Piped water is available. Leashed pets are permitted. Boat docks, launching facilities and rentals are nearby.

Reservations, fee: No reservations; $11-$13 fee per night. Open late May to late October.

Who to contact: Phone Northwest Land Management at (541) 536-8344 or write P.O. Box 1917, Laping, OR 97739. Or phone the Fort Rock Ranger District at (541) 388-5664 or write to Deschutes National Forest, 1230 NE Third Street, Bend, OR 97701.

Location: From Interstate 5 south of Eugene, take exit 188 and turn east on Highway 58. Drive 86 miles, then turn north on US 97 and drive 26 miles to LaPine. Continue five miles northeast on US 97, then 13 miles east on County Road 21.

Trip note: This campground is set along the south shore of Paulina Lake at 6,300 feet. The recreation options here include boating, sailing, fishing and hiking. Nearby trails provide access to the remains of volcanic activity, including craters and obsidian flows.

39. CHIEF PAULINA HORSE CAMP **RV**

Reference: **On Paulina Lake in Deschutes National Forest; map D3, grid f1.**

Campsites, facilities: There are 14 sites for tents, trailers or RVs up to 30 feet long. Picnic tables and fire grills are provided. Piped water and vault toilets are available. Leashed pets are permitted. Boat docks and rentals are nearby.

Reservations, fee: Reservations required, phone (800) 280-2267; $10 fee per night; the entire camp can be reserved for $45 per night. Open late May to late October.

Who to contact: Phone Northwest Land Management at (541) 536-8344 or write P.O. Box 1917, Laping, OR 97739. Or phone the Fort Rock Ranger District at (541) 388-5664 or write to Deschutes National Forest, 1230 NE Third Street, Bend, OR 97701.

Location: From Interstate 5 south of Eugene, take exit 188 and turn east on Highway 58. Drive 86 miles, then turn north on US 97 and drive 26 miles to LaPine. Continue five miles northeast on US 97, then 15 miles east on County Road 21.

Trip note: This campground is set near the south shore of Paulina Lake. Horse trails and a vista point are nearby. See the trip note for Paulina Lake for additional recreation information.

40. LITTLE CRATER **RV**

Reference: **Near Paulina Lake in Deschutes National Forest; map D3, grid f1.**

Campsites, facilities: There are 50 sites for tents, trailers or RVs up to 30 feet long. Picnic tables and fire grills are provided. Piped water and vault toilets are available. Leashed pets are permitted. Boat docks, launching facilities and rentals are available nearby.

Reservations, fee: No reservations; $11-$13 fee per night. Open late May to late October.

Who to contact: Phone Northwest Land Management at (541) 536-8344 or write P.O. Box 1917, Laping, OR 97739. Or phone the Fort Rock Ranger District at (541) 386-5664 or write to Deschutes National Forest, 1230 NE Third Street, Bend, OR 97701.

Location: From Interstate 5 south of Eugene, take exit 188 and turn east on Highway 58. Drive 86 miles, then turn north on US 97 and drive 26 miles to LaPine. Continue five miles northeast on US 97, then 15 miles east on County Road 21.

Trip note: This campground is set near the east shore of Paulina Lake in Newberry Crater, a caldera. See the trip note for Paulina Lake.

41. CINDER HILL **RV**

Reference: **On East Lake in Deschutes National Forest; map D3, grid f1.**

Campsites, facilities: There are 110 sites for tents, trailers or RVs up to 30 feet long. Picnic tables and fire grills are provided. Piped water and flush and vault toilets are available. Leashed pets are permitted. Boat docks, launching facilities and rentals are nearby.

Reservations, fee: No reservations; $11-$13 fee per night. Open late May to late October.

Who to contact: Phone Northwest Land Management at (541) 536-8344 or write P.O. Box 1917, Laping, OR 97739. Or phone the Fort Rock Ranger District at

(541) 388-5664 or write to Deschutes National Forest, 1230 NE Third Street, Bend, OR 97701.

Location: From Interstate 5 south of Eugene, take exit 188 and turn east on Highway 58. Drive 86 miles, then turn north on US 97 and drive 26 miles to LaPine. Continue five miles northeast on US 97, then 18 miles east on County Road 21.

Trip note: This campground is set along the northeast shore of East Lake at an elevation of 6,400 feet. Boating, fishing and hiking are among the recreation options here.

---

42.   EAST LAKE   🚐

Reference: **On East Lake in Deschutes National Forest; map D3, grid f1.**

Campsites, facilities: There are 29 sites for tents, trailers or RVs up to 30 feet long. Picnic tables and fire grills are provided. Piped water and flush and vault toilets are available. Leashed pets are permitted. Boat docks, launching facilities and rentals are nearby.

Reservations, fee: No reservations; $11-$13 fee per night. Open late May to late October.

Who to contact: Phone Northwest Land Management at (541) 536-8344 or write P.O. Box 1917, Laping, OR 97739. Or phone the Fort Rock Ranger District at (541) 388-5664 or write to Deschutes National Forest, 1230 NE Third Street, Bend, OR 97701.

Location: From Interstate 5 south of Eugene, take exit 188 and turn east on Highway 58. Drive 86 miles, then turn north on US 97 and drive 26 miles to LaPine. Continue five miles northeast on US 97, then 17 miles east on County Road 21.

Trip note: This campground is set along the south shore of East Lake. Boating and fishing are popular here, and hiking trails provide access to signs of former volcanic activity in the area.

---

43.   HOT SPRINGS   🚐

Reference: **Near East Lake in Deschutes National Forest; map D3, grid f1.**

Campsites, facilities: There are 42 sites for tents, trailers or RVs up to 30 feet long. Picnic tables and fire grills are provided. Piped water and vault toilets are available. Leashed pets are permitted. Boat docks, launching facilities and rentals are nearby.

Reservations, fee: No reservations; $11-$13 fee per night. Open late May to late October.

Who to contact: Phone Northwest Land Management at (541) 536-8344 or write P.O. Box 1917, Laping, OR 97739. Or phone the Fort Rock Ranger District at (541) 388-5664 or write to Deschutes National Forest, 1230 NE Third Street, Bend, OR 97701.

Location: From Interstate 5 south of Eugene, take exit 188 and turn east on Highway 58. Drive 86 miles, then turn north on US 97 and drive 26 miles to LaPine. Continue five miles northeast on US 97, then 17.5 miles east on County Road 21.

Trip note: This campground is set across the road from East Lake. See the trip note for East Lake for additional recreation information.

44.   EAST LAKE RESORT & RV PARK   RV.

Reference: On East Lake; map D3, grid f1.

Campsites, facilities: There are 32 sites for trailers or RVs of any length. Electricity, piped water and picnic tables are provided. Flush toilets, bottled gas, sanitary services, showers, firewood, a store, a cafe, a laundromat, ice and a playground are available. Pets and are permitted. Boat launching facilities and rentals are nearby.

Reservations, fee: Reservations accepted; $12 fee per night. Open mid-May to mid-October, weather permitting.

Who to contact: Phone (541) 536-2230 or write to P.O. Box 95, LaPine, OR 97739.

Location: From Interstate 5 south of Eugene, take exit 188 and turn east on Highway 58. Drive 86 miles, then turn north on US 97 and drive 26 miles to LaPine. Continue six miles northeast on US 97, then 18 miles east on East Lake-Paulina Lake Road which deadends at the campground.

Trip note: This resort is set along the east shore of East Lake, with opportunities for fishing, boating and swimming. It is in a wooded, mountainous setting with shaded sites.

45.   CHINA HAT   RV.

Reference: In Deschutes National Forest; map D3, grid f2.

Campsites, facilities: There are 14 sites for tents, trailers or RVs up to 30 feet long. Picnic tables and fire grills are provided. Vault toilets are available. There is **no piped water**. Leashed pets are permitted.

Reservations, fee: No reservations; no fee. Open May to late October.

Who to contact: Phone the Fort Rock Ranger District at (541) 388-5664 or write to Deschutes National Forest, 1230 NE Third Street, Bend, OR 97701.

Location: From Interstate 5 south of Eugene, take exit 188 and turn east on Highway 58. Drive 86 miles, then turn north on US 97 and drive 26 miles to LaPine. Drive east on Forest Service Road 22 for about 30 miles, then north for six miles on Forest Service Road 18.

Trip note: This remote campground is set at 5,100 feet in a rugged, primitive setting. Hunters use it as a base camp in the fall. There are hiking and birdwatching opportunities, too.

46.   CABIN LAKE   RV.

Reference: In Deschutes National Forest; map D3, grid f2.

Campsites, facilities: There are 14 sites for tents, trailers or RVs up to 30 feet long. Picnic tables and fire grills are provided. Vault toilets are available. There is **no piped water**. Leashed pets are permitted.

Reservations, fee: No reservations; no fee. Open mid-May to late October.

Who to contact: Phone the Fort Rock Ranger District at (541) 388-5664 or write to Deschutes National Forest, 1230 NE Third Street, Bend, OR 97701.

Location: From Interstate 5 at Eugene, take exit 188 and turn east on Highway 58. Drive 86 miles, then turn north on US 97 and drive 26 miles to LaPine. Continue about 30 miles east on Forest Service Road 22, then south on Forest Service Road 18 for six miles.

Trip note: This remote campground is set at 4,500 feet. Adjacent to the campground is an 80-year-old bird blind—a great place to watch birds. This spot is primitive and secluded, receiving little use even in the busy summer months.

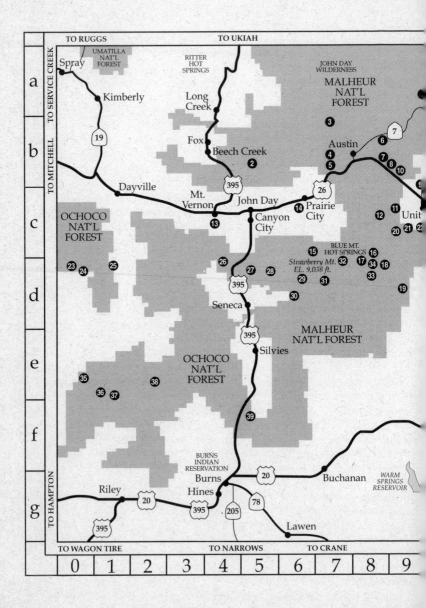

Oregon Map D4 featuring: Olive Lake, Umatilla National Forest, Wallowa-Whitman National Forest, Unity Reservoir, John Day River, Burnt River, Malheur National Forest, Magone Lake, Starr Ridge, Ochoco National Forest, Strawberry Mountain Wilderness, Canyon Meadows Reservoir, Malheur River, Prairie City, Divine Canyon, Yellowjacket Lake, Delintment Lake

1. McCULLY FORKS

Reference: **On McCully Creek in Wallowa-Whitman National Forest; map D4, grid a9.**

Campsites, facilities: There are six tent sites. Picnic tables and fire grills are provided. Firewood and vault toilets are available. There is **no piped water**. Leashed pets are permitted.

Reservations, fee: No reservations; no fee. Open late May to late October.

Who to contact: Phone the Baker Ranger District at (541) 523-1932 or write to Wallowa-Whitman National Forest, P.O. Box 907, Baker City, OR 97814.

Location: From Interstate 84 at Baker City, travel southwest on Highway 7 to the 410 junction. Turn right and travel six miles northwest on Highway 410. The campground is located three miles past Sumpter.

Trip note: This campground is set along the banks of McCully Creek. It is an easy access campground that is tiny, free and primitive. Recreational goldpanning is allowed in the creek (within the campground only). The camp gets moderately heavy use and is often full on weekends.

2. MAGONE LAKE   RV

Reference: **On Magone Lake in Malheur National Forest; map D4, grid b5.**

Campsites, facilities: There are 19 sites for tents, trailers or RVs up to 16 feet long. There is a separate group camping area designed for six families. Some facilities are **wheelchair-accessible**. Picnic tables and fire grills are provided. Piped water and composting toilets are available. Leashed pets are permitted. Boat docks and launching facilities are nearby.

Reservations, fee: No reservations; no fee. Open mid-May to November.

Who to contact: Phone Long Creek Ranger District at (541) 575-2110 or write to Malheur National Forest, 528 East Main, John Day, OR 97845.

Location: From John Day on US 26, travel eight miles west on US 26, then drive nine miles north on US 395. Turn northeast on Forest Service Road 36 and drive eight miles. The camp is two miles north on Forest Service Road 3618.

Trip note: This campground is set along the shore of little Magone Lake. A 1.5-mile trail rings the lake, and a half-mile trail is routed to Magone Slide, a unique geological formation. See a Forest Service map for other trails in the area. Swimming, fishing, sailing and canoeing are some of the popular activities at this lake. There is also an easy-access bike trail within one-quarter mile of the campground.

3. OLIVE LAKE   RV

Reference: **On Olive Lake in Umatilla National Forest; map D4, grid b7.**

Campsites, facilities: There are 24 sites for tents, trailers or RVs up to at least 31 feet long (four can handle up to 45 feet). **No piped water** is available. Picnic tables and fire grills are provided. Vault toilets are available. Leashed pets are permitted. Boat docks and launching facilities are available.

Reservations, fee: No reservations; no fee; 14-day limit. Open June to mid-October, weather permitting.

Who to contact: Phone the North Fork John Day Ranger District at (541) 427-3231 or write to Umatilla National Forest, P.O. Box 158, Ukiah, OR 97880.

Location: From Pendleton on Interstate 84, turn south on US 395 and drive 62 miles to Forest Service Road 55 (one mile north of Dale). Turn right and drive one-half mile, then turn right on Forest Service Road 10 and continue for 26 miles to the park on the right.

Trip note: This campground is set at 6,100 feet along the shore of Olive Lake, located between two sections of the North Fork John Day Wilderness. Nearby trails provide access to the wilderness. Motorbikes and mountain bikes are not permitted in the wilderness.

---

4.   MIDDLE FORK   RV

Reference: **On the Middle Fork of John Day River in Malheur National Forest; map D4, grid b7.**

Campsites, facilities: There are nine sites for tents, trailers or RVs up to 20 feet long. Picnic tables and fire grills are provided. Vault toilets are available. There is **no piped water**. Leashed pets are permitted.

Reservations, fee: No reservations; no fee. Open mid-June to November.

Who to contact: Phone Long Creek Ranger District at (541) 575-2110 or write to Malheur National Forest, 528 East Main, John Day, OR 97845.

Location: From Prairie City on US 26, travel 15 miles northeast on US 26, then one mile north on Highway 7 to its junction with County Road 20. The camp is five miles northwest on County Road 20.

Trip note: This campground is set along the banks of the Middle Fork of the John Day River. It is a rustic spot that is easy to reach off a paved road. Besides wildlife-watching and berry picking, the main activity at this camp is fishing, so bring along your fly rod.

---

5.   DIXIE   RV

Reference: **Near Dixie Summit in Malheur National Forest; map D4, grid b7.**

Campsites, facilities: There are 10 sites for tents, trailers or RVs up to 20 feet long. Picnic tables, vault toilets and fire grills are provided. A store, cafe, gas and ice are available within six miles. Hand-pumped well water is available. Leashed pets are permitted.

Reservations, fee: No reservations; no fee. Open June to November.

Who to contact: Phone Long Creek Ranger District at (541) 575-2110 or write to Malheur National Forest, 528 East Main, John Day, OR 97845.

Location: From Prairie City on US 26, travel 11 miles northeast on US 26, then one-half mile north on Forest Service Road 365.

Trip note: This campground is set at Dixie Summit at 5,300 feet, near Bridge Creek. It is just off US 26, close enough to provide easy access. Fishing is available in Bridge Creek.

---

6.   ANTLERS GUARD STATION

Reference: **On the North Fork of Burnt River in Wallowa-Whitman National Forest; map D4, grid b8.**

Campsites, facilities: There is one four-bed cabin available. Picnic tables and fire grills are provided. Piped water and vault toilets are available. Leashed pets are permitted.

Reservations, fee: No reservations; no fee. Open May to mid-September.

Who to contact: Phone the Unity Ranger District at (541) 448-3351 or write to Wallowa-Whitman National Forest, P.O. Box 907, Baker City, OR 97814.

Location: From Pendleton on Interstate 84, take exit 304, turn south (left) on Highway 7 and drive 20 miles to Whitney. Turn south on County Road 529 and drive three miles along the North Fork Burnt River to the cabin site.

Trip note: This spot is just off Highway 26 and is a staging site for ATV trails.

7.   OREGON   [RV]

Reference: **Near Austin Junction in Wallowa-Whitman National Forest; map D4, grid b8.**

Campsites, facilities: There are 11 sites for tents, trailers or RVs up to 28 feet long. Picnic tables and fire grills are provided. Piped water and vault toilets are available. Leashed pets are permitted.

Reservations, fee: No reservations; no fee. Open May to mid-September.

Who to contact: Phone the Unity Ranger District at (541) 448-3351 or write to Wallowa-Whitman National Forest, P.O. Box 907, Baker City, OR 97814.

Location: From Pendleton on Interstate 84, take Baker City exit 304 and drive 32 miles on Highway 7 to Austin Junction. Turn east on Highway 26 and drive 20 miles to the campground.

Trip note: This campground is just off Highway 26 and is a staging site for ATV trails.

8.   YELLOW PINE   [RV]

Reference: **On Road Creek in Wallowa-Whitman National Forest; map D4, grid b8.**

Campsites, facilities: There are 21 sites for tents, trailers or RVs up to 28 feet long. Picnic tables and fire grills are provided. Piped water, a waste disposal station and vault toilets are available. Leashed pets are permitted.

Reservations, fee: No reservations; no fee. Open late May to mid-September.

Who to contact: Phone the Unity Ranger District at (541) 446-3351 or write to Wallowa-Whitman National Forest, P.O. Box 907, Baker City, OR 97814.

Location: From Pendleton on Interstate 84, take exit 209 and turn south on US 395. Drive 120 miles, then turn east on US 26 and drive 47 miles to the campground (11 miles northwest of Unity).

Trip note: This campground is set along the banks of Road Creek. There are hiking trails in the area, including a one-mile trail that is **wheelchair accessible** that connects to the preceding camp. There is easy access with good recreation potential.

9.   UNITY LAKE STATE PARK   [RV]

Reference: **On Unity Reservoir; map D4, grid b9.**

Campsites, facilities: There are 21 sites with water and electrical hookups for tents or RVs up to 60 feet long, and a special camping area for hikers and bicyclists. Picnic tables and fire grills are provided. Piped water, flush toilets, showers, sanitary disposal station and firewood are available. Some facilities are **wheelchair accessible**. Leashed pets are permitted. Boat docks and launching facilities are nearby.

Reservations, fee: No reservations; $15 fee per night; $4 for hikers/bikers. Open mid-April to late October.

Who to contact: Phone (541) 575-2773 or (800) 452-5687 or write to P.O. Box 9 Canyon City, OR 97820.

Location: From Pendleton on Interstate 84, take exit 209 and turn south on US 395. Drive 120 miles, then turn east on US 26 and drive 56 miles. Turn north (left) on Highway 245 and drive three miles to the park on the left.

Trip note: This campground is set along the east shore of Unity Reservoir. It's easy to reach and a popular spot when the weather is good. Campers can choose from hiking, swimming, boating, fishing, picnicking or enjoying the scenic views.

10.   WETMORE   RV

Reference: **On the Middle Fork of Burnt River in Wallowa-Whitman National Forest; map D4, grid b9.**

Campsites, facilities: There are 16 sites for tents, trailers or RVs up to 28 feet long. Picnic tables and fire grills are provided. Piped water, firewood and vault toilets are available. Some facilities are **wheelchair accessible**. Leashed pets are permitted.

Reservations, fee: No reservations; no fee. Open late May to mid-September.

Who to contact: Phone the Unity Ranger District at (541) 446-3351 or write to Wallowa-Whitman National Forest, P.O. Box 907, Baker City, OR 97814.

Location: From Pendleton on Interstate 84, take exit 209 and turn south on US 395. Drive 120 miles, then turn east on US 26 and drive 48 miles to the campground (10 miles northwest of Unity).

Trip note: This campground is set near the Middle Fork of Burnt River. It's a good base camp for a fishing or hiking trip. The stream can provide good trout fishing. Trails are detailed on a map of Wallowa-Whitman National Forest. In addition, an excellent one-half mile **wheelchair accessible** trail passes through old growth forest.

11.   AMELIA   RV

Reference: **Near Table Rock Lookout in Wallowa-Whitman National Forest; map D4, grid b8.**

Campsites, facilities: There are three sites for tents, trailers or RVs up to 28 feet long. Picnic tables and fire grills are provided. A vault toilet is available. Leashed pets are permitted.

Reservations, fee: No reservations; no fee. Open May to mid-September.

Who to contact: Phone the Unity Ranger District at (541) 448-3351 or write to Wallowa-Whitman National Forest, P.O. Box 907, Baker City, OR 97814.

Location: From Pendleton on Interstate 84, take exit 304 and drive 32 miles on Highway 7 to Austin Junction. Turn east on Highway 26 and drive 23 miles to Unity. Turn west on Highway 600 and turn left on Forest Service Road 6005 and left again on Forest Service Road 6010. Drive on Forest Service Road 6010 to the wilderness trail sign and the campground. (Forest Service Road 6010 is very narrow and rough.)

Trip note: A trail leads from the campground to the Monument Rock Wilderness area and is closed to motorized and mechanized vehicles. This difficult 2.6-mile trail is for hikers and horseback riders. Scenic areas on the route are Mine Ridge, Bullrun Rock and Bullrun Mountain.

12. TABLE ROCK   RV

Reference: **Near Table Rock Lookout in Wallowa-Whitman National Forest; map D4, grid b8.**

Campsites, facilities: There are three sites for tents, trailers or RVs up to 28 feet long. Picnic tables and fire grills are provided. A vault toilet is available. Leashed pets are permitted.

Reservations, fee: No reservations; no fee. Open May to mid-September.

Who to contact: Phone the Unity Ranger District at (541) 448-3351 or write to Wallowa-Whitman National Forest, P.O. Box 907, Baker City, OR 97814.

Location: From Pendleton on Interstate 84, take Baker City exit 304 and drive 32 miles on Highway 7 to Austin Junction. Turn east on Highway 26 and drive 23 miles to Unity. Turn west on Highway 600 and take, in succession, Forest Service Roads 6005, 6010, 6005.030, 6005.035 and 6005.045 to the wilderness trail sign and the campground. (Note that these roads are primitive and narrow. From Unity, it is about 10 miles to the campground. A Forest Service map is recommended.)

Trip note: A trail leads from the campground to the Monument Rock Wilderness area and is closed to motorized and mechanized vehicles. This difficult 2.2-mile trail is for hikers and horseback riders. Scenic areas on the route are the Elkhorn Range, the Greenhorn Range, Deardorf Mountain, Glacier Mountain and the Strawberry Mountain Range.

13. CLYDE HOLLIDAY STATE PARK   RV

Reference: **Near John Day River; map D4, grid c4.**

Campsites, facilities: There are 30 sites for trailers or RVs up to 60 feet long. Electricity, picnic tables and fire grills are provided. Piped water, firewood, sanitary disposal services, showers and flush toilets are available. Some facilities are **wheelchair accessible**. Leashed pets are permitted.

Reservations, fee: No reservations; $17 fee per night. Open March through November.

Who to contact: Phone to (541) 575-2773 or (800) 452-5687, or write to P.O. Box 9, Canyon City, OR 97820.

Location: From John Day at the intersection of US 395 and US 26, travel seven miles west on US 26 to the park on the left.

Trip note: This state park is set near the John Day River. Fishing is popular here, with river access available to visitors. Of special interest in John Day is Kam Wah Chung, a Chinese herbalist's office from the 1880s that is now a museum administered by the State Parks Department.

14. DEPOT PARK   RV

Reference: **On John Day River; map D4, grid c6.**

Campsites, facilities: There are 20 sites for tents, trailers or RVs up to 35 feet. Restrooms, showers, a sanitary dump and a public phone are provided. Leashed pets are permitted.

Reservations, fee: No reservations; $13 fee per night. Open from May 1 to October 31.

Who to contact: Phone Prairie City Hall at (541) 820-3605 or write to P.O. Box 370, Prairie City, OR 97869.

Location: From the junction of Highway 26 and Main Street in Prairie City, drive south on Main Street for one-half mile to the park (signed).

Trip note: This is an urban park on grassy flatlands. The park has access to the John Day River, which has good trout fishing. This is a more developed option to the many forest service campgrounds in the area. Nearby attractions include Strawberry Mountain Wilderness area (prime hiking trails) and Clyde Holliday State Park.

15.   STRAWBERRY

Reference: **On Strawberry Creek in Malheur National Forest; map D4, grid c7.**

Campsites, facilities: There are 11 sites for tents. Picnic tables and fire grills are provided. Piped water, vault toilets and some corrals are available. Leashed pets are permitted.

Reservations, fee: No reservations; no fee. Open June to mid-October.

Who to contact: Phone Prairie City Ranger District at (541) 820-3311 or write to Malheur National Forest, P.O. Box 337, Prairie City, OR 97869.

Location: From John Day at the intersection of US 395 and US 26, travel 13 miles east on US 26. Drive one-half mile southeast on County Road 62 to County Road 60. Turn south on County Road 60 and drive 8.5 miles to Forest Service Road 6001 and drive 2.5 miles to the campground on the left.

Trip note: This campground is set along the bank of Strawberry Creek at 5,700 feet elevation. Nearby trails provide access into the Strawberry Mountain Wilderness, to Strawberry Lake and Strawberry Falls. It is a pretty area with hiking and hunting options. There is fishing in Strawberry Creek.

16.   ELK CREEK

Reference: **On Elk Creek in Malheur National Forest; map D4, grid c8.**

Campsites, facilities: There are five tent sites. Picnic tables and fire grills are provided. Vault toilets are available. There is **no piped water**. Leashed pets are permitted.

Reservations, fee: No reservations; no fee. Open mid-May to mid-November.

Who to contact: Phone Prairie City Ranger District at (541) 820-3311 or write to Malheur National Forest, P.O. Box 337, Prairie City, OR 97869.

Location: From Pendleton on Interstate 84, take exit 209 and turn south on US 395. Drive 120 miles, then turn east on US 26 and drive 21 miles to Prairie City. Turn southeast on County Road 62 and drive 8.5 miles, then 16 miles southeast on Forest Service Road 13. The camp is 1.5 miles south on Forest Service Road 16.

Trip note: This pretty, tiny campground is set at the confluence of the North and South Forks of Elk Creek at 5,000 feet elevation, with hunting and fishing opportunities. It is advisable to obtain a map of Malheur National Forest that details the back country roads. North Fork Malheur is an alternate camp in the area.

17.   MAMMOTH   **RV**

Reference: **On South Fork of Burnt River in Wallowa-Whitman National Forest; map D4, grid c7.**

Campsites, facilities: There are two sites for tents, trailers or RVs up to 28 feet long. Picnic tables and fire grills are provided. Vault toilets are available. Leashed pets are permitted.

Reservations, fee: No reservations; no fee. Open May to mid-September.

Who to contact: Phone the Unity Ranger District at (541) 448-3351 or write to Wallowa-Whitman National Forest, P.O. Box 907, Baker City, OR 97814.

Location: From Pendleton on Interstate 84, take Baker City exit 304 and drive 32 miles on Highway 7 to Austin Junction. Turn east on Highway 26 and drive 23 miles to Unity. Turn west on Highway 600, west again on Forest Service Road 6005, and west a final time on Forest Service Road 2640. (The camp is nine miles from Unity.)

Trip note: South Fork is a nice trout creek with, according to the local ranger, "good evening bites for anglers who know how to sneak-fish." The camp is private and scenic.

18.　　　　　　　LONG CREEK　　　　　　　RV

Reference: On Long Creek Reservoir in Wallowa-Whitman National Forest; map D4, grid c8.

Campsites, facilities: There are three sites for tents, trailers or RVs up to 28 feet long. Picnic tables and fire grills are provided. A vault toilet is available. Leashed pets are permitted.

Reservations, fee: No reservations; no fee. Open May to mid-September.

Who to contact: Phone the Unity Ranger District at (541) 448-3351 or write to Wallowa-Whitman National Forest, P.O. Box 907, Baker City, OR 97814.

Location: From Pendleton on Interstate 84, take exit 304 , turning south (left) on Highway 7 and drive 32 miles to Austin Junction. Turn east on Highway 26 and drive 23 miles to Unity. Drive through Unity, turn south on Forest Service Road 1680 and drive nine miles to the campground on the left.

Trip note: This small, little known camp boasts good trout fishing in the Long Creek Reservoir.

19.　　　　　　　ELDORADO　　　　　　　RV

Reference: On East Camp Creek in Wallowa-Whitman National Forest; map D4, grid c9.

Campsites, facilities: There are six sites for tents, trailers or RVs up to 28 feet long. Picnic tables and fire grills are provided. Vault toilets are available. Leashed pets are permitted.

Reservations, fee: No reservations; no fee. Open May to mid-September.

Who to contact: Phone the Unity Ranger District at (541) 448-3351 or write to Wallowa-Whitman National Forest, P.O. Box 907, Baker City, OR 97814.

Location: From Pendleton on Interstate 84, take exit 304, turning south (left) on Highway 7 and drive 32 miles to Austin Junction. Turn east on Highway 26 and drive 23 miles to Unity. Drive through Unity, and continue another 10 miles on Highway 26. Turn south on Forest Service Road 1680 and drive three miles to the campground on the south side of the road.

Trip note: There is trout fishing in spring and early summer in East Camp Creek. The campground is also convenient for fishing Murray Reservoir.

20.　　　　　　　ELK CREEK #2　　　　　　　RV

Reference: On the South Fork of Burnt River in Wallowa-Whitman National Forest; map D4, grid c9.

Campsites, facilities: There is one group area for up to six tents, trailers or RVs up to 28 feet long. Picnic tables and fire grills are provided. Firewood and vault toilets are available. There is **no piped water.** Leashed pets are permitted.

Reservations, fee: No reservations; no fee. Open late May to mid-September.

Who to contact: Phone the Unity Ranger District at (541) 446-3351 or write to Wallowa-Whitman National Forest, P.O. Box 907, Baker City, OR 97814.

Location: From Pendleton on Interstate 84, take exit 209 and turn south on US 395. Drive 120 miles, then turn east on US 26 and drive 58 miles to Unity. In Unity, turn southwest on Forest Road 6005 (South Fork Road) and drive 10 miles to the campground.

Trip note: This campground is set along the bank of the South Fork of Burnt River. It is a small, obscure camp, a good base camp for fishing and hiking.

21.   SOUTH FORK   RV

Reference: On the South Fork of Burnt River in Wallowa-Whitman National Forest; map D4, grid c9.

Campsites, facilities: There are 14 sites for tents, trailers or RVs up to 28 feet long. Picnic tables and fire grills are provided. Piped water, firewood and vault toilets are available. Leashed pets are permitted.

Reservations, fee: No reservations; no fee. Open late May to mid-September.

Who to contact: Phone the Unity Ranger District at (541) 446-3351 or write to Wallowa-Whitman National Forest, P.O. Box 907, Baker City, OR 97814.

Location: From Pendleton on Interstate 84, take exit 209 and turn south on US 395. Drive 120 miles, then turn east on US 26 and drive 58 miles to Unity. From Unity, drive six miles southwest on Forest Service Road 6005 (South Fork Road) to the campground.

Trip note: This campground is set along the banks of the South Fork of Burnt River. It's a nice trout creek with good evening bites for anglers who know how to sneak-fish. This is a gem of a spot, with piped water, privacy and scenery, all for free.

22.   STEVENS CREEK   RV

Reference: On the South Fork of Burnt River in Wallowa-Whitman National Forest; map D4, grid c9.

Campsites, facilities: There is one group area for up to six tents, trailers or RVs of any length. Picnic tables and fire grills are provided, but there is **no piped water**. Firewood and vault toilets are available. Leashed pets are permitted.

Reservations, fee: No reservations; no fee. Open late May to mid-September.

Who to contact: Phone the Unity Ranger District at (541) 446-3351 or write to Wallowa-Whitman National Forest, P.O. Box 907, Baker City, OR 97814.

Location: From Pendleton on Interstate 84, take exit 209 and turn south on US 395. Drive 120 miles, then turn east on US 26 and drive 58 miles to Unity. Turn south on South Fork Road (Forest Service Road 6005) and drive seven miles to the campground.

Trip note: This campground is set along the banks of the South Fork of Burnt River and is an option to the other small camps along Burnt River. The trout fishing is good here. See the trip note for South Fork Campground.

23.   WOLF CREEK   RV

Reference: On Wolf Creek in Ochoco National Forest; map D4, grid d0.

Campsites, facilities: There are 17 sites for tents, trailers or RVs up to 22 feet long. Picnic tables and fire grills are provided, but there is **no piped water**. Vault toilets are available. Leashed pets are permitted.

Reservations, fee: No reservations; $6 fee per night. Open mid-April to late October.

Who to contact: Phone the Paulina Ranger District at (541) 416-6643 or write to Ochoco National Forest, 171500 Beaver Creek Road, Paulina, OR 97751.

Location: From Interstate 5 at Albany, take exit 233 and turn east on US 20. Drive 74 miles, then turn east on Highway 126 and continue southeast for 65 miles to Prineville. Turn south on County Road 380 and drive 55 miles to Paulina. Continue 3.5 miles east on County Road 380, then 6.5 miles north on County Road 113. The camp is 1.5 miles north on Forest Service Road 42.

Trip note: This campground is set along the banks of Wolf Creek, a nice stream that runs through Ochoco National Forest. It's a quality spot. Some excellent hiking trails are available to the northeast in Black Canyon Wilderness.

---

24. SUGAR CREEK

Reference: **On Sugar Creek in Ochoco National Forest; map D4, grid d0.**

Campsites, facilities: There are 10 sites for tents, trailers or RVs up to 21 feet long. Picnic tables and fire grills are provided. Well water and vault toilets are available. Some facilities are **wheelchair accessible.** Pets are permitted.

Reservations, fee: No reservations; $6 fee per night. Open June to late October.

Who to contact: Phone the Paulina Ranger District at (541) 416-6643 or write to Ochoco National Forest, 171500 Beaver Creek Road, Paulina, OR 97751.

Location: From Interstate 5 at Albany, take exit 233 and turn east on US 20. Drive 74 miles, then turn east on Highway 126 and continue southeast for 65 miles to Prineville. Turn south on County Road 380 and drive 55 miles to Paulina. Continue 3.5 miles east on County Road 380, then 6.5 miles north on County Road 113. The camp is two miles east on Forest Service Road 58.

Trip note: This campground is on the banks of Sugar Creek and is small, quiet and remote. There's a covered group shelter here, in the new day-use area.

---

25. FRAZIER

Reference: **On Frazier Creek in Ochoco National Forest; map D4, grid d1.**

Campsites, facilities: There are 18 sites for tents, trailers or RVs up to 21 feet long. Picnic tables and fire grills are provided. Firewood, vault toilets and a group shelter are available. There is **no piped water**. Leashed pets are permitted.

Reservations, fee: No reservations; no fee; 14-day limit. Open June through October.

Who to contact: Phone the Paulina Ranger District at (541) 477-3713 or write to Ochoco National Forest, 171500 Beaver Creek Road, Paulina, OR 97751.

Location: From Interstate 5 at Albany, take exit 233 and turn east on US 20. Drive 74 miles, then turn east on Highway 126 and continue southeast for 65 miles to Prineville. Turn south on County Road 380 and drive 55 miles to Paulina. Continue 3.5 miles east on County Road 380, then two miles north on County Road 113. Turn east on County Road 135 and drive ten miles, then six miles on Forest Service Road 58. Continue for two miles on Forest Service Road 58-500.

Trip note: This campground is set along the banks of Frazier Creek at 4,300 feet elevation. There are some dirt roads adjacent to camp that are good for mountain biking in summer and cross-country skiing and snowmobiling in winter. There are also hot springs nearby. It is advisable to obtain a map of Ochoco National Forest. It is a small, remote and little-used camp.

26.　　　　　　　　STARR　　　　　　　　🚐

Reference: **On Starr Ridge in Malheur National Forest; map D4, grid d4.**

Campsites, facilities: There are five tent sites and nine sites for trailers or RVs up to 25 feet long. Picnic tables and fire grills are provided. Vault toilets are available. There is **no piped water**. Leashed pets are permitted.

Reservations, fee: No reservations; no fee. Open early May to November.

Who to contact: Phone Bear Valley Ranger District at (541) 575-2110 or write to Malheur National Forest, 528 East Main, John Day, OR 97845.

Location: From John Day at the junction of US 395 and US 26, travel 15 miles south on US 395.

Trip note: This is a good layover for travelers on US 395. It is set adjacent to Starr Ski Bowl, which is popular in winter for skiing and sledding. The camp itself doesn't offer much in the way of recreation options, but to the northeast is Strawberry Mountain Wilderness, which has a number of trails, lakes and streams.

27.　　　　　　　　WICKIUP　　　　　　　🚐

Reference: **On Wickiup Creek in Malheur National Forest; map D4, grid d5.**

Campsites, facilities: There are eight sites for tents, trailers or RVs up to 16 feet long. Picnic tables and fire grills are provided. Piped water and vault toilets are available. Leashed pets are permitted. Horse corrals are available.

Reservations, fee: No reservations; no fee. Open early May to November.

Who to contact: Phone Bear Valley Ranger District at (541) 575-2110 or write to Malheur National Forest, 528 East Main, John Day, OR 97845.

Location: From John Day at the intersection of US 395 and US 26, travel 10 miles south on US 395 and eight miles southeast on Forest Service Road 15.

Trip note: This campground is set along the bank of Wickiup Creek. It is a historic site, with many original structures still in place. There is good fishing in the creek. To the north are many trails that are routed into the Strawberry Mountain Wilderness.

28.　　　　　　CANYON MEADOWS　　　　　🚐

Reference: **On Canyon Meadows Reservoir in Malheur National Forest; map D4, grid d5.**

Campsites, facilities: There are 15 sites for tents, trailers or RVs up to 16 feet long. Picnic tables and fire grills are provided. Piped water and vault toilets are available. Leashed pets are permitted. Boat launching facilities are nearby.

Reservations, fee: No reservations; no fee. Open mid-May to late October.

Who to contact: Phone Bear Valley Ranger District at (541) 575-2110 or write to Malheur National Forest, 528 East Main, John Day, OR 97845.

Location: From John Day at the intersection of US 395 and US 26, drive south on US 395 for 10 miles, then nine miles southeast on Forest Service Road 15. The camp is five miles northeast on Forest Service Road 1520.

Trip note: This campground is on the shore of Canyon Meadows Reservoir, where non-motorized boating, swimming, sailing, fishing and hiking are recreation options. There are several hiking trails nearby that lead north into the Strawberry Mountain Wilderness.

29.   INDIAN SPRINGS

Reference: **Near Strawberry Mountain Wilderness in Malheur National Forest; map D4, grid d6.**

Campsites, facilities: This is a primitive campground with no designated sites. **No piped water** or pit toilets are available. Leashed pets are permitted.

Reservations, fee: No reservations; no fee. Open June to mid-October.

Who to contact: Phone Bear Valley Ranger District at (541) 575-2110 or write to Malheur National Forest, 528 East Main, John Day, OR 97845.

Location: From John Day at the intersection of US 395 and US 26, travel 10 miles south on US 395, then east on Forest Service Road 15 for about 15 miles to Forest Service Road 16. Turn left and drive 2.5 miles, then turn left on Forest Service Road 1640 and continue seven miles north on a gravel then dirt road.

Trip note: This campground is set at Indian Springs, a pretty spot near Bear Creek. A side trip option is to drive the 77-mile loop around the Strawberry Mountain Wilderness. A map of Malheur National Forest details the back roads. Backpackers and hikers will find many trailheads along the Forest Service road.

30.   PARISH CABIN   **RV**

Reference: **On Little Bear Creek in Malheur National Forest; map D4, grid d6.**

Campsites, facilities: There are three tent sites and 16 sites for tents, trailers or RVs up to 32 feet long. Picnic tables and fire grills are provided. Piped water and vault toilets are available. Leashed pets are permitted.

Reservations, fee: No reservations; no fee. Open mid-May to late November.

Who to contact: Phone Bear Valley Ranger District at (541) 575-2110 or write to Malheur National Forest, 528 East Main, John Day, OR 97845.

Location: From John Day at the intersection of US 395 and US 26, travel 10 miles south on US 395, then 16 miles southeast on Forest Service Road 15 to the campground.

Trip note: This campground is set along the bank of Little Bear Creek. It's a pretty spot that is not heavily used. Fishing is available in Little Bear Creek. See a Forest Service map for hiking trails in the area.

31.   BIG CREEK   **RV**

Reference: **Near Strawberry Mountain Wilderness in Malheur National Forest; map D4, grid d7.**

Campsites, facilities: There are 15 sites for tents, trailers or RVs up to 16 feet long. Picnic tables and fire grills are provided. Hand-pumped water and vault toilets are available. Leashed pets are permitted.

Reservations, fee: No reservations; no fee. Open mid-May to mid-November.

Who to contact: Phone Prairie City Ranger District at (541) 820-3311 or write to Malheur National Forest, P.O. Box 337, Prairie City, OR 97869.

Location: From John Day at the intersection of US 395 and US 26, travel 10 miles south on US 395, then southeast on Forest Service Road 15 for 16 miles. Turn east and drive eight miles on Forest Service Road 16 (which becomes Forest Service Road 815). Continue one-half mile north on Forest Service Road 815 to the campground.

Trip note: This campground is set along the bank of Big Creek. Nearby Forest Service roads provide access into Strawberry Mountain Wilderness. Fishing and mountain biking are other recreational options. In the appropriate seasons, elk, bear, coyote and deer are hunted here.

32.   TROUT FARM   🆁🆅

Reference: **Near Prairie City in Malheur National Forest; map D4, grid d7.**

Campsites, facilities: There are six sites for tents, trailers or RVs up to 21 feet long. Picnic tables and fire grills are provided. Piped water and vault toilets are available. Leashed pets are permitted.

Reservations, fee: No reservations; no fee. Open June to mid-October.

Who to contact: Phone Prairie City Ranger District at (541) 820-3311 or write to Malheur National Forest, P.O. Box 337, Prairie City, OR 97869.

Location: From Pendleton on Interstate 84, take exit 209 and turn south on US 395. Drive 120 miles, then turn east on US 26 and drive 21 miles to Prairie City. Turn southeast on County Road 62 and drive 15 miles to the entrance on the right.

Trip note: This campground is set along the upper John Day River, which provides good trout fishing with easy access for people who do not wish to travel off paved roads. A picnic shelter is available for family picnics and there is a small pond at the campground with a trail that is **wheelchair accessible**.

33.   NORTH FORK MALHEUR

Reference: **On North Fork Malheur River in Malheur National Forest; map D4, grid d8.**

Campsites, facilities: There are five tent or trailer sites. Picnic tables and fire grills are provided. Vault toilets are available. There is **no piped water**. Leashed pets are permitted.

Reservations, fee: No reservations; no fee. Open mid-May to mid-November.

Who to contact: Phone Prairie City Ranger District at (541) 820-3311 or write to Malheur National Forest, P.O. Box 337, Prairie City, OR 97869.

Location: From Pendleton on Interstate 84, take exit 209 and turn south on US 395. Drive 120 miles, then turn east on US 26 and drive 21 miles to Prairie City. Turn southeast on County Road 62 and drive 8.5 miles, then 16 miles southeast on Forest Service Road 13. Drive two miles south on Forest Service Road 16, then take the left fork (Forest Road 1675) and drive two miles to the camp.

Trip note: This secluded campground is set along the banks of the North Fork of Malheur River, a designated Wild and Scenic River. Hiking trails and dirt roads provide additional access to the river and backcountry streams. It is essential to obtain a Forest Service map. There are good fishing, hunting and mountain biking opportunities in the area.

34.   LITTLE CRANE

Reference: **On Little Wet Creek in Malheur National Forest; map D4, grid d8.**

Campsites, facilities: There are five tent and trailer sites. Picnic tables and fire grills are provided. Vault toilets are available. There is **no piped water**. Leashed pets are permitted.

Reservations, fee: No reservations; no fee. Open June to mid-November.

Who to contact: Phone Prairie City Ranger District at (541) 820-3311 or write to Malheur National Forest, P.O. Box 337, Prairie City, OR 97869.

Location: From Pendleton on Interstate 84, take exit 209 and turn south on US 395. Drive 120 miles, then turn east on US 26 and drive 21 miles to Prairie City.

Turn southeast on County Road 62 and drive 8.5 miles, then 16 miles southeast on Forest Service Road 13. The camp is 5.5 miles south on Forest Service 16.

Trip note: This campground is set along the banks of Little Crane Creek, a good stream for sneak-fishing for trout. It is small and primitive, but quiet and private as well. There are also some good hiking trails in the area, the closest one at the North Fork Malheur River, detailed on a Forest Service map.

35. DELINTMENT LAKE   🚐

Reference: **On Delintment Lake in Ochoco National Forest; map D4, grid e0.**

Campsites, facilities: There are 24 sites for tents, trailers or RVs up to 30 feet long. Picnic tables and fire grills are provided. Piped water, and vault toilets are available. Some facilities are **wheelchair accessible**. Leashed pets are permitted. Boat docks and launching facilities are nearby.

Reservations, fee: No reservations; $6 fee per night. Open June to mid-October.

Who to contact: Phone the Snow Mountain Ranger District at (541) 573-4300 or write to Ochoco National Forest, HC 74, P.O. Box 12870, Burns, OR 97738.

Location: From the intersection of US 20 and US 395 at Burns, turn south on US 20 and drive 3 miles, then turn north on County Road 127 (which turns into Forest Service Road 47) and drive about 10 miles. Turn left on Forest Service Road 41 and travel about 30 miles to the campground.

Trip note: Not many people know about this one. This campground is set along the shore of Delintment Lake, originally a beaver pond which was gradually developed into a lake covering 57 acres. Here's a secret: rainbow trout here average 12 to 18 inches.

36. EMIGRANT   🚐

Reference: **Near Emigrant Creek in Ochoco National Forest; map D4, grid e1.**

Campsites, facilities: There are five sites for tents, trailers or RVs up to 30 feet long. Picnic tables and fire grills are provided, but there is **no piped water**. Vault toilets are available. Leashed pets are permitted.

Reservations, fee: No reservations; $6 fee per night. Open June to mid-October.

Who to contact: Phone the Snow Mountain Ranger District at (541) 573-4300 or write to Ochoco National Forest, HC 74, P.O. Box 12870, Burns, OR 97738.

Location: From the intersection of US 20 and US 395 at Burns, turn south on US 20 and drive three miles. Turn northwest on Forest Service Road 47 and drive 25 miles, then another 10 miles west on Forest Service Road 43.

Trip note: This campground is set on the border of Ochoco and Malheur national forests in a meadow near Emigrant Creek. This is one of three camps in the immediate area. There are several nearby backcountry dirt roads that are good for mountain biking. See a Forest Service map for details.

37. FALLS   🚐

Reference: **On Emigrant Creek in Ochoco National Forest; map D4, grid e1.**

Campsites, facilities: There are five sites for tents, trailers or RVs up to 30 feet long. Picnic tables and fire grills are provided. Piped water and vault toilets are available. Leashed pets are permitted.

Reservations, fee: No reservations; $6 fee per night. Open June to mid-October.

Who to contact: Phone the Snow Mountain Ranger District at (541) 573-4300 or write to Ochoco National Forest, Star Route 4, P.O. Box 12870 Highway 20, Burns, OR 97720.

Location: From the intersection of US 20 and US 395 at Burns, turn south on US 20 and drive three miles. Turn northwest on Forest Service Road 47 and drive 25 miles. The camp is another 8.5 miles west on Forest Service Road 43.

Trip note: This campground is set along the banks of Emigrant Creek, not far from Emigrant Campground. It's a small, quiet spot and receives relatively little use. There is fishing access to the creek nearby.

38. YELLOWJACKET **RV**

Reference: **On Yellowjacket Lake in Malheur National Forest; map D4, grid e2.**

Campsites, facilities: There are 20 sites for tents, trailers or RVs up to 22 feet long. Picnic tables, hand-pumped well water and vault toilets are available. Leashed pets are permitted. A boat launch is nearby.

Reservations, fee: No reservations; no fee. Open late May to mid-October.

Who to contact: Phone the Burns Ranger District at (541) 573-4300 or write to Malheur National Forest, HC 74, Box 12870, Hines, OR 97738.

Location: Travel one mile south of Burns on US 20, then 32 miles northwest on Forest Service Road 47. The camp is another four miles east on Forest Service Road 37 on the right.

Trip note: This campground is set along the shore of Yellowjacket Lake. Fishing can be very good in the summer. Boats without motors are encouraged, and the price of the camp is definitely a bonus.

39. IDLEWILD **RV**

Reference: **In Divine Canyon in Malheur National Forest; map D4, grid f5.**

Campsites, facilities: There are 26 sites for tents, trailers or RVs up to 30 feet long. Picnic tables, fire grills and a picnic shelter are provided. Piped water, a group shelter and vault toilets are available. Some facilities are **wheelchair accessible**. Leashed pets are permitted.

Reservations, fee: No reservations; no fee. Open late May to mid-October.

Who to contact: Phone the Burns Ranger District at (541) 573-4300 or write to Malheur National Forest, HC 74, Box 12870, Hines, OR 97738.

Location: From Burns on US 20, travel 17 miles north on US 395 to the campground on the right.

Trip note: This campground is set in Divine Canyon, a designated snow park in the winter, popular with locals for snowmobiling and cross-country skiing. Several trailheads initiate in this camp, including the Divine Summit Interpretive Loop Trail and the Idlewild Loop Trail. It's also a popular spot for visitors traveling up US 395 and in need of a stopover. It provides easy access and a pretty setting. See a Forest Service map for backcountry roads that make great mountain biking trails.

LEAVE NO TRACE TIPS

Keep the wilderness wild.

• Treat our natural heritage with respect.
Leave plants, rocks, and historical artifacts as you found them.

• Good campsites are found, not made. Do not alter a campsite.

• Let nature's sounds prevail; keep loud voices and noises to a minimum.

• Do not build structures or furniture or dig trenches.

OREGON MAP .... see page 380
Adjoining Maps
NORTH (C5) .... see page 458
EAST .... no map
SOUTH (E5) .... see page 684
WEST (D4) .... see page 580

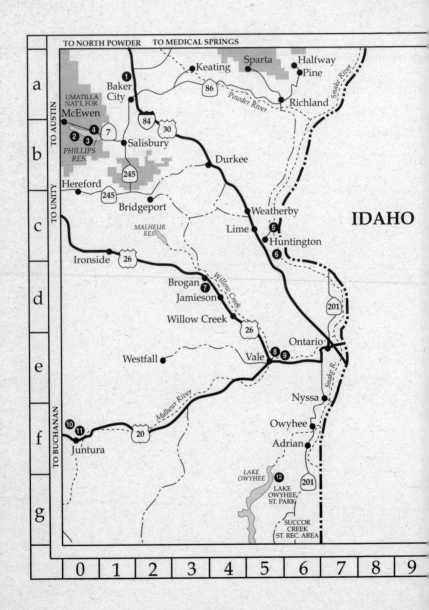

Oregon Map D5 featuring: Wallowa-Whitman National Forest, Phillips Lake, Vale, Snake River, Juntura, Owyhee Lake, Malheur River

1. MOUNTAIN VIEW TRAV-L PARK 🚐

Reference: **In Baker City; map D5, grid a2.**

Campsites, facilities: There are 11 tent sites and 69 full hookup sites (mostly pull-through) for trailers or RVs of any length. Electricity, piped water, sewer hookups, cable TV hookups, and picnic tables are provided. Flush toilets, sanitary disposal services, showers, a laundromat, ice, a playground and a swimming pool are available. Bottled gas, a store and a cafe are located within one mile. Pets and motorbikes are permitted.

Reservations, fee: Reservations accepted; $14-$17.95 fee per night. Open all year with limited winter facilities.

Who to contact: Phone (541) 523-4824 or write to 2845 Hughes Lane, Baker City, OR 97814. Call (800) 323-8899 for reservations only; ask for Best Holiday.

Location: From Interstate 84 at Baker City, take exit 304 and drive 1.5 miles west on Campbell Street. Take a right and drive one mile north on 10th Street to Hughes Lane. The camp is one block east on Hughes Lane.

Trip note: This grassy campground is "the gateway to camping on the Oregon Trail." There is an Oregon Trail Interpretive Center for those with a historical bent. It is a clean, cool park, with spacious sites and many recreation options nearby.

2. SOUTHWEST SHORE 🚐

Reference: **On Phillips Lake in Wallowa-Whitman National Forest; map D5, grid b0.**

Campsites, facilities: There are 20 sites for tents, trailers or RVs up to 24 feet long. Fire grills and vault toilets are available. There is **no piped water**. Leashed pets are permitted. A boat ramp is nearby.

Reservations, fee: No reservations; no fee. Open May to mid-November.

Who to contact: Phone the Baker Ranger District at (541) 523-1932 or write to Wallowa-Whitman National Forest, P.O. Box 907, Baker City, OR 97814.

Location: From Interstate 84 at Baker City, drive southwest on Highway 7 for 24 miles. Turn south on Hudspath Lane and drive two miles. Turn southeast on Forest Service Road 2220 and drive 2.5 miles to the campground entrance.

Trip note: This campground is set along the south shore of Phillips Lake, a four-mile long reservoir created by the Mason Dam on the Powder River. It's one of two primitive camps on the lake. The boat ramp is usable only when water is high in the reservoir. Nearby Union Creek has piped water.

3. MILLERS LANE 🚐

Reference: **On Phillips Lake in Wallowa-Whitman National Forest; map D5, grid b1.**

Campsites, facilities: There are seven sites for tents, trailers or RVs up to 20 feet long. Picnic tables and fire grills are provided. Firewood and vault toilets are available. There is **no piped water**. Leashed pets are permitted. A boat ramp is nearby.

Reservations, fee: No reservations; no fee. Open May to mid-November.

Who to contact: Phone the Baker Ranger District at (541) 523-1932 or write to Wallowa-Whitman National Forest, P.O. Box 907, Baker City, OR 97814.

Location: From Interstate 84 at Baker City, drive southwest on Highway 7 for 24 miles (just past Phillips Lake). Turn south on Hudspath Lane and drive two miles. Turn southeast on Forest Service Road 2220 and drive 3.5 miles to the campground entrance.

Trip note: This campground is set along the south shore of Phillips Lake. It is a long, narrow reservoir, the largest in the region. This is one of two camps on the lake.

4.   UNION CREEK   RV

Reference: **On Phillips Lake in Wallowa-Whitman National Forest; map D5, grid b1.**

Campsites, facilities: There are 58 sites for tents, trailers or RVs up to 32 feet long. Electricity, piped water, sewer hookups and picnic tables are provided. Flush toilets, firewood and ice are available. There is a small concession stand for packaged goods and fishing tackle. Some facilities are **wheelchair accessible**. Leashed pets are permitted. Boat docks and launching facilities are nearby.

Reservations, fee: No reservations; $8-$15 fee per night. Open mid-April to mid-November.

Who to contact: Phone the Baker Ranger District at (541) 523-4476 or write to Wallowa-Whitman National Forest, P.O. Box 907, Baker City, OR 97814.

Location: From Interstate 84 at Baker City, travel southwest on Highway 7 for 20 miles.

Trip note: This campground is set along the north shore of Phillips Lake. It is easy to reach, yet missed by most travelers on Interstate 84. It's the largest of three camps on the lake; this is also the only one with piped water.

5.   FAREWELL BEND STATE PARK   RV

Reference: **On Snake River; map D5, grid c5.**

Campsites, facilities: There are 43 primitive tent sites and 93 sites with partial hookups for trailers or RVs of any length. There are also some teepees and sleeper wagons available. Piped water, barbecues and picnic tables are provided. Flush toilets, sanitary disposal services, showers and firewood are available. Leashed pets are permitted. Boat launching facilities are nearby.

Reservations, fee: Contact Reservations Northwest at (800) 452-5687 ($6 reservation fee); $12-$16 fee per night; $25 teepee or sleeper wagon fee. Open all year with limited winter facilities.

Who to contact: Phone (541) 869-2365 or (800) 452-5687 or write to the park at Star Route, Huntington, OR 97907.

Location: From Ontario (near the Oregon/Idaho border), travel 25 miles northwest on Interstate 84 to the park entrance on the right.

Trip note: This campground is set along the banks of the majestic Snake River and is known as the "catfish capital" of Oregon. It is the site of a historic wagon train camp, and there is an exhibit on the Oregon Trail detailing its history. Recreation options include boating, swimming and picnicking.

6.   SPRING   RV

Reference: **On Snake River; map D5, grid c5.**

Campsites, facilities: There are 44 sites for tents, trailers or RVs. Picnic tables and fire grills are provided. Piped water, sanitary disposal services and vault toilets are available. Leashed pets are permitted. Boat launching facilities are nearby.

Reservations, fee: No reservations; $4 fee per night (14-day limit). Open March through October and some off-season weekends.

Who to contact: Phone (541) 523-6391 or write to Bureau of Land Management, P.O. Box 987, Baker City, OR 97814.

Location: From Interstate 84 on the Oregon/Idaho border, drive to Huntington. Turn northeast on Snake River Road and drive 3.5 miles northeast to the campground.

Trip note: This campground is set along the banks of the Snake River Reservoir. It's one of two camps in or near Huntington. A more developed alternative is Farewell Bend State Park, which offers showers and all the other luxuries a camper could want. Fishing and hunting opportunities are nearby.

---

7.   BROGAN TRAILER PARK & CAMP   RV

Reference: **Near Willow Creek; map D5, grid d3.**

Campsites, facilities: There are four tent sites and 15 drive-through sites for trailers or RVs of any length. Electricity, piped water, sewer hookups and picnic tables are provided. Flush toilets, showers, a laundromat and ice are available. Bottled gas, a store and a cafe are located within one mile. Leashed pets are permitted.

Reservations, fee: Reservations accepted; $6-$10 fee per night. Open April through December.

Who to contact: Phone (541) 473-3062 or write to P.O. Box 23, Brogan, OR 97903.

Location: From Interstate 84 at Ontario, turn west on US 20/26 and drive 12 miles to Vale. Turn northwest on US 26 and drive 24 miles to Brogan. The campground is in town on the left.

Trip note: This rural campground is set on the inner edge of the west's Great Basin. Nearby side trips include Willow Creek, which runs along US 26, or Malheur Reservoir, set northwest of Brogan.

---

8.   PROSPECTOR TRAVEL TRAILER PARK   RV

Reference: **In Vale; map D5, grid e5.**

Campsites, facilities: There are five tent sites and 28 drive-through sites for trailers or RVs of any length, plus a separate area for tents. Picnic tables are provided. Flush toilets, bottled gas, sanitary disposal services, showers, a laundromat and ice are available. A store and a cafe are located within one mile. Pets and motorbikes are permitted.

Reservations, fee: Reservations accepted; $10-$15 fee per night. Open all year, weather permitting.

Who to contact: Phone (541) 473-3879 or write to 511 North 11th Street East, Vale, OR 97918.

Location: From Interstate 84 at Ontario, turn west on US 20/26 and drive 12 miles to Vale. Turn north on US 26 and drive one-half mile, then one block east on Hope Street to the campground on the left.

Trip note: This is one of two camps (Westerner Trailer Park is the other) for travelers in the Vale area. This one is more comfortable for tents, with a specifically designated grassy area. It claims to be a fishing and hunting paradise, and even has a fish and game cleaning room.

9.   WESTERNER TRAILER PARK   RV

Reference: **On Willow Creek; map D5, grid e5.**

Campsites, facilities: There are 10 sites for tents, trailers or RVs of any length. Electricity, piped water, sewer hookups and picnic tables are provided. Flush toilets, showers, a laundromat and ice are available. Bottled gas, a store, a cafe and a swimming pool are located within two blocks. Pets and motorbikes are permitted.

Reservations, fee: Reservations accepted; $10 fee per night; MasterCard and Visa accepted. Open all year.

Who to contact: Phone (541) 473-3947 or write to 317 A Street East, Vale, OR 97918.

Location: From Interstate 84 at Ontario, turn west on US 20/26 and drive 12 miles to Vale. The campground is located on the left side at the junction of US 20 and US 26 in town.

Trip note: This campground is set along the banks of Willow Creek, a good layover spot for travelers heading to or from Idaho on US 20. See trip note for Prospector Travel Trailer Park.

10.   CHUKAR PARK   RV

Reference: **Near North Fork of Malheur River; map D5, grid f0.**

Campsites, facilities: There are 18 sites for tents, trailers or RVs up to 30 feet long. Picnic tables and fire grills are provided. Piped water and vault toilets are available. Leashed pets are permitted.

Reservations, fee: No reservations; $4 fee per night (14-day limit). Open mid-April through November.

Who to contact: Phone (541) 473-3144 or write to Bureau of Land Management, 100 Oregon Street, Vale, OR 97918.

Location: From Interstate 84 at Ontario, turn west on US 20 and drive 73 miles to Juntura. Continue six miles northwest of Juntura on Beulah Reservoir Road.

Trip note: This campground is set along the banks of the North Fork of the Malheur River. The area in general provides habitat for chukar, an upland game species. Hunting can be good in season during the fall, but requires much hiking in rugged terrain.

11.   OASIS RV PARK   RV

Reference: **In Juntura; map D5, grid f0.**

Campsites, facilities: There are 22 drive-through sites for trailers or RVs of any length. Electricity, piped water and sewer hookups are provided. Flush toilets, showers, a cafe and ice are available. Bottled gas and a store are located within one mile.

Reservations, fee: No reservations; $11 fee per night; MasterCard and Visa accepted. Open all year.

Who to contact: Phone (541) 277-3605 or write to P.O. Box 277, Juntura, OR 97911.

Location: From Interstate 84 at Ontario, turn west on US 20 and drive 73 miles to Juntura. The park is located in town.

Trip note: This is one of two camp possibilities in this area; the other is Idlewild, which is in a more primitive setting. Other than these two camps, the closest options are almost an hour's drive away.

12.   OWYHEE LAKE STATE PARK   RV

Reference: **On Owyhee Lake; map D5, grid f5.**

Campsites, facilities: There are 30 sites for tents or self-contained RVs, and 10 sites with water and electrical hookups for trailers or RVs of any length. Picnic tables and fire grills are provided. Flush toilets, a sanitary disposal station and showers are available. Leashed pets are permitted. Boat docks and launching facilities are available nearby.

Reservations, fee: No reservations; $14-$15 fee per night. Open April 12 through October.

Who to contact: Phone (541) 339-2331 or (800) 452-5687 or write to c/o 3012 Island Avenue, LaGrande, OR 97850.

Location: From Interstate 84 at Ontario (near the Oregon/Idaho border), turn south on Highway 201. Drive 19 miles to Owyhee Junction, then turn southwest on Owyhee Lake Road and drive 28 miles to the road's end and the entrance to the park.

Trip note: This state park is set along the shore of Owyhee Lake. This is a good lake for waterskiing in the day and for fishing for warm water species in the morning and evening. Owyhee is famous for its superb bass fishing. There are views of unique geological formations and huge rock pinnacles from the park. Leslie Gulch provides the only other camping option at the lake.

MAP E1

OREGON MAP .... see page 380

Adjoining Maps

NORTH (D1) .... see page 472

EAST (E2) .... see page 636

SOUTH .... no map

WEST .... no map

86 LISTINGS
PAGES 602-635

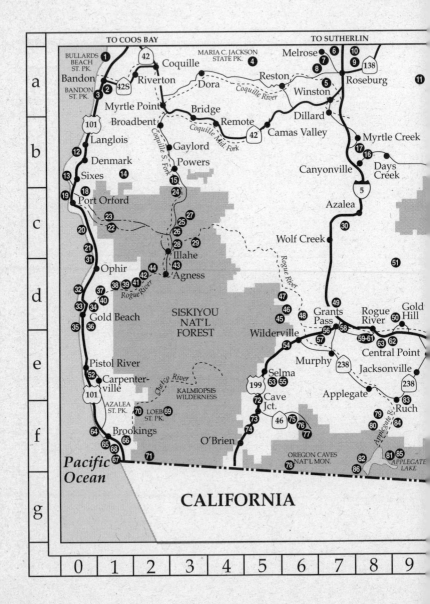

Oregon Map E1 featuring: Coquille River, Bandon State Park, Umpqua River, Roseburg, Elk River, Sixes River, Siskiyou National Forest, Laird Lake, Gold Beach, Glendale, Rogue River, Squaw Lake, Grants Pass, Oregon Caves National Monument, Chetco River, Illinois River, Lake Selmac, Applegate River, Winchuck River, Rogue River National Forest, Bolan Lake

---

1. BULLARDS BEACH STATE PARK   **RV**

Reference: **On Coquille River; map E1, grid a1.**

Campsites, facilities: There are 192 sites with full or partial hookups for trailers or RVs up to 64 feet long. There are four yurts available, one of which is **wheelchair accessible.** Each yurt can sleep five people. A special area for horses is also available, as well as an area reserved for hikers and bicyclists. Piped water, picnic tables and fire grills are provided. Flush toilets, sanitary disposal station, showers, firewood, and a loading ramp for horses are available. Some facilities are **wheelchair accessible.** Leashed pets are permitted. Boat docks and launching facilities are located in the park on the Coquille River.

Reservations, fee: Contact Reservations Northwest at (800)452-5687 ($6 reservation fee); $16-$19 fee per night; yurts are $25 per night; $4 for hikers/bikers; Open all year.

Who to contact: Phone (541) 347-2209 or (800) 452-5687 or write to P.O. Box 25, Bandon, OR 97411.

Location: In Coos Bay, drive south on US 101 for about 22 miles to the park on the right (located two miles north of Bandon).

Trip note: The Coquille River is the centerpiece for this park. It offers good fishing in season, both for boaters and crabbers, with four miles of shore access. If fishing isn't your thing, the park has several hiking trails. An historic lighthouse built in 1896 provides a side trip option. Equestrians can explore the seven-mile horse trail.

---

2. BANDON RV PARK   **RV**

Reference: **Near Bandon State Park; map E1, grid a1.**

Campsites, facilities: There are 40 drive-through sites for trailers or RVs of any length. Electricity, piped water and sewer hookups are provided. Flush toilets, sanitary services, showers, a cafe and a laundromat are available. Bottled gas and a store are located within one mile. Leashed pets are permitted. Boat docks and launching facilities are nearby.

Reservations, fee: Reservations accepted; phone (800) 393-4122; $15-$16.50 fee per night. Open all year.

Who to contact: Phone (541) 347-4122 or write to 935 East Second Street, Bandon, OR 97411.

Location: From US 101 at Coos Bay, drive 23 miles south to Bandon. Bandon RV Park is on Highway 101, one block south of the Highway 42S junction.

Trip note: This is an in-town motor home park that can be a base point for many adventures. Rockhounds will enjoy beachcombing for agates and other semi-precious stones hidden along the beaches. Kids will enjoy the West Coast Game Park Walk-Through Safari petting zoo seven miles south of town, and Bandon State Park, which is four miles south of town and offers a good wading spot in the creek at the north end of the park. Nearby recreation opportunities include an 18-hole golf course, riding stable and tennis courts.

3.   BLUE JAY CAMPGROUND   **RV**

Reference: **Near the Pacific Ocean; map E1, grid a1.**

Campsites, facilities: There are 19 tent sites and 22 sites for trailers or RVs up to 30 feet long. Electricity, piped water and picnic tables are provided. Flush toilets, bottled gas, sanitary services, showers, firewood, a store, a cafe, a laundromat, ice and a playground are available. Pets and motorbikes are permitted. Boat launching facilities are nearby.

Reservations, fee: Reservations accepted; $12-$14 fee per night. Open all year.

Who to contact: Phone (541) 347-3258 or write to P.O. Box 281, Bandon, OR 97411.

Location: Drive two miles south of Bandon on US 101, then drive one-half mile west on Beach Loop Road to the campground entrance.

Trip note: The trip note for Bandon RV Park offers side trip information in Bandon. This park is near the beach and close to an 18-hole golf course and hiking trails.

4.   PARK CREEK

Reference: **Near Coquille; map E1, grid a5.**

Campsites, facilities: There are eight sites for tents, small trailers or camping vans. Picnic tables and fire grills are provided. Vault toilets are available. There is **no piped water**. Leashed pets are permitted.

Reservations, fee: No reservations; no fee (14-day stay limit). Open all year.

Who to contact: Phone (541) 756-0100 or write to Bureau of Land Management, 1300 Airport Lane, North Bend, OR 97459.

Location: From Interstate 5 south of Roseburg, turn west on Highway 42 and drive approximately 64 miles to Coquille. Turn east on Coquille Fairview Road and travel 7.5 miles to Fairview. Turn right on Coos Bay Wagon Road. Drive 3.5 miles, turn east on Middle Creek Access Road and proceed 11 miles to the campground.

Trip note: You want to be by yourself? You came to the right place. This pretty little campground is set along Park Creek out in the middle of nowhere. It is very primitive, so don't forget your drinking water.

5.   WILDLIFE SAFARI RV PARK   **RV**

Reference: **Near Roseburg; map E1, grid a7.**

Campsites, facilities: There are 18 drive-through sites for self-contained trailers or RVs. Electricity, a gift shop and a cafe are available. There is **no piped water**. Pets and motorbikes are permitted.

Reservations, fee: No reservations; $3-$5 fee per night. Closed in winter.

Who to contact: Phone (541) 679-6761 or write to P.O. Box 1600, Winston, OR 97496.

Location: From Interstate 5 south of Roseburg, take exit 119 and drive 3.5 miles southwest on Highway 42 to the park at the end of the road.

Trip note: This park is part of the Wildlife Safari Park in Winston (near Roseburg), which offers a walk-through petting zoo. Nearby recreation options include an 18-hole golf course, hiking trails and marked bike trails.

6. JOHN P. AMACHER COUNTY PARK RV

Reference: **On Umpqua River; map E1, grid a7.**

Campsites, facilities: There are 20 sites for tents, and 30 sites for trailers or RVs up to 30 feet long. Electricity, piped water, sewer hookups and picnic tables are provided. Flush toilets, showers, and a playground are available. Bottled gas, a store, a cafe, a laundromat and ice are located within one mile. Pets and motorbikes are permitted. Boat launching facilities are nearby.

Reservations, fee: No reservations; $9-$12 fee per night. Open all year.

Who to contact: Phone (541) 672-4901 or write to P.O. Box 800, Winchester, OR 97495.

Location: From Roseburg, drive five miles north on Interstate 5. Take exit 129, turning south on Old Highway 99 and drive one-quarter mile to the park on the right.

Trip note: This is a prime layover spot for Interstate 5 motor home cruisers. It is a wooded county park set along the banks of the North Umpqua River, just enough off the beaten track to be missed by most out-of-towners. Nearby recreation options include an 18-hole golf course and tennis courts.

7. TWIN RIVERS VACATION PARK RV

Reference: **Near Umpqua River; map E1, grid a7.**

Campsites, facilities: There are 11 tent sites and 72 drive-through sites for trailers or RVs of any length. Electricity, piped water, sewer hookups and picnic tables are provided. Flush toilets, bottled gas, showers, firewood, a store, a laundromat, ice and a playground are available. Pets and motorbikes are permitted. Boat launching facilities are nearby.

Reservations, fee: Reservations accepted; $15-$20 fee per night. Open all year.

Who to contact: Phone (541) 673-3811 or write to 433 River Forks Park, Roseburg, OR 97470.

Location: From Roseburg on Interstate 5, take exit 125 and travel west for five miles. Turn south on Old Garden Valley Road and drive 1.5 miles to the end of the road and the entrance to the campground.

Trip note: This is the only campground in Roseburg with tent sites as well as motor home sites. It's a wooded campground near the Umpqua River. Nearby recreation options include a golf course, a county park and bike paths.

8. DOUGLAS COUNTY FAIRGROUNDS RV RV

Reference: **Near Umpqua River; map E1, grid a7.**

Campsites, facilities: There are 50 sites for tents, trailers or RVs of any length. Tent camping is limited to two nights. Electricity, piped water and picnic tables are provided. Flush toilets, sanitary services, showers and a playground are available. A store, a cafe, a laundromat and ice are located within one mile. Leashed pets are permitted.

Reservations, fee: No reservations; $15 fee per night; $2 dump station fee. Open all year, except one week in August during the county fair. Phone ahead to confirm that they're open.

Who to contact: Phone (541) 957-7010 or write to 2110 Southwest Frear Street, Roseburg, OR 97470.

Location: From Interstate 5 in Roseburg, take exit 123 and drive south, following signs, to the campground.

Trip note: This county park is near the Umpqua River, one of Oregon's prettiest rivers. There is often good fishing in season. Nearby recreation options include a golf course, bike paths and tennis courts.

9. ALAMEDA AVENUE TRAILER PARK   RV

Reference: **Near Umpqua River; map E1, grid a8.**

Campsites, facilities: There are 35 sites for trailers or RVs up to 30 feet long. Electricity, piped water and sewer hookups are provided. Flush toilets, sanitary services, showers and a laundromat are available. Bottled gas, a store, a cafe and ice are located within one mile. Leashed pets are permitted.

Reservations, fee: Reservations accepted; $10-$15 fee per night. Open all year.

Who to contact: Phone (541) 672-2348 or write to 581 Northeast Alameda, Roseburg, OR 97470.

Location: In Roseburg, take the Garden Valley exit off Interstate 5 and travel east to Business Route 99. Drive one-quarter mile north to Northeast Alameda Avenue. The park is on the left.

Trip note: This is one of four parks in Roseburg. This park is near the Umpqua River. Nearby recreation options include a golf course, bike paths and tennis courts.

10. MT. NEBO TRAILER PARK   RV

Reference: **Near Umpqua River; map E1, grid a8.**

Campsites, facilities: There are 20 drive-through sites for trailers or RVs of any length. Electricity, piped water and sewer hookups are provided. Flush toilets, sanitary services, showers and a laundromat are available. Bottled gas, a store and a cafe are within one mile. Leashed pets are permitted.

Reservations, fee: Reservations accepted; $16 fee per night. Open all year.

Who to contact: Phone (541) 673-4108 or write to 2071 Northeast Stephens, Roseburg, OR 97470.

Location: From Interstate 5 at Roseburg, take exit 125 and drive northeast to Stephens Street. Turn north and drive less than a mile to the park on the right.

Trip note: This is an option for motor home campers stopping in Roseburg. The park is near the Umpqua River. Nearby recreation options include a golf course, bike paths and tennis courts.

11. CAVITT CREEK   RV

Reference: **On Cavitt Creek; map E1, grid a9.**

Campsites, facilities: There are eight sites for trailers or RVs up to 20 feet long. Picnic tables and fire grills are provided. Pit toilets, piped water and firewood are available. Leashed pets are permitted.

Reservations, fee: No reservations; $5 fee per night (14-day stay limit). Open May 16 through Labor Day.

Who to contact: Phone (541) 440-4930 or write to Bureau of Land Management, 777 NW Garden Valley Boulevard, Roseburg, OR 97470.

Location: From Interstate 5 at Roseburg drive 18 miles east on Highway 138 to Glide. From Glide, travel seven miles southeast on Little River Road, then three miles south on Cavitt Creek Road to the campground.

Trip note: This campground is set along the bank of Cavitt Creek about three miles from its confluence with Little River. It is wooded, primitive and private. If you want to get deeper into the woods, the following camps provide options farther down the same road: Coolwater, White Creek (see Chapter E2) and Wolf Creek (see Chapter D4).

12. KOA BANDON-PORT ORFORD $\boxed{\text{RV}}$

Reference: **Near Elk River; map E1, grid b0.**

Campsites, facilities: There are 46 tent sites and 26 drive-through sites for trailers or RVs of any length. Picnic tables are provided. Cabins are also available. Flush toilets, bottled gas, sanitary services, showers, firewood, a recreation hall, a store, a cafe, a laundromat, ice, a playground, electricity, piped water and sewer hookups are available. Pets and motorbikes are permitted.

Reservations, fee: Reservations accepted; $15-$20 fee per night; $26 cabin fee. MasterCard and Visa accepted. Open all year.

Who to contact: Phone (541) 348-2358 or write to 46612 Highway 101, Langlois, OR 97450.

Location: From US 101 at Coos Bay, turn south and drive approximately 50 miles to the campground at milepost 286, on the right.

Trip note: This spot is considered to be just a layover camp, but it offers large, secluded sites set among big trees and coastal ferns. It is minutes away from Elk River and Sixes River, where the fishing can be good and Cape Blanco State Park is just a few miles away.

13. CAPE BLANCO STATE PARK $\boxed{\text{RV}}$

Reference: **Between Sixes and Elk Rivers; map E1, grid b0.**

Campsites, facilities: There are 58 sites with water and electrical hookups for tents, trailers or RVs up to 70 feet long. There is a special camp for horses, a camping area reserved for hikers and bicyclists, and one primitive group site which can accommodate 25 people. Picnic tables, piped water, electrical hookups and fire grills are provided. Firewood, flush toilets, showers and a sanitary disposal station are available. Leashed pets are permitted. Some facilities are **wheelchair accessible**.

Reservations, fee: Contact Reservations Northwest at (800) 452-5687 ($6 reservation fee); $15-$18 fee per night; yurts are $25 per night; $4 for hikers/bikers. Open all year.

Who to contact: Phone Humbug Mountain State Park at (541) 332-6774 or write c/o P.O. Box 1345, Port Orford, OR 97465.

Location: From Coos Bay, turn south on US 101 and drive approximately 46 miles to Cape Blanco Road. Turn northwest and drive five miles to the campground on the left.

Trip note: This large park is named for the white ("blanco") chalk appearance of the sea cliffs, which rise 200 feet above the ocean. Sea lions inhabit the offshore rocks, and there are trails and a road that leads to the black sand beach below the cliffs. There is good access to the Sixes River, which runs for over two miles through the meadows and forests of the park. Of historical interest are the lighthouse and Hughes House Museum, both located within the park. There are also trails for horseback riding.

14. SIXES RIVER $\boxed{\text{RV}}$

Reference: **On Sixes River; map E1, grid b1.**

Campsites, facilities: There are 22 sites for tents, trailers or RVs up to 30 feet long. Picnic tables and fire grills are provided. Pit toilets are available. There is **no**

piped water. Leashed pets are permitted.

Reservations, fee: No reservations; no fee (14-day stay limit). Open all year.

Who to contact: Phone (541) 756-0100 or write to Bureau of Land Management, 1300 Airport Lane, North Bend, OR 97459.

Location: From US 101 at Coos Bay, turn south and drive about 40 miles to Sixes. Turn east on Sixes River Road and drive 11.5 miles to the campground. The last one-half mile is unpaved.

Trip note: This is a primitive, secluded campground for people who want quiet and a free, rustic spot. It is set along the banks of Sixes River. Cape Blanco State Park provides a camping or side trip option.

15.　　　　POWERS COUNTY PARK　　　　RV

Reference: **Near South Fork of Coquille River; map E1, grid b3.**

Campsites, facilities: There are 30 sites for tents, trailers or RVs. Restrooms, showers, a sanitary dump and a public phone are provided. Other facilities include a boat ramp, horseshoes, a playground and a recreation field.

Reservations, fee: No reservations; $9-$11 fee per night. Open all year.

Who to contact: Phone the park at (541) 439-2791.

Location: From Interstate 5 south of Roseburg, take exit 120 and turn west on Highway 42. Drive about 50 miles to the Powers Highway exit (before Myrtle Point). Drive west on Powers Highway for 19 miles to the park on the right.

Trip note: This public park is set in a wooded, mountainous area. It is private and secluded, a great stop for travelers going from Interstate 5 to the coast. There is a small pond at the park where visitors can boat, swim and fish for trout.

16.　　　　CHARLES V. STANTON PARK　　　　RV

Reference: **On South Umpqua River; map E1, grid b8.**

Campsites, facilities: There are 20 tent sites and 20 sites for trailers or RVs up to 30 feet long. Electricity, piped water, sewer hookups and picnic tables are provided. Flush toilets, showers and a playground are available. Bottled gas, sanitary disposal services, a store, a cafe, a laundromat and ice are located within one mile. Pets and motorbikes are permitted.

Reservations, fee: No reservations; $9-$12 fee per night. Open all year.

Who to contact: Phone (541) 839-4483 or write to 1540 Stanton Park Road, Canyonville, OR 97417.

Location: Take exit 99 off Interstate 5 in Canyonville (follow the sign), then drive one mile north on the frontage road to the campground on the right.

Trip note: This campground is set along the banks of the South Umpqua River. It is an all-season spot with a good beach for swimming in the summer, good steelhead fishing in the winter and wild grape picking in the fall.

17.　　　　SURPRISE VALLEY RV PARK　　　　RV

Reference: **On South Umpqua River; map E1, grid b8.**

Campsites, facilities: There are 15 tent sites and 25 drive-through sites for trailers or RVs of any length. Electricity, piped water, sewer hookups and picnic tables are provided. Flush toilets, showers and a laundromat are available. Leashed pets are permitted.

Reservations, fee: No reservations; $10-$15 fee per night. Open all year.

Who to contact: Phone (541) 839-6634 or write to P.O. Box 909, Canyonville, OR 97417.

Location: From Interstate 5 at Canyonville, drive three miles north to exit 102, then one mile east on Gazley Road.

Trip note: This motor home park is set near the South Umpqua River about two miles from a gambling casino. For a more remote setting, the following sites are the answer: Dumont Creek, Boulder Creek and Camp Comfort (see Chapter E2).

18.   ELK RIVER CAMPGROUND   **RV**

Reference: **Near Elk River; map E1, grid c0.**

Campsites, facilities: There are 70 sites for tents, trailers or RVs up to 60 feet. Restrooms, showers, a sanitary dump, a public phone and a laundromat are available. Recreational facilities include a recreation field, horseshoes, a recreation hall and a boat ramp. Some facilities are **wheelchair accessible**. Pets are permitted on leashes.

Reservations, fee: Reservations recommended; $12-$14 fee per night.

Who to contact: Phone the park at (541) 332-2255 or write to 93363 Elk River Road, Port Orford, OR 97465.

Location: From the north end of Port Orford, continue north on Highway 101 for 1.5 miles to Elk River Road (milepost 297). Turn east on Elk River Road and drive for 1.8 miles to the campground on the left.

Trip note: This campground is quiet and restful. It is excellent for fall and winter fishing on the Elk River, which is known for its premier salmon fishing. There is a one-mile private access road to the river, so guests get their own personal fishing hole.

19.   PORT ORFORD TRAILER VILLAGE   **RV**

Reference: **Near Elk and Sixes rivers; map E1, grid c0.**

Campsites, facilities: There are seven tent sites and 49 drive-through sites for trailers or RVs of any length. Electricity, piped water, sewer hookups and picnic tables are provided. Flush toilets, bottled gas, sanitary services, showers, a recreation hall, a cafe, a laundromat and ice are available. Pets and motorbikes are permitted. Boat docks and launching facilities are nearby.

Reservations, fee: Reservations accepted; $15 fee per night. Open all year.

Who to contact: Phone (541) 332-1041 or write to P.O. Box 697, Port Orford, OR 97465.

Location: From US 101 at Coos Bay, turn south and drive approximately 50 miles to Port Orford. Drive one block east on Madrona Avenue, then one-half mile north on Port Orford Loop on the left side.

Trip note: This is a friendly, mom-and-pop campground in Port Orford, where the hosts make you feel at home. An informal group campfire and happy hour is scheduled each evening. There is a small gazebo where you can get coffee in the morning and a patio where you can sit. Fishing is good during the fall and winter on the nearby Elk and Sixes rivers, and the campground has a smokehouse, a freezer and a cleaning table.

20.   HUMBUG MOUNTAIN STATE PARK   **RV**

Reference: **Near the Pacific Ocean; map E1, grid c0.**

Campsites, facilities: There are 78 tent sites and 30 sites with full hookups for trailers or RVs up to 55 feet long. A special camping area is provided for hikers and bicyclists. Fire grills and picnic tables are provided. Flush toilets, showers and firewood are available. Leashed pets are permitted.

Reservations, fee: Contact Reservations Northwest at (800) 452-5687 ($6 reservation fee); $15-$18 fee per night; $4 for hikers/bikers. Open all year.

Who to contact: Phone (541) 332-6774 or write to P.O. Box 1345, Port Orford, OR 97465.

Location: From Coos Bay, turn south on US 101 and drive 50 miles to Port Orford. Continue six miles south on US 101 to the park entrance on the left.

Trip note: This park is named after the mountain that towers almost 2,000 feet above the nearby coastline. A three-mile trail leads to its peak. This is a special place because both the Pacific Ocean and nearby Brush Creek are accessible. You can fish in either. Beautiful evening sunsets can be seen at this park.

21.   ARIZONA BEACH CAMPGROUND   **RV**

Reference: **Near Gold Beach; map E1, grid c0.**

Campsites, facilities: There are 48 tent sites and 78 drive-through sites for trailers or RVs of any length. There is also a motel on the grounds. Electricity, piped water, sewer hookups and picnic tables are provided. Flush toilets, bottled gas, sanitary services, showers, firewood, a store, a laundromat and a playground are available. Pets and motorbikes are permitted.

Reservations, fee: No reservations; $10-$20 fee per night; $29-$69 motel fee. MasterCard and Visa accepted. Open all year.

Who to contact: Phone (541) 332-6491 or write to P.O. Box 621, Gold Beach, OR 97444.

Location: From US 101 at the town of Gold Beach, drive 14 miles north to the campground on the right.

Trip note: This pleasant campground offers grassy, tree-lined sites set along a half mile of ocean beach frontage. A creek runs through the campground and people swim at the mouth of it in the summer. The elk and deer roam nearby. An 11-unit motel is available for campers who need some cleanup time.

22.   LAIRD LAKE

Reference: **On Laird Lake in Siskiyou National Forest; map E1, grid c1.**

Campsites, facilities: There are undeveloped, dispersed tent sites available, with no designated sites. There is **no piped water**. Leashed pets are permitted.

Reservations, fee: No reservations; no fee. Open all year.

Who to contact: Phone the Siskiyou National Forest at (541) 439-3011 or write to Powers Ranger District, Powers, OR 97466.

Location: From US 101 at Coos Bay, turn south and drive 47 miles to County Road 208 (three miles north of Port Orford). Turn right and drive 7.5 miles southeast, then take Forest Service Road 5325 southeast and drive 15.5 miles to the campground. The road is paved all the way to the campground.

Trip note: This secluded campground is set along the shore of Laird Lake in a very private and scenic spot. Most campers have no idea that such a spot is available here. This can be just what you're looking for if you're tired of fighting the crowds for the more developed camps along US 101.

23.   BUTLER BAR   **RV**

Reference: **On Elk River in Siskiyou National Forest; map E1, grid c1.**

Campsites, facilities: There are nine sites for tents, trailers or RVs up to 16 feet long. Picnic tables and fire grills are provided. Piped water and pit toilets are available. Leashed pets are permitted.

Reservations, fee: No reservations; no fee. Open all year.

Who to contact: Phone the Siskiyou National Forest at (541) 439-3011 or write to Powers Ranger District, Port Orford, OR 97465.

Location: From US 101 at Coos Bay, turn south and drive 47 miles to County Road 208 (three miles north of Port Orford). Turn right and drive 7.5 miles southeast, then take Forest Service Road 5325 southeast and drive 11 miles to the campground. The road is paved all the way to the campground.

Trip note: This campground is set back from the shore of the Elk River and is surrounded by old growth forest, with some reforested areas nearby. Across the river is the Grassy Knob Wilderness Area, but it has no trails and is too rugged to hike. Elk River has native trout and steelhead in the winter.

---

24. MYRTLE GROVE

Reference: **On the South Fork of Coquille River in Siskiyou National Forest; map E1, grid c3.**

Campsites, facilities: There are five tent sites. Picnic tables and fire grills are provided. Pit toilets are available. There is **no piped water**. Leashed pets are permitted.

Reservations, fee: No reservations; no fee. Open all year.

Who to contact: Phone the Siskiyou National Forest at (541) 439-3011 or write to Powers Ranger District, Powers, OR 97466.

Location: From US 101 south of Coos Bay, turn west on Highway 42 and drive 20 miles, then turn south on Highway 242 and drive approximately 10 miles to Powers. Continue south on Highway 242 for 4.3 miles, then drive 4.5 miles south on Forest Service Road 33, and you'll see the campground. The road is paved all the way to the campground.

Trip note: This Forest Service campground is set along the South Fork of the Coquille River, a little downstream from Daphne Grove and in similar surroundings. Big Tree Recreation Site is a few miles away; there is a huge Port Orford cedar there. A prime hike can be made on the trail that runs adjacent to Elk Creek. (The road to Big Tree may be closed due to slides—be sure to check with the ranger district in advance.)

---

25. DAPHNE GROVE   RV

Reference: **On the South Fork of Coquille River in Siskiyou National Forest; map E1, grid c3.**

Campsites, facilities: There are 13 sites for tents, trailers or RVs up to 35 feet long. Picnic tables and fire grills are provided. Vault toilets and hand-pumped water are available. Leashed pets are permitted. Some facilities are **wheelchair accessible**.

Reservations, fee: No reservations; $5 fee per night from late May to late September. Open all year, with limited winter facilities.

Who to contact: Phone the Siskiyou National Forest at (541) 439-3011 or write to Powers Ranger District, Powers, OR 97466.

Location: From Interstate 5 south of Roseburg, take exit 120 and drive 55 miles east on Highway 42. Turn south on Highway 242 and drive to Powers. Continue 4.5 miles southeast on Highway 242, then 10.5 miles south on Forest Service Road 33, and you'll see the campground entrance.

Trip note: This prime spot is far enough out of the way that it attracts little attention. It is set along the South Fork of the Coquille River and is surrounded by old growth Douglas fir and cedar. The road is paved all the way to the campground as well as in the campground, a plus for RVs and "city cars."

26. ROCK CREEK [RV]

Reference: **Near the South Fork of Coquille River in Siskiyou National Forest; map E1, grid c3.**

Campsites, facilities: There are seven sites for tents, trailers or RVs. Picnic tables, hand-pumped water, and fire grills are provided. Vault toilets and firewood are available. Leashed pets are permitted.

Reservations, fee: No reservations; $5 fee per night from late May to late September. Open all year, with limited winter facilities.

Who to contact: Phone the Siskiyou National Forest at (541) 439-3011 or write to Powers Ranger District, Powers, OR 97466.

Location: From Interstate 5 south of Roseburg, take exit 120 and drive 55 miles east on Highway 42. Turn south on Highway 242 and drive to Powers. Continue 4.5 miles southeast on Highway 242 to Forest Service Road 33. Drive south for 13 miles, then 1.5 miles southwest on Forest Service Road 3347 to the campground. The road is paved all the way.

Trip note: This little-known camp is set along Rock Creek, just upstream from its confluence with the South Fork of the Coquille River. It is surrounded by old growth forest and some reforested areas. One good side trip here is the one-mile climb to Azalea Lake, which is stocked with trout. There are some hike-in campsites at the lake, but they have no piped drinking water. In July, the azalea blooms are spectacular.

27. SQUAW LAKE [RV]

Reference: **On Squaw Lake in Siskiyou National Forest; map E1, grid c3.**

Campsites, facilities: There are seven partially-developed sites for tents, trailers or RVs up to 21 feet. Pit toilets are provide. There is **no piped water.**

Reservations, fee: No reservations; no fee. Open all year.

Who to contact: Phone the Siskiyou National Forest at (541) 439-3011 or write to Powers Ranger District, Powers, OR 97466.

Location: From Interstate 5 south of Roseburg, take exit 120 and drive 55 miles east on Highway 42. Turn south on Highway 242 and drive to Powers. Continue 4.5 miles southeast on Highway 242. At Forest Service Road 33 drive south for 12.5 miles, then southeast on Forest Service Road 3348 for 4.5 miles. Turn east on Forest Service Road 3342 and drive one mile to the campground. The road is paved for all but the last half mile.

Trip note: This campground is set along the shore of five-acre Squaw Lake, set in rich, old-growth forest. The trailheads for Panther Ridge Trail and Coquille River Falls Trail are a 10-minute drive from the campground. It is strongly advised that you obtain a Forest Service map that details the backcountry roads and trails.

28. ILLAHE [RV]

Reference: **On Rogue River in Siskiyou National Forest; map E1, grid c3.**

Campsites, facilities: There are 14 sites for tents, trailers or RVs up to 21 feet long. Piped water, fire rings and picnic tables are provided. Flush toilets are available. A store is located within five miles. Leashed pets are permitted. Boat docks are nearby.

Reservations, fee: No reservations; $5 fee per night. Open mid-May to mid-October.

Who to contact: Phone the Siskiyou National Forest at (541) 247-3600 or write to Gold Beach Ranger District, 1225 South Ellensburg Avenue, Gold Beach, OR 97444.

Location: From the town of Gold Beach on US 101, take Agness-Gold Beach Road east for 30 miles to the turnoff to Agness. From Agness, travel five miles north on County Road 375 to the campground entrance.

Trip note: This campground is quiet and isolated with great hiking opportunities, yet boating and fishing opportunities are just a mile away at Foster Bar campground. It's a pretty spot and hidden from the majority of tourists who come through.

---

29.   TUCKER FLAT

Reference: **On Rogue River; map E1, grid c4.**

Campsites, facilities: There are 10 primitive tent sites. Picnic tables and fire grills are provided. Pit toilets and bear-proof trash cans are available. There is **no piped water**. Leashed pets are permitted.

Reservations, fee: No reservations; no fee. Open May to late October, weather permitting.

Who to contact: Phone (541) 770-2200 or write to Bureau of Land Management, 3040 Biddle Road, Medford, OR 97504.

Location: From Interstate 5 near Grants Pass, take exit 61 and travel 20 miles west on Merlin-Galice Access Road to the Grave Creek Bridge (second bridge over the Rogue River). Turn left after crossing the bridge onto BLM Road 34-8-1. Continue 16 miles and turn left onto BLM Road 32-8-31 for another seven miles. Turn left onto BLM Road 32-9-14.2 for 15 miles. The campground is just around the corner from the Rogue River Ranch.

Trip note: This campground is set in the Zane Grey Bureau of Land Management tract, covering 18,460 acres. The Rogue River passes through the tract, and the Rogue River Trail runs alongside the river for 26 miles. This is rugged country, with steep canyons and many small waterfalls. There is a riding stable nearby.

---

30.   MEADOW WOOD RV RESORT & CAMP RV

Reference: **In Glendale; map E1, grid c7.**

Campsites, facilities: There are 100 tent sites and 20 drive-through sites (11 with full hookups) for trailers or RVs of any length. Electricity, piped water and picnic tables are provided. Flush toilets, bottled gas, sanitary disposal services, showers, firewood, a recreation hall, a store, a laundromat, ice, a playground and a heated swimming pool are available. No pets or motorbikes.

Reservations, fee: Reservations accepted; $11-$16 fee per night. MasterCard and Visa accepted. Open all year. All camping membership cards accepted.

Who to contact: Phone (541) 832-3114 or write to 862 Autumn Lane, Glendale, OR 97442.

Location: Traveling southbound on Interstate 5, take exit 86 north of Glendale and drive three miles south on the frontage road to Barton Road. Turn east and drive two-tenths of a mile. Drive south on Autumn Lane for three-quarters of a mile to the park. Traveling northbound on Interstate 5, take exit 83 and travel two-tenths of a mile east. Turn south on Autumn Lane and drive three-quarters of a mile to the camp.

Trip note: This is a good option for motor home campers looking for a spot along Interstate 5. All the amenities are available. Nearby attractions include an old ghost town, gold panning and Wolf Creek Tavern.

---

31. HONEYBEAR CAMPGROUND `RV`

Reference: **Near Gold Beach; map E1, grid d0.**

Campsites, facilities: There are 20 tent sites and 58 drive-through sites for trailers or RVs of any length. Picnic tables are provided. Flush toilets, electricity, piped water, cable TV, sanitary services, showers, firewood, a recreation hall, a store, a laundromat, ice and a playground are available. Pets and motorbikes are permitted.

Reservations, fee: Reservations accepted; $12-$17 fee per night. MasterCard and Visa accepted. Open all year, weather permitting.

Who to contact: Phone (541) 247-2765 or write to P.O. Box 97, Ophir, OR 97464.

Location: From US 101 at the town of Gold Beach, drive nine miles north to Ophir Road. The campground is two miles north on the right side of Ophir Road.

Trip note: This campground offers wooded sites with ocean views. The owners have built a huge, authentic chalet which contains a German deli, a recreation area and a big dance floor. On summer nights, they hold dances with live music.

---

32. NESIKA BEACH TRAILER PARK `RV`

Reference: **Near Gold Beach; map E1, grid d0.**

Campsites, facilities: There are six tent sites and 30 sites for trailers or RVs of any length. Electricity, piped water, sewer hookups and picnic tables are provided. Flush toilets, sanitary services, showers, a store, a laundromat and ice are available. There is a cafe within walking distance. Pets and motorbikes are permitted.

Reservations, fee: Reservations accepted; $12-$14 fee per night. Open all year.

Who to contact: Phone (541) 247-6077 or write to 32887 Nesika Road, Gold Beach, OR 97444.

Location: Take US 101 six miles north of the town of Gold Beach to Nesika Road. Drive one-half mile west on Nesika Road to the campground on the left.

Trip note: This campground is next to Nesika Beach, a good layover spot for Highway 101 cruisers. An 18-hole golf course is available nearby.

---

33. IRELAND'S OCEAN VIEW RV PARK `RV`

Reference: **On Pacific Ocean; map E1, grid d0.**

Campsites, facilities: There are 32 sites for trailers or RVs up to 40 feet. Tent camping permitted only in combination with an RV. Cable TV, phones, showers, restrooms, a laundromat, recreation room, horseshoe pits and picnic areas are available. Pets are permitted on leashes.

Reservations, fee: Reservations recommended; $12.50-$20 fee per night. Open all year.

Who to contact: Phone the park at (541) 247-0148 or write to 1230 South Ellensburg, P.O. Box 727, Gold Beach, OR 97444.

Location: This camp is in the town of Gold Beach on US 101. The camp is located across from the U.S. Forest Service Office.

Trip note: This is one of the newest RV parks in the area. It is set on the beach in the quaint little town of Gold Beach, and is only one mile from the famous

Rogue River. Recreation options include beachcombing, fishing and boating.
An observatory/lighthouse is available for great ocean views.

34. INDIAN CREEK RECREATION PARK RV

Reference: **On Rogue River; map E1, grid d0.**

Campsites, facilities: There are 25 tent sites and 100 sites for trailers or RVs of
any length. Electricity, piped water, sewer and cable TV hookups and picnic
tables are provided. Flush toilets, showers, firewood, a recreation hall, a store,
sauna, a cafe, a laundromat, ice and a playground are available. Bottled gas is
located within two miles. Pets and motorbikes are permitted. Boat docks,
launching facilities and rentals are nearby.

Reservations, fee: Reservations accepted; $15-$22 fee per night; MasterCard and
Visa accepted. Open all year.

Who to contact: Phone (541) 247-7704 or write to 94680 Jerry's Flat Road, Gold
Beach, OR 97444.

Location: In the town of Gold Beach on US 101, look for Jerry's Flat Road and
drive one-half mile east to the campground.

Trip note: This campground is set along the Rogue River on the outskirts of the
town of Gold Beach. Nearby recreation options include a riding stable, riding
trails, and boat trips on the Rogue.

35. OCEANSIDE RV PARK RV

Reference: **On the Pacific Ocean; map E1, grid d0.**

Campsites, facilities: There are 90 drive-through sites for trailers or RVs of any
length. Electricity, piped water, sewer hookups and picnic tables are provided.
Flush toilets, showers, cable TV, a small store and ice are available. Bottled
gas, sanitary services, a store, a cafe and a laundromat are located within two
miles. Pets and motorbikes are permitted. Boat docks, launching facilities and
rentals are nearby.

Reservations, fee: Reservations recommended in summer; $15-$20 fee per night.
MasterCard and Visa accepted. Open all year.

Who to contact: Phone (541) 247-2301 or write to P.O. Box 1107, Gold Beach,
OR 97444.

Location: This park is in the town of Gold Beach, at the south jetty of the Port of
Gold Beach.

Trip note: This park is set right on the ocean. Nearby recreation options include
beachcombing, marked bike trails and boating facilities.

36. HUNTER CREEK RV PARK RV

Reference: **On Hunter Creek; map E1, grid d0.**

Campsites, facilities: There are a total of 60 sites for tents, trailers and RVs.
Restrooms, showers, a public phone, a laundromat, limited groceries, RV
supplies, LP gas, a playground and a game room are available.

Reservations, fee: Reservations recommended; $11-$16 fee per night. Open all
year.

Who to contact: Phone the park at (541) 247-2322 or write to 28555 Hunter Creek
Road, Gold Beach, OR 97444.

Location: From US 101 at the south end of the town of Gold Beach, turn east on
Hunter Creek Road and drive seven-tenths of a mile southeast. The campground is located on the left side of the road.

Trip note: This camp is set amidst wooded mountains on a small stream, in the town of Gold Beach. Of the several campgrounds in the area, this one is preferred by tent campers. It is a bit more private and secluded than other camps in town. From January through March, steelhead fishing is excellent.

37.   FOUR SEASONS RV RESORT   RV

Reference: **On Rogue River; map E1, grid d1.**

Campsites, facilities: There are 45 drive-through sites for trailers or RVs up to 35 feet long. Electricity, piped water, sewer hookups and picnic tables are provided. Flush toilets, bottled gas, sanitary services, showers, firewood, a recreation hall, a store, a laundromat and ice are available. Pets and motorbikes are permitted. Boat docks and launching facilities are nearby.

Reservations, fee: Reservations accepted; $21.50-$26.50 fee per night. Open all year.

Who to contact: Phone (800) 248-4541 or (541) 247-4541 or write to 96526 North Bank Rogue, Gold Beach, OR 97444.

Location: Drive one mile north of the town of Gold Beach on US 101, then three miles northeast on Rogue River Road. Then follow the signs on North Bank Rogue Road to the campground.

Trip note: This resort is set along the shore of the Rogue River. Nearby recreation options include a nine-hole golf course and boat trips on the Wild and Scenic Rogue—on anything from a raft to a jet boat. The sites are well-kept, with nice lawns and lots of trees.

38.   KIMBALL CREEK BEND   RV

Reference: **On Rogue River; map E1, grid d1.**

Campsites, facilities: There are 13 tent sites and 56 drive-through sites for trailers or RVs of any length. Electricity, piped water, sewer hookups and picnic tables are provided. Flush toilets, bottled gas, sanitary services, showers, a recreation hall, a store, a laundromat, ice and a playground are available. Leashed pets are permitted. Boat docks and launching facilities are nearby.

Reservations, fee: Reservations accepted; $19-$25.50 fee per night; MasterCard and Visa accepted. Open all year.

Who to contact: Phone (541) 247-7580 or write to 97136 North Bank Rogue, Gold Beach, OR 97444.

Location: From the town of Gold Beach, drive one mile north on US 101, then 3.5 miles northeast on Rogue River Road to North Bank Rogue Road and head 4.5 miles to the campground.

Trip note: This campground is set along the scenic Rogue River, just far enough from the coast to provide quiet and its own distinct character. Nearby recreation options include an 18-hole golf course, hiking trails and boating facilities.

39.   LUCKY LODGE RV PARK   RV

Reference: **On Rogue River; map E1, grid d1.**

Campsites, facilities: There are seven tent sites and 36 drive-through sites for trailers or RVs of any length. Electricity, piped water, sewer hookups and picnic tables are provided. Flush toilets, bottled gas, sanitary services, showers, firewood, a recreation hall and a laundromat are available. Pets and motorbikes are permitted. Boat docks and rentals are nearby.

Reservations, fee: Reservations accepted; $17 fee per night. Open all year.

Who to contact: Phone (541) 247-7618 or write to 32040 Watson Lane, Gold Beach, OR 97444.

Location: Drive one mile north of Gold Beach on US 101. At Rogue River Road, continue northeast 3.5 miles to North Bank Rogue Road and follow it 4.5 more miles.

Trip note: This is a good layover spot for US 101 travelers who want to get off the highway circuit. It is set on the shore of the river and offers opportunities for fishing, boating and swimming. Nearby recreation options include hiking trails.

40.   ANGLERS TRAILER VILLAGE   RV

Reference: **On Rogue River; map E1, grid d1.**

Campsites, facilities: There are two tent sites and 36 drive-through sites for trailers or RVs of any length. No tents are allowed. Electricity, piped water and sewer hookups are provided. Flush toilets, showers, a recreation hall and a laundromat are available. Pets and motorbikes are permitted.

Reservations, fee: Reservations accepted; $15 fee per night. Open all year.

Who to contact: Phone (541) 247-7922 or write to 95706 Jerry's Flat, Gold Beach, OR 97444.

Location: In Gold Beach on US 101, turn east at the south end of Rogue River Bridge, then drive 3.5 miles north on Jerry's Flat Road to the campground.

Trip note: This is one of seven campgrounds set along the lower Rogue River near Gold Beach. This camp is best used as a layover spot.

41.   LOBSTER CREEK   RV

Reference: **On Rogue River in Siskiyou National Forest; map E1, grid d2.**

Campsites, facilities: There are six sites for tents, trailers or RVs up to 21 feet long. Fire rings and picnic tables are provided. Flush toilets and piped water are available. Leashed pets are permitted. A boat launch is also available.

Reservations, fee: No reservations; $5 fee per night. Open mid-April to mid-October.

Who to contact: Phone the Siskiyou National Forest at (541) 247-3600 or write to Gold Beach Ranger District, 1225 South Ellensburg Avenue, Gold Beach, OR 97444.

Location: From the town of Gold Beach on US 101, take County Road 595 (which becomes Forest Service Road 33) and drive about 10 miles northeast to the campground on the left.

Trip note: This small campground is set on a river bar along the Rogue River, about a 15-minute drive from Gold Beach. It's a good base camp for a fishing trip. Camping is permitted on a gravel bar area for $2 per night.

42.   QUOSATANA   RV

Reference: **On Rogue River in Siskiyou National Forest; map E1, grid d2.**

Campsites, facilities: There are 42 sites for tents, trailers or RVs up to 32 feet long. Piped water, fire grills and picnic tables are provided. Flush toilets and a sanitary disposal station are available. Leashed pets are permitted. A boat ramp is available.

Reservations, fee: No reservations; $7 fee per night. Open year-round.

Who to contact: Phone the Siskiyou National Forest at (541) 247-3600 or write to Gold Beach Ranger District, 1225 South Ellensburger Avenue, Gold Beach, OR 97444.

Location: From the town of Gold Beach on US 101, drive on County Road 595 (which becomes Forest Service Road 33) for 13 miles northeast to the campground on the left.

Trip note: This campground is set along the banks of the Rogue River, upriver from the much smaller Lobster Creek. Ocean access is just a short drive away, and the quaint town of Gold Beach offers a decent side trip. Nearby Otter Point State Park (day-use only) has further recreation options. This is a good base camp for hiking or a fishing trip.

---

43. FOSTER BAR   **RV**

Reference: **On Rogue River in Siskiyou National Forest; map E1, grid d3.**

Campsites, facilities: There are several dispersed sites for tents, trailers or RVs up to 16 feet long, though access is difficult for RVs and trailers. Fire rings and picnic tables are provided. Pit toilets are available, but there is **no piped water**. Leashed pets are permitted. Boat launching facilities are available.

Reservations, fee: No reservations; no fee. Open year-round.

Who to contact: Phone the Siskiyou National Forest at (541) 247-3600 or write to Gold Beach Ranger District, 1225 South Ellensburger Avenue, Gold Beach, OR 97444.

Location: From the town of Gold Beach on US 101, take Agness-Gold Beach Road east for 30 miles to the turnoff to Agness. Turn right on Illahe-Agness Road and drive three miles to the campground.

Trip note: This campground is located on the banks of the Rogue River, a popular put-in spot for the eight-mile inner tube ride to Agness. Life jackets are mandatory because of rough rapids. Hiking opportunities are good and you can also fish from the river bar. Illahe and Agness RV Park provide nearby options.

---

44. AGNESS RV PARK   **RV**

Reference: **On Rogue River; map E1, grid d3.**

Campsites, facilities: There are 81 drive-through sites for trailers or RVs of any length. Electricity, piped water, sewer hookups and picnic tables are provided. Flush toilets, sanitary services, showers and a laundromat are available. A store, a cafe, bottled gas and ice are located within 100 yards. Pets and motorbikes are permitted. Boat launching facilities are nearby.

Reservations, fee: Reservations accepted; $15 fee per night; MasterCard and Visa accepted. Open all year.

Who to contact: Phone (541) 247-2813 or write to 4215 Agness Road, Agness, OR 97406.

Location: From Gold Beach on US 101, drive 28 miles east on Jerry's Flat Road and you'll see the entrance to the campground on the left.

Trip note: This is a destination campground set along the scenic Rogue River, in the middle of the Siskiyou National Forest. Fishing is the main focus here. Boating is sharply limited because the nearest pullout is 12 miles downstream. It is advisable to obtain a Forest Service map detailing the backcountry.

---

45. SAM BROWN   **RV**

Reference: **Near Grants Pass in Siskiyou National Forest; map E1, grid d5.**

Campsites, facilities: There are 40 sites for tents, trailers, or RVs of any length, as well as seven remote sites designated for campers with horses. Picnic tables, fire grills, hand-pumped water and vault toilets are provided. Firewood is available. Leashed pets are permitted. Small corrals are provided with the horse campsites. Many sites are **wheelchair-accessible.**

Reservations, fee: No reservations; $5 fee per night. Open late May to mid-September.

Who to contact: Phone the Siskiyou National Forest at (541) 476-3830, or write to Galice Ranger District, 1465 NE Seventh Street, Grants Pass, OR 97526.

Location: From Grants Pass, drive 3.5 miles north on Interstate 5, then take exit 61 and turn northwest on County Road 2-6. Drive 12.5 miles, then turn left on Forest Service Road 25 and head southwest for 14 miles to the campground.

Trip note: This campground is located in an isolated area near Grants Pass, set along Briggs Creek in a valley of old-growth pine and Douglas fir. Many sites lie in the shade of the old-growth trees, and many others are set right on the banks of the creek. There are several hiking and horseback riding trails in the vicinity. An amphitheater is available for small group presentations.

---

46.   BIG PINE

Reference: **On Myers Creek in Siskiyou National Forest; map E1, grid d5.**

Campsites, facilities: There are 14 tent sites. Picnic tables and fire grills are provided. Vault toilets, hand-pumped water and firewood are available. Leashed pets are permitted. The facilities are **wheelchair accessible**.

Reservations, fee: No reservations; $5 fee per night. Open late May to mid-September.

Who to contact: Phone the Siskiyou National Forest at (541) 476-3830 or write to Galice Ranger District, 1465 NE 7th Street, Grants Pass, OR 97526.

Location: From Grants Pass, drive 3.5 miles north on Interstate 5, then take exit 61 and turn northwest on County Road 2-6. Drive 12.5 miles, then turn left on Forest Service Road 25 and head southwest for 12.8 miles to the campground.

Trip note: This little campground is set near the banks of Myers Creek, amidst a valley of old-growth pine and Douglas fir. Many sites are right on the creek, and all are shaded. One of the world's tallest Ponderosa pine trees is located in the campground. A **wheelchair-accessible** nature trail is provided. It is advisable to obtain a national forest map.

---

47.   BEND O' THE RIVER RV PARK   RV

Reference: **On Rogue River; map E1, grid d6.**

Campsites, facilities: There are five tent sites and 22 sites for trailers or RVs of any length (two drive-through). Electricity, piped water, sewer hookups and picnic tables are provided. Flush toilets, sanitary disposal services, showers, firewood, a cafe, a laundromat and ice are available. Pets are permitted.

Reservations, fee: Reservations accepted; $7-$15 fee per night. Open all year.

Who to contact: Phone (541) 479-2547 or write to 7501 Lower River Road, Grants Pass, OR 97526.

Location: Take exit 58 off Interstate 5 in Grants Pass, then drive south on 6th Street to G Street (which becomes Upper River Road and then Lower River Road). The park is located seven miles west on Lower River Road.

Trip note: This campground is set along the banks of the Rogue River. It's a pretty spot far enough out of Grants Pass to have its own unique feel.

48.   WHITE HORSE   RV

Reference: **On the Rogue River; map E1, grid d7.**

Campsites, facilities: There are 45 sites for tents, trailers and RVs up to 35 feet. Piped water and picnic tables are provided. Restrooms, showers, a public phone, fire grills, horseshoes and a playground are available.

Reservations, fee: No reservations; $12-$17 fee per night; $3 each additional vehicle. Open all year.

Who to contact: Phone Josephine County Parks at (541) 474-5285 or write to 101 NW A Street, Grants Pass, OR 97526.

Location: From Grants Pass on Interstate 5 drive in town to the junction of Sixth Street and G Street. Turn west on G Street and drive one mile (G Street turns into Upper River Road). Continue for seven miles on Upper River Road to the campground on the left.

Trip note: This is a pleasant county park set along the banks of the Rogue River. It is one of several parks in the Grants Pass area that provides opportunities for trout fishing, swimming, hiking and boating. Take your pick.

49.   GRANTS PASS OVERNITERS   RV

Reference: **Near Grants Pass; map E1, grid d7.**

Campsites, facilities: There are 40 tent sites and 63 drive-through sites for trailers or RVs of any length. Electricity, piped water, sewer hookups and picnic tables are provided. Flush toilets, bottled gas, showers, a laundromat, ice and a swimming pool are available. A store is located within one mile. Pets and motorbikes are permitted.

Reservations, fee: Reservations accepted; $12-$16 fee per night. Open all year.

Who to contact: Phone (541) 479-7289 or write to 5941 Highland Avenue, Grants Pass, OR 97526.

Location: From Grants Pass, drive three miles north on Interstate 5 to exit 61E, then drive north on the frontage road to the park.

Trip note: This wooded park is set in a rural area just outside Grants Pass. There are several other campgrounds in the area.

50.   LAZY ACRES RV   RV

Reference: **On Rogue River; map E1, grid d9.**

Campsites, facilities: There are 50 sites for trailers or RVs of any length. Electricity, piped water, sewer hookups and picnic tables are provided. Flush toilets, bottled gas, cable TV, a dump station, a playground and a laundromat are available. Boat docks are nearby.

Reservations, fee: No reservations; $12-$15 fee per night; MasterCard and Visa accepted. Open all year.

Who to contact: Phone (541) 855-7000 or write to 1550 Second Avenue, Gold Hill, OR 97525.

Location: In Gold Hill on Interstate 5, take the South Gold Hill exit and drive one-quarter mile north, then 1.2 miles west on Second Avenue to the campground on the left.

Trip note: This wooded campground is set along the Rogue River, adjacent to a motel. It is less scenic, but it offers the same recreation options as KOA Medford-Gold Hill.

51.   ELDERBERRY FLAT

Reference: **On Evans Creek; map E1, grid d9.**

Campsites, facilities: There are 10 primitive tent sites. Picnic tables and fire grills are provided. Vault toilets are available. There is **no piped water**. Leashed pets are permitted. Toilets are **wheelchair accessible**.

Reservations, fee: No reservations; no fee. Open late May to early November.

Who to contact: Phone (541) 770-2200 or write to Bureau of Land Management, 3040 Biddle Road, Medford, OR 97501.

Location: From Interstate 5, take the City of Rogue River exit into town. Turn right on East Evans Creek Road and drive 18 miles to West Fork Evans Creek Road. Turn left and drive nine miles to the campground.

Trip note: This campground is set along the banks of Evans Creek. Virtually unknown, it's only about a 30-minute drive from Interstate 5. It's small, primitive and private—a perfect layover spot for weary highway cruisers who want to get away from the crowds for a while.

52.   WHALESHEAD BEACH RESORT   **RV**

Reference: **Near the Pacific Ocean; map E1, grid e0.**

Campsites, facilities: There are a total of 115 sites for tents, trailers or RVs of any length. Ten cabins are also available. Cable TV, restrooms, showers, a sanitary dump, a public phone, a laundromat, limited groceries, ice, snacks, RV supplies and LP gas are available. Recreational facilities include horseshoe pits, a recreation hall and a game room. Some facilities are **wheelchair accessible**. Pets are permitted on leashes.

Reservations, fee: Reservations recommended; $15-$20 fee per night. Cabins are $85 per night. Visa and MasterCard are accepted. Open year-round.

Who to contact: Contact the park at (541) 469-7446 or write to 19921 Whaleshead Road, Brookings, OR 97415.

Location: From the north end of the Chetco River Bridge in Brookings, drive 8.5 miles north on US 101. The campground is at milepost 349.5, on the right.

Trip note: This resort is about one-quarter of a mile from the beach. It is set in a forested environment with a small stream nearby. Activities at and nearby the camp include ocean and river fishing, jet boat trips, whale watching trips and, 30 minutes away, a golf course.

53.   LAKE SELMAC   **RV**

Reference: **On Lake Selmac; map E1, grid e5.**

Campsites, facilities: There are 81 sites for tents, trailers or RVs up to 32 feet. Piped water and picnic tables are provided. Facilities include restrooms, showers, a sanitary dump, a public phone, snacks, a barbecue, horseshoes, a playground, a recreation field and a boat ramp and dock. Facilities are **wheelchair accessible**. Pets are permitted on leashes.

Reservations, fee: Reservations recommended; $12-$17 fee per night; $3 each additional vehicle. Open all year.

Who to contact: Phone Josephine County Parks at (541) 474-5285 or write to 101 NW A Street, Grants Pass, OR 97526.

Location: From Interstate 5 at Grants Pass, take exit 58 and drive southwest on US 199 for 23 miles to Selma. The camp is located in town (well signed).

Trip note: Set in a wooded, mountainous area, this park offers swimming, hiking, boating and good trout fishing on beautiful Lake Selmac. See the trip note for Lake Selmac RV Resort for details about the area.

54.   GRANTS PASS/REDWOOD KOA   RV

Reference: **Near Grants Pass; map E1, grid e6.**

Campsites, facilities: There are 40 sites for tents, trailers or RVs. Restrooms, showers, a sanitary dump, security, a public phone, a laundromat, limited groceries, ice, RV supplies, LP gas and a barbecue are available. There is also a recreation hall, a playground and a recreation field. Pets are permitted on leashes.

Reservations, fee: Reservations recommended; $16-$21 fee per night. Visa, MasterCard and Discover are accepted.

Who to contact: Phone the park at (541) 476-6508 or write to 13370 Redwood Highway, Wilderville, OR 97543.

Location: From Interstate 5 at the south end of Grants Pass, turn southwest on Highway 199 and drive 14 miles. The campground is located on the right at milepost 14.5.

Trip note: This KOA campground is set on a stream in the hills outside of Grants Pass and is popular with birdwatchers. It is a perfect layover spot for travelers who want to get away from the highway for a while. For an interesting side trip, drive south down scenic Highway 199 to Cave Junction or Illinois River State Park.

55.   LAKE SELMAC RV RESORT   RV

Reference: **On Lake Selmac; map E1, grid e6.**

Campsites, facilities: There are 18 tent sites and 25 sites for trailers or RVs of any length. Electricity, piped water, sewer hookups and picnic tables are provided. Flush toilets, bottled gas, sanitary services, showers, firewood, a store, a cafe, a laundromat, ice and a playground are available. Pets and motorbikes are permitted. Boat docks, launching facilities and rentals are nearby. Horseback riding trails are available in the summer.

Reservations, fee: Reservations accepted; $11-$15 fee per night. Open all year.

Who to contact: Phone (541) 597-4989 or write to 2700 Lake Shore Drive, Selma, OR 97538.

Location: From Interstate 5 at Grants Pass, turn southwest on US 199 and drive approximately 25 miles to Selma. Take the Lake Selmac exit and drive two miles east on Lake Selmac Road to the resort on the left.

Trip note: This resort is set along the shore of Lake Selmac. A golf course is nearby. A unique tour is available at Oregon Caves National Monument, about 30 miles away. To get there, drive 20 miles east of Cave Junction on Highway 46. This road gets narrow near the end and is not recommended for trailers. A 75-minute guided tour is available. The caves are a long, winding trail through a series of amazing caverns. Dress warmly; it can be cold and clammy.

56.   ROGUE VALLEY OVERNITERS   RV

Reference: **Near Rogue River; map E1, grid e7.**

Campsites, facilities: There are two tent sites and 26 drive-through sites for trailers or RVs of any length. Electricity, piped water and sewer hookups are provided. Flush toilets, sanitary disposal services, showers and a laundromat are available. Bottled gas, a store, a cafe and ice are available within one mile. Pets are permitted.

Reservations, fee: Reservations accepted; $17-$19 fee per night. Open all year. Credit cards accepted.

Who to contact: Phone (541) 479-2208 or write to 1806 Northwest 6th Street, Grants Pass, OR 97526.

Location: Take exit 58 off Interstate 5 in Grants Pass, then follow 6th Street south for about 400 yards.

Trip note: This park is just off the freeway in Grants Pass, the jumpoff point for trips down the Rogue River. The summer heat in this part of Oregon can surprise visitors in late June and early July.

---

57.   SCHROEDER   RV

Reference: **On Rogue River; map E1, grid e7.**

Campsites, facilities: There are two tent sites and 28 sites for trailers and RVs. Restrooms, showers and a public phone are available. Recreational facilities include horseshoes, a recreation field, a barbecue, a playground and a boat ramp.

Reservations, fee: No reservations; $12-$17 fee per night. Open all year, with limited winter facilities.

Who to contact: Phone Josephine County Parks at (541) 474-5285 or write to 101 NW A Street, Grants Pass, OR 97526.

Location: From Interstate 5 at Grants Pass, take exit 58 and drive four miles west on Highway 199 to the campground.

Trip note: Set along the Rogue River, this camp has opportunities for trout fishing, swimming and boating. Just a short jog off the highway, this makes an excellent layover camp for Interstate 5 travelers. It is not a highly-publicized camp, so many tourists pass by it in favor of the more commercial camps in the area. Note: No reservations are accepted; plan on arriving early in the day to claim a prime spot.

---

58.   RIVER PARK RV RESORT   RV

Reference: **On Rogue River; map E1, grid e7.**

Campsites, facilities: There are 47 sites for tents, trailers or RVs. Cable TV, restrooms, showers, a sanitary dump, a public phone, a laundromat and ice are available.

Reservations, fee: Reservations recommended; $18-$20 fee per night. Visa and MasterCard are accepted.

Who to contact: Phone the park at (541) 479-0046 or (800) 677-8857 or write to 2956 Rogue River Highway, Grants Pass, OR 97527.

Location: From Interstate 5 at Grants Pass, take exit 58 (Highway 99/Rogue River Highway). Drive south on Highway 99 (Sixth Street) for 2.7 miles to the junction with Highway 199. Turn east on Highway 99/Rogue River Highway and drive 2.5 miles to the park on the left.

Trip note: This park is in a quiet, serene riverfront setting, yet it is close to all the conveniences of a small city. It has 700 feet of Rogue River frontage for trout fishing and swimming. It is one of several parks in the immediate area.

---

59.   CIRCLE W CAMPGROUND   RV

Reference: **On Rogue River; map E1, grid e8.**

Campsites, facilities: There are two tent sites and 23 drive-through sites for trailers or RVs of any length. Electricity, piped water, sewer hookups and picnic tables are provided. Flush toilets, sanitary disposal services, showers, a store, a laundromat, ice and a playground are available. Bottled gas and a cafe are located within one mile. Leashed pets are permitted. Boat docks are nearby.

Reservations, fee: Reservations accepted; $15-$20 fee per night. Open all year.

Who to contact: Phone (541) 582-1686 or write to P.O. Box 1320, Rogue River, OR 97537.

Location: Take the Rogue River exit (exit 48) off Interstate 5, then drive one mile west on Highway 99.

Trip note: This campground is set along the Rogue River. Nearby options include chartered boat trips down the Rogue River, a golf course and tennis courts. Fishing and swimming access are available from the campground.

---

60.   HAVE A NICE DAY CAMPGROUND   `RV`

Reference: **On Rogue River; map E1, grid e8.**

Campsites, facilities: There are 16 tent sites and 30 drive-through sites for trailers or RVs of any length. Electricity, piped water, sewer hookups and picnic tables are provided. Flush toilets, bottled gas, sanitary disposal services, showers, a laundromat, ice and a playground are available. A store and a cafe are located within one mile. Pets and motorbikes are permitted. Boat docks and launching facilities are nearby.

Reservations, fee: Reservations accepted; $16 fee per night. Open all year with limited winter facilities.

Who to contact: Phone (541) 582-1421 or write to 7275 Rogue River Highway, Grants Pass, OR 97527.

Location: Take exit 48 off Interstate 5, cross the river and travel 1.5 miles west on Highway 99.

Trip note: This campground is set along the Rogue River, where fishing, swimming and boating are options. It has grassy, shaded sites.

---

61.   RIVERFRONT TRAILER PARK   `RV`

Reference: **On Rogue River; map E1, grid e8.**

Campsites, facilities: There are 10 tent sites and 20 sites for trailers or RVs of any length. Electricity, piped water, sewer and cable TV hookups and picnic tables are provided. Flush toilets, sanitary disposal services, showers, a laundromat and ice are available. Bottled gas, a store and a cafe are located within one mile. Small pets are permitted. Fishing docks boat docks and launching facilities are nearby.

Reservations, fee: Reservations accepted; $15-$20 fee per night. Open all year.

Who to contact: Phone (541) 582-0985 or write to 7060 Rogue River, Grants Pass, OR 97527.

Location: From Interstate 5 south of Grants Pass, turn west at exit 48 and drive two miles on Highway 99 to the park.

Trip note: There is good fishing, swimming and boating on the Rogue River.

---

62.   VALLEY OF THE ROGUE STATE PARK   `RV`

Reference: **On Rogue River; map E1, grid e8.**

Campsites, facilities: There are 21 sites for tents or self-contained RVs and 152 sites with full or partial hookups for trailers or RVs up to 75 feet long. Picnic tables and fire grills are provided. Flush toilets, sanitary disposal services, showers, firewood, a laundromat, a meeting hall and group campsites are available. A restaurant is nearby. Some facilities are **wheelchair accessible**.

Leashed pets are permitted. Boat launching facilities are nearby.

Reservations, fee: Contact Reservations Northwest at (800) 452-5687 ($6 reservation fee); $13-$18 per night. (Weekly and monthly rates available in the winter months.) Open all year with limited winter facilities.

Who to contact: Phone (541) 582-1118 or write to 3792 North River Road, Gold Hill, OR 97525.

Location: From Grants Pass, turn south on Interstate 5 and travel 12 miles. Turn right at exit 45B and drive to the park on the right.

Trip note: This state park is set along the banks of the Rogue River. Recreation options include fishing, hiking, swimming and boating. With easy highway access, it's a popular spot, often filled to near capacity during summer months. A large picnic shelter is available for groups.

---

63. KOA MEDFORD-GOLD HILL RV

Reference: **On Rogue River; map E1, grid e8.**

Campsites, facilities: There are 30 tent sites and 45 drive-through sites for trailers or RVs of any length. Electricity, piped water, sewer hookups and picnic tables are provided. Flush toilets, bottled gas, sanitary disposal services, showers, firewood, a store, a laundromat, ice, a playground and a swimming pool are available. A cafe is located within one mile. Pets and motorbikes are permitted. Boat launching facilities are nearby.

Reservations, fee: Reservations accepted; $15-$20 fee per night. MasterCard and Visa accepted. Open all year.

Who to contact: Phone (541) 855-7710 or write to P.O. Box 320, Gold Hill, OR 97525.

Location: In Gold Hill on Interstate 5, take the South Gold Hill exit (exit 40) and drive 400 yards to Blackwell Road. The camp is about another 400 yards south on the right.

Trip note: This campground is set along the banks of the Rogue River and near a golf course, bike paths, tennis courts and the Oregon Vortex. It's one of the many camps located between Gold Hill and Grants Pass.

---

64. HARRIS BEACH STATE PARK RV

Reference: **On the Pacific Ocean; map E1, grid f1.**

Campsites, facilities: There are 66 sites for tents or self-contained RVs, and 86 sites with full or partial hookups for trailers or RVs up to 50 feet long. There are four yurts, each accommodating 5 people and a special camping area for hikers and bicyclists. Picnic tables and fire grills are provided. Electricity, piped water, sewer and cable TV hookups, flush toilets, sanitary services, showers and firewood are available. Some facilities are **wheelchair accessible**. Leashed pets are permitted.

Reservations, fee: Contact Reservations Northwest at (800) 452-5687 ($6 reservation fee); $12-$20 fee per night; yurts are $25 per night; $4 for hikers/bikers. Open all year.

Who to contact: Phone (541) 469-2021 or (800) 452-5687 or write to 1655 Highway 101, Brookings, OR 97415.

Location: From Brookings on US 101, drive two miles north to the park entrance on the left.

Trip note: This campground is set along the beach. Beachcombing, hiking and fishing are a few activities available in the park. Goat Rock, a migratory bird sanctuary is just offshore. There are numerous trout streams in the area. For details, pick up a Siskiyou Forest Service map in Brookings at 555 Fifth Street. In the fall and winter, the nearby Chetco River attracts good runs of salmon and steelhead, respectively.

---

65.   PORT OF BROOKINGS HARBOR BEACHFRONT RV PARK RV

Reference: **On the Pacific Ocean; map E1, grid f1.**

Campsites, facilities: There are 25 tent sites and 131 spaces for trailers or RVs of any length. Restrooms, showers, a sanitary dump, a public phone, a laundromat, ice, horseshoes, snacks and LP gas are available. A marina with a boat ramp and dock is nearby. The facilities are **wheelchair accessible**. Pets are permitted on leashes.

Reservations, fee: Reservations recommended; $9-$14 fee per night. Visa and MasterCard are accepted. Open year round.

Who to contact: Phone the park at (541) 469-5867 or, in Oregon, (800) 441-0856. Or, write to 16035 Boat Basin Road, Brookings, OR 97415.

Location: From Brookings on US 101, turn south and drive approximately 2.5 miles to Benham Road. Drive west on Benham Road for six-tenths of a mile to Boat Basin Road. The park is one block north on the left side.

Trip note: Located just past the Oregon/California border, this park is a great layover spot. It is set on the Pacific Ocean, with oceanfront sites available. Recreational activities include boating, fishing and swimming. Nearby Harris Beach State Park provides a good side trip option, with beach access and hiking trails.

---

66.   AT RIVERS EDGE RV RESORT RV

Reference: **On Chetco River; map E1, grid f1.**

Campsites, facilities: There are 90 drive-through sites for trailers or RVs of any length. Electricity, piped water, sewer hookups and picnic tables are provided. Flush toilets, bottled gas, sanitary services, showers, a recreation hall with exercise equipment, a laundromat and cable TV are available. Pets and motorbikes are permitted. Boat launching facilities are also available.

Reservations, fee: Reservations accepted; $20 fee per night. Open all year.

Who to contact: Phone (541) 469-3356 or write to 98203 South Bank Chetco Road, Brookings, OR 97415.

Location: From Brookings on US 101, drive 1.5 miles east on South Bank Chetco River Road and follow the signs to the park.

Trip note: This campground is set along the banks of the Chetco River and offers complete fishing services including guided salmon and steelhead trips on the Chetco in fall and winter. Deep sea trips for salmon or rockfish are available in the summer. Bait, tackle and a free fishing class for campers is offered. There is a beach for sunbathing and swimming.

---

67.   CHETCO RV PARK RV

Reference: **Near Chetco River; map E1, grid f1.**

Campsites, facilities: There are 117 drive-through sites for trailers or RVs of any length. Electricity, piped water, sewer hookups and picnic tables are provided. Flush toilets, sanitary services, showers, a recreation hall, a laundromat and ice are available. Small pets are permitted. Boat docks, launching facilities and rentals are nearby.

Reservations, fee: Reservations accepted; $12-$15 fee per night; MasterCard and Visa accepted. Open all year.

Who to contact: Phone (541) 469-3863 or write to 16117 Highway 101 South, Brookings, OR 97415.

Location: In Brookings on US 101, drive one mile south of the Chetco River bridge on US 101 and you'll see the park entrance.

Trip note: This park is near both the Chetco River, known for its winter steelhead run, and the beach. Whale watching is good from January through May. Nature trails are a good side trip; they are located a short drive up the river road.

---

68. SEA BIRD RV 🚐

Reference: **On the Pacific Ocean; map E1, grid f1.**

Campsites, facilities: There are 70 drive-through sites for trailers or RVs of any length. Electricity, piped water, sewer hookups and picnic tables are provided. Flush toilets, sanitary services, showers, a recreation hall and a laundromat are available. Pets and motorbikes are permitted. Boat docks, launching facilities and rentals are nearby.

Reservations, fee: Reservations accepted; $15 fee per night. Open all year.

Who to contact: Phone (541) 469-3512 or write to P.O. Box 1026, Brookings, OR 97415.

Location: From Brookings on US 101, drive one-quarter mile south of the Chetco River Bridge on US 101 and you'll see the park entrance.

Trip note: This is one of several campgrounds set along the beach here. Nearby recreation options include marked bike trails, a full-service marina and tennis courts.

---

69. LITTLE REDWOOD 🚐

Reference: **On Chetco River in Siskiyou National Forest; map E1, grid f2.**

Campsites, facilities: There are 12 sites for tents, trailers or RVs up to 16 feet long. Picnic tables and fire grills are provided. Piped water and vault toilets are available. Leashed pets are permitted.

Reservations, fee: No reservations; $6 fee per night. Open late May to mid-September.

Who to contact: Phone the Siskiyou National Forest at (541) 469-2196 or write to Chetco Ranger District, 555 Fifth Street, Brookings, OR 97415.

Location: From Brookings on US 101, drive one-half mile south to County Road 784 (North Bank Chetco River Road). Turn northeast and drive 7.5 miles. At Forest Service Road 1376, proceed six miles to the campground.

Trip note: This campground is set among old-growth fir trees near the bank of the Chetco River. The primary water sport here in the summer is swimming, although there is some trout worth fishing for. The camp is also on the main western access route to the Kalmiopsis Wilderness, which is about 20 miles away.

---

70. LOEB STATE PARK 🚐

Reference: **Near Chetco River; map E1, grid f2.**

Campsites, facilities: There are 53 sites with water and electrical hookups for trailers or RVs up to 50 feet long. Picnic tables and fire grills are provided. Flush toilets and firewood are available. Leashed pets are permitted.

Reservations, fee: No reservations; $13-$15 fee per night. (Weekly and monthly rates available from November through March.) Open all year.

Who to contact: Phone (541) 469-2021 or write c/o Harris Beach State Park, 1655 Highway 101, Brookings, OR 97415.

Location: From Brookings on US 101, drive eight miles northeast on North Bank Road to the entrance to the park on the right.

Trip note: This park is located in a canyon formed by the Chetco River, and is adjacent to Siskiyou National Forest. There is a beautiful myrtlewood grove, and a short spur trail that leads to the Forest Service's Redwood Nature Trail. A Forest Service map details other nearby trailheads.

---

71.   WINCHUCK   **RV**

Reference: On Winchuck River in Siskiyou National Forest; map E1, grid f2.

Campsites, facilities: There are 15 sites for tents, trailers or RVs of any length. Picnic tables and fire grills are provided. Vault toilets and piped water are available. Leashed pets are permitted.

Reservations, fee: No reservations; $5 fee per night. Open late May to mid-September.

Who to contact: Phone the Siskiyou National Forest at (541) 469-2196 or write to Chetco Ranger District, 555 Fifth Street, Brookings, OR 97415.

Location: From Brookings, drive 5.5 miles south on US 101, then six miles east on County Road 896. From there, take Forest Service Road 1107 and drive one mile east to the campground.

Trip note: This forested campground is set along the banks of the Winchuck River, an out-of-the-way stream that out-of-towners don't have a clue about. It's quiet, remote and not that far from the coast, although it feels like an inland spot. This site was recently reconstructed, and now offers clean, spacious sites.

---

72.   KERBY TRAILER PARK & CAMPGROUND   **RV**

Reference: Near Illinois River; map E1, grid f5.

Campsites, facilities: There are 13 sites for trailers and RVs (four are full and nine are partial hookups). Electricity, piped water, sewer hookups and picnic tables are provided. Flush toilets, bottled gas, showers and a laundromat are available. A store and ice are located within 1.5 miles. Pets and motorbikes are permitted.

Reservations, fee: Reservations accepted; $10-$11 fee per night. Open April through late October.

Who to contact: Phone (541) 592-2897 or write to P.O. Box 256, Kerby, OR 97531.

Location: From Interstate 5 at Grants Pass, turn south on US 199 and drive approximately 30 miles to Kerby. This campground is about 400 yards south of Kerby on US 199.

Trip note: This small campground is set near the Illinois River, a good stream during the summer for swimming. See the trip note for Lake Selmac RV Resort for side trip information. Other recreation options include an 18-hole golf course, hiking trails and tennis courts.

---

73.   SHADY ACRES   **RV**

Reference: On Illinois River; map E1, grid f5.

Campsites, facilities: There are four tent sites and 27 drive-through sites for trailers or RVs of any length. Electricity, piped water, sewer hookups and picnic tables are provided. Cable TV is available for a fee. Flush toilets, bottled gas, sanitary services, showers and firewood are available. A store, a cafe, a laundromat and ice are located within one mile. Small, leashed pets are permitted.

Reservations, fee: Reservations accepted; $14 fee per night. Open all year.

Who to contact: Phone (541) 592-3702 or write to 27550 Redwood Highway, Cave Junction, OR 97523.

Location: From Interstate 5 at Grants Pass, turn southwest on US 199 and drive approximately 20 miles to Cave Junction. Continue one mile south on US 199 and you'll see the entrance.

Trip note: This park is set in a forested area near the banks of the Illinois River. See the trip note for Lake Selmac RV Resort (camp number 55) for information on Oregon Caves National Monument.

---

74.   TOWN AND COUNTRY RV PARK   RV

Reference: On the Illinois River; map E1, grid f5.

Campsites, facilities: There are 43 sites for tents, trailers or RVs. Cable TV, showers, restrooms, a sanitary dump, a public phone, a laundromat and ice are available. Horseshoe pits, a club house and a playground are also provided. Pets are permitted on leashes.

Reservations, fee: Reservations recommended; $15 fee per night. Open year-round.

Who to contact: Phone the park at (541) 592-2656 or write to 2828 Redwood Highway, Cave Junction, OR 97523.

Location: From Interstate 5 at Grants Pass, take exit 55 and turn south on US 199. Drive about 35 miles to Cave Junction. From the junction of US 199 and Highway 46, continue two miles south on US 199. The campground is on the right.

Trip note: This park is located on the Illinois River and provides opportunities for swimming, fishing and boating (no motors permitted). Nearby side trips include the Oregon Caves (21 miles) and Grants Pass (31 miles). Crescent City is located 50 miles away.

---

75.   WOODLAND ECHOES RESORT   RV

Reference: Near Oregon Caves National Monument; map E1, grid f6.

Campsites, facilities: There are 18 drive-through sites for trailers or RVs of any length. Picnic tables are provided. Flush toilets, showers, firewood, a cafe, a small store, a laundromat and ice are available. Leashed pets are permitted.

Reservations, fee: Reservations accepted; $10-$15 fee per night. MasterCard, Visa, American Express and Discover accepted. Open all year.

Who to contact: Phone (541) 592-3406 or write to 7901 Caves Highway, Cave Junction, OR 97523.

Location: From Interstate 5 at Grants Pass, take exit 58 and turn south on US 199. Drive 33 miles to the town of Cave Junction. Turn east on Highway 46 and drive eight miles.

Trip note: See the trip note for Lake Selmac RV Resort (camp number 55) for information about the nearby Oregon Caves National Monument.

76. GRAYBACK RV.

Reference: **Near Oregon Caves National Monument in Siskiyou National Forest; map E1, grid f6.**

Campsites, facilities: There are 37 sites for tents, trailers or RVs up to 22 feet long. Picnic tables and fire grills are provided. Flush toilets and piped water are available. Leashed pets are permitted. Facilities are **wheelchair accessible**.

Reservations, fee: Reserve some sites by calling (800) 280-CAMP ($7.75 reservation fee); $8 fee per night. Open May through October.

Who to contact: Phone the Siskiyou National Forest at (541) 592-2166 or write to Illinois Valley Ranger District, P.O. Box 389, Cave Junction, OR 97523.

Location: From Interstate 5 at Grants Pass, take exit 58 and turn south on US 199. Drive 33 miles to the town of Cave Junction, then turn east on Highway 46 and drive 12 miles to the campground.

Trip note: This wooded campground is set along the banks of Sucker Creek, about 10 miles from Oregon Caves National Monument. The sites offer ample shade, and this is a good spot to camp if you're planning to visit the caves. The camp is set in a grove of old-growth firs, and is a prime place for birdwatching. There is a one-half mile barrier-free trail in camp.

77. CAVE CREEK

Reference: **Near Oregon Caves National Monument in Siskiyou National Forest; map E1, grid f6.**

Campsites, facilities: There are 18 tent sites. Piped water, vault toilets, picnic tables are provided. Showers are located within eight miles. Leashed pets are permitted.

Reservations, fee: For reservation and fee information, phone (541) 592-3400. Open June through September.

Who to contact: Phone the Siskiyou National Forest at (541) 592-2166 or write to Illinois Valley Ranger District, P.O. Box 389, Cave Junction, OR 97523.

Location: From Interstate 5 at Grants Pass, take exit 58 and turn south on US 199. Drive 33 miles to the town of Cave Junction, then turn east on Highway 46 and drive 16 miles. Turn right on Forest Service Road 4032 and drive one mile south to the campground.

Trip note: This Forest Service camp is just four miles from the Oregon Caves National Monument; no campground is closer. There is even a trail out of camp that leads directly to the caves. See the trip note for Lake Selmac RV Resort for details on the monument. The camp is set in a grove of old-growth timber along the banks of Cave Creek, a small creek with some trout fishing opportunities. The sites are shaded, and an abundance of wildlife can be spotted in the area. There are hiking trails in the area.

78. BOLAN LAKE RV.

Reference: **On Bolan Lake in Siskiyou National Forest; map E1, grid f6.**

Campsites, facilities: There are 12 sites for tents, trailers or RVs up to 16 feet long. Picnic tables and fire grills are provided. Pit toilets and firewood are available, but there is **no piped water**. Leashed pets are permitted.

Reservations, fee: No reservations; no fee. Open July to November.

Who to contact: Phone the Siskiyou National Forest at (541) 592-2166 or write to Illinois Valley Ranger District, P.O. Box 389, Cave Junction, OR 97523.

Location: From Cave Junction, take County Road 12 eight miles southeast, then go 14 miles southeast on County Road 4007. Located at Forest Service Road 408. Note: It is not advisable to pull large trailers or RVs on the access road in; the road is very narrow and rough.

Trip note: This campground is set along the shore of 15-acre Bolan Lake, with pretty, shaded sites. Very few out-of-towners know about this spot. A trail from the lake leads up to a fire lookout and ties into miles of other trails. See a Forest Service map for trailhead locations. This spot is truly a birdwatcher's paradise, with a variety of species to view. The fishing can be good here as well.

---

79.   JACKSON   📷RV

Reference: **On the Applegate River in Rogue River National Forest; map E2, grid f8.**

Campsites, facilities: There are 10 sites for tents, trailers or RVs up to 20 feet long. Piped water and flush toilets are available. Leashed pets permitted.

Reservations, fee: No reservations; $7 fee per night; $3 second vehicle per night. Open May through October.

Who to contact: Phone Rogue Recreation at (541) 770-5146 or (541) 560-3400 or write to 2990 North Pacific Highway, Medford, OR 97501.

Location: From Interstate 5 south of Medford, take the Jacksonville exit and drive the few miles to Jacksonville. Turn southwest on Highway 238 and drive eight miles, then turn southwest on County Road 10 and continue for nine miles to the camp on the right. Jackson is directly across from Flumet Flat campground.

Trip note: This camp is at 1,500 feet elevation, nestled in an old mining area. Right on the Applegate River, there's a swimming hole and good trout fishing.

---

80.   FLUMET FLAT   📷RV

Reference: **On Applegate River in Rogue River National Forest; map E1, grid f8.**

Campsites, facilities: There are 23 sites for tents, trailers or RVs up to 30 feet long. Picnic tables and fire grills are provided. Piped water and flush toilets are available. Showers, a store, a cafe, a laundromat and ice are available nearby at McKee Bridge. Leashed pets are permitted.

Reservations, fee: Reservations available for groups only; $7 fee per night; $3.50 per extra vehicle. Open year-round.

Who to contact: Phone Rogue Recreation at (541) 770-5146 or write 2990 North Pacific Highway, Medford, OR 97501.

Location: From Interstate 5 south of Medford, take the Jacksonville exit and drive the few miles to Jacksonville. Turn southwest on Highway 238 and drive eight miles, then turn southwest on County Road 10 and continue for nine miles. Turn southwest on Forest Service Road 1095 and proceed one mile to the campground.

Trip note: This campground is set along the banks of the Applegate River about six miles north of Applegate Reservoir. The Gin-Lin nature trail, named for the Chinese miner who struck it rich in local gold mines, is nearby. There is a large park-like lawn area with facilities for volleyball, badminton and horseshoes. But the best thing is that because the camp is set at a low 1,500 feet in elevation, it's relatively warm in the swimming hole.

81. FRENCH GULCH

Reference: On Applegate Reservoir (walk-in only) in Rogue River National Forest; map E1, grid f8.

Campsites, facilities: There are nine walk-in sites for tents. Picnic tables and fire grills are provided. Hand-pumped water and vault toilets are available. Leashed pets are permitted. Boat docks and launching facilities are within one to two miles.

Reservations, fee: No reservations; $7 fee per night; $3.50 per extra vehicle. Open May to November. Golden Age and Access discounts.

Who to contact: Phone Rogue Recreation at (541) 770-5146 or write 2990 North Pacific Highway, Medford, OR 97501.

Location: From Interstate 5 south of Medford, take the Jacksonville exit and drive the few miles to Jacksonville. Turn southwest on Highway 238 and drive eight miles, then turn south on County Road 10 and continue for 14 miles. Then drive 1.5 miles east on Forest Service Road 1075 and park. A short walk is required.

Trip note: This campground is set along the shore of Applegate Reservoir. It's a popular summer fishing spot for Ashland anglers. It is also a good boat-in campground when the lake level allows; the launch ramp is not far from the campground.

82. WATKINS

Reference: On Applegate Reservoir (walk-in only) in Rogue River National Forest; map E1, grid f8.

Campsites, facilities: There are 14 walk-in sites for tents. Picnic tables, hand-pumped water and fire grills are provided. Vault toilets are available. Leashed pets are permitted. Boat docks and launching facilities are within one mile.

Reservations, fee: No reservations; $7 fee per night; $3.50 per extra vehicle. Open May to November. Golden Age and Access discounts.

Who to contact: Phone Rogue Recreation at (541) 770-5146 or write 2990 North Pacific Highway, Medford, OR 97501.

Location: From Interstate 5 south of Medford, take the Jacksonville exit and drive a few miles to Jacksonville. Turn southwest on Highway 238 and drive eight miles, then turn southwest on County Road 10 and continue for 17 miles.

Trip note: This campground is set along the southwest shore of Applegate Reservoir. This site, like Carberry Campground, is small and quite primitive, but it's pretty and offers all the same recreation options. It is little-known so it usually doesn't fill up quickly.

83. CANTRALL-BUCKLEY PARK   RV

Reference: On Applegate River; map E1, grid f9.

Campsites, facilities: There are 25 sites for tents, trailers and RVs up to 25 feet. Restrooms, showers and a public phone are provided. Recreational facilities include horseshoes, a playground, a recreation field and a barbecue.

Reservations, fee: No reservations; $10 fee per night. Open May to mid-October.

Who to contact: Phone Jackson County Parks at (541) 776-7001 or write to 400 Antelope Road, White City, OR 97541.

Location: From Interstate 5 at Medford, turn west on Highway 238 and drive 18 miles to Hamilton Road. Turn south on Hamilton Road and drive one mile to the camp (signed).

Trip note: This county park is set in the outside of Medford. It offers pleasant, shady sites in a wooded setting. The Applegate River, which provides good trout fishing, runs nearby.

84. BEAVER SULPHUR

Reference: **On Beaver Creek in Rogue River National Forest; map E1, grid f9.**

Campsites, facilities: There are 10 sites for tents. Picnic tables and fire grills are provided. Vault toilets and hand-pumped water are available. Leashed pets are permitted.

Reservations, fee: No reservations; $4 fee per night; $2 per extra vehicle. Open May to December. Golden Age and Access discounts.

Who to contact: Phone the Star Ranger District at (541) 899-1812 or write to Rogue River National Forest, 6941 Upper Applegate Road, Jacksonville, OR 97530.

Location: From Interstate 5 south of Medford, take the Jacksonville exit and drive a few miles to Jacksonville. Turn southwest on Highway 238 and drive eight miles, then turn southwest on County Road 10 and continue nine miles. Turn east on Forest Service Road 20 and proceed three miles to the campground.

Trip note: This campground is set along the banks of Beaver Creek, about nine miles from Applegate Reservoir. It's tiny and hidden, with pretty, shaded sites and easy access to the creek. Fishing is a possibility. A Forest Service map will detail the roads and trails in the area.

85. SQUAW LAKE

Reference: **On Squaw Lake (walk-in only) in Rogue River National Forest; map E1, grid f9.**

Campsites, facilities: There are 17 walk-in sites for tents. Hand-pumped water is available. Two family group sites are available; each site accommodates up to 10 people. Picnic tables and fire grills are provided. Vault toilets are available. Leashed pets are permitted.

Reservations, fee: Reservations required (phone the ranger district); $5 fee per night. Open all year. Golden Age and Access discounts.

Who to contact: Phone Rogue Recreation at (541) 770-5146 or write 2990 North Pacific Highway, Medford, OR 97501.

Location: From Interstate 5 south of Medford, take the Jacksonville exit and drive the few miles to Jacksonville. Turn southwest on Highway 238 and drive eight miles, then turn southwest on County Road 10 and continue for 14 miles. Turn south on Forest Service Road 1075 and drive eight miles to the campground.

Trip note: This campground is set along the shore of Squaw Lake. Numerous trails are in the area. It's a more intimate setting than the larger Applegate Reservoir to the west. It is also more popular, and the only campground in the district that requires reservations. Be sure to call ahead for available space.

86. CARBERRY   RV

Reference: **On Applegate Reservoir (walk-in only) in Rogue River National Forest; map E1, grid g8.**

Campsites, facilities: There are 10 walk-in sites for tents. Space is available in the parking lot for trailers or RVs. Picnic tables and fire grills are provided. Vault toilets and hand-pumped water are available. Leashed pets are permitted. Boat docks and launching facilities are within two miles.

Reservations, fee: No reservations; $7 fee per night; $3.50 per extra vehicle. Open May to November.

Who to contact: Phone the Star Ranger District at (541) 899-1812 or write to Rogue River National Forest, 6941 Upper Applegate Road, Jacksonville, OR 97530.

Location: From Interstate 5 south of Medford, take the Jacksonville exit and drive a few miles to Jacksonville. Turn southwest on Highway 238 and drive eight miles, then turn southwest on County Road 10 and continue 18 miles. A short walk is required.

Trip note: This campground is set along the southwest shore of Applegate Reservoir. Many recreation options are available to campers, including fishing, boating and swimming. This is a smaller and more primitive option to French Gulch.

LEAVE NO TRACE TIPS

Minimize use and impact of fires.

• Campfires can have a lasting impact on the backcountry. Always carry a lightweight stove for cooking, and use a candle lantern instead of building a fire whenever possible.

• Where fires are permitted, use established fire rings only. Do not scar large rocks or overhangs.

• Gather sticks for your campfire that are no larger than the diameter of your wrist. Do not scar the natural setting by snapping the branches off live, dead, or downed trees.

• Completely extinguish your campfire and make sure it is cold before departing. Remove all unburned trash from the fire ring and scatter the cold ashes over a large area well away from any camp.

MAP E2

OREGON MAP .... see page 380
Adjoining Maps
NORTH (D2) .... see page 500
EAST (E3) .... see page 670

84 LISTINGS
PAGES 636-669

SOUTH .... no map
WEST (E1) .... see page 602

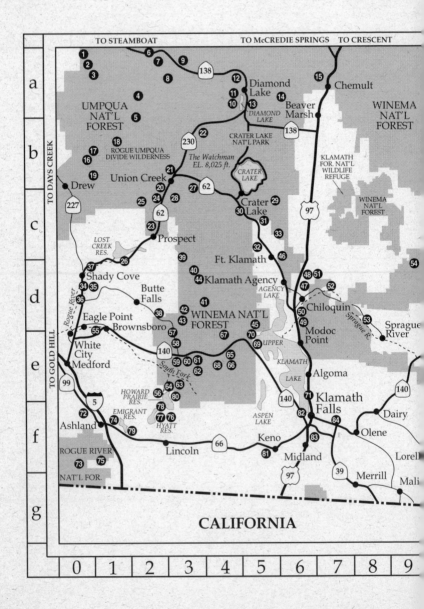

Oregon Map E2 featuring: Little River, Umpqua National Forest, Umpqua River, Lake of the Woods, Hemlock Lake, Big Twin Lake, Lemolo Lake, Rogue River National Forest, Rogue River, Diamond Lake, Clearwater River, Miller Lake, Winema National Forest, Rogue River Trail, Crater Lake National Park, Crater Lake Pinnacles, Sky Lakes Wilderness, Lost Creek Lake, Pacific Crest Trail, Williamson River, Wood River, Collier Memorial State Park, Snowshoe Butte, Parker River, Willow Lake, Fish Lake, Klamath Lake, Fourmile Lake, Sprague River, Hyatt Lake, Howard Prairie Lake, Ashland, Emigrant Lake, Tingley Lake

---

1. WOLF CREEK   RV

Reference: **On Little River in Umpqua National Forest; map E2, grid a0.**

Campsites, facilities: There are seven sites for tents, trailers or RVs up to 30 feet long. Picnic tables and fire grills are provided. Flush toilets and piped water are available. Some facilities are **wheelchair accessible**. Pets are permitted.

Reservations, fee: Reservations required for groups; $45 fee per night. Open mid-May to late October.

Who to contact: Phone the North Umpqua Ranger District at (541) 496-3532 or write to Umpqua National Forest, 18782 North Umpqua Highway, Glide, OR 97443.

Location: From Roseburg on Interstate 5, take exit 120 and drive 18 miles east on Highway 138 to Glide. From Glide, travel 12 miles southeast on County Road 17 to the campground.

Trip note: This campground is set at the entrance to the national forest along the banks of the Little River. It is near the Wolf Creek Civilian Conservation Center. It's a pretty camp, close to civilization with easy access. If you want to get deeper into the interior of the Cascades, Hemlock Lake and Lake of the Woods camps are two choices that are about 15 miles east.

---

2. COOLWATER   RV

Reference: **On Little River in Umpqua National Forest; map E2, grid a1.**

Campsites, facilities: There are seven sites for tents, trailers or RVs up to 24 feet long. Picnic tables and fire grills are provided. Vault toilets and hand-pumped water are available. Leashed pets are permitted.

Reservations, fee: No reservations; no fee. Open year-round.

Who to contact: Phone the North Umpqua Ranger District at (541) 496-3532 or write to Umpqua National Forest, 18782 North Umpqua Highway, Glide, OR 97443.

Location: From Roseburg on Interstate 5, take exit 120 and drive 18 miles east on Highway 138 to Glide. From Glide, travel 17 miles southeast on County Road 17 to the campground.

Trip note: This campground gets relatively little use and is set along the banks of Little River. Fishing and swimming are two options here. Grotto Falls, a scenic waterfall, can be reached by traveling north on Forest Service Road 2703 (across the road from the camp). Near there is Emile Grove, home of a thicket of old-growth Douglas firs and the huge "Bill Taft Tree," named after the former President.

3.　　　　　　　　WHITE CREEK　　　　　　　　**RV**

Reference: **On Little River in Umpqua National Forest; map E2, grid a1.**

Campsites, facilities: There are three sites for tents, trailers or RVs up to 31 feet long. Picnic tables and fire grills are provided. Vault toilets and hand-pumped well water are available. Leashed pets are permitted.

Reservations, fee: No reservations; no fee. Open year-round.

Who to contact: Phone the North Umpqua Ranger District at (541) 496-3532 or write to Umpqua National Forest, 18782 North Umpqua Highway, Glide, OR 97443.

Location: From Roseburg on Interstate 5, take exit 120 and drive 18 miles east on Highway 138 to Glide. From Glide, continue for 17 miles on Little River Road to Forest Service Road 2792 (Red Butte Road). Proceed one-quarter mile to the campground.

Trip note: This campground is set at the confluence of White Creek and Little River. Hiking and fishing are two of the recreation options here. See the trip note for Coolwater campground for other details about the area.

4.　　　　　　　　HEMLOCK LAKE　　　　　　　　**RV**

Reference: **On Hemlock Lake in Umpqua National Forest; map E2, grid a2.**

Campsites, facilities: There are 13 sites for tents, trailers or RVs up to 35 feet long. **No piped water** is available. Picnic tables and fire grills are provided. Vault toilets are available. Leashed pets are permitted. Boat docks and launching facilities are nearby. No motors are permitted on the lake.

Reservations, fee: No reservations; no fee. Open June to late October.

Who to contact: Phone the North Umpqua Ranger District at (541) 496-3532 or write to Umpqua National Forest, 18782 North Umpqua Highway, Glide, OR 97443.

Location: From Roseburg on Interstate 5, take exit 120 and drive 18 miles east on Highway 138 to Glide. Travel on County Road 17 east from Glide for 16.5 miles, then drive 15.5 miles east on Forest Service Road 27.

Trip note: This is a little-known jewel of a spot. For starters, it is set along the shore of Hemlock Lake. An eight-mile loop trail called the Yellow Jacket Loop is just south of the campground. For finishers, another trail leaves camp and heads north for about three miles to the Lake of the Woods Campground. From there, it is just a short hike to either Hemlock Falls or Yakso Falls, both spectacular scenery.

5.　　　　　　　LAKE OF THE WOODS　　　　　　　**RV**

Reference: **On Lake of the Woods in Umpqua National Forest; map E2, grid a2.**

Campsites, facilities: There are 11 sites for tents, trailers or RVs up to 35 feet long. Picnic tables and fire grills are provided. Flush toilets and hand-pumped well water are available. Leashed pets are permitted.

Reservations, fee: No reservations; $3 to $5 fee per night. Open June to late October.

Who to contact: Phone the North Umpqua Ranger District at (541) 496-3532 or write to Umpqua National Forest, 18782 North Umpqua Highway, Glide, OR 97443.

Location: From Roseburg on Interstate 5, take exit 120 and drive 18 miles east on Highway 138 to Glide. Travel on County Road 17 east from Glide for 16.5

miles, then drive 11 miles east on Forest Service Road 27.

Trip note: This campground is set along the shore of little Lake of the Woods. There are several good hikes available. One of them leaves the camp and heads south for about three miles to the Hemlock Lake Campground. Two other nearby trails provide short, scenic hikes to either Hemlock Falls or Yakso Falls.

---

6. APPLE CREEK   RV

Reference: **On Umpqua River in Umpqua National Forest; map E2, grid a2.**

Campsites, facilities: There are eight sites for tents, trailers or RVs up to 21 feet long. Picnic tables and fire grills are provided. Vault toilets are available. There is **no piped water**. Leashed pets are permitted.

Reservations, fee: No reservations; no fee. Open year-round.

Who to contact: Phone the North Umpqua Ranger District at (541) 496-3532 or write to Umpqua National Forest, 18782 North Umpqua Highway, Glide, OR 97443.

Location: From Interstate 5 at Roseburg, take exit 120 and travel east on Highway 138 for 43 miles. The camp is next to the highway.

Trip note: This campground is set along the banks of the Umpqua River at a popular spot for rafting and fly fishing. The North Umpqua River Trail runs east and west along the river for many miles. This camp is pretty, small and primitive, with easy highway access. If it's full, try Horseshoe Bend.

---

7. HORSESHOE BEND   RV

Reference: **On Umpqua River in Umpqua National Forest; map E2, grid a2.**

Campsites, facilities: There are 24 sites for tents, trailers or RVs up to 35 feet long. Picnic tables, fire grills, piped water and flush toilets are provided. A laundromat, a store, gas and propane are available one mile east. Some facilities are **wheelchair accessible**; the camp is partially modified for the disabled. Leashed pets are permitted. Raft launching facilities are nearby.

Reservations, fee: No reservations; $10 fee per night, except for a separate nine-unit reservation area, $40 fee per night. Open mid-May to late September.

Who to contact: Phone the North Umpqua Ranger District at (541) 496-3532 or write to Umpqua National Forest, 18782 North Umpqua Highway, Glide, OR 97443.

Location: From Roseburg on Interstate 5, take exit 120 and drive 47 miles east on Highway 138, then turn right at the signed entrance and follow the road south a short distance to the campground.

Trip note: This campground is set in the middle of a big bend in the North Umpqua River. Rafting and fly fishing are both popular here. See Apple Creek trip note for area information.

---

8. TWIN LAKES

Reference: **On Big Twin Lake (hike-in only) in Umpqua National Forest; map E2, grid a3.**

Campsites, facilities: There are six tent sites. Picnic tables and fire pits are provided. A pit toilet is available. There is **no piped water**. Leashed pets are permitted.

Reservations, fee: No reservations; no fee. Open mid-June to late October, depending on weather.

Who to contact: Phone the North Umpqua Ranger District at (541) 496-3532 or write to Umpqua National Forest, 18782 North Umpqua Highway, Glide, OR 97443.

Location: From Roseburg on Interstate 5, take exit 120 and drive 14 miles east to Glide. From the North Umpqua Ranger Station, take Highway 138 east 33 miles to Marsters Bridge. Cross the bridge and turn right on Forest Service Road 4770. Follow Forest Service Road 4770 for 10 miles to the trailhead for Twin Lakes Tráil No. 1500. It is a 1.25-mile hike to the campground.

Trip note: If you can find it, you'll love it. This remote campground is set along the shore of Big Twin Lake at 5,100 feet. The lake covers 14 acres and is 48 feet deep. It's a place of quiet and great beauty. It is known by few and gets little use, so you may have the whole camp to yourself. There are some excellent hiking trails and two trail shelters in the area. One trail leads to Twin Lakes Mountain (5,879 feet).

9.　　　　　WHITEHORSE FALLS

Reference: **On Clearwater River in Umpqua National Forest; map E2, grid a3.**

Campsites, facilities: There are five tent sites. **No piped water** is available. Picnic tables and fire grills are provided. Vault toilets are available. Leashed pets are permitted.

Reservations, fee: No reservations; no fee. Open June to late October.

Who to contact: Phone the Diamond Lake Ranger District at (541) 498-2531 or write to Umpqua National Forest, HC 60, Box 101, Idleyld Park, OR 97447.

Location: From Roseburg on Interstate 5, take exit 120 and drive 67 miles east on Highway 138 to the campground.

Trip note: This campground is set along the Clearwater River, one of the coldest streams in Umpqua National Forest. The small camp is in a primitive setting, yet it's adjacent to the highway. Pretty Clearwater Falls are located a few miles east, providing a good side trip option. Fishing, hiking, rafting and swimming are some of your recreation options in the area.

10.　　　　　BROKEN ARROW　　　　RV

Reference: **On Diamond Lake in Umpqua National Forest; map E2, grid a4.**

Campsites, facilities: There are 148 sites for tents, trailers or RVs up to 35 feet long. Picnic tables and fire grills are provided. Flush toilets, showers and piped water are available. Leashed pets are permitted. Some facilities are **wheelchair accessible**. Boat docks, launching facilities and rentals are nearby.

Reservations, fee: Reserve group sites only by calling (800) 280-CAMP ($7.50 reservation fee); $8 fee per night for single units. Open late May to mid-September.

Who to contact: Phone the Diamond Lake Ranger District at (541) 498-2531 or write to Umpqua National Forest at HC 60, Box 101, Idleyld Park, OR 97447.

Location: From Roseburg on Interstate 5, take exit 120 and drive 80 miles east on Highway 138. Turn on Forest Service Road 4795 and drive to the campground.

Trip note: This campground is set at 5,200 feet near the south shore of Diamond Lake, the largest natural lake in Umpqua National Forest. Boating, fishing, swimming, hiking and bicycling are among the options here. Diamond Lake is adjacent to the Mount Thielsen Wilderness, Crater Lake National Park and Mount Bailey, all of which offer a variety of recreation opportunities year-round. Diamond Lake is quite popular with anglers because of its good trout trolling, particularly in early summer.

11. THIELSEN VIEW

Reference: On Diamond Lake in Umpqua National Forest; map E2, grid a4.

Campsites, facilities: There are 60 sites for tents, trailers or RVs up to 30 feet long. Picnic tables and fire grills are provided. Piped water and vault toilets are available. Leashed pets are permitted. Some facilities are **wheelchair accessible**. Boat docks, launching facilities and rentals are nearby.

Reservations, fee: No reservations; $7-$10 fee per night. Open late May to late September.

Who to contact: Phone the Diamond Lake Ranger District at (541) 498-2531 or write to Umpqua National Forest, HC 60, Box 101, Idleyld Park, OR 97447.

Location: From Roseburg on Interstate 5, take exit 120 and drive 80 miles east on Highway 138. Then turn south onto Forest Service Road 4795 and drive to the campground.

Trip note: This campground is set along the west shore of Diamond Lake. See the trip note for Broken Arrow for information on recreation opportunities.

12. CLEARWATER FALLS

Reference: On Clearwater River in Umpqua National Forest; map E2, grid a5.

Campsites, facilities: There are nine tent sites. There is **no piped water**. Picnic tables and fire grills are provided. Vault toilets are available. Leashed pets are permitted.

Reservations, fee: No reservations; no fee. Open mid-May to late October.

Who to contact: Phone the Diamond Lake Ranger District at (541) 498-2531 or write to Umpqua National Forest, HC 60, P.O. Box 101, Idleyld Park, OR 97447.

Location: From Roseburg on Interstate 5, take exit 120 and drive 70 miles west on Highway 138. At Forest Service Road 4785 head south to the campground.

Trip note: This campground is set along the banks of the Clearwater River. The attraction here is the cascading section of stream called Clearwater Falls. See the trip note for Whitehorse Falls for area details.

13. DIAMOND LAKE

Reference: On Diamond Lake in Umpqua National Forest; map E2, grid a5.

Campsites, facilities: There are 238 sites for tents, trailers or RVs up to 35 feet long. Picnic tables and fire grills are provided. Flush toilets, showers, piped water and firewood are available. Leashed pets are permitted. Boat docks, launching facilities and rentals are nearby.

Reservations, fee: Reserve some sites by calling (800) 280-CAMP ($7.50 reservation fee); $7-$10 fee per night. Open late April to late October.

Who to contact: Phone the Diamond Lake Ranger District at (541) 498-2531 or write to Umpqua National Forest, HC 60, Box 101, Idleyld Park, OR 97447.

Location: From Roseburg on Interstate 5, take exit 120 and drive 78 miles east on Highway 138. Turn at the sign for Diamond Lake Resort and follow the road (keep straight, don't turn toward the resort) to the campground.

Trip note: This campground is set along the east shore of Diamond Lake. This is an extremely popular camp with all the luxuries: flush toilets, showers and piped water. See the trip note for Broken Arrow for recreation information.

14.   DIGIT POINT   RV

Reference: **On Miller Lake in Winema National Forest; map E2, grid a6.**

Campsites, facilities: There are 64 sites for tents, trailers or RVs up to 30 feet long. Picnic tables and fire grills are provided. Piped water, a sanitary disposal station and flush toilets are available. Leashed pets are permitted. Boat docks and launching facilities are nearby.

Reservations, fee: No reservations; $6 fee per night. Open mid-June to October.

Who to contact: Phone the Chemult Ranger District at (541) 365-7001 or write to Winema National Forest, P.O. Box 150, Chemult, OR 97731.

Location: From Interstate 5 south of Eugene, take exit 188 and turn east on Highway 58. Drive 86 miles, then turn south on US 97 and drive seven miles to Forest Service Road 9772 (one mile north of Chemult). Turn right and drive 12 miles west to the campground.

Trip note: This campground is set along the shore of Miller Lake, a popular spot for boating, fishing, swimming and waterskiing. Nearby trails provide access to the Mount Thielsen Wilderness, and the Pacific Crest Trail passes two miles from camp.

15.   CORRAL SPRING   RV

Reference: **In Winema National Forest; map E2, grid a7.**

Campsites, facilities: There are seven sites for tents, trailers or RVs up to 22 feet long. Picnic tables and fire grills are provided. Vault toilets are available. There is **no piped water**. A store, a cafe, a laundromat and ice are located within five miles. Leashed pets are permitted.

Reservations, fee: No reservations; no fee. Open mid-May to late October.

Who to contact: Phone the Chemult Ranger District at (541) 365-7001 or write to Winema National Forest, P.O. Box 150, Chemult, OR 97731.

Location: From Interstate 5 south of Eugene, take exit 188 and turn east on Highway 58. Drive 86 miles, then turn south on US 97 and drive 6.5 miles to Forest Service Road 9774 (2.5 miles north of Chemult). Turn right and drive two miles west to the campground.

Trip note: This campground is set next to Corral Spring. It's primitive, remote and quiet. There's not much out here, but it's just what some people cruising US 97 want.

16.   DUMONT CREEK   RV

Reference: **On South Umpqua River in Umpqua National Forest; map E2, grid b1.**

Campsites, facilities: There are five sites for tents, trailers or RVs up to 16 feet long. Picnic tables and fire grills are provided. Vault toilets are available. There is **no piped water**. Leashed pets are permitted.

Reservations, fee: No reservations; no fee. Open late May to late October.

Who to contact: Phone the Tiller Ranger District at (541) 825-3201 or write to Umpqua National Forest, 28712 Tiller Trail Highway, Tiller, OR 97484.

Location: From Interstate 5 at Canyonville (exits 99 or 100), travel 25 miles east on County Road 1 to Tiller. Turn left on County Road 46 and drive six miles northeast. The camp is 5.5 miles northeast on Forest Service Road 28.

Trip note: This campground is set along the banks of the South Umpqua River and Dumont Creek. It's quiet, primitive and remote. Boulder Creek camp, just a few miles east, provides an option. A good side trip is to visit nearby South Umpqua Falls, a beautiful, wide waterfall. It features a fish ladder, and a platform is provided so you can watch the fish struggle upstream.

---

17. BOULDER CREEK RV

Reference: **On South Umpqua River in Umpqua National Forest; map E2, grid b1.**

Campsites, facilities: There are 12 sites for tents, trailers or RVs up to 15 feet long. Picnic tables and fire grills are provided. Vault toilets are available. There is **no piped water**. Leashed pets are permitted.

Reservations, fee: No reservations; no fee. Open late May to late October.

Who to contact: Phone the Tiller Ranger District at (541) 825-3201 or write to Umpqua National Forest, 27812 Tiller Trail Highway, Tiller, OR 97484.

Location: From Interstate 5 at Canyonville (exits 99 or 100), travel 25 miles east on County Road 1 to Tiller, then turn left on County Road 46 and drive six miles northeast. The camp is seven miles northeast on Forest Service Road 28.

Trip note: This campground is set along the banks of the South Umpqua River, near Boulder Creek. See Dumont Creek for information on the area.

---

18. CAMP COMFORT RV

Reference: **On the South Fork of Umpqua River in Umpqua National Forest; map E2, grid b1.**

Campsites, facilities: There are five sites for tents, trailers or RVs up to 15 feet long. Picnic tables and fire grills are provided. Vault toilets are available. There is **no piped water**. Leashed pets are permitted.

Reservations, fee: No reservations; no fee. Open late May to late October.

Who to contact: Phone the Tiller Ranger District at (541) 825-3201 or write to Umpqua National Forest, 27812 Tiller Trail Highway, Tiller, OR 97484.

Location: From Interstate 5 at Canyonville (exits 99 or 100), travel 25 miles east on County Road 1 to Tiller, then turn left on County Road 46 and drive six miles northeast. Continue about 18 miles northeast on Forest Service Road 28 to the campground.

Trip note: This campground is set along the banks of the South Umpqua River, deep in the Umpqua National Forest. Trailheads providing access to the Rogue-Umpqua Divide Wilderness can be found at the ends of the Forest Service roads west of the camp. A good side trip is South Umpqua Falls, which you pass on the drive in.

---

19. COVER RV

Reference: **On Jackson Creek in Umpqua National Forest; E2, grid b1.**

Campsites, facilities: There are seven sites for tents, trailers or RVs up to 16 feet long. Picnic tables and fire grills are provided. Vault toilets are available. There is **no piped water**. Leashed pets are permitted.

Reservations, fee: No reservations; no fee. Open late May to late October.

Who to contact: Phone the Tiller Ranger District at (541) 825-3201 or write to Umpqua National Forest, 27812 Tiller Trail Highway, Tiller, OR 97484.

Location: From Interstate 5 at Canyonville (exits 99 or 100), travel 25 miles east on County Road 1 to Tiller, then turn left on County Road 46 and drive five miles northeast. Turn right on Forest Service Road 29 and drive 12 miles east to the campground.

Trip note: This campground is set along the banks of Jackson Creek. If you want quiet, this is the right place. Just about nobody knows about this one. If you head east to Forest Service Road 30 and follow it south, you can access a major trail into the Rogue-Umpqua Divide Wilderness. Be sure not to miss the world's largest sugar pine tree (a few miles west of camp).

20. UNION CREEK   RV

Reference: **Near Upper Rogue River in Rogue River National Forest; map E2, grid b2.**

Campsites, facilities: There are 78 sites for tents, trailers or RVs up to 25 feet long. Picnic tables and fire grills are provided. Potable piped water, vault toilets and firewood are available. Leashed pets are permitted. A store and a restaurant are within walking distance.

Reservations, fee: No reservations; $8 fee per night; $4 second vehicle per night. Golden Age and Access discounts. Open mid-May to mid-October.

Who to contact: Phone Rogue Recreation at (541) 770-5146 or (541) 560-3400 or write to 2990 North Pacific Highway, Medford, OR 97501.

Location: From Medford on Interstate 5, travel 56 miles north on Highway 62 to the campground on the left.

Trip note: This campground is more developed than the nearby camps of Mill Creek, River Bridge and Natural Bridge. It is set along the bank of Union Creek where it joins the Upper Rogue River. The Upper Rogue River Trail passes near camp. This is one of the most popular camps in the district, with interpretive programs in the summer and a convenience store and a restaurant within walking distance.

21. FAREWELL BEND   RV

Reference: **On Upper Rogue River in Rogue River National Forest; map E2, grid b3.**

Campsites, facilities: There are 61 sites for tents, trailers or RVs up to 35 feet long. Picnic tables, fire grills and fire rings are provided. Potable piped water, firewood and flush toilets are available. Some facilities are **wheelchair accessible**. Leashed pets are permitted.

Reservations, fee: No reservations; $10 fee per night; $5 second vehicle per night. Golden Age and Access discounts. Open late May to late October.

Who to contact: Phone Rogue Recreation at (541) 770-5146 or (541) 560-3400 or write to 2990 North Pacific Highway, Medford, OR 97501.

Location: From Medford on Interstate 5, travel 59 miles north on Highway 62 to the campground on the left.

Trip note: This extremely popular campground is set along the bank of the Upper Rogue River near the Rogue River Gorge. There is a one-quarter mile barrier-free trail that leads to the Rogue Gorge Viewpoint, definitely worth the trip. The Upper Rogue River Trail passes near camp. It attracts a lot of the campers who also visit Crater Lake.

22. HAMAKER   RV

Reference: **Near Upper Rogue River in Rogue River National Forest; map E2, grid b4.**

Campsites, facilities: There are 10 sites for tents, trailers or RVs up to 25 feet long. Picnic tables, fire grills and stoves are provided. Potable pumped water and vault toilets are available. Leashed pets are permitted.

Reservations, fee: No reservations; $6 fee per night; $3 second vehicle per night. Golden Age and Access discounts. Open late May to late October.

Who to contact: Phone Rogue Recreation at (541) 770-5146 or (541) 560-3400 or write to 2990 North Pacific Highway, Medford, OR 97501.

Location: From Medford on Interstate 5, travel 57 miles northeast on Highway 62 and then 11 miles north on Highway 230. Continue 600 yards east on Forest Service Road 6530.

Trip note: This campground is set at 4,000 feet near the Upper Rogue River. It is a beautiful little spot, set in a high mountain meadow. In the spring and early summer, wildflowers and wildlife abound. It is one of the least-used camps in the area. This is a prime spot for Crater Lake visitors.

---

23.   RIVER BRIDGE   RV

Reference: **On Upper Rogue River in Rogue River National Forest; map E2, grid c2.**

Campsites, facilities: There are six sites for tents, trailers and RVs up to 30 feet long. Picnic tables and fireplaces are provided. Vault toilets are available. There is **no piped water**. Leashed pets are permitted.

Reservations, fee: No reservations; no fee. Open April to November.

Who to contact: Phone the Prospect Ranger District at (541) 560-3400 or write to Rogue River National Forest, Prospect, OR 97536.

Location: From Medford on Interstate 5, travel 42 miles northeast on Highway 62. Turn left and drive one mile north on Forest Service Road 6210 to the campground on the left.

Trip note: This campground is set along the banks of the Upper Rogue River. It's a particularly scenic spot, with private and secluded sites with river views. This is a calmer part of the Wild and Scenic Upper Rogue, though no swimming or rafting is recommended. The Upper Rogue River Trail passes the camp and follows the river for many miles to the Pacific Crest Trail in Crater Lake National Park.

---

24.   NATURAL BRIDGE   RV

Reference: **On Upper Rogue River Trail in Rogue River National Forest; map E2, grid c2.**

Campsites, facilities: There are 17 sites for tents, trailers or RVs up to 30 feet long. Picnic tables and fire grills are provided. Vault toilets are available. There is **no piped water**. Leashed pets are permitted.

Reservations, fee: No reservations; no fee. Open early May to early November.

Who to contact: Phone the Prospect Ranger District at (541) 560-3400 or write to Rogue River National Forest, Prospect, OR 97536.

Location: From Medford on Interstate 5, travel 54 miles north on Highway 62. Turn left and drive one mile west on Forest Service Road 300 to the campground on the left.

Trip note: The Upper Rogue River runs underground at this spot. The Upper Rogue River Trail passes camp and follows the river for many miles to the Pacific Crest Trail in Crater Lake National Park. There is an interpretive area and a spectacular geological viewpoint adjacent to camp. A one-quarter mile barrier-free trail is also available. This is a popular camp, and you can expect company in the midsummer months.

25.　　　　　ABBOTT CREEK　　　　　**RV**

Reference: On Abbott and Woodruff creeks in Rogue River National Forest; map E2, grid c2.

Campsites, facilities: There are 28 sites for tents, trailers or RVs up to 30 feet long. Picnic tables and fire grills are provided. Potable pump water and vault toilets are available. Leashed pets are permitted.

Reservations, fee: No reservations; $6 fee per night; $3 second vehicle per night. Golden Age and Access discounts. Open late May to late October.

Who to contact: Phone Rogue Recreation at (541) 770-5146 or (541) 560-3400 or write to 2990 North Pacific Highway, Medford, OR 97501.

Location: From Medford on Interstate 5, travel 47 miles northeast on Highway 62. Turn left and drive 3.5 miles northwest on Forest Service Road 68 to the campground on the left.

Trip note: This campground is set at the confluence of Abbott and Woodruff creeks about two miles from the Upper Rogue River. This is a better camp for visitors with children than some of the others along the Rogue River; Abbott Creek is small and tame compared to the roaring Rogue. The kids probably still won't be tempted to dip their toes, however, because the water usually runs at a body-numbing 42 degrees, even in the summer.

26.　　　JOSEPH P. STEWART STATE PARK　　　**RV**

Reference: On Lost Creek Lake; map E2, grid c2.

Campsites, facilities: There are 50 sites for tents or self-contained RVs and 151 sites with water and electrical hookups for trailers or RVs of any length. Picnic tables and fire grills are provided. Flush toilets, sanitary disposal services, showers, firewood and a playground are available. Some facilities are **wheelchair accessible**. Leashed pets are permitted. Boat launching facilities are nearby.

Reservations, fee: No reservations; $13-$14 per night. Open mid-April to late October.

Who to contact: Phone (541) 560-3334 or (800) 452-5687 or write to 35251 Highway 62, Trail, OR 97524.

Location: From Interstate 5 at Medford, drive 34 miles northeast on Highway 62.

Trip note: This state park is set along the shore of Lost Creek Lake, a reservoir with a marina, a beach and boat rentals. There are 5.5 miles of hiking trails and a six-mile bike path available in the park. This nice spot gets attention from Oregonians in the area but is missed by most other people.

27.　　　　HUCKLEBERRY MOUNTAIN　　　　**RV**

Reference: Near Crater Lake National Park in Rogue River National Forest; map E2, grid c3.

Campsites, facilities: There are 27 primitive sites for tents, trailers or RVs up to 21 feet long. Picnic tables and fireplaces are provided. Hand-pumped water and vault toilets are available. Leashed pets are permitted.

Reservations, fee: No reservations; no fee. Open June to late October.

Who to contact: Phone the Prospect Ranger District at (541) 560-3400 or write to Rogue River National Forest, Prospect, OR 97536.

Location: From Medford on Interstate 5, turn north on Highway 62 and drive 35 miles to Prospect. From Prospect, continue 17.5 miles northeast on Highway

62, then four miles south on Forest Service Road 60. Note: The access road is quite rough; trailers are not recommended.

Trip note: This campground is set at 5,400 feet, about 15 miles from the entrance to Crater Lake National Park. It is a prime hideaway for people who visit Crater Lake, and it really does get overlooked by highway travelers, so you have a better chance at privacy and quiet. The camp is located at the site of an old 1930s Civilian Conservation Corps camp, and the Forest Service has even refurbished the original fireplaces to keep the historic aura intact.

28.   MILL CREEK   RV

Reference: **Near Upper Rogue River in Rogue River National Forest; map E2, grid c3.**

Campsites, facilities: There are eight sites for tents, trailers or RVs up to 25 feet long. Picnic tables and fire grills are provided. Vault toilets are available. There is **no piped water**. Leashed pets are permitted.

Reservations, fee: No reservations; no fee. Open April to November.

Who to contact: Phone the Prospect Ranger District at (541) 560-3400 or write to Rogue River National Forest, Prospect, OR 97536.

Location: From Medford on Interstate 5, travel 47 miles northeast on Highway 62, then one mile east on Forest Service Road 30.

Trip note: This campground is set along the bank of Mill Creek about two miles from the Upper Rogue River. It has beautiful, private sites and is heavily vegetated. It is one in a series of remote, primitive camps near Highway 62 that is missed by out-of-towners. It is an excellent camp for tents.

29.   LOST CREEK   RV

Reference: **Near the Crater Lake Pinnacles in Crater Lake National Park; map E2, grid c5.**

Campsites, facilities: There are 16 sites for tents. Picnic tables and fire grills are provided. Piped water and vault toilets are available. Leashed pets and motorbikes are permitted (on paved roads only).

Reservations, fee: No reservations; $5 fee per night. Open mid-July to mid-September.

Who to contact: Phone Crater Lake National Park at (541) 594-2211 or write to P.O. Box 7, Crater Lake, OR 97604.

Location: From Interstate 5 at Medford, turn east on Highway 62 and drive 77 miles to the Annie Springs junction. Take Rim Drive around the lake until the road to the Pinnacles, turn left and drive five miles to the campground.

Trip note: In good weather, this is a prime spot in Crater Lake National Park—you avoid most of the crowd that is driving the Rim Road. This primitive campground is set near little Lost Creek and the Pinnacles, a series of spires. The only trail access down to Crater Lake is at Cleetwood Cove. Some of the park facilities are open in the winter for cross-country skiing along the unplowed roadways. Winter access to the park is available only from the south and west on Highway 62 to Rim Village.

30.   MAZAMA   RV

Reference: **Near Pacific Crest Trail in Crater Lake National Park; map E2, grid c5.**

Campsites, facilities: There are 198 sites for tents, trailers or RVs up to 32 feet long. Picnic tables and fire grills are provided. Piped water, flush toilets, sanitary disposal services, showers, a store, firewood and ice are available. Some facilities are **wheelchair accessible**. Leashed pets are permitted. Motorbikes are permitted on paved roads only.

Reservations, fee: No reservations; $11 fee per night. Open late June to early October.

Who to contact: Phone (541) 830-8700 or write to P.O. Box 128, Crater Lake, OR 97604.

Location: From Medford on Interstate 5, turn east on Highway 62 and drive 77 miles to the Annie Springs entrance. The campground is just past the entrance.

Trip note: The Pacific Crest Trail passes near camp. The only trail access down to Crater Lake is at Cleetwood Cove. Some of the park facilities are open in the winter for cross-country skiing along the unplowed roadways. Winter access to the park is available only from the west on Highway 62 to Rim Village. This is one of the two campgrounds at Crater Lake.

---

31.   CRATER LAKE CAMP & RV PARK   ⚫RV

Reference: **Near Crater Lake National Park; map E2, grid c5.**

Campsites, facilities: There are 50 tent sites and 36 drive-through sites for trailers or RVs of any length. Electricity, piped water, sewer hookups and picnic tables are provided. Flush toilets, showers, firewood, a store, a laundromat, ice and a playground are available. Pets and motorbikes are permitted.

Reservations, fee: Reservations accepted; $12-$16 fee per night. MasterCard and Visa accepted. Open mid-May to October.

Who to contact: Phone (541) 381-2275 or write to P.O. Box 485, Fort Klamath, OR 97626.

Location: From Medford on Interstate 5, turn north on Highway 62 and drive 88 miles north and east to the campground.

Trip note: This campground is located near the south entrance to Crater Lake National Park, the nearest private park in the area. It gets heavy traffic during the summer months, but can be a good option to the packed national park camps. The campground features tepees and trout ponds for fishing.

---

32.   FORT KLAMATH LODGE & RV PARK   ⚫RV

Reference: **On Wood River; map E2, grid c5.**

Campsites, facilities: There are five tent sites and 11 sites for trailers or RVs of any length. Electricity, piped water, sewer hookups and picnic tables are provided. Flush toilets, bottled gas, showers and a laundromat are available. A store and ice are located within one mile. Pets and motorbikes are permitted.

Reservations, fee: Reservations accepted; $9-$12 fee per night; MasterCard and Visa accepted. Open all year.

Who to contact: Phone (541) 381-2234 or write to P.O. Box 428, Fort Klamath, OR 97626.

Location: From Interstate 5 at Medford, take the Jackson County Airport exit and drive five miles north to White City. Turn east on Highway 140 and drive 74 miles to Klamath Falls. From Klamath Falls, travel 21 miles north on US 97, then 14.5 miles north on Highway 62. The campground is 1.5 miles northwest of Fort Klamath.

Trip note: This campground is on the banks of the Wood River, just outside Fort Klamath, the site of numerous military campaigns in the late 1800s against the Modoc Indians.

33.   JACKSON F. KIMBALL STATE PARK   RV

Reference: **On Wood River; map E2, grid c6.**

Campsites, facilities: There are six primitive sites for tents, trailers or self-contained RVs up to 45 feet long. Picnic tables and fire grills are provided. Firewood and vault toilets are available. There is **no piped water**. Leashed pets are permitted.

Reservations, fee: No reservations; $7 fee per night. Open mid-April to late October.

Who to contact: Phone (541) 388-6211 or (800) 452-5687 or write to c/o 63030 O. B. Riley Road, Suite A, Bend, OR 97701.

Location: From Interstate 5 at Medford, take the Jackson County Airport exit and drive five miles north to White City. Turn east on Highway 140 and drive 74 miles to Klamath Falls. Turn north on US 97 and drive 24 miles, then 13 miles north on Highway 62 to Fort Klamath. From Fort Klamath, drive three miles north on Highway 232.

Trip note: This primitive state campground is set near the Wood River. It's another nice spot just far enough off the main drag that most tourists don't have a clue about it. There is a nice hiking trail that leads to the headwaters of the Wood River, which has decent fishing.

34.   FLY-CASTERS RV PARK   RV

Reference: **On Rogue River; map E2, grid d0.**

Campsites, facilities: There are 30 sites for trailers or RVs of any length. Electricity, piped water, sewer hookups and picnic tables are provided. Flush toilets, bottled gas, showers and a laundromat are available. A store, a cafe and ice are located within one mile. Leashed pets are permitted. Boat launching facilities are nearby.

Reservations, fee: Reservations accepted; $16-$20 fee per night. Open all year.

Who to contact: Phone (541) 878-2749 or write to P.O. Box 699, Shady Cove, OR 97539.

Location: From Interstate 5 at Medford, drive north on Highway 62 for 23 miles and you will see the camp along the highway. It is set 2.7 miles south of the junction of Highways 62 and 227.

Trip note: This is a good base camp for motor home drivers who want to fish or hike. It is set along the banks of the Rogue River. The county park in Shady Cove offers picnic facilities and a boat ramp. Lost Creek Lake is about a 15-minute drive northeast.

35.   SHADY TRAILS RV PARK & CAMP   RV

Reference: **On Rogue River; map E2, grid d0.**

Campsites, facilities: There are 27 tent sites and 48 drive-through sites for trailers or RVs of any length. Electricity, piped water, sewer hookups and picnic tables are provided. Flush toilets, cable TV, bottled gas, sanitary disposal services, showers, a store, ice and a playground are available. A cafe is located within one mile. Pets and motorbikes are permitted. Boat launching facilities are nearby.

Reservations, fee: Reservations accepted; $16-$20 fee per night. Open all year.

Who to contact: Phone (541) 878-2206 or write to 1 Meadow Lane, Shady Cove, OR 97539.

Location: From Interstate 5 at Medford, drive 23 miles north on Highway 62 to the campground.

Trip note: This park is set along the banks of the Rogue River. It is in a wooded, mountainous area, with many shaded sites. Recreation options include fishing on the Rogue River or exploring Casey State Park.

36. ROGUE RIVER RV PARK

Reference: **On Rogue River; map E2, grid d0.**

Campsites, facilities: There are 70 sites for tents, trailers or RVs up to 60 feet. Free cable TV, restrooms, showers, a sanitary dump, security, a public phone, a laundromat, limited groceries, ice and RV supplies are available. Other facilities include a barbecue pavilion, green lawns, horseshoe pits, nearby restaurants and a boat ramp. The facilities are **wheelchair accessible**.

Reservations, fee: Reservations recommended; $10-$19 fee per night. Visa and MasterCard are accepted.

Who to contact: Phone the park at (541) 878-2404 or (800) 775-0367 or write to 21800 Crater Lake Highway 62, Shady Cove, OR 97539.

Location: From Interstate 5 at Medford, turn north on Highway 62 and drive 20 miles northeast. The park is located on the right.

Trip note: This resort provides access to mountain lakes, the surrounding wilderness and the Rogue River. The setting is beautiful, lush and heavily wooded. Activities on the river include riverbank fishing, rafting and guided trips. Hunting facilities and winter sports are also available at this resort.

37. BEAR MOUNTAIN RV PARK

Reference: **On Rogue River; map E2, grid d1.**

Campsites, facilities: There are 10 tent sites and 37 drive-through sites for trailers or RVs of any length. Electricity, piped water, sewer hookups and picnic tables are provided. Flush toilets, bottled gas, sanitary disposal services, showers, a laundromat, ice and a playground are available. A store and a cafe are located within one mile. Pets and motorbikes are permitted. Boat docks and launching facilities are nearby.

Reservations, fee: Reservations accepted; $10-$15 fee per night. Discounts are given to Good Sam members. Open all year.

Who to contact: Phone (541) 878-2400 or write to 27301 Highway 62, Trail, OR 97541.

Location: From Interstate 5 at Medford, drive north on Highway 62. From the junction of Highways 62 and 227, continue east on Highway 62 for three more miles to the campground.

Trip note: This campground is set along the Rogue River about six miles from Lost Creek Lake, where boat ramps and picnic areas are available for day use. It is set in an open grassy area, with spacious shaded sites.

38. WHISKEY SPRINGS A AND B

Reference: **Near Willow Lake in Rogue River National Forest; map E2, grid d2.**

Campsites, facilities: There are 35 sites for tents, trailers or RVs up to 16 feet long. Picnic tables and fire grills are provided. Potable piped water and vault toilets are available. Leashed pets are permitted. Boat docks, launching facilities and rentals are within 1.5 miles. Some facilities are **wheelchair-accessible**.

Reservations, fee: No reservations; $6 fee per night; $3 second vehicle per night. Golden Age and Access discounts. Open late May through September.

Who to contact: Phone Rogue Recreation at (541) 770-5146 or (541) 560-3400 or write to 2990 North Pacific Highway, Medford, OR 97501.

Location: From Medford on Interstate 5, travel 15 miles northeast on Highway 62. Turn right and drive 18 miles east on Butte Falls Highway to the town of Butte Falls. From Butte Falls, travel nine miles southeast on Butte Falls Highway/County Road 30. Turn left on Forest Service Road 3317 and drive 300 yards to the campground on the left.

Trip note: This campground is at Whiskey Springs, near Fourbit Creek. A **wheelchair-accessible** nature trail is nearby. This is one of the larger, more developed backwoods Forest Service camps in the area.

---

39. IMNAHA

Reference: **Near Sky Lakes Wilderness in Rogue River National Forest; map E2, grid d3.**

Campsites, facilities: There are four sites for tents. Picnic tables and fire grills are provided. Vault toilets are available. There is **no piped water**. Leashed pets are permitted.

Reservations, fee: No reservations; no fee. Open all year.

Who to contact: Phone the Butte Falls Ranger District at (541) 865-2700 or write to Rogue River National Forest, P.O. Box 227, Butte Falls, OR 97522.

Location: From Medford on Interstate 5, travel 35 miles northeast on Highway 62 to Prospect, then drive 12 miles east on Forest Service Road 37 to the campground.

Trip note: This campground is set along Imnaha Creek. Trailheads at the ends of the nearby Forest Service roads lead east into the Sky Lakes Wilderness. It's a good base camp for a wilderness trip.

---

40. SOUTH FORK RV

Reference: **On the South Fork of Rogue River in Rogue River National Forest; map E2, grid d3.**

Campsites, facilities: There are six sites for tents, trailers or RVs up to 15 feet long. Picnic tables, well water and fire grills are provided. Vault toilets are available. Leashed pets are permitted.

Reservations, fee: No reservations; $3 fee per night. Open all year.

Who to contact: Phone the Butte Falls Ranger District at (541) 865-2700 or write to Rogue River National Forest, P.O. Box 227, Butte Falls, OR 97522.

Location: From Medford on Interstate 5, travel 15 miles north on Highway 62, then 32 miles east on Forest Service Road 34.

Trip note: This campground is set along the South Fork of the Rogue River. To the east, trails at the ends of the nearby Forest Service roads provide access to the Sky Lakes Wilderness. A map of Rogue River National Forest details all back roads, trails and waters.

---

41. PARKER MEADOWS RV

Reference: **On Parker Meadow in Rogue River National Forest; map E2, grid d3.**

Campsites, facilities: There are eight sites for tents, trailers or RVs up to 15 feet long. Picnic tables and fire grills are provided and pumped water and vault toilets are available. Leashed pets are permitted.

Reservations, fee: No reservations; $3 fee per night. Open mid-June to late September.

Who to contact: Phone the Butte Falls Ranger District at (541) 865-2700 or write to Rogue River National Forest, P.O. Box 227, Butte Falls, OR 97522.

Location: From Medford on Interstate 5, travel 14 miles northeast on Highway 62, then 18 miles east to Butte Falls. Continue 10 miles southeast of Butte Falls on County Road 30, then 11 miles northeast on Forest Service Road 37.

Trip note: This campground is set at 5,000 feet on a beautiful meadow with a fantastic view nearby of Mount McLoughlin. Nearby, at the ends of the Forest Service roads, are trailheads that lead into to the Sky Lakes Wilderness. This is a nice spot, complete with water.

---

42. SNOWSHOE   RV

Reference: **Near Snowshoe Butte in Rogue River National Forest; map E2, grid d3.**

Campsites, facilities: There are five sites for tents, trailers or RVs. Picnic tables and fire grills are provided. Vault toilets are available. There is **no piped water.** Leashed pets are permitted.

Reservations, fee: No reservations; no fee. Open all year.

Who to contact: Phone the Butte Falls Ranger District at (541) 865-2700 or write to Rogue River National Forest, P.O. Box 227, Butte Falls, OR 97522.

Location: From Medford on Interstate 5, travel 14 miles northeast on Highway 62, then 18 miles east to Butte Falls. Travel nine miles southeast of Butte Falls on County Road 30, then five miles northeast on Forest Service Road 3065.

Trip note: This campground is set at 4,000 feet near Snowshoe Butte and is a nice, secluded spot that is missed by many.

---

43. FOURBIT FORD

Reference: **On Fourbit Creek in Rogue River National Forest; map E2, grid d3.**

Campsites, facilities: There are seven sites for tents. Picnic tables and fire grills are provided. Potable pumped water and vault toilets are available. A store, a cafe and ice are located within five miles. Leashed pets are permitted. Boat docks, launching facilities and rentals are nearby.

Reservations, fee: No reservations; $6 fee per night; $3 second vehicle per night. Golden Age and Access discounts. Open late May to late September.

Who to contact: Phone Rogue Recreation at (541) 770-5146 or (541) 560-3400 or write to 2990 North Pacific Highway, Medford, OR 97501.

Location: From Medford on Interstate 5, travel 15 miles northeast on Highway 62. Turn left and drive 18 miles east on Butte Falls Highway to the town of Butte Falls. In Butte Falls, turn left and drive nine miles southeast on County Road 30. Turn left on Forest Service Road 3065 and drive one mile to the campground on the left.

Trip note: This campground is set along Fourbit Creek. It's one in a series of hidden spots tucked away near County Road 30.

---

44. BIG BEN   RV

Reference: **Near the South Fork of Rogue River in Rogue River National Forest; map E2, grid d4.**

Campsites, facilities: There are two sites for tents, trailers or RVs up to 15 feet long. Picnic tables and fire grills are provided. Vault toilets are available. There is **no piped water**. Leashed pets are permitted.

Reservations, fee: No reservations; no fee. Open all year.

Who to contact: Phone the Butte Falls Ranger District at (541) 865-2700 or write to Rogue River National Forest, P.O. Box 227, Butte Falls, OR 97522.

Location: From Medford on Interstate 5, travel 15 miles northeast on Highway 62, then 33 miles east on Forest Service Road 34. Drive south one mile on Forest Service Road 37 to the campground.

Trip note: This is one of the smallest official campgrounds in the western U.S. and most folks don't have a clue that it exists. It is set along Big Ben Creek near its confluence with the South Fork of the Rogue River. Nearby trails at the ends of nearby Forest Service roads provide access to the Sky Lakes Wilderness to the east.

---

45. ROCKY POINT RESORT RV

Reference: **On Upper Klamath Lake; map E2, grid d5.**

Campsites, facilities: There are five tent sites and 28 drive-through sites for trailers or RVs of any length. Electricity, piped water, sewer hookups and picnic tables are provided. Flush toilets, bottled gas, sanitary disposal services, showers, firewood, a recreation hall, a store, a cafe, a laundromat, ice and a playground are available. Leashed pets are permitted. Boat docks, launching facilities and rentals are nearby.

Reservations, fee: Reservations accepted; $12-$17 fee per night. Open April to mid-November.

Who to contact: Phone (541) 356-2287 or write to Harriman Route, P.O. Box 92, Klamath Falls, OR 97601.

Location: From Interstate 5 at Medford, take the Jackson County Airport exit and drive five miles north to White City. Turn east on Highway 140 and drive approximately 47 miles, then drive three miles north on Rocky Point Road.

Trip note: This camp is set a mile past Harriman Springs Resort on Upper Klamath Lake, with opportunities for fishing, boating and swimming. See the trip note for Harriman Springs Resort & Marina for more details about the area.

---

46. FORT CREEK RESORT RV

Reference: **On Wood River; map E2, grid d6.**

Campsites, facilities: There are 10 tent sites and 18 sites for trailers or RVs of any length. Electricity, piped water, sewer hookups and picnic tables are provided. Flush toilets, showers, a recreation hall, a laundromat and a swimming pool are available. Bottled gas, a store, a cafe and ice are located within one mile. Pets and motorbikes are permitted.

Reservations, fee: Reservations accepted; $10-$15 fee per night. Open mid-May to October.

Who to contact: Phone (541) 381-2349 or write to P.O. Box 457, Fort Klamath, OR 97626.

Location: From Interstate 5 at Medford, take the Jackson County Airport exit and drive five miles north to White City. Turn east on Highway 140 and drive 74 miles to Klamath Falls. From Klamath Falls, travel 21 miles north on US 97, then 12.5 miles north on Highway 62. The campground is just before Fort Klamath on Highway 62.

Trip note: This campground is on the banks of the Wood River, just outside Fort

Klamath, the site of numerous military campaigns in the late 1800s against the Modoc Indians.

---

47. WALT'S COZY CAMP RV

Reference: **On Williamson River; map E2, grid d6.**

Campsites, facilities: There are 20 tent sites and 34 drive-through sites for trailers or RVs of any length. Electricity, piped water, sewer hookups and picnic tables are provided. Flush toilets, bottled gas, showers and firewood are available. A store, a cafe, a laundromat and ice are available. Pets and motorbikes are permitted.

Reservations, fee: Reservations accepted; $8-$12 fee per night. Open April to early November.

Who to contact: Phone (541) 783-2537 or write to P.O. Box 243, Chiloquin, OR 97624.

Location: From Interstate 5 at Medford, take the Jackson County Airport exit and drive five miles north to White City. Turn east on Highway 140 and drive 79 miles to US 97, then turn north and drive 25 miles to Chiloquin. Continue three miles north on US 97.

Trip note: This campground is set along the banks of the Williamson River, near Collier State Park. It is one of three camps in the immediate area. For a more remote setting, Potter's Trailer Park and Head of the River camps are available to the east.

---

48. COLLIER MEMORIAL STATE PARK RV

Reference: **On Williamson River; map E2, grid d6.**

Campsites, facilities: There are 18 sites for tents or self-contained RVs and 50 sites with full hookups for trailers or RVs up to 60 feet long. Picnic tables and fire grills are provided. Flush toilets, sanitary disposal services, showers, firewood, a laundromat and a playground are available. Some facilities are **wheelchair accessible.** Leashed pets are permitted. A day-use hitching area is also available.

Reservations, fee: No reservations; $12-$16 fee per night. Open mid-April to late October.

Who to contact: Phone (541) 388-6211 or (800) 452-5687 or write to 63030 O. B. Riley Road, Suite A, Bend, OR 97701.

Location: From Interstate 5 at Medford, take the Jackson County Airport exit and drive five miles north to White City. Turn east on Highway 140 and drive 79 miles to Klamath Falls. Turn north on US 97 and drive 30 miles to the park entrance.

Trip note: This campground is set at the confluence of Spring Creek and the Williamson River, both of which are superior trout streams. A nature trail is also available. An open-air museum detailing Oregon's logging history is in the park, and pioneer log cabins still stand nearby.

---

49. NEPTUNE PARK RESORT RV

Reference: **On Upper Klamath Lake; map E2, grid d6.**

Campsites, facilities: There are 15 tent sites and 18 sites for trailers or RVs of any length. Electricity, piped water, sewer hookups and picnic tables are provided. Flush toilets, bottled gas, showers, a store, and ice are available. Pets and motorbikes are permitted. Boat docks and launching facilities are nearby.

Reservations, fee: Reservations accepted; $8-$15 fee per night. MasterCard and Visa accepted. Open all year.

Who to contact: Phone (541) 783-2489 or write to HC 30, P.O. Box 115, Chiloquin, OR 97624.

Location: From Interstate 5 at Medford, take the Jackson County Airport exit and drive five miles north to White City. Turn east on Highway 140 and drive approximately 74 miles to Klamath Falls, then turn north on US 97 and drive about 30 miles to Chiloquin. Turn west at the Modoc Point sign and drive four miles north. From there, follow the signs.

Trip note: This campground is set along Upper Klamath Lake, in an open, grassy area with some shaded sites. See the trip note for Rocky Point, camp number 45, for more information.

50.　　　WATERWHEEL CAMP & RV PARK　　　RV

Reference: **On Williamson River; map E2, grid d6.**

Campsites, facilities: There are 20 tent sites and 24 drive-through sites for trailers or RVs of any length. Electricity, piped water, sewer hookups and picnic tables are provided. Flush toilets, bottled gas, sanitary disposal services, showers, firewood, a store, a laundromat, ice and a playground are available. A cafe is available within one mile. Pets and motorbikes are permitted. Boat docks and launching facilities are nearby.

Reservations, fee: Reservations accepted; $12-$15 fee per night. MasterCard and Visa accepted. Open all year.

Who to contact: Phone (541) 783-2738 or write to HC 30, P.O. Box 91, Chiloquin, OR 97624.

Location: From Interstate 5 at Medford, take the Jackson County Airport exit and drive five miles north to White City. Turn east on Highway 140 and drive approximately 74 miles to Klamath Falls, then turn north on US 97 and drive about 30 miles to the park, located one-half mile south of Chiloquin.

Trip note: This rural campground is set along the banks of the Williamson River. Hiking trails are nearby. Fishing can be excellent here, with a boat ramp and fishing tackle available at the camp.

51.　　　WILLIAMSON RIVER　　　RV

Reference: **Near Collier Memorial State Park in Winema National Forest; map E2, grid d7.**

Campsites, facilities: There are three tent sites and seven sites for trailers or RVs up to 30 feet long. Picnic tables and fire grills are provided. Hand-pumped well water and vault toilets are available. Some facilities are **wheelchair accessible**. A restaurant is located within five miles. Leashed pets are permitted.

Reservations, fee: No reservations; $5 fee per night; $2 each additional vehicle. Open May 15 to November 25, weather permitting.

Who to contact: Phone the Chiloquin Ranger District at (541) 783-4001 or write Winema National Forest, 38500 Highway 97 North, Chiloquin, OR 97624.

Location: From Interstate 5 at Medford, take the Jackson County Airport exit and drive five miles north to White City. Turn east on Highway 140 and drive 79 miles to US 97, then turn north and drive 25 miles to Chiloquin. Continue 5.5 miles north on US 97, then drive one mile northeast on Forest Service Road 9730.

Trip note: Another great little spot is discovered, this one with excellent trout fishing. This campground is set along the banks of the Williamson River. A map of Winema National Forest details the back roads and trails. Collier State Park provides a nearby side trip option.

52. WILLIAMSON RIVER RESORT   **RV**

Reference: **On Williamson River; map E2, grid d7.**

Campsites, facilities: There are eight sites for trailers or RVs of any length. Electricity, piped water and picnic tables are provided. Bottled gas, sanitary disposal services, a store and ice are available. A cafe is located within one mile. Leashed pets are permitted. Boat docks, launching facilities and rentals are nearby.

Reservations, fee: Reservations accepted; $10 fee per night; MasterCard and Visa accepted. Open all year.

Who to contact: Phone (541) 783-2071 or write to 31900 Modoc Point Road, Chiloquin, OR 97624.

Location: From Interstate 5 at Medford, take the Jackson County Airport exit and drive five miles north to White City. Turn east on Highway 140 and drive approximately 74 miles to Klamath Falls, then turn north on US 97 and drive about 29.5 miles to Chiloquin. Turn on Modoc Point Road and continue 5.5 miles to the park.

Trip note: This little RV park is set along the banks of the Williamson River. The Williamson is one of Oregon's famous fishing streams, attracting anglers from many miles away, and can be fished by drift boat. A boat ramp is available at Camp 52, but you can also just put on your waders and wander out into the stream.

53. POTTER'S TRAILER PARK   **RV**

Reference: **On Sprague River; map E2, grid d8.**

Campsites, facilities: There are 17 tent sites and 23 drive-through sites for trailers or RVs of any length. Electricity, piped water, sewer hookups and picnic tables are provided. Flush toilets, bottled gas, showers, firewood, a recreation hall, a store, a cafe, a laundromat and ice are available. Pets and motorbikes are permitted.

Reservations, fee: Reservations accepted; $12 fee per night. Open all year with limited winter facilities.

Who to contact: Phone (541) 783-2253 or write to Star Route 2, Chiloquin, OR 97624.

Location: From Interstate 5 at Medford, take the Jackson County Airport exit and drive five miles north to White City. Turn east on Highway 140 and drive approximately 74 miles to Klamath Falls, then turn north on US 97 and drive 24 miles to Chiloquin. Turn east on Sprague River Highway and continue 12 miles to the resort.

Trip note: This campground is set along the banks of the Sprague River. For the most part, the area east of Klamath Lake doesn't get much attention. But if you want to check out a relatively nearby spot that is out in booger country, check out the Head of the River camp.

54.   HEAD OF THE RIVER   RV

Reference: **On Williamson River in Winema National Forest; map E2, grid d9.**

Campsites, facilities: There are five sites for tents, trailers or RVs up to 30 feet long. Picnic tables and fire pits are provided. Vault toilets are available. There is **no piped water**. Leashed pets are permitted.

Reservations, fee: No reservations; no fee. Open Memorial Day through late November.

Who to contact: Phone the Chiloquin Ranger District at (541) 783-4001 or write to Winema National Forest, 38500 Highway 97 North, Chiloquin, OR 97624.

Location: From Interstate 5 at Medford, take the Jackson County Airport exit and drive five miles north to White City. Turn east on Highway 140 and drive 79 miles to US 97, then turn north and drive 25 miles to Chiloquin. Turn and drive five miles northeast on County Road 858/Sprague River Highway. Turn northeast on County Road 600/Williamson River Highway and drive 27 miles. Turn north on Forest Service Road 4648 and drive one mile to the campground.

Trip note: This campground is set along the headwaters of the Williamson River, where the fishing can be excellent. Almost nobody knows about this small, lonely spot. It is the only camp for miles around.

---

55.   MEDFORD OAKS CAMPARK   RV

Reference: **Map E2, grid e1.**

Campsites, facilities: There are 60 sites for tents, trailers or RVs of any length. Restrooms, showers, a sanitary dump, a public phone, a laundromat, limited groceries, ice, RV supplies and LP gas are available. Recreational facilities include a heated swimming pool, a game room, movies, a dance floor, horseshoe pits, a recreation field and a playground.

Reservations, fee: Reservations recommended; $8-$11 fee per night. Group rates are available. Visa and MasterCard are accepted. Open all year.

Who to contact: Phone the park at (541) 826-5103 or write to 7049 State Highway 140, Eagle Point, OR 97524.

Location: From Interstate 5 at Medford, turn north on Highway 62 and drive five miles to Highway 140. Turn east on Highway 140 and drive 6.8 miles to the campground on the left.

Trip note: This park is in a quiet rural setting among the trees. Just a short hop off Interstate 5, it's an excellent choice for travelers heading south to California. The campground is located along the shore of a pond that provides good pan fishing.

---

56.   LILY GLEN CAMPGROUND   RV

Reference: **On Howard Prairie Lake; map E2, grid e2.**

Campsites, facilities: There are 20 sites for tents, trailers or RVs. Picnic tables, piped water and restrooms are provided. There are no RV hookups available. Pets are permitted on leashes.

Reservations, fee: No reservations; $3 fee per night. Open from April 15 to October 15.

Who to contact: Phone Jackson County Parks at (541) 776-7001 or write to 400 Antelope Road, White City, OR 97503.

Location: From Interstate 5 at Medford, turn east on Dead Indian Road and drive 21 miles to the campground.

Trip note: Set along the shore of Howard Prairie Lake, this campground is a secluded, primitive getaway. Trout fishing is available. Tubb Springs Wayside State Park and the nearby Rogue River National Forest provide possible side trips.

---

57. WILLOW LAKE RESORT RV

Reference: **On Willow Lake; map E2, grid e3.**

Campsites, facilities: There are 37 tent sites and 45 drive-through sites for trailers or RVs up to 30 feet long. Electricity, piped water, sewer hookups and picnic tables are provided. Flush toilets, sanitary disposal services, showers, firewood, a store, a cafe, LP gas, ice and a playground are available. Pets are permitted. Boat docks, launching facilities and rentals are nearby.

Reservations, fee: Reservations accepted; $12-$16 fee per night. MasterCard and Visa accepted. Open all year.

Who to contact: Phone (541) 865-3229 or write to 7800 Fish Lake, Butte Falls, OR 97533.

Location: From Medford on Interstate 5, travel 15 miles northeast on Highway 62, then 25 miles east on Butte Falls Highway. Then drive two miles southeast on Willow Lake Road.

Trip note: This campground is on the shore of Willow Lake. Nearby recreation options include hiking trails and a small marina.

---

58. WILLOW PRAIRIE RV

Reference: **Near Fish Lake in Rogue River National Forest; map E2, grid e3.**

Campsites, facilities: There are 10 sites for tents, trailers or RVs up to 15 feet long. Picnic tables and fire grills are provided. Pumped water and vault toilets are available. A store, a cafe and ice are located within five miles. Leashed pets are permitted. Boat docks, launching facilities and rentals are nearby.

Reservations, fee: Reservations required; $6 fee per night. Open late May to late September.

Who to contact: Phone the Butte Falls Ranger District at (541) 865-2700 or write to Rogue River National Forest, P.O. Box 227, Butte Falls, OR 97522.

Location: From Medford on Interstate 5, travel 31.5 miles east on Highway 140, then 1.5 miles north on Forest Service Road 37. The camp is one mile west on Forest Service Road 3738.

Trip note: This spot is primarily used as a horse camp. A map of Rogue River National Forest details the back roads and can help you get here. The campground is set near the origin of the west branch of Willow Creek. Fish Lake is four miles south.

---

59. NORTH FORK RV

Reference: **Near Fish Lake in Rogue River National Forest; map E2, grid e3.**

Campsites, facilities: There are five tent sites and four sites for trailers or RVs up to 24 feet long. Picnic tables and fire grills are provided. Vault toilets and hand-pumped water are available. Leashed pets are permitted. Boat docks, launching facilities and rentals are nearby. Some facilities are **wheelchair-accessible**.

Reservations, fee: No reservations; no fee, but donations are accepted. Open early May to early November.

Who to contact: Phone the Ashland Ranger District at (541) 482-3333 or write to Rogue River National Forest, 645 Washington Street, Ashland, OR 97520.

Location: From Interstate 5 at Medford, take the Jackson County Airport exit (the last Medford exit) and drive five miles north to White City. Turn east on Highway 140 and drive 31.5 miles, then one-half mile south on Forest Service Road 37 to the campground.

Trip note: Here is a small, pretty campground with easy access from the highway and close proximity to Fish Lake. It's fairly popular, so reserve your spot early. Excellent fly fishing can be found along the Fish Lake Trail, which leads directly out of camp.

---

60.   FISH LAKE   RV

Reference: **On Fish Lake in Rogue River National Forest; map E2, grid e3.**

Campsites, facilities: There 20 sites for tents, trailers or RVs up to 24 feet long. Picnic tables and fire grills are provided. A **wheelchair-accessible** picnic shelter is also available. Piped water, flush toilets, a store, a cafe and ice are available. Leashed pets are permitted. Boat docks, launching facilities and rentals are nearby.

Reservations, fee: No reservations; $10 fee per night; $5 second vehicle per night. Golden Age and Access discounts. Open mid-May to mid-October.

Who to contact: Phone Rogue Recreation at (541) 770-5146 or (541) 560-3400 or write to 2990 North Pacific Highway, Medford, OR 97501.

Location: From Interstate 5 at Medford, take the Jackson County Airport exit (the last Medford exit) and drive five miles north to White City. Turn east on Highway 140 and drive 30 miles to the campground on the right.

Trip note: This campground is on the north shore of Fish Lake. Recreation options include boating, fishing, hiking and bicycling. There is easy one-mile access to the Pacific Crest Trail. If this campground is full, Doe Point and Fish Lake Resort sites provide options.

---

61.   DOE POINT   RV

Reference: **On Fish Lake in Rogue River National Forest; map E2, grid e3.**

Campsites, facilities: There are five walk-in tent sites and 25 sites for tents, trailers or RVs up to 24 feet long. Picnic tables and fire grills are provided. Potable piped water, flush toilets, a store, a cafe and ice are available. Leashed pets are permitted. Boat docks, launching facilities and rentals are nearby.

Reservations, fee: No reservations; $10 fee per night; $5 second vehicle per night. Golden Age and Access discounts. Open mid-May to mid-October.

Who to contact: Phone Rogue Recreation at (541) 770-5146 or (541) 560-3400 or write to 2990 North Pacific Highway, Medford, OR 97501.

Location: From Interstate 5 at Medford, take the Jackson County Airport exit (the last Medford exit) and drive five miles north to White City. Turn east on Highway 140 and drive 30 miles to the campground on the right.

Trip note: This campground is set along the north shore of Fish Lake, nearly adjacent to Fish Lake Camp. This campground is slightly preferable because it is densely vegetated, offering shaded, well-screened sites. Privacy, rare at many campgrounds, can be found here. Recreation options include boating, fishing, hiking and bicycling. There is an easy one-mile access trail to the Pacific Crest Trail.

62. **FISH LAKE RESORT** **RV**

Reference: **On Fish Lake; map E2, grid e3.**

Campsites, facilities: There are five tent sites and 45 sites for trailers or RVs up to 30 feet long. There are also 10 cabins available. Electricity, piped water, sewer hookups and picnic tables are provided. Flush toilets, bottled gas, sanitary disposal services, showers, a recreation hall, a store, a cafe, a laundromat and ice are available. Pets and motorbikes are permitted. Boat docks, launching facilities and rentals are nearby.

Reservations, fee: Reservations accepted; $10-$16 fee per night. Call for cabin fee information. MasterCard and Visa accepted. Open year-round (weather permitting).

Who to contact: Phone (541) 949-8500 or write to P.O. Box 40, Medford, OR 97501.

Location: From Interstate 5 at Medford, take the Jackson County Airport exit (the last Medford exit) and drive five miles north to White City. Turn east on Highway 140 and drive 30 miles to Fish Lake Road. Turn south and drive one-half mile to the camp.

Trip note: This campground is set along Fish Lake, where hiking, bicycling, fishing and boating are some of the options. It is operated privately under permit by the Forest Service, and offers a resort-type feel, catering primarily to families. This is the largest and most developed of the three camps at Fish Lake. It is also the only one open year-round, though the snow keeps away all but the most rugged campers in the winter. Cozy cabins are available for rental, however, and the resort is quite active in winter, with opportunities for cross-country skiing, ice fishing and snowmobiling.

63. **DALEY CREEK** **RV**

Reference: **On Daley Creek in Rogue River National Forest; map E2, grid e3.**

Campsites, facilities: There are five tent sites and two sites for trailers or RVs up to 24 feet. **No piped water** is available. Picnic tables and fire grills are provided. A vault toilet is available. Leashed pets are permitted. The facilities are **wheelchair accessible**.

Reservations, fee: No reservations; no fee, but donations are accepted. Open early May to early November.

Who to contact: Phone the Ashland Ranger District at (541) 482-3333 or write to Rogue River National Forest, 645 Washington, Ashland, OR 97520.

Location: From Ashland, drive 22 miles northeast on Dead Indian Memorial Road, then 1.5 miles north on Forest Service Road 37.

Trip note: This campground is set along the banks of Daley Creek. It is a primitive and free alternative to camping at some of the nearby, more developed campsites. The Beaver Dam Trail heads right out of camp, leading along the creek. Fishing can be decent downstream from here.

64. **BEAVER DAM** **RV**

Reference: **On Daley Creek in Rogue River National Forest; map E2, grid e3.**

Campsites, facilities: There are two primitive tent sites and two sites for trailers or RVs up to 18 feet long. **No piped water** is available. Picnic tables and fire grills are provided. Vault toilets are available. Leashed pets are permitted.

Reservations, fee: No reservations; no fee, but donations are accepted. Open early

May to early November.

Who to contact: Phone the Ashland Ranger District at (541) 482-3333 or write to Rogue River National Forest, 645 Washington, Ashland, OR 97520.

Location: From Ashland, drive 22 miles northeast on Dead Indian Memorial Road, then 1.5 miles north on Forest Service Road 37.

Trip note: This campground is adjacent to Daley Creek Campground, pretty and shaded. It is quiet and rustic, with unique vegetation along the creekside for botany fans. This is the trailhead for Beaver Dam Trail.

---

65. ASPEN POINT RV

Reference: On Lake of the Woods in Winema National Forest; map E2, grid e4.

Campsites, facilities: There are 60 sites for tents, trailers or RVs up to 55 feet long. Picnic tables and fire grills are provided. Piped water and flush toilets are available. Leashed pets are permitted. Boat docks, launching facilities and rentals are nearby.

Reservations, fee: Reserve sites by phoning (800) 280-CAMP ($7.75 reservation fee); $8-$10 fee per night. Open late May to late September.

Who to contact: Phone the Klamath Ranger District at (541) 885-3400 or write to Winema National Forest, 1936 California Avenue, Klamath Falls, OR 97601.

Location: From Interstate 5 at Medford, take the Jackson County Airport exit and drive five miles north to White City. Turn east on Highway 140 and drive approximately 41.5 miles to Forest Service Road 3704. Drive one-half mile, then proceed 100 yards west at the signed entrance.

Trip note: This campground is near the north shore of Lake of the Woods, adjacent to Lake of the Woods Resort. A hiking trail just north of camp leads north for several miles, wandering around Fourmile Lake and extending into the Sky Lakes Wilderness. Other trails nearby head into the Mountain Lakes Wilderness. Fishing, swimming, boating and waterskiing are among your options.

---

66. SUNSET RV

Reference: Near Lake of the Woods in Winema National Forest; map E2, grid e4.

Campsites, facilities: There are 67 sites for tents, trailers or RVs up to 55 feet long. Picnic tables and fire grills are provided. Piped water and flush toilets are available. Some facilities are **wheelchair accessible**. Leashed pets are permitted. Boat docks, launching facilities and rentals are nearby.

Reservations, fee: Reserve sites by phoning (800) 280-CAMP ($7.75 reservation fee); $8-$10 fee per night. Open June to mid-September.

Who to contact: Phone the Klamath Ranger District at (541) 885-3400 or write to Winema National Forest, 1936 California Avenue, Klamath Falls, OR 97601.

Location: From Interstate 5 at Medford, take the Jackson County Airport exit and drive five miles north to White City. Turn east on Highway 140 and drive approximately 41.5 miles to Forest Service Road 3704. Turn south and drive two miles. The camp is one-half mile west on Forest Service Road 3738.

Trip note: This campground is near the eastern shore of Lake of the Woods. It is fully developed and offers a myriad of recreation options. It is popular for both fishing and rafting. A hiking trail that leads east and west along the river is accessible from camp. Serious hikers can access a trail routed into the Boulder Creek Wilderness by driving a short distance west. See a Forest Service map for details. A few miles east on Forest Service Road 38 is Steamboat Falls, a pretty waterfall where you can watch fish swim up a fish ladder. No fishing is allowed, though.

---

67.   FOURMILE LAKE   RV

Reference: **At Fourmile Lake in Winema National Forest; map E2, grid e4.**

Campsites, facilities: There are 25 sites for tents, trailers or RVs up to 22 feet long. Picnic tables and fire grills are provided. Hand-pumped well water and vault toilets are available. Leashed pets are permitted.

Reservations, fee: No reservations; $5-$10 fee per night. Open June to late September.

Who to contact: Phone the Klamath Ranger District at (541) 885-3400 or write to Winema National Forest, 1936 California Avenue, Klamath Falls, OR 97601.

Location: From Interstate 5 at Medford, take the Jackson County Airport exit and drive five miles north to White City. Turn east on Highway 140 and drive approximately 40 miles, then continue six miles north on Forest Service Road 3661.

Trip note: This campground is the only camp on the shore of Fourmile Lake. There are several trails nearby that provide access to Sky Lakes Wilderness. The Pacific Crest Trail passes about two miles from camp. This is a beautiful spot.

---

68.   LAKE OF THE WOODS RESORT   RV

Reference: **On Lake of the Woods; map E2, grid e4.**

Campsites, facilities: There are 27 sites for tents, trailers or RVs up to 35 feet. There are also eight cabins that can accommodate from three to eight people. Restrooms, showers, a sanitary dump, a public phone, a laundromat, ice, snacks, a restaurant, a lounge and LP gas bottles are available. There is also a boat ramp, dock, marina, rentals, and a barbecue.

Reservations, fee: Reservations recommended; $14-$16 fee per night; $58.30-$84.80 cabin fee. Visa, MasterCard and Discover accepted.

Who to contact: Phone the park at (541) 949-8300 or write to 950 Harriman Route, Klamath Falls, OR 97601.

Location: From Interstate 5 at Medford, turn north on Highway 62 and drive five miles, then turn east on Highway 140 and drive approximately 41 miles to Lake of the Woods Road. Turn south and continue to the resort on the right.

Trip note: Set on beautiful Lake of the Woods, this resort offers fishing (four kinds of trout, catfish, bass) and boating in a secluded forest setting. It is a family-oriented campground with all the amenities. In the winter, snowmobiling and cross-country skiing are popular and you can rent equipment at the resort. Attractions in the area include Mountain Lakes Wilderness and the Pacific Crest Trail.

---

69.   ODESSA

Reference: **Near Klamath Lake in Winema National Forest; map E2, grid e5.**

Campsites, facilities: There are five tent sites. Picnic tables and fire grills are provided. Vault toilets are available. There is **no piped water**. Leashed pets are permitted.

Reservations, fee: Reserve sites by phoning (800) 280-CAMP ($7.75 reservation fee); $5-$10 fee per night. Open mid-May to late September.

Who to contact: Phone the Klamath Ranger District at (541) 885-3400 or write to Winema National Forest, 1936 California Avenue, Klamath Falls, OR 97601.

Location: From Interstate 5 at Medford, take the Jackson County Airport exit and drive five miles north to White City. Turn east on Highway 140 and drive approximately 57.5 miles, then one mile northeast on Forest Service Road 3639.

Trip note: This campground is set along Odessa Creek, near the shore of Upper Klamath Lake. Boating and fishing are allowed, but not waterskiing. This lake can provide excellent fishing for rainbow trout on both flies and Rapalas.

70.   HARRIMAN SPRINGS RESORT & MARINA   RV

Reference: **On Upper Klamath Lake; map E2, grid e5.**

Campsites, facilities: There are six tent sites and 17 drive-through sites for trailers or RVs. There are also four cabins, two with kitchens. Electricity, piped water, sewer hookups and picnic tables are provided. Flush toilets, showers, firewood, a restaurant, a lounge, a laundromat and ice are available. Bottled gas, sanitary disposal services and a store are located within one mile. Pets and motorbikes are permitted. Boat docks, launching facilities and rentals are nearby.

Reservations, fee: Reservations accepted; $10-$15 fee per night; $48 cabin fee. Open all year.

Who to contact: Phone (541) 356-2331 or write to Harriman Route, P.O. Box 79, Klamath Falls, OR 97601.

Location: From Interstate 5 at Medford, take the Jackson County Airport exit and drive five miles north to White City. Turn east on Highway 140 and drive approximately 47 miles, then two miles north on Rocky Point Road.

Trip note: This resort is set along the shore of Pelican Bay at the north end of Upper Klamath Lake, adjacent to the Upper Klamath National Wildlife Refuge. Trout fishing is good, especially from a canoe.

71.   MALLARD CAMPGROUND   RV

Reference: **On Upper Klamath Lake; map E2, grid e6.**

Campsites, facilities: There are 10 tent sites and 43 drive-through sites for trailers or RVs of any length. Electricity, piped water, sewer hookups and picnic tables are provided. Flush toilets, showers, a recreation hall, a laundromat, ice and a swimming pool are available. Bottled gas, a store and a cafe are located within one mile. Pets and motorbikes are permitted.

Reservations, fee: Reservations accepted; $10-$15 fee per night. MasterCard and Visa accepted. Open all year with limited winter facilities.

Who to contact: Phone (541) 882-0482 or write to Route 5, P.O. Box 1348, Klamath Falls, OR 97601.

Location: From Interstate 5 at Medford, turn north on Highway 62 and drive five miles, then turn east on Highway 140 and drive 74 miles to Klamath Falls. From Klamath Falls, travel 3.5 miles north on US 97.

Trip note: This campground is near Hanks Marsh on the southeast shore of Upper Klamath Lake, within 50 miles of Crater Lake. Nearby recreation options include a golf course, bike paths and a marina.

72.   JACKSON HOT SPRINGS   RV

Reference: **Near Ashland; map E2, grid f0.**

Campsites, facilities: There are 30 tent sites and 20 drive-through sites for trailers or RVs of any length. Electricity, piped water, sewer hookups and picnic tables are provided. Flush toilets, showers, a cafe, a laundromat, ice and a swimming pool are available. Bottled gas is located within one mile. No pets permitted.

Reservations, fee: No reservations; $13-$18 fee per night. Open all year.

Who to contact: Phone (541) 482-3776 or write to 2253 Highway 99 North, Ashland, OR 97520.

Location: Near Ashland, take exit 19 off Interstate 5 and travel west for one-quarter mile to the stoplight. Turn right and drive 500 feet.

Trip note: This campground has mineral hot springs that empty into a swimming pool, not a hot pool (76 degrees). Hot mineral baths are available in private rooms. Nearby recreation options include a golf course, hiking trails, bike paths and tennis courts.

---

73.   WRANGLE

Reference: **Near Pacific Crest Trail in Rogue River National Forest; map E2, grid f0.**

Campsites, facilities: There are five sites for tents. Picnic tables and fire grills are provided. Vault toilets, hand-pumped water and a community kitchen are available. Leashed pets are permitted.

Reservations, fee: No reservations; no fee. Open early June to late October.

Who to contact: Phone the Star Ranger District at (541) 899-1812 or write to Rogue River National Forest, 6941 Upper Applegate Road, Jacksonville, OR 97530.

Location: From Interstate 5 at Ashland, travel three miles north on Highway 99 to Talent, then drive south on Forest Service Road 22 for 17 miles until it ends at Forest Service Road 20. Head west on Road 20 for 4.5 miles. The entrance road to the campground is on the right.

Trip note: This campground is set at the headwaters of Wrangle Creek in the Siskiyou Mountains. The Pacific Crest Trail passes near camp. A map of Rogue River National Forest details hiking trails and streams, as well as backcountry roads. Dutchman Peak Lookout, built in the late 1920s and featured in the historical register, is located within five miles of the park. This is a lovely campground, and unique with its combination of no fee and drinking water.

---

74.   KOA GLENYAN   RV

Reference: **Near Emigrant Lake; map E2, grid f1.**

Campsites, facilities: There are 30 tent sites and 38 sites for trailers or RVs of any length. Electricity, piped water, sewer hookups and picnic tables are provided. Flush toilets, bottled gas, sanitary disposal services, showers, firewood, a recreation hall, a store, a laundromat, ice, a playground and a swimming pool are available. Pets are permitted.

Reservations, fee: Reservations accepted; $17-$21.50 fee per night. MasterCard and Visa accepted. Open March through October.

Who to contact: Phone (541) 482-4138 or write to 5310 Highway 66, Ashland, OR 97520.

Location: From Interstate 5 at Ashland, turn east on Highway 66 and drive 3.5 miles to the campground on the right.

Trip note: This campground offers shady sites near Emigrant Lake and is within seven miles of Ashland. Nearby recreation options include a golf course, hiking trails, bike paths and tennis courts. It's an easy jump from Interstate 5 at Ashland.

75.   MOUNT ASHLAND   🚐

Reference: **On Pacific Crest Trail in Rogue River National Forest; map E2, grid f1.**

Campsites, facilities: There are eight sites for tents, trailers or RVs up to 15 feet long. Picnic tables and fire grills are provided. Vault toilets are available. There is **no piped water**. Leashed pets are permitted.

Reservations, fee: No reservations; no fee. Open July to late October.

Who to contact: Phone the Oak Knoll Ranger District at (916) 465-2241 or write to Klamath National Forest, 1312 Fairlane Road, Yreka, CA 96097. (Yes, the address and phone number are correct.)

Location: From Ashland, travel 12 miles south on Interstate 5. Turn west on County Road 993 and drive one mile. Turn on Forest Service Road 20 and drive nine miles to the campground.

Trip note: This campground is set at 6,000 feet along the Pacific Crest Trail. This is a beautiful site, heavily wooded with abundant wildlife. On clear days, there are great lookouts, particularly to the south where California's 14,000-foot Mount Shasta is an awesome sight.

---

76.   HYATT LAKE   🚐

Reference: **On Hyatt Lake; map E2, grid f2.**

Campsites, facilities: There are 10 tent sites and 36 sites for tents, trailers or RVs of any length. Picnic tables and fire grills are provided. Piped water, showers, flush toilets, a sanitary disposal station are available. A boat ramp is nearby. Leashed pets are permitted.

Reservations, fee: No reservations; $10 fee per night per family; 14-day limit. Open April 26 through October.

Who to contact: Phone (541) 770-2200 or write to Bureau of Land Management, 3040 Biddle Road, Medford, OR 97504.

Location: From Interstate 5 at Ashland, drive 16 miles east on Highway 66, then four miles north on East Hyatt Lake Road. Turn right into the campground.

Trip note: This campground is on the south end of Hyatt Lake. Nearby recreation options include a marina and a stable. A swimming beach is nearby and the lake has become good for fishing. There are some excellent hiking trails not far from camp.

---

77.   HYATT LAKE RESORT   🚐

Reference: **On Hyatt Lake; map E2, grid f2.**

Campsites, facilities: There are 13 tent sites and 22 sites for trailers or RVs of any length (four drive-through). Electricity, piped water, sewer hookups and picnic tables are provided. Flush toilets, bottled gas, sanitary disposal services, showers, a store, a cafe, a laundromat, ice and a playground are available. Pets and motorbikes are permitted. Boat docks, launching facilities and rentals are nearby.

Reservations, fee: Reservations accepted; $9-$14 fee per night; monthly rates available. MasterCard and Visa accepted. Open April through October.

Who to contact: Phone (541) 482-3331 or write to P.O. Box 447, Ashland, OR 97520.

Location: From Interstate 5 at Ashland, drive 17 miles east on Highway 66, then three miles northeast on Hyatt Lake Road. The camp is one mile further on Hyatt Prairie Road.

Trip note: This campground is set along the shore of Hyatt Lake, where hiking and fishing are some of the recreation options. This is a scaled down option to the resort at adjacent Howard Prairie Lake.

---

78.   CAMPER'S COVE   RV

Reference: **On Hyatt Lake; map E2, grid f2.**

Campsites, facilities: There are 25 drive-through sites for trailers or RVs up to 30 feet long. Electricity, piped water, sewer hookups and picnic tables are provided. Flush toilets, showers, firewood, a store, a cafe and ice are available. Leashed pets are permitted. Boat docks are nearby.

Reservations, fee: Reservations accepted; $12.50 fee per night. MasterCard and Visa accepted. Open all year.

Who to contact: Phone (541) 482-1201 or write to P.O. Box 222, Ashland, OR 97520.

Location: From Interstate 5 at Ashland, drive 18 miles east on Highway 66, then three miles northeast on Hyatt Lake Road. The camp is 2.5 miles further on Hyatt Prairie Road.

Trip note: This campground is set along the shore of Hyatt Lake. The Pacific Crest Trail passes about one mile away.

---

79.   EMIGRANT CAMPGROUND   RV

Reference: **On Emigrant Lake; map E2, grid f2.**

Campsites, facilities: There are 42 sites for tents, trailers and self-contained RVs. There is also an overflow area. There are two group camp areas and picnic and barbecue areas which can be reserved. Restrooms, showers, a sanitary dump, a public phone, a laundromat, snacks and a barbecue are available. Recreational facilities include horseshoe pits, a playground, and a recreation field. A boat ramp is provided. Some facilities are **wheelchair accessible**. Pets are permitted in designated areas only, $1 fee for pets.

Reservations, fee: No reservations (except for the group camps and picnic areas); $14 fee per night. Children 15 and under are free. Open from mid-March to mid-October.

Who to contact: Phone Jackson County Parks at (541) 776-7001 or write to 400 Antelope Road, White City, OR 97503.

Location: From Interstate 5 at Ashland, turn southeast on Highway 66 and drive five miles to the campground.

Trip note: This campground is set among trees on Emigrant Lake. This camp holds a unique "no turn away" policy, so you're just about guaranteed a site. Emigrant Lake is a well-known recreational area, and activities at this park include swimming, hiking, boating, waterskiing and fishing. There are also two super water slides available. The park has its own swimming cove. Side trip possibilities include exploring nearby Mount Ashland, where a ski area operates in the winter, and visiting the world-renowned Shakespeare Festival in Ashland.

---

80.   HOWARD PRAIRIE LAKE RESORT   RV

Reference: **On Howard Prairie Lake; map E2, grid f3.**

Campsites, facilities: There are 155 tent sites and 285 sites for trailers or RVs of any length. Electricity, piped water, sewer hookups, 24-hour security and picnic tables are provided. Flush toilets, bottled gas, sanitary disposal services, showers, firewood, a store, a cafe, a laundromat and ice are available. Pets are permitted. Boat docks, launching and mooring facilities and rentals are nearby.

Reservations, fee: No reservations; $10-$16 fee per night. MasterCard and Visa accepted. Open mid-April through October.

Who to contact: Phone (541) 482-1979 or write to P.O. Box 4709, Medford, OR 97501.

Location: From Interstate 5 at Ashland, take Highway 66 east to Dead Indian Road, go 19 miles east to Howard Prairie Road and drive five miles south to the reservoir.

Trip note: This wooded campground is set along the shore of Howard Prairie Lake, where hiking, swimming, fishing and boating are among the recreation options. This is one of the largest campgrounds within more than a hundred miles.

---

81. TOPSY   RV

Reference: **On Upper Klamath River; map E2, grid f5.**

Campsites, facilities: There are 15 sites for trailers or RVs up to 40 feet. Picnic tables and fire grills are provided. Pit toilets and piped water are available. Facilities are **wheelchair accessible.** Leashed pets are permitted. Boat launching facilities are nearby.

Reservations, fee: No reservations; $5 fee per night; 14-day limit. Open mid-May to mid-November.

Who to contact: Phone (541) 883-6916 or write to Bureau of Land Management, 2795 Anderson Avenue, Building 25, Klamath Falls, OR 97603.

Location: From Klamath Falls on Highway 66, travel west for 14.5 miles. Turn south on Topsy Road and travel 1.5 miles to the recreation site.

Trip note: This campground is set along the Upper Klamath River. This is a good spot for trout fishing and a top river for rafters (for experts only). There is Class IV and V whitewater at Caldera, Satan's Gate, Hell's Corner and Three Rocks. This is a good mountain biking area, too.

---

82. KOA KLAMATH FALLS   RV

Reference: **On Upper Klamath Lake; map E2, grid f6.**

Campsites, facilities: There are 18 tent sites and 73 drive-through sites for trailers or RVs of any length. Electricity, piped water, sewer hookups and picnic tables are provided. Flush toilets, bottled gas, sanitary disposal services, showers, a recreation hall, a store, a laundromat, ice, a playground and a swimming pool are available. A cafe is located within one mile. Pets and motorbikes are permitted. Boat docks and launching facilities are nearby.

Reservations, fee: Reservations accepted; $15-$20 fee per night. MasterCard, Visa and Discover accepted. Open all year with limited winter facilities.

Who to contact: Phone (800) 522-9086 (reservations only) or (541) 884-4644 or write to 3435 Shasta Way, Klamath Falls, OR 97601.

Location: From Interstate 5 at Medford, turn north on Highway 62 and drive five miles, then turn east on Highway 140 and drive 74 miles to Klamath Falls. From Klamath Falls, travel 1.5 miles northwest on US 97, then one block west on Shasta Way.

Trip note: This campground is set along the shore of Upper Klamath Lake, near the marina. Hiking trails and tennis courts are nearby. This is a good base camp if you're planning on exploring the Crater Lake area.

83.　　　TINGLEY LAKE ESTATES　　　RV

Reference: **On Tingley Lake; map E2, grid f6.**

Campsites, facilities: There are six tent sites and 10 drive-through sites for trailers or RVs of any length. Electricity, piped water, sewer hookups and picnic tables are provided. Telephone and cable TV hookups, flush toilets, sanitary disposal services, showers, a laundromat and a playground are available. A store, a cafe and ice are located within two miles. Pets are permitted. Boat docks are nearby.

Reservations, fee: Reservations accepted; $14-$16 fee per night. Open all year, weather permitting.

Who to contact: Phone (541) 882-8386 or write to 11800 Tingley, Klamath Falls, OR 07603.

Location: From Interstate 5 at Medford, turn north on Highway 62 and drive five miles, then turn east on Highway 140 and drive 74 miles to Klamath Falls. From Klamath Falls, drive seven miles southwest on US 97, then two miles east on Old Midland Road. The camp is one-half mile south on Tingley Road.

Trip note: This privately-operated mobile home park provides a layover spot for travelers crossing the Oregon border on US 97. Tingley Lake provides opportunities for bass fishing, boating and swimming.

84.　　　WISEMAN'S MOBILE COURT & RV　　　RV

Reference: **Near Upper Klamath Lake; map E2, grid f7.**

Campsites, facilities: There are eight tent sites and 12 sites for trailers or RVs of any length. Electricity, piped water and sewer hookups are provided. Flush toilets, sanitary disposal services, showers and a laundromat are available. Bottled gas is located within one mile. Leashed pets are permitted.

Reservations, fee: Reservations accepted; $12-$15 fee per night. Open all year.

Who to contact: Phone (541) 884-4327 or write to 6800 South 6th, Klamath Falls, OR 97603.

Location: From Interstate 5 at Medford, turn north on Highway 62 and drive five miles, then turn east on Highway 140 and drive 74 miles to Klamath Falls. Continue 4.5 miles east on Highway 140 to the park.

Trip note: This is a suburban motor home park with the barest essentials. It makes a decent layover spot if you need a quick place to stay.

LEAVE NO TRACE TIPS

Plan ahead and prepare.

• Learn about the regulations and special concerns
of the area you are visiting.

• Visit the backcountry in small groups.

• Avoid popular areas during peak-use periods.

• Choose equipment and clothing in subdued colors.

• Pack food in reusable containers.

MAP E3

 OREGON MAP .... see page 380
Adjoining Maps
NORTH (D3) .... see page 562
EAST (E4) .... see page 680
SOUTH .... no map
WEST (E2) .... see page 636

22 LISTINGS
PAGES 670-679

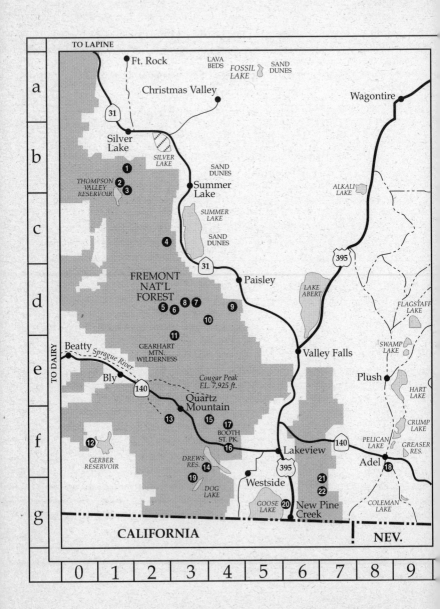

Oregon Map E3 featuring: Fremont National Forest, Thompson Reservoir, Sprague River, Chewaucan River, Gearhart Mountain Wilderness, Campbell Lake, Deadhorse Lake, Gerber Reservoir, Lofton Lake, Cottonwood Meadow Lake, Adel, Goose Lake, Junipers Reservoir, Dog Lake, Lakeview

1.   SILVER CREEK MARSH

Reference: **Near Silver Creek in Fremont National Forest; map E3, grid b1.**

Campsites, facilities: There are 17 tent sites. Picnic tables and fire grills are provided. Well water, firewood and vault toilets are available. Leashed pets are permitted. Hitching trails and corrals for horses are available.

Reservations, fee: No reservations; no fee. Open May to late October.

Who to contact: Phone the Silver Lake Ranger District at (541) 576-2107 or write to Fremont National Forest, P.O. Box 129, Silver Lake, OR 97638.

Location: From Interstate 5 south of Eugene, take exit 188 and turn east on Highway 58. Drive 86 miles, then turn north on US 97 and drive 26 miles. Turn east on Highway 31 and drive 48 miles to Forest Service Road 27 (one mile west of the town of Silver Lake). Turn south and drive 10 miles. The camp is 200 yards southwest on Forest Service Road 27.

Trip note: This campground is set adjacent to Silver Creek Marsh near Silver Creek. A trailhead and terminus for segments of the National Recreational Trail are located here. It's a small, quiet and primitive spot that gets little attention.

2.   THOMPSON RESERVOIR   RV

Reference: **On Thompson Reservoir in Fremont National Forest; map E3, grid b1.**

Campsites, facilities: There are 19 sites for tents, trailers or RVs up to 22 feet long and a separate group camping area. Picnic tables and fire grills are provided. Hand-pumped water and vault toilets are available. Leashed pets are permitted. Boat launching facilities are nearby.

Reservations, fee: No reservations; no fee. Open May to mid-November.

Who to contact: Phone the Silver Lake Ranger District at (541) 576-2107 or write to Fremont National Forest, P.O. Box 129, Silver Lake, OR 97638.

Location: From US 395 at the town of Valley Falls, turn west on Highway 31 and drive 73 miles to the town of Silver Lake. Continue one mile west on Highway 31, then 14 miles south on Forest Service Road 27. The camp is one mile east on Forest Service Road 021.

Trip note: This campground is set along the north shore of Thompson Reservoir. It's simple and pretty, with shaded sites close to the shore. Fishing and boating are permitted. See the trip note for East Bay Campground.

3.   EAST BAY   RV

Reference: **On Thompson Reservoir in Fremont National Forest; map E3, grid c1.**

Campsites, facilities: There are 17 sites for tents, trailers or RVs. Picnic tables and fire grills are provided. Well water and vault toilets are available. Leashed pets are permitted. The facilities are **wheelchair accessible**. Boat launching facilities are nearby.

Reservations, fee: No reservations; $6 fee per night. Open May to mid-November.

Who to contact: Phone the Silver Lake Ranger District at (541) 576-2107 or write to Fremont National Forest, P.O. Box 129, Silver Lake, OR 97638.

Location: From US 395 at the town of Valley Falls, turn west on Highway 31 and drive 73 miles to the town of Silver Lake. Continue one-half mile west on Highway 31, then 13 miles south on Forest Service Road 28. From there, drive 1.5 miles west on Forest Service Road 014.

Trip note: This campground is set along the east shore of Thompson Reservoir. It is a long way from home and you'd best bring all your supplies with you. This campground has been revamped and improved, with paved roads and sites and better toilet facilities. There is a day-use area adjacent to camp. Silver Creek Marsh is an even more primitive setting along a stream.

4.   DAIRY POINT

Reference: **On Dairy Creek in Fremont National Forest; map E3, grid c3.**

Campsites, facilities: There are four sites for tents or trailers. Picnic tables, fire grills, a vault toilet and hand-pumped water are provided. All garbage must be packed out. Leashed pets are permitted.

Reservations, fee: No reservations; no fee. Open April 15 to October 31.

Who to contact: Phone the Paisley Ranger District at (541) 943-3114 or write to Fremont National Forest, P.O. Box 67, Paisley, OR 97636.

Location: From US 395 at the town of Valley Falls, turn west on Highway 31 and drive 22 miles to Paisley. Continue one-half mile west on Highway 31, then turn left on Mill Street and continue to Forest Service Road 33. Drive 19.8 miles, then turn right on Forest Service Road 28 and drive 2.3 miles to the campground.

Trip note: This campground, set at 5,800 feet, is located next to the Dairy Creek Bridge. It is a beautiful, peaceful setting, with a towering backdrop of mountains. Fishing and inner tubing are popular activities at Dairy Creek.

5.   SANDHILL CROSSING   **RV**

Reference: **On Sprague River in Fremont National Forest; map E3, grid d2.**

Campsites, facilities: There are five sites for tents, trailers or RVs (some drive-through). Picnic tables, fire grills, vault toilets and hand-pumped water are provided. All garbage must be packed out. Leashed pets are permitted.

Reservations, fee: No reservations; no fee. Open April 15 to October 31.

Who to contact: Phone the Paisley Ranger District at (541) 943-3114 or write to Fremont National Forest, P.O. Box 67, Paisley, OR 97636.

Location: From US 395 at the town of Valley Falls, turn west on Highway 31 and drive 22 miles to Paisley. Continue one-half mile west on Highway 31, then turn left on Mill Street and continue to Forest Service Road 33. Drive 19.8 miles, then turn right on Forest Service Road 28 and drive 11 miles. Turn left on Forest Service Road 3411 and drive eight miles to the campground.

Trip note: If you're looking for a combination of beauty and solitude, you've found it. This camp is set at 6,100 feet on the banks of the Wild and Scenic Sprague River, where fishing is superior. This is a popular camp with anglers and hunters in the fall.

6.   LEE THOMAS   RV

Reference: On the North Fork of Sprague River in Fremont National Forest; map E3, grid d3.

Campsites, facilities: There are seven sites for tents, trailers or RVs up to 16 feet long. Picnic tables and fire grills are provided. Well water and vault toilets are available. Leashed pets are permitted. All garbage must be packed out.

Reservations, fee: No reservations; no fee. Open April to late October.

Who to contact: Phone the Paisley Ranger District at (541) 943-3114 or write to Fremont National Forest, P.O. Box 67, Paisley, OR 97636.

Location: From US 395 at the town of Valley Falls, turn west on Highway 31 and drive 22 miles to Paisley. Continue one-half mile west on Highway 31, then turn left on Mill Street and continue to Forest Service Road 33. Drive 19.8 miles, then turn right on Forest Service Road 28 and drive 11 miles. Turn left on Forest Service Road 3411 and proceed five miles to the campground.

Trip note: This campground is set along the North Fork of the Sprague River in the interior of Fremont National Forest, a genuine hideaway. The camp is small and cozy, with all the necessities provided.

7.   CAMPBELL LAKE   RV

Reference: On Campbell Lake in Fremont National Forest; map E3, grid d3.

Campsites, facilities: There are 15 sites for tents, trailers or RVs up to 16 feet long. Picnic tables and fire grills are provided. Well water and vault toilets are available. Leashed pets are permitted. A boat launch is adjacent. No gas motors are permitted on the lake; electric motors only. All garbage must be packed out.

Reservations, fee: No reservations; no fee. Open July to late September.

Who to contact: Phone the Paisley Ranger District at (541) 943-3114 or write to Fremont National Forest, P.O. Box 67, Paisley, OR 97636.

Location: From US 395 at the town of Valley Falls, turn west on Highway 31 and drive 22 miles to Paisley. Continue one-half mile west on Highway 31, then turn left on Mill Street and continue to Forest Service Road 33. Drive 19.8 miles, then turn right on Forest Service Road 28 and drive 10 miles. Turn left on Forest Service Road 033 and proceed to the campground.

Trip note: This campground is set along the shore of Campbell Lake. It is near Deadhorse Lake Campground. Both are very busy campgrounds, full most weekends in July and August. No boats with gas motors are permitted on Campbell Lake. Good sidetrips are available in Fremont National Forest. A Forest Service map details the back roads.

8.   DEADHORSE LAKE   RV

Reference: On Deadhorse Lake in Fremont National Forest; map E3, grid d3.

Campsites, facilities: There are five hike-in sites, 10 sites for tents, trailers or RVs up to 16 feet long and a separate area for group camping. Picnic tables and fire grills are provided. Well water and vault toilets are available. Leashed pets are permitted. A boat launch is nearby. Boats with electric motors are permitted, but gasoline motors are prohibited. All garbage must be packed out.

Reservations, fee: No reservations; no fee. Open July to September.

Who to contact: Phone the Paisley Ranger District at (541) 943-3114 or write to Fremont National Forest, P.O. Box 67, Paisley, OR 97636.

Location: From US 395 at the town of Valley Falls, turn west on Highway 31 and drive 22 miles to Paisley. Continue one-half mile west on Highway 31, then turn left on Mill Street and continue to Forest Service Road 33. Drive 19.8 miles, then turn right on Forest Service Road 28 and drive 10 miles. Turn left on Forest Service Road 033 and proceed to the campground.

Trip note: This campground is set along the shore of Deadhorse Lake. There is a hiking trail that leads around the perimeter of the lake, hooking up with other trails along the way. There is one original Civilian Conservation Corps canoe left in the lake, a relic of the 1930s. Good sidetrips are available in Fremont National Forest.

---

9. MARSTERS SPRING   RV

Reference: **On Chewaucan River in Fremont National Forest; map E3, grid d4.**

Campsites, facilities: There are 10 sites for tents, trailers or RVs up to 22 feet long. Picnic tables and fire grills are provided. Well water and vault toilets are available. Leashed pets are permitted.

Reservations, fee: No reservations; no fee. Open April to mid-November.

Who to contact: Phone the Paisley Ranger District at (541) 943-3114 or write to Fremont National Forest, P.O. Box 67, Paisley, OR 97636.

Location: From US 395 at the town of Valley Falls, turn west on Highway 31 and drive 22 miles to Paisley. Continue one-half mile west on Highway 31, then turn left on Mill Street and drive to Forest Service Road 33. Turn south and drive seven miles to the campground.

Trip note: This pretty campground is set along the banks of the Chewaucan River, a good fishing area. It is the largest of several popular camps in this river corridor.

---

10. HAPPY CAMP   RV

Reference: **On Dairy Creek in Fremont National Forest; map E3, grid d4.**

Campsites, facilities: There are nine sites for tents, trailers or RVs up to 16 feet long. Picnic tables and fire grills are provided. Piped water and vault toilets are available. Leashed pets are permitted.

Reservations, fee: No reservations; no fee. Open mid-May to late October.

Who to contact: Phone the Paisley Ranger District at (541) 943-3114 or write to Fremont National Forest, P.O. Box 67, Paisley, OR 97636.

Location: From US 395 at the town of Valley Falls, turn west on Highway 31 and drive 22 miles to Paisley. Continue one-half mile west on Highway 31, then turn left on Mill Street and continue to Forest Service Road 33. Drive 19.8 miles, then turn right on Forest Service Road 28 and drive two miles. Continue 2.4 miles on Forest Service Road 047 to the campground.

Trip note: This campground is set along Dairy Creek. It is a pleasant spot, with open sites. The camp houses some old Depression-era Civilian Conservation Corps shelters, preserved in their original state. Horseshoe pits are provided.

---

11. CORRAL CREEK   RV

Reference: **Near Gearhart Mountain Wilderness in Fremont National Forest; map E3, grid e3.**

Campsites, facilities: There are five sites for tents, trailers or RVs up to 16 feet long. Picnic tables and fire grills are provided. Vault toilets are available. There is **no potable water**. Leashed pets are permitted. Hitching posts and corrals for horses are provided.

Reservations, fee: No reservations; no fee. Open mid-May to late October.

Who to contact: Phone the Bly Ranger District at (541) 353-2427 or write to Fremont National Forest, Bly, OR 97622.

Location: From Interstate 5 at Medford, turn north on Highway 62 and drive five miles, then turn east on Highway 140 and drive 79 miles to Klamath Falls. Continue 67 miles east on Highway 140 to the town of Quartz Mountain, then head northeast on Forest Service Road 3660 for about 16 miles to the junction of Forest Service Road 34. Turn right on Forest Service Road 12 and drive to the campground.

Trip note: This campground is set along Corral Creek adjacent to a trailhead that provides access into the Gearhart Mountain Wilderness, making it a prime base camp for a backpacking trip. There is also access from camp to the Palasade Rocks, a worthwhile sidetrip.

---

12. GERBER RESERVOIR RV

Reference: **On Gerber Reservoir; map E3, grid f0.**

Campsites, facilities: There are 50 sites for tents, trailers or RVs up to 30 feet long. Picnic tables and fire grills are provided. Piped water, firewood, a sanitary dump station and vault toilets are available. Leashed pets are permitted. Boat launching facilities are nearby.

Reservations, fee: No reservations; $5 fee per night. Open mid-May to mid-October.

Who to contact: Phone (541) 947-2177 or write to Bureau of Land Management, P.O. Box 151, Lakeview, OR 97630.

Location: From Interstate 5 at Medford, turn north on Highway 62 and drive five miles, then turn east on Highway 140 and drive 40 miles to Dairy. Turn south on Highway 70 and drive seven miles to Bonanza. Turn east on East Langell Valley Road for 11 miles. Turn north on Gerber Road and drive eight miles to the campground.

Trip note: This campground is set at 4,800 feet along the west shore of Gerber Reservoir. Almost nobody has heard of Gerber Reservoir, since it's set out in the middle of nowhere. And that's just how we like it, right? Recreation options include swimming, fishing, boating and hiking.

---

3. LOFTON RESERVOIR RV

Reference: **On Lofton Lake in Fremont National Forest; map E3, grid f3.**

Campsites, facilities: There are 26 sites for tents, trailers or RVs up to 22 feet long. Picnic tables and fire grills are provided. Well water and vault toilets are available. Leashed pets are permitted. Boat docks and launching facilities are nearby.

Reservations, fee: No reservations; no fee. Open mid-May to late October.

Who to contact: Phone the Bly Ranger District at (541) 353-2427 or write to Fremont National Forest, P.O. Box 25, Bly, OR 97622.

Location: From Interstate 5 at Medford, turn north on Highway 62 and drive five miles, then turn east on Highway 140 and drive 74 miles to Klamath Falls. Continue 54 miles east on Highway 140 to Bly. From Bly, continue 13 miles southeast on Highway 140, then seven miles south on Forest Service Road 3715. From there, go 1.5 miles northeast on Forest Service Road 3715A.

Trip note: This remote campground is set along the shore of Lofton Reservoir. Other lakes are nearby and are accessible by Forest Service roads. This area marks the beginning of the Great Basin, a high-desert area that extends to Idaho.

14. DREWS CREEK   **RV**

Reference: **Near Lakeview in Fremont National Forest; map E3, grid f3.**

Campsites, facilities: There are five sites for tents, trailers or RVs. Picnic tables, fire grills, vault toilets and piped water are provided. All garbage must be packed out. Leashed pets are permitted.

Reservations, fee: No reservations; no fee. Open early June to mid-October.

Who to contact: Phone the Lakeview Ranger District at (541) 947-3334 or write to Fremont National Forest, HC 64, Box 60, Lakeview, OR 97630.

Location: From Lakeview, travel 10 miles west on Highway 140, then turn left on County Road 1-13. Drive four miles, then turn right and drive six miles on County Road 1-11D and Forest Service Road 4017 to the campground.

Trip note: Set along Drews Creek at 4,900 feet, this is an exceptionally beautiful campground. Wild roses grow near the creek, and there are several unmarked trails that lead to nearby hills where campers can enjoy scenic views. This is a great spot for a family trip, with horseshoe pits, an area for baseball and a large group barbecue. Fishing is available in nearby Dog Lake, which also provides facilities for boating. Waterskiing is another option at Drews Reservoir, two miles to the west.

15. COTTONWOOD MEADOWS   **RV**

Reference: **On Cottonwood Meadow Lake in Fremont National Forest; map E3, grid f4.**

Campsites, facilities: There are 21 sites for tents, small trailers or RVs. Picnic tables and fire grills are provided. Piped water and vault toilets are available. Leashed pets are permitted. Boat docks are nearby. Electric motors are permitted, but gasoline motors are prohibited on the lake.

Reservations, fee: No reservations; no fee. Open mid-May to late October.

Who to contact: Phone the Lakeview Ranger District at (541) 947-3334 or write to Fremont National Forest, HC 64, Box 60, Lakeview, OR 97630.

Location: From Lakeview, travel 24 miles west on Highway 140, then eight miles northeast on Forest Service Road 3870.

Trip note: This campground is set along the shore of Cottonwood Meadow Lake. It is one of the better spots in the vicinity for fishing and hiking. Boats with electric motors are allowed on the lake, but gas motors are prohibited. There are three hiking trails around the lake and facilities for horses including hitching posts, feeders, water and corrals.

16. JUNIPERS RESERVOIR RV RESORT   **RV**

Reference: **On Junipers Reservoir; map E3, grid f4.**

Campsites, facilities: There are 15 tent sites and 40 sites for trailers or RVs. Restrooms, showers, a sanitary dump, a public phone, a laundromat and ice are available. Recreational facilities include a recreation hall and horseshoe pits. Some of the facilities are **wheelchair accessible**.

Reservations, fee: Reservations recommended; $14-$17 fee per night. Open from May to mid-October.

Who to contact: Phone the park at (541) 947-2050 or write to HC 60, P.O. Box 1994A, Lakeview, OR 97630.

Location: From Burns on US 20, drive approximately 135 miles south on US 395 to Lakeview. From the junction of Interstate 395 and Highway 140 (in Lakeview), drive west on Highway 140 for 10 miles. The resort is on the right at milepost 86.5.

Trip note: This resort is set on an 8,000-acre cattle ranch. It is a designated Oregon Wildlife Viewing Area, and campers may catch glimpses of seldom-seen species. There are many nature walking trails at the park, and driving tours are offered for guests. Fishing for catfish is good in the vicinity (though not at the reservoir) and the summer climate is mild and pleasant.

17. MUD CREEK   RV

Reference: **On Mud Creek in Fremont National Forest; map E3, grid f4.**

Campsites, facilities: There are seven sites for tents, trailers or RVs up to 16 feet long. Picnic tables, fire grills and vault toilets are available. Leashed pets are permitted. There is **no piped water.**

Reservations, fee: No reservations; no fee. Open June to mid-October.

Who to contact: Phone the Lakeview Ranger District at (541) 947-3334 or write to Fremont National Forest, HC 64, Box 60, Lakeview, OR 97630.

Location: From Lakeview on US 395, continue five miles north, then eight miles east on Highway 140. The camp is seven miles north on Forest Service Road 3615.

Trip note: This campground is set along the banks of Mud Creek. Drake Peak (8,405 feet) is nearby. The camp is remote, in an isolated stand of lodgepole pines. There are no other camps in the immediate vicinity.

18. ADEL STORE & PARK   RV

Reference: **In Adel; map E3, grid f8.**

Campsites, facilities: There are eight sites for trailers or RVs of any length. Electricity, piped water and sewer hookups are provided. Flush toilets, showers, a store, a cafe and ice are available. Pets and motorbikes are permitted.

Reservations, fee: No reservations; $15 fee per night.

Who to contact: Phone (541) 947-3850 or write to P.O. Box 19, Adel, OR 97620.

Location: From Lakeview on US 395, drive five miles north, then turn east on Highway 140 and drive 28 miles to Adel. The motor home park is in town.

Trip note: This is the only game in town, so you'd better grab it while you can. Recreation options in the area include hang gliding, rockhounding or visiting the Hart Mountain National Antelope Refuge, 40 miles north of town.

19. DOG LAKE   RV

Reference: **On Dog Lake in Fremont National Forest; map E3, grid g3.**

Campsites, facilities: There are eight sites for tents, trailers or RVs up to 16 feet long. Piped water, picnic tables and fire grills are provided. Vault toilets are available. Leashed pets are permitted. A boat launch is nearby.

Reservations, fee: No reservations; no fee. Open mid-April to mid-October.

Who to contact: Phone the Lakeview Ranger District at (541) 947-3334 or write to Fremont National Forest, HC 64, Box 60, Lakeview, OR 97630.

Location: From Lakeview, travel 10 miles west on Highway 140, then turn left on County Road 1-13. Drive four miles, then turn right on County Road 1-11D and drive to Forest Service Road 4017. Continue 12 miles on Forest Service Road 4017.

Trip note: This campground is set along the west shore of Dog Lake. Fishing and boats with motors are permitted. Dog Lake is a warm-water and cold-water fishery. There are good prospects of seeing waterfowl and eagles.

---

20.   GOOSE LAKE STATE PARK   **RV**

Reference: **On Goose Lake; map E3, grid g6.**

Campsites, facilities: There are 48 sites with water and electrical hookups for trailers or RVs up to 50 feet long. Picnic tables and fire grills are provided. Flush toilets, showers, a dump station and firewood are available. Leashed pets are permitted. Boat launching facilities are nearby.

Reservations, fee: No reservations; $7-$20 fee per night. Open mid-April to late October.

Who to contact: Phone (541) 947-3111 or (800) 452-5687 or write to the park at P.O. Box 207, New Pine Creek, OR 97635.

Location: From the junction of Highway 140 and US 395 at Lakeview, turn south on US 395 and drive 14 miles. Turn west at the park entrance road and drive one mile to the campground entrance.

Trip note: This park is set along the east shore of Goose Lake, a unique lake which lies half in Oregon and half in California. This out-of-the way area attracts waterfowl from the Pacific Flyway. Boating is popular here.

---

21.   WILLOW CREEK   **RV**

Reference: **On Willow Creek in Fremont National Forest; map E3, grid g7.**

Campsites, facilities: There are eight sites for tents, trailers or RVs up to 22 feet long. Picnic tables and fire grills are provided. Well water and vault toilets are available. Leashed pets are permitted.

Reservations, fee: No reservations; no fee. Open June to mid-October.

Who to contact: Phone the Lakeview Ranger District at (541) 947-3334 or write to Fremont National Forest, HC 64, Box 60, Lakeview, OR 97630.

Location: From US 395 at Lakeview, travel six miles north, then eight miles east on Highway 140. Turn right on Forest Service Road 3915 and drive nine miles, then turn right on Forest Service Road 4011 and continue to the campground.

Trip note: This campground is set along the banks of Willow Creek, not far from a dirt road that heads north to Burnt Creek. There is a hiking trail that accesses the Crane Mountain Trail. A Forest Service map details the back roads.

---

22.   DEEP CREEK   **RV**

Reference: **On Deep Creek in Fremont National Forest; map E3, grid g7.**

Campsites, facilities: There are two sites for tents and four sites for trailers or RVs up to 22 feet long. Picnic tables and fire grills are provided. Vault toilets are available. There is **no piped water**. Leashed pets are permitted.

Reservations, fee: No reservations; no fee. Open June to mid-October.

Who to contact: Phone the Lakeview Ranger District at (541) 947-3334 or write to Fremont National Forest, HC 64, Box 60, Lakeview, OR 97630.

Location: From US 395 at Lakeview, travel six miles north, then eight miles east on Highway 140. Turn right on Forest Service Road 3915 and drive 14 miles, then turn right on Forest Service Road 4015 and drive one mile to the campground.

Trip note: This campground is set along the banks of Deep Creek. It is pretty, shaded by huge ponderosa pine and quaking aspen, and private, receiving little use. Magnificent spring wildflowers are a feature here.

LEAVE NO TRACE TIPS

Travel and camp with care.

On the trail:

• Stay on designated trails.
Walk single file in the middle of the path.

• Do not take shortcuts on switchbacks.

• When traveling cross-country where there are no trails,
follow animal trails or spread out your group so no new routes are created.
Walk along the most durable surfaces available,
such as rock, gravel, dry grasses, or snow.

• Use a map and compass to eliminate the need for
rock cairns, tree scars, or ribbons.

• If you encounter pack animals, step to the downhill side
of the trail and speak softly to avoid startling them.

At camp:

• Choose an established, legal site that will not be damaged by your stay.

• Restrict activities to areas where vegetation is compacted or absent.

• Control pets at all times, or leave them at home
with a sitter. Remove dog feces.

OREGON MAP .... see page 380
Adjoining Maps
NORTH (D4) .... see page 580
EAST (E5) .... see page 684
SOUTH .... no map
WEST (E3) .... see page 670

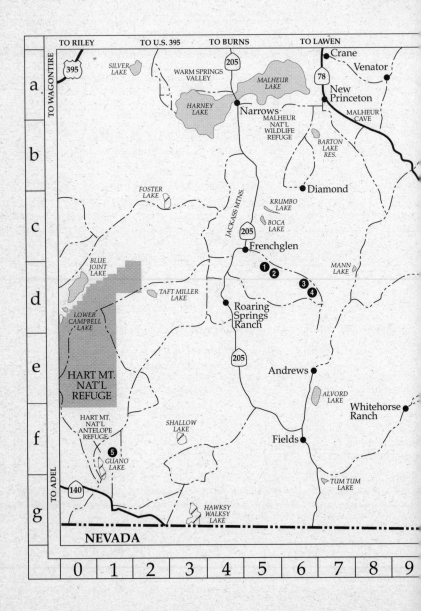

Oregon Map E4 featuring: Fish Lake, Malheur National Wildlife Refuge, Blitzen River, Adel

1. STEENS MOUNTAIN RESORT   RV

Reference: **On the Blitzen River; map E4, grid d5.**

Campsites, facilities: There are 99 sites for tents, trailers or RVs. Restrooms, showers, a sanitary dump, a public phone, a laundromat and ice are available. Leashed pets are permitted.

Reservations, fee: Reservations recommended; $10-$14 fee per night. Visa and MasterCard are accepted.

Who to contact: Phone the park at (541) 493-2415 or write to North Loop Road, Frenchglen, OR 97738.

Location: From Burns on US 20, travel southeast on Highway 78 for 1.8 miles to Highway 205. Turn south on Highway 205 and drive for 59 miles to Steens Mountain Road in the town of Frenchglen. Turn southeast on Steens Mountain Road and drive for three miles to the resort.

Trip note: The self-proclaimed "gateway to the Steens Mountains," this resort has a great view of the surrounding gorges, providing excellent photographic opportunities. Hiking and hunting are other possibilities in the area. Fishing is available on the Blitzen River, with easy access from the camp.

2. PAGE SPRINGS   RV

Reference: **Near Malheur National Wildlife Refuge; map E4, grid d5.**

Campsites, facilities: There are 36 sites for tents, trailers or RVs up to 24 feet long. Picnic tables and fire grills are provided. Piped water, firewood and vault toilets are available. Some facilities are **wheelchair accessible**. Pets are permitted.

Reservations, fee: No reservations; $4 per vehicle per night. Open year-round.

Who to contact: Phone (541) 573-4400 or write to Bureau of Land Management, HC 74-12533, Highway 20 West, Burns, OR 97738.

Location: From Burns on US 20, turn south on Highway 205 and drive 61 miles to Frenchglen, then drive three miles east on Steens Mountain Road to the campground.

Trip note: This campground is set adjacent to Page Springs and the Malheur National Wildlife Refuge. The Frenchglen Hotel is administered by the state parks department and offers overnight accommodations and food. There are a few hiking trails in the area, and birdwatching, fishing, hunting and sightseeing are other recreational opportunities.

3. FISH LAKE   RV

Reference: **On Fish Lake; map E4, grid d6.**

Campsites, facilities: There are 23 sites for tents, trailers or RVs up to 24 feet long. Picnic tables and fire grills are provided. Piped water, firewood and vault toilets are available. Leashed pets are permitted. Boat launching facilities are nearby. Some facilities are **wheelchair accessible**.

Reservations, fee: No reservations; $4 per vehicle per night. Open June through October, weather permitting.

Who to contact: Phone (541) 573-4400 or write to Bureau of Land Management, HC 74-12533, Highway 20 West, Burns, OR 97738.

Location: From Interstate 5 at Albany, turn east on US 20 and drive 254 miles to the town of Burns. Turn south on Highway 205 and drive 61 miles to

Frenchglen, then 16 miles east on Steens Mountain Road to the campground.

Trip note: Located at 7,400 feet, this campground is set along the shore of little Fish Lake. It is primitive but pretty, and not known to many. It can make an excellent weekend getaway spot for backpacking and sight-seeing. Fishing is an option, made easier by the boat ramp near camp.

---

4.   JACKMAN PARK   RV

Reference: **Near Malheur National Wildlife Refuge; map E4, grid d7.**

Campsites, facilities: There are six primitive sites for tents, trailers or RVs up to 24 feet long. Picnic tables are provided. Firewood, hand-pumped water and pit toilets are available. Leashed pets are permitted.

Reservations, fee: No reservations; $4 per vehicle per night. Open July to late October, weather permitting.

Who to contact: Phone (541) 573-4400 or write to Bureau of Land Management, HC 74-12533, Highway 20 West, Burns, OR 97738.

Location: From Interstate 5 at Albany, turn east on US 20 and drive 254 miles to the town of Burns. Turn south on Highway 205 and drive 61 miles to Frenchglen, then drive 20 miles east on Steens Mountain Road to the camp.

Trip note: Set at 8,100 feet in the eastern Oregon desert, this is one of four camps in the area. Page Springs is nearby (see camp number 2) and Adel Store (for supplies) is about 15 miles northeast at the southeastern end of the Malheur National Wildlife Refuge.

---

5.   HART ANTELOPE REFUGE   RV

Reference: **Near Adel; map E4, grid f1.**

Campsites, facilities: There are 12 primitive sites for tents, trailers or RVs up to 20 feet long. Pit toilets are provided. Leashed pets are permitted.

Reservations, fee: No reservations; no fee. Open May to November with limited facilities in the winter.

Who to contact: Phone (541) 947-3315 or write to Plush, OR 97637.

Location: From US 395 at Lakeview, drive five miles north, then turn east on Highway 140 and drive 28 miles to Adel. At the sign for Hart Antelope Refuge, turn north and drive 43 miles northeast on a paved, then gravel road to the refuge headquarters. The campground is four miles beyond that. The road is often impassable in the winter.

Trip note: This unique refuge offers canyons and hot springs. There is no drinking water at the campground, but it can be obtained at the headquarters, which you pass on the way in. Some of Oregon's largest antelope herds roam this large area. The nearest place for supplies is in Adel at the Adel Store.

LEAVE NO TRACE TIPS

Pack it in and pack it out.

• Take everything you bring into the wild back out with you.

• Protect wildlife and your food by storing
rations securely. Pick up all spilled foods.

• Use toilet paper or wipes sparingly; pack them out.

• Inspect your campsite for trash and any evidence of your stay.
Pack out all trash—even if it's not yours!

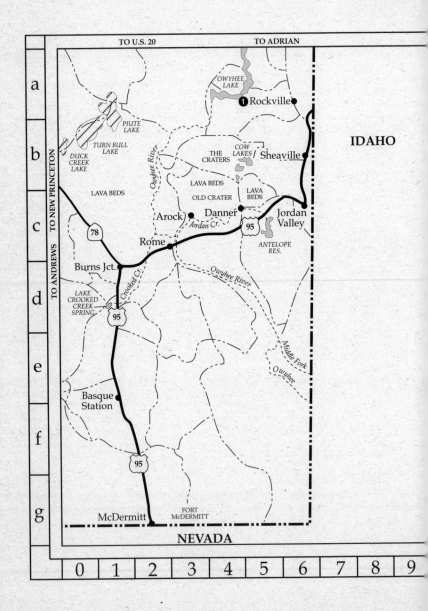

1. LESLIE GULCH

RV

Reference: **On Owyhee Lake; map E5, grid a5.**

Campsites, facilities: There are eight undeveloped sites for tents, trailers or RVs up to 20 feet long. Picnic tables are provided. Vault toilets are available. There is **no piped water**. Leashed pets are permitted. Boat launching facilities are available on site.

Reservations, fee: No reservations; no fee. Open April to November.

Who to contact: Phone (541) 473-3144 or write to Bureau of Land Management, 100 Oregon Street, Vale, OR 97918.

Location: From Homedale, Idaho, drive south on US 95 to the Leslie Gulch Recreation Area turnoff (McBride Creek Road) and travel west for 25 miles to the campground.

Trip note: This campground is set along the eastern shore of Owyhee Lake, not far from the Oregon/Idaho border. Warm-water fishing, waterskiing and hiking are among the recreation options in this high desert area. Owyhee Lake State Park provides the other recreation destination at this lake. There are no other campgrounds located within a one-hour drive.

INDEX

CAMPGROUND LISTINGS ARE IN CAPITAL LETTERS

CAMPGROUND LISTINGS ARE IN CAPITAL LETTERS

CAMPGROUND LISTINGS ARE IN CAPITAL LETTERS

CAMPGROUND LISTINGS ARE IN CAPITAL LETTERS

CAMPGROUND LISTINGS ARE IN CAPITAL LETTERS

CAMPGROUND LISTINGS ARE IN CAPITAL LETTERS

CAMPGROUND LISTINGS ARE IN CAPITAL LETTERS

CAMPGROUND LISTINGS ARE IN CAPITAL LETTERS

ABOUT THE AUTHOR

Tom Stienstra is an outdoors writer and the author of nine books with Foghorn Press. In 1995, he was named National Outdoor Writer of the Year (Newspaper Division), and also won first place for best camping writing in America from the Outdoor Writers Association of America. Other books by Tom Stienstra include:

Rocky Mountain Camping (with Robyn Schlueter)
Epic Trips of the West: Tom Stienstra's 10 Best
California Camping
Easy Camping in Northern California
California Hiking (with Michael Hodgson)
California Fishing
Careers in the Outdoors
Great Outdoor Getaways to the Bay Area and Beyond

Leave No Trace

Leave No Trace, Inc., is a program dedicated to maintaining the integrity of outdoor recreation areas through education and public awareness. Foghorn Press is a proud supporter of this program and its ethics.

Here's how you can Leave No Trace:

Plan Ahead and Prepare
- Learn about the regulations and special concerns of the area you are visiting.
- Visit the backcountry in small groups.
- Avoid popular areas during peak-use periods.
- Choose equipment and clothing in subdued colors.
- Pack food in reusable containers.

Travel and Camp with Care
On the trail:
- Stay on designated trails. Walk single file in the middle of the path.
- Do not take shortcuts on switchbacks.
- When traveling cross-country where there are no trails, follow animal trails or spread out your group so no new routes are created. Walk along the most durable surfaces available, such as rock, gravel, dry grasses, or snow.
- Use a map and compass to eliminate the need for rock cairns, tree scars, or ribbons.
- If you encounter pack animals, step to the downhill side of the trail and speak softly to avoid startling them.

At camp:
- Choose an established, legal site that will not be damaged by your stay.
- Restrict activities to areas where vegetation is compacted or absent.
- Keep pollutants out of the water by camping at least 200 feet (about 70 adult steps) from lakes and streams.
- Control pets at all times, or leave them at home with a sitter. Remove dog feces.

Pack It In and Pack It Out
- Take everything you bring into the wild back out with you.
- Protect wildlife and your food by storing rations securely. Pick up all spilled foods.
- Use toilet paper or wipes sparingly; pack them out.
- Inspect your campsite for trash and any evidence of your stay. Pack out all trash—even if it's not yours!

Properly Dispose of What You Can't Pack Out
- If no refuse facility is available, deposit human waste in catholes dug six to eight inches deep at least 200 feet from water, camps, or trails. Cover and disguise the catholes when you're finished.
- To wash yourself or your dishes, carry the water 200 feet from streams or lakes and use small amounts of biodegradable soap. Scatter the strained dishwater.

Keep the Wilderness Wild
- Treat our natural heritage with respect. Leave plants, rocks, and historical artifacts as you found them.
- Good campsites are found, not made. Do not alter a campsite.
- Let nature's sounds prevail; keep loud voices and noises to a minimum.
- Do not build structures or furniture or dig trenches.

Minimize Use and Impact of Fires
- Campfires can have a lasting impact on the backcountry. Always carry a lightweight stove for cooking, and use a candle lantern instead of building a fire whenever possible.
- Where fires are permitted, use established fire rings only.
- Do not scar the natural setting by snapping the branches off live, dead, or downed trees.
- Completely extinguish your campfire and make sure it is cold before departing. Remove all unburned trash from the fire ring and scatter the cold ashes over a large area well away from any camp.

For more information, call 1-800-332-4100.

FOGHORN PRESS

Founded in 1985, Foghorn Press has quickly become one of the country's premier publishers of outdoor recreation guidebooks. Through its unique Books Building Community program, Foghorn Press supports community environmental issues, such as park, trail, and water ecosystem preservation. Foghorn Press is also committed to printing its books on recycled paper.

Foghorn Press books are sold throughout the United States. Call 1-800-FOGHORN (9:00–5:00 PST) for the location of a bookstore near you that carries Foghorn Press titles. You may also place an order directly with Foghorn Press using your Visa or MasterCard. All of the titles listed below are now available, unless otherwise noted.

The Complete Guide Series

The Complete Guides are the books that have given Foghorn Press its reputation for excellence. Each book is a comprehensive resource for its subject, from *every* golf course in California to *every* fishing spot in the state of Washington. With extensive cross-references and detailed maps, the Complete Guides offer readers a quick and easy way to get the best information available.

California titles include:
- *The Bay Area Dog Lover's Companion* (352 pp) $13.95
- *California Beaches* (640 pp) $19.95
- *California Boating and Water Sports* (608 pp) $19.95, available 6/96
- *California Camping* (848 pp) $19.95
- *The California Dog Lover's Companion* (720 pp) $19.95
- *California Fishing* (832 pp) $19.95
- *California Golf* (896 pp) $19.95
- *California Hiking* (856 pp) $18.95
- *California In-Line Skating* (496 pp) $19.95, available 5/96
- *Great Outdoor Getaways to the Bay Area & Beyond* (632 pp) $16.95
- *Great Outdoor Getaways to Southern California* (512 pp) $17.95, available 12/96
- *Tahoe* (704 pp) $18.95

The Easy Series

The Easy books are perfect for families, seniors, or anyone looking for easy, fun weekend adventures. No special effort or advance planning is necessary—just get outside, relax, and enjoy. Look for Easy guides to Southern California and other favorite destinations in the winter of 1997.

Easy titles include:
- *Easy Biking in Northern California* (224 pp) $12.95
- *Easy Camping in Northern California* (240 pp) $12.95
- *Easy Hiking in Northern California* (240 pp) $12.95

ook's page length and availability are subject to change.

information, call 1-800-FOGHORN or write to:
rn Press, 555 DeHaro Street, Suite 220
San Francisco, CA 94107

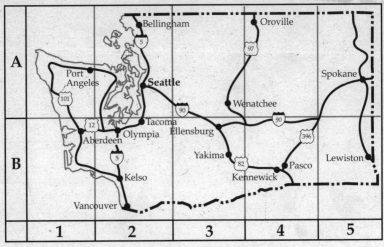

Washington map page 90

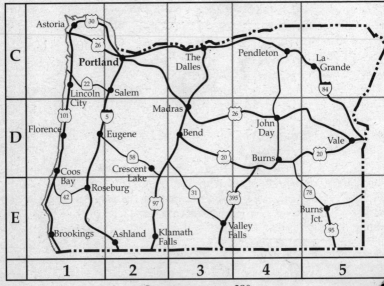

Oregon map page 380